# Scottish Literature

PETER LANG
New York • Washington, D.C./Baltimore
Bern • Frankfurt am Main • Berlin • Vienna • Paris

# Scottish Literature

## An Anthology
## Volume II

David McCordick, editor

PETER LANG
New York • Washington, D.C./Baltimore
Bern • Frankfurt am Main • Berlin • Vienna • Paris

ıg-in-Publication Data

David McCordick, editor.

Scottish literature

ences (p.) and index.
ıd—Literary collections.
David.
PR8636.5.S36s38 820.8'09411—dc20 95-35346
ISBN 0-8204-2880-9 (vol. I)
ISBN 0-8204-3399-3 (vol. II)

**Die Deutsche Bibliothek-CIP-Einheitsaufnahme**

Scottish literature: an anthology/ David McCordick, ed. –New York;
Washington, D.C./ Baltimore; San Francisco; Bern; Frankfurt
am Main; Berlin; Vienna; Paris: Lang.
ISBN 0-8204-2880-9 (Vol. I)
ISBN 0-8204-3399-3 (Vol. II)
NE: McCordick, David [Hrsg.]

Cover design by James F. Brisson

The paper in this book meets the guidelines for permanence and durability
of the Committee on Production Guidelines for Book Longevity
of the Council of Library Resources.

Printed in the United States of America.

# TABLE OF CONTENTS

## THE PRE-ROMANTIC AGE IN SCOTLAND

During the latter part of the eighteenth century, the aesthetic ideals of the Age of Reason were in conflict with the beginnings of Romanticism. The selections of this part of the Anthology contain striking examples of both styles, and of course of writers in whom the two styles were mixed, as with the greatest Scottish poet of the century, Robert Burns.

"Romanticism" is a term used by historians of culture to describe an ideological and aesthetic movement that reached fruition in Europe about 1800–1830, and died out slowly over the remainder of the century. The movement is based upon a view that sees civilization as an unnatural and hostile force that has stifled man's rapport with the universe, one that should be instinctive, and based on feeling. Rather than having a fixed place in the scheme of things, Romantic man is a dynamic creature, striving toward godhead, struggling to achieve a place in the world that is not yet determined, but which may be only a little below the angels. The great good is nature, including the natural man. The essential truths are neither logical nor material, but instinctive and spiritual. Man's route to this ineffable lies often through a mystical empathy with the "oversoul" that is part of all things, which links us to God, and from which we have been sundered since the Fall (i.e., the collapse into civilization).

The primary focus of Romantic literature is upon man as a feeling and imaginative animal, one working through largely instinctive means.

The Romantic aesthetic can be seen as a reaction against eighteenth century ideals, and can be depicted in the following diagram, in which the values of the left-hand side are gradually translated into the right-hand ones (allowing for simplification and exaggeration).

| *18th cent. ("Age of Reason")* | *Romanticism* |
|---|---|
| rationality | sentiment, dreams |
| stability | dynamism, thrust |
| clarity | pursuit of the ineffable |
| balance | intensity |
| regularity | the unusual, irregular |
| simplicity | complexity, Gothicism |
| polish, craftsmanship | ardor, enthusiasm |
| imitation | originality |
| artistic control | inspiration |
| social utility | individualism, catharsis |
| aesthetic response ("taste") | emotion, empathy |
| satire | lyric poetry |
| common sense | the human heart |

One aspect of the Romantic movement which was much welcome in Scotland was its interest in common people—shepherds, farmers—and in rustic scenes and language. In Scotland this took the form of a tremendous outpouring of song, usually written in Scots and with rural settings. Even Robert Fergusson, so much a neo-classicist in his urban focus, satiric detachment, and verbal polish, displays a fascination with the common Scots people of his day, and with their speech. The other major poets of this section are Burns—the greatest songwriter of any age—and John Mayne, whose long poem, "The Siller Gun," is, following a long Scottish tradition, a good-natured celebration of a rustic festival.

## SUSAN BLAMIRE (1747–1794)

["The Siller Croun" is one of the best-loved Scots lyrics from this period. But the author can be only a guest in this anthology. Susan Blamire was born in Carlisle, across the border from Scotland. However, she lived in Scotland for some years, and her Scottish lyrics are virtually the only ones for which she is known.]

### The Siller Croun

"And ye sall walk in silk attire,
And siller* hae to spare, "silver"
Gin* ye'll consent to be his bride, if
Nor think o' Donald mair."

Oh wha wad buy a silken goun
Wi' a puir broken heart?
Or what's to me a siller croun
Gin frae my love I part?

The mind, whose meanest wish is pure,
Far dearest is to me,
And ere I'm forced to break my faith,
I'll lay me doun an' dee.

For I hae vowed a virgin's vow
My lover's fate to share;
An' he has gi'en to me his heart,
And what can man do mair?

His mind and manners won my heart:
He gratefu' took the gift;
And did I wish to seek it back,
It wad be waur than theft.

The langest life can ne'er repay
The love he bears to me,
And ere I'm forced to break my faith,
I'll lay me doun an' dee.

## JAMES TYTLER (1747–1805)

### Lass, Gin Ye Loe Me

I hae laid a herring in saut,
Lass, gin ye loe me, tell me now.
I hae brewed a forpit o maut,
And I canna come ilka day to woo.
I hae a calf will soon be a cow;
Lass, gin ye loe me, tell me now.

I hae a pig will soon be a sow,
And I canna come ilka day to woo.

I've a house on yonder muir,
Lass, gin ye loe me, tell me now.
Three sparrows may dance upon the floor,
And I canna come ilka day to woo.
I hae a but and I hae a ben;[1]
Lass, gin ye loe me, tell me now.
I hae three chickens and a fat hen,
And I canna come ilka day to woo.

I've a hen wi' a happity leg,
Lass, gin ye loe me, tell me now,
Which ilka day lays me an egg,
And I canna come ilka day to woo.
I hae a kebbuck* upon my shelf, cheese
Lass gin ye loe me tak me now.
I downa eat it all myself;
And I winna come ony mair to woo.

## Loch Erroch Side

As I cam' by Loch Erroch side,
The lofty hills surveying,
The water clear, the heather blooms,
Their fragrance sweet conveying;
I met, unsought, my lovely maid,
I found her like May morning;
With graces sweet, and charms so rare,
Her person all adorning.

How kind her looks, how blest was I,
While in my arms I prest her.
And she her wishes scarce concealed
As fondly I caressed her.
She said, "If that your heart be true,
If constantly you'll love me,
I heed not care, nor fortune's frowns,
For nought but death shall move me.

"But faithful, loving, true, and kind
For ever shalt thou find me;
And of our meeting here so sweet
Loch Erroch sweet shall mind me."
Enraptured then, "My lovely lass,"
I cried, "no more we'll tarry.
We'll leave the fair Loch Erroch side,
For lovers soon should marry."

---

[1] An outer and inner room (i.e. a two-room house).

## The Bonnie Bruckit Lassie

The bonnie bruckit* lassie, pale
She's blue beneath the een.
She was the fairest lassie
That dansit on the green.
A lad he lo'ed her dearly,
She did his love return;
But he his vows has broken,
And left her for to mourn.

"My shape," she says, "was handsome,
My face was fair and clean:
But now I'm bonnie bruckit,
And blue beneath the een.
My eyes were bright and sparkling
Before that they turned blue;
But now they're dull wi' weeping,
And a' my love, for you.

"O could I live in darkness,
Or hide me in the sea,
Since my love is unfaithful,
And has forsaken me.
No other love I suffered
Within my breast to dwell;
In nought I have offended,
But loving him too well."

Her lover heard her mourning,
As by he chanced to pass,
And pressed unto his bosom
The lovely bruckit lass.
"My dear," he said, "cease grieving.
Since that ye lo'ed so true,
My bonnie, bruckit lassie,
I'll faithfu' prove to you."

# JOHN LOGAN (1748–1788)

## The Braes of Yarrow

Thy braes were bonny, Yarrow stream,
When first on them I met my lover.
Thy braes how dreary, Yarrow stream,
When now thy waves his body cover.
For ever now, O Yarrow stream,
Thou art to me a stream of sorrow,
For never on thy banks shall I
Behold my love, the flower of Yarrow.

He promised me a milk-white steed,
To bear me to his father's bowers;

He promised me a little page,
To squire me to his father's towers;
He promised me a wedding-ring—
The wedding-day was fixed tomorrow—
Now he is wedded to his grave,
Alas, his watery grave in Yarrow.

Sweet were his words when last we met.
My passion I as freely told him.
Clasped in his arms, I little thought
That I should never more behold him.
Scarce was he gone, I saw his ghost;
It vanished with a shriek of sorrow.
Thrice did the water-wraith ascend,
And gave a doleful groan through Yarrow.

His mother from the window looked,
With all the longing of a mother.
His little sister weeping walked
The green-wood path to meet her brother.
They sought him east, they sought him west,
They sought him all the Forest thorough.
They only saw the cloud of night,
They only heard the roar of Yarrow.

No longer from thy window look.
Thou hast no son, thou tender mother.
No longer walk, thou little maid.
Alas, thou hast no more a brother.
No longer seek him east or west,
And search no more the Forest thorough,
For, wandering in the night so dark,
He fell a lifeless corse in Yarrow.

The tear shall never leave my cheek,
No other youth shall be my marrow*; mate
I'll seek thy body in the stream,
And then with thee I'll sleep in Yarrow.
—The tear did never leave her cheek,
No other youth became her marrow:
She found his body in the stream,
And now with him she sleeps in Yarrow.

## The Complaint of Nature

Few are thy days, and full of woe,
O man, of woman born.
Thy doom is written, "Dust thou art,
And shalt to dust return."

Determined are the days that fly
Successive oer thy head.

The numbered hour is on the wing
That lays thee with the dead.

Alas, the little day of life
Is shorter than a span;
Yet black with thousand hidden ills
To miserable man.

Gay is thy morning; flattering hope
Thy sprightly step attends;
But soon the tempest howls behind,
And the dark night descends.

Before its splendid hour, the cloud
Comes oer the beam of light.
A pilgrim in a weary land,
Man tarries but a night.

Behold, sad emblem of thy state,
The flowers that paint the field,
Or trees, that crown the mountain's brow,
And boughs and blossoms yield.

When chill the blast of winter blows,
Away the summer flies,
The flowers resign their sunny robes,
And all their beauty dies.

Nipt by the year, the forest fades;
And, shaking to the wind,
The leaves toss to and fro, and streak
The wilderness behind.

The winter past, reviving flowers
Anew shall paint the plain.
The woods shall hear the voice of spring,
And flourish green again.

But man departs this earthly scene,
Ah, never to return.
No second spring shall e'er revive
The ashes of the urn.

The inexorable doors of death
What hand can e'er unfold?
Who from the cerements of the tomb
Can raise the human mold?

The mighty flood that rolls along
Its torrents to the main,
The waters lost can ne'er recall
From that abyss again.

The days, the years, the ages, dark
Descending down to night,
Can never, never be redeemed
Back to the gates of light.

So man departs the living scene,
To night's perpetual gloom.
The voice of morning ne'er shall break
The slumbers of the tomb.

Where are our fathers? whither gone
The mighty men of old?
The patriarchs, prophets, princes, kings,
In sacred books enrolled?

Gone to the resting-place of man,
The everlasting home,
Where ages past have gone before,
Where future ages come.

Thus nature poured the wail of woe,
And urged her earnest cry.
Her voice in agony extreme
Ascended to the sky.

The Almighty heard; then from his throne
In majesty he rose;
And from the heaven, that opened wide,
His voice in mercy flows.

"When mortal man resigns his breath,
And falls a clod of clay,
The soul immortal wings its flight
To never-setting day.

"Prepared of old for wicked men
The bed of torment lies.
The just shall enter into bliss
Immortal in the skies."

## JAMES GRAEME (1749–1772)

### The Mortified Genius

What now avails to gain a woman's heart
The sage's wisdom or the poet's art?
Pox on the times! the genius of old
Would whip you off a girl in spite of gold,
In spite of liv'ries, equipage and lace,
And all the Gothic grandeur of a race.
But now the mill'ner's 'prentice with a sneer,
Blessing herself, cries, "Heav'ns, what have we here?

A man of rhyme, worth—fifty lines a year."
  Our wit still pleases; but tis dev'lish hard
What saves the elegy should damn the bard;
That gains access to dressing—drawing-rooms,
A wished-for, welcome guest where'er it comes;
But me, the luckless author, scorned and poor,
Each surly porter drives from ev'ry door.
  Conscious of secret worth, I hurry home,
And now the master damn and now the dome;
Firmly resolved, whatever shall betide,
No more to ask what has been once denied;
Resolved, indeed, but ev'ry pow'r above
Laughs at our weak resolves, and chiefly Love:
"Brush the brown hat, and darn the breeches' knee;
The wealthy pride may suit, but suits not thee.
Papa, I own, looked mighty sour and grim,
But, if the daughter smile, a fig for him.
Marked you the secret motions of her eye?
How kind yon glance had been, had none been by.
Yon proud reserve, yon shyness, I could swear
Is prudence all, and pure pretense with her.
Tis right—old fellows, that can thousands give,
May claim at least some rev'rence while they live;
A few, few years lays Fuscus in his grave,
And Mira's yours perhaps, and all he gave."
  Intent on future harm, thus said the god,
Who bends the stubborn purpose with a nod,
Constrains the stiffest gladly to obey,
Makes the gay gloomy and the gloomy gay.
Resist who will, I knew too well his pow'r,
In vain resisted, to resist it more.
My hands instinctive, at the forceful call,
At once seize gloves, and hat, and staff, and all.
Then forth I walk and ever, as I go,
Con oer my manners and practice a bow;
Spread, careful spread, the cravat on my breast,
As prim and formal as a parish priest.
  The knocker clacks.—"Who's there"—"Is Miss within?"
"Confound the booby, what a monstrous din.
She has no time, she says, to speak with you,
For Mr. Florimel came here just now."
My heart beat thick, and ev'ry word he said
Distained my hollow cheeks with foreign red;
O brutish times, and is that thing of silk,
That sapless sipper of an ass's milk,
That tea-nursed grinner, whose consumptive cough,
Should he but mint a laugh, would cut him off,
Preferred to me! in whose athletic grasp
Ten thousand buzzing beaux were but a wasp.
Sure, wit and learning greater honor claim;
No wit, no learning, ever smiled on him,
I'll lay my lexicon, for all his airs,
That fellow cannot read the arms he bears,

Nor, kneeling, Mira, on his trembling knee,
Explain one half of all he says to thee.
"No matter, he has gold, whose precious hue
Is beauty, virtue, wit and learning too.
O blind to worth, what lovelier than a chaise,
Two bowing footmen and a pair of bays?
What virtue like an handsome country-seat,
A good *per annum*, and a course of plate?
And then for wit—a clever library:
He cannot read a book, but he can buy.
A fig for learning! Learning does he lack,
Whose factor both can write and sign—a tack?
Besides, you know, for ten or less *per ann.*
Even you, or any scholar, is his man."
  Bear me, ye gods, O bear me where you please,
To unknown regions, over unknown seas;
Place me where dews refreshing never drop,
On Niger's banks, a swarthy Aethiop;
Or melt me to the fashionable size,
Below the scorching heat of Indian skies.
No, there, ev'n there, the lust of gold prevails,
Each river groans with ships, each breeze with sails;
The land abounds, nay ocean's fartherst creeks,
With dirt that's sought for, or with dirt that seeks.
Fix me an icen statue at the pole,
Where winds can't carry and where waves can't roll;
To man, to greedy man, your bard prefers
White foxes, sables, ermines, cats and bears,
And all the furry monsters Greenland can call hers.
  Or is the boon too great for gods to give?
Recall the mighty word that bade me live.
So in the dust forever shall I shun
That worst of evils that affronts the sun,
A fool, whose crimes, or father's, have made great,
Spurning true genius prostrate at his feet.

## THOMAS ERSKINE (1750–1823)

[Erskine, youngest son of the Earl of Buchan, was born in Edinburgh in 1750. After a brief stint at the University of St. Andrews and some years in the military he was called to the bar in 1778. He quickly became a huge success. In 1783, he entered the House of Parliament. In 1806 he was made Lord Chancellor.

A brilliant orator, he was especially at home in the court. The following is his spirited defense of a Mr. Bingham, later the Earl of Lucan, in a 1784 trial for adultery, in which Bingham was accused of alienating the affections of Lady Elizabeth Fauconberg from her husband, the Duke of Norfolk. The marriage had been made against Lady Elizabeth's will. Notable in this speech is Erskine's position on the obligations of the upper classes.]

### In Behalf of Bingham

Gentlemen of the Jury—

My learned friend, as counsel for the plaintiff, has bespoke an address from me, as counsel for the defendant, which you must not, I assure you, expect to hear.

He has thought it right (partly in courtesy to me, as I am willing to believe, and in part for the purposes of his cause) that you should suppose you are to be addressed with eloquence which I never possessed and which, if I did, I should be incapable at this moment of exerting; because the most eloquent man, in order to exert his eloquence, must have his mind free from embarrassment on the occasion on which he is to speak. I am not in that condition. My learned friend has expressed himself as the friend of the plaintiff's family. He does not regard that family more than I do; and I stand in the same predicament toward my own honorable client and his relations. I know him and them, and because I know them, I regard them also: my embarrassment, however, only arises at being obliged to discuss this question in a public court of justice, because; could it have been the subject of private reference, I should have felt none at all in being called upon to settle it.

Gentlemen, my embarrassment is abundantly increased, when I see present a noble person, high, very high in rank in this kingdom, but not higher in rank than he is in my estimation: I speak of the noble Duke of Norfolk, who most undoubtedly must feel not a little at being obliged to come here as a witness for the defendant in the cause of a plaintiff so nearly allied to himself. I am persuaded no man can have so little sensibility, as not to feel that a person in my situation must be greatly embarrassed in discussing a question of this nature before such an audience, and between such parties as I have described.

Gentlemen, my learned friend desired you would take care not to suffer argument, or observation, or eloquence to be called into the field, to detach your attention from the evidence in the cause, upon which alone you ought to decide; I wish my learned friend, at the moment he gave you that caution, had not himself given testimony of a fact to which he stood the solitary witness. I wish he had not introduced his own evidence, without the ordinary ceremony of being sworn. I will not follow his example. I will not tell you what I know from the conversation of my client, nor give evidence of what I know myself.

My learned friend tells you that nothing can exceed the agony of mind his client has suffered, and that no words can describe his adoration of the lady he has lost: these most material points of the cause rest, however, altogether on the single, unsupported, unsworn evidence of the counsel for the plaintiff. No relation has been called upon to confirm them, though we are told that the whole house of Fauconberg, Bellasyse, and Norfolk are in the avenues of the court, ready, it seems, to be called at my discretion: and yet my learned friend is himself the only witness; though the facts (and most material facts, indeed, they would have been) might have been proved by so many illustrious persons.

Now, to show you how little disposed I am to work upon you by anything but by proof; to convince you how little desirous I am to practice the arts of speech as my only artillery in this cause, I will begin with a few plain dates, and, as you have pens in your hands, I will thank you to write them down. I shall begin with stating to you what my cause is, and shall then prove it—-not by myself, but by witnesses.

The parties were married on the 24th of April, 1789. The child that has been spoken of, and in terms which gave me great satisfaction, as the admitted son of the plaintiff, blessed with the affection of his parent, and whom the noble person to whom he may become heir can look upon without any unpleasant reflection—that child was born on the 12th of August, 1791. Take that date, and my learned friend's admission, that this child must have been the child of Mr. Howard; an admission which could not have been rationally or consistently made, but upon the implied admission that no illicit connection had existed previously by which its existence might have been referred to the defendant.

On this subject, therefore, the plaintiff must be silent. He can not say the parental mind has been wrung; he can not say hereafter, "No son of mine succeeding." He can say none of these things. This child was born on the 12th of August, 1791, and as Mr. Howard is admitted to be the author of its existence (which he must have been, if at all, in 1790), I have a right to say that, during all that interval, this gentleman could not have had the least reasonable cause of complaint against Mr. Bingham. His jealousy must, of course, have begun after that period; for, had there been grounds for it before, there could be no sense in the admission of his counsel, nor any foundation for that parental consolation which was brought forward in the very front of the cause.

The next dry date is, therefore, the 24th of July, 1793; and I put it to his Lordship, that there is no manner of evidence which can be pressed into this cause previous to that time. Let me next disembarrass the cause from another assertion of my learned friend, namely, that a divorce can not take place before the birth of this child; and that, if the child happens to be a son, which is one contingency—and if the child so born does not die, which is another contingency—and if the noble Duke dies without issue, which is a third contingency—then this child might inherit the honors of the house of Norfolk. That I deny. My recent experience tells me the contrary. In a case where Mr. Stewart, a gentleman of Ireland, stood in a similar predicament, the Lords and Commons of England not only passed an Act of Divorce between him and his lady, but, on finding there was no access on the part of the husband, and that the child was not his, they bastardized the issue.

What, then, remains in this cause? Gentlemen, there remains only this: In what manner, when you have heard my evidence (for this is a cause which, like all others must stand upon evidence), the plaintiff shall be able to prove, what I have the noble judge's authority for saying he must prove, namely the loss of the comfort and society of his wife, by the seduction of the defendant. That is the very gist of the action. The loss of her affection, and of domestic happiness, are the only legal foundations of his complaint.

Now, before any thing can be lost, it must have existed; before any thing can be taken away from a man, he must have had it; before the seduction of a woman's affections from her husband can take place, he must have possessed her affections.

Gentlemen, my friend, Mr. Mingay, acknowledges this to be the law, and he shapes his case accordingly. He represents his client, a branch of a most illustrious house, as casting the eyes of affection upon a disengaged woman, and of rank equal to, or, at least, suitable to his own. He states a marriage of mutual affection, and endeavors to show that this young couple, with all the ardor of love, flew into each other's embraces. He shows a child, the fruit of that affection, and finishes with introducing the seductive adulterer coming to disturb all this happiness, and to destroy the blessings which he describes. He exhibits the defendant coming with all the rashness and impetuosity of youth, careless of the consequences, and thinking of nothing but how be could indulge his own lustful appetite at the expense of another man's honor; while the unhappy husband is represented as watching with anxiety over his beloved wife, anxious to secure her affections, and on his guard to preserve her virtue. Gentlemen, if such a case, or anything resembling it, is established, I shall leave the defendant to whatever measure of damage you choose, in your resentment, to inflict.

In order, therefore, to examine this matter (and I shall support every syllable that I utter with the most precise and uncontrovertible proofs), I will begin with drawing up the curtains of this blessed marriage-bed, whose joys are supposed to have been nipped in the bud by the defendant's adulterous seduction.

Nothing, certainly, is more delightful to the human fancy than the possession of a beautiful woman in the prime of health and youthful passion; it is beyond all doubt the highest enjoyment which God, in his benevolence, and for the wisest purposes, has bestowed upon his own image. I reverence, as I ought, that mysterious union of mind and body which, while it continues our species, is the source of all our affections; which builds up and dignifies the condition of human life; which binds the husband to the wife by ties more indissoluble than laws can possibly create, and which, by the reciprocal endearments arising from a mutual passion, a mutual interest, and a mutual honor, lays the foundation of that parental affection which dies in the brutes with the necessities of nature, but which reflects back again upon the human parents the unspeakable sympathies of their offspring, and all the sweet, delightful relations of social existence.

While the curtains, therefore, are yet closed upon this bridal scene, your imaginations will naturally represent to you this charming woman endeavoring to conceal sensations which modesty forbids the sex, however enamored, too openly to reveal, wishing, beyond adequate expression, what she must not even attempt to express, and seemingly resisting what she burns to enjoy.

Alas, gentlemen, you must now prepare to see in the room of this a scene of horror and of sorrow. You must prepare to see a noble lady, whose birth surely required no further illustration; who had been courted to marriage before she ever heard even her husband's name; and whose affections were irretrievably bestowed upon, and pledged to my honorable and unfortunate client; you must behold her given up to the plaintiff by the infatuation of parents, and stretched upon this bridal-bed as upon a rack; torn from the arms of a beloved and impassioned youth, himself of noble birth, only to secure the honors of a higher title; a legal victim on the altar of Heraldry.

Gentlemen, this is no high coloring for the purposes of a cause; no words of an advocate can go beyond the plain, unadorned effect of the evidence. I will prove to you that when she prepared to retire to her chamber she threw her desponding arms around the neck of her confidential attendant, and wept upon her as a criminal preparing for execution. I will prove to you that she met her bridegroom with sighs and tears—the sighs and tears of afflicted love for Mr. Bingham, and of rooted aversion to her husband.

I think I almost hear her addressing him in the language of the poet—

I tell thee, Howard,
Such hearts as ours were never paired above:
Ill suited to each other; joined, not matched;
Some sullen influence, a foe to both,
Has wrought this fatal marriage to undo us.
Mark but the frame and temper of our minds,
How very much we differ. Ev'n this day,
That fills thee with such ecstasy and transport,
To me brings nothing that should make me bless it,
To think it better than the day before,
Or any other in the course of time,
That duly took its turn, and was forgotten.

Gentlemen, this was not the sudden burst of youthful disappointment but the fixed and settled habit of a mind deserving of a happier fate. I shall prove that she frequently spent her nights upon a couch, in her own apartments, dissolved in tears; that she frequently declared to her woman that she would rather go to Newgate than to Mr. Howard's bed; and it will appear, by his own confession that for months subsequent to the marriage she obstinately refused him the privileges of a husband.

To all this, it will be said by the plaintiff's counsel (as it has, indeed, been hinted already) that disgust and alienation from her husband could not but be expected; but that it arose from her affection for Mr. Bingham. Be it so gentlemen. I readily admit, that if Mr. Bingham's acquaintance with the lady had commenced subsequent to the marriage, the argument would be irresistible, and the criminal conclusion against him unanswerable.

But has Mr. Howard a right to instruct his counsel to charge my honorable client with seduction, when he himself was the seducer? My learned friend deprecates the power of what he terms my pathetic eloquence. Alas, gentlemen, if I possessed it, the occasion forbids its exertion, because Mr. Bingham has only to defend himself, and can not demand damages from Mr. Howard for depriving him of what was his by a title superior to any law which man bas a moral right to make. Mr. Howard was never married! God and nature forbid the bans of such a marriage. If, therefore, Mr. Bingham this day could have, by me, addressed to you his wrongs in the character of a plaintiff demanding reparation, what damages might I not have asked for him; and, without the aid of this imputed eloquence, what damages might I not have expected?

I would have brought before you a noble youth, who had fixed his affections upon one of the most beautiful of her sex, and who enjoyed hers in return. I would have shown you their suitable condition; I would have painted the expectation of an honorable union; and would have concluded by showing her to you in the arms of another, by the legal prostitution of parental choice in the teeth of affection; with child by a rival, and only reclaimed at last, after so cruel and so afflicting a divorce, with her freshest charms despoiled, and her very morals in a manner impeached, by asserting the purity and virtue of her original and spotless choice. Good God! imagine my client to be plaintiff, and what damages are you not prepared to give him? and yet he is here as defendant and damages are demanded against him. Oh, monstrous conclusion!

Gentlemen, considering my client as perfectly safe under these circumstances, I may spare a moment to render this cause beneficial to the public.

It involves in it an awful lesson; and more instructive lessons are taught in courts of justice than the Church is able to inculcate. Morals come in the cold abstract from pulpit; but men smart under them practically when we lawyers are the preachers.

Let the aristocracy of England, which trembles so much for itself, take heed to its own security. Let the nobles of England, if they mean to preserve that pre-eminence which, in some shape or other, must exist in every social community, take care to support it by aiming at that which is creative, and alone creative, of real superiority. Instead of matching themselves to supply wealth, to be again idly squandered in debauching excesses, or to round the quarters of a family shield; instead of continuing their names and honors in cold and alienated embraces, amid the enervating rounds of shallow dissipation, let them live as their fathers of old lived before them. Let them marry as affection and prudence lead the way, and in the ardors of mutual love, and in the simplicities of rural life, let them lay the foundation of a vigorous race of men, firm in their bodies, and moral from early habits; and instead of wasting their fortunes and their strength in the tasteless circles of debauchery, let them light up their magnificent and hospitable halls to the gentry and peasantry of the country, extending the consolations of wealth and influence to the poor.

Let them but do this; and, instead of those dangerous and distracting divisions between the different ranks of life, and those jealousies of the multitude so often blindly painted as big with destruction, we should see our country as one large and harmonious family, which can never be accomplished amid vice and corruption, by wars or treaties, by informations *ex officio* for libels, or by any of the tricks and artifices of the state. Would to God this system had been followed in the instance before us! Surely the noble house of Fauconberg needed no further illustration; nor the still nobler house of Howard, with blood enough to have inoculated half the kingdom. I desire to be understood to make these observations as general moral reflections, and not personally to the families in question; least of all to the noble house of Norfolk, the head of which is now present; since no man, in my opinion, has more at heart the liberty of the subject and the honor of our country.

Having shown the feeble expectation of happiness from this marriage, the next point to be considered is this: Did Mr. Bingham take advantage of that circumstance to increase the disunion? I answer, No. I will prove to you that he conducted himself with a moderation and restraint, and with a command over his passions, which I confess I did not expect to find, and which in young men is not to be expected. I shall prove to you, by Mr. Grevillet that, on this marriage taking place with the betrothed object of his affections, he went away a desponding man. His health declined; he retired into the country to restore it; and it will appear that for months afterward he never saw this lady until by mere accident he met her. And then, so far was he from endeavoring to renew his connection with her, that she came home in tears, and said he frowned at her as he passed. This I shall prove to you by the evidence in the cause.

Gentlemen, that is not all. It will appear that, when he returned to town, he took no manner of notice of her; and that her unhappiness was beyond all power of expression. How, indeed, could it be otherwise, after the account I have given you of the marriage? I shall prove, besides, by a gentleman who married one of the daughters of a person to whom this country is deeply indebted for his eminent and meritorious service that, from her utter reluctance to her husband, although in every respect honorable and correct in his manners and behavior, he was not allowed even the privileges of a husband, for months after the marriage. This I mentioned to you before, and only now repeat it in the statement of the proofs. Nothing better, indeed, could be expected. Who can control the will of a mismatched, disappointed woman? Who can restrain or direct her passions? I beg leave to assure Mr. Howard (and I hope he will believe me when I say it), that I think his conduct toward this lady was just such as might have been expected from a husband who saw himself to be the object of disgust to the woman he had chosen for his wife, and it is with this view only that I shall call a gentleman to say how Mr. Howard spoke of this supposed, but, in my mind, impossible object of his adoration.

How, indeed, is it possible to adore a woman when you know her affections are riveted to another? It is unnatural! A man may have that appetite which is common to the brutes, and too indelicate to be described; but he can never retain an affection which is returned with detestation. Lady Elizabeth, I understand, was, at one time going out in a phaeton. "There she goes," said Mr. Howard; "God damn her—-I wish she may break her neck; I should take care how I got another." This may seem unfeeling behavior; but in Mr. Howard's situation, gentlemen, it was the most natural thing in the world, for they cordially hated one another.

At last, however, the period arrived when this scene of discord became insupportable, and nothing could exceed the generosity and manly feeling of the noble person[1] whose name I have been obliged to use in the course of this cause, in his interference to effect that separation which is falsely imputed to Mr. Bingham. He felt so much commiseration for this unhappy lady, that he wrote to her in the most affecting style. I believe I have got a letter from his Grace to Lady Elizabeth, dated Sunderland, July the 27th, that is, three days after their separation; but before be knew it had actually taken place; it was written in consequence of one received from Mr. Howard upon the subject.

Among other things be says, "I sincerely feel for you." Now if the Duke had not known at that time that Mr. Bingham had her earliest and legitimate affections, she could not have been an object of that pity which she received. She was, indeed, an object of the sincerest pity; and the sum and substance of this mighty seduction will

---

[1]That is, the Duke of Norfolk.

turn out to be no more than this, that she was affectionately received by Mr. Bingham after the final period of voluntary separation. At four o'clock this miserable couple had parted by consent and the chaise was not ordered till she might be considered as a single woman by the abandonment of her husband.

Had this separation been legal and formal I should have applied to his Lordship, upon the most unquestionable authorities, to nonsuit the plaintiff; for this action being founded upon the loss of the wife's society, it must necessarily fall to the ground if it appeared that the society, though not the marriage union, was interrupted by a previous act of his own. In that hour of separation, I am persuaded he never considered Mr. Bingham as an object of resentment or reproach. He was the author of his own misfortunes, and I can conceive him to have exclaimed, in the language of the poet, as they parted,

> Elizabeth never loved me.
> Let no man, after me, a woman wed
> Whose heart he knows he has not; though she brings
> A mine of gold, a kingdom, for her dowry.
> For let her seem, like the night's shadowy queen,
> Cold and contemplative—he can not trust her.
> She may, she will, bring shame and sorrow on him;
> The worst of sorrows, and the worst of shames.

You have, therefore, before you, gentlemen, two young men of fashion, both of noble families, and in the flower of youth: the proceedings, though not collusive, can not possibly be vindictive; they are indispensibly preliminary to the dissolution of an inauspicious marriage, which never should have existed. Mr. Howard may, then, profit by a useful though an unpleasant experience, and be happier with a woman whose mind he may find disengaged; while the parents of the rising generation, taking warning from the lesson which the business of the day so forcibly teaches, may avert from their families, and the public, that bitterness of disunion, which, while human nature continues to be itself, will ever be produced to the end of time, from similar conjunctures.

Gentlemen, I have endeavored so to conduct this cause as to offend no man. I have guarded against every expression which could inflict unnecessary pain; and, in doing so I know that I have not only served my client's interest, but truly represented his honorable and manly disposition.

As the case before you can not be considered by any reasonable man as an occasion for damages, I might here properly conclude. Yet, that I may omit nothing which might apply to any possible view of the subject, I will close by reminding you that my client is a member of a numerous family; that, though Lord Lucan's fortune is considerable, his rank calls for a corresponding equipage and expense; be has other children—-one already married to an illustrious nobleman, another yet to be married to some man who must be happy indeed if he shall know her value. Mr. Bingham, therefore, is a man of no fortune; but the heir only of, I trust, a very distant expectation.

Under all these circumstances, it is but fair to believe that Mr. Howard comes here for the reasons I have assigned, and not to take money out of the pocket of Mr. Bingham to put into his own. You will, therefore, consider, gentlemen, whether it would be creditable for you to offer what it would be disgraceful for Mr. Howard to receive.[1]

---

[1]Despite this brilliant plea, the judge's subsequent instructions to the jury were such that they could not but bring damages against Bingham, which they did, for five hundred pounds. That sum, given the circumstances and the rank of the two contestants, indicates the jury sided, in fact, with Erskine's client.

## ROBERT FERGUSSON (1750–1774)

[Fergusson is Scotland's most neglected major poet. One reason for his lack of fame, even in Scotland, is that he wrote chiefly in Scots at a time when that was not yet acceptable—certainly not for serious poetry. Another is that he died so young, at not quite twenty-four, that his poetic personality had no chance to establish itself with the reading public.

Fergusson, a resident of Edinburgh—now one of the intellectual centers of Europe—with some years of university behind him, and much acquaintance with the philosophical and artistic circles of the former capital, was a relative sophisticate who wrote poems in both English and Scots. The latter are the sole source of his reputation. The Scots poems are vigorous, often rollicking expressions of Edinburgh communal life, with a heavy emphasis upon "street-people," and upon the rhythms of the seasons as a city dweller would experience them. Their tone is both racy and wry—a combination which Burns would echo just a few years later. Fergusson's detached irony and his urban settings may have prevented him from profiting from the pastoral, pre-Romantic interest in the "common man" which was to prove so valuable to Burns. He does lack Burns' musical talents and his knack for the memorable phrase, but Fergusson is one of the most gifted of Scottish eighteenth century poets, and his influence on Burns was significant and salutary. The younger poet acknowledged a major debt to his predecessor. "Auld Reikie," a properly ambiguous tribute to the great Scottish capital, is Fergusson's longest poem, and probably his masterpiece.]

### The Daft Days[1]

Now mirk December's dowie* face  sad
Glow'rs owre the rigs* wi' sour grimace,  fields
While, through his minimum o' space
The bleer-e'ed sun,
Wi' blinkin' light and stealin' pace,
His race doth run.

Frae naked groves nae birdie sings;
To shepherd's pipe nae hillock rings;
The breeze nae od'rous flavor brings
Frae Borean cave;
And dwynin' Nature droops her wings,
Wi' visage grave.

Mankind but scanty pleasure glean
Frae snawy hill or barren plain,
Whan Winter, midst his nippin' train,
Wi' frozen spear,
Sends drift owre a' his bleak domain,
And guides the weir*.  war, struggle

Auld Reikie,[2] thou'rt the canty* hole;  pleasant
A bield* for mony a cauldrife* soul,  shelter/chilly
Wha snugly at thine ingle* loll,  fireside

---

[1] Christmas holidays.

[2] "Old Smoky"—Edinburgh.

Baith warm and couth*; cosy
While round they gar the bicker* roll, beaker
To weet their mouth.

Whan merry Yule-day comes, I trow*, trust
You'll scantlins find a hungry mou;
Sma' are our cares, our stamacks fou* "full"
O' gusty* gear, tasty
And kickshaws*, strangers to our view "quelques-choses"
Sin' fairn-year*. last year

Ye browster wives, now busk* ye braw, dress
And fling your sorrows far awa;
Then, come and gie's the tither blaw
O' reaming* ale. foaming
Mair precious than the well o' Spa,
Our hearts to heal.

Then, though at odds wi' a' the warl',
Amang oursels we'll never quarrel;
Though discord gie a cankered snarl,
To spoil our glee,
As lang's there's pith* into the barrel, strength
We'll drink and gree*. "agree"

Fiddlers, your pins in temper fix,
And roset weel your fiddlesticks;
But banish vile Italian tricks
Frae out your quorum;
Nor fortes wi' pianos mix;—
Gie's Tullochgorum.[1]

For nought can cheer the heart sae weel,
As can a canty* Highland reel; lively
It even vivifies the heel
To skip and dance:
Lifeless is he wha canna feel
Its influence.

Let mirth abound; let social cheer
Invest the dawnin' o' the year;
Let blithesome innocence appear,
To crown our joy:
Nor envy, wi' sarcastic sneer,
Our bliss destroy.

And thou, great god of aquavitae*. whiskey
Wha sways the empire o' this city;—
Whan fou, we're sometimes capernoity*;— muddled, peevish
Be thou prepared

[1] A popular air.

To hedge us frae that black banditti,
The City Guard.

## Braid Claith

Ye wha are fain to hae your name
Wrote in the bonny book of fame,
Let merit nae pretension claim
To laureled wreath,
But hap* ye weel, baith back and wame*, — clothe/stomach
In gude Braid Claith.

He that some ells o' this may fa,
An' slae-black hat on pow* like snaw, — head
Bids bauld to bear the gree* awa', — prize, rank
Wi' a' this graith*, — equipment
Whan bienly clad wi' shell fu' braw
O' gude Braid Claith.

Waesuck* for him wha has nae fek* o't. — pity/amount
For he's a gowk* they're sure to geck* at, — fool/sneer
A chiel* that ne'er will be respekit — base fellow
While he draws breath,
Till his four quarters are bedeckit
Wi' gude Braid Claith.

On Sabbath-days the barber spark,
When he has done wi' scrapin wark,
Wi' siller broachie in his sark,
Gangs trigly*, faith, — smartly
Or to the Meadow, or the Park,
In gude Braid Claith.

Weel might ye trow, to see them there,
That they to shave your haffits* bare, — side whiskers
Or curl an' sleek a pickle* hair, — little
Would be right laith*, — "loath"
Whan pacing wi' a gawsy* air — proud
In gude Braid Claith.

If ony mettled stirrah* green* — gallant/long
For favor frae a lady's een
He maunna care for being seen
Before he sheath
His body in a scabbard clean
O' gude Braid Claith.

For, gin* he come wi' coat thread-bare, — if
A feg for him she winna care,
But crook her bonny mou'fu' sair,
And scald him baith.

Wooers should ay their travel spare
Without Braid Claith.

Braid Claith lends fock an unco heese*, uplift
Makes many kail*-worms butter-flies, cabbage
Gies mony a doctor his degrees
For little skaith*: effort
In short, you may be what you please
Wi' gude Braid Claith.

For though ye had as wise a snout on
As Shakespeare or Sir Isaac Newton,
Your judgment fouk would hae a doubt on,
I'll tak my aith,
Till they could see ye wi' a suit on
O' gude Braid Claith.

## Ode to the Gowdspink

Frae fields whare Spring her sweets has blawn,
Wi' cauler* verdure owre the lawn, fresh
The Gowdspink* comes, in new attire, goldfinch
The brawest mang the whistling choir,
That, ere the sun can clear his een,
Wi' glib notes sain* the Simmer's green. bless
Sure Nature herried mony a tree,
For sprainings* and bonnie spats to thee. stripes
Nae mair the rainbow can impart
Sic glowin' ferlies* o' her art, wonders
Whase pencil wrought its freaks at will
On thee, the sey-piece* o' her skill. showpiece
Nae mair through straths in Simmer dight
We seek the rose to bless our sight;
Or bid the bonnie wa'-flowers sprout
On yonder ruin's lofty snout.
Thy shining garments far outstrip
The cherries upo' Hebe's lip,
And fool the tints that Nature chose,
To busk* and paint the crimson rose. dress

Mang men, wae's heart, we aften find
The brawest dressed want peace o' mind;
While he that gangs wi' ragged coat
Is weel contented wi' his lot.
Whan wand wi' gluey birdlime's set,
To steal far off your dautit* mate, cherished
Blithe wad you change your cleeding gay
In lieu of lav'rock's* sober gray. lark's
In vain, through woods, you sair may ban*. curse
The envious treachery o' man,
That, wi' your gowden glister ta'en,
Still haunts you on the Simmer's plain,

And traps you mang the sudden fa's,
O' Winter's dreary dreepin, snaws.
Now steekit* frae the gowany* field, shut off/daisied
Frae ilka fav'rite houff* and bield* resort/shelter
But mergh*, alas, to disengage weakened
Your bonnie buik* frae fett'ring cage, bulk
Your freeborn bosom beats in vain,
For darlin' liberty again.
In window hung, how aft we see
Thee keek* around at warblers free, peek
That carol saft, and sweetly sing
Wi' a' the blithness o' the Spring?
Like Tantalus they hing you here
To spy the glories o' the year;
And, though you're at the burnie's brink,
They downa suffer you to drink.

Ah, Liberty, thou bonnie dame,
How wildly wanton is thy stream,
Round whilk the birdies a' rejoice,
And hail you wi' a gratefu' voice.
The Gowdspink chatters joyous here,
And courts wi' gleesome sangs his peer.
The mavis*, frae the new-bloomed thorn, thrush
Begins his lauds at earest morn;
And herd louns*, louping owre the grass, yokels
Need far less fleetching* to their lass, flattering
Than paughty* damsels bred at courts, saucy
Wha throw their mou's and tak' the dorts*; pets
But, reft of thee, fient* flee* we care scarcely/a jot
For a' that life ahint can spare.
The Gowdspink, that sae lang has kenned
Thy happy sweets (thy wonted friend),
Her sad confinement ill can brook
In some dark chaumer's dowie* nook; gloomy
Though Mary's hand his neb supplies,
Unkenned to hunger's painfu' cries.
Ev'n beauty canna cheer the heart
Frae life, frae liberty apart;
For now we tyne* its wonted lay, lose
Sae lightsome sweet, sae blithely gay.
Thus Fortune aft a curse can gi'e
To wile us far frae liberty:
Then tent* her siren smiles wha list, care
I'll ne'er envy your girnel's* grist; granary's
For whan fair Freedom smiles nae mair,
Care I for life? Shame fa' the hair*. trifle
A field oer grown wi' rankest stubble,
The essence of a paltry bubble.

## The Farmer's Ingle

Whan gloamin' gray out-owre the welkin keeks*; — peeks
Whan Batie ca's his owsen to the byre*; — barn
When Thrasher John, sair dung*, his barn-door steeks*, — beaten/shuts
And lustly lasses at the dightin*' tire; — corn-cleaning
What bangs* fu' leal the e'enings coming cauld, — overcomes
And gars snaw-tappit Winter freeze in vain;
Gars dowie* mortals look baith blithe and bauld, — sad
Nor fleyed wi' a' the poortith* o' the plain; — poverty
Begin, my Muse and chant in hamely strain.

Frae the big stack, weel winnow't on the hill,
Wi' divots theekit* frae the weet and drift; — thatched
Sods, peats, and heathery turfs the chimley fill,
And gar their thickening smeek salute the lift*. — sky
The gudeman, new come hame, is blithe to find,
Whan he out-owre the hallan* flings his een, — partition
That ilka turn is handled to his mind;
That a' his housie looks sae cosh* and clean; — snug
For cleanly house loes he, though e'er sae mean.

Weel kens the gudewife, that the pleughs require
A heartsome meltith*, and refreshin' synd* — meal/draught
O' nappy* liquor, owre a bleezin' fire. — foaming
Sair wark and poortith downa weel be joined.
Wi' buttered bannocks now the girdle reeks;
I' the far nook the bowie* briskly reams; — cask
The readied kail* stands by the chimley cheeks, — cabbage, broth
And haud the riggin*' bet wi' welcome streams, — rafters
Whilk than the daintiest kitchen* nicer seems. — relish

Frae this, lat gentler gabs* a lesson lear: — mouths
Wad they to labouring lend an eident* hand, — eager, diligent
They'd rax* fell strang upo' the simplest fare, — prosper
Nor find their stamacks ever at a stand.
Fu' hale and healthy wad they pass the day;
At night, in calmest slumbers dose fu' sound;
Nor doctor need their weary life to spae*, — predict
Nor drogs their noddle and their sense confound,
Till death slip sleely on, and gie the hindmost wound.

On sicken* food has mony a doughty deed — such
By Caledonia's ancestors been done;
By this did mony a wight fu' weirlike bleed
In brulzies* frae the dawn to set o' sun. — broils
Twas this that braced their gardies* stiff and strang; — arms
That bent the deadly yew in ancient days;
Laid Denmark's daring sons on yird* alang; — earth
Gar'd Scottish thristles bang the Roman bays;
For near our crest their heads they doughtna raise.

The couthy cracks* begin when supper's owre; jests, chat
The cheering bicker gars them glibly gash* gab
O' Simmer's showery blinks, and Winter sour,
Whase floods did erst their mailin's* produce hash. farm's
Bout kirk and market eke their tales gae on;
How Jock woo'd Jenny here to be his bride;
And there, how Marion, for a bastard son,
Upo' the cutty-stool was forced to ride;
The waefu' scould o' our Mess John* to bide. (minister)

The fient* a cheep's amang the bairnies now; devil
For a' their anger's wi' their hunger gane.
Ay maun the childer, wi' a fastin mou,
Grumble and greet*, and mak an unco* mane. weep/great
In rangles* round, before the ingle's lowe*, groups/fire
Frae Gudame's* mouth auld-warld tales they hear, grandmother's
O' warlocks loupin round the wirrikow*: evil spirit
O' ghaists that win* in glen and kirkyard drear, live
Whilk touzles a' their tap*, and gars them shake wi' fear! hair

For weel she trows that fiends and fairies be
Sent frae the deil to fleetch* us to our ill; wheedle
That kye hae tint their milk wi' evil ee;
And corn been scowdered* on the glowin kill. scorched
O mock na this, my friends, but rather mourn,
Ye in life's brawest spring wi' reason clear;
Wi' eild* our idle fancies a' return, age
And dim our dolefu' days wi' bairnly fear;
The mind's ay cradled whan the grave is near.

Yet thrift, industrious, bides her latest days,
Though age her sair-dowed* front wi' runcles* wave; faded/ "wrinkles"
Yet frae the russet lap the spindle plays;
Her e'enin stent reels she as weel's the lave.
On some feast-day, the wee things, buskit* braw, dressed
Shall heeze* her heart up wi' a silent joy, lift
Fu' cadgie* that her head was up, and saw proud
Her ain spun cleedin* on a darlin oy*; clothing/grandchild
Careless though death should mak the feast her foy*. farewell

In its auld lerroch* yet the deas* remains, place/couch
Whare the gudeman aft streeks him at his ease;
A warm and canny lean for weary banes
O' lab'rers doiled* upon the wintry leas. tried
Round him will baudrins* and the collie come, (the cat)
To wag their tail, and cast a thankfu' ee
To him wha kindly flings them mony a crumb
O' kebbuck* whanged, and dainty fadge* to prie; cheese/bread
This a' the boon they crave, and a' the fee.

Frae him the lads their mornin' counsel tak;
What stacks he wants to thrash; what rigs to till;
How big a birn* maun lie on Bassie's* back, weight/(the horse's)

For meal and mu'ter* to the thirlin* mill. feegrinding/bound
Neist, the gudewife her hirelin damsels bids
Glow'r through the byre, and see the hawkies* bound; cattle
Tak tent, 'case Crummy tak her wonted tids*, impulses
And ca' the laiglen's* treasure on the ground, milk-pail
Whilk spills a kebbuck nice, or yellow pound.

Than a' the house for sleep begin to grien*, wish
Their joints to slack frae industry a-while;
The leaden god fa's heavy on their een,
And hafflins* steeks them frae their daily toil; half-way
The cruizie* too can only blink and bleer; lamp
The restit ingle's done the maist it dow*; can
Tacksman and cotter eke to bed maun steer,
Upo' the cod* to clear their drumly* pow, pillow/dull
Till waukened by the dawnin's ruddy glow.

Peace to the husbandman and a' his tribe,
Whase care fells a' our wants frae year to year.
Lang may his sock* and cou'ter turn the glebe, plowshare
And bauks* o' corn bend down wi' laded ear. ridges
May Scotia's simmers ay look gay and green;
Her yellow har'sts* frae scowry* blasts decreed. harvests/showery
May a' her tenants sit fu' snug and bien*, cosy
Frae the hard grip o' ails, and poortith freed;
And a lang lasting train o' peacefu' hours succeed.

## The Rising of the Sessions

To a' men living be it kend,
The session now is at an end.
Writers, your finger-nebs unbend,
And quat the pen,
Till time wi' lyart* pow* shall send hoary/head
Blythe June again.

Tired o' the law, and a' its phrases,
The wylie writers, rich as Croesus,
Hurl frae the town in hackney chaises,
For country cheer.
The powny that in spring-time grazes,
Thrives a' the year.

Ye lawyers, bid fareweel to lies,
Fareweel to din, fareweel to fees,
The canny hours o' rest may please
Instead o' siller.
Hained multer* hads the mill at ease, meal
And finds the miller.

Blyth they may be wha wanton play
In fortune's bonny blinkin ray,

Fu' weel can they ding* dool* away strike/dole
Wi' comrades couthy,
And never dree* a hungert day, endure
Or e'ening drouthy*. thirsty

Ohon the day for him that's laid,
In dowie* poortith's* caldrife shade, sad/poverty's
Ablins* owr honest for his trade, perhaps
He racks his wits,
How he may get his buick weel clad,
And fill his guts.

The farmers sons, as yap* as sparrows, bold
Are glad, I trow, to flee the barras*, enclosure
And whistle to the plough and harrows
At barley seed.
What writer wadna gang as far as
He cou'd for bread.

After their yokin, I wat weel
They'll stoo* the kebbuck* to the heel*; nibble/cheese/rind
Eith* can the plough-stilts gar a chiel easily
Be unco vogie*, glad
Clean to lick aff his crowdy-meal,
And scart* his cogie*. scrape/plate

Now mony a fallow's dung adrift
To a' the blasts beneath the lift,
And though their stamack's aft in tift
In vacance time,
Yet seenil* do they ken the rift seldom
O' stappit wame*. belly

Now gin* a notar shou'd be wanted, if
You'll find the pillars gayly planted;
For little thing protests are granted
Upo' a bill,
And weightiest matters covenanted
For haf a gill*. glass, drink

Nae body takes a morning dribb
O Halland gin frae Robin Gibb;
And though a dram to Rob's mair sib
Than is his wife,
He maun take time to daut* his rib pet
Till siller's rife.

This vacance is a heavy doom
On Indian Peter's coffee-room,
For a' his china pigs are toom*; empty
Nor do we see
In wine the sucker biskets soom* "swim"
As light's a flee.

But stop, my Muse, nor make a main*, "moan"
Pate disna fend on that alane;
He can fell twa dogs wi ae bane*, "bone"
While ither fock
Maun rest themselves content wi' ane,
Nor farer trock*. deal

Ye changehouse keepers never grumble
Though you a while your bickers whumble*, turn down
Be unco patientfu' and humble,
Nor make a din,
Though gude joot* binna kend to rumble liquor
Your weym within.

You needna grudge to draw your breath
For little mair than haf a reath,
Than, gin we a' be spared frae death,
We'll gladly prie* taste, prove
Fresh noggans o' your reaming graith* goods
Wi' blythsome glee.

## Leith Races

In July month, ae bonnie morn,
Whan Nature's rokelay* green cloak
Was spread owre ilka rig o' corn,
To charm our rovin' een,
Glow'ring about, I saw a quean* girl
The fairest neath the lift*: sky
Her een were o' the siller sheen;
Her skin, like snawy drift,
Sae white that day.

Quo' she, "I ferly* unco sair wonder
That ye sould musand gae,
Ye wha hae sung o' Hallowfair,
Her winter's pranks, and play;
When on Leith sands the racers rare
Wi' jockey louns* are met, fellows, rascals
Their orrow* pennies there to ware, odd
And drown themsel's in debt
Fu' deep that day."

"And wha are ye, my winsome dear,
That tak's the gate sae early?
Whare do ye win*, gin ane may speer*, live/ask
For I right meikle ferly
That sic braw buskit* laughin' lass dressed
Thir bonnie blinks* should gi'e, glances
And loup, like Hebe, owre the grass,
As wanton and as free
Frae dule this day?"

"I dwall amang the cauler* springs    fresh
That weet the Land o' Cakes,
And aften tune my canty* strings    lively
At bridals and late-wakes.
They ca' me Mirth:—I ne'er was kenned
To grumble or look sour;
But blithe wad be a lift to lend,
Gif ye wad sey my power
    And pith this day."

"A bargain be't; and, by my fegs!
Gif ye will be my mate,
Wi' you I'll screw the cheery pegs;
Ye shanna find me blate*:    shy
We'll reel and ramble through the sands,
And jeer wi' a' we meet;
Nor hip* the daft and gleesome bands    miss
That fill Edina's* street    (Edinburgh's)
    Sae thrang* this day."    busy

Ere servant-maid had wont to rise
To seethe the breakfast kettle,
Ilk dame her brawest ribbons tries,
To put her on her mettle,
Wi' wiles some silly chiel* to trap,    lad
(And troth he's fain to get her)
But she'll craw kniefly* in his crap*,    spiritedly/belly
Whan, wow! he canna flit her
    Frae hame that day.

Now, mony a scawed* and bare-arsed loun    pimply
Rise early to their wark;
Eneugh to fley a meikle town,
Wi' dinsome squeal and bark:
"Here is the true and faithfu' list
O' noblemen and horses;
Their eild*, their weight, their hight, their grist*,    age/price
That rin for plates or purses
    Fu' fleet this day."

To whisky plooks* that brunt for ouks*    pimples/ "weeks"
On town-guard sodgers' faces,
Their barber bauld his whittle crooks,
And scrapes them for the races.
Their stumps*, erst used to filibegs,    legs
Are dight in spatterdashes,
Whase barkent* hides scarce fend their legs    crusted
Frae weet and weary plashes
    O' dirt that day.

"Come, hafe a care," the Captain cries,
"On guns your bagnets* thraw*;    bayonets/twist
Now mind your manual exercise,

And marsh down raw by raw."
And, as they march, he'll glower about,
Tent a' their cuts and scars;
Mang them fell mony a gaucy* snout   big-looking
Has gusht in birth-day wars
Wi' bluid that day.

Her nainsel* maun be carefu' now,   own self
Nor maun she be mislear'd,
Sin' baxter* lads hae sealed a vow   baker
To skelp and clout the guard.[1]
I'm sure Auld Reekie kens o' nane
That would be sorry at it,
Though they should dearly pay the kane*,   price, rent
And get their tails weel sautit,
And sair, thir days.

The tinkler* billies* i' the Bow   tinsmith/fellows
Are now less eident* clinkin';   diligently
As lang's their pith or siller dow*,   lasts
They're daffin'*, and they're drinkin'.   fooling
Bedown Leith Walk what burrachs* reel   crowds
O' ilka trade and station,
That gar their wives and childer feel
Toom* wames*, for their libation   empty/bellies
O' drink thir days!

The browster* wives thegither harl*   brewer/drag
A' trash that they can fa' on;
They tak' the grounds o' ilka barrel,
To profit by the lawin'*:   reckoning
For weel wat they, a skin leal het
For drinkin' needs nae hire:
At drumly gear they tak' nae pet;
Foul water slokens fire
And drouth* thir days.   thirst

They say, ill ale has been the dead
O' mony a beirdly* loun;   strong
Then dinna gape like gleds*, wi' greed,   kites
To sweel hale bickers doun.
Gin Lord send mony ane the morn,
They'll ban* fu' sair the time   curse
That e'er they toutit aff the horn
Which wambles* through their wame   waves
Wi' pain that day.

The Buchan bodies through the beach
Their bunch of Findrams* cry;   smoked haddock
And skirl out bauld, in Norlan' speech,

[1]The City Guard (the police).

"Guid speldings*;—fa will buy?" (a fish)
And, by my saul, they're nae wrang gear
To gust* a stirrah's mou'; please
Weel staw'd wi' them, he'll never speer* ask
The price o' being fu'
    Wi' drink that day.

Now wily wights at rowly powl,[1]
And flingin' o' the dice,
Here brak' the banes o' mony a soul
Wi' fa's upo' the ice.
At first, the gate* seems fair and straught; way
Sae they ha'd fairly till her;
But wow! in spite o' a' their maught,
They're rookit o' their siller
    And gowd thir days.

Around whare'er you fling your een
The haiks*, like wind, are scourin': horses
Some chaises honest folk contain,
And some hae mony a whore in.
Wi' rose and lily, red and white,
They gi'e themsel's sic fit airs;
Like Dian, they will seem perfite;
But it's nae gowd that glitters
    Wi' them thir days.

The Lion here, wi' open paw,
May cleek* in mony hunder, hook
Wha geck* at Scotland and her law, sneer
His wily talons under.
For ken, though Jamie's laws are auld,
(Thanks to the wise recorder)
His lion yet roars loud and bauld,
To ha'd the Whigs in order
    Sae prime this day.

To town-guard drum of clangour clear,
Baith men and steeds are rangit:
Some liveries red or yellow wear,
And some are tartan spraingit*. striped
And now the red,—the blue e'en now, —
Bids fairest for the market;
But, ere the sport be done, I trow,
Their skins are gaily yarkit* beaten
    And peeled thir days.

Siclike in Robin Hood debates,
When twa chiels hae a pingle*; argument
E'en now, some coulie* gets his aits, "collegian"

---

[1]Ninepins.

And dirt wi' words they mingle;
Till up loups he, wi' diction fu',
There's lang and dreich contestin';
For now they're near the point in view,
Now ten miles frae the question
In hand that night.

The races owre, they hale* the dules "heal"
Wi' drink o' a' kinkind;
Great feck gae hirpling* hame, like fules; limping
The cripple lead the blind.
May ne'er the canker o' the drink
Mak' our bauld spirits thrawart,
'Case we get wharewitha' to wink
Wi' een as blue's a blawart
Wi' straiks* thir days! "strokes"

## Elegy on the Death of Scots Music

On Scotia's plains, in days of yore,
When lads and lasses tartan wore,
Saft music rang on ilka* shore every
In hamely weid;
But harmony is now no more,
And music dead.

Round her the feathered choir would wing,
Sae bonnily she wont to sing,
And sleely wake the sleeping string,
Their sang to lead,
Sweet as the zephyrs of the spring;
But now she's dead.

Mourn ilka nymph and ilka swain,
Ilk sunny hill and dowie* glen; somber
Let weeping streams and Naiads drain
Their fountain head;
Let echo swell the dolefu' strain,
Since music's dead.

Whan the saft vernal breezes ca'
The gray-haired Winter's fogs awa',
Naebody then is heard to blaw,
Near hill or mead,
On chaunter or on aiten* straw, "oaten"
Since music's dead.

Nae lasses now, on simmer days,
Will lilt at bleaching of their claes;
Nae herds on Yarrow's bonny braes,
Or banks of Tweed,

Delight to chant their hameil* lays, home-bred
Since music's dead.

At gloamin', now, the bagpipe's dumb,
Whan weary owsen haemeward come;
Sae sweetly as it wont to bum,
And pibrachs[1] skreed;
We never hear its warlike hum,
For music's dead.

Macgibbon's gane:[2] Ah, waes my heart.
The man in music maist expert,
Wha could sweet melody impart,
And tune the reed,
Wi' sic a slee and pawky* art; clever
But now he's dead.

Ilk carline* now may grunt and grane, old woman
Ilk bonny lassie make great mane;
Since he's awa', I trow* there's nane trust
Can fill his stead;
The blithest sangster on the plain—
Alack, he's dead.

Now foreign sonnets bear the gree*, prize
And crabit queer variety
Of sounds fresh sprung frae Italy,
A bastard breed!
Unlike that saft-tongued melody
Which now lies dead.

Can lav'rocks* at the dawning day, larks
Can linties chirming frae the spray,
Or todling burns that smoothly play
O'er gowden bed,
Compare wi' "Birks of Indermay?"
But now they're dead.

O Scotland, that could yence* afford "once"
To bang the pith* of Roman sword, might
Winna your sons, wi' joint accord,
To battle sped,
And fight till music be restored,
Which now lies dead?

## To the Tron-Kirk Bell

Wanwordy*, crazy, dinsome thing, unworthy
As e'er was framed to jow* or ring, swing

---

[1]Old-style bagpipe airs.

[2]A celebrated violinist and orchestra leader, William McGibbon died in 1756.

What garred them sic in steeple hing
    They ken themsel',
But weel wat I they coudna bring
    War sounds frae hell.

What de'il are ye? that I should bann,
You're neither kin to pat* nor pan; "pot"
Nor uly* pig, nor maister-cann*, "oily"/chamber-pot
    But weel may gie
Mair pleasure to the ear o' man
    Than stroke o' thee.

Fleece merchants may look bald*, I trow, "bold"
Since a' Auld Reikie's childer now
Maun stap their lugs* wi' teats* o' woo, ears/bits
    Thy sound to bang,
And keep it frae gawn through and through
    Wi' jarrin' twang.

Your noisy tongue, there's nae abideint,
Like scaulding wife's, there is nae guideint.
Whan I'm bout ony bus'ness eident*, eager
    It's sair to thole*; endure
To deave* me, than, ye tak' a pride in't deafen
    Wi' senseless knoll.

O, war I provost o' the town,
I swear by a' the pow'rs aboon,
I'd bring ye wi' a reesle down;
    Nor shud you think
(Sae sair I'd crack and clour* your crown) bruise
    Again to clink.

For whan I've toomed* the muckle cap, emptied
An' fain wad fa' owr in a nap,
Troth I could doze as soun's a tap*, "top"
    Wer't na for thee,
That gies the tither weary chap
    To waukin me.

I dreamt ae night I saw Auld Nick;
Quo he, "This bell o' mine's a trick,
A wylie piece o' politic,
    A cunnin snare
To trap fock in a cloven stick,
    Ere they're aware.

"As lang's my dautit* bell hings there, pet
A' body at the kirk will skair*; share
Quo they, gif he that preaches there
    Like it can wound,
We douna care a single hair
    For joyfu' sound."

If magistrates wi' me wud' gree,
For ay tongue-tackit shud you be,
Nor fleg* wi' anti-melody    frighten
Sic honest fock,
Whase lugs were never made to dree*    endure
Thy doolfu' shock.

But far frae thee the bailies dwell,
Or they wud scunner* at your knell,    feel disgust
Gie the foul thief his riven bell,
And than, I trow,
The by-word hads, "The de'il himsel'
Has got his due."

## Auld Reikie

Auld Reikie! wale* o' ilka town    choice
That Scotland kens beneath the moon;
Whare couthy* chiels* at e'ening meet    friendly/fellows
Their bizzing craigs* and mou's to weet:    throats
And blithely gar auld care gae bye
Wi' blinkit and wi' bleering eye.
O'er lang frae thee the Muse has been
Sae frisky on the simmer's green,
Whan flowers and gowans* wont to glent    daisies
In bonny blinks up' the bent*;    field, grass
But now the leaves a yellow die,
Peeled frae the branches, quickly fly;
And now frae nouther bush nor brier
The sprecled mavis* greets your ear;    thrush
Nor bony blackbird skims and roves
To seek his love in yonder groves.
Then, Reikie, welcome! Thou canst charm
Unfliggit by the year's alarm.
Not Boreas, that sae snelly blows,
Dare here pap in his angry nose:
Thanks to our dads, whase biggin* stands    building
A shelter to surrounding lands.
Now morn, with bonny purpie-smiles,
Kisses the air-cock o' St. Giles;
Rakin their ein, the servant lasses
Early begin their lies and clashes;
Ilk tells her friend of saddest distress,
That still she brooks frae scouling mistress;
And wi' her joe* in turnpike stair    sweetheart
She'd rather snuff the stinking air,
As be subjected to her tongue,
When justly censured in the wrong.
On stair wi' tub, or pat in hand,
The barefoot housemaids looe to stand,
That antrin* fock may ken how snell    strange
Auld Reikie will at morning smell.

Then, with an inundation big as
The burn that neath the Nore Loch Brig* is, "bridge"
They kindly shower Edina's roses,
To quicken and regale our noses.
Now some for this, wi' satyr's leesh,
Hae gi'en auld Edinburgh a creesh*: beating
But without souring nocht is sweet.
The morning smells that hail our street,
Prepare, and gently lead the way
To simmer canty, braw and gay.
Edina's sons mair eithly share
Her spices and her dainties rare,
Than he that's never yet been called
Aff frae his plaidie or his fauld.
Now stairhead critics, senseless fools,
Censure their aim, and pride their rules,
In Luckenbooths,[1] wi' glouring eye,
Their neighbours sma'est faults descry.
If ony loun* should dander there, fellow, rascal
Of aukward gate, and foreign air,
They trace his steps, till they can tell
His pedigree as weel's himsell.
When Phoebus blinks wi' warmer ray,
And schools at noonday get the play,
Then bus'ness, weighty bus'ness comes.
The trader glours; he doubts, he hums.
The lawyers eke to Cross repair,
Their wigs to shaw, and toss an air;
While busy agent closely plies,
And a' his kittle* cases tries. ticklish
Now night, that's cunzied chief for fun,
Is wi' her usual rites begun.
Through ilka gate the torches blaze,
And globes send out their blinking rays.
The usefu' cadie* plies in street, errand-boy
To bide the profits o' his feet;
For by thir lads Auld Reikie's fock
Ken but a sample, o' the stock
O' thieves, that nightly wad oppress,
And make baith goods and gear* the less. money
Near him the lazy chairman stands,
And wats na how to turn his hands,
Till some daft birky*, ranting fu', dandy
Has matters somewhere else to do.
The chairman willing, gi'es his light
To deeds o' darkness and o' night.
It's never sax pence for a lift
That gars thir lads wi' fu'ness rift;
For they wi' better gear are paid,
And whores and culls support their trade.

---

[1] A row of Main Street shops.

Near some lamp-post, wi' dowy* face, gloomy
Wi' heavy een, and sour grimace,
Stands she that beauty lang had kend,
Whoredom her trade, and vice her end.
But see whare now she wuns her bread,
By that which nature ne'er decreed;
And sings sad music to the lugs*, ears
Mang burachs o' damn'd whores and rogues.
Whane'er we reputation loss,
Fair chastity's transparent gloss.
Redemption seenil* kens the name seldom
But a's black misery and shame.
Frae joyous tavern, reeling drunk,
Wi' fiery phizz, and ein half sunk,
Behald the bruiser, fae to a'
That in the reek o' gardies* fa': guardsmen (police)
Close by his side, a feckless race
O' macaronies* shew their face, dandies
And think they're free frae skaith or harm,
While pith* befriends their leaders arm. strength
Yet fearfu' aften o' their maught,
They quatt the glory o' the faught
To this same warrior wha led
Thae heroes to bright honor's bed:
And aft the hack o' honor shines
In bruiser's face wi' broken lines.
Of them sad tales he tells anon,
Whan ramble and whan fighting's done;
And, like Hectorian, ne'er impairs
The brag and glory o' his sairs.
Whan feet in dirty gutters plash,
And fock to wale* their fitstaps fash*; choose/trouble
At night the macaroni drunk,
In pools or gutters aftimes sunk:
Hegh! what a fright he now appears,
Whan he his corpse dejected rears.
Look at that head, and think if there
The pomet slaistered up his hair.
The cheeks observe, where now could shine
The scancing glories o' carmine?
Ah, legs, in vain the silk-worm there
Displayed to view her eidant* care; diligent
For stink, instead of perfumes, grow,
And clarty odours fragrant flow.

Now some to porter, some to punch,
Some to their wife, and some their wench,
Retire, while noisy ten-hours drum
Gars a' your trades gae dandring home.
Now mony a club, jocose and free,
Gie a' to merriment and glee.
Wi' sang and glass, they fley the pow'r
O' care that wad harrass the hour.

For wine and Bacchus still bear down
Our thrawart fortunes wildest frown.
It maks you stark, and bauld, and brave,
Ev'n whan descending to the grave.
Now some, in Pandemonium's shade,
Resume the gormandizing trade;
Whare eager looks, and glancing ein,
Forespeak a heart and stamack keen.
Gang on, my lads; it's lang sin syne
We kent auld Epicurus' line.
Save you, the board wad cease to rise;
Bedight wi' daintiths to the skies;
And salamanders cease to swill
The comforts of a burning gill*. — glass, drink
But chief, O Cape![1] we crave thy aid,
To get our cares and poortith* laid. — poverty
Sincerity, and genius true,
Of knights have ever been the due.
Mirth, music, porter deepest dyed,
Are never here to worth denied:
And health, o' happiness the queen,
Blinks bonny, wi' her smile serene.

Though joy maist part Auld Reikie owns,
Eftsoons she kens sad sorrows frowns.
What group is yon sae dismal grim,
Wi' horrid aspect, cleeding dim?
Says Death, "They'r mine, a dowy crew,
To me they'll quickly pay their last adieu."
How come mankind, whan lacking woe,
In saulie's[2] face their heart to show,
As if they were a clock, to tell
That grief in them had rung her bell?
Then, what is man? why a' this phraze?
Life's spunk decayed, nae mair can blaze.
Let sober grief alone declare
Our fond anxiety and care.
Nor let the undertakers be
The only waefu' friends we see.
Come on, my Muse, and then rehearse
The gloomiest theme in a' your verse:
In morning, when ane keeks about
Fu' blyth and free frae ail, ne doubt
He lippens* not to be misled — trusts
Amang the regions of the dead:
But straight a painted corp he sees,
Lang steekit* neath its canopies. — shut, stretched
Soon, soon will this his mirth controul,
And send damnation to his soul.

---

[1]The men's club to which Fergusson belonged.
[2]Hired mourners.

Or when the dead-deal,[1] (awful shape)
Makes frighted mankind girn* and gape, grimace, grin
Reflection then his reason sours,
For the niest dead-deal may be ours.
Whan Sybil led the Trojan down
To haggard Pluto's dreary town,
Shapes war nor thae, I freely ween,
Could never meet the soldier's ein.
If kail* sae green, or herbs delight, cabbage
Edina's street attracts the sight.
Not Covent-garden, clad sae braw,
Mair fouth o' herbs can eithly shaw.
For mony a yeard is here sair sought,
That kail and cabbage may be bought;
And healthfu' sallad to regale,
Whan pampered wi' a heavy meal.
Glour up the street in simmer morn,
The birks sae green, and sweet brier-thorn,
Wi' sprangit flow'rs that scent the gale,
Ca' far awa' the morning smell,
Wi' which our ladies flow'r-pat's filled,
And every noxious vapour killed.

O Nature! canty*, blyth and free, pleasant, lively
Whare is there keeking-glass like thee?
Is there on earth that can compare
Wi' Mary's shape, and Mary's air,
Save the empurpled speck, that grows
In the saft faulds of yonder rose?
How bonny seems the virgin breast,
Whan by the lillies here carest,
And leaves the mind in doubt to tell
Which maist in sweets and hue excel?
Gillespies' snuff should prime the nose
Of her that to the market goes,
If they wad like to shun the smells
That buoy up frae markest cells;
Whare wames o' paunches sav'ry scent
To nostrils gi'e great discontent.
Now wha in Albion could expect
O' cleanliness sic great neglect?
Nae Hottentot that daily lairs
Mang tripe, or ither clarty wares,
Hath ever yet conceived, or seen
Beyond the Line*, sic scenes unclean. equator

On Sunday here, an altered scene
O' men and manners meets our ein.
Ane wad maist trow some people chose
To change their faces wi' their clo'es,

[1] The laying-out board.

And fain wad gar ilk neighbour think
They thirst for goodness, as for drink.
But there's an unco dearth o' grace,
That has nae mansion but the face,
And never can obtain a part
In benmost* corner of the heart. inmost
Why should religion make us sad,
If good frae virtue's to be had?
Na, rather gleefu' turn your face;
Forsake hypocrisy, grimace;
And never have it understood
You fleg* mankind frae being good. frighten
In afternoon, a' brawly buskit*, dressed
The joes and lasses loe to frisk it.
Some take a great delight to place
The modest bongrace* oer the face; straw bonnet
Though you may see, if so inclined,
The turning o' the leg behind.
Now Comely-Garden and the Park
Refresh them after forenoon's wark.
Newhaven, Leith or Canonmills,
Supply them in their Sunday's gills;
Whare writers aften spend their pence,
To stock their heads wi' drink and sense.
While dandring cits delight to stray
To Castlehill, or public way,
Whare thay nae other purpose mean,
Than that fool cause o' being seen.
Let me to Arthur's Seat pursue,
Whare bonny pastures meet the view;
And mony a wild-lorn scene accrues,
Befitting Willie Shakespeare's muse.
If Fancy there would join the thrang,
The desart rocks and hills amang,
To echoes we should lilt and play,
And gie to mirth the lee-lang day.
Or should some cankered biting show'r
The day and a' her sweets deflour,
To Holy-rood-house let me stray,
And gie to musing a' the day;
Lamenting what auld Scotland knew,
Bien days for ever frae her view.
O Hamilton, for shame! the Muse
Would pay to thee her couthy* vows, friendly, sociable
Gin ye wad tent the humble strain,
And gie's our dignity again.
For O, waes me, the thistle springs
In domicile of ancient kings,
Without a patriot to regrete
Our palace, and our ancient state.
Blest place, whare debtors daily run,
To rid themselves frae jail and dun;
Here, though sequestered frae the din

That rings Auld Reikie's waas within,
Yet they may tread the sunny braes,
And brook Apollo's cheery rays;
Glour frae St. Anthon's grassy hight,
O'er vales in simmer claise bedight,
Nor ever hing their head, I ween,
Wi' jealous fear o' being seen.
May I, whanever duns* come nigh, bill-collectors
And shake my garret wi' their cry,
Scour here wi' haste, protection get,
To screen mysell frae them and debt;
To breathe the bliss of open sky,
And Simon Fraser's[1] bolts defy.

Now gin a lown should hae his clase* "clothes"
In thread-bare autumn o' their days,
St. Mary, brokers' guardian saint,
Will satisfy ilk ail and want;
For mony a hungry writer, there
Dives down at night, wi' cleading bare,
And quickly rises to the view
A gentleman, perfyte and new.
Ye rich fock, look no wi' disdain
Upo' this ancient brokage lane.
For naked poets are supplied
With what you to their wants denied.

Peace to thy shade, thou wale* o' men, choice
Drummond![2] relief to poortith's pain.
To thee the greatest bliss we owe;
And tribute's tear shall grateful flow.
The sick are cured, the hungry fed,
And dreams of comfort tend their bed.
As lang as Forth weets Lothians shore,
As lang's on Fife her billows roar,
Sae lang shall ilk whase country's dear,
To thy remembrance gie a tear.
By thee Auld Reikie thrave, and grew
Delightfu' to her childer's view.
Nae mair shall Glasgow striplings threap* boast
Their city's beauty and its shape,
While our new city spreads around
Her bonny wings on fairy ground.
But Provosts now that ne'er afford
The smaest dignity to "Lord,"
Ne'er care though every scheme gae wild
That Drummond's sacred hand has culled.
The spacious Brig neglected lies,

---

[1]The town's jailer.

[2]George Drummond (1687-1766), Lord Provost. He was much credited with the building of the New Town.

Though plagued wi' pamphlets, dunned wi' cries.
They heed not though destruction come
To gulp us in her gaunting womb.
O shame, that safety canna claim
Protection from a provost's name,
But hidden danger lies behind
To torture and to fleg* the mind. disturb
I may as weel bid Arthur's Seat
To Berwick-Law make gleg* retreat, sharp
As think that either will or art
Shall get the gate to win their heart.
For politics are a' their mark,
Bribes latent, and corruption dark.
If they can neithly* turn the pence, easily
Wi' city's good they will dispense;
Nor care though a' her sons were laired
Ten fathom i' the auld kirk-yard.

To sing yet meickle does remain,
Undecent for a modest strain;
And since the poet's daily bread is
The favour of the Muse or ladies,
He downa like to gie offence
To delicacy's bonny sense;
Therefore the stews* remain unsung, brothels
And bawds in silence drop their tongue.

Reikie, farewell. I ne'er could part
Wi' thee but wi' a dowy heart;
Aft frae the Fifan coast I've seen
Thee tow'ring on thy summit green.
So glowr the saints when first is given,
A fav'rite keek o' glore and heaven.
On earth nae mair they bend their ein,
But quick assume angelic mein.
So I on Fife wad glowr no more,
But galloped to Edina's shore.

## ROBERT GRAHAM (1750–1797)

### O Tell Me How to Woo Thee

Then tell me how to woo thee, love;
O tell me how to woo thee.
For thy dear sake, nae care I'll take,
Though ne'er another trow* me. trust

If doughty deeds my lady please,
Right soon I'll mount my steed;
And strong his arm, and fast his seat,
That bears frae me the meed*. prize
I'll wear thy colors in my cap,

Thy picture in my heart;
And he that bends not to thine eye
Shall rue it to his smart.

If gay attire delight thine eye,
I'll dight me in array;
I'll tend thy chamber door all night,
And squire thee all the day.
If sweetest sounds can win thine ear,
These sounds I'll strive to catch;
Thy voice I'll steal to woo thysel',
That voice that nane can match.

But if fond love thy heart can gain,
I never broke a vow;
Nae maiden lays her skaith* to me; harm
I never loved but you.
For you alone I ride the ring,
For you I wear the blue;
For you alone I strive to sing,
O tell me how to woo!

## RICHARD HEWITT ( ? –1794 )

### Roslin Castle

Twas in that season of the year
When all things gay and sweet appear,
That Colin, with the morning ray,
Arose and sung his rural lay.
Of Nanny's charms the shepherd sung.
The hills and dales with Nanny rung;
While Roslin Castle heard the swain,
And echoed back his cheerful strain.

Awake, sweet muse. The breathing spring
With rapture warms: awake and sing.
Awake and join the vocal throng,
And hail the morning with a song.
To Nanny raise the cheerful lay.
O, bid her haste and come away,
In sweetest smiles herself adorn,
And add new graces to the morn.

O look, my love: on every spray
Each feathered warbler tunes his lay.
Tis beauty fires the ravished throng,
And love inspires the melting song.
Then let the raptured notes arise,
For beauty darts from Nanny's eyes,
And love my rising bosom warms,
And fills my soul with sweet alarms.

O come, my love. Thy Colin's lay
With rapture calls, O come away.
Come while the muse this wreath shall twine
Around that modest brow of thine.
O hither haste, and with thee bring
That beauty blooming like the spring—
Those graces that divinely shine,
And charm this ravished heart of mine.

## ANNE LINDSAY (1750–1825)

### Auld Robin Gray

When the sheep are in the fauld, and the kye a' at hame,
When a' the weary warld to sleep are gane,
The waes o' my heart fa' in showers frae my e'e,
While my gudeman lies sound by me.

Young Jamie lo'ed me weel, and sought me for his bride,
But saving a croun he had naething else beside;
To mak' the croun a pound my Jamie gaed to sea,
And the croun and the pound, they were baith for me.

He hadna been awa' a week but only twa,
When my mither she fell sick, and the cow was stown awa';
My father brak' his arm—my Jamie at the sea—
And auld Robin Gray cam' a-courtin' me.

My father couldna wark, my mither couldna spin;
I toiled day and night, but their bread I couldna win:
Auld Rob maintained them baith, and, wi' tears in his e'e,
Said, "Jeanie, for their sakes, will ye marry me?"

My heart it said na—I looked for Jamie back;
But the wind it blew hie, and the ship it was a wrack;
His ship it was a wrack—why didna Jeanie dee?
And why do I live to cry, Wae's me?

My father urged me sair; my mither didna speak,
But she looked in my face till my heart was like to break.
They gi'ed him my hand—my heart was at the sea;
Sae auld Robin Gray, he was gudeman to me.

I hadna been a wife a week but only four,
When, mournfu' as I sat on the stane at the door,
I saw my Jamie's wraith—I couldna think it he,
Till he said, "I'm come hame, my love, to marry thee."

O sair did we greet*, and meikle did we say: weep
We took but ae kiss, and I bade him gang away.

I wish that I were dead, but I'm no like to dee;
And why was I born to say, Wae's me?

I gang like a ghaist, and I carena to spin;
I daurna think o' Jamie, for that wad be a sin.
But I'll do my best a gude wife to be,
For auld Robin Gray, he is kind to me.

### My Heart Is a Lute

Alas, that my heart is a lute,
Whereon you have learned to play.
For a many years it was mute,
Until one summer's day
You took it, and touched it, and made it thrill,
And it thrills and throbs, and quivers still.

I had known you, dear, so long.
Yet my heart did not tell me why
It should burst one morn into song,
And wake to new life with a cry,
Like a babe that sees the light of the sun,
And for whom this great world has just begun.

Your lute is enshrined, cased in,
Kept close with love's magic key,
So no hand but yours can win
And wake it to minstrelsy.
Yet leave it not silent too long, nor alone,
Lest the strings should break, and the music be done.

## JOHN LOWE (1750–1798)

### Mary's Dream

The moon had climbed the highest hill
Which rises oer the source of Dee,
And from the eastern summit shed
Her silver light on tower and tree;
When Mary laid her down to sleep,
Her thoughts on Sandy far at sea;
When soft and low a voice was heard,
Saying, "Mary, weep no more for me."

She from her pillow gently raised
Her head, to ask who there might be.
She saw young Sandy shivering stand
With visage pale and hollow e'e.
"O Mary dear, cold is my clay,
It lies beneath a stormy sea.
Far, far from thee I sleep in death,
So Mary, weep no more for me.

"Three stormy nights and stormy days
We tossed upon the raging main,
And long we strove our bark to save,
But all our striving was in vain.
Even then, when horror chilled my blood,
My heart was filled with love for thee.
The storm is past, and I at rest,
So, Mary, weep no more for me.

"O maiden dear, thyself prepare,
We soon shall meet upon that shore
Where love is free from doubt and care,
And thou and I shall part no more."
Loud crowed the cock, the shadows fled.
No more of Sandy could she see;
But soft the passing spirit said,
"Sweet Mary, weep no more for me."

## JOHN TAIT (C.1750–1817)

### The Banks of the Dee

Twas summer, and softly the breezes were blowing,
And sweetly the nightingale sung from the tree.
At the foot of a rock where the river was flowing,
I sat myself down on the banks of the Dee.
Flow on, lovely Dee, flow on, thou sweet river,
Thy banks' purest stream shall be dear to me ever,
For there first I gained the affection and favor
Of Jamie, the glory and pride of the Dee.

But now he's gone from me, and left me thus mourning,
To quell the proud rebels—for valiant is he;
And, ah, there's no hope of his speedy returning,
To wander again on the banks of the Dee.
He's gone, hapless youth, oer the rude roaring billows,
The kindest and sweetest of all the gay fellows,
And left me to wander mongst those once loved willows,
The loneliest maid on the banks of the Dee.

But time and my prayers may perhaps yet restore him,
Blest peace may restore my dear shepherd to me;
And when he returns, with such care I'll watch oer him,
He never shall leave the sweet banks of the Dee.
The Dee then shall flow, all its beauties displaying,
The lambs on its banks shall again be seen playing,
While I with my Jamie am carelessly straying,
And tasting again all the sweets of the Dee.

## ESSAYS FROM THE *MIRROR* AND THE *LOUNGER*

[The Mirror Club was an organization of Edinburgh intellectuals, which published the first two literary journals in Scotland, the *Mirror* (1779–1780), and the *Lounger* (1785–1787). The editor of each was Henry Mackenzie (see Volume I) who also contributed about half of the two hundred or so essays, three of which are presented in the selection under his name. Most of the essayists were, like Mackenzie, from Edinburgh's legal society. They kept their identity as authors a strict secret. The essays are of a fairly wide variety of types, by turns sentimental, humorous, satiric, philosophical, or sketches of the manners of the age. There was a general intent to provide a Scottish counterpart to the greatly influential and admired English essayists Addison and Steele. The complete essays from the *Mirror* and *Lounger* are printed as volumes 34-37 in Lionel Berguer's forty-five volume edition of *The British Essayists* (1823).]

### The Manners of Our Age

*Mirror* 26 (April 24, 1779)
—W. Craig

Nothing can give a truer picture of the manners of any particular age, or point out more strongly those circumstances which distinguish it from others, than the change that takes place in the rules established as to the external conduct of men in society, or in what may be called the system of politeness.

It were absurd to say that from a man's external conduct we are always to judge of the feelings of his mind; but certainly when there are rules laid down for men's external behavior to one another, we may conclude, that there are some general feelings prevalent among the people which dictate those rules, and make a deviation from them to be considered as improper. When at any time, therefore, an alteration in those general rules takes place, it is reasonable to suppose that the change has been produced by some alteration in the feelings, and in the ideas of propriety and impropriety of the people.

Whoever considers the rules of external behavior established about a century ago must be convinced that much less attention was then paid by men of high rank to the feelings of those beneath them than in the present age. In that era, a man used to measure out his complaisance to others according to the degree of rank in which they stood compared with his own. A Peer had a certain manner of address and salutation to a Peer of equal rank, a different one to a Peer of an inferior order, and, to a commoner, the mode of address was diversified according to the antiquity of his family, or the extent of his possessions; so that a stranger, who happened to be present at the levee of a great man, could, with tolerable certainty, by examining his features, or attending to the lowness of his bow, judge of the different degrees of dignity among his visitors.

Were it the purpose of the present paper, this might be traced back to a very remote period. By the *Earl of Northumberland's Household Book*, begun in the year 1512, it appears that my Lord's board-end, that is to say, the end of the table where he and his principal guests were seated, was served with a different and more delicate sort of viands, than those allotted to the lower end.

"It is thought good," says that curious record, "that no pluvers be brought at no time but only in Christmas, and principal feasts, and my Lord to be served therewith, and his board-end, and no other."

The line of distinction was marked by a large saltcellar, placed in the middle of the table, above which, at my lord's board-end, sat the distinguished guests, and below it those of an inferior class.

In this country, and in a period nearer our own times, we have heard of a Highland chieftain, who died not half a century ago, remarkable for his hospitality, and for having his table constantly crowded with a number of guests; possessing a high idea of the dignity of his family, and warmly attached to ancient manners. He was in use very nicely to discriminate by his behavior to them, the ranks of the different persons he entertained. The head of the table was occupied by himself, and the rest of the company sat nearer or more remote from him according to their respective ranks. All, indeed, were allowed to partake of the same food; but when the liquor was produced, which was, at that time, and perhaps still is, in some parts of Scotland, accounted the principal part of a feast, a different sort of beverage was assigned to the guests, according to their different dignities. The chieftain himself, and his family, or near relations, drank wine of the best kind; to persons next in degree was allotted wine of an inferior sort, and to guests of a still lower rank were allowed only those liquors which were the natural produce of the country. This distinction was agreeable to the rules of politeness at that time established: the entertainer did not feel any thing disagreeable in making it; nor did any of the entertained think themselves entitled to take this treatment amiss.

It must be admitted, that a behavior of this sort would not be consonant to the rules of politeness established in the present age. A man of good breeding now considers the same degree of attention to be due to every man in the rank of a gentleman, be his fortune, or the antiquity of his family what it may; nay, a man of real politeness will feel it rather more incumbent on him to be attentive and complaisant to his inferiors in these respects, than to his equals. The idea which in modern times is entertained of politeness, points out such a conduct. It is founded on this, that a man of a cultivated mind is taught to feel a greater degree of pleasure in attending to the ease and happiness of people with whom he mixes in society, than in studying his own. On this account he gives up what would be agreeable to his own taste, because he finds more satisfaction in humoring the taste of others. Thus a gentleman nowadays takes the lowest place at his own table; and if there be any delicacy there, it is set apart for his guests. The entertainer finds a much more sensible pleasure in bestowing it on them than in taking it to himself.

From the same cause, if a gentleman be in company with another, not so opulent as himself, or however worthy, not possessed of the same degree of those adventitious honors which are held in esteem by the world, politeness will teach the former to pay peculiar attention and observation to the latter. Men, even of the highest minds, when they are first introduced into company with their superiors in rank or fortune, are apt to feel a certain degree of awkwardness and uneasiness which it requires some time and habit to wear off. A man of fortune or of rank, if possessed of a sensible mind and real politeness, will feel, and be at particular pains to remove this. Hence he will be led to be rather more attentive to those who, in the eyes of the multitude, are reckoned his inferiors, than to others who are more on a footing with him.

It is not proposed, in this paper, to inquire what are the causes of the difference of men's ideas, as to the rules of politeness in this and the former age. It is sufficient to observe, and the reflection is a very pleasant one, that the modern rules of good breeding must give us a higher idea of the humanity and refinement of this age than of the former: and, though the mode of behavior above mentioned may not be universally observed in practice, yet it is hoped it will not be disputed that it is consonant to the rules which are now pretty generally established.

It ought, however, to be observed, that when we speak, even at this day, of good-breeding, of politeness, of complaisance, these expressions are always confined to our behavior towards those who are considered to be in the rank of gentlemen; but no system of politeness or of complaisance is established, at least in this country, for our behavior to those of a lower station. The rules of good breeding do not extend to them; and he may be esteemed the best-bred man in the world who is a very brute to his servants and dependents.

This I cannot help considering as a matter of regret, and it were to be wished that the same humanity and refinement which recommends an equal attention to all in the rank of gentlemen would extend some degree of that attention to those who are in stations below them.

It will require but little observation to be satisfied, that all men, in whatever situation, are endowed with the same feelings (though education or example may give them a different modification); and that one in the lowest rank of life may be sensible of a piece of insolence, or an affront, as well as one in the highest. Nay, it ought to be considered that the greater the disproportion of rank, the affront will be the more sensibly felt; the greater the distance from which it comes, and the more unable the person affronted to revenge it, by so much the heavier will it fall.

It is not meant, that in our transactions with men of a very low station, and who, from their circumstances, and the wants of society must be employed in servile labor, we are to behave in all respects as to those who are in the rank of gentlemen. The thing is impossible, and such men do not expect it. But in all our intercourse with them, we ought to consider that they are men possessed of like feelings with ourselves, which nature has given them, and which no situation can or ought to eradicate. When we employ them in the labor of life, it ought to be our study to demand that labor in the manner easiest to them, and we should never forget that gentleness is part of the wages we owe them for their service.

Yet how many men, in other respects of the best and most respectable characters, are, from inadvertency or the force of habit, deaf to those considerations. And, indeed, the thing has been so little attended to, that in this, which has been called a polite age, complaisance to servants and dependents is not, as I have already observed, at least in this country, considered as making any part of politeness.

But there is another set of persons still more exposed to be treated roughly than even domestic servants, and these are, the waiters at inns and taverns. Between a master and servant a certain connection subsists, which prevents the former from using the latter very ill. The servant, if he is good for any thing, naturally forms an attachment to his master and to his interests, which produces a natural intercourse of kindness between them. But no connection of this sort can be formed with the temporary attendants above mentioned. Hence the monstrous abuse which such persons frequently suffer. Every traveler, and every man who enters a tavern, thinks he is entitled to vent his own ill-humor upon them and volleys of curses are too often the only language they meet with.

Having mentioned the waiters in inns and taverns, I cannot avoid taking particular notice of the treatment to which those of the female sex, who are employed in places of that sort, are often exposed. Their situation is, indeed, peculiarly unfortunate. If a girl in an inn happen to be handsome, and a parcel of young thoughtless fellows cast their eyes upon her, she is immediately made the subject of taunt and merriment; coarse and indecent jokes are often uttered in her hearing, and conversation shocking to modest ears is frequently addressed to her.

The poor girl all the while is at a loss how to behave. If she venture on a spirited answer, the probable consequence will be to raise the mirth of the facetious company, and to expose her to a repetition of insults. If, guided by the feelings of modesty, she avoid the presence of the impertinent guests she is complained of for neglecting her duty; she loses the little perquisite which, otherwise, she would be entitled to; perhaps disobliges her mistress, and loses her place. Whoever attends but for a moment to the case of a poor girl so situated, if he be not lost to all sense of virtue, must feel his heart relent at the cruelty of taking advantage of such a situation. But the misfortune is that we seldom attend to such cases at all; we sometimes think of the fatigues and sufferings incident to the bodies of our inferiors; but we scarcely ever allow any sense of pain to their minds.

Among the French, whom we mimic in much false politeness, without learning from them, as we might do, much of the true, the observances of good breeding are not confined merely to gentlemen, but extend to persons of the lowest ranks. Thus a Frenchman hardly ever addresses any man, however mean his condition, without calling him Monsieur, and the poorest woman in a country village is addressed by the appellation of Madame. The accosting, in this manner, people of so very low a rank, in the same terms with those so much their superiors, may perhaps appear extravagant; but the practice shews how much that refined and elegant people are attentive to the feelings of the meanest, when they have extended the rules and ceremonial of politeness even to them.—S.

## Michael Bruce

*Mirror* 36 (May 29, 1779)
—W. Craig

Nothing has a greater tendency to elevate and affect the heart than the reflection upon those personages who have performed a distinguished part on the theater of life, whose actions were attended with important consequences to the world around them, or whose writings have animated or instructed mankind. The thought that they are now no more, that their ashes are mingled with those of the meanest and most worthless affords a subject of contemplation, which, however melancholy, the mind, in a moment of pensiveness, may feel a secret sort of delight to indulge.

"Tell her," says Hamlet, "that she may paint an inch thick; yet to this she must come at last."

When Xerxes, at the head of his numerous army, saw all his troops ranged in order before him, he burst into tears at the thought that in a short time they would be sweeped from the face of the earth, and be removed to give place to those who would fill other armies, and rank under other generals.

Something of what Xerxes felt from the consideration that those who then were should cease to be, it is equally natural to feel from the reflection that all who have formerly lived have ceased to live, and that nothing more remains than the memory of a very few who have left some memorial which keeps alive their names, and the fame with which those names are accompanied.

But serious as this reflection may be, it is not so deep as the thought that even of those persons who were possessed of talents for distinguishing themselves in the world, for having their memories handed down from age to age, much the greater part, it is likely, from hard necessity, or by some of the various fatal accidents of life, have been excluded from the possibility of exerting themselves, or of being useful either to those who lived in the same age or to posterity. Poverty in many, and "disastrous chance" in others, have chilled the genial current of the soul, and numbers have been cut off by premature death in the midst of project and ambition. How many have there been in the ages that are past, how many may exist at this very moment who, with all the talents fitted to shine in the world to guide or to instruct it, may by some secret misfortune have had their minds depressed, or the fire of their genius extinguished?

I have been led into these reflections from the perusal of a small volume of poems which happens now to lie before me, which though possessed of very considerable merit, and composed in this country, are, I believe, very little known. In a well-written preface, the reader is told that most of them are the production of Michael Bruce: that this Michael Bruce was born in a remote village in Kinrosshire, and descended from parents remarkable for nothing but the innocence and simplicity of their lives: that, in the twenty-first year of his age, he was seized with a consumption, which put an end to his life.

Nothing, methinks, has more the power of awakening benevolence than the consideration of genius thus depressed by situation, suffered to pine in obscurity, and sometimes, as in the case of this unfortunate young man, to perish, it may be, for want of those comforts and conveniences which might have fostered a delicacy of frame or of mind, ill calculated to bear the hardships which poverty lays on both. For my own part, I never pass the place (a little hamlet skirted with a circle of old ash trees, about three miles on this side of Kinross) where Michael Bruce resided; I never look on his dwelling,—a small thatched house, distinguished from the cottages of the other inhabitants only by a sashed window at the end, instead of a lattice, fringed with a honeysuckle plant, which the poor youth had trained around it;—I never find myself in that spot, but I stop my horse involuntarily; and looking on the window, which the honey-suckle has now almost covered, in the dream of the moment, I picture out a figure for the gentle tenant of the mansion. I wish, and my heart swells while I do so, that he were alive, and that I were a great man to have the luxury of visiting him there, and bidding him be happy. I cannot carry my readers thither; hut that they may share some of my feelings, I will present them with an extract from the last poem in the little volume before me, which, from its subject, and the manner in which it is written, cannot fail of touching the heart of every one who reads it.

A young man of genius, in a deep consumption, at the age of twenty-one, feeling himself every moment going faster to decline, is an object sufficiently interesting; but how much must every feeling on the occasion be heightened, when we know that this person possessed so much dignity and composure of mind as not only to contemplate his approaching fate, but even to write a poem on the subject.

In the French language there is a much admired poem of the Abbe de Chaulieu, written in expectation of his own death, to the Marquis la Farre, lamenting his approaching separation from his friend. Michael Bruce, who, it is probable, never heard of the Abbe de Chaulieu, has also written a poem on his own approaching death; with the latter part of which I shall conclude this paper.

Now Spring returns; but not to me returns
The vernal joy my better years have known:
Dim in my breast life's dying taper burns,
And all the joys of life with health are flown.

Starting and shivering in th' unconstant wind,
Meager and pale—the ghost of what I was,
Beneath some blasted tree I lie reclined,
And count the silent moments as they pass—

The winged moments, whose unstaying speed
No art can stop, or in their course arrest,
Whose flight shall shortly count me with the dead,
And lay me down in peace with them that rest.

Oft morning dreams presage approaching fate;—
And morning dreams, as poets tell, are true:

Led by pale ghosts, I enter Death's dark gate,
And bid the realms of light and life adieu.

I hear the helpless wail, the shriek of woe;
I see the muddy wave, the dreary shore,
The sluggish streams that slowly creep below,
Which mortals visit—and return no more.

Farewell, ye blooming fields, ye cheerful plains.
Enough for me the churchyard's lonely mound,
Where Melancholy with still Silence reigns,
And the rank grass waves oer the cheerless ground.

There let me wander at the close of eve,
When Sleep sits dewy on the laborer's eyes,—
The world and all its busy follies leave,
And talk with Wisdom where my Daphnis lies.

There let me sleep, forgotten, in the clay,
When death shall shut these weary aching eyes,
Rest in the hopes of an eternal day,
Till the long night is gone, and the last morn arise.

## The Death of Mrs. Wentworth

*Mirror* 27 (April 27, 1779)
—Robert Cullen

A very amiable and much respected friend of mine, whose real name I shall conceal under that of Wentworth, had lately the misfortune of losing a wife, who was not only peculiarly beautiful, but whose soul was the mansion of every virtue, and of every elegant accomplishment. She was suddenly cut off in the flower of her age, after having lived twelve years with the best and most affectionate of husbands. A perfect similarity of temper and disposition, a kindred delicacy of taste and sentiment, had linked their hearts together in early youth, and each succeeding year seemed but to add new strength to their affection. Though possessed of an affluent fortune, they preferred the tranquillity of the country to all the gay pleasures of the capital. In the cultivation of their estate, in cherishing the virtuous industry of its inhabitants, in ornamenting a beautiful seat, in the society of one another, in the innocent prattle of their little children, and in the company of a few friends, Mr. Wentworth and his Amelia found every wish gratified, and their happiness complete.

My readers will judge then what must have been Mr. Wentworth's feelings, when Amelia was thus suddenly torn from him, in the very prime of her life, and in the midst of her felicity. I dreaded the effects of it upon a mind of his nice and delicate sensibility; and receiving a letter from his brother requesting me to come to them, I hasted thither, to endeavor by my presence to assuage his grief, and prevent those fatal consequences of which I was so apprehensive.

As I approached the house, the sight of all the well-known scenes brought fresh into my mind the remembrance of Amelia; and I felt myself but ill qualified to act the part of a comforter. When my carriage stopped at the gate, I trembled, and would have given the world to go back. A heart-felt sorrow sat on the countenance of every servant, and I walked into the house without a word being uttered. In the hall I was met by the old butler, who has grown gray-headed in the family, and he hastened to conduct me up stairs.

As I walked up, I commanded firmness enough to say, "Well, William, how is Mr. Wentworth?" The old man, turning about with a look that pierced my heart, said, "O, Sir, our excellent lady!"

Here his grief overwhelmed him; and it was with difficulty he was able to open to me the door of the apartment.

Mr. Wentworth ran and embraced me with the warmest affection; and, after a few moments, assumed a firmness, and even an ease, that surprised me. His brother, with a sister of Amelia's, and some other friends that were in the room, appeared more overpowered than my friend himself, who, by the fortitude of his behavior, seemed rather to moderate the grief of those around him than to demand their compassion for himself. By his gentle and kind attentions he seemed anxious to relieve their sorrow; and by a sort of concerted tranquillity, strove to prevent their discovering any symptoms of the bitter anguish which preyed upon his mind. His countenance was pale, and his eyes betrayed that his heart was ill at ease; but it was that silent and majestic sorrow which commands our reverence and our admiration.

Next morning after breakfast I chanced to take up a volume of Metastasio, that lay amongst other books upon a table; and as I was turning over the leaves, a slip of paper with something written on it dropped upon the floor. Mr. Wentworth picked it up, and as he looked at it, I saw the tears start from his eyes, and, fetching a deep sigh, he uttered in a low and broken voice, "My poor Amelia. Poor Amelia!"

It was the translation of a favorite passage which she had been attempting, but had left unfinished. As if uneasy lest I had perceived his emotion, he carelessly threw his arm over my shoulder, and reading aloud a few lines of the page, which I held open in my hand, he went into some remarks on the poetry of that elegant author. Some time after, I observed him take up the book, and carefully replacing the slip of paper where it had been, put the volume in his pocket.

Mr. Wentworth proposed that we should walk out, and that he himself would accompany us. As we stepped through the hall, one of my friend's youngest boys came running up, and catching his Papa by the hand, cried out with joy that "Mamma's Rover was returned."

This was a spaniel who had been the favorite of Amelia, and had followed her in all her walks; but after her death, had been sent to the house of a villager, to be out of the immediate sight of the family. Having somehow made its escape from thence, the dog had that morning found his way home, and as soon as he saw Mr. Wentworth, leaped upon him with an excess of fondness. I saw my friend's lips and cheeks quiver. He catched his little Frank in his arms; and for a few moments hid his face in his neck.

As we traversed his delightful grounds, many different scenes naturally recalled the remembrance of Amelia. My friend, indeed, in order to avoid some of her favorite walks, had conducted us an unusual road; but what corner could be found that did not bear the traces of her hand? Her elegant taste had marked the peculiar beauty of each different scene, and had brought it forth to view with such a happy delicacy of art, as to make it seem the work of nature alone. As we crossed certain paths in the woods, and passed by some rustic buildings, I could sometimes discern an emotion in my friend's countenance; but he instantly stifled it with a firmness and dignity that made me careful not to seem to observe it.

Towards night, Mr. Wentworth having stolen out of the room, his brother and I stepped out to a terrace behind the house. It was the dusk of the evening, the air was mild and serene, and the moon was rising in all her brightness from the cloud of the east. The fineness of the night made us extend our walk, and we strayed into a hollow valley, whose sides are covered with trees overhanging a brook that pours itself along over broken rocks. We approached a rustic grotto, placed in a sequestered corner, under a half impending rock. My companion stopped.

"This," said he, "was one of Amelia's walks, and that grotto was her favorite evening retreat. The last night she ever walked out, and the very evening she caught that fatal fever, I was with my brother and her, while we sat and read to each other in that very place."

While he spoke, we perceived a man steal out of the grotto, and, avoiding us, take his way by a path through a thicket of trees on the other side. "It is my brother," said young Wentworth. "He has been here in his Amelia's favorite grove, indulging that grief he so carefully conceals from us."

We returned to the house, and found Mr. Wentworth with the rest of the company. He forced on some conversation, and even affected a degree of gentle pleasantry during the whole evening.

Such in short, is the noble deportment of my friend, that, in place of finding it necessary to temper and moderate his grief, I must avoid seeming to perceive it, and dare scarcely appear even to think of the heavy calamity which has befallen him. I too well know what he feels, but the more I know this, the more does the dignity of his recollection and fortitude excite my admiration, and command my silent attention and respect.

How very different is this dignified and reserved sorrow, from that weak and teasing grief which disgusts, by its sighs and tears, and clamorous lamentations? How much does such noble fortitude of deportment call forth our regard and reverence? How much is a character in other respects estimable, degraded by a contrary demeanor? How much does the excessive, the importunate, and unmanly grief of Cicero diminish the very high respect which we should otherwise entertain for the exalted character of that illustrious Roman?

Writers on practical morality have described and analyzed the passion of grief, and have pretended to prescribe remedies for restoring the mind to tranquillity; but, I believe, little benefit has been derived from any thing they have advised. To tell a person in grief that time will relieve him is truly applying no remedy; and to bid him reflect how many others there may be who are more wretched is a very inefficacious one. The truth is that the excess of this, as well as of other passions, must be prevented rather than cured. It must be obviated by our attaining that evenness and equality of temper which can arise only from an improved understanding, and an habitual intercourse with refined society. These will not, indeed, exempt us from the pangs of sorrow, but will enable us to bear them with a noble grace and propriety, and will render the presence of our friends (which is the only remedy) a very effectual cure.

This is well explained by a philosopher, who is no less eloquent than he is profound. He justly observes, that we naturally, on all occasions, endeavor to bring down our own passions, to that pitch which those about us can correspond with. We view ourselves in the light in which we think they view us, and seek to suit our behavior to what we think their feelings can go along with. With an intimate friend, acquainted with every circumstance of oar situation, we can, in some measure, give way to our grief, but are more calm than when by ourselves. Before a common acquaintance, we assume a greater sedateness. Before a mixed assembly, we affect a still more considerable degree of composure. Thus, by the company of our friends at first, and afterward by a mingling with society, we come to suit our deportment to what we think they will approve of; we gradually abate the violence of our passion, and restore our mind to its wonted tranquillity.—V .

## A Fashionable Education

*Lounger* 13 (April 30, 1785)
—Michael Bannatyne

To the Author of the *Lounger*.
Sir,

I inherited from my ancestors an estate of about 1000£ a-year; and as I never had any desire for figuring in the world, I married, early in life, the daughter of a neighboring gentleman, and till of late years lived at home, satisfied with the society of my friends and neighbors. I found my fortune fully sufficient for my purposes, and was in hopes that I might provide decently for my younger children, who are four in number, without its being necessary to part with an estate, which, as it had been some centuries in our family, I had an old-fashioned inclination to preserve in it.

I am sorry, however, to add that from the circumstances I am now to take the liberty of mentioning, those hopes have given way to prospects of a very different kind, prospects unspeakably mortifying to me, and which ought to be still more distressing to the rest of my family.

My eldest son, as he possessed but a very limited genius, and shewed no propensity to any particular profession, I wished to follow my own example and become a country gentleman. But a winter in your city, after having passed a few years at one of our universities, taught him that this was a plan quite unfit for a young man of spirit. As he had there acquired a taste for what he was pleased to call genteel life, by hunting, drinking, wenching, and gambling with all the idle young men about town, at a greater expense than what supported all the rest of the family at home, I was persuaded to purchase for him a cornetcy of horse, in compliance with his own earnest desire, and in hopes that by a removal from his present companions, he might learn to retrench his expenses and be gradually reclaimed from the dangerous habits he had contracted in their society.

While my son was thus learning to be a gentleman, my wife thought it no less necessary that my daughters should learn to be ladies.

Accordingly, when the eldest was about thirteen and the other about twelve years of age, they both left my house in the country, and were placed in a boarding-school of the first reputation in Edinburgh.

At home they had passed their time, as I imagined, usefully in learning to read, to write, to work, to keep accounts, and to assist their mother in the little cares of our household. They had been taught to dance; and they sang, not perhaps with much art or skill, but in such a manner as most people listened to with pleasure. These attainments, however, were of a very inferior kind to what was now thought necessary they should acquire. They were quickly provided with masters for all the polite and fashionable branches of education. They were taught dancing (for they would not allow what they had learned in the country to deserve that name), drawing, French, Italian and music; and a female relation, who was kind enough to take some charge of them, sent us the most flattering accounts of their progress in those various accomplishments.

When I received the bills of the boarding-mistress, even for the first season, I was, I must confess somewhat out of humor; and it required all the eloquence of my wife, and the flattering accounts of her kinswoman, to persuade me that the expense was quite so well bestowed as they seemed to imagine. It was, however, a trifle, compared to that which followed. In a few years my young misses were transformed into young ladies; and as the kindness of our female friend procured them an introduction, as she told us, to all the genteel families in town, what between private parties and public places, where they now began to figure, they very seldom found leisure to be at home. The expense which this occasioned, added to that of their education (for they still continued to improve themselves), was such as I could by no means afford to bestow on two members of my family; especially as it now became necessary to fit my two younger boys for the professions they chose to follow; Jack, the elder, being destined for the bar, and Bob for the East Indies, where, under the protection of an uncle, it was hoped he might one day become a Nabob.

The beauty and accomplishments of my daughters had now become a favorite topic with my wife and other friends of my family; and to have buried them in a country retirement would have been deemed the height of folly and barbarity. For their sakes, therefore, as well as the education of my sons, I was now told it was absolutely necessary we should pass a considerable part of the year in Edinburgh. The separate board I must otherwise bestow on my boys and girls was supposed to render this a plan of economy; and the few objections I made to it were silenced, by telling me of many gentlemen from all parts of the country who had found this the only method of giving their children a genteel education, without the absolute ruin of their fortunes.

To these reasons, though not altogether satisfied, I gave way. We provided ourselves with a house in town; and, for these five years past, have spent our winters in Edinburgh and only retired to the country, like other fashionable people, at the end of the season, when it becomes necessary that one part of the family should provide health, and another money, for the gaiety of the next.

During this period I have witnessed the full effect of that fashionable education I had bestowed on my daughters; and it is now some years that they have joined to the other pleasures of a town-life, the envied distinction of beauties and toasts.

You will easily conceive how much this must have gratified the vanity of a mother. My own, Sir, was not altogether proof against it; nor can I deny the pleasure it gave me, to find the company of my daughters universally sought after, and to see their beauty attract all eyes, in every company, and at every public place in which they appeared.

I soon, however, found the effects of this distinction to be very different from those which the sanguine expectations of some of us had suggested. Our house indeed was filled with visitors in the morning, and in the evening my girls were attended at public places by many of the gay young men of rank and fortune. But the fashion of beauties is scarce more lasting than that of the dress they wear. The admiration which my daughters for some time attracted, now sensibly declines, and amidst the crowd of admirers which turned their heads, I do not find there has been one whose admiration led to any other consequence, than that of gratifying his own vanity and feeding theirs by a temporary homage to their fashion and their beauty. My poor girls, meanwhile, have contracted a habit of living, and a turn of thinking, which will prevent any sensible man of their own station from thinking of them as companions for life; and which, I fear, would ill qualify them for such a situation, if it should be offered them, or if their own vanity could allow them to stoop to it.

Jack has been now some time at the bar, and at first gave hopes of such application as would probably have ensured success. But he has not been proof against the vanity of keeping that fashionable company to which the situation of my family gave him access; and now spends his time in a continued circle of idleness and expense, with such young men of fortune as think it an honor done him to admit him of their parties and will despise him, perhaps too justly, when he can no longer afford to partake of them.

My eldest son, far from profiting by his military plans, has retained the same taste of life which gave rise to them. Besides advancing the price of two commissions, I have repeatedly discharged debts which he is pleased to call debts of honor.

After all, he is now obliged to sell out of the army, and end where he should have begun, in the life of a country gentleman, with the advantage of having contracted a thorough distaste for it; of having thrown away, in a round of fashionable vice and extravagance, the plain talents, the honest sentiments, and the sober dispositions that qualify men for a station which they are too apt to despise.

The profusion of this thoughtless boy, added to the expenses of my family, has consumed the savings of my happier years; and not only disabled me from continuing our present style of life, but obliged me to dispose of a considerable part of my estate, and leaves it very uncertain what residue I shall be able to preserve for my own support, and for the provision of my family.

Thus, in place of those flattering hopes we had once formed, my wife and I, now in the decline of life, have before us the melancholy prospect of leaving, as companions for each other, a bankrupt gambler, living embarrassed and distressed on the shattered remains of a fortune; and two neglected beauties, paying, I am afraid, much too dear the pleasure they once derived from that envied distinction, while the most promising of our younger sons has fallen a prey to the same fashionable folly and extravagance; and the whole hopes of a once-flourishing family are left to depend on the doubtful success of an Eastern adventurer.

Such, Sir, are the consequences of that preposterous fashion which leads men of moderate fortunes to give their children an education and taste of life altogether unsuited to the situations they are likely to occupy.

Even to those whose fortunes enable them to move in the sphere of fashionable dissipation and expense, the real pleasures and privileges of their situation are much less considerable than they are commonly imagined; but to men of more limited circumstances, an attempt to rise into that region of extravagance is fatal indeed; it leads them from the moderate station where every happiness was to be found, and abandons them to want embittered by discontent, and to distresses heightened by self-reproach. —Agrestis.

## Miss Lucy Lumber

*Lounger* 16 (May 21, 1785)
—Fraser Tytler

To the Author of the Lounger.
Sir,

Your correspondent Mrs. Careful has given a very just picture of the female Loungers, in her entertaining letter. The disturbance which the morning visits of those idlers give to sober families is become matter of very serious concern to many a mother in this town, who would wish to educate their daughters in such a way as to qualify them for performing their parts with propriety, in whatever rank they may be called to.

Idleness and frivolity seem to form the character of the times. According to the present system of female education amongst as, the culture of the mind and heart, the knowledge of those useful duties which a good wife and a good mother owes to her husband and her children, are but slightly attended to, if not altogether neglected, for those exterior accomplishments which ought properly to be the handmaids of the former. Hence the dissipation of individuals, and the final wreck we often see of families!

The task I am going upon is a melancholy one; to illustrate the truth of the above observation from my own woeful experience; yet, as it may be a caution to others I think it a duty on me to communicate to you the following narrative.

I was married, a few years ago, to an amiable young woman, the only daughter of a wealthy and respectable merchant. My father-in-law, Mr. Lumber, had gone early to the West Indies, where he was so successful in trade as to make a very considerable fortune, with which he returned to settle in his own country. As he had raised himself, and had few relations to supply that want, he married a daughter of the honorable Mr. Stingy, younger brother to the Earl of Loftus, by which connection he at once acquired relationship with a score of honorable and right honorable cousins, some of whom did him the honor to breakfast, dine, or sup with him almost every day.

Mr. Lumber was a sensible man in his way, and had seen a good deal of the world; he might therefore have managed his family in a manner much more to its advantage than that in which it was conducted, had he been allowed the perfect guidance of it. But in this he was a good deal restrained from the circumstance of his inferior birth. It was impossible for the son of a plain citizen to understand any thing so well as the granddaughter of a Peer. He was contented, therefore, to maintain a sort of divided empire: he was allowed to superintend the education of his two boys, who after having been some time in a respectable house in Holland, now assist in carrying on the business in their father's counting house. As to his daughter, he left her to the management of her mother, and of her aunt, Miss Bridget Stingy, a maiden lady who lived in the family. As my grievances all took rise from that root, I must be indulged in mentioning the character of these ladies.

The circumstances of Mr. Stingy did not perhaps allow of giving his daughters the most liberal education, but what he might have given, he did not think it necessary to give: to be the daughters of the honorable Mr. Stingy, and grand-daughters of the Earl of Loftus, was enough without any other endowment. Bred with high ideas of birth and rank, they were ignorant of almost every branch of useful knowledge; and as most of their time passed alternately amongst their quality relations, they had learned to despise taking any concern in the useful employments of domestic life.

On the death of the honorable Mr. Stingy, Miss Bridget, his eldest daughter, was left to the care of her relations: but as they appeared rather cool with regard to her, she was by the benignity of Mr. Lumber brought home to his house, and to ease and plenty if she could have used them with good humor and discretion.

This lady was several years older than her sister, Mrs. Lumber, a weak, good natured woman, over whom she asserted a superiority and direction more than was consistent with her situation, and which Mr. Lumber, though a good-humored man, did not at all times approve of. In place of making herself and her sister happy in the enjoyment of the real blessings which they possessed, Miss Stingy's chief study was to teach her sister a number of wants to which she was not entitled as the wife of a merchant. To many of these Mr. Lumber gave way; such as adding another servant to the table arrangement, who plied behind his lady's chair in a plain suit and ruffles; changing the post-chaise into a body coach, and promoting Jack the driver to the rank of John, coachman. But, to the no small disquiet of Miss Bridget, Lumber was inflexible to his wife's demand of a weekly route and card assembly. This, and several other indulgences, she did not find Mr. Lumber silly enough to grant; but she generally found Mrs. Lumber silly enough to resent the refusal.

But, to end this digression, which I am afraid has already tired you, and to proceed to my own story. Mr. Lumber being my banker while I was abroad, on coming to Scotland, I was often invited to his house, where I was treated with great hospitality and attention. Miss Lucy Lumber, his only daughter, was young, handsome, good-natured, and sprightly. Her vivacity, her good-humor, and her good-looks, attracted my attentions, and I thought I discovered that she was not displeased with them. I was in that situation in which the world suggests the propriety of a man's looking out for a wife, and in which he begins to think it his duty to be married. The qualities Miss Lumber possessed were attractive; and I never thought of those she might want. In short, I was in love: I courted; I was accepted of; and as every man in my situation would say, made completely happy.

After passing some weeks in a round of mirth and dissipation, I carried my Lucy, with a companion of hers, to my house in the north.

The visits of my neighbors, and our returns to them, with the little parties which we made, gave me but little opportunity for observation, or a thorough knowledge of my wife's qualities or turn of mind. She wanted not sense at bottom, had good nature, and, bating a little tincture of that pride of ancestry, or rather vanity, for it never was offensive, which had early been inculcated into her by her aunt Bridget, she had a sweetness and affability that was extremely engaging.

We passed the summer very agreeably. When winter set in, I began to know more intimately my wife's disposition. I had presented her with a small selection of books for her closet; the best of the British poets and historians, some of moral entertainment, such as the Spectators, Guardians, &c. and some for mere amusement. But I soon found that my Lucy was no reader. She read *Tom Jones*, indeed: and on my recommendation to her and Miss Flounce, they went through the greatest part of *Gil Blas*; but of the two scholars of Salamanca, I am afraid they ranked with the first.

By the good management of an experienced housekeeper, who had been brought up in the family by my mother, and who, I knew, had a real liking to the family, my house, table, and domestics had been regulated. On my marriage, I was in hopes that, without entering into the executive part, my Lucy would now, as mistress of the family, superintend the whole domestic economy. But in this I was disappointed. She never had been used to look into household management; it was a province, she said she was not adapted for, and wished not to engage in. She would now and then quote maxims which I could perceive she had learned in the Loftus school. They signified that household cares might become ordinary women, but were degrading to the descendants of people of quality.

When we were not engaged with company, my farm and planting, my dog and my gun, kept me a great part of the day in the field. When I returned, I did not always find from my wife that cheerful, animated look that used to welcome me home. When at times I remarked this, she would suddenly resume a gaiety of countenance, and endeavor to smile away my observation. But as this gaiety was assumed, its continuance was short; and with great uneasiness I now began to see a change of disposition in my Lucy, and that a lowness of spirits at times hung upon her. This I attributed, however, to her situation, as to my great joy, she was, as my friend John Home expresses it, "as women wish to be who love their lords." Mr. Lumber had kindly invited us to town, and we determined to pass the winter with him. We were received with great joy, and found that family much the same as we had left it.

My Lucy brought me a fine boy and while she recovered her health, I flattered myself that she would soon also regain her former sprightliness and good humor. In this I was not disappointed; we got into the fashionable circle of company, and that continual round of dissipation that goes on in the metropolis: the whole forenoon generally spent amidst a succession of visitants, a mob of idlers; the rest of the day in dinners, public places, and evening parties.

Although in my own mind I despised the giddy, restless insignificants that figured in this perpetual drama; yet as I considered myself as a passenger only for the time, I submitted to be carried along with the stream, and partook of the flying amusements as they occurred. I did not lose sight, however, of my own scheme: as the spring approached I gave hints of my return to Homely Castle, and announced the day for our departure. My Lucy, who never disputed my will, prepared herself; but I could observe that she became grave and thoughtful, as the time approached for our setting out. We left our friends, and got safely home.

The smiles of our little infant were for some time his mother's sole amusement; but this, as mere amusement, for it carried no active employment along with it, after some months began to lose its relish. The feeble exertions, which too late she endeavored to call to her aid, were too weak to resist the demon of indolence, with languor and melancholy in his train, that now had invaded her.

Such are the fruits of an education now, I am afraid, but too common. Good natural parts, in place of being trained to exercise, in the several branches of knowledge, and useful employments of life, had either been neglected, or misapplied to frivolous and desultory amusements. Now, when out of the giddy round of the fashionable town entertainments that used to fill up her hours, my Lucy feels a vacant mind that affords no resources within itself. Her reflections of course are painful and bitter or if lulled at all, only sink into a lassitude, and listless unconcern for every thing around her. Her few former amusements, her tambour and harpsichord, have long become insipid and even the smiles of her child, which used to give delight, now I can observe, force a sigh from her, and sometimes the tear will start into her eye, from the painful reflection, no doubt, of her inability to perform to him the duty of a mother.

In this situation, Mr. Lounger, judge of my distress and disappointment. Instead of family happiness and domestic enjoyment, I find at home a constant source of disquiet and melancholy. Perhaps I am more unhappy than husbands whose wives are more blamable. In the greater offenses against the marriage duty, the injured party has the privilege of complaint, the support of resentment, the consolation of indifference, or of hatred. I have no contradiction of which to complain, no injuries to resent: I pity, nay I still love my wife; and yet I am most unhappy.

Tell my situation, Sir, to those young men, who like me—or rather tell it to mothers, who, like Mrs. Lumber, have daughters to educate. Remind them that, however important the education may be that teaches to adorn the mistress, and captivate the lover, there is still another, and a higher, which requires some little attention, that which instructs them to perform the duties of the wife, to retain the affections, and to constitute the happiness of the husband. I am, &c. —Horatius.

## The Mirror Club

*Lounger* 30 (August 27, 1785)
—Alexander Abercromby

To The Lounger.
Sir,

Although a stranger to your person, I have the honor of being pretty near allied to you. When you know who I am, I flatter myself you will not think yourself disgraced by the alliance, and that you will permit me to claim kindred with you. Of this you may be assured, I would not do it, did I not entertain a favorable opinion of you; and having nothing to ask, you may consider my desire to be ranked among your friends as a mark of approbation. Know then, Sir, that the person who has now the honor to address you is a member of the Mirror Club.

Although long since dead as an author, you will readily believe that I am interested in the success of the Lounger. Persons placed in the same situations naturally feel a sympathetic sort of attachment for each other. When the Lounger was first advertised, I could not help recollecting the sensations I experienced when the publication of the Mirror was first announced in the papers; and when your introductory number appeared, I sent for it with an impatience, and a solicitude, which I should not have felt in the same degree had I not once been in a situation similar to yours.

You, Sir, started with many advantages which we did not possess. The public are now taught to know that it is possible to carry on a periodical work of this kind in Edinburgh; and that, if tolerably executed, it will be read, and will hold its place with other works of the same kind. But when we boldly gave the Mirror to the world, a very different notion prevailed. It was supposed that no such work could be conducted with any propriety on this side of the Tweed. Accordingly, the Mirror was received with the most perfect indifference in our own country; and during the publication, it was indebted for any little reputation it received in Scotland, to the notice that happened to be taken of it by some persons of rank and of taste in England. Nay, Sir, strange as you may think it, it is certainly true that narrow as Edinburgh is, there were men who consider themselves as men of letters who never read a number of it while it was going on.

But although in this and in many other respects the Lounger may possess advantages over the Mirror, there is one particular in which I am apt to believe, that we, the members of the Mirror Club, possessed an advantage over the author of the Lounger. You, Sir, if I mistake not, conduct your work single and alone, unconnected with any person whatever. We, Sir, were a society, consisting of a few friends, closely united by long habits of intimacy. Not only, therefore, is your task much more arduous than ours, but, in the way of amusement, we certainly had the advantage of you. I can never forget the pleasure we enjoyed in meeting to read our papers in the Club. There they were criticized with perfect freedom, but with the greatest good humor. When any of us produced a paper, which either from the style or manner of it, or from the nature of the subject seemed inadmissible, it was condemned without hesitation, and the author, putting it in his pocket, drank a bumper to its manes.

We had stated meetings to receive the communications with which we were honored, which afforded another source of amusement. This pleasure, however, was not without alloy. We were often, from particular circumstances, obliged to reject compositions of real merit; and what perhaps was equally distressing, we were sometimes obliged to abridge or to alter the papers which we published. Might I presume to give you an advice, it would be, to use this liberty as rarely as possible. We authors know that there is a certain complacency, not to call it vanity, which a man feels for his own compositions, which makes him unwilling to submit them to the correction of he does not know whom, or to acquiesce in an alteration made he does not know why. In justice, however, to our correspondents I must add, that they continued to honor us with their favors, notwithstanding the liberties we took with their compositions, and although it was not in our power to explain the reasons which induced us to take those liberties.

But, Sir, one never-ceasing fund of amusement to us was communicating the observations we had occasion to hear, in different societies and different companies, upon the Mirror and its supposed authors. The supercilious, who despised the paper because they did not know by whom it was written, talked of it as a catchpenny performance, carried on by a set of needy and obscure scribblers. Those who entertained a more favorable opinion of it, were apt to fall into an opposite mistake, and to suppose that the Mirror was the production of all the men of letters in Scotland.

This last opinion is not yet entirely exploded, and perhaps has rather gained ground from the favorable reception of the Mirror since its publication in volumes. The last time I was in London I happened to step into Mr. Cadell's shop, and while I was amusing myself in turning over the prints in Cook's last voyage, Lord B— came in, and taking up a volume of the Mirror, asked Mr. Cadell, who were the authors of it. Cadell, who did not suspect that I knew any more of the matter than the Great

Mogul, answered, "that he could not mention particular names; but he believed that all the literati of Scotland were concerned in it." Lord B— walked off, satisfied that this was truly the case; and about a week alter I heard him say at Lord M—'s levee, that he was well assured the Mirror was the joint production of all the men of letters in Scotland.

I will now, Sir, tell you in confidence, that (one of our number excepted, whose writings have long been read with admiration and delight, and whose exquisite pencil every reader of taste and discernment must distinguish in the Mirror) there was not one of our Club who ever published a single sentence, or in all likelihood ever would have done it, had it not been for the accidental publication of the Mirror.

But the most amusing part of the whole was the application of the characters in the Mirror to real life; and I verily believe many a charitable lady and well-disposed gentleman read it with no other view than to find out characters which they might apply to their friends and acquaintances. I dined in a large company the day on which the first letter signed John Homespun was published. At table Lady— asked if any body had seen the Mirror of that day.

"Yes," answered Mrs.—, "it is a charming paper, but there is a great lady in the west, that won't be very fond of it. She is drawn to the life; I knew her before I had read half the paper."

"In the west?" replied Lady—. "In the south, you mean. I agree with you that the picture is well drawn; and if you knew the Countess of— as well as I have the honor to know her, you could not doubt that she is truly the original."

"Pardon me, ladies," said a little, sharp-looking man, in a northern accent, "I believe you are both mistaken. I have read the paper, and I think the great lady so well pointed out in it is neither from the west nor from the south, but from my country; at least I am sure we have two or three very like the woman in the Mirror, who do no good to us small folks when we get among them, and are apt to turn the heads of our wives and our daughters;—ay, and of our sons too," added he, with a significant nod.

The ladies, however, would not yield their opinion; and a dispute ensued, which was to me not a little amusing, as I knew that the author had no particular lady in view, either from the west or from the east, from the south or from the north.

One morning I called upon a lady, and found her reading N° 47 of the Mirror, a paper of mine. "Well," said she, "I know every person described here as well as if they had given us their names at full length."

She then named some of her acquaintance, whose persons and characters were equally unknown to me, and even whose names I never heard mentioned before.

But the most dangerous application of this sort was that of the character of Sir Bobby Button. Of our forty-five members it may, without offense, be said that some of them are manu quam lingua promptiores, readier at a blow than a word; and we were told that they seriously intended to make the author of the Mirror speak out, and say, whether, in the modern language of parliament, he meant any thing personal. This intelligence produced some little uneasiness in our society, but we resolved to act with becoming dignity and spirit, had the respectable body of our representatives called upon us for an explanation.

Thus, in the hands of many, the Mirror, innocent and well intended as it was, became a vehicle of slander; and the envious, the splenetic, and the malicious, found an entertainment in it which never was intended for them. Be not you, Sir, discouraged by this. Go on boldly to correct our follies and our vices, by painting them truly as they are. To attain this purpose, I would advise you in the words of the bloody Renault,—"to spare neither age, nor sex, nor condition."

But while I say this, I must add, that it is only the vices and the follies themselves which you are entitled to attack, and not the individuals who may be guilty of

them. You, Sir, will not prostitute your paper to make it the vehicle of slander or of censure against private characters: you will describe the general manners of the age, not those of this or that private person. Hitherto you have not offended in this way; and if you continue in the same proper course, I shall drink success to the Lounger at our next anniversary meeting; for you must know, that our Club still meets once a year on the day our first number was published. There it would do your heart good to hear us talk over the little anecdotes which gave us so much pleasure in the Mirror. I shall propose, Sir, that you be received as a guest at our anniversary next year, that you may see what sort of folks your predecessors were. There is one point in which I trust you will agree with us, and that in preferring good claret to port wine. Hoping to have the honor of drinking a glass of our favorite liquor with you, I am, &c.
a Member of the Mirror Club

---

I feel myself much honored by this mark of attention from one of my predecessors, and much flattered by his approbation. At the same time I hesitated whether I ought or ought not to publish his letter. Indeed I am not at this moment perfectly clear in my own mind, whether he meant or wished that it should be published. It is written so much in the style of private confidence and friendship, that it seems not to have been intended for the public.— Besides, I was aware that the scoffers might be apt to smile at that air of importance with which "we authors," even of periodical sheets, are apt to regard every thing which concerns ourselves and our works, and of which, it must be owned, there are some plain enough marks in this letter.

Notwithstanding all this, I at length resolved to publish it, partly to gratify my own vanity, and partly because I could in no other shape return my acknowledgments to my correspondent for the notice with which he has been so kind as to honor me. I have only to add, that I have long felt a strong desire to be personally acquainted with the members of the Mirror Club, and therefore I am much pleased with the hint given in the close of the letter, of an invitation to attend their anniversary meeting.—

## WILLIAM CAMERON (1751–1811)

### As Oer the Highland Hills I Hied

As oer the Highland hills I hied,
The Camerons in array I spied;
Lochiel's proud standard waving wide,
In all its ancient glory.
The martial pipe loud pierced the sky,
The bard arose, resounding high
Their valor, faith, and loyalty,
That shine in Scottish story.

No more the trumpet calls to arms,
Awaking battle's fierce alarms,
But every hero's bosom warms
With songs of exultation.
While brave Lochiel at length regains,
Through toils of war, his native plains,
And, won by glorious wounds, attains
His high paternal station.

Let now the voice of joy prevail,
And echo wide from hill to vale;

Ye warlike clans, arise and hail
Your laureled chiefs returning.
Oer every mountain, every isle,
Let peace in all her luster smile,
And discord ne'er her day defile
With sullen shades of mourning.

M'Leod, M'Donald, join the strain,
M'Pherson, Fraser, and M'Lean.
Through all your bounds let gladness reign,
Both prince and patriot praising,
Whose generous bounty richly pours
The streams of plenty round your shores,
To Scotia's hills their pride restores,
Her faded honors raising.

Let all the joyous banquet share,
Nor e'er let Gothic grandeur dare,
With scowling brow, to overbear,
A vassal's right invading.
Let freedom's conscious sons disdain
To crowd his fawning, timid train,
Nor even own his haughty reign,
Their dignity degrading.

Ye northern chiefs, whose rage unbroke
Has still repelled the tyrant's shock;
Who ne'er have bowed beneath his yoke,
With servile base prostration:—
Let each now train his trusty band,
Gainst foreign foes alone to stand,
With undivided heart and hand,
For freedom, king, and nation.

## ROBERT COUPER (1753–1818)

### Kinrara

Red gleams the sun on yon hill-tap,
The dew sits on the gowan.
Deep murmurs through her glens the Spey,
Around Kinrara rowan.
Where art thou, fairest, kindest lass?
Alas, wert thou but near me,
Thy gentle soul, thy melting eye,
Would ever, ever cheer me.

The lav'rock sings among the clouds,
The lambs they sport so cheerie,
And I sit weepin by the birk.
O where art thou, my dearie?
Aft may I meet the morning dew,

Lang greet* till I be weary. weep
Thou canna, winna, gentle maid,
Thou canna be my dearie.

## The Sheeling

Oh, grand bounds the deer oer the mountain,
And smooth skims the hare oer the plain.
At noon, the cool shade by the fountain
Is sweet to the lass and her swain.
The ev'ning sits down dark and dreary.
Oh, yon's the loud joys of the ha'.
The laird sings his dogs and his dearie—
Oh, he kens na his singin' ava.

But oh, my dear lassie, when wi' thee,
What's the deer and the maukin* to me? hare
The storm soughin' wild drives me to thee,
And the plaid shelters baith me and thee.
The wild warld then may be reeling,
Pride and riches may lift up their ee.
My plaid haps* us baith in the sheeling*— shelters/cottage
That's a' to my lassie and me.

## WILLIAM DUDGEON (1753–1813)

## The Maid That Tends the Goats

Up amang yon cliffy rocks,
Sweetly rings the rising echo
To the maid that tends the goats,
Lilting oer her native notes.
Hark, she sings, "Young Sandy's kind
And he's promised aye to loe me.
Here's a brooch I ne'er shall tine*, lose
Till he's fairly married to me.
Drive away, ye drone, time,
And bring about our bridal day.

"Sandy herds a flock o' sheep.
Aften does he blaw the whistle
In a strain sae saftly sweet,
Lammies list'ning daurna bleat.
He's as fleet's the mountain roe,
Hardy as the Highland heather,
Wading through the winter snow,
Keeping aye his flock together.
But a plaid, wi' bare houghs*, hollows
He braves the bleakest norlan' blast.

"Brawly* can he dance and sing with flair
Canty* glee, or Highland cronach. pleasant

Nane can ever match his fling
At a reel, or round a ring.
Wightly can he wield a rung*. staff, club
In a brawl he's aye the bangster.
A' his praise can ne'er be sung
By the langest-winded sangster.
Sangs that sing o' Sandy
Come short, though they were e'er sae lang."

## JOHN DUNLOP (1755–1820)

### The Year That's Awa'

Here's to the year that's awa'.
We will drink it in strong and in sma'.
And here's to ilk bonnie young lassie we lo'ed,
While swift flew the year that's awa'.

Here's to the sodger who bled,
And the sailor who bravely did fa'.
Their fame is alive though their spirits are fled
On the wings of the year that's awa'.

Here's to the friends we can trust
When storms of adversity blaw.
May they live in our songs and be nearest our hearts,
Nor depart like the year that's awa'.

### Oh, Dinna Ask Me gin I Loe Ye

Oh, dinna ask me gin* I loe ye. if
Troth, I dar'na tell.
Dinna ask me gin I loe ye—
Ask it o' yersel'.

Oh, dinna look sae sair at me,
For weel ye ken me true.
Oh, gin ye look sae sair at me,
I dar'na look at you.

When ye gang to yon braw, braw toun,
And bonnier lasses see,
Oh, dinna, Jamie, look at them,
Lest you should mind na me.

For I could never bide the lass
That ye'd loe mair than me,
And oh, I'm sure my heart would break
Gin ye'd prove false to me.

## ANN MACVICAR GRANT (1755–1838)

[Born in Glasgow, the daughter of an army officer, Ann Grant lived for a time in North America. In 1778 her father was posted to Fort Augustus, where Ann married the barrack chaplain, with whom she lived in his neighboring ministry at Laggan, until his death in 1801. Her *Letters From the Mountains* was published two years later. The letters are addressed to several persons and are on many subjects. Only a precious few offer the intimate and detailed account of Highland life later given by the *Memoirs* of Elizabeth Grant (1797–1885). Many are of the abstract moralizing kind associated with the eighteenth century formal essay. Printed here, besides some charming lyrics, are one outstanding example of each kind. The two letters offer, as well, interestingly complementary views on the place of women in the Age of Enlightenment. The second letter was prompted by the recent publication of Mary Wollstonecraft's feminist classic, *A Vindication of the Rights of Woman.*]

### Could I Find a Bonnie Glen

Could I find a bonnie glen,
Warm and calm, warm and calm:
Could I find a bonnie glen,
    Warm and calm;
Free frae din, and far frae men,
There my wanton kids I'd pen,
Where woodbines shade some den,
Breathing balm, breathing balm;
Where woodbines shade some den,
    Breathing balm.

Where the steep and woody hill
Shields the deer, shields the deer;
Where the steep and woody hill
    Shields the deer;
Where the woodlark, singing shrill,
Guards his nest beside the rill,
And the thrush, with tawny bill,
Warbles clear, warbles clear;
And the thrush, with tawny bill,
    Warbles clear.

Where the dashing waterfall
Echoes round, echoes round;
Where the dashing waterfall
    Echoes round;
And the rustling aspen tall,
And the owl, at evening's call,
Plaining from the ivied wall,
Joins the sound, joins the sound;
Plaining from the ivied wall,
    Joins the sound.

There my only love I'd own,
All unseen, all unseen:

There my only love I'd own,
All unseen;
There I'd live for her alone,
To the restless world unknown,
And my heart should be the throne
For my queen, for my queen;
And my heart should be the throne
For my queen.

## On a Sprig of Heath

Flower of the waste! the heathfowl shuns
For thee the brake and tangled wood.
To thy protecting shade she runs.
Thy tender buds supply her food.
Her young forsake her downy plumes
To rest upon thy opening blooms.

Flower of the desert though thou art!
The deer that range the mountain free,
The graceful doe, the stately hart,
Their food and shelter seek from thee.
The bee thy earliest blossom greets,
And draws from thee her choicest sweets.

Gem of the heath! whose modest bloom
Sheds beauty oer the lonely moor,
Though thou dispense no rich perfume,
Nor yet with splendid tints allure,
Both valor's crest and beauty's bower
Oft has thou decked, a favorite flower.

Flower of the wild! whose purple glow
Adorns the dusky mountain's side,
Not the gay hues of Iris' bow,
Nor garden's artful varied pride,
With all its wealth of sweets, could cheer,
Like thee, the hardy mountaineer.

Flower of his heart! thy fragrance mild
Of peace and freedom seems to breathe.
To pluck thy blossoms in the wild,
And deck his bonnet with the wreath,
Where dwelt of old his rustic sires,
Is all his simple wish requires.

Flower of his dear-loved native land!
Alas, when distant, far more dear.
When he from some cold foreign strand
Looks homeward through the blinding tear,
How must his aching heart deplore,
That home and thee he sees no more.

## The Highland Housewife

from *Letters From the Mountains*, August 27, 1787

To Mrs. Smith, Lint-House, Laggan

My dear Friend,

The long Lint-house letter you promised me is not yet arrived. I have been for a month at my *Linthouse,* alias Fort George; where being in some measure disengaged from the perpetual hurry which always surrounds me at home, I find leisure to gratify the strong inclination I always feel, to write to you. Taking it for granted, that in the present case, you not only excuse but require egoism, I will endeavor to explain to you the nature of that bustle, and perplexity of affairs, which I complain of so often, and so justly.

Having a great deal to do is not altogether the thing; that, too, abridges my time for amusements of this nature; but tis having a great deal to think of, to contrive, and to plan out, that plagues me. Tis acting in a variety of characters and capacities scarce compatible with each other. I must, after seven years experience, confess, with deep mortification, and due reverence for that exalted character, that the person who would be a notable housewife, must be that individual thing only, and not mar the main affair by an attempt to introduce separate and subordinate excellencies.

She must not even, in any sense, be a tender wife, or attentive mother. She must not walk about with her husband, or be his evening companion in conversation or other amusements; she must not spend her time in instructing her children, nor attend to the forming of their minds: their food, clothing. and health, is all she must attend to.

You Lowlanders have no idea of the complicated nature of Highland farming, and of the odd customs which prevail here. Formerly, from the wild and warlike nature of the men, and their haughty indolence, they thought no rural employment compatible with their dignity, unless, indeed, the plow. Fighting, hunting, lounging in the sun, music, and poetry, were their occupations. For the latter, though you would not think it, their language is admirably adapted.

This naturally extended the women's province both of labor and management. The care of the cattle was peculiarly theirs. Changing their residence so often, as they did in summer, from one bothy or glen to another, gave a romantic peculiarity to their turn of thought and language. Their manner of life, in fact, wanted nothing but the shades of palm, the olives, the vines, and the fervid sun of the East, to resemble the patriarchal one. Yet, as they must carry their beds, food, and utensils, the housewife, who furnishes and divides these matters, has enough to do when her shepherd is in one glen, and her dairy-maid in another with her milk cattle. Not to mention some of the children, who are marched off to the glen as a discipline, to inure them early to hardiness and simplicity of life.

Meanwhile, His Reverence,[1] with my kitchen damsel and the plowman, constitute another family at home, from which all the rest are flying detachments, occasionally sent out and recalled, and regularly furnished with provisions and forage. The effect, you know, often continues when the cause has ceased; the men are now civilized in comparison to what they were, yet the custom of leaving the weight of every thing on the more helpless sex continues, and has produced this one good effect, that they are from this habit less helpless and dependent. The men think they preserve dignity by this mode of management; the women find a degree of power or conse-

[1]Our sense of this teasing reference may be made more ambiguous if we remember her husband was, in fact, a minister.

quence in having such an extensive department, which they would not willingly exchange for inglorious ease.

What these occupations are, you cannot comprehend from a general description; but, as it is an hour to breakfast-time, and I find myself in the humour of journalizing and particularizing, I shall, between fancy and memory, sketch out the diary of one July Monday. I mention Monday, being the day that all dwellers in glens come down for the supplies. Item, at four o'clock, Donald arrives with a horse loaded with butter, cheese, and milk. The former I must weigh instantly. He only asks an additional blanket for the children, a covering for himself; two milk tubs, a cog, and another spoon, because little Peter threw one of the set in the burn; two stones of meal, a quart of salt; two pounds of flax; for the spinners, for the grass continues so good that they will stay a week longer. He brings the intelligence of the old sow's being the joyful mother of a dozen of pigs, and requests something to feed her with. All this must be ready in an hour; before the conclusion of which comes Ronald, from the high hills, where our sheep and young horses are all summer, and only desires meal, salt, and women with shears, to clip the lambs, and tar to smear them.

He informs me that the black mare has a foal, a very fine one; but she is very low, and I must instantly send one to bring her to the meadows. Before he departs, the tenants who do us services come; they are going to stay two days in the oak wood, cutting timber for our new byre, and must have a competent provision of bread, cheese, and ale for the time they stay.

Then I have Caro's breakfast to get, Janet's hank to reel, and a basket of clues to dispatch to the weaver; K—'s lesson to hear, her sampler to rectify; and all must be over before eleven: while His Reverence, calm and regardless of all this bustle, wonders what detains me, urging me out to walk, while the soaring larks, the smiling meadows, and opening flowers, second the invitation; and my imagination, if it gets a moment loose from care, kindles at these objects with all the eagerness of youthful enthusiasm. My tottering constitution, my faded form and multiplying cares are all forgotten, and I enjoy the pause from keen exertion, as others do gaiety and mirth.

How happy, in my circumstances, is that versatile and sanguine temper, which is hoping for a rainbow in every cloud; nay, so prevalent is this disposition, that were a fire to break out in the offices, and burn them all down, I dare say the first thing that would occur to me, would be to console myself by considering how much ground would be manured by all these fine ashes.

Now I will not plague you with the detail of the whole day, of which the above is a competent specimen. Yet spare your pity; for this day is succeeded by an evening so sweetly serene, our walk by the river is so calmly pleasing, our lounge by the burnside so indolently easy, our conversation in the long-wished for hour of leisure so interesting, sliding so imperceptibly from grave to gay; and then our children! Say you wish me more ease and leisure, but do not pity me. Pity with me is like advice with some; I am readier to give than to take it. Adieu! dear and true friend.

## Reply to Mary Wolstonecraft

from *Letters From the Mountains*, January 2, 1794

To Miss Ourry, Glasgow

I am far from imputing neglect to you after your two spirited efforts from F—bridge and London, and the other very pleasing testimonies of attention to my dear friends at Laggan, of which I heard as they passed through the town. After this elegant exordium, with which you must be greatly edified, it remains with me to account for staying so long here, contrary to my mate's tender injunction and your entreaties. First, then, my father has been very ill, and had I been much inclined, which I honestly confess was not the case, I could not, till now, have thought of returning. Then I have not put B. to school, or done half of what I meant.

I have seen Mary Wolstoncraft's book, which is so run after here, that there is no keeping it long enough to read it leisurely, though one had leisure. It has produced no other conviction in my mind, but that of the author's possessing considerable abilities, and greatly misapplying them. To refute her arguments would be to write another and a larger book; for there is more pains and skill required to refute ill-founded assertions, than to make them. Nothing can be more specious and plausible, for nothing can delight Misses more, than to tell them they are as wise as their masters. Though, after all, they will, in every emergency, be like Trinculo in the storm, when he crept under Caliban's gabardine for shelter.

I consider this work as every way dangerous. First, because the author to considerable powers adds feeling, and I dare say a degree of rectitude of intention. She speaks from conviction on her own part, and has completely imposed on herself, before she attempts to mislead you. Then she speaks in such a strain of seeming piety, and quotes Scripture in a manner so applicable and emphatic, that you are thrown off your guard, and surprised into partial acquiescence, before you observe that the deduction to be drawn from her position, is in direct contradiction, not only to Scripture, reason, the common sense and universal custom of the world, but even to parts of her own system, and many of her own assertions.

Some women of a good capacity, with the advantage of superior education, have no doubt acted and reasoned more consequentially and judiciously than some weak men; but, take the whole sex through, this seldom happens; and were the principal departments, where strong thinking and acting become necessary, allotted to females, it would evidently happen so much the more rarely, that there would be little room for triumph, and less for inverting the common order of things, to give room for the exercise of female intellect. It sometimes happens, especially in our climate, that a gloomy dismal winter day, when all without and within is comfortless, is succeeded by a beautiful starlight evening, embellished with aurora borealis, as quick as splendid and as transient, as the play of the brightest female imagination: of these bad days succeeded by good nights, there may perhaps be a dozen in the season.

What should we think of a projector, that to enjoy the benefit of the one, and avoid the oppression of the other, should insist that people should sleep all day and work all night, the whole year round? I think the great advantage that women, taken upon the whole, have over men is that they are more gentle, benevolent, and virtuous. Much of this only superiority they owe to living secure and protected in the shade. Let them loose to go impudently through all the justling paths of politics and business and they will encounter all the corruptions that men are subject to, without the same powers either of resistance or recovery; for, the delicacy of the female mind is like other fine things; in attempting to rub out a stain, you destroy the texture.

I am sorry to tell you, *in a very low whisper,* that this intellectual equality that the Misses make such a rout about, has no real existence. The ladies of talents would not feel so overburdened, and at a loss what to do with them, if they were not quite out of the common course of things.

Mary W. and some others put me in mind of a kitten we had last winter, who, finding a small tea-pot without a lid, put in its head, but not finding it so easy to take it out again, she broke the pot in the struggle; her head, however, still remained in the opening, and she retained as much of the broken utensil round her neck, as made a kind of moveable pillory. She ran about the house in alarm and astonishment. She did not know what was the matter; felt she was not like other cats, but had acquired a greater power of making disturbance, which she was resolved to use to the very utmost, and so would neither be quiet herself, nor suffer any one else to remain so. I leave the application to you.

Our powers are extremely well adapted to the purposes for which they are intended; and if now and then faculties of a superior order are bestowed upon us, they too are, no doubt, given for good and wise purposes, and we have as good a right to use them as a linnet has to sing; but this so seldom happens, and it is of so little consequence whether it happens or not, that there is no reason why Scripture, custom, and nature, should be set at defiance to erect a system of education for qualifying women to act parts which Providence has not assigned to the sex.

Where a woman has those superior powers of mind to which we give the name of genius, she will exert them under all disadvantages: Jean Jacques says truly, that genius will educate itself, and, like flame, burst through all obstructions. Certainly in the present state of society, when knowledge is so very attainable, a strong and vigorous intellect may soon find its level. Creating hotbeds for female genius is merely another way of forcing exotic productions, which, after all, are mere luxuries, indifferent in their kind, and cost more time and expense than they are worth.

As to superiority of mental powers, Mrs. W. is doubtless the empress of female philosophers; yet what has she done for philosophy, or for the sex, but closed a ditch, to open a gulf? There is a degree of boldness in her conceptions, and masculine energy in her style, that is very imposing. There is a gloomy grandeur in her imagination while she explores the regions of intellect without chart or compass which gives one the idea of genius wandering through chaos. Yet her continual self-contradiction and quoting with such-seeming reverence that very Scripture one of whose first and clearest principles it is the avowed object of her work to controvert; her considering religion as an adjunct to virtue, so far and no farther than suits her hypothesis; the taking up and laying down of revelation with the same facility; make me think of a line in an old song

One foot on sea, and one on shore,
To one thing constant never.

What, as I said before has she done? shewed us all the miseries of our condition; robbed us of the only sure remedy for the evils of life, the sure hope of a blessed immortality; and left for our comfort the rudiments of crude unfinished systems that crumble to nothing whenever you begin to examine the materials of which they are constructed.

Come, let us for a moment shut the Bible, and listen to Mary. Let us suppose intellect equally divided between the sexes. We may deceive the understanding, but it would be a very bold effort of sophistry to attempt to impose on the senses. We know too well that our imaginations are more awake, our senses more acute, our feelings more delicate, than those of our *tyrants*. Say, then, we are otherwise equal. These qualities or defects would still leave the advantage on their side; we should much oftener resolve and act, before we called reason to counsel, than they would.

Besides, I foresee that the balance will go in the old fashioned way at last, if Mary carries her point. When the desired revolution is brought about, will not the most sanguine advocates of equality be satisfied, in the first national council, with having an equal number of each sex elected? Now I foresee that when this is done, (as girls, or very old women, will not be eligible for the duties of legislation, and mothers have certainly a greater stake in the commonwealth) a third of the female members will be lying-in, recovering, or nursing; for you can never admit the idea of a female philosopher giving her child to be nursed.

Whatever other changes may be found proper I hope they will recall the wool sacks in the upper house and add some more. The membresses of course, will bring their infants into the house; this will interrupt no debate; for children that suck in philosophy with their milk will not cry like the vulgar brats under the old regime but they may possibly sleep during a long debate, and then the wool-sacks will be very convenient to lay them upon.

There is no end either of reasoning or ridicule on this truly ridiculous subject. If the powers of a very superior female mind prove so inadequate to its own purposes, when thus absurdly exerted, what will become of those who adopt her vanity and skepticism without her knowledge and genius to support them?

To conclude; I see tis a great custom now for people to dabble in skepticism and speculative impiety keeping all the while a slight hold of their original principles, that they may return when they please, as if *thus far and no farther* belonged to finite natures. Yet these same people would be very unhappy, if they saw their young children going out of their depth into a current trusting to a slight hold of a twig on the brink; though the worst that could happen in this latter case were only drowning.

In fact the Bible is or is not the charter of our salvation. It is necessary both for our peace of mind and consistency of conduct that we should either believe, or not believe it. The nature of the subject admits no wavering; it is all true, or all false. Let us then seriously regard the most important object that can ever be presented to our view. These truths must be either wedded or renounced. If we mingle daring innovations and unwarranted practices with a feeble and dubious belief, haunted with pungent remorse or gloomy uncertainty, we shall not even enjoy the fleeting day that is passing from us. Let us then grasp hard our principles, or let them go. As the reformers manage, they have the fears without the hopes that religion inspires.

Let us at any rate, in these important concerns, be guided by the common sense that directs us in ordinary bargains. Let us examine well what we are to get before we part with what we have. My poor brains could never support the rotation of opinions which seems to delight some people here. They remind me of Hotspur, when he talks of living in a windmill. What a pleasing transition I am about to make from those who believe too little, to those who believe rather too much. With what delight and reverence I shall listen to dear Moome's *awe compelling tales,* after all this farrago.

Adieu. May you reap the fruits of steady principle and consistent conduct, both here and hereafter. Farewell, kindly.

## STUART LEWIS (1756–1818)

### Annan's Winding Stream

On Annan's banks, in life's gay morn,
I tuned "my wood-notes wild";
I sung of flocks and flow'ry plains,
Like nature's simple child.
Some talked of wealth—I heard of fame,
But thought twas all a dream,
For dear I loved a village maid
By Annan's winding stream.

The dew-bespangled blushing rose,
The garden's joy and pride,
Was ne'er so fragrant nor so fair
As her I wished my bride.
The sparkling radiance of her eye
Was bright as Phoebus' beam.
Each grace adorned my village maid
By Annan's winding stream.

But war's shrill clarion fiercely blew—
The sound alarmed mine ear.
My country's wrongs called for redress—
Could I my aid forbear?
No. Soon, in warlike garb arrayed,
With arms that bright did gleam,
I sighed, and left my village maid
By Annan's winding stream.

Perhaps blest peace may soon return,
With all her smiling train;
For Britain's conquests still proclaim
Her sovereign of the main.
Whene'er that wished event appears,
I'll hail the auspicious gleam,
And haste to clasp my village maid
Near Annan's winding stream.

## ANDREW SCOTT (1757–1839)

### Rural Content

I'm now a gude farmer, I've acres o' land,
An' my heart aye loups licht when I'm viewin' o't,
An' I hae servants at my command,
An' twa dainty cowts* for the plowin' o't. "colts"
My farm is a snug ane, lies high on a muir,
The muir-cocks and plivers aft skirl at my door,
An' when the sky lowers, I'm sure o' a show'r,
To moisten my land for the plowin' o't.

Leeze me on the mailin,[1] that's fa'n to my share,
It takes sax muckle bowes* for the sawin' o't. measures
I've sax braid acres for pasture, an' mair,
An' a dainty bit bog for the mawin' o't.
A spence* and a kitchen my mansion house gies, inner room
I've a cantie wee wifie to dot whan I please; pleasant
Twa bairnies, twa callans*, that skelp owre the leas, lads
An' they'll soon can assist at the plowin' o't.

My bigging* stands sweet on this south slopin' hill, house
An' the sun shines sae bonnily beamin' on't;
An' past my door trots a clear prattlin' rill
Frae the loch, where the wild ducks are swimmin' on't.
An' on its green banks, on the gay simmer days,
My wifie trips barefit, a-bleachin' her claes,
An' on the dear creature wi' rapture I gaze,
While I whistle and sing at the plowin' o't.

---

[1] A blessing on the farm.

To rank among farmers I hae muckle pride,
But I maunna speak high when I'm tellin' o't,
How brawly I strut on my shelty* to ride, pony
Wi' a sample to show for the sellin' o't.
In blue worset boots that my auld mither span
I've aft been fu' vantie* sin' I was a man, proud
But now they're flung by, and I've bought cordovan,
And my wifie ne'er grudged me a shillin' o't.

Sae now when to kirk or to market I gae,
My weelfare what need I be hidin' o't?
In braw leather boots shinin' black as the slae* sloe-berry
I dink* me to try the ridin' o't. dress
Last towmond* I sell't off four bowes o' gude bere*, year/barley
An' thankfu' I was, for the victual was dear,
An' I cam hame wi' spurs on my heels shinin' clear,
I had sic gude luck at the sellin' o't.

Now hairst-tame is oer, an' a fig for the laird,
My rent's now secure for the toilin' o't;
My fields are a' bare, and my crap's in th' yard,
And I'm nae mair in doubts o' the spoilin' o't.
Now welcome gude weather, or wind, or come weet,
Or bauld ragin' Winter, wi' hail, snaw or sleet,
Nae mair can he draigle my crap mang his feet,
Nor wraik his mischief, and be spoilin' o't.

An' on the dowf* days, when loud hurricanes blaw, dull
Fu' snug i' the spence I'll be viewin' o't,
And jink* the rude blast in my rush-theikit* ha', dodge/thatched
When fields are sealed up frae the plowin' o't.
My bonnie wee wifie, the bairnies, and me,
The peat-stack and turf-stack our Phoebus shall be,
Till day close the scoul o' its angry e'e,
And we'll rest in gude hopes o' the plowin' o't.

## Symon and Janet

Surrounded wi' bent* and wi' heather, grass
Where muircocks and plivers are rife,
For mony a long towmont* thegither year
There lived an auld man and his wife.

About the affairs o' the nation
The twasome they seldom were mute;
Bonaparte, the French, and invasion,
Did saur in their wizens like soot.

In winter, when deep are the gutters,
And night's gloomy canopy spread,
Auld Symon sat luntin'* his cuttie*, lighting/pipe
And lowsin' his buttons for bed.

Auld Janet, his wife, out a-gazin'
(To lock in the door was her care),
She, seeing our signals a-blazin',
Cam' running in rivin' her hair.

"O Symon, the Frenchmen are landit!
Gae look, man, and slip on your shoon;
Our signals I see them extendit,
Like the red rising blaze o' the moon!'

"What plague, the French landit!" quo Symon,
And clash! gaed his pipe to the wa';
"Faith, then there's be loadin' and primin',"
Quo he, "if they're landit ava.'

"Our youngest son's in the militia;
Our eldest grandson's volunteer;
And the French to be fu' o' the flesh o',
I too in the ranks will appear."

His waistcoat-pouch filled he wi' pouther,
And banged down his rusty auld gun;
His bullets he put in the other,
That he for the purpose had run.

Then humpled he out in a hurry,
While Janet his courage bewails,
And cries out, "Dear Symon, be wary,"
Whilst teughly she hung by his tails.

"Let be wi' your kindness," quo Symon,
"Nor vex me wi' tears and your cares;
If now I be ruled by a woman,
Nae laurels shall crown my gray hairs."

Quo Janet, "O keep frae the riot.
Last night, man, I dreamt ye was dead;—
This aught days I've tentit* a pyot
Sit chatterin' upon the house-head.

*heeded

"And yesterday, workin' my stockin',
And you wi' your sheep on the hill,
A muckle black corbie sat croakin',—
I kenned it foreboded some ill."

"Hout, cheer up, dear Janet, be hearty;
For, ere the next sun may gae doun,
Wha kens but I'll shoot Bonaparte,
And end my auld days in renown?"

"Then, hear me," quo Janet, "I pray thee;
I'll tend thee, love, livin' or dead;

And if thou should fa' I'll die wi' thee,
Or tie up thy wounds if thou bleed."

Syne aff in a hurry he stumpled,
Wi' bullets, and pouther, and gun;
At's curpin auld Janet too himpled,—
Awa' to the neighboring toon.

There footmen and yeomen, paradin',
To scour aff in dirdum* were seen— tumult
Auld wives and young lassies a-sheddin'
The briny saut tears frae their een.

Then aff wi' his bonnet gat Symon,
And to the commander he gaes;
Quo he, "Sir, I mean to go wi' ye, man,
And help ye to lounder our faes*. "foes"

"I'm auld, yet I'm teugh as the wire;
Sae we'll at the rogues have a dash—
And, fegs, if my gun winna fire,
I'll turn her butt-end and I'll thrash."

"Well spoken, my hearty auld hero."
The Captain did smiling reply;
But begged he would stay till tomorrow,
Till daylight should glent in the sky.

What reck? a' the stour* cam' to naething; fuss
Sae Symon and Janet, his dame,
Hale-skart frae the wars, without skaithing* harm
Gaed bannin'* the French again hame. cursing

## The Fiddler's Widow

There was a musician wha played a good stick,
He had a sweet wife an' a fiddle,
An' in his profession he had right good luck
At bridals his elbow to diddle.

But ah, the poor fiddler soon chanced to dee,
As a' men to dust must return;
An' the poor widow cried, wi' the tear in her e'e,
That as lang as she lived she wad mourn.

Alane by the hearth she disconsolate sat,
Lamenting the day that she saw;
An' aye as she looked on the fiddle she grat*, wept
That silent now hung on the wa'.

Fair shane the red rose on the young widow's cheek,
Sae newly weel washen wi' tears,

As in cam a younker* some comfort to speak, youngster
Wha whispered fond love in her ears.

"Dear lassie," he cried, "I am smit wi' your charms,
Consent but to marry me now.
I'm as good as ever laid hair upon thairms*, guts (strings)
An' I'll cheer baith the fiddle an' you."

The young widow blushed, but sweet smiling she said,
"Dear sir, to dissemble I hate.
If we twa thegither are doomed to be wed,
Folks needna contend against fate."

He took down the fiddle, as dowie* it hung, sad
An' put a' the thairms in tune.
The young widow dighted* her cheeks an' she sung, cleaned up
For her heart lap her sorrows aboon.

Now sound sleep the dead in his cauld bed o' clay,
For death still the dearest maun sever;
For now he's forgot, an' his widow's fu' gay,
An' his fiddle's as merry as ever.

## Coquet Water

Whan winter winds forget to blaw,
An' vernal suns revive pale nature,
A shepherd lad by chance I saw
Feeding his flocks by Coquet Water.

Saft, saft he sung, in melting lays,
His Mary's charms an' matchless feature;
While echoes answered frae the braes
That skirt the banks of Coquet Water.

"Oh, were that bonnie lassie mine,"
Quoth he, "in love's saft wiles I'd daut* her, pet
An' deem mysel' as happy syne,
As landit laird on Coquet Water.

"Let wealthy rakes for pleasure roam,
In foreign lands their fortune fritter;
But love's pure joys be mine at home,
Wi' my dear lass on Coquet Water.

"Gie fine folks wealth, yet what care I?
Gie me her smiles whom I loe better;
Blest wi' her love an' life's calm joy,
Tending my flocks by Coquet Water.

"Flow fair an' clear, thou bonnie stream,
For on thy banks aft hae I met her.

Fair may the bonnie wild flowers gleam,
That busk* the banks of Coquet Water." dress, adorn

## JEAN GLOVER (1758–1801)

### O'er the Muir Amang the Heather

Coming through the Craigs o' Kyle,
Amang the bonnie blooming heather,
There I met a bonnie lassie,
Keeping a' her ewes thegither.

O'er the muir amang the heather,
O'er the muir amang the heather,
There I met a bonnie lassie,
Keeping a' her ewes thegither.

Says I, "My dear, where is thy hame?
In muir or dale, pray tell me whether."
Says she, "I tent* the fleecy flocks tend
That feed amang the blooming heather."

We laid us down upon a bank,
Sae warm and sunny was the weather.
She left her flocks at large to rove
Amang the bonnie blooming heather.

While thus we lay she sung a sang,
Till echo rang a mile and farther;
And aye the burden o' the sang
Was "O'er the muir amang the heather."

She charmed my heart, and aye sinsyne
I couldna think on ony ither:
By sea and sky she shall be mine,
The bonnie lass amang the heather.

O'er the muir amang the heather,
Down amang the blooming heather:—
By sea and sky she shall be mine,
The bonnie lass amang the heather.

## ELIZABETH HAMILTON (1758–1816)

### My Ain Fireside.

I hae seen great anes and sat in great ha's,
Mang lords and fine ladies a' covered wi' braws*, fine things
At feasts made for princes wi' princes I've been,
When the grand shine o' splendor has dazzled my een.
But a sight sae delightfu' I trow I ne'er spied
As the bonny blithe blink* o' my ain fireside. glimpse

My ain fireside, my ain fireside,
O, cheery's the blink o' my ain fireside.
  My ain fireside, my ain fireside,
  O, there's naught to compare wi' ane's ain fireside.

Ance mair, Gude be thankit, round my ain heartsome ingle*, hearth
Wi' the friends o' my youth I cordially mingle.
Nae forms to compel me to seem wae or glad,
I may laugh when I'm merry, and sigh when I'm sad.
Nae falsehood to dread, and nae malice to fear,
But truth to delight me, and friendship to cheer.
Of a' roads to happiness ever were tried,
There's nane half so sure as ane's ain fireside.
  My ain fireside, my ain fireside,
  O, there's naught to compare wi' ane's ain fireside.

When I draw in my stool on my cozy hearth-stane,
My heart loups* sae light I scarce ken't for my ain. "leaps" (beats)
Care's down on the wind, it is clean out o' sight,
Past troubles they seem but as dreams o' the night.
I hear but kend* voices, kend faces I see, familiar
And mark saft affection glent fond frae ilk ee.
Nae fleechings o' flattery, nae boastings o' pride,
Tis heart speaks to heart at ane's ain fireside.
  My ain fireside, my ain fireside,
  O, there's naught to compare wi' ane's ain fireside.

## JOHN PINKERTON (1758–1826)

### Bothwell Bank

On the blithe Beltane, as I went
By mysel' out oer the green bent*, grass
Whereby the crystal waves of Clyde
Through saughs* and hanging hazels glide, willows
There, sadly sitting on a brae,
I heard a damsel speak her wae.

"O Bothwell bank, thou bloomest fair,
But ah, thou mak'st my heart fu' sair.
For a' beneath thy holts sae green
My love and I wad sit at e'en,
While primroses and daisies, mixed
Wi' blue-bells, in my locks he fixed.

"But he left me ae dreary day,
And haply* now sleeps in the clay, perhaps
Without ae sigh his death to rune,
Without ae flower his grave to croun.
O Bothwell Bank, thou bloomest fair,
But ah, thou mak'st my heart fu' sair."

## ROBERT BURNS (1759–1796)

[Burns is known for two normally opposite kinds of poetry, lyric and satiric, though in his hands the two complement each other. Burns, who loved to emphasize his pastoral roots—he was employed as a farmer most of his life—pictured himself as the poet of the common man, and indeed since the upper classes in Scotland were often perceived as English in their sympathies and language, Burns was soon seen as the most "Scottish" of poets. Burns wrote or revised 250 songs, which he set to popular airs. His characteristic lyrics are love songs, though he writes also patriotic verse, drinking songs, and a small variety of other types. "A Red Red Rose" is as well known a love poem as any in the English language. His "Scots Wha Hae" is probably the most famous patriotic verse in Scottish literature. And "Auld Lang Syne" is surely the best loved of all drinking songs. It functions as the informal national anthem.

Though Burns' *persona,* thanks partly to his own efforts, was that of the unschooled poet of nature, he is in fact an outstanding example of the eighteenth century literary craftsman, a writer of consistent polish and wit. Also of his age was his love of satire, and his clear understanding that a major function of poetry was social correction. Not really a Romantic, his love of nature was of the most abstract and unspecified kind. There is little close observation and scarcely any rapture.

His satiric verse is written primarily against "stuffed shirts" and hypocrites, especially in the Presbyterian Kirk (the established church in Scotland since 1690). "Holy Willie's Prayer," an excoriation of the Kirk's Calvinist theory of predestination, is an especially fine example of his work in that area. Clearly, the poem advocates the same "natural" virtues of sex, drink and companionship as do his lyrics.

Oddly enough, Burns' finest poem is one of a kind, virtually his only narrative—"Tam o' Shanter." This tale, a hilarious account of a meeting between a genial drunk and the forces of the supernatural, is an undoubted masterpiece.

Though Burns had great influence in restoring Scots as a literary medium, his "low-life" image, both in his own person and in his poems, did not contradict the sense of the age that Scots was a country dialect. Burns himself published a glossary in the first, Kilmarnock, edition of his poems—though he surely expected to have his readership restricted largely to Scotland. And throughout the century to come, Scots was used, almost condescendingly, as an instrument of local color. Not until the "Scottish Renaissance" of the twentieth century, led by Hugh MacDiarmid, was a claim made that Scots was the appropriate vehicle for serious, intellectual art, and even then only with modifications. Burns' place as the poet of the common man was thus an ironic achievement.

Burns was often a splendid prose writer. Included here are five of his letters. Almost all of his correspondence, even that written to cronies, is in English (i.e. rather than in Scots), and these demonstrate that, in contrast to what is often said of him, Burns could, when addressing those with whom he felt comfortable, write a perfectly idiomatic, natural English style. Of the included letters, the one to John Moore, in which Burns gave his autobiography, has become famous. The numbers are those of the Clarendon Press edition of 1931.]

### Corn Rigs

It was upon a Lammas night
When corn rigs* are bonnie — "ridges," fields
Beneath the moon's unclouded light,
I held awa to Annie:

The time flew by, wi' tentless* heed, careless
Till tween the late and early;
Wi' sma' persuasion she agreed,
To see me through the barley.

The sky was blue, the wind was still,
The moon was shining clearly;
I set her down, wi' right good will,
Amang the rigs o' barley:
I kent her heart wa a' my ain;
I loved her most sincerely;
I kissed her owre and owre again,
Amang the rigs o' barley.

I locked her in my fond embrace;
Her heart was beating rarely:
My blessings on that happy place,
Amang the rigs o' barley.
But by the moon and stars so bright,
That shone that hour so clearly,
She ay shall bless that happy night
Amang the rigs o' barley.

I hae been blithe wi' comrades dear;
I hae been merry drinking;
I hae been joyfu' gath'rin gear*; goods (money)
I hae been happy thinking:
But a' the pleasure e'er I saw,
Though three times doubled fairly,
That happy night was worth them a',
Amang the rigs o' barley.

Corn rigs, an' barley rigs,
An' corn rigs are bonnie:
I'll ne'er forget that happy night,
Amang the rigs wi' Annie.

## Holy Willie's Prayer[1]

O thou that in the heavens dost dwell,
Wha, as it pleases best thysel,
Sends ane to heaven an' ten to hell
A' for thy glory,
And no for onie guid or ill
They've done before thee.

---

[1] This poem, an attack upon William Fisher, one of the elders of the Mauchline kirk, circulated widely in manuscript, but was not published in Burns' lifetime. The story tells partly of "Holy Willie's" besting by Gavin Hamilton (Burns' landlord) and Hamilton's lawyer, Robert Aiken, in an action in the church court. More significantly, the poem is intended to ridicule the Calvinist doctrine of election.

I bless and praise thy matchless might,
When thousands thou has left in night,
That I am here before thy sight
For gifts an' grace,
A burning and a shining light
To a' this place.

What was I, or my generation,
That I should get sic* exaltation? "such"
I, wha deserved most just damnation
For broken laws
Sax thousand years ere my creation,
Through Adam's cause.

When from my mither's womb I fell,
Thou might hae plunged me deep in hell
To gnash my gooms*, and weep, and wail "gums"
In burning lakes,
Where damned devils roar and yell,
Chained to their stakes.

Yet I am here, a chosen sample,
To show thy grace is great and ample.
I'm here a pillar o' thy temple,
Strong as a rock,
A guide, a buckler, and example
To a' thy flock.

But yet, O Lord! confess I must:
At times I'm fashed* wi' fleshly lust: troubled
An' sometimes, too, in warldly trust
Vile self gets in;
But Thou remembers we are dust,
Defiled wi' sin.

O Lord! yestreen, Thou kens, wi' Meg—
Thy pardon I sincerely beg—
O, may't ne'er be a living plague
To my dishonor,
An' I'll ne'er lift a lawless leg
Again upon her.

Besides, I farther maun avow—
We' Leezie's lass, three times, I trow—
But, Lord, that Friday I was fou*, "full" (drunk)
When I cam near her,
Or else, thou kens, thy servant true
Wad never steer her.

Maybe thou lets this fleshly thorn
Buffet thy servant e'en and morn,
Lest he owre-proud and high should turn
That he's sae gifted:

If sae, Thy han' maun e'en be borne
Intil thou lift it.

Lord, bless thy chosen in this place,
For here thou has a chosen race.
But God confound their stubborn face
An' blast their name,
Wha brings thy elders to disgrace
An' open shame.

Lord, mind Gau'n Hamilton's deserts:
He drinks, an' swears, an' plays at cartes,
Yet has sae monie takin arts
Wi' great and sma',
Frae God's ain priest the people's hearts
He steals awa.

And when we chastened him therefore,
Thou kens how he bred sic a splore*, riot
And set the warld in a roar
O' laughin at us:
Curse thou his basket and his store,
Kail* an' potatoes. cabbage, broth

Lord, hear my earnest cry and pray'r
Against that presbyt'ry of Ayr.
Thy strong right hand, Lord, make it bare
Upo' their heads.
Lord, visit them, an' dinna spare
For their misdeeds.

O Lord, my God, that glib-tongued Aiken,
My very heart and flesh are quakin
To think how we stood sweatin, shakin,
And' pissed wi' dread,
While he, wi' hingin lip an' snakin*, sneering
Held up his head.

Lord, in thy day o' vengeance try him.
Lord, visit him wha did employ him.
And pass not in thy mercy by them
Nor hear their pray'r,
But for thy people's sake destroy them,
An' dinna spare.

But Lord, remember me and mine
Wi' mercies temporal and divine,
That I for grace an' gear* may shine goods (wealth)
Excelled by nane;
And a' the glory shall be thine—
Amen, Amen!

## Epistle To J. Lapraik
### An Old Scottish Bard
### April 1st, 1785

While briers and woodbines budding green,
And paitricks scraichin' loud at e'en,
And morning poussie whiddin'* seen, scudding
Inspire my muse,
This freedom in an unknown frien'
I pray excuse.

On Fasten-e'en we had a rockin'* gathering
To ca' the crack* and weave our stockin'; chat
And there was meikle fun and jokin',
Ye need na' doubt;
At length we had a hearty yokin'
At sang about.

There was ae sang, amang the rest,
Aboon them a' it pleased me best,
That some kind husband had addrest
To some sweet wife:
It thirled the heart-strings through the breast,
A' to the life.

I've scarce heard aught describe sae weel
What generous manly bosoms feel;
Thought I, "Can this be Pope, or Steele,
Or Beattie's wark?"
They tauld me twas an odd kind chiel
About Muirkirk.

It pat me fidgin'-fain to hear't,
And sae about him there I spier't*, asked
Then a' that kent him, round declared
He had ingine,
That nane excelled it, few cam' near't,
It was sae fine.

That, set him to a pint of ale,
And either douce* or merry tale, sober
Or rhymes and sangs he'd made himsel',
Or witty catches,
Tween Inverness and Teviotdale,
He had few matches.

Then up I gat, and swoor an aith,
Though I should pawn my pleugh and graith*, gear
Or die a cadger-pownie's* death, peddler-pony's
At some dyke-back,
A pint and gill I'd gi'e them baith
To hear your crack.

But, first and foremost, I should tell,
A'maist as soon as I could spell,
I to the crambojingle* fell; doggerel
Though rude and rough,
Yet crooning to a body's sel',
Does weel eneugh.

I am nae poet, in a sense,
But just a rhymer, like, by chance,
And hae to learning nae pretense,
Yet, what the matter?
Whene'er my muse does on me glance,
I jingle at her.

Your critic folk may cock their nose,
And say, "How can you e'er propose,
You, wha ken hardly verse frae prose,
To mak' a sang?"
But, by your leaves, my learned foes,
Ye're maybe wrang.

What's a' your jargon o' your schools,
Your Latin names for horns and stools;
If honest nature made you fools,
What sairs* your grammars? "serves"
Ye'd better ta'en up spades and shools*, "shovels"
Or knappin'* hammers. stone breaking

A set o' dull, conceited hashes* hacks
Confuse their brains in college classes!
They gang in stirks*, and come out asses, year-old bullocks
Plain truth to speak;
And syne they think to climb Parnassus
By dint o' Greek!

Gi'e me ae spark o' Nature's fire!
That's a' the learning I desire:
Then though I drudge through dub and mire
At pleugh or cart,
My muse, though hamely in attire,
May touch the heart.

Oh for a spunk o' Allan's glee,
Or Fergusson's, the bauld and slee,
Or bright Lapraik's, my friend to be,
If I can hit it!
That would be lear* enough for me! "learning"
If I could get it.

Now, Sir, if ye hae friends enow—
Though real friends, I believe, are few;
Yet, if your catalogue be fu'
I'se no insist;

But gif ye want ae friend that's true,
    I'm on your list.

I winna blaw about mysel';
As ill I like my fauts to tell:
But friends, and folk that wish me well,
    They sometimes roose* me, — praise
Though I maun own, as mony still
    As far abuse me.

There's ae wee faut they whiles lay to me,
I like the lasses—Gude forgi'e me!
For mony a plack* they wheedle frae me, — (a small coin)
    At dance or fair;
Maybe some ither thing they gi'e me
    They weel can spare.

But, Mauchline race, or Mauchline fair,
I should be proud to meet you there;
We'se gi'e ae night's discharge to care,
    If we foregather,
And hae a swap o' rhymin' ware
    Wi' ane anither.

The four-gill chap, we'se gar* him clatter, — make
And kirsen him wi' reekin' water;
Syne we'll sit down and tak' our whitter*, — large drink
    To cheer our heart;
And faith, we'se be acquainted better
    Before we part.

Awa', ye selfish warldly race,
Wha think that havins*, sense, and grace, — manners
Ev'n love and friendship should give place
    To catch-the-plack!
I dinna like to see your face,
    Nor hear your crack.

But ye whom social pleasure charms,
Whose heart the tide of kindness warms,
Who hold your being on the terms,
    "Each aid the others."
Come to my bowl, come to my arms,
    My friends, my brothers!

But, to conclude my lang epistle,
As my auld pen's worn to the gristle:
Twa lines frae you wad gar me fissle,
    Who am, most fervent,
While I can either sing or whistle
    Your friend and servant.

## Second Epistle to J. Lapraik
April 21, 1785

While new-ca'd kye rowt* at the stake bellow
An' pownies reek in pleugh or braik,
This hour on e'enin's edge I take,
To own I'm debtor
To honest-hearted, auld Lapraik,
For his kind letter.

Forjesket* sair, with weary legs, jaded
Rattlin the corn out-owre the rigs,
Or dealing through amang the naigs
Their ten-hours' bite,
My awkart Muse sair pleads and begs
I would na write.

The tapetless*, ramfeezl'd* hizzie, senseless/exhausted
She's saft at best an' something lazy:
Quo' she, "Ye ken we've been sae busy
This month an' mair,
That trowth, my head is grown right dizzy,
An' something sair."

Her dowff* excuses pat me mad; dull
"Conscience," says I, "ye thowless* jade! useless
I'll write, an' that a hearty blaud*, amount
This vera night;
So dinna ye affront your trade,
But rhyme it right.

"Shall bauld Lapraik, the king o' hearts,
Though mankind were a pack o' cartes,
Roose* you sae weel for your deserts, praise
In terms sae friendly;
Yet ye'll neglect to shaw your parts
An' thank him kindly?"

Sae I gat paper in a blink,
An' down gaed stumpy in the ink:
Quoth I, "Before I sleep a wink,
I vow I'll close it;
An' if ye winna mak it clink,
By Jove, I'll prose it!"

Sae I've begun to scrawl, but whether
In rhyme, or prose, or baith thegither;
Or some hotch-potch that's rightly neither,
Let time mak proof;
But I shall scribble down some blether
Just clean aff-loof*. offhand

My worthy friend, ne'er grudge an' carp,
Though fortune use you hard an' sharp;
Come, kittle* up your moorland harp      tickle
    Wi' gleesome touch.
Ne'er mind how fortune waft and warp;
    She's but a bitch.

She's gien me mony a jirt* and fleg*,      jerk/scare
Sin' I could striddle owre a rig;
But, by the L—d, thou I should beg
    Wi' lyart* pow*,      gray/head
I'll laugh an' sing, an' shake my leg,
    As lang's I dow*.      can

Now comes the sax-an-twentieth simmer
I've seen the bud upon the timmer*,      "timber" (tree)
Still persecuted by the limmer*      jade
    Frae year to year;
But yet, despite the kittle kimmer*,      wench
    I, Rob, am here.

Do ye envy the city gent,
Behint a kist* to lie an' sklent*;      chest/cheat
Or purse-proud, big wi' cent. per cent.
    An' muckle wame*,      belly
In some bit brugh* to represent      "borough"
    A bailie's name?

Or is't the paughty* feudal thane,      haughty
Wi' ruffled sark an' glancing cane,
Wha thinks himsel nae sheep-shank bane,
    But lordly stalks;
While caps and bonnets aff are taen,
    As by he walks?

"O Thou wha gies us each guid gift,
Gie me o' wit an' sense a lift,
Then turn me, if thou please, adrift,
    Through Scotland wide;
Wi' cits nor lairds I wadna shift,
    In a' their pride."

Were this the charter of our state,
"On pain o' hell be rich an' great,"
Damnation then would be our fate,
    Beyond remead;
But, thanks to heaven, that's no the gate*      way
    We learn our creed.

For thus the royal mandate ran,
When first the human race began;
"The social, friendly, honest man,
    Whate'er he be—

Tis he fulfills great nature's plan,
    And none but he."

O mandate glorious and divine!
The followers o' the ragged Nine,
Poor, thoughtless devils, yet may shine
    In glorious light,
While sordid sons o' Mammon's line
    Are dark as night.

Though here they scrape, an' squeeze, an' growl,
Their worthless nievefu'* of a soul    fistful
May in some future carcase howl,
    The forest's fright;
Or in some day-detesting owl
    May shun the light.

Then may Lapraik and Burns arise,
To reach their native, kindred skies,
And sing their pleasures, hopes an' joys,
    In some mild sphere;
Still closer knit in friendship's ties,
    Each passing year.

## One Night as I Did Wander

One night as I did wander,
When corn begins to shoot,
I sat me down to ponder
Upon an auld tree root:
Auld Aire ran by before me,
And bickered to the seas;
A cushat* crouded* oer me    pigeon/cooed
That echoed through the braes.

## The Holy Fair[1]

Upon a simmer Sunday morn,
When Nature's face is fair,
I walked forth to view the corn,
An' snuff the callor* air.    fresh
The rising sun, oer Galston Muirs,
Wi' glorious light was glintan.
The hares were hirplan* down the furrs*,    hopping/ "furrows"
The lav'rocks* they were chantan    larks
    Fu' sweet that day.

[1] "Holy Fair" is a common Scots term for a popular religious festival. The annual Communion service was a major event in which field preaching took place, usually in a tent near a tavern. Scottish literature has a long tradition of celebrating such festivals, for example, "Christ's Kirk on the Green."

As lightsomely I glowred abroad,
To see a scene sae gay,
Three hizzies*, early at the road, — wenches
Cam skelpan* up the way. — skipping
Twa had mantles o' dolefu' black,
But ane wi' lyart* lining; — gray
The third, that gaed a wee a-back,
Was in the fashion shining
Fu' gay that day.

The twa appeared like sisters twin,
In feature, form an' claes;
Their visage withered, lang an' thin,
An' sour as ony slaes*. — sloe-berries
The third cam up, hap-step-an'-loup,
As light as ony lambie,
An' wi' a curchie low did stoop,
As soon as e'er she saw me,
Fu' kind that day.

Wi' bonnet aff, quoth I,
"Sweet lass, I think ye seem to ken me;
I'm sure I've seen that bonnie face,
But yet I canna name ye."
Quo' she, an' laughan as she spak,
An' taks me by the han's.
"Ye, for my sake, hae gien the feck* — bulk
Of a' the ten comman's
A screed* some day. — rip

"My name is Fun—your crony dear,
The nearest friend ye hae;
An' this is Superstition here,
An' that's Hypocrisy,
I'm gaun to Mauchline holy fair,
To spend an hour in daffin*. — fooling
Gin ye'll go there, yon runkled* pair, — "wrinkled"
We will get famous laughin
At them this day."

Quoth I, "With a' my heart, I'll do 't:
I'll get my Sunday's sark on,
An' meet you on the holy spot.
Faith, we'se hae fine remarkin!"
Then I gaied hame at crowdie-time*, — breakfast
An' soon I made me ready;
For roads were clad, frae side to side,
Wi' monie a weary body,
In droves that day.

Here, farmers gash*, in ridin graith*, — vain/gear
Gaed hoddan* by their cotters*; — jogging/cottagers
There, swankies* young, in braw braid-claith, — strong men

Are springan owre the gutters.
The lasses, skelpan barefit, throng,
In silks an' scarlets glitter;
Wi' sweet-milk cheese, in monie a whang*, slice
An' farls*, baked wi' butter, oatcakes
    Fu' crump* that day. crisp

When by the plate we set our nose,
Weel heaped up wi' ha' pence,
A greedy glowr black-bonnet* throws, collection holder
An' we maun draw our tippence.
Then in we go to see the show,
On ev'ry side they're gath'ran.
Some carryan dails*, some chairs an' stools, planks
An' some are busy bleth'ran'
    Right loud that day.

Here stands a shed to fend the show'rs,
An' screen our countra gentry.
There, racer Jess, an' tw'three whores,
Are blinkan at the entry.
Here sits a raw o' tittlan* jads, whispering
Wi' heaving breasts an' bare neck.
An' there, a batch o' wabster* lads, weaver
Blackguarding frae Kilmarnock
    For fun this day.

Here, some are thinkan on their sins,
An' some upo' their claes.
Ane curses feet that fyled* his shins, soiled
Anither sighs an' Fays.
On this hand sits a Chosen swatch*, sample
Wi' screwed-up, grace-proud faces.
On that, a set o' chaps, at watch,
Thrang winkan on the lasses
    To chairs that day.

O happy is that man, an' blest,
Nae wonder that it pride him,
Whase ain dear lass, that he likes best,
Comes clinkan down beside him.
Wi' arm reposed on the chair-back,
He sweetly does compose him;
Which, by degrees, slips round her neck,
An's loof* upon her bosom palm
    Unkend that day.

Now a' the congregation oer
In silent expectation;
For Moodie speels* the holy door, enters
Wi' tidings o' damnation.
Should Hornie*, as in ancient days, (the devil)
Mang sons o God present him,

The vera sight o' Moodie's face.
To's ain het hame had sent him
Wi' fright that day.

Hear how he clears the points o' Faith
Wi' rattlin an' thumpin.
Now meekly calm, now wild in wrath,
He's stampan, an' he's jumpan.
His lengthened chin, his turned up snout,
His eldritch squeal an' gestures,
O how they fire the heart devout,
Like cantharidian* plaisters — aphrodisiac
On sic a day.

But hark, the tent has changed its voice;
There's peace an' rest nae langer,
For a' the real judges rise,
They canna sit for anger.
Smith[1] opes out his cauld harangues,
On practice and on morals;
A' aff the godly pour in thrangs,
To gie the jars an' barrels
A lift that day.

What signifies his barren shine,
Of moral pow'rs an' reason?
His English style, an' gesture fine,
Are a' clean out o' season.
Like Socrates or Antonine,
Or some auld pagan heathen,
The moral man he does define,
But ne'er a word o' faith in
That's right that day.

In guid time comes an antidote
Against sic poisoned nostrum;
For Peebles, frae the water fit*, — river mouth
Ascends the holy rostrum:
See, up he's got the word o' God,
An' meek an' mim* has viewed it, — prim
While common-sense has taen the road,
An' aff, an' up the Cowgate
Fast, fast that day.

Wee Miller niest* the Guard relieves, — next
An' orthodoxy raibles*, — rambles
Though in his heart he weel believes,
An' thinks it auld wives' fables:
But faith, the birkie* wants a Manse — fellow
So, cannily he hums* them; — humbugs

---

[1]The Reverend George Smith, a church liberal.

Although his carnal wit an' sense
Like hafflins-wise* o'ercomes him almost half
At times that day.

Now, butt* an' ben*, the change-house* fills, out/in/tavern
Wi' yill-caup commentators:
Here's crying out for bakes an' gills*, half-pints
An' there the pint-stowp* clatters; pint-cup
While thick an' thrang, an' loud an' lang,
Wi' logic, an' wi' scripture,
They raise a din, that, in the end,
Is like to breed a rupture
O' wrath that day.

Leeze me on drink.[1] It gies us mair
Than either school or college:
It kindles wit, it waukens lear*, learning
It pangs* us fou o' knowledge. crams
Be't whisky-gill or penny-wheep,
Or ony stronger potion,
It never fails, on drinkin deep,
To kittle* up our notion, tickle
By night or day.

The lads an' lasses, blithely bent
To mind baith saul an' body,
Sit round the table, weel content,
An' steer* about the toddy. "stir"
On this ane's dress, an' that ane's leuk,
They're makin observations;
While some are cozy i' the neuk,
An' forming assignations
To meet some day.

But now the Lord's ain trumpet touts,
Till a' the hills are rairan,
An' echoes back return the shouts;
Black Russel is na spairan:
His piercin words, like Highlan swords,
Divide the joints an' marrow:
His talk o' H—ll, whare devils swell,
Our very "Sauls does harrow"
Wi' fright that day.

A vast, unbottomed, boundless pit,
Filled fou o' lowan* brunstane, flaming
Whase raging flame, an' scorching heat,
Wad melt the hardest whun-stane*. granite
The half-asleep start up wi' fear,
An' think they hear it roaran,

[1] Leeze me on: "let me have," or "here's to—."

When presently it does appear,
Twas but some nebor snoran
    Asleep that day.

Twad be owre lang a tale to tell,
How monie stories past,
An' how they crouded to the yill,
When they were a' dismist:
How drink gaed round, in cogs an' caups,
Amang the furms* and benches; seats
An' cheese an' bread, frae women's laps,
Was dealt about in lunches*, large portions
    An' dawds* that day. pieces

In comes a gawsie*, gash* guidwife, jolly/pleasant
An' sits down by the fire,
Syne draws her kibbuck* an' her knife; cheese
The lasses they are shyer.
The auld guidmen, about the grace,
Frae side to side they bother,
Till some ane by his bonnet lays,
An' gies them 't, like a tether*, rope
    Fu' lang that day.

Waesucks* for him that gets nae lass, pity
Or lasses that hae neathing.
Sma' need has he to say a grace,
Or melvie* his braw claithing. soil
O wives be mindfu', ance yoursel,
How bonnie lads ye wanted,
An' dinna, for a kebbuck-heel,
Let lasses be affronted
    On sic a day.

Now Clinkumbell*, wi' rattlan tow*, bell-ringer/rope
Begins to jow* an' croon; swing
Some swagger hame, the best they dow*, can
Some wait the afternoon.
At slaps* the billies halt a blink, hedge-openings
Till lasses strip their shoon:
Wi' faith an' hope, an' love an' drink,
They're a' in famous tune
    For crack* that day. chatter

How monie hearts this days converts,
O' sinners and o' lasses.
Their hearts o' stane, gin* night are gane, by
As saft as ony flesh is.
There's some are fou o' love divine;
There's some are fou o' brandy;
An' monie jobs that day begin,
May end in houghmagandie* fornication
    Some ither day.

## To a Mouse

On turning her up in her nest with the plough, November 1785

Wee, sleekit, cow’rin’, tim’rous beastie,
Oh, what a panic’s in thy breastie.
Thou need na start awa sae hasty,
        Wi’ bickering brattle.
I wad be laith to rin an’ chase thee,
        Wi’ murd’ring pattle*.        plow-staff

I’m truly sorry man’s dominion
Has broken nature’s social union,
An’ justifies that ill opinion
        Which makes thee startle
At me, thy poor earth-born companion,
        An’ fellow-mortal.

I doubt na, whyles, but thou may thieve;
What then? poor beastie, thou maun live.
A daimen* icker* in a thrave*        odd/ear/shock
        ’S a sma’ request:
I’ll get a blessin’ wi’ the lave*,        rest
        And never miss’t.

Thy wee bit housie, too, in ruin.
Its silly wa’s the win’s are strewin’.
An’ naething, now, to big a new ane,
        O’ foggage* green.        foliage
An’ bleak December’s winds ensuin’,
        Baith snell* and keen?        fierce

Thou saw the fields laid bare an’ waste,
An’ weary winter comin’ fast,
An’ cozy here, beneath the blast,
        Thou thought to dwell,
Till crash! the cruel coulter* past        plow-blade
        Out through thy cell.

That wee bit heap o’ leaves an’ stibble
Has cost thee mony a weary nibble.
Now thou’s turned out, for a’ thy trouble,
        But* house or hald,        (without)
To thole the winter’s sleety dribble,
        An’ cranreuch* cauld.        hoarfrost

But, Mousie, thou art no thy lane*,        (not alone)
In proving foresight may be vain:
The best-laid schemes o’ mice an’ men,
        Gang aft agley*,        awry
An’ lea’e us nought but grief and pain
        For promised joy.

Still thou art blest, compared wi' me.
The present only toucheth thee:
But, och, I backward cast my ee,
On prospects drear.
An' forward, though I canna see,
I guess an' fear.

## The Jolly Beggars
### A Cantata

*Recitativo*

When lyart* leaves bestrow the yird, gray
Or wavering like the bauckie-bird*, bat
Bedim cauld Boreas' blast;
When hailstanes drive wi' bitter skyte,
And infant frosts begin to bite,
In hoary cranreuch* drest; frost
Ae night at e'en a merry core
O' randy, gangrel bodies,
In Poosie-Nansie's held the splore,
To drink their orra* duddies; odd
Wi' quaffing an' laughing,
They ranted an' they sang,
Wi' jumping an' thumping,
The vera girdle rang.

First, neist the fire, in auld red rags,
Ane sat, weel braced wi' mealy bags,
And knapsack a' in order.
His doxy lay within his arm.
Wi' usquebae* an' blankets warm whiskey
She blinkit on her sodger;
An' aye he gies the tozie* drab intoxicated
The tither skelpin kiss,
While she held up her greedy gab*, mouth
Just like an aumous dish;
Ilk smack still did crack still,
Just like a cadger's whip.
Then staggering an' swaggering
He roared this ditty up—

*Air*

I am a son of Mars who have been in many wars,
And show my cuts and scars wherever I come;
This here was for a wench, and that other in a trench,
When welcoming the French at the sound of the drum.
Lad de daudle, &c.

My prenticeship I past where my leader breathed his last,
When the bloody die was cast on the heights of Abram;

And I served out my trade when the gallant game was played,
And the Moro low was laid at the sound of the drum.

I lastly was with Curtis among the floating batt'ries,
And there I left for witness an arm and a limb;
Yet let my country need me, with Elliot to head me,
I'd clatter on my stumps at the sound of the drum.

And now though I must beg, with a wooden arm and leg,
And many a tattered rag hanging over my bum,
I'm as happy with my wallet, my bottle and my callet,
As when I used in scarlet to follow a drum.

What though, with hoary locks, I must stand the winter shocks,
Beneath the woods and rocks oftentimes for a home,
When the tother bag I sell, and the tother bottle tell,
I could meet a troop of hell, at the sound of a drum.

*Recitativo*

He ended; and the kebars* sheuk,     rafters
   Aboon the chorus roar;
While frighted rattons* backward leuk,     rats
   An' seek the benmost* bore.     inmost
A fairy fiddler frae the neuk,
   He skirled out, encore!
But up arose the martial chuck,
   An' laid the loud uproar.

*Air*

I once was a maid, though I cannot tell when,
And still my delight is in proper young men.
Some one of a troop of dragoons was my daddy,
No wonder I'm fond of a sodger laddie,
      Sing, lal de lal, &c.

The first of my loves was a swaggering blade,
To rattle the thundering drum was his trade.
His leg was so tight, and his cheek was so ruddy,
Transported I was with my sodger laddie.

But the godly old chaplain left him in the lurch.
The sword I forsook for the sake of the church.
He risked the soul, and I ventured the body.
Twas then I proved false to my sodger laddie.

Full soon I grew sick of my sanctified sot.
The regiment at large for a husband I got.
From the gilded spontoon to the fife I was ready.
I asked no more but a sodger laddie.

But the peace it reduced me to beg in despair,
Till I met my old boy in a Cunningham fair,

His rags regimental, they fluttered so gaudy,
My heart it rejoiced at a sodger laddie.

And now I have lived—I know not how long,
But still I can join in a cup and a song;
But whilst with both hands I can hold the glass steady,
Here's to thee, my hero, my sodger laddie.

*Recitativo*

Poor Merry-Andrew, in the neuk,
Sat guzzling wi' a tinkler-hizzie.
They mind't na wha the chorus teuk,
Between themselves they were sae busy.
At length, wi' drink an' courting dizzy,
He stoitered up an' made a face;
Then turned an' laid a smack on Grizzie,
Syne tuned his pipes wi' grave grimace.

*Air*

Sir Wisdom's a fool when he's fou.
Sir Knave is a fool in a session.
He's there but a prentice I trow,
But I am a fool by profession.

My granny she bought me a beuk,
An' I held awa to the school.
I fear I my talent misteuk,
But what will ye hae of a fool?

For drink I would venture my neck;
A hizzie's the half of my craft;
But what could ye other expect
Of ane that's avowedly daft?

I ance was tied up like a stirk*, young bullock
For civilly swearing and quaffin.
I ance was abused i' the kirk,
For towsing a lass i' my daffin*. fooling

Poor Andrew that tumbles for sport,
Let naebody name wi' a jeer.
There's even, I'm tauld, i' the Court
A tumbler ca'd the Premier.

Observed ye yon reverend lad
Mak faces to tickle the mob.
He rails at our mountebank squad,—
It's rivalship just i' the job.

And now my conclusion I'll tell,
For faith I'm confoundedly dry.

The chiel that's a fool for himsel',
Guid Lord, he's far dafter than I.

*Recitativo*

Then niest outspak a raucle* carlin*, rough/old woman
Wha kent fu' weel to cleek* the sterlin. hook, trick
For mony a pursie she had hooked,
An' had in mony a well been douked.
Her love had been a Highland laddie,
But weary fa' the waefu' woodie.
Wi' sighs an' sobs she thus began
To wail her braw John Highlandman.

*Air*

A Highland lad my love was born,
The Lalland* laws he held in scorn. "Lowland"
But he still was faithfu' to his clan,
My gallant, braw John Highlandman.

*Chorus*

Sing hey my braw John Highlandman.
Sing ho my braw John Highlandman.
There's not a lad in a' the lan'
Was match for my John Highlandman.

With his philibeg an' tartan plaid,
An' guid claymore down by his side,
The ladies' hearts he did trepan,
My gallant, braw John Highlandman,
Sing hey, &c.

We ranged a' from Tweed to Spey,
An' lived like lords an' ladies gay;
For a Lalland face he feared none,—
My gallant, braw John Highlandman.
Sing hey, &c.

They banished him beyond the sea.
But ere the bud was on the tree,
Adown my cheeks the pearls ran,
Embracing my John Highlandman.
Sing hey, &c.

But, och, they catched him at the last,
And bound him in a dungeon fast.
My curse upon them every one,
They've hanged my braw John Highlandman.
Sing hey, &c.

And now a widow, I must mourn
The pleasures that will ne'er return.
No comfort but a hearty can,

When I think on John Highlandman.
Sing hey, &c.

*Recitativo*

A pigmy scraper on his fiddle,
Wha used at trystes an' fairs to driddle,
Her strappin limb and gausy* middle jolly
(He reached nae higher)
Had holed his heartie like a riddle,
An' blawn't on fire.

Wi' hand on hainch, and upward e'e
He crooned his gamut, one, two, three,
Then in an arioso key
The wee Apollo
Set off wi' allegretto glee
His giga solo.

*Air*

Let me ryke up to dight that tear,
An' go wi' me an' be my dear;
An' then your every care an' fear
May whistle owre the lave o't.

*Chorus*

I am a fiddler to my trade,
An' a' the tunes that e'er I played,
The sweetest still to wife or maid,
Was whistle owre the lave o't.

At kirns an' weddins we'se be there,
An' O sae nicely's we will fare.
We'll bowse about till Daddy Care
Sing whistle owre the lave o't.
I am, &c.

Sae merrily's the banes we'll pyke,
An' sun oursels about the dyke;
An' at our leisure, when ye like,
We'll whistle owre the lave o't.
I am, &c.

But bless me wi' your heav'n o' charms,
An' while I kittle* hair on thairms*, tickle/guts
Hunger, cauld, an' a' sic harms,
May whistle owre the lave o't
I am, &c.

*Recitativo*

Her charms had struck a sturdy caird*, tinker
As weel as poor gut-scraper.
He taks the fiddler by the beard,
An' draws a roosty rapier—

He swoor by a' was swearing worth,
To speet him like a pliver*, "plover"
Unless he would from that time forth
Relinquish her for ever.

Wi' ghastly e'e, poor tweedle-dee
Upon his hunkers bended
An' prayed for grace wi' ruefu' face,
An' sae the quarrel ended.
But though his little heart did grieve
When round the tinkler prest her,
He feigned to snirtle in his sleeve,
When thus the caird addressed her:

*Air*

My bonnie lass, I work in brass,
A tinkler is my station.
I've traveled round all Christian ground
In this my occupation.
I've taen the gold, an' been enrolled
In many a noble squadron;
But vain they searched when off I marched
To go an' clout the cauldron.
I've taen the gold, &c.

Despise that shrimp, that withered imp,
With a' his noise an' cap'rin;
An' take a share with those that bear
The budget and the apron.
And by that stowp my faith an' houp,
And by that dear Kilbaigie*, (whiskey)
If e'er ye want, or meet wi' scant,
May I ne'er weet my craigie*. throat
And by that stowp, &c.

*Recitativo*

The caird prevailed—th' unblushing fair
In his embraces sunk;
Partly wi' love e'er come sae sair,
An' partly she was drunk.
Sir Violino, with an air
That showed a man o' spunk,
Wished unison between the pair,
An' made the bottle clunk
  To their health that night.

But hurchin* Cupid shot a shaft, uncouth
That played a dame a shavie*— trick
The fiddler raked her, fore and aft,
Behint the chicken cavie.
Her lord, a wight of Homer's craft,
Though limpin wi' the spavie,
He hirpled up, and lap like daft,

An' shored them *Dainty Davie*
O' boot that night.

He was a care-defying blade
As ever Bacchus listed.
Though Fortune sair upon him laid,
His heart, she ever missed it.
He had no wish but—to be glad,
Nor want but—when he thirsted.
He hated nought but—to be sad,
An' thus the muse suggested
His sang that night.

*Air*

I am a bard of no regard,
Wi' gentle folks an' a' that;
But Homer-like, the glowrin byke*, swarm
Frae town to town I draw that.

*Chorus*

For a' that, an' a' that,
An' twice as muckle's a' that;
I've lost but ane, I've twa behin',
I've wife eneugh for a' that.

I never drank the muses' stank,
Castalia's burn, an' a' that;
But there it streams an' richly reams,
My Helicon I ca' that.
For a' that, &c.

Great love I bear to a' the fair,
Their humble slave an' a' that;
But lordly will, I hold it still
A mortal sin to thraw* that. twist
For a' that, &c.

In raptures sweet, this hour we meet,
Wi' mutual love an' a' that;
But for how lang the flie may stang,
Let inclination law that.
For a' that, &c.

Their tricks an' craft hae put me daft,
They've taen me in, an' a' that;
But clear your decks, and here's —"The Sex."
I like the jads for a' that.

*Chorus*

For a' that, an' a' that,'
An' twice as muckle's a' that;
My dearest bluid, to do them guid,
They're welcome till't for a' that.

*Recitativo*

So sang the bard—and Nansie's wa's
Shook with a thunder of applause,
Re-echoed from each mouth.
They toomed* their pocks, they pawned their duds, emptied
They scarcely left to co'er their fuds*, rabbit tails
To quench their lowin drouth.
Then owre again, the jovial thrang
The poet did request
To lowse his pack an' wale* a sang, choose
A ballad o' the best.
He rising, rejoicing,
Between his twa Deborahs,
Looks round him, an' found them
Impatient for the chorus.

*Air*

See the smoking bowl before us,
Mark our jovial ragged ring.
Round and round take up the chorus,
And in raptures let us sing—

*Chorus*

A fig for those by law protected.
Liberty's a glorious feast.
Courts for cowards were erected,
Churches built to please the priest.

What is title, what is treasure,
What is reputation's care?
If we lead a life of pleasure,
Tis no matter how or where.
A fig for, &c.

With the ready trick and fable,
Round we wander all the day;
And at night in barn or stable,
Hug our doxies on the hay.
A fig for, &c.

Does the train-attended carriage
Through the country lighter rove?
Does the sober bed of marriage
Witness brighter scenes of love?
A fig for, &c.

Life is all a variorum,
We regard not how it goes.
Let them cant about decorum,
Who have character to lose.
A fig for, &c.

Here's to budgets, bags and wallets.
Here's to all the wandering train.
Here's our ragged brats and callets*, trollops
One and all cry out, Amen.

*Chorus*

A fig for those by law protected.
Liberty's a glorious feast.
Courts for cowards were erected,
Churches built to please the priest.

## Address to the Deil

O thou, whatever title suit thee—
Auld Hornie, Satan, Nick, or clootie—
Wha in yon cavern grim an' sootie,
Closed under hatches,
Spairges* about the brunstane cootie*, spatters/tub
To scaud poor wretches.

Hear me, Auld Hangie, for a wee,
An' let poor, damned bodies be;
I'm sure sma' pleasure it can gie
Ev'n to a deil,
To skelp an' scaud poor dogs like me
An' hear us squeal.

Great is thy pow'r, an' great thy fame;
Far kend an' noted is thy name;
An though yon lowan* heugh's* thy hame, burning/hollow
Thou travels far;
An' faith, thou's neither lag, nor lame,
Nor blate*, nor scaur. shy

Whyles, ranging like a roaran lion,
For prey, a' holes an' corners tryin;
Whyles, on the strong-winged tempest flyin,
Tirlan* the kirks; striking
Whyles, in the human bosom pryin,
Unseen thou lurks.

I've heard my rev'rend graunie say,
In lanely glens ye like to stray;
Or, where auld, ruined castles, gray
Nod to the moon,
Ye fright the nightly wand'rer's way,
Wi' eldritch croon.

When twilight did my graunie summon,
To say her pray'rs, douse*, honest woman, sober
Aft yont the dyke she's heard you bumman
Wi' eerie drone;

Or, rustlin, through the boortrees coman,
Wi' heavy groan.

Ae dreary windy, winter night,
The stars shot down wi' sklentan* light, slanting
Wi' you, mysel, I gat a fright:
Ayont the lough,
Ye, like a rash-buss, stood in sight,
Wi' waving sugh.

The cudgel in my nieve* did shake, fist
Each bristled hair stood like a stake:
When wi' an eldritch stoor, "quaick, quaick,"
Among the springs,
Awa ye squattered like a drake,
On whistling wings.

Let warlocks grim, an' withered hags,
Tell how wi' you, on ragweed nags,
They skim the muirs an' dizzy crags,
Wi' wicked speed;
And in kirk-yards renew their leagues,
Owre howkit* dead. disinterred

Thence, countra wives, wi' toil an' pain,
May plunge an' plunge the kirn in vain;
For O, the yellow treasure's taen
By witching skill;
An' dawtet, twal-pint hawkie's* gane cow's
As yell's the bill.

Thence, mystic knots mak grat abuse
On young guidmen, fond, keen an' croose*; confident
When the best wark-lume* i' the house, tool
By cantraip* wit, tricky
Is instant made no worth a louse,
Just at the bit.

When thowes dissolve the snawy hoord,
An' float the jinglan icy boord,
Then, water-kelpies* haunt the foord, spirits
By your direction,
An' nighted trav'llers are allured
To their destruction.

And aft your moss-traversing spunkies* will-o-the-wisps
Decoy the wight that late an' drunk is:
The bleezen, curst, mischievous monkeys
Delude his eyes,
Till in some miry slough he sunk is
Ne'er mair to rise.

When Masons' mystic words an' grip
In storms an' tempests raise you up,
Some cock or cat your rage maun stop,
Or, strange to tell,
The youngest brother ye wad whip
Aff straught to Hell.

Lang syne in Eden's bonnie yard,
When youthfu' lovers first were paired,
An' all the soul of love they shared,
The raptured hour
Sweet on the fragrant flow'ry swaird,
In shady bow'r;

Then you, ye auld, snick-drawing dog,
Ye cam to Paradise incog,
An' played on man a cursed brogue* trick
(Black be your fa'!),
An' gied the infant warld a shog*, jolt
"Maist ruined a'."

D'ye mind that day when in a bizz
Wi' reeket duds, an' reestet gizz,
Ye did present your smoutie phiz
Mang better folk;
An' sklented on the man of Uzz
Your spitefu' joke?

An' how ye gat him i' your thrall,
An' brak him out o' house an' hall,
While scabs an' botches did him gall,
Wi bitter claw;
An' lowsed his ill-tongued, wicked scaul—
Was warst ava?

But a' your doings to rehearse,
Your wily snares an' fechtin fierce,
Sin' that day Michael did you pierce
Down to this time,
Wad ding a Lallan* tongue, or Erse, "Lowland"
In prose or rhyme.

An' now, Auld Cloots, I ken ye're thinkan,
A certain bardie's rantin, drinkin,
Some luckless hour will send him linkan
To your black pit;
But, faith, he'll turn a corner jinkan,
An' cheat you yet.

But fare-you-weel, Auld Nickie-Ben,
O, wad ye tak a thought an' men',
Ye aiblins* micht—I dinna ken— perhaps
Still hae a stake:

I'm wae to think upo' yon den,
Ev'n for your sake.

## Hallowe'en

[The Scottish countryside celebration of this ancient holiday is rich in folk customs, lovingly reproduced and mildly satirized in this poem. Most of the rituals here recorded are connected with love games, especially predicting one's future spouse, or at least one's marriage prospects. Here too are many references to the harvest season.]

> "Yes! let the rich deride, the proud disdain,
> The simple pleasures of the lowly train;
> To me more dear, congenial to my heart,
> One native charm, than all the gloss of art."
> —*Goldsmith.*

Upon that night, when fairies light,
On Cassilis Downans dance,
Or owre the leas in splendid blaze,
On sprightly coursers prance;
Or for Colean the route is ta'en,
Beneath the moon's pale beams!
There, up the cove, to stray and rove
Among the rocks and streams,
    To sport that night.

Amang the bonnie winding banks
Where Doon rins, wimplin', clear,
Where Bruce ance ruled the martial ranks,
And shook his Carrick spear,
Some merry, friendly, countra folks,
Together did convene,
To burn their nits, and pu' their stocks,
And haud their Hallowe'en,
    Fu' blithe that night.

The lasses feat, and cleanly neat,
Mair braw than when they're fine;
Their faces blithe, fu' sweetly kythe
Hearts leal*, and warm, and kin':    true
The lads sae trig*, wi' wooer-babs,[1]    neat
Weel knotted on their garten,
Some unco blate*, and some wi' gabs*,    shy/mouths
Gar* lasses' hearts gang startin'    make
    Whyles fast that night.

Then first and foremost through the kail*    cabbage
Their stocks maun a' be sought ance.
They steek* their een, and graip, and wale*,    shut/choose

---

[1] Signaled by double loops.

For meikle anes and straught anes.
Poor hav'rel* Will fell aff the drift,    dim-witted
And wandered through the bow-kail,
And pu't, for want o' better shift,
A runt* was like a sow-tail,    stalk
    Sae bow't that night.

Then, straught or crooked, yird* or nane,    earth
They roar and cry a' throu'ther*;    with haste
The vera wee things, todlin', rin
Wi' stocks out-owre their shouther;
And gif the custock's sweet or sour,
Wi' joctelegs* they taste them;    kail-hearts
Syne cozily, aboon the door,
Wi' canny care, they place them
    To lie that night.[1]

The lasses staw frae mang them a'
To pu' their stalks o' corn;
But Rab slips out, and jinks about,
Behind the meikle thorn;
He grippit Nelly hard and fast;
Loud skirled a' the lasses;
But her tap-pickle maist was lost,
When kittlin'* in the fause-house[2]    tickling
    Wi' him that night.

The auld guidwife's weel-hoordet nits
Are round and round divided,
And mony lads' and lasses' fates
Are there that night decided:
Some kindle, couthie, side by side,
And burn thegither trimly;
Some start awa' wi' saucy pride,
And jump out-owre the chimlie
    Fu' high that night.

Jean slips in twa wi' tentie* e'e;    careful
Wha twas, she wadna tell;
But this is Jock, and this is me,
She says in to hersel':
He bleezed owre her, and she owre him,
As they wad never mair part;
Till, fuff! he started up the lum*,    chimney
And Jean had e'en a sair heart
    To see't that night.

Poor Willie, wi' his bow-kail runt,
Was brunt wi' primsie* Mallie;    prissy, demure

---

[1]The cabbage tasting and placement are part of a ritual for determining the future spouse.
[2]The inside of a stack (where lovers could hide).

And Mary, nae doubt, took the drunt*, pet
To be compared to Willie:
Mall's nit lap out wi' pridefu' fling,
And her ain fit it brunt it;
While Willie lap, and swoor by jing,
Twas just the way he wanted
 To be that night.

Nell had the fause-house in her min',
She pits hersel' an Rob in;
In loving bleeze they sweetly join,
Till white in ase they're sobbin';
Nell's heart was dancin' at the view,
She whispered Rob to look for't:
Rob, stowlins*, prie'd* her bonnie mou' sneakily/tasted
Fu' cozy in the neuk for't,
 Unseen that night.

But Merran sat behint their backs,
Her thoughts on Andrew Bell;
She lea'es them gashin' at their cracks*, chatter
And slips out by hersel':
She through the yard the nearest taks,
And to the kiln she goes then,
And darklins graipit for the bauks,
And in the blue clue throws then,
 Right fear't that night.[1]

And aye she win't, and aye she swat,
I wat she made nae jaukin'*: idling
Till something held within the pat,
Gude Lord! but she was quakin.'
But whether twas the deil himsel',
Or whether twas a bauk*-en'! rafter
Or whether it was Andrew Bell,
She did na' wait on talkin'
 To spier that night.

Wee Jenny to her granny says,
"Will ye go wi' me, granny?
I'll eat the apple at the glass,
I gat frae uncle Johnnie."
She fuff't her pipe wi' sic a lunt*, smoke
In wrath she was sae vap'rin',
She notic't na, an aizle* brunt cinder
Her braw new worset apron
 Out through that night.

"Ye little skelpie-limmer's* face! rascal's
I daur ye try sic sportin',

[1] Another ritual to predict the future spouse.

As seek the foul thief ony place,
For him to spae* your fortune? predict
Nae doubt but ye may get a sight!
Great cause ye hae to fear it;
For mony a ane has gotten a fright,
And lived and died deleeret* "delirious"
On sic a night.

"Ae hairst* afore the Sherra-muir, harvest
I mind 't as weel's yestreen,
I was a gilpey* then, young girl
I'm sure I was na past fifteen:
The simmer had been cauld and wat,
And stuff was unco green:
And aye a rantin'* kirn we gat, poor
And just on Hallowe'en
It fell that night.

"Our stibble-rig* was Rab M'Graen, best reaper
A clever, sturdy fallow;
His sin gat Eppie Sim wi' wean,
That lived in Achmacalla:
He gat hemp-seed, I mind it weel,
And he made unco light o't;
But mony a day was by himsel',
He was sae sairly frightened
That vera night."

Than up gat fechtin' Jamie Fleck,
And he swore by his conscience,
That he could saw hemp-seed a peck;
For it was a' but nonsense!
The auld guid-man raught down the pock,
And out a handfu' gied him;
Syne bade him slip frae mang the folk,
Sometime when nae ane see'd him,
And try't that night.

He marches through amang the stacks,
Though he was something sturtin'*, afraid
The grape he for a harrow taks,
And haurls* at his curpin*: drags/crupper
And ev'ry now and then he says,
"Hemp-seed, I saw thee,
And her that is to be my lass,
Come after me, and draw thee,
As fast this night."

He whistled up Lord Lennox' march,
To keep his courage cheery;
Although his hair began to arch,
He was sae fleyed* and eerie; frightened
Till presently he hears a squeak,

And then a grane and gruntle;
He by his shouther ga'e a keek*, peek
And tumbled wi' a wintle* stagger
    Out-owre that night.

He roared a horrid murder shout,
In dreadfu' desperation;
And young and auld come rinnin' out,
To hear the sad narration:
He swoor twas hilchin' Jean M'Craw,
Or crouchie Merran Humphie,
Till stop! she trotted through them a';
And wha was it but Grumphies* (the pig)
    Asteer that night!

Meg fain wad to the barn gane,
To win three wechts* o' naething; weights
But for to meet the deil her lane*, (alone)
She pat but little faith in.
She gi'es the herd a pickle* nits, few
And twa red-cheekit apples,
To watch, while for the barn she sets,
In hopes to see Tam Kipples
    That vera night.

She turns the key wi' canny thraw*, twist
And owre the threshold ventures;
But first on Sawnie gi'es a ca',
Syne bauldly in she enters.
A ratton* rattled up the wa', rat
And she cried "Lord preserve her!"
And ran through midden-hole and a',
And prayed wi' zeal and fervor,
    Fu' fast that night.

They hoy't* out Will, wi' sair advice: urged
They hecht* him some fine braw ane: promised
It chanced the stack he faddomed* thrice, "fathomed"
Was timmer-propt for thrawin'.
He taks a swirlie auld moss-oak,
For some black, gruesome carline*; old woman
And loot a winze*, and drew a stroke, oath
Till skin in blypes* cam' haurlin' pieces
    Aff's nieves* that night. fists

A wanton widow Leezie was,
As canty as a kittlin'*; "kitten"
But Och! that night, amang the shaws*, woods
She got a fearfu' settlin'!
She through the whins*, and by the cairn, furze
And owre the hill gaed scrievin'*, (quickly)
Whare three lairds' lands met at a burn,

To dip her left sark-sleeve in,
Was bent that night.

Whyles owre a linn* the burnie plays, waterfall
As through the glen it wimpl't;
Whyles round a rocky scaur it strays;
Whyles in a wiell* it dimpl't: eddy
Whyles glittered to the nightly rays
Wi' bickering dancin dazzle;
Whyles cookit underneath the braes,
Below the spreading hazel,
Unseen that night.

Amang the brackens, on the brae,
Between her and the moon,
The deil, or else an outler quey*, young cow
Gat up and gae a croon.
Poor Leezie's heart maist lap the hool*; shell
Near lav'rock height she jumpit,
But missed a fit, and in the pool
Out-owre the lugs* she plumpit, ears
Wi' a plunge that night.

In order, on the clean hearth-stane,
The luggies* three are ranged, dishes
And ev'ry time great care is ta'en,
To see them duly changed;
Auld uncle John, wha wedlock's joys
Sin' Mar's year did desire,
Because he gat the toom* dish thrice,[1] empty
He heaved them on the fire,
In wrath that night.

Wi' merry sangs, and friendly cracks,
I wat they didna weary;
And unco tales, and funny jokes,
Their sports were cheap and cheery;
Till buttered sow'ns*, wi' fragrant lunt*, porridge/odor
Set a' their gabs a-steerin';
Syne, wi' a social glass o' strunt*, liquor
They parted aff careerin'
Fu' blithe that night.

## Tam Glen

My heart is a breaking, dear Tittie*, sister
Some counsel unto me come len';
To anger them a' is a pity,
But what will I do wi' Tam Glen?

[1] Implying he would never marry.

I'm thinking, wi' sic a braw fellow,
In poortith* I might mak a fen':    poverty
What care I in riches to wallow,
If I mauna marry Tam Glen.

There's Lowrie the laird o' Dumeller,
"Gude day to you" brute, he comes ben*:    in
He brags and he blaws o' his siller,
But when will he dance like Tam Glen?

My minnie* does constantly deave* me,    mother/deafen
And bids me beware o' young men;
They flatter, she says, to deceive me,
But wha can think sae o' Tam Glen?

My daddy says, gin* I'll forsake him,    if
He'll gie me gude hunder marks ten:
But, if it's ordained I maun take him,
O wha will I get but Tam Glen?

Yestreen at the Valentines' dealing,
My heart to my mou* gied a sten*;    mouth/leap
For thrice I drew ane without failing,
And thrice it was written, Tam Glen.

The last Halloween I was waukin
My droukit* sark-sleeve, as ye ken;[1]    drenched
His likeness came up the house staukin*,    "stalking"
And the very gray breeks o' Tam Glen!

Come counsel, dear Tittie, don't tarry;
I'll give you my bonnie black hen,
Gif ye will advise me to marry
The lad I loe dearly, Tam Glen.

## The Twa Dogs
### A Tale

Twas in that place o' Scotland's isle,
That bears the name o' auld King Coil,
Upon a bonnie day in June,
When wearing through the afternoon,
Twa dogs, that were na thrang* at hame,    busy
Forgathered ance upon a time.
The first I'll name they ca'd him Caesar,
Was keepit for His Honor's pleasure.
His hair, his size, his mouth, his lugs*,    ears
Shewed he was nane o' Scotland's dogs
But whalpit some place far abroad,

---

[1] Part of a ceremony to predict one's future husband.

Whare sailors gang to fish for cod.
His locked, lettered, braw brass collar
Shewed him the gentleman an' scholar;
But though he was o' high degree,
The fient* a pride nae pride had he; devil
But wad hae spent an hour caressin,
Ev'n wi' a tinkler-gypsy's messan.
At kirk or market, mill or smiddie,
Nae tawted tyke*, though e'er sae duddie, dog
But he wad stan't, as glad to see him,
An' stroan't on stanes an' hillocks wi' him.
The tither was a plowman's collie—
A rhyming, ranting, raving billie,
Wha for his friend an' comrade had him,
And in his freaks had Luath ca'd him,
After some dog in Highland sang,
Was made lang syne—Lord knows how lang.
He was a gash* an' faithfu' tyke, friendly
As ever lap a sheugh* or dyke. ditch
His honest, sonsie*, baws'nt face pleasant
Aye gat him friends in ilka place.
His breast was white, his touzie back
Weel clad wi' coat o' glossy black;
His gawsie* tail, wi' upward curl, jolly
Hung owre his hurdies* wi' a swirl. backside
Nae doubt but they were fain o' ither,
And unco pack an' thick thegither;
Wi' social nose whiles snuffed an' snowkit;
Whiles mice an' moudieworts* they howkit* moles/dug up
Whiles scoured awa' in lang excursion,
An' worried ither in diversion;
Until wi' daffin'* weary grown fooling
Upon a knowe they set them down.
An' there began a lang digression
About the "lords o' the creation."

Caesar

I've aften wondered, honest Luath,
What sort o' life poor dogs like you have.
An' when the gentry's life I saw,
What way poor bodies lived ava.
Our laird gets in his racked rents,
His coals, his kane*, an' a' his stents*. rents/dues
He rises when he likes himsel';
His flunkies answer at the bell;
He ca's his coach; he ca's his horse.
He draws a bonnie silken purse,
As lang's my tail, where, through the steeks,
The yellow lettered Geordie* keeks. guineas
Frae morn to e'en it's nought but toiling
At baking, roasting, frying, boiling;
An' though the gentry first are stechin,
Yet ev'n the ha' folk fill their pechen* stomach

Wi' sauce, ragouts, an' sic like trashtrie,
That's little short o' down right wastrie.
Our whipper-in, wee, blasted wonner*, "wonder"
Poor, worthless elf, it eats a dinner,
Better than ony tenant-man
His honor has in a' the lan':
An' what poor cot-folk pit their painch in,
I own it's past my comprehension.

Luath

Trowth, Caesar, whiles they're fash't* eneugh: troubled
A cottar howkin in a sheugh,
Wi' dirty stanes biggin a dyke,
Baring a quarry, an' sic like,
Himsel', a wife, he thus sustains,
A smytrie* o' wee duddie weans, collection
An' nought but his handwark, to keep
Them right an' tight in thack an' rape.
An' when they meet wi' sair disasters,
Like loss o' health or want o' masters,
Ye maist wad think, a wee touch langer,
An' they maun starve o' cauld an' hunger.
But how it comes, I never kent yet,
They're maistly wonderfu' contented;
An' buirdly* chiels, an' clever hizzies, stalwart
Are bred in sic a way as this is.

Caesar

But then to see how ye're negleckit,
How huffed and cuffed, an' disrespeckit.
Lord man, our gentry care as little
For delvers, ditchers, an' sic cattle.
They gang as saucy by poor folk,
As I wad by a stinkin brock.
I've noticed, on our laird's court-day—
An' mony a time my heart's been wae—
Poor tenant bodies, scant o' cash,
How they maun thole* a factor's snash. endure
He'll stamp an' threaten, curse an' swear
He'll apprehend them, poind* their gear, impound
While they maun stan', wi' aspect humble,
An' hear it a', an' fear an' tremble.
I see how folk live that hae riches,
But surely poor-folk maun be wretches.

Luath

They're no sae wretched 's ane wad think.
Though constantly on poortith's* brink, poverty's
They're sae accustomed wi' the sight,
The view o't gies them little fright.
Then chance and fortune are sae guided,
They're aye in less or mair provided,
An' though fatigued wi' close employment,

A blink o' rest's a sweet enjoyment.
The dearest comfort o' their lives,
Their grushie* weans an' faithfu' wives. thriving
The prattling things are just their pride,
That sweetens a' their fire-side.
An' whiles twalpennie worth o' nappy* ale
Can mak the bodies unco happy,
They lay aside their private cares,
To mind the kirk and state affairs.
They'll talk o' patronage an' priests,
Wi' kindling fury i' their breasts,
Or tell what new taxation's comin,
An' ferlie* at the folk in Lon'on. wonder
As bleak-faced Hallowmass returns,
They get the jovial, rantin kirns,
When rural life, of ev'ry station,
Unite in common recreation.
Love blinks, wit slaps, an' social mirth
Forgets there's care upo' the earth.
That merry day the year begins,
They bar the door on frosty win's.
The nappy reeks wi' mantling ream,
An' sheds a heart-inspiring steam.
The luntin* pipe, an' sneeshin mill*, smoking/snuffbox
Are handed round wi' right guid will.
The canty auld folks crackin* crouse*, chattering/bold
The young anes rantin through the house—
My heart has been sae fain to see them,
That I for joy hae barkit wi' them.
Still it's owre true that ye hae said,
Sic game is now owre aften played.
There's mony a creditable stock
O' decent, honest, fawsont* folk, seemly
Are riven out baith root an' branch,
Some rascal's pridefu' greed to quench,
Wha thinks to knit himsel the faster
In favor wi' some gentle master,
Wha, aiblins* thrang a parliamentin, perhaps
For Britain's guid his saul indentin—

Caesar

Haith, lad, ye little ken about it.
For Britain's guid! guid faith, I doubt it.
Say rather, gaun as premiers lead him,
An' saying ay or no's they bid him.
At operas an' plays parading,
Mortgaging, gambling, masquerading,
Or maybe, in a frolic daft,
To Hague or Calais takes a waft,
To mak a tour an' tak a whirk,
To learn *bon ton,* an' see the worl'.
There, at Vienna, or Versailles,
He rives his father's auld entails;

Or by Madrid he takes the rout,
To thrum guitars an' fecht wi' nowt*; cattle
Or down Italian vista startles,
Whorehunting amang groves o' myrtles.
Then bowses drumly German-water,
To mak himsel look fair an' fatter,
An' clear the consequential sorrows,
Love-gifts of Carnival signoras.
For Britain's guid! for her destruction,
Wi' dissipation, feud an' faction.

Luath

Hech man! dear sirs, is that the gate* way
They waste sae mony a braw estate?
Are we sae foughten an' harassed
For gear to gang that gate at last?
O would they stay aback frae courts,
An' please themsels wi' countra sports,
It wad for ev'ry ane be better,
The laird, the tenant, an' the cotter.
For thae frank, rantin, ramblin billies,
Feint haet o' them's ill-hearted fellows;
Except for breaken o' their timmer*, (furniture)
Or speakin lightly o' their limmer*, doxy
Or shootin of a hare or moor-cock,
The ne'er a bit they're ill to poor folk.
But will ye tell me, master Caesar,
Sure great folk's life's a life o' pleasure?
Nae cauld nor hunger e'er can steer them,
The vera thought o't need na fear them.

Caesar

Lord, man, were ye but whiles whare I am,
The gentles, ye wad ne'er envy them.
It's true, they need na starve or sweat,
Through winter's cauld, or simmer's heat.
They've nae sair walk to craze their banes,
An' fill auld age wi' grips an' granes.
But human bodies are sic fools,
For a' their colleges an' schools,
That when nae real ills perplex them,
They mak enow themsel's to vex them,
An' aye the less they hae to sturt* them, trouble
In like proportion, less will hurt them.
A country fellow at the pleugh,
His acre's tilled, he's right eneugh;
A country girl at her wheel,
Her dizzen's dune, she's unco weel;
But gentlemen, an' ladies warst,
Wi' ev'n-down want o' wark are curst.
They loiter, lounging, lank an' lazy;
Though deil-haet ails them, yet uneasy.
Their days insipid, dull an' tasteless;

Their nights unquiet, lang an' restless.
An' ev'n their sports, their balls an' races,
Their galloping through public places,
There's sic parade, sic pomp an' art,
The joy can scarcely reach the heart.
The men cast out in party-matches,
Then sowther* a' in deep debauches. soldier
Ae night they're mad wi' drink an' whoring,
Neist day their life is past enduring.
The ladies arm-in-arm in clusters,
As great an' gracious a' as sisters;
But hear their absent thoughts o' ither,
They're a' run-deils an' jads thegither.
Whiles, owre the wee bit cup an' platie,
They sip the scandal-potion pretty;
Or lee-lang nights, wi crabbit leuks
Pore owre the devil's pictured beuks;
Stake on a chance a farmer's stackyard,
An' cheat like ony unhanged blackguard.
There's some exceptions, man an' woman;
But this is gentry's life in common.

By this, the sun was out of sight,
An' darker gloamin brought the night.
The bum-clock hummed wi' lazy drone;
The kye stood rowtin* i' the loan; lowing
When up they gat an' shook their lugs,
Rejoiced they werena men but dogs,
An' each took aff his several way,
Resolved to meet some ither day.

## To a Louse

On seeing one on a lady's bonnet at church

Ha! whare ye gaun, ye crowlan ferlie!
Your impudence protects you sairly:
I canna say but ye strunt* rarely, "strut"
    Owre gawze and lace;
Though faith, I fear ye dine but snarely
    On sic a place.

Ye ugly, creepan, blastet wonner*, "wonder"
Detestet, shunned, by saunt an' sinner,
How daur ye set your fit* upon her, "foot"
    Sae fine a Lady.
Gae somewhere else and seek your dinner,
    On some poor body.

Swith*, in some beggar's haffet* squattle; quick/whisker
There ye may creep, and sprawl, and sprattle,
Wi' ither kindred, jumping cattle,

In shoals and nations;
Whare horn* nor bane* na'er daur unsettle (combs)
Your thick plantations.

Now haud you there, ye're out o' sight,
Below the fatt'rels*, snug and tight, ribbons
Na, faith ye yet, ye'll no be right,
Till ye've got on it,
The vera tapmost, towrin height
O' Miss's bonnet.

My sooth, right bauld ye set your nose out,
As plump an' gray as onie grozet*: gooseberry
O for some rank, mercurial rozet*, "resin"
Or fell, red smeddum*, powder
I'd gie you sic a hearty dose o't,
Wad dress your droddum*! rear end

I wad na been surprised to spy
You on an auld wife's flainen* toy*; "flannel"/cap
Or aiblins* some bit duddie boy, perhaps
On's wyle* coat; waist
But Miss's fine Lunardi*, fye! bonnet
How daur ye do't?

O Jenny dinna toss your head,
An' set your beauties a' abread*. "abroad"
Ye little ken what cursed speed
The blastie's* makin. small creature
Thae winks and finger-ends, I dread,
Are notice takin.

O wad some Pow'r the giftie gie us
To see oursels as others see us.
It wad frae monie a blunder free us
An' foolish notion:
What airs in dress an' gait wad lea'e us,
And ev'n devotion.

## To a Mountain Daisy

On turning one down, with the plow, in
April —1786

Wee, modest, crimson-tipped flower,
Thou's met me in an evil hour;
For I maun crush amang the stoure* struggle
Thy slender stem:
To spare thee now is past my power,
Thou bonnie gem.

Alas! it's no thy neebor sweet,
The bonnie Lark, companion meet.
Bending thee mang the dewy weet.
Wi's spreckled breast,
When upward-springing, blithe, to greet
The purpling East.

Cauld blew the bitter-biting North
Upon thy early, humble birth;
Yet cheerfully thou glinted forth
Amid the storm,
Scarce reared above the parent-earth
Thy tender form.

The flaunting flow'rs our gardens yield,
High-shelt'ring woods and wa's maun shield,
But thou, beneath the random bield* shelter
O' clod or stane,
Adorns the histie* stibble-field, barren
Unseen, alane.

There, in thy scanty mantle clad,
Thy snawy bosom sunward spread,
Thou lifts thy unassuming head
In humble guise;
But now the share uptears thy bed,
And low thou lies.

Such is the fate of artless maid,
Sweet flow'ret of the rural shade.
By love's simplicity betrayed,
And guileless trust,
Till she, like thee, all soiled, is laid
Low i' the dust.

Such is the fate of simple bard,
On life's rough ocean luckless starred.
Unskillful he to note the card
Of prudent lore,
Till billows rage, and gales blow hard,
And whelm him oer.

Such fate to suffering worth is giv'n,
Who long with wants and woes has striv'n,
By human pride or cunning driv'n
To mis'ry's brink,
Till wrenched of ev'ry stay but heav'n,
He, ruined, sink.

Ev'n thou who mourn'st the daisy's fate,
That fate is thine—no distant date;
Stern ruin's plowshare drives, elate,
Full on thy bloom,

Till crushed beneath the furrow's weight,
Shall be thy doom.

## John Barleycorn
### A Ballad

There was three kings into the east,
Three kings both great and high,
And they hae sworn a solemn oath
John Barleycorn should die.

They took a plow and plowed him down,
Put clods upon his head,
And they hae sworn a solemn oath
John Barleycorn was dead.

But the cheerful spring came kindly on,
And show'rs began to fall.
John Barleycorn got up again,
And sore surprised them all.

The sultry suns of Summer came,
And he grew thick and strong,
His head weel armed wi' pointed spears,
That no one should him wrong.

The sober autumn entered mild,
When he grew wan and pale.
His bending joints and drooping head
Showed he began to fail.

His color sickened more and more,
He faded into age;
And then his enemies began
To show their deadly rage.

They've taen a weapon, long and sharp,
And cut him by the knee;
Then tied him fast upon a cart,
Like a rogue for forgery.

They laid him down upon his back,
And cudgeled him full sore.
They hung him up before the storm,
And turned him oer and oer.

They filled up a darksome pit
With water to the brim,
They heaved in John Barleycorn,
There let him sink or swim.

They laid him out upon the floor,
To work him farther woe,
And still, as signs of life appeared,
They tossed him to and fro.

They wasted, oer a scorching flame,
The marrow of his bones;
But a miller used him worst of all,
For he crushed him between two stones.

And they hae taen his very heart's blood,
And drank it round and round;
And still the more and more they drank,
Their joy did more abound.

John Barleycorn was a hero bold,
Of noble enterprise,
For if you do but taste his blood,
Twill make your courage rise.

Twill make a man forget his woe;
Twill heighten all his joy.
Twill make the widow's heart to sing,
Though the tear were in her eye.

Then let us toast John Barleycorn,
Each man a glass in hand;
And may his great posterity
Ne'er fail in old Scotland.

## Green Grow the Rashes

Green grow the rashes*, O; rushes
Green grow the rashes, O;
The sweetest hours that e'er I spend,
Are spent amang the lasses, O.

There's nought but care on ev'ry han',
In ev'ry hour that passes, O.
What signifies the life o' man,
An' twere na for the lasses, O.

The warly race may riches chase,
An' riches still may fly them, O;
An' though at last they catch them fast,
Their hearts can ne'er enjoy them. O.

But gie me a canny* hour at e'en, quiet
My arms about my dearie, O;
An' warly cares, an warly men,
May a' gae tapsalteerie*, O. topsy-turvy

For you sae douse*, ye sneer at this, grave
Ye're nought but senseless asses, O.
The wisest man the warl' e'er saw,[1]
He dearly loved the lasses, O.

Ald nature swears, the lovely dears
Her noblest work she classes, O.
Her prentice han' she tried on man,
An' then she made the lasses, O.

## I'm Oer Young to Marry Yet[2]

I am my mammy's ae bairn,
Wi' unco* folk I weary, Sir, strange
And lying in a man's bed,
I'm fleyed* it make me irie*, Sir. afraid/nervous

I'm oer young, I'm oer young,
I'm oer young to marry yet.
I'm oer young, twad be a sin
To tak me frae my mammy yet.

Hallowmass* is come and gane, (Oct. 31)
The nights are lang in winter, Sir;
And you an' I in ae bed,
In trowth, I dare na venture, Sir.

I'm oer young, I'm oer young,
I'm oer young to marry yet.
I'm oer young, twad be a sin
To tak me frae my mammy yet.

Fu' loud and shrill the frosty wind
Blaws through the leafless timmer*, Sir; "timber"
But if ye come this gate* again, way
I'll aulder be gin* simmer, Sir. by

I'm oer young, I'm oer young,
I'm oer young to marry yet.
I'm oer young, twad be a sin
To tak me frae my mammy yet.

## The Rantin Dog, the Daddy o't[3]

O wha my baby-clouts* will buy? clothes
O wha will tent* me when I cry? care for
Wha will kiss me where I lie?
—The rantin* dog the daddy o't. pleasure-loving

---

[1]Presumably Solomon.

[2]The chorus of this song is old.

[3]Burns wrote this song for Jean Armour, whom he had gotten pregnant. He later married her.

O wha will own he did the faut*? "fault"
O wha will buy the groanin maut?[1]
O wha will tell me how to ca't?
—The rantin dog the daddy o't.

When I mount the creepie-chair?[2]
Wha will sit beside me there?
Gie me Rob, I'll seek nae mair,
—The rantin dog the daddy o't.

Wha will crack* to me my lane*? chat/alone
Wha will mak me fidgin* fain? tingling
Wha will kiss me oer again?
—The rantin dog the daddy o't.

## It Was A' for Our Rightfu' King

It was a' for our rightfu' King
We left fair Scotland's strand;
It was a' for our rightfu' King
We e'er saw Irish land, my dear,
We e'er saw Irish land.

Now a' is done that men can do,
And a' is done in vain;
My love and native land fareweel,
For I maun cross the main, my dear
For I maun cross the main.

He turned him right and round about,
Upon the Irish shore;
And gae his bridle reins a shake,
With adieu for evermore, my dear
And adieu for evermore.

The sodger frae the wars returns,
The sailor frae the main;
But I hae parted frae my love,
Never to meet again, my dear,
Never to meet again.

When day is gane, and night is come,
And a' folk bound to sleep;
I think on him that's far awa',
The lee-lang night and weep, my dear,
The lee-lang night and weep.

---

[1] Ale to be given to the midwife.

[2] The stool of repentance—part of the spectacle of public chastisement and repentance.

## Macpherson's Farewell[1]

Farewell, ye dungeons dark and strong,
The wretch's destiny.
Macpherson's time will not be long
On yonder gallows-tree.

Sae rantingly, sae wantonly,
Sae dauntingly gaed he;
He played a spring*, and danced it round, tune
Below the gallows-tree.

Oh, what is death but parting breath?—
On mony a bloody plain
I've dared his face, and in this place
I scorn him yet again.

Untie these bands from off my hands,
And bring to me my sword,
And there's no a man in all Scotland
But I'll brave him at a word.

I've lived a life of sturt* and strife; trouble
I die by treachery:
It burns my heart I must depart,
And not avenged be.

Now farewell light—thou sunshine bright,
And all beneath the sky.
May coward shame distain his name,
The wretch that dares not die.

## Auld Lang Syne

Should auld acquaintance be forgot,
And never brought to mind?
Should auld acquaintance be forgot,
And auld lang syne?

For auld lang syne, my dear,
For auld lang syne,
We'll tak a cup o' kindness yet
For auld lang syne.

And surely you'll be* your pint-stowp, "buy"
And surely I'll be mine,
And we'll tak a cup o' kindness yet
For auld lang syne.

---

[1]Burns' version of a song supposedly first composed by its subject, a Highland robber named James Macpherson, hanged about 1700.

For auld lang syne, my dear,
For auld lang syne,
We'll tak a cup o' kindness yet
For auld lang syne.

We twa hae run about the braes,
And pou'd* the gowans* fine, "pulled"/daisies
But we've wandered monie a weary fit* "foot"
Sin' auld lang syne.

For auld lang syne, my dear,
For auld lang syne,
We'll tak a cup o' kindness yet
For auld lang syne.

We twa hae paidled in the burn
Frae morning sun till dine,
But seas between us braid hae roared
Sin' auld lang syne.

For auld lang syne, my dear,
For auld lang syne,
We'll tak a cup o' kindness yet
For auld lang syne.

And there's a hand, my trusty fiere*, brother, pal
And gie's a hand o' thine,
And we'll tak a right guid-willie waught* "good will draught"
For auld lang syne.

## John Anderson My Jo

John Anderson my jo*, John, sweetheart
When we were first acquent;
Your locks were like the raven,
Your bony brow was brent*; smooth
But now your brow is beld*, John, "bald"
Your locks are like the snaw;
But blessings on your frosty pow*, head
John Anderson my jo.

John Anderson my jo, John,
We clamb the hill the gither;
And mony a canty* day John, lively
We've had wi' ane anither.
Now we maun totter down, John,
And hand in hand we'll go:
And sleep the gither at the foot,
John Anderson my jo.

## Whistle o'er the Lave o't

First when Maggie was my care,
Heav'n I thought, was in her air;
Now we're married, spier* nae mair, ask
But—whistle oer the lave* o't! rest (remainder)
Meg was meek, and Meg was mild,
Sweet and harmless as a child;
Wiser men then me's beguiled—
Whistle oer the lave o't!

How we live, my Meg and me,
How we love, and how we gree*, weep
I care na by how few may see—
Whistle oer the lave o't!
Wha I wish were maggot's meat,
Dished up in her winding-sheet,
I could write (but Meg wad see't)—
Whistle oer the lave o't.

## Willie Brewed a Peck o' Maut

O Willie brewed a peck o' maut,
And Rob and Allan cam to see.
Three blither hearts, that lee lang night,
Ye wad na found in Christendie.

We are na fou*, we're nae that fou, "full" (drunk)
But just a drappie in our e'e;
The cock may craw, the day may daw,
And ay we'll taste the barley bree.

Here are we met, three merry boys,
Three merry boys I trow are we;
And mony a night we've merry been,
And mony mae we hope to be.

It is the moon, I ken her horn,
That's blinkin in the lift* sae hie. sky
She shines sae bright to wyle us hame,
But by my sooth she'll wait a wee.

Wha first shall rise to gang awa,
A cuckold, coward loun* is he. rascal
Wha first beside his chair shall fa',
He is the king amang us three.

## My Heart's in the Highlands

My heart's in the Highlands, my heart is not here;
My heart's in the Highlands a chasing the deer;
Chasing the wild deer, and following the roe;
My heart's in the Highlands, wherever I go.

Farewell to the Highlands, farewell to the North;
The birth-place of valor, the country of worth.
Wherever I wander, wherever I rove,
The hills of the Highlands for ever I love.

Farewell to the mountains high covered with snow;
Farewell to the straths and green valleys below;
Farewell to the forests and wild-hanging woods;
Farewell to the torrents and loud-pouring floods.

My heart's in the Highlands, my heart is not here,
My heart's in the Highlands a chasing the deer.
Chasing the wild deer, and following the roe;
My heart's in the Highlands, wherever I go.

## Tam o' Shanter[1]

When chapman* billies* leave the street, peddler/fellows
And drouthy* neebors neebors meet; thirsty
As market-days are wearing late,
An' folk begin to tak the gate;
While we sit bousing at the nappy*, ale
An' getting fou* and unco happy, "full" (drunk)
We think na on the lang Scots miles,
The mosses, waters, slaps*, and styles, fence-gaps
That lie between us and our hame
Whare sits our sulky sullen dame,
Gathering her brows like gathering storm,
Nursing her wrath to keep it warm;
This truth fand honest Tam o' Shanter,
As he frae Ayr ae night did canter
(Auld Ayr, wham ne'er a town surpasses,
For honest men and bonnie lasses).

O Tam, had's thou been sae wise,
As taen thy ain wife Kate's advice.
She tauld thee weel thou was a skellum*, scamp
A blethering, blustering, drunken blellum*; babbler
That frae November till October,
Ae market-day thou was na sober;
That ilka* melder* wi' the miller, every/grinding
Thou sat as lang as thou had siller*; "silver"
That ev'ry naig was ca'd* a shoe on, driven
The smith and thee gat roaring fou on;
That at the Lord's house, even on Sunday,
Thou drank wi' Kirkton Jean till Monday.
She prophesied, that, late or soon,
Thou would be found deep drowned in Doon,
Or catched wi' warlocks in the mirk

---

[1]Burns wrote this splendid poem to accompany an illustration of Kirk Alloway in the *Antiquities of Scotland* by Francis Grose. See Burns' letter to Grose, on page 148.

By Alloway's auld, haunted kirk.
Ah gentle dames, it gars* me greet*, makes/weep
To think how monie counsels sweet,
How monie lengthened, sage advices
The husband frae the wife despises.

But to our tale:—Ae market-night,
Tam had got planted unco right,
Fast by an ingle*, bleezing finely, fireside
Wi' reaming swats*, that drank divinely; ale
And at his elbow, Souter* Johnie, cobbler
His ancient, trusty, drouthy crony:
Tam lo'ed him like a very brither;
They had been fou for weeks thegither.
The night drave on wi' sangs and clatter;
And ay the ale was growing better:
The landlady and Tam grew gracious
Wi' secret favors, sweet and precious:
The Souter tauld his queerest stories;
The landlord's laugh was ready chorus:
The storm without might rair and rustle,
Tam did na mind the storm a whistle.
Care, mad to see a man sae happy,
E'en drowned himsel amang the nappy.
As bees flee hame wi' lades o' treasure,
The minutes winged their way wi' pleasure:
Kings may be blest but Tam was glorious,
O'er a' the ills o' life victorious.

But pleasures are like poppies spread:
You seize the flow'r, its bloom is shed;
Or like the snow falls in the river,
A moment white—then melts for ever;
Or like the borealis race,
That flit ere you can point their place;
Or like the rainbow's lovely form
Evanishing amid the storm.
Nae man can tether time or tide;
The hour approaches Tam maun ride:
That hour, o' night's black arch the key-stane,
That dreary hour Tam mounts his beast in,
And sic a night he taks the road in,
As ne'er poor sinner was abroad in.
The wind blew as twad blawn its last;
The rattling showers rose on the blast;
The speedy gleams the darkness swallowed;
Loud, deep, and lang the thunder bellowed:
That night, a child might understand,
The Deil had business on his hand.
Well mounted on his gray mare Meg,
A better never lifted leg,
Tam skelpit on through dub and mire,
Despising wind, and rain, and fire;

Whiles holding fast his guid blue bonnet,
Whiles crooning oer some auld Scots sonnet,
Whiles glow'ring round wi' prudent cares,
Lest bogles catch him unawares:
Kirk-Alloway was drawing nigh,
Whare ghaists and houlets nightly cry.
By this time he was cross the ford,
Whare in the snaw the chapman smoored*; "smothered"
And past the birks* and meikle* stane, "birches"/big
Whare drunken Charlie braks neck-bane;
And through the whins*, and by the cairn, furze
Where hunters fand the murdered bairn;
And neer the thorn, aboon the well,
Whare Mungo's mither hanged hersel.
Before him Doon pours all his floods;
The doubling storm roars through the woods;
The lightnings flash from pole to pole;
Near and more near the thunders roll:
When, glimmering through the groaning trees,
Kirk-Alloway seemed in a bleeze,
Through ilka* bore* the beams were glancing, every/hole
And loud resounded mirth and dancing.

Inspiring bold John Barleycorn,
What dangers thou canst make us scorn.
Wi' tippenny, we fear nae evil;
Wi' usquabae*, we'll face the Devil. whiskey
The swats sae reamed in Tammie's noddle,
Fair play, he cared na deils a boddle*. (small coin)
But Maggie stood, right sair astonished,
Till, by the heel and hand admonished,
She ventured forward on the light;
And, wow! Tam saw an unco* sight. strange
Warlocks and witches in a dance:
Nae cotillion, brent new frae France,
But hornpipes, jigs, strathspeys, and reels,
Put life and mettle in their heels.
A winnock-bunker* in the east, window-seat
There sat Auld Nick, in shape o' beast;
A tousie* tyke*, black, grim, and large, tousled/cur
To gie them music was his charge:
He screwed the pipes and gart* them skirl, made
Till roof and rafters a' did dirl*. ring
Coffins stood round, like open presses,
That shawed the dead in their last dresses;
And, by some devilish cantraip* sleight, magic
Each in its cauld hand held a light:
By which heroic Tam was able
To note upon the haly table*, (altar)
A murderer's banes, in gibbet-airns;
Twa span-lang, wee, unchristened bairns;
A thief new-cutted frae a rape—
Wi' his last gasp his gab did gape;

Five tomahawks wi' bluid red-rusted;
Five scimitars wi' murder crusted;
A garter which a babe had strangled;
A knife a father's throat had mangled—
Whom his ain son o' life bereft—
The gray hairs yet stack to the heft;
Three lawyers' tongues, turned inside out,
Wi' lies seamed like a beggar's clout;
Three priests' hearts, rotten, black as muck,
Lay stinking, vile, in every neuk.[1]
Wi' mair o' horrible and awfu',
Which even to name wad be unlawfu'.
As Tammie glowred, amazed, and curious,
The mirth and fun grew fast and furious;
The piper loud and louder blew,
The dancers quick and quicker flew,
They reeled, they set, they crossed, they cleekit,
Till ilka carlin* swat and reekit, old woman
And coost her duddies* to the wark, rags
And linket* at it in her sark! went

Now Tam, O Tam! had thae been queans,
A' plump and strapping in their teens!
Their sarks, instead o' creeshie* flannen, greasy
Been snaw-white seventeen hunder linen,[2]—
Thir breeks* o' mine, my only pair, britches
That ance were plush, o' guid blue hair,
I wad hae gi'en them off my hurdies* buttocks
For ae blink o' the bonnie burdies*. lasses
But withered beldams, auld and droll,
Rigwoodie* hags wad spean* a foal, skinny/wean
Louping and flinging on a crummock*, staff
I wonder didna turn thy stomach.

But Tam kend what was fu' brawlie*: handsome
There was ae winsome wench and wawlie*, vigorous
That night enlisted in the core,
Lang after kend on Carrick shore
(For monie a beast to dead she shot,
An' perished monie a bonnie boat,
And shook baith meikle corn and bear* barley
And kept the country-side in fear).
Her cutty sark, o' Paisley harn,
That while a lassie she had worn,
In longitude though sorely scanty,
It was her best, and she was vauntie*. proud
Ah! little kend thy reverend granny,
That sark she coft* for her wee Nannie, bought

---

[1] Burns dropped lines 141-144 from later editions, and added lines 145-146.

[2] 177 threads per width (i.e. very fine linen).

Wi' twa pund Scots (twas a' her riches),
Wad ever graced a dance o' witches.

But here my Muse her wing maun cour*,     stoop
Sic flights are far beyond her power:
To sing how Nannie lap and flang
(A souple jade she was and strang),
And how Tam stood like ane bewitched,
And thought his very een enriched;
Ev'n Satan glowred, and fidged* fu' fain,     fidgeted
And hotched and blew wi' might and main;
Till first ae caper, syne anither,
Tam tint* his reason a' thegither,     lost
And roars out: "Weel done, Cutty-sark!"
And in an instant all was dark;
And scarcely had he Maggie rallied,
When out the hellish legion sallied.

As bees bizz out wi' angry fyke*,     fuss
When plundering herds assail their byke*;     hive
As open pussy's mortal foes,
When, pop! she starts before their nose;
As eager runs the market-crowd,
When "Catch the thief!" resounds aloud:
So Maggie runs, the witches follow,
Wi' monie an eldritch screech and hollo.
Ah, Tam! Ah, Tam! thou'll get thy fairin*.     reward
In hell they'll roast thee like a herrin.
In vain thy Kate awaits thy comin.
Kate soon will be a woefu' woman.
Now, do thy speedy utmost, Meg,
And win the key-stane of the brig;
There, at them thou thy tail may toss,
A running stream they dare na cross!
But ere the key-stane she could make,
The fient* a tail she had to shake;     devil
For Nannie, far before the rest,
Hard upon noble Maggie prest,
And flew at Tam wi' furious ettle*;     intent
But little wist she Maggie's mettle.
Ae spring brought off her master hale,
But left behind her ain gray tail:
The carlin* caught her by the rump,     witch
And left poor Maggie scarce a stump.

Now, wha this tale o' truth shall read,
Ilk* man, and mother's son, take heed:     each
Whene'er to drink you are inclined,
Or cutty sarks run in your mind,
Think! ye may buy the joys oer dear:
Remember Tam o' Shanter's mare.

## The Banks o' Doon[1]

Ye banks and braes o' bonnie Doon,
How can ye bloom sae fresh and fair;
How can ye chant, ye little birds,
And I sae weary fu' o' care.
Thou'll break my heart thou warbling bird,
That wantons through the flowering thorn.
Thou minds me o' departed joys,
Departed never to return.

Oft hae I roved by bonnie Doon,
To see the rose and woodbine twine;
And ilka bird sang o' its luve,
And fondly sae did I o' mine.
Wi' lightsome heart I pu'd a rose,
Fu' sweet upon its thorny tree;
And my fause luver staw* my rose, stole
But, ah! he left the thorn wi' me.

## Ye Flowery Banks

Ye flowery banks o' bonnie Doon,
How can ye bloom sae fair;
How can ye chant, ye little birds,
And I sae fu' o' care.

Thou'll break my heart, thou bonnie bird
That sings upon the bough;
Thou minds me o' the happy days
When my fause luve was true.

Thou'll break my heart, thou bonnie bird
That sings beside thy mate;
For sae I sat, and sae I sang,
And wist na o' my fate.

Aft hae I roved by bonnie Doon,
To see the wood-bine twine,
And ilka* bird sang o' its love, every
And sae did I o' mine.

Wi' lightsome heart I pu'd a rose
Frae aff its thorny tree,
And my fause luver staw* the rose, stole
But left the thorn wi' me.

Wi' lightsome heart I pu'd a rose,
Upon a morn in June:
And sae I flourished on the morn,
And sae was pu'd or* noon. "ere"

---

[1] Burns wrote three versions of this song. The poem which follows this is the final one.

## Such a Parcel of Rogues in a Nation

Fareweel to a' our Scottish fame,
Fareweel our ancient glory.
Fareweel ev'n to the Scottish name,
Sae famed in martial story.
Now Sark rins over Solway sands,
An' Tweed rins to the ocean,
To mark where England's province stands—
Such a parcel of rogues in a nation.

What force or guile could not subdue
Through many warlike ages
Is wrought now by a coward few
For hireling traitor's wages.
The English steel we could disdain,
Secure in valor's station;
But English gold has been our bane—
Such a parcel of rogues in a nation.

O, would, or I had seen the day
That Treason thus could sell us,
My auld gray head had lien in clay
Wi' Bruce and loyal Wallace.
But pith and power, till my last hour
I'll mak this declaration:—
"We're bought and sold for English gold"—
Such a parcel of rogues in a nation.

## Afton Water

Flow gently, sweet Afton, among thy green braes,
Flow gently, I'll sing thee a song in thy praise.
My Mary's asleep by thy murmuring stream,
Flow gently, sweet Afton, disturb not her dream.

Thou stock dove whose echo resounds through the glen,
Ye wild whistling blackbirds in yon thorny den,
Thou green crested lapwing thy screaming forbear,
I charge you disturb not my slumbering Fair.

How lofty, sweet Afton, thy neighboring hills,
Far marked with the courses of clear, winding rills.
There daily I wander as noon rises high,
My flocks and my Mary's sweet cot in my eye.

How pleasant thy banks and green valleys below,
Where wild in the woodlands the primroses blow.
There oft as mild ev'ning weeps over the lea,
The sweet scented birk shades my Mary and me.

Thy crystal stream, Afton, how lovely it glides,
And winds by the cot where my Mary resides.

How wanton thy waters her snowy feet lave*, wash
As gathering sweet flowerets she stems thy clear wave.

Flow gently, sweet Afton, among thy green braes,
Flow gently, sweet river, the theme of my lays.
My Mary's asleep by thy murmuring stream,
Flow gently, sweet Afton, disturb not her dream.

## I Hae Been at Crookieden

I hae been at Crookieden,
My bonnie laddie, Highland laddie,
Viewing Willie and his men,
My bonnie laddie, Highland laddie.
There our faes* that brunt and slew, "foes"
My bonnie laddie, Highland laddie,
There, at last, they gat their due,
My bonnie laddie, Highland laddie.

Satan sits in his black neuk,
My bonnie laddie, Highland laddie.
Breaking sticks to roast the Duke,
My bonnie laddie, Highland laddie.
The bloody monster gae a yell,
My bonnie laddie, Highland laddie.
And loud the laugh gaed round a' hell!
My bonnie laddie, Highland laddie.

## Ae Fond Kiss

Ae fond kiss, and then we sever;
Ae farewell and then for ever.
Deep in heart-wrung tears I'll pledge thee,
Warring sighs and groans I'll wage thee.
Who shall say that fortune grieves him
While the star of hope she leaves him?
Me, nae cheerfu' twinkle lights me;
Dark despair around benights me.

I'll ne'er blame my partial fancy,
Naething could resist my Nancy.
But to see her, was to love her,
Love but her, and love for ever.
Had we never loved sae kindly,
Had we never loved sae blindly,
Never met—or never parted,
We had ne'er been broken-hearted.

Fare thee weel, thou first and fairest.
Fare thee weel, thou best and dearest.
Thine be ilka* joy and treasure, every
Peace, enjoyment, love and pleasure.

Ae fond kiss, and then we sever,
Ae fareweel, alas, for ever.
Deep in heart-wrung tears I'll pledge thee,
Warring sighs and groans I'll wage thee.

## Scots, Wha Hae[1]

Scots, wha hae wi' Wallace bled,
Scots, wham Bruce has aften led,
Welcome to your gory bed
Or to victory.

Now's the day, and now's the hour:
See the front o' battle lour,
See approach proud Edward's power—[2]
Chains and slavery.

Wha will be a traitor knave?
Wha can fill a coward's grave?
Wha sae base as be a slave?—
Let him turn, and flee.

Wha for Scotland's king and law
Freedom's sword will strongly draw,
Freeman stand, for freeman fa',
Let him follow me.

By oppression's woes and pains,
By your sons in servile chains,
We will drain our dearest veins
But they shall be free.

Lay the proud usurpers low.
Tyrants fall in every foe.
Liberty's in every blow.
Let us do, or die.

## A Red Red Rose

O my luve is like a red red rose,
That's newly sprung in June.
O, my luve is like the melody,
That's sweetly played in tune.

As fair art thou, my bonnie lass,
So deep in luve am I,
And I will luve thee still, my dear,
Till a' the seas gang dry.

---

[1]The speaker is Robert the Bruce, addressing his troops before the battle of Bannockburn, June, 1314.

[2]Edward II of England.

Till a' the seas gang dry, my dear,
And the rocks melt wi' the sun.
And I will luve thee still, my dear,
While the sands o' life shall run.

And fare thee weel, my only luve,
And fare thee weel a while.
And I will come again, my luve,
Though it were ten thousand mile.

## A Man's a Man for A' That[1]

Is there for honest poverty
That hings his head, an' a' that?
The coward slave, we pass him by—
We dare be poor for a' that.
For a' that, an' a' that.
Our toils obscure, an' a' that,
The rank is but the guinea's stamp,
The man's the gowd for a' that.

What though on hamely fare we dine,
Wear hoddin* gray an' a' that? homespun
Gie fools their silks, and knaves their wine—
A man's a man for a' that.
For a' that, an' a' that,
Their tinsel show, an' a' that,
The honest man, though e'er sae poor,
Is king o' men for a' that.

Ye see yon birkie* ca'd "a lord," dandy
What struts, an' stares, an' a' that?
Though hundreds worship at his word,
He's but a cuif* for a' that. fool
For a' that, an' a' that,
His ribband, star, an' a' that,
The man o' independent mind,
He looks an' laughs at a' that.

A prince can mak a belted knight,
A marquis, duke, an' a' that;
But an honest man's aboon his might—
Guid faith, he mauna fa'* that. do, take
For a' that, an' a' that,
Their dignities, an' a' that,
The pith o' sense an' pride o' worth
Are higher rank than a' that.

Then let us pray that come it may
(As come it will for a' that)

---

[1] The phrase "for a' that" was a proverbial one.

That sense and worth oer a' the earth
Shall bear the gree* an' a' that. prize
For a' that, an' a' that,
It's comin yet for a' that,
That man to man the world oer
Shall brithers be for a' that.

## Wee Willie Gray

Wee Willie Gray, an' his leather wallet;
Peel a willie* wand, to be him boots and jacket. willow
The rose upon the breer will be him trouse an' doublet.
The rose upon the breer will be him trouse an' doublet.

Wee Willie Gray and his leather wallet;
Twice a lily flower will be him sark* and cravat. shirt
Feathers of a flee* wad feather up his bonnet, fly
Feathers of a flee wad feather up his bonnet.

## O Wert Thou in the Cauld Blast

O wert thou in the cauld blast
On yonder lea, on yonder lea,
My plaidie to the angry airt*, direction
I'd shelter thee, I'd shelter thee.
Or did misfortune's bitter storms
Around thee blaw, around thee blaw,
Thy bield* should be my bosom, shelter
To share it a', to share it a'.

Or were I in the wildest waste,
Sea black and bare, sae black and bare,
The desert were a paradise,
If thou wert there, if thou wert there.
Or were I monarch of the globe,
Wi' thee to reign, wi' thee to reign,
The brightest jewel in my crown
Wad be my queen, wad be my queen.

## Comin Through the Rye

Comin through the rye, poor body
Comin through the rye,
She draigl't a' her petticoatie,
Comin through the rye.

O, Jenny's a' weet, poor body,
Jenny's seldom dry:
She draigl't a' her petticoatie,
Comin through the rye.

Gin* a body meet a body
Comin through the rye,
Gin a body kiss a body,
Need a body cry?

*if

O, Jenny's a' weet, poor body,
Jenny's seldom dry:
She draigl't a' her petticoatie,
Comin through the rye.

Gin a body meet a body
Comin through the glen,
Gin a body kiss a body,
Need the warld ken?

O, Jenny's a' weet, poor body,
Jenny's seldom dry:
She draigl't a' her petticoatie,
Comin through the rye.

## Dedication to the Second Edition

To the Noblemen and Gentlemen of the Caledonian Hunt

My Lords and Gentlemen:

A Scottish bard, proud of the name, and whose highest ambition is to sing in his country's service—where shall he so properly look for patronage as to the illustrious names of his native land; those who bear the honors and inherit the virtues of their ancestors? The poetic genius of my country found me, as the prophetic bard Elijah did Elisha—at the plow;[1] and threw her inspiring mantle over me. She bade me sing the loves, the joys, the rural scenes and rural pleasures of my natal soil, in my native tongue: I tuned my wild, artless notes, as she inspired. She whispered me to come to this ancient metropolis of Caledonia and lay my songs under your honored protection: I now obey her dictates.

Though much indebted to your goodness, I do not approach you, my Lords and Gentlemen, in the usual style of dedication, to thank you for past favors: that path is so hackneyed by prostituted learning that honest rusticity is ashamed of it. Nor do I present this address with the venal soul of a servile author, looking for a continuation of those favors: I was bred to the plow, and am independent. I come to claim the common Scottish name with you, my illustrious countrymen; and to tell the world that I glory in the title. I come to congratulate my country, that the blood of her ancient heroes still runs uncontaminated; and that from your courage, knowledge, and public spirit, she may expect protection, wealth, and liberty. In the last place, I come to proffer my warmest wishes to the great fountain of honor, the monarch of the universe, for your welfare and happiness.

When you go forth to waken the echoes, in the ancient and favorite amusement of your forefathers, may pleasure ever be of your party: and may social joy await your return! When harassed in courts or camps with the jostlings of bad men and bad measures, may the honest consciousness of injured worth attend your return to your native seats; and may domestic happiness, with a smiling welcome, meet you at your gates!

---

[1] 1 Kings, 19:19.

May corruption shrink at your kindling, indignant glance; and may tyranny in the ruler, and licentiousness in the people, equally find you an inexorable foe!

I have the honor to be, with the sincerest gratitude and highest respect,
My Lords and Gentlemen,
Your most devoted humble servant,
Robert Burns.
Edinburgh, April 4, 1787

## 29. To John Arnot

The following was to one of the most accomplished of the sons of men that I ever met with—John Arnot of Dalquhatswood in Ayr-shire—alas! had he been equally prudent!—It is a damning circumstance in human-life, that prudence, insular and alone, without another virtue will conduct a man to the most envied eminences in life while having every other good quality, and wanting that one, which at best is itself but a half virtue, will not save a man from the world's contempt, and real misery, perhaps perdition.—

The story of the letter was this—I had got deeply in love with a young fair-one, of which proofs were every day *arising* more and more to view.—I would gladly have covered my inamorata from the darts of calumny with the conjugal shield, nay, had actually made up some sort of wedlock; but I was at that time deep in the guilt of being unfortunate, for which good and lawful objection, the lady's friends broke all our measures, and drove me au desespoir.—

I think that the letter was written sometime about the latter end of 1785, as I was meditating to publish my Poems.—

To John Arnot of Dalquhatswood, Esquire, inclosing a subscription-bill for my first edition, which was printed at Kilmarnock—

Sir, I have long wished for some kind of claim to the honor of your acquaintance, and since it is out of my power to make that claim by the least service of mine to you, I shall do it by asking a friendly office of you to me.—I should be much hurt, Sir, if any one should view my poor Parnassian Pegasus in the light of a spur-galled hack, and think that I wish to make a shilling or two by him.—I spurn the thought.—

It may-do—maun-do, Sir, wi' them wha
Maun please the great folk for a wame*-fou; belly
For me, sae laigh I need na bow,
For, Lord be thankit! I can plow:
And when I downa* yoke a naig, cannot
Then, Lord be thankit. I can beg—

You will then, I hope Sir, forgive my troubling you with the inclosed; and spare a poor heart-crushed devil a world of apologies: a business he is very unfit for at any time; but at present, widowed as he is of every woman-giving comfort, he is utterly incapable of.— sad and grievous, of late, Sir, has been my tribulation, and many and piercing my sorrows; and had it not been for the loss the world would have sustained in losing so great a poet, I had, ere now, done as a much wiser man, the famous Achitophel of long-headed memory, did before me, when he went home and set his house in order.— I have lost, Sir, that dearest earthly treasure, that greatest blessing here below, that last, best gift which completed Adam's happiness in the garden of bliss, I have lost—I have lost—my trembling hand refuses its office, the frighted ink recoils up the quill—Tell it not in Gath—I have lost—a—a—a wife!

Fairest of God's creation, last and best!
*How art thou lost!*

You have doubtless, Sir, heard my story, heard it with all its exaggerations; but as my actions, and my motives for action, are peculiarly like myself, and that is peculiarly like nobody else, I shall just beg a leisure-moment and a spare-tear of you, until I tell my own story my own way.—

I have been all my life, Sir, one of the rueful-looking, long-visaged sons of disappointment.—A damned star has always kept my zenith, and shed its baleful influence, in that emphatic curse of the Prophet—"And behold whatsoever he doth, it shall not prosper!"—I rarely hit where I aim: and if I want anything, I am almost sure never to find it where I seek it.—For instance, if my pen-knife is needed, I pull out twenty things—a plowwedge, a horse-nail, an old letter or a tattered rhyme, in short, everything but my pen-knife; and that at last, after a painful, fruitless search, will be found in the unsuspected corner of an unsuspected pocket, as if on purpose thrust out of the way.

—Still, Sir, I had long had a wishing eye to that inestimable blessing, a wife.—My mouth watered deliciously, to see a young fellow, after a few idle, commonplace stories from a gentleman in black, strip and go to bed with a young girl, and no one durst say, black was his eye; while I, for just doing the same thing, only wanting that ceremony, am made a Sunday's laughing-stock, and abused like a pick-pocket.

I was well aware though, that if my ill-starred fortune got the least hint of my connubial wish, my schemes would go to nothing.—To prevent this, I determined to take my measures with such thought and forethought, such a caution and precaution, that all the malignant planets in the hemisphere should be unable to blight my designs.

—Not content with, to use the words of the celebrated Westminster Divines, "The outward and ordinary means," I left no *stone* unturned; sounded every unfathomed *depth;* stopped up every *hole and bore* of an objection: but, how shall I tell it! notwithstanding all this turning of stones, stopping of bores, etc.—whilst I, with secret pleasure, marked my project *swelling* to the proper crisis, and was singing te Deum in my own fancy; or, to change the metaphor, whilst I was vigorously pressing on the siege; had carried the counter-scarp, and made a practicable breach behind the curtain in the gorge of the very principal bastion; nay, having mastered the covered way, I had found means to slip a choice detachment into the very citadel; while I had nothing less in view than displaying my victorious banners on the top of the walls—Heaven and Earth must I "remember"! my damned star wheeled about to the zenith, by whose baleful rays fortune took the alarm, and pouring in her forces on all quarters, front, flank, and rear, I was utterly routed, my baggage lost, my military chest in the hands of the enemy; and your poor devil of a humble servant, commander in chief forsooth, was obliged to scamper away, without either arms or honors of war, except his bare bayonet and cartridge-pouch; nor in all probability had he escaped even with them, had he not made a shift to hide them under the lap of his military cloak.—

In short, Pharaoh at the Red Sea, Darius at Arbela, Pompey at Pharsalia, Edward at Bannockburn, Charles at Pultaway, Burgoyne at Saratoga—no prince, potentate, or commander of ancient or modern unfortunate memory, ever got a more shameful or more total defeat—

"O horrible! O horrible! Most horrible!"

How I bore this, can only be conceived.—All powers of recital labor far, far behind.—There is a pretty large portion of bedlam in the composition of a poet at any time; but on this occasion I was nine parts and nine tenths, out of ten, stark staring mad.

—At first, I was fixed in stuporific insensibility, silent, sullen, staring like Lot's wife besaltified in the plains of Gomorra.— But my second paroxysm chiefly beggars description.— The rifted northern ocean when returning suns dissolve the chains of winter, and loosening precipices of long accumulated ice tempest with hideous crash the foaming deep—images like these may give some faint shadow of what was the situation of my bosom.—

My chained faculties broke loose; my maddening passions, roused to ten-fold fury, bore over their banks with impetuous, resistless force, carrying every check and principle before them—Counsel, was an unheeded call to the passing hurricane; reason, a screaming elk in the vortex of Moskoestrom; and religion, a feebly-struggling beaver down the roarings of Niagara.—I reprobated the first moment of my existence; execrated Adam's folly-infatuated wish for that goodly-looking, but poison-breathing, gift, which had ruined him, and undone me; and called on the womb of uncreated night to close over me and all my sorrows.—

A storm naturally overblows itself.—My spent passions gradually sank into a lurid calm; and by degrees I have subsided into the time-settled sorrow of the sable widower, who, wiping away the decent tear, lifts up his grief-worn eye to look—for another wife.—

Such is the state of man; today he buds
His tender leaves of hope; tomorrow blossoms,
And bears his blushing honors thick upon him;
The third day comes a frost, a killing frost.
And nips his root, and then he falls as I do.[1]

Such, Sir, has been this fatal era of my life.—"And it came to pass that when I looked for sweet, behold bitter; and for light, behold darkness."—

But this is not all.—Already the holy beagles, the houghmagandie[2] pack, begin to snuff the scent, and I expect every moment to see them cast off, and hear them after me in full cry: but as I am an old fox, I shall give them dodging and doubling for it; and by and bye, I intend to earth among the mountains of Jamaica.—

I am so struck, on a review, with the impertinent length of this letter, that I shall not increase it with one single word of apology; but abruptly conclude with assuring you that I am,

Sir, Your and misery's most humble servant
Robert Burns
—[April 1786]

## 112. To William Nicol

Carlisle lst June 1787—or I believe the 39th o' May rather

Kind, honest-hearted Willie,

I'm sitten down here, after seven and forty miles ridin, e'en as forjesket and for-

---

[1]Cf. *Henry VIII*. III.ii.352-358.

[2]Fornication.

niaw'd as a forfoughten cock, to gie you some notion o' my landlowper-like stravaguin sin the sorrowfu' hour that I sheuk hands and parted wi' auld Reekie.[1]—

My auld, ga'd Gleyde o' a meere has huchyall'd up hill and down brae, in Scotland and England, as teugh and birnie as a vera devil wi' me.—It's true, she's as poor's a sang-maker and as hard's a kirk, and tipper-taipers when she taks the gate first like a lady's gentlewoman in a minuwae, or a hen on a het girdle, but she's a yauld, poutherie girran for a' that; and has a stomach like Willie Stalker's meere that wad hae digested tumbler-wheels, for she'll whip me aff her five stimparts o' the best aits[2] at a down-sittin and ne'er fash[3] her thumb.—When ance her ringbanes and spavies, her crucks and cramps, are fairly soupl'd, she beets to, beets to, and ay the hindmost hour the tightest. I could wager her price to a thretty pennies that, for twa or three wooks ridin at fifty mile a day, the deil-sticket a five gallopers acqueesh Clyde and Whithorn could cast saut in her tail.—

I hae dander'd owre a' the kintra frae Dumbar to Selcraig, and hae forgather'd wi' monie a guid fallow, and monie a weel-far'd hizzie.—I met wi' twa dink quines[4] in particlar, ane o' them a sonsie, fine fodgel lass, baith braw and bonnie; the tither was a clean-shankit, straught, tight, weel-far'd winch, as blythe's a lintwhite on a flowery thorn, and as sweet and modest's a new blawn plumrose in a hazle shaw.[5]—They were baith bred to mainers by the beuk, and onie ane o' them has as muckle smeddum[6] and rumblegumtion as the half o' some Presbytries that you and I baith ken.

—They played me sik a deevil o' a shavie that I daur say if my harigals were turned out, ye wad see twa nicks i' the heart o' me like the mark o' a kail-whittle in a castock.—

I was gaun to write you a lang pistle, but, Gude forgie me, I gat myself sae noutouriously bitchify'd the day after kail-time that I can hardly stoiter but and ben.[7]—

My best respecks to the guidwife and a' our common friens, especiall Mr and Mrs Cruikshank and the honest Guidman o' Jock's Lodge.—

I'll be in Dumfries the morn gif the beast be to the fore and the branks bide hale.—

Gude be wi' you, Willie! Amen
Robt Burns

## 125. To Dr. John Moore

Sir

For some months past I have been rambling over the country, partly on account of some little business I have to settle in various places; but of late I have been confined with some lingering complaints originating as I take it in the stomach.—To divert my spirits a little in this miserable fog of ennui, I have taken a whim to give you a history of myself.

My name has made a small noise in the country; you have done me the honor to interest yourself very warmly in my behalf; and I think a faithful account of, what

---

[1]Edinburgh.
[2]"Oats."
[3]Trouble.
[4]Lasses.
[5]Wood.
[6]Spunk.
[7]Out and in.

character of a man I am, and how I came by that character, may perhaps amuse you in an idle moment.

I will give you an honest narrative, though I know it will be at the expense of frequently being laughed at; for I assure you, Sir, I have, like Solomon whose character, excepting the trifling affair of wisdom, I sometimes think I resemble, I have, I say like him "turned my eyes to behold madness and folly"; and like him too, frequently shaken hands with their intoxicating friendship.

In the very polite letter Miss Williams did me the honor to write me, she tells me you have got a complaint in your eyes.—I pray God that it may be removed; for considering that lady and you are my common friends, you will probably employ her to read this letter; and then goodnight to that esteem with which she was pleased to honor the Scotch Bard.— After you have perused these pages, should you think them trifling and impertinent, I only beg leave to tell you that the poor author wrote them under some very twitching qualms of conscience, that, perhaps he was doing what he ought not to do: a predicament he has more than once been in before.—

I have not the most distant pretensions to what the pye-coated guardians of escutcheons call, A Gentleman. —When at Edinburgh last winter, I got acquainted in the herald's office, and looking through that granary of honors I there found almost every name in the kingdom; but for me,

"—My ancient but ignoble blood has crept through scoundrels ever since the flood"—

Gules, Purpure, Argent, etc. quite disowned me.—My fathers rented land of the noble Kieths of Marshal, and had the honor to share their fate.—I do not use the word, honor, with any reference to political principles; loyal and disloyal I take to be merely relative terms in that ancient and formidable court known in this country by the name of club-law.

Those who dare welcome ruin and shake hands with infamy for what they sincerely believe to be the cause of their God or their King—"Brutus and Cassius are honorable men."—I mention this circumstance because it threw my father on the world at large; where after many years' wanderings and sojournings, he pickt up a pretty large quantity of observation and experience, to which I am indebted for most of my little pretensions to wisdom.

I have met with few who understood "Men, their manners and their ways" equal to him; but stubborn, ungainly integrity, and headlong, ungovernable irascibility are disqualifying circumstances: consequently I was born a very poor man's son.

For the first six or seven years of my life my father was gardener to a worthy gentleman of small estate in the neighborhood of Ayr.—had my father continued in that situation, I must have marched off to be one of the little underlings about a farm-house; but it was his dearest wish and prayer to have it in his power to keep his children under his own eye till they could discern between good and evil; so with the assistance of his generous master my father ventured on a small farm in his estate.

At these years I was by no means a favorite with any body.—I was a good deal noted for a retentive memory, a stubborn, sturdy something in my disposition, and an enthusiastic, idiot piety. —I say idiot piety, because I was then but a child.— Though I cost the schoolmaster some thrashings, I made an excellent English scholar; and against the years of ten or eleven, I was absolutely a critic in substantives, verbs and particles.—In my infant and boyish days too, I owed much to an old maid of my mother's, remarkable for her ignorance, credulity and superstition.

She had, I suppose, the largest collection in the county of tales and songs concerning devils, ghosts, fairies, brownies, witches, warlocks, spunkies, kelpies, elf-candles, deadlights, wraiths, apparitions, cantraips, giants, enchanted towers, dragons and other trumpery. —This cultivated the latent seeds of poesy; but had so strong an effect on my imagination, that to this hour, in my nocturnal rambles, I sometimes keep a sharp look-out in suspicious places; and though nobody can be more skeptical in these matters than I, yet it often takes an effort of philosophy to shake off these idle terrors.

The earliest thing of composition that I recollect taking pleasure in was, The vision of Mirza and a hymn of Addison's beginning—"How are Thy servants blest, O Lord!" I particularly remember one half-stanza which was music to my boyish ear—

For though in dreadful whirls we hung,
High on the broken wave—

I met with these pieces in Mason's English Collection, one of my school-books—The two first books I ever read in private, and which gave me more pleasure than any two books I ever read again, were, the life of Hannibal and the history of Sir William Wallace.— Hannibal gave my young ideas such a turn that I used to strut in raptures up and down after the recruiting drum and bagpipe, and wish myself tall enough to be a soldier; while the story of Wallace poured a Scottish prejudice in my veins which will boil along there till the flood-gates of life shut in eternal rest.

Polemical divinity about this time was putting the country half mad; and I, ambitious of shining in conversation parties on Sundays between sermons, funerals, etc. used in a few years more to puzzle Calvinism with so much heat and indiscretion that I raised a hue and cry of heresy against me which has not ceased to this hour.

My vicinity to Ayr was of great advantage to me.— My social disposition, when not checked by some modification of spited pride, like our catechism definition of Infinitude, was "without bounds or limits."—I formed many connections with other youngkers who possessed superior advantages, the youngling actors who were busy with the rehearsal of parts in which they were shortly to appear on that stage where, Alas! I was destined to drudge behind the scenes.

It is not commonly at these green years that the young noblesse and gentry have a just sense of the immense distance between them and their ragged play-fellows.—It takes a few dashes into the world to give the young great man that proper, decent, unnoticing disregard for the poor, insignificant, stupid devils, the mechanics and peasantry around him; who perhaps were born in the same village.—My young superiors never insulted the clouterly appearance of my plowboy carcass, the two extremes of which were often exposed to all the inclemencies of all the seasons.

They would give me stray volumes of books; among them, even then, I could pick up some observations; and one, whose heart I am sure not even the munny begum's scenes have tainted, helped me to a little French.—Parting with these, my young friends and benefactors, as they dropped off for the east or west Indies, was often to me a sore affliction; but I was soon called to more serious evils.—My father's generous master died; the farm proved a ruinous bargain; and, to clench the curse, we fell into the hands of a factor who sat for the picture I have drawn of one in my tale of two dogs.

My father was advanced in life when he married; I was the eldest of seven children; and he, worn out by early hardship, was unfit for labor.—My father's spirit was soon irritated, but not easily broken.—There was a freedom in his lease in two years more, and to weather these two years we retrenched expenses.—We lived very poorly; I was a dextrous plowman for my years and the next eldest to me was a brother, who could drive the plow very well and help me to thrash— A novel-writer might perhaps have viewed these scenes with some satisfaction, but so did not I: my indignation yet boils at the recollection of the scoundrel tyrant's insolent, threatening epistles, which used to set us all in tears.—

This kind of life, the cheerless gloom of a hermit with the unceasing moil of a galley-slave, brought me to my sixteenth year; a little before which period I first committed the sin of rhyme.—You know our country custom of coupling a man and woman together as partners in the labors of harvest—In my fifteenth autumn, my partner was a bewitching creature who just counted an autumn less—my scarcity of English denies me the power of doing her justice in that language; but you know the Scotch idiom She was a bonnie, sweet, sonsie lass.—In short, she altogether unwittingly to herself, initiated me in a certain delicious passion which in spite of acid disappointment, ginhorse prudence and bookworm philosophy, I hold to be the first of human joys, our dearest pleasure here below.

How she caught the contagion I can't say; you medical folks talk much of infection by breathing the same air, the touch, etc. but I never expressly told her that I loved her.—Indeed I did not well know myself, why I liked so much to loiter behind with her, when returning the evening from our labors; why the tones of her voice made my heartstrings thrill like an Eolian harp; and particularly, why my pulse beat such a furious ratann when I looked and fingered over her hand, to pick out the nettle-stings and thistles.

Among her other love-inspiring qualifications, she sung sweetly; and twas her favorite reel to which I attempted giving an embodied vehicle in rhyme.—I was not so presumptive as to imagine that I could make verses like printed ones, composed by men who had Greek and Latin; but my girl sung a song which was said to be composed by a small country laird's son, on one of his father's maids, with whom he was in love; and I saw no reason why I might not rhyme as well as he, for excepting smearing sheep and casting peats, his father living in the moors, he had no more scholarcraft than I had.—

Thus with me began love and poesy; which at times have been my only, and till within this last twelvemonth have been my highest enjoyment.

My father struggled on till he reached the freedom in his lease, when he entered on a larger farm about ten miles farther in the country.—The nature of the bargain was such as to throw a little ready money in his hand at the commencement, otherwise the affair would have been impractible.—For four years we lived comfortably here; but a lawsuit between him and his landlord commencing, after three years tossing and whirling in the vortex of litigation, my father was just saved from absorption in a jail by phthisical consumption, which after two years promises, kindly stept in and snatched him away—"To where the wicked cease from troubling, and where the weary be at rest."

It is during this climacteric that my little story is most eventful.—I was, at the beginning of this period, perhaps the most ungainly, awkward being in the parish. —No solitaire was less acquainted with the ways of the world.—My knowledge of ancient story was gathered from Salmon's and Guthrie's geographical grammars; my knowledge of modern manners, and of literature and criticism, I got from the Spectator.—These, with Pope's works, some plays of Shakespeare, Tull and Dickson on agriculture, The Pantheon, Locke's essay on the human understanding, Stackhouse's history of the Bible, Justice's British gardener's directory, Boyle's lectures, Allan Ramsay's works, Taylor's scripture doctrine of original sin, a select Collection of English Songs and Hervey's Meditations had been the extent of my reading.

The Collection of Songs was my vade mecum.—I poured over them, driving my cart or walking to labor, song by song, verse by verse; carefully noting the true tender or sublime from affectation and fustian. —I am convinced I owe much to this for my critic-craft such as it is.—

In my seventeenth year, to give my manners a brush, I went to a country dancing school.—My father had an unaccountable antipathy against these meetings; and my going was, what to this hour I repent, in absolute defiance of his commands.—My father, as I said before was the sport of strong passions: from that instance of rebellion he took a kind of dislike to me, which, I believe was one cause of that dissipation which marked my future years.—I only say, dissipation, comparative with the strictness and sobriety of Presbyterian country life; for though the will-o'-wisp meteors of thoughtless whim were almost the sole lights of my path, yet early ingrained piety and virtue never failed to point me out the line of innocence.

The great misfortune of my life was, never to have an aim.—I had felt early some stirrings of ambition, but they were the blind gropins of Homer's Cyclops round the walls of his cave: I saw my father's situation entailed on me perpetual labor. —The only two doors by which I could enter the fields of fortune were, the most niggardly economy, or the little chicaning art of bargain-making: the first is so contracted an aperture, I never could squeeze myself into it; the last, I always hated the contamination of the threshold.

Thus, abandoned of aim or view in life; with a strong appetite for sociability, as well from native hilarity as from a pride of observation and remark; a constitutional hypochondriac taint which made me fly solitude; add to all these incentives to social life, my reputation for bookish knowledge, a certain wild, logical talent, and a strength of thought something like the rudiments of good sense, made me generally a welcome guest; so tis no great wonder that always "where two or three were met together, there was I in the midst of them."

But far beyond all the other impulses of my heart was, un penchant l'adorable moitiee du genre humain.—My heart was completely tender, and was eternally lighted up by some goddess or other: and like every warfare in this world, I was sometimes crowned with success, and sometimes mortified with defeat.—At the plow, scythe or reap-hook I feared no competitor, and set want at defiance; and as I never cared farther for my labors than while I was in actual exercise, I spent the evening in the way after my own heart.

A country lad rarely carries on an amour without an assisting confident.—I possessed a curiosity, zeal and intrepid dexterity in these matters which recommended me a proper second in duels of that kind; and I dare say, I felt as much pleasure at being in the secret of half the amours in the parish, as ever did premier at knowing the intrigues of half the courts of Europe.—

The very goosefeather in my hand seems instinctively to know the well-worn path of my imagination, the favorite theme of my song; and is with difficulty restrained from giving you a couple of paragraphs on the amours of my compeers, the humble inmates of the farmhouse and cottage; but the grave sons of science, ambition or avarice baptize these things by the name of follies.—To the sons and daughters of labor and poverty they are matters of the most serious nature: to them, the ardent hope, the stolen interview, the tender farewell, are the greatest and most delicious part of their enjoyments.—

Another circumstance in my life which made very considerable alterations in my mind and manners was, I spent my seventeenth summer on a smuggling coast a good distance from home at a noted school, to learn mensuration, surveying, dialing, etc. in which I made a pretty good progress.—But I made greater progress in the knowledge of mankind.—The contraband trade was at that time very successful; scenes of swaggering riot and roaring dissipation were as yet new to me; and I was no enemy to social life.—Here, though I learned to look unconcernedly on a large tavern-bill, and mix without fear in a drunken squabble, yet I went on with a high hand in my geometry; till the sun entered Virgo, a month which is always a carnival in my bosom, a charming Fillette who lived next door to the school overset my trigonometry, and set me off in a tangent from the sphere of my studies.

I struggled on with my sines and co-sines for a few days more; but stepping out to the garden one charming noon, to take the sun's altitude, I met with my angel,

> Like Proserpine gathering flowers,
> Herself a fairer flower—

It was vain to think of doing any more good at school.

The remaining week I stayed, I did nothing but craze the faculties of my soul about her, or steal out to meet with her; and the two last nights of my stay in the country, had sleep been a mortal sin, I was innocent.—

I returned home very considerably improved.—my reading was enlarged with the very important addition of Thomson's and Shenstone's works; I had seen mankind in a new phasis; and I engaged several of my schoolfellows to keep up a literary correspondence with me.—This last helped me much on in composition.— I had met with a collection of letters by the Wits of Queen Ann's reign, and I pored over them most devoutly.—I kept copies of any of my own letters that pleased me, and a comparison between them and the composition of most of my correspondents flattered my vanity.—I carried this whim so far that though I had not three farthings worth of business in the world, yet every post brought me as many letters as if I had been a broad, plodding son of day-book and ledger.—

My life flowed on much in the same tenor till my twenty third year.—Vive l' amour et vive la bagatelle, were my sole principles of action.—The addition of two more authors to my library gave me great pleasure; Sterne and Mackenzie.—Tristram Shandy and the Man of Feeling were my bosom favorites.

—Poesy was still a darling walk for my mind, but twas only the humour of the hour.—I had usually half a dozen or more pieces on hand; I took up one or other as it suited the momentary tone of the mind, and dismissed it as it bordered on fatigue.— My passions when once they were lighted up, raged like so many devils, till they got vent in rhyme; and then conning over my verses, like a spell, soothed all into quiet. None of the rhymes of those days are in print, except, Winter, a Dirge, the eldest of my printed pieces; The death of Poor Mailie, John Barleycorn, and songs first, second and third: song second was the ebullition of that passion which ended the forementioned school-business.—

My twenty third year was to me an important era.— Partly through whim, and partly that I wished to set about doing something in life, I joined with a flax-dresser in a neighboring town, to learn his trade and carry on the business of manufacturing and retailing flax.—This turned out a sadly unlucky affair.—My partner was a scoundrel of the first water who made money by the mystery of thieving; and to finish the whole, while we were giving a welcoming carousal to the New year, our shop, by the drunken carelessness of my partner's wife, took fire and was burnt to ashes; and left me like a true poet, not worth sixpence.

I was obliged to give up business; the clouds of misfortune were gathering thick round my father's head, the darkest of which was, he was visibly far gone in a consumption; and to crown all, a belle-fille whom I adored and who had pledged her soul to meet me in the field of matrimony, jilted me with peculiar circumstances of mortification.—The finishing evil that brought up the rear of this infernal file was my hypochondriac complaint being irritated to such a degree, that for three months I was in a diseased state of body and mind, scarcely to be envied by the hopeless wretches who have just got their mittimus, "Depart from me, ye Cursed."—

From this adventure I learned something of a town life.—But the principal thing which gave my mind a turn was, I formed a bosom-friendship with a young fellow, the first created being I had ever seen, but a hapless son of misfortune.—He was the son of a plain mechanic; but a great man in the neighborhood taking him under his patronage gave him a genteel education with a view to bettering his situation in life.— The patron dying just as he was ready to launch forth into the world, the poor fellow in despair went to sea; where after a variety of good and bad fortune, a little before I was acquainted with him, he had been set ashore by an American privateer on the wild coast of Connaught, stript of every thing.—I cannot quit this poor fellow's story without adding that he is at this moment Captain of a large westIndiaman belonging to the Thames.—

This gentleman's mind was fraught with courage, independence, magnanimity, and every noble, manly virtue.—I loved him, I admired him, to a degree of enthusiasm, and I strove to imitate him.—In some measure I succeeded: I had the pride before, but he taught it to flow in proper channels.—His knowledge of the world was vastly superior to mine, and I was all attention to learn.—He was the only man I ever saw who was a greater fool than myself when woman was the presiding star; but he spoke of a certain fashionable failing with levity, which hitherto I had regarded with horror.

Here his friendship did me a mischief; and the consequence was, that soon after I resumed the plow, I wrote the welcome inclosed.—My reading was only increased by two stray volumes of Pamela, and one of Ferdinand Count Fathom, which gave me some idea of novels.—Rhyme, except some religious pieces which are in print, I had given up; but meeting with Fergusson's Scotch poems, I strung anew my wildly-sounding, rustic lyre with emulating vigor.

When my father died, his all went among the rapacious hell-hounds that growl in the kennel of justice; but we made a shift to scrape a little money in the family amongst us, with which, to keep us together, my brother and I took a neighboring farm.—My brother wanted my harebrained imagination as well as my social and amorous madness, but in good sense and every sober qualification he was far my superior.— I entered on this farm with a full resolution, "Come, go to, I will be wise!"—I read farming books; I calculated crops; I attended markets; and in short, in spite of "The devil, the world and the flesh," I believe I would have been a wise man; but the first year from unfortunately buying in bad seed, the second from a late harvest, we lost half of both our crops: this overset all my wisdom, and I returned "Like the dog to his vomit, and the sow that was washed to her wallowing in the mire.—"

I now began to be known in the neighborhood as a maker of rhymes.—The first of my poetic offspring that saw the light was a burlesque lamentation on a quarrel between two reverend Calvinists, both of them dramatis person in my Holy Fair.—I had an idea myself that the piece had some merit; but to prevent the worst, I gave a copy of it to a friend who was very fond of these things, and told him I could not guess who was the author of it, but that I thought it pretty clever.—With a certain side of both clergy and laity it met with a roar of applause.—Holy Willie's Prayer next made its appearance, and alarmed the kirk-Session so much that they held three several meetings to look over their holy artillery, if any of it was pointed against profane rhymers. Unluckily for me, my idle wanderings led me, on another side, point-blank within the reach of their heaviest metal.—This is the unfortunate story alluded to in my printed poem, The Lament.—'Twas a shocking affair, which I cannot yet bear to recollect; and had very nearly given me one or two of the principal qualifications for a place among those who have lost the chart and mistake the reckoning of rationality.—I gave up my part of the farm to my brother, as in truth it was only nominally mine; and made what little preparation was in my power for Jamaica.

Before leaving my native country for ever, I resolved to publish my poems. —I weighed my productions as impartially as in my power; I thought they had merit; and twas a delicious idea that I would be called a clever fellow, even though it should never reach my ears a poor Negro-driver, or perhaps a victim to that inhospitable clime gone to the world of spirits.

I can truly say that pauvre inconnu as I then was, I had pretty nearly as high an idea of myself and my works as I have at this moment.—It is ever my opinion that the great, unhappy mistakes and blunders, both in a rational and religious point of view, of which we see thousands daily guilty, are owing to their ignorance, or mistaken notions of themselves.—To know myself had been all along my constant study.—I weighed myself alone; I balanced myself with others; I watched every means of information how much ground I occupied both as a man and as a poet: I studied assiduously Nature's design where she seemed to have intended the various lights and shades in my character.—I was pretty sure my poems would meet with some applause; but at the worst, the roar of the Atlantic would deafen the voice of censure, and the novelty of west-Indian scenes make me forget neglect.—

I threw off six hundred copies, of which I had got subscriptions for about three hundred and fifty.—My vanity was highly gratified by the reception I met with from the public, besides pocketing, all expenses deducted near twenty pounds.—This last came very seasonable, as I was about to indent myself for want of money to pay my freight.—So soon as I was master of nine guineas, the price of wafting me to the torrid zone, I bespoke a passage in the very first ship that was to sail, for—"Hungry ruin had me in the wind."

I had for some time been skulking from covert to covert under all the terrors of a jail; as some ill-advised, ungrateful people had uncoupled the merciless legal pack at my heels.—I had taken the last farewell of my few friends; my chest was on the road to Greenock; I had composed my last song I should ever measure in Caledonia, "The gloomy night is gathering fast," when a letter from Dr. Blacklock to a friend of mine overthrew all my schemes by rousing my poetic ambition.

The Doctor belonged to a set of critics for whose applause I had not even dared to hope.—His idea that I would meet with every encouragement for a second edition fired me so much that away I posted to Edinburgh without a single acquaintance in town, or a single letter of introduction in my pocket.—The baneful star that had so long shed its blasting influence in my zenith, for once made a revolution to the nadir; and the providential care of a good God placed me under the patronage of one of his noblest creatures, the Earl of Glencairn: "Oublie moi, Grand Dieu, si jamais je l'oublie!"—

I need relate no farther.—At Edinburgh I was in a new world: I mingled among many classes of men, but all of them new to me; and I was all attention "to catch the manners living as they rise."—

You can now, Sir, form a pretty near guess what sort of a wight he is whom for some time you have honored with your correspondence.—That fancy and whim, keen sensibility and riotous passions may still make him zig-zag in his future path of life, is far from being improbable; but come what will, I shall answer for him the most determinate integrity and honor; and though his evil star should again blaze in his meridian with tenfold more direful influence, he may reluctantly tax friendship with pity but no more.—

My most respectful compliments to Miss Williams. —Her very elegant and friendly letter I cannot answer at present, as my presence is requisite in Edinburgh, and I set off tomorrow.—

If you will oblige me so highly and do me so much honor as now and then to drop me a letter, Please direct to me at Mauchline, Ayrshire—

Mauchline I have the honor to be, Sir,
2d August your ever grateful humble servant
1787 Robert Burns

## 401. To Francis Grose

Among the many witch stories I have heard relating to Aloway Kirk, I distinctly remember only two or three.

Upon a stormy night, amid whirling squalls of wind and bitter blasts of hail, in short, on such a night as the devil would choose to take the air in, a farmer or a farmer's servant was plodding and plashing homeward with his plow-irons on his shoulder, having been getting some repairs on them at a neighboring smithy. His way lay by the Kirk of Aloway, and being rather on the anxious look-out in approaching a place so well known to be a favorite haunt of the devil and the devil's friends and emissaries, he was struck aghast by discovering, through the horrors of the storm and stormy night, a light, which, on his nearer approach, plainly shewed itself to proceed from the haunted edifice.

Whether he had been fortified from above on his devout supplication, as is customary with people when they suspect the immediate presence of Satan; or whether, according to another custom, he had got courageously drunk at the smithy, I will not pretend to determine; but so it was that he ventured to go up to, nay into the very Kirk.—As good luck would have it, his temerity came off unpunished. The members of the infernal junto were all out on some midnight business or other, and he saw nothing but a kind of kettle or caldron, depending from the roof, over the fire, simmering some heads of unchristened children, limbs of executed malefactors, etc. for the business of the night. It was, in for a penny, in for a pound, with the honest plowman; so without ceremony he unhooked the caldron from off the fire, and pouring out the damnable ingredients, inverted it on his head, and carried it fairly home, where it remained long in the family a living evidence of the truth of the story.

Another story, which I can prove to be equally authentic, was as follows.

On a market day in the town of Ayr, a farmer from Carrick, and consequently whose way lay by the very gate of Aloway kirk-yard, in order to cross the river Doon at the old bridge, which is about two or three hundred yards farther on than the said gate, had been detained by his business till by the time he reached Aloway it was the wizard hour, between night and morning.

Though he was terrified with a blaze streaming from the kirk, yet as it is a well known fact, that to turn back on these occasions is running by far the greatest risk of mischief, he prudently advanced on his road. When he had reached the gate of the kirk-yard, he was surprised and entertained, through the ribs and arches of an old gothic window which still faces the highway, to see a dance of witches merrily footing it round their old sooty blackguard master, who was keeping them all alive with the power of his bagpipe.

The farmer stopping his horse to observe them a little, could plainly descry the faces of many old women of his acquaintance and neighborhood. How the gentleman was dressed, tradition does not say; but the ladies were all in their smocks; and one of them happening unluckily to have a smock which was considerably too short to answer all the purpose of that piece of dress, our farmer was so tickled that he involuntarily burst out, with a loud laugh, "Weel luppen, Maggy wi' the short sark!" and recollecting himself, instantly spurred his horse to the top of his speed.

I need not mention the universally known fact, that no diabolical power can pursue you beyond the middle of a running stream. Lucky it was for the poor farmer that the river Doon was so near, for notwithstanding the speed of his horse, which was a good one, against he reached the middle of the arch of the bridge, and consequently the middle of the stream, the pursuing, vengeful hags were so close at his heels that one of them actually sprung to seize him: but it was too late; nothing was on her side of the stream but the horse's tail, which immediately gave way to her infernal grip, as if blasted by a stroke of lightning; but the farmer was beyond her reach. However, the unsightly, tailless condition of the vigorous steed was to the last hours of the noble creature's life, an awful warning to the Carrick farmers not to stay too late in Ayr markets.—

The last relation I shall give, though equally true, is not so well identified as the two former, with regard to the scene; but as the best authorities give it for Aloway, I shall relate it.

On a summer's evening, about the time that nature puts on her sables to mourn the expiry of the cheerful day, a shepherd boy belonging to a farmer in the immediate neighborhood of Aloway Kirk, had just folded his charge, and was returning home. As he passed the kirk, in the adjoining field, he fell in with a crew of men and women, who were busy pulling stems of the plant ragwort.

He observed that as each person pulled a ragwort, he or she got astride of it, and called out, "Up horsie!" on which the ragwort flew off, like Pegasus, through the air with its rider. The foolish boy likewise pulled his ragwort, and cried, with the rest, "Up horsie!" and, strange to tell, away he flew with the company.

The first stage at which the cavalcade stopt, was a merchant's wine cellar in Bourdeaux, where, without saying, by your leave, they quaffed away at the best the cellar could afford, until the morning, foe to the imps and works of darkness, threatened to throw light on the matter, and frightened them from their carousals.—

The poor shepherd lad, being equally a stranger to the scene and the liquor, heedlessly got himself drunk; and when the rest took horse, he fell asleep and was found so next day by some of the people belonging to the merchant. Somebody that understood Scotch, asking him what he was, he said he was such-a-one's herd in Aloway, and by some means or other getting home again, he lived long to tell the world the wondrous tale— I am, Dr. Sir,

Robert Burns

## 631. To Samuel Clark

Sunday Morning—

Dear Sir,

I was, I know, drunk last night, but I am sober this morning.—From the expressions Captain Dods made use of to me, had I had nobody's welfare to care for but my own, we should certainly have come, according to the manners of the world, to the necessity of murdering one another about the business.—The words were such as generally, I believe, end in a brace of pistols; but I am still pleased to think that I did not ruin the peace and welfare of a wife and a family of children in a drunken squabble.—Farther, you know that the report of certain political opinions being mine, has already once before brought me to the brink of destruction.—I dread lest last night's business may be misrepresented in the same way.—You, I beg, will take care to prevent it.—I tax your wish for Mr. Burns' welfare with the task of waiting as soon as possible, on every gentleman who was present, and state this to him, and as you please, shew him this letter.—

What after all was the obnoxious toast?—"May our success in the present war be equal to the justice of our cause"—a toast that the most outrageous frenzy of loyalty cannot object to.— I request and beg that this morning you will wait on the parties present at the foolish dispute.—The least delay may be of unlucky consequence to me.—I shall only add, that I am truly sorry that a man who stood so high in my estimation as Mr. Dods, should use me in the manner in which I conceive he has done.—

I am, Dear Sir, yours sincerely,

Robert Burns

## JOHN MAYNE (1759–1836)

[John Mayne, born in the same year as Robert Burns, wrote the charming comic poem *The Siller Gun*, which he sketched as a brief work of 1777, and then augmented several times over the years, publishing it in three cantos in 1780, four cantos in 1808 and five cantos in 1836. The "gun" was a ten-inch silver tube which had been donated as a prize by James VI for a Dumfries shooting contest or "waponshaw", and which had become a ceremonial prize (to be returned to the city fathers after each contest) in the traditional renewals of this event. The occasion described in Mayne's poem is the Dumfries waponshaw of 1777, but the author acknowledged he "has not scrupled to introduce events which occurred at festivals subsequent to that which suggested the original effort." The celebration of rustic festivals is a tradition of Scottish poetry, as for example in "Christ's Kirk on the Green."]

## Logan Braes

By Logan's streams that rin sae deep
Fu' aft, wi' glee, I've herded sheep—
I've herded sheep, or gathered slaes* — sloe berries
Wi' my dear lad on Logan Braes.
But wae's my heart, thae days are gane
And fu' o' grief, I herd my lane*, — (alone)
While my dear lad maun face his faes*, — "foes"
Far, far frae me and Logan Braes.

Nae mair, at Logan Kirk will he,
Atween the preachings, meet wi' me—
Meet wi' me, or, when it's mirk,
Convoy me hame frae Logan Kirk.
I weel may sing, thae days are gane;
Frae kirk and fair I come alane,
While my dear lad maun face his faes,
Far, far frae me and Logan Braes.

## Hallowe'en

Of a' the festivals we hear,
Frae Handsel-Monday[1] till New-Year,
There's few in Scotland held mair dear
    For mirth, I ween,
Or yet can boast o' better cheer,
    Than Hallowe'en.

Langsyne indeed, as now in climes
Where priests for siller pardon crimes,
The kintry round in Popish rhymes
    Did pray and graen;
But customs vary wi' the times
    At Hallowe'en.

Ranged round a bleezing ingleside, — fireside
Where nowther cauld nor hunger bide,
The farmer's house, wi' secret pride,
    Will a' convene;

---

[1] The first Monday of the year.

For that day's wark is thrawn aside
At Hallowe'en.

Placed at their head the gudewife sits,
And deals round apples, pears, and nits;
Syne tells her guests, how, at sic bits
Where she has been,
Bogle's hae gart* folk tyne* their wits    made/lose
At Hallowe'en.

Grieved, she recounts how, by mischance,
Puir pussy's forced a' night to prance
Wi' fairies, wha in thousands dance
Upon the green,
Or sail wi' witches ower to France
At Hallowe'en.

Syne, issued frae the gardy-chair*,    armchair
For that's the seat of empire there,
To co'er the table wi' what's rare,
Commands are gi'en;
That a' fu' daintily may fare
At Hallowe'en.

And when they've toomed* ilk heapit plate,    emptied
And a' things are laid out o' gate*,    (the way)
To ken their matrimonial mate,
The youngsters keen
Search a' the dark decrees o' fate
At Hallowe'en.

A' things prepared in order due,
Gosh guide's! what fearfu' pranks ensue!
Some i' the kiln-pat thraw a clew,
At whilk, bedene*,    at once
Their sweethearts by the far end pu'
At Hallowe'en.

Ithers, wi' some uncanny gift,
In an auld barn a riddle lift,
Where, thrice pretending corn to sift,
Wi' charms between,
Their joe* appears, as white as drift,    sweetheart
At Hallowe'en.

But twere a langsome tale to tell
The gates o' ilka charm and spell.
Ance, gaen to saw hempseed himsel,
Puir Jock Maclean,
Plump in a filthy peat-pot fell
At Hallowe'en.

Half filled wi' fear, and droukit* weel, drenched
He frae the mire dught hardly speel*; climb
But frae that time the silly chiel* fellow
Did never grien* yearn
To cast his cantrips* wi' the Deil tricks
At Hallowe'en.

O Scotland! famed for scenes like this,
That thy sons walk where wisdom is,
Till death in everlasting bliss
Shall steek* their e'en, close
Will ever be the constant wish of
Jockie Mein.

## Helen of Kirkconnel[1]

I wish I were where Helen lies,
For, night and day, on me she cries;
And, like an angel, to the skies,
Still seems to beckon me.
For me she lived, for me she sighed,
For me she wished to be a bride;
For me, in life's sweet morn, she died
On fair Kirkconnel-Lee.

Where Kirtle-waters gently wind,
As Helen on my arm reclined,
A rival, with a ruthless mind,
Took deadly aim at me.
My love, to disappoint the foe,
Rushed in between me and the blow;
And now her corse is lying low
On fair Kirkconnel-Lee.

Though heaven forbids my wrath to swell,
I curse the hand by which she fell—
The fiend, who made my heaven a hell,
And tore my love from me.
For if, where all the graces shine—
O, if on earth there's aught divine,
My Helen, all these charms were thine—
They centered all in thee.

Ah, what avails it that, amain,
I clove th' assassin's head in twain?
No peace of mind, my Helen slain,
No resting-place for me.
I see her spirit in the air—
I hear the shriek of wild despair,

---

[1] Mayne's version of a popular song. Compare with the similarly-titled poem under "Anonymous" in the Renaissance section in Volume I.

When murder laid her bosom bare,
On fair Kirkconnel-Lee.

O, when I’m sleeping in my grave,
And oer my head the rank weeds wave,
May He who life and spirit gave
Unite my love and me.
Then from this world of doubts and sighs,
My soul on wings of peace shall rise;
And, joining Helen in the skies,
Forget Kirkconnel-Lee.

## The Siller Gun

### Canto First. The Gathering, and the March

For loyal feats, and trophies won,
Dumfries shall live till time be done.
Ae simmer’s morning, wi’ the sun,
The seven trades there,
Forgathered, for their Siller Gun
To shoot ance mair.

To shoot ance mair in grand array,
And celebrate the king’s birthday,
Crowds, happy in the gentle sway
Of ane sae dear,
Were proud their fealty to display,
And marshal here.

O, George, the wale* o’ kings and men, choice
For thee, in daily prayer, we bend.
With ilka* blessing heaven can send every
May’st thou be crowned;
And may thy race our rights defend,
The warld around.

For weeks before this fete sae clever,
The fowk were in a perfect fever,
Scouring gun-barrels in the river—
At marks practicing—
Marching wi’ drums and fifes for ever—
A’ sodgerizing.

And turning coats, and mending breeks*, britches
New seating where the sark-tail keeks*; peeps
(Nae matter though the clout that eeks
Be black or blue;)
And darning, with a thousand steeks*, stitches
The hose anew.

Between the last and this occasion,
Lang, unco* lang, seemed the vacation    very
To him wha woos sweet recreation
In nature's prime;
And him wha likes a day's potation
At ony time.

The lift* was clear, the morn serene,    sky
The sun just glinting owr the scene,
When James McNoe began again
To beat to arms,
Rousing the heart o' man and wean
Wi' war's alarms.

Frae far and near, the country lads,
(Their joes* ahint them on their yads*)    sweethearts/horses
Flocked in to see the show in squads;
And, what was dafter,
Their pawky* mithers and their dads    clever, sly
Cam trotting after.

And mony a beau and belle were there,
Doited* wi' dozing on a chair;    stupefied
For, lest they'd, sleeping, spoil their hair,
Or miss the sight,
The gowks*, like bairns before a fair,    fools
Sat up a' night.

Wi' hats as black as ony raven,
Fresh as the rose, their beards new shaven,
And a' their Sunday's cleeding having
Sae trim and gay,
Forth cam our trades, some ora* saving    odd things
To wair that day.

Fair fa' ilk canny, caidgy carl*,    peasant
Weel may be bruik his new apparel.
And never dree* the bitter snarl    suffer
O' scowling wife.
But, blest in pantry, barn, and barrel,
Be blithe through life.

Hegh, sirs! what crowds cam into town,
To see them must'ring up and down.
Lasses and lads, sun-burnt and brown—
Women and weans,
Gentle and semple, mingling, crown,
The gladsome scenes.

At first, forenent ilk deacon's hallan,
His ain brigade was made to fall in;
And, while the muster-roll was calling,
And joybells jowing,

Het-pints, weel spiced, to keep the saul in,
Around were flowing.

Broiled kipper, cheese and bread, and ham,
Laid the foundation for a dram
O' whisky, gin frae Rotterdam,
Or cherry brandy;
Whilk after, a' was fish that cam
To Jock, or Sandy.

O, weel ken they wha loo their chappin*, — half-pints
Drink maks the auldest swack and strappin;
Gars* care forget the ills that happen— — makes
The blate* look spruce— — shy
And ev'n the thowless cock their tappin,
And craw fu' croose*. — boldly

The muster owr, the diff'rent bands
File aff, in parties, to the Sands:
Where, mid loud laughs and clapping hands,
Gleyed* Geordy Smith — squint-eyed
Reviews them, and their line expands
Alang the Nith.

But ne'er, for uniform or air,
Was sic a group reviewed elsewhere.
The short, the tall; fat fowk, and spare;
Side coats, and dockit;
Wigs, queues, and clubs, and curly hair;
Round hats, and cockit.

As to their guns—thae fell engines,
Borrowed or begged, were of a' kinds
For bloody war, or bad designs,
Or shooting cushies*— — pigeons
Lang fowling-pieces, carabines,
And blunder-busses.

Maist feck, though oiled to mak them glimmer,
Hidna been shot for mony a simmer;
And fame, the story-telling kimmer*, — gossip
Jocosely hints
That some o' them had bits o' timmer*, — wood ("timber")
Instead o' flints.

Some guns, she threeps*, within her ken, — rumors
Were spiked, to let nae priming ben*; — in
And, as in twenty there were ten
Worm-eaten stocks,
Sae, here and there, a rozit-end
Held on their locks.

And then, to show what diffrence stands
Atween the leaders and their bands,
Swords that, unsheathed, since Prestonpans,[1]
    Neglected lay,
Were furbished up, to grace the hands
    O chiefs, this day.

"Ohon!" says George, and ga'e a grane,
"The age o' chivalry is gane."
Syne, having owr and owr again
    The hale surveyed,
Their route, and a' things else, made plain,
    He snuffed, and said:

"Now, Gentlemen, now mind the motion,
And dinna, this time, mak a botion.
Shouther your arms, O, ha'd them tosh on,
    And not athraw.
Wheel wi' your left-hands to the ocean,
    And march awa."

Wi' that, the dinlin drums rebound,
Fifes, clarionets, and hautboys sound.
Through crowds on crowds, collected round,
    The corporations
Trudge aff, while echo's self is drowned
    In acclamations.

Their steps to martial airs agreeing,
And a' the seven-trades' colors fleeing,
Bent for the Criags*, O, weel worth seeing. "crags"
    They hied awa;
Their bauld convener proud o' being
    The chief owr a'.

Attended by his body-guard,
He stepped in gracefu'ness unpaired.
Straught as the poplar on the swaird,
    And strong as Sampson,
Nae ee could look without regard
    On Robin Tamson.

His craft, the hammermen, fu' braw*, handsome
Led the procession, twa and twa.
The leddies waved their napkins a',
    And boys huzzayed,
As onward, to the waponshaw,
    They stately strade.

---

[1] Battle of September, 1745, in which Bonnie Prince Charlie defeated the forces of Sir John Cope.

Close to the hammermen, behold,
The squaremen come like chiefs of old.
The weavers, syne, their flags unfold;
And, after them,
The tailors walk, erect and bold,
Intent on fame.

The souters*, o' King Crispin vain, cobblers
March next in turn to the campaign;
And, while the crowd applauds again,
See, too, the tanners,
Extending far the glitt'ring train
O' guns and banners.

The fleshers, on this joyous day,
Bring up the rearward in array.
Enarmed, they mak a grand display—
A' jolly chiels*, fellows
Able, in ony desp'rate fray,
To feght like de'ils.

The journeymen were a' sae gaucy*, imposing
Th' apprentices sae kir and saucy,
That, as they gaed alang the causey,
Ahint* them a', behind
Th' applauding heart o' mony a lassie
Was stown* awa. stolen

Brisk as a bridegroom gawn to wed,
Ilk deacon his battalion led.
Foggies the zig-zag followers sped,
But scarce had pow'r
To keep some, fitter for their bed,
Frae stoit'ring* owr. staggering

For, blithsome Sir John Barleycorn
Had charmed them sae, this simmer's morn,
That, what wi' drams, and mony a horn,
And reaming bicker*, beaker
The ferly* is, withouten scorn, wonder
They walked sae sicker*. sure

As through the town their banners fly,
Frae windows low, frae windows high,
A' that could find a neuk* to spy, "nook"
Were leaning oer.
The streets, stair-heads, and carts, forbye,
Were a' uproar.

Frae the Freer's Vennel, through and through,
Care seemed to've bid Dumfries adieu.
Housewives forgat to bake, or brew,
Owrjoyed, the while,

To view their friends, a’ marching now
In warlike style.

To see his face whom she loo’d best,
Hab’s wife was there amang the rest;
And, as, wi’ joy, her sides she prest,
Like mony mae,
Her exultation was exprest
In words like thae:

“Wow, but it maks ane’s heart lowp* light    leap
To see auld fowk sae cleanly dight*.    dressed
E’en now, our Habby seems as tight
As when, lang syne,
His looks were first the young delight
And pride o’ mine.”

But on the meeker maiden’s part,
Deep sighs alane her love assert.
Deep sighs, the language o’ the heart,
Will aft reveal
A flame whilk a’ the gloss of art
Can ne’er conceal.

Frae rank to rank while thousands hustle,
In front, like waving corn, they rustle;
Where, dangling like a baby’s whustle,
The siller gun,
The royal cause of a’ this bustle,
Gleamed in the sun.

Suspended frae a painted pole,
A glimpse o’t sae inspired the whole,
That auld and young, wi’ heart and soul,
Their heads were cocking,
Keen as ye’ve seen, at bridals droll,
Maids catch the stocking.

In honor o’ this gaudy thing,
And eke in honor o’ the King,
A fouth o’ flo’rs the gard’ners bring,
And frame sweet posies
Of a’ the relics o’ the spring,
And simmer’s roses.

Amang the flow’ry forms they weave,
There’s Adam to the life, and Eve.
She, wi’ the apple in her neeve*,    fist
Enticing Adam;
While Satan’s laughing in his sleeve,
At him and madam.

The lily white, the vi'let blue,
The heather-bells of azure hue,
Heart's-ease for lovers kind and true,
Whate'er their lot,
And that dear flow'r, to friendship due,
"Forget me not."

A' thae, and wi' them mingled now,
Pinks and carnations, not a few,
Fresh garlands, glitt'ring wi' the dew,
And yellow broom,
Athort* the scented welkin threw "athwart"
A rich perfume.

Perfume, congenial to the clime,
The sweetest in the sweetest time.
The merry bells, in jocund chime,
Rang through the air,
And minstrels played, in strains sublime,
To charm the fair.

And fairer than our Nithsdale fair,
Or handsomer, there's nane elsewhere.
Pure as the streams that murmur there,
In them ye'll find
That virtue and the graces rare
Are a' enshrined.

Lang may the bonny bairns recline
On plenty's bosom, saft and kind.
And, O, may I, ere life shall dwine
To its last scene,
Return, and a' my sorrows tine* lose
At hame again.

Canto Second. Arrival at the field—beginning of the competition—surrounding scenery.

Now, through the Kirkgate Port, the thrang
O' men in arms proceed alang.
Behold them, while the cymbals' clang
Resounds afar,
In a' the pomp, without the pang,
Or waes of war.

Aff to the Craigs, the hale forenoon,
By the best paths to get there soon,
Crowds after crowds were flocking down,
In nines, and tens,
Deserting, fast, the bonniest town
That Scotia kens.

O, happy they wha, up twa story,
Saw the procession in its glory.
Alang the roads it left out oer ye,
Sic clouds o' stoor*, dust
Ye couldna see ye'r thoom before ye
For half an hour.

Where the lang train of armor gleams,
Bright Phoebus shone in scorching beams.
Parched up wi' heat, nae caller* streams fresh
To weet their hasses*, throats
The squadrons greined for ale that reams
Frae jenny Gass's.

They wha had corns, or broken wind,
Begood to pegh and limp behind:
Laith* to sit down, and still inclined "loath"
To try their pith*, strength
"I hope we'll dance yet, ere we've dined,"
Cries Geordy Smith.

To cheer them wha began to fag,
The minstrels lowsed* Apollo's bag, "loosened"
And lilted up, though still they lag,
*The Reel o' Boggie,*
And *Willy Was a Wanton Wag*,
Wi' *Kath'rine Oggie.*

But *Bruce's March to Bannockburn*,
To leave his banes in freedom's urn,
Or, glorious and triumphant, spurn
Intended thraldom,
Sae raised their hearts, at ilka turn,
That nought could hald them.

O, blessings on King Robert's name.
On Wallace, and Sir John the Graeme.
While freedom dare assert her claim,
Or virtue blossom,
Wallace and Bruce will aye enflame
The patriot bosom.

A' this and mair, baith ane and a',
They seemed to say, and croosely* craw: bravely
*Out Owr the Hills and Far Awa,*
The pipers played;
And, roaring like a water-fa',
The crowd huzzayed.

The Craigs, with ivy mantled round,
Re-echoed back the jocund sound;
And, as the troops approached the ground,
Araise to view

Like some sweet islands, newly found,
In fair Pelew.

Syne, louder grew the busy hum
O' friends rejoicing as they come:
Wi' double vir* the drummers drum — vigor
The pint-stoups* clatter, — containers
And bowls o' negus, milk and rum,
Flow round like water.

"Tak a gude waught*—I'm sure ye're weary," — drought
Says Anny Kaillie to her dearie.
John, fain to see his wife sae cheery,
Indulged the fun,
Gat fu'*, and dandered lang and eerie, — drunk
And tint* his gun— — lost

And missed, mair owr, th' endearing charms
(The very thought ilk bosom warms)
Of auld acquaintaces in swarms,
Meeting like brithers,
And wee-things giggling in the arms
O' their fond mithers.

And bonny lasses, tight and clean,
Buskit* to please their ain lads' een— — dressed
Lasses, whase faces, as the scene
Its tints discloses,
In glowing sweetness intervene,
Like living roses.

Convener Tamson's troop, the while,
Prepare for action in great style.
The lave* their various firelocks pile, — rest
By three and three,
And, tween ilk corps, for half a mile,
Their banners flee.

The drums and fifes a flourish made;
Three loud huzzas the menyie* gaed, — group
And cleared the stance, that ilka blade
The mark might view,
Far glist'ning, circled white and red,
Wi' sprainings o' blue.

In mingled prospect, on the plain
That parts the Maiden-Craigs in twain,
Craems, ginge-bread-stawns, legerdemain,
And raree-shows,
Enticed young sparks to entertain,
And treat their joes*. — sweethearts

For fear o' scant, whilk aften mars
The best o' projects in the wars,
Provisions, Ferrintosh in jars,
And casks o' beer,
Were ranged, like batteries, on cars,
In front and rear.

Then there were tents, where, frank and free,
On divot-seats, sae cozily,
Auld birkies*, innocently slee, — sparks
Wi' cap* and stowp*, — "cup"/beaker
Were e'en as blithe as blithe could be—
A' fit to loup*. — "leap"

Pleased, they recount, wi' meikle joy,
How aft they've been at sic a ploy*; — affair
Descrive past scenes; re-act the boy,
And a' his wheems:
Sweet days of youth, without alloy,
Like fairy dreams.

And mony a crack*, and gallant tale, — chat
Bout bauld forebears, sae stark and hale,
Inspired their breasts with ardent zeal,
While, circling round,
The reaming cogs o' nappy* ale — foaming
Gaed glibber down.

Yet now and then, a silent tear,
For friends departed, kindred dear,
Friends, wha were aye the foremost here,
Bedewed ilk cheek,
Mair eloquent, in grief sincere,
Than tongue can speak.

Amang auld cronies, Geordy Smith
Discoursed of war with a' his pith*: — strength
Siege followed siege, till kin and kith
Were grown sae frisky,
They would have drank the river Nith
Had it been whisky.

To war accustomed when a boy,
A sodger's life was still his joy—
First, in the ranks at Fontenoy,
And, mony a year,
Like Hector on the plains o' Troy,
A gen'ral here.

When a' the hammermen, sae bright,
Had charged their guns, like men o' might,
Convener Tamson, wi' delight,
The sport began;

And never yet was belted knight
A blither man.

Meantime, the younkers on the green,
In merry rounds are dancing seen.
Wi' rapture sparkling in their een,
They mind, fu' weel,
The sappy kiss, and squeeze, between
Ilk blithesome reel.

And, as the Highland flings begin,
Their heels grow lighter wi' the din.
They smack their hands; and, chin to chin,
They cut and caper.
Ev'n the bye-standers figure in,
And flounce, and vapor.

The minstrels there were Sandy Brown,
The Piper o' Lochmaben town:
Though whoozling sair, and cruppen* down, "creeping"
Ald Sanders seemed,
His chaunter, for its cheering sound,
Was aye esteemed.

Jock Willison, a souter* bred, cobbler
Wha, for the fiddle, left his trade,
Jigged it far better than he sped,
For, oh, poor Jock
Could ne'er gang soberly to bed,
Like other folk.

Blind-fu,' at weddings, or a dance,
He'd play, though like ane in a trance;
And then, for feghting, Jock would prance
At fair, or market,
And box whaever durst advance,
Till they were yarkit*. whipped

Yet Jock was as humane as brave,
And aften for the helpless strave.
To snatch the drowning frae the wave,
He'd quickly dive,
And to a weeping mither save
Her bairn alive.

To hear John Bruce exert his skill,
Ye'd never grudge anither gill*. glass
O, how he scorned th' Italian trill,
And variations;
And gart his thairm-strings speak, at will,
True Scots vibrations.

Nor was it only for a reel
That Johnny was beloved sae weel.
He loo'd his friend, was aye genteel,
And, what's far mair,
John to his prince was true and leal,
Ev'n in despair.

But wha's he lilting in the rear,
Sae saft, sae tunefu', and sae clear?
It's Dingwall, to the Muses dear,
Whase modest merit
Was sae represt for want o' gear*, money
Care crushed his spirit.

Aft, when the Waits* were playing by, Watch?
I've marked his viol with a sigh,
Soothing lorn lovers, where they lie,
To visions sweet—
Saft as a mither's lullaby,
When babies greet*. weep

*The Bonny Bush Abune Traquair,*
And *Mary Scott of Yarrow, Fair*;
*Tweedside*, and *O, I Wish I Were*
*Where Helen Lie*s,
He played in tones that suit despair,
When beauty dies.

But, twere owr lang to reckon a'
The strains he played, sae saft and slaw—
Strains o' the minstrels, now awa,
Sweetest and last
Memorials, like our waponshaw,
Of ages past.

By this time, now, wi' mony a dunder,
Auld guns were brattling aff like thunder,
Three parts o' whilk, in ilka hunder,
Did sae recoil,
That collar-banes gat mony a lunder,
In this turmoil.

Wide o' the mark, as if to scar us,
The bullets ripped the swaird like harrows;
And, fright'ning a' the craws and sparrows
About the place,
Ramrods were fleeing thick as arrows
At Chevy Chace.

Yet still, as through the tents we steer,
Unmoved the festive groups appear:
Lads oxter* lasses, without fear, walk arm in arm
Or dance like wud*; crazy

Blithe, when the guns gaed aff sae queer,
    To hear the thud.

Disporting in the sunny beam,
When gentler mates are in a breem,
Some seek the shade, and some the stream,
    And banquet there
On strawberries, or cruds* and cream, "curds"
    And country fare.

O, wi' what glee the muse stravaigs* wanders
Owr a' the beauties o' the Craigs—
Forgetting a' the ills and plagues
    That aft harass us,
She scours the hills and dales, for leagues,
    Round this Parnassus.

Sweet spot, how happy hae I been
Seeking birds-nests with eager een;
Or, pu'ing gowans* on the green, daisies
    Where waving corn,
Blue-bells and roses, fringe the scene,
    And flow'ring thorn.

Yonder the lads and lasses group,
To see the luckless lover's-lowp.
Wae's me that disappointed houp*, "hope"
    That cruel blight,
Should drive fowk frae this warld to scoup
    To endless night.

Beneath yon cliff, high beetling owr,
Is chaste Diana's Maiden-Bow'r.
There, sacred to the guardian pow'r,
    A tablet stands,
Inscribed by a' wha make that tour,
    In true-love's bands.

Sae strait and narrow is the way,
Nane but pure virgins enter may.
And, O, it's droll, in this essay,
    When flirts, alack,
Their wee infirmities betray,
    By turning back.

Censorious Bess, that dorty* dame, huffy
Cam here to carve her lover's name.
But Bessy, having been to blame
    For failings, too,
Had nearly gane to her lang hame,
    In squeezing through.

Hither, forbye the young and fair,
Grave matrons come to tak the air.
Ev'n gentry, and the sons o' care,
Resort, a-wee,
To view, around, the beauties rare
By land and sea.

At tide-time, with an anxious mind,
The sailor's wife, lang left behind,
Looks for her love with ilka wind,
And watches here
Ship after ship, to Nith consigned,
Till he appear.

Behold, far hence, in sylvan charms,
Cots, country-seats, kirk-towns, and farms,
Hills, circling wide, wi' sheep in swarms;
And mould'ring tow'rs,
Famous, langsyne, for chiefs in arms,
And potent pow'rs.

Imbowered around, how sweet to spy
Corn-rigs* and orchards laughing lie. rows
Dumfries, wi' steeples to the sky,
And ships in crowds,
And Criffel-hill ascending high
Amang the clouds.

Lo, glitt'ring onward to the sea,
The stream that gave the Muse to me.
Pure stream, on whase green banks, wi' glee,
In life's sweet morn,
I chased the gaudy butterflee,
Ere care was born.

O, though it's mony a langsome year,
Since, fu' o' care, and scant o' gear,
I left thy banks, sweet Nith, sae dear,
This heart o' mine
Lowps light whene'er I think or hear
O' thee, or thine.

In seed-time, when thy farmers saw*, "sew"
In simmer, when thy roses blaw;
In harvest, or in frost and snaw,
When winter low'rs,
My heart and mind are with ye a'—
For ever yours.

Canto Third. The multitude assembled—Most prominent characters—The feast—Continuation of the Competition—Noble daring of the people under the threat of invasion

Still crowding to the waponshaw,
O, what a swarm o' great and sma'.
See them, owr ditches, dykes, and a',
Exulting, sprang,
Eager to join, wi' loud huzza,
The jocund thrang.

As customers cam flocking in,
The ale-wives thought it nae great sin
To order fresh supplies o' gin,
For, drouthy* throttles thirsty
Had left nought o' the meikle bin
But empty bottles.

Hegh! what a concourse now appears
O' horse, and foot, and charioteers:
Farmers, and lairds, and a' their dears—
A' ranks, and stations,
Parading on, while music cheers
The corporations.

Wi' scores o' gentlemen, and mair,
Wha come their townsmen's joys to share,
See brave Sir Robert Laurie there,
And Eldlershaw,
And young Terraughtie, worthies rare,
Beloved by a'.

Terraughtie, here a welcome guest,
Was hailed wi' raptures aft exprest.
Ten thousand tongues his worth confest—
A patriot leal*, "loyal"
The object dearest to his breast
The commonweal.

Amang the crowd was Johnny Gass,
Kend through Dumfries by lad and lass.
Revered abune the common class,
Up late and air,
John had seen saxty simmers pass,
A barber there.

The chronicle o' former years,
At him ilk ane some question speers*; asks
But when they spak of auld forebears,
Now dead and gane,
John answered only wi' his tears,
Or made a mane.

"Oh, Sirs," says he, wi' heavy granes,
"How quickly man to age attains.
I mind yon leddies when but weans,
In leading-strings,

And now their oys can dance their lanes,[1]
    In fairy-rings."

O, wha, amang the wrights, is he
That seems, for grace, to bear the gree*? prize
"It's Roby Kemp. In him you see,
    On virtue's plan,
The traits o' true nobility—
    An honest man."

For honest men, the crowd exclaim,
Lang may our trades* preserve their name. guilds, tradesmen
"And if," cries John, "at wealth they aim,
    Like Richie Hawat,
May they bring gowd-in-gowpins hame,
    And credit to it.

"To mak a spune, or spoil a horn,
He left Dumfries ae dowy* morn, gloomy
Gaed far frae hame, returned wi' corn,
    And wine, and oil,
And, glad to live where he was born,
    Tills his ain soil."

And wha's he on the milk-white steed?
"Wae's me," quo' John, and shook his head.
"The gout has marred George Johnston's speed,
    Since, in our garden,
We ran, when boys, for gingerbread,
    Wi' Johnny Jardine.

"Cracking his jokes wi' friends sae kirry,
Here's Deacon Threshie, wise and merry.
And yonder's blameless Willy Berry,
    The leddies' glover,
At five and fifty, bright as sherry,
    And still a lover.

"Sedately joining in the game,
James Hutchison now taks his aim:
An architect o' meikle fame,
    Wha plans wi' care,
And builds his hopes o' bliss supreme
    On praise and pray'r.

"Neist rank to him, see Deacon Gowdy,
In velvet coat as black's a mowdy*, mole-catcher
A gawcier man ne'er suppit crowdy,
    Did what was right,

---

[1]Oys = grandsons. Their lanes = by themselves.

Or loved freemasonry, uncloudy,
Wi' mair delight.

"See, also, armed wi' sword and spear,
M'Ghee, our ain town's-bairn, draws near.
Sirs, when the Highlandmen were here,
In Forty-five,
His father gart them flee for fear,
And skulk belive*. quickly

"Sent out disguised in Bedesman's gown,
To watch the foe near Annan town,
There, ere he weel had sitten down,
Or fed his filly,
Unwelcome news was buzzed around,
About Duke Willie.

"Back to Dumfries, in dread the while,
He brought in word, that, mony a mile,
King George's army, frae Carlisle,
Had crossed the border.
They come, cried he, in rank and file,
And battle order.

"This news, first told him as a hum,
Suin gart the Highlanders look glum.
At night, when a' was dark and dumb,
They vanished fairly,
And never mair, wi' pipe and drum,
Saw we Prince Charlie.

"Yet, ere his flight, to our great skaith*, harm
He levied fines; and, by my faith,
Glenriddel and our Provost, baith,
Awa were ta'en,
As hostages, on pain o' death,
To pay the kain*. price

"Albeit they werena lang detained,
Our purse, to ransom them, was drained.
Syne, having liberty regained,
They cantered hame,
And, through a weel-spent life, sustained
An honored name.

"True to their country, king, and law,
My blessings on our burghers a'.
O, never, in their kirk or ha'*, "hall"
May party-strife,
Dissolving bosom friends in twa,
Vex man or wife."

But wha, amang the lookers-on,
With aspect meek and mild is yon?
He's, sure, the sire o' mony a son,
If ane may guess
By them wha seem to watch the tone
He would express.

"That's Doctor Chapman—shaved by me,"
Quo' John, "thir thretty years and three.
He and his boarders come to see,
Ere a' be done,
Our ance-in-seven-years' jubilee,
The siller gun!"

A scholar there, wi' loud acclaim,
Did homage to the good man's name.
Led by the luster o' his fame,
Frae far and near,
Lords, lairds, and nabobs, quit their hame,
To study here.

Nor is it only classic lair*, learning
Mere Greek and Latin, and nae mair.
Chapman, wi' fond parental care,
Has lair combined
With a' the gems and jewels rare
That deck the mind.

"O, had I followed up the plan
His sage instructions first began,
The race which my school-fellows ran,
Like stars to shine,
And a' that elevates the man,
Had now been mine."

Full o' his auld preceptor's praise,
Around the Craigs the scholar strays,
Blithe, after a' his thorny ways,
Retracing here
The gowden scenes of early days—
For ever dear.

Returning hame, when time and care
Ha'e bleached, in foreign lands, our hair,
How sweet to breathe our native air,
And talk of joys,
And pleasures past, and friendships rare,
When we were boys.

Thrice happy they wha claim our meed,
As men of worth, or friends in need.
Lang has thy name, benignant Reid,
Exalted stood,

For thou, in heart, and mind, and deed,
Art great, and good.

The next, for worth, endeared to me,
And dear to a', is Sandy Key,
Like Reid, benevolent and free,
Withouten pride,
Kind to his countrymen is he,
And a' beside.

With other friends, o' great desert,
Wha nobly act, through life, their part,
There's Hutchison, wi' kindly heart,
And right gude-will,
A master o' the healing art,
Wi' meikle skill.

At Hampton, jocular and gay,
Is health-restoring Halliday,
Wha, making providence his stay,
Wi' firm endeavor,
Frae camps to courts, attained his way
To royal favor.

Linked in th' Aesculapian train,
Whom Nithsdale boasts of as her ain,
Hyslop, wha ne'er prescribes in vain,
Affords a sample
How much a family may gain
By gude example.

O' men belanging to the law,
John Aikin was the flow'r owr a'.
Like Andrew Crosbie, now awa,
His auld class-fellow,
Through kittle* points he clearly saw, ticklish
Though sometimes mellow.

O, for a muse, upon her throne,
To sing o' vent'rous Clapperton,
Intrepid Ross, and Richardson,
Wha bade defiance
To ice-bergs, or the torrid zone,
In aid o' science.

Frae India, to our bonny town,
Craigdarroch comes wi' high renown.
The Malcolms, too, we proudly own—
Four brother-wights,
A' steadfast servants o' the crown—
A' belted knights.

In times when war, frae year to year,
Called forth our armies, far and near,
Learned Pasley, vict'ry's pioneer,
 Before them sped,
Or joined them in their brave career,
 Where glory led.

To rank amang our men o' fame,
Telford upholds a double claim:
O' fabrics of a splendid frame,
 The engineer—
In poesy, a poet's name,
 To Eskdale dear.

But what has been a source o' gain
To commerce and her num'rous train,
Sage Miller, o' Dalswinton's plain,
 By Nith's sweet stream,
First broached the art to plow the main,
 Propelled by steam.

Sons o' the soil frae whilk we came,
We've mony mae whom we could name,
And, wi' them, Allan Cunningham,
 Wha fondly try
To reach the pinnacle o' fame,
 However high.

Hail, kindred spirits, ane and a',
Men of account, without a flaw,
Pushing your fortunes, far awa,
 Or, fu' o' glee,
Rejoicing at our waponshaw,
 Dumfries, wi' thee.

How beautiful, on yonder green,
The tents wi' dancing pairs between.
In front, though banners intervene,
 And guns are rattling,
There's nought but happiness, I ween,
 In a' this battling.

For miles, by people over-run,
The air resounds wi' mirth and fun.
Frae grave to gay, frae sire to son,
 And great to sma',
The shooting for the siller gun
 Delights them a.

Behold the concourse, here and there,
Gaffawing till their sides are sair.
See, as the balls whiz through the air,
 Yon thoughtless wights

Careering till they find out where
Ilk bullet lights.

A chosen band, at twelve at noon,
Drew up to fire in grand platoon.
The troops that garrisoned the town
Returned ilk volley,
And never, on the fourth o' June,
Were fowk mair jolly.

The cocks-and-pales were on the run.
Rum punch was flowing by the tun.
Trenchers were handed round wi' bun,
Cookies and baiks,
Short-bread, wi' carvy nicely done,
And ait-meal cakes.

Ait-meal, the staff o' life! Through thee,
Our sires were hearty, brave, and free.
And, still preferring brose[1] to tea,
Their sons are gallant,
And bear, in arms and arts, the gree*— prize
Humane and valiant.

But there was nought like feasting, till
The grace was said by James Mackill.
For, though our townsmen feast and fill,
Without much pressing,
They keep the gude auld custom still—
To ask a blessing.

Convener Tamson mensed* the board, honored, blessed
Where sat ilk deacon like a lord.
John Blackstock raise, and waved his sword
In loyal glee—
"*God save the King!*" was twice encored,
Wi' three times three.

Of a' the toasts that scour their hasses*, throats
*The Kirk o' Scotland*, foremost passes.
*Dumfries, and a' her bonny lasses,*
*And gallant lads,*
Were drank in magnum-bonum glasses,
Wi' ruffs and dads.

And, when the loud applause had ceast,
"Let's fill," exclaimed a score at least.
"Fill, fill to him, for his bequeest,
In wine unmixt,

[1]A famous Scottish dish: oatmeal mixed with boiling water or milk, or sometimes liquor.

*The royal founder o' the feast—*
*Gude James the Sixt!"*

"Peace to his saul!" cries Deacon Gibb,
And drained the goblet ilka drib.
Syne, *George the Third—the royal rib—*
*The Prince, and a'—*
Were drank sae aft, that tongues, ance glib,
Scarce wagged ava.

Where gladness beamed in ilka face,
Wha could be dowf*, whate'er his case? gloomy
The gravest gentry o' the place
In tents convene,
Mix wi' their friends, and blithely grace
The festive scene.

Ev'n Maister Auld, our letter-gae,
And English teacher, mony a day,
Forgat the cares that made him wae,
And lilted here
Sangs that shall live till time decay,
To Scotia dear.

He sang, wi' matchless taste and skill,
*The Cowden-Knowes*, and *Paty's Mill—*
*My Nanny, O!*—and sweeter still,
In life's decline,
*We'll tak a cup*, in kind gude-will,
*For auld lang syne.*

But, hark, throughout the tented plain,
Where mirth, and wine, and music, reign,
Bellona, wi' her stalwart train
O' men in arms,
Recalls the wond'ring Muse again
To war's alarms.

There, still, instead o' marksmen true,
To shoot at yonder target now,
Some fallows hald their guns askew,
And some let fly
Clean owr the Craigs, ayont our view—
A mile owr high.

Rob Simson, sportsman bred and born,
To won the royal prize had sworn,
But windy Robin's powder-horn
Blew up in air,
And he had nought but skaith* and scorn, harm
And meikle care.

Some chaps, bumbazed amid the yowder*, fumes
Pat in the ball before the powder.
Some clapped their guns to the wrang shou'der,
Where, frae the priming,
Their cheeks and whiskers gat a scowder,
Their een, a styming.

Steeking* his een, big John M'Maff shutting
Held out his musket like a staff,
Turned, though the chiel* was half-and-half, fellow
His head away,
And, panting, cried, "Sirs, is she aff?"
In wild dismay.

Puir gowk*, ne'er used to war's alarms, fool
Though love o' fame his bosom warms,
His fears foresaw a thousand harms—
But here the Muse
Propones, for twa-three friends in arms,
A short excuse:

Peace and gude-will had been sae lang
The burthen o the people's sang,
Their arms like useless lumber hang.
Nor fife, nor drum,
Was heard, save when the fire-bell rang
For some foul lum*. chimney

Yet though, like children after play,
In calm repose the people lay,
That flame whilk lighted Bruce's way
To freedom's shrine,
Cloudless as yon bright orb o' day,
Ne'er ceased to shine.

For, when the French, in aftertimes,
Mad wi' success, and drunk wi' crimes,
Vowed to infest our happy climes,
And scourge the nation,
Then, with a spirit that sublimes
The humblest station—

Then, ere our king could gi'e command,
Up raise the Genius o' the Land.
Dumfries, in mony a chosen band,
Enarmed appears,
Fit, in ae phalanx, to withstand
A host o' spears.

Men of a' ranks, on foot and horse,
Assembled at the market-corss;
Where, looking up to virtue's source,
The people swore

Never to let a foreign force
Pollute their shore.

Nor was this fervor only here.
It spread, like wild-fire, far and near.
Scotland, to ilka virtue dear,
Though aft sair mauled,
Scotland was never in the rear
When danger called.

At hame, afield, or far awa,
She bore the brunt in front of a'.
The last to sheathe, the first to draw
Her auld claymore,
For liberty, her king, and law,
And native shore.

O, in his king and country's cause,
How blest is he wha nobly fa's.
Bright fame her gowden trumpet blaws,
And deathless story
Devotes his name, wi' loud huzzas,
To endless glory.

Canto Fourth. Episodes of love and quarrel—gaining of the prize

Tween boozing, dancing, sangs, and laughing,
The afternoon drew on wi' daffin*. fooling
Auld fowk seemed young again wi' quaffing
Some fav'rite's name,
And love, in youthfu' breasts, was flaffing,
A mutual flame.

Sic shaking hands, and kind enquiries,
Tween Uncle Johns, and Auntie Maries.
Grave dames, in a' their nice feegaries,
And ancient beaus,
Whistling and singing, like canaries—
Blithe and jocose.

Croose* as a cock in his ain cavy, brave
Wha should be there but Hinny Davy?
*The Gee*, and *Fare ye weel, Killavy,*
He sang sae sweet,
His friends, though knuckle-deep in gravy,
Forgat to eat.

Some ballad-singers, lilting lang,
Paraded round and round the thrang.
I wat they were a canty* gang, pleasant
And sung sae fine,
Fowk followed till they learnt some sang,
Like this o' mine:

Crawfordjohn

As I was gawn to Crawfordjohn,
Amang the bonny blooming heather,
A blithsome laddy, passing on,
Proposed that we should gang together.
For, O my bonny lass, says he,
I'm quite in love wi' you already,
And, if ye'll trust yoursel' wi' me,
When I'm a laird, ye'se be a leddy.

He spak sae kind, as we gaed on,
We didna mind the wind or weather,
For, ere we cam to Crawfordjohn,
We pledged our troth to ane anither.
Through life he vows he'll gang wi' me,
And a' my thoughts are now about him,
His simple wife I'd rather dee,
Than live a titled dame without him.

Then, weel's me aye on Crawfordjohn,
And, O, when kindly hearts forgather,
May never lad nor lassie moan
That ere they met amang the heather.
For, as to my lad and mysel',
Our lots are cast with ane anither;
And, hence, our bairns's bairns shall tell
How weel we lived and loved together.

But wha can paint yon matron's fears,
Whase daughter in the dance appears?
Boding nae gude frae young men's leers,
She, wi' concern,
Starts at ilk glance, and thinks she hears
Her ruined bairn.

She sees, wi' meikle grief and pain,
Jock getting fu', and Jenny fain,
And sighs for fear that guilt should stain
Yon spotless face,
Flushed, like red roses after rain,
Wi' modest grace.

Aft to the whins*, frae mang the thrang, furze, fields
Some laddy and his lassie gang;
But, O, the sports sae sweet and lang,
Within that shade,
Beguile to mony a future pang
The yielding maid.

Among the lave* was country Johnny, rest
Wi' his joe Meg as braw* as ony. handsome
Nae doubt she thought hersel' as bonny

As ony there;
But, lang ere e'en, her cockernonny[1]
Was toozeled sair.

For, when the slee intriguing clown
Had fairly danced his partner down,
Cauld whisky-punch, and ale, nut-brown,
He gart* her sweel, made
Till, dizzy, a' the warld ran round,
As in a reel.

Twas then, in ecstasy, he saw
Her well-turned ankle, straught and sma',
Her neck, her heaving breast, and a'.
O, strange delight.
Wow, what is man or maid ava,
In sic a plight?

For, owr the mind, when drink presides,
In pranks o' sin and shame it prides.
To wisdom's ways it never guides,
But brings to view
A thousand fau'ts whilk temp'rance hides
In me and you.

Still, where encamped the sev'n trades lie,
Their gilded banners proudly fly.
Still to the stance detachments hie,
And cock their guns,
While troops o' friends are standing by,
To see wha wons.

Elsewhere, the youth of ilka trade,
Their first attempt, as marksmen, made;
And, to their credit, be it said,
That this day's muster
Conferred distinction on their grade,
And nae sma' luster.

Contending for a bran new hat,
To wear on Sundays, and a' that,
Like riflemen, they were sae pat,
And aimed sae true,
The mark whilk they were shooting at
Was riddled through.

Till now, while thund'ring guns resound,
The feast prevails, the glass gaes round,
Pastime and harmony abound,
And fond entreating—

---

[1]Either the top-pile of a woman's hair or a woman's cap with a crown.

Pleasures that hae, for ages, crowned
    This merry meeting.

Bright Phoebus, frae his azure clime,
Shone sweetly radiant a' the time.
Nature hersel' was in her prime—
    When fruits and flow'rs
Fill the glad heart wi' thoughts sublime
    Of heavenly powers.

But word was brought to Deacon Greer,
Intrenched wi' friends, pies, bread, and beer,
That, counter to a mandate clear,
    Ane o' the snobs,
Vain as a peacock, strutted here
    In crimson robes.

This news, though nought could happen droller,
Bred the hale party meikle dolor.
A tailor, mair frae spleen than valor,
    Assailed the man,
And, taking Crispin by the collar,
    To carp began:

"Ye gude-for-naething soutor* hash, cobbler
Though muisted* is your carrot pash*, powdered/head
Tell me, I say, thou Captain Flash,
    Withouten charter,
What right hae ye to wear this sash,
    And star and garter?"

"It sets ye weel, indeed to speer*," ask
The soutor answered with a sneer.
"I represent King Crispin here.
    While, fye for shame,
Your lousy craft to manhood ne'er
    Could yet lay claim!"

Cut to the quick wi' this rebuff,
The captious tailor grew mair gruff,
And, swearing he was better stuff
    Than sic a foutre*, (term of abuse)
Stripped, in a twinkling, to the buff,
    And braved the soutor.

"A ring, a ring!" the soutors cried.
"A ring, a ring!" the snips replied.
Some egged them on, and, while some tried
    To stop their flyting*, quarreling
The crowd fell back, encircling wide
    A space for fighting.

In dread for what might happen neist,
Around the ring the clamor ceast.
Sae croose* the twa set up their creest, manly
Before the toolie*, brawl
Fowk thought in other's wames*, at least, bellies
They'd sheath a goolie*. knife

Wi' looks that ill concealed his fears,
The tailor in the lists appears:
King Crispin, wha in nobler weirs* "wars"
Had aften bled,
His brawny arm, indignant, rears,
And, dauntless, said:

"Now tak, thou warst o' worthless things,
The vengeance due frae slighted kings!"
Wi' that, his garments aff he flings,
And, as he strack,
The supple tailor skips and springs—
Aye jeuking* back. "juking," swerving

To see fair play, or help a frien',
Fowk stoitered frae a' airts, bedeen.[1]
Auld wives, to red* them, ran between, part
Like Amazons,
And nought was heard, syne, owr the green,
But scraighs and groans.

The tailor lad, forfoughten* sair, exhausted
Was knockit down, ance, twice, and mair.
His baffled comrades, in despair,
Draw quickly near him,
Heeze* up his carcass on a chair, raise
Revive, and cheer him.

Besprent wi' blood, besprent wi' glar*, mud
His een japanned, his chafts* ajar, jaws
"Be thankfu', man, it is nae war,"
Says Edom Bryon,
"A living dog is better far
Than a dead lion."

Mid loud huzzas, and women's squeels,
A dawn of hope the tailor feels,
Feghts like a cock that rins and wheels,
While, dunt, dunt, dunting*, pounding
Crispin pursues, trips up his heels,
And leaves him grunting.

---

[1] Stoitered = staggered. Airts = quarters. Bedeen = at once.

Vexed at the upshot o' this fray,
The tailors bore their friend away.
Crispin remained in kingly sway,
And, loud and lang,
Bursts of wild joy, "hurray! hurray!"
Exulting, rang.

Frae Johnny Groats's[1] to the Border,
Was ne'er sic tumult and disorder.
Here discord strave new broils to forder.
There, beagles[2] flew
To haud the soutor lads in order,
But nought would do.

Rob Kinnie, Clench, and Jeamy Strong,
And twa-three mae, the feght prolong.
Where'er they cam, aff flew the throng
O' country billies*, — chaps
Like cattle prodit with a prong,
Or cleg*-stung fillies. — gadfly

There's little wisdom in his pow* — head
Wha lights a candle at the lowe*: — flame
To bell the cat wi' sic a scrow*, — mob
Some swankies* ettled*; — blades/endeavored
But, O, they gat a fearfu' cowe* — cut, rebuke
Ere a' was settled.

Rushing like droves o' maddened nowt*, — cattle
Rob's party caused a gen'ral rout:
Foul play or fair; kick, cuff, and clout;
Right side, or wrang,
Friends feghting friends, rampaged about,
A drucken thrang.

In vain Convener Tamson raised
And waved his hand, like ane half crazed.
In vain his heralds fleeched* and phrased, — implored
Where strife, lang brewing,
Threatened, like Ilium when it blazed,
Baith wreck and ruin.

To furnish weapons for th' affray,
Craems, tents, and stawns, were swept away.
Puist fowk, unused to cudgel play,
And douce* spectators, — sober
Were a' involved in this deray*, — disarray
Like gladiators.

[1] John o' Groats, northernmost town on the Scottish mainland. The "border" is, naturally, the extreme southern one shared with England.
[2] "Beadles" —town officers.

Nor could ye ken, wi' nicest care,
The victors frae the vanquished there:
Like Kelton-Hill, that feghting fair,
The hubbleshew,
Wi' neeves*, and staffs, and rugging* hair, fists/pulling
Sae awesome grew.

And aft, as ye may weel suppose,
In broils where women interpose,
Baith parties gat the sairest blows,
Blows that were gi'en them
While pu'd and hauled by their ain joes*, sweethearts
Striving to screen them.

Thus, lang and sair, our pleasures crost,
The battle raged frae host to host.
The turbulent, when uppermost,
Tint* a' decorum, lost
And, like the ocean, tempest-tost,
Drave a' before them.

At length a parley is decreed—
Parties shake hands, and are agreed.
The crowd, dispersing, join wi' speed
In nobler fun,
The shooting for that royal meed*— reward
The siller gun.

Amid the scenes, depainted here,
O' love, and war, and social cheer,
Auld sportsmen fired correct and clear;
And Samuel Clark,
Mild as the spring, when flow'rs appear,
Just missed the mark.

Auld sodgers, too, and honest tars,
Returned triumphant frae the wars,
Leveled their guns like sons o' Mars,
While mony a dame
Extoled the glory o' their scars,
And deeds o' fame.

Yet, oh, examples were but few
Of hardiment, like theirs, I trow;
When Geordy Rae his trigger drew,
The bowel-hive
Gart meickle Geordy change his hue
Four times or five.

When his gun snappit, James M'Kee,
Charge after charge, charged to the ee.
At length she bounced out owr a tree,
In mony a flinner*— splinter

"For Gude's sake, bairns, keep back!" cries he.
"There's sax shot in her!"

Loud leugh the crowd at Watty Lock,
Whase gun exploded at half-cock.
"Hoot," cries a friend, by way o' joke,
"My honest carl*, — peasant, fellow
Your gun wants only a new stock,
New lock, and barrel!"

Wull Shanklin brought his firelock hither,
And cocked it in an unco swither.
Ae drucken soutor jeered anither
To come and learn—
Fuff played the priming—heels owr ither,
They fell in shairn*. — pieces

Just in the moment o' disgrace,
Convener Tamson saw their case.
O, how he hid his manly face,
And fleeched* thae fallows — implored
To think upon the glorious race
O' godlike Wallace.

William M'Nish, a tailor slee,
Rouzed at the thought, charged his fuzee;
Took but ae vizzy wi' his ee—
The bullet flies
Clean through the target to a tee,
And wons the prize!

His winsome wife, wha lang had missed him,
Pressed through the crowd, caressed and kissed him.
Less furthy dames (wha could resist them?)
Th' example take,
And some held up his bairns, and blessed them,
For daddy's sake.

In William's hat, wi' ribbons bound,
The gunny was wi' laurel crowned;
And, while in triumph owr the ground
They bore him tenty*, — carefully
His health in streams o' punch gaed round,
"Lang life and plenty!"

Wi' loud applause, frae man and woman,
His fame spread like a spate wide foaming.
Warse deeds hae gi'en to mony a Roman
Immortal fame;
But prodigies are grown sae common,
They've tint the name.

Canto Fifth. Return home—Birth Day banquet in the town's-hall, under the direction of the magistrates—assemblies and the play—bonfires and other rejoicings conclude the festivity

While round the victor and his prize,
Shouts frae applauding crowds arise—
While to Dumfries the rumor flies,
    "M'Nish has won!"
And minstrel-harps immortalize
    The siller gun—

Our troops, ance mair, frae warfare free,
Resolve to ground their arms a-wee,
Ilk squadron, in their grand marquee,
    To chant a chorus,
And drink, wi' heart-enduring glee,
    A deochandorus*. (farewell-toast)

Meanwhile, like midges in the sun,
Frae tent to tent the wee-things run.
Lasses, to dance wi' him wha won,
    Are forward pressing;
And meikle, meikle is their fun,
    And fond caressing.

But soon, to finish the campaign,
"To arms! to arms!" resounds amain.
The seven trades, syne, a' ranked again
    In due gradation,
March frae the Craigs, a glitt'ring train—
    A grand ovation.

The crowd, in token of applause,
Threw up their hats as black as craws;
And followed fast, wi' loud huzzas,
    Except a few
Whase hearts, owr zealous in the cause,
    Were squeamish now.

Far as the keenest ee could run,
The waving flags, and mony a gun,
Buskit wi' flow'rs, and yellow whun*, furze
    Sae sweetly shining,
Streamed like a rainbow, while the sun
    Was just declining.

And, as the troops drew near the town,
With a' the ensigns o' renown,
The magistrates paraded down,
    And a' the gentry,
And love and friendship vied to crown
    Their joyous entry.

"See, see the conq'ring hero comes!"
The band struck up with a' their drums.
Louder the big bass-fiddle bums,
    The cymbals jingle,
And, in ten thousand thousand hums,
    Glad voices mingle.

Close by Convener Tamson's side,
The victor marched wi' stately stride.
The seven-trades' flag, unfurled sae wide,
    Was borne before;
And the lang train advanced wi' pride,
    By corps and corps.

To Mistress Corsane's when they came,
The deacons hailed the comely dame;
Took aff their hats; extolled her name,
    And, marching on,
Lowered their flags to worth and fame,
    Where'er they shone.

Like roses on a castle-wa',
The leddies smiled upon them a'.
Frae the Auld Kirk to the Trades'-Ha',
    And New Kirk steeple,
Ye might have walked a mile or twa
    On heads o' people.

"O, what can keep our John sae lang?"
Cries Meggy Muncy, in the thrang.
"I left him happy, hale, and strang,
    Wi' sash and sword on.
Gude grant there may be naething wrang
    Wi' Johnny Gordon!"

Lang, lang they dandered* to and fro          sauntered
Wha missed a kinsman or a beau,
The pomp and splendor o' the show,
    To them and theirs,
Brought nought but apprehensive woe,
    And fruitless cares.

Back to the Craigs they hie again,
To seek their friends amang the slain.
By the road sides, and on the plain,
    The drucken crew,
Heart-sick, and penitent in vain,
    Were unco fu'.

The muse is sorry to portray
The fuddled heroes o' the day.
Nae camp, when war has reft away
    Her brightest sons,

Could sic a ruefu' scene display
O' men and guns.

Their firelocks broke, their doublets torn,
And eke King Crispin a' forlorn,
Here lay, beside the bugle-horn,
A cat-gut strummer,
And there, blithe herald o' the morn,
The parish drummer.

Ev'n Geordy Smith, though stark* and slee, strong
Was there as fu' as fu' could be:
Reviewing still, in fancy's ee,
The martial train—
"Now, Gentlemen, tak tent—" cries he,
And snored again.

Carts, syne, wi' sic as dughtna gae,
Were panged* till they could haud nae mae. stuffed
Rob Kinnie, Clench, and sic as thae,
Now blind and lame,
Sad wights, wi' ribs baith black and blae,
Were hareled hame.

When fowk are in a merry pin,
Weel fortified wi' Highland gin,
They'll eithly thole* a weel-peyd skin, suffer
Or crackit crown;
And nowther care nor sorrow fin',
Though streaming down.

Yet, soon as sober sense returns,
Yestreen's debauch the drunkard mourns.
His feckless body aft he turns,
O, dool and wae.
Sair grieved, a fev'rish heart-ache burns
Wi' him next day.

But turn, my muse, frae scenes debasing,
To windows filled wi' beauty gazing,
To streets wi' happy thousands praising
The passing show;
And bonfires crackling loud, and blazing,
As on they go.

Ding, ding, ding, dang, the bells ring in,
The minstrels screw their merriest pin.
The magistrates, wi' loyal din,
Tak aff their cau'kers;[1]

---

[1]Drink off their pledges.

And boys their annual pranks begin,
Wi' squibs and crackers.

Wae's me for Deacon Ronald's jeezy*, wig
That sat sae orthodox and easy.
For, while he smiled at his ain Leezy,
A squib cam whizzing,
Set a' its ringlets in a bleezy,
And left them bizzing.

And wae's me, likewise, for the folly,
That fowk, half-fu', should fire a volley.
As through the town they marched sae jolly,
A *feu de joie*
Had nearly led to melancholy,
And great annoy.

Tat, tat, a-rat-tat, clitter, clatter,
Gun after gun played blitter, blatter.
A random shot, not leveled at her,
Hit Nanny Nairm,
Gart bonny Nanny's blue een water,
And hurt her arm.

This, when Convener Tamson saw,
He grieved, and soon dismissed them a'.
Syne, wi' the Deacons, scoured awa,
By Maister Wylie's,
And took his seat at the town's-ha',
Amang the bailies.

Arriving in an unco* flutter, rare
The coffee cups began to clutter;
But first, Mass John,[1] grave Doctor Mutter,
Wi' pious care,
And a' the zeal that grace could utter,
Preferred this pray'r:

"O Thou, by whose resistless law,
Kings, kingdoms, empires, stand or fa',
Watch owr this realm; bless great and sma';
Keep, keep us free.
And fill our hearts wi' rev'rend awe
For truth and thee."

The town clerk next, a fallow fine,
Wha ne'er loo'd water in his wine,
Gart bring the great big gardevine,[2]
And fill the glasses.

---

[1] Mass John—generic name for a minister.

[2] Either a large wine bottle or a chest of wine bottles.

Wi' thrice three cheers, in bumpers, syne,
The claret passes.

*The King*, and other loyal toasts;
*Health, peace, and plenty, round our coasts;*
*Our fleets*, and *a' our armed hosts*,
Were drank aloud;
And names of whilk the country boasts,
And may be proud—

The Johnstons, Lords of Annandale,
The Douglasses, and Murrays, hale,
The Maxwells, famed through Nith's sweet vale,
Kirkpatricks, too,
And him, of a' that's gude, the wale*, choice
The great Buccleugh.

Duncan's, a never-dying name;
And Abercromby's, dear to fame;
Wallace, and Bruce, Sir John the Graeme,
And names like theirs,
Heroes and Patriots shall proclaim
To Scotland's heirs.

Scotland, my ain dear native land,
England, her sister, great and grand,
Would Ireland join us, heart and hand,
Without commotion,
Our faes would crumble like the sand
Before the ocean.

The provost spoke a speech belive:
"Wha can the valiant Scots descrive?
Aye foremost where the bravest strive,
And aye victorious;
Or, hindmost, wi' the few alive,
Retreating glorious."

Of early scenes the singers sung,
In days of yore, when life was young,
When music dwelt on ilka tongue,
And a' the arts
To peace their gowden harps had strung,
Wi' lightsome hearts.

The bailies caught the welcome strain,
And made the ha' resound again.
*God save the King, and bless his reign,*
*And still watch oer us*—
And *Rule Britannia, rule the main*—
Were sung in chorus.

When healths were drank to friends awa,
And benisons invoked on a',
The court house rang wi "Sir James Shaw,"
A pattern, bright,
Of virtue, reverential awe,
And truth upright.

But vain is a' the poet's art
To paint this banquet o' the heart—
The town's fowk a' on the alert,
The grave, the gay,
Happy to meet, and laith to part,
On sic a day.

And where could love or fealty trace
A mansion like this bonny place?
Where manliness, in a' its grace,
Protects the land—
Where beauty's saft enchanting face
Is blithe and bland.

Nor is it only, here and there,
Ae bonny lassie, and nae mair.
O' beauties, gracefu' as they are
Throughout the nation,
Dumfries can boast, beyond compare,
A constellation.

For them, assemblies and the play
Conclude the pleasures o' the day.
In birthday dress, sae fine and gay,
The belle and beau,
In chairs and chariots, stop the way—
A splendid show.

A' ranks in loyal freaks* agreeing, notions
The mingled scene was weel worth seeing:
Big bonfires here—there, boys tee-heeing—
Crowds on the streets—
Dead cats, and duddy* doublets fleeing, ragged
And burning peats.

But Bailie Clark, wha seldom brooks
The pastime that like mischief looks,
Sent for John Doogan frae the Neuks,
And, at his ca',
John quenched the fires, and fleyed*, like rooks, scared
The boys awa.

Lang had the callans*, morn and noon, youngsters
Looked forward to the fourth o' June,
And sair they grudge, when now, in tune,
The joy-bells chime,

Their pleasures cropt, like flow'rs owr soon,
    This happy time.

Yes, happy time, and scenes renowned,
Now only in remembrance found.
For, oh, though terms and tides come round,
    The days of yore,
Like water sprinkled on the ground,
    Are seen no more.

Hame, as the gloaming nearer draws,
Convener Tamson slips his wa's,
Where wife and weans, in a' their braws*, bravery
    And best complexion,
Crown the last transports of applause
    Wi' sweet affection.

Jocosely, in the gardy-chair*, armchair
He tells the day's adventures there;
Syne, ere the bairns to bed repair,
    For mercies given,
His gratefu' thoughts, in fervent pray'r,
    Ascend to Heaven.

With his, our closing strain shall be,
May Scotland, happy, brave, and free,
Aye flourish like the green bay tree;
    And may Dumfries,
In a' her revelry and glee,
    Blend love and peace.

And may this day, whate'er befa',
The king's birthday, our waponshaw,
Be hailed wi' joy by great and sma',
    And through the land,
May concord, liberty, and law,
    Gae hand in hand.

What though, Dumfries, some awkward blades
Compeared wi' muskets and cockades,
Thy Waponshaw, in a' its shades
    O' praise or blame,
Shall memorize thy seven trades,
    And gild their name.

To gild thy name, may ilka grace
Adorn the annals o' thy race,
May steadfast justice rule the place
    With equal scales,
And tender mercy shew her face
    Where doubt prevails.

And should the fates, till death ensue,
Detain me still, sweet Nith, frae you,
O, if, frae yon bright realms, anew,
    The state o' bliss,
Departed spirits may review
    A warld like this—

Then, when Dumfries, thy siller gun,
In future times, is lost and won,
The spirit o' the bard, thy son,
    Shall hover near,
And flighter, till the day be done,
    Round scenes sae dear.

## GAVIN TURNBULL (FL. 1788–1794)

### May

Begin, sweet lass, a merry lay,
And sing the bonnie month of May,
When chantin' birds, on ilka spray
    And hawthorn sing,
And larks salute the rising day
    On restless wing.

And hark, the cuckoo through his throat
Pours out a sweet but simple note,
The gowdspink, in her painted coat
    And trim array,
Gars echo answer, frae the grot,
    The praise of May.

Now wha wad tine* this joyous hour, lose
Beneath the drowsy monarch's power,
To snore and sleep in lockit bower,
    While, sad to tell,
Terrific dreams our peace devour,
    Like hags of hell?

The sun, emerging frae the sea,
Lifts up his radiant head on hie.
Mirk clouds and dusky shadows flee
    Before his beam.
The tap of ilka tower and tree
    Like siller gleam.

A' nature blooming charms the view—
The greensward earth, and welkin blue,
The bent*, refreshed wi' morning dew, grass
    And spreading thorn,
Gay vernal flowers, of motley hue,
    The braes adorn.

The music of the westlin breeze,
That soughs* amang the nodding trees, sighs
The drowsy croon of busy bees
In waxen cell,
Can lull the passions into ease,
And cares expel.

Sweet smile the woodland and the plain.
Joy fills the heart of ilka swain,
And rouses up the village train
By creek o' dawn.
Eident* on rustic toils again diligent
They seek the lawn.

Furth frae the theekit* cot is seen thatched
The landwart* lasses, braw and clean, country
Skiff lightly oer the dewy green.
Withouten art;
In native innocence, I ween,
They charm the heart.

Now come, my pleasure-loving maid,
And tent* the beauties of the shade— note
The thicket gaudily arrayed
In rokelay* green, (a cloak)
And burnies hurling through the glade
Their waters sheen.

Now is the time for those who love
To woo the muses in the grove,
Or wi' the nymph, sweet Fancy, rove
Her flowery way.
Then come, ye tunefu' swains, and prove
The joys of May.

## Nancy

The fop may praise the city belle
In verse that charms the fancy, O.
Wi' simple croon I'll please mysel',
And praise my bonnie Nancy, O;
Wha, without dress, and foreign aid,
Which at the first alarm ye, O,
In hamely russet weeds arrayed,
Like magic art can charm ye, O.

Sic native dignity and grace,
But* other arts, invite ye, O. without
Sic modest looks adorn her face,
And gentle smiles delight ye, O.
Her blushing cheeks the crimson scorn;
Her e'en sae clear and glancy, O.

The rose refreshed wi' dews of morn
Is nought compared wi' Nancy, O.

Then cease to muse, ye witless beaux.
Nae mair torment the fancy, O;
But join wi' me, and sing wi' glee
The praise of lovely Nancy, O.

## To Melancholy

Maiden of the downcast eye,
Who, when evening draweth nigh,
Windest oft thy devious way
Beneath the sober twilight gray,
Pursuing still the lonely road
By human footsteps seldom trod,
By the hills or shady woods,
Dreary dells and haunted floods,
By the churchyard's lonely bound,
Wand'ring oer the cheerless round,
Where oft, as vulgar stories tell,
From aisles the midnight specters yell,
Or where some stalwart ruins nod,
Of wealth and grandeur once th' abode,
Delighted with the dismal howl
Of ravens and the screaming owl:—
Come Melancholy, sober maid,
In all thy winning charms arrayed.
Come, sober nymph, nor once disdain
To take me in thy pensive train.

## THE ROMANTIC AGE

In the early part of the nineteenth century, Romanticism reached fruition, especially in the works of the great poets of England—Wordsworth, Coleridge, Byron (part Scottish), Shelley, Keats. Strangely, the spirit of the great Romantic movement in Britain, which the Scots had done so much to ferment in the eighteenth century, with the nature writings of Ramsay, Thomson, Beattie, Macpherson and Burns, burned feebly in Scotland itself, apart perhaps from Scott, and even Scott, fine poet though he was, was a mild Romantic. He and the other leading poet of his country, James Hogg, wrote romantically picturesque lyrics or narratives but with little of the intensity of feeling or appreciation of nature celebrated by Wordsworth or Shelley. Perhaps only the minor poet Thomas Campbell, writing for the English market, displays the "wild" romantic style—plus, of course, that half-Scot, Lord Byron. Symptomatic of the Scottish tendency to stand outside Romanticism is the poetry of William Aytoun, whose *Lays of the Scottish Cavaliers*, a picturesque but genteel rendering of the Scottish narrative tradition, is balanced by his Bon Gaultier Ballads, a burlesque of the same. The Scots did not seem to have their hearts in it.

What the Scots borrowed from Romanticism was the dressing—the natural settings and poetic personae, the love of the unusual, the picturesque, the appeal to emotion—often the pleasantly sentimental. During the last two-thirds of the nineteenth century in Europe, Romanticism itself turned in this same direction, so that one sees a marked softening of aesthetic and spiritual intensity as the Victorian era progresses: by the end of the century the Romantic movement had become effete and world-weary.

During the nineteenth century Scotland produced a remarkable number of talented and successful writers, who created something of a recognizable literary genre, so that a "Scottish" author might be expected to write in as predictable a fashion as, say, a modern detective novelist. However, Scotland produced few *great* writers during this period—as though something was being held back. Indeed, a large and influential group of angry Scottish writers and critics of the twentieth century would sneer at the age which preceded them as shallow, imitative and timid. Now that these "angry young men" have somewhat passed into history themselves, it is perhaps possible to view Scottish Romanticism and Victorian Post-Romanticism as simply an aesthetic phenomenon which was faithful to at least one view of Scotland and which is still capable of giving much pleasure to readers of Scottish literature.

## CHARLES KEITH ( ?–1807)

### The Har'st Rig

The har'st* time is a time o' thrang* — "harvest"/busyness
For which we hae sma' cause to lang,
For hard sair wark, wi' mony a bang
    Does ay attend it;
And weather aft does bruckle gang
    As we hae kend it.

But wha has pleasure wanting pain?
What though we hae baith wind and rain,
Let nane tyne* heart, nor hand refrain, — lose
But try their mettle,
For good sunshine may come again,
And weather settle.

In mouth o' har'st, whan corns do fill,
And ripen fast, let nane sit still,
But try their strength, and show their will,
In being handy.
Let Lowland John then match his skill
Wi' Highland Sandie.

Let cottar wives hae washings ended,
Their houses cleaned, and claes weel mended,
And a' their ither wark suspended,
Whan har'st begins,
For ilka wife maun now attend it
That cards or spins.

For now the farmer views his corn,
To see what's fittest to be shorn,
For yellow fields do now adorn
The country-side;
And har'st may e'en begin the morn,
It winnae bide.

But a the servants dounae bear,
That har'st should be sae very near;
They ken the wark, and sair they fear,
It gars them quake:
And ay they tell, that, "a green shear
Is an ill shake."

But now the master gie's nae heed
To their auld sayings, wise indeed,
But answers them wi' pith and speed;
"The proverb says
That scaith* and danger baith proceed — harm
Ay from delays."

And straught he bids them a' turn out,
Baith auld and young; baith frail and stout;
But ere they hae begun to lout*, — bend
In comes a bang
O' Highlanders, a fendy* rout, — able, energetic
Baith yawl* and strang. — loud?

O' these some frae Lochaber come
Lang thretty miles ayont* Tyndrum, — beyond
And some frae Mull; and ither some
Frae wild Lochiel,

Whare mountain goats and roebucks roam
And Camerons dwell.

Frae Keppoch's and Glengarie's lands
There comes a power o' special hands;
Or eastward thence, whare Carie stands
By Rannoch loch,
Comes Struan's clan, and numerous bands
Frae Badenoch.

Oh, much behaden the Lowdons are
To this supply o' reapers rare,
Without their aid ill wad we fare
In time o' need;
Industrious fowk beyond compare
In har'st indeed.

They now spear* gin the fam'ly's weel, ask
And "fu gaes a'," most kind atweel;
That they shore here, they no conceal,
This time fernyear*; last year
Then Duncan brags how meikle meal
She's eaten here.

They vow they'll work as weel's they can,
And tak sic wages as are gaen,
For weel do they loe the gudeman;
For, now they tell,
That his clan cam frae the same clan
They cam their sell.

And then they vow they'll never steer
Sae lang's he has a cut to shear,
But bide wi' him till fields are clear;
But—wait awee!
Till ance some windy days appear,
And then ye'll see.

And forthwith then they a' down clank
Upon the green; and rank by rank
Tak what's to gi'e; for which they thank
And mak nae fike*, fuss
For some o' them are e'en right lank,
And hungry-like.

This being done, they straughtway gang
Into the barn, which they've kent lang,
And there they sing a highland sang,
And dance awa';
The fiddler gi'es his strings a twang,
Which pleases a'.

Upon the morn the master looks
To see gin a' his fowk hae hooks;
For now sair wark amang the stooks
Is biding them;
Whae'er he be frae this that jouks* ducks, avoids
Is fair to blame.

The hamelan' servants tak the lead;
The cotters next come on wi' speed,
And next to them the Embrugh* breed; "Edinburgh"
A randy race!
Of ill-tongued limmers*, that exceed no-goods
In want o' grace.

To spur them on, and had them gaen,
Behind is placed the highland clan,
Led on by Malcom, honest man,
Wha taks his snish*, snuff
And cries, whan they a clattering stan,'
"Curish Curish*!" hurry!

Whan they hae a' their places ta'en,
The master gangs frae ane to ane,
And reds* them to "shear laigh and clean, counsels
For corn is dear,
And fother's scant, as will be seen
Throughout the year."

And then he bids them eident* be, diligent
And no like drones work sluggardly,
For he nae wages has to gi'e
To idle folk;
Which if they be, he'll let them see
He disnae joke.

The ha-rig rins fu' fast awa,'
For they're newfangle, ane and a',
But Donald thinks, for a' their blaw,
That he will fend*, prevail
He says, their pride will get a fa'
Ere the week end.

The next rig reds them to tak care
To cut their fur, and tak their share
O' their nane rig. But ony mair?
The fient* ae stime! "fiend"
"For fowk ay wond'rous honest are
In the har'st time."[1]

---

[1]That is, they would not take sheaves from their neighbor's rig ("ridge," row, harvest area).

And now some learner tries to shear,
But comes right little speed I fear;
"The corn lies ill," and aye we hear
"The sickle's bad."
The bye-word says, "Ill shearer ne'er
A good hook had."

O' gath'rers* next, unruly bands, gleaners
Do spread themsel's athwart the lands;
And sair they green to try their hands
Amang the sheaves,
But that's against express commands;
For they're great thieves.

For which they're ordered far behind,
To mak such singles as they find;
But gin the master little mind,
They'll come again,
And plague him sair, till in the end
They pay the kain*. payment, rent

For they hae come sae aften back,
And their auld trade begin to tak,
The master now gies them a thwack
Wi' his lang staff,
And syne they're ordered a' to pack
Frae the field aff.

But now the parridge comes a-field,
Which joy to ilka ane does yield:
For now ilk yap* and hungry chield* eager/fellow
Fu' blithe does look,
Wi's lass and coggie* in the bield* bowl/shelter
O' some high stook.

For now the bickers* weel they cram beakers, cups
Wi' good steeve brochin*, braw an' warm, gruel
Wi' which themsels they daily pang*; stuff
Tis halesome cheer,
And halesome wark it is to gang
Afield and shear.

The Embrugh wives can hardly brook
To tak their breakfast 'side a stook,
But ay at ane anither look
As they thought shame;
Quo they, "It wasnae thus we took
Our tea at hame."

The highlanders are no sae blate*, shy
But are fu blithe at sight o' meat;
They a' their weans around them seat,
And gi'em a share,

For weel ken they twas but o' late
They had to spare.

Now whan the stented time is past
Which they're allowed to break their fast,
The master comes, and calls wi' haste,
"Come, come awa'!
Airoch, airoch*! get up fast — get up
Fhala fhala*!" — get going

Wi' spirit bauld they work I trow,
And mony a strange tale they tell now,
Of ilka thing that's rare or new
They never fag;
Auld proverb says, "When wames* are fu' — bellies
The tongues maun wag."

Yet chiefly they their cracks* confine — chat, jests
To things that happened lang since syne,
In days whan they war in their prime;
O how they'll blaw!
"The sun in these days warm did shine,"
Even that's awa'!

Some carle* that's weel kenned to rift, — fellow, peasant
Declares, whan in a blasting tift,
In days o' yore, how he cud lift
Twa bows o' bear,
And how he was amaist as swift
As ony deer!

Frae this he tells anither blaw;
"Some rogues war reeving* in the ha' — stealing
Whan he brak in upon them a'
And catched a thief";
But ere he wist he gets a fa'
Attour a sheaf.

Some flairing wife now tells how she
Did win a kemp[1] most manfully,
By which she nettled twa or three,
And garred them gloom.
A flust'ring stroke now she does gi'e,
And cuts her thumb.

But nane sae mony braw things says
As does the Chelsea man, whase phrase
Exceeds them a', and wins the bays;
He shews them scars

---

[1] Fight, contest, prize. In this context, the "game" is to finish first in the harvest.

Which he in George the Second's days
Got in the wars!

For to his colors he was staunch,
In time o' battle ne'er did flinch,
But bravely fought in field or trench:
At Fontenoy,
He wi' Duc William fought the French;
The brave old boy!

Sometimes he'll speak o' Minden plain,
Whar siccan* heaps o' French war slain, such
For he did bravely mak campaign
Wi' Ferdinan',
And there saw Granby glory gain,
That gallant man!

O he has seen great battles win,
And mony a fort and town ta'en in,
And aft he'll tell, if he begin,
How Prussia's king
Did gar the Austrians scud and rin
Like ony thing.

"But now," says he, "sic fightin's rare,
Your officers themsels can spare,
Your K--p--l naething did but stare,
The H——s* an' a': "Howe's"
Wi' Wolfe and Hawk the'll ne'er compare,
Awa' awa!

"But yet," he owns, "we've some that's brave,
Auld Rodney bauldly did behave;
He didnae loiter like the lave*, rest
But fought outright,
Till a' his faes war fain to save
Themsels by flight.

"And there," says he, "is Elliot too,
Wha garred the Spaniard sadly rue
That e'er he came wi' sic ado
To tak his fort;
He sent him fire and flames enow;
It bred braw sport!"

O weel sic tales they like to hear!
And lend to him an itching ear;
And whiles about the King they'll spear,
Or yet the Queen;
"Gin* e'er he saw them, and how near if
To them he's been?"

"And whether he was e'er amang
The nigres wild? or e'er got wrang
Frae bloody Turks?" for sair they lang
To ken ilk ferlie*, wonder
And marvel much, nae news does gang
'Bout Popish Charlie?

But something else does now attract
The gen'ral notice and the crack:
They reckon now how mony a stack
This year they'll be;
For they suspect they'll be a lack
O' twa or three.

Frae this they tell, as how the rent
O' sic a room was overstent,
The back-ga'en tenant fell ahint* behind
And coudnae stand;
So he to pigs and whistles went,
And left the land.

And how anither man they saw
Did slip a fit and get a fa',
And after him a third did draw
To the sam' side;
But soon tint heart and ran awa,
And wadnae bide.

Again it taks anither turn;
Some drucken* wife wi' drouth* does burn, drunken/thirst
And sair does mutter and does mourn
For good sma' beer;
The lave advise her to the burn,
That caller* cheer. fresh

To this at last she's fain to rin,
But louting down, does tumble in,
By which she gets a good wet skin;
They, jeering, say,
"She'll no be on sae dry a pin
Again this day."

Some wife whase rig now lingering stands,
On her gudeman lays her commands
To gie her help—He understands,
But says wi' speed,
"Gif like your tongue war your twa hands,
Nae help you'd need."

Sculdudry next comes on right het;
'Bout wanton Lowrie Loupie's get,
Or Jenny Jounkers, wha upset
Ayont the cairn,

Whar she wi' a misfortune met
And had a bairn.

And how some feckless man an's wife
The tither day had a great strife:
Some lown* as sharp set as a knife — rascal
Was lurking bye:
The filthy-fallow ran for's life:
"Howt-out," they cry.

At lesser matters now they mint*; — aim
They tell how Maggy lately tint
Her leathern purse and naething in't;
But how that she
Pretends there was: But then they hint
She tells a lie.

And how the packman Rabie Gray,
Beguiled a wife the tither day;
For he did gar her sweetly pay
For crackit gear,
But ay since syne he's tint the way
For her to spear.

Frae this to different ither talk
A quick transition they will mak
O' clavers* they hae never lack; — gossip
"For tongues are free,
On the har'st rig to gab an' crack
Whate'er it be."

The Embrugh wives them a' exceed
For sad misleared ill words indeed!
They never stand to say wi' speed
Some ill-fared name,
And ban*!—but* either fear or dread, — curse/without
O shame! O shame!

Sometimes twa havrel* wives cast out, — foolish, chattering
Wi' tongues sae gleg* might clip a clout, — sharp
Wi' which they mak a mighty rout:
But yet whase wyte?
They're wise that wits.—but sair they lout,
And sair they flyte*. — scold, argue

They bitterly cast up whase kin
Maist feckless are.—And ilka sin,
They e'er cud do, is now brought in,
To the dispute:
The bansters* redd them "cease their din," — binders
But they'll no do't.

At length whan they hae wracked their wrath
Wi' sad ill-words, till out o' breath
They stop at last, but still look laith* “loath”
The threap* to yield, quarrel
Though ilka ane laughs at them baith
Throughout the field.

This wicked flyte being laid at last,
Some rig now strives for to get past
The ithers; and wi' flaring haste
To shew its strength;
This sets the lave a working fast;
They kemp* at length. race, contest

Gainst this the master is set sair,
And vows bedeen*, that he will share at once
His staff amang them; and no spare
Sic daft fool-folk.
Whan-a'be, they but kemp the mair,
—He does but joke.

A windy tailor leads the van,
A clean-houghed nimble, little man:
And sair this nettles Wabster* Tam, weaver
And gars him girn*; scowl
He vows he'll ne'er rest till he can
Wind him a pirn*. spool

The blasty Smith does brook it ill
That he maun stand sae study still,
For sair it is against his will
To lose the strife,
And a' for fault o' pith and skill
O's glaikit* wife. foolish

Yet her tongue clinks through a' the field:
She sair misca's the supple chield,
And ay casts-up whate'er's been stealed
By prick-the-louse,
But yet, for a' that, he'll no yield,
But gabs fu' crouse*. boldly

He says, “Her manners need a patch,
(“For this her tongue is an ill swatch”)
Her borders ne'er with his will match;
And then he jeers,
That he cud mak as quick dispatch
Wi' his auld sheers.

Auld Tamie Speals, the cowan-wright*, (low-skilled mason)
Now strives gainst him with a' his might,
But he is doung*, clean out o' sight beaten
“His edge is gane,”

The tailor jeering bids him hight,
To 'grinding stane.

Then he sic measures does display:
And skreed sic blads o' corn away,
That he had fairly gained the day,
But that a soutor*, cobbler
Most manfully about does lay;
A tough auld f—t—r.

He strives as't had been for his last;
And a' his airs about does cast,
That now he had him surely past
As clean's a lingle*; shoemaker's thread
The tailor now clips lang and fast;—
He's in a pingle*. struggle, contest

Till now the master does stand still,
And lets them tak o' wark their will,
But now they shear sae very ill,
Sae foul and lang;
The bansters too hae tint their mill,
And a' gaes wrang.

The master dounae langer bear
To see sae high and rough a shear,
But cries with haste, "Come, lads, forbear,
This kemp let be;
To let you work this way, I fear
You'd ruin me."

The tailor first does tak the hint,
For he's a remnant fa'n ahint;
The soutor now his ends maun stint,
Syne dight his cheeks,
For a' this foul wark cam' by dint
O' his lang steeks.

They're a' right glad the kemp is done;
For they're forfoughten* ilka ane; exhausted
At which the master maks nae mane,
But speaks o' scaith;
The bansters, too, are out o' tune,
And maun hae breath.

For they've been right sair haden to,
And kept their place wi' great ado;
Now kempen fowk they dinnae loe,
They work sae stark,
"For naething does," as they say now,
"Like eident wark."

They a' declare the vi'ttal's good,
As by their hands they've understood;
It should bleed weel, and mak' prime food
Frae neath the flails;
The strae's sae hard 't'as brought the blood
Frae 'bout their nails.

Auld William says, (that canny man,
The same that wont to thresh the barn)
"In truth a-tweel they're sair to blame
That guide corn ill:
Nae gude I e'er kent come o' them
Gude food that spill.

"To shear sae foul is ill to brook,
For better corn ne'er cam' oer hook,
Ise warrant they'll be in ilka stook
Four pecks an' mair."
Syne he does the pickle* look— a (sample of) grain
"Tis wondrous fair!"

Then does auld highland Malcom say,
That "they should also mind the strae,
To cut him laigh, for he'd be wae
To waste good fothers,
For nowts* and horse their foods maun hae cattle
As weel as ithers."

But raking* clouds now gather fast, moving
And a' the lift* does soon oer-cast: sky
Some ane now cries, "We'll hae a blast,
The skies do lower";
Anither says, "It winna last—
A flying shower."

Mair scouthry*-like it still does look, showery
At length comes on a mochy* rook*: misty/wrack
The Embrugh wives rin to a stook;
It were nae fau't;
But Highlanders ne'er mind a douk*, wetting
"For they're na saut."

Say they, "What needs we be afraid?
For tis a blout* will soon be laid, burst
And we may hap' us in our plaid
Till it blaws oer.
Tis pity for to break our bread
For a sma' shower!"

But now it rains sae very fast,
They're a' obliged to rin at last:
Their claes on hastily they cast,
And aff they scour;

For now it turns an eident blast,
An even-down pour.

The cotters a' rin to their hames;
For them there needs to mak' nae maens.
The Embrugh tribe scarce crawl their lanes,
Sae sair they're droukit*: drenched
For wet's their claes, and cauld's their banes,
They're sadly doukit.

Quo they, "We're murdered clean aff hand,"
As in the kitchen now they stand,
"For sic a blast we never fand;
And O!" quo' they,
"We're sadly skaithed and sair we're wranged,
This rainy day!"

They sair bemane some paitlich-gown*— kerchief
Some yellow-dippit stained wi' brown—
Which they brought, claithlike, frae the town;
But now, a seat
By th' ingle*-side, they clank them down, fire
For they're ne'er blate.

And now it is na very lang
Till a' the "Trout-shows,"[1] in a bang,
Do come, and to the barn they thrang,
For that's their hame:
Into the ha' they never gang,
For they think shame.

But straught into the barn they hie,
And hang their claes to dreep and dry,
Syne sit them down a sang to try,
To pass the time:
Up springs the pipes, and a' do vie
Wi' them to chime.

Now dances Neil wi' little Nell,
And comely Kate wi' "her nainsel'";
But Donald Dhu bears off the bell
Wi' Flora Fair:
In sprightly dancing they excel
Beyond compare.

Thus do they pass the time away,
Even every night or rainy day.
Cold shivering blasts do not dismay
The Celtic race:

---

[1] Highlanders (Gaelic for "come over here").

Their native vigor they display
In every place.

But now, whileas the shower does last,
Tis na thought proper they should fast,
The scogie* lass does rin wi' haste, servant
And bring the kail,
On which they dine, and mak' repast,
Or baps* and ale. cakes

Nae sooner is the dinner oer,
Than Highland Malcolm gangs to glower,
And see the weather, gin the shower
Be blawn awa'.
Sae soon's the sky looks nae mair sour
He tells them a'.

They ask now gin the master please
To let them gang and shear the pease;
For they are laith to lose their fees
By broken days.
They're glad when he permission gi'es
To gae their ways.

But sair it grieves the Embrugh breed
That they maun troop wi' siccan speed.
They cry wi' haste, "What is the need
To shear ava'?
It will be soon enough indeed
This hour or twa!"

The Highlanders ne'er mind their din,
But fast afield awa' do rin,
And there they straughtway do begin
To work their wa's.
The townsfolk draigle far ahin',
By anes and twas.

At length they are a' gotten out,
And syne they work anither bout;
But as they ettle* for to lout struggle, intend
The pease to shear,
The wives fill weel their laps, nae doubt,
Ye needna speer.

Frae this it isna very lang
Till they do lilt some canty* sang, pleasant
Sic as *Pease Strae,* or *Jenny dang*
*The weaver,* braw,
*The tailor through the bed did gang*
*Thimble and a'.*

The Embrugh lass fu' loud does cry
Gin ony will _Broom Besoms*_ buy? brooms
The _Grey Breeks_ next, and then she'll try
    _The Sodger Laddie._
Tis her delight. Then, _O! to lie_
    _In 's Highland plaidie._

The Highland lasses raise the song
In music wild and sweet and strong:
All join in chorus, as along
    The subject strays;
The hills and dales resounding long
    The cheerful lays.

At length the sun does wear down low,
Which a' the field fu' weel does know.
The Embrugh wives cry "Let us go,
    And quit our wark!
Tis after six, and mirk does grow;
    Twill soon be dark."

To this the master gi'es nae heed,
But reds them "mind their wark" indeed.
Quo they, "Wha, deil, can shear wi' speed
    That hasna light?
Come, light the candles! for there's need
    O' them this night."

But yet, for a' their clamor, still
They are kept sair against their will.
They ever and anon stand still,
    And yamor sair:
"We're sure we do our day fulfill,
    And meikle mair!

"To keep's sae late is a great wrang,
When now the day's sae very lang!"
But they might as weel sing a sang
    Wi' a' their sikes*; sighs
The master lets his shearers gang
    Just when he likes.

But glad are they when he does say,
"Now fill your raips* and get away! ropes
This shall be held nae broken day,"
    _"Tchoukin*, tchoukin!_ come away!
_Gaghe*, Gaghe!"_ the clans now cry; home!
    _"O tchoukin brochin!"_

The bedding time does now begin,
Whan ilka ane does wale* their kin, choose
And for their bed awa' do rin
    To get some strae.

And here there is nae little din
Till it they hae.

This being had, the blankets next
They seek wi' haste, and share betwixt
Themsel's in manner as is fixed
By usage lang.
Now, though they're a' together mixed,
There's naething wrang.

But still the dorty* Embrugh crew quarrelsome
Declare they've got o' claes too few:
O' blankets they hae not enow.
"A pair apiece
They a' should hae; twill hardly do,
For folk's no beas's."

And now on this their just demand
They are determined for to stand,
And ere they flinch they will aff-hand
E'en gae their ways,
For never was there yet a land
But folk got claes.

The master now does carena be
Though he were red o' twa or three,
So, unexpectedly, does he
Gi'e his consent
To let them gang, and wages gi'e;
But they repent.

Quo they, "The night is now grown dark,
And well eneugh we like your wark;
But Oh, it's hard that in our sark
We use sic cleading*! clothing
For we're no used to siccan stark
And naked bedding."

And syne some sleekit-gabbit wife
Declares, "she never likit strife;
For she was aye for a quiet life.
Tis but ae night;
We'll e'en stay, (maybe get the rife*), itch
Till tis daylight."

Some wally-dragles* pay for a', lazybones
Wha little dreamt o' this ava',
For they wi' scorn are set awa',
To their great shame.
The byword says, "Ill bairns are a'
Best heard at hame."

Now whan they a' to bed are gane,
Auld Seonet comes in sark alane,
Beseeching for a dram o' gin,
    Or what you please;
For Duncan has a sare wame ta'en
    Wi' eating pease.

At length they a' sleep very sound,
In slumber sweet and eke profound:
In idle dreams they ne'er abound
    That hae sair wark;
Yet ilka morn are cheerfu' found
    As ony lark.

Now whan the day breaks through the sky
They're raised again wi' hasty cry,
The master calls, "Why do ye lie?
    The sun does shine!
Come, get up fast, and shearing try,
    The weather's fine."

Yet they get up but very slow,
For now some lubber* cries, "Oh no! lout
Let's e'en lie still, for now to go
    I wad be wae";
Then down he slinks, and hides him low
    Amang the strae.

Yet they are a' got up at last,
Although it isnae very fast,
Their claes most leisurely they cast
    About their shouthers,
The master calls "Mak haste, mak haste!
    Ye lazy louthers*." idlers

Their sickles now they straughtway tak,
And gae their wa's to the field back;
Yet commonly there is some lack;
    Some Embrugh quean
Is sickly grown, and dounae mak
    A-field again.

Whan a' the week is past and gane,
It joy affords to ilka ane;
Weel pleased are they, and are right fain
    Wi' mirth and glee;
Nor rich nor poor e'er mak a mane
    To pouch their fee.

They're set in orderly array;
And ane by ane now get their pay,
And mony a blessing now they say,
    For they are glad,

Their very weans around them play
As they were mad.

The Highlanders now count their gain:
The skillin sassenach* makes them fain, English
Syne fleetch* the master no to hain*, coax/spare
(For weel they've shorn)
But gi'e a penny to ilk ane
The *skillin khorun*.[1]

The Embrugh tribe do ay insist,
That they should get their wages first;
For now they ken of ither grist
Into their mill:
Gaen hame there is nae pease-field mist
But which they spill.

Frae this the corns do faster fill,
And har'st next week is thranger still;
The shearers now come not a will,
But maun be sought,
And now they a' exert their skill
To be dear bought.

For they relate what wages they
Do gi'e at Embrugh Port ilk day,
And how there was a great affray;
Some master-man
Was soundly swinged, and then, they say,
He fled and ran!

Wi' that some Embrugh wife does tell,
How a' the hobble-shew* befell; hubbub
For she was there, and saw't hersell:
She heard his offer;
And how the chairmen on him fell,
For his sma' proffer.

And now anither tells bedeen,
(That went into the town yestreen)
How siccan wages ne'er were seen
As gangs this day;
For masters far and near hae been
At port, they say.

Says she (and to the master looks)
"What think ye they were gien for hooks*? reapers
As sure's I stand among the stooks,
A shillin's gaen!"

---

[1]"Hook-Penny," which each shearer is in use to ask and receive weekly over and above their pay (1801 editor's note).

The master ill the story brooks,
    But answers nane.

Then she does tell how mony came,
And how they a' did bid the same;
And well her story she does frame,
    For now she tells,
There were sae mony, some thought shame,
    And hid themsels!

Nae sooner does her story end,
Than boist'rous winds mayhap portend
That the ripe-corn will hardly fend,
    But shaken be,
Weel may the shearers now pretend
    To height their fee!

Now murmurs gang frae side to side;
"For our sma' wage, O wha wad bide,
For scabbit aughtpence! woe betide
    That we should shear;
And then to hae sair wark beside!
    We're oer lang here."

And now ilk ane some faut does find—
The parridge arenae to their mind.
The ale is sour, and ill o' kind:
    The blankets too
Are riven, or ill-together joined:
    They'll naething do!

The stout-anes now a' dounae bear,
Wi' silly feckless anes to shear,
But maun hae their nain-folk, that's clear;
    And they'll no part,
Or they will stay nae langer here,
    But will depart!

The master hardly can restrain
Their thrawart humour and cross-grain,
Which breeds him nae sma' toil and pain,
    And gars him chide;
He almost wishes for some rain
    To lay their pride.

The Highland clans are roused at last,
For stormy growls the howling blast,
To *Dun-Eudain** they hie with haste (Edinburgh)
    The next port-day,
In hopes some better cheer to taste,
    And get mair pay.

At length the har'st draws to a close,
The stately stooks stand thick in rows,
And now the honest farmer knows
Whata crop he'll hae,
When tis a' in, he bounty shows,
And feast does gie.

For now the *maiden** has been win, last cartful
And *winter** is at last brought in: harvest-home
And syne they dance and had the kirn* feast
In farmer's ha',
Whare mirth and joy does now begin
To gladden a'.

For there baith man, and wife, and wean,
Are steghed* while they dou' stand their lane, stayed, stop work
For a' the langboard now does grane
Wi' swacks o' kale.
And mony a dainty rough fat bane,
And reaming ale.

Auld William sits at the board-head,
And says the grace wi' grace indeed!
To which they a' tak special heed,
Till he does close;
Syne to they fa' wi' might and speed
Keen to the brose.

Auld John, the stalwart Chelsea-man,
(Whase now taen in to redd the barn)
Sits here and drives about the can
Well filled wi' stout;
He drinks, "The King—him prosper lang!"
Syne toots it out.

To turn the timmer* they're no sweer, dish, cup
And mony a tale they'll tell or spear,
Or reckon up what time fernyear
The kirn was held,
And how the mickle ox or steer,
That time was felled.

Frae this they speak o' har'sts that's gane,
And cast them a' up ane by ane,
And how they dreed baith skaith and pain
In aughty-twa,
When they could hardly stan' their lane
For frost and snaw!

O that year was a year forlorn!
Lang was the har'st and little corn!
And, sad mischance! the Maid was shorn
After sunset!

As rank a witch as e'er was born,
    They'll ne'er forget!

But now they throw aside a' care,
And on sair-wark they think nae mair,
But tak wi' joy a hearty share
    Of ilka thing,
Till they as blithe and happy are
    As ony king.

## JOHN HAMILTON (1761–1814)

### Up in the Mornin' Early

Cauld blaws the wind frae north to south,
The drift is driving sairly;
The sheep are cowerin' in the heugh*;    hollow
Oh, sirs, it's winter fairly!
Now, up in the mornin's no for me,
Up in the mornin' early;
I'd rather gae supperless to my bed
Than rise in the mornin' early.

Loud roars the blast amang the woods,
And tirls* the branches barely;    strips
On hill and house hear how it thuds!
The frost is nippin' sairly.
Now, up in the mornin's no for me,
Up in the mornin' early;
To sit a' nicht wad better agree
Than rise in the mornin' early.

The sun peeps ower yon southland hills,
Like ony timorous carlie*;    peasant
Just blinks awee, then sinks again;
And that we find severely.
Now, up in the mornin's no for me,
Up in the mornin' early;
When snaw blaws in at the chimney cheek
Wha'd rise in the mornin' early?

Nae linties lilt on hedge or bush:
Poor things, they suffer sairly;
In cauldrife* quarters a' the nicht,    chilly
A' day they feed but sparely.
Now, up in the morning's no for me,
Up in the mornin' early;
A penniless purse I wad rather dree*    suffer
Than rise in the mornin' early.

A cozy house and canty* wife    pleasant
Aye keep a body cheerly;

And pantries stowed wi' meat and drink,
They answer unco* rarely. quite
But up in the mornin'—na, na, na!
Up in the mornin' early!
The gowans* maun glint on bank and brae daisies
When I rise in the mornin' early.

## Oh, Blaw, Ye Westlin' Winds

Oh, blaw, ye westlin' winds, blaw saft
Amang the leafy trees.
Wi' gentle gale, frae muir and dale
Bring hame the laden bees;
And bring the lassie back to me
That's aye sae neat and clean.
Ae blink of her wad banish care,
Sae lovely is my Jean.

What sighs and vows amang the knowes* "knolls"
Hae passed atween us twa.
How fain to meet, how wae to part,
That day she gaed awa.
The powers abune can only ken,
To whom the heart is seen,
That nane can be sae dear to me
As my sweet lovely Jean.

## The Rantin' Highlandman

Ae morn, last ouk*, as I gaed out "week"
To flit a tethered ewe and lamb,
I met, as skiflin' ower the green,
A jolly, rantin'* Highlandman. boisterous
His shape was neat, wi' feature sweet,
And ilka smile my favor wan.
I ne'er had seen sae braw a lad
As this young rantin' Highlandman.

He said, "My dear, ye're soon asteer.
Cam ye to hear the laverock's sang?
Oh, wad ye gang and wed wi' me,
And wed a rantin' Highlandman?
In summer days, on flow'ry braes,
When frisky are the ewe and lamb,
I'se row ye in my tartan plaid,
And be your rantin' Highlandman.

"Wi' heather bells, that sweetly smell,
I'll deck your hair, sae fair and lang,
If ye'll consent to scour the bent* grass, field
Wi' me, a rantin' Highlandman.
We'll big* a cot, and buy a stock, build

Syne do the best that e'er we can.
Then come, my dear, ye needna fear
To trust a rantin' Highlandman."

His words, sae sweet, gaed to my heart,
And fain I wad hae gi'en my han'.
Yet durstna, lest my mither should
Dislike a rantin' Highlandman.
But I expect he will come back.
Then, though my kin should scauld and ban*, curse
I'll ower the hill, or whare he will,
Wi' my young rantin' Highlandman.

## JOANNA BAILLIE (1762–1851)

### Disappointment

On village green, whose smooth and well-worn sod,
Cross-pathed, with every gossip's foot is trod;
By cottage door where playful children run,
And cats and curs sit basking in the sun:
Where oer the earthen seat the thorn is bent,
Cross-armed, and back to wall, poor William leant.
His bonnet broad drawn oer his gathered brow,
His hanging lip and lengthened visage show
A mind but ill at ease. With motions strange,
His listless limbs their wayward postures change;
Whilst many a crooked line and curious maze,
With clouted shoon, he on the sand portrays.
The half-chewed straw fell slowly from his mouth,
And to himself low muttring spoke the youth.
"How simple is the lad, and reft of skill,
Who thinks with love to fix a woman's will:
Who ev'ry Sunday morn, to please her sight,
Knots up his neck-cloth gay and hosen white:
Who for her pleasure keeps his pockets bare,
And half his wages spends on peddler's ware;
When every niggard clown or dotard old,
Who hides in secret nooks his oft-told gold,
Whose field or orchard tempts with all her pride,
At little cost may win her for his bride;
Whilst all the meed her silly lover gains
Is but the neighbors' jeering for his pains.
On Sunday last when Susan's banns were read,
And I astonished sat with hanging head,
Cold grew my shrinking limbs and loose my knee,
Whilst every neighbor's eye was fixed on me.
Ah, Sue, when last we worked at Hodge's hay,
And still at me you jeered in wanton play;
When last at fair, well pleased by showman's stand,
You took the new bought fairing* from my hand; gift, trinket
When at old Hobb's you sung that song so gay,

"Sweet William" still the burthen of the lay,
I little thought, alas, the lots were cast,
That thou should'st be another's bride at last:
And had, when last we tripped it on the green
And laughed at stiff-backed Rob, small thought, I ween,
Ere yet another scanty month was flown,
To see thee wedded to the hateful clown.
Ay, lucky swain, more gold thy pockets line;
But did these shapely limbs resemble thine,
I'd stay at home and tend the household gear,
Nor on the green with other lads appear.
Ay, lucky swain, no store thy cottage lacks,
And round thy barn thick stand the sheltered stacks;
But did such features hard my visage grace,
I'd never budge the bonnet from my face.
Yet let it be: it shall not break my ease;
He best deserves who doth the maiden please.
Such silly cause no more shall give me pain,
Nor ever maiden cross my rest again.
Such grizzly suitors with their taste agree,
And the black fiend may take them all for me!"
  Now through the village rise confused sounds,
Hoarse lads, and children shrill, and yelping hounds.
Straight ev'ry matron at the door is seen,
And pausing hedgers on their mattocks lean.
At every narrow lane and alley mouth,
Loud laughing lasses stand, and joking youth.
A near approaching band in colors gay,
With minstrels blithe before to cheer the way,
From clouds of curling dust which onward fly,
In rural splendor break upon the eye.
As in their way they hold so gaily on,
Caps, beads and buttons glancing in the sun,
Each village wag, with eye of roguish cast,
Some maiden jogs and vents the ready jest;
Whilst village toasts the passing belles deride,
And sober matrons marvel at their pride.
But William, head erect, with settled brow,
In sullen silence viewed the passing show:
And oft he scratched his pate with manful grace,
And scorned to pull the bonnet oer his face;
But did with steady look unmoved wait,
Till hindmost man had turned the church-yard gate;
Then turned him to his cot with visage flat,
Where honest Tray upon the threshold sat.
Up jumped the kindly beast his hand to lick,
And, for his pains, received an angry kick.
Loud shuts the flapping door with thund'ring din;
The echoes round their circling course begin,
From cot to cot in wide progressive swell;
Deep groans the church-yard wall and neighb'ring dell,
And Tray responsive joins with long and piteous yell.

## Woo'd and Married and A'

The bride she is winsome and bonny,
Her hair it is snooded* sae sleek — bound up
And faithfu' and kind is her Johnny,
Yet fast fa' the tears on her cheek.
New pearlins* are cause of her sorrow, — finery
New pearlins and plenishing* too; — furnishings
The bride that has a' to borrow
Has e'en right mickle ado.
Woo'd and married and a'.
Woo'd and married and a'.
Is na' she very weel aff
To be woo'd and married at a'?

Her mither then hastily spak,
"The lassie is glaikit* wi' pride; — foolish
In my pouch I had never a plack* — (a small coin)
On the day when I was a bride.
E'en tak to your wheel and be clever,
And draw out your thread in the sun;
The gear* that is gifted it never — goods, money
Will last like the gear that is won.
Woo'd and married and a',
Wi' havins and tocher* sae sma'; — dowry
I think ye are very well aff
To be woo'd and married at a'."

"Toot, toot," quo her gray-headed faither,
"She's less o' a bride than a bairn,
She's ta'en like a cout* frae the heather, — "colt"
Wi' sense and discretion to learn.
Half husband, I trow, and half daddy,
As humor inconstantly leans,
The chiel* maun be patient and steady — fellow
That yokes wi' a mate in her teens.
A kerchief sae douce* and sae neat — sober
Oer her locks that the wind used to blaw.
I'm baith like to laugh and to greet* — weep
When I think of her married at a'."

Then out spak the wily bridegroom,
Weel waled* were his wordies, I wean, — chosen
"I'm rich, though my coffer be toom*, — empty
Wi' the blinks o' your bonny blue een.
I'm prouder o' thee by my side,
Though thy ruffles or ribbons be few,
Than if Kate o' the Croft were my bride
Wi' purfles* and pearlins enow. — trimmings
Dear and dearest of ony,
Ye're woo'd and buikit[1] and a'.

---

[1] Proclaimed for marriage.

And do ye think scorn o' your Johnny,
And grieve to be married at a'?"

She turned, and she blushed, and she smiled,
And she looked sae bashfully down;
The pride o' her heart was beguiled,
And she played wi' the sleeves o' her gown.
She twirled the tag o' her lace,
And she nipped her bodice sae blue,
She blinkit sae sweet in his face,
And aff like a maukin* she flew, — hare
Woo'd and married and a',
Wi' Johnny to roose* her and a'. — praise
She thinks hersel very weel aff
To be woo'd and married at a'.

## Fy, Let Us A' to the Wedding[1]

Fy, let us a' to the wedding,
For they will be lilting there;
For Jock's to be married to Maggie,
The lass wi' the gowden hair.
And there will be jilting and jeering,
And glancing of bonnie dark een;
Loud laughing and smooth-gabbit speering* — asking
O' questions, baith pawky* and keen. — sly

And there will be Bessie, the beauty,
Wha raises her cock-up sae hie,
And giggles at preachings and duty;
Gude grant that she gang nae ajee!
And there will be auld Geordie Tanner,
Wha coft* a young wife wi' his gowd; — bought
She'll flaunt wi' a silk gown upon her,
But, wow! he looks dowie* and cowed. — sad

And braw Tibby Fowler, the heiress,
Will perk at the top o' the ha',
Encircled wi' suitors, whase care is
To catch up the gloves when they fa',
Repeat a' her jokes as they're cleckit,
And haver and glower in her face,
When tocherless* Mays are negleckit— — dowry-less
A crying and scandalous case.

And Mysie, whase clavering* aunty — gossiping
Wad match her wi' Jamie, the laird;
And learn the young fouk to be vaunty,
But neither to spin nor to caird;

---

[1]Joanna Baillie's version of an old song. Compare with the similarly-titled poem in the Renaissance "Anonymous" section of Volume I.

And Andrew, whase granny is yearning
To see him a clerical blade,
Was sent to the college for learning,
And cam' back a coof*, as he gaed. fool

And there will be auld Widow Martin,
That ca's hersel' thretty and twa!
And thrawn*-gabbit Marge, wha for certain twisted
Was jilted by Hab o' the Shaw.
And Elspy, the sewster, sae genty—
A pattern of havens and sense—
Will straik on her mittens sae dainty,
And crack* wi' Mess John in the spence*. chat/pantry

And Angus, the seer o' ferlies*, wonders
That sits on the stane at his door,
And tells about bogles, and mair lies
Than tongue ever uttered before.
And there will be Bauldy, the boaster,
Sae ready wi' hands and wi' tongue;
Proud Pattie and silly Sam Foster,
Wha quarrel wi' auld and wi' young.

And Hugh, the town-writer, I'm thinking,
That trades in his lawyerly skill,
Will egg on the fighting and drinking,
To bring after grist to his mill.
And Maggie—na, na! we'll be civil,
And let the wee bridie abee;
A vilipend tongue it is evil,
And ne'er was encouraged by me.

Then fy, let us a' to the wedding,
For they will be lilting there,
Frae mony a far-distant ha'ding*, "holding"
The fun and the feasting to share;
For they will get sheep's-head and haggis,
And browst o' the barley-mow;
E'en he that comes latest and lag is
May feast upon dainties enow.

Veal florentines, in the o'en baken,
Weel plenished wi' raisins and fat;
Beef, mutton, and chuckies*, a' taken chickens
Het reekin' frae spit and frae pat.
And glasses (I trow 'tis nae said ill)
To drink the young couple gude luck,
Weel filled wi' a braw beechen ladle,
Frae punch-bowl as big as Dumbuck.

And then will come dancing and daffing*, teasing
And reelin' and crossin' o' han's,
Till even auld Lucky is laughing,

As back by the aumry* she stan's.    cupboard
Sic bobbing, and flinging, and whirling,
While fiddlers are making their din;
And pipers are droning and skirling,
As loud as the roar o' the linn*.    waterfall

Then fy, let us a' to the wedding,
For they will be lilting there;
For Jock's to be married to Maggie,
The lass wi' the gowden hair.

## It Fell on a Morning

It fell on a morning when we were thrang*—    busy, crowded
Our kirn was gaun, our cheese was making,
And bannocks on the girdle baking—
That ane at the door chapped loud and lang:
But the auld goodwife, and her mays* sae tight,    maidens
Of this stirrin' an' din took sma' notice, I ween;
For a chap at the door in braid daylight
Is no like a chap when heard at e'en.

Then the clocksie auld laird of the warlock glen,
Wha stood without, half cowed, half cheery,
And yearned for a sight of his winsome dearie,
Raised up the latch and came crousely ben*.    in
His coat was new, and his owrelay* was white,    collar, necktie
And his hose and his mittens were cozy and bein*;    snug
But a wooer that comes in braid daylight
Is no like a wooer that comes at e'en.

He greeted the carlin*' and lasses sae braw,    old woman
And his bare lyart* paw* he smoothly straikit,    gray/face
And looked about, like a body half glaikit*,    silly
On bonny sweet Nanny, the youngest of a' :
"Ha, ha!" quo the carlin', "and look ye that way?
Hoot! let na sic fancies bewilder ye clean—
An elderlin' man, i' the noon o' the day,
Should be wiser than youngsters that come at e'en."

"Na, na," quo the pawky* auld wife: "I trow    sly
You'll fash* na your head wi' a youthfu' gilly,    trouble
As wild and as skeigh* as a muirland filly.    frisky
Black Madge is far better and fitter for you."
He hemmed and he hawed and he screwed in his mouth,
And he squeezed his blue bonnet his twa hands between.
For wooers that come when the sun's in the south
Are mair awkward than wooers that come at e'en.

"Black Madge she is prudent." "What's that to me?"
"She is eident* and sober, has sense in her noddle—    diligent
Is douce* and respeckit." "I carena a boddle;    sober

I'll baulk na my luve, and my fancy's free."
Madge tossed back her head wi' a saucy slight,
And Nanny ran laughing out to the green;
For wooers that come when the sun shines bright
Are no like the wooers that come at e'en.

Awa' flung the laird, and loud muttered he,
"All the daughters of Eve, between Orkney and Tweed, O,
Black and fair, young and old, dame, damsel, and widow,
May gang, wi' their pride, to the wuddy* for me." halter, gallows
But the auld gudewife, and her mays sae tight,
For a' his loud banning* cared little, I ween; cursing
For a wooer that comes in braid daylight
Is no like a wooer that comes at e'en.

## A Scotch Song

The gowan* glitters on the sward, daisy
The laverock's* in the sky, lark's
And collie on my plaid keeps ward,
And time is passing by.
Oh no, sad and slow
And lengthened on the ground,
The shadow of our trysting bush,
It wears so slowly round.

My sheep-bell tinkles frae the west,
My lambs are bleating near,
But still the sound that I loe best,
Alack, I canna' hear.
Oh no, sad and slow,
The shadow lingers still,
And like a lonely ghaist I stand
And croon* upon the hill. wail

I hear below the water roar,
The mill wi' clacking din,
And Lucky scolding frae her door,
To ca' the bairnies in.
Oh no, sad and slow,
These are na' sounds for me,
The shadow of our trysting bush,
It creeps sae drearily.

I coft* yestreen from Chapman Tam, bought
A snood* of bonny blue, hairband
And promised when our trysting cam',
To lie it round her brow.
Oh no, sad and slow,
The mark it winna' pass;
The shadow of that weary thorn
Is tethered on the grass.

O now I see her on the way,
She's past the witch's knowe*, "knoll"
She's climbing up the Browny's brae,
My heart is in a lowe*. flame
Oh no, tis no' so,
Tis glam'rie* I have seen; magic
The shadow of that hawthorn bush
Will move na' mair till e'en.

My book o' grace I'll try to read,
Though conned wi' little skill,
When collie barks I'll raise my head,
And find her on the hill;
Oh no, sad and slow,
The time will ne'er be gane,
The shadow of the trysting bush
Is fixed like ony stane.

## Love's Wistful Tale

They who may tell love's wistful tale,
Of half its cares are lightened.
Their bark is tacking to the gale,
The severed cloud is brightened.

Love, like the silent stream, is found
Beneath the willows lurking,
The deeper, that it hath no sound
To tell its ceaseless working.

Submit, my heart; thy lot is cast,
I feel its inward token.
I feel this misery will not last,
Yet last till thou art broken.

## Wake, Lady

Up, quit thy bower, late wears the hour,
Long have the rooks cawed round the tower.
Oer flower and tree loud hums the bee,
And the wild kid sports merrily.
The sun is bright, the sky is clear.
Wake, lady, wake, and hasten here.

Up, maiden fair, and bind thy hair,
And rouse thee in the breezy air.
The lulling stream that soothed thy dream
Is dancing in the sunny beam.
Waste not these hours, so fresh and gay.
Leave thy soft couch, and haste away.

Up! Time will tell the morning bell
Its service-sound has chimèd well.
The aged crone keeps house alone,
The reapers to the fields are gone.
Lose not these hours, so cool and gay.
Lo, while thou sleep’st they haste away.

### The Black Cock

Good-morrow to thy sable beak,
And glossy plumage dark and sleek,
Thy crimson moon and azure eye,
Cock of the heath, so wildly shy.
I see thee, slyly cowering, through
That wiry web of silvery dew,
That twinkles in the morning air,
Like casement of my lady fair.

A maid there is in yonder tower,
Who, peeping from her early bower,
Half shows, like thee, with simple wile,
Her braided hair and morning smile.
The rarest things, with wayward will,
Beneath the covert hide them still.
The rarest things to light of day
Look shortly forth, and shrink away.

One fleeting moment of delight
I sunned me in her cheering sight;
And short, I ween, the term will be
That I shall parley hold with thee.
Through Snowdon’s mist red beams the day,
The climbing herd-boy chants his lay,
The gnat-flies dance their sunny ring—
Thou art already on the wing.

## WILLIAM BEATTIE (1762–1815)

### The Winter’s Night

Ye gentle folk ’at win* in touns, — dwell
At canty* fires, in well-boxed bouns, — pleasant
When blust’ring hailstanes rattle,
Consider how the village swain,
Unsheltered, on the open plain,
Maun bide the bickerin brattle*. — assault

Or if perforce of endrift* styth, — driving snow
He is obliged to seek a lyth* — shelter
Amo’ the byres and barns,
For fear the poor dumb brutes sud smore*, — “smother”

He staps wistrae ilk navus-bore*, knot-hole
And ilka crevice darns*. hides

Syne atter he has done his best,
The sheep sought hame, and a' at rest,
He bouns* him to the house, addresses
And sits him down upo' the bink*, settle
And plaits a theet*, or mends a mink*, rope/noose
To sair* an after use. serve

The young-man now casts on his plaid,
To gang and seek an ewe that's strayed;
But has a tryste wi Nell.
He thinks they winna be foun' out;
But ere a twalmonth come about,
Young Jock'll maybe tell.

Sae blithe's he lilts out-oer the lea,
Wi bonnet cocked somewhat ajee,
And whistlin Nelly Symon;
Between hands thinkin wi himsel'
How blest he'll be when he and Nell
Are linked in bands of Hymen.

And Nell comes out to milk the kye,
Glowering atweese her and the sky,
To see gin he be comin;
She sees him leeshin* up the craft, loping
And thinks her whittle's i' the shaft,—
I wish her joy, poor 'oman.

But now they're met, we'se leave them there,
And back again we sall repair;
The sky begins to darken;
Gin* you or I were i' their plight, if
I guess we would no think it right,
Were ony ane to harken.

The shankers* hamphise* the fireside; knitters/surround
The little anes play at seek and hide
Ahint the kists* and tables; chests
The farmer sits anent the light,
And reads a piece o' Wallace Wight
Or maybe Aesop's Fables.

And little Pate sits i' the nook,
And but-a-house* dare hardly look, (outside)
But had* and snuff the fir*; "hold"/candle
And whan the farmer tines* the line, loses
He says, "Yer light casts little shine,—
Had in the candle, sir."

The goodwife sits and spins a thread,
And now and then, to red* her head, clear
She taks a pickle* snuff; little
And first she counts how meikle tow,
And syne how meikle carded woo'
She'll need for apron stuff.

At last she cries, "Gi'e oer yer ploys,
Ye geets, or else mak some less noise!
I think ye may be douce*. sober
Ou! gaen like gaunties* in a sty! pigs
The folk'll think, 'at's gaen by,
We keep a bordel house.

"I'll wager, gin I need to rise,
I'll shortly gar you turn the guize*; play
Ye filthy, fashous* teds*! troublesome/kids
See, here's yer father comin but*; out
I'll wad* my lug*, he'll teach ye wit! bet/ear
Come, come, and mak for beds."

Syne she sets by the spinning wheel,
Taks them in-oer, and warms them weel,
And pits them to their hammock;
Syne haps them up, and says, "Now boys,
Lie still and sleep, and mak nae noise";
And bribes them wi a bannock.

Syne she comes ben* the house, and says, in
"Dear me, that stoun's amo' my taes
Will pit my heart awa'!
That weary corns gi'e me sic pain,
I ken we'll hae a blash* o' rain, downpour
Or else a skirl o' snaw.

"What keeps that hallyrakus* scum*, foolish/fellow
The tailor, 'at he winna come,
And men' the bairns' duds?
He promised aught days syne, I'm sear,
Foul fa' him, gin I had him here
But he sud get his thuds.

"They never had sae meikle need,
I'm really feart they'll get their dead,
Their duds are turned sae auld
And, silly things, they hae na wit,
A moment i' the house to sit;
And now the weather's cauld.

"Believe me, sirs, troth, I admire
What comes o' folk 'at's scant o' fire;
For really this night's thirlin*; piercing
I never 'maist fand sic a frost;

Troth, I believe my taes will roast
And yet my heels are dirlin*. tingling

"Sirs, I believe it's wearin late;
Lat's see in-oer the ladle, Pate,
And ye'se get out a castock*. cabbage-stem
Gang roun' about by Geordy's hack,
Ye'll get it lyin i' the rack,
Aside the cutty basket.

"O Peter, ye're a careless loun*! rascal
What sorrow's that ye're dingin doun?
That's surely something broken.
I think ye might tak better care;
Ye ken we hae nae things to spare:
They're nae sae easy gotten."

The merry merchant* jokes the lasses, (peddler)
And gars them trow he kens what passes
Atweesh them and their lads;
And reads their fortunes o' the cards,
Weirds* some to farmers, some to lairds, fates
To some he weirds cockades.

But, wi his cunnin magic spell,
He weirds the maiden to himsel,
And gi'es her twa-three needles,
Or buttons for her Sunday's sleeves—
Delf set in tin, which she believes
Is silver set wi pebbles.

The merchant kens what he's about;
He has nae will to lie throughout,
Or yet to tramp the gutter.
He's nae a stranger to his trade;—
For this he gets the chamber bed,
And raff* o' brose and butter. lots

But now the lave* are i' the bung*, rest/peeve
And Kate says, "See, ye stupid slung*, fool
What way ye've fyled* my kurch! soiled
Ye think auld Bobby's at your will;
But faith I'm red*, for a' your skill convinced
He'll leave you i' the lurch.

"Just keep yer hands upo' yoursel.
Sirs, fand ye ever sic a smell
O' brimstane and nit saw*? salve
Feich! dear be here! I b'lieve I'll spue.
Troth, laddie, they that tig* wi you, fool
Will soon hae cause to claw.

"Jean, we'll need to wear* hame, I doubt; head
We'll baith be pranned* for biding out. blamed
Na, lassie, we're a fright.
The shame be on's for ae clean rag,
And washing's naething but a drag
We hae sae short daylight.

"Though we were dressed, this creeshy woo'
Wad soon rub out the mangle* hue, calendar
Ye never saw sic trash.
We tak it out frae Robbie More,
But troth, we'll need to gi'e him oer,
He's really sic a fash*." trouble

The gaudman sits and toasts his nose,
Or awkwardly heelcaps his hose,
Or maks yoke-sticks o' rodden*. rowan
Auld Luckydaddy* winds at brutches*, grandfather/ropes
And Granny tells them tales o' witches,
Until the kail be sodden*. cooked

Syne quoth the horseman, "I suppose
It's wearin late; we'll hae our brose.
I saw the seven starns,
Whan I gaed forth to sup the naigs,
Hyne*, oer ayont the millstane craigs, hence
Aboon the Parson's barns.

"The morn's *gentle* Christmas day,
As rattlin Robbie used to say,
And we hae scarce ae starn* small amount
O' fardel* strae laid by gain Yeel; gathered
But ere the sky, gin I be weel,
I sall be i' the barn."

Wi this the farmer says the grace,
Wi bonnet up afore his face;
And whan the brose* are suppit, (oatmeal dish)
They mak for bed, and them 'at's dry
Just tak a drink, as they gae by
The cauler* water bucket. fresh

And still, as Sabbath night comes roun,
The chapter's read, wi holy soun;
And, for their past offenses,
The chapter read, they join in prayer;—
But I half think, wi some 'at's there
It's naething but pretenses.

For Jock taks Jenny by the snout,
And Jenny halflins* snickers out, half
Syne sic a cushle-mushle* whispering
Is heard, that ane wad really think

Some pigs had got behind the bink,
Or in beneath a bushel.

Thus does the rustic's evening end.
Saft slumbers now their cares suspend;
Dark silence fills the house:
Unless slee badrins*, on the watch, (the cat)
Intent his little prey to catch,
Surprise a hungry mouse.

Till thrice the cock extends his wings,
And thrice th' unwelcome tidings brings,
Of Sol's approaching light;
The lads, unwilling yet to stir,
Fire aff their morning guns wi vir,
And gaunt* wi a' their might. yawn

At length the farmer steals out-oer
Frae Kitty's side. He hears her snore,
And thinks 't would be a sin
To wake her, sae the host* he crubs*, cough/ "curbs"
And frae his hose rubs aff the dubs,
Pits on wi little din.

Syne he'll gang forth and look about,
And raise the lads, ye need no doubt,
To yoke them to the flail.
But soon as he sets forth his nose
The first thing meets him is a dose
Of styth endrift and hail.

"Bless me! it's been a dismal night,"
He says; "I wish I may be right,
I hear the stirkies roustin*. bellowing
Rise, boys, you'll sleep awa' your sight,
Ye've sleepit till it's fair daylight,
For a' your last night's voustin*. bragging

"Weel fells us 'at's in biggit bouns!
I pity them 'at's far frae touns;
They canno' do but smore;
For mark nor meith* ye wadna ken— landmark
The greenswaird how*, and seggy* den hollow/sedgy
Are streiked* even-oer. smoothed

"O haste ye, boys, look forth and see
The Tap o' Noth and Bennachie,
What heaps o' snaw lie o' them.
Lord help the tenants i' the hills!
For neither plows, nor kilns, nor mills,
I'm sure, can gae amo' them.

"The hills look white, the woods look blue
Nae hidlins for a hungry ewe—
They're sae beset wi drift.
We'll gi'e the sheep a rip* o' corn    handful
The day, and aiblins* gin the morn    perhaps
They'll a' win forth to shift.

"And Jock and Tam, ye'll yoke and thrash,
For troth, I dinna think we'll fash
To yoke a plow the day.
As Bruxy says, 'Gin ye had heal',
I think ye'll hae laid by gin Yeel
A fouth* o' fordel strae.'    plenty

"And Pate, as soon's ye get your pottage,
Ye'll look gin there be ony stoppage
About the Litster's burn.
The horse are gaen daft for water;
Gin she be closed, we maun be at her,
Afore we do a turn.

"And are ye hearin, Geordy Lithy?
Ye'll tak the cou'ter to the smithy,
And get her laid and sharped;
And haste ye hame afore't be night,
Ye ken ye winna hae moonlight;
And mind to get her marked.

"The smith'll ken the mark himsel —
Twa double letters, T and L,
And mak it right and tight.
And tell him I'll be oer the morn,
And he and I sall hae a horn,
Gin ilka thing had* right."    hold

Now a' thing's settled for the time,
Nor needs the farmer sair repine,
Wi a' his girnels* fu';    granaries
But what comes o' the cotter folk,
And sic as hae nae fordel stock
But just frae hand to mou?

For they 'at hae a gueed peat-stack,
And claise to hap* baith bed and back,    dress
I think hae nae grit pingle*—    problem
Wi a brown bickerfu' to graff*,    bury
To gar baith cauld and care had aff,
Afore a bleezin ingle.

## ROBERT LOCHORE (1762–1852)

### Marriage and the Care o't

Quoth Rab to Kate, My sonsy dear,
I've wooed ye mair than ha' a year,
An' if ye'd wed me ne'er could speer*, ask
Wi blateness*, an' the care o't. shyness
Now to the point: sincere I'm wi't:
Will ye be my ha'f-marrow, sweet?
Shake han's, and say a bargain be't
An' ne'er think on the care o't.

Na, na, quo Kate, I winna wed,
O' sic a snare I'll aye be rede*. wary
How mony, thochtless, are misled
By marriage, an' the care o't.
A single life's a life o' glee,
A wife ne'er think to mak' o' me,
Frae toil an' sorrow I'll keep free,
An' a' the dool* an' care o't. sorrow

Weel, weel, said Robin, in reply,
Ye ne'er again shall me deny,
Ye may a toothless maiden die;
For me, I'll tak nae care o't.
Fareweel for ever!—aff I hie.
—Sae took his leave without a sigh.
Oh, stop, quo Kate, I'm yours, I'll try
The married life, an' care o't.

Rab wheel't about, to Kate cam' back,
An' ga'e her mou a hearty smack,
Syne lengthened out a lovin crack* chat
'Bout marriage an' the care o't.
Though as she thocht she didna speak,
An' lookit unco mim an' meek,
Yet blithe was she wi Rab to cleek*, shut
In marriage, wi the care o't.

### Walter's Waddin'

#### Part I

Near yon bank neuk*, aboon the mill, "nook"
Beside the fir plantation,
The laigh* farm house, wi wings there till, low
Is Walter's habitation.
Some time he there a widower dwelt,
But sae he wadna tarry,
For he the force o' love sae felt

He Helen wished to marry,
          Some chosen day.

'Bout five miles back, by a burn side
That wimples through a meadow,
Lived Helen, ere she was a bride,
A gausey*, wanton widow. jovial, handsome
The bargain firm between the twa,
For baith their gude was ettel't,
That wha liv't langest wad get a'
The gear they had, was settl't
          Quite sure that day.

A' parties pleased—the day was set
To have them joined thegither.
That morn arrived—his frien's were met
To fetch his consort hither:
Convened a' in the bridegroom's house,
Dressed braw wi gaudy cleedin*, clothing
Except a few folks, auld an' douse*, respectable
That was na very heedin
          'Bout dress nae day.

Social they roun' a table sat,
Was covered oer wi plenty
O' fine milk saps, buns, cheese, an what
Was thought a breakfast dainty.
Whanever John the grace had said,
A spoon each eager gruppit,
Nae prim, punctilious rites were paid,
But mensfu' eat an' suppit
          Wi gust that day.

Thus lib'ral, whan they'd a' been fed,
Drams circlin' made them cracky*, talkative
Raised was their hearts, an unco glad,
Fu' couthy, crouse*, an knacky. lively
But for the bride they must awa'.
Their horse were saddled ready,
They mount, an' ranged were in a raw*, "row"
Then aff—quick trot, fu' gaudy,
          They rode that day.

The bridegroom rode a dapple gray
Smart geldin', plump an sleekit,
Upo' the front, an he, fu' gay,
Frae tap to tae was decket.
Sae vogie* Walter did appear, imposing
When on the way advancin',
That whan the bride's house they drew near
He set the beast a prancin,
          Right vain, that day.

The bride, wi'r party, in a room
Was waitin', buskit* finely, dressed
An' courteous welcomed the bridegroom
An' a' his frien's fu' kin'ly.
Now bridegroom, bride, best maid an' man,
Stood in a raw thegither,
The priest then joined the pair in one,
An' duties to ilk other
Enjoined that day.

While he linked them in Hymen's ban's,
They mute, mim* were, an' blushin', prim
But soon they smiled, when frien's shook han's,
An' wished them ilka blessin'.
The company courteous sat or stood,
While drams an' cake they tasted,
Engaged in frien'ly jocular mood,
A wee while's time they wasted
I' the house that day.

Than to the loan they a' cam out,
Wi bustlin', hasty bicker,
An' quick upo' their horses stout
Were mounted a' fu' sicker*; sure
Except some females fear't to ride,
Spent some time wi their fykin*, fidgeting
While some palavered wi the bride,
To get things to their likin'.
Wi a fraise, that day.

When for the road they were set right,
An' just began a steerin',
The *broose*[1] wi fury took the flight,
An' splutterin' flew careerin'.
Thus on they drave, contendin' keen,
Which made spectators cheery,
Till Tam's horse stumled on a stane,
An' he fell tapsalteerie* head over heels
I' the dirt that day.

Behin', wi birr, cam Bauldy Bell,
Wha rushed in contact thither,
While whirlin' heels owre head he fell,
Se they lay baith thegither;
Baith free o' skaith*, they mount again, harm
But, by their luckless fallin',
The broose was won wi vauntin' vain,
But easy, by Jock Allan,
That bustlin' day.

---

[1] A race to see who could first reach the bridegroom's house, the winner to get a bottle of rum or whisky.

The bulk an' body cam belive*,    quickly
A' hobblin' at the canter,
An' did at Walter's house arrive
Without the least mishanter.
A barn, set roun' wi furms an' planks,
Was ranged for their admission,
To which threescore at least, in ranks,
Walked inward, in procession,
        Fu' gay that day.

For dinner stood—kail* in tureens,    cabbage
An' legs o' mutton roasted;
Wheat bread in heaps, pies, beef an' greens,
An' peeled potatoes toasted.
The grace was said, an' wi gude will
All fared most delicious.
They syn't a' down wi nappy* yill    foaming
An' crowned the feast facetious
        Wi drams that day.

Collection for the poor was made,
Frae use an' wont not swerving,
Bestowed on such as were decayed,
Aged, needfu', an' deservin'.
The bridegroom's pride was raised to see
Sae big an' braw a party
Show them respeck—an a' to be
Agreeable an' hearty
        On sic a day.

The tables to a side were flung,
The barn floor gat a clearin',
While groups o' couples auld an' young
Took to themsels an airin'.
Baith out an' in confusion reigned—
The barn resound wi clatter,
In neuk o' whilk a tub contained
Punch made wi rum, cauld water,
        An' limes that day.

Part II

'Bout e'enin's edge they met again,
—Then day an' night was equal—
Still incidents, yet in a train,
Ye'll meet wi in the sequel.
At ilka corner tables stood,
To sit at, talk, an' fuddle,
An' Ned now scrunts an interlude,
Wi short springs on his fiddle,
        To tune' t that night.

Youngsters, wi anxious whisperin bizz,
Wished to begin their dances,
But at a waddin custom is
Best man an bride commences.
Though she ne'er learned steps, nor to wheel
Wi flirds* an airs new fasont, flutterings
Yet she kept time, sailed through the reel,
An played her part fu' decent
        An prim that night.

Lasses wi lads were now asteer,
Joy in their faces gleamin;
An happily each lovin pair
Went through the dances sweemin.
Poor Frank in love, wi beatin heart,
There spent the e'enin dreary,
For Sam his rival's crafty art,
Decoyed from him his dearie
        The lee lang night.

Betimes there was a bickrin fray
Tween Davie Gray an Sandie,
For each keen wished without delay
To dance wi comely Annie.
They pulled—held—fleetchit*—lang they strave, cajoled
Till she had cause to wail at,
For her new muslin gown they rave* tore
Frae headban' to the tail o't,
        Wi a screed* that night. tear

This sad mishap her mither saw,
Her wrath she could na smother,
But bitter scawl't them ane an a',
An urged the fallows hither.
The chiels* went to a drinkin houff*, fellows/shelter
But she affronted Annie
By gi'en wi'r neeve* her chafts* a gouff, fist/jaws
To learn her to be canny
        'Mang lads that night.

Amang the stir kind feelin's were,
Talkin owre drink an laughin,—
The dancin drivin on wi birr,
Some bauk-heigh loup't in daffin*; fooling
What bowin, scrapin, skips, an flings,
Crossin and cleekin* ither, linking
Settin an shufflin, formed in rings,
An whirlin roun thegither,
        Wi glee that night.

Even runkled wives an' carles* looked gay, old men
Though stiff wi age an stoopin,
Fidg't, leugh, an crack't their thumbs when they

Through foursome reels gaed loupin:
An whan they toom't* their horns, loud cheers    lost
They gae at droll narrations
O' frolics in their youthfu' years,
At sicken* blithe occasions,    such
By day or night.

The bridegroom, muchle pressed to dance,
A' fleech* and praise rejecket.    cajolery
He wadna do't , he said at once,
Twas certain he wad stick it.
Some wags then schemed to fill him fou*,    "full" (drunk)
An in their scheme persisted;
But he their base design saw through,
An cautiously resisted
The trick that night.

Inspired wi punch an love, some chiels
Slipt cautious out a little,
Each wi his jo* to house or fiel's,    sweetheart
Some points o' love to settle.
Straught to the kill* gaed Rab an Kate,    kiln
But slyly Geordie Logie
Firm locked them in, poor Rab, when late
Crap out by the kill-ogie,
Ill pleased that night.

He sought the key like one deleert,
We's face an clais a' sootie,
While Kate within the kill was fear't
She'd see a ghaist or clootie*;    ogre
Rab's coomie* face, an sic a trick,    sooty
Amused the merry meetin,
Whilst Tam the smith the lock did pick
To let out Katie, sweatin'
Wi fricht that night.

Three brisk young lairds, wha lost their hearts,
An nearly lost their senses,
Their partners' charms an winnin' arts
Stole them in kintra dances:—
The lairds withdrew to a snug crove,
Wi their bewitchin beauties;
They wooed an feasted there on love,
Punch, cardemum, an sweeties,
Till late that night.

Some greedy grunks* wi menseless maws    pigs?
Took mair than nature wanted,
Baith in an out, held by the wa's,
Twafold hatch-potch decanted:
Sic flavort dainties hungry tykes
Fu' greedily gulped all in,

Syne on the loan*, an side o dykes, green
Some o' them drunk lay sprawlin
An sick that night.

Tam, Sawney, Charlie, Will, and Hugh,
When tipplin yill* an whisky, ale
Filled Ned the fiddler roarin fou,
An played a waggish pliskie*; joke
They in his fiddle poured some yill,
Which made him boist'rous surly,
Forby they hid his sneshin* mill, snuff
An raised a hurly-burly
Wi' him that night.

The fiddler fou—his wark he struck,
Dancin of course was ended.
Then drinkin parties in ilk neuk
Their clashmaclaver* vended,— tales, gossip
Domestic gossip, public clash,
Were copiously detailed;
While bustle, din, an balderdash
Through a' the barn prevailed
That unco night.

Twas late—the elder guests retired,
In groups they hameward airted*; headed
Anon the young, wi daffin tired,
In merry mood depairted;
Sae after sic a rantin rare,
Frien'ship an harmless wrangle,
They left the newly kipp'lt pair,
Baith loving an newfangle
That noted night.

## AGNES L' AMY LYON (1762-1840)

### Neil Gow's Farewell to Whisky

You've surely heard of famous Neil,
The man who played the fiddle weel.
He was a heartsome merry chiel*, fellow
And weel he lo'ed the whisky, O.
For e'er since he wore the tartan hose
He dearly liket Athole brose,
And grieved was, you may suppose,
To bid "Farewell to whisky," O.

Alas, says Neil, I'm frail and auld,
And whiles my hame is unco cauld,
I think it makes me blithe and bauld,
A wee drap Highland whisky, O.
But a' the doctors do agree

That whisky's no the drink for me.
I'm fleyed* they'll gar me tyne* my glee, afraid/lose
By parting me and whisky, O.

But I should mind on "auld lang syne,"
How Paradise our friends did tyne,
Because something ran in their mind—
Forbid—like Highland whisky, O.
Whilst I can get good wine and ale,
And find my heart, and fingers hale,
I'll be content, though legs should fail,
And though forbidden whisky, O.

I'll tak my fiddle in my hand,
And screw its strings whilst they can stand,
And mak a lamentation grand
For guid auld Highland whisky, O.
Oh all ye powers of music, come,
For, 'deed, I think I'm mighty glum,
My fiddle-strings will hardly bum,
To say, "Farewell to whisky," O.

## ANDREW SHIRREFS (1762–1800)

### A Cogie o' Yill

Then hey for the whisky, and hey for the meal,
And hey for the cogie, and hey for the yill*; ale
Gin ye steir a' thegither they'll do unco weel
To keep a chiel* cheery and brisk aye. fellow

A cogie o' yill
And a pickle* aitmeal, little
And a dainty wee drappie o' whisky,
Was our forefathers' dose
For to sweel down their brose,
And keep them eye cheery and frisky.

When I see our Scots lads,
Wi their kilts and cockàdes,
That sae aften hae loundered* our foes, man, walloped
I think to mysel',
On the meal and the yill,
And the fruits o' our Scottish kail-brose*, man. cabbage soup

When our brave Highland blades,
Wi their claymores and plaids,
In the field drive like sheep a' our foes, man,
Their courage and pow'r
Spring frae this, to be sure,
They're the noble effects o' the brose, man.

But your spindle-shanked sparks,
Wha sae ill fill their sarks,
Your pale-visaged milksops and beaux, man,
I think when I see them,
'Twere kindness to gi'e them
A cogie o' yill or o' brose, man.

What John Bull despises,
Our better sense prizes.
He denies eatin' blanter* ava, man, oats
But by eatin' o' blanter,
His mare's grown, I'll warrant her,
The manliest brute o' the twa, man.

## ALEXANDER CAMPBELL (1764–1824)

### The Hawk Whoops on High

The hawk whoops on high, and keen, keen from yon cliff,
Lo, the eagle on watch eyes the stag cold and stiff;
The deerhound, majestic, looks lofty around,
While he lists with delight to the harp's distant sound;
Is it swept by the gale, as it slow wafts along,
The heart-soothing tones of an olden times' song?
Or is it some Druid who touches, unseen,
"The Harp of the North," newly strung now I ween?

Tis Albyn's own minstrel, and, proud of his name,
He proclaims him chief bard, and immortal his fame—
He gives tongue to those wild lilts that ravished of old,
And soul to the tales that so oft have been told.
Hence Walter the Minstrel shall flourish for aye,
Will breathe in sweet airs, and live long as his "Lay,"
To ages unnumbered thus yielding delight,
Which will last till the gloaming of Time's endless night.

### Now Winter's Wind Sweeps

Now winter's wind sweeps oer the mountains,
Deeply clad in drifting snow.
Soundly sleep the frozen fountains.
Icebound streams forget to flow.
The piercing blast howls loud and long,
The leafless forest oaks among.

Down the glen, lo, comes a stranger,
Wayworn, drooping, all alone;—
Haply, tis the deer-haunt ranger,
But alas, his strength is gone.
He stoops, he totters on with pain,
The hill he'll never climb again.

Age is being's winter season,
Fitful, gloomy, piercing cold.
Passion, weakened, yields to reason,
Man feels then himself grown old.
His senses one by one have fled,
His very soul seems almost dead.

## WILLIAM REID (1764–1831)

### Kate o' Gowrie

When Katie was scarce out nineteen
Oh, but she had twa coal-black een.
A bonnier lass ye wadna seen
In a' the Carse o' Gowrie.
Quite tired o' livin' a' his lane*, (alone)
Pate did to her his love explain,
And swore he'd be, were she his ain,
The happiest lad in Gowrie.

Quo she, "I winna marry thee,
For a' the gear that ye can gi'e,
Nor will I gang a step ajee
For a' the gowd in Gowrie.
My father will gi'e me twa kye:
My mother's gaun some yarn to dye:
I'll get a gown just like the sky,
Gif I'll no gang to Gowrie."

"Oh, my dear Katie, say nae sae.
Ye little ken a heart that's wae.
Hae, there's my hand; hear me, I pray,
Sin' thou'lt no gang to Gowrie.
Since first I met thee at the shiel*, hut
My saul to thee's been true and leal*. loyal
The darkest night I near nae deil,
Warlock, or witch in Gowrie.

"I fear nae want o' claes* nor nocht, "clothes"
Sic silly things my mind ne'er taught.
I dream a' nicht, and start about,
And wish for thee in Gowrie.
I loe thee better, Kate, my dear,
Than a' my rigs and out-gaun gear.
Sit doun by me till ance I swear,
Thou'rt worth the Carse o' Gowrie."

Syne on her mou sweet kisses laid,
Till blushes a' her cheeks oerspread;
She sighed, and in soft whispers said,
"O, Pate, tak me to Gowrie."
Quo he, "Let's to the auld folk gang.

Say what they like, I'll bide their bang*, abuse
And bide a' night, though beds be thrang*, crowded
But I'll have thee to Gowrie."

The auld folk syne baith gi'ed consent.
The priest was ca'd. A' were content.
And Katie never did repent
That she gaed hame to Gowrie.
For routh* o' bonnie bairns had she. quantities
Mair strapping lads ye wadna see;
And her braw lasses bore the gree* prize
Frae a' the rest o' Gowrie.

## JAMES GRAHAME (1765–1811)

### The Sabbath

[This poem was one of the most popular of the age.]

How still the morning of the hallowed day.
Mute is the voice of rural labor, hushed
The plowboy's whistle and the milkmaid's song.
The scythe lies glittering in the dewy wreath
Of tedded grass, mingled with fading flowers,
That yestermorn bloomed waving in the breeze.
Sounds the most faint attract the ear—the hum
Of early bee, the trickling of the dew,
The distant bleating, midway up the hill.
Calmness sits throned on yon unmoving cloud.
To him who wanders oer the upland leas
The blackbird's note comes mellower from the dale;
And sweeter from the sky the gladsome lark
Warbles his heaven-tuned song; the lulling brook
Murmurs more gently down the deep-worn glen;
While from yon lowly roof, whose circling smoke
Oermounts the mist, is heard at intervals
The voice of psalms, the simple song of praise.
With dovelike wings peace oer yon village broods;
The dizzying mill-wheel rests; the anvil's din
Hath ceased; all, all around is quietness.
Less fearful on this day, the limping hare
Stops, and looks back, and stops, and looks on man,
Her deadliest foe. The toil-worn horse, set free,
Unheedful of the pasture, roams at large;
And as his stiff, unwieldy bulk he rolls,
His iron-armed hoofs gleam in the morning ray.
But chiefly man the day of rest enjoys;
Hail, Sabbath! thee I hail, the poor man's day.
On other days the man of toil is doomed
To eat his joyless bread, lonely, the ground
Both seat and board, screened from the winter's cold

And summer's heat by neighboring hedge or tree;
But on this day, embosomed in his home,
He shares the frugal meal with those he loves.
With those he loves he shares the heartfelt joy
Of giving thanks to God—not thanks of form,
A word and a grimace, but rev'rently,
With covered face and upward, earnest eye.
Hail, Sabbath! thee I hail, the poor man's day.
The pale mechanic now has leave to breathe
The morning air pure from the city's smoke,
While, wandering slowly up the river side,
He meditates on Him whose power he marks
In each green tree that proudly spreads the bough,
As in the tiny dew-bent flowers that bloom
Around the roots; and while he thus surveys
With elevated joy each rural charm,
He hopes (yet fears presumption in the hope)
To reach those realms where Sabbath never ends.
But now his steps a welcome sound recalls.
Solemn the knell, from yonder ancient pile,
Fills all the air, inspiring joyful awe.
Slowly the throng moves oer the tomb-paved ground.
The aged man, the bowed down, the blind
Led by the thoughtless boy, and he who breathes
With pain, and eyes the new-made grave, well pleased;
These, mingled with the young, the gay, approach
The house of God. These, spite of all their ills,
A glow of gladness feel. With silent praise
They enter in. A placid stillness reigns,
Until the man of God, worthy the name,
Opens the book, and reverentially
The stated portion reads. A pause ensues.
The organ breathes its distant thunder-notes,
Then swells into a diapason full.
The people rising, sing, "With harp, with harp,
And voice of psalms." Harmoniously attuned
The various voices blend; the long-drawn aisles,
At every close, the lingering strain prolong.
And now the tubes a softened stop controls.
In softer harmony the people join,
While liquid whispers from yon orphan band
Recall the soul from adoration's trance,
And fill the eye with pity's gentle tears.
Again the organ-peal, loud rolling, meets
The hallelujahs of the choir. Sublime
A thousand notes symphoniously ascend,
As if the whole were one, suspended high
In air, soaring heavenward. Afar they float,
Wafting glad tidings to the sick man's couch.
Raised on his arm, he lists the cadence close,
Yet thinks he hears it still. His heart is cheered.
He smiles on death; but, ah, a wish will rise—
"Would I were now beneath that echoing roof.

No lukewarm accents from my lips should flow.
My heart would sing; and many a Sabbath-day
My steps should thither turn; or, wand'ring far
In solitary paths, where wild flowers blow,
There would I bless His name who led me forth
From death's dark vale, to walk amid those sweets,
Who gives the bloom of health once more to glow
Upon this cheek, and lights this languid eye."

It is not only in the sacred fane
That homage should be paid to the Most High;
There is a temple, one not made with hands,
The vaulted firmament: far in the woods,
Almost beyond the sound of city chime,
At intervals heard through the breezeless air;
Where not the limberest leaf is seen to move,
Save where the linnet lights upon the spray;
Where not a floweret bends its little stalk,
Save when the bee alights upon the bloom;
There, rapt in gratitude, in joy, and love,
The man of God will pass the Sabbath-noon;
Silence his praise: his disembodied thoughts,
Loosed from the load of words, will high ascend
Beyond the empyreal.—
Nor yet less pleasing at the heavenly throne,
The Sabbath-service of the shepherd boy.
In some lone glen, where every sound is lulled
To slumber, save the tinkling of the rill,
Or bleat of lamb, or hovering falcon's cry,
Stretched on the sward, he reads of Jesse's son;
Or sheds a tear oer him to Egypt sold,
And wonders why he weeps. The volume closed,
With thyme-sprig laid between the leaves, he sings
The sacred lays, his weekly lesson, conned
With meikle care beneath the lowly roof,
Where humble lore is learned, where humble worth
Pines unrewarded by a thankless State.
Thus reading, hymning, all alone, unseen,
The shepherd boy the Sabbath holy keeps,
Till on the heights he marks the straggling bands
Returning homeward from the house of prayer.
In peace they home resort. Oh blissful days,
When all men worship God as conscience wills.
Far other times our fathers' grandsires knew,
A virtuous race, to godliness devote.
What though the skeptic's scorn hath dared to soil
The record of their fame. What though the men
Of worldly minds have dared to stigmatize
The sister-cause, religion and the law,
With superstition's name. Yet, yet their deeds,
Their constancy in torture and in death,
These on tradition's tongue still live, these shall
On history's honest page be pictured bright

To latest times. Perhaps some bard, whose muse
Disdains the servile strain of fashion's choir,
May celebrate their unambitious names.
With them each day was holy, every hour
They stood prepared to die, a people doomed
To death; old men, and youths, and simple maids.
With them each day was holy; but that morn
On which the angel said, "See where the Lord
Was laid," joyous arose; to die that day
Was bliss. Long ere the dawn, by devious ways,
Oer hills, through woods, oer dreary wastes, they sought
The upland moors, where rivers, there but brooks,
Dispart to different seas: fast by such brooks,
A little glen is sometimes scooped, a plat
With greensward gay, and flowers that strangers seem
Amid the heathery wild, that all around
Fatigues the eye: in solitudes like these
Thy persecuted children, Scotia, foiled
A tyrant's and a bigot's bloody laws.
There, leaning on his spear (one of the array
That, in the times of old, had scathed the rose
On England's banner, and had powerless struck
The infatuate monarch and his wavering host,
Yet ranged itself to aid his son dethroned),
The lyart* veteran heard the word of God    gray
By Cameron thundered, or by Renwick poured
In gentle stream: then rose the song, the loud
Acclaim of praise; the wheeling plover ceased
Her plaint; the solitary place was glad,
And on the distant cairns, the watcher's ear
Caught doubtfully at times the breeze-borne note.
But years more gloomy followed; and no more
The assembled people dared, in face of day,
To worship God, or even at the dead
Of night, save when the wintry storm raved fierce,
And thunder-peals compelled the men of blood
To couch within their dens; then dauntlessly
The scattered few would meet, in some deep dell
By rocks oer-canopied, to hear the voice,
Their faithful pastor's voice. He by the gleam
Of sheeted lightning oped the sacred book,
And words of comfort spake: over their souls
His accents soothing came, as to her young
The heathfowl's plumes, when at the close of eve
She gathers in, mournful, her brood dispersed
By murderous sport, and oer the remnant spreads
Fondly her wings; close nestling neath her breast
They cherished cower amid the purple blooms.

But wood and wild, the mountain and the dale,
The house of prayer itself, no place inspires
Emotions more accordant with the day,
Than does the field of graves, the land of rest.

Oft at the close of evening prayer, the toll,
The funeral toll, announces solemnly
The service of the tomb; the homeward crowds
Divide on either hand; the pomp draws near.
The choir to meet the dead go forth, and sing,
"I am the resurrection and the life."
Ah me, these youthful bearers robed in white,
They tell a mournful tale: some blooming friend
Is gone, dead in her prime of years. Twas she,
The poor man's friend, who, when she could not give,
With angel tongue pleaded to those who could,
With angel tongue and mild beseeching eye,
That ne'er besought in vain, save when she prayed
For longer life, with heart resigned to die,
Rejoiced to die; for happy visions blessed
Her voyage's last days, and, hovering round,
Alighted on her soul, giving presage
That heaven was nigh. Oh what a burst
Of rapture from her lips! what tears of joy
Her heavenward eyes suffused. Those eyes are closed:
Yet all her loveliness is not yet flown.
She smiled in death, and still her cold pale face
Retains that smile; as when a waveless lake,
In which the wintry stars all bright appear,
Is sheeted by a nightly frost with ice,
Still it reflects the face of heaven unchanged,
Unruffled by the breeze or sweeping blast.
Again that knell! The slow procession stops;
The pall withdrawn, death's altar, thick embossed
With melancholy ornaments (the name,
The record of her blossoming age), appears
Unveiled, and on it dust to dust is thrown,
The final rite. Oh, hark that sullen sound.
Upon the lowered bier the shoveled clay
Falls fast, and fills the void. But who is he
That stands aloof, with haggard wistful eye,
As if he coveted the closing grave?
And he does covet it; his wish is death.
The dread resolve is fixed. His own right hand
Is sworn to do the deed. The day of rest
No peace, no comfort, brings his woe-worn spirit.
Self-cursed, the hallowed dome he dreads to enter.
He dares not pray; he dares not sigh a hope.
Annihilation is his only heaven.
Loathsome the converse of his friends! he shuns
The human face. In every careless eye
Suspicion of his purpose seems to lurk.
Deep piny shades he loves, where no sweet note
Is warbled, where the rook unceasing caws:
Or far in moors, remote from house or hut,
Where animated nature seems extinct,
Where even the hum of wandering bee ne'er breaks
The quiet slumber of the level waste;

Where vegetation's traces almost fail,
Save where the leafless cannachs wave their tufts
Of silky white, or massy oaken trunks
Half buried lie, and tell where greenwoods grew.
There on the heathless moss outstretched, he broods
Oer all his ever changing plans of death:
The time, place, means, sweep, like a moonlight rack,
In fleet succession, oer his clouded soul—
The poniard, and the opium draught, that brings
Death by degrees, but leaves an awful chasm
Between the act and consequence; the flash
Sulphureous, fraught with instantaneous death;
The ruined tower perched on some jutting rock,
So high that, tween the leap and dash below,
The breath might take its flight in midway air;
This pleases for a time; but on the brink,
Back from the toppling edge his fancy shrinks
In horror; sleep at last his breast becalms;
He dreams tis done; but starting wild awakes,
Resigning to despair his dream of joy.
Then hope, faint hope revives, hope that despair
May to his aid let loose the demon frenzy,
To lead scared conscience blindfold oer the brink
Of self-destruction's cataract of blood.
Most miserable, most incongruous wretch,
Dar'st thou to spurn thy life, the boon of God,
Yet dreadest to approach his holy place?
Oh dare to enter in. Maybe some word,
Or sweetly chanted strain, will in thy heart
Awake a chord in unison with life.
What are thy fancied woes to his whose fate
Is (sentence dire) incurable disease,
The outcast of a lazar-house, homeless,
Or with a home where eyes do scowl on him?
Yet he, even he, with feeble step draws near,
With trembling voice joins in the song of praise.
Patient he waits the hour of his release.
He knows he has a home beyond the grave.

Or turn thee to that house, with studded doors,
And iron visored windows, even there
The Sabbath sheds a beam of bliss, though faint;
The debtor's friends (for still he has some friends)
Have time to visit him; the blossoming pea,
That climbs the rust-worn bar, seems fresher tinged;
And on the little turf, this day renewed,
The lark, his prison mate, quivers the wing
With more than wonted joy. See, through the bars,
That pallid face retreating from the view,
That glittering eye following, with hopeless look,
The friends of former years, now passing by
In peaceful fellowship to worship God.
With them, in days of youthful years, he roamed

Oer hill and dale, oer broomy knowe*; and wist "knoll"
As little as the blithest of the band
Of this his lot; condemned, condemned unheard,
The party for his judge. Among the throng,
The Pharisaical hard hearted man
He sees pass on, to join the heaven taught prayer,
"Forgive our debts, as we forgive our debtors."
From unforgiving lips most impious prayer.
Oh happier far the victim, than the hand
That deals the legal stab. The injured man
Enjoys internal, settled calm; to him
The Sabbath-bell sounds peace; he loves to meet
His fellow-sufferers, to pray and praise.
And many a prayer, as pure as e'er was breathed
In holy fanes, is sighed in prison halls.
Ah me, that clank of chains, as kneel and rise
The death-doomed row. But see, a smile illumes
The face of some; perhaps they're guiltless. Oh,
And must high minded honesty endure
The ignominy of a felon's fate?
No, tis not ignominious to be wronged.
No, conscious exultation swells their hearts,
To think the day draws nigh, when in the view
Of angels, and of just men perfect made,
The mark which rashness branded on their names
Shall be effaced; when, wafted on life's storm,
Their souls shall reach the Sabbath of the skies;
As birds, from bleak Norwegia's wintry coast,
Blown out to sea, strive to regain the shore.
But, vainly striving, yield them to the blast,
Swept oer the deep to Albion's genial isle,
Amazed they light amid the bloomy sprays
Of some green vale, there to enjoy new loves,
And join in harmony unheard before.

Relentless justice, with fate-furrowed brow,
Wherefore to various crimes, of various guilt,
One penalty, the most severe, allot?
Why, palled in state, and mitered with a wreath
Of nightshade, dost thou sit portentously,
Beneath a cloudy canopy of sighs,
Of fears, of trembling hopes, of boding doubts,
Death's dart thy mace? Why are the laws of God,
Statutes promulged in characters of fire,
Despised in deep concerns, where heavenly guidance
Is most required: the murd'rer—let him die
And him who lifts his arm against his parent,
His country, or his voice against his God.
Let crimes less heinous, dooms less dreadful meet
Than loss of life. So said the law divine,
That law beneficent, which mildly stretched
To the forgotten and forlorn the hand
Of restitution: yes, the trumpet's voice

The Sabbath of the jubilee announced:
The freedom-freighted blast, through all the land
At once, in every city, echoing rings,
From Lebanon to Carmel's woody cliffs,
So loud, that far within the desert's verge
The couching lion starts, and glares around.
Free is the bondman now; each one returns
To his inheritance. The man grown old
In servitude, far from his native fields,
Hastes joyous on his way; no hills are steep,
Smooth is each rugged path; his little ones
Sport as they go, while oft the mother chides
The lingering step, lured by the wayside flowers.
At length the hill from which a farewell look,
And still another parting look, he threw
On his paternal vale, appears in sight:
The summit gained, throbs hard his heart with joy
And sorrow blent, to see that vale once more.
Instant his eager eye darts to the roof
Where first he saw the light; his youngest born
He lifts, and, pointing to the much-loved spot,
Says, "There thy fathers lived, and there they sleep."
Onward he wends; near and more near he draws.
How sweet the tinkle of the palm-bowered brook.
The sunbeam slanting through the cedar grove
How lovely, and how mild. But lovelier still
The welcome in the eye of ancient friends,
Scarce known at first; and dear the fig tree shade
Neath which on Sabbath eve his father told
Of Israel from the house of bondage freed,
Led through the desert to the promised land.
With eager arms the aged stem he clasps,
And with his tears the furrowed bark bedews.
And still, at midnight hour, he thinks he hears
The blissful sound that brake the bondman's chains,
The glorious peal of freedom and of joy.
Did ever law of man a power like this
Display? Power marvelous as merciful,
Which, though in other ordinances still
Most plainly seen, is yet but little marked
For what it truly is—a miracle.
Stupendous, ever new, performed at once
In every region, yea, on every sea
Which Europe's navies plow;—yes, in all lands
From pole to pole, or civilized or rude,
People there are to whom the Sabbath morn
Dawns, shedding dews into their drooping hearts:
Yes, far beyond the high-heaved western wave,
Amid Columbia's wildernesses vast,
The words which God in thunder from the mount
Of Sinai spake, are heard, and are obeyed.
Thy children, Scotia, in the desert land,
Driven from their homes by fell monopoly,

Keep holy to the Lord the seventh day.
Assembled under loftiest canopy
Of trees primeval (soon to be laid low),
They sing, "By Babel's streams we sat and wept."

What strong mysterious links enchain the heart
To regions where the morn of life was spent.
In foreign lands, though happier be the clime,
Though round our board smile all the friends we love,
The face of nature wears a stranger's look.
Yea, though the valley which we love be swept
Of its inhabitants, none left behind,
Not even the poor blind man who sought his bread
From door to door still, still there is a want.
Yes, even he, round whom a night that knows
No dawn is ever spread, whose native vale
Presented to his closed eyes a blank,
Deplores its distance now. There well he knew
Each object, though unseen; there could he wend
His way guideless through wilds and mazy woods;
Each aged tree, spared when the forest fell,
Was his familiar friend, from the smooth birch,
With rind of silken touch, to the rough elm;
The three gray stones, that marked where heroes lay,
Mourned by the harp, mourned by the melting voice
Of Cona, oft his resting place had been.
Oft had they told him that his home was near:
The tinkle of the rill, the murmuring
So gentle of the brook, the torrent's rush,
The cataract's din, the ocean's distant roar,
The echo's answer to his foot or voice,
All spoke a language which he understood,
All warned him of his way. But most he feels
Upon the hallowed morn the saddening change.
No more he hears the gladsome village bell
Ring the blessed summons to the house of God.
And for the voice of psalms, loud, solemn, grand,
That cheered his darkling path, as with slow step
And feeble he toiled up the spire-topped hill,
A few faint notes ascend among the trees.
What though the clustered vine there hardly tempts
The traveler's hand; though birds of dazzling plume
Perch on the loaded boughs; "Give me thy woods,
(Exclaims the banished man) thy barren woods,
Poor Scotland; sweeter there the reddening haw,
The sloe, or rowan's bitter bunch, than here
The purple grape; more dear the redbreast's note,
That mourns the fading year in Scotia's vales,
Than Philomel's where spring is ever new;
More dear to me the redbreast's sober suit,
So like a withered leaflet, than the glare
Of gaudy wings that make the iris dim."
Nor is regret exclusive to the old;

The boy, whose birth was midway oer the main,
A ship his cradle, by the billows rocked,
"The nursling of the storm,"—although he claims
No native land, yet does he wistful hear
Of some far distant country still called home,
Where lambs of whitest fleece sport on the hills,
Where gold specked fishes wanton in the streams;
Where little birds, when snowflakes dim the air,
Light on the floor, and peck the table crumbs,
And with their singing cheer the winter day.

But what the loss of country to the woes
Of banishment and solitude combined?
Oh, my heart bleeds to think there now may live
One hapless man, the remnant of a wreck,
Cast on some desert island of that main
Immense, which stretches from the Cochin shore
To Acapulco. Motionless he sits,
As is the rock his seat, gazing whole days
With wandering eye oer all the watery waste;
Now striving to believe the albatross
A sail appearing on the horizon's verge;
Now vowing ne'er to cherish other hope
Than hope of death. Thus pass his weary hours,
Till welcome evening warn him that tis time,
Upon the shell-notched calendar to mark
Another day—another dreary day—
Changeless—for in these regions of the sun,
The wholesome law that dooms mankind to toil,
Bestowing grateful interchange of rest
And labor, is annulled; for there the trees,
Adorned at once with bud, and flower, and fruit,
Drop, as the breezes blow, a shower of bread
And blossoms on the ground. But yet by him,
The hermit of the deep, not unobserved
The Sabbath passes,—tis his great delight.
Each seventh eve he marks the farewell ray,
And loves and sighs to think that setting sun
Is now empurpling Scotland's mountain tops,
Or, higher risen, slants athwart her vales,
Tinting with yellow light the quivering throat
Of day-spring lark, while woodland birds below
Chant in the dewy shade. Thus, all night long
He watches while the rising moon describes
The progress of the day in happier lands.
And now he almost fancies that he hears
The chiming from his native village church;
And now he sings, and fondly hopes the strain
May be the same that sweet ascends at home
In congregation full,—where, not without a tear,
They are remembered who in ships behold
The wonders of the deep. He sees the hand,
The widowed hand, that veils the eye suffused.

He sees his orphan boy look up, and strive
The widowed heart to soothe. His spirit leans
On God. Nor does he leave his weekly vigil,
Though tempests ride oer welkin-lashing waves
On winds of cloudless wing; though lightnings burst
So vivid, that the stars are hid and seen
In awful alternation. Calm he views
The far-exploding firmament, and dares
To hope—one bolt in mercy is reserved
For his release; and yet he is resigned
To live; because full well he is assured
Thy hand does lead him, thy right hand upholds.

And thy right hand does lead him. Lo, at last,
One sacred eve, he hears, faint from the deep,
Music remote, swelling at intervals,
As if th' embodied spirit of sweet sounds
Came slowly floating on the shoreward wave.
The cadence well he knows—a hymn of old,
Where sweetly is rehearsed the lowly state
Of Jesus, when his birth was first announced,
In midnight music, by an angel choir,
To Bethlehem's shepherds, as they watched their flocks.
Breathless, the man forlorn listens, and thinks
It is a dream. Fuller the voices swell.
He looks, and starts to see, moving along,
The semblance of a fiery wave, in crescent form,
Approaching to the land; straightway he sees
A towering whiteness. Tis the heaven-filled sails
That waft the missioned men, who have renounced
Their homes, their country, nay, almost the world,
Bearing glad tidings to the furthest isles
Of ocean, that the dead shall rise again.
Forward the gleam-girt castle coastwise glides.
It seems as it would pass away. To cry
The wretched man in vain attempts, in vain,
Powerless his voice, as in a fearful dream.
Not so his hand; he strikes the flint, a blaze
Mounts from the ready heap of withered leaves.
The music ceases; accents harsh succeed,
Harsh, but most grateful; downward drop sails;
Engulfed the anchor sinks; the boat is launched,
But cautious lies aloof till morning dawn.
Oh then the transport of the man, unused
To other human voice beside his own,
His native tongue to hear. He breathes at home,
Though earth's diameter is interposed.
Of perils of the sea he has no dread,
Full well assured the missioned bark is safe,
Held in the hollow of th' Almighty's hand;
(And signal thy deliverances have been
Of those thy messengers of peace and joy).
From storms that loudly threaten to unfix

Islands rock-rooted in the ocean's bed,
Thou dost deliver them—and from the calm,
More dreadful than the storm, when motionless
Upon the purple deep the vessel lies
For days, for nights, illumed by phosphor lamps;
When sea-birds seem in nests of flame to float;
When backward starts the boldest mariner
To see, while oer the side he leans, his face
As if deep-tinged with blood. Let worldly men
The cause and combatants contemptuous scorn,
And call fanatics them who hazard health
And life, in testifying of the truth,
Who joy and glory in the cross of Christ.
What were the Galilean fishermen
But messengers commissioned to announce
The resurrection and the life to come?
They too, though clothed with power of mighty works
Miraculous, were oft received with scorn;
Oft did their words fall powerless, though enforced
By deeds that marked omnipotence their friend.
But when their efforts failed, unweariedly
They onward went, rejoicing in their course.
Like helianthus, borne on downy wings
To distant realms, they frequent fell on soils
Barren and thankless; yet ofttimes they saw
Their labors crowned with fruit an hundred fold,
Saw the new converts testify their faith
By works of love, the slave set free, the sick
Attended, prisoners visited, the poor
Received as brothers at the rich man's board.
Alas, how different now the deeds of men
Nursed in the faith of Christ—the free made slaves,
Stolen from their country, borne across the deep,
Enchained, endungeoned, forced by stripes to live,
Doomed to behold their wives, their little ones,
Tremble beneath the white man's fiend-like frown.
Yet even to scenes like this, the Sabbath brings
Alleviation of the enormous woe:
The oft-reiterated stroke is still;
The clotted scourge hangs hardening in the shrouds.
But see, the demon man, whose trade is blood,
With dauntless front, convene his ruffian crew,
To hear the sacred service read. Accursed,
The wretch's bile-tinged lips profane the Word
Of God. Accursed, he ventures to pronounce
The decalogue, nor falters at that law
Wherein tis written, Thou shalt do no murder.
Perhaps, while yet the words are on his lips,
He hears a dying mother's parting groan;
He hears her orphaned child, with lisping plaint,
Attempt to rouse her from the sleep of death.

Oh England, England, wash thy purpled hands
Of this foul sin, and never dip them more
In guilt so damnable; then lift them up
In supplication to that God whose name
Is mercy; then thou may'st, without the risk
Of drawing vengeance from the surcharged clouds,
Implore protection to thy menaced shores;
Then God will blast the tyrant's arm that grasps
The thunderbolt of ruin oer thy head;
Then will he turn the wolfish race to prey
Upon each other; then will he arrest
The lava torrent, causing it regorge
Back to its source with fiery desolation.

Of all the murderous trades by mortals plied,
Tis war alone that never violates
The hallowed day by simulate respect,
By hypocritic rest: no, no, the work proceeds.
From sacred pinnacles are hung the flags
That give the sign to slip the leash from slaughter;
The bells whose knoll a holy calmness poured
Into the good man's breast, whose sound consoled
The sick, the poor, the old—perversion dire—
Pealing with sulph'rous tongue, speak death-fraught words.
From morn to eve destruction revels frenzied,
Till at the hour when peaceful vesper chimes
Were wont to sooth the ear, the trumpet sounds
Pursuit and flight altern; and for the song
Of larks descending to their grass-bowered homes,
The croak of flesh-gorged ravens, as they slake
Their thirst in hoof prints filled with gore, disturbs
The stupor of the dying man: while death
Triumphantly sails down th' ensanguined stream,
On corses throned, and crowned with shivered boughs,
That erst hung imaged in the crystal tide.

And what the harvest of these bloody fields?
A double weight of fetters to the slave,
And chains on arms that wielded freedom's sword.
Spirit of Tell, and art thou doomed to see
Thy mountains, that confessed no other chains
Than what the wintry elements had forged—
Thy vales, where freedom, and her stern compeer,
Proud virtuous poverty, their noble state
Maintained, amid surrounding threats of wealth,
Of superstition, and tyrannic sway—
Spirit of Tell, and art thou doomed to see
That land subdued by slavery's basest slaves,
By men whose lips pronounce the sacred name
Of liberty, then kiss the despot's foot?
Helvetia, hadst thou to thyself been true,
Thy dying sons had triumphed as they fell.
But twas a glorious effort, though in vain.

Aloft thy genius, mid the sweeping clouds,
The flag of freedom spread; bright in the storm
The streaming meteor waved, and far it gleamed;
But, ah, twas transient as the iris' arch,
Glanced from leviathan's ascending shower,
When mid the mountain waves heaving his head.
Already had the friendly-seeming foe
Possessed the snow-piled ramparts of the land;
Down like an avalanche they rolled, they crushed;
The temple, palace, cottage, every work
Of art and nature, in one common ruin.
The dreadful crash is oer, and peace ensues—
The peace of desolation, gloomy, still.
Each day is like a Sabbath, but, alas,
No Sabbath service glads the seventh day;
No more the happy villagers are seen,
Winding adown the rock-hewn paths that wont
To lead their footsteps to the house of prayer;
But, far apart, assembled in the depth
Of solitudes, perhaps a little group
Of aged men, and orphan boys, and maids
Bereft, list to the breathings of the holy man
Who spurns an oath of fealty to the power
Of rulers chosen by a tyrant's nod.
No more, as dies the rustling of the breeze,
Is heard the distant vesper hymn; no more
At gloaming hour the plaintive strain, that links
His country in the Switzer's heart, delights
The loosening team; or if some shepherd-boy
Attempt the strain, his voice soon faltering stops;
He feels his country now a foreign land.

O Scotland, canst thou for a moment brook
The mere imagination, that a fate
Like this can e'er be thine, that oer those hills,
And dear-bought vales, whence Wallace, Douglas, Bruce,
Repelled proud Edward's multitudinous hordes,
A Gallic foe, that abject race, should rule?
No, no, let never hostile standard touch
Thy shore: rush, rush into the dashing brine,
And crest each wave with steel; and should the stamp
Of slavery's footstep violate the strand,
Let not the tardy tide efface the mark:
Sweep off the stigma with a sea of blood.

But truce with war, at best a dismal theme;
Thrice happy he who, far in Scottish glen
Retired (yet ready at his country's call),
Has left the restless emmet-hill of man.
He never longs to read the saddening tale
Of endless wars; and seldom does he hear
The tale of woe; and ere it reaches him,
Rumor, so loud when new, has died away

Into a whisper, on the memory borne
Of casual traveler; as on the deep,
Far from the sight of land, when all around
Is waveless calm, the sudden tremulous swell,
That gently heaves the ship, tells, as it rolls,
Of earthquakes dread, and cities overthrown.

Oh Scotland, much I love thy tranquil dales;
But most, on Sabbath eve, when low the sun
Slants through the upland copse, tis my delight,
Wandering, and stopping oft, to hear the song
Of kindred praise arise from humble roofs;
Or when the simple service ends, to hear
The lifted latch, and mark the gray-haired man,
The father and the priest, walk forth alone
Into his garden plat or little field,
To commune with his God in secret prayer—
To bless the Lord that in his downward years
His children are about him; sweet meantime,
The thrush, that sings upon the aged thorn,
Brings to his view the days of youthful years,
When that same aged thorn was but a bush.
Nor is the contrast between youth and age
To him a painful thought; he joys to think
His journey near a close; heaven is his home.
More happy far that man, though bowed down,
Though feeble be his gait, and dim his eye,
Than they, the favorites of youth and health,
Of riches and of fame, who have renounced
The glorious promise of the life to come,
Clinging to death. Or mark that female face,
The faded picture of its former self,
The garments coarse but clean; frequent at church,
I've noted such a one, feeble and pale,
Yet standing, with a look of mild content,
Till beckoned by some kindly hand to sit.
She had seen better days; there was a time
Her hands cold earn her bread, and freely give
To those who were in want; but now old age
And lingering disease have made her helpless.
Yet she is happy, aye, and she is wise
(Philosophers may sneer, and pedants frown),
Although her Bible be her only book;
And she is rich, although her only wealth
Be recollection of a well-spent life—
Be expectation of the life to come.
Examine here, explore the narrow path
In which she walks; look not for virtuous deeds
In history's arena, where the prize
Of fame or power prompts to heroic acts.
Peruse the lives themselves of men obscure;
There charity, that robs itself to give,
There fortitude in sickness nursed by want,

There courage that expects no tongue to praise,
There virtue lurks, like purest gold deep hid
With no alloy of selfish motive mixed.
The poor man's boon, that stints him of his bread,
Is prized more highly in the sight of Him
Who sees the heart, than golden gifts from hands
That scarce can know their countless treasures loss:
Yes, the deep sigh that heaves the poor man's breast
To see distress, and feel his willing arm
Palsied by penury, ascends to heaven,
While ponderous bequests of lands and goods
Ne'er rise above their earthly origin.

And should all bounty that is clothed with power
Be deemed unworthy? Far be such a thought.
Even when the rich bestow, there are sure tests
Of genuine charity: yes, yes, let wealth
Give other alms than silver or than gold—
Time, trouble, toil, attendance, watchfulness,
Exposure to disease—yes, let the rich
Be often seen beneath the sick man's roof;
Or cheering, with inquiries from the heart,
And hopes of health, the melancholy range
Of couches in the public wards of woe:
There let them often bless the sick man's bed,
With kind assurances that all is well
At home, that plenty smiles upon the board,
The while the hand that earned the frugal meal
Can hardly raise itself in sign of thanks.
Above all duties, let the rich man search
Into the cause he knoweth not, nor spurn
The suppliant wretch as guilty of a crime.

Ye blessed with wealth (another name for power
Of doing good), oh would ye but devote
A little portion of each seventh day
To acts of justice to your fellow men.
The house of mourning silently invites.
Shun not the crowded alley; prompt descend
Into the half sunk cell, darksome and damp,
Nor seem impatient to be gone; inquire,
Console, instruct, encourage, soothe, assist;
Read, pray, and sing a new song to the Lord;
Make tears of joy down grief-worn furrows flow.

O health, thou sun of life, without whose beam
The fairest scenes of nature seem involved
In darkness, shine upon my dreary path
Once more; or, with thy faintest dawn, give hope
That I may yet enjoy thy vital ray;
Though transient be the hope, twill be most sweet,
Like midnight music, stealing on the ear,
Then gliding past, and dying slow away.

Music, thou soothing power, thy charm is proved
Most vividly when clouds oercast the soul.
So light displays its loveliest effect
In lowering skies, when through the murky rack
A slanting sunbeam shoots, and instant limns
Th' ethereal curve of seven harmonious dyes,
Eliciting a splendor from the gloom.
O music, still vouchsafe to tranquilize
This breast perturbed; thy voice, though mournful, soothes;
And mournful aye are thy most beauteous lays,
Like fall of blossoms from the orchard boughs,
The autumn of the spring: enchanting power,
Who, by thy airy spell, canst whirl the mind
Far from the busy hints of men, to vales
Where Tweed or Yarrow flows; or, spurning time,
Recall red Flodden field; or suddenly
Transport, with altered strain, the deafened ear
To Lindon's plain.—But what the pastoral lay,
The melting dirge, the battle's trumpet peal,
Compared to notes with sacred numbers linked
In union, solemn, grand. Oh then the spirit,
Upborne on pinions of celestial sound,
Soars to the throne of God, and ravished hears
Ten thousand times ten thousand voices rise
In slow explosion—voices that erewhile
Were feebly tuned, perhaps, to low-breathed hymns
Of solace in the chambers of the poor,
The Sabbath worship of the friendless sick.

Blessed be the female votaries,[1] whose days
No Sabbath of their pious labors prove,
Whose lives are consecrated to the toil
Of minist'ring around the uncurtained couch
Of pain and poverty: blessed be the hands,
The lovely hands (for beauty, youth, and grace
Are oft concealed by pity's closest veil),
That mix the cup medicinal, that bind
The wounds which ruthless warfare and disease
Have to the loathsome lazar-house consigned.
Fierce superstition of the mitered king!
Almost I could forget thy torch and stake,
When I this blessed sisterhood survey,
Compassion's priestesses, disciples true
Of him whose touch was health, whose single word
Electrified with life the palsied arm,
Of him who said, "Take up thy bed, and walk"—
Of him who cried to Lazarus, "Come forth."

And he who cried to Lazarus, "Come forth,"
Will, when the Sabbath of the tomb is past,

---

[1]Beguine nuns.

Call forth the dead, and reunite the dust
(Transformed and purified) to angel souls.
Ecstatic hope, belief, conviction firm.
How grateful tis to recollect the time
When hope arose to faith. Faintly at first
The heavenly voice is heard. Then by degrees
Its music sounds perpetual in the heart.
Thus he, who all the gloomy winter long
Has dwelt in city-crowds, wandering afield
Betimes on Sabbath morn, ere yet the spring
Unfold the daisy's bud, delighted hears
The first lark's note, faint yet, and short the song,
Checked by the chill ungenial northern breeze;
But, as the sun ascends, another springs,
And still another soars on loftier wing,
Till all oer head, the joyous choir unseen,
Poised welkin-high, harmonious fills the air,
As if it were a link tween earth and heaven.

### The Wild Duck and Her Brood

How calm that little lake. No breath of wind
Sighs through the reeds. A clear abyss it seems,
Held in the concave of the inverted sky,—
In which is seen the rook's dull flagging wing
Move oer the silvery clouds. How peaceful sails
Yon little fleet, the wild duck and her brood.
Fearless of harm, they row their easy way.
The water lily, 'neath the plumy prows,
Dips, reappearing in their dimpled track.
Yet, even amid that scene of peace, the noise
Of war, unequal, dastard war, intrudes.
Yon revel rout of men, and boys, and dogs,
Boisterous approach; the spaniel dashes in.
Quick he decries the prey; and faster swims,
And eager barks. The harmless flock, dismayed,
Hasten to gain the thickest grove of reeds,
All but the parent pair. They, floating, wait
To lure the foe, and lead him from their young;
But soon themselves are forced to seek the shore.
Vain then the buoyant wing; the leaden storm
Arrests their flight; they, fluttering, bleeding fall,
And tinge the troubled bosom of the lake.

## JAMES MACKINTOSH (1765–1832)

### In Defense of Jean Peltier (February 21, 1803)

[The following is one of the most celebrated orations by any Scotsman. Its author, a noted attorney and public speaker, who served as a member of parliament, was called upon to defend one Jean Peltier, publisher of a French newspaper in

London called "L' Ambigu." Peltier used the paper to attack Napoleon Bonaparte, who demanded, as England and France were then at peace, that the English government should prosecute Peltier for "a libel on a friendly government," a serious offense at the time. Mackintosh's defense of his client is one of the most memorable pleas for the freedom of the press in English.]

Gentlemen of the Jury:—The time is now come for me to address you in behalf of the unfortunate gentleman who is the defendant on this record.

I must begin with observing that though I know myself too well to ascribe to anything but to the kindness and good nature of my learned friend, the Attorney General, the unmerited praises which he has been pleased to bestow on me, yet, I will venture to say, he has done me no more than justice in supposing that in this place and on this occasion, where I exercise the functions of an inferior minister of justice,—an inferior minister, indeed, but a minister of justice still,—I am incapable of lending myself to the passions of any client, and that I will not make the proceedings of this court subservient to any political purpose. Whatever is respected by the laws and government of my country shall in this place be respected by me. In considering matters that deeply interest the quiet, the safety, and the liberty of all mankind, it is impossible for me not to feel warmly and strongly; but I shall make an effort to control my feelings, however painful that effort may be, and where I cannot speak out but at the risk of offending either sincerity or prudence I shall labor to contain myself and be silent.

I cannot but feel, gentlemen, how much I stand in need of your favorable attention and indulgence. The charge which I have to defend is surrounded with the most invidious topics of discussion; but they are not of my seeking. The case and the topics which are inseparable from it are brought here by the prosecutor. Here I find them, and here it is my duty to deal with them as the interests of Mr. Peltier seem to me to require. He, by his choice and confidence, has cast on me a very arduous duty which I could not decline and which I can still less betray. He has a right to expect from me a faithful, a zealous, and a fearless defense; and this his just expectation, according to the measure of my humble abilities, shall be fulfilled.

I have said a fearless defense. Perhaps that word was unnecessary in the place where I now stand. Intrepidity in the discharge of professional duty is so common a quality at the English bar that it has, thank God, long ceased to be a matter of boast or praise. If it had been otherwise, gentlemen, if the bar could have been silenced or overawed by power, I may presume to say that an English jury would not this day have been met to administer justice. Perhaps I need scarce say that my defense shall be fearless in a place where fear never entered any heart but that of a criminal. But you will pardon me for having said so much when you consider who the real parties before you are.

Gentlemen, the real prosecutor is the master of the greatest empire the civilized world ever saw. The defendant is a defenseless, proscribed exile. He is a French Royalist, who fled from his country in the autumn of 1792, at the period of that memorable and awful emigration when all the proprietors and magistrates of the greatest civilized country of Europe were driven from their homes by the daggers of assassins; when our shores were covered, as with the wreck of a great tempest, with old men, and women, and children, and ministers of religion, who fled from the ferocity of their countrymen as before an army of invading barbarians.

The greatest part of these unfortunate exiles—of those, I mean, who have been spared by the sword, who have survived the effect of pestilential climates or broken hearts—have been since permitted to revisit their country. Though despoiled of their all, they have eagerly embraced even the sad privilege of being suffered to die in their native land.

Even this miserable indulgence was to be purchased by compliances, by declarations of allegiance to the new government, which some of these suffering Royalists deemed incompatible with their consciences, with their dearest attachments, and their most sacred duties. Among these last is Mr. Peltier. I do not presume to blame those who submitted, and I trust you will not judge harshly of those who refused. You will not think unfavorably of a man who stands before you as the voluntary victim of his loyalty and honor. If a revolution (which God avert) were to drive us into exile and to cast us on a foreign shore, we should expect, at least, to be pardoned by generous men for stubborn loyalty and unseasonable fidelity to the laws and government of our fathers.

This unfortunate gentleman had devoted a great part of his life to literature. It was the amusement and ornament of his better days. Since his own ruin and the desolation of his country he has been compelled to employ it as a means of support. For the last ten years he has been engaged in a variety of publications of considerable importance; but since the peace he has desisted from serious political discussion and confined himself to the obscure journal which is now before you, the least calculated, surely, of any publication that ever issued from the press, to rouse the alarms of the most jealous government; which will not be read in England because it is not written in our language; which cannot be read in France because its entry into that country is prohibited by a power whose mandates are not very supinely enforced nor often evaded with impunity; which can have no other object than that of amusing the companions of the author's principles and misfortunes, by pleasantries and sarcasms on their victorious enemies.

There is, indeed, gentlemen, one remarkable circumstance in this unfortunate publication; it is the only, or almost the only journal which still dares to espouse the cause of that royal and illustrious family which but fourteen years ago was flattered by every press and guarded by every tribunal in Europe. Even the court in which we are met affords an example of the vicissitudes of their fortune. My learned friend has reminded you that the last prosecution tried in this place at the instance of a French government was for a libel on that magnanimous princess who has since been butchered in sight of her palace.

I do not make these observations with any purpose of questioning the general principles which have been laid down by my learned friend. I must admit his right to bring before you those who libel any government recognized by his Majesty and at peace with the British empire. I admit that whether such a government be of yesterday or a thousand years old, whether it be a crude and bloody usurpation or the most ancient, just, and paternal authority upon earth, we are here equally bound, by his Majesty's recognition, to protect it against libelous attacks. I admit that if, during our usurpation, Lord Clarendon had published his history at Paris, or the Marquess of Montrose his verses on the murder of his sovereign, or Mr. Crowley his "Discourse on Cromwell's Government," and if the English ambassador had complained, the President De Moli, or any other of the great magistrates who then adorned the Parliament of Paris, however reluctantly, painfully, and indignantly, might have been compelled to have condemned these illustrious men to the punishment of libelers. I say this only for the sake of bespeaking a favorable attention, from your generosity and compassion, to what will be feebly urged in behalf of my unfortunate client, who has sacrificed his fortune, his hopes, his connections, his country, to his conscience; who seems marked out for destruction in this his last asylum.

That he still enjoys the security of this asylum, that he has not been sacrificed to the resentment of his powerful enemies, is perhaps owing to the firmness of the king's government. If that be the fact, gentlemen; if his Majesty's ministers have resisted applications to expel this unfortunate gentleman from England, I should publicly thank them for their firmness if it were not unseemly and improper to suppose that they could have acted otherwise—to thank an English government for not violating the most sacred duties of hospitality; for not bringing indelible disgrace on their country.

But be that as it may, gentlemen, he now comes before you perfectly satisfied that an English jury is the most refreshing prospect that the eye of accused innocence ever met in a human tribunal; and he feels with me the most fervent gratitude to the Protector of empires that, surrounded as we are with the ruins of principalities and powers, we still continue to meet together, after the manner of our fathers, to administer justice in this her ancient sanctuary.

There is another point of view in which this case seems to me to merit your most serious attention. I consider it as the first of a long series of conflicts between the greatest power in the world and the only free press remaining in Europe. No man living is more thoroughly convinced than I am that my learned friend, Mr. Attorney General, will never degrade his excellent character; that he will never disgrace his high magistracy by mean compliances, by an immoderate and unconscientious exercise of power; yet I am convinced, by circumstances, which I shall now abstain from discussing, that I am to consider this as the first of a long series of conflicts between the greatest power in the world and the only free press now remaining in Europe.

Gentlemen, this distinction of the English press is new; it is a proud and melancholy distinction. Before the great earthquake of the French Revolution had swallowed up all the asylums of free discussion on the continent, we enjoyed that privilege indeed more fully than others; but we did not enjoy it exclusively. In great monarchies the press has always been considered as too formidable an engine to be entrusted to unlicensed individuals.

But in other continental countries, either by the laws of the state or by long habits of liberality and toleration in magistrates, a liberty of discussion has been enjoyed perhaps sufficient for most useful purposes. It existed, in fact, where it was not protected by law; and the wise and generous connivance of governments was daily more and more secured by the growing civilization of their subjects. In Holland, in Switzerland, in the imperial towns of Germany, the press was either legally or practically free. Holland and Switzerland are no more; and since the commencement of this prosecution fifty imperial towns have been erased from the list of independent states by one dash of the pen. Three or four still preserve a precarious and trembling existence. I will not say by what compliances they must purchase its continuance. I will not insult the feebleness of states whose unmerited fall I do most bitterly deplore.

These governments were in many respects one of the most interesting parts of the ancient system of Europe. Unfortunately for the repose of mankind, great states are compelled, by regard to their own safety, to consider the military spirit and martial habits of their people as one of the main objects of their polices. Frequent hostilities seem almost the necessary condition of their greatness; and without being great they cannot long remain safe. Smaller states, exempted from this cruel necessity—a hard condition of greatness, a bitter satire on human nature—devoted themselves to the arts of peace, to the cultivation of literature, and the improvement of reason. They became places of refuge for free and fearless discussion; they were the impartial spectators and judges of the various contests of ambition which from time to time disturbed the quiet of the world.

They thus became peculiarly qualified to be the organs of that public opinion which converted Europe into a great republic with laws which mitigated though they could not extinguish ambition, and with moral tribunals to which even the most despotic sovereigns were amenable. If wars of aggrandizement were undertaken. their authors were arraigned in the face of Europe.

If acts of internal tyranny were perpetrated, they resounded from a thousand presses throughout all civilized countries. Princes on whose will there were no legal checks thus found a moral restraint which the most powerful of them could not brave with absolute impunity. They acted before a vast audience to whose applause or condemnation they could not be utterly indifferent. The very constitution of human nature, the unalterable laws of the mind of man, against which all rebellion is fruitless, subjected the proudest tyrants to this control. No elevation of power, no depravity however consummate, no innocence however spotless, can render man wholly independent of the praise or blame of his fellow men.

These governments were in other respects one of the most beautiful and interesting parts of our ancient system. The perfect security of such inconsiderable and feeble states, their undisturbed tranquillity amid the wars and conquests that surrounded them, attested, beyond any other part of the European system, the moderation, the justice, the civilization to which Christian Europe had reached in modern times.

Their weakness was protected only by the habitual reverence for justice which during a long series of ages had grown up in Christendom. This was the only fortification which defended them against those mighty monarchs to whom they offered so easy a prey; and till the French Revolution this was sufficient.

Consider, for instance, the situation of the Republic of Geneva. Think of her defenseless position, in the very jaws of France; but think also of her undisturbed security; of her profound quiet, of the brilliant success with which she applied to industry and literature while Louis XIV was pouring his myriads into Italy before her gates. Call to mind, if ages crowded into years have not effaced them from your memory, that happy period when we scarcely dreamed more of the subjugation of the feeblest republic of Europe than of the conquest of her mightiest empire; and tell me if you can imagine a spectacle more beautiful to the moral eye, or a more striking proof of progress in the noblest principles of true civilization.

These feeble states—these monuments of the justice of Europe—the asylum of peace, of industry, and of literature—the organs of public reason—the refuge of oppressed innocence and persecuted truth, have perished with those ancient principles which were their sole guardians and protectors. They have been swallowed up by that fearful convulsion which has shaken the uttermost corners of the earth. They are destroyed and gone forever.

One asylum of free discussion is still inviolate. There is still one spot in Europe where man can freely exercise his reason on the most important concerns of society, where he can boldly publish his judgment on the acts of the proudest and most powerful tyrants. The press of England is still free. It is guarded by the free constitution of our forefathers. It is guarded by the hearts and arms of Englishmen, and I trust I may venture to say that if it be to fall it will fall only under the ruins of the British empire.

It is an awful consideration, gentlemen. Every other monument of European liberty has perished. That ancient fabric which has been gradually reared by the wisdom and virtue of our fathers still stands. It stands, thanks be to God, solid and entire; but it stands alone, and it stands amid ruins.

In these extraordinary circumstances I repeat that I must consider this as the first of a long series of conflicts between the greatest power in the world and the only free press remaining in Europe. And I trust that you will consider yourselves as the advanced guard of liberty, as having this day to fight the first battle of free discussion against the most formidable enemy that it ever encountered. You will therefore excuse me if, on so important an occasion, I remind you, at more length than is usual, of those general principles of law and policy on this subject which have been handed down to us by our ancestors.

Those who slowly built up the fabric of our laws never attempted anything so absurd as to define, by any precise rule, the obscure and shifting boundaries which divide libel from history or discussion. It is a subject which, from its nature, admits neither rules nor definitions. The same words may be perfectly innocent in one case and most mischievous and libelous in another. A change of circumstances, often apparently slight, is sufficient to make the whole difference.

These changes, which may be as numerous as the variety of human intentions and conditions, can never be foreseen nor comprehended under any legal definitions, and the framers of our law have never attempted to subject them to such definitions. They left such ridiculous attempts to those who call themselves philosophers, but who have, in fact, proved themselves most grossly and stupidly ignorant of that philosophy which is conversant with human affairs.

The principles of the law of England on the subject of political libel are few and simple, and they are necessarily so broad that without an habitually mild administration of justice they might encroach materially on the liberty of political discussion. Every publication which is intended to vilify either our own government or the government of any foreign state in amity with this kingdom is, by the law of England, a libel. To protect political discussion from the danger to which it would be exposed by these wide principles, if they were severely and literally enforced, our ancestors trusted to various securities—some growing out of the law and constitution, and others arising from the character of those public officers whom the constitution had formed, and to whom its administration is committed.

They trusted, in the first place, to the moderation of the legal officers of the Crown, educated in the maxims and imbued with the spirit of a free government, controlled by the superintending power of Parliament, and peculiarly watched in all political prosecutions by the reasonable and wholesome jealousy of their fellow subjects. And I am bound to admit that, since the glorious era of the revolution, making due allowance for the frailties, the faults, and the occasional vices of men, they have, upon the whole, not been disappointed.

I know that in the hands of my learned friend that trust will never be abused. But, above all, they confided in the moderation and good sense of juries, popular in their origin, popular in their feelings, popular in their very prejudices, taken from the mass of the people, and immediately returning to that mass again. By these checks and temperaments they hoped that they should sufficiently repress malignant libels without endangering that freedom of inquiry which is the first security of a free state.

They knew that the offense of a political libel is of a very peculiar nature and differing in the most important particulars from all other crimes. In all other cases the most severe execution of law can only spread terror among the guilty; but in political libels it inspires even the innocent with fear. This striking peculiarity arises from the same circumstances which make it impossible to define the limits of libel and innocent discussion; which make it impossible for a man of the purest and most honorable mind to be always perfectly certain whether he be within the territory of fair argument and honest narrative, or whether he may not have unwittingly overstepped the faint and varying line which bounds them.

But, gentlemen, I will go further. This is the only offense where severe and frequent punishments not only intimidate the innocent, but deter men from the most meritorious acts and from rendering the most important services to their country. They indispose and disqualify men for the discharge of the most sacred duties which they owe to mankind. To inform the public on the conduct of those who administer public affairs requires courage and conscious security. It is always an invidious and obnoxious office; but it is often the most necessary of all public duties. If it is not done boldly it cannot be done effectually, and it is not from writers trembling under the uplifted scourge that we are to hope for it.

There are other matters, gentlemen, to which I am desirous of particularly calling your attention. These are the circumstances in the condition of this country which have induced our ancestors, at all times, to handle with more than ordinary tenderness that branch of the liberty of discussion which is applied to the conduct of foreign states. The relation of this kingdom to the commonwealth of Europe is so peculiar that no history, I think, furnishes a parallel to it.

From the moment in which we abandoned all projects of Continental aggrandizement we could have no interest respecting the state of the continent but the interests of national safety and of commercial prosperity. The paramount interest of every state—that which comprehends every other—is security. And the security of Great Britain requires nothing on the continent but the uniform observance of justice. It requires nothing but the inviolability of ancient boundaries and the sacredness of ancient possessions, which, on these subjects, is but another form of words for justice. A nation which is herself shut out from the possibility of Continental aggrandizement can have no interest but that of preventing such aggrandizement in others. We can have no interest of safety but the preventing of those encroachments which, by their immediate effects or by their example, may be dangerous to ourselves. We can have no interest or ambition respecting the Continent. So that neither our real nor even our apparent interest can ever be at variance with justice.

As to commercial prosperity, it is indeed a secondary, but it is still a very important branch of our national interests, and it requires nothing on the continent of Europe but the maintenance of peace as far as the paramount interest of security will allow.

Whatever ignorant or prejudiced men may affirm, no war was ever gainful to a commercial nation. Losses may be less in some, and incidental profits may arise in others. But no such profits ever formed an adequate compensation for the waste of capital and industry which all wars must produce. Next to peace, our commercial greatness depends chiefly on the affluence and prosperity of our neighbors. A commercial nation has, indeed, the same interest in the wealth of her neighbors that a tradesman has in the wealth of his customers.

The prosperity of England has been chiefly owing to the general progress of civilized nations in the arts and improvements of social life. Not an acre of land has been brought into cultivation in the wilds of Siberia or on the shores of the Mississippi which has not widened the market for English industry. It is nourished by the progressive prosperity of the world, and it amply repays all that it has received. It can only be employed in spreading civilization and enjoyment over the earth; and by the unchangeable laws of nature, in spite of the impotent tricks of government, it is now partly applied to revive the industry of those very nations who are the loudest in their senseless clamors against its pretended mischiefs. If the blind and barbarous project of destroying English prosperity could be accomplished, it could have no other effect than that of completely beggaring the very countries who now stupidly ascribe their own poverty to our wealth.

Under these circumstances, gentlemen, it became the obvious policy of the kingdom, a policy in unison with the maxims of a free government, to consider with great indulgence even the boldest animadversions of our political writers on the ambitious projects of foreign states.

Bold, and sometimes indiscreet as these animadversions might be, they had at least the effect of warning the people of their danger, and of rousing the national indignation against those encroachments which England has almost always been compelled in the end to resist by arms. Seldom, indeed, has she been allowed to wait till a provident regard to her own safety should compel her to take up arms in defense of others. For as it was said by a great orator of antiquity that no man ever was the enemy of the republic who had not first declared war against him, so I may say with truth that no man ever meditated the subjugation of Europe who did not consider the destruction or the corruption of England as the first condition of his success.

If you examine history you will find that no such project was ever formed in which it was not deemed a necessary preliminary either to detach England from the common cause or to destroy her. It seems as if all the conspirators against the independence of nations might have sufficiently taught other states that England is their natural guardian and protector; that she alone has no interest but their preservation; that her safety is interwoven with their own.

When vast projects of aggrandizement are manifested, when schemes of criminal ambition are carried into effect, the day of battle is fast approaching for England. Her free government cannot engage in dangerous wars without the hearty and affectionate support of her people. A state thus situated cannot without the utmost peril silence those public discussions which are to point the popular indignation against those who must soon be enemies. In domestic dissensions it may sometimes be the supposed interest of government to overawe the press. But it never can be even their apparent interest when the danger is purely foreign.

A king of England who in such circumstances should conspire against the free press of this country would undermine the foundations of his own throne; he would silence the trumpet which is to call his people round his standard.

Our ancestors never thought it their policy to avert the resentment of foreign tyrants by enjoining English writers to contain and repress their just abhorrence of the criminal enterprises of ambition. This great and gallant nation, which has fought in the front of every battle against the oppressors of Europe, has sometimes inspired fear, but, thank God, she has never felt it. We know that they are our real, and must soon become our declared foes. We know that there can be no cordial amity between the natural enemies and the independence of nations. We have never adopted the cowardly and short-sighted policy of silencing our press, of breaking the spirit and palsying the hearts of our people, for the sake of a hollow and precarious truce. We have never been base enough to purchase a short respite from hostilities by sacrificing the first means of defense,—the means of rousing the public spirit of the people and directing it against the enemies of their country and of Europe.

Gentlemen, the public spirit of a people, by which I mean the whole body of those affections which unite men's hearts to the commonwealth, is in various countries composed of various elements and depends on a great variety of causes. In this country I may venture to say that it mainly depends on the vigor of the popular parts and principles of our government, and that the sprit of liberty is one of its most important elements. Perhaps it may depend less on those advantages of a free government which are most highly estimated by calm reason than upon those parts of it which delight the imagination and flatter the just and natural pride of mankind.

Among these we are certainly not to forget the political rights which are not uniformly withheld from the lowest classes, and the continual appeal made to them in public discussion upon the greatest interests of the state. These are undoubtedly among the circumstances which endear to Englishmen their government and their country, and animate their zeal for that glorious institution which confers on the meanest of them a sort of distinction and nobility unknown to the most illustrious slaves who tremble at the frown of a tyrant.

Whoever were unwarily and rashly to abolish or narrow these privileges, which it must be owned are liable to great abuse and to very specious objections, might perhaps discover too late that he had been dismantling his country. Of whatever elements public spirit is composed, it is always and everywhere the chief defensive principle of a State. It is perfectly distinct from courage. Perhaps no nation, certainly no European nation, ever perished from an inferiority of courage. And undoubtedly no considerable nation was ever subdued in which the public affections were sound and vigorous. It is public spirit which binds together the dispersed courage of individuals and fastens it to the commonwealth.

It is, therefore, as I have said, the chief defensive principle of every country. Of all the stimulants which arouse it into action, the most powerful among us is certainly the press; and it cannot be restrained or weakened without imminent danger that the national spirit may languish, and that the people may act with less zeal and affection for their country in the hour of its danger.

These principles, gentlemen, are not new—they are genuine old English principles. And though in our days they have been disgraced and abused by ruffians and fanatics, they are in themselves as just and sound as they are liberal; and they are the only principles on which a free state can be safely governed. These principles I have adopted since I first learned the use of reason, and I think I shall abandon them only with life.

On these principles I am now to call your attention to the libel with which this unfortunate gentleman is charged. I heartily rejoice that I concur with the greatest part of what has been said by my learned friend, Mr. Attorney General, who has done honor even to his character by the generous and liberal principles which he has laid down. He has told you that he does not mean to attack historical narrative. He has told you that he does not mean to attack political discussion. He has told you, also, that he does not consider every intemperate word into which a writer, fairly engaged in narration or reasoning, might be betrayed, as a fit subject for prosecution.

The essence of the crime of libel consists in the malignant mind which the publication proves and from which it flows. A jury must be convinced, before they find a man guilty of libel, that his intention was to libel, not to state facts which he believed to be true, or reasonings which he thought just. My learned friend has told you that the liberty of history includes the right of publishing those observations which occur to intelligent men when they consider the affairs of the world; and I think he will not deny that it includes also the right of expressing those sentiments which all good men feel on the contemplation of extraordinary examples of depravity or excellence.

One more privilege of the historian, which the Attorney General has not named, but to which his principles extend, it is now my duty to claim on behalf of my client; I mean the right of republishing, historically, those documents, whatever their original malignity may be, which display the character and unfold the intentions of governments, or factions, or individuals.

I think my learned friend will not deny that a historical compiler may innocently republish in England the most insolent and outrageous declaration of war ever published against his Majesty by a foreign government. The intention of the original author was to vilify and degrade his Majesty's government; but the intention of the compiler is only to gratify curiosity, or, perhaps, to rouse just indignation against the calumniator whose production he republishes. His intention is not libelous; his republication is therefore not a libel. Suppose this to be the case with Mr. Peltier. Suppose him to have republished libels with a merely historical intention. In that case it cannot be pretended that he is more a libeler than my learned friend, Mr. Abbott, who read these supposed libels to you when he opened the pleadings. Mr. Abbott republished them to you, that you might know and judge of them: Mr. Peltier, on the supposition I have made, also republished them, that the public might know and judge of them.

You already know that the general plan of Mr. Peltier's publication was to give a picture of the cabals and intrigues, of the hopes and projects of French factions. It is undoubtedly a natural and necessary part of this plan to republish all the serious and ludicrous pieces which these factions circulate against each other. The ode ascribed to Chenier or Ginguene I do really believe to have been written at Paris, to have been circulated there, to have been there attributed to some one of these writers, to have been sent to England as their work, and as such to have been republished by Mr. Peltier. But I am not sure that I have evidence to convince you of the truth of this. Suppose that I have not; will my learned friend say that my client must necessarily be convicted? I, on the contrary, contend that it is for my learned friend to show that it is not a historical republication. Such it professes to be, and that profession it is for him to disprove. The profession may indeed be "a mask"; but it is for my friend to pluck off the mask and expose the libeler before he calls upon you for a verdict of guilty.

If the general lawfulness of such republications be denied, then I must ask Mr. Attorney General to account for the long impunity which English newspapers have enjoyed. I must request him to tell you why they have been suffered to republish all the atrocious official and unofficial libels which have been published against his Majesty for the last ten years by the Brissots, the Marats, the Dantons, the Robespierres, the Barreres, the Talliens, the Reubells, the Merlins, the Barrases, and all that long line of bloody tyrants who oppressed their own country and insulted every other which they had not the power to rob.

What must be the answer?

That the English publishers were either innocent, if their motive was to gratify curiosity; or praiseworthy, if their intention was to rouse indignation against the calumniators of their country. If any other answer be made, I must remind my friend of a most sacred part of his duty—the duty of protecting the honest fame of those who are absent in the service of their country.

Within these few days we have seen, in every newspaper in England, a publication, called the report of Colonel Sebastiani, in which a gallant British officer is charged with writing letters to procure assassination. The publishers of that infamous report are not and will not be prosecuted, because their intention is not to libel General Stuart.

On any other principle, why have all our newspapers been suffered to circulate that most atrocious of all libels against the king and people of England, which purports to be translated from the "Moniteur" of the 9th of August, 1802, a libel against a prince who has passed through a factious and stormy reign of forty-three years without a single imputation on his personal character; against a people who have passed through the severest trials of national virtue with unimpaired glory—who alone in the world can boast of mutinies without murder, of triumphant mobs without massacre, of bloodless revolutions, and of civil wars unstained by a single assassination.

That most impudent and malignant libel which charges such a king of such a people, not only with having hired assassins, but with being so shameless, so lost to all sense of character, as to have bestowed on these assassins, if their murderous projects had succeeded, the highest badges of public honor, the rewards reserved for statesmen and heroes,—the order of the Garter: the order which was founded by the heroes of Cressy and Poitiers; the garter which was worn by Henry the Great and Gustavus Adolphus; which might now be worn by the hero who, on the shores of Syria —the ancient theater of English chivalry— has revived the renown of English valor and of English humanity,—that unsullied garter which a detestable libeler dares to say is to be paid as the price of murder.

I am aware, gentlemen, that I have already abused your indulgence, but I must entreat you to bear with me for a short time longer, to allow me to suppose a case which might have occurred, in which you will see the horrible consequences of enforcing rigorously principles of law, which I cannot counteract, against political writers. We might have been at peace with France during the whole of that terrible period which elapsed between August, 1792 and 1794, which has been usually called the reign of Robespierre, the only series of crimes, perhaps, in history, which, in spite of the common disposition to exaggerate extraordinary facts, has been beyond measure underrated in public opinion.

I say this, gentlemen, after an investigation which I think entitles me to affirm it with confidence. Men's minds were oppressed by atrocity and the multitude of crimes; their humanity and their indolence took refuge in skepticism from such an overwhelming mass of guilt; and the consequence was that all these unparalleled enormities, though proved not only with the fullest historical but with the strictest judicial evidence, were at the time only half believed and are now scarcely half remembered.

When these atrocities were daily perpetrating, of which the greatest part are as little known to the public in general as the campaigns of Genghis Khan, but are still protected from the scrutiny of men by the immensity of those voluminous records of guilt in which they are related, and under the mass of which they will be buried till some historian be found with patience and courage enough to drag them forth into light, for the shame, indeed, but for the instruction of mankind— when these crimes were perpetrating, which had the peculiar malignity, from the pretexts with which they were covered, of making the noblest objects of human pursuit seem odious and detestable; which has almost made the names of liberty, reformation, and humanity synonymous with anarchy, robbery, and murder; which thus threatened not only to extinguish every principle of improvement, to arrest the progress of civilized society, and to disinherit future generations of that rich succession which they were entitled to expect from the knowledge and wisdom of the present, but to destroy the civilization of Europe, which never gave such a proof of its vigor and robustness as in being able to resist their destructive power —when all these horrors were acting in the greatest empire of the continent, I will ask my learned friend, if we had then been at peace with France, how English writers were to relate them so as to escape the charge of libeling a friendly government.

When Robespierre, in the debates in the national Convention on the mode of murdering their blameless sovereign, objected to the formal and tedious mode of murder called a trial, and proposed to put him immediately to death, "on the principles of insurrection," because to doubt the guilt of the king would be to doubt the innocence of the Convention; and if the king were not a traitor, the convention must be rebels; would my learned friend have had an English writer state all this with "decorum and moderation?" Would he have had an English writer state that though this reasoning was not perfectly agreeable to our national laws, or perhaps to our national prejudices, yet it was not for him to make any observations on the judicial proceedings of foreign states?

When Marat, in the same convention, called for two hundred and seventy thousand heads, must our English writers have said that the remedy did indeed seem to their weak judgment rather severe; but that it was not for them to judge the conduct of so illustrious an assembly as the National Convention, or the suggestions of so enlightened a statesman as M. Marat?

When that Convention resounded with applause at the news of several hundred aged priests being thrown into the Loire, and particularly at the exclamation of Carrier, who communicated the intelligence, "What a revolutionary torrent is the Loire,"—when these suggestions and narrations of murder, which have hitherto been only hinted and whispered in the most secret cabals, in the darkest caverns of banditti, were triumphantly uttered, patiently endured, and even loudly applauded by an assembly of seven hundred men, acting in the sight of all Europe, would my learned friend have wished that there had been found in England a single writer so base as to deliberate upon the most safe, decorous, and polite manner of relating all these things to his countrymen?

When Carrier ordered five hundred children under fourteen years of age to be shot, the greater part of whom escaped the fire from their size; when the poor victims ran for protection to the soldiers and were bayoneted clinging round their knees! —would my friend—but I cannot pursue the strain of interrogation. It is too much. It would be a violence which I cannot practice on my own feelings. It would be an outrage to my friend. It would be an insult to humanity. No! Better, ten thousand times better, would it be that every press in the world were burned; that the very use of letters were abolished; that we were returned to the honest ignorance of the rudest times, than that the results of civilization should be made subservient to the purposes of barbarism; than that literature should be employed to teach a toleration for cruelty, to weaken moral hatred for guilt, to deprave and brutalize the human mind. I know that I speak my friend's feelings as well as my own when I say God forbid that the dread of any punishment should ever make any Englishman an accomplice in so corrupting his countrymen, a public teacher of depravity and barbarity!

Mortifying and horrible as the idea is, I must remind you, gentlemen that even at that time, even under the reign of Robespierre, my learned friend, if he had then been Attorney General, might have been compelled by some most deplorable necessity to have come into this court to ask your verdict against the libelers of Barrere and Collot d' Herbois. Mr. Peltier then employed his talents against the enemies of the human race, as he has uniformly and bravely done. I do not believe that any peace, any political considerations, any fear of punishment would have silenced him. He has shown too much honor, and constancy and intrepidity, to be shaken by such circumstances as these.

My learned friend might then have been compelled to have filed a criminal information against Mr. Peltier for "wickedly and maliciously intending to vilify and degrade Maximilian Robespierre, President of the Committee of Public Safety of the French Republic!" He might have been reduced to the sad necessity of appearing before you to belie his own better feelings, to prosecute Mr. Peltier for publishing those sentiments which my friend himself had a thousand times felt, and a thousand times expressed. He might have been obliged even to call for punishment upon Mr. Peltier for language which he and all mankind would forever despise Mr. Peltier if he were not to employ. Then, indeed, gentlemen, we should have seen the last humiliation fall on England; the tribunals, the spotless and venerable tribunals of this free country reduced to be the ministers of the vengeance of Robespierre! What could have rescued us from this last disgrace? The honesty and courage of a jury. They would have delivered the judges of this country from the dire necessity of inflicting punishment on a brave and virtuous man because he spoke truth of a monster. They would have despised the threats of a foreign tyrant, as their ancestors braved the power of oppression at home.

In the court where we are now met, Cromwell twice sent a satirist on his tyranny to be convicted and punished as a libeler; and in this court, almost in sight of the scaffold streaming with the blood of his sovereign, within hearing of the clash of his bayonets which drove out Parliament with contumely, two successive juries rescued the intrepid satirist from his fangs, and sent out with defeat and disgrace the usurper's Attorney General from what he had the insolence to call his court!

Even then, gentlemen, when all law and liberty were trampled under the feet of a military banditti; when those great crimes were perpetrated on a high place and with a high hand against those who were the objects of public veneration, which, more than anything else, break their spirits and confound their moral sentiments, obliterate the distinctions between right and wrong in their understanding, and teach the multitude to feel no longer any reverence for that justice which they thus see triumphantly dragged at the chariot-wheels of a tyrant; even then, when this unhappy country, triumphant, indeed, abroad, but enslaved at home, had no prospect but that of a long succession of tyrants wading through slaughter to a throne,—even then, I say, when all seemed lost, the unconquerable spirit of English liberty survived in the hearts of English jurors. That Spirit is, I trust in God, not extinct; and if any modern tyrant were, in the drunkenness of his insolence, to hope to overawe an English jury, I trust and I believe that they would tell him, "Our ancestors braved the bayonets of Cromwell; we bid defiance to yours." "Contempsi Catilinae gladios—non pertimescam tuos!" [I have held the daggers of Cataline in contempt; I shall not fear yours.]

What could be such a tyrant's means of overawing a jury? As long as their country exists they are girt round with impenetrable armor. Till the destruction of their country, no danger can fall upon them for the performance of their duty, and I do trust that there is no Englishman so unworthy of life as to desire to outlive England. But if any of us are condemned to the cruel punishment of surviving our country; if, in the inscrutable councils of Providence, this favored seat of justice and liberty, this noblest work of human wisdom and virtue, be destined to destruction, which I shall not be charged with national prejudice for saying would be the most dangerous wound ever inflicted on civilization; at least let us carry with us into our sad exile the consolation that we ourselves have not violated the rights of hospitality to exiles, that we have not torn from the altar the suppliant who claimed protection as the voluntary victim of loyalty and conscience.

Gentlemen, I now leave this unfortunate gentleman in your hands. His character and his situation might interest your humanity; but on his behalf I only ask justice from you. I only ask a favorable construction of what cannot be said to be more than ambiguous language, and this you will soon be told, from the highest authority, is a part of justice.

[Despite this eloquence, the jury found Peltier guilty. However, since England and France were soon at war again, Peltier was not punished.]

## HELEN STEWART (1765–1838)

### The Tears I Shed Must Ever Fall

The tears I shed must ever fall.
I weep not for an absent swain,
For time may happier hours recall,
And parted lovers meet again.

I weep not for the silent dead.
Their pains are past, their sorrows oer,
And those they loved their steps shall tread,
And death shall join to part no more.

Though boundless oceans roll between,
If certain that his heart is near,
A conscious transport glads each scene,
Soft is the sigh and sweet the tear.

E'en when by death's cold hand removed,
We mourn the tenant of the tomb,
To think that e'en in death he loved,
Can gild the horrors of the gloom.

But bitter, bitter are the tears
Of her who slighted love bewails.

No hope her dreary prospect cheers,
No pleasing melancholy hails.

Hers are the pangs of wounded pride,
Of blasted hope, of withered joy.
The flattering veil is rent aside;
The flame of love burns to destroy.

In vain does memory renew
The hours once tinged in transport's dye.
The sad reverse soon starts to view,
And turns the past to agony.

E'en time itself despairs to cure
Those pangs to every feeling due.
Ungenerous youth, thy boast how poor,
To win a heart—and break it too.

No cold approach, no altered mien,
Just what would make suspicion start;
No pause the dire extremes between,
He made me blest—and broke my heart.

From hope, the wretched's anchor, torn,
Neglected and neglecting all;
Friendless, forsaken and forlorn
The tears I shed must ever fall.

## ALEXANDER WILSON (?1765–1813)

### The Laurel Disputed

Delivered in the Pantheon, at Edinburgh, on Thursday, April 14, 1791, on the question — "Whether have the exertions of Allan Ramsay or Robert Fergusson done more honor to Scottish Poetry?"

Before ye a' hae done, I'd humbly crave
To speak twa words or three amang the lave*; rest
No for mysel, but for an honest carl* peasant, fellow
Wha's seen richt mony changes i' the warl',
But is sae blate*, down here he durstna come, shy
Lest, as he said, his fears might ding* him dumb; strike
And then he's frail—sae begged me to repeat
His simple thoughts about this fell debate.
He gi'ed me this lang scroll; tis e'en right brown.
I'se let you hear't as he has set it down.
Last ouk* our Elspa, wi' some creels o' eggs, week
And three fat earocks* fastent by the legs, young fowls
Gaed down to Embrugh; caft* a new bane kaim, bought
And brought a warl' o' news and clashes* hame. gossip
For she's scarce out a day, and gets a text,
But I'm dung deaf wi' clatter a' the next.

She'll tell a' what she heard frae en' to en',
Her cracks* to wives, wives' cracks to her again;   chatter
Till wi' quo I's, quo she's, and so's, her skirl
Sets my twa lugs* a-ringing like a gir'le.   ears
Mang ither ferlies* whilk my kimmers* saw,   wonders/pals
Was your prent paper batter't on the wa'.
She said she kentna rightly what it meant,
But saw some words o' gowd and poets in't.
This gart* me glower; sae aff sets I my lane*,   made/alone
To Daniel Reid's, an auld frien' o' my ain.
He gets the *News,* and tald me that ye'd hecht*,   promised
A daud o' gowd, on this same Fursday nicht,
To him wha'd show, in clinking verses drest,
Gin Ramsay's sangs, or Fergusson's were best.
Troth, I was glad to hear ye war sae kind
As keep our slee-tongued billies in your mind;
And though our Elspa ca'd me mony a gowk*   cuckoo (fool)
To think to speak amang sae mony folk,
I gat my staff, pat on my bonnet braid,
And best blue breeks, that war but fernyear* made;   last year
A saxpence too, to let me in bedene*,   right away
And thir auld spentacles to help my een;
Sae I'm come here, in houps ye'll a' agree
To hear a frank auld kintra man like me.
In days whan Dryden sang ilk bonnie morn,
And Sandy Pope began to tune his horn,
Whan chiels* round Lon'on chanted a' fu' thrang,   fellows
But poor auld Scotland sat without a sang,
Droll Will Dunbar frae flyting[1] than was freed,
And Douglas too, and Kennedy were dead,
And nane were left in hamely cracks to praise
Our ain sweet lasses, or our ain green braes;
Far aff our gentles for their poets flew,
And scorned to own that Lallan* sangs they knew;   "Lowland"
Till Ramsay rase. O blithesome, hearty days,
When Allan tuned his chanter on the braes!
Auld Reekie than, frae blackest, darkest wa's,
To richest rooms, resounded his applause;
And whan the nights were dreary, lang, and dark,
The beasts a' fother't and the lads frae wark,
The lasses wheels thrang birring* round the ingle*,   whirring/fireplace
The plowman borin' wi' his brogs* and lingle*,   awl/thread
The herd's wires clicking ower the half-wrought hose,
The auld gudeman's e'en halflins like to close,
The "Gentle Shepherd" frae the bole* was ta'en:—   nook
Than sleep, I trow, was banished frae their e'en;
The crankiest than was kittled up to daffin'*,   fooling, gaiety
And sides and chafts* maist riven were wi' laughin'.   jaws
Sic war the joys his cracks could eith* afford   easily
To peer or plowman, barrowman or lord;

---

[1] (Literary) scoldings or disputes.

In ilka clachan* wife, man, wean, and callan* — village/boy
Crackit and sang frae morn to e'en o' Allan.
Learned folk, that lang in colleges and schools
Hae sookit learning to the vera hools*, — husks
And think that naething charms the heart sae weel's
Lang cracks o' gods, Greeks, Paradise, and deils;
Their pows* are cram't sae fu' o' lear and art, — heads
Plain simple nature canna reach their heart;
But whare's the rustic that can, readin', see
Sweet Peggy skippin' ower the dewy lea,
Or, wishfu', stealin' up the sunny howe
To gaze on Pate, laid sleeping on the knowe;
Or hear how Bauldy ventured to the deil,
How thrawn auld carlins skelpit* him afiel', — beat
How Jude wi's hawk met Satan i' the moss,
How Skinflint grain't his pocks o' gowd to loss,
How bloody snouts and bloody beards war gi'en
To smiths and clowns at Christ's Kirk on the Green,
How twa daft herds, wi' little sense or havings,
Dined by the road on honest Hawkie's leavings,
How Hab maist brak the priest's back wi' a rung,
How deathless Addie died, and how he sung;—
Whae'er can thae (o' mae I needna speak)
Read tenty* ower at his ain ingle-cheek, — careful
And no fin' something glowin' through his blood,
That gars his een glower through a siller flood,
May close the buik, poor cuif*! and lift his spoon, — fool
His heart's as hard's the tackets in his shoon.
Lang saxty years hae whiten't ower this pow,
And mony a height I've seen, and mony a howe,
But aye when Elspa flate*, or things gaed wrang, — scolded
Next to my pipe was Allie's sleekit sang.
I thought him blither ilka time I read,
And mony a time wi' unco glee I've said
That ne'er in Scotland wad a chiel appear
Sae droll, sae hearty, sae confoundit queer,
Sae glibly-gabbit*, or sae bauld again;— — mouthed
I said, I swore't, but 'deed I was mista'en.
Up frae auld Reekie Fergusson begoud,
In fell* auld phrase that pleases aye the crowd, — strong
To cheer their hearts whiles wi' an antrin* sang, — rare
Whilk far and near round a' the kintra rang.
At first I thought the swankie* didna ill; — young blade
Again I glower't to hear him better still.
Bauld, slee, and sweet, his lines mair glorious grew,
Glowed round the heart, and glanced the soul out through.
But whan I saw the freaks o' Hallow Fair
Brought a' to view as plain as I'd been there,
And heard, wi' teeth maist chatterin' i' my head,
Twa kirkyard ghaists raised goustly frae the dead;
Dazed Sandy greetin' for the thriftless wife,
How camsheugh* Sammy had been fed in Fife, — crooked
Poor Will and Geordy mournin' for their frien',

The Farmer's Ingle, and the cracks at e'en,
My heart cried out, while tears war drappin' fast,
O Ramsay, Ramsay, art thou beat at last?
Ae night the lift was skinklin' a' wi' starns,
I crossed the burn, and dauner't through the cairns
Down to auld Andrew Ralston's o' Craigneuk,
To hear his thoughts, as he had seen the buik.
Andrew's a gey droll haun',—ye'll aiblins ken him?—
It maks na, I had hecht* some sangs to len' him. promised
"Aweel," quo I, as soon's I reek't the hallan*, partition
"What think ye now o' our bit Embrugh callan?"
"Saf's man!" quo Andrew, "yon's an unco chiel!
He surely has some dealings wi' the deil!
There' no a turn that ony o' us can work at,
At hame, or yet afiel', at kirk, or market,
But he describes't as pawkily* and fell cleverly
As gin he'd been a kintra man himsel'.
Yestreen, I'm sure, beside our auld gudewife,
I never leugh as meikle a' my life,
To read the King's birthday's fell hurry-burry—
How draigle't pussy flies about like fury.
Faith! I ken that's a fact: the last birthday,
As I stood glowerin' up and down the way,
A dead cat's guts, before I could suspec',
Harl't* through the dirt, cam' clash about my neck; dragged
And while, wi' baith my hauns, frae bout I took it,
Wi' perfect stink I thought I wad hae bockit*. vomited
His stories, too, are tell't sae sleek and baul',
Ilk oily word rins jinking through the saul;
What he describes, before your e'en ye see't
As plain and lively as ye see that peat.
It's my opinion, John, that this young fallow
Excels them a', and beats auld Allan hallow,
And shows, at twenty-twa, as great a giftie
For painting just, as Allan did at fifty."
You, Mr. President, ken weel yoursel',
Better by far than kintra folks can tell,
That they wha reach the gleg*, auldfarrant art sharp
In verse to melt and soothe and mend the heart—
To raise up joy, or rage, or courage keen,
And gar ilk passion sparkle in our een—
Sic chiels, whare'er they hae their ha' or hame,
Are true-blue bards, and wordy o' the name.
Sould ane o' thae, by lang experience, man,
To spin out tales frae mony a pawky plan,
And set's a' laughing at his blauds* o' rhyme, large lots
Wi' songs aft polished by the haun o' Time;
And should some stripling, still mair light o' heart,
A livelier humor to his cracks impart;
Wi' careless pencil draw, yet gar us stare,
To see our ain firesides and meadows there—
To see our thoughts, our hearts, our follies drawn,
And Nature's sel fresh starting frae his haun—

Wad mony words, or speeches lang, be needed
To tell whase rhymes war best, wha clearest-headed
Sits there within the four wa's o' this house,
Ae chield o' taste, droll, reprobate, or douce*, sober
Whase blessed lugs* hae heard young Rob himsel'— ears
Light as the lamb wha dances on the dell—
Lay aff his auld Scots crack wi' pawky glee,
And seen the fire that darted frae his e'e;
O let him speak! O let him try t'impart
The joys that than gushed headlang on his heart,
Whan ilka line, and ilka langsyne glower
Sets faes and friends and Pantheons in a roar!
Did e'er auld Scotland fin' a nobler pride
Through a' her veins and glowin' bosom glide,
Than when her Muse's dear young fav'rite bard,
Wi' her hale strength o' wit and fancy fired,
Rase frae the thrang, and kindlin' at the sound,
Spread mirth, conviction, truth, and rapture round?
To set Rob's youth and inexperience by,—
His lines are sweeter, and his flights mair high.
Allan, I own, may show far mair o' art,
Rob pours at once his raptures on the heart.
The first by labor mans* our breast to move, manages
The last exalts to ecstasy and love.
In Allan's verse sage sleeness we admire,
In Rob's the glow of fancy and of fire,
And genius bauld, that nought but deep distress,
And base neglect, and want, could e'er suppress.
O hard, hard fate!—but cease, thou friendly tear!
I daurna mourn my dear-lo'ed Bardie here,
Else I might tell how his great soul had soared.
And nameless ages wondered and adored,
Had friends been kind, and had not his young breath
And rising glory been eclipsed by death.
But lest ower lang I lengthen out my crack,
And Epps be wearying for my coming back,
Let ane and a' here vote as they incline;
Frae heart and saul Rob Fergusson has mine.

## Watty and Meg
### Or, the Wife Reformed

Keen the frosty winds were blawing,
Deep the snaw had wreathed the plows,
Watty, wearied a' day sawing,
Daunert* down to Mungo Blue's. sauntered

Dryster Jock was sitting cracky*, chummy
Wi' Pate Tamson o' the Hill.
"Come awa," quo Johnny, "Watty,
Haith we'se hae anither gill*." glass

Watty, glad to see Jock Jabos,
And sae mony neighbors roun',
Kicket frae his shoon the snawba's,
Syne ayont* the fire sat down. beside

Owre a broad, wi' bannocks heapet,
Cheese, and stoups*, and glasses stood; beakers
Some were roaring, ithers sleepit,
Ithers quietly chewt their cud.

Jock was selling Pate some tallow,
A' the rest a racket hel',
A' but Watty, wha, poor fallow,
Sat and smoket by himsel.

Mungo filled him up a toothfu',
Drank his health and Meg's in ane.
Watty, puffing out a mouthfu',
Pledged him wi' a dreary grane*. groan

"What's the matter, Watty, wi' you?
Trouth your chafts* are fa'ing in. cheeks
Something's wrang—I'm vexed to see you—
Gudesake, but ye're desp'rate thin."

"Ay," quo Watt, "things are altered,
But it's past redemption now.
Lord, I wish I had been haltered
When I married Maggy Howe.

"I've been poor, and vexed, and raggy,
Tried wi' troubles no that sma.
Them I bore—but marrying Maggy
Laid the capstane o' them a'.

"Night and day she's ever yelping.
With the weans she ne'er can gree*. "agree"
When she's tired with perfect skelping*, abusing
Then she flees like fire on me.

"See ye, Mungo, when she'll clash on
With her everlasting clack,
Whiles* I've had my neive* in passion sometimes/fist
Liftet up to break her back."

"O, for gudesake, keep frae cuffets,"
Mungo shook his head and said,
"Weel I ken what sort of life it's.
Ken ye, Watty, how I did?

"After Bess and I were kippled,
Soon she grew like ony bear,

Brak my shins, and when I tippled,
Harl't out my very hair.

"For a wee* I quietly knuckled,     while
But whan naething would prevail,
Up my claes* and cash I buckled,—     "clothes"
'Bess, for ever fare-ye-weel.'

"Then her din grew less and less aye,
Haith I gart* her change her tune.     made
Now a better wife than Bessy
Never stept in leather shoon.

"Try this, Watty—When you see her
Raging like a roaring flood,
Swear that moment that ye'll lea' her,—
That's the way to keep her good."

Laughing, sangs, and lasses' skirls
Echoed now out-through the roof.
"Done," quo Pate, and syne his erls*     advance money
Nailed the Dryster's wauked loof*.     hand

In the thrang of stories telling,
Shaking hauns, and ither cheer,
Swith*, a chap comes on the hallan*,     quick/passage
"Mungo, is our Watty here?"

Maggy's weel kent tongue and hurry
Darted through him like a knife,
Up the door flew—like a fury
In came Watty's scawling wife.

"Nasty, gude-for-naething being!
O ye snuffy, drunken sow!
Bringing wife and weans to ruin,
Drinking here wi' sic a crew!

"Devil nor your legs were broken,
Sic a life nae flesh endures,
Toiling like a slave to sloken
You, ye dyvor*, and your whores.     bankrupt

"Rise, ye drucken beast o' Bethel.
Drink's your night and day's desire.
Rise, this precious hour, or faith I'll
Fling your whiskey i' the fire."

Watty heard her tongue unhallowed,
Paid his groat* wi' little din,     (small coin)
Left the house, while Maggy fallowed,
Flyting* a' the road behin'.     scolding

Fowk frae every door came lamping,
Maggy curst them ane and a',
Clappet wi' her hands, and stamping,
Lost her bauchles i' the sna'*. "snow"

Hame, at length, she turned the gavel,
Wi' a face as white's a clout,
Raging like a very devil,
Kicking stools and chairs about.

"Ye'll sit wi' your limmers* round you. bawds
Hang you, sir, I'll be your death.
Little hands my hands, confound you,
But I'll cleave you to the teeth."

Watty, wha, midst this oration,
Eyed her whiles but durstna speak,
Sat like patient Resignation,
Trem'ling by the ingle* cheek. fireplace

Sad his wee drap brose he sippet,
Maggy's tongue gaed like a bell,
Quietly to his bed he slippet,
Sighing aften to himsel:

"Nane are free frae some vexation,
Ilk ane has his ills to dree*; suffer
But through a' the hale creation
Is a mortal vext like me?"

A' night lang he rowt and gaunted, yawned
Sleep or rest he couldna tak;
Maggy aft wi' horror haunted,
Mumling started at his back.

Soon as e'er the morning peepit,
Up raise Watty, waefu' chiel*, fellow
Kist his weanies, while they sleepet,
Waukened Meg, and sought farewell.

"Farewell, Meg—and, O may heav'n
Keep you aye within his care.
Watty's heart ye've lang been grievin,
Now he'll never fash* you mair. trouble

"Happy could I been beside you,
Happy baith at morn and e'en.
A' the ills did e'er betide you,
Watty aye turned out your frien'.

"But ye ever like to see me
Vext and sighing, late and air.

Farewell, Meg. I've sworn to lea' thee,
So thou'll never see me mair."

Mag, a' sabbing, sae to lose him,
Sic a change had never wist,
Held his hand close to her bosom,
While her heart was like to burst.

"O my Watty, will ye lea' me,
Frien'less, helpless, to despair.
O, for this ae time forgi'e me.
Never will I vex you mair."

"Ay, ye've aft said that, and broken
A' your vows ten times a week.
No, no, Meg, see, there's a token
Glittering on my bonnet cheek.

"Owre the seas I march this morning,
Listed*, tested, sworn and a', "enlisted"
Forced by your confounded girning*— grimacing
Farewell, Meg, for I'm awa."

Then poor Maggy's tears and clamor
Gushed afresh, and louder grew,
While the weans, wi' mournfu' yaumor,
Round their sabbing mother flew.

"Through the yirth I'll wauner wi' you—
Stay, O Watty, stay at hame.
Here, upon my knees, I'll gi'e you
Ony vow you like to name.

"See your poor young lammies pleadin',
Will ye gang and break our heart?
No a house to put our head in,
No a friend to take our part."

Ilka word came like a bullet.
Watty's heart begoud to shake.
On a kist* he laid his wallet, chest
Dighted* baith his een and spake. wiped

"If ance mair I cold by writing
Lea' the sogers and stay still,
Wad you swear to drap your flyting?"
"Yes, O Watty, yes, I will."

"Then," quo Watty, "mind, be honest.
Aye to keep your temper strive.
Gin ye break this dreadfu' promise,
Never mair expect to thrive.

"Marget Howe, this hour ye solemn
Swear by every thing that's gude,
Ne'er again your spouse to scal' him,
While life warms your heart and blood.

"That ye'll ne'er in Mungo's seek me—
Ne'er put "drucken" to my name—
Never out at e'ening steek* me— shut
Never gloom when I come hame.

"That ye'll ne'er, like Bessy Miller,
Kick my shins or rug* my hair— yank
Lastly, I'm to keep the siller.
This upon your saul you swear?"

"O——h," quo Meg, "Aweel," quo Watty,
"Farewell, faith I'll try the seas."
"O stand still," quo Meg, and grat* aye, wept
"Ony, ony way ye please."

Maggy syne, because he prest her,
Swore to a' thing owre again.
Watty lap*, and danced, and kist her. leapt
Wow, but he was won'rous fain.

## A Peddler's Story

I wha stand here in this bare scowry coat,
Was ance a packman, worth mony a groat;
I've carried packs as big's your meikle table.
I've scarted* pats and sleepit in a stable. scraped (for food)
Sax pounds I wadna for my pack ance taen,
And I could bauldly brag twas a' mine ain.
Ay, thae were days indeed that garred* me hope, made
Aiblins*, through time to warsle up a shop. perhaps
And as a wife aye in my noddle ran,
I kenned my Kate wad grapple at me than.
Oh, Kate was past compare. Sic cheeks, sic een!
Sic smiling looks were never, never seen.
Dear, dear I lo'ed her, and whene'er we met,
Pleaded to have the bridal day but set;
Stapped her pouches fu' o' preens and laces,
And thought myself weel paid wi' twa three kisses.
Yet still she put it aff frae day to day,
And aften kindly in my lug* would say, ear
"Ae half year langer's no nae unco* stop, unusual
We'll marry then, and syne set up a shop."
Oh, sir, but lasses' words are saft and fair,
They soothe our griefs and banish ilka* care. every
Wha wadna toil to please the lass he lo'es?
A lover true minds this in all he does.
Finding her mind was thus sae firmly bent,

And that I couldna get her to relent,
There was nought left but quietly to resign,
To heeze* my pack for ae lang, hard campaign; lift
And as the Highlands was the place for meat,
I ventured there in spite o' wind and weet.

Cauld now the winter blew, and deep the snaw
For three hale days incessantly did fa';
Far in a muir, amang the whirling drift,
Where nought was seen but mountains and the lift*, sky
I lost my road, and wandered mony a mile,
Maist dead wi' hunger, cauld, and fright, and toil.
Thus wandering, east or west, I kenned na where,
My mind oercome wi' gloom and black despair,

Wi' a fell ringe I plunged at once, forsooth,
Down through a wreath o' snaw up to my mouth—
Clean ower my head my precious wallet flew,
But whar it gaed, Lord kens—I never knew.
What great misfortunes are poured down on some:
I thought my fearfu' hinder-end was come.
Wi' grief and sorrow was my saul owercast,
Ilk breath I drew was like to be my last;
For aye the mair I warsled roun' and roun',
I fand mysel aye stick the deeper down;
Till ance, at length, wi' a prodigious pull,
I drew my puir cauld carcass frae the hole.
Lang, lang I sought and graped for my pack,
Till night and hunger forced me to come back.
For three lang hours I wandered up and down,
Till chance at last conveyed me to a town.
There, wi' a trembling hand, I wrote my Kate
A sad account of a' my luckless fate,
But bade her aye be kind, and no despair,
Since life was left, I soon would gather mair,
Wi' whilk I hoped, within a towmont's date
To be at hame, and share it a' wi' Kate.
Fool that I was, how little did I think
That love would soon be lost for faut o' clink.
The loss o' fair-won wealth, though hard to bear,
Afore this—ne'er had power to force a tear.
I trusted time would bring things round again,
And Kate, dear Kate, would then be a' mine ain,
Consoled my mind in hopes o' better luck—
But, oh what sad reverse, how thunderstruck,
When ae black day brought word frae Rab my brither,
That—Kate was cried and married on anither.

Though a' my friends, and ilka comrade sweet,
At ance had drapped cauld dead at my feet;
Or though I'd heard the last day's dreadful ca',
Nae deeper horror ower my heart could fa'.
I cursed mysel, I cursed my luckless fate,

And grat*—and sabbing cried, Oh Kate, oh Kate! wept
Frae that day forth I never mair did weel,
But drank, and ran head foremost to the deil.
My siller vanished, far frae hame I pined,
But Kate for ever ran across my mind.
In her were a' my hopes—these hopes were vain,
And now I'll never see her like again.

## Rab and Ringan[1]

### A Tale

#### Introduction

Hech, but its awfu' like to rise up here,
Where sic a sight o' learned folks' pows* appear. heads
Sae mony piercing een a' fixed on ane
Is maist enough to freeze me to a stane.
But it's a mercy—mony thanks to fate,
Peddlers are poor, but unco* seldom blate*. very/shy

(Speaking to the President)

This question, sir, has been right well disputed,
And meikle weel-a-wat's been said about it;
Chiels*, that precisely to the point can speak, fellows
And gallop oer lang blauds* of kittle* Greek, globs/ticklish
Hae sent frae ilka side their sharp opinion,
And peeled it up as ane wad peel an ingon.
I winna plague you lang wi' my poor spale,
But only crave your patience to a tale,
By which ye'll ken on whatna side I'm stanin'
As I perceive your hindmost minute's rinnin'.

#### The Tale

There lived in Fife an auld, stout, worldly chiel*, fellow
Wha's stomach kenned nae fare but milk and meal.
A wife he had, I think they ca'd her Bell,
And twa big sons, amaist as heigh's himsel.
Rab was a gleg*, smart cock, with powdered pash*; sharp/head
Ringan, a slow, feared, bashfu', simple hash.

Baith to the college gaed. At first spruce Rab
At Greek and Latin grew a very dab.
He beat a' round about him, fair and clean,
And ilk ane courted him to be their frien'.
Frae house to house they harled him to dinner,
But cursed poor Ringan for a hum-drum sinner.

---

[1]In an Edinburgh debate on the question, "Whether is diffidence or the allurements of pleasure the greatest bar to the progress in knowledge?" Wilson was the last speaker.

Rab talked now in sic a lofty strain,
As though braid Scotland had been a' his ain.
He ca'd the kirk the church, the yirth the globe,
And changed his name, forsooth, frae Rab to Bob.
Whare'er ye met him flourishing his rung*, — cudgel
The hail discourse was murdered wi' his tongue.
On friends and faes wi' impudence he set,
And rammed his nose in everything he met.

The college now to Rab grew douf* and dull, — weary
He scorned wi' books to stupefy his skull,
But whirled to plays and balls, and sic like places,
And roared awa at fairs and kintra races;
Sent hame for siller frae his mother Bell,
And caft a horse, and rade a race himsel.
Drank day and night, and syne, when mortal fu',
Rowed on the floor, and snored like ony sow;
Lost a' his siller wi' some gambling sparks,
And pawned, for punch, his Bible and his sarks*; — shirts
Till driven at last to own he had eneugh,
Gaed hame a' rags to haud his father's plow.

Poor hum-drum Ringan played anither part,
For Ringan wanted neither wit nor art;
Of mony a far-aff place he kent the gate*; — way
Was deep, deep learned, but unco, unco blate.
He kend how mony mile twas to the moon,
How mony rake wad lave the ocean toom*; — empty
Where a' the swallows gaed in time of snaw;
What gars the thunders roar, and tempests blaw;
Where lumps o' siller grow aneath the grun';
How a' this yirth rows round about the sun;
In short, on books sae meikle time he spent,
Ye couldna's speak o' aught, but Ringan kent.

Sae meikle learning wi' sae little pride,
Soon gained the love o' a' the kintra side;
And Death, at that time, happening to nip aff
The parish minister—a poor, dull calf,
Ringan was sought—he couldna say them nay,
And there he's preaching at this very day.

Moral

Now, Mr. President, I think tis plain,
That a youthfu' diffidence is certain gain.
Instead of blocking up the road to knowledge,
It guides alike, in commerce or at college;
Struggles the bursts of passion to control,
Feeds all the finer feelings of the soul;
Defies the deep-laid stratagems of guile,
And gives even innocence a sweeter smile;
Ennobles all the little worth we have,

And shields our virtue even to the grave.
How vast the difference, then, between the twain,
Since pleasure ever is pursued by pain.
Pleasure's a siren, with inviting arms,
Sweet is her voice and powerful are her charms.
Lured by her call we tread her flowery ground,
Joy wings our steps and music warbles round,
Lulled in her arms we lose the flying hours,
And lie embosomed 'midst her blooming bowers,
Till—armed with death, she watches our undoing,
Stabs while she sings, and triumphs in our ruin.

### Connel and Flora

Dark lowers the night oer the wide stormy main,
Till mild rosy morning rise cheerful again.
Alas, morn returns to revisit the shore,
But Connel returns to his Flora no more.

For see, on yon mountain, the dark cloud of death,
Oer Connel's lone cottage, lies low on the heath;
While bloody and pale, on a far distant shore,
He lies, to return to his Flora no more.

Ye light fleeting spirits, that glide oer the steep,
Oh, would ye but waft me across the wild deep.
There fearless I'd mix in the battle's loud roar,
I'd die with my Connel, and leave him no more.

## CAROLINA OLIPHANT, LADY NAIRNE (1766–1845)

### The Laird o' Cockpen

The Laird o' Cockpen, he's proud an' he's great,
His mind is ta'en up wi' thing o' the State:
He wanted a wife, his braw house to keep;
But favor wi' wooin' was fashous* to seek. troublesome

Down by the dyke-side a lady did dwell;
At his table-head he thought she'd look well—
McClish's ae daughter o' Claverse-ha' Lee,
A penniless lass wi' a lang pedigree.

His wig was weel pouthered and as gude as new;
His waistcoat was white, his coat it was blue:
He put on a ring, a sword, and cocked hat,—
And wha could refuse the Laird wi' a' that?

He took the gray mare, and rade cannily,
An' rapped at the yett* o' Claverse-ha' Lee: gate
"Gae tell Mistress Jean to come speedily ben*, in
She's wanted to speak to the Laird o' Cockpen."

Mistress Jean was makin' the elder-flower wine:
"And what brings the Laird at sic a like time?"
She put aff her apron and on her silk goun,
Her mutch* wi' red ribbons, and gaed awa doun. cap

And when she cam' ben he bowed fu' low;
An' what was his errand he soon let her know.
Amazed was the Laird when the lady said "Na";
And wi' a laigh* curtsey she turned awa. low

Dumbfoundered was he; nae sigh did he gie,
He mounted his mare, he rade cannily;
And aften he thought as he gaed through the glen,
"She's daft to refuse the Laird o' Cockpen!"

## The Lass o' Gowrie

Twas on a simmer's afternoon,
A wee afore the sun gaed doun,
A lassie wi' a braw new goun
Cam' owre the hills to Gowrie.
The rosebud washed in simmer's shower
Bloomed fresh within the sunny bower;
But Kitty was the fairest flower
That e'er was seen in Gowrie.

To see her cousin she cam' there;
And oh the scene was passing fair,
For what in Scotland can compare
Wi' the Carse o' Gowrie?
The sun was setting on the Tay,
The blue hills melting into gray,
The mavis and the blackbird's lay
Were sweetly heard in Gowrie.

O long the lassie I had wooed,
And truth and constancy had vowed,
But cam' nae speed wi' her I lo'ed
Until she saw fair Gowrie.
I pointed to my faither's ha'—
Yon bonnie bield* ayont* the shaw* shelter/beyond/wood
Sae lown* that there nae blast could blaw:— protected
Wad she no bide in Gowrie?

Her faither was baith glad and wae;
Her mither she wad naething say;
The bairnies thocht they wad get play
If Kitty gaed to Gowrie.
She whiles did smile, she whiles did greet*; weep
The blush and tear were on her cheek;
She naething said, and hung her head;—
But now she's Leddy Gowrie.

## The White Rose o' June[1]

Now the bricht sun, and the soft simmer showers,
Deck a' the woods and the gardens wi' flowers;
But bonnie and sweet though the hale o' them be,
There's ane abune a' that is dearest to me;
And O that's the white rose, the white rose o' June,
And may he that should wear it come back again soon.

It's no on my breast, nor yet in my hair
That the emblem dear I venture to wear;
But it blooms in my heart, and its white leaves I weet,
When alane in the gloamin' I wander to greet*, weep
Oer the white rose, the white rose, the white rose o' June;
And may he that should wear it come back again soon.

Mair fragrant and rich the red rose may be,
But there is nae spell to bind it to me;
But dear to my heart and to fond memory,
Though scathed and though blighted the white rose may be.
O the white rose, the white rose, the white rose o' June,
O may he that should wear it come back again soon.

And oh may the true hearts thy perils who share,
Remembered wi' tears and remembered in prayer,
Whom misfortune's rude blast has sent far awa',
Fair breezes bring back soon to cottage and ha';—
Then O sing the white rose, the white rose o' June,
And may he that should wear it wear Scotland's auld croun.

## The Land o' the Leal

I'm wearin' awa', John,
Like snaw-wreaths in thaw, John—
I'm wearin' awa'
To the land o' the leal*. true
There's nae sorrow there, John;
There's neither cauld nor care, John—
The day is aye fair
In the land o' the leal.

Our bonnie bairn's there, John;
She was baith guid and fair, John;
And, oh! we grudged her sair
To the land o' the leal.
But sorrow's sel wears past, John,
And joy is coming fast, John—
The joy that's aye to last
In the land o' the leal.

---

[1] The white rose is the sign of the Jacobites. "He that should wear it" is Bonnie Prince Charlie.

Ye were aye leal and true, John;
Your task's ended now, John,
And I'll welcome you
To the land o' the leal.
Now fare-ye-weel, my ain John:
This warld's cares are vain, John;—
We'll meet and we'll be fain* — happy
In the land o' the leal.

## Caller Herrin'

Wha'll buy my caller* herrin'? — fresh
They're bonnie fish and halesome farin';
Wha'll buy my caller herrin',
New drawn frae the Forth?

When ye were sleepin' on your pillows,
Dreamed ye aught o' our puir fellows—
Darkling as they faced the billows,
A' to fill our woven willows?

Wha'll buy my caller herrin'?
They're no brought here without brave daring:
Buy my caller herrin',
Hauled through wind and rain.

Wha'll buy my caller herrin'?
Oh, ye may ca' them vulgar farin',—
Wives and mithers, 'maist despairin',
Ca' them lives o' men.

When the creel o' herrin' passes,
Ladies clad in silks and laces
Gather in their braw pelisses,
Cast their necks, and screw their faces.

Caller herrin's no got lightly;
Ye can trip the spring fu' tightly;
Spite o' tauntin', flauntin', flingin',
Gow[1] has set you a' a-singin'.

Neebour wives, now tent* my tellin: — heed
When the bonnie fish ye're sellin',
At ae word be in your dealin',—
Truth will stand when a' thing's failin'.

## Bonnie Ran the Burnie Doun

Bonnie ran the burnie doun,
Wand'rin' and windin';

[1] Nathaniel Gow, a composer, for whom this song was written.

Sweetly sang the birds abune,
Care never mindin'.

The gentle simmer wind
Was their nursie saft and kind,
And it rockit them, and rockit them,
All in their bowers sae hie.
Bonnie ran, &c.

The mossy rock was there,
And the water-lily fair,
And the little trout would sport about
All in the sunny beam.
Bonnie ran, &c.

Though simmer days be lang,
And sweet the birdies' sang,
The wintry night and chilling blight
Keep aye their eerie roun'.
Bonnie ran, &c.

And then the burnie's like a sea,
Roarin' and reamin';
Nae wee bit sangster's on the tree,
But wild birds screamin'.

O that the past I might forget,
Wand'rin' and weepin'!
O that aneath the hillock green
Sound I were sleepin'!

## Wha'll Be King but Charlie?

Come through the heather, round him gather,
Ye're a' the welcomer early.
Around him cling wi' a' your kin;
For wha'll be king but Charlie?

Come through the heather, round him gather,
Come Ronald, come Donald, come a' thegither,
And crown your rightfu', lawfu' king;
For wha'll be king but Charlie?

The news frae Moidart cam yestreen,
Will soon gar mony ferlie*; wonders
For ships o' war hae just come in,
And landit Royal Charlie,

The Hieland clans, wi' sword in hand,
Frae John o' Groat's to Airlie,
Hae to a man declared to stand
Or fa' wi' Royal Charlie.

The Lowlands a', baith great an' sma,
Wi' many a lord and laird, hae
Declared for Scotia's king an' law,
And speir* ye wha but Charlie. ask

There's ne'er a lass in a' the lan',
But vows baith late an' early,
She'll ne'er to man gie heart nor han
Wha wadna fecht for Charlie.

Then here's a health to Charlie's cause,
And be't complete an' early;
His very name our heart's blood warms;
To arms for Royal Charlie!

## Row Weel, My Boatie

Row weel, my boatie, row weel,
Row weel, my merry men a',
For there's dool and there's wae in Glenfiorich's bowers,
And there's grief in my father's ha'.

And the skiff it danced light on the merry wee waves,
And it flew owre the water sae blue,
And the wind it blew light, and the moon it shone bright,
But the boatie ne'er reached Allandhu.

Ohon! for fair Ellen, ohon.
Ohon, for the pride of Strathcoe—
In the deep, deep sea, in the salt, salt bree,
Lord Reoch, thy Ellen lies low.

## The Auld House

Oh, the auld house, the auld house.
What though the rooms were wee?
Oh, kind hearts were dwelling there,
And bairnies fu' o' glee.
The wild rose and the jessamine
Still hang upon the wa'.
How mony cherished memories
Do they, sweet flowers, reca'.

Oh, the auld laird, the auld laird,
Sae canty*, kind, and crouse*. cheerful/lively
How mony did he welcome to
His ain wee dear auld house.
And the leddy, too, sae genty*, elegant
That sheltered Scotland's heir,
And clipt a lock wi' her ain hand
Frae his lang yellow hair.

The mavis still doth sweetly sing,
The blue-bells sweetly blaw.
The bonnie Earn's clear winding still,
But the auld house is awa.
The auld house, the auld house,
Deserted though ye be,
There ne'er can be a new house
Will seem sae fair to me.

Still flourishing the auld pear tree,
The bairnies liked to see;
And oh, how often they did speer* — ask
When ripe they a' wad be.
The voices sweet, the wee bit feet
Aye rinnin' here and there;
The merry shout—oh, whiles we greet* — weep
To think we'll hear nae mair.

For they are a' wide scattered now,
Some to the Indies gane,
And ane, alas, to her lang hame;
Not here will meet again.
The kirkyaird, the kirkyaird,
Wi' flowers o' every hue,
Sheltered by the holly's shade,
And the dark, somber yew.

The setting sun, the setting sun,
How glorious it gaed doun.
The cloudy splendor raised our hearts
To cloudless skies abune.
The auld dial, the auld dial,
It tauld how time did pass.
The wintry winds hae dung* it doun, — struck
Now laid 'mang weeds and grass.

## Charlie Is My Darling[1]

Twas on a Monday morning,
Right early in the year,
When Charlie cam to our town,
The young chevalier.

O Charlie is my darling,
My darling, my darling—
O Charlie is my darling,
The young chevalier.

As he cam marching up the street,
The pipes played loud and clear,

[1]One of many versions of this song.

And a' the folk cam running out
To meet the chevalier.

Wi' Hieland bonnets on their heads,
And claymores bright and clear,
They cam to fight for Scotland's right,
And the young chevalier.

They've left their bonnie Hieland hills,
Their wives and bairnies dear,
To draw the sword for Scotland's lord,
The young chevalier.

O there were mony beating hearts,
And mony a hope and fear,
And mony were the prayers put up
For the young chevalier.

## He's Ower the Hills That I Loe Weel

He's ower the hills that I loe weel,
He's ower the hills we daurna name:
He's ower the hills ayont Dunblane,
Wha soon will get his welcome hame.

My father's gane to fight for him,
My brithers winna bide at hame.
My mither greets* and prays for them,
And 'deed she thinks they're no to blame.

weeps

The Whigs may scoff, the Whigs may jeer;
But, ah, that love maun be sincere
Which still keeps true whate'er betide,
An' for his sake leaves a' beside.

His right these hills, his right these plains.
Ower Hieland hearts secure he reigns.
What lads e'er did our laddies will do.
Were I a laddie, I'd follow him too.

Sae noble a look, sae princely an air,
Sae gallant and bold, sae young and sae fair.
Oh, did ye but see him, ye'd do as we've done.
Hear him but ance, to his standard you'll run.

Then draw the claymore, for Charlie then fight;
For your country, religion, and a' that is right.
Were ten thousand lives now given to me,
I'd die as aft for ane o' the three.

## The Attainted Scottish Nobles

Oh, some will tune their mournfu' strains,
To tell o' hame-made sorrow,
And if they cheat you o' your tears,
They'll dry upon the morrow.
Oh, some will sing their airy dreams,
In verity they're sportin';
My sang's o' nae sic thieveless* themes, lifeless
But wakin' true misfortune.

Ye Scottish nobles, ane and a',
For loyalty attainted,[1]
A nameless bardie's wae to see
Your sorrows unlamented;
For if your fathers ne'er had fought
For heirs of ancient royalty,
Ye're down the day that might hae been
At the top o' honor's tree a'.

For old hereditary right,
For conscience' sake they stoutly stood;
And for the crown their valiant sons
Them selves have shed their injured blood;
And if their fathers ne'er had fought
For heirs of ancient royalty,
They're down the day that might hae been
At the top o' honor's tree a'.

## Farewell, O Farewell

Farewell, O farewell.
My heart it is sair.
Farewell, O farewell.
I'll see him nae mair.

Lang, lang was he mine,
Lang, lang—but nae mair.
I mauna repine,
But my heart it is sair.

His staff's at the wa',
Toom*, toom is his chair. empty
His bannet, an' a'
—An' I maun be here.

But oh, he's at rest,
Why sud I complain?
Gin my soul be blest,
I'll meet him again.

---

[1]To "attaint" is to deprive of civil rights following conviction for a crime. The reference is to the penalties given to the Scottish nobles who had followed Bonnie Prince Charlie in 1745-46.

Oh, to meet him again,
Where hearts ne'er were sair;
Oh, to meet him again,
To part never mair.

## ALEXANDER BALFOUR (1767–1829)

### To a Canary Bird

Poor, reckless bird, you'll rue the hour
You rashly left your wiry bower;
Unfit on feckless wing to scour
Alang the sky;
Though, like the lark, you hope to tower,
And mount on high.

I ferly* sair you thought na shame wonder
To leave that snug and cozy hame,
Wi' comforts mair than I can name.
Where friends caressed you.
To play the madly losing game,
What freak possessed you?

On Anna's lap you sat to rest,
And sometimes fondly made your nest
In gentle Mary's virgin breast—
E'en dared to sip
Sweets, might have made a monarch blest,
Frae Emma's lip.

Your comfort was their daily care,
They fed you wi' the daintiest fare;
And now, through fields of trackless air
You've taen your flight;
Left a' your friends wi' hearts fu' sair,
Without Good-night.

Frae morn to e'en you blithely sang,
Till a' the room around you rang.
Your bosom never felt the pang
O' want or fear.
Nor greedy gled*, nor pussy's fang, hawk
Were ever near.

When leeting out, in wanton play,
Some bonnie, calm, and cloudless day,
You cast your ee oer gardens gay,
And skies sae clear,
And deemed that ilka month was May
Throughout the year.

When gay green leaves the woods adorn,
And fields are fair wi' springing corn,
To brush the pearly dews of morn,
And spread your plumes,
Where sweetly smiles the sna-'white thorn,
Or primrose blooms;

On gowany* braes to sit and sing, daisy-filled
While budding birks their odors fling,
And blooming flowers around you spring,
To glad your ee,
To hap* the wild rose wi' your wing,— clothe
The thought was glee.

Poor, flightered thing, you little ken
What passes in the flowery glen;
When you can neither flee nor fen',
You'll wish fu' fain
That you were in your cage again;
But wish in vain.

Nae doubt you think your freedom sweet.
You'll change your mind when blashy weet,
Keen pirling* hail, or chilling sleet, thrusting
Your feathers daidle;
Twad ill befit your slender feet
In dubs* to paidle. puddles

Though summer blooms in beauty rare,
I fear you'll dine but bauchly there.
You canna feed when fields are bare,
On haps and haws*, hawthorn (berries)
Or scart and scrape for coarser fare,
Like corbie craws.

November winds will nip the flower.
Then comes the cauld and pelting shower,
And shivering in the leafless bower,
Wi' droukit* wing, drenched
You, while the dark clouds round you lower,
Forget to sing.

When freezing winds around you bla',
Oer glittering wreaths o' drifted sna',
And robin hides in sheltering ha',
Wi' hardy form,
I fear your chance, poor bird, is sma,
To bang the storm.

But you will never see that day,
Ne'er shiver on the naked spray,
For lang before the leaves decay,
Some hapless morn,

To ruthless hawk you'll fall a prey,
Your plumage torn.

Was't freedom, say, or pleasure's name,
That lured you frae your cozy hame?
Whichever, I can hardly blame,
Though you'll repent it,
For wiser folk have done the same,
And sair lament it.

I've kent the rich, but restless swain,
For liberty, or sordid gain,
Leave Albion's fair and fruitful plain
Wi' scornfu' ee,
To search beyond the western main
For bliss to be;

And in Columbia's forests deep,
Where Indians prowl and serpents creep,
He dreamed of Scotia in his sleep,
Still fondly dear;
Or waking, turned to sigh and weep
The bootless tear.

Tis naething strange for folks to think,
If pleasure for a moment blink,
Her noontide sun will never sink;
And birds and men
She leads to dark destruction's brink
Before they ken.

## The Bonnie Lass o' Leven Water

Though siller Tweed rin oer the lea,
An dark the Dee mang Highland heather,
Yet siller Tweed an drumly* Dee — *muddy
Are not sae dear as Leven Water.
When nature formed our favorite isle,
An a' her sweets began to scatter,
She looked with fond approving smile
Alang the banks o' Leven Water.

On flowery braes, at gloamin gray,
Tis sweet to scent the primrose springin;
Or through the woodlands green to stray,
In ilka buss the mavis singin.
But sweeter than the woodlands green,
Or primrose painted fair by nature,
Is she wha smiles, a rural queen,
The bonnie lass o' Leven Water.

The sunbeam in the siller dew,
That hangs upon the hawthorn's blossom,
Shines faint beside her een sae blue;
An purer is her spotless bosom.
Her smile wad thaw a hermit's breast.
There's love an truth in ilka feature.
For her I'm past baith wark an rest,
The bonnie lass o' Leven Water.

But I'm a lad o' laigh* degree, "low"
Her purse-proud daddy's dour an saucy;
An sair the carl* wad scowl on me rascal
For speakin to his dawtit* lassie; petted
But were I laird o' Leven's glen,
An she a humble shepherd's daughter,
I'd kneel, an court her for my ain,
The bonnie lass o' Leven Water.

## Stanzas

(Written at Midnight, 31st December, 1828)

Hark, time has struck the midnight bell,
Another year has passed away.
His requiem sung—his parting knell—
And, hark, again—that wild hurrah.

Is it because the sire's deposed
That thus they hail the newborn son?
Or, that life's lease is nearer closed,
Their ebbing sands still nearer run?

Just now they wildly lift their voice
In welcome to a puny child;
As gladly will that crowd rejoice,
Some twelve months hence, when he's exiled.

And some will laud, and some revile,
The name of the departed year;
Some oer his grave exulting smile,
And on his turf some drop a tear.

For some will sigh, of friends bereaved,
Those long possessed and dearly loved;
While others mourn oer hopes deceived;
And some rejoice, their fears removed.

And some, with retrospective eye,
Behind a lingering look will cast;
Will fondly gaze on scenes gone by,
And vainly sigh for pleasures past.

Others will calmly look before,
Long tossed on life's tempestuous wave;
By faith and hope will view the shore,
The haven of rest, beyond the grave.

And some will glide along the stream,
Insensible to joy or care:
To eat and drink, and doze and dream,
The highest bliss their souls can share.

Untiring, many will pursue
The pleasures wealth and power impart;
By day and night their toils renew,
And clasp them closer to the heart.

Alas, it is a bootless chase,
And vainly we with time contend.
We shall be distanced in the race,
And breathless to the grave descend.

The hand that pens this simple rhyme
Already wants its wonted skill;
Enfeebled now by age and time,
Shall soon in death lie cold and still.

Reader, does youth light up thine eye?
It sparkled once as bright in mine;
And though the days are long gone by,
My heart was once as light as thine.

Perhaps the cup of love and joy,
Thy raptured heart delights to sip;
But fate may soon that bliss destroy,
Untimely snatch it from thy lip.

Art thou the child of many woes,
Long wandering in life's dreary gloom?
The hour is near that brings repose,
The dreamless slumber of the tomb.

If young, the lengthened train of years,
The boundless landscape, spread before,
An endless vista now appears—
A halcyon sea, without a shore.

If old, perhaps you look behind,
And pensive, muse on what has been;
Though not without surprise, to find
How time has changed the fairy scene.

The prospect, once so fair and vast,
Now dwindled to a point will seem;

And you, like me, will feel at least,
That life is but a morning dream.

## A Lament for Culloden

Alas, for the land of the heath-covered mountains,
Where raves the loud tempest, and rolls the dark flood.
Alas, for the land of the smooth crystal fountains,
The sword of the slayer has stained them with blood.
Ah, me, for the nation, so famous in story,
Where valor, and freedom, and loyalty, shone.
They gathered around the bright star of their glory;
But faded their laurels, their glory is gone.
Weep, Caledonia, mourn for the fallen.

His banner, unfurled, in splendor was streaming,
The sons of the mighty were gathered around;
Their bucklers and broadswords in brightness were gleaming,
And high beat each heart at the loud pibroch's sound.
They came to Culloden, the dark field of danger,
Oh, why will not memory the record efface.
Alas, for their leader, the gallant young stranger.
And woe to the traitors who wrought the disgrace.
Weep, Caledonia, mourn for the fallen.

Alas, for the heroes whom death has enshrouded.
Yet not for the valiant and mighty I weep;
When darkness was lowering, their sun set unclouded,
And loud was the war-shout that lulled them asleep.
Their turf the gay spring with rich verdure shall cover,
The sweet flower of summer in fragrance shall bloom.
In the mist from the mountains bright spirits shall hover.
The shades of their fathers shall glide oer the tomb.
Weep, Caledonia, mourn for the fallen.

Alas, for the stranger, by fortune forsaken,
Who pillows his head on the heath-blossomed hill;
From dreams of delight with the day to awaken,
His cheek pale and wet with the night-dew so chill.
Alas, for my country—her glory's departed—
No more shall the thistle its purple bloom wave.
But shame to the coward, the traitor false-hearted,
And barren the black sod be aye on his grave.
Weep, Caledonia, weep for the fallen.

## JOHN ROBERTSON (1767–1810)

### The Toom Meal Pock

Preserve us a', what shall we do,
Thir* dark, unhallowed times? these
We're surely dreeing* penance now, suffering

For some most awfu' crimes.
Sedition daurna now appear
In reality or joke;
For ilka chiel* maun mourn wi me, fellow
O' a hinging, toom* meal pock, empty
And sing, Oh, waes me.

When lasses braw gaed out at e'en,
For sport and pastime free;
I seemed like ane in paradise,
The moments quick did flee.
Like Venuses they all appeared,
Well pouthered were their locks.
Twas easy dune, when at their hame,
Wi the shaking o' their pocks.
And sing, Oh, waes me.

How happy passed my former days,
Wi' merry heartsome glee;
When smiling fortune held the cup,
And peace sat on my knee.
Nae wants had I but were supplied;
My heart wi joy did knock,
When in the neuk I smiling saw
A gaucie*, weel-filled pock. plump
And sing, Oh, waes me.

Speak no ae word about reform,
Nor petition Parliament.
A wiser scheme I'll now propose,
I'm sure ye'll gi'e consent.
Send up a chiel or twa like me,
As a sample o' the flock,
Whose hollow cheeks will be sure proof
O' a hinging, toom meal pock.
And sing, Oh, waes me.

And should a sicht sae ghastly-like,
Wi rags, and banes, and skin,
Hae nae impression on yon folks,
But tell ye'll stand ahin';
O what a contrast will ye shaw,
To the glow'rin' Lunnun folk,
When in St James' ye tak your stand,
Wi a hinging, toom meal pock.
And sing, Oh, waes me.

Then rear your head, and glow'r, and stare,
Before yon hills o' beef.
Tell them ye are frae Scotland come,
For Scotia's relief.
Tell them ye are the verra best,
Waled* frae the fattest flock; chosen

Then raise your arms, and, oh, display
A hinging, toom meal pock.
And sing, Oh, waes me.

## JAMES NICOL (1769–1819)

### Haluckit Meg

Meg, muckin at Geordie's byre*, barn
Wrought as gin* her judgment was wrang. if
Ilk daud o' the scartle* strake fire, scraping
While loud as a lavrock she sang.
Her Geordie had promised to marry,
An Meg, a sworn fae* to despair, "foe"
Not dreamin the job could miscarry,
Already seemed mistress an mair.

"My neebors," she sang, "aften jeer me,
An ca' me daft haluckit* Meg, hoyden
An say they expect soon to hear me,
I' the kirk, for my fun, get a fleg.[1]
An now, bout my marriage they'll clatter,
An Geordie, puir fallow, they ca'
An ald doited hav'rel*,—nae matter, he-goat
He'll keep me aye brankin* an braw. finely dressed

I grant ye, his face is kenspeckle*, conspicuous
That the white o' his ee is turned out,
That his black beard is rough as a heckle,
That his mou to his lug's* raxed* about; ear's/stretched
But that needna let on that he's crazy,
His pikestaff will ne'er let him fa;
Nor that his hair's white as a daisy,
But fient* a hair has he ava. scarcely

"But a well-plenished mailin* has Geordie, farm
An routh* o' gude gowd in his kist*, plenty/ "chest"
An if siller comes at my wordie,
His beauty I never will miss't.
Daft gowks*, wha catch fire like tinder, fools
Think love-raptures ever will burn.
But wi' poortith*, hearts het as a cinder, poverty
Will cauld as an iceshugle turn.

"There'll just be ae bar to my pleasures,
A bar that's aft filled me wi' fear,
He's sic a hard ne'er-be-gawn miser,
He likes his saul less than his gear*. money
But though I now flatter his failin,

---

[1] Fleg = scare. That is, they expect her to be reproved before the church congregation for licentious behavior.

An swear nought wi' gowd can compare,
Gude sooth, it shall soon get a scailin,
His bag shall be moldy nae mair.

"I dreamt that I rode in a chariot,
A flunky ahint* me in green; behind
While Geordie cried out he was harriet,
An' the saut tear was blindin his een.
But though gainst my spendin he swear aye,
I'll hae frae him what ser's my turn;
Let him slip awa when he grows weary:
Shame fa' me, gin lang I wad mourn."

But Geordie, while Meg was haranguin,
Was cloutin his breeks* in the bauks; britches
An whan a' his failin's she brang in,
His strang hazel pikestaff he taks:
Designin' to rax her a lounder*, blow
He chanced on the lather to shift,
An down frae the bauks, flat's a flouder,
Flew like a shot starn frae the lift*. sky

## Blaw Saftly, Ye Breezes

Blaw saftly, ye breezes, ye streams, smoothly murmur,
Ye sweet scented blossoms, deck every green tree;
Mong yon wild scattered flow'rets aft wanders my charmer,
The sweet lovely lass wi' the black rollin ee.
But round me let nature a wilderness seem,
Blast each flow'ret that catches the sun's early beam,
For pensive I ponder, and languishin' wander,
Far frae the sweet rosebud on Quair's windin stream.

Why, Heaven, wring my heart wi' the hard heart o' anguish?
Why torture my bosom tween hope and despair?
When absent frae Nancy, I ever maun languish.
That dear angel smile, shall it charm me nae mair?
Since here life's a desert, an pleasure's a dream,
Bear me swift to those banks which are ever my theme,
Where, mild as the mornin at simmer's returnin,
Blooms the sweet lovely rosebud on Quair's windin stream.

# EBENEZER PICKEN (1769–1816)

## New Year's Day

Now Simmer's gowden beam withdrawn
Brings hoary Winter oer the lawn,
While, drivin', cauld, in awfu' form,
Bauld Boreas aids the direfu' storm.
Nae langer blooms the flowery thorn,
Whase fragrant sweets perfumed the morn;

Nae mair o' pastime now, I ween—
The dance, the play, has left the green.
Nae mair our e'en blithe prospects cheer;
Stern Winter blin's them wi' a tear.
Ilk thing looks dowie*, dowf*, and wae,     sad/doleful
Just like auld Nature's last decay;
And ilka hill and haugh* and plain     hollow
Scarce hechts* that Spring will come again.     promises
The herd, poor thing! through chillin' air,
Tends in the meads his fleecy care;
Dosened wi' cauld and drivin' sleet,
Rowed in a coarse woo' en muirlan' sheet;
Or maybe, oer the drift-clad brae,
Frae whare he hears the lambkins ba,
He weary winds his road, and slaw,
To howk* them out frae mang the snaw.     dig
Cauld wind soughs through the leafless trees;
His tautie* locks are like to freeze.     shaggy
Stieve* in his plaid ilk hand he rows,     firm
And wi' his breath the cranreuch* thows,     frost
Till ance ilk dinlin' finger glows.
Winter's keen breath has made him yap*;     hungry
He langs to see the parritch cap;
Sae up some hillock-tap or brae,
He bends his way, baith cauld and blae*,     wan
To see gif, oer the neighborin' dale,
The servant brings his mornin' meal.
Thinned is the foliage o' the grove
Whare wissfu' lovers wont to rove:
December sheets wi' ice the knowes*,     "knolls"
And staps the burnie as it rows.
Now on its banks nae verdure shaws,
Nor birdie sings, nor blossom blaws;
But frae ilk bus' the tangles gay
Hang skinklin'* in the mornin' ray,     sparkling
While ilka blast seems to conspire
To blaw out Nature's vital fire.
Yet, though ilk thing without looks cauld,
The ingle* bleezes, warm and bauld,     fireplace
And lang before the cock has crawn,
Or glintin' morn led in the dawn,
I wat there's mony a wight asteer
To glad his heart wi' New'rday cheer.
Now, though the vera skies sould fa'
In heavy flakes o' feathery snaw;
Though wintry rain a deluge pour,
The bitter, bitin' tempest roar,
Whirlin' destruction through the street,
And threatenin' heaven and earth to meet;
Yet spite o' Winter's drearest form,

The "first fit" bauldly fronts the storm.[1]
The maudlin' "het pint's" heavenly power
Has raised a flame that bangs* the shower— overcomes
That heaviest rain, in evendown drench,
And scarce a sea itsel could quench.
The whelmin' ocean couldna choke it,
Nae mair than 't wad a Congreve's rocket.
Scrievin'* awa', he dreads nae harm; racing
The glorious beverage, reekin' warm,
He dauntless bears; and, bent on fun,
Nor kebbuck* hains*, nor curran' bun. cheese/pieces
Thus doubly armed, he onward plods,
Nor envies goddesses or gods.
Weel wat I, on Olympus tap
There's nowther sic a bit nor drap.
Happy that frien' whase door sae blest
Is doomed to welcome sic a guest!
There care nae shilpit* face can shaw: wan
He's boltit out amang the snaw.
Now, bonnie lasses, shun the street;
For ye'll be kissed by a' ye meet.
But aiblins* ye're sae ill to sair o't perhaps
Ye'll no keep in the house the mair o't.
Weel, gang your wa's; love send ye speed!
I'se wat ye'll get your mou's weel pree'd*. proved (tested)
Now the saft maid whase yieldin' heart
O' love's keen flame has dree'd* the smart, endured
Recks na, I trow, her want o' rest,
But dinks her out in a' her best,
Wi' weel-airned mutch* and kirtle clean, cap
To wait the hour o' twal' at e'en.
Blithe hour, that on the passin' bell
Rings out the auld year's partin' knell!
Syne, whan she hears it strike, I wat,
Her modest heart gangs pittie-pat.
Fu' anxious now, she's on the watch,
And thinks, ilk breath, she hears the latch—
Starts frae the stool, wi' waterin' mouth,
To welcome ben* the dear-lo'ed youth, in
For wham 't had been her e'enin' care
Some gusty beverage to prepare.
As aft she finds hersel' mista'en,
And, dowie, sits her down again.
Soon a quick, eager step draws near—
She's no deceived—it is her dear!
Her heart beats quick wi' sweet alarms;
She finds hersel within his arms.
But here nae mair the musie tells:
We leave the lovers to themsels.
The wight oppressed wi' toil and care

---

[1] A new year's visiting custom: the "first foot" across the threshold brings good luck.

Minds poortith* now, and debt, nae mair; poverty
But sweetly bends the reamin' bicker,
To drown dull care in jaws o' liquor.
Now mony a rantin' feast, weel stored,
Saurs* sweetly on the rustic board. "savors"
The table brags its ample store,
That held a simple meal before.
The ale gangs roun', the e'enin' lang;
Auld age unbends, and joins the sang,
And while he blithely slacks his drouth,
Brags o' the feats o' early youth.
The laithfu' wooers' smirkin' e'en
In glints they wiss na to be seen,
Speak the saft language o' the heart,
And dread the minute they maun part;
Or maybe, seated side by side,
The strugglin' sigh they strive to hide,
And, laith love's raptures to delay,
Fix the lang-wissed-for, happy day.
Hail, friendly neighbors, cheerfu' thrang!
To you life's purest joys belang.
Care seinle* sours ye, air or late, seldom
Contentit wi' your humble state.
Far frae ambition's maddin' strife,
Ye spend a blithe and blameless life;
And though neath poortith's sair down-draw
Some o' ye fag your days awa',
And aften hae your ain ado,
Ye hae your blinks o' sunshine too:
The blithe New Year comes sweetly in,
And gi'es misfortune to the win'.
The rich are mair to mean* than you— regret
They've aften pine that scugs* the view; hides
Their joys parade, while yours are true.
E'en let them sport their giddy hours—
The show is theirs, the substance yours.
Your harmless mirth let wealth envy,
In fu'ness fret, and wonder why;
Ambition aye, we ken fu' weel,
Pretends to scorn the joys it canna feel.

## Blithe Are We Set wi' Ither

Blithe are we set wi' ither*; (each) "other"
Fling care ayont* the moon. beyond
Nae sae aft we meet thegither
Wha wad think o' partin' soon?
Though snaw bends down the forest trees,
And burn and river cease to flow,
Though nature's tide has shored to freeze,
And winter withers a' below,
Blithe are we set wi' ither;

Fling care ayont the moon.
Nae sae aft we meet thegither
Wha wad think o' partin' soon?

Now round the ingle* cheerly met, fireplace
We'll scog* the blast, and dread nae harm; dodge
Wi' jows o' toddy, reekin' het,
We'll keep the genial current warm.
The friendly crack*, the cheerfu' sang chat
Shall cheat the happy hours awa',
Gar* pleasure reign the e'enin' lang, make
And laugh at bitin' frost and snaw.
Blithe are we set wi' ither;
Fling care ayont the moon.
Nae sae aft we meet thegither
Wha wad think o' partin' soon?

The cares that cluster roun' the heart,
And gar the bosom stoun'* wi' pain, stun
Shall get a fright afore we part,
Will gar them fear to come again.
Then, fill about, my winsome chiels*, lads
The sparklin' glass will banish pine.
Nae pain the happy bosom feels,
Sae free o' care as yours and mine.
Blithe are we set wi' ither;
Fling care ayont the moon.
Nae sae aft we meet thegither
Wha wad think o' partin' soon?

## Woo Me Again

Whan Jamie first wooed me he was but a youth.
Frae his lips flowed the strains o' persuasion and truth.
His suit I rejected wi' pride and disdain,
But, O wad he offer to woo me again!

He aft wad hae tauld me his love was sincere,
And e'en wad hae ventured to ca' me his dear.
My heart to his tale was as hard as a stane;
But, O wad he offer to woo me again!

He said that he hoped I wad yield and be kind;
But I counted his proffers as light as the wind.
I laughed at his grief whan I heard him complain;
But, O wad he offer to woo me again!

He flattered my locks, that were black as the slae;
And praised my fine shape, frae the tap to the tae.
I flate*, and desired he wad let me alane; scolded
But, O wad he offer to woo me again!

Repulsed, he forsook me, and left me to grieve,
And mourn the sad hour that my swain took his leave.
Now, since I despised and was deaf to his maen,
I fear he'll ne'er offer to woo me again.

O wad he but now to his Jean be inclined,
My heart in a moment wad yield to his mind;
But I fear wi' some ither my laddie is taen,
And sae he'll ne'er offer to woo me again.

Ye bonnie young lasses, be warned by my fate.
Despise not the heart ye may value too late.
Improve the sweet sunshine that now gilds the plain.
With you it ne'er may be sunshine again.

The simmer o' life, ah, it soon flits awa,
And the bloom on your cheek will soon dow* in the snaw. fade
O think, ere you treat a fond youth wi' disdain,
That in age the sweet flowers never blossom again.

## Nan of Logie Green

By pleasure long infected,
Kind heaven, when least expected,
My devious path directed
To Nan of Logie Green;
Where thousand sweets repose 'em
In quiet's unruffled bosom,
I found my peerless blossom
Adorning Logie Green.

The city belle declaiming,
My fancy may be blaming,
But still I'll pride in naming
Sweet Nan of Logie Green.
Her cheek the vermeil rose is,
Her smile a heav'n discloses,
No lily leaf that blows is
So fair on Logie Green.

Ye town bred dames, forgive me,
Your arms must ne'er receive me;
Your charms are all, believe me,
Eclipsed on Logie Green.
Forgive my passion tender;
Heav'n so much grace did lend her,
As made my heart surrender
To Nan of Logie Green.

No more the town delights me,
For love's sweet ardor smites me,
I'll go where he invites me—

To Nan of Logie Green.
My heart shall ne'er deceive her,
I ne'er in life shall leave her;
In love and peace for ever
We'll live at Logie Green.

## Peggy wi the Glancin Ee

Walkin out ae mornin early
Ken ye wha I chanced to see?
But my lassie gay and frisky,
Peggy wi the glancin ee.
Phoebus, left the lap o' Thetis,
Fast was lickin up the dew,
Whan, ayont* a risin hilloc, beyond
First my Peggy came in view.

Hark ye, I gaed up to meet her;
But whane'er my face she sae,
Up her plaidin coat she kiltit,
And in daffin* scoured awa. fooling
Weel kent I that though my Peggy
Ran sae fast out oer the mead,
She was wantin me to follow—
Yes, ye swains, an sae I did.

At yon burnie I oertook her,
Where the shinin pebbles lie:
Where the flowers, that fringe the border,
Soup the stream, that wimples by.
While wi' her I sat reclinin,
Frae her lips I staw a kiss;
While she blushed, I took anither,—
Shepherds, was there ill in this?

Could a lass, sae sweet and comely,
Ever bless a lover's arms?
Could the bonnie wife o' Vulcan
Ever boast o' hauf the charms?
While the zephyrs fan the meadows,
While the flow'rets crown the lea,
While they paint the gowden simmer,
Wha sae blest as her and me?

## JAMES HOGG (1770–1835)

[James Hogg is, along with Walter Scott, the finest Scottish poet of the century. Like Burns, he was from the countryside (he referred to himself as "The Ettrick Shepherd"). He wrote in a wide variety of literary forms, and in both Scots and English. His pastoral fantasy, "Kilmeny," is perhaps his finest sustained piece of verse. The moral theme is straightforward enough, but the work also contains a (somewhat vague) political allegory about Scotland, Mary Queen of Scots, and England. Hogg also wrote much prose fiction, including one of the finest novels in Scottish literature, *The Private Memoirs and Confessions of a Justified Sinner* (1824). Like "Wandering Willie's Tale," the work is an example of the then prevailing Gothic horror story; but it is also a satire on the Presbyterian Church and a psychological novel of real penetration, one of the first examples of that characteristically Scottish preoccupation: the divided personality.]

## When the Kye Comes Hame

Come all ye jolly shepherds
That whistle through the glen,
I'll tell ye of a secret
That courtiers dinna ken:
What is the greatest bliss
That the tongue o' man can name?
Tis to woo a bonny lassie
When the kye* comes hame. cattle

Tis not beneath the coronet,
Nor canopy of state,
Tis not on couch of velvet,
Nor arbor of the great—
Tis beneath the spreading birk*, "birch"
In the glen without the name,
Wi' a bonny, bonny lassie,
When the kye comes hame.

There the blackbird bigs his nest
For the mate he loes to see,
And on the topmost bough,
O, a happy bird is he;
Where he pours his melting ditty,
And love is a' the theme,
And he'll woo his bonny lassie
When the kye comes hame.

When the blewart* bears a pearl, bluebell
And the daisy turns a pea,
And the bonny lucken gowan* globe flower
Has fauldit up her ee,
Then the laverock* frae the blue lift* lark/sky
Drops down, an' thinks nae shame
To woo his bonny lassie
When the kye comes hame.

See yonder pawkie* shepherd, sly
That lingers on the hill,
His ewes are in the fauld,
An' his lambs are lying still;
Yet he downa gang to bed,
For his heart is in a flame,

To meet his bonny lassie
When the kye comes hame.

When the little wee bit heart
Rises high in the breast,
An' the little wee bit starn
Rises red in the east,
O there's a joy sae dear,
That the heart can hardly frame,
Wi' a bonny, bonny lassie,
When the kye comes hame.

Then since all nature joins
In this love without alloy,
O, wha wad prove a traitor
To Nature's dearest joy?
Or wha wad choose a crown,
Wi' its perils and its fame,
And miss his bonny lassie
When the kye comes hame?

## The Skylark

Bird of the wilderness,
Blithesome and cumberless,
Sweet be thy matin oer moorland and lea.
Emblem of happiness,
Blest is thy dwelling-place—
Oh, to abide in the desert with thee.

Wild is thy lay and loud,
Far in the downy cloud,
Love gives it energy, love gave it birth.
Where, on thy dewy wing,
Where art thou journeying?
Thy lay is in heaven, thy love is on earth.

Oer fell and fountain sheen,
Oer moor and mountain green,
Oer the red streamer that heralds the day,
Over the cloudlet dim,
Over the rainbow's rim,
Musical cherub, soar, singing, away.

Then, when the gloaming comes,
Low in the heather blooms
Sweet will thy welcome and bed of love be.
Emblem of happiness,
Blest is thy dwelling-place—
Oh, to abide in the desert with thee.

## When Maggy Gangs Away

Oh, what will a' the lads do
When Maggy gangs away?
Oh, what will a' the lads do
When Maggy gangs away?
There's no a heart in a' the glen
That disna dread the day:
Oh what will a' the lads do
When Maggy gangs away?

Young Jock has ta'en the hill for't—
A waefu' wight is he;
Poor Harry's ta'en the bed for't,
An' laid him down to dee;
An' Sandy's gane into the kirk,
An' learnin' fast to pray;
And oh, what will the lads do
When Maggy gangs away?

The young laird o' the Lang-Shaw
Has drunk her health in wine;
The priest has said—in confidence—
The lassie was divine,
And that is mair in maiden's praise
Than ony priest should say:
But oh, what will the lads do
When Maggy gangs away?

The wailing in our green glen
That day will quaver high;
Twill draw the redbreast frae the wood,
The laverock frae the sky;
The fairies frae their beds o' dew
Will rise an' join the lay:
An' hey! what a day will be
When Maggy gangs away.

## Kilmeny

Bonny Kilmeny gaed up the glen;
But it wasna to meet Duneira's men,
Nor the rosy monk of the isle to see,
For Kilmeny was pure as pure could be.
It was only to hear the Yorlin sing,
And pu' the cress-flower round the spring;
The scarlet hypp and the hyndberrye,
And the nut that hung frae the hazel tree;
For Kilmeny was pure as pure could be.
But lang may her minny* look oer the wa'. mother
And lang may she seek i' the green wood shaw*; copse
Lang the laird of Duneira blame,
And lang, lang greet* or* Kilmeny come hame. weep/ "ere"

When many lang day had come and fled,
When grief grew calm, and hope was dead,
When mass for Kilmeny's soul had been sung,
When the bedes-man had prayed, and the dead bell rung:
Late, late in a gloamin when all was still,
When the fringe was red on the westlin hill,
The wood was sere, the moon i' the wane,
The reek* o' the cot* hung oer the plain, smoke/ "cottage"
Like a little wee cloud in the world its lane;
When the ingle lowed* wi' an eerie leme*, "glowed"/gleam
Late, late in the gloamin Kilmeny came hame.

"Kilmeny, Kilmeny, where have you been?
Lang hae we sought baith holt and dean;
By linn*, by ford, and greenwood tree, waterfall
Yet you are halesome and fair to see.
Where gat you that joup* o' the lily sheen? petticoat
That bonny snood* o' the birk sae green? hair-band
And these roses, the fairest that ever were seen?—
Kilmeny, Kilmeny, where have you been?"

Kilmeny looked up with a lovely grace,
But nae smile was seen on Kilmeny's face;
As still was her look, and as still was her ee,
As the stillness that lay on the emerant* lea, emerald
Or the mist that sleeps on a waveless sea.
For Kilmeny had been she kenned not where,
And Kilmeny had seen what she could not declare:
Kilmeny had been where the cock never crew,
Where the rain never fell, and the wind never blew.
But it seemed as the harp of the sky had rung,
And the airs of heaven played round her tongue,
When she spake of the lovely forms she had seen,
And a land where sin had never been;
A land of love, and a land of light,
Withouten sun, or moon, or night;
Where the river swaed* a living stream, surged
And the light a pure and cloudless beam;
The land of vision it would seem
A still, an everlasting dream.

In yon green wood there is a waik*, glade
And in that waik there is a wene*, recess
And in that wene there is a maike*, mate, person
That neither has flesh, nor blood, nor bane;
And down in yon greenwood he walks his lane*. (alone)
In that green wene Kilmeny lay,
Her bosom happed* wi' flowerets gay; dressed
But the air was soft and the silence deep,
And bonny Kilmeny fell sound asleep.
She kenned nae mair, nor opened her ee,
Till waked by the hymns of a far countrye.
She woke on a couch of the silk sae slim,

All striped wi' the bars of the rainbow's rim;
And lovely beings round were rife,
Who erst had traveled mortal life;
And aye they smiled, and gan to speer*, ask
"What spirit has brought this mortal here?"

"Lang have I ranged the world wide,"
A meek and reverend fere replied;
"Baith night and day I have watched the fair,
Eident* a thousand years and mair. ceaselessly
Yes, I have watched oer ilk* degree, every
Wherever blooms femininity;
And sinless virgin, free of stain
In mind and body, fand I nane.
Never, since the banquet of time,
Found I a virgin in her prime,
Till late this bonnie maiden I saw
As spotless as the morning snaw:
Full twenty years she has lived as free
As the spirits that sojourn in this countrye.
I have brought her away from the snares of men,
That sin or death she never may ken."

They clasped her waist and her hands sae fair,
They kissed her cheek, and they kemed her hair;
And round came many a blooming fere,
Saying, "Bonny Kilmeny, ye're welcome here.
Women are freed of the littand* scorn:— staining
O, blessed be the day Kilmeny was born.
Now shall the land of the spirits see,
Now shall it ken what a woman may be.
Many lang year in sorrow and pain,
Many lang year through the world we've gane,
Commissioned to watch fair womankind,
For it's they who nurse the immortal mind.
We have watched their steps as the dawning shone,
And deep in the greenwood walks alone;
By lily bower and silken bed,
The viewless tears have oer them shed;
Have soothed their ardent minds to sleep,
Or left the couch of love to weep.
We have seen, we have seen, but the time maun* come, "must"
And the angels will weep at the day of doom.

"O, would the fairest of mortal kind
Aye keep these holy truths in mind,
That kindred spirits their motions see,
Who watch their ways with anxious ee,
And grieve for the guilt of humanity.
O, sweet to Heaven the maiden's prayer,
And the sigh that heaves a bosom sae fair.
And dear to Heaven the words of truth,
And the praise of virtue frae beauty's mouth.

And dear to the viewless forms of air,
The mind that kythest* as the body fair. appears
O, bonny Kilmeny, free frae stain,
If ever you seek the world again,
That world of sin, of sorrow, and fear,
O tell of the joys that are waiting here;
And tell of the signs you shall shortly see;
Of the times that are now, and the times that shall be."

They lifted Kilmeny, they led her away,
And she walked in the light of a sunless day:
The sky was a dome of crystal bright,
The fountain of vision, and fountain of light.
The emerant fields were of dazzling glow,
And the flowers of everlasting blow.
Then deep in the stream her body they laid,
That her youth and beauty never might fade;
And they smiled on heaven, when they saw her lie
In the stream of life that wandered by.
And she heard a song, she heard it sung,
She kend not where; but sae sweetly it rung,
It fell on her ear like a dream of the morn:
"O blest be the day Kilmeny was born.
Now shall the land of the spirits see,
Now shall it ken what a woman may be.
The sun that shines on the world sae bright,
A borrowed gleid* frae the fountain of light; spark
And the moon that sleeks* the sky sae dun, smoothes, lightens
Like a gouden bow, or a beamless sun,
Shall wear away and be seen nae mair,
And the angels shall miss them traveling the air.
But lang, lang after baith night and day,
When the sun and the world have fled away;
When the sinner has gane to his waesome doom,
Kilmeny shall smile in eternal bloom."
They bore her away, she wist not how,
For she felt not arm nor rest below:
But so swift they wained* her through the light, carried
Twas like the motion of sound or sight;
They seemed to split the gales of air,
And yet nor gale nor breeze was there.
Unnumbered groves below them grew;
They came, they past, and backward flew,
Like floods of blossoms gliding on,
A moment seen, in a moment gone.
O, never vales to mortal view
Appeared like those oer which they flew,
That land to human spirits given,
The lowermost vales of the storied heaven;
From thence they can view the world below,
And heaven's blue gates with sapphires glow,
More glory yet unmeet to know.

They bore her far to a mountain green,
To see what mortal never had seen;
And they seated her high on a purple sward,
And bade her heed what she saw and heard;
And note the changes the spirits wrought,
For now she lived in the land of thought.
She looked, and she saw nor sun nor skies,
But a crystal dome of a thousand dyes;
She looked, and she saw nae land aright,
But an endless whirl of glory and light:
And radiant beings went and came
Far swifter than wind, or the linked flame.
She hid her een frae the dazzling view;
She looked again, and the scene was new.
She saw a sun on a summer sky,
And clouds of amber sailing by;
A lovely land beneath her lay,
And that land had lakes and mountains gray;
And that land had valleys and hoary piles,
And marled* seas and a thousand isles. multicolored
Its fields were speckled, its forests green,
And its lakes were all of the dazzling sheen,
Like magic mirrors, where slumbering lay
The sun and the sky, and the cloudlet gray;
Which heaved and trembled, and gently swung,
On every shore they seemed to be hung:
For there they were seen on their downward plain
A thousand times, and a thousand again;
In winding lake, and placid firth,
Little peaceful heavens in the bosom of earth.
Kilmeny sighed and seemed to grieve,
For she found her heart to that land did cleave;
She saw the corn wave on the vale,
She saw the deer run down the dale;
She saw the plaid and the broad claymore,
And the brows that the badge of freedom bore;—
And she thought she had seen the land before.

She saw a lady sit on a throne,[1]
The fairest that ever the sun shone on:
A lion[2] licked her hand of milk,
And she held him in a leash of silk;
And a leifu'* maiden stood at her knee, wistful, loyal
With a silver wand and melting ee;
Her sovereign shield till love stole in,
And poisoned all the fount within.
Then a gruff untoward bedes-man came,[3]
And hundit* the lion on his dame; "hounded" (incited)

---

[1]Mary Queen of Scots?

[2]The lion is an emblem of Scotland.

[3]John Knox, the fiery Protestant minister and foe of the Catholic Queen Mary.

And the guardian maid wi' the dauntless ee,
She dropped a tear, and left her knee;
And she saw till the queen frae the lion fled,
Till the bonniest flower of the world lay dead;
A coffin was set on a distant plain,
And she saw the red blood fall like rain:
Then bonny Kilmeny's heart grew sair,
And she turned away, and could look nae mair.
Then the gruff grim carle girned* amain, grimaced
And they trampled him down, but he rose again;
And he baited the lion to deeds of weir*, "war"
Till he lapped the blood to the kingdom dear;
And weening his head was danger-preef,
When crowned with the rose and clover leaf,
He gowled at the carle, and chased him away
To feed wi' the deer on the mountain gray.
He gowled at the carle, and he geeked* at Heaven, mocked
But his mark was set, and his arles[1] given.
Kilmeny a while her een withdrew;
She looked again, and the scene was new.

She saw below her fair unfurled
One half of all the glowing world,
Where oceans rolled, and rivers ran,
To bound the aims of sinful man.
She saw a people, fierce and fell,
Burst frae their bounds like fiends of hell;
There lilies grew, and the eagle flew,
And she herked* on her ravening crew, urged
Till the cities and towers were wrapt in a blaze,
And the thunder it roared oer the lands and the seas.
The widows wailed, and the red blood ran.
And she threatened an end to the race of man.
She never lened*, nor stood in awe, rested
Till caught by the lion's deadly paw.
Oh, then the eagle swinked* for life, struggled
And brainzelled* up a mortal strife; stirred
But flew she north, or flew she south,
She met wi' the gowl* of the lion's mouth. "growl"
With a mooted* wing and waefu' maen, "molted"
The eagle sought her eiry again;
But lang may she cower in her bloody nest,
And lang, lang sleek her wounded breast,
Before she say* another flight, "assay"
To play wi' the norland lion's might.

But to sing the sights Kilmeny saw,
So far surpassing nature's law,
The singer's voice wad sink away,
And the string of his harp wad cease to play.

---

[1]Earnest money ("just deserts").

But she saw till the sorrows of man were by,
And all was love and harmony;
Till the stars of heaven fell calmly away,
Like the flakes of snaw on a winter day.
Then Kilmeny begged again to see
The friends she had left in her ain countrye,
To tell of the place where she had been,
And the glories that lay in the land unseen;
To warn the living maidens fair,
The loved of Heaven, the spirits' care,
That all whose minds unmeled* remain unmixed
Shall bloom in beauty when time is gane.

With distant music, soft and deep,
They lulled Kilmeny sound asleep;
And when she awakened, she lay her lane,
All happed* with flowers in the greenwood wene. clothed
When seven lang years had come and fled;
When grief was calm, and hope was dead;
When scarce was remembered Kilmeny's name,
Late, late in a gloamin Kilmeny came hame.
And O, her beauty was fair to see,
But still and steadfast was her ee.
Such beauty bard may never declare,
For there was no pride nor passion there;
And the soft desire of maiden's een
In that mild face could never be seen.
Her seymar* was the lily flower, robe
And her cheek the moss-rose in the shower;
And her voice like the distant melody,
That floats along the twilight sea.
But she loved to raike* the lanely glen, roam
And keep afar frae the haunts of men;
Her holy hymns unheard to sing,
To suck the flowers and drink the spring.
But wherever her peaceful form appeared,
The wild beasts of the hill were cheered;
The wolf played blithely round the field,
The lordly bison lowed and kneeled;
The dun deer wooed with manner bland,
And cowered aneath her lily hand.
And when at eve the woodlands rung,
When hymns of other worlds she sung
In ecstasy of sweet devotion,
O, then the glen was all in motion.
The wild beasts of the forest came,
Broke from their boughts* and faulds the tame, pens
And goved* around, charmed and amazed; stared
Even the dull cattle crooned and gazed,
And murmured and looked with anxious pain
For something the mystery to explain.
The buzzard came with the throstle-cock;
The corby* left her houf in the rock; raven

The blackbird alang wi' the eagle flew;
The hind came tripping oer the dew;
The wolf and the kid their raike began,
And the tod*, and the lamb, and the leveret* ran; fox/young hare
The hawk and the hern attour them hung,
And the merle and the mavis forhooyed* their young; forsook
And all in a peaceful ring were hurled:
It was like an eve in a sinless world.

When a month and a day had come and gane,
Kilmeny sought the greenwood wene;
There laid her down on the leaves sae green,
And Kilmeny on earth was never mair seen.
But O, the words that fell from her mouth,
Were words of wonder and words of truth.
But all the land were in fear and dread,
For they kendna whether she was living or dead.
It wasna her hame and she couldna remain;
She left this world of sorrow and pain,
And returned to the land of thought again.

## The Witch of Fife

"Whare haif ye been, ye ill woman,
These three lang nights fra hame?
What gars* the sweat drap fra yer brow, makes
Like clots of the saut sea faem?

"It fears me muckil ye haif seen
What guid man never knew;
It fears me muckil ye haif been
Whare the gray cock never crew.

"But the spell may crack, and the bridle breck,
Then sherp yer werd will be;
Ye had better sleep in yer bed at haem,
Wi' yer dear little bairns and me."

"Sit doun, sit doun, my leal* auld man, trusty
Sit doun, and listen to me;
I'll gar the hair stand on yer crown,
And the cauld sweat blind yer ee.

"But tell nae words, my guid auld man,
Tell never word again;
Or dear shall be yer courtesy,
And driche and sair yer pain.

"The first leet night, whan the new moon set,
Whan all was douffe and mirk
We saddled ouir naigs wi' the moon-fern leif,
And rode fra Kilmerrin kirk.

"Some horses ware of the brume-cow framit,
And some of the green bay tree;
But mine was made of ane hemlock shaw*, wood
And a stout stallion was he.

"We raid the tod* doun on the hill, fox
The martin on the law;
And we hunted the hoolet out of breath,
And forcit him doun to fa'."

"What guid was that, ye ill woman?
What guid was that to thee?
Ye wald better haif been in yer bed at home,
Wi' yer dear little bairns and me."

"And aye we raid, and se merrily we raid,
Through the merkist gloffs of the night;
And we swam the flood, and we darnit the wood,
Till we cam to the Lommond height.

"And whan we cam to the Lommond height,
Se lythlye we lychtid doun;
And we drank fra the horns that never grew,
The beer that was never brewin.

"Then up there raise ane wee wee man,
Fra neath the moss-gray stane;
His fece was wan like the cauliflower,
For he nouthir had blude nor bane.

"He set ane reid-pipe til his muthe,
And he playit se bonnily,
Till the gray curlew and the black-cock flew
To listen his melody.

"It rang se sweet through the green Lommond,
That the nicht-wind lowner blew;
And it soupit alang the Loch Leven,
And wakinit the white sea mew.

"It rang se sweet through the green Lommond,
Se sweetly butt and se shill,
That the weasels laup out of their moldy holes,
And dancit on the midnicht hill.

"The corby craw cam gledgin near,
The ern gede veering bye;
And the trouts laup out of the Leven Loch,
Charmit with the melody.

"And aye we dancit on the green Lommond,
Till the dawn on the ocean grew.

Ne wonder I was a weary wicht
When I cam hame to you."

"What guid, what guid, my weird weird wife,
What guid was that to thee?
Ye wald better haif bein in yer bed at hame,
Wi' yer dear little bairnis and me."

"The second nicht, whan the new moon set,
Oer the roaring sea we flew;
The cockle-shell our trusty bark,
Our sails of the green sea-rue.

"And the bauld winds blew, and the fire-flauchts flew,
And the sea ran to the sky;
And the thunner it growlit, and the sea-dogs howlit,
As we gaed scouring bye.

"And aye we mountit the sea-green hills,
Whill we brushit through the cludis of the heaven;
Than sousit dounright like the stern-shot light,
Fra the lifts* blue casement driven. sky's

"But our taickle stood, and our bark was good,
And se pang* was our pearily prow; full
When we couldna speil the brow of the waves,
We needilit them through below.

"As fast as the hail, as fast as the gale,
As fast as the midnicht leme*, (lightning)
We borit the breist of the bursting swale,
Or fluffit i' the flotying faem*. "foam"

"And whan to the Norraway shore we wan,
We muntyed our steeds of the wind,
And we splashit the flood, and we darnit the wood,
And we left the shouir behind.

"Fleit is the roe on the green Lommond,
And swift is the couring grew*; greyhound
The rein-dear dun can eithly run,
Whan the hounds and the horns pursue.

"But nowther the roe, nor the rein-dear dun,
The hind nor the couring grew,
Culde fly owr moutain, muir, and dale,
As our braw steeds they flew.

"The dales war deep, and the Doffrins steep,
And we raise to the skys ee-bree;
White, white was our rode, that was never trode,
Owr the snaws of eternity.

"And whan we cam to the Lapland lone,
The fairies war all in array;
For all the genii of the north
War keeping their holiday.

"The warlock men and the weird wemyng,
And the fays of the wood and the steep,
And the phantom hunters all war there,
And the mermaids of the deep.

"And they washit us all with the witch-water,
Distillit fra the muirland dew,
Whill our beauty blumit like the Lapland rose,
That wild in the forests grew."

"Ye lee, ye lee, ye ill woman,
Se loud as I heir ye lee!
For the warst-faurd* wife on the shores of Fife "favored"
Is cumlye comparit wi' thee."

"Then the mermaids sang and the woodlands rang,
Se sweetly swellit the quire;
On every cliff a herp they hang,
On every tree a lyre.

"And aye they sang, and the woodlands rang,
And we drank, and we drank se deep;
Then saft in the arms of the warlock men,
We laid us dune to sleep."

"Away, away, ye ill woman,
An ill deid met ye dee.
Whan ye hae proovit se false to yer God,
Ye can never prove true to me."

"And there we learnit fra the fairy folk,
And fra our master true,
The words that can bear us through the air,
And locks and bars undo.

"Last nicht we met at Maisry's cot;
Richt weil the words we knew;
And we set a foot on the black cruik-shell,
And out at the lum* we flew. chimney

"And we flew owr hill, and we flew owr dale,
And we flew owr firth an sea,
Until we cam to merry Carlisle,
Whare we lightit on the lea.

"We gaed to the vault beyond the towr,
Whare we enterit free as air;

And we drank, and we drank of the bishops wine
Whill we could drink ne mair."

"Gin* that be true, my guid auld wife, if
Whilk* thou hast tauld to me, which
Betide my death, betide my life,
I'll bear thee company.

"Naist time ye gaung to merry Carlisle
To drink of the blude-reid wine,
Beshrew my heart, I'll fly with thee,
If the deil should fly behind."

"Ah, little do ye ken, my silly auld man,
The dangers we maun dree*; endure
Last nicht we drank of the bishops wine,
Whill near near taen* war we. "taken"

"Afore we wan to the Sandy Ford,
The gor-cocks nichering flew;
The lofty crest of Ettrick Pen
Was wavit about with blue,
And, flichtering through the air, we fand
The chill chill morning dew.

"As we flew owr the hills of Braid,
The sun raise fair and clear;
There gurly James, and his barons braw,
War out to hunt the dear.

"Their bows they drew, their arrows flew,
And piercit the air with speed,
Whill purple fell the morning dew
Wi' witch-blude rank and reid*. "red"

"Little do ye ken, my silly auld man,
The dangers we maun dree;
Ne wonder I am a weary wicht
Whan I come hame to thee."

"But tell me the *word,* my guid auld wife,
Come tell it me speedily;
For I lang to drink of the guid reid wine,
And to wing the air with thee.

"Yer hellish horse I wilna ride,
Nor sail the seas in the wind;
But I can flee as weil as thee,
And I'll drink whill ye be blind."

"O fy, O fy, my leal auld man,
That word I darena tell;

It wald turn this warld all upside down,
And make it warse than hell.

"For all the lassies in the land
Wald munt the wind and fly;
And the men wald doff their doublets side,
And after them wald ply."

But the auld guidman was ane cunning auld man,
And ane cunning auld man was he;
And he watchit, and he watchit for mony a nicht,
The witches' flicht to see.

Ane nicht he darnit* in Maisry's cot; hid
The fearless hags cam in;
And he heard the word of awesome weird*, fate, power
And he saw their deeds of sin.

Than ane by ane they said that word,
As fast to the fire they drew;
Then set a foot on the black cruik-shell,
And out at the lum they flew.

The auld guidman cam fra his hole
With feir and muckil dread,
But yet he couldna think to rue,
For the wine cam in his head.

He set his foot in the black cruik-shell,
With ane fixit and ane wawlying ee;
And he said the word that I darena say,
And out at the lum flew he.

The witches skalit the moonbeam pale;
Deep groanit the trembling wind;
But they never wist till* our auld guidman to
Was hovering them behind.

They flew to the vaults of merry Carlisle,
Whare they enterit free as air;
And they drank and they drank of the bishops wine
Whill they could drink ne mair.

The auld guidman he grew se crouse*, bold
He dancit on the moldy ground,
And he sang the bonniest sangs of Fife,
And he tuzzlit the cerlings* round. old women (witches)

And aye he piercit the ither butt,
And he suckit, and he suckit se lang,
Whill his een they closit, and his voice grew low,
And his tongue wald hardly gang.

The cerlings drank of the bishops wine
Whill they scentit the morning wind;
Then clove again the yielding air,
And left the auld man behind.

And aye he sleepit on the damp damp floor,
He sleepit and he snorit amain;
He never dreamit he was far fra hame,
Or that the auld wives war gane.

And aye he sleepit on the damp damp floor,
Whill past the mid-day hight,
Whan wakenit by five rough Englishmen
That trailit him to the licht.

"Now wha are ye, ye silly auld man,
That sleeps se sound and se weil?
Or how gat ye into the bishops vault
Through locks and bars of steel?"

The auld gudeman he tryit to speak,
But ane word he couldna find;
He tryit to think, but his head whirlit round,
And ane thing he couldna mind:
"I cam fra Fife," the auld man cryit,
"And I cam on the midnicht wind."

They nickit the auld man, and they prickit the auld man,
And they yerkit his limbs with twine,
Whill the reid blude ran in his hose and shoon*, "shoes"
But some cryit it was wine.

They lickit the auld man, and they prickit the auld man,
And they tyit him till ane stone;
And they set ane bele-fire him about,
To burn him skin and bone.

"O woe to me!" said the puir auld man,
"That ever I saw the day.
And wae be to all the ill weming
That lead puir men astray.

"Let never ane auld man after this
To lawless greed incline;
Let never ane auld man after this
Rin post to the deil for wine."

The reike* flew up in the auld mans face, smoke
And choukit him bitterly;
And the lowe* cam up with ane angry blese, fire
And it singit his auld breek-knee.

He lukit to the land fra whence he cam,
For lukis he could get nae mae;
And he thocht of his dear little bairns at hame,
And O the auld man was wae.

But they turnit their faces to the sun,
With gloffe* and wondrous glair, look, glance
For they saw ane thing beth lairge and dun,
Coming swaipin down the air.

That bird it cam fra the lands o' Fife,
And it cam richt timeouslye,
For wha was it but the auld mans wife,
Just commit his death to see?

Scho put ane reid cap on his heid,
And the auld guidman lookit fain,
Then whisperit ane word intil his lug*, ear
And tovit to the air again.

The auld guidman he gae ane bob,
I' th mids o' the burning lowe;
And the sheklis that band him to the ring,
They fell fra his armis like towe*. twine

He drew his breath, and he said the word,
And he said it with muckil glee,
Then set his fit on the burning pile,
And away to the air flew he.

Till aince he clerit the swirling reik,
He lukit beth ferit and sad;
But whan he wan to the licht blue air,
He lauchit as he'd been mad.

His arms war spread, and his heid was hiche,
And his feet stack out behind;
And the laibies of the auld mans coat
War wauffling in the wind.

And aye he neicherit, and aye he flew,
For he thocht the ploy so rare;
It was like the voice of the gainder blue,
Whan he flies through the air.

He lukit back to the Carlisle men
As he borit the norlan sky;
He noddit his heid, and gae ane girn*, "grin"
But he never said guid-bye.

They vanisht far i' the lifts blue wale,
Ne mair the English saw,

But the auld mans lauch cam on the gale,
With a lang and a loud gaffa.

May ever ilke man in the land of Fife
Read what the drinkers dree*; suffer
And never curse his puir auld wife,
Richt wicked although scho be.

## There's Gowd in the Breast

There's gowd in the breast of the primrose pale,
An' siller in every blossom;
There's riches galore in the breeze of the vale,
And health in the wild wood's bosom.
Then come my love, at the hour of joy,
When warbling birds sing oer us;
Sweet nature for us has no alloy,
And the world is all before us.

The courtier joys in bustle and power,
The soldier in war-steeds bounding,
The miser in hoards of treasured ore,
The proud in their pomp surrounding:
But we hae yon heaven, sae bonnie and blue,
And laverocks skimming out oer us;
The breezes of health and the valleys of dew—
Oh, the world is all before us.

## Appie M'Gie

O Love has done muckle in city an' glen,
In tears of the women, an' vows of the men;
But the sweet little rogue, wi' his visions o' bliss,
Has never done aught sae unhallowed as this.
For what do ye think?—at a dance in the green,
Afore the dew fell through the gloamin' yestreen,
He has woundit the bosom, an' blindit the e'e,
Of the flower o' our valley, young Appie M'Gie.

Young Appie was sweet as the zephyr of even,
And blithe as the laverock that carols in heaven;
As bonnie as ever was bud o' the thorn,
Or rose that unfolds to the breath o' the morn.
Her form was the fairest o' nature's design,
And her soul was as pure as her face was divine:
Ah, Love, tis a shame that a model so true,
By thee should be melted and molded anew.

The little pale flow'rets blush deep for thy blame;
The fringe o' the daisy is purple wi' shame;
The heath-breeze that kisses the cheeks o' the free,
Has a tint of the mellow soft-breathings of thee.

Of all the wild wasters of glee and of hue,
And eyes that have depths o' the ocean of blue,
Love, thou art the chief: and a shame upon thee,
For this deed thou hast done to young Appie M'Gie.

## The Witch o' Fife

Hurray, hurray, the jade's away,
Like a rocket of air with her bandalet*. ribbon
I'm up in the air on my bonnie gray mare,
But I see her yet, I see her yet.
I'll ring the skirts o' the gowden wain[1]
Wi' curb an' bit, wi' curb an' bit;
An' catch the Bear, by the frozen mane—
An' I see her yet, I see her yet.

Away, away, oer mountain an' main,
To sing at the morning's rosy yett*; gate
An' water my mare at its fountain clear—
But I see her yet, I see her yet.
Away, thou bonnie witch o' Fife,
On foam of the air to heave an' flit,
An' little reck thou of a poet's life,
For he sees thee yet, he sees thee yet.

## Blithe an' Cheerie

On Ettrick clear there grows a brier,
An mony a bonnie blooming shaw*; grove
But Peggie's grown the fairest flower
The braes o' Ettrick ever saw.
Her cheek is like the woodland rose;
Her ee the violet set wi dew.
The lily's fair without compare,
Yet in her bosom tines* its hue. loses

Had I as muckle gowd an gear* money
As I could lift unto my knee,
Nae ither lass but Peggie dear
Should ever be a bride to me.
Oh she's blithe, an oh she's cheerie,
Oh she's bonnie, frank, an free.
The starnies bright, nae dewy night,
Could ever beam like Peggie's ee.

Had I her hame at my wee house,
That stands aneath yon mountain high,
To help me wi' the kye an ewes,
An in my arms at e'ening lie;
Oh sae blithe, an oh sae cheerie,

---

[1]Wain: cart (a constellation).

Oh sae happy we wad be.
The lammie to the ewe is dear,
But Peggie's dearer far to me.

But I may sigh and stand abeigh*, aloof
An greet* till I tine baith my een; weep
Though Peggie's smile my heart beguiles,
She disna mind my love a preen*. pin
Oh I'm sad, an oh I'm sorry.
Sad an sorry may I be.
I may be sick an very sick
But I'll be desperate sweer* to dee. slow

## I Hae Lost My Jeanie

Oh, I hae seen when fields were green,
An birds sae blithe an' cheerie, O,
How swift the day would pass away
When I was wi my dearie, O.
My heart's now sair, my elbows bare,
My pouch without a guinea, O.
I'll never taste o' pleasure mair,
Since I hae lost my Jeanie, O.

O fortune, thou hast used me ill,
Far waur than my deserving, O.
Thrice oer the crown thou'st knocked me down,
An left me hauflins* starving, O. half
Thy roughest blast has blawn the last,
My lass has used me meanly, O.
Thy keenest dart has pierced my heart,
An ta'en frae me my Jeanie, O.

I'll nae mair strive, while I'm alive,
For aught but missing slavery, O;
This world's a stage, a pilgrimage,
A mass o' guilt an knavery, O.
If fickle fame but save my name,
An frae oblivion screen me, O,
Then farewell fortune, farewell love,
An farewell, bonnie Jeanie, O.

## Gracie Miller

"Little, queer bit auld body,
Whar ye gaun sae late at e'en?
Sic a massy auld body
I saw never wi my een."
"I'm gaun to court the bonniest lass
That e'er stepped in leather shoe."
"But little shabby auld body,
Where's the lass will look at you?

"Ere I war kissed wi ane like you,
Or sic a man cam to my bed,
I'd rather kiss the hawkit* cow, spotted
An in my bosom tak a taed.
Wha ever weds wi sic a stock
Will be a gibe to a the lave*. rest
Little, stupit auld body,
Rather think upon your grave."

"But I'm sae deep in love wi ane,
I'll wed or die, it maks na whether.
Oh, she's the prettiest, sweetest queen
That ever brushed the dew frae heather.
The fairest Venus ever drawn
Is naething but a bogle till* her. to
She's fresher than the morning dawn,
An hark—her name is Gracie Miller."

She raised her hands; her een they reeled,
Then wi a skirl outoer she fell,
An aye she leuch*, an aye she squealed, laughed
"Hey, mercy, body, that's mysel!"
Then down he hurkled* by her side, crouched
An kissed her hand, an warmly wooed her;
An whiles* she leuch, an whiles she sighed, at times
An leaned her head upon his shoulder.

"O pity me, my bonnie Grace.
My words are true, ye needna doubt 'em.
Nae man can see your bonnie face
An keep his senses a' about him."
"Troth, honest man, I kenned langsyne
Nae ither lass could equal wi me;
But yet the brag sae justly mine
Was tint*, till you hae chanced to see me. lost

"Thou ye want yudith, gear, an mense*, dignity, manners
Ye hae a dash o' amorous fire;
Ye hae good taste, an sterling sense,
An ye sall hae your hearts desire."
Oh woman, woman, after death,
If that vain nature still is given,
An deils* get leave to use their breath, "devils"
They'll flatter ye into hell frae heaven.

## Bauldy Frazer

My name is Bauldy Frazer, man.
I'm puir, an auld, an pale, an wan.
I brak my shin, an tint* a han' lost
Upon Culloden lea, man.
Our Hielan' clans were bauld and stout,

An' thought to turn their faes about,
But gat that day a desperate rout,
An owre the hills did flee, man.

Sic hurly-burly ne'er was seen,
Wi cuffs, an buffs, an blindit een,
While Hielan' swords o' metal keen
War gleamin' grand to see, man.
The cannons routit* in our face, roared
An brak our banes an raive* our claes. tore
Twas then we saw our ticklish case
Atween the deil an sea, man.

Sure Charlie an the brave Lochiel
Had been that time beside theirsel,
To plant us in the open fell,
In the artillery's ee, man;
For had we met wi Cumberland
By Athol braes or yonder strand,
The bluid o' a' the savage band
Had dyed the German sea, man.

But down we drappit dadd* for dadd; blow
I thought it should hae put me mad,
To see sae mony a Hielan' lad
Lie bluthrin'* on the brae, man. disfigured
I thought we ance had won the fray;
We smasht ae wing till it gae way;
But the other side had lost the day,
An skelpit fast awa, man.

When Charlie wi Macpherson met,
Like Hay he thought him back to get.
"We'll turn," quo he, "an try them yet.
We'll conquer or we'll dee, man."
But Donald shumpit oer the purn,
An sware an aith* she wadna turn, "oath"
Or sure she wad hae cause to mourn;
Then fast awa did flee, man.

Oh, had you seen that hunt o' death.
We ran until we tint our breath,
Aye looking back for fear o' skaith*, harm
Wi hopeless shinin ee, man.
But Britain ever may deplore
That day upon Drumossie moor,
Whar thousands taen war drenched in gore,
Or hanged outoer a tree, man.

O Cumberland, what meaned ye then,
To ravage ilka Hielan' glen?
Our crime was truth, an love to ane,
We had nae spite at thee, man.

An you or yours may yet be glad,
To trust the honest Hieland lad.
The bonnet blue, and belted plaid,
Will stand the last o' three, man.

## Connel of Dee

[This poem, rough but lively, is notable for its author's progressive abandonment of the thick Scots diction with which it begins.]

Connel went out by a blink of the moon
To his light little bower in the deane;
He thought they had gi'en him his supper owre soon,
And that still it was long, until e'en.
Oh, the air was so sweet, and the sky so serene,
And so high his soft languishment grew—
That visions of happiness danced oer his mind;
He longed to leave parent and sisters behind,
For he thought that his Maker to him was unkind:
For that high were his merits he knew.

Sooth, Connel was halesome, and stalwart to see,
The bloom of fair yudith he wore;
But the lirk of displeasure hang over his bree,
Nae glisk of contentment it bore;
He langed for a wife with a mailen* and store; farm
He grevit in idleness to lie;
Afar from his cottage he wished to remove
To wassail and wake, and unchided to rove,
And beik in the cordial transports of love
All under a kindlier sky.

Oh sweet was the fa' of that gloaming to view.
The day-light crap laigh on the doon,
And left its pale borders abeigh on the blue,
To mix wi' the beams of the moon.
The hill hang its skaddaw the greenwood aboon,
The houf* of the bodyng Benshee; vale
Slow oer him were sailing the cloudlets of June;
The beetle began his wild airel to tune,
And sang on the wind with ane eirysome croon,
Away on the breeze of the Dee.

With haffat* on lufe poor Connel lay lorn, side-locks
He languishit for muckle and mair;
His bed of green heather he eynit to scorn,
The bygane he doughtna weel bear.
Attour him the green leif was fannyng the air,
In noiseless and flychtering play;
The hush of the water fell saft on his ear,
And he fand as gin sleep, wi' her gairies, war near,

Wi' her freaks and her ferlies* and phantoms of fear, wonders
But he eidently* wysit her away. thoroughly

Short time had he sped in that sellible strife
Ere he saw a young maiden stand by,
Who seemed in the bloom and the bell of her life;
He wist not that ane was sae nigh.
But sae sweet was her look, and sae saft was her eye,
That his heart was all quaking with love;
And then there was kything* a dimple sae sly, provoking
At play on her cheek, of the moss-rose's dye,
That kindled the heart of poor Connel on high
With ravishment deadly to prove.

He deemed her a beautiful spirit of night,
And eiry was he to assay;
But he found she was mortal with thrilling delight,
For her breath was like zephyr of May;
Her eye was the dew-bell, the beam of the day,
And her arm it was softer than silk;
Her hand was so warm, and her lip was so red,
Her slim taper waist so enchantingly made,
And some beauties moreover that cannot be said—
Of bosom far whiter than milk.

Poor Connel was reaved* of all power and of speech, bereft
His frame grew all powerless and weak;
He neither could stir, nor caress her, nor fleech*; flirt
He trembled, but word couldna speak.
But oh, when his lips touched her soft rosy cheek,
The channels of feeling ran dry.
He found that like emmets his life-blood it crept,
His liths turned as limber as dud* that is steeped; coarse cloth
He streekit his limbs, and he moaned and he wept,
And for love he was just gaun to die.

The damsel beheld, and she raised him so kind,
And she said, "My dear beautiful swain,
Take heart till I tell you the hark of my mind;
I'm weary of living my-lane*; alone
I have castles, and lands, and flocks of my ain,
But want ane my gillour* to share; attendant
A man that is hale as the hart on the hill,
As stark, and as kind, is the man to my will,
Who has slept on the heather and drank of the rill,
And, like you, gentle, amorous, and fair.

"I often hae heard, that like you there was nane,
And I ance got a glisk of thy face;
Now far have I ridden, and far have I gane,
In hopes thou wilt nurice the grace
To make me thy ain—Oh, come to my embrace,
For I love thee as dear as my life.

I'll make thee a laird of the boonmost degree,
My castles and lands I'll give freely to thee;
Though rich and abundant, thine own they shall be,
If thou wilt but make me thy wife."

Oh, never was man sae delighted and fain.
He bowed a consent to her will;
Kind providence thankit again and again,
And gan to display his rude skill
In leifu'* endearment; and thought it nae ill "lawful"
To kiss the sweet lips of the fair,
And press her to lie, in that gloamin' sae still,
Adown by his side in the howe* of the hill, vale
For the water flowed sweet, and the sound of the rill
Would soothe every sorrow and care.

No—she wadna lie by the side of a man
Till the rites of the marriage were bye.
Away they hae sped; but soon Connel began,
For his heart it was worn to a sigh,
To fondle, and simper, and look in her eye,
Oh, direful to bear was his wound,
When on her fair neck fell his fingers sae dun—
It strak through his heart like the shot of a gun.
He felt as the sand of existence were run:
He trembled, and fell to the ground.

O Connel, dear Connel, be patient a while.
These wounds of thy bosom will heal,
And thou with thy love mayest walk many a mile
Nor transport nor passion once feel.
Thy spirits once broke on electeric wheel,
Cool reason her empire shall gain;
And haply, repentance in dowy* array, soft
And laithly disgust may arise in thy way,
Encumbering the night, and o'ercasting the day,
And turn all those pleasures to pain.

The mansion is gained, and the bridal is past,
And the transports of wedlock prevail;
The lot of poor Connel the shepherd is cast
Mid pleasures that never can fail.
The balms of Arabia sweeten the gale,
The tables for ever are spread
With damask, and viands and heart-cheering wine
Their splendor and elegance fully combine;
His lawns they are ample, his bride is divine,
And of goud-fringed silk is his bed.

The transports of love gave rapture, and flew;
The banquet soon sated and cloyed;
Nae mair they delighted, nae langer were new,
They could not be ever enjoyed.

He felt in his bosom a fathomless void,
A yearning again to be free.
Than all that voluptuous sickening store,
The wine that he drank and the robes that he wore,
His diet of milk had delighted him more
Afar on the hills of the Dee.

Oh, oft had he sat by the clear springing well,
And dined from his wallet full fain.
Then sweet was the scent of the blue heather-bell,
And free was his bosom of pain.
The laverock was lost in the lift*, but her strain sky
Came trilling so sweetly from far,
To rapture the hour he would wholly resign,
He would listen, and watch, till he saw her decline
And the sun's yellow beam on her dappled breast shine,
Like some little musical star.

And then he wad lay his blue bonnet aside,
And turn his rapt eyes to the heaven,
And bless his kind maker who all did provide;
And beg that he might be forgiven,
For his sins were like crimson—all bent and uneven
The path he had wilesomely trod;
Then who the delight of his bosom could tell.
Oh, sweet was that meal by his pure mountain well;
And sweet was its water he drank from the shell,
And peaceful his moorland abode.

But now was he deaved* and babbled outright, deafened
By gossips in endless array,
Who thought not of sin nor of Satan aright,
Nor the dangers that mankind belay;
Who joked about heaven, and scorned to pray,
And gloried in that was a shame.
Oh, Connel was troubled at things that befell,
So different from scenes he had once loved so well,
He deemed he was placed on the confines of hell,
And fand like the sa'ur of its flame.

Of bonds and of law-suits he still was in doubt,
And old debts coming due every day;
And a thousand odd things he kenned naething about
Kept him in continued dismay.
At board he was awkward, nor wist what to say,
Nor what his new honors became;
His guests they wad mimic and laugh in their sleeve;
He blushed, and he faltered, and scarce dought believe
That men were so base as to smile and deceive;
Or eynied of him to make game.

Still franker and freer his gossipers grew,
And preyed upon him and his dame.

Their jests and their language to Connel were new,
It was slander, and cursing, and shame.
He groaned in his heart, and he thought them to blame
For revel and rout without end.
He saw himself destined to pamper and feed
A race whom he hated, a profligate breed,
The scum of existence to vengeance decreed,
Who laughed at their God and their friend.

He saw that in wickedness all did delight,
And he kenned na what length it might bear;
They drew him to evil by day and by night,
To scenes that he trembled to share.
His heart it grew sick, and his head it grew sair,
And he thought what he dared not to tell:
He thought of the far distant hills of the Dee;
Of his cake, and his cheese, and his lair on the lea;
Of the laverock that hung on the heaven's e'e-bree;
His prayer, and his clear mountain well.

His breast he durst sparingly trust wi' the thought
Of the virtuous days that were fled;
Yet still his kind lady he loved as he ought,
Or soon from that scene he had fled.
It now was but rarely she honored his bed—
Twas modesty, heightening her charms!
A delicate feeling that man cannot ween:
O Heaven! each night from his side she had been—
He found it at length—nay, he saw't wi' his een,
She slept in a paramour's arms.

It was the last pang, that the spirit could bear,
Destruction and death was the meed:
For forfeited vows there was nought too severe;
Even conscience applauded the deed.
His mind was decided, her doom was decreed;
He led her to chamber apart,
To give her to know of his wrongs he had sense,
To chide and upbraid her in language intense,
And kill her, at least, for her heinous offense—
A crime at which demons would start.

With grievous reproaches, in agonized zeal,
Stern Connel his lecture began;
He mentioned her crime.—She turned on her heel
And her mirth to extremity ran.
"Why, that was the fashion!—no sensible man
Could e'er of such freedom complain.
What was it to him? there were maidens enow
Of the loveliest forms, and the loveliest hue,
Who blithely would be his companions, he knew,
If he wearied of lying his lane."

How Connel was shocked!—but his fury still rose,
He shivered from toe to the crown;
His hair stood like heath on the mountain that grows,
And each hair had a life of its own.
"O thou most"—But whereto his passion had flown
No man to this day can declare,
For his dame, with a frown, laid her hand on his mouth,
That hand once as sweet as the breeze of the south;
That hand that gave pleasures and honor and routh;
And she said, with a dignified air:—

"Peace, booby! if life thou regardest, beware;
I have had some fair husbands ere now;
They wooed, and they flattered, they sighed and they sware,
At length they grew irksome like you.
Come hither one moment, a sight I will show
That will teach thee some breeding and grace."
She opened a door, and there Connel beheld
A sight that to trembling his spirit impelled;
A man standing chained, who nor 'plained, nor rebelled,
And that man had a sorrowful face.

Down creaked a trap-door, on which he was placed,
Right softly and slowly it fell;
And the man seemed in terror, and strangely amazed,
But why, Connel could not then tell.
He sunk and he sunk as the vice did impel;
At length, as far downward he drew,
Good Lord! In a trice, with the pull of a string,
A pair of dread shears, like the thunderbolt's wing,
Came snap on his neck, with a terrible spring,
And severed it neatly in two.

Adown fell the body—the head lay in sight,
The lips in a moment grew wan;
The temple just quivered, the eye it grew white,
And upward the purple threads span.
The dark crooked streamlets along the boards ran,
Thin pipings of reek could be seen;
Poor Connel was blinded, his lugs how they sung.
He looked once again, and he saw like the tongue,
That motionless out twixt the livid lips hung;
Then mirkness set over his e'en.

He turned and he dashed his fair lady aside;
And off like the lightning he broke,
By staircase and gallery, with horrified stride;
He turned not, he staid not, nor spoke;
The iron-spiked court-gate he could not unlock,
His haste was beyond that of man;
He stopped not to rap, and he staid not to call,
With ram-race he cleared at a bensil* the wall,

*great effort

And headlong beyond got a grievous fall,
But he rose, and he ran, and he ran!

As stag of the forest, when fraudfully coiled,
And mured up in barn for a prey,
Sees his dappled comrades dishonored and soiled
In their blood, on some festival day,
Bursts all intervention, and hies him away,
Like the wind over holt, over lea;
So Connel pressed on, all encumbrance he threw,
Over height, over hollow, he lessened to view:
It may not be said that he ran, for he flew,
Straight on for the hills of the Dee.

The contrair of all other runners in life,
His swiftness increased as he flew,
But be it remembered, he ran from a wife,
And a trap-door that sunk on a screw.
His prowess he felt and decidedly knew,
So much did his swiftness excel,
That he skimmed the wild paths like a thing of the mind,
And the stour* from each footstep was seen on the wind, dust
Distinct by itself for a furlong behind,
Before that it mingled or fell.

He came to a hill, the ascent it was steep,
And much did he fear for his breath;
He halted, he ventured behind him to peep,—
The sight was a vision of death!
His wife and her paramours came on the path,
Well mounted, with devilish speed;
O Connel, poor Connel, thy hope is a wreck.
Sir, run for thy life, without stumble or check,
It is thy only stake, the last chance for thy neck,—
Strain Connel, or death is thy meed!

Oh wend to the right, to the woodland betake;
Gain that, and yet safe thou may'st be;
How fast they are gaining! Oh stretch to the brake.
Poor Connel, tis over with thee!
In the breath of the horses his yellow locks flee,
The voice of his wife's in the van;
Even that was not needful to heighten his fears.
He sprung oer the bushes, he dashed through the briers,
For he thought of the trap-door and damnable shears,
And he cried to his God, and he ran.

Through gallwood and bramble he floundered amain,
No bar his advancement could stay;
Though heels-over-head whirled again and again,
Still faster he gained on his way.
This moment on swinging bough powerless he lay,
The next was flying along

So lightly, he scarce made the green leaf to quake;
Impetuous he splashed through the bog and the lake,
He rainbowed the hawthorn, he needled the brake,
With power supernaturally strong.

The riders are foiled, and far lagging behind,
Poor Connel has leisure to pray.
He hears their dread voices around on the wind,
Still farther and farther away—
"O Thou who sit'st throned oer the fields of the day,
Have pity this once upon me.
Deliver from those that are hunting my life,
From traps of the wicked that round me are rife,
And oh, above all, from the rage of a wife,
And guide to the hills of the Dee!

"And if ever I grumble at providence more,
Or scorn my own mountains of heath;
If ever I yearn for that sin-breeding ore,
Or shape to complaining a breath.
Then may I be nipt with the scissors of death."—
No farther could Connel proceed:
He thought of the snap that he saw in the nook;
Of the tongue that came out, and the temple that shook,
Of the blood and the reek, and the deadening look:
He lifted his bonnet and fled.

He wandered and wandered through woodlands of gloom,
And sorely he sobbed and he wept;
At cherk of the pyat, or bee's passing boom,
He started, he listened, he leaped.
With eye and with ear a strict guardship he kept;
No scene could his sorrows beguile:
At length he stood lone by the side of the Dee;
It was placid and deep, and as broad as a sea;
Oh, could he get over, how safe he might be,
And gain his own mountains the while.

Twas dangerous to turn, but proceeding was worse,
For the country grew open and bare,
No forest appeared, neither broomwood nor gorse,
Nor furze that would shelter a hare.
Ah, could he get over how safe he might fare;
At length he resolved to try;
At worst twas but drowning, and what was a life
Compared to confinement in sin and in strife,
Beside a trap-door and a scandalous wife?
Twas nothing,—he'd swim, or he'd die.

Ah, he could not swim, and was loath to resign
This life for a world unknown;
For he had been sinning, and misery condign
Would sure be his portion alone.

How sweetly the sun on the green mountain shone;
And the flocks they were resting, in peace,
Or bleating along on each parallel path:
The lambs they were skipping on fringe of the heath—
How different might kythe the lone valleys of death,
And cheerfulness evermore cease?

All wistful he stood on the brink of the pool,
And dropt on its surface the tear;
He started at something, that boded him dool,
And his mouth fell wide open with fear.
The trample of gallopers fell on his ear;
One look was too much for his eye;
For there was his wife, and her paramours twain,
With whip and with spur coming over the plain;
Bent forward, revengeful, they galloped amain,
They hasten, they quicken, they fly!

Short time was there now to deliberate, I ween,
And shortly did Connel decree;
He shut up his mouth, and he closed his een,
And he pointed his arms like a V,
And like a scared otter, he dived in the Dee,
His heels pointed up to the sky;
Like bolt from the firmament downward he bears;
The still liquid element startled uprears,
It bubbled, and bullered, and roared in his ears,
Like thunder that bellows on high.

He soon found the symptoms of drowning begin,
And painful the feeling be sure,
For his breath it gaed out, and the water gaed in,
With drumble and mudwart impure;
It was most unpleasant, and hard to endure,
And he struggled its inroads to wear;
But it rushed by his mouth, and it rushed by his nose,
His joints grew benumbed, all his fingers and toes,
And his een turned they neither would open nor close,
And he found his departure was near.

One time he came up, like a porpoise, above,
He breathed and he lifted his eye,
It was the last glance of the land of his love,
Of the world, and the beautiful sky:
How bright looked the sun from his window on high,
Through furs of the light golden grain.
Oh, Connel was sad, but he thought with a sigh,
That far above yon peaceful vales of the sky,
In bowers of the morning he shortly might lie,
Though very unlike it just then.

He sunk to the bottom, no more he arose,
The waters for ever his body inclose;

The horse-mussel clasped on his fingers and toes,
All passive he suffered the scathe.
But oh, there was one thing his heart could not brook,
Even in his last struggles his spirit it shook;
The eels, with their cursed equivocal look,
Redoubled the horrors of death.
Oh, aye since the time that he was but a bairn,
When catching his trouts in the Cluny or Gairn,
At sight of an eel he would shudder and darn!
It almost deprived him of breath.

He died, but he found that he never would be
So dead to all feeling and smart,
No, not though his flesh were consumed in the Dee,
But that eels would some horror impart.
With all other fishes he yielded to mart,
Resistance became not the dead;
The minnow, with gushet sae gowden and braw,
The siller-ribbed perch, and the indolent craw,
And the ravenous ged, with his teeth like a saw,
Came all on poor Connel to feed.

They rave and they rugged*, he cared not a speal, tore
Though they preyed on his vitals alone;
But, Lord, when he felt the cold nose of an eel,
A quaking seized every bone;
Their slid slimy forms lay his bosom upon,
His mouth that was ope, they came near;
They guddled his loins, and they bored through his side,
They warped all his bowels about on the tide.

Young Connel was missed, and his mother was sad,
But his sisters consoled her mind;
And said, he was wooing some favorite maid,
For Connel was amorous and kind.
Ah, little weened they that their Connel reclined
On a couch that was loathful to see.
Twas mud—and the water-bells oer him did heave;
The lampreys passed through him without law or leave,
And windowed his frame like a riddle or sieve,
Afar in the deeps of the Dee.

It was but a night, and a midsummer night,
And next morning when rose the red sun,
His sisters in haste their fair bodies bedight,
And, ere the day's work was begun,
They sought for their Connel, for they were undone
If aught should their brother befall:
And first they went straight to the bower in the deane,
For there he of late had been frequently seen:
For nature he loved, and her evening scene
To him was the dearest of all.

And when within view of his bourack* they came, cow-fetter
It lay in the skaddow so still,
They lift up their voices and called his name,
And their forms they shone white on the hill;
When, trow you, that hallo so erlisch and shrill
Arose from those maids on the heath?
It was just as poor Connel most poignant did feel,
As reptiles he loved not of him made a meal,
Just when the misleered and unmannerly eel
Waked him from the slumbers of death.

He opened his eyes, and with wonder beheld
The sky and the hills once again;
But still he was haunted, for over the field
Two females came running, amain.
No form but his spouse's remained on his brain;
His sisters to see him were glad;
But he started bolt upright in horror and fear,
He deemed that his wife and her minions were near,
He flung off his plaid, and he fled like a deer,
And they thought their poor brother was mad.

He 'scaped; but he halted on top of the rock;
And his wonder and pleasure still grew;
For his clothes were not wet, and his skin was unbroke,
But he scarce could believe it was true
That no eels were within; and too strictly he knew
He was married and buckled for life.
It could not be a dream; for he slept and awoke;
Was drunken, and sober; had sung, and had spoke;
For months and for days he had dragged in the yoke
With an unconscientious wife.

However it was, he was sure he was there,
On his own native cliffs of the Dee:
Oh never before looked a morning so fair,
Or the sun-beam so sweet on the lea!
The song of the merle from her old hawthorn tree,
And the blackbird's melodious lay,
All sounded to him like an anthem of love;
A song that the spirit of nature did move;
A kind little hymn to their maker above,
Who gave them the beauties of day.

So deep the impression was stamped on his brain;
The image was never defaced;
Whene'er he saw riders that galloped amain,
He darned* in some bush till they passed. hid
At kirk or at market sharp glances he cast,
Lest haply his wife might be there;
And once, when the liquor had kindled his e'e,
It never was known who or what he did see,

But he made a miraculous flight from Dundee,
The moment he entered the fair.

But never again was his bosom estranged
From his simple and primitive fare;
No longer his wishes or appetite ranged
With the gay and voluptuous to share.
He viewed every luxury of life as a snare:
He drank of his pure mountain spring;
He watched all the flowers of the wild as they sprung;
He blest his sweet laverock, like fairy that sung,
Aloft on the hem of the morning cloud hung,
Light fanning its down with her wing.

And oft on the shelve of the rock he reclined,
Light caroling humorsome rhyme,
Of his midsummer dream, of his feelings refined,
Or some song of the good olden time.
And even in age was his spirit in prime,
Still reverenced on Dee is his name;
His wishes were few, his enjoyments were rife,
He loved and he cherished each thing that had life,
With two small exceptions, an eel and a wife,
Whose commerce he dreaded the same.

## The Mermaid

"Oh where won* ye, my bonnie lass, dwell
Wi look sae wild an cheery?
There's something in that witching face
That I loe wonder dearly."

"I live where the harebell never grew,
Where the streamlet never ran,
Where the winds o' heaven never blew;
Now find me gin* you can." if

"Tis but your wild an wily way,
The gloaming maks you eirie,
For ye are the lass o' the Braken-Brae,
An nae lad maun come near ye;

"But I am sick, an very sick
Wi a passion strange an new,
For ae kiss o' thy rosy cheek
An lips o' the coral hue."

"O laith, laith wad a wanderer be
To do your youth sic wrang;
Were you to reave* a kiss from me steal
Your life would not be lang.

"Go, hie you from this lonely brake,
Nor dare your walk renew;
For I'm the Maid of the Mountain Lake,
An I come wi the falling dew."

"Be you the Maid of the Crystal Wave,
Or she of the Braken-Brae,
One tender kiss I mean to have.
You shall not say me nay.

"For beauty's like the daisy's vest
That shrinks from the early dew,
But soon it opes its bonnie breast,
An sae may it fare wi you."

"Kiss but this hand, I humbly sue,
Even there I'll rue the stain;
Or the breath of man will dim its hue,
It will ne'er be pure again.

"For passion's like the burning beal* boil
Upon the mountain's brow,
That wastes itself to ashes pale;
An sae will it fare wi you."

______________________________[1]

"O mother, mother, make my bed,
An make it soft and easy;
An with the cold dew bathe my head,
For pains of anguish seize me:

"Or stretch me in the chill blue lake,
To quench this bosom's burning;
An lay me by yon lonely brake,
For hope there's none returning.

"I've been where man should not have been,
Oft in my lonely roaming;
And seen what man should not have seen,
By green wood in the gloaming.

"O, passion's deadlier than the grave,
A' human things undoing.
The Maiden of the Mountain Wave
Has lured me to my ruin."

______________________

[1](Sic.)

Tis now an hundred years an more,
An all these scenes are over,
Since rose his grave on yonder shore,
Beneath the wild wood cover;

An late I saw the Maiden there,
Just as the daylight faded,
Braiding her locks of gowden hair,
An singing as she braided:

The Mermaid's Song

Lie still, my love, lie still and sleep,
Long is thy night of sorrow;
Thy maiden of the mountain deep
Shall meet thee on the morrow.

But oh, when shall that morrow be,
That my true love shall waken;
When shall we meet, refined and free,
Amid the moorland braken?

Full low and lonely is thy bed,
The worm even flies thy pillow;
Where now the lips, so comely red,
That kissed me 'neath the willow?

Oh, I must smile, and weep the while,
Amid my song of mourning,
At freaks of man in life's short span,
To which there's no returning.

Lie still, my love, lie still and sleep,
Hope lingers oer thy slumber:
What though thy years beneath the steep
Should all its flowers outnumber;

Though moons steal oer, and seasons fly
On time-swift wing unstaying?
Yet there's a spirit in the sky,
That lives oer thy decaying.

In domes beneath the water springs,
No end hath my sojourning;
And to this land of fading things
Far hence be my returning;

For all the spirits of the deep
Their long last leave are taking.
Lie still, my love, lie still and sleep,
Till the last morn is breaking.

## A Witch's Chant

Thou art weary, weary, weary,
Thou art weary and far away.
Hear me, gentle spirit, hear me;
Come before the dawn of day.

I hear a small voice from the hill,
The vapor is deadly, pale, and still—
A murmuring sough* is on the wood, swish, sigh
And the witching star is red as blood.

And in the cleft of heaven I scan
The giant form of a naked man.
His eye is like the burning brand,
And he holds a sword in his right hand.

All is not well: by dint of spell,
Somewhere between the heaven and hell
There is this night a wild deray*; ado
The spirits have wandered from their way.

The purple drops shall tinge the moon,
As she wanders through the midnight noon;
And the dawning heaven shall all be red
With blood by guilty angels shed.

Be as it will, I have the skill
To work by good or work by ill;
Then here's for pain, and here's for thrall,
And here's for conscience, worst of all.

Another chant, and then, and then,
Spirits shall come or Christian men—
Come from the earth, the air, or the sea:
Great Gil-Moules, I cry to thee.

Sleep'st thou, wakest thou, lord of the wind?
Mount thy steeds and gallop them blind;
And the long-tailed fiery dragon outfly,
The rocket of heaven, the bomb of the sky.

Over the dog-star, over the wain,[1]
Over the cloud, and the rainbow's mane,
Over the mountain, and over the sea,
Haste—haste—haste to me.

Then here's for trouble, and here's for smart,
And here's for the pang that seeks the heart.
Here's for madness, and here's for thrall,
And here's for conscience, the worst of all.

---

[1]Wagon (a constellation).

## The Lassie of Yarrow

"What makes my heart beat high,
What makes me heave the sigh,
When yon green den I spy,
Lonely and narrow?
Sure on your braken lea
Under the hawthorn tree,
Thou hast bewitched me,
Lassie of Yarrow."

"Yon braken den so lone,
Rueful I ponder on;
Lad, though my vow ye won,
Twas to deceive thee.
Sore, sore I rue the day
When in your arms I lay,
And swore by the hawthorn gray,
Never to leave thee."

"Mary, thy will is free;
All my fond vows to thee
Were but in jest and glee;
Could'st thou believe me:
I have another love
Kind as the woodland dove;
False to that maid to prove,
Oh, it would grieve me."

Mary's full eye so blue,
Mild as the evening dew,
Quick from his glance withdrew,
Soft was her sighing;
Keen he the jest renewed,
Hard for his freedom sued—
When her sweet face he viewed,
Mary was crying.

"Cheer thee," the lover said,
"Now thy sharp scorn repaid,
Never shall other maid
Call me her marrow*. mate
Far sweeter than sun or sea,
Or aught in this world I see,
Is thy love-smile to me,
Lassie of Yarrow."

## The Minstrel Boy

The minstrel boy to the glen is gone,
In its deepest dells you'll find him,
Where echoes sing to his music's tone,
And fairies listen behind him.

And fairies listen behind him.
He sings of nature all in her prime,
Of sweets that around him hover,
Of mountain heath and moorland thyme,
And trifles that tell the lover.

How wildly sweet is the minstrel's lay,
Through cliffs and wild woods ringing;
For ah, there is love to beacon his way,
And hope in the song he's singing.
The bard may indite, and the minstrel sing,
And maidens may chorus it rarely;
But unless there be love in the heart within,
The ditty will charm but sparely.

## The Village of Balmaquhapple

D'ye ken the big village of Balmaquhapple,
The great muckle village of Balmaquhapple?
Tis steeped in iniquity up to the thrapple*, throat
An what's to become o' poor Balmaquhapple?
Fling a' aff your bannets, an kneel for your life, folks,
And pray to St. Andrew, the god o' the Fife folks;
Gar* a' the hills yout wi sheer vociferation, make
And thus you may cry on sic needfu' occasion:

"O blessed St. Andrew, if e'er ye could pity folk,
Men folk or women folk, country or city folk,
Come for this aince wi the auld thief to grapple,
An save the great village of Balmaquhapple
Frae drinking an leeing, an flyting* an swearing, scolding
An sins that ye wad be affrontit at hearing,
An cheating an stealing; oh, grant them redemption,
All save an except the few after to mention;

"There's Johnny the elder, wha hopes ne'er to need ye,
Sae pawkie*, sae holy, sae gruff, an sae greedy; sly
Wha prays every hour as the wayfarer passes,
But aye at a hole where he watches the lasses:
He's cheated a thousand, an e'en to this day yet
Can cheat a young lass, or they're leears that say it.
Then gie him his gate*; he's sae slee an sae civil, way
Perhaps in the end he may wheedle the devil.

"There's Cappie the cobbler, an Tammie the tinman,
An Dickie the brewer, an Peter the skinman,
An Geordie our deacon for want of a better,
An Bess, wha delights in the sins that beset her.
O worthy St. Andrew, we canna compel ye,
But ye ken as weel as a body can tell ye,
If these gang to heaven, we'll a' be sae shockit,
Your garret o' blue will but thinly be stockit.

"But for a' the rest, for the women's sake, save them,
Their bodies at least, an their sauls, if they have them.
But it puzzles Jock Lesly, an sma it avails,
If they dwell in their stamocks, their heads, or their tails.
An save, without word of confession auricular,
The clerk's bonny daughters, an Bell in particular;
For ye ken that their beauty's the pride an the staple
Of the great wicked village of Balmaquhapple.

## The Women Folk

Oh sairly may I rue the day
I fancied first the womankind;
For aye sinsyne I ne'er can hae
Ae quiet thought or peace o' mind.
They hae plagued my heart an pleased my ee,
An teased an flattered me at will,
But aye for a their witchery,
The pawky* things I loe them still. sly

Oh the women folk; oh, the women folk;
But they hae been the wreck o' me;
Oh weary fa' the women folk,
For they winna let a body be.

I hae thought an thought, but darena tell,
I've studied them wi a' my skill,
I've lo'ed them better than mysel,
I've tried again to like them ill.
Wha sairest strives, will sairest rue,
To comprehend what nae man can;
When he has done what man can do,
He'll end at last where he began.

That they hae gentle forms and meet,
A man wi half a look may see;
An gracefu' airs, and faces sweet,
An waving curls aboon the bree;
An smiles as soft as the young rose bud;
An een sae pawky, bright, an rare,
Wad lure the laverock frae the cludd—
But laddie, seek to ken nae mair.

Even but this night nae farther gane,
The date is neither lost nor lang;
I tak ye witness ilka ane,
How fell they fought an fairly dang*. strike
Their point they've carried right or wrang,
Without a reason, rhyme, or law,
An forced a man to sing a sang,
That ne'er could sing a verse ava*. at all

## The Harp of Ossian

I have been sorely blamed by some friends for a sentiment expressed in this song; but I have always felt it painfully that the name of Scotland, the superior nation in everything but wealth, should be lost, not in Britain, for that is proper, but in England. In all despatches we are denominated *the English*, forsooth! We know ourselves, however, that we are not English, nor never intend to be.

Old harp of the Highlands, how long hast thou slumbered
In cave of the correi, ungarnished, unstrung.
Thy minstrels no more with thy heroes are numbered,
Or deeds of thy heroes no more dare be sung.
A seer late heard, from thy cavern ascending,
A low sounding chime, as of sorrow and dole;
Some spirit unseen on the relic attending,
Thus sung the last strain of the warrior's soul:

"My country, farewell, for the days are expired
On which I could hallow the deeds of the free.
Thy heroes have all to new honors aspired,
They fight, but they fight not for Scotia nor me.
All lost is our sway, and the name of our nation
Is sunk in the name of our old mortal foe.
Then why should the lay of our last degradation
Be forced from the harp of old Ossian to flow?

"My country, farewell, for the murmurs of sorrow
Alone the dark mountains of Scotia become.
Her sons condescend from new models to borrow,
And voices of strangers prevail in the hum.
Before the smooth face of our Saxon invaders,
Is quenched the last ray in the eye of the free.
Then oh, let me rest in the caves of my fathers,
Forgetful of them as forgetful of thee."

## Why Weeps Yon Highland Maid?

Why weeps yon Highland maid
Over the tartan plaid—
Is it a pledge of care,
Or are the blood drops there?
Tell me, thou hind of humble seeming,
Why the tears on her cheek are gleaming?
Why should the young and fair
Thus weep unpitied there?

Stranger, that Highland plaid
Low in the dust was laid.
He who the relic wore,
He is, alas, no more.
He and his loyal clan were trodden
Down by slaves on dark Culloden.

Well oer a lover's pall,
Well may the tear drops fall.

Where now her clansman true?
Where is the bonnet blue?
Where the claymore that broke
Fearless through fire and smoke?
Not one gleam by glen or river;
It lies dropped from the hand for ever.
Stranger, our fate deplore,
Our ancient name's no more.

## I Hae Lost My Love

I hae lost my love, an I dinna ken how,
I hae lost my love, an I carena.
For laith will I be just to lie down an dee,
And to sit down an greet* wad be bairnly*. — weep/childish
But a screed* o' ill-nature I canna weel help. — piece
At having been guidit unfairly;
An weel wad I like to gie women a skelp,
An yerk* their sweet haffits* fu' yarely. — pull/side-locks

Oh plague on the limmers*, sae sly and demure, — wretches
As pawkie* as deils wi their smiling; — sly
As fickle as winter, in sunshine and shower,
The hearts o' a' mankind beguiling;
As sour as December, as soothing as May,
To suit their ain ends, never doubt them.
Their ill faults I coudna tell ower in a day,
But their beauty's the warst thing about them.

Ay, that's what sets up the hail warld in a lowe*, — flame
Makes kingdoms to rise and expire;
Man's micht is nae mair than a flaughten* o' tow*, — lock/twine
Opposed to a bleeze o' reid fire.
Twas women at first made creation to bend,
And of nature's prime lord made the fellow;
An tis her that will bring this ill warld to an end,
An that will be seen an heard tell o'.

## Love's Visit

Love came to the door o' my heart ae night,
And he called wi a whining din—
"Oh, open the door, for it is but thy part
To let an old crony come in."
"Thou sly little elf, I have opened to thee
Far aftener than I dare say;
An dear hae the opening been to me,
Before I could wile you away."

"Fear not," quo Love, "for my bow's in the rest,
And my arrows are ilk ane gane;
For you sent me to wound a lovely breast,
Which has proved o' the marble stane.
I am sair forspent, then let me come in
To the nook where I wont* to lie, used
For sae aft hae I been this door within,
That I downa* think to gang by." cannot

I opened the door, though I weened it a sin,
To the sweet little whimpering fay;
But he raised sic a buzz the cove within,
That he filled me with wild dismay;
For first I felt sic a thrilling smart,
And then sic an ardent glow,
That I feared the chords o' my sanguine heart
War a' gaun to flee in a lowe*. flame

"Gae away, gae away, thou wicked wean,"
I cried, wi the tear in my ee.
"Ay, sae ye may say," quo he, "but I ken
Ye'll be laith now to part wi me."
And what do you think—by day and by night,
For these ten lang years and twain,
I have cherished the urchin with fondest delight,
And we'll never mair part again.

## Song of the Times of Charles I

See now, my brethren, heaven is clear,
And all the clouds are gone;
The righteous man shall flourish now—
Brave days are coming on.
Come then, dear comrades, and be glad,
And eke rejoice with me;
Lawn sleeves and rochets shall go down,
And hey, then up go we!

Whate'er the bishops' hands have built,
Our hammers shall undo;
We'll break their pipes, and burn their copes,
And burn their churches too.
We'll exercise within the groves,
And preach beneath the tree.
We'll make a pulpit of a cask,
And hey, then up go we!

We'll down with deans and prebends too,
And I rejoice to tell ye,
How we shall eat good pigs our fill,
And capons stewed in jelly.
We'll burn the fathers' learned books,

And make the schoolmen flee;
We'll down with all that smells of wit,
And hey, then up go we!

If once the greedy churchmen crew
Be crushed and overthrown,
We'll teach the nobles how to stoop,
And keep the gentry down.
Good manners have an ill report,
And turn to pride we see;
We'll therefore cry good manners down,
And hey, then up go we!

The name of lord shall be abhorred,
For every man's a brother;
No reason why, in church or state,
One man should rule another.
Now when this change of government
Has set our fingers free,
We'll make their saucy dames come down,
And hey, then up go we!

What though the king and parliament
Do now accord together?
We have more cause to be content,
This is our sunshine weather.
For if that reason should take place,
And they should disagree,
For us there would be little grace;
For hey, then up go we!

What should we do then in such case?
Let's put it to a venture;
If we can hold out seven years' space,
We'll sue out our indenture.
A time may come to make us rue,
Yet time may set us free,
Unless the gallows claim his due,
And hey, then up go we!

## Sir David Graeme

The dow* flew east, the dow flew west, dove
The dow flew far ayont* the fell*; beyond/hill
An sair at e'en she seemed distrest,
But what perplexed her could not tell.

But aye she cooed wi mournfu' croon,
An ruffled a' her feathers fair;
An lookit sad as she war boun
To leave the land for evermair.

The lady wept, an some did blame,—
She didna blame the bonnie dow,
But sair she blamed Sir David Graeme,
Because the knight had broke his vow.

For he had sworn by the starns sae bright,
An by their bed on the dewy green,
To meet her there on St. Lambert's night,
Whatever dangers lay between;

To risk his fortune an his life
In bearing her frae her father's towers,
To gae her a' the lands o' Dryfe,
An the Enzie-holm wi its bonnie bowers.

The day arrived, the evening came,
The lady looked wi wistful ee;
But, O, alas, her noble Graeme
Frae e'en to morn she didna see.

An she has sat her down an' grat*; wept
The warld to her like a desert seemed;
An she wited* this, an she wited that, thought, blamed
But o' the real cause never dreamed.

The sun had drunk frae Keilder Fell
His beverage o' the morning dew.
The deer had crouched her in the dell,
The heather oped its bells o' blue.

The lambs were skipping on the brae,
The laverock hiche attour them sang,
An aye she hailed the jocund day,
Till the wee, wee tabors o' heaven rung.

The lady to her window hied,
And it opened owre the banks o' Tyne.
"An, O, alack," she said, and sighed,
"Sure ilka breast is blithe but mine.

"Where hae ye been, my bonnie dow,
That I hae fed wi' the bread an' wine?
As roving a' the country through,
O, saw ye this fause knight o' mine?"

The dow sat down on the window tree,
An she carried a lock o' yellow hair.
Then she perched upon that lady's knee,
An carefully she placed it there.

"What can this mean? This lock's the same
That aince was mine. Whate'er betide,

This lock I gae to Sir David Graeme,
The flower of a' the Border side.

"He might hae sent it by squire or page,
An no letten the wily dow steal't awa.
Tis a matter for the lore and the counsels of age,
But the thing I canna read at a'."

The dow flew east, the dow flew west,
The dow she flew far ayont the fell,
An back she came wi panting breast
Ere the ringing o' the castle bell.

She lighted ahiche on the holly-tap,
An she cried, "cur-dow," an fluttered her wing,
Then flew into that lady's lap,
An there she placed a diamond ring.

"What can this mean? This ring is the same
That aince was mine. Whate'er betide,
This ring I gae to Sir David Graeme,
The flower of a' the Border side.

"He sends me back the love-tokens true.
Was ever poor maiden perplexed like me?
Twould seem he's reclaimed his faith an his vow,
But all is fauldit in mystery."

An she has sat her down an grat;
The warld to her like a desert seemed;
An she wited this, an she wited that,
But o' the real cause never dreamed.

When, lo, Sir David's trusty hound,
Wi humbling back, an a waefu' ee,
Came crining* in and lookit around, shrinking
But his look was hopeless as could be.

He laid his head on that lady's knee,
An he lookit as somebody he would name,
An there was a language in his howe* ee hollow
That was stronger than a tongue could frame.

She fed him wi the milk an the bread,
An ilka good thing that he wad hae.
He lickit her hand, he coured his head,
Then slowly, slowly he slunkered away.

But she has eyed her fause knight's hound,
An a' to see where he wad gae.
He whined, an he howled, an lookit around,
Then slowly, slowly he trudged away.

Then she's casten aff her coal black shoon,
An her bonnie silken hose, sae glancin an sheen;
She kiltit her wilye coat an broidered gown,
An away she has linkit over the green.

She followed the hound owre muirs an rocks,
Through mony a dell and dowie* glen, gloomy
Till frae her brow an bonnie goud locks,
The dew dreepit down like the drops o' rain.

An aye she said, "My love may be hid,
An darena come to the castle to me;
But him I will find and dearly I'll chide,
For lack o' stout heart an courtesy.

"But ae kind press to his manly breast,
An ae kind kiss in the moorland glen,
Will weel atone for a' that is past;—
O wae to the paukie* snares o' men." wily

An aye she eyed the gray sloth hound,
As he windit owre Deadwater Fell,
Till he came to the den wi the moss inbound,
An O, but it kithed* a lonesome dell. revealed

An he waggit his tail, an he fawned about,
Then he coured him down sae wearily;
"Ah, yon's my love, I hae found him out,
He's lying waiting in the dell for me.

"To meet a knight near the fall of night
Alone in this untrodden wild,
It scarcely becomes a lady bright,
But I'll vow that the hound my steps beguiled."

Alack, whatever a maiden may say,
True has't been said, an often been sung,
The ee her heart's love will betray,
An the secret will sirple frae her tongue.

"What ails my love, that he looks nae roun,
A lady's stately step to view?
Ah me, I hae neither stockings nor shoon,
An my feet are sae white wi the moorland dew.

"Sae sound as he sleeps in his hunting gear,
To waken him great pity would be.
Deaf is the man that caresna to hear,
And blind is he wha wantsna to see."

Sae saftly she treads the wee green swaird,
Wi the lichens an the ling* a' fringed around. heather

"My een are darkened wi some wul-weird*, "wild witch"
What ails my love he sleeps sae sound?"

She gae ae look, she needit but ane,
For it left nae sweet uncertainty.
She saw a wound through his shoulder bane
An in his brave breast two or three.

There wasna sic een on the Border green,
As the piercing een o' Sir David Graeme.
She glisked wi her ee where these een should be,
But the raven had been there afore she came.

There's a cloud that fa's darker than the night,
An darkly on that lady it came.
There's a sleep as deep as the sleep outright,—
Tis without a feeling or a name.

Tis a dull and a dreamless lethargy,
For the spirit strays owre vale an hill,
An the bosom is left a vacancy,
An when it comes back it is darker still.

O shepherd lift that comely corpse,
Well you may see no wound is there.
There's a faint rose mid the bright dew drops,
An they have not wet her glossy hair.

There's a lady has lived in Hoswood tower,
Tis seven years past on St. Lambert's day,
An aye when comes the vesper hour
These words an no more can she say:

"They slew my love on the wild swaird green,
As he was on his way to me.
An the ravens picked his bonnie blue een,
An the tongue that was formed for courtesy.

"My brothers they slew my comely knight,
An his grave is red blood to the brim.
I thought to have slept out the lang, lang night,
But they've wakened me, and wakened not him."

## Lass, an Ye Lo'e Me, Tell Me Now[1]

"Afore the muircock begin to craw,
Lass, an ye loe me, tell me now
The bonniest thing that ever ye saw,
For I canna come every night to woo."
"The gowden broom is bonny to see,

[1] Hogg's version of a popular song.

And sae is the milk-white flower o' the haw*, river meadow land
The daisy's wee freeng is sweet on the lea,
But the bud of the rose is the bonniest of a'."

"Now, wae light on a' your flow'ry chat,
Lass, an ye loe me, tell me now;
It's no the thing that I would be at,
An' I canna come every night to woo.
The lamb is bonny upon the brae,
The leveret friskin' oer the knowe*, knoll
The bird is bonny upon the tree—
But which is the dearest of a' to you?

"The thing that I loe best of a',
Lass, an ye loe me, tell me now;
The dearest thing that ever I saw,
Though I canna come every night to woo,
Is the kindly smile that beams on me
Whenever a gentle hand I press,
And the wily blink frae the dark blue ee
Of a deer, dear lassie that they ca' Bess."

"Aha, young man, but I couldna see;
What I loe best I'll tell you now,
The compliment that ye sought frae me,
Though ye canna come every night to woo;
Yet I would rather hae frae you
A kindly look, an a word witha',
Than a' the flowers o' the forest pu',
Than a' the lads that ever I saw."

"Then, dear, dear Bessie, you shall be mine,
Sin' a' the truth ye hae tauld me now,
Our hearts an' fortunes we'll entwine,
An I'll aye come every night to woo.
For O, I canna descrive to thee
The feeling o' love's and nature's law,
How dear this world appears to me,
Wi Bessie my ain for good an for a'."

## Ah, Peggie, Since Thou'rt Gane Away

Ah, Peggie, since thou'rt gane away,
An left me here to languish,
I canna fend anither day
In sic regretfu' anguish.
My mind's the aspen o' the vale,
In ceaseless waving motion.
Tis like a ship without a sail,
On life's unstable ocean.

I downna* bide to see the moon — cannot
Blink* owre the glen sae clearly; — glance
Aince on a bonny face she shone—
A face that I lo'ed dearly.
An when beside yon water clear,
At e'en I'm lanely roaming,
I sigh and think, if ane was here,
How sweet wad fa' the gloaming.

When I think o' thy cheerfu' smile,
Thy words sae free an' kindly,
Thy pawkie* ee's bewitching wile, — sly
The unbidden tear will blind me.
The rose's deepest blushing hue
Thy cheek could eithly* borrow, — easily
But ae kiss o' thy cheery mou
Was worth a year o' sorrow.

Oh, in the slippery paths of love,
Let prudence aye direct thee.
Let virtue every step approve,
An virtue will respect thee.
To ilka pleasure, ilka pang,
Alack, I am nae stranger;
An he wha aince has wandered wrang
Is best aware o' danger.

May still thy heart be kind an true,
A' ither maids excelling.
May heaven distill its purest dew
Around thy rural dwelling.
May flow'rets spring an wild birds sing
Around thee late an early,
An oft to thy remembrance bring
The lad that loved thee dearly.

## Gang to the Brakens wi Me

I'll sing of yon glen of red heather,
An a dear thing that ca's it her hame,
Wha's a' made o' love-life thegither,
Frae the tie o' the shoe to the kaime;
Love beckons in every sweet motion,
Commanding due homage to gie;
But the shrine o' my dearest devotion
Is the bend o' her bonnie e'ebree.

I fleeched* an' I prayed the dear lassie — coaxed
To gang to the brakens wi me;
But though neither lordly nor saucy,
Her answer was—"Laith wad I be.
I neither hae father nor mither,

Sage counsel or caution to gie;
An prudence has whispered me never
To gang to the brakens wi thee."

"Dear lassie, how can ye upbraid me,
An try your ain love to beguile?
For ye are the richest young lady
That ever gaed oer the kirk-stile.
Your smile that is blither than ony,
The bend o' your cheerfu' e'ebree.
An the sweet blinks o' love they're sae bonny,
Are five hundred thousand to me."

She turned her around and said, smiling,
While the tear in her blue ee shone clear,
"Your welcome, kind sir, to your mailing*, farm
For, O, you have valued it dear.
Gae make out the lease, do not linger,
Let the parson endorse the decree;
An then, for a wave of your finger,
I'll gang to the brakens wi thee."

There's joy in the bright blooming feature,
When love lurks in every young line,
There's joys in the beauties of nature,
There's joy in the dance and the wine:
But there's a delight will ne'er perish,
Mang pleasures all fleeting and vain,
Ane that is to love and to cherish
The fond little heart that's our ain.

## A Boy's Song

Where the pools are bright and deep,
Where the gray trout lies asleep,
Up the river and oer the lea,
That's the way for Billy and me.

Where the blackbird sings the latest,
Where the hawthorn blooms the sweetest,
Where the nestlings chirp and flee,
That's the way for Billy and me.

Where the mowers mow the cleanest,
Where the hay lies thick and greenest;
There to trace the homeward bee,
That's the way for Billy and me.

Where the hazel bank is steepest,
Where the shadow falls the deepest,
Where the clustering nuts fall free,
That's the way for Billy and me.

Why the boys should drive away
Little maidens from their play,
Or love to banter and fight so well,
That's the thing I never could tell.

But this I know, I love to play,
Through the meadow, among the hay:
Up the water and oer the lea,
That's the way for Billy and me.

## Lock the Door, Lariston

"Lock the door, Lariston, lion of Liddesdale.
Lock the door, Lariston, Lowther comes on.
The Armstrongs are flying,
The widows are crying,
The Castletown's burning, and Oliver's gone!

"Lock the door, Lariston—high on the weather-gleam
See how the Saxon plumes bob on the sky—
Yeomen and carbineer,
Billman and halberdier,[1]
Fierce is the foray, and far is the cry.

"Bewcastle brandishes high his broad scimitar.
Ridley is riding his fleet-footed gray;
Hidley and Howard there,
Wandale and Windermere;
Lock the door, Lariston; hold them at bay.

"Why doest thou smile, noble Elliot of Lariston?
Why does the joy-candle gleam in thine eye?
Thou bold Border ranger,
Beware of thy danger.
Thy foes are relentless, determined, and nigh."

Jack Elliot raised up his steel bonnet and lookit,
His hand grasped the sword with a nervous embrace.
"Ah, welcome, brave foemen,
On earth thee are no men
More gallant to meet in the foray or chase.

"Little know you of the hearts I have hidden here.
Little know you of our moss-troopers'[2] might—
Linhope and Sorbie true,
Sundhope and Milburn too,
Gentle in manner, but lions in fight.

---

[1]Carbineers, billmen and halberdiers are cavalrymen armed with carbines, bills and halberds respectively. Bills are long staffs with a hook-shaped blade attached. A halberd is also a long staff, with an ax-like blade and a sharp spike at the end.

[2]Freebooters riding the Border country.

"I've Mangerton, Ogilvie, Raeburn, and Netherbie,
Old Sim of Whitram, and all his array;
Come all Northumberland,
Teesdale and Cumberland,
Here at the Breaken tower end shall the fray."

Scowled the broad sun oer the links of green Liddesdale,
Red as the beacon-light tipped he the wold*; hill
Many a bold martial eye
Mirrored that morning sky,
Never more oped on its orbit of gold.

Shrill was the bugle's note, dreadful the warrior's shout,
Lances and halberds in splinters were borne;
Helmet and hauberk* then (coat of mail)
Braved the claymore in vain,
Buckler and armlet in shivers were shorn.

See how they wane—the proud files of Windermere.
Howard, ah, woe to thy hopes of the day.
Hear the wide welkin rend,
While the Scots' shouts ascend—
"Elliot of Lariston, Elliot for aye!"

## The Maid of the Sea

Come from the sea,
Maiden, to me,
Maiden of mystery, love, and pain.
Wake from thy sleep,
Low in the deep,
Over thy green waves sport again.
Come to this sequestered spot, love.
Death's where thou art, as where thou art not, love.
Then come unto me,
Maid of the sea,
Rise from the wild and stormy main.
Wake from thy sleep;
Calm in the deep,
Over thy green waves sport again.

Is not the wave
Made for the slave,
Tyrant's chains, and stern control;
Land for the free
Spirit like thee?
Thing of delight to a minstrel's soul,
Come, with thy song of love and of sadness,
Beauty of face and rapture of madness.
O, come unto me,
Maid of the sea,
Rise from the wild and surging main.

Wake from thy sleep,
Calm in the deep,
Over thy green waves sport again.

## The Liddel Bower

"Oh, will ye walk the wood, lady?
Or will ye walk the lea?
Or will ye gae to the Liddel Bower,
An' rest a while wi' me?"

"The deer lies in the wood, Douglas,
The wind blaws on the lea;
An' when I gae to Liddel Bower
It shall not be wi' thee."

"The stag bells on my hills, lady,
The hart but and the hind.
My flocks lie in the Border dale,
My steeds outstrip the wind;

"At ae blast o' my bugle horn,
A thousand tend the ca':
Oh, gae wi' me to Liddel Bower—
What ill can thee befa'?

"D'ye mind when in that lonely bower
We met at even tide,
I kissed your young an' rosy lips,
An' wooed you for my bride?

"I saw the blush break on your cheek,
The tear stand in your e'e.
Oh, could I ween, fair Lady Jane,
That then ye lo'ed na me?"

"But sair, sair hae I rued that day,
An' sairer yet may rue.
Ye thought na on my maiden love,
Nor yet my rosy hue.

"Ye thought na' on my bridal bed,
Nor vow nor tear o' mine.
Ye thought upon the lands o' Nith,
An' how they might be thine.

"Away! away! ye fause leman*, lover
Nae mair my bosom wring.
There is a bird within yon bower,
Oh, gin* ye heard it sing!" if

Red grew the Douglas' dusky cheek,
He turned his eye away,
The gowden hilt fell to his hand;
"What can the wee bird say?"

It hirpled* on the bough an' sang, limped
"Oh, wae's me, dame, for thee,
An' wae's me for the comely knight
That sleeps aneath the tree.

"His cheek lies on the cauld, cauld clay,
Nae belt nor brand has he.
His blood is on a kinsman's spear.
Oh, wae's me, dame, for thee."

"My yeomen line the wood, lady,
My steed stands at the tree;
An' ye maun dree* a dulefu' weird*, suffer/fate
Or mount and fly wi' me."

What gars Caerlaverock yeomen ride
Sae fast in belt an' steel?
Wha gars the Jardine mount his steed,
And scour owre muir and dale?

Why seek they up by Liddel Ford,
An' down by Tarras linn*? waterfall
The heiress o' the lands o' Nith,
Is lost to a' her kin.

Oh, lang, lang may her mother greet*, weep
Down by the salt sea faem;
An' lang, lang may the Maxwells look,
Afore their bride come hame.

An' lang may every Douglas rue,
An' ban the deed for aye;—
The deed was done at Liddel Bower
About the break of day.

## The Laird o' Lamington

Can I bear to part wi' thee,
Never mair your face to see?
Can I bear to part wi' thee,
Drunken Laird o' Lamington?
Canty* were ye oer your kale, pleasant
Toddy jugs, an' caups o' ale.
Heart aye kind, an' leal*, an' hale, true
Honest Laird o' Lamington.

He that swears is but so so,
He that lies to hell must go,
He that falls in bagnio
Falls in the devil's frying-pan.
Wha was't ne'er pat aith to word,
Never lied for duke nor lord,
Never sat at sinfu' board?
The honest Laird o' Lamington.

He that cheats can ne'er be just;
He that prays is ne'er to trust;
He that drinks to drauck* his dust, assuage
Wha can say that wrang is done?
Wha was't, ne'er to fraud inclined,
Never prayed sin' he can mind?
Ane wha's drouth* there's few can find, thirst
The honest Laird o' Lamington.

I like a man to tak his glass,
Toast a friend or bonnie lass;
He that winna is an ass—
Deil send him ane to gallop on!
I like a man that's frank an' kind,
Meets me when I have a mind,
Sings his sang, an' drinks me blind,
Like the Laird o' Lamington.

## I Lately Lived in Quiet Ease

I lately lived in quiet ease,
An' never wished to marry, O.
But when I saw my Peggy's face,
I felt a sad quandary, O.
Though wild as ony Athol deer,
She has trepanned* me fairly, O. knocked out
Her cherry cheeks an' een sae clear
Torment me late an' early, O.

O love, love, love!
Love is like a dizziness.
It winna let a poor body
Gang about his biziness.

To tell my feats this single week
Wad mak a daft-like diary, O.
I drave my cart out owre a dike,
My horses in a miry, O.
I wear my stockings white an' blue,
My love's sae fierce an' fiery, O.
I drill the land that I should pleugh,
An' pleugh the drills entirely, O.

Ae morning, by the dawn o' day,
I rase to theek* the stable, O. thatch
I cuist my coat, an' plied away
As fast as I was able, O.
I wrought that morning out an' out,
As I'd been redding fire, O.
When I had done an' looked about,
Gudefaith it was the byre*, O. barn

Her wily glance I'll ne'er forget,
The dear, the lovely blinkin' o't
Has pierced me through an' through the heart,
An' plagues me wi' the prinkling o't.
I tried to sing, I tried to pray,
I tried to drown't wi' drinkin' o't,
I tried wi' sport to drive 't away,
But ne'er can sleep for thinkin' o't.

Nae man can tell what pains I prove,
Or how severe my pliskie, O.
I swear I'm sairer drunk wi' love
Than ever I was wi' whiskey, O.
For love has raked me fore an' aft,
I scarce can lift a leggie, O.
I first grew dizzy, then gaed daft,
An' soon I'll dee for Peggy, O.

## Good Night, and Joy

The year is wearing to the wane,
An' day is fading west awa';
Loud raves the torrent an' the rain,
And dark the cloud comes down the shaw*; wood
But let the tempest tout an' blaw
Upon his loudest winter horn,
Good night, an' joy be wi' you a';
We'll maybe meet again the morn.

Oh, we hae wandered far an' wide
Oer Scotia's hills, oer firth an' fell,
An' mony a simple flower we've culled,
An' trimmed them wi' the heather bell.
We've ranged the dingle an' the dell,
The hamlet an' the baron's ha';
Now let us take a kind farewell,—
Good night, an' joy be wi' you a'.

Though I was wayward, you were kind,
And sorrowed when I went astray;
For oh, my strains were often wild
As winds upon a winter day.
If e'er I led you from the way,

Forgie your minstrel aince for a';
A tear fa's wi' his parting lay,—
Good night, and joy be wi' you a'.

## Bonnie Jean

Sing on, sing on my bonnie bird,
The sang ye sang yestreen, O,
When here, aneath the hawthorn wild,
I met my bonnie Jean, O.
My blude ran prinklin through my veins,
My hair began to steer, O;
My heart played deep against my breast,
As I beheld my dear, O.

O weels me on my happy lot,
O weels me on my dearie,
O weels me on the charmin spot
Where a' combined to cheer me.
The mavis liltit on the bush,
The laverock on the green, O.
The lily bloomed, the daisy blushed,
But a' was nought to Jean, O.

Sing on, sing on my bonnie thrush,
Be neither fleed or eerie,
I'll wad your love sits in the bush
That gars ye sing sae cheerie.
She may be kind, she may be sweet,
She may be neat and clean, O,
But oh she's but a drysome mate
Compared with bonnie Jean, O.

If love would open a' her stores,
An a' her blooming treasures,
An bid me rise, and turn and choose,
An taste her chiefest pleasures;
My choice would be the rosy cheek,
The modest beaming eye, O,
The yellow hair, the bosom fair,
The lips o' coral dye, O.

A bramble shade around her head,
A burnie poplin by, O;
Our bed the swaird, our sheet the plaid,
Our canopy the sky, O.
An here's the burn, an there's the bush
Around the flowery green, O,
An this the plaid, an sure the lass
Wad be my bonnie Jean, O.

Hear me, thou bonnie modest moon,
Ye sternies twinklin high, O,
An a' ye gentle powers aboon
That roam athwart the sky, O;
Ye see me grateful for the past,
Ye saw me blest yestreen, O;
An ever till I breathe my last
Ye'll see me true to Jean, O.

## Flora Macdonald's Farewell[1]

Far over yon hills of the heather sae green,
An down by the corrie* that sings to the sea, mountain hollow
The bonny young Flora sat sighing her lane*, (alone)
The dew on her plaid, and the tear in her ee.
She looked at a boat wi the breezes that swung,
Away on the wave, like a bird of the main;
An aye as it lessened she signed and she sung,
Fareweel to the lad I shall ne'er see again.
Fareweel to my hero, the gallant and young,
Fareweel to the lad I shall ne'er see again.

The moorcock that craws on the brows of Ben-Connal,
He kens of his bed in a sweet mossy hame;
The eagle that soars oer the cliffs of Clan-Ronald,
Unawed and unhunted his eyrie can claim;
The solan* can sleep on the shelve of the shore, gannet
The cormorant roost on his rock of the sea,
But, ah, there is one whose hard fate I deplore.
Nor house, ha', nor hame in his country has he.
The conflict is past, and our name is no more—
There's nought left but sorrow for Scotland and me.

The target* is torn from the arm of the just, shield
The helmet is cleft on the brow of the brave,
The claymore for ever in darkness must rust,
But red is the sword of the stranger and slave.
The hoof of the horse, and the foot of the proud,
Have trod oer the plumes on the bonnet of blue,
Why slept the red bolt in the breast of the cloud,
When tyranny reveled in blood of the true?
Fareweel, my young hero, the gallant and good;
The crown of thy fathers is torn from thy brow.

## Bonnie Prince Charlie

Cam ye by Athol, lad wi the philabeg,
Down by the Tummel or banks o' the Garry,

---

[1] Flora Macdonald was the young Scotswoman who sheltered Bonnie Prince Charlie during his romantically improbable flight from capture after the battle of Culloden.

Saw ye our lads wi their bonnets and white cockades,[1]
Leaving their mountains to follow Prince Charlie?

Follow thee, follow thee, wha wadna follow thee?
Lang hast thou loved and trusted us fairly.
Charlie, Charlie, wha wadna follow thee,
King o' the Highland hearts, bonnie Prince Charlie?

I have but ae son, my gallant young Donald;
But if I had ten they should follow Glengarry.
Health to M'donell and gallant Clan-Ronald—
For these are the men that will die for their Charlie.

I'll to Lochiel and Appin, and kneel to them,
Down by Lord Murray, and Roy of Kildarlie;
Brave McIntosh, he shall fly to the field with them,
These are the lads I can trust wi my Charlie.

Down through the Lowlands, down wi the Whigamore,[2]
Loyal true Highlanders, down wi them rarely.
Ronald and Donald, drive on, wi the broad claymore,
Over the necks o' the foes o' Prince Charlie.

## Lucky Shaw's Tale

[The following is an inset story from Hogg's splendid novel, *Private Memoirs and Confessions of a Justified Sinner* (1824).]

"Now, Penpunt, you may tell me all that passed between you and the wives of the clachan.[3] I am better of that stomach-qualm, with which I am sometimes seized, and shall be much amused by hearing the sentiments of noted witches regarding myself and my connections."

"Weel, you see, sir," I says to them, "It will be lang afore the deil intermeddle wi' as serious a professor, and as fervent a prayer as my master, for gin he gets the upper hand o' sickan men, wha's to be safe?" An, what think ye they said, sir? There was ane Lucky Shaw set up her lang lantern chafts, an' answered me, an' a' the rest shanned and noddit in assent an' approbation.

"Ye silly, sauchless, Cameronian cuif!"[4] quo she, "is that a' that ye ken about the wiles and doings o' the prince o' the air, that rules an' works in the bairns of disobedience? Gin ever he observes a proud professor, wha has mae than ordinary pretensions to a divine calling, and that reards and prays till the very howlets learn his preambles, *that's* the man Auld Simmie fixes on to mak a dishclout o'. He canna get rest in hell, if he sees a man, or a set of men o' this stamp, an' when he sets fairly to wark, it is seldom that he disna bring them round till his ain measures by hook or by crook. Then, O it is a grand prize for him, an' a proud deil he is, when he gangs hame to his ain ha', wi' a batch o' the souls o' sic strenuous professors on his back. Ay, I

[1]The emblem of the Jacobites.

[2]Persons loyal to the (Hanoverian) king.

[3]Village.

[4]Fool.

trow, auld Ingleby, the Liverpool packman, never came up Glasco street wi' prouder pomp, when he had ten horse-laids afore him o' Flanders lace, an' Hollin lawn, an' silks an' satins frae the eastern Indians, than Satan wad strodge into hell with a pack-laid o' the souls o' proud professors on his braid shoulders. Ha, ha, ha!

"I think I see how the auld thief wad be gaun through his gizened dominions, crying his wares, in derision, 'Wha will buy a fresh, cauler[1] divine, a bouzy bishop, a fasting zealot, or a piping priest? For a' their prayers an' their praises, their aumuses, an' their penances, their whinings, their howlings, their rantings, an' their ravings, here they come at last. Behold the end. Here go the rare and precious wares. A fat professor for a bodle,[2] an' a lean ane for half a merk."

I declare, I trembled at the auld hag's ravings but the lave[3] o' the kimmers[4] applauded the sayings as sacred truths. An' then Lucky went on.

"There are many wolves in sheep's clathing, among us my man; mony deils aneath the masks o' zealous professors, roaming about in kirks and meeting-houses o' the land. It was but the year afore the last, that the people o' the town o' Auchtermuchty grew so rigidly righteous, that the meanest hind among them became a shining light in ither towns an' parishes. There was nought to be heard, neither night nor day, but preaching, praying, argumentation, an' catechizing in a' the famous town o' Auchtermuchty. The young men wooed their sweethearts out o' the Song o' Solomon, an' the girls returned answers in strings o' verses out o' the Psalms. At the lint-swinglings,[5] they said questions round; and read chapters, and sang hymns at bridals; auld and young prayed in their dreams, an' prophesied in their sleep, till the deils in the farrest nooks o' hell were alarmed, and moved to commotion.

"Gin it hadna been an auld carl,[6] Robin Ruthven, Auchtermuchty wad at that time hae been ruined and lost for ever. But Robin was a cunning man, an' had rather mae wits than his ain, for he had been in the hands o' the fairies when he was young, an' a' kinds o' spirits were visible to his een, an' their language as familiar to him as his ain mother tongue. Robin was sitting on the side o' the West Lowmond, ae still gloomy night in September, when he saw a bridal o' corbie craws coming east the lift, just on the edge o' the gloaming. The moment that Robin saw them, he kenned, by their movements, that they were craws o' some ither warld than this; so he signed himself, and crap into the middle o' his bourock.[7]

"The corbie craws came a' an' sat down round about him, an' they poukit their black sooty wings, an' spread them out to the breeze to cool; and Robin heard ae corbie speaking, an' another answering him; and the tane said to the tither: 'Where will the ravens find a prey the night?' 'On the lean crazy souls o' Auchtermuchty,' quo the tither.

'I fear they will be oer weel wrappit up in the warm flannens o' faith, an' clouted wi' the dirty duds o' repentance, for us to mak a meal o',' quo the first.

'Whaten vile sounds are these that I hear coming and bumming up the hill?'

'O these are the hymns and praises o' the auld wives and creeshy louns[8] o' Auchtermuchty, wha are gaun crooning their way to heaven; an' gin it warna for the shame o' being beat, we might let our great enemy tak them. For sic a prize as he

---

[1]Newly caught, fresh.

[2]A small coin.

[3]Rest, remainder.

[4]Gossips, village women.

[5]Flax beating.

[6]Peasant.

[7]Cow-tether.

[8]"Loons," fools.

will hae! Heaven, forsooth. What shall we think o' heaven, if it is to be filled wi' vermin like thae, amang whom there is mair poverty and pollution, than I can name.'

"'No matter for that,' said the first, 'we cannot have our power set at defiance; though we should put them in the thief's hole, we must catch them, and catch them with their own bait too. Come all to church to-morrow, and I'll let you hear how I'll gull the saints of Auchtermuchty. In the mean time, there is a feast on the Sidlaw hills tonight, below the hill of Macbeth,—Mount, Diabolus, and fly.'

"Then, with loud croaking and crowing, the bridal of corbies again scaled the dusky air, and left Robin Ruthven in the middle of his cairn.

"The next day the congregation met in the kirk of Auchtermuchty, but the minister made not his appearance. The elders ran out and in, making inquiries; but they could learn nothing, save that the minister was missing. They ordered the clerk to sing a part of the 119th Psalm, until they saw if the minister would cast up. The clerk did as he was ordered, and by the time he reached the 77th verse, a strange divine entered the church, by the *western door,* and advanced solemnly up to the pulpit. The eyes of all the congregation were riveted on the sublime stranger, who was clothed in a robe of black sackcloth, that flowed all around him, and trailed far behind, and they weened him an angel, come to exhort them, in disguise. He read out his text from the Prophecies of Ezekiel, which consisted of these singular words: 'I will overturn, overturn, overturn it; and it shall be no more, until he come, whose right it is, and I will give it him.'

"From these words he preached such a sermon as never was heard by human ears, at least never by ears of Auchtermuchty. It was a true, sterling, gospel sermon—it was striking, sublime, and awful in the extreme. He finally made out the IT, mentioned in the text, to mean, properly and positively, the notable town of Auchtermuchty. He proved all the people in it, to their perfect satisfaction, to be in the gall of bitterness and bond of iniquity, and he assured them, that God would overturn them, their principles, and professions; and that they should be no more, until the devil, the town's greatest enemy, came, and then it should be given unto him for a prey, for it was his right, and to him it belonged, if there was not forthwith a radical change made in all their opinions and modes of worship.

"The inhabitants of Auchtermuchty were electrified—they were charmed; they were actually raving mad about the grand and sublime truths delivered to them, by this eloquent and impressive preacher of Christianity.

"'He is a prophet of the Lord,' said one, 'sent to warn us, as Jonah was sent to the Ninevites.'

"'O, he is an angel sent from heaven, to instruct this great city,' said another, 'for no man ever uttered truths so sublime before.'

"The good people of Auchtermuchty were in perfect raptures with the preacher, who had thus sent them to hell by the slump, tag, rag, and bobtail. Nothing in the world delights a truly religious people so much, as consigning them to eternal damnation. They wondered after the preacher— they crowded together, and spoke of his sermon with admiration, and still as they conversed, the wonder and the admiration increased; so that honest Robin Ruthven's words would not be listened to. It was in vain that he told them he heard a raven speaking, and another raven answering him: the people laughed him to scorn, and kicked him out of their assemblies, as a one who spoke evil of dignities; and they called him a warlock, an' a daft body, to think to mak language out o' the crouping o' craws.

"The sublime preacher could not be heard of, although all the country was sought for him, even to the minutest corner of St. Johnston and Dundee; but as he had announced another sermon on the same text, on a certain day, all the inhabitants of that populous country, far and near, flocked to Auchtermuchty. Cupar, Newburgh, and Strathmiglo, turned out men, women, and children. Perth and Dundee gave their thousands; and from the East Nook of Fife to the foot of the Grampian hills, there was nothing but running and riding that morning to Auchtermuchty.

"The kirk would not hold the thousandth part of them. A splendid tent was erected on the brae north of the town, and round that the countless congregation assembled. When they were all waiting anxiously for the great preacher, behold, Robin Ruthven set up his head in the tent, and warned his countrymen to beware of the doctrines they were about to hear, for he could prove, to their satisfaction, that they were all false, and tended to their destruction.

"The whole multitude raised a cry of indignation against Robin, and dragged him from the tent, the elders rebuking him, and the multitude threatening to resort to stronger measures; and though he told them a plain and unsophisticated tale of the black corbies, he was only derided.

"The great preacher appeared once more, and went through his two discourses with increased energy and approbation. All who heard him were amazed, and many of them went into fits, writhing and foaming in a state of the most horrid agitation.

"Robin Ruthven sat on the outskirts of the great assembly, listening with the rest, and perceived what they, in the height of their enthusiasm, perceived not,—the ruinous tendency of the tenets so sublimely inculcated. Robin kenned the voice of his friend the corby-craw again, and was sure he could not be wrang: sae when public worship was finished, a' the elders an' a' the gentry flocked about the great preacher, as he stood on the green brae in the sight of the hale congregation, an' a' war alike anxious to pay him some mark o' respect. Robin Ruthven came in amang the thrang, to try to effect what he had promised; and, with the greatest readiness and simplicity, just took haud o' the side an' wide gown, an' in sight of a' present, held it aside as high as the preacher's knee, and behold there was a pair o' cloven feet.

"The auld thief was fairly catched in the very height o' his proud conquest, an' put down by an auld carl. He could feign nae mair, but gnashing on Robin wi' his teeth, he dartit into the air like a fiery dragon, an' keust a reid rainbow our the taps o' the Lowmonds.

"A' the auld wives an' weavers o' Auchtermuchty fell down flat wi' affright, an' betook them to their prayers aince again, for they saw the dreadfu' danger they had escapit, an' frae that day to this it is a hard matter to gar an Auchtermuchty man listen to a sermon at a', an' a harder ane still to gar him applaud ane, for he thinks aye that he sees the cloven foot peeping out frae aneath ilka sentence.

"Now, this is a true story, my man," quo the auld wife; "an' whenever you are doubtfu' of a man, take auld Robin Ruthven's plan, an' look for the cloven foot, for it's a thing that winna weel hide; an' it appears whiles where ane wadna think o't. It will keek[1] out frae aneath the parson's gown, the lawyer's wig, and the Cameronian's blue bannet: but still there is a gouden rule whereby to detect it, an' that never, never fails."

The auld witch didna gie me the rule, an' though I hae heard tell o't often an' often shame fa' me an I ken what it is!

## Mr. Adamson of Laverhope

One of those events that have made the deepest impression on the shepherds' minds for a century bygone, seems to have been the fate of Mr. Adamson, who was tenant in Laverhope for the space of twenty-seven years. It stands in their calendar as an era from which to date summer floods, water-spouts, hail and thunder storms, &c., and appears from tradition to have been attended with some awful circumstances ex-

[1]Peek.

pressive of divine vengeance. This Adamson is represented as having been a man of an ungovernable temper; of irritability so extreme, that no person could be for a moment certain to what excesses he might be hurried. He was otherwise accounted a good and upright man, and a sincere Christian; but in these outbreakings of temper, he often committed acts of cruelty and injustice for which any good man ought to have been ashamed. Among other qualities he had an obliging disposition, there being few to whom a poor man would sooner have applied in a strait. Accordingly, he had been in the habit of assisting a less wealthy neighbor of his with a little credit for many years. This man's name was Irvine, and though he had a number of rich relations, he was never out of difficulties. Adamson, from some whim or caprice, sued this poor farmer for a few hundred merks, taking legal steps against him, even to the very last measures short of poinding[1] and imprisonment. Irvine paid little attention to this, taking it for granted that his neighbor took these steps only for the purpose of inducing his debtor's friends to come forward and support him.

It happened one day about this period, that a thoughtless boy, belonging to Irvine's farm, hunted Adamson's cattle in a way that gave great offense to their owner, on which the two farmers differed, and some hard words passed between them. The next day Irvine was seized and thrown into jail; and shortly after his effects were poinded and sold by auction for ready money. They were consequently thrown away, as the neighbors, not having been forewarned, were wholly unprovided with ready money, and unable to purchase at any price. Mrs. Irvine came to the enraged creditor with a child in her arms, and implored him to put off the sale for a month, that she might try what could be done amongst her friends, to prevent a wreck so irretrievable. He was at one time on the very point of yielding; but some bitter recollections coming over his mind at the moment, stimulated his spleen against her husband, and he resolved that the sale should go on. William Carruders of Grindistone heard the following dialogue between them; and he said that his heart almost trembled within him: for Mrs. Irvine was a violent woman, and her eloquence did more harm than good.

"Are ye really gaun to act the part of a devil, the day, Mr. Adamson, and turn me and thae bairns out to the bare highroad, helpless as we are? Oh, man if your bowels binna seared in hell-fire already, take some compassion; for an ye dinna, they *will* be seared afore baith men and angels yet, till that hard and cruel heart o' yours be nealed to an izle."

"I'm gaun to act nae part of a devil, Mrs. Irvine; I'm only gaun to take my ain in the only way I can get it. I'm no baith gaun to tine my siller, and hae my beasts abused into the bargain."

"Ye sall neither lose plack[2] nor bawbee[3] o' your siller, man, if you will gie me but a month to make a shift for it—I swear to you, ye sall neither lose, nor rue the deed. But if ye winna grant me that wee, wee while, when the bread of a hail family depends on it, ye're waur than ony deil that's yammering and cursing i' the bottomless pit."

"Keep your ravings to yoursel, Mrs. Irvine, for I hae made up my mind what I'm to do, and I'll do it; sae it's needless for ye to pit yoursel into a bleeze; for the surest promisers are aye the slackest payers. It isna likely that your bad language will gar me alter my purpose."

"If that *be* your purpose, Mr. Adamson, and if you put that purpose in execution, I wadna change conditions wi' you the day for ten thousand times a' the gear ye

---

[1] Seizing at law.

[2] Small coin.

[3] Small coin.

are worth. Ye're gaun to do the thing that ye'll repent only aince, for a' the time that ye hae to exist baith in this world and the neist, and that's a lang, lang forrit and ayond. Ye have assisted a poor honest family for the purpose of taking them at a disadvantage, and crushing them to beggars; and when ane thinks o' that, what a heart you must hae? Ye hae first put my poor man in prison, a place where he little thought and less deserved ever to be; and now ye are reaving[1] his sackless family out o' their last bit o' bread. Look at this bit bonny innocent thing in my arms, how it is smiling on ye. Look at a' the rest standing leaning against the wa's, ilka ane wi' his een fixed on you by way o' imploring your pity! If ye reject thae looks, ye'll see them again in some trying moments, that will bring this ane back to your mind—ye will see them i' your dreams; ye will see them on your death-bed, and ye will *think* ye see them gleaming on ye through the reek o' hell; but it winna be them."

"Haud your tongue, woman, for ye make me feared to hear ye."

"Ay, but better be feared in time, than torfelled[2] for ever. Better conquess your bad humour for aince, than be conquessed for it through sae mony lang ages. Ye pretend to be a religious man, Mr. Adamson, and a great deal mair sae than your neighbors; do you think that religion teaches you acts o' cruelty like this? Will ye hae the face to kneel afore your Maker this night, and pray for a blessing on you and yours, and that He will forgive you your debts as you forgive your debtors? I hae nae doubt but you will. But aih! how sic an appeal will heap the coals o' divine vengeance on your head, and tighten the belts o' burning yettlin[3] ower your hard heart! Come forrit, bairns, and speak for yourselves, ilk ane o' ye."

"O, Maister Adamson, ye mauna turn my father and mother out o' their house and their farm; or what think ye is to come o' us?" said Thomas.

No consideration, however, was strong enough to turn Adamson from his purpose. The sale went on; and still, on the calling off of every favorite animal, Mrs. Irvine renewed her anathemas.

"Gentlemen, this is the mistress's favorite cow, and gives thirteen pints of milk every day. She is valued in my roup-roll at fifteen pounds; but we shall begin her at ten. Does any body say ten pounds for this excellent cow? ten pounds—ten pounds? nobody says ten pounds. Gentlemen, this is extraordinary! Money is surely a scarce article here to-day. Well, then, does any gentleman say five pounds to begin this excellent cow that gives twelve pints of milk daily? Five pounds—only five pounds!—nobody bids five pounds. Well the stock must positively be sold without reserve. Ten shillings for the cow—ten shillings—ten shillings—Will nobody bid ten shillings to set the sale agoing?"

"I'll gie five-and-twenty shillings for her," cried Adamson.

"Thank you, sir. One pound five—one pound five, and just a-going. Once—twice—thrice. Mr. Adamson, one pound five."

Mrs. Irvine came forward, drowned in tears, with the babe in her arms, and patting the cow, she said, "Ah, poor lady Bell, this is my last sight o' you, and the last time I'll clap your honest side! And hae we really been deprived o' your support for the miserable sum o' five-and-twenty shillings? My curse light on the head o' him that has done it! In the name of my destitute bairns I curse him; and does he think that a mother's curse will sink fizzenless to the ground? Na, na! I see an ee that's looking down here in pity and in anger; and I see a hand that's gathering the bolts o' Heaven thegither, for some purpose that I could divine, but daurna utter. But that hand is unerring, and where it throws the bolt, there it will strike. Fareweel, puir

[1]Swindling, stealing.

[2]Lost.

[3]Iron.

beast, ye hae supplied us wi' mony a meal, but ye will never supply us wi' another."

This sale at Kirkheugh was on the 11th of July. On the day following, Mr. Adamson went up to the folds in the Hope to shear his sheep, with no fewer than twenty-five attendants, consisting of all his own servants and cotters, and about as many neighboring shepherds whom he had collected, it being customary for the farmers to assist one another reciprocally on these occasions. Adamson continued more than usually capricious and unreasonable all that forenoon. He was discontented with himself, and when a man is ill pleased with himself, he is seldom well pleased with others. He seemed altogether left to the influences of the wicked one, running about in a rage, finding fault with everything and every person, and at times cursing bitterly, a practice to which he was not addicted; so that the sheep-shearing, that used to be a scene of hilarity among so many young and old shepherds, lads, lasses, wives, and callants,[1] was that day turned into one of gloom and dissatisfaction.

After a number of other provoking outrages, Adamson at length, with the buisting-iron[2] which he held in his hand, struck a dog belonging to one of his own shepherd boys, till the poor animal fell senseless on the ground, and lay sprawling as in the last extremity. This brought matters to a point which threatened nothing but anarchy and confusion; for every shepherd's blood boiled with indignation, and each almost wished in his heart that the dog had been his own, that he might have retaliated on the tyrant. At the time the blow was struck, the boy was tending one of the fold-doors, and perceiving the plight of his faithful animal, he ran to its assistance, lifted it in his arms, and holding it up to recover its breath, he wept and lamented over it most piteously. "My poor little Nimble!" he cried; "I am feared that mad body has killed ye, and then what am I to do wanting ye. I wad ten times rather he had strucken mysel."

He had scarce said the words ere his master caught him by the hair of the head with the one hand, and began to drag him about, while with the other he struck him most unmercifully. When the boy left the fold-door, the unshorn sheep broke out, and got away to the hill among the lambs and the clippies, and the farmer being in one of his "mad tantrums," as the servants called them, the mischance had almost put him beside himself; and that boy or man either is in a ticklish case who is in the hands of an enraged person far above him in strength.

The sheep-shearers paused, and the girls screamed, when they saw their master lay hold of the boy. But Robert Johnston, a shepherd from an adjoining farm, flung the sheep from his knee, made the shears ring against the fold dike, and in an instant had the farmer by both wrists, and these he held with such a grasp, that he took the power out of his arms; for Johnston was as far above the farmer in might as the latter was above the boy.

"Mr. Adamson, what are ye about?" he cried; "hae ye tint your reason a'thegither, that ye are gaun on rampauging like a madman that gate? Ye hae done the thing, sir, in your ill-timed rage that ye ought to be ashamed of baith afore God aud man."

"Are ye for fighting, Rob Johnston?" said the farmer, struggling to free himself. "Do ye want to hae a fight, lad? Because if ye do, I'll maybe gie you enough o' that."

"Na, sir, I dinna want to fight; but I winna let you fight either, unless wi' ane that's your equal; Sae gie ower spraughling,[3] and stand still till I speak to ye; for an ye winna stand to hear reason, I'll gar ye lie till ye hear it. Do ye consider what ye hae been doing even now? Do ye consider that ye hae been striking a poor orphan

---

[1]Youths.

[2]Instrument for marking sheep.

[3]Struggling.

callant, wha has neither father nor mother to protect him or to right his wrangs? and a' for naething but a bit start o' natural affection? How wad you like, sir, an ony body were to guide a bairn o' yours that gate? and ye as little ken what they are to come to afore their deaths, as that boy's parents did when they were rearing and fondling ower him. Fie for shame, Mr. Adamson! fie for shame! Ye first strak his poor dumb brute, which was a greater sin than the tither, for it didna ken what ye were striking it for; and then, because the callant ran to assist the only creature he has on the earth, and I'm feared the only true and faithfu' friend beside, ye claught him by the hair o' the head, and fell to the dadding[1] him as he war your slave! 'Od, sir, my blood rises at sic an act o' cruelty and injustice; and gin I thought ye worth my while, I wad tan ye like a pellet for it."

The farmer struggled and fought so viciously, that Johnston was obliged to throw him down twice over, somewhat roughly, and hold him by main force. But on laying him down the second time, Johnston said, "Now, sir, I just tell ye, that ye deserve to hae your banes weel throoshen; but ye're nae match for me, and I'll scorn to lay a tip on ye. I'll leave ye to Him who has declared himself the stay and shield of the orphan; and gin some visible testimony o' his displeasure dinna come ower ye for the abusing of his ward, I am right sair mista'en."

Adamson, finding himself fairly mastered, and that no one seemed disposed to take his part, was obliged to give in, and went sullenly away to tend the hirsel[2] that stood beside the fold. In the meantime the sheep-shearing went on as before, with a little more of hilarity and glee. It is the business of the lasses to take the ewes, and carry them from the fold to the clippers; and now might be seen every young shepherd's sweetheart or favorite waiting beside him, helping him to clip, or holding the ewes by the hind legs to make them lie easy, a great matter for the furtherance of the operator. Others, again, who thought themselves slighted or loved a joke, would continue to act in a different manner, and plague the youths by bringing them such sheep as it was next to impossible to clip.

"Aih, Jock lad, I hae brought you a grand ane this time! Ye will clank the shears ower her, and be the first done o' them a'!"

"My truly, Jessy, but ye hae gi'en me ane! I declare the beast is woo to the cloots and the een holes; and afore I get the fleece broken up, the rest will be done. Ah, Jessy, Jessy! ye're working for a mischief the day; and ye'll maybe get it."

"She's a braw sonsie sheep, Jock. I ken ye like to hae your arms weel filled. She'll amaist fill them as weel as Tibby Tod."

"There's for it now! there's for it! What care I for Tibby Tod, dame? Ye are the most jealous elf, Jessy, that ever drew coat ower head. But wha was't that sat half a night at the side of a gray stane wi' a crazy cooper? And wha was't that gae the poor precentor the whiskings, and reduced a' his sharps to downright flats? An ye cast up Tibby Tod ony mair to me, I'll tell something that will gar thae wild een reel i' your head, Mistress Jessy."

"Wow, Jock, but I'm unco wae for ye now. Poor fellow! It's really very hard usage! If ye canna clip the ewe, man, gie me her, and I'll tak her to anither; for I canna bide to see ye sae sair put about. I winna bring ye anither Tibby Tod the day, take my word on it. The neist shall be a real May Henderson o' Firthhopecleuch—ane, ye ken, wi' lang legs, and a good lamb at her fit."

"Gudesake, lassie, haud your tongue, and dinna affront baith yoursel and me. Ye are fit to gar ane's cheek burn to the bane. I'm fairly quashed, and daurna say anither word. Let us therefore hae let-a-be for let-a-be, which is good bairns'

---

[1]Beating.

[2]Flock.

agreement, till after the close o' the day sky; and then I'll tell ye my mind."

"Ay, but whilk o' your minds will ye tell me, Jock? For ye will be in five or six different anes afore that time. Ane, to ken your mind, wad need to be tauld it every hour o' the day, and then cast up the account at the year's end. But how wad she settle it then, Jock? I fancy she wad hae to multiply ilk years minds by dozens, and divide by four, and then we a' ken what wad be the quotients."

"Aih wow, sirs! heard ever ony o' ye the like o' that. For three things the sheepfauld is disquieted, and there are four which it cannot bear."

"And what are they, Jock?"

"A witty wench, a woughing dog, waukit-wood[1] wedder, and a pair o' shambling shears."

After this manner did the gleesome chat go on, now that the surly goodman had withdraw from the scene. But this was but one couple; every pair being engaged according to their biases, and after their kind—some settling the knotty points of divinity; others telling auld warld stories about persecutions, forays, and fairy raids; and some whispering, in half sentences, the soft breathings of pastoral love.

But the farmer's bad humour in the meanwhile was only smothered, not extinguished; and, like a flame that is kept down by an overpowering weight of fuel, wanted but a breath to rekindle it; or like a barrel of gunpowder, that the smallest spark will set in a blaze. That spark unfortunately fell upon it too soon. It came in the form of an old beggar, yclept Patie Maxwell, a well known, and generally a welcome guest, over all that district. He came to the folds for his annual present of a fleece of wool which had never before been denied him; and the farmer being the first person he came to, he approached him as in respect bound, accosting him in his wonted obsequious way.

"Weel, gudeman, how's a' wi' ye the day?"— (no answer.)—"This will be a thrang[2] day w' ye? How are ye getting on wi' the clipping?"

"Nae the better o' you, or the like o' you. Gang away back the gate ye came. What are you coming doiting up through amang the sheep that gate for, putting them a' tersyversy?"

"Tut, gudeman, what does the sheep mind an auld creeping body like me? I hae done nae ill to your pickle[3] sheep; and as for ganging back the road I cam, I'll do that whan I like, and no till than."

"But I'll make you blithe to turn back, auld vagabond! Do ye imagine I'm gaun to hae a' my clippers and grippers, buisters and binders, laid half idle, gaffing and giggling wi' you?"

"Why, then, speak like a reasonable man and a courteous Christian, as ye used to do, and I'se crack[4] wi' yoursel, and no gang near them."

"I'll keep my Christian cracks for others than auld Papist dogs, I trow."

"Wha do ye ca' auld Papist dogs, Mr. Adamson? Wha is it that ye mean to denominate by that fine-sounding title?"

"Just you, and the like o' ye, Pate. It is weel kenned that ye are as rank a Papist as ever kissed a crosier, and that ye were out in the very fore-end o' the unnatural Rebellion, in order to subvert our religion and place a Popish tyrant on the throne. It is a shame for a Protestant parish like this to support ye, and gie you as liberal awmosses as ye were a Christian saint. For me, I can tell you, ye'll get nae

---

[1]Crazed, angry.

[2]Busy.

[3]Few.

[4]Chatter.

mae at my hand; nor nae rebel Papist loun[1] amang ye."

"Dear sir, ye're surely no yoursel the day. Ye hae kenned I professed the Catholic religion these thretty years—it was the faith I was brought up in, and that in which I shall dee; and ye kenned a' that time that I was out in the Forty-Five wi' Prince Charles, and yet ye never made mention o' the facts nor refused me any awmos till the day. But as I hae been obliged t'ye, I'll haud my tongue; only, I wad advise ye as a friend, whenever ye hae occasion to speak of ony community of brother Christians, that ye will in future hardly make use o' siccan harsh terms. Or, if ye will do't, tak care wha ye use them afore, and let it no be to the face o' an auld veteran."

"What, ye auld profane water-eater and worshipper of graven images, dare ye heave your pikit kent at me?"

"I hae heaved baith sword and spear against mony a better man; and, in the cause o' my religion, I'll do it again."

He was proceeding, but Adamson's choler rising to an ungovernable height, he drew a race, and, running against the gaberlunzie[2] with his whole force, made him fly heels-over-head down the hill. The old man's bonnet flew off, his meal-pocks were scattered about, and his mantle, with two or three small fleeces of wool in it, rolled down into the burn.

The servants observed what had been done, and one elderly shepherd said, "In troth, sirs, our master is no himsel the day. He maun really be looked to. It appears to me, that sin' he roupit out yon poor family yesterday, the Lord has ta'en his guiding arm frae about him. Rob Johnston, ye'll be obliged to rin to the assistance o' the auld man."

"I'll trust the auld Jacobite for another shake wi' him yet," said Rob, "afore I steer my fit; for it strikes me if he hadna been ta'en unawares, he wad hardly hae been sae easily coupit."

The gaberlunzie was considerably astounded and stupefied when he first got up his head; but finding all his bones whole, and his old frame disencumbered of every superfluous load, he sprang to his feet, shook his gray burly locks, and cursed the aggressor in the name of the Holy Trinity, the Mother of our Lord, and all the blessed Saints above. Then approaching him with his cudgel heaved, he warned him to be on his guard, or make out of his reach else he would send him to eternity in the twinkling of an eye. The farmer held up his staff across to defend his head against the descent of old Patie's piked kent, and at the same time made a break in with intent to close with his assailant; but, in so doing, he held down his head for a moment, on which the gaberlunzie made a swing to one side, and lent Adamson such a blow over the neck, or back part of the head, that he fell violently on his face, after running two or three steps precipitately forward. The beggar, whose eyes gleamed with wild fury, while his gray locks floated over them like a winter cloud over two meteors of the night, was about to follow up his blow with another more efficient one on his prostrate foe; but the farmer, perceiving these unequivocal symptoms of danger wisely judged that there was no time to lose in providing for his own safety, and, rolling himself rapidly two or three times over, he got to his feet, and made his escape, though not before Patie had hit him what he called "a stiff lounder across the rumple."

The farmer fled along the brae, and the gaberlunzie pursued, while the people at the fold were convulsed with laughter. The scene was highly picturesque, for the beggar could run none, and still the faster that he essayed to run, he made the less

[1]Fellow, rascal.

[2]Beggar.

speed. But ever and anon he stood still, and cursed Adamson in the name of one or other of the saints or apostles, brandishing his cudgel, and stamping with his foot. The other, keeping still at a small distance, pretended to laugh at him, and at the same time uttered such bitter abuse against the Papists in general, and old Patie in particular, that after the latter had cursed himself into a proper pitch of indignation, he always broke at him again, making vain efforts to reach him one more blow. At length, after chasing him by these starts about half a mile, the beggar returned, gathered up the scattered implements and fruits of his occupation and came to the fold to the busy group.

Patie's general character was that of a patient jocular, sarcastic old man, whom people liked, but dared not much to contradict; but that day his manner and mien had become so much altered, in consequence of the altercation and conflict which had just taken place, that the people were almost frightened to look at him; and as for social converse, there was none to be had with him. His countenance was grim, haughty, and had something satanic in its lines and deep wrinkles, and ever and anon, as he stood leaning against the fold, he uttered a kind of hollow growl, with a broken interrupted sound, like a war-horse neighing in his sleep, and then muttered curses on the farmer.

The old shepherd before mentioned ventured, at length, to caution him against such profanity, saying, "Dear Patie, man, dinna sin away your soul, venting siccan curses as these. They will a' turn back on your ain head; for what harm can the curses of a poor sinfu' worm do to our master?"

"My curse, sir, has blasted the hopes of better men than either you or him," said the gaberlunzie in an earthquake voice, and shivering with vehemence as he spoke. "Ye may think the like o' me can hae nae power wi' Heaven; but an I hae power wi' hell, it is sufficient to cow ony that's here. I sanna brag what effect my curse will have, but I shall say this, that either your master or ony o' his men had as good have auld Patie Maxwell's blessing as his curse ony time, Jacobite and Roman Catholic though he be."

It now became necessary to bring into the fold the sheep that the farmer was tending, and they were the last hirsel that was to shear that day. The farmer's face was reddened with ill-nature; but yet he now appeared to be somewhat humbled, by reflecting on the ridiculous figure he had made. Patie sat on the top of the fold-dike, and from the bold and hardy asseverations that he made, he seemed disposed to provoke a dispute with any one present who chose to take up the cudgels. While the shepherds, under fire of the gaberlunzie's bitter speeches, were sharping their shears, a thick black cloud began to rear itself over the height to the southward, the front of which seemed to be boiling —both its outsides rolling rapidly forward, and again wheeling in toward the center. I have heard old Robin Johnston, the stout young man mentioned above, but who was a very old man when I knew him, describe the appearance of the cloud as greatly resembling a whirlpool made by the eddy of a rapid tide or flooded river; and he declared, to his dying day, that he never saw aught in nature have a more ominous appearance. The gaberlunzie was the first to notice it, and drew the attention of the rest towards that point of the heavens by the following singular and profane remark:—"Aha, lads, see what's coming yonder. Yonder's Patie Maxwell's curse coming rowing and reeling on ye already; and what will ye say an the curse of God be coming backing it."

"Gudesake, haud your tongue, ye profane body; ye mak me feared to hear ye," said one. "It's a strange delusion to think that a Papish can hae ony influence wi' the Almighty, either to bring down his blessing or his curse."

"Ye speak ye ken nae what, man," answered Pate, "ye hae learned some rhames frae your poor cauld-rife Protestant Whigs about Papists and Antichrist and children of perdition; yet it is plain that ye haena ae spark o' the life or power o' religion in your whole frame, and dinna ken either what's truth or what's falsehood. Ah! yonder it is coming, grim and gurly! Now I hae called for it, and it is coming; let me see if a' the Protestants that are of ye can order it back, or pray it away again! Down on your knees, ye dogs, and set your mows up against it, like as many spiritual cannon, and let me see if you have influence to turn aside ane o' the hailstanes that the deils are playing at chucks[1] wi' in yon dark chamber!"

"I wadna wonder if our clipping were cuttit short," said one.

"Na, but I wadna wonder if something else were cuttit short," said Patie; "What will ye say an some o' your weazons[2] be cuttit short? Hurraw yonder it comes! Now, there will be sic a hurlyburly in Laverhope as never was sin' the creation o' man!"

The folds of Laverhope were situated on a gentle, sloping plain, in what is called "the forkings of a burn." Laver-burn runs to the eastward, and Widehope-burn runs north, meeting the other at a right angle, a little below the folds. It was around the head of this Widehope that the cloud first made its appearance, and there its vortex seemed to be impending. It descended lower and lower, with uncommon celerity, for the elements were in a turmoil. The cloud laid first hold of one height, then of another, till at length it closed over and around the pastoral group, and the dark Hope had the appearance of a huge chamber hung with sackcloth. The big clear drops of rain soon began to descend, on which the shepherds covered up the wool with blankets, then huddled together under their plaids at the side of the fold, to eschew the speat, which they saw was going to be a terrible one. Patie still kept undauntedly to the top of the dike, and Mr. Adamson stood cowering at the side of it, with his plaid over his head, at a little distance from the rest. The hail and rain mingled, now began to descend in a way that had been seldom witnessed; but it was apparent to them all that the tempest raged with much greater fury in Widehope-head to the southward. Anon a whole volume of lightning burst from the bosom of the darkness, and quivered through the gloom, dazzling the eyes of every beholder—even old Maxwell clapped both his hands on his eyes for a space; a crash of thunder followed the flash, that made all the mountains chatter, and shook the firmament so, that the density of the cloud was broken up; for, on the instant that the thunder ceased, a rushing sound began in Widehope, that soon increased to a loudness equal to the thunder itself; but it resembled the noise made by the sea in a storm.

"Holy Virgin!" exclaimed Patie Maxwell, "What is this? What is this? I declare we're a' ower lang here, for the dams of heaven are broken up"; and with that he flung himself from the dike, and fled toward the top of a rising ground. He knew that the sound proceeded from the descent of a tremendous waterspout; but the rest, not conceiving what it was, remained where they were. The storm increased every minute, and in less than a quarter of an hour after the retreat of the gaberlunzie, they heard him calling out with the utmost earnestness; and when they eyed him, he was jumping like a madman on the top of the hillock, waving his bonnet, and screaming out, "Run, ye deil's buckies! Run for your bare lives!" One of the shepherds, jumping up on the dyke to see what was the matter, beheld the burn of Widehope coming down in a manner that could be compared to nothing but an ocean, whose boundaries had given way, descending into the abyss. It came with a cataract front more than twenty feet deep, as was afterwards ascertained by measurement; for it left sufficient marks to enable men to do this with precision. The shepherd called for assistance, and leaped into the fold to drive out the sheep; and just as he got the foremost of them to take the door, the flood came upon the head of the fold, on which he threw

[1]Tossing stones.

[2]Windpipes.

himself over the side-wall, and escaped in safety, as did all the rest of the people.

Not so Mr. Adamson's ewes; the greater part of the hirsel being involved in this mighty current. The large fold nearest the burn was leveled with the earth in one second. Stones, ewes, and sheephouse, all were carried before it, and all seemed to bear the same weight. It must have been a dismal sight to see so many fine animals tumbling and rolling in one irresistible mass. They were strong, however, and a few plunged out, and made their escape to the eastward; a great number were carried headlong down, and thrown out on the other side of Laver-burn, upon the side of a dry hill, to which they all escaped, some of them considerably maimed; but the greatest number of all were lost, being overwhelmed among the rubbish of the fold, and entangled so among the falling dykes, and the torrent wheeling and boiling amongst them, that escape was impossible. The wool was totally swept away, and all either lost or so much spoiled, that, when afterwards recovered, it was unsaleable.

When first the flood broke in among the sheep, and the women began to run screaming to the hills, and the despairing shepherds to fly about, unable to do anything, Patie began a laughing with a loud and hellish guffaw, and in that he continued to indulge till quite exhausted.

"Ha, ha, ha, ha! what think ye o' the auld beggar's curse now? Ha, ha, ha, ha! I think it has been backit wi' heaven's e and the deil's e baith. Ha, ha, ha, ha!"

And then he mimicked the thunder with the most outrageous and ludicrous jabberings, turning occasionally up to the cloud streaming with lightning and hail, and calling out—"Louder yet, deils! louder yet! kindle up your crackers, and yerk away! Rap, rap, rap, rap—Ro-ro, ro, ro—Roo—Whush."

"I daresay that body's the vera deevil himsel in the shape o' the auld papish beggar!" said one, not thinking that Patie could hear at such a distance.

"Na, na, lad, I'm no the deil," cried he in answer, "but an I war, I would let you see a stramash![1] It is a sublime thing to be a Roman Catholic among sae mony weak apostates; but it is a sublimer thing still to be a deil—a master-spirit in a forge like yon. Ha, ha, ha, ha! Take care o' your heads, ye cockchickens o' Calvin; take care o' the auld coppersmith o' the Black Cludd!"

From the moment that the first thunder-bolt shot from the cloud, the countenance of the farmer was changed. He was manifestly alarmed in no ordinary degree; and when the flood came rushing from the dry mountains, and took away his sheep and his folds before his eyes, he became as a dead man, making no effort to save his store, or to give directions how it might be done. He ran away in a cowering posture, as he had been standing, and took shelter in a little green hollow, out of his servant's view.

The thunder came nearer and nearer the place where the astonished hinds were, till at length they perceived the bolts of flame striking the earth around them in every direction; at one time tearing up its bosom, and at another splintering the rocks. Robin Johnston, in describing it, said that "the thunnerbolts came shimmering out o' the cludd sae thick, that they appeared to be linkit thegither, and fleeing in a' directions. There war some o' them blue, some o' them red, and some o' them like the color o' the lowe of a candle; some o' them diving into the earth, and some o' them springing up out o' the earth and darting into the heaven." I cannot vouch for the truth of this, but I am sure my informer thought it true, or he would not have told it; and he said further, that when old Patie Maxwell saw it, he cried—"Fie, tak care, cubs o' hell! fie, tak care! cower laigh, and sit sicker; for your auld dam is aboon ye, and aneath ye, and a' round about ye. O for a good wat nurse to spean ye, like John Adamson's lambs! Ha, ha, ha!" The lambs, it must be observed, had been turned out

---

[1]Commotion, row.

of the fold at first, and none of them perished with their dams.

But just when the storm was at the height, and apparently passing the bounds ever witnessed in these northern climes; when the embroiled elements were in the state of hottest convulsion, and when our little pastoral group were every moment expecting the next to be their last, all at once a lovely "blue bore," fringed with downy gold, opened in the cloud behind, and in five minutes more the sun appeared, and all was beauty and serenity. What a contrast to the scene so lately witnessed!

The most remarkable circumstance of the whole was perhaps the contrast between the two burns. The burn of Laverhope never changed its color, but continued pure, limpid, and so shallow, that a boy might have stepped over it dry-shod, all the while that the other burn was coming in upon it like an ocean broken loose, and carrying all before it. In mountainous districts, however, instances of the same kind are not unfrequent in time of summer speats. Some other circumstance connected with this storm were also described to me; the storm coming from the south, over a low-lying, wooded, and populous district, the whole of the crows inhabiting it posted away up the glen of Laverhope to avoid the fire and fury of the tempest.

"There were thoosands and thoosands came up by us," said Robin, "a' laying theirsels out as they had been mad. And then, whanever the bright bolt played flash through the darkness, ilk ane o' them made a dive and a wheel to avoid the shot; for I was persuaded that they thought a' the artillery and musketry o' the hail country were loosed on them, and that it was time for them to tak the gate. There were likewise several collie dogs came by us in great extremity, hinging out their tongues, and looking aye ower their shouthers, rinning straight on they kenned na where; and amang other things, there was a black Highland cow came roaring up the glen, wi' her stake hanging at her neck."

When the gush of waters subsided, all the group, men and women, were soon employed in pulling out dead sheep from among rubbish of stones, banks of gravel, and pools of the burn; and many a row of carcasses was laid out, which at that season were of no use whatever, and of course utterly lost. But all the time they were so engaged, Mr. Adamson came not near them; at which they wondered, and some of them remarked, that "they thought their master was fey the day, mae ways than ane."

"Ay, never mind him," said the old shepherd, "he'll come when he thinks it his ain time; he's a right sair humbled man the day, and I hope by this time he has been brought to see his errors in a right light. But the gaberlunzie is lost too. I think he be sandit in the yird, for I hae never seen him sin' the last great crash o' thunner."

"He'll be gane into the howe[1] to wring his duds," said Robert Johnston, "or maybe to make up matters wi' your master. Gude sauf us, what a profane wretch the auld creature is! I didna think the muckle-horned deil himself could hae set up his mou' to the heaven, and braggit and blasphemed in sic a way. He gart my heart a' grue within me, and dirle[2] as it had been bored wi' red-het elsins."[3]

"Oh, what can ye expect else of a Papish?" said the old shepherd, with a deep sigh: "they're a' deil's bairns ilk ane, and a' employed in carrying on their father's wark. It is needless to expect gude branches frae sic a stock, or gude fruit frae siccan branches."

"There's ae wee bit text that folks should never lose sight o'," said Robin, "and it's this: 'Judge not, that ye be not judged.' I think," remarked Robin, when he told the story, "I think that steekit their gabs!"

The evening at length drew on; the women had gone away home, and the

---

[1]Hollow.

[2]Reverberate, tingle.

[3]Awls.

neighboring shepherds had scattered here and there to look after their own flocks. Mr. Adamson's men alone remained, lingering about the brook and the folds, waiting for their master. They had seen him go into the little green hollow, and they knew he was gone to his prayers, and were unwilling to disturb him. But they at length began to think it extraordinary that he should continue at his prayers the whole afternoon. As for the beggar, though acknowledged to be a man of strong sense and sound judgment, he had never been known to say prayers all his life, except in the way of cursing and swearing a little sometimes; and none of them could conjecture what was become of him. Some of the rest, as it grew late, applied to the old shepherd before oft-mentioned, whose name I have forgot, but he had herded with Adamson twenty years—some of the rest, I say, applied to him to go and bring their master away home, thinking that perhaps he was taken ill.

"O, I'm unco laith to disturb him," said the old man; "he sees that the hand o' the Lord has fa'en heavy on him the day, and he's humbling himsel afore him in great bitterness o' spirit, I daresay. I count it a sin to break in on sic devotions as thae."

"Na, I carena if he should lie and pray yonder till the morn," said a young lad; "only I wadna like to gang hame and leave him lying on the hill, if he should hae chanced to turn no weel. Sae, if nane o' ye will gang and bring him, or see what ails him, I'll e'en gang mysel"; and away he went, the rest standing still to await the issue.

When the lad went first to the brink of the little slack where Adamson lay, he stood a few moments, as if gazing or listening, and then turned his back and fled. The rest, who were standing watching his motions, wondered at this; and they said one to another, that their master was angry at being disturbed, and had been threatening the lad so rudely that it had caused him to take to his heels. But what they thought most strange was, that the lad did not fly towards them, but straight to the hill; nor did he ever so much as cast his eyes in their direction, so deeply did he seem to be impressed with what had passed between him and his master; Indeed it rather appeared that he did not know what he was doing; for, after running a space with great violence, he stood and looked back, and then broke to the hill again—always looking first over the one shoulder, and then over the other. Then he stopped a second time, and returned cautiously towards the spot where his master reclined; and all the while he never so much as once turned his eyes in the direction of his neighbors, or seemed to remember that they were there. His motions were strikingly erratic; for all the way, as he returned to the spot where his master was, he continued to advance by a zigzag course, like a vessel beating up by short tacks; and several times he stood still, as on the very point of retreating. At length he vanished from their sight in the little hollow.

It was not long till the lad again made his appearance, shouting and waving his cap for them to come likewise; on which they all went away to him as fast as they could, in great amazement what could be the matter. When they came to the green hollow, a shocking spectacle presented itself: there lay the body of their master, who had been struck dead by the lightning, and his right side having been torn open, his bowels had gushed out, and were lying beside the body. The earth was rutted and plowed close to his side, and at his feet there was a hole scooped out, a full yard in depth, and very much resembling a grave. He had been cut off in the act of prayer, and the body was still lying in the position of a man praying in the field. He had been on his knees, with his elbows leaning on the brae, and his brow laid on his folded hands; his plaid was drawn over his head, and his hat below his arm; and this affecting circumstance proved a great source of comfort to his widow afterwards, when the extremity of her suffering had somewhat abated.

No such awful visitation of Providence had ever been witnessed, or handed down to our hinds on the ample records of tradition, and the impression which it made, and the interest it excited, were also without a parallel. Thousands visited the spot, to view the devastations made by the flood, and the furrows formed by the electric matter; and the smallest circumstances were inquired into with the most minute curiosity: above all, the still and drowsy embers of superstition were rekindled by it into a flame, than which none had ever burned brighter, not even in the darkest days of ignorance; and by the help of it a theory was made out and believed, that for horror is absolutely unequaled. But as it was credited in its fullest latitude by my informant, and always added by him at the conclusion of the tale, I am bound to mention the circumstances, though far from vouching them to be authentic.

It was asserted, and pretended to have been proved, that old Peter Maxwell was not *in the glen of Laverhope that day,* but at a great distance in a different county, and that it was the devil who attended the folds in his likeness. It was further believed by all the people at the folds, that it was the last explosion of the whole that had slain Mr. Adamson; for they had at that time observed the side of the brae, where the little green slack was situated, covered with a sheet of flame for a moment. And it so happened that thereafter the profane gaberlunzie had been no more seen, and therefore they said—and here was the most horrible part of the story—there was no doubt of his being the devil, waiting for his prey, and that he fled away in that sheet of flame, carrying the soul of John Adamson along with him.

I never saw old Pate Maxwell—for I believe he died before I was born; but Robin Johnston said, that to his dying day, he denied having been within forty miles of the folds of Laverhope on the day of the thunder-storm, and was exceedingly angry when any one pretended to doubt the assertion. It was likewise reported, that at six o'clock in the afternoon a stranger had called on Mrs. Irvine, and told her that John Adamson and a great part of his stock had been destroyed by the lightning and the hail. Mrs. Irvine's house was five miles distant from the folds; and more than that, the farmer's death was not so much as known of by mortal man until two hours after Mrs. Irvine received this information. The storm exceeded anything remembered, either for its violence or consequences, and these mysterious circumstances having been bruited abroad, gave it a hold on the minds of the populace, never to be erased but by the erasure of their existence. It fell out on the 12th of July, 1753.

## GEORGE MACINDOE (1771–1848)

### The Burn Trout

Brither Jamie cam west, wi a braw burn trout,
An speered* how acquaintance were greeing; — asked
He brought it frae Peebles, tied up in a clout*, — cloth
An said it wad just be a preeing*, a preeing, — sample, taste
An said it wad just be a preeing.

In the burn that rins by his grandmother's door
This trout had lang been a dweller,
Ae night fell asleep a wee piece frae the shore,
An was killed wi a stane by the miller, the miller,
An was killed wi a stane by the miller.

This trout it was gutted an dried on a nail
Weel rubbed wi saut, frae the head to the tail,

An kippered as 't had been a salmon, a salmon,
An kippered as 't had been a salmon.

This trout it was boiled an set ben* on a plate, in
Ne fewer than ten made a feast o't.
The banes and the tail, they were gi'en to the cat.
But we lickit our lips at the rest o't, the rest o't,
But we lickit our lips at the rest o't.

When this trout it was eaten, we were a' like to rive*, burst
Sae ye mauna think it was a wee ane.
May ilk trout in the burn grow muckle an thrive,
An Jamie bring west aye a preeing, a preeing,
An Jamie bring west aye a preeing.

## JAMES MONTGOMERY (1771–1854)

### The Common Lot

Once, in the flight of ages past,
There lived a man—and who was he?—
Mortal, howe'er thy lot be cast,
That man resembled thee.

Unknown the region of his birth,
The land in which he died unknown.
His name hath perished from the earth.
This truth survives alone:

That joy and grief, and hope and fear,
Alternate triumphed in his breast.
His bliss and woe—a smile, a tear—
Oblivion hides the rest.

The bounding pulse, the languid limb,
The changing spirits' rise and fall—
We know that these were felt by him,
For these are felt by all.

He suffered—but his pangs are oer;
Enjoyed—but his delights are fled;
Had friends—his friends are now no more;
And foes—his foes are dead.

He loved—but whom he loved, the grave
Hath lost in its unconscious womb.
O, she was fair—but nought could save
Her beauty from the tomb.

He saw whatever thou hast seen;
Encountered all that troubles thee.

He was—whatever thou hast been.
He is—what thou shalt be.

The rolling seasons, day and night,
Sun, moon, and stars, the earth and main,
Erewhile his portion, life, and light,
To him exist in vain.

The clouds and sunbeams, oer his eye
That once their shades and glory threw,
Have left in yonder silent sky
No vestige where they flew.

The annals of the human race,
Their ruins, since the world began,
Of him afford no other trace
Than this—there lived a man.

## The Daisy

There is a flower, a little flower
With silver crest and golden eye,
That welcomes every changing hour,
And weathers every sky.

The prouder beauties of the field
In gay but quick succession shine.
Race after race their honors yield,
They flourish and decline.

But this small flower, to nature dear,
While moons and stars their courses run,
In-wreathes the circle of the year,
Companion of the sun.

It smiles upon the lap of May,
To sultry August spreads its charm,
Lights pale October on his way,
And twines December's arm.

The purple heath and golden broom
On moory mountains catch the gale;
Oer lawns the lily sheds perfume,
The violet in the vale.

But this bold floweret climbs the hill,
Hides in the forest, haunts the glen,
Plays on the margin of the rill,
Peeps round the fox's den.

Within the garden's cultured round
It shares the sweet carnation's bed;

And blooms on consecrated ground
In honor of the dead.

The lambkin crops its crimson gem;
The wild bee murmurs on its breast.
The blue-fly bends its pensile stem
Light oer the skylark's nest.

Tis Flora's page—in every place,
In every season, fresh and fair,
It opens with perennial grace,
And blossoms everywhere.

On waste and woodland, rock and plain,
Its humble buds unheeded rise.
The rose has but a summer reign;
The daisy never dies.

## Night

Night is the time for rest:
How sweet, when labors close,
To gather round an aching breast
The curtain of repose,
Stretch the tired limbs, and lay the head
Upon our own delightful bed.

Night is the time for dreams:
The gay romance of life,
When truth that is, and truth that seems,
Blend in fantastic strife.
Ah, visions, less beguiling far
Than waking dreams by daylight are.

Night is the time for toil:
To plow the classic field,
Intent to find the buried spoil
Its wealthy furrows yield;
Till all is ours that sages taught,
That poets sang or heroes wrought.

Night is the time to weep:
To wet with unseen tears
Those graves of memory, where sleep
The joys of other years;
Hopes, that were angels at their birth,
But perished young, like things of earth.

Night is the time to watch:
Oer ocean's dark expanse,
To hail the Pleiades, or catch
The full moon's earliest glance,

That brings into the homesick mind
All we have loved and left behind.

Night is the time for care:
Brooding on hours misspent,
To see the specter of despair
Come to our lonely tent;
Like Brutus, midst his slumbering host,
Startled by Caesar's stalwart ghost.

Night is the time to muse:
When, from the eye, the soul
Takes flight; and, with expanding views,
Beyond the starry pole
Descries athwart the abyss of night
The dawn of uncreated light.

Night is the time to pray:
Our Savior oft withdrew
To desert mountains far away.
So will his followers do,
Steal from the throng to haunts untrod,
And hold communion there with God.

Night is the time for death:
When all around is peace,
Calmly to yield the weary breath,
From sin and suffering cease,
Think of heaven's bliss, and give the sign
To parting friends;—such death be mine!

## At Home in Heaven

"Forever with the Lord!"
Amen, so let it be.
Life from the dead is in that word:
Tis immortality.

Here in the body pent,
Absent from him I roam,
Yet nightly pitch my moving tent
A day's march nearer home.

My Father's house on high,
Home of my soul, how near
At times, to faith's foreseeing eye,
Thy golden gates appear.

Ah, then my spirit faints
To reach the land I love,
The bright inheritance of saints,
Jerusalem above.

Yet clouds will intervene,
And all my prospect flies.
Like Noah's dove, I flit between
Rough seas and stormy skies.

Anon the clouds dispart,
The winds and waters cease,
While sweetly oer my gladdened heart
Expands the bow of peace.

Beneath its glowing arch,
Along the hallowed ground,
I see cherubic armies march,
A camp of fire around.

I hear at morn and even,
At noon and midnight hour,
The choral harmonies of heaven
Earth's Babel-tongues oerpower.

Then, then I feel that He,
Remembered or forgot,
The Lord, is never far from me,
Though I perceive him not.

## The Recluse

A fountain issuing into light
Before a marble palace, threw
To heaven its column, pure and bright,
Returning thence in showers of dew;
But soon a humble course it took,
And glid away a nameless brook.

Flowers on its grassy margin sprang,
Flies oer its eddying surface played,
Birds midst the older branches sang,
Flocks through the verdant meadows strayed.
The weary there lay down to rest,
And there the halcyon built her nest.

Twas beautiful to stand and watch
The fountains' crystal turn to gems,
And from the sky such colors catch
As if twere raining diadems;
Yet all was cold and curious art,
That charmed the eye, but missed the heart.

Dearer to me the little stream
Whose unimprisoned waters run,
Wild as the changes of a dream,
By rock and glen, through shade and sun.

Its lovely links had power to bind
In welcome chains my wandering mind.

So thought I when I saw the face
By happy portraiture revealed,
Of one adorned with every grace,
Her name and date from me concealed,
But not her story. She had been
The pride of many a splendid scene.

She cast her glory round a court,
And frolicked in the gayest ring,
Where fashion's high-born minions sport
Like sparkling fire-flies on the wing;
But thence, when love had touched her soul,
To nature and to truth she stole.

From din, and pageantry and strife,
Midst woods and mountains, vales and plains,
She treads the paths of lowly life,
Yet in a bosom-circle reigns,—
No fountain scattering diamond-showers,
But the sweet streamlet watering flowers.

## Evening in the Alps

Come, golden evening in the west
Enthrone the storm-dispelling sun,
And let the triple rainbow rest
Oer all the mountain tops. Tis done:—
The tempest ceases; bold and bright,
The rainbow shoots from hill to hill;
Down sinks the sun; on presses night;—
Mount Blanc is lovely still.

There take thy stand, my spirit; spread
The world of shadows at thy feet;
And mark how calmly overhead
The stars, like saints in glory, meet.
While hid in solitude sublime,
Methinks I muse on nature's tomb,
And hear the passing foot of time
Step through the silent gloom.

All in a moment, crash on crash,
From precipice to precipice,
An avalanche's ruins dash
Down to nethermost abyss.
Invisible, the ear alone
Pursues the uproar till it dies;

Echo to echo, groan for groan,
From deep to deep replies.

Silence again the darkness seals,
Darkness that may be felt;—but soon
The silver-clouded east reveals
The midnight specter of the moon.
In half eclipse she lifts her horn,
Yet oer the host of heaven supreme
Brings the faint semblance of a morn,
With her awakening beam.

Ah, at her touch these Alpine heights
Unreal mockeries appear;
With blacker shadows, ghastlier lights,
Emerging as she climbs the sphere,
A crowd of apparitions pale.
I hold my breath in child suspense—
They seem so exquisitely frail—
Lest they should vanish thence.

I breathe again, I freely breathe;
Thee, Leman's Lake, once more I trace,
Like Dian's crescent, far beneath,
As beautiful as Dian's face:
Pride of the land that gave me birth,
All that thy waves reflect I love,
Where heaven itself, brought down to earth,
Looks fairer than above.

Safe on thy banks again I stray;
The trance of poesy is oer,
And I am here at down of day,
Gazing on mountains as before,
Where all the strange mutations wrought
Were magic feats of my own mind;
For, in that fairy land of thought,
Whate'er I seek, I find.

Yet, O ye everlasting hills,
Buildings of God, not made with hands,
Whose word performs whate'er He wills,
Whose word, though ye shall perish, stands;
Can there be eyes that look on you,
Till tears of rapture make them dim,
Nor in his works the Maker view,
Then lose his works in Him?

By me, when I behold Him not,
Or love Him not when I behold,
Be all I ever knew forgot—
My pulse stand still, my heart grow cold;
Transformed to ice, twixt earth and sky,

On yonder cliff my form be seen,
That all may ask, but none reply,
What my offense hath been.

## WALTER SCOTT (1771–1832)

[The nineteenth century is dominated by the gigantic figure of Walter Scott. Scott's series of long narrative poems, mostly on subjects from Scottish history, made him at one time the most read poet in Britain. When his popularity waned, he turned to writing novels—then a form of literature regarded as "common" and thus somewhat uncouth. His success was immediate and enormous. His novels are virtually all set in historical eras. He began a vogue for both the historical novel, and the "regional novel" which makes him in fact one of the seminal figures in the development of literature. He was much imitated; his influence can be detected in almost every Western literature. For example, the "Leatherstocking Tales," the works of the popular American novelist, James Fenimore Cooper, owe much to him.

Almost as importantly, nineteen of his twenty-seven novels are set in Scotland itself. They helped spark an interest in Scottish history throughout Britain and indeed the world at large, one which has to some degree endured. The Romantic figure of the Highland Scot, with bagpipe, tartan, and kilt, derives primarily from Scott. Throughout the nineteenth century, Scotland was to be an acceptable subject for the popular novel, that is, for Scottish novelists attempting to sell their books in England and the United States as well as in their own country. One of the most striking characteristics of Scottish literature—its tendency to look to its own history as its primary subject matter—becomes dominant in this century. Very much of Scottish literature in this age was "backwards looking."

Like every Scottish writer who wished to achieve popularity outside his native country, while still writing about Scotland, Scott was forced to a kind of compromise in his diction. He simply used standard English (a somewhat literary variety, in his case), for the narration, and the speech of his upper-class characters, and reserved Scots for the diction of the common people. That way, his English readers would be able to read his works without too much difficulty, while still catching the flavor of the native Scottish dialect. For much of the nineteenth century, Scottish novelists wrote in this fashion. Even to this day, the practice is common. One inevitable result, however, is that the practice reinforced the notion, even in Scotland, that Scots was the speech of the lower or uneducated classes. Thus, paradoxically, Scott's novels made Scots both more acceptable in literature and less acceptable in society. Perhaps another result of Scott's practice and his influence is the tendency of the lesser nineteenth century Scots novelist to emphasize the "quaint" Scotsman—countryfied, fixated, canny, mildly ridiculous but lovable, sort of a "stage Irishman" in kilts.

Included here is perhaps the finest short story in Scottish literature, "Wandering Willie's Tale," which is a self-sustaining inset in his novel, *Redgauntlet.*

Scott, one of the best essayists of his time, was a regular contributor to magazines. His study of "King George III" appeared in the *Edinburgh Weekly Journal* on February 8, 1820, shortly after the King's death. While tinged with the sentimental and patriotic touches expected in an article about the death of the monarch (especially coming from one of Scott's Tory principles), the essay reveals its author's remarkably evenhanded historical insight, as it does his grasp of character and his flair for salient detail.

In his later years, he kept a journal—from November, 1825, to April, 1832—though he eventually found it difficult to remain faithful to the task. He is among the finest diarists in English. The excerpts from the *Journal* printed below reveal his manliness, humor and wide range of interests and insights. The first two express his reaction to the news of his (quite undeserved) financial ruin; the others show us something of his notorious working methods. Also included is his famous and generous tribute to his contemporary and great literary opposite, Jane Austen.]

## The Violet

The violet in her greenwood bower,
Where birchen boughs with hazels mingle,
May boast itself the fairest flower
In glen, or copse, or forest dingle.

Though fair her gems of azure hue,
Beneath the dewdrop's weight reclining;
I've seen an eye of lovelier blue,
More sweet through wat'ry luster shining.

The summer sun that dew shall dry,
Ere yet the day be past its morrow;
Nor longer in my false love's eye
Remained the tear of parting sorrow.

## To a Lady

With Flowers from the Roman Wall

Take these flowers which, purple waving,
On the ruined rampart grew,
Where, the sons of freedom braving,
Rome's imperial standards flew.

Warriors from the breach of danger
Pluck no longer laurels there;
They but yield the passing stranger
Wild-flower wreaths for Beauty's hair.

## Glenfinlas

O hone a rie'! O hone a rie'![1]
The pride of Albin's line is o'er.
And fall'n Glenartney's stateliest tree;
We ne'er shall see Lord Ronald more.

O, sprung from great Macgillianore,
The chief that never feared a foe,
How matchless was thy broad claymore,
How deadly thine unerring bow.

[1] "Alas for the chief!"

Well can the Saxon widows tell,
How, on the Teith's resounding shore,
The boldest Lowland warriors fell,
As down from Lenny's pass you bore.

But oer his hills, in festal day,
How blazed Lord Ronald's beltane tree,
While youths and maids the light strathspey
So nimbly danced with Highland glee.

Cheered by the strength of Ronald's shell,
E'en age forgot his tresses hoar;
But now the loud lament we swell,
O ne'er to see Lord Ronald more.

From distant isles a chieftain came,
The joys of Ronald's halls to find,
And chase with him the dark-brown game,
That bounds oer Albin's hills of wind.

Twas Moy; whom in Columba's isle
The Seer's prophetic spirit found,
As, with a minstrel's fire the while,
He waked his harp's harmonious sound.

Full many a spell to him was known,
Which wandering spirits shrink to hear;
And many a lay of potent tone,
Was never meant for mortal ear.

For there, tis said, in mystic mood,
High converse with the dead they hold,
And oft espy the fated shroud,
That shall the future corpse enfold.

O so it fell, that on a day,
To rouse the red deer from their den,
The Chiefs have ta'en their distant way,
And scoured the deep Glenfinlas glen.

No vassals wait their sports to aid,
To watch their safety, deck their board;
Their simple dress, the Highland plaid,
Their trusty guard, the Highland sword.

Three summer days, through brake and dell,
Their whistling shafts successful flew;
And still, when dewy evening fell,
The quarry to their hut they drew.

In gray Glenfinlas' deepest nook
The solitary cabin stood,

Fast by Moneira's sullen brook,
Which murmurs through that lonely wood.

Soft fell the night, the sky was calm,
When three successive days had flown;
And summer mist in dewy balm
Steeped heathy bank and mossy stone.

The moon, half-hid in silvery flake,
Afar her dubious radiance shed,
Quivering on Katrine's distant lakes
And resting on Benledi's head.

Now in their hut, in social guise,
Their sylvan fare the Chiefs enjoy;
And pleasure laughs in Ronald's eyes,
As many a pledge he quaffs to Moy.

"What lack we here to crown our bliss,
While thus the pulse of joy beats high?
What, but fair woman's yielding kiss,
Her panting breath and melting eye?

"To chase the deer of yonder shades,
This morning left their father's pile
The fairest of our mountain maids,
The daughters of the proud Glengyle.

"Long have I sought sweet Mary's heart,
And dropped the tear and heaved the sigh;
But vain the lover's wily art,
Beneath a sister's watchful eye.

"But thou mayst teach that guardian fair,
While far with Mary I am flown,
Of other hearts to cease her care,
And find it hard to guard her own.

"Touch but thy harp, thou soon shalt see
The lovely Flora of Glengyle,
Unmindful of her charge and me,
Hang on thy notes, twixt tear and smile.

"Or, if she choose a melting tale,
All underneath the greenwood bough,
Will good St. Oran's rule prevail,
Stern huntsman of the rigid brow."

"Since Enrick's fight, since Morna's death,
No more on me shall rapture rise,
Responsive to the panting breath,
Or yielding kiss, or melting eyes.

"E'en then, when oer the heath of woe,
Where sunk my hopes of love and fame,
I bade my harp's wild wailings flow,
On me the Seer's sad spirit came.

"The last dread curse of angry heaven,
With ghastly sights and sounds of woe,
To dash each glimpse of joy was given—
The gift, the future ill to know.

"The bark thou saw'st, yon summer morn,
So gaily part from Oban's bay,
My eye beheld her dashed and torn,
Far on the rocky Colonsay.

"Thy Fergus too—thy sister's son,
Thou saw'st, with pride, the gallant's power,
As marching gainst the Lord of Downe,
He left the skirts of huge Benmore.

"Thou only saw'st their tartans wave,
As down Benvoirlich's side they wound,
Heard'st but the pibroch, answering brave
To many a target clanking round.

"I heard the groans, I marked the tears,
I saw the wound his bosom bore,
When on the serried Saxon spears
He poured his clan's resistless roar.

"And thou, who bidst me think of bliss,
And bidst my heart awake to glee,
And court, like thee, the wanton kiss—
That heart, O Ronald, bleeds for thee!

"I see the death-damps chill thy brow,
I hear thy Warning Spirit cry:
The corpse-lights dance—they're gone, and now . . . .
No more is given to gifted eye!"—

"Alone enjoy thy dreary dreams,
Sad prophet of the evil hour.
Say, should we scorn joy's transient beams,
Because tomorrow's storm may lour?

"Or false, or sooth, thy words of woe,
Clangillian's Chieftain ne'er shall fear;
His blood shall bound at rapture's glow,
Though doomed to stain the Saxon spear.

"E'en now, to meet me in yon dell
My Mary's buskins brush the dew."

He spoke, nor bade the Chief farewell,
But called his dogs, and gay withdrew.

Within an hour returned each hound;
In rushed the rousers of the deer;
They howled in melancholy sound,
Then closely couched beside the Seer.

No Ronald yet, though midnight came;
And sad were Moy's prophetic dreams,
As, bending oer the dying flame,
He fed the watch-fire's quivering gleams.

Sudden the hounds erect their ears,
And sudden cease their moaning howl;
Close pressed to Moy, they mark their fears
By shivering limbs and stifled growl.

Untouched, the harp began to ring,
As softly, slowly, oped the door;
And shook responsive every string,
As light a footstep pressed the floor.

And by the watch-fire's glimmering light,
Close by the minstrel's side was seen
An huntress maid, in beauty bright,
All dropping wet her robes of green.

All dropping wet her garments seem;
Chilled was her cheek, her bosom bare,
As, bending oer the dying gleam,
She wrung the moisture from her hair.

With maiden blush, she softly said:—
"O gentle huntsman, hast thou seen,
In deep Glenfinlas' moonlight glade,
A lovely maid in vest of green;

"With her a Chief in Highland pride;
His shoulders bear the hunter's bow,
The mountain dirk adorns his side,
Far on the wind his tartans flow?"—

"And who art thou? and who are they?"
All ghastly gazing, Moy replied.
"And why, beneath the moon's pale ray,
Dare ye thus roam Glenfinlas' side?"—

"Where wild Loch Katrine pours her tide,
Blue, dark, and deep, round many an isle,
Our father's towers o'erhang her side,
The castle of the bold Glengyle.

"To chase the dun Glenfinlas deer,
Our woodland course this morn we bore,
And haply met, while wandering here,
The son of great Macgillianore.

"O aid me, then, to seek the pair,
Whom, loitering in the woods, I lost;
Alone, I dare not venture there,
Where walks, they say, the shrieking ghost."—

"Yes, many a shrieking ghost walks there;
Then, first, my own sad vow to keep,
Here will I pour my midnight prayer,
Which still must rise when mortals sleep."—

"O first, for pity's gentle sake,
Guide a lone wanderer on her way.
For I must cross the haunted brake,
And reach my father's towers ere day."

"First, three times tell each Ave-bead,
And thrice a Pater-noster say;
Then kiss with me the holy rede;
So shall we safely wend our way."—

"O shame to knighthood, strange and foul!
Go, doff the bonnet from thy brow,
And shroud thee in the monkish cowl,
Which best befits thy sullen vow,

"Not so, by high Dunlathmon's fire,
Thy heart was froze to love and joy,
When gaily rung thy raptured lyre
To wanton Morna's melting eye."

Wild stared the minstrel's eyes of flame,
And high his sable locks arose,
And quick his color went and came,
As fear and rage alternate rose.

"And thou, when by the blazing oak
I lay, to her and love resigned,
Say, rode ye on the eddying smoke,
Or sailed ye on the midnight wind?

"Not thine a race of mortal blood,
Nor old Glengyle's pretended line;
Thy dame, the Lady of the Flood—
Thy sire, the Monarch of the Mine."

He muttered thrice St. Oran's rhyme,
And thrice St. Fillan's powerful prayer;

Then turned him to the eastern clime,
And sternly shook his coal black hair.

And, bending oer the harp, he flung
His wildest witch-notes on the wind;
And loud, and high, and strange, they rung
As many a magic change they find.

Tall waxed the Spirit's altering form,
Till to the roof her stature grew;
Then, mingling with the rising storm,
With one wild yell away she flew.

Rain beats, hail rattles, whirlwinds tear;
The slender hut in fragments flew;
But not a lock of Moy's loose hair
Was waved by wind, or wet by dew.

Wild mingling with the howling gale,
Loud bursts of ghastly laughter rise;
High oer the minstrel's head they sail,
And die amid the northern skies.

The voice of thunder shook the wood,
As ceased the more than mortal yell;
And, spattering foul, a shower of blood
Upon the hissing firebrands fell.

Next dropped from high a mangled arm;
The fingers strained at half-drawn blade;
And last, the life-blood streaming warm,
Torn from the trunk, a gasping head.

Oft oer that head, in battling field
Streamed the proud crest of high Benmore;
That arm the broad claymore could wield,
Which dyed the Teith with Saxon gore.

Woe to Moneira's sullen rills.
Woe to Glenfinlas' dreary glen.
There never son of Albin's hills
Shall draw the hunter's shaft agen.

E'en the tired pilgrim's burning feet
At noon shall shun that sheltering den,
Lest, journeying in their rage, he meet
The wayward Ladies of the Glen.

And we—behind the Chieftain's shield,
No more shall we in safety dwell;
None leads the people to the field—
And we the loud lament must swell.

O hone a rie'! O hone a rie'!
The pride of Albin's line is oer.
And fall'n Glenartney's stateliest tree;
We ne'er shall see Lord Ronald more.

## Harold's Song[1]

Then from his seat with lofty air
Rose Harold, bard of brave Saint Clair,
Saint Clair, who, feasting high at Home,
Had with that lord to battle come.
Harold was born where restless seas
Howl round the storm-swept Orcades:
Where erst Saint Clairs held princely sway
Oer isle and islet, strait and bay;
Still nods their palace to its fall,
Thy pride and sorrow, fair Kirkwall.
Thence oft he marked fierce Pentland rave,
As if grim Odin rode her wave,
And watched the whilst, with visage pale
And throbbing heart, the struggling sail;
For all of wonderful and wild
Had rapture for the lonely child.
And much of wild and wonderful
In these rude isles might Fancy cull,
For thither came in times afar
Stern Lochlin's sons of roving war,
The Norsemen, trained to spoil and blood,
Skilled to prepare the raven's food,
Kings of the main their leaders brave,
Their barks the dragons of the wave;
And there, in many a stormy vale,
The Scald had told his wondrous tale,
And many a runic column high
Had witnessed grim idolatry.
And thus had Harold in his youth
Learned many a Saga's rhyme uncouth,
Of that sea-snake, tremendous curled,
Whose monstrous circle girds the world;
Of those dread maids whose hideous yell
Maddens the battle's bloody swell:
Of chiefs who, guided through the gloom
By the pale death-lights of the tomb,
Ransacked the graves of warriors old,
Their falchions wrenched from corpses' hold,
Waked the deaf tomb with war's alarms,
And bade the dead arise to arms.
With war and wonder all on flame,
To Roslin's bowers young Harold came,
Where, by sweet glen and greenwood tree,

[1]From *The Lay of the Last Minstrel*, VI, 306-403.

He learned a milder minstrelsy;
Yet something of the Northern spell
Mixed with the softer numbers well.—

O, listen, listen, ladies gay,
No haughty feat of arms I tell;
Soft is the note, and sad the lay,
That mourns the lovely Rosabelle.

"Moor, moor the barge, ye gallant crew,
And, gentle lady, deign to stay.
Rest thee in Castle Ravensheuch,
Nor tempt the stormy firth today.

"The blackening wave is edged with white;
To inch and rock the sea-mews fly;
The fishers have heard the water sprite,
Whose screams forebode that wreck is nigh.

"Last night the gifted seer did view
A wet shroud swathed round lady gay;
Then stay thee, fair, in Ravensheuch.
Why cross the gloomy firth today?''

"Tis not because Lord Lindesay's heir
Tonight at Roslin leads the ball,
But that my lady-mother there
Sits lonely in her castle-hall.

"Tis not because the ring they ride,
And Lindesay at the ring rides well,
But that my sire the wine will chide,
If 't is not filled by Rosabelle."

Oer Roslin all that dreary night
A wondrous blaze was seen to gleam;
Twas broader than the watch-fire light,
And redder than the bright moonbeam.

It glared on Roslin's castled rock,
It ruddied all the copsewood glen;
Twas seen from Dreyden's groves of oak,
And seen from caverned Hawthornden.

Seemed all on fire that chapel proud
Where Roslin's chiefs uncoffined lie,
Each baron, for a sable shroud,
Sheathed in his iron panoply.

Seemed all on fire within, around,
Deep sacristy and altar's pale;
Shone every pillar foliage-bound,
And glimmered all the dead men's mail.

Blazed battlement and pinnet high,
Blazed every rose-carved buttress fair—
So still they blaze when fate is nigh
The lordly line of high Saint Clair.

There are twenty of Roslin's barons bold
Lie buried within that proud chapelle;
Each one the holy vault doth hold—
But the sea holds lovely Rosabelle.

And each Saint Clair was buried there,
With candle, with book, and with knell;
But the sea-caves rung and the wild winds sung
The dirge of lovely Rosabelle.

## Lochinvar[1]

O, young Lochinvar is come out of the west.
Through all the wide Border his steed was the best;
And save his good broadsword he weapons had none;
He rode all unarmed, and he rode all alone.
So faithful in love, and so dauntless in war,
There never was knight like the young Lochinvar.

He stayed not for brake*, and he stopped not for stone; thickets
He swam the Eske river where ford there was none;
But ere he alighted at Netherby gate,
The bride had consented, the gallant came late:
For a laggard in love, and a dastard in war,
Was to wed the fair Ellen of brave Lochinvar.

So boldly he entered the Netherby Hall,
Among bridesmen, and kinsmen, and brothers, and all.
Then spoke the bride's father, his hand on his sword,
(For the poor craven bridegroom said never a word):
"O come ye in peace here, or come ye in war,
Or to dance at our bridal, young Lord Lochinvar?"

"I long wooed your daughter; my suit you denied;
Love swells like the Solway, but ebbs like its tide;
And now am I come, with this lost love of mine
To lead but one measure, drink one cup of wine.
There are maidens in Scotland more lovely by far,
That would gladly be bride to the young Lochinvar."

The bride kissed the goblet; the knight took it up,
He quaffed off the wine, and he threw down the cup.
She looked down to blush, and she looked up to sigh,
With a smile on her lips, and a tear in her eye.

---

[1]From *Marmion* (1808).

He took her soft hand, ere her mother could bar—
"Now tread we a measure," said young Lochinvar.

So stately his form, and so lovely her face,
That never a hall such a galliard did grace;
While her mother did fret, and her father did fume,
And the bridegroom stood dangling his bonnet and plume;
And the bride-maidens whispered, "Twere better by far
To have matched our fair cousin with young Lochinvar."

One touch to her hand, and one word in her ear,
When they reached the hall-door, and the charger stood near;
So light to the croupe* the fair lady he swung, saddle
So light to the saddle before her he sprung.
"She is won! We are gone, over bank, bush, and scaur*. rock
They'll have fleet steeds that follow," quoth young Lochinvar.

There was mounting mong Graemes of the Netherby clan;
Forsters, Fenwicks, and Musgraves, they rode and they ran;
There was racing and chasing, on Cannobie Lee,
But the lost bride of Netherby ne'er did they see.
So daring in love and so dauntless in war,
Have ye e'er heard of gallant like young Lochinvar?

## Brignall Banks[1]

O, Brignall banks are wild and fair,
And Greta woods are green,
And you may gather garlands there
Would grace a summer queen.
And as I rode by Dalton-hall,
Beneath the turrets high,
A maiden on the castle wall
Was singing merrily:—
"O Brignall banks are fresh and fair,
And Greta woods are green;
I'd rather rove with Edmund there,
Than reign our English queen."

"If, maiden, thou wouldst wend with me,
To leave both tower and town,
Thou first must guess what life lead we,
That dwell by dale and down.
And if thou canst that riddle read,
As read full well you may,
Then to the greenwood shalt thou speed,
As blithe as Queen of May."
Yet sung she, "Brignall banks are fair,
And Greta woods are green;

---

1 From *Rokeby* (1813)

I'd rather rove with Edmund there,
Then reign our English queen.

"I read you, by your bugle-horn,
And by your palfrey good,
I read you for a ranger sworn,
To keep the king's greenwood."
"A ranger, lady, winds his horn,
And tis at peep of light;
His blast is heard at merry morn,
And mine at dead of night."
Yet sung she, "Brignall banks are fair,
And Greta woods are gay;
I would I were with Edmund there,
To reign his Queen of May.

"With burnished brand and musketoon,
So gallantly you come,
I read you for a bold dragoon,
That lists the tuck* of drum." beat
"I list no more the tuck of drum,
No more the trumpet hear;
But when the beetle sounds his hum,
My comrades take the spear.
And O, though Brignall banks be fair,
And Greta woods be gay,
Yet mickle must the maiden dare,
Would reign my Queen of May.

"Maiden, a nameless life I lead,
A nameless death I'll die;
The fiend, whose lantern lights the mead,
Were better mate than I.
And when I'm with my comrades met
Beneath the greenwood bough,
What once we were we all forget,
Nor think what we are now.
Yet Brignall banks are fresh and fair,
And Greta woods are green,
And you may gather garlands there
Would grace a summer queen."

## Hie Away, Hie Away[1]

Hie away, hie away,
Over bank and over brae,
Where the copsewood is the greenest,
Where the fountains glisten sheenest,
Where the lady-fern grows strongest,
Where the morning dew lies longest,
Where the black-cock sweetest sips it,

[1]From *Waverley* (1814).

Where the fairy latest trips it:
Hie to haunts right seldom seen,
Lovely, lonesome, cool, and green
Over bank and over brae,
Hie away, hie away.

## Wasted, Weary, Wherefore Stay[1]

Wasted, weary, wherefore stay,
Wrestling thus with earth and clay?
From the body pass away:—
Hark, the mass is singing.

From thee doff thy mortal weed,
Mary Mother be thy speed,
Saints to help thee at thy need;—
Hark, the knell is ringing.

Fear not snowdrift driving fast,
Sleet, or hail, or levin* blast; lightning
Soon the shroud shall lap thee fast,
And the sleep be on thee cast
That shall ne'er know waking.

Haste thee, haste thee, to be gone,
Earth flits fast, and time draws on,—
Gasp thy gasp, and groan thy groan,
Day is near the breaking.

## Twist Ye, Twine Ye[2]

Twist ye, twine ye; even so,
Mingle shades of joy and woe,
Hope and fear and peace and strife,
In the thread of human life.

While the mystic twist is spinning,
And the infant's life beginning,
Dimly seen through twilight bending,
Lo, what varied shapes attending.

Passions wild and follies vain,
Pleasures soon exchanged for pain;
Doubt and jealousy and fear,
In the magic dance appear.

Now they wax and now they dwindle,
Whirling with the whirling spindle,

---

[1]From *Guy Mannering* (1815).
[2]From *Guy Mannering* (1815).

Twist ye, twine ye; even so,
Mingle human bliss and woe.

## Cavalier Song[1]

And what though winter will pinch severe
Through locks of gray and a cloak that's old,
Yet keep up thy heart, bold cavalier,
For a cup of sack* shall fence the cold. wine

For time will rust the brightest blade,
And years will break the strongest bow;
Was never wight so starkly* made, strongly
But time and years would overthrow.

## Why Sit'st Thou by That Ruined Hall[2]

"Why sit'st thou by that ruined hall,
Thou aged carle* so stern and gray? peasant
Dost thou its former pride recall,
Or ponder how it passed away?"

"Know'st thou not me?" the Deep Voice cried:
"So long enjoyed, so oft misused—
Alternate, in thy fickle pride,
Desired, neglected, and accused.

"Before my breath, like blazing flax,
Man and his marvels pass away.
And changing empires wane and wax,
Are founded, flourish, and decay.

"Redeem mine hours—the space is brief—
While in my glass the sand-grains shiver,
And measureless thy joy or grief,
When Time and thou shalt part forever."

## Jock of Hazeldean[3]

"Why weep ye by the tide, ladie?
Why weep ye by the tide?
I'll wed ye to my youngest son,
And ye sall be his bride:
And ye sall be his bride, ladie,
Sae comely to be seen"—
But aye she loot the tears down fa'
For Jock of Hazeldean.

---

[1]From *Old Mortality* (1816).
[2]From *The Antiquary* (1816).
[3]The first stanza is from a folk ballad.

"Now let this wilfu' grief be done,
And dry that cheek so pale;
Young Frank is chief of Errington,
And lord of Langley-dale;
His step is first in peaceful ha',
His sword in battle keen"—
But aye she loot the tears down fa'
For Jock of Hazeldean.

"A chain of gold ye sall not lack,
Nor braid to bind your hair;
Nor mettled hound, nor managed hawk,
Nor palfrey fresh and fair;
And you, the foremost o' them a',
Shall ride our forest queen"—
But aye she loot the tears down fa'
For Jock of Hazeldean.

The kirk was decked at morning-tide,
The tapers glimmered fair;
The priest and bridegroom wait the bride,
And dame and knight are there.
They sought her baith by bower and ha';
The ladie was not seen.
She's oer the Border, and awa'
Wi' Jock of Hazeldean.

## Proud Maisie[1]

Proud Maisie is in the wood,
Walking so early;
Sweet Robin sits on the bush,
Singing so rarely.

"Tell me, thou bonny bird,
When shall I marry me?"
"When six braw* gentlemen — handsome
Kirkward shall carry ye."

"Who makes the bridal bed,
Birdie, say truly?"
"The gray-headed sexton
That delves the grave duly.

"The glow-worm oer grave and stone
Shall light thee steady.
The owl from the steeple sing,
'Welcome, proud lady'."

[1]This ballad is from chapter 40 of *The Heart of Midlothian*, (1818) where it is sung by the madwoman, Madge Wildfire, on her deathbed.

## The Dreary Change

The sun upon the Weirdlaw Hill,
In Ettrick's vale, is sinking sweet;
The westland wind is hush and still,
The lake lies sleeping at my feet.
Yet not the landscape to mine eye
Bears those bright hues that once it bore;
Though evening, with her richest dye,
Flames oer the hills of Ettrick's shore.

With listless look along the plain,
I see Tweed's silver current glide,
And coldly mark the holy fane
Of Melrose rise in ruined pride.
The quiet lake, the balmy air,
The hill, the stream, the tower, the tree,—
Are they still such as once they were?
Or is the dreary change in me?

Alas, the warped and broken board,
How can it bear the painter's dye.
The harp of strained and tuneless chord,
How to the minstrel's skill reply?
To aching eyes each landscape lowers,
To feverish pulse each gale blows chill;
And Araby's or Eden's bowers
Were barren as this moorland hill.

## Lucy Ashton's Song[1]

Look not thou on beauty's charming,
Sit thou still when kings are arming,
Taste not when the wine-cup glistens,
Speak not when the people listens,
Stop thine ear against the singer,
From the red gold keep thy finger;
Vacant heart and hand and eye,
Easy live and quiet die.

## Border March[2]

March, march, Ettrick and Teviot-dale,
Why the deil dinna ye march forward in order?
March, march, Eskdale and Liddesdale,
All the blue bonnets are bound for the Border.
Many a banner spread,
Flutters above your head,
Many a crest that is famous in story.
Mount and make ready then,

[1]From *The Bride of Lammermoor* (1819).

[2]From *The Monastery* (1820).

Sons of the mountain glen,
Fight for the Queen[1] and the old Scottish glory.

Come from the hills where your hirsels* are grazing, herds, flocks
Come from the glen of the buck and the roe;
Come to the crag where the beacon is blazing,
Come with the buckler, the lance, and the bow.
Trumpets are sounding,
War steeds are bounding,
Stand to your arms, and march in good order;
England shall many a day
Tell of the bloody fray,
When the blue bonnets came over the Border.

## On Ettrick Forest's Mountains Dun

On Ettrick Forest's mountains dun
Tis blithe to hear the sportsman's gun,
And seek the heath-frequenting brood
Far through the noonday solitude;
By many a cairn and trenched mound
Where chiefs of yore sleep lone and sound,
And springs where gray-haired shepherds tell
That still the fairies love to dwell.

Along the silver streams of Tweed
Tis blithe the mimic fly to lead,
When to the hook the salmon springs,
And the line whistles through the rings;
The boiling eddy see him try,
Then dashing from the current high,
Till watchful eye and cautious hand
Have led his wasted strength to land.

Tis blithe along the midnight tide
With stalwart arm the boat to guide;
On high the dazzling blaze to rear,
And heedful plunge the barbed spear;
Rock, wood, and scaur, emerging bright,
Fling on the stream their ruddy light,
And from the bank our band appears
Like Genii armed with fiery spears.

Tis blithe at eve to tell the tale
How we succeed and how we fail,
Whether at Alwyn's lordly meal,
Or lowlier board of Ashestiel;
While the gay tapers cheerly shine,
Bickers the fire and flows the wine—

[1] Mary, Queen of Scots.

Days free from thought and nights from care,
My blessing on the Forest fair.

## The Maid of Neidpath

O lover's eyes are sharp to see,
And lovers' ears in hearing;
And love, in life's extremity,
Can lend an hour of cheering.
Disease had been in Mary's bower,
And slow decay from mourning,
Though now she sits on Neidpath's tower
To watch her love's returning.

All sunk and dim her eyes so bright,
Her form decayed by pining,
Till through her wasted hand, at night,
You saw the taper shining;
By fits, a sultry hectic hue
Across her cheek was flying;
By fits, so ashy pale she grew,
Her maidens thought her dying.

Yet keenest powers to see and hear
Seemed in her frame residing;
Before the watch-dog pricked his ear
She heard her lover's riding;
Ere scarce a distant form was kend,
She knew, and waved to greet him;
And oer the battlement did bend,
As on the wing to meet him.

He came—he passed—-an heedless gaze,
As oer some stranger glancing;
Her welcome, spoke in faltering phrase,
Lost in the courser's prancing.
The castle arch, whose hollow tone
Returns each whisper spoken,
Could scarcely catch the feeble moan
Which told her heart was broken.

## Woman's Faith[1]

Woman's faith, and woman's trust:
Write the characters in dust,
Stamp them on the running stream,
Print them on the moon's pale beam,
And each evanescent letter
Shall be clearer, firmer, better,

---

[1]From *The Betrothed* (1825).

And more permanent, I ween,
Than the things those letters mean.

I have strained the spider's thread
Gainst the promise of a maid;
I have weighed a grain of sand
Gainst her plight of heart and hand;
I told my true love of the token,
How her faith proved light, and her word was broken:
Again her word and truth she plight,
And I believed them again ere night.

## The Sun Upon the Lake[1]

The sun upon the lake is low,
The wild birds hush their song,
The hills have evening's deepest glow,
Yet Leonard tarries long.
Now all whom varied toil and care
From home and love divide,
In the calm sunset may repair
Each to the loved one's side.

The noble dame, on turret high
Who waits her gallant knight,
Looks to the western beam to spy
The flash of armor bright.
The village maid, with hand on brow
The level ray to shade,
Upon the footpath watches now
For Colin's darkening plaid.

Now to their mates the wild swans row,
By day they swam apart;
And to the thicket wanders slow
The hind beside the hart.
The woodlark at his partner's side
Twitters his closing song—
All meet whom day and care divide,
But Leonard tarrie long.

## When Friends Are Met[2]

When friends are met oer merry cheer,
And lovely eyes are laughing near,
And in the goblet's bosom clear
The cares of day are drowned;

---

[1]From Scott's play, *The Doom of Devergoil* (published 1830, written apparently many years before).

[2]From *The Doom of Devergoil* (1830).

When puns are made, and bumpers quaffed,
And wild wit shoots his roving shaft,
And mirth his jovial laugh has laughed,
Then is our banquet crowned,
Ah gay,
Then is our banquet crowned.

When glees are sung, and catches trolled,
And bashfulness grows bright and bold,
And beauty is no longer cold,
And age no longer dull;
When chimes are brief, and cocks do crow,
To tell us it is time to go,
Yet how to part we do not know,
Then is our feast at full,
Ah gay,
Then is our feast at full.

## King George III

[From the *Edinburgh Weekly Journal*, February 8, 1820]

Our last Journal acquainted our readers, that our venerable sovereign had closed his long and varied part in the mortal drama. Death has dropped the curtain on a reign of sixty years, the longest in the British annals, and the most marked with public events; and, at the same time, a life spent in the most conscientious, virtuous, and self-denying efforts to perform the arduous duties of a monarch, has been closed in sickness, in sorrow, and in comparative obscurity. Were a voice from Heaven to proclaim aloud to us, that there is another and a better world, in which virtue may expect its assured reward, the testimony of a miracle could not impress the awful truth more deeply upon the mind than the life and death of George the Third.

Our readers will forgive us, if, in recording this striking event, we forget for a space our character as journalists in the more important duty of the moral teacher. A very brief review of the character of our late beloved sovereign, though long in reference to our limits, is all we are enabled to give. We trust to perform it with the veneration due to the memory of the dead, and, at the same time, with the truth and sincerity which the living have a right to expect from us.

George the Third was the first of his family who could be termed a British monarch; for his father, grandfather, and great-grandfather, were foreigners both in language and manners; and without its being possible to impute blame to them for a predilection so natural, the two former loved their German hereditary dominions better than they did the more powerful and wealthy kingdoms, which fortune, and the misconduct of the Stuarts, had called them to govern.

Accordingly, the accession of our late sovereign, in 1760, was hailed by most of his subjects as the commencement of a new dynasty of kings, Britain's genuine offspring. The *morgue germanique*, the military pedantry and awkward formality, which characterized the court of George the Second, gave way, under the young sovereign, to manners and an etiquette of a more easy nature, which better fitted the genius of a free and high-spirited people. Even the caustic Walpole has recorded favorably the impression made upon him by the change.

"I was surprised," says he, "to find the levee room had lost so entirely the air of the lion's den. This sovereign don't stand with his eyes fixed royally on the ground, and dropping bits of German news: he walks about and speaks to everybody. I saw him afterwards on the throne, where he is graceful and genteel, sits with dignity, and reads his answers to addresses well."

Of his Majesty's personal appearance and demeanor we need only add to the testimony of this acute observer, that George the Third continued till the close of the active part of his reign, to be distinguished by his graceful and dignified elocution in public. The rapture of the celebrated Quin, who had been his tutor, broke out upon the first royal speech from the throne, in the familiar exclamation, "I taught the boy to speak!" In private conversation, George the Third's manner was too much hurried to be graceful; but his desire to please and oblige was seconded by a memory tenacious in a most flattering degree, of all the minute particulars which could interest those who had been once introduced to him.

Of the King's person, it is only necessary to say, it indicated more of muscular strength than of grace; and with his features, his whole subjects are well acquainted; for not only the most ordinary prints, but even the effigies on his coin, however deplorable in other respects, have not failed to preserve a striking likeness of the royal original. We return to the impression made by the King's accession.

A short acquaintance with the new sovereign showed that morals, as well as courtesy, had ascended the throne with him. His early marriage with the late Queen, by a happy union of temper, and of virtues on both sides, made the royal household a model of domestic affection. The pleasures of the monarch were as simple as they were innocent. Without doors, they were limited to the chase, and to the improvement of his farm; the first of which afforded a healthy exercise, and the second a profitable example to his subjects. At home, he filled up the few intervals which the laborious duties of his station left him, with music (the only one of the fine arts to which he was powerfully attached), with mechanical pursuits and scientific experiments, and with the collecting, improving, and arranging that most valuable library, which the munificence of his royal successor graciously bestowed on the public.

George III. might be termed a bibliographer rather than a student, yet he read a good deal also, and rather for improvement than amusement. The King's habits were temperate even to abstemiousness, and his chief delight was in the conversation of his own family, and a very few of the nobles about his person, who were most devotedly attached to him. Among those who held that distinction, John, Duke of Roxburghe, was particularly distinguished. He was, as is well known, a bibliomaniac, like his Majesty. Each was the happy possessor of a copy of Caxton's Book of Troy; but the King examined his own with such accuracy, as enabled him to prove to demonstration, that though both copies were of the same edition, that in the Royal Library must have been more early thrown off than the Duke's, because a leaf in the former was what is technically called locked, an error which had been discerned and corrected in the Duke's copy. So that his Majesty triumphed that his own copy of the first book (we believe) of the English press was also the earliest printed.

Mechanics were also a favorite study of the King, who used to amuse himself with the construction of optical and other philosophical instruments. It will give an idea of his good-nature to mention, that his Majesty had bespoken a complicated instrument from the celebrated Ramsden, and had directed the artist, who was not so much renowned for punctuality as for talents, to have it ready against a particular day. When at length it was sent home, the only notice which the King took of the want of punctuality, was by telling the optician, good-humoredly, that "he had observed the day of the week and month accurately, he had only forgotten the year."

Yet, with all the pretensions to popularity afforded by a life devoted to duty, and relieved only by such innocent amusements, George the Third, at the commencement of his reign, and for a long period after, was by no means popular.

His character was respected and his merits appreciated by those who approached his person; but he was not a favorite of the people at large, to whom his merits were only known by report.

One of his first acts of royalty was to call to his administration a nobleman who had been his own tutor; a person of worth and honor, a patron of literature and the arts, but not possessing political talents comparable to those of the celebrated Earl of Chatham, whom he succeeded in power. That daring minister had engaged the country, for no very adequate cause, in a bloody war with France, whom Britain had humbled in every part of the globe. The new minister made a peace so much inferior to the high-blown expectations of the country, that it seemed he had willfully thrown away the advantages which had been gained so dearly; and the King's support of this unfortunate nobleman gave the utmost dissatisfaction to the country, and led the way to a spirit of mobbish license, which in British history had never been so directly leveled against the person of the monarch.

This cause of discontent, skillfully kept up by demagogues, did not by any means subside at the dismissal of the obnoxious servant of the crown. The breach between the King and his favorite is now well known to have been absolute; from the dissolution of the ministry they never afterwards saw each other, except in public, and then in the most formal manner, insomuch, that we are aware of Lord Bute having expressed with some vehemence his sense of the King's harshness, when his Majesty, on an occasion when his lordship appeared at court, did not even ask after the health of his lady, which was then in a precarious condition.

Whether the King thought that Lord Bute had too early given way to the popular clamor, and in some degree deserted him, by giving in his resignation before it was required by the royal mandate, we do not pretend to decide. One thing is certain, that if his Majesty's breach with his late favorite had been made so total with the purpose of disarming the obloquy attending the connection (which we do not believe to have been the case), the intended consequence was not attained. For several years afterwards, the watchword for discontent was, that ministers actually in office were merely puppets, and all was managed by Lord Bute behind the curtain. Such assertions served long to excite factious clamors against the King; while the ex minister, with more reason, complained of the inexorable displeasure, which did not permit his Majesty to use even ordinary civility towards his early and faithful servant.

The disputes with the colonies, and the war which ensued, kept up and encouraged the spirit of public disaffection. This unhappy war might have a great color of justice in theory; but in practice it was so ill conducted, and on the whole was so very impolitic, that all will now allow we had better have manumitted the Americans on their first exhibiting symptoms of discontent.

But it is no less clear, that the King, in honor and conscience, deemed himself obliged to carry on the unhappy struggle to the very last; and being in a remarkable degree the *justus et tenax propositi* of the moral poet, he would not consent to the dismemberment of his dominions until necessity absolutely compelled him to that sacrifice. His speech to Adams, envoy from the American States, after the peace, was singularly expressive of his character. The ambassador naturally felt that the first interview betwixt him and his late sovereign must be unpleasant; when the King at once relieved him of his painful feelings, by saying to him, with the utmost frankness, "Mr. Adams, I was the last man to consent to the peace with America; but that peace being made, I will be the first in my dominions to oppose any attempts which may be made to disturb its conditions."

Still the people of Britain only saw that an unsuccessful war had been carried on with pertinacity, until it was concluded by a peace, which was only short of being disgraceful; and remembering the victories of Chatham's administration under George the Second, were in proportion discontented with the ministers and measures, and even with the person, of their present sovereign.

It might have been thought that the personal character of the monarch would have alleviated the strong censure arising from public misfortunes. But candor must admit, that, with the advantages which we have mentioned, George the Third labored under some disadvantages, which for a long time obscured his highly estimable qualities. Notwithstanding what we have said of his personal qualities, his education had been narrow and confined in an unusual degree, and no adequate pains had been taken either to form his external manners, or to cultivate his mind in classical or polite literature.

The King felt these wants, and in the earlier part of his reign was shy and reserved, admitting very few to his familiar society, and avoiding rather than courting the opportunities of appearing in public. The general voice of an Opposition, distinguished for talents and for wit, accused the King of affecting the retired state of an Eastern sultan, rather than the social dignity of a British monarch. The qualities which ought to have counterbalanced those impressions, the firmness and soundness of his judgment, the steadiness of his courage, the high principle upon which he regulated his conduct, the sacrifices of ease, of amusement, of indulgence, even of health, which, with unostentatious perseverance, George III. offered up year after year to the regular discharge of his regal duties, were long in forcing their way to the public. But at length they made their due impression.

The first act of the King's life which obtained him the general expression of the people's gratitude, was his conduct during the riots in 1780. The then Lord Mayor of London (a man of deep political research, like high civic authorities in the present day), was so steady a friend to the right of petitioning parliament, that, instead of dispersing a body of 60,000 men, who had assembled to exercise this constitutional privilege, he suffered them to occupy the city, which they set on fire in twenty different places. The confusion was yet upon the increase, and the petitioners had already destroyed a million's worth of houses, goods, and furniture, before the constitutional sages could satisfy their scrupulous consciences, when or how government ought to exercise that important function for which of all others it is chiefly intended,—the protection, namely, of the peaceable subject in his life and property.

The King cut the knot, by offering to march into the city at the head of his Guards, and, at every personal risk, to put down this disgraceful commotion. The common sense and manly spirit which dictated his decision, gave energy to the timid counselors around him—London was saved—no one complained of the infringement of the right of petitioning—and we cannot observe that our liberties suffered much by the forcible dispersion of those who had assembled to exercise it in so tremendous a manner.

But the great burst of public feeling in favor of George the Third, took place at a period somewhat later, when the coalition was formed betwixt the parties of North and Fox; when these two leaders, who had long stood in such inveterate hostility to each other, joined their forces for the purpose of taking the cabinet by storm, and placing the King at their discretion. In this emergency, the King made an appeal, which might be termed a personal one, to the public opinion of the nation, in opposition to a parliamentary majority, obtained by a union of parties so incongruous.

A sense of the real worth and unostentatious merits of the Monarch had by degrees sunk into the minds of the middle classes of the people (in whose voice, and neither in that of the highest nor of the lowest orders, public opinion really lodges), and now that their feelings also were interested in the behalf of the sovereign, the King's cause was adopted by general acclamation; nor did he ever afterwards lose the firm hold which he then attained on the hearts of his subjects.

Scotland may boast that she took the lead of the sister country, in perceiving, and rewarding by her affection, the virtues of the sovereign. This did not, however, arise either entirely from the moral character or the sagacity usually imputed to our countrymen; it sprung from honest gratitude, for the King had been a friend to Scotland. Much of the abuse leveled against George III by Wilkes, Churchill, and others, accused him of partiality to the northern part of his dominions; and the imputation designed to irritate the English, served to attach their neighbors to the person of their prince. Besides, the gentleness and kindness of his disposition were well qualified to reclaim to their allegiance the adherents of the unhappy house of Stuart, who now found themselves objects rather of compassionate respect than of political hatred and persecution. The restoration of the forfeited estates completed the reconciliation of a bold and enthusiastic class of subjects with the reigning monarch; which was not the less perfect, that many, with an amiable inconsistency, retained in theory their old political tenets, and could not in conscience have taken the oath of allegiance to George the Third, while they would have spent in his defense the last drop of their blood.

These causes of the King's popularity were peculiar to those who dwelt "benorth the Roman Wall"; but that popularity soon became universal through Britain. It was in vain that the most indecent satire was directed against the harmless peculiarities of a manner and mode of expression, too precipitate to be graceful; and equally in vain that his private life and amusements were ransacked to serve the purposes of slander. It seemed as if men loved the King the better for knowing, that all which "much malice mingled with a little wit" could say against him, was exaggerated ridicule directed against trifling personal peculiarities, or the quiet pleasures of his inoffensive domestic life. His Majesty even gained by this rigorous examination: he was loved in proportion as he was known.

The King's virtuous and exemplary conduct as a parent and husband, his dislike of the pomp of attendance, and apparatus of royalty, the quiet and innocent tenor of his amusements, the exemplary diligence and precision with which he despatched the load of public business attached to his functions, were qualities of English growth, and made him dear to the hearts of Englishmen. It became known, though the King studied to conceal it, that if a strict economy regulated the expenditure of his palace, at least a fifth part of the income assigned to his Majesty by the state, was devoted to public and private charity, with a munificence truly royal. It became known also, that if, in his solitary rambles around Windsor, his conversation with those whom he casually encountered was marked by his usual rapidity of inquiry, it was also distinguished by traits of benevolence and good-nature, which might well atone for want of grace, or occasional departure from etiquette.

In the most trifling instances, as well as in the most important, his Majesty's conduct towards those with whom he was placed in casual contact, was marked by that amiable bonhommie and wish to oblige, which indicated the most genuine good-nature. He respected age, and he loved childhood. Many anecdotes have been given of his private walks in Windsor Forest. That which follows is trivial, but we know it to be correct; and it shows the kindly benevolence which wished to make every one happy: Two Eton boys were spending their holidays with a friend at Sunning-hill, and had wandered into the Forest, where they met a fresh-looking old gentleman in the Windsor uniform, who stopped them, and jestingly asked if they were playing truant. They gave an account of themselves, and said they had come to see the King's stag-hounds throw off.

"The King does not hunt to-day," said the kind stranger, "but when he does, I will let you know; and you must not come to the ground by yourselves, lest you should meet with some accident." They parted; and two or three days after, while the family were at breakfast, one of the Royal Yeomanry-prickers rode up to the gate, to acquaint them that the King was waiting till he brought the two young gentlemen to a place of safety, where they might see the hounds thrown off: it is probable this little trait of overflowing good-nature made two royalists for life.

All these anecdotes got abroad, and all told to the King's advantage. Great bounties may be bestowed in policy, and striking occasions may be chosen to do generous actions out of vanity and ostentation; but the bounty and the kindness which marked the King's disposition in the calm tenor of his privacy, could not be assumed as a disguise, and were appreciated as the generous effusions of his excellent heart. Known popularly and familiarly by the name of Farmer George, the British people at once loved him as a father, respected him as their sovereign, and regarded even his peculiarities as something belonging to the character and humour of the nation, of whom he might be termed at once the king and the representative.

The deplorable circumstances of the malady with which he was seized, showed the regard of the subjects to their sovereign, and served to increase it by interesting their compassion in his behalf; and we are persuaded that, from the period of his recovery to that of his death, there never lived a monarch so firmly enthroned in the hearts of his subjects. His conduct during the stormy period which followed that event, served to rivet their affections to him firmly and indissolubly. His name was the rallying word of patriotism and gallantry; and when Britons were called upon to fight for their all, it was the more willingly obeyed because they were also to fight for their good old king.

No human voice was more fit to call a nation to arms, for no man possessed more courage in his own person than George the Third. During the period when disaffected and misguided men were forming daily plots against his person and life, he could not be persuaded to adopt any of the precautions which were recommended by his anxious counselors.

"My life," he said, "assume what precautions I may, must always be in the power of every man desperate enough to throw away his own; and to appear apprehensive on the topic, would be to invite the attempt."

When the danger was imminent, his courage was as steady as his understanding was correct in judging of it at a distance. Upon one occasion, when his Majesty was assaulted by a furious rabble in the Park, and the carriage-doors nearly forced open, he was not observed to change countenance, or to alter a single muscle; and when the maniac Hatfield fired a pistol at him in the theater, he was, when the smoke cleared off, discovered standing in the front of the box upright and unmoved, the only composed man in the crowded and convulsed assembly, and anxious only to prevent the Queen from being alarmed. This personal courage was the inalienable inheritance of the house of Brunswick, which is distinguished for a constitutional fearlessness of danger: the kind and generous affection with which it was united was his Majesty's own.

We have spoken of our lamented sovereign as a man; it remains to speak of him as a king. We do not at present pretend either to question or to defend the principles on which his foreign and domestic policy were conducted, further than in illustration of his personal character. In both the great and predominant events of his reign, he was guided by a sense of justice and of duty. In the American, and afterwards in the Revolutionary war, he was actuated by no pique against his neighbor, nor by any ambitious wish to extend his own dominions.

The former was unfortunate from the commencement to the conclusion, and the latter was so during the whole period in which George the Third exercised the government. But it was never hinted that the King, in encouraging and supporting the ministers who carried on the one or the other, had any other object but that of maintaining the lawful rights of his crown, and of upholding the constitution of the country which he governed. Even the tongue of slander went no farther than to charge him with an obstinate adherence to what it termed an extravagant opinion.

And there was that firmness and hardihood in the King's mind which, even when things seemed most desperate, refused the unmanly expedient which sovereigns have sometimes resorted to, in casting off an unfortunate minister to shelter themselves from popular indignation, as a sultan causes the head of the grand vizier to be thrown over the gates of the seraglio, to appease a mutiny among the Janizaries. In the situation of Charles the First, George the Third would never have abandoned the Earl of Strafford. The obnoxious Earl of Bute retreated from his post of premier, giving way to a storm, which he perhaps foresaw would be dangerous to his master as well as to himself. But he was not dismissed by the King, who seems rather to have resented than approved of his resignation.

Taking his full share of the responsibility of the actions of his ministers when censured, George III was equally ready to ascribe to them the full measure of merit which they could justly claim, even when he did them this justice at his own expense. The following anecdote is a remarkable proof of what we have said. The Egyptian expedition was planned almost exclusively by the late Lord Melville, and did not receive a cordial assent even from Mr. Pitt himself. It was resolved upon in the council by the narrowest majority, and the sovereign gave his written assent in words like the following: "I consent with the utmost reluctance, to a measure, which seems to me calculated to peril the flower of my army upon a distant and hazardous expedition."

Under such discouraging auspices that expedition was undertaken, which was the first in the lengthened war that served distinctly to show, that, whether the encounter be by land or sea, the Briton is more than a match for his enemies. On occasion of the King's breakfasting with Lord Melville at Wimbledon, during his retirement from office, in Lord Sidmouth's administration, he took a public and generous mode of acknowledging that minister's merit. He filled a glass of wine, and, having desired the Queen and company to follow his example, he drank "to the health of the minister, who, in opposition to the opinion of his colleagues, and under the avowed reluctance of his sovereign, dared to plan, and carry into execution, the Egyptian expedition."

The King's conduct towards the Coalition ministry, and afterwards to Fox and Grenville's administration, both of which were well understood to be forced upon him by parliament, in opposition to his own choice and wishes, was equally candid, open, and manly. He used no arts to circumvent or deceive the counselors whom he unwillingly received into the cabinet; nor did he, on the other hand, impede their measures by petty opposition. While they were ministers, he gave them the full power of their situation; not affecting, at the same time, to conceal, that they were not those whose assistance he would voluntarily have chosen.

It is very well known, that many of the distinguished statesmen, who were called upon these occasions to approach the King's person, were surprised to find that they had formed a false estimate of his character. They had repeated it so often, that they were themselves convinced that the king's firmness was but the pertinacity of an obstinate unpersuadable man, of small abilities and a contracted judgment. They found on a nearer approach to the sovereign, that it was the resolution of a man of strong intellectual capacity, a shrewd and excellent judge of mankind, well acquainted with the constitution of Great Britain, and yet better with the peculiar character of her inhabitants.

"They may say what they will of the King," said a Scottish Whig, of great and deserved esteem in that party, "but he has more sense than the whole bunch of them." Indeed, however inferior George the Third might be to many of the ministers whom the voice of Parliament had recommended, in theoretical or general information, he possessed in a degree far superior to most, perhaps to all of them, an accurate practical acquaintance with the temper and opinions of the people of Great Britain.

"Charles Fox," said a lady of great sagacity, when speaking of that accomplished statesman, "is a very clever and highly-gifted man, but he has never discovered the great secret that John Bull is a Tory by nature."

The King, however, had made this discovery. He knew that the sense of the kingdom could not be expressed by the mob, to whom the Whigs made too frequent appeals, and who swallow by wholesale whatever flatters their passions for the time; nor by the highest order of society, whom political connections lead to form preconceived and unalterable opinions, or whom the eager pursuit of some favorite political scheme sometimes renders callous to the choice of the means by which it may be served; but by those numerous classes, whose education has prepared their minds for deciding on points which their leisure and habits give them opportunity and inclination to consider, and who, themselves unengaged in the game, can the more soundly judge of the manner in which it is played.

The King was aware of the weight which his personal character gave him amongst that middling but independent portion of the community; and trusting to his influence amongst them, he watched for, and embraced, the opportunities when he could make a successful appeal to their judgment and feelings. He availed himself, perhaps equally, of his natural tact, and of the experience which the miscarriages of the early part of his reign had taught him, to wait for the moment when the popular gale shifted against an unacceptable ministry, to make this appeal; and he chose his time so judiciously, that he was always successful, because, like an able general, he never commenced the contest until he had gained the advantage-ground on which the struggle was to be made. The two remarkable changes of administration which followed on Fox's India Bill and on the Catholic question, manifested the King's skill in this species of tactics.

We have purposely delayed to mention one marked feature in George the Third's character. We have endeavored to show him in his private and in his public capacity; but it remains to mention his sentiments and conduct in that relation, in which the King of the Islands, and of the Ocean which surrounds them, was of no higher importance than one of his meanest subjects. His conduct as a Christian indicated the firmest belief in the doctrines of our holy religion, as well as the deepest reverence for its practical precepts.

He was conscientiously scrupulous, even where the grounds of his scruples might seem questionable; and his dismissing the Fox and Grenville administration, on the subject of Catholic Emancipation, could not be wondered at, since he had parted with Pitt on the same grounds. In both cases, the nation gave him credit for the utmost sincerity; and many sympathized with his feelings, who doubted the solidity of the grounds on which they were awakened. His Majesty set, in his own conduct, as well as in the regulation of his family and household, the example of a sincere and pious Christian. His faith illustrated his conduct, and his conduct did credit to the doctrines which he received and defended.

Here, then, we pause, arrived by a circular path at the point from which we commenced. This Monarch, so worthy of affection, so devoted to his people, so faithful in the discharge of every duty, so blameless in his private conduct, whose greatest errors were the fruits of the best intentions, opened his career amid a storm of turbulence and calumny, and closed it, virtually at least, amidst national calamity, amounting nearly to despair.

He nailed the colors of Britain to the mast; but he was not rewarded by seeing them float triumphant over all her enemies. He reaped not in this world the reward of his firmness, his virtue, his enduring patriotism; but was stricken with mental alienation, while he wept, broken-hearted, over the bed of a beloved and amiable daughter, and died the secluded inhabitant of a private apartment, in darkness, mental as well as bodily.

Deep, therefore, is our conviction, while comparing the life of George III. with its termination, that Heaven had destined for our beloved sovereign a far richer reward, in the applause of his own conscience, whilst struggling with so many difficulties; and when these, with all the troubles of life, had disappeared, in the exchange of a temporal crown, entwined with thorns, for that glory which passeth not away.

## Wandering Willie's Tale[1]

Ye maun have heard of Sir Robert Redgauntlet of that ilk, who lived in these parts before the dear years. The country will lang mind him; and our fathers used to draw breath thick if ever they heard him named. He was out wi' the Hielandmen in Montrose's time, and again he was in the hills wi' Glencairn in the saxteen hundred and fifty-twa; and sae when King Charles the Second came in, wha was in sic favor as the Laird of Redgauntlet? He was knighted at Lonon court, wi' the King's ain sword; and being a red-hot prelatist, he came down here, rampauging like a lion, with commissions of lieutenancy (and of lunacy, for what I ken), to put down a' the Whigs and Covenanters in the country.[2] Wild wark they made of it, for the Whigs were as dour as the Cavaliers were fierce, and it was which should first tire the other. Redgauntlet was aye for the strong hand; and his name is kenned as wide in the country as Claverhouse's or Tam Dalyell's. Glen, nor dargle, nor mountain, nor cave could hide the puir Hill-folk when Redgauntlet was out with bugle and bloodhound after them, as if they had been sae mony deer. And troth when they fand them, they didna mak muckle mair ceremony than a Hielandman wi' a roebuck. It was just, "Will ye tak the test?" If not, "Make ready—present—fire!" and there lay the recusant.

Far and wide was Sir Robert hated and feared. Men thought he had a direct compact with Satan; that he was proof against steel, and that bullets happed aff his buff-coat like hailstanes from a hearth; that he had a mear that would turn a hare on the side of Carrifra Gauns—and muckle to the same purpose, of whilk mair anon. The best blessing they wared on him was, "deil scowp wi' Redgauntlet!" He wasna a bad maister to his ain folk though, and was weel aneugh liked by his tenants, and as for the lackies and troopers that raid out wi' him to the persecutions, as the Whigs ca'd those killing times, they wad hae drunken themsells blind to his health at ony time.

Now you are to ken that my gudesire lived on Redgauntlet's grund; they ca' the place Primrose Knowe. We had lived on the grund, and under the Redgauntlets, since the riding days, and lang before. It was a pleasant bit, and I think the air is callerer and fresher there than onywhere else in the country. It's a' deserted now; and I sat on the broken door-cheek three days since, and was glad I couldna see the plight the place was in, but that's a' wide o' the mark. There dwelt my gudesire, Steenie Steenson, a rambling, rattling chiel he had been in his young days, and could play weel on the pipes; he was famous at "Hoopers and Girders", a' Cumberland couldna touch him at "Jockie Lattin", and he had the finest finger for the back-lilt between Berwick and Carlisle. The like o' Steenie wasna the sort that they made Whigs o'. And so he became a Tory, as they ca' it, which we now ca' Jacobites, just out of a kind of needcessity, that he might belang to some side or other. He had nae ill-will to the Whig bodies, and liked little to see the blude rin, though, being obliged to follow Sir Robert in hunting and hosting,[3] watching and warding, he saw muckle mischief,

---

[1]The tale is a self-contained chapter in Scott's novel, *Redgauntlet* (1824).

[2]Redgauntlet was a supporter of Charles II in the latter's often brutal attempts to restore Episcopacy to Scotland. This involved a harsh suppression of the fiercely Presbyterian Covenanters. These are the "killing times" referred to.

[3]Military service.

and maybe did some, that he couldna avoid.

Now Steenie was a kind of favorite with his master, and kenned a' the folks about the castle, and was often sent for to play the pipes when they were at their merriment. Auld Dougal MacCallum, the butler, that had followed Sir Robert through gude and ill, thick and thin, pool and stream, was specially fond of the pipes, and aye gae my gudesire his gude word wi' the laird; for Dougal could turn his master round his finger.

Weel, round came the Revolution,[1] and it had like to have broken the hearts baith of Dougal and his master. But the change was not a' thegither sae great as they feared, and other folk thought for. The Whigs made an unco crawing what they wad do with their auld enemies, and in special wi' Sir Robert Redgauntlet. But there were ower mony great folks dipped in the same doings to mak a spick and span new warld. So Parliament passed it a' ower easy; and Sir Robert, bating that he was held to hunting foxes instead of Covenanters, remained just the man he was. His revel was as loud, and his hall as weel lighted, as ever it had been, though maybe he lacked the fines of the Nonconformists, that used to come to stock his larder and cellar, for it is certain he began to be keener about the rents than his tenants used to find him before, and they behoved to be prompt to the rentday, or else the laird wasna pleased. And he was sic an awesome body that naebody cared to anger him; for the oaths he swore, and the rage that he used to get into, and the looks that he put on, made men sometimes think him a devil incarnate.

Weel, my gudesire was nae manager—no that he was a very great misguider—but he hadna the saving gift, and he got twa terms' rent in arrear. He got the first brash at Whitsunday put ower wi' fair word and piping, but when Martinmas came, there was a summons from the grundofficer to come wi' the rent on a day preceese,[2] or else Steenie behoved to flit. Sair wark he had to get the siller; but he was weel-freended, and at last he got the haill scraped thegither—a thousand merks; the maist of it was from a neighbor they ca'd Laurie Lapraik—a sly tod.[3] Laurie had walth o' gear[4]— could hunt wi' the hound and rin wi' the hare—and be Whig or Tory, saunt or sinner, as the wind stood. He was a professor in this Revolution warld; but he liked an orra[5] sough of this warld, and a tune on the pipes weel aneugh at a byetime; and abune a', he thought he had gude security for the siller he lent my gudesire ower the stocking at Primrose Knowe.

Away trots my gudesire to Redgauntlet Castle, wi' a heavy purse and a light heart, glad to be out of the laird's danger.

Weel, the first thing he learned at the castle was that Sir Robert had fretted himsell into a fit of the gout, because he did not appear before twelve o'clock. It wasna a' thegither for sake of the money, Dougal thought; but because he didna like to part wi' my gudesire aff the grund. Dougal was glad to see Steenie, and brought him into the great oak parlor, and there sat the laird his leesome lane,[6] excepting that he had beside him a great ill-favored jackanape,[7] that was a special pet of his—a cankered beast it was, and mony an illnatured trick it played; ill to please it was, and easily angered—ran about the haill castle, chattering and yowling, and pinching and biting folk, especially before ill weather, or disturbances in the state. Sir Robert

[1]Of 1688, which returned low-church Protestants to favor.

[2]"Precise."

[3]Fox.

[4]Money

[5]Odd, occasional.

[6]"His lane": alone.

[7]Monkey.

ca'd it Major Weir after the warlock that was burnt; and few folk liked either the name or the conditions of the creature—they thought there was something in it by ordinar—and my gudesire was not just easy in his mind when the door shut on him, and he saw himself in the room wi' naebody but the laird, Dougal MacCallum, and the major, a thing that hadna chanced to him before.

Sir Robert sat, or, I should say, lay, in a great armed chair, wi' his grand velvet gown, and his feet on a cradle; for he had baith gout and gravel, and his face looked as gash and ghastly as Satan's. Major Weir sat opposite to him, in a red laced coat, and the laird's wig on his head; and aye as Sir Robert girned wi' pain, the jackanape girned too, like a sheep's-head between a pair of tangs—an ill-faured, fearsome couple they were. The laird's buff-coat was hung on a pin behind him, and his broadsword and his pistols within reach; for he keepit up the auld fashion of having the weapons ready, and a horse saddled day and night, just as he used to do when he was able to loup on horseback, and away after ony of the Hill-folk he could get speerings of. Some said it was for fear of the Whigs taking vengeance, but I judge it was just his auld custom—he wasna gien to fear onything. The rentalbook, wi' its black cover and brass clasps, was lying beside him; and a book of sculduddry sangs was put betwixt the leaves, to keep it open at the place where it bore evidence against the goodman of Primrose Knowe, as behind the hand with his mails and duties. Sir Robert gave my gudesire a look as if he would have withered his heart in his bosom. Ye maun ken he had a way of bending his brows that men saw the visible mark of a horse-shoe in his forehead, deep-dinted, as if it had been stamped there.

"Are ye come light-handed, ye son of a toom whistle?" said Sir Robert. "Zounds! if you are—"

My gudesire, with as gude a countenance as he could put on, made a leg,[1] and placed the bag of money on the table wi' a dash, like a man that does something clever. The laird drew it to him hastily. "Is it all here, Steenie, man?"

"Your honor will find it right," said my gudesire.

"Here, Dougal," said the laird, "gie Steenie a tass of brandy downstairs, till I count the siller and write the receipt."

But they werena weel out of the room when Sir Robert gied a yelloch that garred the castle rock. Back ran Dougal— in flew the livery-men yell on yell gied the laird, ilk ane mair awfu' than the ither. My gudesire knew not whether to stand or flee, but he ventured back into the parlor, where a' was gaun hirdie-girdie, naebody to say "come in" or "gae out". Terribly the laird roared for cauld water to his feet, and wine to cool his throat; and "Hell, hell, hell, and its flames", was aye the word in his mouth. They brought him water, and when they plunged his swoln feet into the tub, he cried out it was burning; and folk say that it *did* bubble and sparkle like a seething cauldron. He flung the cup at Dougal's head, and said he had given him blood instead of burgundy; and, sure aneugh, the lass washed clotted blood aff the carpet the neist day. The jackanape they ca'd Major Weir, it jibbered and cried as if it was mocking its master. My gudesire's head was like to turn: he forgot baith siller and receipt, and downstairs he banged; but as he ran, the shrieks came faint and fainter; there was a deep-drawn shivering groan, and word gaed through the castle that the laird was dead.

Weel, away came my gudesire wi' his finger in his mouth, and his best hope was that Dougal had seen the money-bag, and heard the laird speak of writing the receipt. The young laird, now Sir John, came from Edinburgh to see things put to rights. Sir John and his father never gree'd weel. Sir John had been bred an advocate, and afterwards sat in the last Scots Parliament and voted for the Union, having gotten, it

[1]Bowed.

was thought, a rug of the compensations;[1] if his father could have come out of his grave he would have brained him for it on his awn hearthstane. Some thought it was easier counting with the auld rough knight than the fair-spoken young ane—but mair of that anon.

Dougal MacCallum, poor body, neither grat[2] nor graned but gaed about the house looking like a corpse, but directing as was his duty, a' the order of the grand funeral. Now, Dougal looked aye waur and waur when night was coming, and was aye the last to gang to his bed, whilk was in a little round just opposite the chamber of dais, whilk his master occupied while he was living, and where he now lay in state, as they ca'd it, weel-a-day! The night before the funeral Dougal could keep his awn counsel nae langer: he came doun with his proud spirit, and fairly asked auld Hutcheon to sit in his room with him for an hour. When they were in the round, Dougal took ae tass of brandy to himsell and gave another to Hutcheon, and wished him all health and lang life, and said that, for himsell, he wasna lang for this world; for that, every night since Sir Robert's death, his silver call had sounded from the state chamber, just as it used to do at nights in his lifetime, to call Dougal to help to turn him in his bed. Dougal said that, being alone with the dead on that floor of the tower (for naebody cared to wake Sir Robert Redgauntlet like another corpse), he had never daured to answer the call, but that now his conscience checked him for neglecting his duty; for, "though death breaks service," said MacCallum, "it shall never break my service to Sir Robert; and I will answer his next whistle, so be you will stand by me, Hutcheon."

Hutcheon had nae will to the wark, but he had stood by Dougal in battle and broil, and he wad not fail him at this pinch; so down the carles[3] sat ower a stoup of brandy, and Hutcheon, who was something of a clerk, would have read a chapter of the Bible; but Dougal would hear naething but a blaud[4] of Davie Lindsay, whilk was the waur preparation.

When midnight came, and the house was quiet as the grave, sure aneugh the silver whistle sounded as sharp and shrill as if Sir Robert was blowing it, and up gat the twa auld serving-men and tottered into the room where the dead man lay. Hutcheon saw aneugh at the first glance; for there were torches in the room, which showed him the foul fiend in his ain shape, sitting on the laird's coffin! Ower he couped as if he had been dead. He could not tell how lang he lay in a trance at the door, but when he gathered himself he cried on his neighbor, and getting nae answer, raised the house, when Dougal was found lying dead within twa steps of the bed where his master's coffin was placed. As for the whistle, it was gaen anes and aye; but mony a time was it heard at the top of the house on the bartizan,[5] and amang the auld chimneys and turrets, where the howlets have their nests. Sir John hushed the matter up, and the funeral passed over without mair bogle-wark.

But when a' was ower, and the laird was beginning to settle his affairs, every tenant was called up for his arrears and my gudesire for the full sum that stood against him in the rental-book. Weel, away he trots to the castle, to tell his story, and there he is introduced to Sir John, sitting in his father's chair, in deep mourning, with weepers and hanging cravat, and a small walking rapier by his side, instead of the auld broadsword that had a hundredweight of steel about it, what with blade, chape, and basket-hilt. I have heard their communing so often tauld ower, that I almost think

---

[1]That is, a bribe from the English interests.

[2]Wept.

[3]Men, fellows.

[4]Piece.

[5]Battlement.

I was there mysel, though I couldna be born at the time.

"I wuss ye joy, sir, of the head seat, and the white loaf, and the braid lairdship. Your father was a kind man to friends and followers; muckle grace to you, Sir John, to fill his shoon —his boots, I suld say, for he seldom wore shoon, unless it were muils when he had the gout."

"Ay, Steenie," quoth the laird, sighing deeply, and putting his napkin to his een, "his was a sudden call, and he will be missed in the country, no time to set his house in order : weel prepared Godward, no doubt, which is the root of the matter but left us behind a tangled hesp to wind, Steenie. Hem! hem! We maun go to business, Steenie; much to do, and little time to do it in."

Here he opened the fatal volume. I have heard of a thing they call Doomsday Book—I am clear it has been a rental of back-ganging tenants.

"Stephen," said Sir John, still in the same soft, sleekit tone of voice—"Stephen Stevenson, or Steenson, ye are down here for a year's rent behind the hand, due at last term."

*Stephen.* "Please your honor, Sir John, I paid it to your father."

*Sir John.* "Ye took a receipt then, doubtless, Stephen, and can produce it?"

*Stephen.* "Indeed I hadna time, an it like your honor; for nae sooner had I set doun the siller, and just as his honor Sir Robert, that's gaen, drew it till him to count it, and write out the receipt, he was ta'en wi' the pains that removed him."

"That was unlucky," said Sir John, after a pause. "But ye maybe paid it in the presence of somebody. I want but a *talis qualis* evidence, Stephen. I would go ower strictly to work with no poor man."

*Stephen.* "Troth, Sir John, there was naebody in the room but Douglas MacCallum, the butler. But, as your honor kens, he has e'en followed his auld master."

"Very unlucky again, Stephen," said Sir John, without altering his voice a single note. "The man to whom ye paid the money is dead, and the man who witnessed the payment is dead too; and the siller, which should have been to the fore, is neither seen nor heard tell of in the repositories. How am I to believe a' this?"

*Stephen. "I* dinna ken, your honor; but there is a bit memorandum note of the very coins—for, God help me! I had to borrow out of twenty purses—and I am sure that ilka man there set down will take his grit oath for what purpose I borrowed the money."

*Sir John. "I* have little doubt ye *borrowed* the money, Steenie. It is the *payment* to my father that I want to have some proof of."

*Stephen.* "The siller maun be about the house, Sir John. And since your honor never got it, and his honor that was canna have ta'en it wi' him, maybe some of the family may have seen it."

*Sir John.* "We will examine the servants, Stephen; that is but reasonable."

But lackey and lass, and page and groom, all denied stoutly that they had ever seen such a bag of money as my gudesire described. What was waur, he had unluckily not mentioned to any living soul of them his purpose of paying his rent. Ae quean[1] had noticed something under his arm, but she took it for the pipes.

Sir John Redgauntlet ordered the servants out of the room, and then said to my gudesire, "Now, Steenie, ye see you have fair play; and, as I have little doubt ye ken better where to find the siller than ony other body, I beg, in fair terms, and for your own sake, that you will end this fasherie for, Stephen, ye maun pay or flit."

"The Lord forgie your opinion," said Stephen, driven almost to his wit's end—"I am an honest man."

---

[1]Girl.

"So am I, Stephen," said his honor; "and so are all the folks in the house, I hope. But if there be a knave amongst us, it must be he that tells the story he cannot prove." He paused, and then added, mair sternly, "If I understand your trick, sir, you want to take advantage of some malicious reports concerning things in this family, and particularly respecting my father's sudden death, thereby to cheat me out of the money, and perhaps take away my character, by insinuating that I have received the rent I am demanding. Where do you suppose this money to be? I insist upon knowing."

My gudesire saw everything look sae muckle against him that he grew nearly desperate; however, he shifted from one foot to another, looked to every corner of the room, and made no answer.

"Speak out, sirrah," said the laird, assuming a look of his father's—a very particular ane, which he had when he was angry: it seemed as if the wrinkles of his frown made that selfsame fearful shape of a horse's shoe in the middle of his brow—"speak out, sir! I will know your thoughts. Do you suppose that I have this money?"

"Far be it frae me to say so," said Stephen.

"Do you charge any of my people with having taken it?"

"I wad be laith to charge them that may be innocent," said my gudesire; "and if there be any one that is guilty, I have nae proof."

"Somewhere the money must be, if there is a word of truth in your story," said Sir John; "I ask where you think it is and demand a correct answer?"

"In hell, if you *will* have my thoughts of it," said my gudesire, driven to extremity—"in hell! with your father, his jackanape, and his silver whistle."

Down the stairs he ran, for the parlor was nae place for him after such a word, and he heard the laird swearing blood and wounds behind him, as fast as ever did Sir Robert, and roaring for the bailie and the baron-officer.

Away rode my gudesire to his chief creditor, him they ca'd Laurie Lapraik, to try if he could make onything out of him; but when he tauld his story he got but the warst word in his wame[1]—thief, beggar, and dyvour[2] were the saftest terms; and to the boot of these hard terms, Laurie brought up the auld story of his dipping his hand in the blood of God's saunts, just as if a tenant could have helped riding with the laird, and that a laird like Sir Robert Redgauntlet. My gudesire was by this time far beyond the bounds of patience, and while he and Laurie were at deil speed the liars, he was wanchancie[3] aneugh to abuse Lapraik's doctrine as weel as the man, and said things that garred folks' flesh grue that heard them; he wasna just himsell, and he had lived wi' a wild set in his day.

At last they parted, and my gudesire was to ride hame through the wood of Pitmurkie, that is a' fou of black firs, as they say. I ken the wood, but the firs may be black or white for what I can tell. At the entry of the wood there is a wild common, and on the edge of the common a little lonely change-house, that was keepit then by a hostler-wife they suld hae ca'd her Tibbie Faw—and there puir Steenie cried for a mutchkin of brandy, for he had had no refreshment the haill day. Tibbie was earnest wi' him to take a bite o' meat, but he couldna think o't, nor would he take his foot out of the stirrup, and took off the brandy wholly at two draughts and named a toast at each—the first was, the memory of Sir Robert Redgauntlet, and might he never lie quiet in his grave till he had righted his poor bond-tenant; and the second was, a health to Man's Enemy, if he would but get him back the pock of siller, or tell him what came o't, for he saw the haill world was like to regard him as a thief and a

---

[1]Stomach.

[2]Bankrupt, good-for-nothing.

[3]Unfortunate.

cheat, and he took that waur than even the ruin of his house and hauld.

On he rode, little caring where. It was a dark night turned, and the trees made it yet darker, and he let the beast take its ain road through the wood; when, all of a sudden, from tired and wearied that it was before, the nag began to spring, and flee, and stend, that my gudesire could hardly keep the saddle; upon the whilk, a horseman, suddenly riding up beside him, said, "That's a mettle beast of yours, freend; will you sell him?" So saying, he touched the horse's neck with his riding-wand, and it fell into its auld heigh-ho of a stumbling trot. "But his spunk's soon out of him, I think," continued the stranger, "and that is like mony a man's courage, that thinks he wad do great things till he come to the proof."

My gudesire scarce listened to this, but spurred his horse, with "Gude e'en to you, freend."

But it's like the stranger was ane that doesna lightly yield his point; for, ride as Steenie liked, he was aye beside him at the selfsame pace. At last my gudesire, Steenie Steenson, grew half angry, and, to say the truth, half feared.

"What is it that ye want with me, freend?" he said. "If ye be a robber, I have nae money; if ye be a leal[1] man, wanting company, I have nae heart to mirth or speaking; and if ye want to ken the road, I scarce ken it mysel."

"If you will tell me your grief," said the stranger, "I am one that, though I have been sair misca'd in the world, am the only hand for helping my freends."

So my gudesire, to ease his ain heart, mair than from any hope of help, told him the story from beginning to end.

"It's a hard pinch," said the stranger; "but I think I can help you."

"If you could lend the money, sir, and take a lang day—I ken nae other help on earth," said my gudesire.

"But there may be some under the earth," said the stranger. "Come, I'll be frank wi' you, I could lend you the money on bond, but you would maybe scruple my terms. Now, I can tell you that your auld laird is disturbed in his grave by your curses, and the wailing of your family, and if ye daur venture to go to see him, he will give you the receipt."

My gudesire's hair stood on end at this proposal, but he thought his companion might be some humorsome chield that was trying to frighten him, and might end with lending him the money. Besides, he was bauld wi' brandy, and desperate wi' distress, and he said he had courage to go to the gate of hell, and a step farther, for that receipt.

The stranger laughed.

Weel, they rode on through the thickest of the wood, when, all of a sudden, the horse stopped at the door of a great house, and but that he knew the place was ten miles off, my father would have thought he was at Redgauntlet Castle. They rode into the outer courtyard, through the muckle faulding yetts,[2] and aneath the auld portcullis; and the whole front of the house was lighted, and there were pipes and fiddles, and as much dancing and deray within as used to be in Sir Robert's house at Pace and Yule, and such high seasons. They lap off, and my gudesire, as seemed to him, fastened his horse to the very ring he had tied him to that morning, when he gaed to wait on the young Sir John.

"God!" said my gudesire, "if Sir Robert's death be but a dream!"

He knocked at the ha' door just as he was wont, and his auld acquaintance, Dougal MacCallum, just after his wont, too, came to open the door, and said, "Piper Steenie, are ye there, lad? Sir Robert has been crying for you."

---

[1]Loyal, trustworthy.

[2]Gates.

My gudesire was like a man in a dream; he looked for the stranger, but he was gane for the time. At last he just tried to say, "Ha! Dougal Driveower, are ye living? I thought ye had been dead."

"Never fash[1] yoursel wi' me," said Dougal, "but look to yoursell; and see ye tak naething frae onybody here, neither meat, drink, or siller, except just the receipt that is your ain."

So saying, he led the way out through halls and trances that were weel kenned to my gudesire, and into the auld oak parlor; and there was as much singing of profane sangs, and birling of red wine, and speaking blasphemy and sculduddry, as had ever been in Redgauntlet Castle when it was at the blithest.

But, Lord take us in keeping! what a set of ghastly revelers they were that sat round that table! My gudesire kenned mony that had long before gane to their place, for often had he piped to the most part in the hall of Redgauntlet. There was the fierce Middleton, and the dissolute Rothes, and the crafty Lauderdale and Dalyell, with his bald head and a beard to his girdie; and Earlshall, with Cameron's blude on his hand; and wild Bonshaw, that tied blessed Mr. Cargill's limbs till the blude sprung; and Dumbarton Douglas, the twice-turned traitor baith to country and king. There was the Bluidy Advocate MacKenyie, who, for his worldly wit and wisdom, had been to the rest as a god. And there was Claverhouse,[2] as beautiful as when he lived, with his long, dark, curled locks, streaming down over his laced buff-coat, and his left-hand always on his right spuleblade, to hide the wound that the silver bullet had made. He sat apart from them all, and looked at them with a melancholy, haughty countenance; while the rest hallooed, and sung, and laughed, that the room rang. But their smiles were fearfully contorted from time to time, and their laughter passed into such wild sounds as made my gudesire's very nails grow blue and chilled the marrow in his banes.

They that waited at the table were just the wicked servingmen and troopers that had done their work and cruel bidding on earth. There was the Lang Lad of the Nethertown, that helped to take Argyle; and the bishop's summoner, that they called the Deil's Rattle-bag; and the wicked guardsmen, in their laced coats; and the savage Highland Amorites, that shed blood like water, and mony a proud servingman, haughty of heart and bloody of hand, cringing to the rich, and making them wickeder than they would be; grinding the poor to powder, when the rich had broken them to fragments. And mony, mony mair were coming and ganging, a' as busy in their vocation as if they had been alive.

Sir Robert Redgauntlet, in the midst of a' this fearful riot, cried, wi' a voice like thunder, on Steenie Piper to come to the board-head where he was sitting, his legs stretched out before him, and swathed up with flannel, with his holster pistols aside him, while the great broadsword rested against his chair, just as my gudesire had seen him the last time upon earth—the very cushion for the jackanape was close to him, but the creature itsel was not there; it wasna its hour, it's likely; for he heard them say as he came forward, "Is not the major come yet?" And another answered, "The jackanape will be here betimes the morn." And when my gudesire came forward Sir Robert or his ghaist, or the deevil in his likeness, said, "Weel, piper, hae ye settled wi' my son for the year's rent?"

With much ado my father gat breath to say that Sir John would not settle without his honor's receipt.

---

[1]Trouble.

[2]John Graham of Claverhouse, 1st Viscount Dundee (1649-1689), for years a vigilant and ruthless enemy of the low-church Presbyterians called Covenanters. "Bonnie Dundee" was killed at the battle of Killiecrankie (July, 1689).

"Ye shall hae that for a tune of the pipes, Steenie," said the appearance of Sir Robert. "Play us up, 'Weel hoddled, Luckie'."

Now this was a tune my gudesire learned frae a warlock, that heard it when they were worshipping Satan at their meetings, and my gudesire had sometimes played it at the ranting suppers in Redgauntlet Castle, but never very willingly; and now he grew cauld at the very name of it, and said, for excuse, he hadna his pipes wi' him.

"MacCallum, ye limb of Beelzebub," said the fearfu' Sir Robert, "bring Steenie the pipes that I am keeping for him!"

MacCallum brought a pair of pipes might have served the piper of Donald of the Isles. But he gave my gudesire a nudge as he offered them; and looking secretly and closely, Steenie saw that the chanter was of steel, and heated to a white heat; so he had fair warning not to trust his fingers with it. So he excused himself again, and said he was faint and frightened, and had not wind aneugh to fill the bag.

"Then ye maun eat and drink, Steenie," said the figure; "for we do little else here; and it's ill speaking between a fou man and a fasting."

Now these were the very words that the bloody Earl of Douglas said to keep the king's messenger in hand, while he cut the head off MacLellan of Bombie, at the Threave Castle, and that put Steenie mair and mair on his guard. So he spoke up like a man, and said he came neither to eat, or drink, or make minstrelsy, but simply for his ain—to ken what was come o' the money he had paid, and to get a discharge for it; and he was so stout-hearted by this time, that he charged Sir Robert for conscience' sake (he had no power to say the holy name), and as he hoped for peace and rest, to spread no snares for him, but just to give him his ain.

The appearance gnashed its teeth and laughed, but it took from a large pocket-book the receipt, and handed it to Steenie. "There is your receipt, ye pitiful cur; and for the money, my dog-whelp of a son may go look for it in the Cat's Cradle."

My gudesire uttered mony thanks, and was about to retire when Sir Robert roared aloud, "stop though, thou sackdoudling son of a whore! I am not done with thee. HERE we do nothing for nothing; and you must return on this very day twelve-month to pay your master the homage that you owe me for my protection."

My father's tongue was loosed of a suddenty, and he said aloud, "I refer mysel to God's pleasure, and not to yours."

He had no sooner uttered the word than all was dark around him, and he sunk on the earth with such a sudden shock, that he lost both breath and sense.

How lang Steenie lay there, he could not tell, but when he came to himsell, he was lying in the auld kirkyard of Redgauntlet parochine, just at the door of the family aisle, and the scutcheon of the auld knight, Sir Robert, hanging over his head. There was a deep morning fog on grass and gravestane around him, and his horse was feeding quietly beside the minister's twa cows. Steenie would have thought the whole was a dream, but he had the receipt in his hand, fairly written and signed by the auld laird; only the last letters of his name were a little disorderly, written like one seized with sudden pain.

Sorely troubled in his mind, he left that dreary place, rode through the mist to Redgauntlet Castle, and with much ado he got speech of the laird.

"Well, you dyvour bankrupt," was the first word, "have you brought me my rent?"

"No," answered my gudesire, "I have not; but I have brought your honor Sir Robert's receipt for it."

"How, sirrah? Sir Robert's receipt! You told me he had not given you one."

"Will your honor please to see if that bit line is right?"

Sir John looked at every line, and at every letter, with much attention, and at last at the date, which my gudesire had not observed— "From my appointed place," he read, "this twenty-fifth of November." "What! That is yesterday! Villain, thou must have gone to Hell for this!"

"I got it from your honor's father; whether he be in Heaven or Hell, I know not," said Steenie.

"I will delate you for a warlock to the privy council!" said Sir John. "I will send you to your master, the devil, with the help of a tar-barrel and a torch!"

"I intend to delate mysel to the presbytery," said Steenie, "and tell them all I have seen last night, whilk are things fitter for them to judge of than a borrel[1] man like me."

Sir John paused, composed himsell, and desired to hear the full history; and my gudesire told it him from point to point, as I have told it you—word for word, neither more nor less.

Sir John was silent again for a long time, and at last he said, very composedly, "Steenie, this story of yours concerns the honor of many a noble family besides mine; and if it be a leasing-making, to keep yourself out of my danger, the least you can expect is to have a red-hot iron driven through your tongue, and that will be as bad as scauding your fingers with a red-hot chanter. But yet it may be true, Steenie; and if the money cast up, I shall not know what to think of it. But where shall we find the Cat's Cradle? There are cats enough about the old house, but I think they kitten without the ceremony of bed or cradle."

"We were best ask Hutcheon," said my gudesire; "he kens a' the odd corners about as weel as—another serving-man that is now gane, and that I wad not like to name."

Aweel, Hutcheon, when he was asked, told them that a ruinous turret, lang disused, next to the clock-house, only accessible by a ladder, for the opening was on the outside, and far above the battlements, was called of old the Cat's Cradle.

"There will I go immediately," said Sir John; and he took (with what purpose, Heaven kens) one of his father's pistols from the hall-table, where they had lain since the night he died, and hastened to the battlements.

It was a dangerous place to climb, for the ladder was auld and frail, and wanted ane or twa rounds. However, up got Sir John, and entered at the turret door, where his body stopped the only little light that was in the bit turret. Something flees at him wi' a vengeance, maist dang him back ower; bang gaed the knight's pistol, and Hutcheon, that held the ladder, and my gudesire that stood beside him, hears a loud skelloch. A minute after, Sir John flings the body of the jackanape down to them, and cries that the siller is fund, and that they should come up and help him. And there was the bag of siller sure aneugh, and mony orra things besides that had been missing for mony a day. And Sir John, when he had ripped the turret weel, led my gudesire into the dining-parlor, and took him by the hand, and spoke kindly to him, and said he was sorry he should have doubted his word, and that he would hereafter be a good master to him, to make amends.

"And now, Steenie," said Sir John, "although this vision of yours tends, on the whole, to my father's credit, as an honest man, that he should, even after his death, desire to see justice done to a poor man like you, yet you are sensible that illdispositioned men might make bad constructions upon it, concerning his soul's health. So, I think, we had better lay the haill dirdum on that ill-deedie creature, Major Weir, and say naething about your dream in the wood of Pitmurkie. You had taken ower muckle brandy to be very certain about ony thing; and, Steenie, this receipt (his hand shook while he held it out), it's but a queer kind of document, and we will do best, I think, to put it quietly in the fire."

---

[1]Rough, crude.

"Od, but for as queer as it is, it's a' the voucher I have for my rent," said my gudesire, who was afraid, it may be, of losing the benefit of Sir Robert's discharge.

"I will bear the contents to your credit in the rental-book and give you a discharge under my own hand," said Sir John, "and that on the spot. And, Steenie, if you can hold your tongue about this matter, you shall sit, from this term downward, at an easier rent."

"Mony thanks to your honor," said Steenie, who saw easily in what corner the wind was; "doubtless I will be conformable to all your honor's commands; only I would willingly speak wi' some powerful minister on the subject for I do not like the sort of soumons of appointment whilk your honor's father—"

"Do not call the phantom my father!" said Sir John, interrupting him.

"Weel, then, the thing that was so like him," said my gudesire, "he spoke of my coming back to him this time twelvemonth, and it's a weight on my conscience."

"Aweel, then," said Sir John, "if you be so much distressed in mind, you may speak to our minister of the parish; he is a douce[1] man, regards the honor of our family, and the mair that he may look for some patronage from me."

Wi' that my gudesire readily agreed that the receipt should be burnt, and the laird threw it into the chimney with his ain hand. Burn it would not for them, though; but away it flew up the lum,[2] wi' a lang train of sparks at its tail, and a hissing noise like a squib.

My gudesire gaed down to the manse, and the minister, when he had heard the story, said it was his real opinion that, though my gudesire had gaen very far in tampering with dangerous matters, yet, as he had refused the devil's arles[3] (for such was the offer of meat and drink), and had refused to do homage by piping at his bidding, he hoped, that if he held a circumspect walk hereafter, Satan could take little advantage by what was come and gane. And, indeed, my gudesire, of his ain accord, lang forswore baith the pipes and the brandy; it was not even till the year was out, and the fatal day passed, that he would so much as take the fiddle, or drink usquebaugh or tippenny.

Sir John made up his story about the jackanape as he liked himsell, and some believe till this day there was no more in the matter than the filching nature of the brute. Indeed, ye'll no hinder some to threap[4] that it was nane o' the Auld Enemy that Dougal and Hutcheon saw in the laird's room, but only that wanchancie creature, the major, capering on the coffin; and that, as to the blawing on the laird's whistle that was heard after he was dead, the filthy brute could do that as weel as the laird himsell, if no better. But Heaven kens the truth, whilk first came out by the minister's wife, after Sir John and her ain gudeman were baith in the molds. And then, my gudesire, wha was failed in his limbs, but not in his judgment or memory—at least nothing to speak of—was obliged to tell the real narrative to his freends for the credit of his good name. He might else have been charged for a warlock.

## From *The Journal*

### "The Bad News" —January 22, 1826

I feel neither dishonored nor broken down by the bad—miserably bad news I have received. I have walked my last on the domains I have planted—sate the last

---

[1] Sober, respectable.

[2] Chimney.

[3] Earnest money (contract binder).

[4] Argue.

time in the halls I have built. But death would have taken them from me if misfortune had spared them. My poor people whom I loved so well! There is just another dye to turn up against me in this run of ill-luck— *i.e.* if I should break my magic wand in the fall from this elephant, and lose my popularity with my fortune. Then *Woodstock* and *Boney* may both go to the paper-maker, and I may take to smoking cigars and drinking grog, or turn devotee, and intoxicate the brain another way. In prospect of absolute ruin, I wonder if they would let me leave the Court of Session. I would like, methinks, to go abroad, "And lay my bones far from the Tweed." But I find my eyes moistening, and that will not do. I will not yield without a fight for it. It is odd, when I set myself to work *doggedly,* as Dr. Johnson would say, I am exactly the same man that I ever was, neither low-spirited nor *distrait.* In prosperous times I have sometimes felt my fancy and powers of language flag, but adversity is to me at least a tonic and bracer; the fountain is awakened from its inmost recesses, as if the spirit of affliction had troubled it in his passage.

Poor Mr. Pole the harper sent to offer me £500 or £600, probably his all. There is much good in the world, after all. But I will involve no friend, either rich or poor. My own right hand shall do it—else will I be *done* in the slang language, and *undone* in common parlance.

I am glad that, beyond my own family, who are, excepting L. S., young and able to bear sorrow, of which this is the first taste to some of them, most of the hearts are past aching which would have been inconsolable on this occasion. I do not mean that many will not seriously regret, and some perhaps lament, my misfortunes. But my dear mother, my almost sister, Christy R-d, poor Will Erskine—these would have been mourners indeed.

Well—exertion—exertion. O Invention, rouse thyself! May man be kind! May God be propitious! The worst is, I never quite know when I am right or wrong and Ballantyne, who does know in some degree, will fear to tell me. Lockhart would be worth gold just now, but he too would be too diffident to speak broad out. All my hope is in the continued indulgence of the public.

I have a funeral-letter to the burial of the Chevalier Yelin, a foreigner of learning and talent, who has died at the Royal Hotel. He wished to be introduced to me, and was to have read a paper before the Royal Society when this introduction was to have taken place. I was not at the Society that evening, and the poor gentleman was taken ill in the meeting and unable to proceed. He went to his bed and never arose again; and now his funeral will be the first public place that I shall appear at. He dead, and I ruined. This is what you call a meeting.

## "The Troubles" —February 3, 1826

—This is the first morning since my troubles that I felt at awaking

"I had drunken deep
Of all the blessedness of sleep."

I made not the slightest pause, nor dreamed a single dream, nor even changed my side. This is a blessing to be grateful for. There is to be a meeting of the creditors today, but I care not for the issue. If they drag me into the Court *obtorto collo,* instead of going into this scheme of arrangement, they will do themselves a great injury and perhaps eventually do me good though it would give me much pain.

J. B. is severely critical on what he calls imitations of Mrs. Radcliffe in *Woodstock.* Many will think with him— yet I am of opinion he is quite wrong, or, as friend J. F. says, *vrong.* In the first place, I am to look on the mere fact of another author having treated a subject happily as a bird looks on a potato-bogle which scares it away from a field otherwise as free to its depredations as any one's else!

In 2d place, I have taken a wide difference —my object is not to excite fear of supernatural things in my reader, but to show the effect of such fear upon the agents in the story—one a man of sense and firmness—one a man unhinged by remorse—one a stupid uninquiring clown—one a learned and worthy but superstitious divine.

In 3d place, the book turns on this hinge and cannot want it. But I will try to insinuate the refutation of Aldiboronti's exception into the prefatory matter.

From the 19 January to the 2d February inclusive is exactly fifteen days, during which time (with the intervention of some days' idleness, to let imagination brood on the task a little) I have written a volume. I think, for a bet, I could have done it in ten days. Then I must have had no Court of Session to take me up two or three hours every morning, and dissipate my attention and powers of working for the rest of the day. A volume, at cheapest, is worth £1000. This is working at the rate of £24,000 a year; but then we must not bake buns faster than people have appetite to eat them. They are not essential to the market, like potatoes. . . .

### "Woodstock" —February 12, 1826

Having ended the Second Vol. of *Woodstock* last night, I have to begin the Third this morning. Now I have not the slightest idea how the story is to be wound up to a catastrophe. I am just in the same case as I used to be when I lost myself in former days in some country to which I was a stranger. I always pushed for the pleasantest road, and either found or made it the nearest. It is the same in writing, I never could lay down a plan—or, having laid it down, I never could adhere to it; the action of composition always dilated some passages, and abridged or omitted others; and personages were rendered important or insignificant, not according to their agency in the original conception of the plan, but according to the success or otherwise with which I was able to bring them out. I only tried to make that which I was actually writing diverting and interesting, leaving the rest to fate. I have been often amused with the critics distinguishing some passages as particularly labored, when the pen passed over the whole as fast as it could move, and the eye never again saw them, excepting in proof. Verse I write twice, and sometimes three times over. This may be called in Spanish the *Der donde diere* mode of composition, in English *hab nab at a venture.*

It is a perilous style, I grant, but I cannot help. When I chain my mind to ideas which are purely imaginative—for argument is a different thing—it seems to me that the sun leaves the landscape, that I think away the whole vivacity and spirit of my original conception, and that the results are cold, tame, and spiritless. It is the difference between a written oration and one bursting from the unpremeditated exertions of the speaker, which have always something of the air of enthusiasm and inspiration. I would not have young authors imitate my carelessness, however—*consilium non currum cape.*

Read a few pages of Will D'Avenant, who was fond of having it supposed that Shakespeare intrigued with his mother. I think the pretension can only be treated as Phaeton's was, according to Fielding's farce—

"Besides, by all the village boys I'm shamed,
You, the sun's son, you rascal?—you be damned."

Egad—I'll put that into *Woodstock.* It might come well from the old admirer of Shakespeare. Then Fielding's lines were not written. What then?—it is an anachronism for some sly rogue to detect. Besides, it is easy to swear they were written, and that Fielding adopted them from tradition. Walked with Skene on the Calton Hill.

### "Jane Austen" —(from) March 14, 1826

. . . . Also read again and for the third time at least Miss Austen's very finely written novel of *Pride and Prejudice.* That young lady had a talent for describing the involvements and feelings and characters of ordinary life which is to me the most wonderful I ever met with. The Big Bow-wow strain I can do myself like any now going, but the exquisite touch which renders ordinary commonplace things and characters interesting from the truth of the description and the sentiment is denied to me. What a pity such a gifted creature died so early.

### "Duty" —August 2, 1826

Well, and to-day I finished before dinner five leaves more, and I would crow a little about it, but here comes Duty like an old housekeeper on an idle chamber-maid. Hear her very words:—

DUTY.—Oh! you crow, do you? Pray, can you deny that your sitting so quiet at work was owing to its raining heavily all the forenoon, and indeed till dinner-time, so that nothing would have stirred out that could help it, save a duck or a goose? I trow, if it had been a fine day, by noon there would have been aching of the head, throbbing, shaking, and so forth, to make an apology for going out.

EGOMET IPSE.—And whose head ever throbbed to go out when it rained, Mrs. Duty?

DUTY.—*Answer not to me with a fool-born jest,* as your poor friend Erskine used to say to you when you escaped from his good advice under the fire of some silly pun. You smoke a cigar after dinner, and I never check you—drink tea, too, which is loss of time; and then, instead of writing one other page, or correcting those you have written out, you rollick into the woods till you have not a dry thread about you; and here you sit writing down my words in your foolish journal instead of minding my advice.

EGO.—Why, Mrs. Duty, I would as gladly be friends with you as Crabbe's tradesman fellow with his conscience; but you should have some consideration with human frailty.

DUTY.—Reckon not on that. But, however, good-night for the present. I would only recommend to you to think no thoughts in which I am not mingled—to read no books in which I have no concern—to write three sheets of botheration all the six days of the week *per diem,* and on the seventh to send them to the printer. Thus advising, I heartily bid you farewell.

EGO.—Farewell, madam (exit Duty) and be d—d to ye for an unreasonable bitch! "The devil must be in this greedy gled!" as the Earl of Angus said to his hawk; "will she never be satisfied?" I believe in my soul she is the very hag who haunted the merchant Abudah.

I'll have my great chest upstairs exorcised, but first I'll take a nap till supper, which must take place within ten minutes.

August 3.—Wrote half a task in the morning. From eleven till half-past eight in Selkirk taking precognitions about a *row* on Selkirk-hill-fair, and came home famished and tired. Now, Mrs. Duty, do you think there is no other Duty of the family but yourself? Or can the Sheriff-deputy neglect his Duty, that the author may mind *his?* The thing cannot be; the people of Selkirk must have justice as well as the people of England books. So the two Duties may go pull caps about it. My conscience is clear.

## JAMES GLASSFORD (1772–1845)

### Murtagh Malowney's Complaint

And why was you beguiling
My heart so soon from me?

O why was Oonah smiling
On Murtie at Tralee?

When they figged it at Fitz-Symond's,
O why was Oonah there?
Were your feet not two diamonds,
And your steps tuned air?

What bird so sweet as this bird
Of all, on summer tree?
And your eyes how they whispered
Then to me at Tralee?

She told me, too, O mind her,
That she scorned young O'shee;
But Boggra Rocks are kinder
Now than Oonah to me.

No more must I be going
My nightingale to see.
O why is daybreak showing
Me your smoke at Tralee?

The boys all say I'm spooney,
And bring me poteen.
Bad luck, they cry to Oonie,
Bad luck to Mic Maclean.

But wait till Corker Fair come,
And then I'll tell you more
Of who's the boy that's welcome
Yet to darken Oonie's door.

## FRANCIS JEFFREY (1773–1850)

[Somewhat implausibly, Scotland was the home of the most important literary criticism of the nineteenth century, primarily through the influence of the first major critical journal in Britain, the *Edinburgh Review*. Its editor was Francis Jeffrey, who was also a major contributor, known for his vigor, honesty and high standards. His review of Walter Scott's novel, *Waverley*, should be read with the understanding that Scott had kept his authorship secret. It is clear from the review to what extent Jeffrey was taken in. This editor has excised a rather long section in which Jeffrey summarizes the plot of the novel.]

### Why Write My Name

Why write my name midst songs and flowers,
To meet the eye of lady gay?
I have no voice for lady's bowers—
For page like this no fitting lay.

Yet though my heart no more must bound
At witching call of sprightly joys,
Mine is the brow that never frowned
On laughing lips, or sparkling eyes.

No—though behind me now is closed
The youthful paradise of love,
Yet can I bless, with soul composed,
The lingerers in that happy grove.

Take, then, fair girls, my blessing take.
Where'er amid its charms you roam;
Or where, by western hill or lake,
You brighten a serener home.

And while the youthful lover's name
Here with the sister beauty's blends,
Laugh not to scorn the humbler aim,
That to their list would add a friend's.

## Review of *Waverley*

*Edinburgh Review,* 24 November 1814

It is wonderful what genius and adherence to nature will do, in spite of all disadvantages. Here is a thing obviously very hastily, and, in many places, somewhat unskillfully written—composed, one half of it, in a dialect unintelligible to four-fifths of the reading population of the country—relating to a period too recent to be romantic, and too far gone by to be familiar—and published, moreover, in a quarter of the island where materials and talents for novel-writing have been supposed to be equally wanting: And yet, by the mere force and truth and vivacity of its coloring, already casting the whole tribe of ordinary novels into the shade, and taking its place rather with the most popular of our modern poems, than with the rubbish of provincial romances.

The secret of this success, we take it, is merely that the author is a man of Genius; and that he has, notwithstanding, had virtue enough to be true to Nature throughout; and to content himself, even in the marvelous parts of his story, with copying from actual existences, rather than from the phantasms of his own imagination. The charm which this communicates to all works that deal in the representation of human actions and character, is more readily felt than understood; and operates with unfailing efficacy even upon those who have no acquaintance with the originals from which the picture has been borrowed. It requires no ordinary talent, indeed, to choose such realities as may outshine the bright imaginations of the inventive, and so to combine them as to produce the most advantageous effect; but when this is once accomplished, the result is sure to be something more firm, impressive, and engaging, than can ever be produced by mere fiction.

The object of the work before us, was evidently to present a faithful and animated picture of the manners and state of society that prevailed in this northern part of the island, in the earlier part of last century; and the author has judiciously fixed upon the era of the Rebellion in 1745, not only as enriching his pages with the interest inseparably attached to the narration of such occurrences, but as affording a fair opportunity for bringing out all the contrasted principles and habits which distinguished the different classes of persons who then divided the country, and formed among them the basis of almost all that was peculiar in the national character. That unfortunate contention brought conspicuously to light, and, for the last time, the fading image of feudal chivalry in the mountains, and vulgar fanaticism in the plains; and startled the more polished parts of the land with the wild but brilliant picture of the devoted valor, incorruptible fidelity, patriarchal brotherhood, and savage habits, of the Celtic Clans, on the one hand,—and the dark, intractable, and domineering bigotry of the Covenanters on the other. Both aspects of society had indeed been formerly prevalent in other parts of the country,—but had there been so long superseded by more peaceable habits, and milder manners, that their vestiges were almost effaced, and their very memory nearly extinguished. The feudal principalities had been destroyed in the South, for near 300 years,—and the dominion of the Puritans from the time of the Restoration. When the glens, and banded clans, of the central Highlands, therefore, were opened up to the gaze of the English, in the course of that insurrection, it seemed as if they were carried back to the days of the Heptarchy;—and when they saw the array of the West country Whigs, they might imagine themselves transported to the age of Cromwell. The effect, indeed, is almost as startling at the present moment; and one great source of the interest which the volumes before us undoubtedly possess, is to be sought in the surprise that is excited by discovering, that in our own country, and almost in our own age, manners and characters existed, and were conspicuous, which we had been accustomed to consider as belonging to remote antiquity, or extravagant romance.

The way in which they are here represented must satisfy every reader, we think, by an inward *tact* and conviction, that the delineation has been made from actual experience and observation;— experience and observation employed perhaps only on a few surviving relics and specimens of what was familiar a little earlier—but generalized from instances sufficiently numerous and complete, to warrant all that may have been added to the portrait:—And, indeed, the existing records and vestiges of the more extraordinary parts of the representation are still sufficiently abundant, to satisfy all who have the means of consulting them, as to the perfect accuracy of the picture.

The great traits of Clannish dependence, pride and fidelity, may still be detected in many districts of the Highlands, though they do not now adhere to the chieftains when they mingle in general society; and the existing contentions of Burghers and Antiburghers, and Cameronians, though shrunk into comparative insignificance, and left, indeed, without protection to the ridicule of the profane, may still be referred to, as complete verifications of all that is here stated about Gifted Gilfillan, or Ebenezer Cruickshank.

The traits of Scottish national character in the lower ranks, can still less be regarded as antiquated or traditional; nor is there any thing in the whole compass of the work which gives us a stronger impression of the nice observation and graphical talent of the author, than the extraordinary fidelity and felicity with which all the inferior agents in the story are represented. No one who has not lived extensively among the lower orders of all descriptions. and made himself familiar with their various tempers and dialects, can perceive the full merit of those rapid and characteristic sketches; but it requires only a general knowledge of human nature, to feel that they must be faithful copies from known originals; and to be aware of the extraordinary facility and flexibility of hand which has touched, for instance, with such discriminating shades, the various gradations of the Celtic character, from the savage imperturbability of Dugald Mahony, who stalks grimly about with his battle-axe on his shoulder, without speaking a word to any one,—to the lively unprincipled activity of Callum Beg,—the coarse unreflecting hardihood and heroism of Evan Maccombich,—and the pride, gallantry, elegance, and ambition of Fergus himself. In the lower class of the Lowland characters, again, the vulgarity of Mrs. Flockhart and of Lieutenant Jinker is perfectly distinct and original;—as well as the Puritanism of Gilfillan and Cruickshank—the atrocity of Mrs. Mucklewrath—and the slow solemnity of Alexander Saunderson. The Baron of Bradwardine, and Baillie Macwheeble, are caricatures no doubt, after the fashion of the caricatures in the novels of Smollett,—or pictures, at the best, of individuals who must always have been unique and extraordinary: but almost all the other personages in the history are fair representatives of classes that are still existing, or may be remembered at least to have existed, by many whose recollections do not extend quite so far back as to the year 1745. . . .

The gay scenes of the Adventurer's court—the breaking up of his army from Edinburgh—the battle of Preston—and the whole process of his disastrous advance and retreat from the English provinces, are given with the greatest brilliancy and effect—as well as the scenes of internal disorder and rising disunion that prevail in his scanty army—the quarrel with Fergus—and the mystical visions by which that devoted chieftain foresees his disastrous fate. The lower scenes again with Mrs. Flockhart, Mrs. Nosebag, Callum-Beg, and the Cumberland peasants, though to some fastidious readers they may appear coarse and disgusting, are painted with a force and a truth to nature, which equally bespeak the powers of the artist, and are incomparably superior to any thing of the sort which has been offered to the public for the last "sixty years." There are also various copies of verses scattered through the work, which indicate poetical talents of no ordinary description—though bearing, perhaps still more distinctly than the prose, the traces of considerable carelessness and haste.

The worst part of the book by far is that portion of the first volume which contains the history of the hero's residence in England—and next to it is the laborious, tardy, and obscure explanation of some puzzling occurrences in the story, which the reader would, in general, be much better pleased to be permitted to forget—and which are neither well explained after all, nor at all worth explaining.

There has been much speculation, at least in this quarter of the island, about the authorship of this singular performance—and certainly it is not easy to conjecture why it is still anonymous.— Judging by internal evidence, to which alone we pretend to have access, we should not scruple to ascribe it to the highest of those authors to whom it has been assigned by the sagacious conjectures of the public;—and this at least we will venture to say, that if it be indeed the work of an author hitherto unknown, Mr. Scott would do well to look to his laurels, and to rouse himself for a sturdier competition than any he has yet had to encounter!

## HAMILTON PAUL (1773–1854)

### The Bonnie Lass of Barr

Of streams that down the valley run,
Or through the meadow glide,
Or glitter to the summer sun,
The Stinchar is the pride.
Tis not his banks of verdant hue,
Though famed they be afar;
Nor grassy hill, nor mountain blue,
Nor flower bedropt with diamond dew:
Tis she that chiefly charms the view,
The bonnie lass of Barr.

When rose the lark on early wing,
The vernal tide to hail,
When daisies decked the breast of spring,
I sought her native vale.
The beam that gilds the evening sky,
And brighter morning star,
That tells the king of day is nigh,
With mimic splendor vainly try
To reach the luster of thine eye,
Thou bonnie lass of Barr.

The sun behind yon misty isle
Did sweetly set yestreen,
But not his parting dewy smile
Could match the smile of Jean.
Her bosom swelled with gentle woe,
Mine strove with tender war.
On Stinchar's banks, while wild woods grow,
While rivers to the ocean flow,
With love of thee my heart shall glow,
Thou bonnie lass of Barr.

## Petition of the Auld Brig o' Doon

[The bridge, of course, is the one made celebrated by Burns' "Tam o' Shanter." Paul's poem was successful. The bridge still stands.]

Must I, like modern fabrics of a day,
Decline, unwept, the victim of decay?
Shall my bold arch, which proudly stretches oer
Doon's classic stream, from Kyle to Carrick's shore,
Be suffered in oblivion's gulf to fall,
And hurl to wreck my venerable wall?
Forbid it, every tutelary power,
That guards my keystone at the midnight hour;
Forbid it ye, who, charmed by Burns's lay,
Amid those scenes can linger out the day,
Let Nanny's sark and Maggie's mangled tail
Plead in my cause, and in the cause prevail.
The man of taste who comes my form to see,
And curious asks, but asks in vain, for me,
With tears of sorrow will my fate deplore,
When he is told "the Auld Brig is no more."
Stop then; stop the more than Vandal rage
That marks this revolutionary age,
And bid the structure of your fathers last,
The pride of this, the boast of ages past;
For never let your children's children tell
By your decree the fine old fabric fell.

## ROBERT ALLAN (1774–1841)

### To a Linnet

Chaunt no more thy roundelay,
Lovely minstrel of the grove.
Charm no more the hours away
With thine artless tale of love.
Chaunt no more thy roundelay,
Sad it steals upon mine ear.
Leave, O leave thy leafy spray,
Till the smiling morn appear.

Light of heart, thou quit'st thy song,
As the welkin's shadows lour,
Whilst the beetle wheels along,
Humming to the twilight hour.
Not like thee I quit the scene
To enjoy night's balmy dream;
Not like thee I wake again,
Smiling with the morning beam.

### The Twa Martyrs' Widows[1]

Sit down, sit down by thy martyr's side,
And I'se sit down by mine;
And I shall speak o' him to my Gude*, "God"
And thou may speak o' thine.

It's wae to thee, and it's wae wi me,
For our day o' peace is gane,
And we maun sit wi a tearfu ee,
In our bouroch-ha'* alane. "hall"

O Scotland, Scotland, it's wae to thee,
When thy lichts are taen awa;
And it's wae, it's wae to a sinfu' lan'
When the righteous sae maun fa'.

It was a halie covenant aith* "oath"
We made wi our Gude to keep;
And it's for the halie covenant vow
That we maun sit and weep.

O wha will gang to yon hill-side,
To sing the psalm at een?
And wha will speak o' the luve o' our gude?
For the covenant reft hath been.

[1] This—and the following poem—refers to the seventeenth century struggles in Scotland between the Presbyterian signers of various "covenants" to maintain their religion, and their Episcopalian opponents. For a long time the battle went against the Covenanters, and the bloody consequences came to be called the "killing times."

The gerse* may grow on yon bonnie hill-tap, "grass"
And the heather sweetly bloom;
But there nae mair we sall sit at een,
For our hearts are in the tomb.

The hectic glow is upo' my cheek,
And the lily hue on thine.
Thou soon will lie by thy martyr's side,
And soon I sall sleep by mine.

## The Covenanter's Lament

There's nae Covenant noo, lassie.
There's nae Covenant noo.
The Solemn League and Covenant
Are a' fallen through.
There's nae Renwick noo, lassie.
There's nae gude Cargill,
Nor holy Sabbath preaching
Upon the Martyrs' Hill.

It's naething but a sword, lassie,
A bluidy, bluidy ane,
Waving owre puir Scotland
For her rebellious sin;
Scotland's a' wrang, lassie,
Scotland's a' wrang—
It's neither to the hill nor glen,
Lassie, we daur gang.

The Martyrs' Hill's forsaken
In simmer's dusk sae calm;
There's nae gathering noo, lassie,
To sing the sacred psalm.
But the martyr's grave will rise, lassie,
Aboon the warrior's cairn;
And the martyr sound will sleep, lassie,
Aneath the waving fern.

## The Cypress and the Yew

O I hae twined wi' mickle love
A garland for ye're brow,
But withered are its sweetest flowers,
And broken is ye're vow.
Syne I will tak the cypress wreath,
And weave it wi' the yew.

The gladsome hours of love are gone,
I wist na ere they sped,
The lily pale has stained my cheek,
Tint is the damask red;

The cypress shall my chaplet be
To bind around my head.

O why does love sae sweetly smile,
And gayest flow'rets strew?
O why does love, the fairest flower,
Still twine about with rue?
The rue was thine—but aye is mine,
The Cypress and the Yew.

## The Mermaid

O heard you the mermaid of the sea,
When the ship by the rock was sinking?
Saw you the maid with her coral cup,
A health to the sea-nymphs drinking?
The morning was fair, and the ocean calm,
Not a breath awoke the billow,
The foam that played in the clefted rock
Was the mermaid's resting pillow.

As round the cave where the mermaid slept,
The vessel light was sailing,
A voice was heard in the gathering storm,
Of mariners deeply wailing,
And loud came the deep'ning thunder-peal,
The white waves around were dashing,
And the light that illumined the pathless way,
Was the gleam of lightning flashing.

The sails are torn, the ship a wreck;
The Mermaid sweet is singing.
And the crystal halls where the sea-nymphs bathe,
Are merrily, merrily ringing.
And many a tear for these mariners lost,
From maidens' eyes are streaming,
While reckless they sleep in their wat'ry shroud,
Nor of ought that's earthly dreaming.

## The Sun Is Setting on Sweet Glengarry

The sun is setting on sweet Glengarry,
The flow'rs are fair and the leaves are green;
O, bonnie lassie, ye maun be my dearie,
And the rose is sweet in the dew at e'en.

Doun yon glen ye never will weary,
The flow'rs are fair and the leaves are green;
Bonnie lassie, ye maun be my dearie,
And the rose is sweet in the dew at e'en.

Birds are singing fu' blithe and cheery,
The flow'rs are fair and the leaves are green,
Bonnie lassie, on bank sae briery,
And the rose is sweet in the dew at e'en.

In yonder glen there's nathing to fear ye,
The flow'rs are fair and the leaves are green;
Ye canna be sad, ye canna be eerie,
And the rose is sweet in the dew at e'en.

The water is wimpling by fu' clearly,
The flow'rs are fair, and the leaves are green.
Oh, ye sall ever be my dearie,
And the rose is sweet in the dew at e'en.

## A Lassie Cam' to Our Gate

A lassie cam' to our gate yestreen,
An low she curtsied doun.
She was lovelier far, an fairer to see
Than a' our ladies roun'.

Oh, whar do ye wend*, my sweet winsome doo? go
An whar may your dwelling be?
But her heart, I trow, was liken to break,
An the teardrap dimmed her ee.

I haena a hame, quo the bonnie lassie—
I haena a hame, nor ha'*; "hall"
Fain here wad I rest my weary feet,
For the night begins to fa'.

I took her into our tapestry ha',
An we drank the ruddy wine;
An aye I strave, but fand my heart
Fast bound wi love's silken twine.

I weened she might be the fairies' queen,
She was sae jimp* and sma; slender
And the tear that dimmed her bonnie blue ee
Fell owre twa heaps o' snaw.

Oh, whar do ye wend, my sweet winsome doo?
An whar may your dwelling be?
Can the winter's rain an the winter's wind
Blaw cauld on sic as ye?

I haena a hame, quo the bonnie lassie—
I haena a ha' nor hame.
My father was one o' Charlie's men,
An him I daurna name.

Whate'er be your kith, whate'er be your kin,
Frae this ye mauna gae;
An gin* ye'll consent to be my ain, if
Nae marrow ye shall hae.

Sweet maiden, tak the siller cup,
Sae fu' o' the damask wine,
An press it to your cherry lip,
For ye shall aye be mine.

An drink, sweet doo, young Charlie's health,
An a' your kin sae dear.
Culloden has dimmed mony an ee
Wi mony a saut, saut tear.

## HENRY DUNCAN (1774–1846)

### Curling Song

The music o' the year is hushed
In bonny glen and shaw*, man; wood
And winter spreads oer nature dead
A winding sheet o' snaw, man.
Oer burn and loch, the warlike frost,
A crystal brig* has laid, man. bridge
The wild geese screaming wi surprise,
The ice-bound wave hae fled, man.

Up, curler, frae your bed sae warm,
And leave your coaxing wife, man.
Gae get your besom*, tramps, and stanes, broom
And join the friendly strife, man.
For on the water's face are met,
Wi mony a merry joke, man,
The tenant and his jolly laird,
The pastor and his flock, man.

The rink is swept, the tees are marked,
The bonspiel is begun, man.
The ice is true, the stanes are keen,
Huzza for glorious fun, man!
The skips are standing at the tee,
To guide the eager game, man.
Hush, not a word, but mark the broom,
And tak a steady aim, man.

There draw a shot, there lay a guard,
And here beside him lie, man.
Now let him feel a gamester's hand,
Now in his bosom die, man.
Then fill the port, and block the ice,
We sit upon the tee, man.

Now tak this in-ring, sharp and neat,
And mak their winner flee, man.

How stands the game? It's eight and eight,
Now for the winning shot, man.
Draw slow and sure, and tak your aim,
I'll sweep you to the spot, man.
The stane is thrown, it glides along,
The besoms ply it in, man.
Wi twisting back the player stands,
And eager, breathless grin, man.

A moment's silence, still as death,
Pervades the anxious thrang, man,
When sudden bursts the victor's shout,
With holla's loud and lang, man.
Triumphant besoms wave in air,
And friendly banters fly, man.
Whilst, cold and hungry, to the inn,
Wi eager steps they hie, man.

Now fill ae bumper, fill but ane,
And drink wi social glee, man.
May curlers on life's slippery rink,
Frae cruel rubs be free, man.
Or should a treacherous bias lead
Their erring course ajee, man,
Some friendly in-ring may they meet,
To guide them to the tee, man.

## Thou Ken'st, Mary Hay

Thou ken'st, Mary Hay, that I loe thee weel,
My ain auld wife sae canty* and leal*, lively/true
Then what gars thee stand wi the tear in thine ee,
And look aye sae wae, when thou look'st at me?

Dost thou miss, Mary Hay, the saft bloom o' my cheek,
And the hair curling round it, sae gentie and sleek?
For the snaw's on my head, and the roses are gane,
Since that day o' days I first ca'd thee my ain.

But though, Mary Hay, my auld een be grown dim,
An age, wi its frost, maks cauld every limb,
My heart, thou kens weel, has nae cauldness for thee,
For simmer returns at the blink o' thine ee.

The miser hauds firmer and firmer his gold,
Thy ivy sticks close to the tree when it's old,
And still thou grow'st dearer to me, Mary Hay,
As a' else turns eerie, and life wears away.

We maun part, Mary Hay, when our journey is done,
But I'll meet thee again in the bright world aboon,
Then what gars thee stand wi the tear in thine ee,
And look aye sae wae when thou look'st at me?

## MARGARET MAXWELL INGLIS (1774–1843)

### Sweet Bard of Ettrick's Glen

Sweet bard of Ettrick's glen,
Where art thou wandering?
Missed is thy foot on the mountain and lea.
Why round yon craggy rocks
Wander thy heedless flocks,
While lambies are list'ning and bleating for thee?
Cold as the mountain stream,
Pale as the moonlight beam,
Still is thy bosom, and closed is thine ee.
Wild may the tempest's wave
Sweep oer thy lonely grave.
Thou art deaf to the storm—it is harmless to thee.

Like a meteor's brief light,
Like the breath of the morning,
Thy life's dream hath passed as a shadow gone by;
Till thy soft numbers stealing
Oer memory's warm feeling,
Each line is embalmed with a tear or a sigh.
Sweet was thy melody,
Rich as the rose's dye,
Shedding its odors oer sorrow or glee;
Love laughed on golden wing,
Pleasure's hand touched the string,
All taught the strain to sing, shepherd, by thee.

Cold on Benlomond's brow
Flickers the drifted snow,
While down its sides the wild cataracts foam;
Winter's mad winds may sweep
Fierce oer each glen and steep,
Thy rest is unbroken, and peaceful thy home.
And when on dewy wing
Comes the sweet bird of spring,
Chanting its notes on the bush or the tree,
The bird of the wilderness,
Low in the waving grass,
Shall, cow'ring, sing sadly its farewell to thee.

## Heard Ye the Bagpipe?

Heard ye the bagpipe, or saw ye the banners
That floated sae light oer the fields o' Kildairlie?
Saw ye the broadswords, the shields, and the tartan hose,
Heard ye the muster-roll sworn to Prince Charlie?
Saw ye brave Appin, wi bonnet and belted plaid,
Or saw ye the lords o' Seaforth and Airlie?
Saw ye the Glengarry, M'Leod, and Clandonachil,
Plant the white rose in their bonnets for Charlie?

Saw ye the halls o' auld Holyrood lighted up,
Kenned ye the nobles that reveled sae rarely?
Saw ye the chiefs of Lochiel and Clanronald,
Wha rushed frae their mountains to follow Prince Charlie?
But saw ye the blood-streaming fields of Culloden,
Or kenned ye the banners were tattered sae sairly?
Heard ye the pibroch sae wild and sae wailing,
That mourned for the chieftains that fell for Prince Charlie?

Wha in yon Highland glen, weary and shelterless,
Pillows his head on the heather sae barely?
Wha seeks the darkest night, wha maunna face the light,
Borne down by lawless might—gallant Prince Charlie?
Wha, like the stricken deer, chased by the hunter's spear,
Fled frae the hills o' his father sae scaredly;
But wha, by affection's chart, reigns in auld Scotland's heart?
Wha but the royal, the gallant Prince Charlie.

## When Shall We Meet Again?

When shall we meet again,
Meet ne'er to sever?
When shall peace wreathe her chain
Round us for ever?
When shall our hearts repose,
Safe from each breath that blows,
In this dark world of woes?
Never, oh never.

Fate's unrelenting hand
Long may divide us,
Yet in one holy land
One god shall guide us.
Then, on that happy shore,
Care ne'er shall reach us more,
Earth's vain delusions oer,
Angels beside us.

There, where no storms can chill,
False friends deceive us,
Where, with protracted thrill,
Hope cannot grieve us;

There with the pure in heart,
Far from fate's venomed dart,
There shall we meet to part
Never, oh never.

### Charlie's Bonnet's Down, Laddie

Let Highland lads, wi belted plaids,
And bonnets blue and white cockades,
Put on their shields, unsheathe their blades,
And conquest fell begin;
And let the word be Scotland's heir:
And when their swords can do nae mair,
Lang bowstrings o' their yellow hair
Let Hieland lasses spin, laddie.

Charlie's bonnet's down, laddie,
Kilt yer plaid and scour the heather;
Charlie's bonnet's down, laddie,
Draw yer kirk and rin.

Mind Wallace wight, auld Scotland's light,
And Douglas bright, and Scrymgeour's might,
And Murray Bothwell's gallant knight,
And Ruthven light and trim—
Kirkpatrick black, wha in a crack
Laid Cressingham upon his back,
Garred Edward gather up his pack,
And ply his spurs and rin, laddie.

Charlie's bonnet's down, laddie,
Kilt yer plaid and scour the heather;
Charlie's bonnet's down, laddie,
Draw yer kirk and rin.

## ROBERT TANNAHILL (1774–1810)

### O, Are Ye Sleepin', Maggie?

"O, are ye sleepin', Maggie?
O, are ye sleepin', Maggie?
Let me in, for loud the linn* waterfall
Is roarin' oer the warlock cragie.

"Mirk an' rainy is the nicht,
No a starn in a' the carry*; sky
Lightnin's gleam athwart the lift*, sky
An' win's drive on wi' winter's fury.

"Fearfu' soughs the bour-tree bank,
The rifted wood roars wild an' dreary,

Loud the iron yett* does clank, gate
The cry o' howlets maks me eerie.

"Aboon my breath I daurna speak,
For fear I rouse your waukrife* daddy. wakeful
Cauld's the blast upon my cheek,—
O rise, rise, my bonnie lady."

She oped the door, she loot him in:
He cuist aside his dreepin' plaidie.
"Blaw your warst, ye rain an' win',
Since, Maggie, now I'm in beside ye.

"Now, since ye're waukin', Maggie,
Now, since ye're waukin', Maggie,
What care I for howlet's cry,
For bour-tree bank, or warlock craigie?"

## Gloomy Winter's Now Awa'

Gloomy Winter's now awa',
Saft the westlan' breezes blaw;
'Mang the birks o' Stanley shaw* wood
The mavis sings fu' cheerie, O.

Sweet the crawflower's carly bell
Decks Gleniffer's dewy dell,
Blooming like thy bonny sel',
My young, my artless dearie, O.

Come, my lassie, let us stray
Oer Glenkilloch's sunny brae,
Blithely spend the gowden day,
Midst joys that never weary, O.

Tow'ring oer the Newton woods,
Laverocks fan the snaw-white clouds,
Siller saughs*, wi' downy buds, willows
Adorn the banks sae briery, O.

Round the sylvan fairy nooks,
Feath'ry breckans fringe the rocks,
Neath the brae the burnie jouks*, runs in and out
And ilka thing is cheerie, O.

Trees may bud, and birds may sing,
Flowers may bloom, and verdure spring,
Joy to me they canna bring,
Unless wi' thee, my dearie, O.

## Towser: A True Tale

In mony an instance, without doubt,
The man may copy frae the brute,
And by th' example grow much wiser.
Then read the short memoirs of Towser.
With deference to our great Lavaters,
Wha judge o' mankind by their features,
There's mony a smiling, pleasant-faced cock
That wears a heart no worth a custock,
While mony a visage, antic, droll,
Oerveils a noble, gen'rous soul.
With Towser this was just the case;
He had an ill-faured, tawtie* face. stupid
His make was something like a messin*, cur
But big, and quite unprepossessin'.
His master coft* him frae some fallows, bought
Wha had him doomed unto the gallows,
Because—sae happed poor Towser's lot—
He wadna tear a comrade's throat.
Yet in affairs of love or honor
He'd stand his part amang a hun'er,
An where'er fighting was a merit,
He never failed to shaw his spirit.
He never girned* in neighbor's face, grimaced
Wi wild ill-natured scant o' grace,
Nor e'er accosted ane wi smiles,
Then, soon as turned, wad bite his heels;
Nor ever kent the courtier art,
To fawn wi rancor at his heart,
Nor aught kent he o' cankert quarreling,
Nor snarlin just for sake o' snarlin,
Ye'd pinch him sair afore he'd growl,
Whilk shows he had a mighty soul.
But what adds maistly to his fame,
An will immortalize his name—
"Immortalize!—presumptuous wight!
Thy lines are dull as darkest night,
Without ae spark o' wit or glee,
To licht them through futurity."
E'en be it; sae poor Towser's story,
Though lamely tauld, will speak his glory.
Twas in the month o' cauld December,
When nature's fire seemed just an ember,
An growlin winter bellowed forth
In storms and tempests frae the north—
When honest Towser's loving master,
Regardless o' the surly bluster,
Set out to the neist* burrow town, "nearest"
To buy some needments o' his own:
An case some purse-pest should waylay him,
He took his trusty servant wi' him.
His business done, twas near the gloamin,

An aye the king o' storms was foamin,
The doors did ring—lum-pigs down tumbled,
The strawns gushed big, the sinks loud rumbled,
Auld grannies spread their looves* and sighed, palms
Wi "O, sirs, what an awfu' night!"
Poor Towser shook his sides a' draigled*, bedraggled
And's master grudged that he had taigled*; dawdled
But wi his merchandising load;
Come weal, come wae, he took the road.
Now clouds drave oer the fields like drift,
Night flung her black cleuk oer the lift*; sky
An through the naked trees and hedges
The horrid storm redoubled rages;
An to complete his piteous case,
It blew directly in his face.—
Whiles* gainst the footpath stabs he thumped, sometimes
Whiles oer the coots in holes he plumped;
But on he gaed, and on he waded;
Till he at length turned faint and jaded.
To gang he could nae langer bide,
But lay doun by the bare dyke-side.
Now, wife an bairns rushed on his soul,
He groaned—poor Towser loud did howl,
An' mourning cowered doun aside him.
But, oh, his master couldna heed him,
For now his senses gan to dozen,
His verra life-streams maist were frozen,
An't seemed as if the cruel skies
Exulted oer their sacrifice;
For fierce the winds did oer him hiss,
An dashed the sleet on his cauld face.
As on a rock, far, far frae land,
Twa shipwrecked sailors shiv'ring stand,
If chance a vessel they descry,
Their hearts exult with instant joy,
Sac was poor Towser joyed to hear
The tread o' travelers drawing near;
He ran an yowled, and fawned upon 'em,
But couldna make them understand him,
Till tugging at the foremost's coat,
He led them to the mournfu' spot
Where, cauld and stiff, his master lay,
To the rude storm a helpless prey.
Wi Caledonian sympathy,
They bore him kindly on the way,
Until they reached a cottage bein*, shelter
They tauld the case, were welcomed in—
The rousin fire, the cordial drop,
Restored him soon to life and hope.
Fond raptures beamed in Towser's eye,
An' antic gambols spake his joy.
Wha reads this simple tale may see
The worth of sensibility,

And learn frae it to be humane—
In Towser's life he saved his ain.

## Jessie, the Flower of Dumblane

The sun has gane down oer the lofty Benlomond,
And left the red clouds to preside oer the scene,
While lanely I stray in the calm simmer gloamin'
To muse on sweet Jessie, the flower o' Dumblane.
How sweet is the brier, wi its saft faulding blossom,
And sweet is the birk, wi its mantle o' green;
Yet sweeter and fairer, and dear to this bosom,
Is lovely young Jessie, the flower o' Dumblane.

She's modest as ony, and blithe as she's bonny;
For guileless simplicity marks her its ain;
And far be the villain, divested of feeling,
Wha'd blight, in its bloom, the sweet flower o' Dumblane.
Sing on, thou sweet mavis, thy hymn to the e'ening,
Thou'rt dear to the echoes of Calderwood glen;
Sae dear to this bosom, sae artless and winning,
Is charming young Jessie, the flower o' Dumblane.

How lost were my days till I met wi my Jessie,
The sports o' the city seemed foolish and vain.
I ne'er saw a nymph I would ca' my dear lassie,
Till charmed wi sweet Jessie, the flower o' Dumblane.
Though mine were the station o' loftiest grandeur,
Amidst its profusion I'd languish in pain;
And reckon as naething the height o' its splendor,
If wanting sweet Jessie, the flower o' Dumblane.

## Good Night, and Joy

The evening sun's gaen down the west,
The birds sit nodding on the tree.
All nature now prepares for rest,
But rest prepared there's none for me.
The trumpet sounds to war's alarms,
The drums they beat, the fifes they play,
Come, Mary, cheer me wi thy charms,
For the morn I will be far away.

Good night, and joy—good night, and joy,
Good night, and joy be wi you a';
For since it's so that I must go,
Good night, and joy be wi you a'.

I grieve to leave my comrades dear,
I mourn to leave my native shore;
To leave my aged parents here,
And the bonnie lass whom I adore.

But tender thoughts maun now be hushed,
When danger calls I must obey,
The transport waits us on the coast,
And the morn I will be far away.

Adieu, dear Scotia's sea-beat coast.
Though bleak and drear thy mountains be,
When on the heaving ocean tost
I'll cast a wishful look to thee.
And now, dear Mary, fare thee well,
May providence thy guardian be.
Or in the camp, or on the field,
I'll heave a sigh, and think on thee.

## The Wood of Craigie Lea

Thou bonny wood of Craigie Lea,
Thou bonny wood of Craigie Lea,
Near thee I passed life's early day,
And won my Mary's heart in thee.

The broom, the brier, the birken bush,
Bloom bonny oer thy flowery lea,
And a' the sweets that ane can wish
Frae nature's hand, are strewed on thee.

Far ben* thy dark green plantain's shade — in
The cushat croodles am'rously,
The mavis, down thy bughted glade,
Gars* echo ring frae every tree. — makes

Awa, ye thoughtless, murd'ring gang,
Wha tear the nestlings ere they flee.
They'll sing you yet a canty* sang, — lively
Then O, in pity, let them be.

When winter blaws in sleety showers
Frae aff the Norlan' hills sae hie,
He lightly skiffs thy bonny bowers,
As laith to harm a flower in thee.

Though fate should drag me south the line,
Or oer the wide Atlantic sea,
The happy hours I'll ever mind
That I, in youth, hae spent in thee.

## The Lass o' Arranteenie

Far lone amang the Highland hills,
Midst nature's wildest grandeur,
By rocky dens, an' woody glens,
With weary steps I wander.

The langsome way, the darksome day,
The mountain mist sae rainy,
Are naught to me when gaun to thee,
Sweet lass o' Arranteenie.

Yon mossy rosebud down the howe* hollow
Just op'ning fresh an' bonnie,
Blinks sweetly neath the hazel bough,
An 's scarcely seen by ony:
Sae, sweet amidst her native hills,
Obscurely blooms my Jeanie—
Mair fair an' gay than rosy May,
The flower o' Arranteenie.

Now from the mountain's lofty brow,
I view the distant ocean;
There av'rice guides the bounding prow,
Ambition courts promotion:
Let fortune pour her golden store,
Her laurelled favors many;
Give me but this, my soul's first wish,
The lass o' Arranteenie!

## The Braes o' Balquhither

Let us go, lassie, go
To the braes o' Balquhither,
Where the blaeberries grow
'Mang the bonnie Highland heather;
Where the deer and the rae,
Lightly bounding together,
Sport the lang simmer day
On the braes o' Balquhither.

I will twine thee a bow'r
By the clear siller* fountain, "silver"
And I'll cover it oer
Wi' the flowers o' the mountain;
I will range through the wilds
And the deep glens sae dreary,
And return wi' their spoils
To the bow'r o' my dearie.

When the rude wintry win'
Idly raves round our dwelling,
And the roar of the linn* waterfall
On the night breeze is swelling
So merrily we'll sing,
As the storm rattles oer us,
Till the dear shieling* ring cottage
Wi' the light lilting chorus.

Now the Simmer is in prime,
Wi' the flowers richly blooming,
And the wild mountain thyme
A' the moorlands perfuming;
To our dear native scenes
Let us journey together,
Whar glad innocence reigns
'Mang the braes o' Balquhither.

## The Midges Dance Aboon the Burn

The midges dance aboon the burn,
The dews begin to fa',
The pairtricks* doun the rushy holm, partridges
Set up their e'ening ca':
Now loud and clear the blackbird's sang
Rings throuth the briery shaw*, wood
While, flitting gay, the swallows play
Around the castle wa'.

Beneath the golden gloamin' sky
The mavis mends her lay.
The redbreast pours his sweetest strains
To charm the lingering day;
While weary yeldrins* seem to wail yellow-hammers
Their little nestlings torn,
The merry wren, frae den to den,
Gaes jinking through the thorn.

The roses fauld their silken leaves,
The foxsglove shuts its bell,
The honeysuckle and the birk* birch
Spread fragrance through the dell.
Let others crowd the giddy court
Of mirth and revelry,
The simple joys that Nature yields
Are dearer far to me.

## The Lament of Wallace
### After the Battle of Falkirk

Thou dark winding Carron, once pleasing to see,
To me thou canst never give pleasure again,
My brave Caledonians lie low on the lea,
And thy streams are deep tinged with the blood of the slain.
Ah, base-hearted treach'ry has doomed our undoing,
My poor bleeding country, what more can I do?
Even valor looks pale oer the red field of ruin,
And freedom beholds her best warriors laid low.

Farewell, ye dear partners of peril, farewell.
Though buried ye lie in one wide bloody grave,
Your deeds shall ennoble the place where ye fell,
And your names be enrolled with the sons of the brave.
But I, a poor outcast, in exile must wander,
Perhaps, like a traitor, ignobly must die.
On thy wrongs, O my country, indignant I ponder,
Ah, woe to the hour when thy Wallace must fly.

## Langsyne, Beside the Woodland Burn

Langsyne, beside the woodland burn,
Amang the broom sae yellow,
I leaned me neath the milk-white thorn,
On nature's mossy pillow.
A' round my seat the flowers were strewed
That frae the wild wood I had pu'd,
To weave mysel a summer snood*, hair-ribbon
To pleasure my dear fellow.

I twined the woodbine round the rose,
Its richer hues to mellow.
Green sprigs of fragrant birk I chose
To busk* the sedge sae yellow. dress
The crow-flow'r blue, and meadow pink,
I wove in primrose-braided link;
But little, little did I think
I should have wove the willow.

My bonnie lad was forced afar,
Tost on the raging billow.
Perhaps he's fa'en in bloody war,
Or wrecked on rocky shallow.
Yet aye I hope for his return,
As round our wonted haunts I mourn;
And often by the woodland burn
I pu' the weeping willow.

## The Harper of Mull

When Rosie was faithful, how happy was I.
Still gladsome as summer the time glided by.
I played my harp cheery, while fondly I sang
Of the charms of my Rosie the winter nights lang.
But now I'm as waefu' as waefu' can be,
Come simmer, come winter, tis a' ane to me,
For the dark gloom of falsehood sae clouds my sad soul,
That cheerless for aye is the harper of Mull.

I wander the glens and the wild woods alane,
In their deepest recesses I make my sad mane;
My harp's mournful melody joins in the strain,

While sadly I sing of the days that are gane.
Though Rosie is faithless, she's no the less fair,
And the thoughts of her beauty but feed my despair.
With painful remembrance my bosom is full,
And weary of life is the harper of Mull.

As slumb'ring I lay by the dark mountain stream,
My lovely young Rosie appeared in my dream.
I thought her still kind, and I ne'er was sae blest,
As in fancy I clasped the dear nymph to my breast.
Thou false fleeting vision, too soon thou wert oer.
Thou wak'dst me to tortures unequaled before;
But death's silent slumbers my griefs soon shall lull,
And the green grass wave over the harper of Mull.

## ALEXANDER BOSWELL (1775–1841)[1]

### Jenny Dang the Weaver

At Willie's wedding o' the green,
The lasses, bonnie witches,
Were busked* out in aprons clean, — dressed
And snaw-white Sunday's mutches*. — caps
Auld Maisie bade the lads tak tent*, — care
But Jock wad na believe her;
But soon the fool his folly kent,
For Jenny dang* the weaver. — struck

In ilka countra dance and reel,
Wi' her he wad be babbin'*. — dancing
When she sat doun, then he sat doun,
An till her wad be gabbin'.
Where'er she gaed, or butt or ben*, — out or in
The coof* wad never leave her, — fool
Aye cacklin' like a clockin' hen,
But Jenny dang the weaver.

Quo he, "My lass, to speak my mind,
Gude haith, I needna swither*; — hesitate
Ye've bonnie een, and gif ye're kind,
I needna court anither."
He hummed and hawed, the lass cried Pheugh!
And bade the fool no deave* her. — deafen
Syne cracked her thumb, and lap, and leuch*, — laughed
And dang the silly weaver.

### Good Night, and Joy Be wi' Ye A'

Gude night, and joy be wi' ye a',
Your harmless mirth has cheered my heart;

---

[1] Alexander Boswell is the son of James Boswell, the author of the great *Life of Johnson*.

May life's fell blasts out oer ye blaw.
In sorrow may ye never part.
My spirit lives, but strength is gone,
The mountain-fires now blaze in vain.
Remember, sons, the deeds I've done,
And in your deeds I'll live again.

When on yon muir our gallant clan,
Frae boasting foes their banners tore,
Wha showed himself a better man,
Or fiercer waved the red claymore?
But when in peace—then mark me there—
When through the glen the wand'rer came,
I gave him of our hardy fare—
I gave him here a welcome hame.

The auld will speak, the young maun hear;
Be cantie*, but be gude and leal*. lively/loyal
Yer ain ills aye hae heart to bear,
Anither's aye hae heart to feel.
So ere I set I'll see you shine.
I'll see you triumph ere I fa'.
My parting breath shall boast you mine—
Good night, and joy be wi' ye a'.

## JOHN LEYDEN (1775–1811)

### The Sabbath Morning

With silent awe I hail the sacred morn,
That slowly wakes while all the fields are still.
A soothing calm on every breeze is borne.
A graver murmur gurgles from the rill;
And echo answers softer from the hill;
And sweeter sings the linnet from the thorn.
The skylark warbles in a tone less shrill:
Hail, light serene! hail, sacred Sabbath morn!
The rooks float silent by in airy drove.
The sun a placid yellow luster throws.
The gales that lately sighed along the grove
Have hushed their downy wings in dead repose.
The hovering rack of clouds forgets to move—
So smiled the day when the first morn arose.

### Noontide

Beneath a shivering canopy reclined,
Of aspen leaves that wave without a wind,
I love to lie, when lulling breezes stir
The spiry cones that tremble on the fir;
Or wander mid the dark green fields of broom,
When peers in scattered tufts the yellow bloom;

Or trace the path with tangling furze o'errun,
When bursting seed-bells crackle in the sun,
And pittering grasshoppers, confus'dly shrill,
Pipe giddily along the glowing hill.
Sweet grasshopper, who lov'st at noon to lie
Serenely in the green-ribbed clover's eye,
To sun thy filmy wings and emerald vest,
Unseen thy form, and undisturbed thy rest,
Oft have I listening mused the sultry day,
And wondered what thy chirping song might say,
When naught was heard along the blossomed lea,
To join thy music, save the listless bee.

## To the Evening Star

How sweet thy modest light to view,
Fair star, to love and lovers dear,
While trembling on the falling dew,
Like beauty shining through a tear.

Or hanging oer that mirror-stream,
To mark that image trembling there,
Thou seem'st to smile with softer gleam,
To see thy lovely face so fair.

Though, blazing oer the arch of night,
The moon thy timid beams outshine
As far as thine each starry light,—
Her rays can never vie with thine.

Thine are the soft enchanting hours
When twilight lingers on the plain,
And whispers to the closing flowers
That soon the sun will rise again.

Thine is the breeze that, murmuring bland
As music, wafts the lover's sigh,
And bids the yielding heart expand
In love's delicious ecstasy.

Fair star, though I be doomed to prove
That rapture's tears are mixed with pain,
Ah, still I feel tis sweet to love,—
But sweeter to be loved again.

## The Elfin King

"O swift, and swifter far he speeds
Than earthly steed can run;
But I hear not the feet of his courser fleet,
As he glides oer the moorland dun."

Lone was the strath* where he crossed their path,
And wide did the heath extend,
The knight in green on that moor is seen
At every seven years' end.

river valley

And swift is the speed of his coal-black steed,
As the leaf before the gale,
But never yet have that courser's feet
Been heard on hill or dale.

But woe to the wight who meets the green knight,
Except on his faulchion arm
Spell-proof he bear, like the brave St. Clair,
The holy Trefoil's charm.

For then shall fly his gifted eye,
Delusions false and dim;
And each unblessed shade shall stand portrayed
In ghostly form and limb.

O swift, and swifter far he speeds
Than earthly steed can run.
"He skims the blue air," said the brave St. Clair,
"Instead of the heath so dun.

"His locks are bright as the streamer's light,
His cheeks like the rose's hue.
The elfin-king, like the merlin's wing
Are his pinions of glossy blue."

"No elfin-king, with azure wing,
On the dark brown moor I see;
But a courser keen, and a knight in green,
And full fair I ween is he.

"Nor elfin-king, nor azure wing,
Nor ringlets sparkling bright,"
Sir Geoffry cried, and forward hied
To join the stranger knight.

He knew not the path of the lonely strath,
Where the elfin-king went his round;
Or he never had gone with the green knight on,
Nor trod the charmed ground.

How swift they flew! no eye could view
Their track on heath or hill.
Yet swift across both moor and moss
St. Clair did follow still.

And soon was seen a circle green,
Where a shadowy wassel* crew

"wassail"

Amid the ring did dance and sing,
In weeds of watchet blue.

And the windlestrae*, so limber and gray, rye-grass
Did shiver beneath the tread
Of the coursers' feet, as they rushed to meet
The morrice* of the dead. morris-dance?

"Come here, come here, with thy green fere,
Before the bread be stale;
To roundel dance with speed advance,
And taste our wassel ale."

Then up to the knight came a grizzly wight,
And sounded in his ear,
"Sir Knight, eschew this goblin crew,
Nor taste their ghostly cheer."

The tabors rung, the lilts were sung,
And the knight the dance did lead;
But the maidens fair seemed round him to stare,
With eyes like the glassy bead.

The glance of their eye, so cold and so dry,
Did almost his heart appall.
Their motion is swift, but their limbs they lift
Like stony statues all.

Again to the knight came the grizzly wight,
When the roundel dance was oer.
"Sir Knight, eschew this goblin crew,
Or rue for evermore."

But forward pressed the dauntless guest
To the tables of ezlar* red, (a stone)
And there was seen the knight in green,
To grace the fair board head.

And before that knight was a goblet bright
Of emerald smooth and green,
The fretted brim was studded full trim
With mountain rubies' sheen.

Sir Geoffry the Bold of the cup laid hold,
With health-ale mantling oer;
And he saw as he drank that the ale never shrank,
But mantled as before.

Then Sir Geoffry grew pale as he quaffed the ale,
And cold as the corpse of clay;
And with horny beak the ravens did shriek,
And fluttered oer their prey.

But soon throughout the revel rout,
A strange commotion ran,
For beyond the round, they heard the sound
Of the steps of an uncharmed man.

And soon to St. Clair the grim wight did repair,
From the midst of the wassel crew.
"Sir Knight, beware of the revelers there,
Nor do as they bid thee do."

"What woeful wight art thou," said the knight,
"To haunt this wassel fray?"
"I was once," quoth he, "a mortal, like thee,
Though now I'm an elfin gray.

"And the knight so bold as the corpse lies cold,
Who trode the greensward ring.
He must wander along with that restless throng,
For aye, with the elfin-king.

"With the restless crew, in weed so blue,
The hapless knight must wend;
Nor ever be seen on haunted green
Till the weary seven years' end.

"Fair is the mien of the knight in green,
And bright his sparkling hair.
Tis hard to believe how malice can live
In the breast of aught so fair.

"And light and fair are the fields of air,
Where he wanders to and fro;
Still doomed to fleet from the regions of heat,
To the realms of endless snow.

"When high overhead fall the streamers red,[1]
He views the blessed afar;
And in stern despair darts through the air
To earth, like a falling star.

"With his shadowy crew, in weeds so blue,
That knight for aye must run;
Except thou succeed in a perilous deed,
Unseen by the holy sun.

"Who ventures the deed, and fails to succeed,
Perforce must join the crew."
"Then brief, declare," said the brave St. Clair,
"A deed that a knight may do."

---

[1]The northern lights.

"Mid the sleet and the rain thou must here remain,
By the haunted greensward ring,
Till the dance wax slow, and the song faint and low,
Which the crew unearthly sing.

"Then right at the time of the matin chime,
Thou must tread the unhallowed ground,
And with mystic pace the circles trace,
That enclose it nine times round.

"And next must thou pass the rank green grass
To the tables of ezlar red;
And the goblet clear away must thou bear,
Nor behind thee turn thy head.

"And ever anon as thou treadst upon
The sward of the green charmed ring,
Be no word expressed in that space unblessed
That 'longeth of holy thing.

"For the charmed ground is all unsound,
And the lake spreads wide below,
And the water-fiend there, with the fiend of air,
Is leagued for mortals' woe."

Mid the sleet and the rain did St. Clair remain
Till the evening star did rise;
And the rout so gay did dwindle away
To the elritch dwarfy size.

When the moonbeams pale fell through the white hail,
With a wan and a watery ray,
Sad notes of woe seemed round him to grow—
The dirge of the elfins gray.

And right at the time of the matin chime
His mystic pace began,
And murmurs deep around him did creep,
Like the moans of a murdered man.

The matin bell was tolling farewell,
When he reached the central ring,
And there he beheld, to ice congealed,
That crew, with the elfin king.

For aye, at the knell of the matin bell,
When the black monks wend to pray,
The spirits unblessed have a glimpse of rest
Before the dawn of day.

The sigh of the trees, and the rush of the breeze,
Then pause on the lonely hill;

And the frost of the dead clings round their head,
And they slumber cold and still.

The knight took up the emerald cup,
And the ravens hoarse did scream,
And the shuddering elfins half rose up,
And murmured in their dream.

They inwardly mourned, and the thin blood returned
To every icy limb;
And each frozen eye, so cold and so dry,
Gan roll with luster dim.

Then brave St. Clair did turn him there,
To retrace the mystic track,
He heard the sigh of his lady fair,
Who sobbed behind his back.

He started quick, and his heart beat thick,
And he listened in wild amaze;
But the parting bell on his ear it fell,
And he did not turn to gaze.

With panting breast, as he forward pressed,
He trode on a mangled head;
And the skull did scream, and the voice did seem
The voice of his mother dead.

He shuddering trode: on the great name of God
He thought—but he nought did say;
And the greensward did shrink, as about to sink,
And loud laughed the elfins gray.

And loud did resound, oer the unblessed ground,
The wings of the blue elf-king;
And the ghostly crew to reach him flew,
But he crossed the charmed ring.

The morning was gray, and dying away
Was the sound of the matin bell;
And far to the west the fays that ne'er rest,
Fled where the moonbeams fell.

And Sir Geoffry the Bold, on the unhallowed mold,
Arose from the green witch-grass;
And he felt his limbs like a dead man's cold,
And he wist not where he was.

And that cup so rare, which the brave St. Clair
Did bear from the ghostly crew,
Was suddenly changed, from the emerald fair,
To the ragged whinstone blue;

And instead of the ale that mantled there,
Was the murky midnight dew.

## The Mermaid

On Jura's heath how sweetly swell
The murmurs of the mountain bee.
How softly mourns the writhed shell
Of Jura's shore, its parent sea.

But softer floating oer the deep,
The mermaid's sweet sea-soothing lay,
That charmed the dancing waves to sleep
Before the bark of Colonsay.

Aloft the purple pennons wave,
As, parting gay from Crinan's shore,
From Morven's wars, the seamen brave
Their gallant chieftain homeward bore.

In youth's gay bloom, the brave Macphail
Still blamed the lingering bark's delay:
For her he chid the flagging sail,
The lovely maid of Colonsay.

"And raise," he cried, "the song of love
The maiden sung with tearful smile,
When first, oer Jura's hills to rove,
We left afar the lonely isle.

"'When on this ring of ruby red
Shall die,' she said, 'the crimson hue,
Know that thy favorite fair is dead,
Or proves to thee and love untrue.'"

Now, lightly poised, the rising oar
Disperses wide the foamy spray,
And echoing far oer Crinan's shore,
Resounds the song of Colonsay.

"Softly blow, thou western breeze,
Softly rustle through the sail.
Soothe to rest the furrowy seas
Before my love, sweet western gale.

"Where the wave is tinged with red,
And the russet sea-leaves grow,
Mariners, with prudent dread,
Shun the shelving reefs below.

"As you pass through Jura's sound,
Bend your course by Scarba's shore.

Shun, O shun the gulf profound,
Where Corrievreckin's surges roar.

"If from that unbottomed deep,
With wrinkled form and writhed train,
Oer the verge of Scarba's steep,
The sea-snake heave his snowy mane;

"Unwarp, unwind his oozy coils,
Sea-green sisters of the main,
And in the gulf where ocean boils,
The unwieldy wallowing monster chain.

"Softly blow, thou western breeze,
Softly rustle through the sail.
Soothe to rest the furrowed seas
Before my love, sweet western gale."

Thus all to soothe the chieftain's woe,
Far from the maid he loved so dear,
The song arose, so soft and slow,
He seemed her parting sigh to hear.

The lonely deck he paces oer,
Impatient for the rising day,
And still from Crinan's moonlight shore
He turns his eyes to Colonsay.

The moonbeams crisp the curling surge
That streaks with foam the ocean green;
While forward still the rowers urge
Their course, a female form was seen.

That sea-maid's form, of pearly light,
Was whiter than the downy spray,
And round her bosom, heaving bright,
Her glossy yellow ringlets play.

Borne on a foamy crested wave,
She reached amain the bounding prow.
Then clasping fast the chieftain brave,
She, plunging, sought the deep below.

Ah, long beside thy feigned bier,
The monks the prayers of death shall say,
And long for thee, the fruitless tear,
Shall weep the maid of Colonsay.

But downwards, like a powerless corse,
The eddying waves the chieftain bear.
He only heard the moaning hoarse
Of waters murmuring in his ear.

The murmurs sink by slow degrees,
No more the surges round him rave.
Lulled by the music of the seas,
He lies within a coral cave.

In dreamy mood reclines he long,
Nor dares his tranced eyes unclose,
Till, warbling wild, the sea-maid's song
Far in the crystal cavern rose;

Soft as that harp's unseen control
In morning dreams that lovers hear,
Whose strains steal sweetly oer the soul,
But never reach the waking ear.

As sunbeams through the tepid air,
When clouds dissolve in dews unseen,
Smile on the flowers that bloom more fair,
And fields that glow with livelier green—

So melting soft the music fell.
It seemed to soothe the fluttering spray—
"Say, heard'st thou not these wild notes swell?
Ah, tis the song of Colonsay."

Like one that from a fearful dream
Awakes, the morning light to view,
And joys to see the purple beam,
Yet fears to find the vision true,

He heard that strain, so wildly sweet,
Which bade his torpid languor fly.
He feared some spell had bound his feet,
And hardly dared his limbs to try.

"This yellow sand, this sparry cave,
Shall bend thy soul to beauty's sway.
Canst thou the maiden of the wave
Compare to her of Colonsay?"

Roused by that voice of silver sound,
From the paved floor he lightly sprung,
And glancing wild his eyes around
Where the fair nymph her tresses wrung,

No form he saw of mortal mold.
It shone like ocean's snowy foam.
Her ringlets waved in living gold,
Her mirror crystal, pearl her comb.

Her pearly comb the siren took,
And careless bound her tresses wild.

Still oer the mirror stole her look,
As on the wondering youth she smiled.

Like music from the greenwood tree,
Again she raised the melting lay.
"Fair warrior, wilt thou dwell with me,
And leave the maid of Colonsay?

"Fair is the crystal hall for me
With rubies and with emeralds set;
And sweet the music of the sea
Shall sing, when we for love are met.

"How sweet to dance with gliding feet
Along the level tide so green,
Responsive to the cadence sweet
That breathes along the moonlight scene.

"And soft the music of the main
Rings from the motley tortoise-shell,
While moonbeams oer the watery plain
Seem trembling in its fitful swell.

"How sweet, when billows heave their head,
And shake their snowy crests on high,
Serene in Ocean's sapphire bed
Beneath the tumbling surge to lie;

"To trace, with tranquil step, the deep,
Where pearly drops of frozen dew
In concave shells unconscious sleep,
Or shine with luster, silvery blue.

"Then shall the summer sun, from far,
Pour through the wave a softer ray;
While diamonds in a bower of spar,
At eve shall shed a brighter day.

"Nor stormy wind, nor wintry gale,
That oer the angry ocean sweep,
Shall e'er our coral groves assail,
Calm in the bosom of the deep.

"Through the green meads beneath the sea,
Enamored we shall fondly stray—
Then, gentle warrior, dwell with me,
And leave the maid of Colonsay."

"Though bright thy locks of glistering gold,
Fair maiden of the foamy main,
Thy life-blood is the water cold,
While mine beats high in every vein.

"If I, beneath thy sparry cave,
Should in thy snowy arms recline,
Inconstant as the restless wave,
My heart would grow as cold as thine."

As cygnet-down, proud swelled her breast,
Her eye confessed the pearly tear.
His hand she to her bosom pressed,
"Is there no heart for rapture here?

"These limbs sprung from the lucid sea,
Does no warm blood their currents fill,
No heart-pulse riot, wild and free,
To joy, to love's delirious thrill?"

"Though all the splendor of the sea
Around thy faultless beauty shine,
That heart, that riots wild and free,
Can hold no sympathy with mine."

"These sparkling eyes, so wild and gay,
They swim not in the light of love.
The beauteous maid of Colonsay,
Her eyes are milder than the dove.

"E'en now, within the lonely isle,
Her eyes are dim with tears for me;
And canst thou think that siren smile
Can lure my soul to dwell with thee?"

An oozy film her limbs oerspread,
Unfolds in length her scaly train.
She tossed in proud disdain her head,
And lashed with webbed fin the main.

"Dwell here alone!" the mermaid cried,
"And view far off the sea nymphs play.
The prison wall, the azure tide,
Shall bar thy steps from Colonsay.

"Whene'er, like ocean's scaly brood,
I cleave with rapid fin the wave,
Far from the daughter of the flood,
Conceal thee in this coral cave.

"I feel my former soul return,
It kindles at thy cold disdain,
And has a mortal dared to spurn
A daughter of the foamy main?"

She fled; around the crystal cave
The rolling waves resume their road;

On the broad portal idly rave,
But enter not the nymph's abode.

And many a weary night went by,
As in the lonely cave he lay;
And many a sun rolled through the sky,
And poured its beams on Colonsay.

And oft beneath the silver moon
He heard afar the mermaid sing;
And oft to many a melting tune
The shell-formed lyres of ocean ring.

And when the moon went down the sky,
Still rose, in dreams, his native plain;
And oft he thought his love was by,
And charmed him with some tender strain.

And heartsick, oft he waked to weep,
When ceased that voice of silver sound,
And thought to plunge him in the deep
That walled his crystal cavern round.

But still the ring, of ruby red,
Retained its vivid crimson hue,
And each despairing accent fled,
To find his gentle love so true.

When seven long lonely months were gone,
The mermaid to his cavern came,
No more misshapen from the zone,
But like a maid of mortal frame.

"O give to me that ruby ring
That on thy finger glances gay,
And thou shalt hear the mermaid sing
The song thou lov'st of Colonsay."

"This ruby ring, of crimson grain,
Shall on thy finger glitter gay,
If thou wilt bear me through the main
Again to visit Colonsay."

"Except thou quit thy former love,
Content to dwell for aye with me,
Thy scorn my finny frame might move
To tear thy limbs amid the sea."

"Then bear me swift along the main,
The lonely isle again to see;
And when I here return again,
I plight my faith to dwell with thee."

An oozy film her limbs oerspread,
While slow unfolds her scaly train.
With gluey fangs her hands were clad.
She lashed with webbed fin the main.

He grasps the mermaid's scaly sides,
As with broad fin she oars her way.
Beneath the silent moon she glides,
That sweetly sleeps on Colonsay.

Proud swells her heart. She deems at last
To lure him with her silver tongue,
And, as the shelving rocks she passed,
She raised her voice, and sweetly sung.

In softer, sweeter strains she sung,
Slow gliding oer the moonlight bay,
When light to land the chieftain sprung,
To hail the maid of Colonsay.

O sad the mermaid's gay notes fell,
And sadly sink remote at sea.
So sadly mourns the writhed shell
Of Jura's shore, its parent sea.

And ever as the year returns
The charm-bound sailors know the day:
For sadly still the mermaid mourns
The lovely chief of Colonsay.

## JAMES SCADLOCK (1775–1818)

### Hark, Hark, the Skylark Singing

Hark, hark, the skylark singing,
While the early clouds are bringing
Fragrance on their wings;
Still, still on high he's soaring,
Through the liquid haze exploring,
Fainter now he sings.
Where the purple dawn is breaking,
Fast approaches morning's ray;
From his wings the dew he's shaking
As he joyful hails the day,
While echo, from his slumbers waking,
Imitates his lay.

See, see the ruddy morning,
With his blushing locks adorning
Mountain, wood, and vale;
Clear, clear the dewdrop's glancing,
As the rising sun's advancing

Oer the eastern hill;
Now the distant summits clearing,
As the vapors steal their way,
And his heath-clad breast's appearing,
Tinged with Phoebus' golden ray.
Far down the glen the blackbird's cheering
Morning with her lay.

Come, then, let us be straying,
Where the hazel boughs are playing
Oer yon summits gray:
Mild now the breeze is blowing,
And the crystal streamlet's flowing
Gently on its way.
On its banks the wild rose springing,
Welcomes in the sunny ray.
Wet with dew its head is hinging,
Bending low the prickly spray.
Then haste, my love, while birds are singing
To the new born day.

## October Winds

October winds, wi biting breath,
Now nip the leaves that's yellow fading.
Nae gowans glint upon the green;
Alas, they're co'ered wi winter's cleading.
As through the woods I musing gang
Nae birdies cheer me frae the bushes,
Save little robin's lanely sang,
Wild warbling where the burnie gushes.

The sun is jogging down the brae,
Dimly through the mist he's shining,
And cranreuch* hoar creeps oer the grass
As day resigns his throne to e'ening.
Oft let me walk at twilight gray,
To view the face of dying nature,
Till spring again, wi mantle green,
Delights the heart o' ilka creature.

* frost

## Retrospect Recollections of Youth

Yon high tow'ring hill with its broom-skirted vale,
Where the redbreast at eve warbles sweet his love song,
And the sound of the streamlet is heard on the gale,
As it gurgling meanders the dark woods among—
There oft have I wondered, when eve's mellow beams
Had tinged the brown heath on the bleak jutting steep,
Where round the gray summit the seafowl loud screams
To the hoarse dashing waves of the wild foaming deep.

And still as I pass the old tree by the burn,
Whose bark is half stript, and whose leaves now are few,
I linger awhile—for gay life's blooming morn,
With its tender emotions, recurs to my view.
Near the wild shrubs that hang oer yon storm-beaten rocks,
And lift their gray sides from the heath-covered way,
My Mary and I oft have tended our flocks,
Ere the sun drank the dew from the leaf-budding spray.

When summer with verdure the fields had arrayed,
And ocean's rude billows were sunk into rest,
Along by the banks of the stream have I strayed,
No anxious forebodings disturbing my breast,
Even here, as I view her lone cot in the vale,
Where hawthorns are blooming, and flow'rs deck the plain,
The dear native spot still with rapture I hail,
And to Mary my wand'rings tell over again.

## THOMAS CUNNINGHAM (1776–1834)

### The Hills o' Gallowa'

Amang the birks, sae blithe an gay,
I met my Julia hameward gaun;
The linties chantit on the spray,
The lammies loupit* on the lawn. leaped
On ilka swaird the hay was mawn,
The braes wi gowans buskit* bra'; dressed
An' ev'ning's plaid o' gray was thrawn
Out-owre the hills o' Gallowa'.

Wi music wild the woodlands rang,
An fragrance winged alang the lea,
As down we sat the flowers amang,
Upon the banks o' stately Dee.
My Julia's arms encircled me,
An saftly slade the hours awa,
Till dawning coost a glimmerin' e'e
Upon the hills o' Gallowa'.

It isna owsen, sheep, and kye,
It isna gowd, it isna gear*, money
This lifted e'e wad hae, quoth I,
The warld's drumlie* gloom to cheer; sad
But gie to me my Julia dear,
Ye powers wha row this yirthen ba'*, "ball"
An oh, sae blithe through life I'll steer
Amang the hills o' Gallowa'.

Whan gloamin danders up the hill,
An our gudeman ca's hame the yowes*, "ewes"
Wi her I'll trace the mossy rill

That through the muir meand'ring rows;
Or, tint* amang the scroggie* knowes, lost/stunted
My birken pipe I'll sweetly blaw,
An sing the streams, the straths, and howes*, hollows
The hills and dales o' Gallowa'.

An whan auld Scotland's heathy hills,
Her rural nymphs an jovial swains,
Her flowery wilds an wimpling rills,
Awake nae mair my canty* strains; lively
Where friendship dwells an freedom reigns,
Where heather blooms an muir-cocks craw,
Oh dig my grave, and lay my banes
Amang the hills o' Gallowa'.

## Mary's Grave

Ye briery bields*, where roses blaw, shelters
Ye flow'ry fells, an sunny braes,
Whase scroggie* bosoms fostered a' stunted
The pleasures o' my youthfu' days,
Amang your leafy simmer claes,
And blushin blooms, the zephyr flies,
Syne wings awa, and wanton plays
Around the grave whar Mary lies.

Nae mair your bonnie birken bowers,
Your streamlets fair, and woodlands gay,
Can cheer the weary winged hours
As up the glen I joyless stray;
For a' my hopes hae flown away,
And when they reached their native skies,
Left me, amid the world o' wae,
To weet the grave whar Mary lies.

It is na beauty's fairest bloom,
It is na maiden charms consigned
And hurried to an early tomb,
That wrings my heart and clouds my mind;
But sparkling wit, and sense refined,
And spotless truth without disguise,
Make me with sighs enrich the wind
That fans the grave whar Mary lies.

## The Braes of Ballahun

Now smiling summer's balmy breeze,
Soft whispering, fans the leafy trees;
The linnet greets the rosy morn,
Sweet in yon fragrant flowery thorn;
The bee hums round the woodbine bower,
Collecting sweets from every flower;

And pure the crystal streamlets run
Amang the braes of Ballahun.

Oh, blissful days for ever fled,
When wandering wild, as fancy led,
I ranged the bushy bosomed glen,
The scroggie shaw*, the rugged linn*, wood/waterfall
And marked each blooming hawthorn bush,
Where nestling sat the speckled thrush;
Or, careless roaming, wandered on
Amang the braes of Ballahun.

Why starts the tear, why bursts the sigh,
When hills and dales rebound with joy?
The flowery glen and lilied lea
In vain display their charms to me.
I joyless roam the heathy waste,
To soothe this sad, this troubled breast;
And seek the haunts of men to shun,
Amang the braes of Ballahun.

The virgin blush of lovely youth,
The angel smile of artless truth,
This breast illumed with heavenly joy,
Which lyart* time can ne'er destroy, gray
Oh, Julia, dear, the parting look,
The sad farewell we sorrowing took,
Still haunt me as I stray alone
Among the braes of Ballahun.

## RICHARD GALL (1776–1801)

### Cradle Song

Baloo, baloo, my wee wee thing,
O saftly close thy blinkin' e'e.
Baloo, baloo, my wee wee thing,
For thou art doubly dear to me.
Thy daddy now is far awa',
A sailor laddie oer the sea;
But hope aye hechts* his safe return promises
To you, my bonnie lamb, and me.

Baloo, baloo, my wee wee thing,
O saftly close thy blinkin' e'e.
Baloo, baloo, my wee wee thing,
For thou art doubly dear to me.
Thy face is simple, sweet, and mild,
Like ony simmer e'ening fa';
Thy sparkling e'e is bonnie black;
Thy neck is like the mountain snaw.

Baloo, baloo, my wee wee thing,
O saftly close thy blinkin' e'e.
Baloo, baloo, my wee wee thing,
For thou art doubly dear to me.
O, but thy daddie's absence, lang,
Might break my dowie* heart in twa, sad
Wert thou na left, a dawtit* pledge, darling
To steal the eerie hours awa.

## The Hazlewood Witch

For many lang year I hae heard frae my granny
Of brownies and bogles by yon castle wa',
Of auld withered hags that were never thought canny,
And fairies that danced till they heard the cock craw.
I leugh* at her tales, and last ouk, i' the gloaming laughed
I dandered, alane, down the Hazelwood green;
Alas, I was reckless, and rue sair my roaming,
For I met a young witch wi' twa bonnie black een.

I thought o' the starns in a frosty night glancing,
Whan a' the lift* round them is cloudless and blue; sky
I lookit again, and my heart fell a dancing;
Whan I was hae spoken she glamoured* my mou', enchanted
O wae to her cantrips*, for dumpish I wander; tricks
At kirk or at market there's nought to be seen;
For she dances before me wherever I dander,
The Hazelwood witch wi' the bonnie black een.

## The Braes o' Drumlee

Ere eild* wi his blatters had warsled me down, age
Or reft me o' life's youthfu' bloom,
How aft hae I gane, wi a heart louping* light, leaping
To the knowes* yellow tappit wi broom. "knolls"
How aft hae I sat in' the bield* o' the knowe, shelter
While the laverock mounted sae hie,
An the mavis sang sweet in the plantings around,
On the bonnie green braes o' Drumlee.

But ah, while we daff* in the sunshine o' youth, play
We see na the blasts that destroy;
We count na upon the fell waes* that may come, "woes"
An' eithly* oercloud a' our joy. easily
I saw na the fause face that fortune can wear,
Till forced from my country to flee;
Wi a heart like to burst, while I sobbed "Farewell
To the bonnie green braes o' Drumlee.

"Farewell, ye dear haunts o' the days o' my youth,
Ye woods and ye valleys sae fair;
Ye'll bloom when I wander abroad like a ghaist,
Sair niddered wi' sorrow an care.

Ye woods an ye valleys, I part wi a sigh,
While the flood gushes down frae my ee;
For never again shall the tear weet my cheek
On the bonnie green braes o' Drumlee.

"O time, could I tether your hours for a wee.
Na, na, for they flit like the wind."
Sae I took my departure, an sauntered awa,
Yet aften looked wistfu' behind.
Oh sair is the heart of the mither to twin* — separate
Wi the baby that sits on her knee;
But sairer the pang when I took a last peep
O' the bonnie green braes o' Drumlee.

I heftit* 'mang strangers years thretty an twa, — settled
But naething could banish my care;
An aften I sighed when I thought on the past,
Whar a' was sae pleasant an fair.
But now, wae's my heart, when I'm lyart* an ald, — gray
An fu' lint-white my haffet* locks flee, — cheek
I'm hamewards returned wi a remnant o' life
To the bonnie green braes o' Drumlee.

Poor body, bewildered, I scarcely do ken
The haunts that were dear ance to me;
I yirded a plant in the day o' my youth,
An the mavis now sings on the tree.
But, haith, there's nae scenes I wad niffer* wi' thae; — trade
For it fills my fond heart fu' o' glee,
To think how at last my auld banes they will rest
Near the bonnie green braes o' Drumlee.

## Farewell to Ayrshire

Scenes of woe and scenes of pleasure,
Scenes that former thoughts renew;
Scenes of woe and scenes of pleasure,
Now a sad and last adieu.
Bonny Doon, sae sweet at gloaming,
Fare-thee-weel before I gang—
Bonny Doon, where, early roaming,
First I weaved the rustic sang.

Bowers, adieu, where love decoying,
First enthralled this heart o' mine
There the saftest sweets enjoying,
Sweets that memory ne'er shall tine*. — lose
Friends so dear my bosom ever,
Ye hae rendered moments dear;
But, alas, when forced to sever,
Then the stroke, oh, how severe.

Friends, that parting tear reserve it,
Though tis double dear to me.
Could I think I did deserve it,
How much happier would I be.
Scenes of woe and scenes of pleasure,
Scenes that former thoughts renew;
Scenes of woe and scenes of pleasure,
Now a sad and last adieu.

## My Only Jo and Dearie O

Thy cheek is o' the rose's hue,
My only jo* and dearie O. sweetheart
Thy neck is like the siller*-dew "silver"
Upon the banks sae briery O.
Thy teeth are o' the ivory,
Oh, sweet's the twinkle o' thine ee.
Nae joy, nae pleasure, blinks* on me, looks
My only jo and dearie O.

The birdie sings upon the thorn
Its sang o' joy, fu' cheerie O,
Rejoicing in the summer morn,
Nae care to mak it eerie O.
Ah, little kens the sangster sweet
Aught o' the care I hae to meet,
That gars* my restless bosom beat, makes
My only jo and dearie O.

When we were bairnies on yon brae,
And youth was blinking bonny O,
Aft we wad daff* the lee-lang day, fool
Our joys fu' sweet and mony O;
Aft I wad chase thee oer the lea,
And round about the thorny tree,
Or pu' the wild-flowers a' for thee,
My only jo and dearie O.

I hae a wish I canna tine*, lose
'Mang a' the cares that grieve me O:
I wish thou wert for ever mine,
And never mair to leave me O;
Then I wad daut* thee night and day, pet, fondle
Nae ither wardly care wad hae,
Till life's warm stream forget to play,
My only jo and dearie O.

## On the Death of Burns

There's waefu' news in yon town,
As e'er the warld heard ava;
There's dolefu' news in yon town,
For Robbie's gane an left them a'.

How blithe it was to see his face
Come keeking* by the hallan* wa'. — peeking/partition
He ne'er was sweir* to say the grace, — slow
But now he's gane an left them a'.

He was the lad wha made them glad,
Whanever he the reed did blaw.
The lasses there may drap a tear,
Their funny friend is now awa'.

Nae daffin* now in yon town; — fooling
The browster*-wife gets leave to draw — brewer
An' drink hersel', in yon town,
Sin Robbie gaed and left them a'.

The lawin*'s canny counted now, — tavern bill
The bell that tinkled ne'er will draw,
The king will never get his due,
Sin Robbie gaed and left them a'.

The squads o' chiels* that lo'ed a splore* — lads/party
On winter e'enings, never ca';
Their blithesome moments a' are oer
Sin Robbie's gane an left them a'.

Frae a' the een in yon town
I see the tears o' sorrow fa',
An weel they may in yon town,
Nae canty* sang they hear ava*. — lively/at all

Their e'ening sky begins to lour,
The murky clouds thegither draw;
Twas but a blink* afore a shower, — look
Ere Robbie gaed and left them a'.

The landwart* hizzy winna speak; — country
Ye'll see her sitting like a craw
Amang the reek*, while rattons* squeak— — smoke/rats
Her dawtit* bard is now awa. — darling

But could I lay my hand upon
His whistle, keenly wad I blaw,
An screw about the ald drone*, — (bagpipe)
An lilt a lightsome spring or twa.

If it were sweetest aye whan wat,
Then wad I ripe my pouch an draw,
An steep it weel amang the maut*, — "malt"
As lang's I'd saxpence at my ca'.

For warld's gear* I dinna care, — money, goods
My stock o' that is unco* sma'. — very

Come, friend, we'll pree* the barley-bree    taste
To his braid fame that's now awa.

## Glendochart Vale

As I came through Glendochart vale,
Whar mists oertap the mountains gray,
A wee bit lassie met my view,
As cantily* she held her way;    lively
But O sic love each feature bore,
She made my saul wi rapture glow.
An aye she spake sae kind and sweet,
I couldna keep my heart in tow.

O speak na o' your courtly queans*.    girls
My wee bit lassie fools them a'.
The little cuttie's done me skaith*,    harm
She's stown my thoughtless heart awa.

Her smile was like the gray-e'ed morn,
Whan spreading on the mountain green;
Her voice saft as the mavis' sang,
An' sweet the twinkle o' her een.
Aboon her brow, sae bonnie brent*,    smooth
Her raven locks waved oer her ee;
An ilka* slee bewitching glance    each
Conveyed a dart o' love to me.

The lasses fair in Scotia's isle,
Their beauties a' what tongue can tell?
But oer the fairest o' them a',
My wee bit lassie bears the bell.
O had I never marked her smile,
Nor seen the twinkle o' her ee,
It might na been my lot the day
A waefu' lade o' care to dree*.    suffer

## The Waits

Wha's this, wi voice o' music sweet,
Sae early wakes the weary wight?
O weel I ken them by their sough*,    lilt, music
The wandering minstrels o' the night.
O weel I ken their bonnie lilts,
Their sweetest notes o' melody,
Fu' aft they've thrilled out through my saul,
And gart* the tear fill ilka ee.    made

O, sweetest minstrels, weet your pipe
A tender, soothin note to blaw.
Syne souf* the "Broom o' Cowdenknowes,"    sing
Or "Rosslyn Castle's" ruined wa'.

They bring to mind the happy days
Fu' aft I've spent wi Jenny dear.—
Ah, now ye touch the very note
That gars me sigh, and drap a tear.

Your fremit* lilts I downa* bide, foreign/cannot
They never yield a charm for me.
Unlike our ain, by nature made,
Unlike the saft delight they gie.
For weel I ween they warm the breast,
Though sair oppressed wi poortith* cauld; poverty
An sae an auld man's heart they cheer,
He tines* the thought that he is auld. loses

O, sweetest minstrels, halt awee,
Anither lilt afore ye gang;
An syne I'll close my waukrife* ee, wakeful
Enraptured wi your bonnie sang.
They're gane—the moon begins to dawn.
They're weary, paidlin through the weet.
They're gane, but on my ravished ear
The dying sounds yet thrill fu' sweet.

## WILLIAM GILLESPIE (1776–1825)

### The Highlander

From the climes of the sun, all war-worn and weary,
The Highlander sped to his youthful abode;
Fair visions of home cheered the desert so dreary,
Though fierce was the noon-beam, and steep was the road.

Till spent with the march that still lengthened before him,
He stopped by the way in a sylvan retreat.
The light shady boughs of the birch tree waved oer him,
The stream of the mountain fell soft at his feet.

He sunk to repose where the red heaths are blended,
On dreams of his childhood his fancy past oer;
But his battles are fought, and his march it is ended,
The sound of the bagpipe shall wake him no more.

No arm in the day of the conflict could wound him,
Though war launched her thunder in fury to kill.
Now the Angel of Death in the desert has found him,
And stretched him in peace by the stream of the hill.

Pale Autumn spreads oer him the leaves of the forest,
The fays of the wild chant the dirge of his rest;
And thou, little brook, still the sleeper deplorest,
And moistens the heath-bell that weeps on his breast.

### Ellen

The moon shone in fits,
And the tempest was roaring,
The storm spirit shrieked,
And the fierce rain was pouring.
Alone in her chamber,
Fair Ellen sat sighing,
The tapers burned dim,
And the embers were dying.

"The drawbridge is down,
That spans the wide river.
Can tempests divide,
Whom death cannot sever?
Unclosed is the gate,
And those arms long to fold thee;
Tis midnight, my love;
O say, what can hold thee?"

But scarce flew her words,
When the ridge reft asunder,
The horseman was crossing,
Mid lightning and thunder,
And loud was the yell,
As he plunged in the billow.
The maid knew it well
As she sprang from her pillow.

She screamed oer the wall,
But no help was beside her;
And thrice to her view
Rose the horse and his rider.
She gazed at the moon,
But the dark cloud passed over.
She plunged in the stream,
And she sank to her lover.

Say, what is that flame,
Oer the midnight deep beaming?
And whose are those forms,
In the wan moonlight gleaming?
That flame gilds the wave,
Which their pale corses cover;
And those forms are the ghosts
Of the maid and her lover.

## JAMES KING (1776–1849)

### Life's Like the Dew

No sound was heard oer the broom-covered valley,
Save the lone stream oer the rock as it fell,

Warm were the sunbeams, and glancing so gaily,
That gold seemed to dazzle along the flowered vale.
At length from the hill I heard,
Plaintively wild, a bard,
Yet pleasant to me was his soul's ardent flow:
"Remember what Morard says,
Morard of many days,
Life's like the dew on the hill of the roe.

"Son of the peaceful vale, keep from the battle plain,
Sad is the song that the bugle-horns sing.
Though lovely the standard it waves oer the mangled slain,
Widows' sighs stretching its broad gilded wing.
Hard are the laws that bind
Poor foolish man and blind;
But free thou may'st walk as the breezes that blow.
Thy cheek's with health's roses spread,
Till time clothes with snow thy head,
Fairer than dew on the hill of the roe.

"Would'st thou have peace in thy mind when thou'rt hoary,
Shun vice's paths in the days of thy bloom.
Innocence leads to the summit of glory,
Innocence gilds the dark shades of the tomb.
The tyrant, whose hands are red,
Trembles alone in bed;
But pure is the peasant's soul, pure as the snow,
No horror fiends haunt his rest,
Hope fills his placid breast,
Hope bright as dew on the hill of the roe."

Ceased the soft voice, for gray mist was descending,
Slow rose the bard, and retired from the hill.
The blackbird's mild notes with the thrush's were blending,
Oft screamed the plover her wild notes and shrill.
Yet still from the hoary bard,
Methought the sweet song I heard,
Mixed with instruction and blended with woe.
And oft as I pass along,
Chimes in mine ear his song,
"Life's like the dew on the hill of the roe."

## JOHN STRUTHERS (1776–1853)

### Admiring Nature's Simple Charms

Admiring nature's simple charms,
I left my humble home,
Awhile my country's peaceful plains,
With pilgrim step to roam.
I marked the leafy summer wave
On flowing Irvine's side,

But richer far's the robe she wears
Within the vale of Clyde.

I roamed the braes o' bonnie Doon,
The winding banks o' Ayr,
Where flutters many a small bird gay,
Blooms many a flow'ret fair.
But dearer far to me the stem
That once was Calder's pride,
And blossoms now the fairest flower
Within the vale of Clyde.

Avaunt, thou life-repressing north,
Ye withering east winds too;
But come, thou all-reviving west,
Breathe soft thy genial dew.
Till at the last, in peaceful age,
This lovely flow'ret shed
Its last green leaf upon my grave,
Within the vale of Clyde.

## Oh, Bonnie Buds Yon Birchen Tree

Oh, bonnie buds yon birchen tree,
The western breeze perfuming;
And softly smiles yon sunny brae,
Wi gowans gaily blooming.
But sweeter than yon birchen tree,
Or gowans gaily blooming,
Is she, in blushing modesty,
Wha meets me there at gloaming.

Oh, happy, happy there yestreen,
In mutual transport ranging,
Among these lovely scenes, unseen,
Our vows of love exchanging.
The moon, with clear, unclouded face,
Seemed bending to behold us;
And breathing birks, with soft embrace,
Most kindly to enfold us.

We bade each tree record our vows,
And each surrounding mountain,
With every star on high that glows
From light's oerflowing fountain.
But gloaming gray bedims the vale,
On day's bright beam encroaching.
With rapture once again I hail
The trysting hour approaching.

## THOMAS CAMPBELL (1777-1844)

### The Pleasures of Hope

#### Part I

At summer eve, when Heaven's ethereal bow
Spans with bright arch the glittering hills below,
Why to yon mountain turns the musing eye,
Whose sunbright summit mingles with the sky?
Why do those cliffs of shadowy tint appear
More sweet than all the landscape smiling near?
Tis distance lends enchantment to the view,
And robes the mountain in its azure hue.
Thus, with delight we linger to survey
The promised joys of life's unmeasured way.
Thus, from afar, each dim-discovered scene
More pleasing seems than all the past hath been;
And every form, that Fancy can repair
From dark oblivion, glows divinely there.
What potent spirit guides the raptured eye
To pierce the shades of dim futurity?
Can wisdom lend, with all her heavenly power,
The pledge of joy's anticipated hour?
Ah, no! she darkly sees the fate of man—
Her dim horizon bounded to a span;
Or, if she hold an image to the view,
Tis nature pictured too severely true.
With thee, sweet Hope! resides the heavenly light
That pours remotest rapture on the sight.
Thine is the charm of life's bewildered way,
That calls each slumbering passion into play.
Waked by thy touch, I see the sister band,
On tiptoe watching, start at thy command,
And fly where'er thy mandate bids them steer,
To pleasure's path, or glory's bright career.
Primeval Hope, the Aonian Muses say,
When man and nature mourned their first decay;
When every form of death, and every woe,
Shot from malignant stars to earth below;
When murder bared his arm, and rampant war
Yoked the red dragons of her iron car;
When peace and mercy, banished from the plain,
Sprung on the viewless winds to heaven again;
All, all forsook the friendless guilty mind,
But Hope, the charmer, lingered still behind.
Thus, while Elijah's burning wheels prepare
From Carmel's height to sweep the fields of air,
The prophet's mantle, ere his flight began,
Dropt on the world—a sacred gift to man.
Auspicious Hope! in thy sweet garden grow
Wreaths for each toil, a charm for every woe:
Won by their sweets, in nature's languid hour

The way-worn pilgrim seeks thy summer bower.
There, as the wild bee murmurs on the wing,
What peaceful dreams thy handmaid spirits bring!
What viewless forms the Aeolian organ play,
And sweep the furrowed lines of anxious thought away!
Angel of life! thy glittering wings explore
Earth's loneliest bounds, and Ocean's wildest shore.
Lo, to the wintry winds the pilot yields
His bark careering oer unfathomed fields;
Now on the Atlantic waves he rides afar,
Where Andes, giant of the western star,
With meteor-standard to the winds unfurled,
Looks from his throne of clouds oer half the world.
Now far he sweeps, where scarce a summer smiles
On Behring's rocks, or Greenland's naked isles:
Cold on his midnight watch the breezes blow
From wastes that slumber in eternal snow,
And waft, across the wave's tumultuous roar,
The wolf's long howl from Oonalaska's shore.
Poor child of danger, nursling of the storm,
Sad are the woes that wreck thy manly form!
Rocks, waves, and winds the shattered bark delay;
Thy heart is sad, thy home is far away.
But hope can here her moonlight vigils keep,
And sing to charm the spirit of the deep.
Swift as yon streamer lights the starry pole,
Her visions warm the watchman's pensive soul;
His native hills that rise in happier climes,
The grot that heard his song of other times,
His cottage home, his bark of slender sail,
His glassy lake, and broomwood-blossomed vale,
Rush on his thought; he sweeps before the wind,
Treads the loved shore he sighed to leave behind;
Meets at each step a friend's familiar face,
And flies at last to Helen's long embrace;
Wipes from her cheek the rapture-speaking tear,
And clasps, with many a sigh, his children dear!
While, long neglected, but at length caressed,
His faithful dog salutes the smiling guest,
Points to his master's eyes (where'er they roam)
His wistful face, and whines a welcome home.

Friend of the brave! in peril's darkest hour
Intrepid virtue looks to thee for power;
To thee the heart its trembling homage yields
On stormy floods, and carnage-covered fields,
When front to front the bannered hosts combine,
Halt ere they close, and form the dreadful line.
When all is still on Death's devoted soil,
The march-worn soldier mingles for the toil;
As rings his glittering tube, he lifts on high
The dauntless brow, and spirit-speaking eye,
Hails in his heart the triumph yet to come,

And hears thy stormy music in the drum!
And such thy strength-inspiring aid that bore
The hardy Byron to his native shore.
In horrid climes, where Chiloe's tempests sweep
Tumultuous murmurs oer the troubled deep,
Twas his to mourn misfortune's rudest shock,
Scourged by the winds, and cradled on the rock,
To wake each joyless morn, and search again
The famished haunts of solitary men,
Whose race, unyielding as their native storm,
Know not a trace of nature but the form:
Yet, at thy call, the hardy tar pursued,
Pale but intrepid, sad but unsubdued,
Pierced the deep woods, and, hailing from afar
The moon's pale planet and the northern star,
Paused at each dreary cry, unheard before,
Hyenas in the wild, and mermaids on the shore;
Till, led by thee oer many a cliff sublime,
He found a warmer world, a milder clime,
A home to rest, a shelter to defend,
Peace and repose, a Briton and a friend!

Congenial Hope! thy passion-kindling power,
How bright, how strong, in youth's untroubled hour!
On yon proud height, with Genius hand in hand,
I see thee light, and wave thy golden wand.
"Go, child of Heaven!" thy winged words proclaim,
"Tis thine to search the boundless fields of fame!
Lo, Newton, priest of nature, shines afar,
Scans the wide world, and numbers every star!
Wilt thou, with him, mysterious rites apply,
And watch the shrine with wonder-beaming eye?
Yes, thou shalt mark, with magic art profound,
The speed of light, the circling march of sound;
With Franklin, grasp the lightning's fiery wing,
Or yield the lyre of Heaven another string.
The Swedish sage admires, in yonder bowers,
His winged insects, and his rosy flowers;
Calls from their woodland haunts the savage train
With sounding horn, and counts them on the plain.
So once, at Heaven's command, the wanderers came
To Eden's shade, and heard their various name.
Far from the world, in yon sequestered clime,
Slow pass the sons of wisdom more sublime;
Calm as the fields of Heaven his sapient eye
The loved Athenian lifts to realms on high;
Admiring Plato, on his spotless page,
Stamps the bright dictates of the father sage:
"Shall nature bound to earth's diurnal span
The fire of God, the immortal soul of man?"
Turn, child of Heaven, thy rapture-lightened eye
To wisdom's walks; the sacred Nine are nigh.
Hark, from bright spires that gild the Delphian height,

From streams that wander in eternal light,
Ranged on their hill, Harmonia's daughters swell
The mingling tones of horn, and harp, and shell;
Deep from his vaults, the Loxian murmurs flow,
And Pythia's awful organ peals below.
Beloved of Heaven! the smiling Muse shall shed
Her moonlight halo on thy beauteous head;
Shall swell thy heart to rapture unconfined,
And breathe a holy madness oer thy mind.
I see thee roam her guardian power beneath,
And talk with spirits on the midnight heath;
Inquire of guilty wanderers whence they came,
And ask each blood-stained form his earthly name;
Then weave in rapid verse the deeds they tell,
And read the trembling world the tales of hell.
When Venus, throned in clouds of rosy hue,
Flings from her golden urn the vesper dew,
And bids fond man her glimmering noon employ,
Sacred to love, and walks of tender joy;
A milder mood the goddess shall recall,
And soft as dew thy tones of music fall;
While beauty's deeply-pictured smiles impart
A pang more dear than pleasure to the heart—
Warm as thy sighs shall flow the Lesbian strain,
And plead in Beauty's ear, nor plead in vain.
Or wilt thou Orphean hymns more sacred deem,
And steep thy song in mercy's mellow stream;
To pensive drops the radiant eye beguile—
For beauty's tears are lovelier than her smile;
On nature's throbbing anguish pour relief
And teach impassioned souls the joy of grief?
Yes; to thy tongue shall seraph words be given,
And power on earth to plead the cause of Heaven;
The proud, the cold untroubled heart of stone,
That never mused on sorrow but its own,
Unlocks a generous store at thy command,
Like Horeb's rocks beneath the prophet's hand.
The living lumber of his kindred earth,
Charmed into soul, receives a second birth,
Feels thy dread power another heart afford,
Whose passion-touched harmonious strings accord
True as the circling spheres to nature's plan;
And man, the brother, lives the friend of man.
"Bright as the pillar rose at Heaven's command,
When Israel marched along the desert land,
Blazed through the night on lonely wilds afar,
And told the path,—a never-setting star;
So, heavenly genius, in thy course divine,
Hope is thy star, her light is ever thine."

Propitious power! when rankling cares annoy
The sacred home of Hymenean joy;
When, doomed to poverty's sequestered dell,

The wedded pair of love and virtue dwell
Unpitied by the world, unknown to fame,
Their woes, their wishes, and their hearts the same—
Oh, there, prophetic Hope, thy smile bestow,
And chase the pangs that worth should never know;
There, as the parent deals his scanty store
To friendless babes, and weeps to give no more,
Tell that his manly race shall yet assuage
Their father's wrongs, and shield his latter age.
What though for him no Hybla sweets distill,
Nor bloomy vines wave purple on the hill?
Tell that when silent years have passed away,
That when his eye grows dim, his tresses gray,
These busy hands a lovelier cot shall build,
And deck with fairer flowers his little field,
And call from Heaven propitious dews to breathe
Arcadian beauty on the barren heath;
Tell that while love's spontaneous smile endears
The days of peace, the Sabbath of his years,
Health shall prolong to many a festive hour
The social pleasures of his humble bower.
Lo, at the couch where infant beauty sleeps,
Her silent watch the mournful mother keeps;
She, while the lovely babe unconscious lies,
Smiles on her slumbering child with pensive eyes,
And weaves a song of melancholy joy—
"Sleep, image of thy father, sleep, my boy.
No lingering hour of sorrow shall be thine;
No sigh that rends thy father's heart and mine;
Bright as his manly sire the son shall be
In form and soul; but, ah, more blest than he.
Thy fame, thy worth, thy filial love, at last,
Shall soothe his aching heart for all the past,
With many a smile my solitude repay,
And chase the world's ungenerous scorn away.
And say, when summoned from the world and thee
I lay my head beneath the willow tree,
Wilt thou, sweet mourner, at my stone appear,
And sooth my parted spirit lingering near?
Oh, wilt thou come, at evening hour to shed
The tears of memory oer my narrow bed;
With aching temples on thy hand reclined,
Muse on the last farewell I leave behind,
Breathe a deep sigh to winds that murmur low,
And think on all my love, and all my woe?"

So speaks affection, ere the infant eye
Can look regard, or brighten in reply;
But when the cherub lip hath learnt to claim
A mother's ear by that endearing name;
Soon as the playful innocent can prove
A tear of pity, or a smile of love,
Or cons his murmuring task beneath her care,

Or lisps with holy look his evening prayer,
Or gazing, mutely pensive, sits to hear
The mournful ballad warbled in his ear;
How fondly looks admiring Hope the while,
At every artless tear, and every smile.
How glows the joyous parent to descry
A guileless bosom, true to sympathy!

Where is the troubled heart, consigned to share
Tumultuous toils, or solitary care,
Unblest by visionary thoughts that stray
To count the joys of fortune's better day?
Lo, nature, life, and liberty relume
The dim-eyed tenant of the dungeon gloom;
A long-lost friend, or hapless child restored,
Smiles at his blazing hearth and social board;
Warm from his heart the tears of rapture flow
And virtue triumphs oer remembered woe.
Chide not his peace, proud reason! nor destroy
The shadowy forms of uncreated joy
That urge the lingering tide of life, and pour
Spontaneous slumber on his midnight hour.

Hark! the wild maniac sings, to chide the gale
That wafts so slow her lover's distant sail;
She, sad spectatress, on the wintry shore
Watched the rude surge his shroudless corse that bore,
Knew the pale form, and, shrieking in amaze,
Clasped her cold hands, and fixed her maddening gaze:
Poor widowed wretch, twas there she wept in vain,
Till memory fled her agonizing brain;
But mercy gave, to charm the sense of woe,
Ideal peace, that truth could ne'er bestow;
Warm on her heart the joys of fancy beam,
And aimless Hope delights her darkest dream.
Oft when yon moon has climbed the midnight sky,
And the lone sea-bird wakes its wildest cry,
Piled on the steep, her blazing faggots burn
To hail the bark that never can return;
And still she waits, but scarce forbears to weep
That constant love can linger on the deep.

And mark the wretch whose wanderings never knew
The world's regard, that soothes though half untrue,
Whose erring heart the lash of sorrow bore,
But found not pity when it erred no more.
Yon friendless man, at whose dejected eye
The unfeeling proud one looks—and passes by,
Condemned on penury's barren path to roam,
Scorned by the world, and left without a home—
Even he, at evening, should he chance to stray
Down by the hamlet's hawthorn-scented way,
Where, round the cot's romantic glade, are seen

The blossomed bean-field, and the sloping green;
Leans oer its humble gate, and thinks the while —
"Oh, that for me some home like this would smile,
Some hamlet shade, to yield my sickly form
Health in the breeze, and shelter in the storm.
There should my hand no stinted boon assign
To wretched hearts with sorrow such as mine."
That generous wish can soothe unpitied care,
And Hope half mingles with the poor man's prayer.
Hope! when I mourn, with sympathizing mind,
The wrongs of fate, the woes of human kind,
Thy blissful omens bid my spirit see
The boundless fields of rapture yet to be;
I watch the wheels of nature's mazy plan,
And learn the future by the past of man.
Come, bright improvement! on the car of time,
And rule the spacious world from clime to clime;
Thy handmaid arts shall every wild explore,
Trace every wave, and culture every shore.
On Erie's banks, where tigers steal along,
And the dread Indian chants a dismal song,
Where human fiends on midnight errands walk,
And bathe in brains the murderous tomahawk—
There shall the flocks on thymy pasture stray,
And shepherds dance at Summer's opening day:
Each wandering genius of the lonely glen
Shall start to view the glittering haunts of men,
And silence watch, on woodland heights around,
The village curfew as it tolls profound.
In Libyan groves, where damned rites are done,
That bathe the rocks in blood, and veil the sun,
Truth shall arrest the murderous arm profane;
Wild Obi flies—the veil is rent in twain.
Where barbarous hordes on Scythian mountains roam,
Truth, mercy, freedom, yet shall find a home;
Where'er degraded nature bleeds and pines,
From Guinea's coast to Sibir's dreary mines,
Truth shall pervade the unfathomed darkness there,
And light the dreadful features of despair.
Hark, the stern captive spurns his heavy load,
And asks the image back that Heaven bestowed.
Fierce in his eye the fire of valor burns,
And, as the slave departs, the man returns.

Oh, sacred truth, thy triumph ceased awhile,
And Hope, thy sister, ceased with thee to smile,
When leagued oppression poured to Northern wars
Her whiskered pandoors and her fierce hussars,
Waved her dread standard to the breeze of morn,
Pealed her loud drum, and twanged her trumpet horn,
Tumultuous horror brooded oer her van,
Presaging wrath to Poland—and to man!
Warsaw's last champion from her height surveyed

Wide oer the fields, a waste of ruin laid.
"Oh, Heaven!" he cried, "my bleeding country save!
Is there no hand on high to shield the brave?
Yet, though destruction sweep these lovely plains,
Rise, fellow men, our country yet remains!
By that dread name we wave the sword on high,
And swear for her to live!—with her to die."
He said, and on the rampart-heights arrayed
His trusty warriors, few but undismayed.
Firm-paced and slow, a horrid front they form,
Still as the breeze, but dreadful as the storm.
Low murmuring sounds along their banners fly,
Revenge, or death,—the watch-word and reply;
Then pealed the notes, omnipotent to charm,
And the loud tocsin tolled their last alarm!
In vain, alas! in vain, ye gallant few!
From rank to rank your volleyed thunder flew.
Oh, bloodiest picture in the book of time,
Sarmatia fell, unwept, without a crime;
Found not a generous friend, a pitying foe,
Strength in her arms, nor mercy in her woe.
Dropped from her nerveless grasp the shattered spear,
Closed her bright eye, and curbed her high career,—
Hope, for a season, bade the world farewell,
And freedom shrieked—as Kosciusko fell!
The sun went down, nor ceased the carnage there.
Tumultuous murder shook the midnight air.
On Prague's proud arch the fires of ruin glow,
His blood-dyed waters murmuring far below:
The storm prevails, the rampart yields a way;
Bursts the wide cry of horror and dismay.
Hark, as the smoldering piles with thunder fall,
A thousand shrieks for hopeless mercy call!
Earth shook; red meteors flashed along the sky,
And conscious nature shuddered at the cry!
Oh! righteous Heaven! ere Freedom found a grave,
Why slept the sword omnipotent to save?
Where was thine arm, O vengeance! where thy rod,
That smote the foes of Zion and of God,
That crushed proud Ammon when his iron car
Was yoked in wrath, and thundered from afar?
Where was the storm that slumbered till the host
Of blood-stained Pharaoh left their trembling coast,
Then bade the deep in wild commotion flow,
And heaved an ocean on their march below?
Departed spirits of the mighty dead!
Ye that at Marathon and Leuctra bled!
Friends of the world, restore your swords to man,
Fight in his sacred cause, and lead the van!
Yet for Sarmatia's tears of blood atone,
And make her arm puissant as your own!
Oh, once again to freedom's cause return
The patriot Tell—the Bruce of Bannockburn!

Yes, thy proud lords, unpitied land, shall see
That man hath yet a soul—and dare be free!
A little while, along thy saddening plains,
The starless night of desolation reigns.
Truth shall restore the light by nature given,
And, like Prometheus, bring the fire of Heaven.
Prone to the dust oppression shall be hurled,
Her name, her nature, withered from the world.
Ye that the rising morn invidious mark,
And hate the light—because your deeds are dark;
Ye that expanding truth invidious view,
And think, or wish, the song of Hope untrue—
Perhaps your little hands presume to span
The march of genius, and the powers of man;
Perhaps ye watch, at pride's unhallowed shrine,
Her victims, newly slain, and thus divine—
"Here shall thy triumph, Genius, cease, and here
Truth, science, virtue, close your short career."
Tyrants! in vain ye trace the wizard ring;
In vain ye limit mind's unwearied spring:
What, can ye lull the winged winds asleep,
Arrest the rolling world, or chain the deep?
No!—the wild wave contemns your sceptered hand;
It rolled not back when Canute gave command.
Man, can thy doom no brighter soul allow?
Still must thou live a blot on nature's brow?
Shall war's polluted banner ne'er be furled?
Shall crimes and tyrants cease but with the world?
What! are thy triumphs, sacred truth, belied?
Why then hath Plato lived—or Sydney died?
Ye fond adorers of departed fame,
Who warm at Scipio's worth, or Tully's name!
Ye that, in fancied vision, can admire
The sword of Brutus, and the Theban lyre,
Rapt in historic ardor, who adore
Each classic haunt, and well-remembered shore,
Where valor tuned, amid her chosen throng,
The Thracian trumpet and the Spartan song;
Or, wandering thence, behold the later charms
Of England's glory, and Helvetia's arms!
See Roman fire in Hampden's bosom swell,
And fate and freedom in the shaft of Tell!
Say, ye fond zealots to the worth of yore,
Hath valor left the world—-to live no more?
No more shall Brutus bid a tyrant die,
And sternly smile with vengeance in his eye?
Hampden no more, when suffering Freedom calls,
Encounter Fate, and triumph as he falls?
Nor Tell disclose, through peril and alarm,
The might that slumbers in a peasant's arm.

Yes! in that generous cause for ever strong,
The patriot's virtue and the poet's song,

Still, as the tide of ages rolls away,
Shall charm the world, unconscious of decay.
Yes! there are hearts, prophetic Hope may trust,
That slumber yet in uncreated dust,
Ordained to fire the adoring sons of earth
With every charm of wisdom and of worth;
Ordained to light, with intellectual day,
The mazy wheels of nature as they play,
Or, warm with fancy's energy, to glow,
And rival all but Shakespeare's name below!
And say, supernal powers! who deeply scan
Heaven's dark decrees, unfathomed yet by man,
When shall the world call down, to cleanse her shame,
That embryo spirit, yet without name,—
That friend of nature, whose avenging hands
Shall burst the Libyan's adamantine bands?
Who, sternly marking on his native soil
The blood, the tears, the anguish, and the toil,
Shall bid each righteous heart exult, to see
Peace to the slave, and vengeance on the free!

Yet, yet, degraded men, the expected day
That breaks your bitter cup is far away;
Trade, wealth, and fashion, ask you still to bleed,
And holy men give Scripture for the deed;
Scourged and debased, no Briton stoops to save
A wretch, a coward; yes, because a slave!
Eternal nature, when thy giant hand
Had heaved the floods, and fixed the trembling land,
When life sprung startling at thy plastic call,
Endless her forms, and man the lord of all!
Say, was that lordly form inspired by thee
To wear eternal chains and bow the knee?
Was man ordained the slave of man to toil,
Yoked with the brutes, and fettered to the soil;
Weighed in a tyrant's balance with his gold?
No!—nature stamped us in a heavenly mold!
She bade no wretch his thankless labor urge,
Nor, trembling, take the pittance and the scourge.
No homeless Libyan, on the stormy deep,
To call upon his country's name, and weep!

Lo, once in triumph on his boundless plain,
The quivered chief of Congo loved to reign;
With fires proportioned to his native sky,
Strength in his arm, and lightning in his eye;
Scoured with wild feet his sun-illumined zone,
The spear, the lion, and the woods his own,
Or led the combat, bold without a plan,
An artless savage, but a fearless man!
The plunderer came!—alas, no glory smiles
For Congo's chief on yonder Indian isles;
For ever fallen! no son of nature now,

With freedom chartered on his manly brow!
Faint, bleeding, bound, he weeps the night away,
And, when the sea-wind wafts the dewless day,
Starts, with a bursting heart, for evermore
To curse the sun that lights their guilty shore.
The shrill horn blew; at that alarum knell
His guardian angel took a last farewell.
That funeral dirge to darkness hath resigned
The fiery grandeur of a generous mind.
Poor fettered man, I hear thee whispering low
Unhallowed vows to guilt, the child of woe.
Friendless thy heart; and canst thou harbor there
A wish but death—-a passion but despair?
The widowed Indian, when her lord expires,
Mounts the dread pile, and braves the funeral fires.
So falls the heart at thralldom's bitter sigh.
So virtue dies, the spouse of liberty!

But not to Libya's barren climes alone,
To Chili, or the wild Siberian zone,
Belong the wretched heart and haggard eye,
Degraded worth, and poor misfortune's sigh.
Ye orient realms, where Ganges' waters run,
Prolific fields, dominions of the sun,
How long your tribes have trembled and obeyed!
How long was Timour's iron scepter swayed!
Whose marshaled hosts, the lions of the plain,
From Scythia's northern mountains to the main,
Raged oer your plundered shrines and altars bare,
With blazing torch and gory scimitar,
Stunned with the cries of death each gentle gale,
And bathed in blood the verdure of the vale!
Yet could no pangs the immortal spirit tame,
When Brama's children perished for his name;
The martyr smiled beneath avenging power,
And braved the tyrant in his torturing hour!
When Europe sought your subject realms to gain,
And stretched her giant scepter oer the main,
Taught her proud barks their winding way to shape,
And braved the stormy spirit of the Cape;
Children of Brama, then was mercy nigh
To wash the stain of blood's eternal dye?
Did peace descend, to triumph and to save
When freeborn Britons crossed the Indian wave?
Ah, no!—to more than Rome's ambition true,
The nurse of freedom gave it not to you.
She the bold route of Europe's guilt began,
And, in the march of nations, led the van.
Rich in the gems of India's gaudy zone
And plunder piled from kingdoms not their own,
Degenerate trade, thy minions could despise
The heart-born anguish of a thousand cries;
Could lock, with impious hands, their teeming store,

While famished nations died along the shore;
Could mock the groans of fellow men, and bear
The curse of kingdoms peopled with despair;
Could stamp disgrace on man's polluted name,
And barter, with their gold, eternal shame!

But hark! as bowed to earth the Bramin kneels,
From heavenly climes propitious thunder peals.
Of India's fate her guardian spirits tell,
Prophetic murmurs breathing on the shell,
And solemn sounds that awe the listening mind,
Roll on the azure paths of every wind.
"Foes of mankind!" her guardian spirits say,
"Revolving ages bring the bitter day,
When Heaven's unerring arm shall fall on you,
And blood for blood these Indian plains bedew;
Nine times have Brama's wheels of lightning hurled
His awful presence oer the alarmed world;
Nine times hath guilt, through all his giant frame,
Convulsive trembled, as the mighty came;
Nine times hath suffering mercy spared in vain.
But Heaven shall burst her starry gates again!
He comes! dread Brama shakes the sunless sky
With murmuring wrath, and thunders from on high;
Heaven's fiery horse, beneath his warrior form,
Paws the light clouds, and gallops on the storm!
Wide waves his flickering sword; his bright arms glow
Like summer suns, and light the world below.
Earth, and her trembling isles in Ocean's bed
Are shook, and nature rocks beneath his tread
To pour redress on India's injured realm,
The oppressor to dethrone, the proud to whelm;
To chase destruction from her plundered shore
With arts and arms that triumphed once before,
The tenth Avatar comes! at Heaven's command
Shall Seriswattee wave her hallowed wand!
And Camdeo bright, and Ganesa sublime,
Shall bless with joy their own propitious clime!
Come, Heavenly Powers! primeval peace restore!
Love!—mercy!—wisdom!—rule for evermore!"

### Part II

In joyous youth, what soul hath never known
Thought, feeling, taste, harmonious to its own?
Who hath not paused while beauty's pensive eye
Asked from his heart the homage of a sigh?
Who hath not owned, with rapture-smitten frame,
The power of grace, the magic of a name?
There be, perhaps, who barren hearts avow,
Cold as the rocks on Torneo's hoary brow;
There be whose loveless wisdom never failed
In self-adoring pride securely mailed;
But triumph not ye peace-enamored few!

Fire, nature, genius never dwelt with you.
For you no fancy consecrates the scene
Where rapture uttered vows and wept between.
Tis yours unmoved to sever and to meet;
No pledge is sacred and no home is sweet!
Who that would ask a heart to dullness wed
The waveless calm, the slumber of the dead?
No, the wild bliss of nature needs alloy,
And fear and sorrow fan the fire of joy;
And say, without our hopes, without our fears,
Without the home that plighted love endears,
Without the smile from partial beauty won
Oh, what were man?—a world without a sun!
Till Hymen brought his love-delighted hour
There dwelt no joy in Eden's rosy bower!
In vain the viewless seraph lingering there
At starry midnight charmed the silent air;
In vain the wild bird caroled on the steep
To hail the sun slow wheeling from the deep;
In vain to soothe the solitary shade
Aerial notes in mingling measure played.
The summer wind that shook the spangled tree
The whispering wave, the murmur of the bee;
Still slowly passed the melancholy day;
And still the stranger wist not where to stray;
The world was sad! the garden was a wild;
And man the hermit sighed—till woman smiled.
True the sad power to generous hearts may bring
Delirious anguish on his fiery wing—
Barred from delight by fate's untimely hand,
By wealthless lot or pitiless command;
Or doomed to gaze on beauties that adorn
The smile of triumph or the frown of scorn;
While memory watches oer the sad review,
Of joys that faded like the morning dew.
Peace may depart; and life and nature seem
A barren path, a wildness, and a dream!
But can the noble mind for ever brood,
The willing victim of a weary mood,
On heartless cares that squander life away,
And cloud young genius brightening into day?
Shame to the coward thought that e'er betrayed
The noon of manhood to a myrtle shade!
If hope's creative spirit cannot raise
One trophy sacred to thy future days,
Scorn the dull crowd that haunt the gloomy shrine
Of hopeless love to murmur and repine!
But, should a sigh of milder mood express
Thy heart-warm wishes, true to happiness;
Should Heaven's fair harbinger delight to pour
Her blissful visions on thy pensive hour,
No tear to blot thy memory's pictured page,
No fears but such as fancy can assuage;

Though thy wild heart some hapless hour may miss
The peaceful tenor of unvaried bliss
(For love pursues an ever-devious race,
True to the winding lineaments of grace),—
Yet still may Hope her talisman employ
To snatch from Heaven anticipated joy,
And all her kindred energies impart
That burn the brightest in the purest heart.
When first the Rhodian's mimic art arrayed
The queen of beauty in her Cyprian shade,
The happy master mingled on his piece
Each look that charmed him in the fair of Greece:
To faultless nature true, he stole a grace
From every finer form and sweeter face;
And, as he sojourned on the Aegean isles,
Wooed all their love, and treasured all their smiles;
Then glowed the tints, pure, precious, and refined,
And mortal charms seemed heavenly when combined.
Love on the picture smiled! Expression poured
Her mingling spirit there—and Greece adored!
So thy fair hand, enamored fancy, gleans
The treasured pictures of a thousand scenes.
Thy pencil traces on the lover's thought
Some cottage-home, from towns and toil remote,
Where love and lore may claim alternate hours,
With peace embosomed in Idalian bowers.
Remote from busy life's bewildered way,
Oer all his heart shall taste and beauty sway.
Free on the sunny slope, or winding shore,
With hermit steps to wander and adore,
There shall he love, when genial morn appears,
Like pensive beauty smiling in her tears,
To watch the brightening roses of the sky,
And muse on nature with a poet's eye.
And when the sun's last splendor lights the deep,
The woods and waves, and murmuring winds asleep;
When fairy harps the Hesperian planet hail,
And the lone cuckoo sighs along the vale,—
His path shall be where streamy mountains swell
Their shadowy grandeur oer the narrow dell,
Where moldering piles and forests intervene,
Mingling with darker tints the living green,—
No circling hills his ravished eye to bound,
Heaven, Earth, and Ocean, blazing all around.
The moon is up—the watchtower dimly burns—
And down the vale his sober step returns;
But pauses oft, as winding rocks convey
The still sweet fall of music far away;
And oft he lingers from his home awhile
To watch the dying notes!—and start, and smile.

Let Winter come! let polar spirits sweep
The darkening world and tempest-troubled deep!

Though boundless snows the withered heath deform,
And the dim sun scarce wanders through the storm,
Yet shall the smile of social love repay
With mental light the melancholy day!
And, when its short and sullen noon is oer,
The ice-chained waters slumbering on the shore,
How bright the faggots in his little hall
Blaze on the hearth, and warm the pictured wall.
How blest he names, in love's familiar tone,
The kind fair friend, by nature marked his own;
And, in the waveless mirror of his mind,
Views the fleet years of pleasure left behind,
Since Anna's empire oer his heart began;
Since first he called her his before the holy man.
Trim the gay taper in his rustic dome,
And light the wintry paradise of home.
And let the half-uncurtained window hail
Some way-worn man benighted in the vale.
Now, while the moaning night-wind rages high,
As sweep the shot-stars down the troubled sky,
While fiery hosts in Heaven's wide circle play,
And bathe in lurid light the milky-way,
Safe from the storm, the meteor, and the shower,
Some pleasing page shall charm the solemn hour—-
With pathos shall command, and wit beguile,
A generous tear of anguish, or a smile;
Thy woes, Arion, and thy simple tale,
Oer all the heart shall triumph and prevail.
Charmed as they read the verse too sadly true,
How gallant Albert and his weary crew[1]
Heaved all their guns, their foundering bark to save,
And toiled—and shrieked—and perished on the wave.
Yes, at the dead of night, by Lonna's steep,
The seaman's cry was heard along the deep;
There, on his funeral waters, dark and wild,
The dying father blessed his darling child.
"Oh, Mercy, shield her innocence," he cried,
Spent on the prayer his bursting heart, and died.
Or they will learn how generous worth sublimes
The robber Moor, and pleads for all his crimes;
How poor Amelia kissed, with many a tear,
His hand blood-stained, but ever, ever dear,
Hung on the tortured bosom of her lord,
And wept, and prayed perdition from his sword.
Nor sought in vain! At that heart-piercing cry
The strings of nature cracked with agony.
He, with delirious laugh, the dagger hurled,
And burst the ties that bound him to the world.
Turn from his dying words, that smite with steel
The shuddering thoughts, or wind them on the wheel;

---

[1]From William Falconer's *Shipwreck* (1762).

Turn to the gentler melodies that suit
Thalia's harp, or Pan's Arcadian lute;
Or, down the stream of truth's historic page
From clime to clime descend, from age to age.
Yet there, perhaps, may darker scenes obtrude
Than fancy fashions in her wildest mood;
There shall he pause with horrent brow, to rate
What millions died—-that Caesar might be great!
Or learn the fate that bleeding thousands bore,
Marched by their Charles to Dneiper's swampy shore:
Faint in his wounds, and shivering in the blast
The Swedish soldier sunk—and groaned his last.
File after file the stormy showers benumb,
Freeze every standard-sheet, and hush the drum.
Horseman and horse confessed the bitter pang,
And arms and warriors fell with hollow clang.
Yet, ere he sunk in nature's last repose,
Ere life's warm torrent to the fountain froze,
The dying man to Sweden turned his eye,
Thought of his home, and closed it with a sigh.
Imperial pride looked sullen on his plight,
And Charles beheld—-nor shuddered at the sight.

Above, below, in Ocean, Earth, and Sky,
Thy fairy worlds, imagination, lie,
And Hope attends, companion of the way,
Thy dream by night, thy visions of the day!
In yonder pensile orb, and every sphere
That gems the starry girdle of the year;
In those unmeasured worlds, she bids thee tell,
Pure from their God, created millions dwell,
Whose names and natures, unrevealed below,
We yet shall learn, and wonder as we know;
For, as Iona's saint, a giant form,
Throned on her towers, conversing with the storm
(When oer each runic altar, weed-entwined,
The vesper clock tolls mournful to the wind),
Counts every wave-worn isle and mountain hoar
From Kilda to the green Ierne's shore;
So, when thy pure and renovated mind
This perishable dust hath left behind,
Thy seraph eye shall count the starry train
Like distant isles embosomed in the main,—
Rapt to the shrine where motion first began,
And light and life in mingling torrents ran,
From whence each bright rotundity was hurled,
The throne of God,—the center of the world.

Oh, vainly wise, the moral Muse hath sung
That suasive Hope hath but a siren tongue.
True; she may sport with life's untutored day,
Nor heed the solace of its last decay,
The guileless heart her happy mansion spurn,

And part like Ajut—never to return.
But yet, methinks, when wisdom shall assuage
The griefs and passions of our greener age,
Though dull the close of life, and far away
Each flower that hailed the dawning of the day;
Yet oer her lovely hopes, that once were dear,
The time-taught spirit, pensive, not severe,
With milder griefs her aged eye shall fill,
And weep their falsehood, though she love them still.
Thus, with forgiving tears, and reconciled,
The king of Judah mourned his rebel child,
Musing on days, when yet the guiltless boy
Smiled on his sire, and filled his heart with joy.
"My Absalom!" the voice of nature cried:
"Oh, that for thee thy father could have died;
For bloody was the deed, and rashly done,
That slew my Absalom!—my son!—my son!"

Unfading Hope! when life's last embers burn,
When soul to soul, and dust to dust return,
Heaven to thy charge resigns the awful hour;
Oh, then thy kingdom comes, immortal power.
What though each spark of earth-born rapture fly
The quivering lip, pale cheek, and closing eye.
Bright to the soul thy seraph hands convey
The morning dream of life's eternal day—-
Then, then, the triumph and the trance begin,
And all the phoenix spirit burns within!

Oh! deep-enchanting prelude to repose,
The dawn of bliss, the twilight of our woes!
Yet half I hear the panting spirit sigh,
It is a dread and awful thing to die—
Mysterious worlds, untraveled by the sun!
Where time's far-wandering tide has never run,
From your unfathomed shades and viewless spheres
A warning comes, unheard by other ears.
Tis Heaven's commanding trumpet, long and loud,
Like Sinai's thunder, pealing from the cloud,
While nature hears, with terror-mingled trust,
The shock that hurls her fabric to the dust;
And, like the trembling Hebrew, when he trod
The roaring waves, and called upon his God,
With mortal terrors clouds immortal bliss,
And shrieks, and hovers oer the dark abyss.

Daughter of faith, awake, arise, illume
The dread unknown, the chaos of the tomb.
Melt, and dispel, ye specter-doubts, that roll
Cimmerian darkness on the parting soul.
Fly, like the moon-eyed herald of dismay,
Chased on his night-steed by the star of day.
The strife is oer—the pangs of nature close,

And life's last rapture triumphs oer her woes.
Hark, as the spirit eyes, with eagle gaze,
The noon of Heaven undazzled by the blaze,
On heavenly winds that waft her to the sky,
Float the sweet tones of star-born melody;
Wild as that hallowed anthem sent to hail
Bethlehem's shepherds in the lonely vale,
When Jordan hushed his waves, and midnight still
Watched on the holy towers of Zion hill!
Soul of the just! companion of the dead!
Where is thy home, and whither art thou fled?
Back to its heavenly source thy being goes,
Swift as the comet wheels to whence he rose;
Doomed on his airy path awhile to burn,
And doomed, like thee, to travel, and return.
Hark, from the world's exploding center driven,
With sounds that shook the firmament of Heaven,
Careers the fiery giant, fast and far,
On bickering wheels, and adamantine car;
From planet whirled to planet more remote,
He visits realms beyond the reach of thought,
But wheeling homeward, when his course is run,
Curbs the red yoke, and mingles with the sun.
So hath the traveler of earth unfurled
Her trembling wings, emerging from the world;
And oer the path by mortal never trod,
Sprung to her source, the bosom of her God.

Oh, lives there, Heaven, beneath thy dread expanse,
One hopeless, dark idolater of chance,
Content to feed, with pleasures unrefined,
The lukewarm passions of a lowly mind;
Who, moldering earthward, reft of every trust,
In joyless union wedded to the dust,
Could all his parting energy dismiss,
And call this barren world sufficient bliss?
There live, alas, of heaven-directed mien,
Of cultured soul, and sapient eye serene,
Who hail thee, Man, the pilgrim of a day,
Spouse of the worm, and brother of the clay,
Frail as a leaf in Autumn's yellow bower,
Dust in the wind, or dew upon the flower;
A friendless slave, a child without a sire,
Whose mortal life and momentary fire
Lights to the grave his chance-created form,
As ocean-wreaks illuminate the storm,
And, when the gun's tremendous flash is oer,
To night and silence sink for evermore.

Are these the pompous tidings ye proclaim,
Lights of the world, and demi-gods of Fame?
Is this your triumph—this your proud applause,
Children of truth, and champions of her cause?

For this hath science searched on weary wing
By shore and sea each mute and living thing?
Launched with Iberia's pilot from the steep,
To worlds unknown, and isles beyond the deep?
Or round the cope her living chariot driven,
And wheeled in triumph through the signs of Heaven?
Oh! star-eyed science, hast thou wandered there,
To waft us home the message of despair?
Then bind the palm, thy sage's brow to suit,
Of blasted leaf, and death-distilling fruit!
Ah me! the laureled wreath that murder rears,
Blood-nursed, and watered by the widow's tears,
Seems not so foul, so tainted, and so dread,
As waves the night-shade round the skeptic's head.
What is the bigot's torch, the tyrant's chain?
I smile on death, if heavenward Hope remain!
But, if the warring winds of nature's strife
Be all the faithless charter of my life,
If chance awaked, inexorable power,
This frail and feverish being of an hour,
Doomed oer the world's precarious scene to sweep,
Swift as the tempest travels on the deep,
To know delight but by her parting smile,
And toil, and wish, and weep a little while;
Then melt, ye elements, that formed in vain
This troubled pulse, and visionary brain.
Fade, ye wild flowers, memorials of my doom,
And sink, ye stars, that light me to the tomb.
Truth, ever lovely,—since the world began
The foe of tyrants, and the friend of man,—
How can thy words from balmy slumber start
Reposing virtue, pillowed on the heart?
Yet, if thy voice the note of thunder rolled,
And that were true which nature never told,
Let wisdom smile not on her conquered field;
No rapture dawns, no treasure is revealed.
Oh, let her read, nor loudly, nor elate,
The doom that bars us from a better fate;
But, sad as angels for the good man's sin,
Weep to record, and blush to give it in!
And well may doubt, the mother of dismay,
Pause at her martyr's tomb, and read the lay.
Down by the wilds of yon deserted vale
It darkly hints a melancholy tale.
There, as the homeless madman sits alone,
In hollow winds he hears a spirit moan.
And there, they say, a wizard orgie crowds,
When the moon lights her watch-tower in the clouds.
Poor lost Alonzo, fate's neglected child.
Mild be the doom of Heaven—as thou wert mild.
For oh, thy heart in holy mold was cast,
And all thy deeds were blameless, but the last.
Poor lost Alonzo! still I seem to hear

The clod that struck thy hollow-sounding bier!
When Friendship paid, in speechless sorrow drowned,
Thy midnight rites, but not on hallowed ground!

Cease, every joy, to glimmer on my mind,
But leave, oh leave the light of Hope behind.
What though my winged hours of bliss have been,
Like angel-visits, few and far between?
Her musing mood shall every pang appease,
And charm—-when pleasures lose the power to please.
Yes, let each rapture, dear to nature, flee;
Close not the light of fortune's stormy sea—
Mirth, music, friendship, love's propitious smile,
Chase every care, and charm a little while,
Ecstatic throbs the fluttering heart employ,
And all her strings are harmonized to joy.
But why so short is love's delighted hour?
Why fades the dew on beauty's sweetest flower?
Why can no hymned charm of music heal
The sleepless woes impassioned spirits feel?
Can fancy's fairy hands no veil create,
To hide the sad realities of fate?
No, not the quaint remark, the sapient rule,
Nor all the pride of wisdom's worldly school
Have power to soothe, unaided and alone,
The heart that vibrates to a feeling tone.
When stepdame nature every bliss recalls,
Fleet as the meteor oer the desert falls;
When, reft of all, yon widowed sire appears
A lonely hermit in the vale of years;
Say, can the world one joyous thought bestow
To friendship weeping at the couch of woe?
No! but a brighter soothes the last adieu,—
Souls of impassioned mold, she speaks to you!
"Weep not," she says, "at Nature's transient pain;
Congenial spirits part to meet again."

What plaintive sobs thy filial spirit drew,
What sorrow choked thy long and last adieu,
Daughter of Conrad! when he heard his knell,
And bade his country and his child farewell.
Doomed the long isles of Sydney Cove to see,
The martyr of his crimes, but true to thee.
Thrice the sad father tore thee from his heart,
And thrice returned, to bless thee, and to part;
Thrice from his trembling lips he murmured low
The plaint that owned unutterable woe;
Till faith, prevailing oer his sullen doom,
As bursts the morn on night's unfathomed gloom,
Lured his dim eye to deathless hopes sublime,
Beyond the realms of nature and of time.
"And weep not thus," he cried, "young Ellenore;
My bosom bleeds, but soon shall bleed no more.

Short shall this half-extinguished spirit burn,
And soon these limbs to kindred dust return.
But not, my child, with life's precarious fire,
The immortal ties of nature shall expire;
These shall resist the triumph of decay,
When time is oer, and worlds have passed away.
Cold in the dust this perished heart may lie,
But that which warmed it once shall never die.
That spark unburied in its mortal frame,
With living light, eternal, and the same,
Shall beam on joy's interminable years,
Unveiled by darkness, unassuaged by tears.
Yet, on the barren shore and stormy deep,
One tedious watch is Conrad doomed to weep;
But when I gain the home without a friend,
And press the uneasy couch where none attend,
This last embrace, still cherished in my heart,
Shall calm the struggling spirit ere it part;
Thy darling form shall seem to hover nigh,
And hush the groan of life's last agony!
Farewell! when strangers lift thy father's bier,
And place my nameless stone without a tear;
When each returning pledge hath told my child
That Conrad's tomb is on the desert piled;
And when the dream of troubled fancy sees
Its lonely rank-grass waving in the breeze;
Who then will soothe thy grief, when mine is oer?
Who will protect thee, helpless Ellenore?
Shall secret scenes thy filial sorrows hide,
Scorned by the world, to factious guilt allied?
Ah, no; methinks the generous and the good
Will woo thee from the shades of solitude.
Oer friendless grief compassion shall awake,
And smile on innocence, for mercy's sake."

Inspiring thought of rapture yet to be,
The tears of love were hopeless, but for thee.
If in that frame no deathless spirit dwell,
If that faint murmur be the last farewell,
If fate unite the faithful but to part,
Why is their memory sacred to the heart?
Why does the brother of my childhood seem
Restored awhile in every pleasing dream?
Why do I joy the lonely spot to view,
By artless friendship blessed when life was new?
Eternal Hope! when yonder spheres sublime
Pealed their first notes to sound the march of time,
Thy joyous youth began—but not to fade.
When all the sister planets have decayed,
When wrapt in fire the realms of ether glow,
And Heaven's last thunder shakes the world below,
Thou, undismayed, shalt oer the ruin smile,
And light thy torch at nature's funeral pile.

## Florine

Could I bring back lost youth again
And be what I have been,
I'd court you in a gallant strain,
My young and fair Florine.
But mine's the chilling age that chides
Devoted rapture's glow,
And Love—that conquers all besides—
Finds Time a conquering foe.

Farewell. We're severed by our fate
As far as night from noon;
You came into the world too late,
And I depart so soon.

## Lochiel's Warning[1]

WIZARD

Lochiel, Lochiel! beware of the day
When the lowlands shall meet thee in battle array.
For a field of the dead rushes red on my sight,
And the clans of Culloden are scattered in fight.
They rally, they bleed, for their kingdom and crown;
Woe, woe to the riders that trample them down.
Proud Cumberland[2] prances, insulting the slain,
And their hoof-beaten bosoms are trod to the plain.
But hark, through the fast-flashing lightning of war,
What steed to the desert flies frantic and far?
Tis thine, oh Glenullin, whose bride shall await,
Like a love-lighted watch-fire, all night at the gate.
A steed comes at morning: no rider is there;
But its bridle is red with the sign of despair.
Weep, Albin, to death and captivity led.
Oh weep, but thy tears cannot number the dead:
For a merciless sword on Culloden shall wave,
Culloden, that reeks with the blood of the brave.

LOCHIEL

Go, preach to the coward, thou death-telling seer.
Or, if gory Culloden so dreadful appear,
Draw, dotard, around thy old wavering sight
This mantle, to cover the phantoms of fright.

WIZARD

Ha! laugh'st thou, Lochiel, my vision to scorn?
Proud bird of the mountain, thy plume shall be torn.
Say, rushed the bold eagle exultingly forth,

---

[1]Lochiel is Donald Cameron, a Highland chief. Fighting in the Jacobite cause, he was wounded at Culloden, fled to France, and died there in 1748.

[2]The Duke of Cumberland, a son of George II, and the ruthless victor at Culloden.

From his home, in the dark, rolling clouds of the north?
Lo, the death-shot of foemen outspeeding, he rode
Companionless, bearing destruction abroad;
But down let him stoop from his havoc on high.
Ah, home let him speed, for the spoiler is nigh.
Why flames the far summit? Why shoot to the blast
Those embers, like stars from the firmament cast?
Tis the fire-shower of ruin, all dreadfully driven
From his eyrie, that beacons the darkness of heaven.
Oh, crested Lochiel, the peerless in might,
Whose banners arise on the battlements' height,
Heaven's fire is around thee, to blast and to burn;
Return to thy dwelling, all lonely return.
For the blackness of ashes shall mark where it stood,
And a wild mother scream oer her famishing brood.

LOCHIEL

False Wizard, avaunt! I have marshaled my clan,
Their swords are a thousand, their bosoms are one.
They are true to the last of their blood and their breath,
And like reapers descend to the harvest of death.
Then welcome be Cumberland's steed to the shock.
Let him dash his proud foam like a wave on the rock.
But woe to his kindred, and woe to his cause,
When Albin her claymore indignantly draws;
When her bonneted chieftains to victory crowd,
Clanronald the dauntless, and Moray the proud,
All plaided and plumed in their tartan array—

WIZARD

Lochiel, Lochiel, beware of the day;
For, dark and despairing, my sight I may seal,
But man cannot cover what God would reveal;
Tis the sunset of life gives me mystical lore,
And coming events cast their shadows before.
I tell thee, Culloden's dread echoes shall ring
With the bloodhounds that bark for thy fugitive king.
Lo! anointed by Heaven with the vials of wrath,
Behold, where he flies on his desolate path.
Now in darkness and billows, he sweeps from my sight:
Rise, rise, ye wild tempests, and cover his flight.
Tis finished. Their thunders are hushed on the moors:
Culloden is lost, and my country deplores.
But where is the iron-bound prisoner? Where?
For the red eye of battle is shut in despair.
Say, mounts he the ocean-wave, banished, forlorn,
Like a limb from his country cast bleeding and torn?
Ah no, for a darker departure is near;
The war-drum is muffled, and black is the bier;
His death-bell is tolling: oh, mercy, dispel
Yon sight, that it freezes my spirit to tell.
Life flutters convulsed in his quivering limbs,
And his blood-streaming nostril in agony swims.

Accursed be the fagots, that blaze at his feet,
Where his heart shall be thrown, ere it ceases to beat,
With the smoke of its ashes to poison the gale—

LOCHIEL

Down, soothless insulter. I trust not the tale:
For never shall Albin a destiny meet,
So black with dishonor, so foul with retreat.
Though my perishing ranks should be strewed in their gore,
Like ocean-weeds heaped on the surf-beaten shore,
Lochiel, untainted by flight or by chains,
While the kindling of life in his bosom remains,
Shall victor exult, or in death be laid low,
With his back to the field, and his feet to the foe.
And leaving in battle no blot on his name,
Look proudly to Heaven from the death-bed of fame.

## Lord Ullin's Daughter

A chieftain to the Highlands bound
Cries "Boatman, do not tarry!
And I'll give thee a silver pound
To row us oer the ferry."

"Now who be ye would cross Lochgyle,
This dark and stormy water?"
"O, I'm the chief of Ulva's isle,
And this Lord Ullin's daughter.

"And fast before her father's men
Three days we've fled together,
For, should he find us in the glen,
My blood would stain the heather.

"His horsemen hard behind us ride;
Should they our steps discover,
Then who will cheer my bonny bride
When they have slain her lover?"

Outspoke the hardy Highland wight,
"I'll go, my chief! I'm ready.
It is not for your silver bright,
But for your winsome lady.

"And, by my word, the bonny bird
In danger shall not tarry;
So, though the waves are raging white
I'll row you oer the ferry."

By this the storm grew loud apace,
The water-wraith was shrieking;

And in the scowl of heaven each face
Grew dark as they were speaking.

But still, as wilder blew the wind,
And as the night grew drearer,
Adown the glen rode armed men—
Their trampling sounded nearer.

"O haste thee, haste!" the lady cries,
"Though tempests round us gather;
I'll meet the raging of the skies,
But not an angry father."

The boat has left a stormy land,
A stormy sea before her,—
When oh, too strong for human hand,
The tempest gathered oer her.

And still they rowed amidst the roar
Of waters fast prevailing;
Lord Ullin reached that fatal shore,—
His wrath was changed to wailing.

For sore dismayed, through storm and shade,
His child he did discover.
One lovely hand she stretched for aid,
And one was round her lover.

"Come back! Come back!" he cried in grief
Across the stormy water:
"And I'll forgive your Highland chief,
My daughter, oh my daughter."

Twas vain. The loud waves lashed the shore,
Return or aid preventing.
The waters wild went oer his child,
And he was left lamenting.

## Earl March

Earl March looked on his dying child,
And, smit with grief to view her—
"The youth," he cried, "whom I exiled
Shall be restored to woo her."

She's at the window many an hour
His coming to discover;
And her love looked up to Ellen's bower,
And she looked on her lover—

But ah, so pale, he knew her not,
Though her smile on him was dwelling.

"And am I then forgot—forgot?"—
It broke the heart of Ellen.

In vain he weeps, in vain he sighs.
Her cheek is cold as ashes.
Nor love's own kiss shall wake those eyes
To lift their silken lashes.

## Glenara

O heard ye yon pibroch sound sad in the gale,
Where a band cometh slowly with weeping and wail?
Tis the chief of Glenara laments for his dear;
And her sire, and the people, are called to her bier.

Glenara came first with the mourners and shroud;
Her kinsmen they followed, but mourned not aloud:
Their plaids all their bosoms were folded around;
They marched all in silence,—they looked on the ground.

In silence they reached over mountain and moor,
To a heath, where the oak-tree grew lonely and hoar:
"Now here let us place the gray stone of her cairn:
Why speak ye no word?"—said Glenara the stern.

"And tell me, I charge you, ye clan of my spouse,
Why fold ye your mantles, why cloud ye your brows?"
So spake the rude chieftain:—no answer is made,
But each mantle unfolding, a dagger displayed.

"I dreamt of my lady, I dreamt of her shroud,"
Cried a voice from the kinsmen, all wrathful and loud;
"And empty that shroud and that coffin did seem:
Glenara! Glenara! now read* me my dream." (explain)

O pale grew the cheek of that chieftain, I ween,
When the shroud was unclosed, and no lady was seen;
When a voice from the kinsmen spoke louder in scorn,
Twas the youth who had loved the fair Ellen of Lorn:

"I dreamt of my lady, I dreamt of her grief,
I dreamt that her lord was a barbarous chief:
On a rock of the ocean fair Ellen did seem:
Glenara! Glenara! now read me my dream."

In dust, low the traitor has knelt to the ground,
And the desert revealed where his lady was found:
From a rock of the ocean that beauty is borne—
Now joy to the house of fair Ellen of Lorn.

## Lines Written on Visiting a Scene in Argyleshire

At the silence of twilight's contemplative hour,
I have mused in a sorrowful mood,
On the wind-shaken weeds that embosom the bower,
Where the home of my forefathers stood.
All ruined and wild is their roofless abode,
And lonely the dark raven's sheltering tree:
And traveled by few is the grass-covered road,
Where the hunter of deer and the warrior trode,
To his hills that encircle the sea.

Yet wandering, I found on my ruinous walk,
By the dial-stone aged and green,
One rose of the wilderness left on its stalk,
To mark where a garden had been:
Like a brotherless hermit, the last of its race,
All wild in the silence of nature, it drew,
From each wandering sun-beam, a lonely embrace,
For the night-weed and thorn overshadowed the place,
Where the flower of my forefathers grew.

Sweet bud of the wilderness, emblem of all
That remains in this desolate heart.
The fabric of bliss to its center may fall,
But patience shall never depart.
Though the wilds of enchantment, all vernal and bright,
In the days of delusion by fancy combined
With the vanishing phantoms of love and delight,
Abandon my soul, like a dream of the night,
And leave but a desert behind.

Be hushed, my dark spirit, for wisdom condemns
When the faint and the feeble deplore;
Be strong as the rock of the ocean that stems
A thousand wild waves on the shore.
Through the perils of chance, and the scowl of disdain,
May thy front be unaltered, thy courage elate.
Yea, even the name I have worshipped in vain
Shall awake not the sigh of remembrance again:
To bear is to conquer our fate.

## The Last Man

All worldly shapes shall melt in gloom,
The sun himself must die,
Before this mortal shall assume
Its immortality.
I saw a vision in my sleep,
That gave my spirit strength to sweep
Adown the gulf of time.
I saw the last of human mold

That shall creation's death behold,
As Adam saw her prime.

The sun's eye had a sickly glare,
The Earth with age was wan,
The skeletons of nations were
Around that lonely man.
Some had expired in fight—the brands
Still rusted in their bony hands,
In plague and famine some.
Earth's cities had no sound nor tread;
And ships were drifting with the dead
To shores where all was dumb.

Yet, prophet-like, that lone one stood,
With dauntless words and high,
That shook the sere leaves from the wood
As if a storm passed by,
Saying, "We are twins in death, proud sun.
Thy face is cold, thy race is run,
Tis mercy bids thee go;
For thou ten thousand thousand years
Hast seen the tide of human tears,
That shall no longer flow.

"What though beneath thee man put forth
His pomp, his pride, his skill;
And arts that made fire, flood, and earth,
The vassals of his will?
Yet mourn I not thy parted sway,
Thou dim discrowned king of day;
For all those trophied arts
And triumphs that beneath thee sprang,
Healed not a passion or a pang
Entailed on human hearts.

"Go, let oblivion's curtain fall
Upon the stage of men,
Nor with thy rising beams recall
Life's tragedy again.
Its piteous pageants bring not back,
Nor waken flesh, upon the rack
Of pain anew to writhe;
Stretched in disease's shapes abhorred,
Or mown in battle by the sword,
Like grass beneath the scythe.

"Ev'n I am weary in yon skies
To watch thy fading fire;
Test of all sumless agonies,
Behold not me expire.
My lips that speak thy dirge of death
Their rounded gasp and gurgling breath

To see thou shalt not boast.
The eclipse of nature spreads my pall,
The majesty of darkness shall
Receive my parting ghost.

"This spirit shall return to Him
Who gave its heavenly spark;
Yet think not, Sun, it shall be dim
When thou thyself art dark.
No, it shall live again, and shine
In bliss unknown to beams of thine.
By him recalled to breath,
Who captive led captivity,
Who robbed the grave of victory,
And took the sting from death.

"Go, sun, while mercy holds me up
On nature's awful waste
To drink this last and bitter cup
Of grief that man shall taste—
Go, tell the night that hides thy face,
Thou saw'st the last of Adam's race.
On Earth's sepulchral clod,
The darkening universe defy
To quench his immortality,
Or shake his trust in God."

## Ode to Winter

When first the fiery-mantled sun
His heavenly race began to run;
Round the earth and ocean blue,
His children four the Seasons flew.
First, in the green apparel dancing,
The young Spring smiled with angel grace;
Rosy Summer next advancing,
Rushed unto her sire's embrace:—
Her bright-haired sire who bade her keep
For ever nearest to his smiles,
On Calpe's olive-shaded steep,
Or India's citron-covered isles:
More remote and buxom-brown,
The Queen of vintage bowed before his throne;
A rich pomegranate gemmed her crown,
A ripe sheaf bound her zone.

But howling Winter fled afar,
To hills that prop the polar star,
And loves on deer-borne car to ride
With barren darkness by his side,
Round the shore where loud Lofoden
Whirls to death the roaring whale,

Round the hall where Runic Odin
Howls his war-song to the gale;
Save when adown the ravaged globe
He travels on his native storm,
Deflowering Nature's grassy robe,
And trampling on her faded form:—
Till light's returning lord assume
The shaft that drives him to his polar field,
Of power to pierce his raven plume
And crystal-covered shield.

Oh, sire of storms, whose savage ear
The Lapland drum delights to hear,
When Frenzy with her blood-shot eye
Implores thy dreadful deity,
Archangel! power of desolation!
Fast descending as thou art,
Say, hath mortal invocation
Spells to touch thy stony heart?
Then, sullen Winter, hear my prayer,
And gently rule the ruined year;
Nor chill the wanderer's bosom bare,
Nor freeze the wretch's falling tear;
To shuddering Want's unmantled bed
Thy horror-breathing agues cease to lend,
And gently on the orphan head
Of innocence descend.—

But chiefly spare, O king of clouds,
The sailor on his airy shrouds;
When wrecks and beacons strew the steep,
And specters walk along the deep.
Milder yet thy snowy breezes
Pour on yonder tented shores,
Where the Rhine's broad billow freezes,
Or the dark-brown Danube roars.
Oh, winds of Winter, list ye there
To many a deep and dying groan;
Or start, ye demons of the midnight air,
At shrieks and thunders louder than your own.
Alas, ev'n your unhallowed breath
May spare the victim fallen low;
But man will ask no truce to death,—
No bounds to human woe.[1]

## Field Flowers

Ye field flowers, the gardens eclipse you, tis true,
Yet, wildings of Nature, I dote upon you,
For ye waft me to summers of old,

[1] A reference to the current stages of the Napoleonic wars.

When the earth teemed around me with fairy delight,
And when daisies and buttercups gladdened my sight,
Like treasures of silver and gold.

I love you for lulling me back into dreams
Of the blue Highland mountains and echoing streams,
And of birchen glades breathing their balm,
While the deer was seen glancing in sunshine remote,
And the deep mellow cursh of the wood-pigeon's note
Made music that sweetened the calm.

Not a pastoral song has a pleasanter tune
Than ye speak to my heart, little wildings of June:
Of old ruinous castles ye tell,
Where I thought it delightful your beauties to find,
When the magic of Nature first breathed on my mind,
And your blossoms were part of her spell.

Even now what affections the violet awakes.
What loved little islands, twice seen in their lakes,
Can the wild water-lily restore.
What landscapes I read in the primrose's looks,
And what pictures of pebbled and minnowy brooks,
In the vetches that tangled their shore.

Earth's cultureless buds, to my heart ye were dear,
Ere the fever of passion, or ague of fear,
Had scathed my existence's bloom;
Once I welcome you more, in life's passionless stage,
With the visions of youth to revisit my age,
And I wish you to grow on my tomb.

## To the Evening Star

Star that bringest home the bee,
And sett'st the weary laborer free,
If any star shed peace, tis thou
That send'st it from above,
Appearing when heaven's breath and brow
Are sweet as hers we love.

Come to the luxuriant skies
Whilst the landscape's odors rise,
Whilst far-off lowing herds are heard,
And songs, when toil is done,
From cottages whose smoke unstirred
Curls yellow in the sun.

Star of love's soft interviews,
Parted lovers on thee muse.
Their remembrancer in heaven
Of thrilling vows thou art,

Too delicious to be riven
By absence from the heart.

# THE VICTORIAN AGE

In the nineteenth century, Scottish literature became famous, initially through the efforts of Walter Scott, one of the most popular and influential writers of the century. The nostalgic interest he created was furthered by a large number of Scottish writers, mostly working in either his historical vein, as with Robert Louis Stevenson, or celebrating a comfortably old-fashioned landscape of pawky shepherds, canny villagers, stubborn but good-hearted ministers and dominies.

During the century, many Scots writers either lived in England or wrote for the international market, as with Thomas Campbell, James Thomson—whose brilliant, morbid *City of Dreadful Night* is one of the major poems of the time—Andrew Lang, or Louis Stevenson himself. The major Scottish novelist aside from Scott and Stevenson was probably Margaret Oliphant whose prodigious literary output is primarily English in setting, most notably in the fine novel sequence, *The Chronicles of Carlingford*. The international success of Conan Doyle, the creator of that most English of detectives, Sherlock Holmes, affords other evidence of the Scottish writer abroad.

But a lot of other Scottish writers stayed home, at least in setting their works, as Scottish writers found a market for their particular brand of sentimental and picturesque regional literature throughout the English speaking world. Again Scott was probably the main influence, as his "Scottish homespun" characters were imitated in hundreds of novels.

John Galt was Scott's leading contemporary. Galt's *Annals of the Parish* (1821) is one of the finest small-town studies of the century. Later in the century, Galt was imitated by James Barrie, whose vastly popular sketches of Scottish village life, it is often said, led to that wave of nostalgic Scots fiction called "kailyard" (cabbage-patch).

The kailyard school is represented here by three of its more effective practitioners, John Watson ("Ian Maclaren"), Samuel Crockett, and William Black. Their short stories reflect the rusticity, and "tough-sadness" which is a cardinal feature of the genre.

The essence of the sentimental view of mankind is usually said to be the belief that all men are essentially good—thus the emphasis in sentimental fiction on reformed villains, prostitutes with hearts of gold, criminals who love their mothers, and so on. And indeed Watson, Crockett and Black reaffirm the essential decency of mankind under even the most trying of conditions (which they also love to depict). This is a view which is out of favor in our hard-boiled age; but it has been a feature of some very great literature at various times. At any rate, the kailyarders entertained and persuaded millions and they held up an image of Scotland which was terrifically influential.

As with Romanticism, that other major influence upon nineteenth century literature, Realism, was also muted in Scotland. Not one significant Scottish writer of the century may be labeled a realist, though of course realistic detail is to some degree a stock in trade of regionalists, and one finds occasional naturalistic moments in the kailyarders, in Margaret Oliphant's studies of the middle-class, and even in pages of the spiritual novelist, George Macdonald. But for the most part Scottish literature was notable, even notorious, for its love of the other states: the heroic past, the "Celtic twilight," the world of children, the ideal world, and at their least literary level, melodrama.

# JOHN GALT (1779–1839)

[John Galt, one of the finest of Scottish novelists, is best known for his stories of small-town Scottish life, especially *Annals of the Parish* (1821), one of the classics of nineteenth century literature. *The Ayrshire Legatees* (1821), and *The Entail* (1823) are other fine examples. Essentially his works are comedies of manners, satiric but usually gentle studies of life in the Provinces. His emphasis on the rustic and the quaint helped pave the way for the late nineteenth century "kailyard school" of sentimental rural sketches. A special characteristic of Galt is his preference for the ironically limited point of view—one in which a story is told by a self-satisfied narrator unaware of how much his story is revealing about himself. "The Gudewife" is such a tale, a smiling satire upon woman as domestic tyrant—the ogre seen from within.]

## The Gudewife

I am inditing the good matter of this book for the instruction of our only daughter when she comes to years of discretion, as she soon will, for her guidance when she has a house of her own, and has to deal with the kittle temper of a gudeman in so couthy a manner as to mollify his sour humour when anything out of doors troubles him. Thanks be and praise I am not ill qualified! indeed, it is a clear ordinance that I was to be of such a benefit to the world; for it would have been a strange thing if the pains taken with my education had been purposeless in the decrees of Providence.

Mr. Desker, the schoolmaster, was my father; and, as he was reckoned in his day a great teacher, and had a pleasure in opening my genie for learning, it is but reasonable to suppose that I in a certain manner profited by his lessons, and made a progress in parts of learning that do not fall often into the lot of womankind. This much it behoves me to say, for there are critical persons in the world that might think it very upsetting of one of my degree to write a book, especially a book which has for its end the bettering of the conjugal condition. If I did not tell them, as I take it upon me to do, how well I have been brought up for the work, they might look down upon my endeavors with a doubtful eye; but when they read this, they will have a new tout to their old horn and reflect with more reverence of others who may be in some things their inferiors, superiors, or equals. It would not become me to say to which of these classes I belong, though I am not without an inward admonition on that head.

It fell out, when I was in my twenties, that Mr. Thrifter came, in the words of the song of Auld Robin Gray, "a-courting to me"; and, to speak a plain matter of fact, in some points he was like that bald-headed carle.[1] For he was a man considering my juvenility, well stricken in years; besides being a bachelor, with a natural inclination (as all old bachelors have) to be dozened, and fond of his own ayes and nays. For my part, when he first came about the house, I was as dawty[2] as Jeanie—as I thought myself entitled to a young man, and did not relish the apparition of him coming in at the gloaming, when the day's darg[3] was done, and before candles were lighted. However, our lot in life is not of our own choosing. I will say—for he is still to the fore—that it could not have been thought he would have proved himself such a satisfactory gudeman as he has been. To be sure, I put my shoulder to the wheel, and likewise prayed to Jupiter; for there never was a rightful head of a family without the concurrence of his wife. These are words of wisdom that my father taught, and I put in practice.

---

[1]Person, old man.

[2]Darling.

[3]Work.

Mr. Thrifter, when he first came about me, was a bein[1] man. He had parts in two vessels, besides his own shop, and was sponsible for a nest-egg of lying money; so that he was not, though rather old, a match to be, as my father thought, discomfited with a flea in the lug[2] instanter. I therefore, according to the best advice, so comported myself that it came to pass in the course of time that we were married; and of my wedded life and experience I intend to treat in this book. Among the last words that my sagacious father said when I took upon me to be the wedded wife of Mr. Thrifter were, that a man never throve unless his wife would let, which is a text that I have not forgotten; for though in a way, and in obedience to the customs of the world, women acknowledge men as their head, yet we all know in our hearts that this is but diplomatical. Do not we see that men work for us, which shews that they are our servants? do we not see that men protect us, are they not therefore our soldiers? do we not see that they go hither and yon at our bidding, which shews that they have that within their nature that teaches them to obey? and do not we feel that we have the command of them in all things, just as they had the upper hand in the world till woman was created? No clearer proof do I want that, although in a sense for policy we call ourselves the weaker vessels—and in that very policy there is power—we know well in our hearts that, as the last made creatures, we necessarily are more perfect, and have all that was made before us, by hook or crook, under our thumb. Well does Robin Burns sing of this truth in the song where he has— *Her 'prentice hand she tried on man,/ And syne she made the lassies oh!*

Accordingly, having a proper conviction of the superiority of my sex, I was not long of making Mr. Thrifter, my gudeman, to know into what hands he had fallen, by correcting many of the bad habits of body to which he had become addicted in his bachelor loneliness. Among these was a custom that I did think ought not to be continued after he had surrendered himself into the custody of a wife, and that was an usage with him in the morning before breakfast to toast his shoes against the fender and forenent the fire. This he did not tell me till I saw it with my own eyes the morning after we were married, which, when I beheld, gave me a sore heart, because, had I known it before we were everlastingly made one, I will not say but there might have been a dubiety as to the paction; for I have ever had a natural dislike to men who toasted their shoes, thinking it was a hussie fellow's custom. However, being endowed with an instinct of prudence, I winked at it for some days; but it could not be borne any longer, and I said in a sweet manner, as it were by and by,

"Dear Mr. Thrifter, that servant lass we have gotten has not a right notion of what is a genteel way of living. Do you see how the misleart creature sets up your shoes in the inside of the fender, keeping the warmth from our feet? really I'll thole[3] this no longer; it's not a custom in a proper house. If a stranger were accidentally coming in and seeing your shoes in that situation, he would not think of me as it is well known he ought to think."

Mr. Thrifter did not say much, nor could he; for I had judiciously laid all the wyte and blame of the thing to the servant; but he said, in a diffident manner, that it was not necessary to be so particular.

"No necessary! Mr. Thrifter, what do you call a particularity, when you would say that toasting shoes is not one? It might do for you when you were a bachelor, but ye should remember that you're so no more, and it's a custom I will not allow."

"But," replied he with a smile, "I am the head of the house; and to make few

[1]Comfortable.

[2]Ear.

[3]Endure

words about it, I say, Mrs. Thrifter, I will have my shoes warmed anyhow, whether or no."

"Very right, my dear," quo I; "I'll ne'er dispute that you are the head of the house; but I think that you need not make a poor wife's life bitter by insisting on toasting your shoes."

And I gave a deep sigh. Mr. Thrifter looked very solemn on hearing this, and as he was a man not void of understanding, he said to me:

"My dawty," said he, "we must not stand on trifles; if you do not like to see my shoes within the parlor fender, they can be toasted in the kitchen."

I was glad to hear him say this; and, ringing the bell, I told the servant-maid at once to take them away and place them before the kitchen fire, well pleased to have carried my point with such debonair suavity; for if you get the substance of a thing, it is not wise to make a piece of work for the shadow likewise. Thus it happened I was conqueror in the controversy; but Mr. Thrifter's shoes have to this day been toasted every morning in the kitchen; and I dare say the poor man is vogie[1] with the thoughts of having gained a victory; for the generality of men have, like parrots, a good conceit of themselves, and cry "Pretty Poll!" when everybody sees they have a crooked neb.[2]

But what I have said was nothing to many other calamities that darkened our honeymoon. Mr. Thrifter having been a long-keepit bachelor, required a consideration in many things besides his shoes; for men of that stamp are so long accustomed to their own ways that it is not easy to hammer them into docility, far less to make them obedient husbands. So that although he is the best of men, yet I cannot say on my conscience that he was altogether free from an ingrained temper, requiring my canniest hand to manage properly. It could not be said that I suffered much from great faults; but he was fiky, and made more work about trifles that didna just please him than I was willing to conform to. Some excuse, however, might be pleaded for him, because he felt that infirmities were growing upon him, which was the cause that made him think of taking a wife; and I was not in my younger days quite so thoughtful, maybe, as was necessary: for I will take blame to myself, when it would be a great breach of truth in me to deny a fault that could be clearly proven.

Mr. Thrifter was a man of great regularity; he went to the shop and did his business there in a most methodical manner; he returned to the house and ate his meals like clockwork; and he went to bed every night at half-past nine o'clock, and slept there like a door nail. In short, all he did and said was as orderly as commodities on chandler pins; but for all that he was at times of a crunkly spirit, fractiously making faults about nothing at all: by which he was neither so smooth as oil nor so sweet as honey to me, whose duty it was to govern him.

At the first outbreaking of the original sin that was in him, I was vexed and grieved, watering the plants in the solitude of the room, when he was discoursing on the news of the day with customers in the shop. At last I said to myself, "This will never do; one of two must obey: and it is not in the course of nature that a gudeman should rule a house, which is the province of a wife and becomes her nature to do."

So I set a stout heart to the stey[3] brae, and being near my time with our daughter, I thought it would be well to try how he would put up with a little sample of womanhood. So that day when he came in to his dinner, I was, maybe, more incommoded with my temper than might be, saying to him, in a way as if I could have fought with the wind, that it was very unsettled weather.

---

[1] Proud.

[2] Beak.

[3] Steep, difficult.

"My dawty," said he, "I wonder what would content you! we have had as delightful a week as ever made the sight of the sun heartsome."

"Well, but," said I, "good weather that is to you may not be so to me; and I say again, that this is most ridiculous weather."

"What would you have, my dawty? Is it not known by a better what is best for us?"

"Oh," cried I, "we can never speak of temporal things but you haul in the grace of the Maker by the lug and the horn. Mr. Thrifter, ye should set a watch on the door of your lips; especially as ye have now such a prospect before you of being the father of a family."

"Mrs. Thrifter," said he, "what has that to do with the state of the weather?"

"Everything," said I. "Isn't the condition that I am in a visibility that I cannot look after the house as I should do? which is the cause of your having such a poor dinner to-day; for the weather wiled out the servant lass, and she has in consequence not been in the kitchen to see to her duty. Doesn't that shew you that, to a woman in the state that I am, fine sunshiny weather is no comfort?"

"Well," said he, "though a shower is at times seasonable, I will say that I prefer days like this."

"What you, Mr. Thrifter, prefer, can make no difference to me; but I will uphold, in spite of everything you can allege to the contrary, that this is not judicious weather."

"Really now, gudewife," said Mr. Thrifter, "what need we quarrel about the weather? neither of us can make it better or worse."

"That's a truth," said I, "but what need you maintain that dry weather is pleasant weather, when I have made it plain to you that it is a great affliction? And how can you say the contrary? does not both wet and dry come from Providence? Which of them is the evil?—for they should be in their visitations both alike."

"Mrs. Thrifter," said he, "what would you be at, summering and wintering on nothing?" Upon which I said, "Oh, Mr. Thrifter, if ye were like me, ye would say anything; for I am not in a condition to be spoken to. I'll not say that ye're far wrong, but till my time is a bygone ye should not contradict me so; for I am no in a state to be contradicted: it may go hard with me if I am. So I beg you to think, for the sake of the baby unborn, to let me have my way in all things for a season." "I have no objection," said he, "if there is a necessity for complying; but really, gudewife, ye're at times a wee fashous[1] just now; and this house has not been a corner in the kingdom of heaven for some time." Thus, from less to more, our argolbargoling was put an end to; and from that time I was the ruling power in our domicile, which has made it the habitation of quiet ever since; for from that moment I never laid down the rod of authority, which I achieved with such a womanly sleight of hand.

Though from the time of the conversation recorded in the preceding chapter I was, in a certain sense, the ruling power in our house, as a wedded wife should be, we did not slide down a glassy brae till long after. For though the gudeman in a compassionate manner allowed me to have my own way till my fullness of time was come, I could discern by the tail of my eye that he meditated to usurp the authority again, when he saw a fit time to effect the machination. Thus it came to pass, when I was delivered of our daughter, I had, as I lay on my bed, my own thoughts anent the evil that I saw barming[2] within him; and I was therefore determined to keep the upper hand, of which I had made a conquest with such dexterity, and the breaking down of difficulties. So when I was some days in a recumbent posture, but in a well-doing

---

[1]Troublesome.

[2]Brewing. Barm = yeast.

way, I said nothing; it made me, however, often grind my teeth in a secrecy when I saw from the bed many a thing that I treasured in remembrance should never be again. But I was very thankful for my deliverance, and assumed a blitheness in my countenance that was far from my heart. In short, I could see that the gudeman, in whose mouth you would have thought sugar would have melted, had from day to day a stratagem in his head subversive of the regency that I had won in my tender state; and as I saw it would never do to let him have his own will, I had recourse to the usual diplomaticals of womankind.

It was a matter before the birth that we settled, him and me, that the child should be baptized on the eighth day after, in order that I might be up and a partaker of the ploy; which, surely, as the mother, I was well entitled to. But from what I saw going on from the bed and jaloused, it occurred to me that the occasion should be postponed, and according as Mr. Thrifter should give his consent, or withhold it, I should comport myself; determined, however, I was to have the matter postponed, just to ascertain the strength and durability of what belonged to me.

On the fifth day I, therefore, said to him, as I was sitting in the easy chair by the fire, with a cod[1] at my shoulders and my mother's fur cloak about me—the baby was in a cradle close by, but not rocking, for the keeper said it was yet too young—and sitting, as I have said, Mr. Thrifter forenent me, "My dear," said I, "it will never do to have the christening on the day we said."

"What for no?" was the reply; "isn't it a very good day?" So I, seeing that he was going to be upon his peremptors, replied, with my usual meekness, "No human being, my dear, can tell what sort of day it will be; but be it good or it bad, the christening is not to be on that day."

"You surprise me!" said he, "I considered it a settled point, and have asked Mr. Sweetie, the grocer, to come to his tea."

"Dear me!" quo I; "ye should not have done that without my consent; for although we set the day before my time was come, it was not then in the power of man to say how I was to get through; and therefore it was just a talk we had on the subject, and by no manner of means a thing that could be fixed."

"In some sort," said Mr. Thrifter, "I cannot but allow that you are speaking truth; but I thought that the only impediment to the day was your illness. Now you have had a most blithe time o't, and there is nothing in the way of an obstacle."

"Ah, Mr. Thrifter!" said I, "it's easy for you, who have such a barren knowledge of the nature of women, so to speak, but I know that I am in no condition to have such a handling as a christening; and besides, I have a scruple of conscience well worth your attention concerning the same—and it's my opinion, formed in the watches of the night, when I was in my bed, that baby should be christened in the kirk on the Lord's day."

"Oh," said he, "that's but a fashion, and you'll be quite well by the eighth; the howdie[2] told me that ye had a most pleasant time o't, and cannot be ill on the eighth day."

I was just provoked into contumacy to hear this; for to tell a new mother that childbirth is a pleasant thing, set me almost in a passion; and I said to him that he might entertain Mr. Sweetie himself, for that I was resolved the christening should not be as had been set.

In short, from less to more, I gained my point; as, indeed, I always settled it in my own mind before broaching the subject: first, by letting him know that I had latent pains, which made me very ill, though I seemed otherwise; and, secondly, that it was

[1]Pillow.

[2]Midwife.

very hard, and next to a martyrdom, to be controverted in religion, as I would be if the bairn was baptized anywhere but in the church.

In due time the christening took place in the kirk, as I had made a point of having; and for some time after we passed a very happy married life. Mr. Thrifter saw that it was of no use to contradict me, and in consequence we lived in great felicity, he never saying nay to me; and I, as became a wife in the rightful possession of her prerogatives, was most condescending. But still he shewed, when he durst, the bull-horn; and would have meddled with our householdry, to the manifest detriment of our conjugal happiness, had I not continued my interdict in the strictest manner. In truth, I was all the time grievously troubled with nursing Nance, our daughter, and could not take the same pains about things that I otherwise would have done; and it is well known that husbands are like mice, that know when the cat is out of the house or her back turned, they take their own way: and I assure the courteous reader, to say no ill of my gudeman, that he was one of the mice genus.

But at last I had a trial that was not to be endured with such a composity as if I had been a black snail. It came to pass that our daughter was to be weaned, and on the day settled—a Sabbath day—we had, of course, much to do, for it behoved in this ceremony that I should keep out of sight; and keeping out of sight it seemed but reasonable, considering his parentage to the wean, that Mr. Thrifter should take my place. So I said to him in the morning that he must do so, and keep Nance for that day; and, to do the poor man justice, he consented at once, for he well knew that it would come to nothing to be contrary.

So I went to the kirk, leaving him rocking the cradle and singing hush, ba! as he saw need. But oh, dule! scarcely had I left the house when the child screamed up in a panic, and would not be pacified. He thereupon lifted it out of the cradle, and with it in his arms went about the house; but it was such a roaring buckie that for a long time he was like to go distracted. Over what ensued I draw the curtain, and must only say that, when I came from the church, there he was, a spectacle, and as sour as a crab apple, blaming me for leaving him with such a devil.

I was really woeful to see him, and sympathised in the most pitiful manner with him, on account of what had happened; but the more I condoled with him the more he would not be comforted, and for all my endeavors to keep matters in a propriety, I saw my jurisdiction over the house was in jeopardy, and every now and then the infant cried out, just as if it had been laid upon a heckle.[1] Oh! such a day as that was for Mr. Thrifter, when he heard the tyrant bairn shrieking like mad, and every now and then drumming with its wee feetie like desperation, he cried:

"For the love of God, give it a drop of the breast! or it will tempt me to wring off its ankles or its head."

But I replied composedly that it could not be done, for the wean must be speant, and what he advised was evendown nonsense.

"What has come to pass, both my mother and other sagacious carlinges[2] told me I had to look for; and so we must bow the head of resignation to our lot. You'll just," said I, "keep the bairn this afternoon; it will not be a long fashery."

He said nothing, but gave a deep sigh.

At this moment the bells of the kirk were ringing for the afternoon's discourse, and I lifted my bonnet to put it on and go; but ere I knew where I was, Mr. Thrifter was out of the door and away, leaving me alone with the torment in the cradle, which the bells at that moment wakened: and it gave a yell that greatly discomposed me.

Once awa and aye awa, Mr. Thrifter went into the fields, and would not come

---

[1]Conical top (of a roof, rick, etc.).

[2]Old women.

back when I lifted the window and called to him, but walked faster and faster, and was a most demented man; so that I was obligated to stay at home, and would have had my own work with the termagant baby if my mother had not come in and advised me to give it sweetened rum and water for a pacificator.

Mr. Thrifter began in time to be a very complying husband, and we had, after the trial of the weaning, no particular confabulation; indeed he was a very reasonable man, and had a rightful instinct of the reverence that is due to the opinion of a wife of discernment. I do not think, to the best of my recollection, that between the time Nance was weaned till she got her walking shoes and was learning to walk, that we had a single controversy; nor can it be said that we had a great ravelment on that occasion. Indeed, saving our daily higling about trifles not worth remembering, we passed a pleasant life. But when Nance came to get her first walking shoes, that was a catastrophe well worthy of being rehearsed for her behoof now.

It happened that for some months before, she had, in place of shoes, red worsted socks; but as she began, from the character of her capering, to kithe that she was coming to her feet, I got a pair of yellow slippers for her; and no mother could take more pains than I did to learn her how to handle her feet. First, I tried to teach her to walk by putting a thimble or an apple beyond her reach, at least a chair's breadth off, and then I endeavored to make the cutty run from me to her father, across the hearth, and he held out his hands to catch her.

This, it will be allowed, was to us pleasant pastime. But it fell out one day, when we were diverting ourselves by making Nance run to and fro between us across the hearth, that the glaiket baudrons[1] chanced to see the seal of her father's watch glittering, and, in coming from him to me, she drew it after her, as if it had been a turnip. He cried, "Oh, Christal and—" I lifted my hands in wonderment; but the tottling creature, with no more sense than a sucking turkey, whirled the watch—the Almighty knows how!—into the fire, and giggled as if she had done an exploit.

"Take it out with the tongs," said I.

"She's an ill-brought-up wean," cried he.

The short and the long of it was, before the watch could be got out, the heat broke the glass and made the face of it dreadful; besides, he wore a riband chain—that was in a blaze before we could make a redemption.

When the straemash was over, I said to him that he could expect no better by wearing a watch in such a manner.

"It is not," said he, "the watch that is to blame, but your bardy[2] bairn that ye have spoiled in the bringing up."

"Mr. Thrifter," quo I, "this is not a time for upbraiding; for if ye mean to insinuate anything to my disparagement, it is what I will not submit to."

"E'en as you like, my dawty," said he; "but what I say is true—that your daughter will just turn out a randy[3] like her mother."

"What's that ye say?" quo I, and I began to wipe my eyes with the corner of my shawl—saying in a pathetic manner, "If I am a randy, I ken who has made me one."

"Ken," said he, "Ken! everybody kens that ye are like a clubby foot, made by the hand of God, and passed the remede of doctors."

Was not this most diabolical to hear? Really my corruption rose at such blasphemy; and starting from my seat, I put my hands on my haunches, and gave a stamp with my foot that made the whole house dirl; "What does the man mean?" said I.

But he replied with a composity as if he had been in liquor, saying, with an ill-

---

[1]Foolish cat.

[2]Impudent, troublesome.

[3]Loud woman, scold.

faured smile, "Sit down, my dawty; you'll do yourself a prejudice if ye allow your passion to get the better of you."

Could mortal woman thole the like of this? It stunned me speechless, and for a time I thought my authority knocked on the head. But presently the spirit that was in my nature mustered courage, and put a new energy within me, which caused me to say nothing, but to stretch out my feet, and stiffen back, with my hands at my sides, as if I was a dead corpse. Whereupon the good man ran for a tumbler of water to jaup on my face; but when he came near me in this posture, I dauded the glass of water in his face, and drummed with my feet and hands in a delirious manner, which convinced him that I was going by myself. Oh, but he was in an awful terrification! At last, seeing his fear and contrition, I began to moderate, as it seemed; which made him as softly and kindly as if I had been a true frantic woman; which I was not, but a practiser of the feminine art, to keep the ruling power.

Thinking by my state that I was not only gone daft, but not without the need of soothing, he began to ask my pardon in a proper humility, and with a most pitiful penitence. Whereupon I said to him, that surely he had not a rightful knowledge of my nature: and then he began to confess a fault, and was such a dejected man that I took the napkin from my eyes and gave a great guffaw, telling him that surely he was silly daft and gi'en to pikery, if he thought he could daunton me. "No, no, Mr. Thrifter," quo I, "while I live, and the iron tongs are by the chumly leg, never expect to get the upper hand of me."

From that time he was as bidable a man as any reasonable woman could desire; but he gave a deep sigh, which was a testificate to me that the leaven of unrighteousness was still within him, and might break out into treason and rebellion if I was not on my guard.

## JOSEPH TRAIN (1779–1852)

### Old Scotia

I've loved thee, old Scotia, and love thee I will,
Till the heart that now beats in my bosom is still.
My forefathers loved thee, for often they drew
Their dirks in defense of thy banners of blue.
Though murky thy glens, where the wolf prowled of yore,
And craggy thy mountains, where cataracts roar,
The race of old Albyn, when danger was nigh,
For thee stood resolved still to conquer or die.

I love yet to roam where the beacon-light rose,
Where echoed thy slogan, or gathered thy foes,
Whilst forth rushed thy heroic sons to the fight,
Opposing the stranger who came in his might.
I love through thy time-fretted castles to stray,
The mold'ring halls of thy chiefs to survey;
To grope through the keep, and the turret explore,
Where waved the blue flag when the battle was oer.

I love yet to roam oer each field of thy fame,
Where valor has gained thee a glorious name.
I love where the cairn or the cromlech is made,
To ponder, for low there the mighty are laid.

Were these fall'n heroes to rise from their graves,
They might deem us dastards, they might deem us slaves;
But let a foe face thee, raise fire on each hill,
Thy sons, my dear Scotia, will fight for thee still.

## Blooming Jessie

On this unfrequented plain,
What can gar thee sigh alane,
Bonnie blue-eyed lassie?
Is thy mammy dead and gane,
Or thy loving Jamie slain?
Wed anither, mak nae main*, "moan"
Bonnie, blooming Jessie.

Though I sob and sigh alane,
I was never wed to ane,
Quo the blue-eyed lassie.
But if loving Jamie's slain,
Farewell pleasure, welcome pain,
A' the joy wi' him is gane,
O' poor hapless Jessie.

Ere he crossed the raging sea,
Was he ever true to thee,
Bonnie, blooming Jessie?
Was he ever frank and free?
Swore he constant aye to be?
Did he on the roseate lea
Ca' thee blooming Jessie?

Ere he crossed the raging sea,
Aft he on the dewy lea
Ca'd me blue-eyed lassie.
Weel I mind his words to me,
Were, if he abroad should die,
His last throb and sigh should be,
Bonnie, blooming Jessie.

Far frae hame, and far frae thee,
I saw loving Jamie die,
Bonnie blue-eyed lassie.
Fast a cannon ball did flee,
Laid him stretched upo' the lea;
Soon in death he closed his e'e,
Crying, "Blooming Jessie."

Swelling with a smothered sigh,
Rose the snowy bosom high
Of the blue-eyed lassie.
Fleeter than the streamers fly,
When they flit athwart the sky,

Went and came the rosy dye
On the cheeks of Jessie.

Longer wi' sic grief oppressed
Jamie couldna sae distressed
See the blue-eyed lassie.
Fast he clasped her to his breast,
Told her a' his dangers past,
Vowed that he would wed at last
Bonnie, blooming Jessie.

## Wi' Drums and Pipes

Wi' drums and pipes the clachan* rang; village
I left my goats to wander wide;
And e'en as fast as I could bang,
I bickered down the mountain side.
My hazel rung* and haslock plaid staff
Awa I flang wi' cauld disdain,
Resolved I would nae langer bide
To do the auld thing oer again.

Ye barons bold, whose turrets rise
Aboon the wild woods white wi' snaw,
I trow the laddies ye may prize
Wha fight your battles far awa.
Wi' them to stan', wi' them to fa',
Courageously I crossed the main,
To see, for Caledonia,
The auld thing weel done oer again.

Right far a-feil' I freely fought
Gainst mony an outlandish loon*; fellow, rascal
An' wi' my good claymore I've brought
Mony a beardy birkie* down. stout fellow
While I had pith* to wield it roun', strength
In battle I ne'er met wi' ane
Cauld danton* me, for Britain's crown, daunt
To do the same thing oer again.

Although I'm marching life's last stage,
Wi' sorrow crowded roun' my brow;
And though the knapsack o' auld age
Hangs heavy on my shoulders now—
Yet recollection, ever new,
Discharges a' my toil and pain,
When fancy figures in my view
The pleasant auld thing oer again.

## Garryhorn

Gin* ye wad gang, lassie, to Garryhorn, if
Ye might be happy, I ween;
Albeit the cuckoo was never heard there,
And a swallow there never was seen.

While cuchats* coo round the mill of Glenlee, pigeons
And little birds sing on the thorn,
Ye might hear the bonnie heather bleat croak
In the wilds of Garryhorn.

Tis bonnie to see at the Garryhorn
Kids skipping the highest rock,
And, wrapt in his plaid at midsummer day,
The moorman tending his flock.

The reaper seldom his sickle whets there,
To gather in standing corn;
But many a sheep is to sheer and smear
In the bughts* of Garryhorn. sheepfolds

There are hams on the bauks at Garryhorn
Of braxy*, and eke a store (salted sheep flesh)
Of cakes in the kist*, and peats in the neuk, "chest"
To put aye the winter oer.

There is aye a clog for the fire at Yule,
With a browst* for New Year's morn; brewing
And gin ye gang up ye may sit like a queen
In the chamber at Garryhorn.

And when ye are lady of Garryhorn,
Ye shall ride to the kirk with me;
Although my mither should skelp through the mire,
With her coats kilted up to the knee.

I woo not for siller, my bonnie May,
Sae dinna my offer scorn.
"No, but ye maun speer at my minny*," quo she, mother
"Ere I gang to Garryhorn."

# WILLIAM DUNBAR (1780–1861)

## The Maid of Islay

Rising oer the heaving billow,
Evening gilds the ocean's swell,
While with thee, on grassy pillow,
Solitude, I love to dwell.
Lonely to the sea-breeze blowing,
Oft I chaunt my love-lorn strain,

To the streamlet sweetly flowing,
Murmur oft a lover's pain.

Twas for her, the maid of Islay,
Time flew oer me winged with joy.
Twas for her, the cheering smile aye
Beamed with rapture in my eye.
Not the tempest raving round me,
Lightning's flash or thunder's roll,
Not the ocean's rage could wound me,
While her image filled my soul.

Farewell days of purest pleasure,
Long your loss my heart shall mourn.
Farewell, hours of bliss the measure,
Bliss that never can return.
Cheerless oer the wild heath wand'ring,
Cheerless oer the wave-worn shore,
On the past with sadness pond'ring,
Hope's fair visions charm no more.

## ROBERT JAMIESON (1780–1844)

### My Wife's a Winsome Wee Thing

My wife's a winsome wee thing,
A bonnie, blithesome wee thing,
My dear, my constant wee thing,
And evermair sall be:
It warms my heart to view her;
I canna choose but lo'e her,
And oh, weel may I trow her
How dearly she lo'es me.

For—though her face sae fair be
As nane could ever mair be,
And though her wit sae rare be
As seenil* do we see— seldom
Her beauty ne'er had gained me,
Her wit had ne'er enchained me,
Nor baith sae lang retained me,
But for her love to me.

When wealth and pride disowned me,
A' views were dark around me;
And sad and laigh she found me
As friendless worth could be:
When ither hope gaed frae me
Her pity kind did stay me,
And love for love she ga'e me;
And that's the love for me.

And, till this heart is cauld, I
That charm of life will hald by;
And, though my wife grow auld, my
Leal love aye young will be;
For she's my winsome wee thing,
My canty*, blithesome wee thing, lively
My tender, constant wee thing,
And evermair sall be.

## WILLIAM LAIDLAW (1780–1845)

### Lucy's Flittin'

Twas when the wan leaf frae the birk tree was fa'in',
And Martinmas dowie* had wound up the year, sadly
That Lucy rowed up her wee kist* wi' her a' in't, chest
And left her auld maister and neebours sae dear,
For Lucy had served in "The Glen" a' the simmer;
She cam' there afore the flower bloomed on the pea;
An orphan was she, and they had been gude till* her, to
Sure that was the thing brocht the tear to her ee.

She gaed by the stable where Jamie was stannin',
Richt sair was his kind heart the flittin' to see.
Fare-ye-weel, Lucy, quo Jamie, and ran in;
The gatherin' tears trickled fast frae his ee.
As down the burn-side she gaed slow wi' the flittin',
Fare-ye-weel, Lucy! was ilka bird's sang.
She heard the craw sayin't, high on the tree sittin',
And robin was chirpin't the brown leaves amang.

Oh, what is't that pits my puir heart in a flutter?
And what gars the tears come sae fast to my ee?
If I wasna ettled* to be ony better, determined
Then what gars me wish ony better to be?
I'm just like a lammie that loses its mither;
Nae mither or friend the puir lammie can see;
I fear I hae tint* my puir heart a' thegither, lost
Nae wonder the tear fa's sae fast frae my ee.

Wi' the rest o' my claes I hae rowed up the ribbon,
The bonnie blue ribbon that Jamie gae me;
Yestreen, when he gae me't, and saw I was sabbin',
I'll never forget the wae blink o' his ee.
Though now he said neathing but Fare-ye-weel, Lucy!
It made me I neither could speak, hear, nor see.
He cudna say mair but just, Fare-ye-weel, Lucy.
Yet that I will mind till the day that I dee.

The lamb likes the gowan wi' dew when it's droukit*; soaked
The hare likes the brake, and the braird on the lea;
But Lucy likes Jamie;—she turned and she lookit,

She thocht the dear place she wad never mair see.
Ah, weel may young Jamie gang dowie and cheerless,
And weel may he greet* on the bank o' the burn; weep
For bonnie sweet Lucy, sae gentle and peerless,
Lies cauld in her grave, and will never return.

## Her Bonnie Black Ee

On the banks o' the burn while I pensively wander,
The mavis sings sweetly, unheeded by me.
I think on my lassie, her gentle mild nature,
I think on the smile o' her bonnie black ee.

When heavy the rain fa's, and loud, loud the win' blaws,
An' simmer's gay cleedin' drives fast frae the tree;
I heedna the win' nor the rain when I think on
The kind lovely smile o' my lassie's black ee.

When swift as the hawk, in the stormy November,
The cauld norlan' win' ca's the drift owre the lea;
Though bidin' its blast on the side o' the mountain,
I think on the smile o' her bonnie black ee.

When braw at a weddin' I see the fine lasses,
Though a' neat an' bonnie, they're naething to me;
I sigh an' sit dowie*, regardless what passes, sadly
When I miss the smile o' her bonnie black ee.

When thin twinklin' sternies* announce the gray gloamin', stars
When a' round the ingle* sae cheery to see; fireplace
Then music delightfu', saft on the heart stealin',
Minds me o' the smile o' her bonnie black ee.

When jokin', an' laughin', the lave* they are merry, rest
Though absent my heart, like the lave I maun be;
Sometimes I laugh wi' them, but aft I turn dowie,
An' think on the smile o' my lassie's black ee.

Her lovely fair form frae my mind's awa' never,
She's dearer than a' this hale warld to me;
An' this is my wish: May I leave it if ever
She row on anither her love-beaming ee.

## JOHN GRIEVE (1781–1836)

### Twas Summer Tide

Twas summer tide; the cushat sang
His am'rous roundelay;
And dews, like clustered diamonds, hang
On flower and leafy spray.
The coverlet of gloaming gray

On everything was seen,
When lads and lasses took their way
To Polwarth on the green.

The spirit-moving dance went on,
And harmless revelry
Of young hearts all in unison,
Wi' love's soft witchery;
Their hall the open-daisied lea,
While frae the welkin sheen
The moon shone brightly on the glee
At Polwarth on the green.

Dark een and raven curls were there,
And cheeks of rosy hue,
And finer forms, without compare,
Than pencil ever drew;
But ane, wi' een of bonnie blue,
A' hearts confessed the queen,
And pride of grace and beauty too,
At Polwarth on the green.

The miser hoards his golden store,
And kings dominion gain;
While others in the battle's roar
For honor's trifles strain.
Away, such pleasures! false and vain.
Far dearer mine have been,
Among the lowly rural train,
At Polwarth on the green.

## ANONYMOUS

### Canadian Boat Song

Fair these broad meads—these hoary woods are grand;
But we are exiles from our fathers' land.

Listen to me, as when you heard our father
Sing long ago the song of other shores—
Listen to me, and then in chorus gather
All your deep voices, as ye pull your oars.

From the lone sheiling* of the misty island
Mountains divide us, and the waste of seas—
Yet still the blood is strong, the heart is Highland,
And we in dreams behold the Hebrides.

* cottage

We ne'er shall tread the fancy-haunted valley,
Where tween the dark hills creeps the small clear stream,
In arms around the patriarch banner rally,
Nor see the moon on royal tombstones gleam.

When the bold kindred, in the time long vanished,
Conquered the soil and fortified the keep,—
No seer foretold the children would be banished
That a degenerate lord might boast his sheep.

Come foreign rage—let discord burst in slaughter.
O then for clansmen true, and stern claymore—
The hearts that would have given their blood like water,
Beat heavily beyond the Atlantic roar.

## Some Say That Kissing's a Sin

Some say that kissing's a sin;
But I think it's nane ava,
For kissing has wonned* in this warld    dwelled
Since ever that there was twa.

O, if it wasna lawfu'
Lawyers wadna allow it.
If it wasna holy,
Ministers wadna do it.

If it wasna modest,
Maidens wadna tak it.
If it wasna plenty,
Puir folk wadna get it.

## Mormond Braes

As I gaed doon by Strichen toon,
I heard a fair maid mournin',
And she was makin' sair complaint
For her true love ne'er returnin'.
It's Mormond Braes where heather grows,
Where aftimes I have been cheery,
It's Mormond Braes where heather grows.
And it's there I've lost my dearie.

Sae fare ye weel, ye Mormond Braes,
Where aftimes I've been cheery,
Fare ye weel, ye Mormond Braes,
For it's there I've lost my dearie.

Oh, I'll put on my goon o' green,
It's a forsaken token,
And that will let the young men know
That the bands o' love are broken.
There's mony a horse has snappert* and fa'an,    stumbled
And risen and gane fu' rarely,
There's mony a lass has lost her lad,
And gotten anither richt early.

There's as guid fish into the sea
As ever yet was taken,
I'll cast my line and try again,
I'm only ance forsaken.
Sae I'll gae doon to Strichen toon
Where I was bred and born,
And there I'll get anither sweetheart,
Will mairy me the morn.

### Martin Elginbrod

Here lie I, Martin Elginbrod.
Hae mercy on my soul, Lord God;
As I would do, were I Lord God,
And Ye were Martin Elginbrod.

## CHARLES SIBLEY (DATES UNKNOWN)

### The Plaidie

Upon ane stormy Sunday,
Coming adoon the lane,
Were a score of bonnie lassies—
And the sweetest I maintain
Was Caddie,
That I took unneath my plaidie,
To shield her from the rain.

She said that the daisies blushed
For the kiss that I had ta'en.
I wadna hae thought the lassie
Wad sae of a kiss complain.
"Now, laddie,
I winna stay under your plaidie,
If I gang hame in the rain!"

But, on an after Sunday,
When cloud there was not ane,
This selfsame winsome lassie
(We chanced to meet in the lane)
Said, "Laddie,
Why dinna ye wear your plaidie?
Wha kens but it may rain?"

## CHARLES GRAY (1782–1851)

### Grim Winter Was Howlin'

Grim winter was howlin' owre muir and owre mountain,
And bleak blew the wind on the wild stormy sea;
The could frost had locked up each riv'let and fountain,
As I took the dreich* road that leads north to Dundee. dreary

Though a' round was dreary, my heart was fu' cheery,
And cantie* I sung as the bird on the tree; cheerful
For when the heart's light, the feet winna soon weary,
Though ane should gang further than bonnie Dundee.

Arrived at the banks o' sweet Tay's flowin' river,
I looked, as it rapidly rowed to the sea;
And fancy, whose fond dream still pleases me ever,
Beguiled the lone passage to bonnie Dundee.
There, glowrin' about, I saw in his station
Ilk bodie as eydent* as midsummer bee; industrious
When fair stood a mark, on the face o' creation,
The lovely young Peggy, the pride o' Dundee.

O, aye since the time I first saw this sweet lassie,
I'm listless, I'm restless, wherever I be;
I'm dowie*, and donnart*, and aften ca'd saucy; sad/dull
They kenna its a' for the lass o' Dundee.
O lang may her guardians be virtue and honor;
Though anither may wed her, yet well may she be;
And blessin's in plenty be showered down upon her—
The lovely young Peggy, the pride o' Dundee.

## When Autumn

When autumn has laid her sickle by,
And the stacks are theekit* to haud them dry; covered
And the sapless leaves comes down frae the trees,
And dance about in the fitfu' breeze;
And the robin again sits burd-alane,
Ane sings his sang on the auld peat stane;
When come is the hour o' gloamin gray,
Oh, sweet is to me the minstrel's lay.

When winter is driving his cloud on the gale,
And spairgin* about his snaw and his hail, sprinkling
And the door is steekit* against the blast, shut
And the winnocks* wi' wedges are firm and fast, windows
And the ribs are rypet, the cannal a-light,
And the fire on the hearth is bleezin bright,
And the bicker* is reamin with pithy brown ale; cup, tankard
Oh, dear is to me a sang or a tale.

Then I tove* awa by the ingle* side, smoke/fire
And tell o' the blasts I was wont to bide,
When the nichts were lang and the sea ran high,
And the moon hid her face in the depths of the sky,
And the mast was strained, and the canvas rent,
By some demon on message of mischief sent;
O, I bless my stars that at hame I can bide,
For dear, dear to me is my ain ingle-side.

## Sequel to Maggie Lauder

The cantie* spring scarce reared her head, pleasant
And winter yet did blaud* her, buffet
When the Ranter cam' to Anster Fair,
And speered* for Maggie Lauder; asked
A snug wee house in the East Green
Its shelter kindly lent her;
Wi' canty ingle*, clean hearth stane, fire
Meg welcomed Rob the Ranter.

Then Rob made bonnie Meg his bride,
An' to the kirk they ranted.
He played the auld "East Nook o' Fife,"
And merry Maggie vaunted,
That Hab himself ne'er played a spring,
Nor blew sae weel his chanter,
For he made Anster town to ring—
An' wha's like Rob the Ranter?

For a' the talk an' loud reports
That ever gaed against her,
Meg proves a true and carefu' wife
As ever was in Anster;
An' since the marriage knot was tied
Rob swears he couldna want her,
For he loes Maggie as his life,
An' Meg loes Rob the Ranter.

## The Minstrel

Keen blaws the wind oer Donocht-head.
The snaw drives snelly* through the dale. fiercely
The gaberlunzie* tirls* my sneek, beggar/rings
And, shivering, tells his waefu' tale:
"Cauld is the night, O let me in,
And dinna let your minstrel fa',
And dinna let his winding sheet
Be naething but a wreath o snaw.

"Full ninety winters hae I seen,
And piped whare gorcocks whirring flew,
And mony a day ye've dance, I ween,
To lilts which frae my drone I blew."
My Eppie waked, and soon she cried,
"Get up, gudeman, and let him in;
For weel ye ken the winter night
Was short when he began his din."

My Eppie's voice, O wow, it's sweet,
E'en though she bans* and scaulds a wee; curses
But when it's tuned to sorrow's tale,
O, haith, it's doubly dear to me.

"Come in, ald carle*, I'll steer my fire,    fellow, peasant
And mak it bleeze a bonnie flame.
Your blude is thin, ye've tint the gate*,    way
Ye should nae stray sae far frae hame."

"Nae hame hae I," the minstrel said,
"Sad party strife oerturned my ha';
And, weeping, at the eve o' life,
I wander through a wreath o' snaw."
"Waes me, auld carle, sad is your tale—
Your wallet's toom*, your cleeding thin;    empty
Mine's no the hand to steek* the door    shut
When want and wae would fain be in."

We took him ben*—we set him doun,    in
And soon the ingle bleezed fu' hie.
The auld man thought himself at hame,
And dried the tear-drap frae his e'e.
He took his pipes and played a spring—
Sad was the strain, and full of woe;
In fancy's ear it seemed to wail
A free-born nation's overthrow.

## The Social Cup

Blithe, blithe, and merry are we!
Blithe are we, ane and a',
Aften hae we canty* been,    lively
But sic a night we never saw.

The gloamin' saw us a' sit down,
And meikle mirth has been our fa';
Then let the sang and toast gae roun',
Till chanticleer begins to craw.
Blithe, blithe, and merry are we—
Pick and wale* o' merry men:    choice
What care we though the cock may craw?
We're masters o' the tappit-hen*.    quart container

The auld kirk bell has chappit twal,—
Wha cares though she had chappit twa?
We're licht o' heart, and winna part,
Though time and tide may rin awa'.
Blithe, blithe, and merry are we—
Hearts that care can never ding:
Then let time pass,—we'll steal his glass,
And pu' a feather frae his wing.

Now is the witching time of nicht,
When ghaists, they say, are to be seen;
And fays dance to the glow-worms' licht,
Wi' fairies in their gowns of green.

Blithe, blithe, and merry are we!
Ghaists may tak their midnicht stroll,
Witches ride, on brooms astride,
While we sit by the witchin' bowl.

Tut, never speer how wears the morn,—
The moon's still blinkin' i' the sky;
And gif, like her, we fill our horn,
I dinna doubt we'll drink it dry.
Blithe, blithe, and merry are we—
Blithe out-owre the barley bree*; brew
Then let me tell, the moon hersel'
Aft dips her toom* horn i' the sea. empty

Then fill us up a social cup,
And never mind the dapple-dawn:
Just sit awhile—the sun may smile,
And licht us a' across the lawn.
Blithe, blithe, and merry are we;
See, the sun is keekin'* ben. peeking
Gi'e time his glass, for months may pass
Ere we hae sic a nicht again.

## WILLIAM NICHOLSON (1782–1849)

### The Braes of Gallowa

O Lassie, wilt thou gang wi' me,
And leave thy frien's i' th' south country—
Thy former frien's and sweethearts a',
And gang wi' me to Gallowa?

O Gallowa braes they wave wi' broom,
And heather-bells in bonnie bloom.
There's lordly seats, and livin's braw*, fine
Amang the braes o' Gallowa.

There's stately woods on mony a brae,
Where burns and birds in concert play;
The waukrife* echo answers a', vigilant
Amang the braes o' Gallowa.

The simmer shiel* I'll build for thee cottage
Alang the bonnie banks o' Dee,
Half circlin' roun' my father's ha',
Amang the braes o' Gallowa.

When autumn waves her flowin' horn,
And fields o' gowden grain are shorn,
I'll busk* thee fine, in pearlins braw, dress
To join the dance in Gallowa.

At e'en, whan darkness shrouds the sight,
And lanely, langsome is the night,
Wi' tentie* care my pipes I'll thraw, special
Play "A' the way to Gallowa."

Should fickle fortune on us frown,
Nae lack o' gear our love should drown.
Content should shield our haddin'* sma, homestead
Amang the braes o' Gallowa.

Come while the blossom's on the broom,
And heather bells sae bonnie bloom;
Come, let us be the happiest twa
On a' the braes o' Gallowa.

## O, Will Ye Go to Yon Burn Side?

O, will ye go to yon burn side,
Amang the new-made hay;
And sport upon the flowery swaird,
My ain dear May?
The sun blinks blithe on yon burn side,
Whare lambkins lightly play,
The wild bird whistles to his mate,
My ain dear May.

The waving woods, wi' mantle green,
Shall shield us in the bower,
Whare I'll pu'* a posy for my May, "pull"
O' mony a bonnie flower.
My father maws ayont* the burn, beyond
My mammy spins at hame;
And should they see thee here wi' me,
I'd better been my lane*. (alone)

The lightsome lammie little kens
What troubles it await—
Whan ance the flush o' spring is oer,
The fause bird lea'es its mate.
The flowers will fade, the woods decay,
And lose their bonnie green;
The sun wi' clouds may be oercast,
Before that it be e'en.

Ilk thing is in its season sweet;
So love is in its noon:
But cankering time may soil the flower,
And spoil its bonnie bloom.
Oh, come then, while the summer shines,
And love is young and gay;
Ere age his withering, wintry blast
Blaws oer me and my May.

For thee I'll tend the fleecy flocks,
Or haud the halesome plow;
And nightly clasp thee to my breast,
And prove aye leal* and true. "loyal"
The blush oerspread her bonnie face,
She had nae mair to say,
But gae her hand and walked alang,
The youthfu', bloomin' May.

## The Brownie of Blednoch

There cam' a strange wight to our town-en',
An' the fient* a body did him ken. (devil)
He tirled* na lang, but he glided ben* knocked/in
Wi' a weary, dreary hum.

His face did glow like the glow o' the west,
When the drumly cloud has it half oercast;
Or the struggling moon when she's sair distrest,
O, sirs, twas Aiken-drum.

I trow* the bauldest stood aback, trust
Wi' a gape an' a glower till their lugs* did crack, ears
As the shapeless phantom mumblin spak—
"Hae ye wark for Aiken-drum?"

O, had ye seen the bairns' fright,
As they stared at this wild and unyirthly wight;
As they skulkit in tween the dark and the light,
And graned out Aiken-drum.

"Sauf us," quoth Jock, "d'ye see sic een?"
Cries Kat, "There's a hole where a nose should ha' been;
An' the mouth's like a gash that a horn had ri'en*. "riven"
Wow, keep's frae Aiken-drum."

The black dog growling cowered his tail,
The lassie swarfed*, loot fa' the pail; swooned
Rob's lingle* brak as he men't the flail, thread
At the sight o' Aiken-drum.

His matted head on his breast did rest,
A long blue beard wan'ered down like a vest;
But the glare o' his e'e hath nae bard exprest,
Nor the skimes* o' Aiken-drum. glances

Roun' his hairy form there was naething seen
But a philabeg o' the rashes green,
An' his knotted knees played aye knoit between—
What a sight was Aiken-drum.

On his wauchie* arms three claws did met, unpleasant
As they trailed on the grun' by his taeless feet;
E'en the auld gudeman himsel' did sweat,
To look at Aiken drum.

But he drew a score, himsel' did sain*, bless
The auld wife tried, but her tongue was gane;
While the young ane closer clasped her wean,
And turned frae Aiken-drum.

But the canty* auld wife cam till her breath, clever
And she thocht the Bible might ward off scaith*, harm
Be it benshee, bogle, ghaist, or wraith—
But it fearned na Aiken-drum.

"His presence protect us!" quoth the auld gudeman;
"What wad ye, whare won* ye, by sea or by lan', dwelt
I conjure ye—speak—by the beuk in my han'."
What a grane* gae Aiken-drum. "groan"

"I lived in a lan' whare we saw nae sky,
I dwalt in a spot whare a burn rins na by;
But I'se dwall now wi' you if ye like to try—
Hae ye wark for Aiken-drum?

"I'll shiel a' your sheep i' the mornin' sune,
I'll berry your crap by the light o' the moon,
An' ba' the bairns wi' an unkenned tune,
If ye'll keep puir Aiken-drum.

"I'll loup the linn* when ye canna wade, waterfall
I'll kirn* the kirn, and I'll turn the bread; "churn"
An' the wildest filly that ever can rede,
I'se tame't," quote Aiken-drum.

"To wear the tod* frae the flock on the fell, fox
To gather the dew frae the heather bell,
An' to look at my face in your clear crystal well,
Might gie pleasure to Aiken-drum.

"I'se seek nae guids, gear, bond, nor mark;
I use nae beddin, shoon, nor sark;
But a cogfu' o' brose tween the light an' the dark,
Is the wage o' Aiken-drum."

Quoth the wylie auld wife, "The thing speaks weel;
Our workers are scant—we hae routh* o' meal; plenty
Gif he'll do as he says—be he man, be he deil—
Wow, we'll try this Aiken-drum."

But the wenches skirled, "He's no be here!
His eldritch look gars us swarf* wi' fear; swoon

An' the feint a ane will the house come near,
If they think but o' Aiken-drum.

"For a foul and a stalwart ghaist is he,
Despair sits broodin aboon his e'e-bree,
And unchancie to light o' a maiden's e'e,
Is the glower o' Aiken-drum."

"Puir clipmalabors,[1] ye hae little wit.
Ist'na Hallowmas now, an' the crap out yet?"
Sae she silenced them a' wi' a stamp o' her fit—
"Sit yer wa's down, Aiken-drum."

Round' a' that side what wark was dune
By the streamer's gleam, or the glance o' the moon;
A word, or a wish, an' the brownie* cam soon, goblin
Sae helpfu' was Aiken-drum.

But he slade aye awa' or* the sun was up, "ere"
He ne'er could look straught on Macmillan's cup.
They watched—but nane saw him his brose ever sup.
Nor a spoon sought Aiken-drum.

On Blednoch banks, an' on crystal Cree,
For mony a day a toiled wight was he;
And the bairns they played harmless roun' his knee.
Sae social was Aiken-drum.

But a new-made wife, fu' o' frippish freaks,
Fond o' a' things feat for the five first weeks,
Laid a moldy pair o' her ain man's breeks
By the brose o' Aiken-drum.

Let the learned decide when they convene,
What spell was him an' the breeks between;
For frae that day forth he was nae mair seen,
An' sair missed was Aiken-drum.

He was heard by a herd gaun by the Thrieve,
Crying, "Lang, lang now may I greet* an' grieve; weep
For alas, I hae gotten baith fee an' leave
—O, luckless Aiken-drum."

Awa', ye wrangling skeptic tribe,
Wi your pro's an' your con's wad ye decide
'Gain the sponsible voice o' a hale country side,
On the facs bout Aiken-drum?"

Though the "Brownie o' Blednoch" lang be gane,
The mark o' his feet's left on mony a stane;

---

[1] Idle talkers, fools.

An' mony a wife an' mony a wean
Tell the feats o' Aiken-drum.

E'en now, light loons that jibe an' sneer
At spiritual guests an' a' sic gear,
At the Glashnoch Mill hae swat wi fear,
An' looked roun' for Aiken-drum.

An' guidly folks hae gotten a fright,
When the moon was set, an' the stars gied nae light;
At the roaring linn, in the howe* o' the night, depth
Wi' sughs like Aiken-drum.

## CLEMENTINA STIRLING GRAHAM (?1783– ? )

### Serenade

Awake, awake, my own true love,
The trysting hour is come.
The lights of Tay are waning low,
And Broughty sands are won.
My skiff is launched and buoyant floats
Upon the light wave borne,
And one fair planet sweetly glows
To herald in the morn.

The dawn now breaking in the east
Is spreading far and wide,
And in a flood of living gold
Is melting in the tide.
From willing oars the sparkling drops
In circling rainbows play,
And merrily, with laughing waves,
We'll cruise the pathless way.

### The Birkie of Bonnie Dundee

Ye fair lands of Angus and bonnie Dundee,
How dear are your echoes, your memories to me.
At gatherings and meetings in a' the braw toons,
I danced wi' the lasses and distanced the loons*; churls
Syne bantered them gaily, and bade the young men
Be mair on their mettle when I cam' again.
They jeered me, they cheered me, and cried ane and a',
He's no an ill fellow that, now he's awa.

When puir beggar bodies cam' making their mane* "moan"
I spak' them aye cheery, for siller I'd nane.
They shook up their duddies, and muttered "wae's me,
Sae lightsome a laddie no worth a bawbee!"
I played wi' the bairnie at bowls and at ba',
And left them a' greetin* when I cam' awa; weeping

Ay, mithers, and bairnies, and lasses and a',
Were a' sobin loudly when I cam' awa.

I feigned a gay laugh, just to keep in the greet,
For ae bonnie lassie, sae douce* and sae sweet, pleasant
How matchless the blink of her deep loving ee,
How soft fell its shade as it glanced upon me.
I flung her a wild rose sae fresh and sae fair,
And bade it bloom on in the bright summer there;
While breathing its fragrance, she aiblins* may gi'e perhaps
A thought to the Birkie* of bonnie Dundee. stout fellow

## ALLAN CUNNINGHAM (1784–1842)

### Hame, Hame, Hame[1]

Hame, hame, hame, O hame fain wad I be—
O hame, hame, hame, to my ain countree.

When the flower is i' the bud and the leaf is on the tree,
The larks shall sing me hame in my ain countree;
Hame, hame, hame, O hame fain wad I be.
O hame, hame, hame, to my ain countree.

The green leaf o' loyalty's beginning for to fa',
The bonnie White Rose[2] it is withering an' a';
But I'll water't wi' the blude of usurping tyranny,
An' green it will graw in my ain countree.

O, there's nocht now frae ruin my country can save,
But the keys o' kind heaven, to open the grave;
That a' the noble martyrs wha died for loyalty
May rise again an' fight for their ain countree.

The great now are gane, a' wha ventured to save,
The new grass is springing on the tap o' their grave;
But the sun through the mirk blinks blithe in my e'e,
"I'll shine on ye yet in your ain countree."

Hame, hame, hame, O hame fain wad I be—
O hame, hame, hame, to my ain countree.

### The Spring of the Year

Gone were but the winter cold,
And gone were but the snow,
I could sleep in the wild woods
Where primroses blow.

---

[1]Cunningham's version of a popular Jacobite song.
[2]Emblem of the exiled Jacobites.

Cold's the snow at my head,
And cold at my feet;
And the finger of death's at my e'en,
Closing them to sleep.

Let none tell my father
Or my mother so dear,—
I'll meet them both in heaven
At the spring of the year.

## A Wet Sheet and a Flowing Sea

A wet sheet and a flowing sea,
A wind that follows fast,
And fills the white and rustling sail
And bends the gallant mast;
And bends the gallant mast, my boys,
While, like the eagle free,
Away the good ship flies, and leaves
Old England on the lee.

"O for a soft and gentle wind!"
I hear a fair one cry;
But give to me the snoring breeze
And white waves heaving high;
And white waves heaving high, my boys,
The good ship tight and free.
The world of waters is our home,
And merry men are we.

There's tempest in yon horned moon,
And lightning in yon cloud;
And hark the music, mariners!
The wind is piping loud;
The wind is piping loud, my boys,
The lightning flashing free,—
While the hollow oak our palace is,
Our heritage the sea.

## The Wee, Wee German Lairdie[1]

Wha the deil hae we got for a King,
But a wee, wee German lairdie.
An' whan we gaed to bring him hame,
He was delving in his kail-yardie*. cabbage-patch
Sheughing* kail an' laying leeks, planting
But* the hose and but the breeks, (without)

---

[1]George I, the Protestant Elector of Hanover, who after the death of Queen Anne in 1714, was invited to become king of England, instead of the exiled Catholic James Stuart ("our gudeman"). George's immediate descendant, George II, is then by implication tarred with the same brush of illegitimacy.

Up his beggar duds he cleeks*, hooks
The wee, wee German lairdie.

An' he's clapt down in our gudeman's chair,
The wee, wee German lairdie;
An' he's brought fouth* o' foreign leeks, plenty
An' dibblet them in his yardie.
He's pu'd the rose o' English louns,
An' brak the harp o' Irish clowns,
But our thistle will jag his thumbs,
The wee, wee German lairdie.

Come up amang the Highland hills,
Thou wee, wee German lairdie;
An' see how Charlie's[1] lang-kail thrive,
He dibblet in his yardie.
An' if a stock ye daur to pu',
Or haud the yoking of a pleugh,
We'll break yere scepter o'er yere mou',
Thou wee bit German lairdie.

Our hills are steep, our glens are deep,
Nae fitting for a yardie;
An' our norlan' thistles winna pu',
Thou wee, wee German lairdie.
An' we've the trenching blades o' weir*, "war"
Was twine ye o' yere German gear;
An' pass ye neath the claymore's shear,
Thou feckless German lairdie.

## The Lovely Lass of Preston Mill

The lark had left the evening cloud,
The dew was saft, the wind was lowne*, calm
The gentle breath amang the flowers,
Scarce stirred the thistle's tap o' down;
The dappled swallow left the pool,
The stars were blinking owre the hill,
As I met, amang the hawthornes green,
The lovely lass of Preston Mill.

Her naked feet, amang the grass,
Seemed like twa dew-gemmed lilies fair;
Her brow shone comely mang her locks,
Dark curling owre her shoulders bare;
Her cheeks were rich wi' bloomy youth;
Her lips had words and wit at will;
And heaven seemed looking through her een,—
The lovely lass of Preston Mill.

---

[1] The Jacobite leader at the time of George II, "Bonnie Prince Charlie."

Quo' I, "Sweet lass, will ye gang wi' me,
Where blackcocks craw, and plovers cry?
Six hills are woolly wi' my sheep,
Six vales are lowing wi' my kye:
I hae looked lang for a weel-faured lass,
By Nithsdale's holmes* an' monie a hill." Lowlands
She hung her head like a dew-bent rose,—
The lovely lass of Preston Mill.

Quo' I, "Sweet maiden, look nae down,
But gie's a kiss, and gang wi' me:"
A lovelier face, O, never looked up,
And the tears were drapping frae her ee.
"I hae a lad, wha's far awa',
That weel could win a woman's will:
My heart's already fu' o' love,"
Quo' the lovely lass of Preston Mill.

"Now wha is he wha could leave sic a lass,
To seek for love in a far countree?"
Her tears drapped down like simmer dew;
I fain wad kissed them frae her ee.
I took but ane o' her comely cheek;
"For pity's sake, kind sir, be still.
My heart is fu' o' ither love,"
Quo' the lovely lass of Preston Mill.

She stretched to heaven her twa white hands,
And lifted up her watery ee:
"Sae lang's my heart kens aught o' God,
Or light is gladsome to my ee;
While woods grow green, and burns rin clear,
Till my last drap o' blood be still,
My heart shall haud nae other love,"
Quo' the lovely lass of Preston Mill.

There's comely maids on Dee's wild banks
And Nith's romantic vale is fu':
By lanely Cluden's hermit stream
Dwells monie a gentle dame, I trow.
O, they are lights of a gladsome kind,
As ever shone on vale or hill:
But there's a light puts them a' out,—
The lovely lass of Preston Mill.

## The Lovely Lass of Inverness

There lived a lass in Inverness,
She was the pride of a' the town;
Blithe as the lark on gowan-tap,
When frae the nest but newly flown.
At kirk she won the auld folks' love,

At dance she was the young men's een.
She was the blithest aye o' the blithe,
At wooster-trystes or Halloween.

As I came in by Inverness,
The simmer sun was sinking down.
Oh, there I saw the weel-faured* lass, "favored"
And she was greeting* through the town: weeping
The gray-haired men were a' i' the streets,
And auld dames crying (sad to see)
"The flower o' the lads of Inverness
Lie dead upon Culloden-lee."[1]

She tore her haffet-links* of gowd, side-curls
And dighted aye her comely ee.
"My father's head's on Carlisle wall,
At Preston sleep my brethren three.
I thought my heart could haud nae mair,
Nae tears could ever blin' my ee;
But the fa' o' ane has burst my heart,
A dearer ane there couldna be.

"He trysted me o' love yestreen,
Of love-tokens he gave me three;
But he's fauldled i' the arms o' weir*, "war"
Oh, ne'er again to think o' me.
The forest flowers shall be my bed,
My food shall be the wild berry,
The fa' o' the leaf shall cover me cauld,
And waukened again I winna be."

Oh weep, oh weep, ye Scottish dames,
Weep till ye blin' a mither's ee.
Nae reeking* ha' in fifty miles, (burning)
But naked corses*, sad to see. "corpses"
Oh spring is blithesome to the year,
Trees sprout, flowers spring, and birds sing hie;
But oh, what spring can raise them up,
That lie on dread Culloden-lee?

The hand o' God hung heavy here,
And lightly touched foul tyranny.
It struck the righteous to the ground,
And lifted the detroyer hie.
"But there's a day," quo my God in prayer,
"When righteousness shall bear the gree*; prize
I'll rake the wicked low i' the dust,
And wauken, in bliss, the gude man's ee."

---

[1]The battlefield of Culloden is only a few miles from Inverness, the unofficial capital of the Highlands.

## My Nanie, O

Red rows the Nith tween bank and brae,
Mirk is the night, and rainy, O;
Though heaven and earth should mix in storm,
I'll gang and see my Nanie, O.
My Nanie, O, my Nanie, O;
My kind and winsome Nanie, O,
She holds my heart in love's dear bands,
And nane can do't but Nanie, O.

In preaching time sae meek she stands,
Sae saintly and sae bonnie, O;
I cannot get ae glimpse of grace,
For thieving looks at Nanie, O.
My Nanie, O, my Nanie, O;
The world's in love with Nanie, O.
That heart is hardly worth the wear
That wadna love my Nanie, O.

My breast can scarce contain my heart,
When dancing she moves finely, O;
I guess what heaven is by her eyes,
They sparkle sae divinely, O.
My Nanie, O, my Nanie, O;
The flower o' Nithsdale's Nanie, O.
Love looks frae neath her lang brown hair,
And says, I dwell with Nanie, O.

Tell not, thou star at gray daylight,
Oer Tinwald-top so bonnie, O,
My footsteps mang the morning dew,
When coming frae my Nanie, O.
My Nanie, O, my Nanie, O,
Nane ken o' me and Nanie, O.
The stars and moon may tell't aboon,
They winna wrang my Nanie, O.

## The Thistle's Grown Aboon the Rose

Full white the Bourbon lily blows,
And fairer haughty England's rose.
Nor shall unsung the symbol smile,
Green Ireland, of thy lovely isle.
In Scotland grows a warlike flower,
Too rough to bloom in lady's bower;
His crest, when high the soldier bears,
And spurs his courser on the spears,
O, there it blossoms—there it blows—
The thistle's grown aboon* the rose. above

Bright like a steadfast star it smiles
Aboon the battle's burning files;

The mirkest cloud, the darkest night,
Shall ne'er make dim that beauteous light;
And the best blood that warms my vein
Shall flow ere it shall catch a stain.
Far has it shone on fields of fame,
From matchless Bruce till dauntless Graeme,
From swarthy Spain to Siber's snows;—
The thistle's grown aboon the rose.

What conquered ay, what nobly spared,
What firm endured, and greatly dared?
What reddened Egypt's burning sand?
What vanquished on Corunna's strand?
What pipe on green Maida blew shrill?
What dyed in blood Barossa hill?
Bade France's dearest life-blood rue
Dark Soignies and dread Waterloo?
That spirit which no terror knows;—
The thistle's grown aboon the rose.

I vow—and let men mete the grass
For his red grave who dares say less—
Men kinder at the festive board,
Men braver with the spear and sword,
Men higher famed for truth—more strong
In virtue, sovereign sense, and song,
Or maids more fair, or wives more true,
Than Scotland's, ne'er trode down the dew.
Round flies the song—the flagon flows,—
The thistle's grown aboon the rose.

## The Sun Rises Bright in France

The sun rises bright in France,
And fair sets he;
But he has tint* the blithe blink he had
In my ain country.
O, gladness comes to many,
But sorrow comes to me,
As I look oer the wide ocean
To my ain country.

O, it's nae my ain ruin
That saddens aye my e'e,
But the love I left in Galloway,
Wi' bonnie bairnies three.
My hamely hearth burnt bonnie,
An' smiled my fair Marie;
I've left my heart behind me
In my ain country.

*lost

The bud comes back to summer,
And the blossom to the bee;
But I'll win back—O never,
To my ain country.
I'm leal* to the high heaven, "loyal"
Which will be leal to me,
An' there I'll meet ye a' soon
Frae my ain country.

### The Bonnie Bairns[1]

The lady she walked in yon wild wood,
Aneath the hollin tree;
And she was aware of two bonnie bairns
Were running at her knee.

The tane it pulled a red, red rose,
With a hand as soft as silk;
The other, it pulled the lily pale,
Wi' a hand mair white than milk.

"Now, why pull ye the red rose, fair bairns?
And why the white lily?"
"O we sue wi' them at the seat of grace
For the soul of thee, lady."

"O bide wi' me, my twa bonnie bairns,
I'll cleid ye rich and fine;
And all for the blaeberries of the wood,
Ye'se hae white bread and wine."

She heard a voice, a sweet low voice,
Say, "Weans, ye tarry lang."
She stretched her hand to the youngest bairn:
"Kiss me before ye gang."

She sought to take a lily hand,
And kiss a rosy chin:—
"O, nought sae pure can bide the touch,
Of a hand red-wet wi' sin."

The stars were shooting to and fro,
And wild-fire filled the air,
As that lady followed thae bonnie bairns
For three lang hours and mair.

"O where dwell ye, my ain sweet bairns?
I'm wae and weary grown."
"O lady, we live where woe never is,
In a land to sin unknown."

---

[1] Cunningham's reworking of a folk ballad.

There came a shape which seemed to her
As a rainbow mang the rain;
And sair these sweet babes pled for her,
And they pled and pled in vain.

"And O, and O," said the youngest babe,
"My mother maun come in."
"And O, and O," said the eldest babe,
"Wash her twa hands frae sin."

"And O, and O," said the youngest babe,
"She nursed me on her knee."
"And O, and O," said the eldest babe,
"She's a mither yet to me."

"And O, and O," said the babes baith,
"Take her where waters rin,
And white as the milk o' her white breast
Wash her twa hands frae sin."

## The Lord's Marie

The lord's Marie has kepped* her locks — caught
Up wi' a gowden kame;
An' she has put on her net-silk hose,
An' awa' to the tryst has gane.
O saft, saft fell the dew on her locks,
An' saft, saft on her brow;—
Ae sweet drap fell on her strawberry lip,
An' I kissed it aff, I trow.

"O where gat ye that leal maiden
Sae jimpy* laced an' sma? — slender
An' where gat ye that young damsel
Wha dings* our lasses a'? — (bests)
O where gat ye that bonny, bonny lass
Wi' heaven in her e'e?
O here's ae drap o' the damask wine;—
Sweet maiden, will ye pree*?" — taste

Fu' white, white was her taper neck,
Twist wi' the satin twine;
But ruddy, ruddy grew her hawse* — throat
While she supped the blude red wine.
"Come, here's thy health, young stranger doo*, — dove
Wha wears the gowden kame.
This night will mony drink thy health,
An' ken na wha to name."

"Play me up *Sweet Marie*," I cried,
An' loud the piper blew;
But the fiddler played aye *Struntum strum*,—

An' down his bow he threw:
"Now here's thy health i' the red, red wine,
Fair dame o' the stranger land,
For never a pair of een before
Could mar my gude bow-hand."

Her lips were a cloven hinny-cherry,
Ripe tempting to the sight;
Her locks o'er alabaster brows
Fell like the morning light;
An' O, her hinny breath raised her locks,
As through the dance she flew;
While love laughed out o' her bright blue e'e,
An' dwalt on her rosy mou'.

"Loose hings yere broidered gowd garter,
Fair lady,—daur I speak?"—
She, trembling, raised her snowy hand
To her red, red flushing cheek.
"Ye hae drapt yere broach o' the beaten gowd,
Thou Lord's daughter sae gay."—
The tears swam bright in her bonny blue ee:
"O come, O come away."

"O haste, unbar the siller bolt—
To my chamber let me win,
An' take this kiss, thou peasant youth,—
For I daurna let ye in.
An' take," quo she, "this kame o' gowd,
Wi' this tress o' yellow hair;
For mickle my beating heart forebodes
I never maun meet ye mair."

## ALEXANDER RODGER (1784–1846)

### Behave Yoursel' Before Folk

Behave yoursel' before folk,
Behave yoursel' before folk,
And dinna be sae rude to me,
As kiss me sae before folk.

It wouldna gie me meikle pain,
Gin we wer seen and heard by nane,
To tak a kiss, or grant you ane;
But gudesake! no before folk.
Behave yoursel' before folk,
Behave yoursel' before folk,
What'er you do when out o' view,
Be cautious aye before folk.

Consider, lad, how folks will crack*, gossip
And what a great affair they'll mak
O' naething but a simple smack,
That's gi'en or ta'en before folk.
Behave yoursel' before folk,
Behave yoursel' before folk,
Nor gie the tongue o' old and young
Occasion to come o'er folk.

It's no through hatred o' a kiss,
That I sae plainly tell you this;
But losh! I tak it sair amiss
To be sae teased before folk.
Behave yoursel' before folk,
Behave yoursel' before folk,
When we're our lane* ye may tak ane, alone
But fient* a ane before folk. devil

I'm sure wi' you I've been as free
As ony modest lass should be;
But yet it doesna do to see
Sic freedom used before folk.
Behave yoursel' before folk,
Behave yoursel' before folk,
I'll ne'er submit again to it.
So mind you that—before folk.

Ye tell me that my face is fair:
It may be sae—I dinna care—
But ne'er again gar't blush so sair
As ye hae done before folk.
Behave yoursel' before folk,
Behave yoursel' before folk,
Nor heat my cheeks wi' your mad freaks,
But aye be douce* before folk. sober

Ye tell me that my lips are sweet.
Sic tales, I doubt, are a' deceit—
At ony rate, it's hardly meet
To prie their sweets before folk.
Behave yoursel' before folk,
Behave yoursel' before folk,
Gin that's the case, there's time and place,
But surely no before folk.

But gin you really do insist
That I should suffer to be kissed,
Gae get a license frae the priest,
And mak me yours before folk.
Behave yoursel' before folk,
Behave yoursel' before folk,
And when we're ane, baith flesh and bane,
Ye may tak ten—before folk.

## My Auld Breeks

My mither men't my auld breeks,
An' wow! but they were duddy*, ragged
And sent me to get Mally shod
At Robin Tamson's smiddy.
The smiddy stands beside the burn
That wimples through the clachan*, village
I never yet gae by the door,
But aye I fa' a-laughin'.

For Robin was a walthy carle* fellow, peasant
An' had ae bonnie dochter,
Yet ne'er wad let her tak a man,
Though mony lads had socht her.
But what think ye o' my exploit?
The time our mare was shoeing,
I slippit up beside the lass,
And briskly fell a-wooing.

An' aye she e'ed my auld breeks,
The time that we sat crackin'*, chatting
Quo I, "My lass, ne'er mind the clouts*, patches
I've new anes for the makin';
But gin ye'll just come hame wi' me,
An' lea'e the carle, your father,
Ye'se get my breeks to keep in trim,
Mysel, an' a' thegither."

"Deed, lad," quo she, "Your offer's fair.
I really think I'll tak it,
Sae, gang awa', get out the mare,
We'll baith slip on the back o't:
For gin I wait my father's time,
I'll wait till I be fifty;
But na, I'll marry in my prime,
An' mak a wife most thrifty."

Wow, Robin was an angry man,
At tyning* o' his dochter. losing
Through a' the kintra-side he ran,
An' far an' near he socht her;
But when he cam to our fire-end,
An' fand us baith thegither,
Quo, I, "Gudeman, I've ta'en your bairn,
An' ye may tak my mither."

Auld Robin girned* an' sheuk his pow*, grinned/head
"Guid sooth," quo he, "Ye're merry,
But I'll just tak ye at your word,
An' end this hurry-burry."
So Robin an' our auld wife
Agreed to creep thegither.

Now, I hae Robin Tamson's pet,
A' Robin has my mither.

## WILLIAM TENNANT (1784–1848)

[Tennant, a lifelong scholar of languages, was born at Anstruther in Fife. He worked for years as a schoolmaster, then in 1834 was appointed Professor of Oriental Languages at the University of St. Andrews. He is known for two fine poems, both mock epics, *Anster Fair* (1812) and *Papistry Stormed* (1827). The first, of 3500 lines, is based on the folk song "Maggie Lauder" which Tennant alters to a story of a four-part contest or tournament at Anstruther ("Anster") in which Rob the Ranter wins the hand of the village beauty, Maggie Lauder. In *Anster Fair*, King James V is himself present to hand over the prize, and elements of the supernatural are of considerable significance. Given below is the poem's finest moment, the third or bagpipe contest (the others are a donkey race, a sack race and a storytelling match).

*Anster Fair*, in more or less standard English, is a charming work, but *Papistry Stormed* is the author's great achievement, one of the most unusual long poems in Scottish literature. Written in Scots, it is a brilliantly funny and iconoclastic treatment of a serious subject, the destruction of the great Cathedral of St. Andrews by a Protestant mob in 1559. The poem is too long (4000 lines) for inclusion, but it does lend itself to excerpting since the sixth "Sang," called here "Kirk-spulyie, Herriement, and Raid," is not only the climax of the poem, but the poem itself in miniature. *Papistry Stormed* ranks with Scott's *Lady of the Lake*, Hogg's "Kilmeny," and Thomson's *The City of Dreadful Night*, as among the best long poems of the Scottish nineteenth century.]

### Tammy Little

Wee Tammy Little, honest man!
I kent the body weel,
As round the kintra-side he gaed,
Careerin' wi' his creel.

He was sae slender and sae wee,
That aye when blasts did blaw,
He ballasted himself wi' stanes
Gainst bein' blawn awa.

A meikle stane the wee bit man
In ilka coat-pouch clappit,
That by the michty gowlin' wind
He michtna doun be swappit.

When he did chance within a wood,
On simmer days to be,
Aye he was frichted lest the craws
Should heise him up on hie;

And aye he, wi' an aiken* cud, "oaken"
The air did thump and beat,

To stap the craws frae liftin' him
Up to their nests for meat.

Ae day, when in a barn he lay,
And thrashers thrang* were thair, crowded
He in a moment vanished aff,
And nae man could tell whair.

They lookit till the riggin' up,
And round and round they lookit,
At last they fand him underneath
A firlot[1] cruyled and crookit.

Ance as big Samuel passed him by,
Big Samuel gave a sneeze,
And wi' the sough* o't he was cast swoosh
Clean doun upon his knees.

His wife and he upon ane day
Did chance to disagree,
And up she took the bellowses,
As wild as wife could be;

She gave ane puff intill his face,
And made him, like a feather,
Flee frae the tae side o' the house,
Resoundin' till the tither.

Ae simmer e'en, when as he through
Pitkirie forest past,
By three braid leaves, blawn aff the trees,
He doun to yird* was cast. earth

A tirl o' wind the three braid leaves
Doun frae the forest dang*: struck
Ane frae an ash, ane frae an elm,
Ane frae an aik-tree strang.

Ane strack him sair on the back-neck,
Ane on the nose him rappit,
Ane smote him on the vera heart,
And doun as dead he drappit.

But ah, but ah, a drearier dool* "dole"
Ance happed at Ounston-dammy,
That heised* him a' thegither up, raised
And maist extinguished Tammy;

For, as he cam slow-daunderin' doun,
In's hand his basket hingin',

[1] A small measure, i.e. a small cask or tub.

And staivered* ower the hei-road's breidth, staggered
Frae side to side a'swingin';

There cam a blast frae Kelly-law,
As bald a blast as ever
Auld snivelin' Boreas blew abraid,
To mak the warld shiver.

It liftit Tammy aff his feet,
Mair easy than a shavin',
And hurled him half a mile complete
Hie up tween earth and heaven.

That day puir Tammy had wi' stanes
No ballasted his body,
So that he flew, maist like a shot,
Ower corn-land and ower cloddy.

You've seen ane tumbler on a stage,
Tumble sax times and mair,
But Tammy weel sax hundred times
Gaed tumbln' through the air.

And whan the whirly-wind gave ower
He frae the lift* fell plumb, sky
And in a blink stood stickin' fast
In Gaffer Glowr-weel's lum*. chimney

Ay—there his legs and body stack
Amang the smotherin' soot,
But, by a wonderfu' good luck,
His head kept peepin' out.

But Gaffer Glowr-weel, when he saw
A man stuck in his lum,
He swarfed* wi' drither clean awa, swooned
And sat some seconds dumb.

It took five masons near an hour
A' riving at the lum
Wi' picks—he was sae jammed therein—
Ere Tammy out could come.

As for his basket—weel I wat,
His basket's fate and fa'
Was, as I've heard douce* neighbors tell, sober
The queerest thing of a'.

The blast took up the body's creel
And laid it on a cloud,
That bare it, sailin' through the sky,
Richt ower the Firth's braid flood.

And whan the cloud did melt awa,
Then, then the creel cam doun,
And felled the toun-clerk o' Dunbar
E'en in his aun gude toun.

The clerk stood yelpin' on the street,
At some bit strife that stirred him,
Doun cam the creel, and to the yird
It dang him wi' a dirdom*. uproar

The Epitaph for Tammy

O Earth, O Earth, if thou hast but
A rabbit-hole to spair,
O grant the graff to Tammy's corp,
That it may nestle thair.

And press thou light on him, now dead,
That was sae slim and wee,
For weel I wat, when he was quick,
He lightly pressed on thee.

## "Their Powers of Piping"
(*Anster Fair*, Canto IV, 400-728)

. . . Nor ceased the business of the day meanwhile;
For as the monarch[1] chewed his sav'ry cake,
The man, whose lungs sustain the trumpet's toil,
Made haste again his noisy tube to take,
And with a cry, which, heard full many a mile,
Caused the young crows on Airdrie's trees to quake,
He bade the suitor-pipers to draw nigh,
That they might, round the knoll, their powers of piping try.

Which when the rabble heard, with sudden sound
They broke their circle's huge circumference,
And, crushing forward to the southern mound,
They pushed their many-headed shoal immense,
Diffusing to an equal depth around
Their mass of bodies wedged compact and dense,
That, standing nigher, they might better hear
The pipers sqeaking loud to charm Miss Maggie's ear.

And soon the pipers, shouldering along
Through the close mob their squeezed uneasy way,
Stood at the hillock's foot, an eager throng,
Each asking license from the king to play;
For with a tempest, turbulent and strong,
Labored their bags impatient of delay,

[1] James V, presiding over the Fair.

Heaving their bloated globes outrageously,
As if in pangs to give their contents to the sky.

And every bag, thus full and tempest-ripe,
Beneath its arm lay ready to be prest,
And, on the holes of each fair-polished pipe,
Each piper's fingers long and white were placed;
Fiercely they burned in jealous rivalship;
Each madding piper scoffed at all the rest,
And fleered and tossed contemptuously his head,
As if his skill alone deserved fair Maggie's bed.

Nor could they wait, so piping-mad they were,
Till James gave each man orders to begin,
But in a moment they displode their air
In one tumultuous and unlicensed din;
Out-flies, in storm of simultaneous blare,
The whizzing wind comprest their bags within,
And, whiffling through the wooden tubes so small,
Growls gladness to be freed from such confining thrall.

Then rose, in burst of hideous symphony,
Of pibrochs and of tunes one mingled roar;
Discordantly the pipes squealed sharp and high,
The drones alone in solemn concord snore;
Five hundred fingers, twinkling funnily,
Play twiddling up and down on hole and bore
Now passage to the shrilly wind denying,
And now a little raised to let it out a-sighing.

Then rung the rocks and caves of Billyness,
Reverberating back that concert's sound,
And half the lurking echoes that possess
The glens and hollows of the Fifan ground,
Their shadowy voices strained into excess
Of outcry, loud huzzaing round and round
To all the Dryads of Pitkirie wood,
That now they round their trees should dance in frisky mood.

As when the sportsman with report of gun
Alarms the sea-fowl of the Isle of May,
Ten thousand mews and gulls that shade the sun
Come flapping down in terrible dismay;
And with a wild and barb'rous concert stun
His ears, and scream, and shriek, and wheel away;
Scarce can the boatman hear his plashing oar;
Yell caves and eyries all, and rings each Maian shore.

Just so around the knoll did pipe and drone
Whistle and hum a discord strange to hear,
Tort'ring with violence of shriek and groan
Kingly, and courtly, and plebeian ear;
And still the men had hummed and whistled on.

Ev'n till each bag had burst its bloated sphere,
Had not the king, uprising, waved his hand,
And checked the boist'rous din of such unmannered band.

On one side of his face a laugh was seen,
On t'other side a half-formed frown lay hid;
He frowned, because they petulantly keen,
Set up their piping forward and unbid;
He laughed, for who could have controlled his mien,
Hearing such crash of pibrochs as he did?
He bade them orderly the strife begin,
And play each man the tune wherewith the fair he'd win.

Whereat the pipers ceased their idle toil
Of windy music wild and deafening,
And made too late (what they forgot e'erwhile)
A general bow to Maggie and their king;
But, as they vailed their bare heads tow'rd the soil,
O then there happed a strange portentous thing,
Which had not good my Muse confirmed for true,
Myself had not believed, far less have told to you.

For lo! whilst all their bodies yet were bent,
Breaks from the spotless blue of eastern sky
A globe of fire, (miraculous ostent!)
Bursten from some celestial cleft on high;
And thrice in circle round the firmament
Trailed its long light the gleamy prodigy,
Till on the ring of pipers down it came,
And set their pipes and drones and chanters in a flame.

Twas quick and sudden as th' electric shock;
One moment lighted and consumed them all;
As is the green hair of the tufted oak
Scathed into blackness by the fulmined ball,
Or, as spark-kindled, into fire and smoke,
Flashes and fumes the nitrous grain so small,
So were their bagpipes, in a twink, like tinder
Fired underneath their arms and burned into a cinder.

Yet so innocuous was the sky-fall'n flame
That, save their twangling instruments alone,
Unsinged their other gear remained the same,
Ev'n to the nap that stuck their coats upon;
Nor did they feel its heat when down it came
On errand to destroy pipe, bag and drone,
But stood in blank surprise, when to the ground
Dropt down in ashes black their furniture of sound.

Crest-fallen they stood, confounded and distrest,
And fixed upon the turf their stupid look,
Conscious that Heav'n forbade them to contest
By such a burning token of rebuke.

The rabble, too, its great alarm confest,
For every face the ruddy blood forsook,
As with their white, uprolling, ghastly eyes
They spied the streaky light wheel whizzing from the skies.

And still they to that spot of orient heav'n,
Whence burst the shining glove, look up aghast,
Expecting when th' empyreal pavement riven
A second splendor to the earth should cast;
But when they saw no repetition given,
Changed from alarm to noisy joy at last,
They set up such a mixed tremendous shout,
As made the girdling heav'ns to bellow round about.

And such a crack and peal of laughter rose,
When the poor pipers bagpipe-less they saw,
As when a flock of inky-feathered crows,
On winter morning when the skies are raw,
Come from their woods in long and sooty rows,
And over Anster through their hoarse throats caw;
The sleepy old-wives, on their warm chaff-beds,
Up from their bolsters rear, afeared, their flanneled heads.

Then did th' affronted pipers slink away,
With faces fixed on earth for very shame,
For not one remnant of those pipes had they
Wherewith they late so arrogantly came,
But in a black and ashy ruin lay
Their glory moldered by the scathing flame;
Yet in their hearts they cursed (and what the wonder?)
That fire to which their pipes so quick were giv'n a plunder.

And scarce they off had slunk, when with a bound
Great Robert Scot sprung forth before the king,
For he alone, when all the pipers round
Stood ranged into their fire-devoted ring,
Had kept snug distance from the fated ground,
As if forewarned of that portentous thing;
He stood and laughed, as underneath his arm
He held his bagpipe safe, unscathed with fiery harm.

His hollow drone, with mouth wide-gaping, lay
Over his shoulder pointing to the sky,
Ready to spew its breath and puff away
The lazy silver clouds that sit on high;
His bag swelled madly to begin the play,
And with its bowel-wind groaned inwardly;
Not higher heaved the wind-bags which of yore
Ulysses got from him who ruled th' Aeolian shore.

He thus the king with reverence bespoke;
My liege, since Heaven with bagpipe-leveled fire
Hath turned my bretheren's gear to dust and smoke,

And testified too glaringly its ire,
It fits me now, as yet my bagpipe's poke
Remains unsinged and every pipe entire,
To play my tune—O king, with your good will—
And to the royal ear to prove my piping skill.

Nodded his liege assent, and straightway bade
Him stand atop o th' hillock at his side;
Atop he stood; and first a bow he made
To all the crowd that shouted far and wide,
Then, like a piper dext'rous at his trade,
His pipes to play adjusted and applied;
Each finger rested on its proper bore;
His arm appeared half raised to wake the bag's uproar.

A space he silent stood, and cast his eye
In meditation upwards to the pole,
As if he prayed some fairy pow'r in sky
To guide his fingers right oer bore and hole,
Then pressing down his arm he gracefully
Awaked the merry bagpipe's slumb'ring soul,
And piped and blew and played so sweet a tune
As might have well unsphered the reeling midnight moon.

His ev'ry finger, to its place assigned,
Moved quiv'ring like the leaf of aspen tree,
Now shutting up the skittish squeaking wind,
Now op'ning to the music passage free;
His cheeks, with windy puffs therein confined,
Were swoln into a red rotundity,
As from his lungs into the bag was blown
Supply of needful air to feed the growling drone.

And such a potent tune did never greet
The drum of human ear with lively strain,
So merry, that from dancing on his feet
No man undeaf could stockishly refrain,
So loud, twas heard a dozen miles complete,
Making old Echo pipe and hum again,
So sweet, that all the birds in air that fly,
Charmed into new delight, come sailing through the sky.

Crow, sparrow, linnet, hawk, and white-winged dove,
Wheel in aerial jig oer Anster loan;
The sea-mews from each Maian cleft and cove
O'er the deep sea come pinion-wafted on;
The light-detesting bats now flap above,
Scaring the sun with wings to day unknown:
Round Robert's head they dance, they cry, they sing,
And shear the subtle sky with broad and playful wing.

And eke the mermaids that in ocean swim,
Drawn by that music from their shelly caves,

Peep now unbashful from the salt-sea brim,
And flounce and plash exulting in the waves;
They spread at large the white and floating limb,
That Neptune amorously clips and laves,
And kem with combs of pearl and coral fair
Their long sleek oozy locks of green redundant hair.

Now was its influence less on human ear;
First from their gilded chairs up-start at once
The royal James and Maggie seated near,
Enthusiastic both and mad to dance;
Her hand he snatched and looked a merry leer,
Then capered high in wild extravagance,
And on the grassy summit of the knoll,
Wagged each monarchial leg in galliard strange and droll.

As when a sunbeam, from the waving face
Of well-filled waterpail reflected bright,
Varies upon the chamber walls its place,
And, quiv'ring, tries to cheat and foil the sight;
So quick did Maggie, with a nimble grace
Skip patt'ring to and fro, alert and light,
And, with her noble colleague in the reel,
Sublimely tossed her arms, and shook the glancing heel.

The lords and ladies, next, who sat or stood,
Near to the piper and the king around,
Smitten with that contagious dancing mood,
Gan hand in hand in high lavolt to bound,
And jigged it on as featly as they could,
Circling in sheeny rows the rising ground,
Each sworded lord a lady's soft palm griping,
And to his mettle roused at such unwonted piping.

Then did th' infectious hopping-mania seize
The circles of the crowd that stood more near,
Till, round and round, far spreading by degrees,
It maddened all the loan to kick and rear;
Men, women, children, lilt and ramp, and squeeze,
Such fascination takes the gen'ral ear.
Ev'n babes, that at their mothers' bosoms hung,
Their little willing limbs fantastically flung.

And hoar-haired men and wives, whose marrow age
Hath from their hollow bones sucked out and drunk,
Canary in unconscionable rage,
Nor feel their sinews withered now and shrunk;
Pellmell in random couples they engage,
And boisterously wag their bodies trunk,
Till from their heated skin the sweat out-squirts,
And soaks with clammy dew their goodly Holland shirts.

And cripples from beneath their shoulders fling
Their despicable crutches far away,
Then, yoked with those of stouter limbs, upspring
In hobbling merriment, uncouthly gay;
And some on one leg stand y-gamboling;
For why? The other short and frail had they;
Some, whose both legs distorted were and weak,
Dance on their poor knee-pans in mad prepost'rous freak.

So on they trip, king, Maggie, knight, and earl,
Green-coated courtier, satin-snooded* dame, kerchiefed
Old men and maidens, man, wife, boy, and girl,
The stiff, the supple, bandylegged, and lame,
All sucked and rapt into the dance's whirl,
Inevitably witched within the same;
Whilst Rob, far-seen, oerlooks the huddling loan,
Rejoicing in his pipes, and squeals serenely on.

But such a whirling and a din there was,
Of bodies and of feet that heeled the ground,
As when the Maelstrom in his craggy jaws
Engluts the Norway waves with hideous sound;
In vain the black sea-monster plies his paws
Gainst the strong eddy that impels him round;
Worked into barm, the torrent surges roar,
And fret their frothy wrath and reel from shore to shore.

So reel the mob, and with their feet up-cast
From the tramped soil a dry and dusty cloud,
That shades the huddling hurly-burly vast
From the warm sun as with an earthy shroud;
Else, had the warm sun spied them wriggling fast,
He sure had laughed at such bewitched crowd,
For never, since heaven's baldric first he trod,
Tripped was such country dance beneath his fiery road.

Then was the shepherd, that on Largo law
Sat idly whistling to his feeding flock,
Dismayed, when looking southeastward he saw
The dusty cloud more black than furnace-smoke;
He leaned his ear, and catched with trembling awe
The dance's sounds that th' ambient ether broke;
He blessed himself, and cried, By sweet St John,
The devil hath got a job in Anster's dirty loan.

At length the mighty piper, honest Rob,
His wonder-working melody gave oer,
When on a sudden all the flouncing mob
Their high commotion ceased and tossed no more;
Trunk, arm, and leg, forgot to shake and bob,
That bobbed and shaked so parlously before;
On ground, fatigued, the panting dancers fall,
Wond'ring what witch's craft had thus embroiled them all.

And some cried out, that oer the piper's head
They had observed a little female fay,
Clad in green gown, and purple-striped plaid,
That fed his wind-bag, aidant* of the play; eager
Some, impotent to speak and almost dead
With jumping, as on earth they sat or lay
Wiped from their brows with napkin, plaid or gown,
The globes of shining sweat that ooze and trickle down.

Nor less with jig oerlabored and oerwrought,
Down on their chairs dropt Maggie and the king,
Amazed what supernat'ral spell had caught
And forced their heels into such frolicking;
And much was Mag astonished when she thought
(As sure it was an odd perplexing thing)
That Robert's tune was to her ear the same
As what Tom Puck late played, when from her pot he came.[1]

But from that hour the monarch and the mob
Gave Maggie Lauder's name to Robert's tune,
And so shall it be called while oer the globe
Travels the waning and the crescent moon:
And from that hour the puissant piper Rob,
Whose bagpipe waked so hot a rigadoon,
From his well-managed bag and drone and chanter,
Obtained the glorious name of Mighty Rob the Ranter.

## "Kirk-spulyie, Herriement, and Raid"

(Sang Sixth of *Papistry Stormed,* being the description of St. Andrews Cathedral sacked by a Protestant mob, in 1559)

. . . This canticle's the best ava;
There's fechtin and there's thwackin;
Canons and freirs frae kirk and ha
Are peltit and sent packin;
Pu'pits and beelds are hackit sma;
There's guttin kists* and hackin; "chests"
And as the finish, to crown a,
Down comes the steeple crackin.

The sun was cockin now upon
The vera pin o mid-day's cone,
And frae his beryl-bernin throne,
That loftily did low
Scatter't his great spring-flude o beams,
That whitened a th' Eastnook wi gleams,

[1]The Anster Fair tournament had been the idea of two behind-the-scenes fairies, Tom and Mrs. Puck. The former had been imprisoned by a magician within Maggie's mustard-pot. Madam Puck had been similarly enchanted into Rob's pepper-box.

And made the Firth's clear glassy streams
In siller dance and row;
Nae cloud owr-head the lift* did dim, sky
But i' the wastern weddir-glim
A black up-castin, with ane rim
O' darkness, laced the yerth*, "earth"
Betakenin by the vapor's form,
That in th' Atlantic flude a storm
Was labrin for a birth.

The hour o denner now was come,
And men grew hungry all and some,
And cravin in their crap;
Frae five o'clock that they had risen
Sorry a flow had cross't their gizen
O' solid or a sap';
In Lothian, and in ither pairts,
They dennered weil, wi cheerfu' hearts,
On tailyies* fat and fine; meat pieces
But in Sanct Androis town that day,
Man, wife, nor bairn, as I've heard say,
Had na a heart to dine;
They were sae bent on cloister-guttin,
And hackin images and cuttin,
Ae thocht on beef or yet on mutton
Nae man could safely spare;
He that was yesterday a glutton,
This day he didna care a button
For belly or for fare:
Hunger and anger are near-kin,
Whilk made them that bauld wark begin
Wi' greater dirdom*, wraith, and din, uproar
Than they wud dune wi panget skin
Plumpet wi vivers* rare. viands

Sae in within the yetts* they ran gates
Ramstam, rampagin, wife and man,
Thousands, wi bitter winze* and ban, curse
Cast at the rotten bang,
That now, confoundit wi the steir*, storm, struggle
Took to their heels in deidly fear,
To shelter them in kirk or queir
Frae that in-pourin thrang;
Canon, the greasy monk, and prior,
Arch-dean, and ilka-colored freir,
The Pape's hail fam'ly, fat and fere,
Did in a mass forgather
Within their sacrified abodes,
Scougin themsel's frae stanes and clods,
Aside their shrines and velvet-cods,
Their Lares and their household-gods,
Frae siccan stalwart weather;
As Trojan wives, upon the nicht

Whan Priam's palace bleezit bricht,
Huggit and kiss't (a doolfu' sicht)
Altars and posts in ghastly fricht,
Makin loud screechs and manes;
Saewise that cowled and girdlet fither,
Astoundit wi dumfounderin drither,
Ran through the hey-kirk hither-thither,
Huggin their beilds and banes:
The doors were steeked* and boltit hard; — shut
Wickets and windocks firmly barred;
But through the doors and wa's they heard,
Ascendin from without,
The terrible stramash o tongues,
And winzes flung fram angry lungs,
And shouts o men wi picks and rungs*, — clubs
That huddlit round about;
Ilk man encouragin his feer*, — pal
Cryin aloud, To weir*! To weir! — "war"
Down wi the Harlot and her gear!
Assailzie, strike, destroy!
Whilst thourgh the windocks they did spy
Wier's wild wud* wappens* wavin by; — crazed/ "weapons"
Cuds*, swerds, and halberts, heavit high, — clubs
Whase shadows tween them and the sky
Forebodit noucht but noy;
And surly faces, warst ava,
Horribly glumshin* ane and a, — scowling
Or girnin* into joy, — grimacing, grinning
As they look't up ilk lofty wa,
Takin their meiths* for its downfa, — boundaries
That they may strike an stroy.

Thairat th' assailzie did begin
Wi' gallyies o loud-blairin din;
A thousand sticks, a thousand stanes,
Are through the windocks dash't at anes;
The garnish't glass, the birnish't lozens,
Are knocket in, and dash't in dozens;
Great iron-sweys, great timmer*-trams, — "timber"
And meicle smitin batterin-rams,
Swinget about by angry squads,
Gaif ilk besiegit door sic dads*, — blows
They garred them crack and flee in blads;
Man, wife, nor bairn, of a that host,
Was idle, or was aff his post;
The little bairns threw little stanes,
And played upon the paintet panes.
The wives, as rampant in their mettle,
With idle foolitch neifs* did ettle*, — fists/struggle
And wi their flytings* fired the battle: — scoldings
The men—here sax, there seven or aucht—
A batterin-ram wi a their maucht,
Were swappin gainst a portal straucht.

Here scores their pinches and their picks
Atween the ayslar* stanes did fix. ashlar
And rugg't and rave them out;
Wi' batter-ax some brak in sma'
The carvit wark and pillars bra,
Sendin the glory of the wa,
In fritter't frush about;
Some to the windocks up did clamber,
And daddit in, wi chappin-hammer,
The staney-frames and lead.
Some delvit down wi spades and shools,
Deep, deep amid the yerth and mools*, "molds" (earth)
Strivin wi howkin* and wi digging' disinterring
To bring th' upsettin pridefu' biggin* building
Laigh down amang the dead.
And some gat ladders large and lang,
On whilk they mountit and did spang,
Chasin ilk ither in a bang
Up to the roofs on hie,
Owr whilk frae end to end they spread,
Like flock o locusts black and braid,
And rave frae rafter and frae riggin
The capper* that owr-clad the biggin, "copper"
Glitterand owr land and sea.

But, saftly, Muse, and tak mair time;
Be mair partic'lar in your rhyme;
I wish to ken what chiftain first
Intill th' expugnate kirk did burst.
What man assailzied with ane kick
The water-vat, and garred it quick
Gang rowin aff its silver styk?
Wha the hey-altar over-coupit?
The graven idols aff wha soupit?
Wha tumbled down the Card'nal's pupit?
And monie ither famous thing,
Worthy o you to say and sing,
Albeit I be to write inding.

The batterin-ram wi jowin* jerk swinging
Nae sooner brak the door o the kirk,
When Caryl's bauld through-gain clerk
Burst in wi sudden spang,
His left hand holdin up on-heicht
The borough-colors wavin bricht;
A halbert in his stalwart richt
Up-stannin clean and lang;
He paused a wee on the dure-stane
Crying, "Hurra, my merry men!
Ha, Satan's toy-shop now is taen!
Look up and see your spulzie.
March, birkies*, ben*, and follow me." men/in
Sae sayin, wi triumphant glee,

He wav't his pennon up on hie,
The sign o march and tulzie,
Whilk whan the Papish folk beheld,
A gallyie* o fierce wraith was yelled     roar
Frae a' within the kirk,
Mixt wi shrill skellochs o despair
As they espied gambadin there
That lion-lookin clerk.
Yet, nat the less for his bauld look,
Great shoals o freirs, frae ilk kirk-nouk*,     "nook"
Men o weil-biggit frame and buik,
Cam down upon him rushin,
Ettlin, wi fuffin and wi pain,
To ding th' assaulter back again,
And hurlin at his head a rain
O creepie, stool, and cushion.
He lowered down his braid-cheek't wapen,
And round and round he held it swappin,
To catch the fallows that mith happen
To come within his cleik.
Will Cranstoun, that deil's-buckie chap
(A tap-thrawn monk wi roundit cap),
Was the first man that caught a wap.
He gat in on his cheek;
Wi its strang swing, the girdlet brither
Flew frae ae pillar to the tither,
Syne in a stound did drap.
Tam Guillaum in his heavy gown
(A bummill* kent through a the town)     idler
Was the neist man whase shaven crown
Was hanseled* wi a swap.     rewarded
The bummil felt the swap sae sair,
Backlins he stagger't wi a rair
To Gamyl's tomb, and hid him thair
Fram onie mair wanhap*;     mishap
And twenty mair sic rotten whelps
Gat on the haffets* famous skelps,     cheeks
That made them utter yells and yelps
And tummle into trances;
Sae that the not'ry through the wrack
O strewit shavelings in a crack
March't wi his legion at his back
With iron-gads and lances.
By this time, too, wi dreidfu' din,
The windocks a were driven in,
And heaps o ragin bodies
Cam streamin in through ilk fenester,
Loupin ilk man than tither faster,
Red-wud* for mischief and disaster,     crazed
And brandishin their cuddies*;     clubs
Sae that the kirk's ilk battered side
Fram a her raggit loop-holes wide,
Lat in ane over-flowin tide

O ragin-wud assaulters,
That forcit into sma'er space
The Paip's canallyie* scant o grace, mob
Garrin them fecht i' th' middle place
For heartstanes now and altars.
And now the hail kirk east and wast
Was but ane hurlie-burlie vast
O fechters and defenders fast
A toylin at the tulyie.
The cross-kirk too was just as thrang
O bangsters that did ither mang
In hideous tulyie-mulyie.
Terrible thumps were gien and taken,
Whairby ten thousand ribs were shaken.
Nae man did spare his faeman's bacon;
Nae man cried, Hoolyie, Hoolyie!
Braid showther-blades now gat their paikin;
Back-banes wi bastinads were shaken
Down, down to their foundation.
Ilk wappen that cam frae the coast,
Was now in action by the host,
Swung round their huddlin heads and tost
In windy agitation.
Battens and a kinkind* o sticks, sort
Clodmells and barrow-trams and picks,
And handspakes that gave lounderin licks,
Flickered in fierce vibration.
The vera wind o siccan werk
Blew down the mouse-webs black and mirk,
That had, up on the tap o th' kirk,
Twa hunder year been stickin;
What wi the mouse-webs fram on hie,
And stour* that frae their feet did flie, dust
Around their heads a canopy
O misty motes did thicken,
Sae that, half-hidden in the dark,
They labored at the fechtin-wark,
But ilka man took weil his mark,
And, as he lounder't strang and stark,
Kent weil wham he was lickin.

Around the bonnie siller-platter,
That did contein the Heilie water,
Twal canons bare the brunt and blatter,
By William Lauder backit,
Whase face wi crabbitness did grin,
And his flyte-poke aneath his chin
Prieved he was in an angry pin
To be thus-gate attacket;
The laird o Barns discern't ere lang
That cankered carl* amid the gang, peasant

Wha wi his accusation dang
Gude Wishart[1] to the dede;
The mem'rie o that wicket thing,
And cruel martyrdom inding
Was to his mind a ready sting,
To prick him up to fede:
Ah, cruel wratch! he thus began,
Yet dost thou live, thou wicket man?
Whan he wham thy black tongue did ban* curse
Lies down amang the dead!
Ah, happy me, if I can pay
Sma vengeance for that michtie wae:
He drew his swerd out, saying sae,
And wi a sturdy straik,
First his richt ear he clean aff-cleft,
And then he sneddit aff his left,
Leavin o baith his lugs* bereft ears
The head of that vile rake:
The wratch ran quiverin aff and quakin,
Leavin his lugs to save his bacon;
Happy it sae had endit,
For had he gat his just desert,
His tongue, the rogue's maist peccant pairt,
Had fra his mou been rendit:
But whan Kilbrachmont by that taken
The water-ewer saw forsaken,
Nor langer weil defendit,
He rushed upon it with a spang,
And wi a monstrous kick down-dang
The styk o silver rich and lang
That did up-hald the platter;
The vat flew mair than twenty paces,
Strenkellin, a round, the fectar's faces,
Wi its out-waffin water;
The stick, extirpate wi the blaw,
Clean owr the flure frae wa to wa
Gaed rowin wi a clatter.

Whilst styk and vat was dingin down,
A troop, saul-thirsty for renown,
The scholars of Sanct Androis town,
Ilk ane in dud o scarlet gown,
Gaed tween the wa's and pillars,
Ravagin on, a furious squade,
The Regent Douglas at their head,
Seekin for beelds to ding them dead,
That they mith spread their name abread
As famous image-killers:
Ilk tirlie-wirlie mawment* bra, idol
That had, for cent'ries ane or twa,

[1] A recent Protestant martyr, whose death was one justification for the assault.

Brankit on pillar or on wa,
Cam tumblin tap-owr-tail;
The gifts o cardinals and paips,
Owr-fret wi spanglet gowden-caps,
And siller vest or veil,
Aneath the straik o learnit gown,
Cam divin on the pavement down,
Ilk ane upon its marble crown
Smashin itsel to splinders;
A saint or image in a niche,
That wont to glitter there sae rich,
Enflamin folk to sic a pitch—
The sorrow ane was left o such:
The haill were frushed to flinders*: splinters
Much glory frae that plunder-bout
Ilk learnit gown, withouten doubt,
May challenge and may claim;
Exceptin Crail's bauld wabster-band*, (weavers)
For idol-breakin strength o hand,
Nane may the guerdon* sae demand, (reward)
Or share sae weil the fame.

Meantime a fier* o lairds, close groupit, group
Besiegit weil the mickle pu'pit;
It was the Cardinal's ain kirk-loom;
He brocht it in a ship frae Rome;
Twas a owr-carved wi saints and fairies,
And tirlie-wirlies and fleegaries,
And cardinals-hats and Virgin Maries;
Fram it he used, on gala-days,
Busk't* in his bravitie o claes, dressed
To pitter -patter and to phrase:
The vera sicht o that vain loom
Recallit Beaton up and Rome;
The liards wox wudder* aye and wudder; madder
They drew their swerds, and, in a pudder*, rage
Attack't it fierce as fire or fudder*; lightning
They hack't it sae wi swerd and dirk,
Splenders and bits at ilka yerk
Gaed fleein round through a the kirk;
Never was sakeless* dask o timmer* innocent/ "timber"
Sae persecute and put to cummer;
What wi their gulligaws* and gashes, hacks
The pu'pit had been driv'n to smashes,
And not ae scrap had scaped that stour
To busk the bein ha' o Balfour,
Had not a laird cried, "Hoolie, hoolie!
Hae mercy ilk man wi his gullie*. retainer
Leave but a crumb o this kirk-loom,
Memorial o the power o Rome,
And my Lord Card'nal's bottom-room!"
This said, they a their showthers stoopit,
And whummeled up the muckle pu'pit.

Thus they; but battle's fiercest beir*    noise
Was ragin the hey-altar near;
That was the crater o the steir*,    storm
The vera navel o the weir;
Lord Prior James had stood there lang,
Rallyin and gen'rallin his gang;
But seein papists' side gae wrang,
Out at the Chanc'llor's-door he flang:
A howdle* o hog-showtherin* freirs,    swarm/shoving
Augustines, Carm'leits, Cordeliers,
He bauldly left ahent,
To be that altar's body-guard,
And bide the buff o' lout and laird,
As he flew owr the bent*:    grass, field
Than skippers, tailzeours, lairds, and hinds,
Fludes o mad burghers a kinkinds,
Dissim'lar men, but sim'lar minds,
In formidable sailyie,
Cam whurrin in like cats on rattens,
Swappin their handspakes and their battens,
And ither mad artailyie;
Then mells cam down on gowden pyx;
Cud quarreled it wi crucifix;
And crosiers and candlesticks
In th' air excambied* furious licks    exchanged
Wi aiken-rungs and chappin-sticks:
Was never sic a squabble.
Hood, cord and round-cap, cowl and clout,
In tatter-wallops flew about;
Trodden were wafers under-foot;
And then sic skellochin and shout,
Frae conquerin and conquered rout.
Was never sic a yabble!
If e'er there was sic strife and clatter,
Fracas o tongues and bellerin blatter,
Twas at the towr o Babel.
The cross-kirk rang wi scolds and flytes;
The main-kirk rang wi slaps and smites;
Pell-mell, thwack! hiddie-giddie!
There were sic gouffs, and youffs, and swaks,
On heads and bellies, sides and backs,
If onie whair are heard sic cracks,
Tis in a blacksmith's smiddie.
Not frae the blacksmith's study rush
Sae thick the sparks and hammer-flush,
As then did devel, dunt, and dusch,[1]
Makin the ee-sicht giddie;
Aiblins* they'd focht till candle-licht,    perhaps
Had not a stieve braid-showthered wicht,
My gret-great-grandsher, in his micht,

[1]Paste, strike, crash down.

Ran on them wi a spang*: rush, blow
Meal-melvied as he was, I wot,
The meal cam fleein aff his coat,
As up the kirk he sprang:
He caucht John Caldcleugh by the thrapple,
And made him tirvie down and tapple
Head-foremest wi a bang:
He clench't Tam Tottis (Johnie's brither),
And garred him waigle hither-thither,
Syne on the flure him flang:
Arch-dean John Wynram he did grip;
He caucht Prior Guthrie on the hip;
He garred fat hoastin* Forman skip; grunting
Principal Cranston he did trip;
He wi' his fingers' furious nip
Half-strangled Canon Strang:
Great Ajax, whan he waxit daft,
Banged na the puir sheep owr the taft,
As my great-grandsher banged and baf't
That rotten papist gang:
Sic doing were owr het to last;
The papists could na bide that blast;
Astonayed, gumple-faced*, aghast, sad-faced
Out at the Dortour-door, fu fast,
Hurry-scurry, they birred and brast,
Wi blastin and wi puffin;
The Chanc'llor's dure was panged alsae;
Ilk man, brain-mad to get away,
Kickin the neist to gar him gae,
On's mooly-heel rapt horny tae;
And out-ran, fisslin*, fuffin*: raging, puffing
Meantime my grandsher and some others,
The Laird o Grange, and John Carruthers,
In chevalrie twin-bairns and brothers,
The altar fierce attacket:
Missal and mawment, pyx and tass*, goblet
The haill machinery o the mass
Were soupit down and swacket;
The marble slabs, the gowden-gilt,
And frettit-wark was stroyed and split;
That great show-shop of idol-ware,
Gather't for near four hundred year,
Graham's, Gamyl's, Pai's, and Arnold's gear,
Rome's michtie mummery heapit there—
Was in a mament wracket.
The kirk, meantime, was turnin thinner
O vile mass-worshipper and sinner;
They saw their capitol now shaken,
Their great palladium tashed and taken;
Sae, out at ilk door, quiverin, quakin,
They birringly did bicker;
Men never, wi sic whoslin breath,
Fram th' instantaneous grip o death

Flew furiouser or quicker:
Doors wadna serve to let them gang:
Furth at the windocks too they sprang;
Terrible stends* they took and lang, leaps
To scape frae that kirk-bicker;
In kirkyard or in abbey-ground
They tarried not ae single stound;
They couldna think their heads their ain
Ere they were fairly fled and gane:
Sae out at ilka abbey-yett
Baith south, and east, and wast, they sett
Out-owr the kintra fast;
Strathtyrum's bonnie banks were black
Wi freirs, all-fleein in a pack,
Wi tatterwallops* at their back, rags
And faces clean down-cast;
Some took the road to Cupar-town;
Some to the Anster coast ran down;
Some bickered to Balmer'nie; some
To Falkland, ere they stapped, did come;
Some landit up at Tullilum
Wi stammachs clung and clappit;
For therty miles a round about,
The land was cover't wi that rout,
That ran and never stappit;
The roads and fields, as if wi buds,
Were strawn wi rags and bits o duds,
That frae their showthers drappit;
Sic wrack, and ruin, and deray,
Was never in Scotland syne that day
When scatter't Southrons in dismay
Frae Bannockburn's eventfu day
Ran on and never stappit.
As they were fleein thus abread,
Kirk-spulyie*, herriement*, and raid, pillage
Gaed on mair fast then ever.
In the main-kirk three thousand folk
Carv't wark and arch and pillar broke.
Through the cross-kirk twa thousand ran
Batterin awa, ilk angry man,
Wi hammer, ax, and lever.
A thousand bodies on the riggin
Tirred and unroof't the pridefu biggin.
Great faulds o capper aff were flypit;
Great sheets o braid lead aff were rippit;
The folk aboon in joy down-lookit
Through holes that their ane hands had howkit,
Halloin them below.
The folk below cast up their een,
Gazin on sky and heevin's sheen,
Through sky-lichts whair late nocht was seen
But ceiling dark and refter-treen,
And shoutit back, Hurro!

Sae ilka man provok't his brither,
And the hail tot gaed on thegither,
Vyin in strife wi ane anither
At ravagin and ruggin.
Nae thing was prosperin there and thrivin,
But tirlin roofs and rafter-rivin,
And pullin down and puggin.
Weil as they thrived aboon in plunder,
I think, they prosper't better under.
For now the vestry was attacket;
Presses and kists* were hewed and hackit, chests
Wi huge rapacity and racket.
Out-flew unwillin to the licht,
The gard-rob's bravities sae bricht,
For haly-days stored up aricht.
Hands of unhallow't men out-dragget
Pai's velvet-cods wi silver taggit,
And wi their swerds them hash't and hagget,
Makin them shabby cods and ragget.
The bawdekyns* and cloth o gold, gold vestments
Stoles, towals, vestments manifold,
The snaw-white albs wi their parures,
Fannouns and ither garnitures,
The chesybyls wi spangles thick,
And Beaton's ain dear dalmatick*, bishop's robe
The hail o them, by lawit fists,
Were haurled and howkit frae their kists.
For Paip's anathema or ban
Cared not a bodle onie man,
And monie ane that day did herrie
Braw spulyie frae the vestiary.
The piper o the brogh o Crail
Ran aff wi ae priest's-vestment hail.
The town's-drummer o Cellardyke
Stole Beaton's ain dear dalmatyke
(He wore it lang on king's birthdays,
Like a cur-sackie owr his claes,
Whan drummin through the public ways).
Twa regents o Sanct Androis town
(Their names I sanna here set down),
Stole ane a stole, and ane a gown,
But David Barclay had mair sense;
In spulyiein he shawed craft and mense:
For albs or priestly vestiments
He didna care a plack*; (small coin)
He saw the styk o th' water-ewer
Glitterin temptation on the flure.
He cleek't it up, and to the dure
He bangit in a crack,
And hame as fast as feet could carry
He hurried fra that fierie-farie.
That siller styk, for monie a year,
Dan David, mang his ither gear

Fu carefully did keep.
His bairn's-bairns lang stored it well;
But now it's gane—as I hear tell.
Tairge* them about it now—they'll say, examine
O sic ane styk until this day
We never heard a cheep.
Time thus wi meicle greedy mou,
Swallows up auncient things and true,
And leaveth nocht to modern hashes
But idle tales and empty clashes.

Whilst Barclay wi the silver styk
Was owr the King's-muir runnin quick,
The kirk was a' displenish't.
Of idols there remain't not ane.
Priest's-claes and busking-clouts were gane.
Capper and thack-lead aff were tane;
Kirk-gutting clean was finish't.
Except bare wa's and lime and stane,
O that kirk's brav'ries left was nane.
Her glory was diminish't.
Neth'less the meikle middle tow'r,
Wi' her lang spindly sisters four,
Stood glowrin a the kintra owr,
Up-struttin in their pride o pow'r
As gawcy* as afore; fine, saucy
As lang as they stood brankin sae
Nae man could safely brag and say
That down into the grund that day
Was brocht the Papal glore.
The gildit crucifix that shone
The great mid-steeple's tap upon,
Sae lang as it near heevin should stand,
Twas but a sign to sea and land,
That shelter't underneath that taken*, "token"
Rome's power, though shaterit and shaken,
Yet in our land micht live.
And aiblins on some after-time,
Blude-nursed by Guise[1] micht yet sublime
Ereck her head and thrive.
Therefor, out frae the huddlin crowd
Ane college-regent bangin, stood
Heigh on a graff-stane up, and loud
Bespak the listnin people:
Gae, get Deaf Meg and Crookit Mou.[2]
Stech their how* hungry stammachs fou, hollow
And wi them batter till it bow
The meikle middle steeple.

---

[1]Mary of Guise, French (and of course, Catholic) mother of the infant Queen Mary, and for many years regent of Scotland.
[2](Cannons).

Gif ance yon cross were yerdlins* come, "earthward"
Than than, I'll think the pride o Rome
To be doun-cast, and sealed her doom
Within our land for ever;
And our twa friends, I'll whisper you,
Dinnelin Deaf Mag and Crookit Mou
Allenarlie* that feat can do. only
There's nane can crack* sae clever. speak
Nae sooner was the hint thrawn out,
Than sax-score fallows swank* and stout, strong
Down till the Castill flew;
And wi great poust* o arm and leg strength
The dinnelin* and dure Deaf Meg, noisy, tingling
And her sour sister lang and big,
Out frae their port-holes drew.
In twenty minutes a the men
Returnt mair hearty back again,
Wi' cords and cables, micht and main,
Haulin the iron sisters twain,
Wi whoopin and halloo.
In thirteen minutes they were plantit
Wi mickle mou's that gap't and gauntit,
Threatnin wi their first puff o breath
To blaw the bottoms out aneath
The steeple's buirdly length.
They needit but ae single spark
To kendle them for that dure wark,
And try their spit-fire strength.
Out frae their throats wi frichsom gowl,
As if a Scylla's dogs did howl,
Baith fire and soot and shot did rowl.
Meg never frae her chokit thrapple
Garred sae the bullets roar and rapple.
Crook-Mou did never in sic ire
Vomit, wi hurly-burly dire,
Her stammach-fu o airn and fire.
The pond'rous steeple wi the brattle
Did vibrate back and fore, and rattle.
Frae her four stuttin pillars stout
Lumps of out-batter't stane fell out
Enwrappit wi their lime,
And meikle pieces mair and mair
Down tumblin' laid the inside bare,
As the re-loadit sister-pair
Aye guller't out wi awfu rair
Their charges ilka time.

As thir* twa bombards* on the ground these/cannons
Were thunderin wi an awesome sound,
Up i the sky, wi michtier clutter,
The clouds begoud their voice to utter,
And correspondingly to mutter;
For now the vapors dark and dim,

That a day in the welkin's rim
Had nursed themsels owr ocean's brim
Wi waters frae her wave,
Now up the sky had spread and run,
And wi ane horrid tempest dun
Had worried up the splendid sun,
Narrowin the ether's bricht expanse
Into a black-hung ugly trance
As gloomy as the grave.
Great, gourlie*, goustrous-lookin clouds — stormy
Seemed jundyin* i the air wi thuds, — shoving
And on the towns, and fields, and woods,
Out frae their fissures poured the floods
They'd borrow't frae the sea.
Whilst thunder-volleys, peal on peal.
And fudder-flashes mixt wi hail,
Garred bodies tremmle and turn pale,
And kye on mountains flee,
And little fishes, in the deep,
Down to their laighest* bottoms creep, — "lowest"
And there their tangly coverts keep,
That they mith not behauld the sweep
O fire-slaucht from on hie.
Owr auld Sanct Androis city maist
The fury o that storm did rest.
Owr her hie-kirk, maist dark and dour
The thunder-vapor seem't to lowr,
As if upon the mid-most tow'r
The cloud concentratit its power.
Men lookit up wi fear and dreid
On the pit-mirkness owr their heid,
Expeckin some fell thing indeed.
And as they lookit, in a stound,
There cam a crack, that wi its sound,
Garred dinnel a the houses round,
And the hail hill to shake.
At that sam mament rent asunder
Frae cross aloft to bottoms under,
By the tremendous pith o thunder,
The cannon-batter't steeple fell,
Spire, arches, bartizan, and bell,
Wi roarin ruin terrible,
Maist like to ane earthquake.
Masses o stane, enormous blads,
Down on the kirk, wi dunderin dads,
Tremendously cam tumblin,
That wa's, roofs, pillars did confound
In ae destruction round and round;
Makin the haill kirk-yard rebound
Wi rattlin and wi rumblin.
A cloud o limy stouff and stour,
In spite o the thick-gushin shower
Flew whirlin up to heevin,

As fain the thunder-cloud to meet
And gratulate on hie, and greet
The fiery-winget levin*. lightning
Wi rubbish and wi frush that flew
Dinnelin Deaf Meg and Crookit Mou
Were maistlins buried up, I trow,
And whelmit clean frae bodies' view.
But it was wonder-luck,
That wi the smashery o stane,
Man, wife, nor bairnie, there was nane
Murder't, or maimit, or owr-tane,
Wi breakin or o skull or bane.
Nae wicht was scaithed or struck,
Sic tent* they'd taken ane and a care
To stand a goodly space awa
Frae that descendin steeple's fa,
And keep themsels scart-free and hail
Frae banes-breakin or ither bale.

Whan they beheld that steeple's ruin
The yird wi smokin shivers strewin,
They kent richt weil their endit wark,
The consummation o their dark,
And hamewarts bairn, and wife, and man,
Helter-skelter they skelp't and ran,
The faster for the hail and rain
That peltit on their pows* wi pain. heads
As they intill their chambers gat,
Down to their suppers then they sat.
They'd need o cheese and bread, I wat,
After the lang darg they'd been at.
But whan the Pape in Vatican
Heard o the puir freirs how they ran,
And how, despisin bull or ban,
Fife's fechtin bodies, wife and man,
His kirk had spulyied sae,
Three days he in his mournin-chalmer,
Sat greetin* wi ane eerie yammer weeping
Makin the Tiber ring wi clamor
And echoes o his wae.
The College too o Cardinals,
They cast aside their fal-de-rals,
And spaciered weepin through their halls
In doolfu claes o black,
And ilka monk wi grane and gaunt
Made a heart-rending mulligrant*, lamentation
And pat on claith o sack.
As throughout Scotland there was joy,
And gladness at that spulyie-ploy,
Sae throughout a the Papal lands,
Was noucht but grief and wringin hands,
And sichan mang the monkish bands,
Alas me, and alack.

## JOHN WILSON (1785–1854)

[John Wilson was a poet, essayist, novelist and editor. He spent many of his early years in England. As a writer of verse, he was much influenced by the Lake poets (Wordsworth, Coleridge). His long poem *The Isle of Palms* (1812) is frequently beautiful, but also dreamy, formless and strangely bloodless. In 1817, he joined with John Lockhart and James Hogg in editing *Blackwood's Magazine*, to which periodical for years he contributed a stream of articles, under the persona "Christopher North." The most notable of his works for *Blackwood's* is a series of sketches, the *Noctes Ambrosianae* ("ambrosial nights" but also "nights at Ambrose's"— a tavern) which the magazine featured between 1822 and 1835. Wilson seems to have been the principal author of the *Noctes*, and to have increased the degree of his authorship as the series went on. In these columns, written as dramatic sketches, the principal "actors" are himself and James Hogg (the "Ettrick Shepherd," usually referred to simply as "the Shepherd"—the latter a rather ambiguous role, and apparently having rather an ambiguous effect on Hogg, though the series made Hogg a name).

"The Haggis Deluge" is a fair sample of the comic verve, picturesque dialect and general shapelessness of most of these essays. One notes that while Wilson could obviously recreate Scots as broad as was with difficulty decipherable, the character he patterned after himself, "Christopher North," speaks impeccably upper-class English. The most original aspect of the series is "The Shepherd," who is, rather like the American figure Davy Crockett, part legend, part real, part homespun philosopher, and part buffoon.]

### Turn Ye to Me

The stars are shining cheerily, cheerily,
Ho ro Mhairi dhu, turn ye to me.
The sea-mew is moaning drearily, drearily,
Ho ro Mhairi dhu, turn ye to me.
Cold is the storm-wind that ruffles his breast,
But warm are the downy plumes lining his nest.
Cold blows the storm there,
Soft falls the snow there,
Ho ro Mhairi dhu, turn ye to me.

The waves are dancing merrily, merrily,
Ho ro Mhairi dhu, turn ye to me.
The sea-birds are wailing wearily, wearily,
Ho ro Mhairi dhu, turn ye to me.
Hushed be thy moaning, lone bird of the sea,
Thy home on the rocks is a shelter to thee,
Thy home is the angry wave,
Mine but the lonely grave,
Ho ro Mhairi dhu, turn ye to me.

### The Evening Cloud

A cloud lay cradled near the setting sun,
A gleam of crimson tinged its braided snow;
Long had I watched the glory moving on
O'er the still radiance of the lake below.
Tranquil its spirit seemed, and floated slow.

Even in its very motion there was rest;
While every breath of eve that chanced to blow
Wafted the traveler to the beauteous west:
Emblem, methought, of the departed soul,
To whose white robe the gleam of bliss is given
And by the breath of mercy made to roll
Right onward to the golden gates of heaven,
Where to the eye of faith it peaceful lies,
And tells to man his glorious destinies.

## On a Highland Glen

To whom belongs this valley fair
That sleeps beneath the filmy air,
Even like a living thing?
Silent, as infant at the breast,
Save a still sound that speaks of rest—
That streamlet's murmuring.

The heavens appear to love this vale.
Her clouds with scarce-seen motion sail,
Or mid the silence lie:
By that blue arch this beauteous earth,
Mid evening's hour of dewy mirth,
Seems bound unto the sky.

O that this lovely vale were mine!
Then, from glad youth to calm decline,
My years would gently glide.
Hope would rejoice in endless dreams,
And memory's oft-returning gleams
By peace be sanctified.

Then would unto my soul be given,
From furnace of that gracious heaven,
A purity sublime;
And thoughts would come of mystic mood
To make in this deep solitude
Eternity of time.

And did I ask to whom belonged
This vale? I feel that I have wronged
Nature's most gracious soul.
She spreads her glories oer the earth,
And all her children from their birth
Are joint heirs of the whole.

Yea, long as nature's humblest child
Hath kept his temple undefiled
By sinful sacrifice,
Earth's fairest scenes are all his own.

He is a monarch, and his throne
Is built amid the skies.

## The Haggis Deluge

*North.* Thank Heaven, my dear Shepherd, Winter is come again, and Edinburgh is beginning once more to look like herself, like her name and her nature, with rain, mist, sleet, haur, hail, snow I hope, wind, storm—-would that we could but add a little thunder and lightning—the Queen of the North.

*Shepherd.* Hoo could you, sir, wi' a' your time at your ain command, keep in and about Embro' frae May to December? The city, for three months in the dead o' simmer, is like a tomb.

*Tickler (in a whisper to the Shepherd).* The widow, James-—the widow.

*Shepherd (aloud).* The weedow—sir—the weedow! Couldna he hae brocht her out wi' him to the Forest? At their time o' life, surely scandal wad hae held her tongue.

*Tickler.* Scandal never holds her tongue, James. She drops her poison upon the dew on the virgin's untimely grave —her breath will not let the gray hairs rest in the mold—

*Shepherd.* Then, Mr. North, marry her at ance, and bring her out in Spring, that you may pass the hinny-moon on the sunny braes o' Mount Benger.

*North.* Why, James, the moment I begin to press matters, she takes out her pocket-handkerchief—and through sighs and sobs recurs to the old topic—that twenty thousand times told tale—the dear old General.

*Shepherd.* Deevil keep the dear old General! Hasna the man been dead these twunty years? And if he had been leevin, wuldna he been aulder than yoursel, and far mair infirm? You're no in the least infirm, sir.

*North.* Ah, James! that's all you know. My infirmities are increasing with years—

*Shepherd.* Wad you be sae unreasonable as to expect them to decrease with years? Are her infirmities—

*North.* Hush—she has no infirmities.

*Shepherd.* Nae infirmities! Then she's no worth a brass button. But let me ask you ae interrogatory.— hae ye ever put the question? Answer me that, sir.

*North.* Why, James, I cannot say that I ever have—

*Shepherd.* What! and you expeck that she wull put the question to you? That would indeed be puttin the cart before the horse. If the women wure to ask the mon, there wad be nae leevin in this warld. Yet let me tell you, Mr. North, that it's a shamefu' thing to keep playin in the way you hae been doin for these ten years past on a young woman's feelings—

*Tickler.* Ha ha ha James! A young woman! Why, she's sixty, if she's an hour.

*North.* You lie.

*Shepherd.* That's a douss[1] on the chops, Mr. Tickler. That's made you as red in the face as a bubbly-jock, Sir. Oh, the power o' ae wee bit single monosyllabic syllable o' a word to awaukun a' the safter and a' the fiercer passions! Dinna keep bitin your thoomb, Mr. Tickler, like an Itawlian! Make an apology to Mr. North—

*North.* I will accept of no apology. The man who calls a woman old deserves death.

*Shepherd.* Did you call her auld, Mr. Tickler?

*Tickler.* To you, sir, I will condescend to reply. I did not. I merely said she was sixty if she was an hour.

*Shepherd.* In the first place, dinna "Sir" me—for it's not only ill-bred, but it's

---

[1] Blow.

stupit. In the second place, dinna talk o' "condescending" to reply to me—for that's language I'll no thole even frae the King on the throne, and I'm sure the King on the throne wadna mak use o't. In the third place, to ca' a woman saxty, and then maintain that ye dinna ca' her auld, is naething short o' a sophism. And in the fourth place, you shouldna hae accompanied your remark wi' a loud haw—haw—haw,—-for on a tender topic a guffaw's an aggravation—-and marryin a widow, let her age be what it wull, is a tender topic, depend on't—sae that on a calm and dispassionate view o' a' the circumstances o' the case, there can be nae doubt that you maun mak an apology; or, if you do not, I leave the room, and there is an end of the Noctes Ambrosianae.

*North.* An end of the Noctes Ambrosianae!

*Tickler.* An end of the Noctes Ambrosianae!

*Shepherd.* An end of the Noctes Ambrosianae!

*Omnes.* An end of the Noctes Ambrosianae!!!

*North.* Rather than that should happen, I will make a thousand apologies—

*Tickler.* And I ten thousand—

*Shepherd.* That's behavin like men and Christians. Embrace—embrace.

*(North and Tickler embrace.)*

*North.* Where were we, James?

*Shepherd.* I was abusin Embro' in simmer.

*North.* Why?

*Shepherd.* Whey? All the lums[1] smokeless! No ae jack turnin a piece o' roastin beef afore ae fire in ony ae kitchen in a' the New Toon. Streets and squares a' grass-grown, sae that they micht he mawn! Shops like beehives that hae dee'd in wunter. Coaches settin aff for Stirlin, and Perth, and Glasgow, and no ae passenger either inside or out—only the driver keepin up his heart wi' flourishing his whip, and the guard sittin in perfect solitude, playin an eerie spring on his bugle-horn! The shut-up playhouse a' covered ower wi' bills that seem to speak o' plays acted in an antediluvian world!

But to return to the near approach o' wunter. Mankind hae again putten on worsted stockins, and flannen drawers—white jeans and yellow nankeen troosers hae disappeared—dooble soles hae gotten a secure footen ower pumps-—big-coats wi' fur, and mantles wi' miniver, gie an agreeable rouchness to the picturesque stream o' life eddyin alang the channel o' the streets—gloves and mittens are sae general that a red hairy haun looks rather singular—every third body ye meet, for fear o' a sudden blash, carries an umbrella—a' folk shave noo wi' hot water—coal-carts are emptyin theirsels into ilka area—-caddies at the corners o' the streets and drivers on coach-boxes are soon warmin themsels by blawin on their fingers, or whuskin themsels wi' their open nieves[2] across the shouthers—skates glitter at shop-windows, prophetic o' frost.

—Mr. Phin may tak in his rod noo, for nae mair thocht o' anglin till spring,—and wi' spring hersel, as wi' ither o' our best and bonniest freens, it may be said, out o' sicht out o' mind,—-you see heaps o' bears hung out for sale—-horses are "a hairier o' the hide"—the bit toon bantam craws nane, and at breakfast you maun tak tent no to pree an egg afore smellin at it,—-you meet hares carryin about in a' quarters—and gemkeepers precedin out into the kintra wi' strings o' grews,[3]—sparrows sit silent and smoky wi' ruffled feathers, waiting for crumbs on the ballustrawds—loud is the cacklin in the fowl-market o' Christmas geese that come a month at least afore the

---

[1]Chimneys.

[2]Fists.

[3]Greyhounds.

day, just like thae annuals, the forget-me-nots, amulets, keepsakes, beejoos, gems, anniversaries, souvenirs, friendship offerings, and wunter-wreaths—-

*Tickler.* Stop, James—stop. Such an accumulation of imagery absolutely confounds—-perplexes—-

*Shepherd.* Folk o' nae fancy. Then for womankind—

*Tickler.* Oh, James, James. I knew you would not long keep off that theme—-

*Shepherd.* Oh, ye pawkie[1] auld carle! What ither theme in a' this wide weary warld is worth ae single thocht or feelin in the poet's heart-—ae single line frae the poet's pen—-a' single—-

*North.* Song from the Shepherd's lyre—of which, as of the Teian Bards of old, it may be said:—

Α βαρβιτοσ δε χορδαιζ
Ερωτα μουνον ηχει.[2]

Do, my dear James, give us John Nicholson's daughter.

*Shepherd.* Wait a wee. The womankind, I say, sirs, never look sae bonny as in wunter, excep indeed it may be in spring—

*Tickler.* Or summer or autumn, James—

*Shepherd.* Haud your tongue. You old bachelors ken naething o' womankind—and hoo should ye, when they treat you wi' but ae feelin, that o' derision? Oh, sirs! but the dear creturs do look weel in muffs—whether they haud them, wi' their invisible hauns clasped thegither in their beauty within the cozy silk linin, close prest to their innocent waists, just aneath the glad beatins o' their first-love-touched hearts—

*Tickler.* There again, James!

*Shepherd.* Or haud them hingin frae their extended richt arms, leavin a' the feegur visible, that seems taller and slimmer as the removed muff reveals the clasps o' the pelisse a' the way doun frae neck till feet.

*North.* Look at Tickler, James—how he moves about in his chair. His restlessness—

*Shepherd.* Is no unnatural. Then, sir, is there, in a' the beautifu' and silent unfauldins o' natur amang plants and flowers, onything sae beautifu' as the white, smooth, saft chafts o' a bit smilin maiden o' saxteen, aughteen, or twunty blossomin out, like some bonny bud o' snaw-white satin, frae a coverin o' rough leaves,—blossomin out, sirs, frae the edge o' the fur tippet, that haply a lover's happy haun had delicately hung ower her gracefu' shouthers—oh, the dear delightfu' little Laplander!

*Tickler.* For a married man, James, you really describe—

*North.* Whisht!

*Shepherd.* I wish you only heard the way the bonny croodin-doos keep murmuring their jeists to ane anither, as soon as a nest o' them gets rid o' an auld bacheleer on Princes Street.

*Tickler.* Gets rid o' an auld bachelor!

*Shepherd.* Booin and scrapin to them after the formal and stately fashion o' the auld school o' politeness, and thinkin himsel the very pink o' courtesy, wi' a gold-headed cane, aiblins,[3] nae lest, in his haun, and buckles on's shoon—for buckles are no quite out yet a'thogither—a frill like a fan at the shirt-neck o' him—and, wad the warld believe't, kneebreeks!—then they titter—and then they lauch—and then, as musical as if they were singin in pairts, the bonny, bloomin, innocent wicked creturs break out into—I mauna say, o' sic rosy lips, and sic snawy breasts, a guffaw—but a guffay, sirs, a guffay—for that's the feminine o' guffaw—

---

[1]Clever, tricky.

[2]The stringed harp plays only of love.

[3]Perhaps.

*North.* Tickler, we really must not allow ourselves to be insulted in this style any longer—

*Shepherd.* And then awa they trip, sirs, flingin an antelope's or gazelle's ee ower their shouther, diverted beyond measure to see their antique beau continuing at a distance to cut capers in his pride—till a' at ance they see a comet in the sky—a young offisher o' dragoons, wi' his helmet a' in a low[1] wi' a flicker o' red feathers—and as he "turns and winds his fiery Pegassus," they are a' mute as death—yet every face at the same time eloquent wi' malting smiles, and wi' blushes that break through and around the blue heaveens o' their een, like crimson clouds to sudden sunlight burning beautiful for a moment, and then melting away like a thocht or a dream.

*North.* Why, my dear James, it does one's heart good even to be ridiculed in the language of poetry. Does it not, Tickler?

*Tickler.* James, your health, my dear fellow.

*Shepherd.* I never ridicule onybody, sirs, that's no fit to bear it. But there's some sense and some satisfaction in makin a fool o' them, that, when the fiend's in them, can mak fools o' a'body, like North and Tickler.

*(Enter Mr. Ambrose with a hot roasted round of beef—King Pepin with a couple of boiled ducks—Sir David Gam with a trencher of tripe a la Meg Dods—and Tappytoorie with a haggis. Pickled salmon, Welsh rabbits, &c, &c.—and, as usual, oysters, raw, stewed, scalloped, roasted, and pickled, of course—rizzards, finzeans, red herrings.)*

*Shepherd.* You've really served up a bonny wee neat bit sooper for three, Mr. Awmrose. I hate, for my ain pairt, to see a table overloaded. It's sae vulgar. I'll carve the haggis.[2]

*North.* I beseech you, James, for the love of all that is dear to you, here and hereafter, to hold your hand. Stop— stop—stop!

*(The Shepherd sticks the haggis, and the table is instantly overflowed.)*

*Shepherd.* Heavens and earth! Is the haggis mad? Tooels! Awmrose—tooels! ,Safe us! we'll a' be drooned!

*(Picardy and his Tail rush out for towels.)*

*North.* Rash man! what ruin have you wrought! See how it has overflown the deck from stem to stern—we shall all be lost.

*Shepherd.* Sweepin everything afore it! Whare's the puir biled dyucks? Only the croon-head o' the roun' visible. Tooels—tooels—tooels! Send roun' the fire-drum through the city.

*(Re-enter Picardy and "the rest" with napery.)*

*Mr. Ambrose.* Mr. North, I look to you for orders in the midst of this alarming calamity. Shall I order in more strength?

*Shepherd.* See—see—sir it's creeping alang the carpet! We're like men left on a sandbank, when the tide's comin in rampaugin. Oh, that I had insured my life. Oh that I had learned to soom! What wull become o' my widow and my fatherless children?

*North.* Silence! Let us die like men.

*Shepherd.* O Lord it's ower our insteps already! Open a' the doors and wundows—and let it find its ain level. I'll up on a chair in the meantime.

*(The Shepherd mounts the back of the chair, and draws Mr. North up after him.)*
Sit on my shouthers, my dear—dear—dearest sir. I insist on't. Mr. Tickler, Mr. Awmrose, King Pepin, Sir David, and Tappitourie—you wee lazy deevil—help Mr. North up— help Mr. North up on my shouthers!

---

[1]Flame.

[2]The famous—or infamous—Scottish dish. It is the stomach of a sheep filled with its heart, liver, etc., and heavily spiced.

*(Mr. North is elevated, crutch and all, astride on the Shepherd's shoulders.)*

*North.* Good God! Where is Mr. Tickler?

*Shepherd.* Look—look—look, sir,—yonner he's staunin on the brace piece—on the mantel! Noo, Awmrose, and a' ye waiters make your escape, and leave us to our fate. Oh, Mr. North, gie us a prayer.—What for do you look so miserable, Mr. Tickler? Death is common—tis but "passing through Natur' to eternity!" and yet—to be drooned in haggis 'ill be waurs than Clarence's dream! Alack and alas a-day! it's up to the ring o' the bell-rope! Speak, Mr. Tickler—oh, speak, sir—men in our dismal condition—Are you sittin easy, Mr. North?

*North.* Quite so, my dear James, I am perfectly resigned. Yet, what is to become of maga—

*Shepherd.* Oh my wee Jamie!

*North.* I fear I am very heavy, James.

*Shepherd.* Dinna say't, sir—dinna say't. I'm like the pious Aeneas bearin his father Ancheeses through the flames o' Troy. The simile doesna haud gude at a' points—I wish it did—oh, haud fast sir, wi' your arms roun' my neck, lest the cruel tyrant o' a haggis swoop ye clean awa under the sideboard to inevitable death!

*North.* Far as the eye can reach it is one wide wilderness of suet.

*Tickler.* Hurra! hurra! hurra!

*Shepherd.* Do you hear the puir gentleman, Christopher? It's affeckin to men in our condition to see the pictur we hae baith read o' in accounts o' shipwrecks realeezed! Timothy's gane mad! Hear till him shoutin wi' horrid glee on the brink o' eternity!

*Tickler.* Hurra! hurra! hurra!

*North.* Horrible! most horrible!

*Tickler.* The haggis is subsiding—the haggis is subsiding! It has fallen an inch by the surbase since the Shepherd's last ejaculation.

*Shepherd.* If you're tellin a lee, Timothy, I'll wade ower to you, and bring you doun aff the mantel wi' the crutch.— Can I believe my een? It is subseedin. Hurraw! hurraw! hurraw! Nine times nine, Mr. North, to our deliverance— and the Protestant ascendancy.

*Omnes.* Hurra! hurraw! hurree!

*Shepherd.* Noo, sir, you may dismunt.

*(Re-enter the household, with the immediate neighborhood.)*

*Shepherd.* High Jinks! High Jinks! High Jinks! The haggis has putton out the fire, and sealed up the boiler—

*(The Shepherd descends upon all fours, and lets Mr. North off gently.)*

*North.* Oh, James, I am a daft old man.

*Shepherd.* No sae silly as Solomon, sir, at your time o' life. Noo for sooper.

*Tickler.* How the devil am I to get down?

*Shepherd.* How the deevil did you get up? Oh, ho, by the gas ladder! And it's been removed in the confusion. Either jump down—or stay where you are, Mr. Tickler.

*Tickler.* Come now, James—shove over the ladder.

*Shepherd.* Oh that Mr. Chantrey was here to sculptur him in that attitude! Streitch out your richt haun. A wee grain heicher! Hoo gran' be looks in basso-relievo!

*Tickler.* Shove over the ladder, you son of the mist, or I'll brain you with the crystal.

*Shepherd.* Sit doun, Mr. North, opposite to me—and Mr. Ambrose, tak roun' my plate for a shave o' the beef.—Isna he the perfeck pictur o' the late Right Honorable William Pitt? Shall I send you, sir, some o' the biled dyuck?

*North.* If you please, James.—rather "Like Patience on a monument smiling at

Grief."

*Shepherd.* Gie us a sang, Mr. Tickler, and then you shall hae the ladder. I never preed[1] a roasted roun' afore—it's real savory.

*North—* "Oh who can tell how hard it is to climb
The height where Fame's proud temple shines afar!"

*Shepherd.* I'll let you doun, Mr. Tickler, if you touch the ceilin wi' your fingers. Itherwise, you maun sing a sang.

(*Tickler tries and fails.)*

*Tickler.* Well, if I must sing let me have a tumbler of toddy.

*Shepherd.* Ye shall hae that, sir

*(The Shepherd fills a tumbler from the jug, and balancing it on the cross of the crutch, reaches it up to Mr. Tickler. Tickler sings* "The Twa Magicians.")

*Shepherd.* Noo—sir—here is the ladder to you—for which you're indebted to Mr. Peter Buchan, o' Peterhead, tha ingenious collector o' the *Ancient Ballads*, frae which ye have chanted so speeritedly the speerited "Twa Magicians." It's a capital collection—and should be added in a' libraries, to Percy, and Ritson, and Headley, and the *Minstrelsy of the Border*, and John Finlay, and Robert Jamieson, and Gilchrist and Kinloch, and the Quarto o' that clever chiel,[2] Motherwell o' Paisley, wha's no only a gude collector and commentator o' ballads, but a gude writer o' them too— as he has proved by that real poetical address o' a Northman to his Swurd in ane o' the Annals. Come awa doun, sir— come awn doun. Tak tent, for the steps are gey shoggly.[3] Noo—sir—fa' to the roun'.

*Tickler.* I have no appetite, James. I have been suffering all night under a complication of capital complaints,—the toothache, which like a fine attenuated red-hot, steel-sting, keeps shooting through an old rugged stump, which to touch with my tongue is agony—the tongue-ache, from a blister on that weapon, that I begin to fear may prove cancerous— the lip-ache, from having accidentally given myself a labial wound in sucking out an oyster—the eye-ache, as if an absolute worm were laying eggs in the pupil—the ear-ache, tingling and stounin[4] to the very brain, till my drum seems heating for evening parade—to which add a headache of the hammer-and-anvil kind—and a stomach-ache, that seems to intimate that dyspepsy is about to be converted into cholera morbus; and you have a partial enumeration of the causes that at present deaden my appetite—and that prevented me from chanting the ballad with my usual vivacity. However —I will trouble you for a duck.

*Shepherd.* You canna be in the least pain, wi' sae mony complaints as these—for they maun neutraleeze ane anither. But even if they dinna, I believe mysel, wi' the Stoics, that pain's nae evil.—Dinna you, Mr. North?

*North.* Certainly. But Tickler, you know, has many odd crotchets.

*Ambrose (entering with his suavest physiognomy).* Beg pardon, Mr. North, for venturing in unrung, but there's a young lady wishing to speak with you—

*Shepherd.* A young lady!—show her ben.

*North.* An anonymous article?

*Ambrose.* No, Sir,—Miss Helen Sandford, from the Lodge.

*North.* Helen! what does she want?

*Ambrose.* Miss Sandford had got alarmed, sir—

*Shepherd.* Safe us! only look at the timepiece! Four o'clock in the mornin!

*Ambrose.* And has walked up from the Lodge—

---

[1]"Proved" (tasted).

[2]Fellow.

[3]Shaky.

[4]Aching.

*North.* What? Alone!

*Ambrose.* No, Sir. Her father is with her—and she bids me say—now she knows her master is well—that here is your Kilmarnock nightcap.

*(Mr. North submits his head to Picardy, who adjusts the nightcap.)*

*Shepherd.* What a cowl!

*North.* A capote, James. Mr. Ambrose,—we three must sleep here all night.

*Shepherd.* A' mornin, ye mean. Tak care o' Tickler amang ye—but recolleck it's no safe to wauken sleepin dowgs.— Oh! man! Mr. North, sir! but that was touchin attention in puir Eelen. She's like a dochter, indeed.—Come awa, yon auld vagabon, to your bed. I'll kick open the door o' your dormitory wi' my fit, as I pass alang the transe in the mornin! The mornin! Faith, I'm beginnin already to get hungry for breakfast. Come awa, you auld vagabon-—come awa.

*(Exeunt North and Shepherd, followed by the Height of Tickler, to roost.)*

*North. (singing as they go)—*

Early to bed, and early to rise,
Is the way to be healthy, wealthy, and wise.
*—Da Capo.*

## GEORGE BEATTIE (1786–1823)

### The Dream

Last night I dreamed a dream of horror. Methought
That, at the hour of midnight, the bell tolled,
With slow and solemn peal; and straight, beneath
The pale cold moon, a thousand specters moved,
In "dread array," along "the church-way path,"
All swathed in winding sheets as white as snow—
A ghastly crew! Methought I saw the graves
Yawn and yield up their charge; and I heard the
Coffins crack, and the deadal drapery
Rustle against their hollow sides, like the
Wing of the renovated chrysoly,
As they flutter against the ruins of
Their winter dormitory, when the voice
Of spring awakes them from their drowsy couch,
To float aloft upon the buxom air.
Although the round full moon shone bright and clear,
Yet did none of these awful phantoms cast
Their shadows on the wan and silent earth,
Nor was the passing breeze interrupted
By their presence. Some skimmed along the earth,
And others sailed aloft on the thin air;
And I observed, when they came between me
And the moon, they interrupted not her
Pale rays; for I saw her majestic orb
Distinct, round, and clear, through their indistinct
And airy forms; and although they moved
Betwixt me and the tomb-stones, yet I read
Their sculpture (deeply shaded by the bright
And piercing beams of the moon) as distinctly
As if nought, dead or living, interposed

Between my eyes and the cold monuments.
The bell ceased to toll; and when the last peal
Died away on the ear, these awful forms
Congregated in various groups, and seemed
To hold converse. The sound of their voices
Was solemn and low, and they spoke the language
Of the "days of other years." In seeming
Woe, they spoke of events long gone by; and
Marveled at the changes that had taken
Place since they left this mortal scene, to sleep
Within the dark and narrow house. Voices
Issued from the mold, where no forms were seen;
These were still more hollow and sepulchral;
They were as the sound of the cold, bleak wind,
In the dark and danky vaults of death, when
It moans low and mournful, through the crannies
Of their massive doors, shattered by the hand
Of time—a serenade for owls most meet,
And such the raven loves, and hoarsely croaks
His hollow response from the blasted yew.
Often have I heard, when but a stripling,
Twas meet to speak a troubled ghost, to give
It peace to sleep within the silent grave.
With clammy brow, and joints palsied with fear,
I said, in broken accents, "What means this
Awful congress, this wild and wan array
Of shadowy shapes, gliding here, and moaning
At the silent, solemn hour of midnight?
Have the crying sins, and unwhipt crimes
Of mortals, in these latter days, reached you
Ev'n in the grave, where silence ever reigns,
At least as we believe? Or complain ye
Of holy rites unpaid,—or of the crowd
Whose careless steps those sacred haunts profane?"
Straight a fleshless hand, cold as ice, was pressed
Upon my lips; and the specters vanished
Like dew before the morning sun: and as
They faded on my sight a sound was heard
Like the peal of many organs, solemn,
Loud, and sonorous; or like the awful
Voice of thunder in the sky—or mighty
Tempest, roaring in a boundless forest,
Uprooting trees, razing habitations,
And sweeping the earth with desolation;
Or like the voice of millions, raised in song;
Or the dark ocean, howling in its wrath;
Or, rather, like all these together, in
One wild concert joined. Now the mighty coil
Died gradually away, till it resembled
The last murmur of the blast on the hill;
Of storms, when it lulls itself to rest; and
The echo of its wrath is faintly heard
In the valley; or the last sigh of the

Aeolian harp, when the breeze, that erewhile
Kissed its trembling strings, is spent and breathless.
The next whisper was still lower; and the last
Was so faint and feeble that nothing seemed
To live between it and silence itself.
The awful stillness was more appalling
Than its dread precursor; and I awoke
In terror. But I never shall forget
What I heard and saw in that horrid dream.

## JOHN CARRICK (1787–1837)

[John Carrick was the principal force behind a well-known Scottish literary miscellany called *The Laird of Logan, or Anecdotes and Tales Illustrative of the Wit and Humour of Scotland.* The title character was an imaginary figure about whom many of the anecdotes are centered. Carrick's main associates in assembling these materials were William Motherwell (1797–1835) and Andrew Henderson (1783–1835). Since Carrick was well acquainted with the Highlands, he is presumed to be the writer, or anthologist, for the selections given here. Also taken from the same collection is Carrick's comic poem, "The Harp and the Haggis." Carrick contributed many pieces in the same vein to the "Whistle-Binkie" series of humorous and popular poetry collections, beginning in 1832 and edited by David Robertson.]

### The Harp and the Haggis

At that tide when the voice of the turtle is dumb,
And winter wi' drap at his nose doth come,—
A whistle to make o' the castle lum* — chimney
To sowf* his music sae sairie, O; — murmur
And the roast on the speet is sapless an' sma,
And meat is scant in chamber and ha',
And the knichts hae ceased their merry gaffaw,
For lack o' their warm canary*, O. — (wine)

Then the Harp and the Haggis began a dispute,
Bout whilk o' their charms were in highest repute.
The Haggis at first as a haddie was mute,
An' the Harp went on wi' her vaporin', O;
An' lofty an' loud were the tones she assumed,
An' boasted how ladies and knichts gaily plumed,
Through rich gilded halls, all so sweetly perfumed,
To the sound of her strings went a caperin', O.

"While the Haggis," she said, "was a beggardly slave,
An' never was seen mang the fair an' the brave."
"Fuff, fuff!" quo the Haggis, "thou vile lying knave,
Come tell us the use of thy twanging, O.
Can it fill a toom* wame*? Can it help a man's pack? — empty/belly
A minstrel when out may come in for his snack,
But when starving at hame, will it keep him, alack,
Frae trying his hand at the hanging, O!"

The twa they grew wud* as wud could be, mad
But a minstrel boy they chanced to see,
Wha stood list'ning bye, an' to settle the plea,
They begged he would try his endeavor, O,
For the twa in their wrath had all reason forgot,
And stood boiling with rage just like peas in a pot,
But a Haggis ye ken, aye looks best when it's hot,
So his bowels were moved in her favor, O.

"Nocht pleases the lug* half sae weel as a tune, ear
An' whar hings the lug wad be fed wi' a spoon?"
The harp in a triumph cried, "Laddie, weel done,"
An' her strings wi' delight feel a tinkling, O.
"The harp's a braw thing," continued the youth,
"But what is a harp to put in the mouth?
It fills na the wame, it slaiks na the drouth*,— thirst
At least,—that is my way o' thinking, O.

"A tune's but an air; but a Haggis is meat;—
An' wha plays the tune that a body can eat?
When a haggis is seen wi' a sheep's head and feet,
My word, she has gallant attendance, O.
A man wi' sic fare ma ne'er pree* the tangs*, taste/pangs
But laugh at lank hunger though sharp be her fangs;
But the bard that maun live by the wind o' his sangs,
Waes me, has a puir dependence, O.

"How aften we hear wi' the tear in our eye,
How the puir starving minstrel, exposed to the sky,
Lays his head on his harp, and breathes out his last sigh,
Without e'er a friend within hearing, O.
But wha ever heard of a minstrel so crost,—
Lay his head on a Haggis to gie up the ghost?
O never, since time took his scythe frae the post,
An' truntled awa to the shearing, O.

"Now I'll settle your plea in the crack o' a whup:
Gie the Haggis the lead, be't to dine or to sup.
Till the bags are weel filled, there can nae drone get up,
Is a saying I learned from my mither, O.
When the feasting is owre, let the harp loudly twang,
An' soothe ilka lug wi' the charms o' her sang,
An' the wish of my heart is, wherever ye gang,
Gud grant ye may aye be thegither, O!"

## Highland Anecdotes
from *The Laird of Logan*

### 1. A Royal Regiment

When the 42d regiment was recruiting at Paisley, early in the present century, the address of the sergeant to the gaping multitude was as follows: "Come noo, lads, enter that auld bauld corps—often tried, never found failing—ca'd the Twa-and-Forty Regiment o' Hieland Feet, commanded by Prince Frederick, king o' Europe, and a' the Europes i' Scotland."

2. Highland Arithmetic

It is said, that when this "auld bauld corps" was recruiting in the Highlands, it was not uncommon in the public houses to hear a sergeant, with a large bunch of notes in his hand, thus addressing his newly-enlisted man: Sax and twa's ten—tak your boonty and awa' wi' ye, you—scoon'rell!"

3. Highland Cure for Rheumatism

"Dear me, Shamis, but you are very pad indeed," said a sympathizing Highlander to a friend who was confined by a severe attack of sciatica; "so long a time, I'm sure mony day and night you are weary, with sore bone and thocht for yourself and family; is there nothing will did you good at all?"

"Och no, nothing, and I'll took every medicine that the Doctor told me to use, and it's all as you'll saw, nothing for my good."

"Well, that's a great vexation and grief— deed is't, Shamis;—I think that I could did you goot, but I needna spoke, for you'll not took it, deed no, so it is of no use to talk."

"You need not spoken that, did I'll not take everything already? and it's may be no likely, is it, that I'll teuck no more that will make me petter."

"I would tell you in a moment, if I just would believe myself, that you would take it, would you?"

"If you are going, to make a fun of me, it is all you appear to me to do; and it is not a friend's part, as you are, to did it."

"Well, then, I think you will take it."

"I think so too," replied the invalid, "but I must know what is't I'm to take pefore I'll teuck it."

"Shamis then, go away, and take hold of the back end of the Paisley coach, and run all the way, and mind to keep up with it, else it will not do, to the half-way to Paisley House; and depend on't, Shamis, whan you do this, you'll never have a stiff body in any of your joints, though you live to the age of Craigangilloch, peside our selves."

4. Highland Thieves

Dugald M'Caul was a professed thief in the Highlands and sometimes took young lads into his service as apprentices to the same business. With one of these hopeful youths, who had recently engaged with him, he agreed one night to proceed upon an excursion; the apprentice to steal a wedder, and Dugald himself to steal kale. It was also agreed that they should, after being in possession of their booty, meet in the kirk-yard, where they were pretty sure of not being molested, as it got the name of being haunted by a ghost.

Dugald, as may well be supposed, arrived first at the place of rendezvous, and, sitting on a grave-stone, amused himself with eating kale-custocks until the apprentice should arrive with the wedder.

In a neighboring farm house, a cripple tailor happened to be at work, and the conversation having turned upon the story of the kirk-yard bring haunted, the tailor boldly censured some young men present, for not having the courage to go and speak to the supposed apparition, adding, that if he had the use of his limbs, he would have no hesitation in doing it himself. One of the young men, nettled at the tailor's remarks, proposed taking the tailor on his back to the kirk-yard; and, as the tailor could not well recede from what he had said, off they went.

The moment they entered the kirk yard, Dugald M'Caul saw them, and thinking it was the apprentice with a wedder on his back, he said, in a low tone of voice, as they approached him, "Is he fat?"

"Whether he be fat or lean," cried the young man, "there he is to ye;" and throwing down the tailor, ran off as hard as he could. On entering the farm-house, to his utter astonishment, he found the tailor close at his heels; intense fear having supplied him with the long-lost use of his limbs, which, it is said, he retained ever after.

5. Notice to Highland Customers

The following intimation was some time ago copied by the writer, from a placard on the walls of the lobby of the inn at the head of Loch-Suinart:

**"Notice—No person will get credit for whisky, in this house, but those that pay money down."**

6. Highland Negatives

Two Highland skippers meeting on the quay of Leith, the one hailed the other with—"Weel Donald, are you going for to sail to night?"—Donald immediately answered with regular norlan' birr, "Perhaps no, and perhaps not!"

7. Highland Distinctions

"Have you had a goot sport to-day, Sir?" said the Bellman to a gentleman with whom he was acquainted, returning from lashing the stream, with the basket slung over back.

"No, Archie, I can't say I have."

"Ay, I am vex for that; but did you'll not catch nothing?"

"Only a few small pars, and a tolerably fine grilse."

"A grulse, did you? it's a ponny fish a grulse, teet is't; would you let me see it, Sir? I like to see a grulse always."

"Most certainly—there it is."

"It's a ponny fish, and, as I'll guess from my eye, six pounds weight, a little more maybe if you were putting it on a weight to try; but I'll thocht you was knew better; it's no a grulse, it's a trout."

"A trout, is it? how do you know?"

"How I knew?—ken in a moment."

"Yes, but how do you know?"

"Weel, will you hearken till I was explain? You see, a grulse and a trout is of a perfect difference; it's not the same fish at all, and if you was seen a trout and a grulse just before you there, you would say tat fish is not the tother, but that's a trout, and tother is a grulse."

"Yes! yes! you can say that, Archie, but in what way am I to distinguish between the two?"

"Is it possible noo that you'll no understood? Its a trout, as I'm telling you ay, an' it's no a trout out o' the water down there, the Echeck, beside oursels neither but a Messon trouts; teet is it."

"That's all very well, but tell me the color, form, or point that I may know again, and how you know that to be a Messon trout?"

"Know't in a moment, mony a tog dee sin' Archie was a whalp;—the burn doun gaun by, you see, is a bigger burn nor the Messon, and consequence the trouts are better made, thicker at the shouthers, more stronger to mak their way through the water, as I could say, and I'll just try again to explain. I will made you know the difference, plain as if you was a fish yourself, and put your nose to your brither fish, as you will see the kindly cratures in the water when they're meeting wi' them they ken; ay, more nor some of our brithers and sisters will do amang themsels, for all that's told them in the kirk, deet ay. I was going to explain to you the perfect difference that there is between a trout and a grulse. You see, if the two were laid down before you there this moment, you would observe, ay before just you would look again, and no pody would need to tell you that they're not the same fish; you would say that a trout and a grulse would be here and there, if they happen to be put down, and you knew that's a trout, ay a trout's not a bit of a grulse about it."

"But Archie, I am just as wise as I was, you have yet given me no idea whatever of the points in which the trout and grilse differ from each other."

"After that, now, it's a perfect astonishment to me, that you'll not understood what I'll made as plain as the schild's A B C to the school laddie. What I'll say in a word to made you ken, I don't know! you see, for I want you to knew, for it's importance to a gentleman like you that's often fish—a grulse and trout belong to a different family, and their father nor mother is not the same, and their offspring canna be the same, but jest resemble their father and mother like ourself—a perfect, altogether difference, never possible to be mistake by any body that will knew a trout; you see, I say again, there noo, that's a trout lying down, you'll say in a moment when you'll saw, well that's a trout, and you'll knew it; a grulse is a difference now, and you look at it too, because it's there, and though they just be awa from one another, not far you'll just say yourself, they're not the same fish at all. Now you are satisfied that it's no possible to be the same, because they are, as I'm saying as perfect plain, not the same; if you'll not understood now, you are a stupid more nor I'll thocht, and I canna put words into your head."

## ALEXANDER LAING (1787–1857)

### Ae Happy Hour

The dark gray o' gloamin',
The lone leafy shaw*, wood
The coo o' the cushat*, pigeon
The scent o' the haw;
The brae o' the burnie
A' bloomin' in flower,
An' twa faithfu' lovers
Make ae happy hour.

A kind winsome wifie,
A clean cantie* hame pleasant
An' smilin' sweet babies,
To lisp the dear name;
Wi' plenty o' labor,
An' health to endure,
Make time to row round aye
The ae happy hour.

Ye, lost to affection
Whom avarice can move
To woo an' to marry
For a' thing but love;
Awa wi' your sorrows,
Awa wi' your store,

Ye ken na the pleasure,
O' ae happy hour.

## Jean of Aberdeen

Ye've seen the blooming rosy brier,
On stately Dee's wild woody knowes*; "knolls"
Ye've seen the op'ning lily fair,
In streamy Don's gay broomy howes*; Lowlands
An' ilka bonnie flower that grows
Amang their banks and braes sae green—
These borrow a' their finest hues
Frae lovely Jean of Aberdeen.

Ye've seen the dew-eyed bloomy haw,
When morning gilds the welkin high;
Ye've heard the breeze o' summer blaw,
When e'ening steals alang the sky.
But brighter far is Jeanie's eye
When we're amang the braes alane,
An' softer is the bosom-sigh
Of lovely Jean of Aberdeen.

Though I had a' the valleys gay
Around the airy Bennochie,
An' a' the fleecy flocks that stray
Amang the lofty hills o' Dee;
While mem'ry lifts her melting ee,
An' hope unfolds her fairy scene,
My heart wi' them I'd freely gie
To lovely Jean of Aberdeen.

## The Brownie of Fearnden

Thair livit ane man on Norinside,
Whan Jamis held his ain;
He had ane mailen* fair and wide, farm
And servants nine or tene.

He had ane servant dwelling near,
Worth all his maids and men;
And wha was this gin ye wald speer?
The Brownie* of Fearnden! goblin

Whan thair was corn to thresh or dicht,
Or barn or byre to clene,
He had ane busy hour at nicht,
Atween the twall and ane;

And thouch the sna' was never so deep,
So wild the wind or rain,

He ran ane errant in a wheip,
The Brownie of Fearnden!

Ae nicht the gudewife of the house
Fell sick as sick could be,
And for the skilly manny-wife
She wantit ane to gae.

The nicht was dark, and never a spark
Wald venture doun the glen,
For fear that he micht hear or see
The Brownie of Fearnden!

But Brownie was na far to seek,
For weil he heard the strife;
And ablins* thocht, as weil he micht, perhaps
They soon wald tine* the wife. lose

He aff and branks* the riding mear, bridles
And throch the wind and rain;
And soon was at the skilly wife's,
Wha livit owre the den.

He pullit the sneke*, and out he spak, latch
That she micht better hear,
"Thair is a mother wald give birth,
But hasna strength to bear.

"O rise, o rise, and hap* you weil, clothe
To keep you fra the rain."
"Whaur do you want me?" quoth the wife.
"O whaur but owre the den."

Whan baith waur mountit on the mear,
And riding up the glen;
"O wat ye, laddy," quoth the wife,
"Gin* we be near the den? if

"Are we come near the den?" she said;
"Tush, wysht*, ye fool," quoth he, silence
"For waur na ye hae in your arms,
This nicht ye winna see."

They soon waur landit at the door,
The wife he handit doun—
"I've left the house but ae half hour,
I am a clever loun*." rascal

"What maks your feet sae brayd?" quoth she,
"And what sae reid your een?"
"I've wandert mony a weary foot,
And unco* sichts I've seen. strange

"But mind the wife, and mind the wean,
And see that all gae right;
And keep the beyld* of biggit land — shelter
Till aynce the morning licht:

"And gin they speer wha brocht you here,
Cause they waur scaunt of men.
Even tell them that ye rade ahint* — behind
The Brownie of Fearnden."

## ALEXANDER CARLILE (1788–1860)

### The Corbie and Craw

The corbie* wi' his roupy throat, — raven
Cried frae the leafless tree,
"Come oer the loch, come oer the loch,
Come oer the loch to me."

The craw put up his sooty head,
And looked oer the nest whare he lay,
And gied a flaf wi' his rousty wings,
And cried, "Whare tae? whare tae?"

"Te pike a dead man that's lying
Ahint* yon meikle stane." — behind
"Is he fat, is he fat, is he fat, is he fat?
If no, we may let him alane."

"He cam frae merry England, to steal
The sheep, and kill the deer."
"I'll come, I'll come, for an Englishman
Is aye the best o' cheer."

"O we may breakfast on his breast,
And on his back may dine;
For the lave* a' fled to their ain country, — rest
And they've ne'er been back sinsyne."

## GEORGE GORDON, LORD BYRON (1788–1824)

[Byron is one of the most famous of British poets, and is usually thought of as English. His English father died shortly after his birth and he was brought up by his Scottish mother in Aberdeen until he was ten, at which age he inherited wealth and title from one of his father's relatives. He moved then to the Byron estate in England. Byron was quite conscious of his mixed heritage, of being different from his peers—all his life he felt somewhat out of place. The following are the few poems in which the youthful author refers to his Scottish background, plus one in which he makes reference to a Scottish folk song.]

## Lachin Y Gair[1]

Away, ye gay landscapes, ye gardens of roses.
In you let the minions of luxury rove;
Restore me the rocks where the snow-flake reposes,
Though still they are sacred to freedom and love:
Yet, Caledonia, beloved are thy mountains,
Round their white summits though elements war;
Though cataracts foam stead of smooth-flowing fountains,
I sigh for the valley of dark Loch na Garr.

Ah! there my young footsteps in infancy wandered;
My cap was the bonnet, my cloak was the plaid;
On chieftains long perished my memory pondered,
As daily I strode through the pine-covered glade;
I sought not my home till the day's dying glory
Gave place to the rays of the bright polar star;
For fancy was cheered by traditional story,
Disclosed by the natives of dark Loch na Garr.

"Shades of the dead! have I not heard your voices
Rise on the night-rolling breath of the gale?"
Surely the soul of the hero rejoices
And rides on the wind o'er his own highland vale.
Round Loch na Garr while the stormy mist gathers,
Winter presides in his cold icy car:
Clouds there encircle the forms of my fathers;
They dwell in the tempests of dark Loch na Garr.

"Ill-starred, though brave, did no visions foreboding
Tell you that fate had forsaken your cause?"
Ah, were you destined to die at Culloden,
Victory crowned not your fall with applause:
Still were you happy in death's earthly slumber,
You rest with your clan in the caves of Braemar:
The pibroch resounds to the piper's loud number,
Your deeds on the echoes of dark Loch na Garr.

Years have rolled on, Loch na Garr, since I left you,
Years must elapse ere I tread you again:
Nature of verdure and flowers has bereft you,
Yet still are you dearer than Albion's plain.
England! thy beauties are tame and domestic
To one who has roved o'er the mountains afar:
Oh for the crags that are wild and majestic.
The steep frowning glories of dark Loch na Garr.

## I Would I Were a Careless Child

I would I were a careless child,
Still dwelling in my Highland cave,

[1]A mountain in the northern Highlands.

Or roaming through the dusky wild,
Or bounding o'er the dark blue wave;
The cumbrous pomp of Saxon pride
Accords not with the freeborn soul,
Which loves the mountain's craggy side,
And seeks the rocks where billows roll.

Fortune, take back these cultured lands,
Take back this name of splendid sound.
I hate the touch of servile hands,
I hate the slaves that cringe around.
Place me among the rocks I love,
Which sound to Ocean's wildest roar;
I ask but this—again to rove
Through scenes my youth hath known before.

Few are my years, and yet I feel
The world was ne'er designed for me:
Ah, why do darkning shades conceal
The hour when man must cease to be?
Once I beheld a splendid dream,
A visionary scene of bliss:
Truth,—wherefore did thy hated beam
Awake me to a world like this?

I loved—but those I loved are gone;
Had friends—my early friends are fled:
How cheerless feels the heart alone,
When all its former hopes are dead.
Though gay companions o'er the bowl
Dispel awhile the sense of ill;
Though pleasure stirs the maddening soul,
The heart—the heart—is lonely still.

How dull, to hear the voice of those
Whom rank or chance, whom wealth or power,
Have made, though neither friends nor foes,
Associates of the festive hour.
Give me again a faithful few,
In years and feelings still the same.
And I will fly the midnight crew,
Where boist'rous joy is but a name.

And woman, lovely woman? thou,
My hope, my comforter, my all.
How cold must be my bosom now,
When e'en thy smiles begin to pall.
Without a sigh would I resign
This busy scene of splendid woe,
To make that calm contentment mine,
Which virtue knows, or seems to know.

Fain would I fly the haunts of men—
I seek to shun, not hate mankind;
My breast requires the sullen glen,
Whose gloom may suit a darkened mind.
Oh, that to me the wings were given
Which bear the turtle to her nest.
Then would I cleave the vault of heaven,
To flee away, and be at rest.

## When I Roved a Young Highlander

When I roved a young Highlander o'er the dark heath,
And climbed thy steep summit, oh Morven of snow,
To gaze on the torrent that thundered beneath,
Or the mist of the tempest that gathered below,
Untutored by science, a stranger to fear,
And rude as the rocks where my infancy grew,
No feeling, save one, to my bosom was dear;
Need I say, my sweet Mary, twas centered in you?

Yet it could not be love, for I knew not the name,—
What passion can dwell in the heart of a child?
But still I perceive an emotion the same
As I felt, when a boy, on the crag-covered wild:
One image alone on my bosom impressed,
I loved my bleak regions, nor panted for new;
And few were my wants, for my wishes were blessed;
And pure were my thoughts, for my soul was with you.

I arose with the dawn; with my dog as my guide,
From mountain to mountain I bounded along;
I breasted the billows of Dee's rushing tide,
And heard at a distance the Highlander's song:
At eve, on my heath-covered couch of repose,
No dreams, save of Mary, were spread to my view;
And warm to the skies my devotions arose,
For the first of my prayers was a blessing on you.

I left my bleak home, and my visions are gone;
The mountains are vanished, my youth is no more;
As the last of my race, I must wither alone,
And delight but in days I have witnessed before:
Ah, splendor has raised but embittered my lot;
More dear were the scenes which my infancy knew:
Though my hopes may have failed, yet they are not forgot;
Though cold is my heart, still it lingers with you.

When I see some dark hill point its crest to the sky,
I think of the rocks that o'ershadow Colbleen;
When I see the soft blue of a love-speaking eye,
I think of those eyes that endeared the rude scene;
When, haply, some light-waving locks I behold,

That faintly resemble my Mary's in hue,
I think on the long, flowing ringlets of gold,
The locks that were sacred to beauty, and you.

Yet the day may arrive when the mountains once more
Shall rise to my sight in their mantles of snow:
But while these soar above me, unchanged as before,
Will Mary be there to receive me?—ah, no.
Adieu, then, ye hills, where my childhood was bred.
Thou sweet flowing Dee, to thy waters adieu.
No home in the forest shall shelter my head, —
Ah Mary, what home could be mine but with you?

## So, We'll Go No More a Roving

[Byron here makes use of Scottish folk lyrics. His first stanza is almost identical to the chorus of the anonymous 15th-16th century song, "The Jolly Beggar," printed in Volume I.]

So, we'll go no more a roving
So late into the night,
Though the heart be still as loving,
And the moon be still as bright.

For the sword outwears its sheath,
And the soul wears out the breast,
And the heart must pause to breathe,
And love itself have rest.

Though the night was made for loving,
And the day returns too soon,
Yet we'll go no more a roving
By the light of the moon.

## WILLIAM GLEN (1789–1826)

### Wae's Me for Prince Charlie

A wee bird came to our ha' door.
He warbled sweet and clearly.
And aye the o'ercome o' his sang
Was "Wae's me for Prince Charlie."
Oh, when I heard the bonny, bonny bird,
The tears came drapping rarely.
I took my bonnet aff my head,
For weel I lo'ed Prince Charlie.

Quoth I, "My bird, my bonny, bonny bird,
Is that a tale ye borrow?
Or is't some words ye've learned by rote,
Or a lilt o' dool* and sorrow?" suffering

"Oh, no, no, no," the wee bird sang,
"I've flown sin' morning early,
But sic a day o' wind and rain!—
Oh, wae's me for Prince Charlie!

"On hills that are by right his ain
He roams a lonely stranger;
On ilka hand he's pressed by want,
On ilka side by danger.
Yestreen I met him in the glen,
My heart near bursted fairly;
For sadly changed indeed was he—
Oh, wae's me for Prince Charlie!

"Dark night came on; the tempest howled
Out owre the hills and valleys;
And where was't that your prince lay down,
Whase hame should be a palace?
He rowed him in a Highland plaid,
Which covered him but sparely,
And slept beneath a bush o' broom—
Oh, wae's me for Prince Charlie!"

But now the bird saw some red-coats,
And he shook his wings wi' anger:
"Oh, this is no a land for me—
I'll tarry here nae langer."
A while he hovered on the wing,
Ere he departed fairly;
But weel I mind the farewell strain,
Twas "Wae's me for Prince Charlie!"

## WILLIAM KNOX (1789–1825)

[This work gained some notoriety in the United States when Abraham Lincoln declared it his favorite poem.]

### Oh Why Should the Spirit of Mortal Be Proud

Oh, why should the spirit of mortal be proud?
Like a fast-flitting meteor, a fast-flying cloud,
A flash of the lightning, a break of the wave,
He passeth from life to his rest in the grave.

The leaves of the oak and the willow shall fade,
Be scattered around and together be laid;
And the young and the old, and the low and the high,
Shall molder to dust and together shall lie.

The child that a mother attended and loved,
The mother that infant's affection who proved,

The husband that mother and infant who blessed,—
Each, all, are away to their dwellings of rest.

The maid on whose cheek, on whose brow, in whose eye,
Shone beauty and pleasure,—her triumphs are by;
And the memory of those who have loved her and praised,
Are alike from the minds of the living erased.

The hand of the king that the scepter hath borne,
The brow of the priest that the miter hath worn,
The eye of the sage, and the heart of the brave,
Are hidden and lost in the depths of the grave.

The peasant whose lot was to sow and to reap,
The herdsman who climbed with his goats to the steep,
The beggar who wandered in search of his bread,
Have faded away like the grass that we tread.

The saint who enjoyed the communion of heaven,
The sinner who dared to remain unforgiven,
The wise and the foolish, the guilty and just,
Have quietly mingled their bones in the dust.

So the multitude goes, like the flower and the weed,
That wither away to let others succeed;
So the multitude comes, even those we behold,
To repeat every tale that hath often been told.

For we are the same things our fathers have been;
We see the same sights that our fathers have seen,—
We drink the same stream, and we feel the same sun,
And run the same course that our fathers have run.

The thoughts we are thinking our fathers would think;
From the death we are shrinking from, they too would shrink;
To the life we are clinging to, they too would cling;
But it speeds from the earth like a bird on the wing.

They loved, but their story we cannot unfold;
They scorned, but the heart of the haughty is cold;
They grieved, but no wail from their slumbers will come;
They joyed, but the voice of their gladness is dumb.

They died,—ay, they died; and we things that are now,
Who walk on the turf that lies over their brow,
Who make in their dwellings a transient abode,
Meet the changes they met on their pilgrimage road.

Yea, hope and despondence, and pleasure and pain,
Are mingled together in sunshine and rain;
And the smile and the tear, the song and the dirge,
Still follow each other, like surge upon surge.

Tis the twink of an eye, tis the draught of a breath,
From the blossom of health to the paleness of death,
From the gilded saloon to the bier and the shroud,—
Oh why should the spirit of mortal be proud?

## THOMAS PRINGLE (1789–1834)

### The Ewe-Buchtin's Bonnie

[This poem is a continuation of Lady Grisell Bailie's verse of the same name, printed in Volume I.]

The ewe-buchtin's* bonnie, baith e'enin' and morn, sheep-folding
When our blithe shepherds play on the bog-reed and horn;
While we're milking, they're lilting, baith pleasant and clear;
But my heart's like to break when I think on my dear.
O the shepherds take pleasure to blow on the horn,
To raise up their flocks o' sheep soon i' the morn.
On the bonnie green banks they feed pleasant and free,
But alas, my dear heart, all my sighing's for thee.

O the sheep-herdin's lightsome amang the green braes,
Where Kale wimples clear neath the white-blossomed slaes,
Where the wild-thyme and meadow-queen scent the soft gale,
And the cushat* croods luesomely down in the dale. pigeon
There the lintwhite and mavis sing sweet frae the thorn,
And blithe lilts the laverock aboon the green corn,
And a' things rejoice in the simmer's glad prime—
But my heart's wi' my love in the far foreign clime.

O the hay-makin's pleasant, in bright sunny June—
The hay-time is cheery when hearts are in tune;
But while others are jokin' and laughin' sae free,
There's a pang at my heart and a tear i' my e'e.
At e'en i' the gloamin', adown by the burn,
Fu' dowie* and wae, aft I daunder* and mourn; sad/ramble
Amang the lang broom I sit greetin* alane, weeping
And sigh for my dear and the days that are gane.

O the days o' our youth-heid were heartsome and gay,
When we herded thegither by sweet Gaitshaw brae,
When we plaited the rushes and pu'd the witch-bells
By the Kale's ferny houms* and on Hownam's green fells. flats
But young Sandy bood* gang to the wars wi' the laird, must
To win honor and gowd—(gif his life it be spared).
Ah, little care I for wealth, favor, or fame,
Gin I had my dear shepherd but safely at hame.

Then round our wee cot though gruff winter s'ould roar,
And poortith* glower in like a wolf at the door; poverty
Though our toom* purse had barely twa boddles to clink, empty

And a barley-meal scone were the best on our bink*; shelf
Yet, he wi' his hirsel*, and I wi' my wheel, flock
Through the howe* o' the year we wad fen' unco weel; middle
Till the lintwhite and the laverock, and lambs bleatin' fain,
Brought back the blithe time o' ewe-buchtin' again.

## The Emigrant's Farewell

Our native land, our native vale,
A long and last adieu.
Farewell to bonny Teviotdale,
And Cheviot mountains blue.

Farewell, ye hills of glorious deeds,
And streams renowned in song;
Farewell, ye braes and blossomed meads,
Our hearts have loved so long.

Farewell, the blithesome broomy knowes*, "knolls"
Where thyme and harebells grow;
Farewell, the hoary, haunted howes*, hollows
O'erhung with birk and sloe.

The mossy cave and moldering tower
That skirt our native dell,
The martyr's grave, and lover's bower,
We bid a sad farewell.

Home of our love, our father's home,
Land of the brave and free!
The sail is flapping on the foam
That bears us far from thee.

We seek a wild and distant shore
Beyond the western main.
We leave thee to return no more,
Nor view thy cliffs again.

But may dishonor blight our fame,
And blast our household fires,
If we or ours forget thy name,
Green island of our sires.

Our native land, our native vale,
A long and last adieu.
Farewell to bonny Teviotdale,
And Scotland's mountains blue.

## DAVID VEDDER (1790–1854)

### Auld Freends

My word! but ye seem nae sheep-shank;
I like your visage free and frank;
That ye're a man o walth and rank
I suldna wonder,
Wi credit in Sir Willie's Bank
For twa-three hunder;

Forbye a sclated* house to bide in, "slated"
A powny cairt to tak a ride in;
Sax guid milk-kye ye'll hae a pride in,
A mare and filly.
This comes o thrift and frugal guidin,
Auld muirland Willie.

And when ye gae to tryst and fair,
Gin ye hae little time to spare,
Ye'll trot the canny auld gray mare
Through dubs and plashes,
Your legs happed in a cozy pair
O splatterdashes.

Nae doubt, but ye hae struggled sair
Through fifty year to gather gear*; money
Your manly brow wi lines o care
Is sair indentit,
But *truth* and *honesty* are there
As deep imprentit.

The parish kens that ye maintained
Through life a character unstained;
The eldership ye'll hae attained,
As is richt meet;—
Or, if ye binna yet ordained,
Ye're on the leet*. (waiting) list

When neebours cam to altercation,
Aspersion and recrimination,
And naething for't but Courts o Session
And judge and jury,
Your mild and richteous arbitration
Aye laid their fury.

When tailor Tam brak yard and shears,
And listit wi the Fusiliers,
His widowed mither, bathed in tears,
Mourned owre the staff
And stay o her declining years,—
Ye bought him aff.

Besides, it's kent that ye can len'
Sma sums to puir but honest men;
But, a' unlike "my uncle" Ben
O Borrowstoun,
Ye never seek a pledge again,
But shools it doun.

I'se wad ye hae ane ample store
O solid theologic lore,
Frae Baillie, Boston, Brown, and More,
And weel can quote them;
And ither worthies, half a score,
Though I've forgot them.

I see ye've trotted owre the green
To meet your valued early freen';
He's sittin on an auld gray stane
Quite at his leisure;
The verra twinkle o his een
Denotes his pleasure.

Ah! had we mony mae like thee
To prop the State's auld randle-tree* roof-beam
And drink the stream o Liberty
In moderation,
In spite o grumblers we wad be
A happy nation.

## Jeanie's Welcome Hame

Let wrapt musicians strike the lyre,
While plaudits shake the vaulted fane*: building
Let warriors rush through flood and fire,
A never dying name to gain;
Let bards, on fancy's fervid wing,
Pursue some high or holy theme:
Be't mine, in simple strains, to sing
My darling Jeanie's welcome hame.

Sweet is the morn of flowery May,
When incense breathes from heath and wold—
When laverocks hymn the matin lay,
And mountain peaks are bathed in gold—
And swallows, frae some foreign strand,
Are wheeling oer the winding stream;
But sweeter to extend my hand,
And bid my Jeanie welcome hame.

Poor collie, our auld-farrant* dog, wise
Will bark wi' joy whene'er she comes;
And baudrons*, on the ingle rug, (the cat)
Will blithely churm at "auld gray-thrums."

The mavis, frae our apple tree,
Shall warble forth a joyous strain;
The blackbird's mellow minstrelsy
Shall welcome Jeanie hame again.

Like dew drops on a fading rose,
Maternal tears shall start for thee,
And low-breathed blessings rise like those
Which soothed thy slumb'ring infancy.
Come to my arms, my timid dove;
I'll kiss thy beauteous brow once more;
The fountain of thy father's love
Is welling all its banks out oer.

## To Orkney

Land of the whirlpool—torrent—foam,
Where oceans meet in maddening shock;
The beetling cliff—the shelving holm—
The dark insidious rock:
Land of the bleak, the treeless moor—
The sterile mountain, sered and riven—
The shapeless cairn, the ruined tower,
Scathed by the bolts of heaven:
The yawning gulf—the treacherous sand—
I love thee still, my native land.

Land of the dark—the Runic rhyme—
The mystic ring—the cavern hoar;
The Scandinavian seer—sublime
In legendary lore:
Land of a thousand Sea-kings' graves—
Those tameless spirits of the past,
Fierce as their subject Arctic waves,
Or hyperborean blast;
Though polar billows round thee foam,
I love thee! Thou wert once my home.

With glowing heart, and island lyre,
Ah, would some native bard arise
To sing with all a poet's fire
Thy stern sublimities;
The roaring flood, the rushing stream,
The promontory wild and bare,
The pyramid where sea-birds scream
Aloft in middle air;
The Druid temple on the heath,
Old, even beyond tradition's breath.

Though I have roamed through verdant glades,
In cloudless climes, neath azure skies;
Or plucked from beauteous orient meads

Flowers of celestial dyes:
Though I have laved in limpid streams,
That murmur over golden sands;
Or basked amid the fulgid beams
That flame o'er fairer lands;
Or stretched me in the sparry grot,—
My country! Thou wert ne'er forgot.

## The First of May

Now the beams of May morn
On the mountains are streaming,
And the dews on the corn
Are like diamond-drops gleaming;
And the birds from the bowers
Are in gladness ascending;
And the breath of sweet flowers
With the zephyrs is blending.

And the rose-linnet's thrill,
Overflowing with gladness,
And the wood-pigeon's bill,
Though their notes seem of sadness;
And the jessamine rich
Its soft tendrils is shooting,
From pear and from peach
The bright blossoms are sprouting.

And the lambs on the lea
Are in playfulness bounding,
And the voice of the sea
Is in harmony sounding;
And the streamlet on high
In the morning beam dances,
For all nature is joy
As sweet summer advances.

Then, my Mary, let's stray
Where the wild-flowers are glowing,
By the banks of the Tay
In its melody flowing;
Thou shalt bathe in May dew,
Like a sweet mountain blossom,
For tis bright like thy brow
And tis pure as thy bosom.

## The Tempest Is Raging

The tempest is raging
And rending the shrouds;
The ocean is waging
A war with the clouds;

The cordage is breaking,
The canvas is torn,
The timbers are creaking—
The seamen forlorn.

The water is gushing
Through hatches and seams;
Tis roaring and rushing
Oer keelson and beams;
And nought save the lightning
On mainmast or boom,
At intervals bright'ning
The palpable gloom.

Though horrors beset me,
And hurricanes howl,
I may not forget thee,
Beloved of my soul.
Though soon I must perish
In ocean beneath,
Thine image I'll cherish,
Adored one, in death.

## The Sun Had Slipped

The sun had slipped ayont* the hill, — beyond
The darg* was done in barn and byre; — day's work
The carle* himself, come hame frae the mill, — peasant
Was luntin'* his cutty before the fire; — smoking
The lads and lasses had just sitten down,
The hearth was sweepit fu' canty* an' clean, — pleasant
When the cadgie* laird o' Windlestraetown — cheerful
Cam' in for till haud his Halloween.

The gudewife becked, and the carle boo'd;
In owre to the deis the laird gaed he;
The swankies[1] a', they glowred like wud*, — crazy
The lasses leugh i' their sleeves sae slee;
An' sweet wee Lilias was unco* feared, — very
Though she bloomed like a rose in a garden green;
An' sair she blushed when she saw the laird
Come there for till haud his Halloween.

"Now haud ye merry," quo Windlestraetown,
"I downa* come here your sport to spill,— — cannot
Rax* down the nits, ye unco like loon, — reach
For though I am auld, I am gleesome still:
An' Lilias, my pet, to burn wi' me,
Ye winna be sweer, right weel I ween,

[1] Strapping young fellows.

However it gangs, my fate I'll dree*, suffer
Since here I am haudin' my Halloween."

The pawky* auld wife, at the chimly-cheek, canny
Took courage an' spak', as a mither should do;
"Noo haud up yer head, my dochter meek,—
A laird comesna ilka night to woo.
He'll make you a lady, and that right soon,
I dreamt it twice owre, I'm sure, yestreen."
"A bargain be't," quo Windlestraetown,—
"It's lucky to book on Halloween."

"I'll stick by the nits for better, for waur,—
Will ye do the like, my bonny May?
Ye sall shine at my board like the gloaming star,
An' gowd in gowpins ye's hae for aye."
The nits are cannily laid on the ingle*, fireplace
Weel, weel are they tented* wi' anxious een, watched
And sweetly in ase* thegither they mingle; ashes
"Noo blessed for aye be this Halloween."

## HEW AINSLIE (1792–1878)

### The Hint o' Hairst

It's dowie* in the hint o' hairst*, sad/autumn
At the wa-gang o' the swallow,
When the wind grows cauld, and the burns grow bauld,
And the wuds are hingin' yellow;
But oh, it's dowier far to see
The wa-gang o' her the heart gangs wi',
The deid-set o' a shinin' e'e—
That darkens the weary world on thee.

There was mickle love atween us twa—
Oh, twa could ne'er be fonder;
And the thing on yird* was never made, earth
That could ha'e gart* us sunder. made
But the way of Heaven's abune a' ken,
And we maun bear what it likes to sen'—
It's comfort, though, to weary men,
That the warst o' this warld's waes maun en'.

There's mony things that come and gae,
Just kent, and syne forgotten;
And the flowers that busk* a bonnie brae, dress
Gin anither year lie rotten.
But the last look o' that lovely e'e,
And the dying grip she gae to me,
They're settled like eternity—
Oh, Mary! that I were wi' thee.

## I Left Ye, Jeanie

I left ye, Jeanie, blooming fair,
Mang the bourocks* o' Bargeny— shacks
I've foun' ye on the banks o' Ayr,
But sair ye're altered, Jeanie.

I left ye mang the woods sae green,
In rustic weed befittin'—
I've foun' ye buskit* like a queen, dressed
In painted chambers sittin'.

Ye're fairer, statelier, I can see,
Ye're wiser, nae doubt, Jeanie;—
But O, I'd rather met wi' thee
Mang the green bowers o' Bargeny!

## Willie and Helen

"Wharefore sou'd ye talk o' love,
Unless it be to pain us?
Wharefore should ye talk o' love
Whan ye say the sea maun twain us?"

"It's no because my love is light,
Nor for your angry deddy;
It's a' to buy ye pearlins bright,
An' to busk* ye like a leddy." dress

"O Willy, I can caird an' spin,
Sae ne'er can want for cleedin';
An' gin I hae my Willy's heart,
I hae a' the pearls I'm heedin'.

"Will it be time to praise this cheek
When years an' tears hae blenched it?
Will it be time to talk o' love
Whan cauld an' care hae quenched it?"

He's laid ae han' about her waist—
The ither's held to heaven;
An' his luik was like the luik o' man
Wha's heart in twa is riven.

## The Ingle-Side

It's rare to see the morning bleeze
Like a bonfire frae the sea,
It's fair to see the burnie kiss
The lip o' the flowery lea;
An' fine it is on green hillside,
Where hums the bonnie bee,

But rarer, fairer, finer far
Is the ingle-side for me.

Glens may be gilt wi' gowans rare,
The birds may fill the tree;
An' haughs hae a' the scented ware
The simmer-growth can gie:
But the canty* hearth where cronies meet, pleasant, snug
An' the darling o' our e'e,
That makes to us a warl' complete:
Oh, the ingle-side for me.

## On wi' the Tartan

Can you loe*, my dear lassie, "love"
The hills wild and free;
Whar the sang o' the shepherd
Gars* a' ring wi' glee? makes
Or the steep rocky glens,
Where the wild falcons bide?
Then on wi' the tartan,
And, fy, let us ride.

Can ye loe the knowes*, lassie, "knolls"
That ne'er war in rigs*? (plowed)
Or the bonnie loune lee,
Where the sweet robin bigs*? builds
Or the sang o' the lintie,
Whan wooin' his bride?
Then on wi' the tartan,
And, fy, let us ride.

Can ye loe the burn, lassie,
That loups amang linns*? waterfalls
O the bonnie green howmes,[1]
Where it cannily rins,
Wi' a canty* bit housie pleasant
Sae snug by its side?
Then on wi' the tartan,
And, fy, let us ride.

## "Stands Scotland Where It Did?"

Hoo's dear auld mither Scotland, lads,
Hoo's kindly Scotland noo?
Are a' her glens as green's of yore,
Her hills as stern an' blue?

I meikle dread the iron steed,
That tears up heugh and fell*, hill

[1] Land by a river.

Has gi'en our canny old folk
A sorry tale to tell.

Hae touns taen a' our bonnie burns
To cool their lowin' craigs*?    throats
Or damned them up in timmer* troughs    (wooden)
To slock their yettlin'* naigs?    iron

Do Southern loons* infest your touns    rascals
Wi' mincing Cockney gab?
Hae "John and Robert" taen the place
O plain ald "Jock an' Rab?"

In sooth, I dread a foreign breed
Noo rules oer "corn an' horn";
An' kith an' kin I'd hardly fin',
Or place whare I was born.

They're houkin* sae in bank an' brae,    digging
An' sheughin' hill an' howe*:    dale
I tremble for the bonny broom,
The whin an' heather cowe*.    twig

I fear the dear auld "deligence"
An' "flies" hae flown the track,
An' cadgers* braw, pocks, creels an' a',    peddlers
Gane i' the ruthless wrack.

Are souple kimmers* kirkward boun,    gossips
On Sabbath to be seen?
Wi' sturdy carles* that talk o' texts,    fellows
Roups, craps, an' days hae been.

Gang lasses yet wi' wares to sell
Barefitit to the toun?
Is wincie still the wiliecoat*    undercoat
An' demitty the goun?

Do wanters[1] try the yarrow leaf
Upon the first o' May?
Are there touslings on the hairst* rig,    harvest
An' houtherings mang the hay?

Are sheepshead dinners on the board,
Wi' gousty* haggis seen?    tasty
Come scones an' farls at four hours;
Are sowens[2] saired at e'en?

---

[1]Widows or unmarried persons.

[2]A dish made from oats and meal, eaten like porridge.

Are winkings tween the preachings rife
Out owre the baps an' yill?
Are there cleekings* i' the kirk gates, latches
An' loans for lovers still?

Gang loving sauls in plaids for shawls
A courtin' to the bent*? grass
Has gude braid lawlins* left the land? (Scots)
Are kail and crowdy[1] kent?

Ah, weel I min', in dear langsyne,
Our rantin's round the green:
The meetings at the trystin' tree,
The "chappings out" at e'en.

Oh bootless queries, vanished scenes;
Oh wan and wintry Time!
Why lay alike, on heart an' dyke,
Thy numbing frost and rime?

E'en noo my day gans doun the brae,
An' tear draps fa' like rain,
To think the fouth* o' gladsome youth plenty
Can ne'er return again.

## The Rover o' Lochryan

The rover o' Lochryan he's gane,
Wi' his merry men sae brave.
Their hearts are o' the steel, and a better keel
Ne'er bowled oer the back o' a wave.

It's no when the loch lies dead in its trough,
When naething disturbs it ava*; at all
But the rack an the ride o' the restless tide,
An' the splash o' the gray sea-maw.

It's no when the yawl an' the light skiffs crawl
Owre the breast o' the siller sea,
That I look to the west for the bark I loe best,
An' the Rover that's dear to me.

But when that the clud lays its cheeks to the flud,
An' the sea lays its shouther to the shore;
When the wind sings high, and the sea-whaups cry,
As they rise frae the deafening roar.

It's then that I look through the thickening rook
An' watch by the midnight tide.

---

[1] An oatmeal dish.

I ken the wind brings my Rover hame,
And the sea that he glories to ride.

Merrily he stands mang his jovial crew,
Wi' the helm heft in his hand,
An' he sings aloud to his boys in blue,
As his e'e's upon Galloway's land—

"Unstent and slack each reef and tack,
Gie her sail, boys, while it may sit;
She has roared through a heavier sea afore,
And she'll roar through a heavier yet.

"When landsmen drouse, or trembling rouse,
To the tempest's angry moan,
We dash through the drift, and sing to the lift
O' the wave that heaves us on.

"It's braw, boys, to see the morn's blithe e'e,
When the night's been dark an' drear;
But it's better far to lie, wi' our storm-locks dry,
In the bosom o' her that is dear.

"Gie her sail, gie her sail, till she buries her wale,
Gie her sail, boys, while it may sit;
She has roared through a heavier sea afore,
An' she'll roar through a heavier yet."

## The Sweetest o' Them A'

When springtime gi'es the heart a lift
Out ower cauld winter's snaw and drift,
An' April's showers begin to sift
Fair flowers on field an' shaw*, wood
Then, Katie, when the dawing's clear—
Fresh as the firstlings o' the year—
Come forth, my joy—my dearest dear—
O, sweetest o' them a'.

When pleasant primrose days are doon—
When linties sing their saftest tune—
And simmer, nearing to his noon,
Gars rarest roses blaw—
Then, sheltered frae the sun an' win',
Beneath the buss, below the linn*, waterfall
I'll tell thee hoo this heart ye win,
Thou sweetest o' them a'.

When flowers hae ripened into fruit—
When plantings wear their Sabbath suit—
When win's grow laud, and birdies mute,
An' swallows flit awa'—

Then, on the lee side o' a stook,
Or in some calm an' cozy nook,
I'll swear I'm thine upon the Book,
Thou sweetest o' them a'.

Though black December bin's the pool
Wi' blasts might e'en a wooer cool,
It's them that brings us canty* Yule    pleasant
As weel's the frost an' snaw.
Then, when auld winter's raging wide,
An' cronies crowd the ingle*-side,    fire
I'll bring them ben* a blooming bride—    in
O, sweetest o' them a'!

## WILLIAM FINLAY (1792–1847)

### The Widow's Excuse

"O, Leezie M'Cutcheon, I canna but say,
Your grief hasna lasted a year and a day;
The crape aff your bannet already ye've tane;
Nae wonner that men ca' us fickle an' fain.
Ye sich't and ye sabbit, that nicht Johnnie dee't,
I thought my ain heart wad hae broken to see't;
But noo ye're as canty* and brisk as a bee;    cheerful
Oh, the frailty o' women I wonner to see;
The frailty o' women I wonner to see;
The frailty o' women I wonner to see;
Ye kissed his cauld gab* wi' the tear in your e'e;    mouth
Oh, the frailty o' women I wonner to see.

"When Johnnie was living, oh little he wist
That the sound o' the mools* as they fell on his kist,    (dirt)
While yet like a knell, ringing loud in your lug*,    ear
By anither man's side ye'd be sleeping sae snug,
O Leezie, my lady, ye've surely been fain,
For an unco*-like man to your arms ye have taen.    strange
John Mc'Cutcheon was buirdly, but this ane, I trow,
The e'e o' your needle ye might draw him through.
O, the e'e o' your needle ye might draw him through.
His nose it is shirpit, his lip it is blue,
Oh, Leezie, ye've surely to wale* on had few,    choose
Ye've looted and lifted but little, I trow."

"Now, Janet wi' jibing and jeering hae dune.
Though it's true that anaither now fills Johnnie's shoon,
He was lang in sair trouble, and Robin, ye ken
Was a handy bit body, and lived but and ben.
He was unco* obliging, and cam' at my wag,    very
Whan wi' grief and fatigue I was liken to fag.
'Deed, John couldna want him—for aften I've seen
His e'e glisten wi' gladness when Robin cam' in.

Then, how can ye wonner I gied him my haun?
Oh, how can ye wonner I gied him my haun?
When I needed his help he was aye at comman';
Then how can ye wonner I gied him my haun?

"At length when John dee't, and was laid in the clay,
My haun it was bare, and my heart it was wae.
I had na a steek, that was black, to put on,
For wark I had plenty wi' guiding o' John.
Now Robin was thrifty, and ought that he wan
He took care o't, and aye had twa notes at comman',
And he lent me as muckle as coft* a black gown,
Sae hoo can ye wonner he's wearing John's shoon?
Then hoo can ye wonner he's wearing John's shoon,
My heart-strings wi' sorrow were a' out o' tune;
A man that has worth and twa notes at comman',
Can soon get a woman to tak him in haun."

*bought

## THOMAS LYLE (1792–1859)

### Kelvin Grove

Let us haste to Kelvin Grove, bonnie lassie, O,
Through its mazes let us rove, bonnie lassie, O,
Where the rose in all her pride
Decks the hollow dingle side,
Where the midnight fairies glide, bonnie lassie, O.

Let us wander by the mill, bonnie lassie, O,
To the cove beside the rill, bonnie lassie, O,
Where the glens rebound the call
Of the roaring waters' fall,
Through the mountain's rocky hall, bonnie lassie, O.

O Kelvin banks are fair, bonnie lassie, O,
When in summer we are there, bonnie lassie, O.
There, the May-pink's crimson plume
Throws a soft, but sweet perfume,
Round the yellow banks of broom, bonnie lassie, O.

Though I dare not call thee mine, bonnie lassie, O,
As the smile of fortune's thine, bonnie lassie, O,
Yet with fortune on my side,
I could stay thy father's pride,
And win thee for my bride, bonnie lassie, O.

But the frowns of fortune lower, bonnie lassie, O,
On thy lover at this hour, bonnie lassie, O.
Ere yon golden orb of day
Wake the warblers on the spray,
From this land I must away, bonnie lassie, O.

Then farewell to Kelvin Grove, bonnie lassie, O,
And adieu to all I love, bonnie lassie, O,
To the river winding clear,
To the fragrant scented brier,
Even to thee of all most dear, bonnie lassie, O.

When upon a foreign shore, bonnie lassie, O,
Should I fall midst battle's roar, bonnie lassie, O,
Then, Helen, shouldst thou hear
Of thy lover on his bier,
To his memory shed a tear, bonnie lassie, O.

### Dark Dunoon

See the glow-worm lits her fairy lamp,
From a beam of the rising moon;
On the heathy shore at evening fall,
Twixt Holy-Loch and dark Dunoon;
Her fairy lamp's pale silvery glare,
From the dew-clad, moorland flower,
Invite my wandering footsteps there,
At the lonely twilight hour.

When the distant beacon's revolving light
Bids my lone steps seek the shore,
There the rush of the flow-tide's rippling wave
Meets the dash of the fisher's oar;
And the dim-seen steamboat's hollow sound,
As she seaward tracks her way.
All else are asleep in the still calm night,
And robed in the misty gray.

When the glow-worm lits her elfin lamp,
And the night breeze sweeps the hill,
It's sweet on thy rock-bound shores, Dunoon,
To wander at fancy's will.
Eliza, with thee in this solitude,
Life's cares would pass away,
Like the fleecy clouds over gray Kilmun,
At the wake of early day.

## JOHN NEVAY (1792–1870)

### The Fall of the Leaf

The summer flowers are gone,
And oer the melancholy sea
The thistledown is strewn.
The brown leaf drops, drops from the tree,
And on the spated river floats,—
That with a sullen spirit flows;
Like lurid dream of troubled thoughts;

While mournfully, all mournfully,
    The rain-wind blows.

The summer birds are mute,
And cheerless is the unsung grove;
Silent the rural flute,
Whose Doric stop was touched to love,
By hedgerow stile at gloaming gray:
Nor heard the milk-maid's melody,
To fountain wending, blithe as gay;
In wain-shed stand, all pensively,
The hamlet fowls,—the cock not crows;
While mournfully, all mournfully,
    The rain-wind blows.

Nor heard the pastoral bleat
Of flocks, that whitened many hills;
Vacant the plaided shepherd's seat—
Far up above the boulder-leaping rills:
Young winter oer the Grampians scowls,
His blasts and snow clouds marshaling;
Beasts of the fields, and forest fowls,
Instinctive see the growing wing of storm
Dark coming oer their social haunts;
Yet fear not they, for Heaven provides
For them; the wild bird never wants;
Want still with luxury resides.
Prophetic, on the rushy lea,
Stalk the dull choughs and crows.
While mournfully, and drearily,
    The rain-wind blows.

Thick on the unsunned lake
Float, murmuringly, its blasted reeds;
And on the pebbles break
To rot among the oozy weeds;
The wreck of summer grand and beauteous spring,
The hearse-like, pensive, chilly fret
Of the bleak water seems to sing
The elegy of bright suns set,
And all their balmy blossoms dead;
Like young life's verdant pastimes fled;
Nor sapphire sky, nor amber cloud,
Lies mirrored in the somber wave,
The gloomy heaven's like nature's shroud;
The water's lurid depth seemeth the grave
Of beauty gone. And beauty's eye
No more with floral pleasure glows;
While mournfully, all mournfully,
    The rain-wind blows.

There long decay hath been;
Through the rank weeds, and nettles vile,

Whistle the surly winds of e'en,
Where Scotland's Queen was wont to smile;
Who, in a dark and savage age,
Was learned and pious; read the sacred page
Unto her lord; taught maids of lowliest home
To know and love the Savior-Lord;
To read his soul-uplifting word,
And understand the kingdom yet to come:
Now sainted Margaret's bonny summer bower
Is reft of all its sylvan joy;
Nor vestige left of the Inch Tower;
Nor that which charmed the roaming boy;
The ancient bush of glossy sloes:
Nought but the lightning-scathed tree
Remains; that, from its leafless boughs
Drops the cold dew incessantly,
Like Eld* weeping for a young maiden's woes; age
While mournfully, all mournfully,
The rain-wind blows.

Browse not the kine and horse;
Rusted the harrow and the plow;
And all day long upon the gorse,
Brown-blighted on the brae's rough brow,
The night-dew and thin gossamer,
Hang chilly; and the weary sun
Seems tired amid the troubled air;
And, long ere his full course be run,
Beneath the Sidlaws wild, sinks down;
Night gathers fast oer cot and town;
Around, and far as eye can see,
Day has a dreary, death-like close;
While mournfully, most mournfully,
The rain-wind blows.

Thick glooms fall on the wood;
A cold and thrilling sough* is there. swoosh
Tis like the heart's mirk mood,
That makes this fleeting world its care;
And hath no joys, nor hope of joys,
Above the vulgar mortal aim
Which all the groveling soul employs,
Till quenched is its ethereal flame.
From sky to earth now all is night.
In every nook old darkness creeps;
And art the halls of wealth must light,
Where beauty smiles; nay, haply weeps,
Amid the grandeur of a station high;
Tears from the fount of sympathy—
For hapless worth, worth which the world not knows;
O, blessed is the tear that flows,
Like manna-dew from a celestial tree,
For uncomplaining woes.

Now happy—O how happy they,
The toil-tired sons of honest industry,
Who, by the cheerful hearth, mid children gay,
In cottage-home, enjoy health's blithe repose,
While mournfully, and drearily,
The rain-wind blows.

## HENRY LYTE (1793–1847)

### Abide With Me

Abide with me! Fast falls the eventide.
The darkness deepens. Lord, with me abide.
When other helpers fail, and comforts flee,
Help of the helpless, O abide with me.

Swift to its close ebbs out life's little day.
Earth's joys grow dim; its glories pass away.
Change and decay in all around I see.
O thou, who changes not, abide with me.

Not a brief glance I beg, a passing word,
But as thou dwell'st with thy disciples, Lord,
Familiar, condescending, patient, free,
Come, not to sojourn, but abide, with me.

Come not in terrors, as the King of Kings;
But kind and good, with healing in thy wings;
Tears for all woes, a heart for every plea.
Come, friend of sinners, and thus bide with me.

Thou on my head in early youth didst smile,
And, though rebellious and perverse meanwhile,
Thou hast not left me, oft as I left thee.
On to the close, O Lord, abide with me.

I need thy presence every passing hour.
What but thy grace can foil the tempter's power?
Who like thyself my guide and stay can be?
Through cloud and sunshine, O abide with me.

I fear no foe with thee at hand to bless.
Ills have no weight, and tears no bitterness.
Where is death's sting, where, grave, thy victory?
I triumph still, if thou abide with me.

Hold thou thy cross before my closing eyes.
Shine through the gloom, and point me to the skies.
Heaven's morning breaks, and earth's vain shadows flee.
In life and death, O Lord, abide with me.

## JAMES NICOL (1793–1819)

### Where Quair Rins Sweet Amang the Flowers

Where Quair rins sweet amang the flowers,
Down by yon woody glen, lassie,
My cottage stands—it shall be yours,
Gin ye will be my ain, lassie.

I'll watch ye wi' a lover's care,
And wi' a lover's e'e, lassie.
I'll weary heaven wi' mony a prayer,
And ilka prayer for thee, lassie.

Tis true I hae na mickle gear*; money
My stock is unco* sma', lassie; very
Nae fine spun foreign claes I wear;
Nae servants tend my ca', lassie.

But had I heired the British crown,
And thou o' low degree, lassie;
A rustic lad I wad hae grown,
Or shared that crown wi' thee, lassie.

I blame the blast, blaws on thy cheek;
The flower that decks thy hair, lassie,
The gales that steal thy breath sae sweet,
My love and envy share, lassie.

Where Quair rins sweet amang the flowers,
Down by yon woody glen, lassie,
I have a cot. It shall be yours,
Gin you will be my ain, lassie.

## EDWARD RAMSAY (1793–1872)

### On Humor Proceeding From Scottish Language

from *Reminiscences of Scottish Life and Character, 6th ed.* (1861)

We come next to reminiscences chiefly connected with peculiarities which turned upon our Scottish language, whether contained in words or in expressions. Now this is a very important change, and affects in a greater degree than many persons would imagine, the general modes and aspects of society. I suppose at one time the two countries of England and Scotland were considered as almost speaking different languages and I suppose also, that from the period of the union of the crowns, the language has been assimilating. We see the process of assimilation going on, and ere long amongst persons of education and birth very little difference will be perceptible.

With regard to that class a great change has taken place in my time. I recollect old Scottish ladies and gentlemen who regularly spoke Scotch. It was not, mark me, speaking English with an accent. No, it was downright Scotch. Every tone and every syllable was Scotch. For example, I recollect old Miss Erskine of Dun, a fine specimen of a real lady, and daughter of an ancient Scottish house. Many people now would not understand her. She was always the lady, notwithstanding her dialect, and to none could the epithet vulgar be less appropriately applied. I speak of thirty years ago, and yet I recollect her accost to me as well as if it were yesterday, "I didna ken ye were i' the toun." Taking words and accent together, an address how totally unlike what we now meet with in society.

Some of the old Scottish words which we can remember are delicious; but how strange they would sound to the ears of the present generation. Fancy that in walking from church, and discussing the sermon, a lady of rank should now express her opinion of it by the description of its being, "but a hummelcorn discourse." Many living persons can remember Angus old ladies who would say to their nieces and daughters, "Whatna hummeldoddie o' a mutch hae ye gotten?" meaning a flat and low-crowned cap. In speaking of the dryness of the soil on a road in Lanarkshire, a farmer said, "It stoors[1] in an orr."[2] How would this be as tersely translated into English? The late Duchess of Gordon sat at dinner next an English gentleman who was carving, and who made it a boast that he was thoroughly master of the Scottish language. Her Grace turned to him and said, "Rax me a spaul o' that bubbly jock.''[3]

The unfortunate man was completely nonplused.

A Scottish gentleman was entertaining at his house an English cousin who professed himself as rather knowing in the language of the north side of the Tweed. He asked him what he supposed to be the meaning of the expression, "ripin' the ribs."[4] To which he readily answered, "Oh, it describes a very fat man."

I profess myself an out and out Scotchman. I have strong national partialities—call them if you will national prejudices. I cherish a great love of old Scottish language. Some of our pure Scottish ballad poetry is unsurpassed in any language for grace and pathos. How expressive, how beautiful are its phrases! You can't translate them. Take an example of power in a Scotch expression, to describe with tenderness and feeling what is in human life. Take one of our most familiar phrases; as thus,—we meet an old friend, we talk over bygone days, and remember many who were dear to us both, once bright and young and gay, of whom some remain honored, prosperous, and happy, of whom some are under a cloud of misfortune or disgrace. some are broken in health and spirits, some sunk into the grave; we recall old familiar places—-old companions, pleasures, and pursuits; as Scotchmen our hearts are touched with these remembrances of AULD LANG SYNE.

Match me the phrase in English. You can't translate it. The fitness and the beauty lie in the felicity of the language. Like many happy expressions, it is not transferable into another tongue, just like the "simplex munditiis" of Horace, which describes the natural grace of female elegance, or the "ανηρι ϑμον γελασμα" of Aeschylus, which describes the bright sparkling of the ocean in the sun.

I think the power of Scottish dialect was happily exemplified by the late Dr. Adam, rector of the High School of Edinburgh, in his translation of the Horatian expression, "desipere in loco," which he turned by the Scotch phrase "weel-timed daffin'."[5] a translation, however, which no one but a Scotchman could appreciate. The following humorous Scottish translation of an old Latin aphorism has been assigned to the late Dr. Hill of St. Andrews, "Qui bene cepit dimidium facti fecit." The witty principal expressed in Scotch: "Weel saipet (well soaped) is half shaven."

---

[1]Storms, kicks up dust.

[2]"Hour."

[3]Reach me a leg of that turkey. [ER]

[4]Clearing ashes out of the bars of the grate. [ER]

[5]Fooling, teasing.

What mere English word could have expressed a distinction so well in such a case as the following: I heard once a lady in Edinburgh objecting to a preacher that she did not understand him. Another lady, his great admirer, insinuated that probably he was too "deep" for her to follow. But her ready answer was, "Na, na, he's no just deep, but he's drumly."[1]

We have just received a testimony to the value of our Scottish language from the illustrious Chancellor of the University of Edinburgh, the force and authority of which no one will be disposed to question. Lord Brougham, in speaking of improvements upon the English language, makes these striking remarks:

> The pure and classical language of Scotland must on no account be regarded as a provincial dialect, any more than French was so regarded in the reign of Henry V., or Italian in that of the first Napoleon, or Greek under the Roman Empire. Nor is it to be in any manner of way considered as a corruption of the Saxon. On the contrary, it contains much of the old and genuine Saxon, with an intermixture from the Northern nations, as Danes and Norse, and some, though a small portion, from the Celtic. But in whatever way composed, or from whatever sources arising, it is a national language, used by the whole people in their early years, by many learned and gifted persons throughout life, and in which are written the laws of the Scotch, their judicial proceedings, their ancient history, above all, their poetry.
>
> There can be no doubt that the English language would greatly gain by being enriched with a number both of words and of phrases, or turns of expression, now peculiar to the Scotch. It was by such a process that the Greek became the first of tongues, as well written as spoken.
>
> Would it not afford means of enriching and improving the English language, if full and accurate glossaries of improved Scotch words and phrases—those successfully used by the best writers, both in prose and verse—were given, with distinct explanation and reference to authorities? This has been done in France and other countries, where some dictionaries accompany the English, in some cases with Scotch synonyms, in others with varieties of expression." *Installation Address*, p. 63.

I cannot help thinking that a change of national language involves to some extent change of national character. Numerous examples of great power in Scottish phraseology, to express the picturesque, the feeling, the wise, and the humorous, might be taken from the works of Robert Burns, Ferguson, or Allan Ramsay, and which lose their charm altogether when unscottified. The speaker certainly seems to take a strength and character from his words. We must now look for specimens of this racy and expressive tongue in the more retired parts of the country. It is no longer to be found in high places. It has disappeared from the social circles of our cities. In my early days the intercourse with the peasantry of Forfarshire, Kincardineshire, and especially of Deeside, was most amusing, not that the things said were so much out of the common, as that the language in which they were conveyed was picturesque, and odd, and taking. And certainly it does appear to me that as the language grows more uniform and conventional, less marked and peculiar in its dialect and expressions, so does the character of those who speak it become so.

I have a rich sample of Mid-Lothian Scotch from a young friend in the country, who describes the conversation of an old woman on the property as amusing her by such specimens of genuine Scottish raciness and humor. On one occasion, for in-

---

[1]Muddled.

stance, the young lady had told her humble friend that she was going to Ireland and would have to undergo a sea voyage.

"Weel, noo, ye dinna mean that! Ance I thocht to gang across to tither side o' the Queensferry wi' some ither folks to a fair, ye ken; but just when e'er I pat my fit in the boat the boat gie wallop, and my heart gie a loup, and I thocht I'd gang oot o' my judgment athegither, so says I, Na, na, ye gang awa by yoursels to tither side, and I'll bide here till sic times as ye come awa back."

When we hear our Scottish language at home, and spoken by our own countrymen, we are not so much struck with any remarkable effects; but it takes a far more impressive character when heard amongst those who speak a different tongue, and when encountered in other lands. I recollect the late Sir Robert Liston expressing this feeling in his own case. When our ambassador at Constantinople, some Scotchmen had been recommended to him for some purpose of private or of government business; and Sir Robert was always ready to do a kind thing for a countryman. He found them out in a barber's shop waiting for being shaved in turn. One came in rather late and seeing he had scarcely room at the end of the seat, addressed his countryman, "Neebour, wad ye sit a bit *wast*." What strong associations must have been called up, by hearing, in a distant land, such an expression in Scottish tones.

We may observe here, that marking the course any person is to take or the direction in which any object is to be met with by the points of the compass, was a prevailing practice amongst the older Scottish race. There could hardly be a more ludicrous application of the test, than was furnished by an honest Highlander in describing the direction which his medicine would *not* take. Jean Cumming, of Altyre, who, in common with her three sisters, was a true soeur de la charite, was one day taking her rounds as usual, visiting the poor sick, among whom there was a certain Donald MacQueen, who had been sometime confined to his bed. Jean Cumming, after asking him how he felt, and finding that he was "no better," of course inquired if he had taken the medicine which she had sent him.

"Troth no, me lady," he replied.

"But why not, Donald," she answered, "it was very wrong; how can you expect to get better if you do not help yourself with the remedies which Heaven provides for you."

"Vright or Vrang," said Donald, "it would na gang wast in spite o' me."

In all the north country, it is always said, "I'm ganging east or west," etc., and it happened that Donald on his sick bed was lying east and west, his feet pointing to the latter direction, hence his reply to indicate that he could not swallow the medicine.

We may fancy the amusement of the officers of a regiment in the West Indies at the innocent remark of a young lad who had just joined from Scotland. On meeting at dinner, his salutation to his colonel was, "Anither het day, Cornal," as if "het days" were in Barbadoes few and far between, as they were in his dear old stormy, cloudy Scotland.

Or take the case of a Scottish saying, which indicated at once the dialect and the economical habits of a hardy and struggling race. A young Scotchman who had been some time in London met his friend recently come up from the north to pursue his fortune in the great metropolis. On discussing matters connected with their new life in London, the more experienced visitor remarked upon the greater expenses there than in the retired Scottish town which they had left.

"Ay," said the other, sighing over the reflection, "when ye get cheenge for a saxpence here, it's soon slippit awa'."

I recollect a story of my father's which illustrates the force of dialect, although confined to the inflections of a single monosyllable. On riding home one evening, he passed a cottage or small farm-house, where there was a considerable assemblage of people, and an evident incipient merry-making for some festive occasion. On asking one of the lasses standing about what it was, she answered, "Ou, it's juist a wedding o' Jock Thamson and Janet Fraser." To the question, "Is the bride rich?" there was a plain quiet "Na." "Is she young?" a more emphatic and decided "Naa!" but to the query, "Is she bonny?" a most elaborate and prolonged shout of "Naaa!"

It has been said that the Scottish dialect is peculiarly powerful in its use of vowels, and the following dialogue between a shopman and a customer has been given as a specimen. The conversation relates to a plaid hanging at the shop door.

*Cus*. (inquiring the material), Oo? (wool?)
*Shop*. Ay, oo (yes, of wool).
*Cus*. A' oo? (all wool?)
*Shop*. Ay, a' oo (yes, all wool).
*Cus*. A' ae oo? (all same wool?)
*Shop*. Ay, a', ae oo (yes, all same wool).

## Scottish Proverbs

A blate* cat maks a proud mouse. — shy
A bonny bride's soon buskit*. — dressed
A burnt bairn fire dreads.
A dry summer ne'er made a dear peck.
Ae bird i' the hand is worth twa fleeing.
Ae swallow makes nae simmer.
A gangang fit is aye gettin.
A green Yule and a white Pay* mak a fat kirkyard. — Easter
All wald have all, all wald forgie.
An air winter maks a sair winter.
Anes payit never cravit.
A Scots mist will weet an Englishman to the skin.
A short horse is soon wispit*. — given hay?
A' Stuarts are na sib to the king.
As sure's deeth.
A wilfu' man should be unco* wise. — very
A year a nurish, seven year a da.
A Yule feast may be done at Pasch*. — Easter, Passover
Bannocks* are better nor nae kind o' bread. — cakes
Better a finger aff than aye waggin.
Better a toom* house than an ill tenant. — empty
Bluid is thicker than water.
Bourd not wi' bawtie*. — dog, rabbit
Bread's house skailed never.
Cadgers are aye cracking* o' crook-saddles. — bragging
Cadgers* maun aye be cracking o' creels. — peddlers
Crabbit was and cause had.
Dame, deem* warily (ye watna wha wytes yoursel). — judge
Do as the cow of Forfar did, tak a standing drink.
Efter lang mint never dint.
Faint heart ne'er wan fair lady.
Fill fou* and haud fou maks a stark man. — "full" (drunk)
Folly is a bonny dog.
Fools mak feasts and wise men eat 'em.
He has got his kail through the reek.
He is worth na weill that may not bide na wae.

He rides on the riggin o' the kirk.
He rives the kirk to theik* the quire. thatch
He should hae a lang shafted spoon that sups kail wi' the deil.
He's not a man to ride the water wi'.
He that crabs without cause, should mease* without mends. calm down
He that has a meikle nose thinks ilka ane speaks o't.
He that teaches himsel has a fool for his maister.
He that will to Cupar maun to Cupar.
His bark is waur nor his bite.
His head will ne'er fill his father's bonnet.
I'll mak Cathkin's covenant with you. Let abee for let abee.
Ill weeds wax weel.
It is an ill cause that the lawyer thinks shame o'.
It's a sin to lee on the deil.
It's aye guid to be ceevil, as the auld wife said when she beckit to the deevil.
It's better to sup wi' a cutty than want a spoon.
It's ill getting the breeks aff the Highlandman.
It's ill to wauken sleeping dogs.
It's nae mair pity to see a woman greit, nor to see a goose go barefit.
Jouk and let the jaw gang by.
Kame* sindle kame sair. "comb"
Kamesters are aye creeshie*. greasy
Keep your ain fish guts to your ain sea maws.
Kindness creeps where it canna gang.
Lang ere the deil dee by the dykeside.
Lang mint little dint.
Leal heart never leed.
Let ae deil ding anither.
Let alone makes mony lurden*. rascals
Let him tak a spring on his ain fiddle.
Let that flee stick to the wa'.
Like a sow playing on a trump.
Lippen* to me, but look to yoursell. trust
Lookit at the moon, and lichtit in the midden*. trash heap
Mair by luck than gude guiding.
Mair whistle than woo, as the souter said when shearing the soo.
Mak a kirk and a mill o't.
Meat and mass hinders nae man.
Monie a thing's made for the penny.
Mony ane speirs* the gate he kens fu' weel. asks about
Mony cooks ne'er made gude kail.
Mony sma's mak a muckle.
Mony tynes the half mark whinger (for the half penny whang).
Na plie is best.
O twa ills choose the least.
Raise nae mair deils than ye are able to lay.
Reavers should not be rewers.
Ruse* the fair day at e'en. praise
Seil* comes not till sorrow be o'er. happiness
Seil o' your face.
Set a knave to grip a knave.
Set a stout heart to a stey* brae. steep
She's better than she's bonny.

Sokand seill is best.
The Deil and the Dean begin wi' ae letter, when the Deil has the Dean, the kirk will be the better.
The deil's a busy bishop in his ain diocie.
The deil's aye gude to his ain.
The deil's bairns hae deil's luck.
The deil's gane ower Jock Wabster.
The deil's nae sae ill as he's caaed.
The e'ening brings a' hame.
The king's errand may come the cadger's gate yet.
The kirk is meikle, but ye may say mass in ae end o't.
The maut* is aboon the meal. malt
The men o' the Mearns manna do mair than they may.
The tod* ne'er sped better than when he gaed his ain errand. fox
The water will never warr the widdie*. noose
There's aye water where the stirkie* drouns. bullock
There's mae madines nor makines.
There's nae fool to an auld fool.
Twa wits are better than ane.
Wha will bell the cat.
When the castle of Stirling gets a hat, the carse of Corntown pays for that.
When the dirt's dry, it will rub out.
Ye are as lang in tuning your pipes as anither would play a spring.
Ye bried of the gouk*, ye have not a rhyme but ane. fool
Ye canna mak a silk purse o' a sow's lug*. ear
Ye gae far about seeking the nearest.
Ye hae tint* the tongue o' the trump. lost
Ye'll mend when ye grow better.
Ye'll no sell your hen in a rainy day.
Ye're nae chicken for a' your cheepin.
Ye wad do little for God an* the deevil was dead. if

## JOHN LOCKHART (1794–1854)

[A childhood resident of Glasgow, Lockhart spent five years at Oxford University, then studied for the bar. He became a writer for the newly-formed *Blackwood's Magazine*, earning for himself a reputation as a somewhat vitriolic satirist. In 1819, Lockhart published *Peter's Letters to His Kinsfolk*, a series of essays and anecdotes purporting to be the letters from a Welsh visitor to Edinburgh to a relative back home. Much of his material attacks the Whigs associated with the *Edinburgh Review*, but the subjects for the "letters" are overall quite varied. Given below are letters 51 and 52, which together describe Peter's "First Meeting With [Walter] Scott." In fact, Lockhart married Scott's daughter Sophia in 1820. Thereafter he wrote, among other things, a series of novels, one of which, a tragedy called *Adam Blair* (1822) is especially powerful. In 1837–1838 he published the work for which he will be longest remembered, *Memoirs of the Life of Scott*, in seven volumes. This is probably second only to Boswell's *Life of Johnson* among British biographies. Of course, like Boswell, Lockhart had a great subject and like Boswell again, a great opportunity to view that subject at close range. After his death in 1854, Lockhart was buried next to Scott at Dryburgh Abbey.]

## The Broadswords of Scotland

Now there's peace on the shore, now there's calm on the sea,
Fill a glass to the heroes whose swords kept us free,
Right descendants of Wallace, Montrose, and Dundee.
Oh, the broadswords of old Scotland!
And oh, the old Scottish broadswords!

Old Sir Ralph Abercromby, the good and the brave—
Let him flee from our board, let him sleep with the slave,
Whose libation comes slow while we honor his grave.
Oh, the broadswords of old Scotland!
And oh, the old Scottish broadswords!

Though he died not, like him, amid victory's roar,
Though disaster and gloom wove his shroud on the shore,
Not the less we remember the spirit of Moore.
Oh, the broadswords of old Scotland!
And oh, the old Scottish broadswords!

Yea, a place with the fallen the living shall claim;
We'll entwine in one wreath every glorious name,
The Gordon, the Ramsay, the Hope, and the Graham,
Oh, the broadswords of old Scotland!
And oh, the old Scottish broadswords!

Count the rocks of the Spey, count the groves of the north,
Count the stars in the clear, cloudless heaven of the north;
Then go blazon their numbers, their names, and their worth,
Oh, the broadswords of old Scotland!
And oh, the old Scottish broadswords!

The highest in splendor, the humblest in place,
Stand united in glory, as kindred in race,
For the private is brother in blood to His Grace.
Oh, the broadswords of old Scotland!
And oh, the old Scottish broadswords!

Then sacred to each and to all let it be,
Fill a glass to the heroes whose swords kept us free,
Right descendants of Wallace, Montrose, and Dundee.
Oh, the broadswords of old Scotland!
And oh, the old Scottish broadswords!

## When Youthful Faith Hath Fled

When youthful faith hath fled,
Of loving take thy leave.
Be constant to the dead—
The dead cannot deceive.

Sweet modest flowers of spring,
How fleet your balmy day.

And man's brief year can bring
No secondary May,

No earthly burst again
Of gladness out of gloom,
Fond hope and vision vain,
Ungrateful to the tomb.

But tis an old belief
That on some solemn shore,
Beyond the sphere of grief,
Dear friends shall meet once more.

Beyond the sphere of time,
And Sin and Fate's control,
Serene in endless prime
Of body and of soul.

That creed I fain would keep,
That hope I'll not forgo,
Eternal be the sleep
Unless to waken so.

## Captain Paton's Lament

Touch once more a sober measure,
And let punch and tears be shed
For a prince of good old fellows
That, alack-a-day, is dead,—
For a prince of worthy fellows,
And a pretty man also,
That has left the Saltmarket
In sorrow, grief, and woe.
Oh, we ne'er shall see the like of Captain Paton no mo'e.

His waistcoat, coat, and breeches
Were all cut off the same web,
Of a beautiful snuff-color,
Or a modest genty drab.
The blue stripe in his stocking
Round his neat slim leg did go,
And his ruffles of the cambric fine
They were whiter than the snow.
Oh, we ne'er shall see the like of Captain Paton no mo'e.

His hair was curled in order,
At the rising of the sun,
In comely rows and buckles smart
That about his ears did run.
And, before, there was a toupee
That some inches up did grow,
And behind there was a long queue

That did o'er his shoulders flow.
Oh, we ne'er shall see the like of Captain Paton no mo'e.

And whenever we foregathered
He took off his wee three-cockit,
And he proffered you his snuff-box,
Which he drew from his side-pocket;
And on Burdett or Bonaparte
He would make a remark or so;
And then along the plainstanes
Like a provost he would go.
Oh, we ne'er shall see the like of Captain Paton no mo'e.

In dirty days he picked well
His footsteps with his rattan.
Oh, you ne'er could see the least speck
On the shoes of Captain Paton.
And on entering the coffee room,
About two, all men did know
They would see him with his *Courier*
In the middle of the row.
Oh, we ne'er shall see the like of Captain Paton no mo'e.

Now and then, upon a Sunday,
He invited me to dine
On a herring and a mutton-chop,
Which his maid dressed very fine;
There was also a little Malmsey
And a bottle of Bordeaux,
Which between me and the Captain
Passed nimbly to and fro.
Oh, I ne'er shall take pot-luck with Captain Paton no mo'e.

Or if a bowl was mentioned,
The Captain he would ring
And bid Nelly rin to the West Port
And a stoup of water bring.
Then would he mix the genuine stuff
As they made it long ago,
With limes that on his property
In Trinidad did grow.
Oh, we ne'er shall taste the like of Captain Paton's punch no mo'e.

And then all the time he would discourse
So sensible and courteous,—
Perhaps talking of last sermon
He had heard from Dr. Porteous,—
Of some little bit of scandal
About Mrs. So-and-so,
Which he scarce could credit, having heard
The con but not the pro.
Oh, we ne'er shall see the like of Captain Paton no mo'e.

Or when the candles were brought forth
And the night was fairly setting in,
He would tell some fine old stories
About Minden-field or Dettingen:
How he fought with a French major
And dispatched him at a blow,
While his blood ran out like water
On the soft grass below.
Oh, we ne'er shall hear the like from Captain Paton no mo'e.

But at last the Captain sickened,
And grew worse from day to day;
And all missed him in the coffee room,
From which now he stayed away.
On Sabbaths, too, the Wynd Kirk
Made a melancholy show,
All for wanting of the presence
Of our venerable beau.
Oh, we ne'er shall see the like of Captain Paton no mo'e.

And, in spite of all that Cleghorn
And Corkindale could do,
It was plain from twenty symptoms,
That death was in his view;
So the Captain made his test'ment
And submitted to his foe,
And we laid him by the Ram's-horn-Kirk.
Tis the way we all must go.
Oh, we ne'er shall see the like of Captain Paton no mo'e.

Join all in chorus, jolly boys,
And let punch and tears be shed
For this prince of good old fellows,
That, alack-a-day, is dead,—
For this prince of worthy fellows,
And a pretty man also,
That has left the Saltmarket
In sorrow, grief, and woe.
Oh, we ne'er shall see the like of Captain Paton no mo'e.

## Lines Written on Tweedside

September the 18th, 1831

A day I've seen whose brightness pierced the cloud
Of pain and sorrow, both for great and small;
A night of flowing cups, and pibrochs[1] loud,
Once more within the minstrel's blazoned hall.

---

[1] Stately bagpipe music.

"Upon this frozen hearth pile crackling trees;
Let every silent clarshach* find its strings; harp
Unfurl once more the banner to the breeze.
No warmer welcome for the blood of kings."

From ear to ear, from eye to glistening eye,
Leap the glad tidings, and the glance of glee.
Perish the hopeless breast that beats not high
At thought beneath his roof that guest to see.

What princely stranger comes?—what exiled lord
From the far East to Scotia's strand returns,
To stir with joy the towers of Abbotsford,
And "wake the minstrel's soul?"—The boy of Burns.

O, sacred genius! blessing on the chains,
Wherein thy sympathy can minds entwine.
Beyond the conscious glow of kindred veins,
A power, a spirit, and a charm are thine.

Thine offspring share them. Thou hast trod the land—
It breathes of thee—and men, through rising tears,
Behold the image of thy manhood stand,
More noble than a galaxy of peers.

And he—his father's bones had quaked, I ween,
But that with holier pride his heart-strings bound,
Than if his host had king or kaiser been,
And star and cross on every bosom round.

High strains were poured of many a Border spear,
While gentle fingers swept a throbbing shell;
A manly voice, in manly notes and clear,
Of lowly love's deep bliss responded well.

The children sang the ballads of their sires:—
Serene among them sat the hoary knight;
And, if dead bards have ears for earthly lyres,
The Peasant's shade was near, and drank delight.

As through the woods we took our homeward way,
Fair shone the moon last night on Eildon Hill;
Soft rippled Tweed's broad wave beneath her ray,
And in sweet murmurs gushed the Huntly rill.

Heaven send the guardian genius of the vale
Health yet, and strength, and length of honored days,
To cheer the world with many a gallant tale,
And hear his children's children chant his lays.

Through seas unruffled may the vessel glide,
That bears her poet far from Melrose' glen.

And may his pulse be steadfast as our pride,
When happy breezes waft him back again.

## "First Meeting with Scott"
### *Peter's Letters to His Kinsfolk*: Letter LI

To the Same Oman's,

After passing the town of Dalkeith, and all along the skirts of the same lovely tract of scenery on the Esk, which I have already described to you, the road to Abbotsford leads for several miles across a bare and sterile district, where the progress of cultivation has not yet been able to change much of the general aspect of the country. There are, however, here and there some beautiful little valleys cutting the desert, in one of which, by the side of a small mountain stream, whose banks are clothed everywhere with a most picturesque abundance of blooming furze, the old Castle of Borthwick is seen projecting its venerable keep, unbroken apparently, and almost undecayed, over the few oaks which still seem to linger like so many frail faithful vassals around the relics of its grandeur. When I passed by this fine ruin, the air was calm and the sky unclouded, and the shadow of the square massy pile lay in all its clear breadth upon the blue stream below; but Turner has caught or created perhaps still more poetical accompaniments, and you may see it to at least as much advantage as I did, in his magnificent delineation.

Shortly after this the view becomes more contracted, and the road winds for some miles between the hills, while, upon the right, you have close by your side a modest little rivulet, increasing, however, every moment in breadth and boldness. This is the infant *Gala Water* so celebrated in the pastoral poetry of Scotland, flowing on to mingle its tributary stream with the more celebrated Tweed. As you approach, with it, the great valley of that delightful river, the hills become more and more beautiful in their outlines, and where they dip into the narrow plain, their lower slopes are diversified with fine groups of natural wood—hazel, ash, and birch—with here and there some drooping, moldering oaks and pines, the scanty relics of that once mighty *Forest,* from which the whole district still takes its name. At last, the Gala makes a sudden turn, and instead of

The grace of forest-charms decayed,
And pastoral melancholy,

you have a rich and fertile vale, covered all over with nodding groves and luxuriant verdure, through which the Gala winds proudly towards the near end of its career. I crossed it at the thriving village of Galashiels, and pursued my journey for a mile or two on its right bank, being told, that I should thus save a considerable distance, for the usual road goes round about for the sake of a bridge, which, in the placid seasons of the Tweed, is quite unnecessary. I saw this far-famed river for the first time, with the turrets of its great poet's mansion immediately beyond it, and the bright foliage of his young larches reflected half-way over in its mirror.

You cannot imagine a more lovely river; it is as clear as the tiniest brook you ever saw, for I could count the white pebbles as I passed and yet it is broad and deep, and above all extremely rapid; and although it rises sometimes to a much greater height, it seems to fill the whole of its bed magnificently. The ford of which I made use, is the same from which the house takes its name, and a few minutes brought me to its gates.

Ere I came to it, however, I had time to see that it is a strange fantastic structure, built in total defiance of all those rules of uniformity to which the modern architects of Scotland are so much attached. It consists of one large tower, with several smaller ones clustering around it, all built of fine gray granite, their roofs diversified abundantly with all manner of antique chimney-tops, battlements, and turrets, the windows placed here and there with appropriate irregularity, both of dimension and position, and the spaces between or above them not unfrequently occupied with saintly niches, and chivalrous coats-of-arms. Altogether it bears a close resemblance to some of our true old English manor-houses, in which the forms of religious and warlike architecture are blended together with no ungraceful mixture.

But I have made a sketch with my pencil, which will give you a better notion of its exterior, than any written description. The interior is perfectly in character, but I dare say, you would turn the leaf were I to detain you any longer from the lord of the place, and I confess you are right in thinking him "metal more attractive."

I did not see Mr. Scott, however, immediately on my arrival; he had gone out with all his family, to shew the Abbey of Melrose to the Count von Bulow, and some other visitors. I was somewhat dusty in my apparel (for the shandrydan had moved in clouds half the journey), so I took the opportunity of making my toilet, and had not quite completed it, when I heard the trampling of their horses' feet beneath the window. But in a short time, having finished my adonization, I descended, and was conducted to Mr. Scott, whom I found alone in his library. Nothing could be kinder than his reception of me, and so simple and unassuming are his manners, that I was quite surprised, after a few minutes had elapsed, to find myself already almost at home in the company of one, whose presence I had approached with feelings so very different from those with which a man of my age and experience is accustomed to meet ordinary strangers.

There is no kind of rank, which I should suppose it so difficult to bear with perfect ease, as the universally-honored nobility of universally-honored genius; but all this sits as lightly and naturally upon this great man, as ever a plumed casque did upon the head of one of his own graceful knights. Perhaps, after all, the very highest dignity may be more easily worn than some of the inferior degrees, as it has often been said of princes. My Lord Duke is commonly a much more homely person than the Squire of the Parish, or your little spick-and-span new Irish Baron. And, good heavens! what a difference between the pompous Apollo of some Cockney coterie, and the plain, manly, thorough-bred courtesy of a Walter Scott!

There was a large party at dinner, for the house was full of company, and much very amusing and delightful conversation passed on every side around me; but you will not wonder that I found comparatively little leisure either to hear or see much of anything besides my host. And as to his person, in the first place, that was almost perfectly new to me, although I must have seen, I should suppose, some dozens of engravings of him before I ever came to Scotland. Never was any physiognomy treated with more scanty justice by the portrait-painters; and yet, after all, I must confess that the physiognomy is of a kind that scarcely falls within the limits of their art.

I have never seen any face which disappointed me less than this, after I had become acquainted with it fully; yet, at the first glance, I certainly saw less than, but for the vile prints, I should have looked for, and I can easily believe that the feelings of the uninitiated—the uncranioscopical observer—might be little different from those of pure disappointment. It is not that there is deficiency of expression in any part of Mr. Scott's face, but the expression which is most prominent, is not of the kind which one who had known his works, and had heard nothing about his appearance, would be inclined to expect. The common language of his features expresses all manner of discernment and acuteness of intellect, and the utmost nerve and decision of character. He smiles frequently, and I never saw any smile which tells so eloquently the union of broad good humor, with the keenest perception of the ridiculous, but all this would scarcely be enough to satisfy one in the physiognomy of Walter Scott. And, indeed, in order to see much finer things in it, it is only necessary to have a little patience,

And tarry for the hour,
When the Wizard shews his power;
The hour of might and mastery,
Which none may shew but only he.

In the course of conversation, he happened to quote a few lines from one of the old Border Ballads, and, looking round, I was quite astonished with the change which seemed to have passed over every feature in his countenance. His eyes seemed no longer to glance quick and gray from beneath his impending brows, but were fixed in their expanded eye-lids with a sober, solemn luster. His mouth (the muscles about which are at all times wonderfully expressive,) instead of its usual language of mirth or benevolence, or shrewdness, was filled with a sad and pensive earnestness. The whole face was tinged with a glow that shewed its lines in new energy and transparence, and the thin hair parting backward displayed in tenfold majesty his Shakespearean pile of forehead. It was now that I recognized the true stamp of nature on the poet of Marmion, and looking back for a moment to the former expression of the same countenance, I could not choose but wonder at the facility with which one set of features could be made to speak things so different. But, after all, what are features unless they form the index to the mind? and how should the eyes of him who commands a thousand kinds of emotion, be themselves confined to beam only with the eloquence of a few?

It was about the Lammas tide,
When husbandmen do win their hay;
The doughty Douglas he would ride
Into England to drive a prey.

I shall certainly never forget the fine heroic enthusiasm of look, with which he spoke these lines, nor the grand melancholy roll of voice, which shewed with what a world of thoughts and feelings every fragment of the old legend was associated within his breast. It seemed as if one single cadence of the ancestral strain had been charm enough to transport his whole spirit back into the very pride and presence of the moment, when the White Lion of the Percies was stained and trampled under foot beside the bloody rushes of Otterbourne. The more than martial fervors of his kindled eye, were almost enough to give to the same lines the same magic in my ears; and I could half fancy that the portion of Scottish blood which is mingled in my veins, had begun to assert, by a more ardent throb, its right to partake in the triumphs of the same primitive allegiance.

While I was thus occupied, one of the most warlike of the Lochaber pibrochs began to be played in the neighborhood of the room in which we were, and, looking towards the window, I saw a noble Highland piper parading to and fro upon the lawn, in front of the house, the plumes of his bonnet, the folds of his plaid, and the streamers of his bag-pipe all floating majestically about him in the light evening breeze.

You have seen this magnificent costume, so I need not trouble you either with its description or its eulogy; but I am quite sure you never saw it where its appearance harmonized so delightfully with all the accompaniments of the scene. It is true, that it was in the Lowlands, and that there are other streams upon which the shadow of the tartans might fall with more of the propriety of mere antiquarianism, than on the Tweed. But the Scotch are right in not now-a-days splitting too much the symbols of their nationality; as they have ceased to be an independent people, they do wisely in striving to be as much as possible an united people. But here, above all, whatever was truly Scottish could not fail to be truly appropriate in the presence of the great genius to whom whatever is Scottish in thought, in feeling, or in recollection, owes so large a share of its prolonged, or reanimated, or ennobled existence. The poet of Roderick Dhu, and under favor the poet of Fergus Mac-Ivor, does well assuredly to have a piper among the retainers of his hospitable mansion. You remember, too, how he has himself described the feast of the Rhymer:

Nor lacked they, as they sat at dine,
*The Music,* nor the tale,
Nor goblets of the blood-red wine,
Nor mantling quaighs of ale.

After the Highlander had played some dozen of his tunes, he was summoned, according to the ancient custom, to receive the thanks of the company. He entered *more militari* without taking off his bonnet, and received a huge tass of aquavita from the hand of his master, after which he withdrew again, the most perfect solemnity all the while being displayed in his weather-beaten, but handsome and warlike Celtic lineaments. The inspiration of the generous fluid prompted one strain merrier than the rest, behind the door of the Hall, and then the piper was silent, his lungs, I dare say, consenting much more than his will, for he has all the appearance of being a fine enthusiast in the delights and dignity of his calling. So much for Roderick of Skye, for such I think is his style.

His performance seemed to diffuse, or rather to heighten, a charming flow of geniality over the whole of the party, but nowhere could I trace its influence so powerfully and so delightfully as in the Master of the Feast. The music of the hills had given a new tone to his fine spirits, and the easy playfulness with which he gave vent to their buoyancy, was the most delicious of contagions. Himself temperate in the extreme (some late ill health has made it necessary he should be so), he sent round his claret more speedily than even I could have wished (you see I am determined to blunt the edge of all your sarcasms), and I assure you we were all too well employed to think of measuring our bumpers.

Do not suppose, however, that there is anything like display or formal leading in Mr. Scott's conversation. On the contrary, every body seemed to speak the more that he was there to hear, and his presence seemed to be enough to make every body speak delightfully, as if it had been that some princely musician had tuned all the strings, and even under the sway of more vulgar fingers, they could not choose but discourse excellent music. His conversation, besides, is for the most part of such a kind, that all can take a lively part in it, although, indeed, none that I ever met with can equal himself. It does not appear as if he ever could be at a loss for a single moment for some new supply of that which constitutes its chief peculiarity, and its chief charm; the most keen perception, the most tenacious memory, and the most brilliant imagination, having been at work throughout the whole of his busy life, in filling his mind with a store of individual traits and anecdotes, serious and comic, individual and national, such as it is probable no man ever before possessed, and such, still more certainly, as no man of great original power ever before possessed in subservience to the purposes of inventive genius.

A youth spent in wandering among the hills and valleys of his country, during which he became intensely familiar with all the lore of those gray-haired shepherds, among whom the traditions of warlike as well as of peaceful times find their securest dwelling-place, or in more equal converse with the relics of that old school of Scottish cavaliers, whose faith had nerved the arms of so many of his own race and kindred, such a boyhood and such a youth laid the foundation, and established the earliest and most lasting sympathies of a mind, which was destined, in after years, to erect upon this foundation, and improve upon these sympathies, in a way of which his young and thirsting spirit could have then contemplated but little.

Through his manhood of active and honored, and now for many years of glorious exertion, he has always lived in the world, and among the men of the world, partaking in all the pleasures and duties of society as fully as any of those who had nothing but such pleasures and such duties to attend to. Uniting, as never before they were united, the habits of an indefatigable student with those of an indefatigable observer, and doing all this with the easy and careless grace of one who is doing so, not to task, but to gratify his inclinations and his nature, is it to be wondered that the riches of his various acquisitions should furnish a never-failing source of admiration even to those who have known him the longest, and who know him the best? As for me, enthusiastic as I had always been in my worship of his genius, and well as his works had prepared me to find his conversation rich to overflowing in all the elements of instruction as well as of amusement, I confess the reality entirely surpassed all my anticipations, and I never despised the maxim *Nil admirari* so heartily as now.

I can now say what I believe very few of my friends can do, that I have conversed with almost all the illustrious poets our contemporaries; indeed, Lord Byron is the only exception that occurs to me. Surely I need not tell you that I met each and all of them with every disposition to be gratified; and now I cannot but derive great pleasure from being able to look back upon what I have so been privileged to witness, and comparing in my own mind their different styles of conversation. The most original and interesting, as might be supposed, in this point of view, are the same whose originality has been most conspicuous in other things—this great poet of Scotland, and the great poet of the Lakes.

It is, indeed, a very striking thing, how much the conversation of each of these men harmonizes with the peculiar vein of his mind, as displayed in more elaborate shapes, how one and entire the impression is, which the totality of each of them is calculated to leave upon the mind of an honoring, but not a bigoted observer. In listening to Wordsworth, it is impossible to forget for a single moment that the author of "The Excursion" is before you. Poetry has been with him the pure sole business of life—he thinks of nothing else, and he speaks of nothing else—and where is the man who hears him, that would for a moment wish it to be otherwise? The deep sonorous voice in which he pours forth his soul upon the high secrets of his divine art, and those tender glimpses which he opens every now and then into the bosom of that lowly life, whose mysteries have been his perpetual inspirations, the sincere earnestness with which he details and expatiates, the innocent confidence which he feels in the heart that is submitted to his working, and the unquestioning command with which he seeks to fasten to him every soul that is capable of understanding his words, all these things are as they should be, in one that has lived the life of a hermit, musing and meditating, and composing in the seclusion of a lonely cottage, loving and worshipping the nature of man, but partaking little in the pursuits, and knowing little of the habits, of the men of the world. There is a noble simplicity in the warmth with which he discourses to all that approach him, on the subject of which he himself knows most, and on which he feels most, and of which he is wise enough to know that every one must be most anxious to hear him speak. His poetry is the poetry of external nature and profound feeling, and such is the hold which these high themes have taken of his intellect, that he seldom dreams of descending to the tone in which the ordinary conversation of men is pitched. Hour after hour his eloquence flows on, by his own simple fireside, or along the breezy slopes of his own mountains, in the same lofty strain as in his loftiest poems:

Of man and Nature, and of human life,
His haunt and the main region of his song.

His enthusiasm is that of a secluded artist; but who is he that would not rejoice in being permitted to peep into the sanctity of such a seclusion, or that, being there, would wish for a moment to see the enthusiasm that has sanctified it, suspended or interrupted in its work? The large, dim, pensive eye, that dwells almost for ever upon the ground, and the smile of placid abstraction, that clothes his long, tremulous, melancholy lips, complete a picture of solemn wrapped-up contemplative genius, to which, amid the dusty concussions of active men and common life, my mind reverts sometimes for repose, as to a fine calm stretch of verdure in the bosom of some dark and hoary forest of venerable trees, where no voice is heard but that of the sweeping wind, and far-off waters, what the Ettrick Shepherd finely calls

> Great Nature's hum,
> Voice of the desert, never dumb.

Scott, again, is the very poet of active life, and that life, in all its varieties, lies for ever stretched out before him, bright and expanded, as in the glass of a magician. Whatever subject he mentioned, he at once steals a beam from his mirror, and scatters such a flood of illustration upon it, that you feel as if it had always been mantled in palpable night before. Every remark gains, as it passes from his lips, the precision of a visible fact, and every incident flashes upon your imagination, as if your bodily eye, by some new gift of nature, had acquired the power of seeing the past as vividly as the present. To talk of exhausting his light of *gramourie* to one that witnessed its play of radiance, would sound as absurd as to talk of drying up the Nile. It streams alike copiously, alike fervently upon all things, like the light of heaven, which "shineth upon the evil and upon the good." The eye, and the voice, and the words, and the gestures, seem all alike to be the ready unconscious interpreters of some imperial spirit, that moves irresistibly their mingled energies from within. There is no effort, no semblance of effort, but everything comes out as is commanded, swift, clear, and radiant through the impartial medium.

The heroes of the old times spring from their graves in panoply, and "drink the red wine through the helmet barried" before us; or

> Shred their foemen's limbs away,
> As lops the woodsman's knife the spray.

But they are honored, not privileged; the humblest retainers quit the dust as full of life as they do; nay, their dogs and horses are partakers in the resurrection, like those of the Teutonic warriors in the Valhalla of Odin. It is no matter what period of his country's story passes in review: Bruce, Douglas, their kingly foe, in whose eye was set

> Some spark of the Plantagenet,

James, Mary, Angus, Montrose, Argyle, Dundee—these are all alike, not names, but realities, living, moving, breathing, feeling, speaking, looking realities, when he speaks of them. The grave loses half its potency when he calls. His own imagination is one majestic sepulcher, where the wizard lamp burns in never-dying splendor, and the charmed blood glows for ever in the cheeks of the embalmed, and every long-sheathed sword is ready to leap from its scabbard, like the Tizona of the Cid in the vault of Cardena. Of all this more anon. P.M.

## LETTER LII

### To the Same

Next morning I got up pretty early, and walked for at least two hours before breakfast through the extensive young woods with which Mr. Scott has already clothed the banks of the Tweed, in every direction about his mansion. Nothing can be more soft and beautiful than the whole of the surrounding scenery; there is scarcely a single house to be seen, and excepting on the rich low lands, close by the river, the country seems to be almost entirely in the hands of the shepherds. The green hills, however, all around the horizon, begin to be skirted with sweeping plantations of larch, pine, and oak; and the shelter which these will soon afford, must no doubt ere long give a more agricultural aspect to the face of Tweeddale. To say the truth. I do not think with much pleasure of the prospect of any such changes. I love to see tracts of countries, as well as races of men, preserving as much as possible of their old characteristics. There hovers at present over the most of this district a certain delicious atmosphere of pastoral loneliness, and I think there would be something like sacrilege in disturbing it, even by things that elsewhere would confer interest as well as ornament.

After a breakfast *a la fourchette,* served up in the true style of old Scottish luxury, which a certain celebrated novelist seems to take a particular pleasure in describing, a breakfast, namely, in which tea, coffee, chocolate, toast, and sweetmeats, officiated as little better than ornamental out-works to more solid and imposing fortifications of mutton-ham, hung-beef, and salmon killed over-night in the same spear and torch-light method, of which Dandie Dinmont was so accomplished a master; after doing all manner of justice to this interesting meal, I spent an hour with Mr. Scott in his library, or rather in his closet; for, though its walls are quite covered with books, I believe the far more valuable part of his library is in Edinburgh. One end seemed to be devoted to books of Scots Law —which are necessary to him no doubt even here; for he is Chief Magistrate of the county —and, indeed, is known among the country people, who passionately love him, by no other name than that of "the Sherra."

The other books, so far as I could see, were just what I should have expected to find Mr. Scott draw round him in his retirement —not the new and flashy productions of the day, but good plain copies of the old English Classics above all, the historians and poets, together with a copious intermixture of black-letter romances, and Spanish ballads of chivalry, and several shelves entirely filled with the best collection I have ever seen of German *Volksmarchen* and *Volkslieder.* Among these, no doubt, his mind has found, at once, useful employment, and delightful relaxation.

We then mounted our horses, a numerous cavalcade, and rode to one of the three summits of the Eildon Hill, which rises out of the plain a little way behind Abbotsford, and forms, in almost every point of view, a glorious back-ground to its towers and rising woods. We passed before leaving Mr. Scott's territories, a deep dingle, quite covered with all manner of wild bushes, through which a little streamlet far below could, for the most part, be rather heard than seen. Mr. Scott paused at the rustic bridge which led us over this ravine, and told me, that I was treading on classical ground —that here was the *Huntly Burn,* by whose side Thomas the Rhymer of old saw the Queen of Faery riding in her glory, and called to this hour by the shepherds, from that very circumstance, the *Bogle* or *Goblin Burn.* He then went on to repeat the fine words of the original *Prophesia Thomae de Ercildoune.*

In a land as I was lent,
In the gryking of the day,
Ay alone as I went
In Huntly bankys me for to play:
I saw the throstyl and the jay,
The mavis moved of her sange,
The wodwale sang notes gay,
That all the wood about range;
In that longing as I lay
Underneath a derne tree,
I was aware of a ladye fair
Cam riding over a fair lee—
Her palfray was dappil graye,
Such one saw never none,
As the sun in somer's day,
All about that ladye shone, &c. &c.

I could not but express my delight to find, that the scene of so many romantic recollections was included within the domains of the great inheritor of the glories of "True Thomas," and promised to myself to pay a more leisurely visit to Huntly Bank and the Goblin Burn. From this we passed right up the hill, the ponies here being as perfectly independent as our own of turnpike ways, and as scornful of perpendicular ascents. I was not a little surprised, however, with Mr. Scott's horsemanship, for, in spite of the lameness in one of his legs, he manages his steed with the most complete mastery, and seems to be as much at home in the saddle, as any of his own rough-riding Deloraines or Lochinvars could have been.

He is, indeed, a very strong man in all the rest of his frame, the breadth and massiness of his iron muscles being evidently cast in the same mold with those of the old "Wats of Harden," and "Bauld Rutherfuirds that were fow stout." We took several ditches that would have astonished nine-tenths of the Epping sportsmen, and he was always foremost at the leap. All around the top of the hill, there may be seen the remains of Roman walls and ditches, which seem to have been brought very low down in one direction, in order to inclose a fine well, and, indeed, the very peculiar outline of the Eildon leaves no doubt, that it was the *Trimontium* of antiquity.

The transitory visits of a few Roman legions, however, did not seem to me to confer much additional interest on this noble mountain, from whose summits the scenes of so many Scottish and English battles may be seen. The name of every hill and every valley all around is poetical, and I felt, as I heard them pointed out one by one, as if so many old friends had been introduced to my acquaintance after a long absence, in which I had thought of them all a thousand times. To the left, at the foot of the hill, lies the picturesque village of Melrose, with the AbbotsLaw, or Court-Mound, swelling close behind, and between it and the Tweed, the long gray arches of the magnificent Abbey itself. The river winds away for some miles among a rich succession of woods and lawns, at the end of which the fraternal towers of Dryburgh lift themselves from among their groves of elm.

Dryborough, where with chiming Tweed
The lintwhites sing in chorus.

The back-ground on this side consists, among other fine hills, of the Colding Knowes, so celebrated in Border song; on the other side, there is Ruberslaw, and the Carter, and Dunyon; and farther off, the Cheviots, and all between the beautiful windings of the Teviot. Right before my eye, Mr. Scott pointed out a small round tower, perched upon some irregular crags, at the distance of some few miles— Smaylholm Tower, the scene of the Eve of St. John, and, what is still better, the scene of the early youth of the poet himself.

It was here, he told me, that in years of feebleness, which afforded little hope of the vigorous manhood which has followed them, he was entrusted to the care of some ancient female relations, who, in watching by his side, were never weary of chanting, to the sad music of the Border, the scattered relics of that Minstrelsy of love and war, which he himself has since gathered and preserved with so pious veneration. The situation of the Tower must be charming. I remember of no poet whose infancy was passed in so poetical a scene. But he has touched all this most gracefully himself:

He passed the court-gate, and he oped the tower-grate,
And he mounted the narrow stair,
To the bartizan seat, where with maids that on her wait,
He found his Lady fair.
That Lady sat in mournful mood,
Looked over hill and vale,
O'er Tweed's fair flood, and Mertoun's wood,
And all down Teviotdale.

Turning again to the left, Mr. Scott pointed out to me an opening in the hills, where the Leader comes down to mingle with the Tweed by whose side the remains of the Rhymer's old castle are yet, I believe, to be seen; although, in conformity with one of the Rhymer's own prophecies, the hall is deserted, and the land has passed to other blood. The whole scene has been embraced by Mr. Scott himself, in the opening of one of his finest ballads:

When seven years more were come and gone,
Was war through Scotland spread;
And Ruberslaw showed high Dunyon
His beacon blazing red.
Then all by bonny Colding Know,
Pitched pallions took their room;
And crested helms and spears a-rowe,
Glanced gaily through the broom.
The Leader, rolling to the Tweed,
Resounds the enzenzie;
They roused the deer from Caddenhead,
To distant Torwoodlee.
The feast was spread in Ercildoune,
In Learmont's high and ancient hall;
And there were knights of high renown,
And ladies laced in pall, &c. &c.

But if I were to quote all the poetry connected with the scenes among which I now stood, in truth, my letter might easily become a volume.

After we had fairly descended the hill, we found that much more time had passed than we had thought of, and with me, indeed, I know not that time ever passed more delightfully —so we made haste and returned at a high trot, the chiding echoes of the dinner-bell coming to us long ere we reached Abbotsford—

Swinging slow with sullen roar.

The evening passed as charmingly as the preceding. The younger part of the company danced reels to the music of the bag-pipe, and I believe I would have been tempted to join them, but for some little twitches I had in my left foot. Indeed, I still fear the good cheer of the North is about to be paid for in the usual way; but Heaven send the reckoning may not be a long one. At all events, I am glad the fit did not overtake me in the country, for I should have been sorry to give my company to anybody but Mr. Oman during the visitation. —P.M.

## THOMAS CARLYLE (1795–1881)

[Perhaps the most influential essayist of the Victorian era, Thomas Carlyle was born of peasant stock in Ecclefechan, a village in the western Lowlands. He graduated from Edinburgh University, studied for the ministry for a time, worked as a schoolmaster, read law in Edinburgh, then finally turned to literature, publishing essays about the arts, history and philosophy. Perhaps his most notable work, dating from early in his career, is *Sartor Resartus* ("The Tailor Retailored," 1833–1834), a novel *cum* spiritual autobiography. Purportedly it is the biography of a Professor Diogenes Teufelsdrockh, a decidedly eccentric specialist in Things-in-General at the University of Utopia. Carlyle's book-length essay is an expression of transcendentalism, a belief which here asserts that man's body is merely the clothing for the divine spirit, just as society's institutions are merely the dress of a universal "Social Idea" which transcends simple utility.

Carlyle's prose style is remarkable, and rather difficult. Forceful, almost explosive in its energy, fervid, dense, sententious, it provides as much of the value from his essays as does the content.

The well-known selection here given from *Sartor Resartus* features a spiritual crisis, in which Professor Teufelsdrockh, mired in a period of moral fermentation, passes from denial to spiritual insight and affirmation.

## Today

So here hath been dawning
Another blue day.
Think, wilt thou let it
Slip useless away?

Out of eternity
This new day is born;
Into eternity,
At night, will return.

Behold it aforetime
No eye ever did:
So soon it forever
From all eyes is hid.

Here hath been dawning
Another blue day.
Think, wilt thou let it
Slip useless away.

## Adieu

Let time and chance combine, combine,
Let time and chance combine;
The fairest love from heaven above,
That love of yours was mine,
My dear,
That love of yours was mine.

The past is fled and gone, and gone,
The past is fled and gone;
If naught but pain to me remain,
I'll fare in memory on,
My dear,
I'll fare in memory on.

The saddest tears must fall, must fall,
The saddest tears must fall;
In weal or woe, in this world below,
I love you ever and all,
My dear,
I love you ever and all.

A long road full of pain, of pain,
A long road full of pain;
One soul, one heart, sworn ne'er to part,—
We ne'er can meet again,

My dear,
We ne'er can meet again.

Hard fate will not allow, allow,
Hard fate will not allow;
We blessed were as the angels are,—
Adieu forever now,
My dear,
Adieu forever now.

## Cui Bono?

What is hope? A smiling rainbow
Children follow through the wet.
Tis not here, still yonder, yonder;
Never urchin found it yet.

What is life? A thawing iceboard
On a sea with sunny shore.
Gay we sail; it melts beneath us;
We are sunk, and seen no more.

What is man? A foolish baby,
Vainly strives, and fights, and frets;
Demanding all, deserving nothing;—
One small grave is what he gets.

## "Towards the Everlasting Yea"
## *Sartor Resartus*, Book II, Chapters 7-9

### THE EVERLASTING NO

Under the strange nebulous envelopment, wherein our professor has now shrouded himself, no doubt but his spiritual nature is nevertheless progressive, and growing; for how can the "son of time," in any case, stand still? We behold him, through those dim years, in a state of crisis, of transition; his mad pilgrimings, and general solution into aimless discontinuity, what is all this but a mad fermentation; wherefrom the fiercer it is, the clearer product will one day evolve itself?

Such transitions are ever full of pain; thus the eagle when he molts is sickly; and, to attain his new beak, must harshly dash off the old one upon rocks. What stoicism soever our wanderer, in his individual acts and motions, may affect, it is clear that there is a hot fever of anarchy and misery raving within; coruscations of which flash out; as, indeed, how could there be other? Have we not seen him disappointed, bemocked of destiny, through long years? All that the young heart might desire and pray for has been denied; nay as in the last worst instance, offered and then snatched away. Ever an "excellent passivity"; but of useful, reasonable activity, essential to the former as food to hunger, nothing granted; till at length, in this wild pilgrimage, he must forcibly seize for himself an activity, though useless, unreasonable.

Alas, his cup of bitterness. which had been filling drop by drop, ever since the first "ruddy morning" in the Hinterschlag Gymnasium was at the very lip; and then with that poison-drop, of the Towgood-and-Blumine business,[1] it runs over, and even hisses over in a deluge of foam.

He himself says once, with more justice than originality: "Man is, properly speaking, based upon hope, he has no other possession but hope; this world of his is emphatically the place of hope." What, then, was our professor's possession? We see him, for the present, quite shut out from hope; looking not into the golden orient, but vaguely all round into a dim copper firmament, pregnant with earthquake and tornado.

Alas, shut out from hope, in a deeper sense than we yet dream of! For, as he wanders wearisomely through this world, he has now lost all tidings of another and higher. Full of religion, or at least of religiosity, as our friend has since exhibited himself, he hides not that, in those days, he was wholly irreligious. "Doubt had darkened into unbelief," says he; "shade after shade goes grimly over your soul, till you have the fixed, starless, Tartarean black."

To such readers as have reflected, what can be called reflecting, on man's life, and happily discovered, in contradiction to much profit-and-loss philosophy, speculative and practical, that soul is not synonymous with stomach; who understand, therefore, in our friend's words, "that, for man's well-being, faith is properly the one thing needful; how, with it, martyrs, otherwise weak, can cheerfully endure the shame and the cross—and without it, worldlings puke up their sick existence, by suicide, in the midst of luxury"—to such, it will be clear that, for a pure moral nature, the loss of his religious belief was the loss of everything.

Unhappy young man! All wounds, the crush of long-continued destitution, the stab of false friendship, and of false love, all wounds in thy so genial heart, would have healed again had not its life-warmth been withdrawn. Well might he exclaim, in his wild way: "Is there no God, then; but at best an absentee God, sitting idle, ever since the first Sabbath, at the outside of his universe, and seeing it go? Has the word *duty* no meaning? is what we call duty no divine messenger and guide, but a false earthly fantasm, made up of desire and fear, of emanations from the gallows and from Doctor Graham's celestial bed?[2] Happiness of an approving conscience! Did not Paul of Tarsus, whom admiring men have since named saint, feel that *he* was "the chief of sinners," and Nero of Rome, jocund in spirit (wohlgemuth), spend much of his time in fiddling?

"Foolish wordmonger, and motivegrinder, who in thy logic-mill hast an earthly mechanism for the godlike itself, and wouldst fain grind me out virtue from the husks of pleasure—I tell thee, Nay! To the unregenerate Prometheus Vinctus of a man, it is ever the bitterest aggravation of his wretchedness that he is conscious of virtue, that he feels himself the victim not of suffering only, but of injustice. What then? Is the heroic inspiration we name virtue but some passion; some bubble of the blood, bubbling in the direction others profit by? I know not; only this I know, if what thou namest happiness be our true aim, then are we all astray. With stupidity and sound digestion man may front much. But what, in these dull unimaginative days, are the terrors of conscience to the diseases of the liver! Not on morality, but on cookery, let us build our stronghold; there brandishing our frying-pan, as censer, let us offer sweet incense to the Devil, and live at ease on the fat things he has provided for his elect!"

Thus has the bewildered wanderer to stand, as so many have done, shouting question after question into the Sibyl-cave of destiny, and receive no answer but an echo. It is all a grim desert, this once-fair world of his; wherein is heard only the howling of wild beasts, or the shrieks of despairing, hate-filled men; and no pillar of

---

[1]Teufelsdrockh here refers to an unhappy love affair.

[2]Said to cure sterility.

cloud by day, and no pillar of fire by night, any longer guides the pilgrim. To such length has the spirit of inquiry carried him. "But what boots it (was thut's)?" cries he; "it is but the common lot in this era. Not having come to spiritual majority prior to the siecle de Louis Quinze, and not being born purely a loghead (dummkopf), thou hadst no other outlook. The whole world is, like thee, sold to unbelief; their old temples of the Godhead, which for long have not been rainproof, crumble down, and men ask now: Where is the Godhead; our eyes never saw him?"

Pitiful enough were it, for all these wild utterances, to call our Diogenes wicked. Unprofitable servants as we all are, perhaps at no era of his life was he more decisively the servant of goodness, the servant of God, than even now when doubting God's existence. "One circumstance I note," says he; "after all the nameless woe that inquiry, which for me, what it is not always, was genuine love of truth, had wrought me, I nevertheless still loved truth. and would bate no jot of my allegiance to her.

'Truth!' I cried, 'though the heavens crush me for following her, no falsehood! though a whole celestial Lubberland[1] were the price of apostasy.' In conduct it was the same. Had a divine messenger from the clouds, or miraculous handwriting on the wall, convincingly proclaimed to me *This thou shalt do*, with what passionate readiness, as I often thought, would I have done it, had it been leaping into the infernal fire. Thus, in spite of all motivegrinders, and mechanical profit-and-loss philosophies, with the sick ophthalmia and hallucination they had brought on, was the infinite nature of duty still dimly present to me; living without God in the world, of God's light I was not utterly bereft; if my as yet sealed eyes, with their unspeakable longing, could nowhere see Him, nevertheless in my heart He was present and His heaven-written law still stood legible and sacred there."

Meanwhile, under all these tribulations, and temporal and spiritual destitutions, what must the wanderer, in his silent soul, have endured! "The painfulest feeling," writes he, "is that of your own feebleness (unkraft); ever, as the English Milton says, to be weak is the true misery. And yet of your strength there is and can be no clear feeling, save by what you have prospered in, by what you have done. Between vague wavering capability and fixed indubitable performance, what a difference! A certain inarticulate self-consciousness dwells dimly in us; which only our works can render articulate and decisively discernible. Our works are the mirror wherein the spirit first sees its natural lineaments. Hence, too, the folly of that impossible precept, know thyself; till it be translated into this partially possible one, know what thou canst work at.

"But for me, so strangely unprosperous had I been, the net-result of my workings amounted as yet simply to—nothing. How then could I believe in my strength, when there was as yet no mirror to see it in? Ever did this agitating, yet, as I now perceive. quite frivolous question, remain to me insoluble: Hast thou a certain faculty, a certain worth, such even as the most have not; or art thou the completest dullard of these modern times? Alas! the fearful unbelief is unbelief in yourself; and how could I believe? Had not my first, last faith in myself, when even to me the heavens seemed laid open, and I dared to love, been all-too cruelly belied?

"The speculative mystery of life grew ever more mysterious to me; neither in the practical mystery had I made the slightest progress but been everywhere buffeted, foiled, and contemptuously cast out. A feeble unit in the middle of a threatening infinitude, I seemed to have nothing given me but eyes, whereby to discern my own wretchedness. Invisible yet impenetrable walls, as of enchantment, divided me from all living; was there, in the wide world, any true bosom I could press trustfully to

---

[1]Cornucopia.

mine? O heaven. No. there was none! I kept a lock upon my lips; why should I speak much with that shifting variety of so-called friends, in whose withered, vain and toohungry souls friendship was but an incredible tradition?

"In such cases, your resource is to talk little, and that little mostly from the newspapers. Now when I look back, it was a strange isolation I then lived in. The men and women around me, even speaking with me, were but figures, I had practically, forgotten that they were alive, that they were not merely automatic. In the midst of their crowded streets and assemblages, I walked solitary; and (except as it was my own heart, not another's, that I kept devouring) savage also, as the tiger in his jungle.

"Some comfort it would have been, could I, like a Faust, have fancied myself tempted and tormented of the Devil, for a Hell, as I imagine, without life, though only diabolic life, were more frightful; but in our age of down-pulling and disbelief, the very Devil has been pulled down, you cannot so much as believe in a Devil. To me the universe was all void of life, of purpose, of volition even of hostility; it was one huge, dead, immeasurable steam-engine, rolling on, in its dead indifference, to grind me limb from limb. O, the vast, gloomy, solitary Golgotha, and mill of death! Why was the living banished thither companionless, conscious? Why, if there is no Devil; nay, unless the Devil is your God?"

A prey incessantly to such corrosions, might not, moreover, as the worst aggravation to them, the iron constitution even of a Teufelsdrockh threaten to fail? We conjecture that he has known sickness; and, in spite of his locomotive habits, perhaps sickness of the chronic sort. Hear this, for example: "How beautiful to die of broken-heart, on paper! Quite another thing in practice; every window of your feeling, even of your intellect, as it were, begrimed and mudbespattered, so that no pure ray can enter; a whole drugshop in your inwards; the fordone soul drowning slowly in quagmires of disgust!"

Putting all which external and internal miseries together, may we not find in the following sentences, quite in our professor's still vein, significance enough? "From suicide a certain aftershine (nachschein) of Christianity withheld me—perhaps also a certain indolence of character; for, was not that a remedy I had at any time within reach? Often, however was there a question present to me: Should someone now, at the turning of that corner, blow thee suddenly out of space, into the other world or other noworld, by pistol-shot—how were it? On which ground, too, I have often, in sea-storms and sieged cities and other death scenes exhibited an imperturbability, which passed, falsely enough, for courage.

"So had it lasted," concludes the wanderer, "so had it lasted, as in bitter protracted death agony, through long years the heart within me, unvisited by any heavenly dewdrop, was smoldering in sulphurous, slow-consuming fire. Almost since earliest memory I had shed no tear; or once only when I, murmuring half-audibly recited Faust's Deathsong, that wild selig der den er im siegesglanze findet (happy whom he finds in battle's splendor), and thought that of this last friend even I was not forsaken, that destiny itself could not doom me not to die. Having no hope, neither had I any definite fear, were it of man or of Devil; nay, I often felt as if it might be solacing, could the arch-devil himself, though in Tartarean terrors, but rise to me that I might tell him a little of my mind. And yet, strangely enough, I lived in a continual, indefinite, pining fear; tremulous, pusillanimous, apprehensive of I knew not what; it seemed as if all things in the heavens above and the earth beneath would hurt me; as if the heavens and the earth were but boundless jaws of a devouring monster, wherein I, palpitating, waited to be devoured.

"Full of such humor, and perhaps the miserablest man in the whole French capital or suburbs, was I, one sultry dog-day, after much perambulation, toiling along the dirty little Rue Saint-Thomas de l'Enfer, among civic rubbish enough, in a close atmosphere, and over pavements hot as Nebuchadnezzar's furnace, whereby doubtless my spirits were little cheered; when, all at once, there rose a thought in me, and I asked myself, 'What art thou afraid of? Wherefore, like a coward, dost thou forever pip and whimper, and go cowering and trembling? Despicable biped! what is the sum total of the worst that lies before thee? death? Well, death; and say the pangs of Tophet[1] too, and all that the Devil and man may, will, or can do against thee! Hast thou not a heart; canst thou not suffer whatsoever it be; and, as a child of freedom, though outcast, trample Tophet itself under thy feet while it consumes thee? Let it come, then—I will meet it and defy it!'

"And as I so thought there rushed like a stream of fire over my whole soul; and I shook base fear away from me forever. I was strong, of unknown strength; a spirit, almost a god. Ever from that time, the temper of my misery was changed; not fear or whining sorrow was it, but indignation and grim fireeyed defiance.

"Thus had the Everlasting No (das ewige nein) pealed authoritatively through all the recesses of my being, of my ME; and then was it that my whole Me stood up, in native Godcreated majesty, and with emphasis recorded its protest. Such a protest, the most important transaction in life, may that same indignation and defiance, in a psychological point of view, be fitly called. The Everlasting No had said: 'Behold, thou art fatherless, outcast, and the universe is mine (the Devil's)'; to which my whole ME now made answer: 'I am not thine, but free, and forever hate thee!'

"It is from this hour that I incline to date my spiritual new-birth, or Baphometic[2] fire-baptism; perhaps I directly thereupon began to be a man."

## CENTER OF INDIFFERENCE

Though, after this "Baphometic fire-baptism" of his, our wanderer signifies that his unrest was but increased, as, indeed, "indignation and defiance," especially against things in general, are not the most peaceable inmates; yet can the psychologist surmise that it was no longer a quite hopeless unrest; that henceforth it had at least a fixed center to revolve round. For the firebaptized soul, long so scathed and thunder-riven, here feels its own freedom, which feeling is its Baphometic baptism; the citadel of its whole kingdom it has thus gained by assault, and will keep inexpugnable; outwards from which the remaining dominions, not indeed without hard battling, will doubtless by degrees be conquered and pacificated. Under another figure, we might say, if in that great moment, in the Rue Saint-Thomas de l'Enfer, the old inward Satanic school was not yet thrown out of doors, it received peremptory judicial notice to quit—whereby, for the rest, its howl-chantings, Ernulphus-cursings, and rebellious gnashings of teeth, might, in the meanwhile, become only the more tumultuous, and difficult to keep secret. Accordingly, if we scrutinize these pilgrimings well, there is perhaps discernible henceforth a certain incipient method in their madness. Not wholly as a specter does Teufelsdrockh now storm through the world; at worst as a specter-fighting man, nay who will one day be a specter-queller. If pilgriming restlessly to so many "Saints' Wells," and ever without quenching of his thirst, he nevertheless finds little secular wells, whereby from time to time some alleviation is ministered. In a word, he is now, if not ceasing, yet intermitting to "eat his own heart," and clutches round him outwardly on the NOT-ME for wholesomer food. Does not the following glimpse exhibit him in a much more natural state?

"Towns also and cities, especially the ancient, I failed not to look upon with interest. How beautiful to see thereby, as through a long vista, into the remote time; to have, as it were, an actual section of almost the earliest past brought safe into the

---

[1]Hell.

[2]Of sudden illumination.

present, and set before your eyes! There, in that old city, was a live ember of culinary fire put down, say only two thousand years ago; and there, burning more or less triumphantly, with such fuel as the region yielded, it has burned, and still burns, and thou thyself seest the very smoke thereof. Ah! and the far more mysterious live ember of vital fire was then also put down there; and still miraculously burns and spreads; and the smoke and ashes thereof (in these judgment-halls and churchyards), and its bellows-engines (in these churches), thou still seest; and its flame, looking out from every kind countenance, and every hateful one, still warms thee or scorches thee.

"Of man's activity and attainment the chief results are aeriform, mystic, and preserved in tradition only; such are his forms of government with the authority they rest on; his customs, or fashions both of cloth-habits and of soul-habits; much more his collective stock of handicrafts, the whole faculty he has acquired of manipulating nature. All these things, as indispensable and priceless as they are, cannot in any way be fixed under lock and key, but must flit, spiritlike, on impalpable vehicles, from father to son; if you demand sight of them, they are nowhere to be met with. Visible plowmen and hammermen there have been, ever from Cain and Tubalcain downwards; but where does your accumulated agricultural, metallurgic, and other manufacturing skill lie warehoused? It transmits itself on the atmospheric air, on the sun's rays (by hearing and vision); it is a thing aeriform, impalpable, of quite spiritual sort. In like manner, ask me not, Where are the laws; where is the government? In vain wilt thou go to Schonbrunn, to Downing Street, to the Palais Bourbon; thou findest nothing there but brick; or stone houses, and some bundles of papers tied with tape. Where, then, is that same cunninglydevised almighty government of theirs to be laid hands on? Everywhere, yet nowhere; seen only in its works, this too is a thing aeriform, invisible; or if you will, mystic and miraculous. So spiritual (geistig) is our whole daily life; all that we do springs out of mystery, Spirit, invisible force; only like a little cloud-image, or Armida's palace, air-built, does the actual body itself forth from the great mystic deep.

"Visible and tangible products of the past, again, I reckon-up to the extent of three: cities, with their cabinets and arsenals; then tilled fields, to either or to both of which divisions roads with their bridges may belong; and thirdly—books. In which third truly, the last-invented, lies a worth far surpassing that of the two others. Wondrous indeed is the virtue of a true book. Not like a dead city of stones, yearly crumbling, yearly needing repair; more like a tilled field, but then a spiritual field—like a spiritual tree, let me rather say, it stands from year to year, and from age to age (we have books that already number some hundred-and-fifty human ages); and yearly comes its new produce of leaves (commentaries, deductions, philosophical, political systems; or were it only sermons, pamphlets, journalistic essays), every one of which is talismanic and thaumaturgic, for it can persuade men. O thou who art able to write a book, which once in the two centuries or oftener there is a man gifted to do, envy not him whom they name city-builder, and inexpressibly pity him whom they name conqueror or city-burner! Thou too art a conqueror and victor; but of the true sort, namely over the Devil; thou too hast built what will outlast all marble and metal, and be a wonder-bringing city of the mind, a temple and seminary and prophetic Mount, whereto all kindreds of the Earth will pilgrim.—Fool! why journeyest thou wearisomely, in thy antiquarian fervor, to gaze on the stone pyramids of Geeza or the clay ones of Sacchara? These stand there, as I can tell thee, idle and inert, looking over the desert, foolishly enough, for the last three-thousand years; but canst thou not open thy Hebrew Bible, then, or even Luther's version thereof?"

No less satisfactory is his sudden appearance not in battle, yet on some battle-field; which, we soon gather, must be that of Wagram; so that here, for once is a certain approximation to distinctness of date. Omitting much let us impart what follows:

"Horrible enough! A whole Marchfeld strewed with shell-splinters, cannon-shot, ruined tumbrels, and dead men and horses; stragglers still remaining not so much as buried. And those red mold heaps; aye, there lie the shells of men, out of which all the life and virtue has been blown and now they are swept together and crammed down out of sight like blown egg-shells!—Did nature when she bade the Donau bring down his mold-cargoes from the Carinthian and Carpathian heights, and spread them out here into the softest richest level—intend thee O Marchfeld, for a corn-bearing nursery, whereon her children might be nursed; or for a cockpit, wherein they might the more commodiously be throttled and tattered? Were thy three broad highways, meeting here from the ends of Europe, made for ammunition-wagons, then? Were thy Wagrams and Stillfrieds but so many readybuilt casemates, wherein the house of Hapsburg might batter with artillery, and with artillery be battered? Konig Ottokar, amid yonder hillocks, dies under Rodolf's truncheon; here Kaiser Franz falls a-swoon under Napoleon's; within which five centuries, to omit the others, how hast thy breast, fair plain, been defaced and defiled! The greensward is torn-up and trampled-down; man's fond care of it, his fruit-trees, hedge-rows, and pleasant dwellings, blown-away with gunpowder; and the kind seedfield lies a desolate, hideous Place of Skulls—Nevertheless, nature is at work; neither shall these powder-devilkins with their utmost devilry gainsay her; but all that gore and carnage will be shrouded-in, absorbed into manure; and next year the Marchfeld will be green, nay greener. Thrifty unwearied nature, ever out of our great waste educing some little profit of thy own—how dost thou, from the very carcass of the killer, bring life for the living!

"What, speaking in quite unofficial language, is the net-purport and upshot of war? To my own knowledge, for example, there dwell and toil, in the British village of Dumdrudge, usually some five hundred souls. From these, by certain 'natural enemies' of the French, there are successively selected, during the French war, say thirty able-bodied men. Dumdrudge, at her own expense, has suckled and nursed them; she has, not without difficulty and sorrow, fed them up to manhood, and even trained them to crafts, so that one can weave, another build, another hammer, and the weakest can stand under thirty stone avoirdupois. Nevertheless, amid much weeping and swearing, they are selected, all dressed in red; and shipped away, at the public charges, some two thousand miles, or say only to the south of Spain; and fed there till wanted.

"And now to that same spot in the south of Spain, are thirty similar French artisans from a French Dumdrudge in like manner wending; till at length, after infinite effort, the two parties come into actual juxtaposition; and Thirty stands fronting Thirty, each with a gun in his hand. Straight-way the word 'Fire!' is given; and they blow the souls out of one another; and in place of sixty brisk useful craftsmen, the world has sixty dead carcasses, which it must bury, and anew shed tears for. Had these men any quarrel? Busy as the Devil is, not the smallest! They lived far enough apart; were the entirest strangers; nay, in so wide a universe, there was even, unconsciously, by commerce, some mutual helpfulness between them. How then? Simpleton! their governors had fallen-out; and, instead of shooting one another, had the cunning to make these poor blockheads shoot.—Alas, so is it in Deutschland, and hitherto in all other lands, still as of old, 'what devilry soever kings do, the Greeks must pay the piper!'—In that fiction of the English Smollett, it is true, the final cessation of war is perhaps prophetically shadowed forth; where the two natural enemies, in person, take each a tobacco-pipe, filled with brimstone; light the same, and smoke in one another's faces till the weaker gives in; but from such predicted peace-era, what blood-filled trenches, and contentious centuries, may still divide us!"

Thus can the professor, at least in lucid intervals, look away from his own sorrows, over the many-colored world, and pertinently enough note what is passing there. We may remark, indeed, that for the matter of spiritual culture, if for nothing else, perhaps few periods of his life were richer than this. Internally, there is the most momentous instructive course of practical philosophy, with experiments, going on; towards the right comprehension of which his peripatetic habits, favorable to meditation, might help him rather than hinder. Externally, again, as he wanders to and fro, there are, if for the longing heart little substance, yet for the seeing eye sights enough; in these so boundless travels of his, granting that the Satanic school was even partially kept down, what an incredible knowledge of our planet, and its inhabitants and their works, that is to say, of all knowable things, might not Teufelsdrockh acquire!

"I have read in most public libraries," says he, "including those of Constantinople and Samarcand; in most colleges, except the Chinese Mandarin ones, I have studied, or seen that there was no studying. Unknown languages have I oftenest gathered from their natural repertory, the air, by my organ of hearing; statistics, geographics, topographics came, through the eye, almost of their own accord. The ways of man, how he seeks food, and warmth, and protection for himself, in most regions, are ocularly known to me. Like the great Hadrian, I meted-out much of the terraqueous globe with a pair of compasses that belonged to myself only.

"Of great scenes why speak? Three summer, days, I lingered reflecting, and composing (dichtete), by the pine-chasms of Vaucluse, and in that clear Lakelet moistened my bread. I have sat under the palm-trees of Tadmor; smoked a pipe among the ruins of Babylon. The Great Wall of China I have seen; and can testify that it is of gray brick, coped and covered with granite, and shows only second-rate masonry. Great events also, have not I witnessed? Kings sweated-down (ausgemergelt) into Berlin-and-Milan customhouse-officers; the world well won, and the world well lost; oftener than once a hundred thousand individuals shot (by each other) in one day. All kindreds and peoples and nations dashed together, and shifted and shoveled into heaps that they might ferment there, and in time unite. The birth-pangs of democracy, wherewith convulsed Europe was groaning in cries that reached heaven, could not escape me.

"For great men I have ever had the warmest predilection; and can perhaps boast that few such in this era have wholly escaped me. Great men are the inspired (speaking and acting) texts of that divine Book of Revelations whereof a chapter is completed from epoch to epoch, and by some named history; to which inspired texts your numerous talented men, and your innumerable untalented men, are the better or worse exegetic commentaries, and wagon load of too-stupid, heretical or orthodox, weekly sermons. For my study, the inspired texts themselves! Thus did not I, in very early days, having disguised me as a tavern-waiter, stand behind the field-chairs, under that shady tree at Triesnitz by the Jena highway; waiting upon the great Schiller and greater Goethe, and hearing what I have not forgotten. For—"

—But at this point the editor recalls his principle of caution, some time ago laid down, and must suppress much. Let not the sacredness of laureled, still more, of crowned heads, be tampered with. Should we, at a future day, find circumstances altered, and the time come for publication, then may these glimpses into the privacy of the Illustrious be conceded; which for the present were little better than treacherous, perhaps traitorous eavesdroppings.

Of Lord Byron therefore, of Pope Pius, Emperor Tarakwang and the "white water-roses" (Chinese Carbonari) with their mysteries, no notice here. Of Napoleon himself we shall only, glancing from afar, remark that Teufelsdrockh's relation to him seems to have been of very varied character. At first we find our poor professor on the point of being shot as a spy; then taken into private conversation, even pinched on the ear, yet presented with no money; at last indignantly dismissed. almost thrown out of doors, as an "ideologist."

"He himself," says the professor, "was among the completest ideologists, at least ideopraxists;[1] in the idea (in der idee) he lived, moved, and fought. The man was a divine missionary, though unconscious of it; and preached, through the cannon's throat, that great doctrine, la carriere ouverte aux talens (the tools to him that can handle them), which is our ultimate political evangel, wherein alone can liberty lie. Madly enough he preached, it is true, as enthusiasts and first missionaries are wont, with imperfect utterance, amid much frothy rant; yet as articulately perhaps as the case admitted. Or call him, if you will an American backwoodsman, who had to fell unpenetrated forests, and battle with innumerable wolves, and did not entirely forbear strong liquor rioting, and even theft; whom, notwithstanding, the peaceful sower will follow, and, as he cuts the boundless harvest, bless."

More legitimate and decisively authentic is Teufelsdrockh's appearance and emergence (we know not well whence) in the solitude of the North Cape, on that June midnight. He has a "light-blue Spanish cloak" hanging round him as his "most commodious, principal, indeed sole upper-garment"; and stands there, on the world-promontory, looking over the infinite brine, like a little blue belfry (as we figure), now motionless indeed, yet ready, if stirred, to ring quaintest changes.

"Silence as of death," writes he; "for midnight, even in the Arctic latitudes, has its character—nothing but the granite cliffs ruddy-tinged, the peaceable gurgle of that slow-heaving polar ocean, over which in the utmost north the great sun hangs low and lazy, as if he too were slumbering. Yet is his cloud-couch wrought of crimson and cloth-of-gold; yet does his light stream over the mirror of waters, like a tremulous firepillar, shooting downwards to the abyss, and hide itself under my feet. In such moments, solitude also is invaluable; for who would speak, or be looked on, when behind him lies all Europe and Africa, fast asleep, except the watchmen; and before him the silent immensity and palace of the Eternal, whereof our sun is but a porch-lamp?

"Nevertheless, in this solemn moment, comes a man, or monster, scrambling from among the rock-hollows; and, shaggy, huge as the Hyperborean bear, hails me in Russian speech—most probably, therefore, a Russian smuggler. With courteous brevity, I signify my indifference to contraband trade, my humane intentions, yet strong wish to be private. In vain; the monster, counting doubtless on his superior stature, and minded to make sport for himself, or perhaps profit, were it with murder, continues to advance; ever assailing me with his importunate train-oil[2] breath; and now has advanced, till we stand both on the verge of the rock, the deep sea rippling greedily down below. What argument will avail? On the thick Hyperborean, cherubic reasoning, seraphic eloquence were lost. Prepared for such extremity, I, deftly enough, whisk aside one step; draw out, from my interior reservoirs, a sufficient Birmingham horse-pistol, and say, 'Be so obliging as retire, Friend (Er ziehe sich zuruck, Freund), and with promptitude!' This logic even the Hyperborean understands; fast enough, with apologetic, petitionary growl, he sidles off; and, except for suicidal as well as homicidal purposes, need not return.

"Such I hold to be the genuine use of gunpowder—that it makes all men alike tall. Nay, if thou be cooler, cleverer than I, if thou have more mind, though all but no body whatever, then canst thou kill me first, and art the taller. Hereby, at last, is the Goliath powerless, and the David resistless; savage animalism is nothing, inventive spiritualism is all.

"With respect to duels, indeed, I have my own ideas. Few things, in this so surprising world, strike me with more surprise. Two little visual spectra of men, hovering with insecure enough cohesion in the midst of the UNFATHOMABLE, and to dis-

---

[1]Those who practice ideas.

[2]Whale oil.

solve therein, at any rate, very soon—make pause at the distance of twelve paces asunder; whirl round; and, simultaneously by the cunningest mechanism, explode one another into dissolution; and off-hand become air, and nonextant! Deuce on it (verdammt), the little spitfires!—Nay, I think with old Hugo von Trimberg: 'God must needs laugh outright, could such a thing be, to see his wondrous manikins here below.'"

But amid these specialties, let us not forget the great generality which is our chief quest here: How prospered the inner man of Teufelsdrockh under so much outward shifting? Does legion still lurk in him, though repressed: or has he exorcised that Devil's brood? We can answer that the symptoms continue promising. Experience is the grand spiritual doctor; and with him Teufelsdrockh has now been long a patient, swallowing many a bitter bolus. Unless our poor friend belong to the numerous class of Incurables, which seems not likely, some cure will doubtless be effected. We should rather say that legion, or the Satanic school, was now pretty well extirpated and cast out, but next to nothing introduced in its room; whereby the heart remains, for the while, in a quiet but no comfortable state.

"At length, after so much roasting," thus writes our autobiographer, "I was what you might name calcined. Pray only that it be not rather, as is the more frequent issue, reduced to a caput-mortuum! But in any case, by mere dint of practice, I had grown familiar with many things. Wretchedness was still wretched—but I could now partly see through it, and despise it. Which highest mortal, in this inane existence, had I not found a shadow-hunter, or shadow-hunted; and, when I looked through his brave garnitures, miserable enough? Thy wishes have all been sniffed aside, thought I; but what, had they even been all granted! Did not the boy Alexander weep because he had not two planets to conquer—or a whole solar system; or after that, a whole universe? Ach Gott, when I gazed into these stars, have they not looked down on me as if with pity, from their serene spaces; like eyes glistening with heavenly tears over the little lot of man! Thousands of human generations, all as noisy as our own, have been swallowed-up of time, and there remains no wreck of them any more; and Arcturus and Orion and Sirius and the Pleiades are still shining in their courses, clear and young, as when the shepherd first noted them in the plain of Shinar. Pshaw! what is this paltry little dogcage of an Earth; what art thou that sittest whining there? Thou art still nothing, nobody; true; but who, then, is something, Somebody? For thee the family of man has no use—it rejects thee; thou art wholly as a dissevered limb—so be it, perhaps it is better so!"

Too-heavy-laden Teufelsdrockh! Yet surely his bands are loosening; one day he will hurl the burden far from him, and bound forth free and with a second youth.

"This," says our professor, "was the CENTER OF INDIFFERENCE I had now reached; through which whoso travels from the negative pole to the positive must necessarily pass."

## THE EVERLASTING YEA

"Temptations in the wilderness!" exclaims Teufelsdrockh: "Have we not all to be tried with such? Not so easily can the old Adam, lodged in us by birth, be dispossessed. Our life is compassed round with necessity; yet is the meaning of life itself no other than freedom, than voluntary force; thus have we a warfare; in the beginning, especially, a hard-fought battle. For the God-given mandate, *Work thou in welldoing*, lies mysteriously written, in Promethean prophetic characters, in our hearts; and leaves us no rest, night or day, till it be deciphered and obeyed; till it burn forth, in our conduct, a visible, acted Gospel of freedom. And as the clay-given mandate, *Eat thou and be filled*, at the same time persuasively proclaims itself through every nerve—must not there be a confusion, a contest, before the better influence can become the upper?

"To me nothing seems more natural than that the Son of Man, when such God-given mandate first prophetically stirs within him, and the clay must now be vanquished or vanquish—should be carried of the spirit into grim solitudes, and there fronting the Tempter do grimmest battle with him; defiantly setting him at naught, till he yield and fly. Name it as we choose—with or without visible Devil, whether in the natural desert of rocks and sands, or in the populous. moral desert of selfishness and baseness—to such temptation are we all called.

"Unhappy if we are not! Unhappy if we are but half-men, in whom that divine handwriting has never blazed forth, all-subduing, in true sun-splendor; but quivers dubiously amid meaner lights; or smolders, in dull pain, in darkness, under earthly vapors! Our wilderness is the wide world in an atheistic century; our forty days are long years of suffering and fasting; nevertheless, to these also comes an end. Yes, to me also was given, if not victory, yet the consciousness of battle, and the resolve to persevere therein while life or faculty is left. To me also, entangled in the enchanted forests, demon-peopled, doleful of sight and of sound, it was given, after weariest wanderings, to work out my way into the higher sunlit slopes—of that mountain which has no summit, or whose summit is in heaven only!"

He says elsewhere, under a less ambitious figure;—as figures are, once for all, natural to him: "Has not thy life been that of most sufficient men (tuchtigen manner) thou hast known in this generation? An outflush of foolish young enthusiasm, like the first fallow-crop, wherein are as many weeds as valuable herbs; this all parched away, under the droughts of practical and spiritual unbelief, as disappointment, in thought and act, often-repeated gave rise to doubt, and doubt gradually settled into denial! If I have had a second-crop, and now see the perennial greensward, and sit under umbrageous cedars, which defy all drought (and doubt); herein too, be the heavens praised, I am not without examples, and even exemplars."

So that, for Teufelsdrockh also, there has been a "glorious revolution"—these mad shadow-hunting and shadow-hunted pilgrimings of his were but some purifying "temptation in the wilderness," before his apostolic work (such as it was) could begin; which temptation is now happily over, and the Devil once more worsted! Was "that high moment in the Rue de l'Enfer," then, properly the turning-point of the battle; when the Fiend said, Worship me, or be torn in shreds; and was answered valiantly with an Apage Satana?

—Singular Teufelsdrockh, would thou hadst told thy singular story in plain words! But it is fruitless to look there, in those paperbags, for such. Nothing but innuendoes, figurative crotchets; a typical shadow, fitfully wavering, prophetico-satiric; no clear logical picture. "How paint to the sensual eye," asks he once, "what passes in the holy-of-holies of man's soul in what words, known to these profane times, speak even afar-off of the unspeakable?" We ask in turn: Why perplex these times, profane as they are, with needless obscurity, by omission and by commission? Not mystical only is our professor, but whimsical; and involves himself, now more than ever, in eye-bewildering chiaroscuro. Successive glimpses, here faithfully imparted, our more gifted readers must endeavor to combine for their own behoof.

He says: "The hot Harmattan wind had raged itself out; its howl went silent within me; and the long-deafened soul could now hear. I paused in my wild wanderings, and sat me down to wait and consider; for it was as if the hour of change drew nigh. I seemed to surrender, to renounce utterly, and say: Fly, then, false shadows of hope; I will chase you no more, I will believe you no more. And ye too, haggard specters of fear, I care not for you; ye too are all shadows and a lie. Let me rest here: for I am way-weary and life-weary; I will rest here, were it but to die—to die or to live is alike to me; alike insignificant." And again: "Here, then, as I lay in that CENTER OF INDIFFERENCE; cast, doubtless by benignant upper influence, into a healing sleep, the heavy dreams rolled gradually away, and I awoke to a new heaven and a new earth. The first preliminary moral act, annihilation of self (selbsttodtung), had been happily accomplished; and my mind's eyes were now unsealed, and its hands ungyved."

Might we not also conjecture that the following passage refers to his locality, during this same "healing sleep" that his pilgrim-staff lies cast aside here, on "the high tableland"; and indeed that the repose is already taking wholesome effect on him? If it were not that the tone, in some parts, has more of riancy, even of levity, than we could have expected! However, in Teufelsdrockh, there is always the strangest dualism: light dancing, with guitar-music, will be going on in the forecourt, while by fits from within comes the faint whimpering of woe and wail. We transcribe the piece entire.

"Beautiful it was to sit there, as in my skyey tent, musing and meditating; on the high tableland, in front of the mountains, over me, as roof the azure dome, and around me, for walls, four azure-flowing curtains—namely, of the four azure winds, on whose bottom-fringes also I have seen gilding. And then to fancy the fair castles that stood sheltered in these mountain hollows with their green flower-lawns, and white dames and damosels, lovely enough; or better still, the straw-roofed cottages, wherein stood many a mother baking bread, with her children round her—all hidden and protectingly folded-up in the valley-folds; yet there and alive, as sure as if I beheld them. Or to see, as well as fancy, the nine towns and villages, that lay round my mountainseat, which, in still weather were wont to speak to me (by their steeple-bells with metal tongue; and, in almost all weather, proclaimed their vitality by repeated smoke-clouds; whereon, as on a culinary horologe, I might read the hour of the day. For it was the smoke of cookery, as kind housewives at morning, midday, eventide, were boiling their husbands' kettles, and ever a blue pillar rose up into the air, successively or simultaneously, from each of the nine, saying, as plainly as smoke could say, Such and such a meal is getting ready here. Not uninteresting! For you have the whole borough, with all its lovemakings and scandal-mongeries, contentions and contentments, as in miniature, and could cover it all with your hat—If, in my wide wayfarings I had learned to look into the business of the world in its details, here perhaps was the place for combining it into general propositions, and deducing inferences therefrom.

"Often also could I see the black tempest marching in anger through the distance; round some Schreckhorn, as yet grim-blue, would the eddying vapor gather, and there tumultuously eddy, and flow down like a mad witch's hair; till, after a space, it vanished, and in the clear sunbeam, your Schreckhorn stood smiling grimwhite, for the vapor had held snow. How thou fermentest and elaboratest in thy great fermenting-vat and laboratory of an atmosphere, of a world, O nature!—Or what is nature? Ha! why do I not name thee God? Art thou not the 'living garment of God'? O heavens, is it, in very deed, HE, then, that ever speaks through thee; that lives and loves in thee, that lives and loves in me?

"Fore-shadows, call them rather fore-splendors, of that truth, and beginning of truths, fell mysteriously over my soul sweeter than dayspring to the shipwrecked in Nova Zembla; ah, like the mother's voice to her little child that strays bewildered, weeping, in unknown tumults; like soft streamings of celestial music to my too exasperated heart, came that evangel. The universe is not dead and demoniacal, a charnel-house with specters; but godlike, and my Father's!

"With other eyes, too, could I now look upon my fellow man—with an infinite love, an infinite pity. Poor, wandering, wayward man! Art thou not tried, and beaten with stripes, even as I am? Ever, whether thou bear the royal mantle or the beggar's gabardine, art thou not so weary, so heavy-laden; and thy bed of rest is but a grave. O my brother, my brother, why cannot I shelter thee in my bosom, and wipe away all tears from thy eyes!—Truly, the din of manyvoiced life, which, in this solitude, with the mind's organ, I could hear, was no longer a maddening discord, but a melting one; like inarticulate cries, and sobbings of a dumb creature, which in the ear of heaven are prayers. The poor Earth, with her poor joys, was now my needy mother, not my cruel stepdame; Man, with his so mad wants and so mean endeavors, had become the dearer to me; and even for his sufferings and his sins, I now first named him brother.

"Thus was I standing in the porch of that 'sanctuary of sorrow'; by strange, steep ways had I too been guided thither; and ere long its sacred gates would open, and the 'divine depth of sorrow' lie disclosed to me."

The professor says, he here first got eye on the knot that had been strangling him and straightway could unfasten it, and was free. "A vain interminable controversy," writes he, "touching what is at present called origin of evil, or some such thing, arises in every soul, since the beginning of the world; and in every soul, that would pass from idle suffering into actual endeavoring must first be put an end to. The most, in our time, have to go content with a simple, incomplete enough suppression of this controversy; to a few, some solution of it is indispensable. In every new era, too, such solution comes-out in different terms, and ever the solution of the last era has become obsolete, and is found unserviceable. For it is man's nature to change his dialect from century to century; he cannot help it though he would. The authentic church-catechism of our present century has not yet fallen into my hands; meanwhile, for my own private behoof, I attempt to elucidate the matter so.

"Man's unhappiness, as I construe, comes of his greatness; it is because there is an infinite in him, which with all his cunning he cannot quite bury under the finite. Will the whole finance ministers and upholsterers and confectioners of modern Europe undertake, in joint-stock company, to make one shoeblack happy? They cannot accomplish it, above an hour or two; for the shoeblack also has a soul quite other than his stomach; and would require, if you consider it, for his permanent satisfaction and saturation, simply this allotment, no more, and no less: God's infinite universe altogether to himself, therein to enjoy infinitely, and fill every wish as fast as it rose. Oceans of Hochheimer, a throat like that of Ophiuchus—speak not of them; to the infinite shoeblack they are as nothing. No sooner is your ocean filled, than he grumbles that it might have been of better vintage. Try him with half of a universe, of an omnipotence, he sets to quarreling with the proprietor of the other half, and declares himself the most maltreated of men.—Always there is a black spot in our sunshine; it is even, as I said, the shadow of ourselves.

"But the whim we have of happiness is somewhat thus. By certain valuations, and averages, of our own striking, we come upon some sort of average terrestrial lot; this we fancy belongs to us by nature, and of indefeasible right. It is simple payment of our wages, of our deserts; requires neither thanks nor complaint; only such overplus as there may be do we account happiness; any deficit again is misery. Now consider that we have the valuation of our own deserts ourselves, and what a fund of self-conceit there is in each of us—do you wonder that the balance should so often dip the wrong way, and many a blockhead cry: See there, what a payment; was ever worthy gentleman so used!—I tell thee, Blockhead, it all comes of thy vanity; of what thou fanciest those same deserts of thine to be. Fancy that thou deservest to be hanged (as is most likely), thou wilt feel it happiness to be only shot; fancy that thou deservest to be hanged in a hair-halter, it will be a luxury to die in hemp.

"So true is it, what I then said, that the fraction of life can be increased in value not so much by increasing your numerator as by lessening your denominator. Nay, unless my algebra deceive me, unity itself divided by zero will give infinity. Make thy claim of wages a zero, then; thou hast the world under thy feet. Well did the wisest of our time write: 'It is only with renunciation (entsagen) that life, properly speaking, can be said to begin.'

"I asked myself: What is this that, ever since earliest years, thou hast been fretting and fuming, and lamenting and self-tormenting, on account of? Say it in a word: is it not because thou art not HAPPY? Because the THOU (sweet gentleman) is not sufficiently honored, nourished, soft-bedded, and lovingly cared for? Foolish soul! What act of legislature was there that thou shouldst be happy? A little while ago thou hadst no right to be at all. What if thou wert born and predestined not to be happy, but to be unhappy! Art thou nothing other than a vulture, then, that fliest through the universe seeking after somewhat to eat; and shrieking dolefully because carrion enough is not given thee? Close thy Byron; open thy Goethe.

"Es leuchtet mir ein, I see a glimpse of it!" cries he elsewhere; "there is in man a HIGHER than love of happiness; he can do without happiness, and instead thereof find blessedness! Was it not to preach-forth this same HIGHER that sages and martyrs, the poet and the priest, in all times, have spoken and suffered; bearing testimony, through life and through death, of the Godlike that is in man, and how in the Godlike only has he strength and freedom? Which God-inspired doctrine art thou also honored to be taught; O heavens! and broken with manifold merciful afflictions, even till thou become contrite, and learn it! O, thank thy destiny for these; thankfully bear what yet remain—thou hadst need of them; the self in thee needed to be annihilated. By benignant fever-paroxysms is life rooting out the deep-seated chronic disease, and triumphs over death. On the roaring billows of time, thou art not engulfed, but borne aloft into the azure of eternity. Love not pleasure; love God. This is the EVERLASTING YEA, wherein all contradiction is solved—wherein whoso walks and works, it is well with him."

And again: "Small is it that thou canst trample the earth with its injuries under thy feet, as old Greek Zeno trained thee; thou canst love the earth while it injures thee, and even because it injures thee; for this a greater than Zeno was needed, and he too was sent. Knowest thou that 'worship of sorrow'?[1] The temple thereof, founded some eighteen centuries ago, now lies in ruins, overgrown with jungle, the habitation of doleful creatures—nevertheless, venture forward; in a low crypt, arched out of falling fragments, thou findest the altar still there, and its sacred lamp perennially burning."

Without pretending to comment on which strange utterances, the editor will only remark, that there lies beside them much of a still more questionable character; unsuited to the general apprehension; nay, wherein he himself does not see his way. Nebulous disquisitions on religion, yet not without bursts of splendor; on the "perennial continuance of inspiration"; on prophecy; that there are "true priests, as well as Baal-priests in our own day"; with more of the like sort. We select some fractions, by way of finish to this farrago.

"Cease, my much-respected Herr von Voltaire," thus apostrophizes the professor; "shut thy sweet voice; for the task appointed thee seems finished. Sufficiently hast thou demonstrated this proposition, considerable or otherwise: That the mythus of the Christian religion looks not in the eighteenth century as it did in the eighth. Alas, were thy six-and-thirty quartos, and the six-and thirty thousand other quartos and folios, and flying sheets or reams, printed before and since on the same subject, all needed to convince us of so little! But what next? Wilt thou help us to embody the divine spirit of that religion in a new mythus, in a new vehicle and vesture, that our souls, otherwise too like perishing, may live? What! thou hast no faculty in that kind? Only a torch for burning, no hammer for building? Take our thanks, then, and thyself away.

"Meanwhile what are antiquated mythuses to me? Or is the God present, felt in

[1]The Christian religion.

my own heart, a thing which Herr von Voltaire will dispute out of me—or dispute into me? To the "worship of sorrow" ascribe what origin and genesis thou pleasest, has not that worship originated, and been generated; is it not here? Feel it in thy heart, and then say whether it is of God! This is belief; all else is opinion—for which latter whoso will, let him worry and be worried."

"Neither," observes he elsewhere. "shall ye tear out one another's eyes, struggling over 'plenary inspiration,' and suchlike; try rather to get a little even partial inspiration, each of you for himself. One bible I know, of whose plenary inspiration doubt is not so much as possible; nay, with my own eyes I saw the God's-hand writing it; thereof all other bibles are but leaves—say, in picture-writing to assist the weaker faculty."

Or, to give the wearied reader relief, and bring it to an end, let him take the following, perhaps more intelligible, passage:

"To me, in this our life," says the professor, "which is an internecine warfare with the timespirit, other warfare seems questionable. Hast thou in any way a contention with thy brother, I advise thee, think well what the meaning thereof is. If thou gauge it to the bottom, it is simply this: 'Fellow, see! thou art taking more than thy share of happiness in the world, something from my share; which, by the heavens, thou shalt not; nay, I will fight thee rather.'—Alas, and the whole lot to be divided is such a beggarly matter, truly a 'feast of shells,' for the substance has been spilled out—not enough to quench one appetite; and the collective human species clutching at them—Can we not, in all such cases, rather say: 'Take it, thou too-ravenous individual, take that pitiful additional fraction of a share, which I reckoned mine, but which thou so wantest, take it with a blessing—would to heaven I had enough for thee!'—If Fichte's wissenschaftslehre be, 'to a certain extent, applied Christianity,' surely to a still greater extent, so is this. We have here not a whole duty of man, yet a half duty, namely, the passive half—could we but do it, as we can demonstrate it!

"But indeed conviction, were it never so excellent, is worthless till it convert itself into conduct. Nay, properly conviction is not possible till then; inasmuch as all speculation is by nature endless, formless, a vortex amid vortices; only by a felt indubitable certainty of experience does it find any center to revolve round, and so fashion itself into a system. Most true is it, as a wise man teaches us, that 'Doubt of any sort cannot be removed except by action.' On which ground, too, let him who gropes painfully in darkness or uncertain light, and prays vehemently that the dawn may ripen into day, lay this other precept well to heart, which to me was of invaluable service: 'Do the duty which lies nearest thee,' which thou knowest to be a duty! Thy second duty will already have become clearer.

"May we not say, however, that the hour of spiritual enfranchisement is even this: When your ideal world, wherein the whole man has been dimly struggling and inexpressibly languishing to work, becomes revealed, and thrown open; and you discover, with amazement enough, like the Lothario in Wilhelm Meister, that your 'America is here or nowhere'? The situation that has not its duty, its ideal was never yet occupied by man. Yes here, in this poor, miserable, hampered, despicable actual, wherein thou even now standest, here or nowhere is thy ideal—work it out therefrom; and working, believe, live, be free. Fool! the ideal is in thyself, the impediment too is in thyself; thy condition is but the stuff thou art to shape that same ideal out of; what matters whether such stuff be of this sort or that, so the form thou give it be heroic, be poetic? O thou that pinest in the imprisonment of the actual, and criest bitterly to the gods for a kingdom wherein to rule and create, know this of a truth: the thing thou seekest is already with thee, 'here or nowhere,' couldst thou only see!

"But it is with man's soul as it was with nature: the beginning of creation is—light. Till the eye have vision, the whole members are in bonds. Divine moment, when over the tempest-tossed soul, as once over the wild-weltering chaos, it is spoken: Let there be light! Ever to the greatest that has felt such moment, is it not miraculous and God-announcing; even as, under simpler figures, to the simplest and least. The mad primeval discord is hushed; the rudely-jumbled conflicting elements bind themselves into separate firmaments; deep silent rock-foundations are built beneath; and the skyey vault with its everlasting luminaries above—instead of a dark wasteful chaos, we have a blooming, fertile, heaven-encompassed world.

"I too could now say to myself: Be no longer a chaos, but a world, or even worldkin. Produce! Produce! Were it but the pitifulest infinitesimal fraction of a product, produce it, in God's name! Tis the utmost thou hast in thee; out with it, then. Up, up! Whatsoever thy hand findeth to do, do it with thy whole might. Work while it is called today; for the night cometh, wherein no man can work."

## DANIEL WEIR (1796–1831)

### See the Moon

See the moon oer cloudless Jura
Shining in the lake below.
See the distant mountain tow'ring
Like a pyramid of snow.
Scenes of grandeur—scenes of childhood—
Scenes so dear to love and me;
Let us roam by bower and wildwood—
All is lovelier when with thee.

On Leman's breast the winds are sighing.
All is silent in the grove;
And the flow'rs, with dew drops glist'ning,
Sparkle like the eye of love.
Night so calm, so clear, so cloudless;
Blessed night to love and me;
Let us roam by bower and fountain—
All is lovelier when with thee.

### The Midnight Wind

I've listened to the midnight wind,
Which seemed, to fancy's ear,
The mournful music of the mind,
The echo of a tear;
And still methought the hollow sound
Which, melting, swept along,
The voice of other days had found,
With all the powers of song.

I've listened to the midnight wind,
And thought of friends untrue—
Of hearts that seemed so fondly twined,
That nought could e'er undo;
Of cherished hopes once fondly bright—
Of joys which fancy gave—

Of youthful eyes, whose lovely light
Were darkened in the grave.

I've listened to the midnight wind,
When all was still as death;
When nought was heard before, behind—
Not e'en the sleeper's breath.
And I have sat at such an hour
And heard the sick man's sigh;
Or seen the babe, like some sweet flow'r,
At that lone moment die.

I've listened to the midnight wind,
And wept for others' woe;
Nor could the heart such music find
To bid its tear drops flow.
The melting voice of one we loved,
Whose voice was heard no more,
Seemed, when those fancied chords were moved,
Still breathing as before.

I've listened to the midnight wind,
And sat beside the dead,
And felt those movings of the mind
Which own a secret dread.
The ticking clock, which told the hour,
Had then a sadder chime;
And these winds seemed an unseen pow'r,
Which sung the dirge of time.

I've listened to the midnight wind,
When, oer the new-made grave
Of one whose heart was true and kind,
Its rudest blasts did rave.
Oh, there was something in the sound—
A mournful, melting tone—
Which led the thoughts to that dark ground
Where he was left alone.

I've listened to the midnight wind,
And courted sleep in vain,
While thoughts like these have oft combined
To rack the wearied brain.
And even when slumber, soft and deep,
Has seen the eyelid close,
The restless soul, which cannot sleep,
Has strayed till morning rose.

## 'Neath the Wave

'Neath the wave thy lover sleeps,
And cold, cold is his pillow.

Oer his bed no maiden weeps,
Where rolls the white billow.
And though the winds have sunk to rest
Upon the troubled ocean's breast,
Yet still, oh still there's left behind
A restless storm in Ellen's mind.

Her heart is on yon dark'ning wave,
Where all she loved is lying,
And where, around her William's grave,
The sea-bird is crying.
And oft on Jura's lonely shore,
Where surges beat and billows roar,
She sat—but grief has nipt her bloom,
And there they made young Ellen's tomb.

## ELIZABETH GRANT (1797–1885)

[Born in Edinburgh of a Highland family, Elizabeth Grant divided her youth among London, Edinburgh and the Highland family estate of Rothiemurchus. Her father, Sir John Grant, a lawyer, Member of Parliament and member of Scottish society, suffered about 1820 severe financial reverses, causing his family to live for some years in the Highlands on a strict economy. In 1827 the family left for India, where her father had been given a judgeship. Here Elizabeth married Colonel Henry Smith, an Irishman. Shortly after, the couple removed to Smith's estate in Ireland and there she lived out her long life. From 1845 to 1854 she wrote *Memoirs of a Highland Lady*, apparently for the benefit of her family. Thirteen years after her death, in 1898, the book was published. It was a major success.

The *Memoirs* are among the most entertaining journals in English. Informal, racy, incisive, witty, they detail her life and the social mores of her age to the time of her return to Britain with her husband in 1830. Among Elizabeth Grant's many literary skills was the gift of portraiture. "Picardy Place," her account of a year at that address during their stay in Edinburgh, is Chapter 20 of the *Memoirs*. It contains several among the book's most notable character sketches, some quite comic, and some seething with vitriol, roasting, for example, Walter Scott, his books, and even his family. One assumes the aristocratic Miss Grant was offended both by Scott's presumption in claiming to know the Highlands, and by his social climbing.

The chapter contains references to the author's family. With Elizabeth lived her parents (the father away in London as a rule), her sisters Mary and Jane, a brother, William, and a Miss Elphick, the governess-duenna.]

### Picardy Place

After a very short stay in the highlands we all came up to Picardy Place the end of October 1817, to meet my father on his return from Ireland. We soon settled ourselves in our spacious house, making ourselves more really at home than we had hitherto felt ourselves to be in town, having the certainty of no removal for three years. Still we younger ones were not soon reconciled to the situation, all our habits being disturbed by the separation from the West End! Three winters we spent here, none of them worthy of particular note, neither indeed can I at this distance of time separate the occurrences of each from the others.

The usual routine seemed to be followed in all. My father and his new, very queer clerk, Mr. Caw, worked away in their law chambers till my father went up to London late in Spring. The second winter he lost his seat for Grimsby, a richer competitor carried all votes, and for a few months he was out of Parliament. How much better it would have been for him had he remained out, stuck to the Bar, at which he really would have done well had he not left ever so many cases in the lurch when attending the "House," where he made no figure—he seldom spoke, said little when he did speak, and never in any way made himself of consequence. Only once, when all his party censured the Speaker, he made a little reputation by the polite severity of his few words, called by Sir Alexander Boswell his bit of brimstone and butter, a witticism that ran through all *coteries*, almost turning the laugh against the really clever speech. He dined out every where with my mother while he was in Edinburgh, but hardly ever went out in an evening. He seemed, from his daily letters to my mother, to go a good deal into society while he was in London, dining at Holland House, Lord Lansdowne's, Lord Grey's, all the Whigs in fact, for he got into Parliament again. The Duke of Bedford gave him Tavistock till one of his own sons should be ready for it.

Five or six dinners, two small evening parties, and one large one, a regular rout, paid my mother's debts in the visiting line each winter. She understood the management of company so well, every assembly of whatever kind always went off admirably at her house. In particular she lighted her rooms brilliantly, had plenty of refreshments, abundance of attendants, always a piece of matting spread from the carriage steps to the house door, and two dressing rooms with toilettes, good fires, hot water, and in the one prepared for the ladies stood a maid with thread and needle in case of accident. Every body praised, though few imitated; such preparations involved a little trouble, besides requiring more rooms than many people had to dispose of.

We dined out a great deal, Jane and I taking the dinners in turns. We both went out in the evenings except when I could manage an escape, which was easier than formerly, my mother having given me up as a matrimonial speculation, and Jane really delighting in society. We got into rather a graver set than we had belonged to while in the sunshine of George Street and Charlotte Square, not quite giving up our gayer companions, but the distance from them was so great our easy sociable intercourse was very much broken. In our own short street we knew only John Clerk, not then a judge, and his truly agreeable sister Miss Bessy. We half lived in their house, William, Jane and I. They never gave a dinner without one of us being wanted to fill the place of an apology, and none of us ever shirked the summons feeling so at home, and meeting always such pleasant people. All the law set of course, judges, barristers, and writers; some of the literary, some of the scientific, and a great many country families. The drawing rooms, four of them, were just a picture gallery, hung with paintings by the "ancient masters," some of them genuine! There were besides portfolios of prints, clever caricatures, and original sketches, these last undoubted and very valuable.

John Clerk was a collector; a thousand curiosities were spread about. He made more of his profession than any man at the Bar, and with his ready money commanded the market to a certain extent. The last purchase was the favorite always, indeed the only one worth possessing, so that it almost seemed as if the enjoyment was in the acquisition, not in the intrinsic merit of the object. A hideous daub called a Rubens, a crowd of fat lumps of children miscalled angels, with as much to spare of "de quoi" as would have supplied the deficiencies of the whole cherubim, was the wonder of the world for ever so long; my wonder too, for if it was a Rubens it must have been a mere sketch, and never finished. I think I have heard that at the sale of this museum on Lord Eldin's death, a great many of his best loved pictures were acknowledged to be trash.

I did not like him; the immorality of his private life was very discreditable; he was cynical too, severe, very, when offended, though of a kindly nature in the main. His talents there was no dispute about, though his reputation certainly was enhanced by his eccentricities and by his personal appearance, which was truly hideous. He was very lame, one leg being many inches shorter than the other, and his countenance, harsh and heavy when composed, became demoniac when illumined by the mocking smile that sometimes relaxed it. I always thought him the personification of the devil on two sticks, a living, actual Mephistopheles. He spoke but little to his guests, uttering some caustic remark, cruelly applicable, at rare intervals, treasured up by every body around as another saying of the wise man's deserving of being written in gold, eastern fashion. When he did rouse up beyond this, his exposition of any subject he warmed on was really luminous, masterly, carried one away. The young men were all frightened to death of him; he did look as if he could bite, and as if the bite would be deadly. The young ladies played with the monster, for he was very gentle to us.

In the parliament house, as the Courts of Justice are called in Scotland, he was a very tiger, seizing on his adversary with tooth and nail, and demolishing him without mercy, often without justice, for he was a true advocate, heart and soul, right or wrong, in his client's cause. Standing very upright on the long leg, half a dozen pair of spectacles shoved up over his forehead, his wickedest countenance on, beaming with energy, he poured forth in his broad Scotch a torrent of flaming rhetoric too bewildering to be often very successfully opposed. There was a story went of his once having mistaken a case, and so in his most vehement manner pleading on the wrong side, the attorneys, called writers with us, in vain whispering and touching and pulling, trying in their agony every possible means of recalling his attention. At last he was made to comprehend the mischief he was doing. So he paused—for breath, readjusted his notes, probably never before looked at, held out his hand for the spectacles his old fat clerk Mr. George had always a packet of ready, put them on, shoved them up over all the series sent up before, and then turning to the Judge resumed his address thus, "Having now, my lord, to the best of my ability stated my opponent's case as strongly as it is possible for even my learned brother"—bowing to the opposite counsel with a peculiar swing of the short leg—"to argue it, I shall proceed point by point to refute every plea advanced, etc. etc."; and he did, amid a convulsion of laughter. As a consulting lawyer he was calm and clear, a favorite arbitrator, making indeed most of his heavy fees by chamber practice.

The sort of tart things he said at dinner were like this. Some one having died, a man of birth and fortune in the West country, rather celebrated during his life for drawing pretty freely with the long bow in conversation, it was remarked that the heir had buried him with much pomp, and had ordered for his remains a handsome monument: "wi' an epitaph," said John Clerk in his broadest border dialect; "he must hae an epitáph, an appropriate epitaph, an' we'll change the exordium out o' respect. Instead o' the usual Here lies, we'll begin his epitaph wi' Here continues to lie" . . .

I wish I could remember more of them; they were scattered broadcast, and too many fell by the wayside. The sister who lived with him and kept his house must in her youth have been a beauty. Indeed she acknowledged this, and told how to enhance it, she had when about fifteen possessed herself of her mother's patch box, and not content with one or two black spots to brighten her complexion, had stuck on a whole shower, and thus speckled had set out on a very satisfactory walk, every one she met staring at her admiringly. A deal of such quiet fun enlivened her conversation, adding considerably to the attraction of a thoroughly well bred manner. She painted a little, modeled in clay beautifully, sometimes finishing her small groups in ivory, and her busts in stone or marble. She was well read in French and English classics, had seen much, suffered some, reflected a good deal. She was a most charming companion, saying often in few words what one could think over at good length. She was very proud—the Clerks of Eldin had every right so to be—and the patronizing pity with which she folded up her ancient skirts from contact with the *snobs*, as we call them now, whom she met and visited and was studiously polite to, was often my amusement to watch. She never disparaged them by a syllable individually, but she would describe a rather fast family as "the sort of people you never see in mourning," "persons likely to make the mistake of being in advance of the fashion—so busy trying to push themselves into a place and not succeeding," added with a smile a trifle akin to her brother's.

There was a younger brother William who, likewise a bachelor, had some office with a small salary and lived in lodgings, dining out every day, for no party was complete without him. He was less kindly than John, but his manner concealed this. He was as clever, if not cleverer, but too indolent to make any use of his great natural abilities. He had never practiced at the Bar, and was quite content with his small income and his large reputation, though I have heard say, when wondering at the extent of his information, that his memory was regularly refreshed for society, it being his habit to read up in the morning for his display in the evening, and then dexterously turn the conversation into the prepared channel. He told a story better than any one in the world, except his friend Sir Adam Ferguson. He one dark winter's evening over the fire gave us a whole murder case so graphically that when he seized me to illustrate the manner of the strangling, I and the whole of the rest of us shrieked. I never trembled so much in my life.

Sir Adam Ferguson was the son of the "Roman Antiquities"; another idler. He was fond in the summer of walking excursions in two or three localities where he had friends, in the Perthshire highlands, along the coasts of Fife and Forfar, and in the border country, the heights along the Tweed, etc. Mark the points well. His acquaintance were of all ranks. He had eyes, ears, observation of all kinds, a wonderful memory, extraordinary powers of imitation, a pleasure in detailing—acting, in fact, all that occurred to him. He was the bosom friend of Walter Scott; he and William Clerk lived half their time with the "great novelist," and it was very ungenerous in him and Mr. Lockhart to have made so little mention of them in the biography, for most undoubtedly Sir Adam Ferguson was the "nature" from which many of these lifelike pictures were drawn. We, who knew all, recognized our old familiar stories, nay, characters, and afterwards accounted for the silence on the subject of the friends from the desire to avoid acknowledging the rich source that had been so constantly drawn on. Walter Scott had never crossed the Firth of Forth as far as I know.[1]

*Waverley* came out, I think it must have been in the autumn of 1814, just before we went first to Edinburgh. It was brought to us to the Doune, I know, by "little Jemmy Simpson," as that good man, since so famous, was then most irreverently called. Some liked the book, he said; he thought himself it was in parts quite beyond the common run, and the determined mystery as to the author added much to its vogue. I did not like it. The opening English scenes were to me intolerably dull, so lengthy, and so prosy, and the persons introduced so uninteresting, the hero contemptible, the two heroines unnatural and disagreeable, and the whole idea given of the highlands so utterly at variance with truth. I read it again long afterwards, and remained of the same mind.

Then burst out *Guy Mannering*, carrying all the world before it, in spite of the very pitiful setting, the gypsies, the smugglers, and Dandie Dinmont are surrounded by. Here again is the copyist, the scenery Dumfries and Galloway, the dialect Forfar. People now began to feel these works could come but from one author, particularly

[1]Not accurate.

as a few acres began to be added to the recent purchase of the old tower of Abbotsford, and Mrs. Scott set up a carriage, a Barouche landau built in London, and which from the time she got it she was seldom out of, appearing indeed to spend her life in driving about the streets all day. I forget which came next, the baronetcy or the *Antiquary*—the one was very quickly succeeded by the other—and were followed by the *Castle* at Abbotsford, that monument of vanity, human absurdity, or madness, William Clerk used to speak of this most melancholy act of folly almost with tears.

I was never in company with Walter Scott; he went very little out, and when he did go he was not agreeable, generally sitting very silent, looking dull and listless, unless an occasional flash lighted up his heavy countenance. In his own house he was another character, especially if he liked his guests. His family were all inferior. I have often thought that this was the reason of the insipidity of his ideal gentlemen and ladies—he knew none better.

Lady Scott, a natural daughter of a Marquis of Downshire, her mother French of low degree, herself half educated in Paris, very silly and very foolish, was a most unfortunate mate for such a man. When I saw her she had no remains of beauty, dressed fantastically, spoke the greatest nonsense in her broken English—and very frequently had taken too much wine. I recollect one evening at the Miss Pringles', she was actually unconscious of her actions, poor Anne Scott vainly trying to conceal her condition, till catching sight of William Clerk they got her to go away. The excuse was asthma, a particular asthmatic affection, which a glass or more of Madeira relieved.

Such a mother could scarcely do much for or with her children. The eldest son, Walter, was a mere good-natured goose forced into a marriage he hated and never able to get over the annoyance his unsuitable partner gave him. The younger, Charles, was thought more of, he died on his travels before being in any way brought to notice. Sophy, Mrs. Lockhart, was an awkward, very ignorant girl, not exactly plain yet scarcely otherwise, her husband did a great deal with her. She was liked in London, her manner remaining simple after it was softened. Anne was odious—very ugly and very pretending and very unpopular, which she should not have been, would not, had she been less exacting, less irritable, for she was a good daughter in different ways to both parents.

It was odd, but Sir Walter never had the reputation in Edinburgh he had elsewhere—was not the Lion, I mean. His wonderful works were looked for, read with avidity, praised on all hands, still the author made far less noise at home than he did abroad. The fat, very vulgar Mrs. Jobson, whose low husband had made his large fortune at Dundee by pickling herrings, on being congratulated at the approaching marriage of her daughter to Sir Walter's son, said the young people were attached, which was not true, otherwise her Jane might have looked higher. It was only a baronetcy, and quite a late creation.

Another family in the Clerk set and ours were the Dalzels; they lived in a small house just behind Picardy Place, in Albany or Forth Street. They were a professor's widow, her sister, and her sons and daughters, reduced in the short space of a few years to the one son and one daughter who still survive. Mary Dalzel played well on the piano forte; there was no other talent among them. The Professor had been a learned but a singularly simple man. He had been tutor to either Lord Lauderdale or to his eldest son, and they had a story of him which Lady Mary told us, that at dinner at Dunbar—a large party—a guest alluding to the profligacy of some prominent political character, Mr. Dalzel burst in with, "There has not been such a rogue unhanged since the days of the wicked Duke of Lauderdale." John Dalzel was a great companion of my brother William's; they had gone through College, and were now studying for their civil law trials together. He was dull but persevering, and might have risen to respectability at least in his profession had he lived.

In York Place we had only the old Miss Pringles, chiefly remarkable for never in the morning going out together—always different ways, that when they met at dinner there might be the more to say; and Miss Kate Sinclair; and two families which, all unguessed by us, were destined to have such close connection with us hereafter, Mrs. Henry Siddons and the Gibson Craigs.

Mrs. Siddons was now a widow living with her two very nice daughters and her two charming little boys, quietly as became her circumstances. She acted regularly, as the main prop of the theater on which the principal part of her income depended. She went a little into society. She had pleasure in seeing her friends in a morning in her own house, and the friends were always delighted to go to see her, she was so very agreeable. The girls were great friends of my sister Mary's. The little boys were my mother's passion, they were with us for ever, quite little pets.

The Gibsons, who were not Craigs then, we got more intimate with after they moved to a fine large house Mr. Gibson was building in Picardy Place when we went there. There were two sons, and seven daughters of every age, all of them younger than the brothers.

Mr. Shannon, the Irish chaplain of the Episcopal chapel we attended, the fashionable one, lived in York Place, and the Gillies's, with whom we were as intimate as with the Clerks, and on the same easy terms; we young people being called on when wanted, and never loath to answer the call, Lord Gillies being kind in his rough way, and Mrs. Gillies then, as now, delightful. Their nieces Mary and Margaret at this time lived with them.

Jane and I added to our private list of so called friends Mr. Kennedy of Dunure, whose sister wrote *Father Clement*, whose mother, beautiful at eighty, was sister to the mother of Lord Brougham, who himself married Sir Samuel Romilly's daughter and held for many years a high situation here in Ireland. Archy Allison, now Sir Archibald, heavy, awkward, plain, and yet foredoomed to greatness by the united testimony of every one sufficiently acquainted with him. His father, one of the Episcopal Chaplains and author of a work on taste, had married Mrs. Montague's Miss Gregory, so there was celebrity on all sides.

Willy and Walter Campbell, uncle and nephew the same age. Willy Campbell of Winton was really a favorite with all the world, and most certainly would have shone in it had he been spared; he died in Greece, bequeathing his immense fortune equally between his two sisters, Lady Ruthven and Lady Belhaven; they were all three the children of a second marriage of old Campbell of Shawfield's with the heiress of Winton. Robert Hay, Captain Dalzel who lent us the whole of M. Jouy's then published works beginning with *L'hermite de la Chaussee d'Antin*, and the *Scots Greys*, completed our first winter's list.

There was always a cavalry regiment at the barracks at Piers Hill, and in this fine corps was a nephew of General Need's, Tom Walker, who was the means of introducing us to the rest of the officers.

The gay set in Edinburgh was increased by the advent of Mr. and Mrs. Inglis, Mr. and Mrs. Horrocks, the McLeods of Harris, and others. Mr. Inglis was but a Writer to the Signet, but a hospitable man reputed to be thriving in business; his wife, sister to Mr. Stein, the rich distiller, with a sister married to General Duff, Lord Fife's brother, kept a sort of open dancing house, thus, as she fancied, ushering her two very pretty little daughters, really nice natural girls, into the world with every advantage. Her aim was to marry them well, that is, highly or wealthily. She fixed on McLeod of Harris for the younger, and got him; the elder fixed on Davidson of Tulloch for herself, and lost him.

Did I forget to name Duncan Davidson among our peculiar friends? A finer, simpler, handsomer, more attractive young man was never ruined. Spoiled by flattery, and not very judiciously managed at home, year by year with sorrow we saw him falling from the better road, till at last no one named him. He was much in love with Catherine Inglis, and there was no doubt meant to marry her. He might perhaps have turned out better had his early inclinations not been thwarted. The old stock broker was as ambitious as Mrs. Inglis, and expected a very much superior connection for his eldest son. Harris, having no father, could choose his own wife, too blind to see how very distasteful he was to her. This miserable beginning had a wretched ending hereafter. Charles McLeod, the brother, would have been more likely to take a young girl's fancy. The McLeod sisters were nothing particular. Mr. Horrocks was the very rich and extremely under bred son of a Liverpool merchant, a handsome little man married to a Glasgow beauty, a cold, reserved woman, who did not care for him a bit. They could do nothing better than give balls.

Of course Miss Baillie gave her annual *fete*, no longer an amusing one. An Ayrshire aunt had died and left her and Mrs. Cumming handsome legacies, upon the strength of which the Lady Logie came up to live in Edinburgh, and Grace Baillie bought a good house, furnished it neatly, and became quite humdrum. She had taken charge of a "decent man," for whom she wanted a proper wife—Sir Ewan Cameron of Fassiefern, made a Baronet as a mark of honor to the reputation of two, if not three, elder brothers all killed in the battlefield, leaving this poor body the only representative of the old family. She offered him both to Jane and me, and that we might not buy a pig in a poke, she paraded him several times before our windows on the opposite side of the street.

These old kind of men were beginning to fancy us. I suppose we were considered, like them, on the decline. Mr. Crawford, of Japan reputation, was seriously attracted first by one and then the other, but Jane carried the day, got all the languishing looks from such bilious eyes, an ivory fan, and the two heavy volumes of his Eastern history. A year or two after, he married Miss Perry, the Morning Chronicle, she being referred to me for his character, like a servant, and getting Mary Gillies to write to me to beg for a candid opinion of her elderly lover. When ladies arrive at asking for such opinions, one only answer can be given. Mine was highly satisfactory. We really knew no ill of the man; his appearance was the worst of him, and there was a drowned wife too, lost on her voyage home. She might have been saved on a desert island, and so start up some day like the old woman in the farce, to destroy the happiness of the younger bride and the bridegroom.

But I had an old lover all to myself, unshared with any rival, won, not by my bright eyes, but by my spirited fingers, from playing the highland marches as Lady Huntly had taught me them. Old Colonel Stuart of Garth, seventy, I should think, always in a green coat, and silver broad rimmed spectacles, was writing the history of the 42nd Regiment, and the slow Black Watch, and the quickstep of the Highland Laddie, given better, he said, than by the band of his old love, so over excited or over enchanted him that he hardly ever quitted my side, and he gave me his precious work on its publication. I had my two thick volumes too, but they were not heavy ones. He was a fine old soldier, though a little of a bore sometimes, so very enthusiastic about the deeds of his warrior country men. He never went further in his love-making than to wish he were a young man for my sake, so that Jane had the advantage over me of a real offer. As for poor little Sir Ewan, we left him to Grace Baillie.

It was a great addition to the quiet home society we were beginning to prefer to the regular gaiety, the having Mrs. Cumming settled near us. Her two elder sons had already gone out to India, Alexander in the Civil Service, Robert in the Artillery, both to Bengal. The three younger it was necessary to educate better, as it was gradually becoming more difficult to get passed through the examinations, and all were destined for the East. Besides, there was May Anne, who had hitherto, happy child, been let to run wild on the beautiful banks of the Findhorn, and who was now declared to be of an age requiring taming and training. John Peter, the third son, whom you know best as the Colonel, soon got his cadetship and sailed away to Bombay. George and Willie, intended for army surgeons, were to study medicine, and were also to have their manners formed by appearing occasionally in society.

Willie made his entrance into fashionable life at a large evening party of my mother's. He was a handsome lad, very desirous of being thought a beau, so he dressed himself in his best carefully, and noticing that all the fine young men were scented, he provided himself with a large white cotton pocket handkerchief of his mother's which he steeped in peppermint water, a large bottle of this useful corrective always standing on the chimney piece in her room. Thus perfumed, and hair and whiskers oiled and curled, Willie, in a flutter of shyness and happiness, entered our brilliant drawing rooms, when he was pounced on by Miss Shearer, the very plain sister of Mrs. James Grant, an oldish woman of no sort of fashion and cruelly marked with the small pox. "We'll keep together, Willie," said Miss Shearer, at every attempt of poor Willie's to shake himself clear of such an encumbrance in the crowd.

How Dr. Cumming laughed at these recollections when he and I met again after a lifetime's separation. Up and down this ill assorted pair paraded, Miss Shearer seeming determined to shew off her beau. "There's an extraordinary smell of peppermint here," said Lord Erskine to Mrs. Henry Siddons, as the couple turned and twirled round to pass them, Willie flourishing the large pocket handkerchief in most approved style. It was really overpowering, nor could we contrive to get rid of it, nor to detect the offending distributor of such pharmaceutical perfume, till next day, talking over the party with the Lady Logie, she enlightened us, more amused herself by the incident than almost any of the rest of us.

She was right to keep the bottle of peppermint where it could easily be found, as the sort of housekeeping she practiced must have made a frequent appeal to it necessary. She bought every Saturday a leg of mutton and a round of beef; when the one was finished, the other was begun; the leg was roasted, the round was boiled, and after the first day they were eaten cold, and served herself, her daughter, her two sons, and her two maid servants the week. There were potatoes, and in summer cabbage, and peas that rattled, in winter oranges, and by the help of the peppermint the family throve.

We never heard of illness among them; the minds expanded too, after their own queer fashion, even George, the most eccentric of human beings, doing credit to the rearing. He was so very singular in his ways, his mother was really uncertain about his getting through the college of surgeons. She made cautious enquiries now and then as to his studies, attention to lectures, notes of them, visits to the hospital, preparation for his thesis and so on, and getting very unsatisfactory replies, grew very fidgety. One day one of the medical examiners stopt her in the street to congratulate her on the admirable appearance made by her son George when he was passed at Surgeon's hall; his answers had been remarkable, and his thesis, dedicated to my father, had been No. 2 or No. 3 out of fifty. She was really amazed.

"George," said she, when they met, "when did you get your degree? When did you pass your trials?"

"Eh," said George, looking up with his most vacant expression. "Oh, just when I was ready for them."

"You never told me a word about it?"

"No? Humph, you'd have heard fast enough if I'd failed."

That was all she could get out of him; but he told us, that seeing the door of the Surgeon's hall open and finding it was an examining day, it just struck him that he would go in and get the job over; it was very easy to pass, he added. He has since at Madras risen high in his profession, been twice publicly thanked for the care of the troops, made money, married a wife; yet when he was at home on furlough he acted more like Dominie Sampson[1] than any other character ever heard of.

George Carr was also a medical student, a very attentive one, making up by diligence for no great natural capacity; he was kept in order by his sister, a young lady lately from Bath, as we were without ceasing reminded. She was a ladylike, rather nice looking person, without being at all handsome; beautifully neat and neat handed, and amiable, I believe, in her home, though dreadfully tiresome in ours; for when asked for a day, she stayed a week, sharing my small room and civilly begging the loan of pins, oils, gloves, ribbons, handkerchiefs, and other small articles with none of which I was particularly well provided, and yet none were ever returned.

We were not comfortably managed with regard to our private expenses, Jane and I. My mother bought for us what she judged necessary, and she was apt to lay out more on handsome gowns than left her sufficient for clean gloves, neat shoes, fresh flowers; a way of proceeding that greatly distressed us—distressed me at least, for I was by nature tidy, had all the Raper methodically pricknickity ways, and a five guinea blonde trimmed dress, with calico or dirty gloves and ill made shoes, made me wretched; besides, there was no pleasure in managing a wardrobe not under my own control.

Out of economy I made most of my own clothes, many of my mother's and Jane's, yet reaped no benefit from this diligence, as what I disliked was often chosen for me, and what I hated I had to wear. The extreme neatness of Miss Carr exactly suited me; all her under clothes, made by herself, were perfection; her dresses of simple materials, except such as had been presents, were well fitting and fresh, so that she looked always nicer in a room than many much more expensively attired. She had the fault of hinting for presents, but then she loved dress, she loved company, she was not very wise, and her purse was very scanty.

She amused us another way. She had such a string of lovers—had had; it was poor Miss Elphick and her early adorers over again; and if any one danced twice with her, she wriggled about like an eel when his name was mentioned. Every now and then we were informed in confidence that she was going to be married, or to try make up her mind to marry—that was the form. However, these affairs never progressed. A Mr. Lloyd did "make his offer"; mother and daughter walked up in pleased agitation to tell us. He was an ugly, little, shabby old man, a friend of Mr. Massie's, who wanted a wife and was taken with her, but when they came to particulars, there was not money enough on either side to make the connection prudent. It was a great feather though in Miss Carr's thirty year cap, and she shook it out on all occasions with much complacency.

Bessie Goodchild likewise favored us with another visit; her teeth again required attention. She did not trust to a request and a favorable answer, but very sagaciously made sure she would be welcome for three days, and then contrived one way or another to stay above a month. She was very entertaining, and made herself very agreeable to my mother with funny gossip about all the old Durham relations. She was no plague in the house, but we had been brought up too honestly to approve of her carrying tales from family to family, and mimicking the oddities of persons from whom she had received kindness.

We had an odd family party sometimes—a Carr, a Goodchild, a Gillio, and Grace Baillie who thrice a week at least walked in at dinner time. My brother's young men friends continued popping in morning and evening, when it suited them. He brought us most frequently William Gibson, Germaine Lavie, Robert Ferguson, now the superfine colonel, Mr. Beauclerk, grandson of Topham's John Dalzel, and the two Lindsays while they remained at College. Mary, now grown into a very

[1]From Scott's *Guy Mannering*.

handsome girl, did her part well in all home company. Johnny also was made a little man of; he had a tutor for Latin, attended the French and dancing classes, and read English history with Jane. We had given up all masters except the Italian and the harp, which last taught us in classes, and thereby hangs a tale.

Monsieur Elouis, the harp master, charged so high for his private lessons, that my mother suggested to him to follow the Edinburgh fashion of classes at so much a quarter, three lessons a week. He made quite a fortune. There were eight pupils in a Class, the lessons lasting two hours. We three, the two Hunters, Grace Stein, afterwards Lady Don, Amelia Gillio and Catherine Inglis were his best scholars. We played concerted pieces doubling the parts. Chorus's arranged by him, and sometimes duets or solos, practicing in other rooms. The fame of our execution spread over the town, and many persons entreated permission to mount up the long common stair to the poor Frenchman's garret to listen to such a number of harps played by such handsome girls. One or two of the mamas would have had no objection, but my mother and Lady Hunter would not hear of their daughters being part of an exhibition. We went there to learn, not to shew off.

Miss Elphick, too, had her own ideas upon the subject. She always went with us, and was extremely annoyed by the group of young men so frequently happening to pass down the street just at the time our class dispersed, some of them our dancing partners, so that there were bows and speeches and attendance home, much to her disgust. She waited once or twice till the Second Class assembled, but the beaux waited too. So then she carried us all of a quarter of an hour too soon, leaving our five companions to their fate; and this not answering long, she set to scold Monsieur Elouis, and called the Edinburgh gentlemen all sorts of vile names.

In the midst of her season of wrath the door of our music room opened one day, and a very large fine looking military man, braided and belted and mustached, entered and was invited to be seated. Every harp was silent.

"Mesdemoiselles," said Monsieur Elouis with his most polished air of command, "recommence if you please; this gentleman is my most particular friend, a musical amateur, etc."

Miss Elphick was all in a flame; up she rose, up she made us rise, gather our music together, and driving us and Amelia Gillio before her, we were shawled and bonneted in less time than I am writing of it, and on our way down stairs before poor Monsieur had finished his apologies to the officer and the other young ladies. Never was little woman in such a fury.

We never returned to the harp classes, neither did the Hunters, and very soon they were given up. It was certainly an unwarrantable liberty, an impertinence, and the man must either have been totally unaware of the sort of pupils he was to find, or else an ill-bred ignorant person. Poor Elouis never recovered the mistake; he had to leave for want of business.

Margaret Gillio and I went shares in another master, mistress rather. She had a sweet, flexible, bird like voice and sang her little English ballads very prettily. I tried higher flights, but my singing was very so so till we had some lessons from Mrs. Bianchi Lacey. She came with her husband and her apprentice, a Miss Simmons, to give a concert or two and take a few pupils by the way. The concerts were delightful, the three sang so well together, the music they gave us was so good, and it was all so simply done; her pianoforte the only accompaniment, and in the small Assembly room so that they were perfectly heard. It was a style of singing, hers, that we may call peculiarly ladylike; no very powerful voice, and it was now going, for she was no longer young; still it was round and true and sweet in the upper notes, and the finish of her whole song, the neatness of every passage, the perfect expression she gave both to music and words, was all new to me. I could now understand it, and it gave to me a different notion of the art from any that had ever entered into my head before.

The first concert she gave we were so much amused with old Sir John Hay, one of the directors, squiring her about, bringing her negus,[1] a shawl, a chair, and what not, and my brother William doing ditto by Miss Simmons, that the first song by that young lady, "*H*angels ever bright and fair," she was Birmingham, made less impression than it should have done, for her voice was splendid. We never heard what became of her; she was pretty, so perhaps she married a pinmaker and led a private, instead of a hazardous public, life. But the moment Mr. Lacey and his wife began their delightful duets we had ears for none else. My father offered me a dozen lessons. We had time for only ten—all, I may say, I ever got—but we went to her three concerts. They dined with us twice, and sang as much as we liked, and my mother gave an evening party for them at which their singing enchanted every body. It was essentially suited to the drawing room.

She was taught by old Bianchi, who made her a perfect musician. She played admirably and had a thorough knowledge of the science. She was his apprentice and he married her. After a short widowhood she rather threw herself away on too young a husband, a very vulgar man with so much presumption of manner as to keep one in a fright lest he should commit some atrocity. It was like sitting on needles and pins, that young monkey our brother Johnny said, to sit in company with him. However, he never offended, and if he had, his fine voice would have secured his pardon.

Mrs. Lacey took a fancy to me, gave me extra long lessons, and the kindest directions for the management of my voice in her absence. She was very particular about the erect position of the head and chest, the smile with which the mouth was to be opened, the clear pronunciation of every word. She gave me a set of exercises to develop the powers of the voice, every tone, every half tone being brought out in every one of them; the inequalities were to be carefully marked and carefully improved. When we came to songs, she made me study one. First the poet's meaning; his intentions were to be accurately ascertained, as accurately expressed aided by the music, which was to accompany the words and follow out the idea. In fact the song was to be acted.

Next it was to be embellished with a few occasional graces, very neatly executed, applied in fit pauses, the whole got up so perfectly as to be poured forth with ease, any effort, such as straining or forcing the voice or unduly emphasizing a passage, being altogether so much out of taste as to produce pain instead of pleasure. Lastly she bid me practice what I liked, but never inflict on other ears what was not completely within my compass—no effort to myself. I owed her much, very much, and yet she did not teach me singing, at least not altogether. Her valuable advice, and her care of the form of the mouth, were the foundation of my after fame. My finishing instructress was Mrs. Robert Campbell. She and her sister Mrs. James Hamilton were two little Jewesses four feet high, whose father had been Consul at some of the Italian ports.

One evening, at a small party at Mrs. Munro's, Mrs. Robert Campbell sang a simple Italian ballad so beautifully, so exactly according to Mrs. Lacey's rules, it was all so easy, so satisfying, my lesson in singing was then, I felt, given me. She was encored by acclamation; this enabled me to follow every note. On going home I sat down to the piano forte, sang the ballad myself with every little grace that she had given it, next day repeated it, took another from a store sent us by Eliza Cottam, Ironside, then decorated it after my own taste, got every little turn to flow as from a flute, and in the evening treated my father to both. His surprise was only equaled by his extreme pleasure. It seemed to be the height of his musical expectations. However, we did more for him than that. He really loved music, he loved us and was

[1] A spiced wine and hot water.

proud of us, and though he could sternly express his dissatisfaction, he was no niggard of praise when praise was due. We worked with a heart for a person so discriminating.

Mr. Loder brought an opera company with him, and gave, not whole operas, he had not strength enough for that, but very well got up scenes from several most in favor. It was a most agreeable variety in a place where public amusements were but scantily supplied to the inhabitants. We had de Begnis and his wife, and scenes from Figaro, Don Giovanni, etc.; the rest of the artists were very fair, but I forget their names.

Going into a music shop we saw on the counter two numbers of a new work—the opera of Don Juan arranged for two performers on the pianoforte; the first attempt in a kind that had such success, and that brought real good music within the power of the family circle. We secured our prize, Jane and I, hurried home, tried the first Scena, were delighted, gave a week to private, very diligent study, and when we had it all by heart, the first afternoon my father came up to spend the gloaming napping in an easy chair, we arrested his sleepy fit by "notte e giorno," to his amazement. He liked our opera better, I think, than "Sul margine dun rio" or "Ninetta cara," for we had so lately heard all the airs we played that we were quite up to the proper style, and had ourselves all the desire in the world to give the music we loved the expression intended by our then favorite composer, Mozart.

William also began to try a few tenor duets with me. Mrs. Lacey had taken the trouble to teach him half a dozen for love. It is surprising how well he could do both tender and buffo. His ear either was slightly defective naturally, or from want of early exercise; this made it difficult to keep his voice in order, otherwise he was a most agreeable singer, and once set out kept the key well, but after a pause might begin flat again, never sharp luckily. Really our home concerts, with Mary Dalzel's help, were very much applauded by our partial audience.

Edinburgh did not afford much public amusement. Except these operas which were a chance, a stray concert now and then, catches and glees being the most popular, and the six Assemblies, there were none other. The Assemblies were very ill attended, the small room never half full, the large, which held with ease twelve hundred people, was never entered except upon occasion of the Caledonian Hunt Ball, when the members presented the tickets, and their friends graciously accepted the free entertainment. The very crowded dances at home, inconvenient, and troublesome and expensive as they were, seemed to be more popular than those easy balls, where for five shillings we had space, spring, a full orchestra, and plenty of slight refreshments.

I heard afterwards that as private houses became more fully and handsomely furnished, the fashion of attending the Assemblies revived. McLeod of Harris did a very sensible thing the winter he married poor, pretty little Richmond Inglis. They were living with her father and mother, and so very much invited out that he did not think Mrs. Inglis' perpetual entertainments sufficient return for the many civilities he and his young wife had received. He therefore hired Smart's rooms where the dancing master had his Academy, asked every one he knew far and near, contracted for a supper, and gave the best ball I was ever at in my young days; a ball that finally established waltzing among us. This much persecuted dance had been struggling on for a season, gaining far less ground than the quadrilles; but a strong band mustering on this occasion, the very "propers" gave in as by magic touch, and the whole large room was one whirligig. Harris himself danced for the first time at his own ball, and beautifully; his brother Charles was the Vestris of our Society—acknowledged. The Laird was even more graceful in his movements.

"Ah," said poor Richmond, "if I had ever seen my husband dance, Mama would not have found it so difficult to get me to marry him."

She saw his perfections too late, I fancy, for she left him and seven children afterwards.

## WILLIAM MOTHERWELL (1797–1835)

### Jeannie Morrison

I've wandered east, I've wandered west,
Through mony a weary way;
But never, never can forget
The luve o' life's young day.
The fire that's blawn on Beltane* e'en, May-day
May weel be black gin Yule;
But blacker fa' awaits the heart
Where first fond luve grows cool.

Oh dear, dear Jeannie Morrison,
The thochts o' bygane years
Still fling their shadows ower my path,
And blind my een wi' tears.
They blind my een wi' saut, saut tears,
And sair and sick I pine,
As memory idly summons up
The blithe blinks o' longsyne.

Twas then we luvit ilk* ither weel, each
Twas then we twa did part.
Sweet time—sad time—twa bairns at scule.
Twa bairns, and but ae heart.
Twas then we sat on ae laugh bink*, bench
To leir* ilk ither lear; "learn" (teach)
And tones, and looks, and smiles were shed,
Remembered evermair.

I wonder, Jeannie, aften yet
When sitting on that bink,
Cheek touchin' cheek, loof* locked in loof, palm
What our wee heads could think.
When baith bent doun ower ae braid page,
Wi' ae buik on our knee
Thy lips were on thy lesson, but
My lesson was in thee.

Oh, mind ye how we hung our heads,
How cheeks brent red wi' shame,
Whene'er the school-weans laughin' said,
We cleeked[1] thegither hame?
And mind ye o' the Saturdays
(The scule then skail't* at noon) broke up

[1] Walked arm in arm.

When we ran aff to speel* the braes— climb
The broomy braes o' June?

My head rins round and round about,
My heart flows like a sea,
As ane by ane the thochts rush back
O' scule-time and o' thee.
Oh, mornin' life, oh, mornin' luve.
Oh lichtsome days and lang,
When hinnied* hopes around our hearts, "honied"
Like simmer blossoms sprang.

O mind ye, luve, how aft we left
The deavin'*, dinsome* toun, deafening/noisy
To wander by the green burnside,
And hear its waters croon.
The simmer leaves hung ower our heads,
The flowers burst round our feet,
And in the gloamin' o' the wood,
The throssil whusslit sweet.

The throssil whusslit in the wood,
The burn sang to the trees,
And we with Nature's heart in tune,
Concerted harmonies.
And on the knowe abune the burn,
For hours thegither sat
In the silentness o' joy, till baith
Wi' very gladness grat*. wept

Aye, aye, dear Jeannie Morrison,
Tears trinkled down your cheek,
Like dew-beads from a rose, yet nane
Had ony power to speak.
That was a time, a blessed time,
When hearts were fresh and young,
When freely gushed all feelings forth,
Unsyllabled—unsung.

I marvel, Jeannie Morrison,
Gin* I hae been to thee if
As closely twined wi' earliest thochts
As ye hae been to me?
Oh, tell me gin their music fills
Thine ear as it does mine.
Oh, say gin e'er your heart grows grit* "great"
Wi' dreamings o' Langsyne?

I've wandered east, I've wandered west,
I've borne a weary lot;
But in my wanderings, far or near,
Ye never were forgot.
The fount that first burst frae this heart,

Still travels on its way;
And channels deeper as it rins,
The luve o' life's young day.

O dear, dear Jeannie Morrison,
Since we were sindered young,
I've never seen your face, nor heard
The music o' your tongue;
But I could hug all wretchedness,
And happy could I die,
Did I but ken your heart still dreamed
O' bygane days and me.

## Song

If to thy heart I were as near
As thou art near to mine,
I'd hardly care though a' the year
Nae sun on earth suld shine, my dear,
Nae sun on earth suld shine.

Twin starnies are thy glancin' een—
A warld they'd licht and mair—
And gin that ye be my Christine,
Ae blink to me ye'll spare, my dear,
Ae blink to me ye'll spare.

My leesome* May I've wooed too lang— pleasant
Aneath the trystin' tree,
I've sung till a' the plantin' rang,
Wi' lays o' love for thee, my dear,
Wi' lays o' love for thee.

The dew-draps glisten on the green,
The laverocks lilt on high,
We'll forth and doun the loan*, Christine, "lane"
And kiss when nane is nigh, my dear,
And kiss when nane is nigh.

## The Wooing Song of Jarl Egill Skallagrim

Bright maiden of Orkney,
Star of the blue sea,
I've swept o'er the waters
To gaze upon thee;
I've left spoil and slaughter,
I've left a far strand,
To sing how I love thee,
To kiss thy small hand,
Fair daughter of Einar,
Golden haired maid.
The lord of yon brown bark,
And lord of this blade;

The joy of the ocean—
Of warfare and wind,
Hath boune him to woo thee,
And thou must be kind.
So stoutly Jarl Egill wooed Torf Einar's daughter.

In Jutland—in Iceland
On Neustria's shore,
Where'er the dark billow
My gallant bark bore,
Songs spoke of thy beauty,
Harps sounded thy praise,
And my heart loved thee long ere
It thrilled in thy gaze;
Ay, daughter of Einar,
Right tall may'st thou stand,
It is a Vikingir
Who kisses thy hand.
It is a Vikingir
That bends his proud knee,
And swears by Great Freya,
His bride thou must be.
So Jarl Egill swore when his great heart was fullest.

Thy white arms are locked in
Broad bracelets of gold;
Thy girdle-stead's gleaming
With treasures untold.
The circlet that binds up
Thy long yellow hair,
Is starred thick with jewels,
That bright are and rare.
But gifts yet more princely
Jarl Egill bestows,
For girdle, his great arm
Around thee he throws;
The bark of a sea-king
For palace, gives he,
While mad waves and winds shall
Thy true subjects be.
So richly Jarl Egill endowed his bright bride.

Nay, frown not, nor shrink thus,
Nor toss so thy head,
Tis a Vikingir asks thee,
Land-maiden, to wed.
He skills not to woo thee,
In trembling and fear,
Though lords of the land may
Thus troop with the deer.
The cradle he rocked in
So sound and so long,
Hath framed him a heart

And a hand that are strong.
He comes then as Jarl should,
Sword belted to side,
To win thee and wear thee
With glory and pride.
So sternly Jarl Egill wooed, and smote his long brand.

Thy father, thy bretheren,
Thy kin keep from me,
The maiden I've sworn shall
Be Queen of the sea.
A truce with that folly—
Yon sea-strand can show
If this eye missed its aim,
Or this arm failed its blow.
I had not well taken
Three strides on this land
Ere a Jarl and his six sons
In death bit the sand.
May, weep not, pale maid, though
In battle should fall
The kemps who would keep thy
Bridegroom from the hall.
So carped Jarl Egill, and kissed the bright weeper.

Through shadows and horrors
In worlds underground,
Through sounds that appall
And through sights that confound,
I sought the weird women
Within their dark cell,
And made them surrender
Futurity's spell.
I made them rune over
The dim scroll so free,
And mutter how fate sped
With lovers like me.
Yes, maiden, I forced them
To read forth my doom,
To say how I should fare
As jolly bridegroom.
So Jarl Egill's love dared the world of grim shadows.

They waxed and they waned,
They passed to and fro,
While lurid fires gleamed o'er
Their faces of snow.
Their stony eyes moveless,
Did glare on me long,
Then sullen they chanted:
"The sword and the song
Prevail with the gentle,
Sore chasten the rude,

And sway to their purpose
Each evil-shaped mood!"
Fair daughter of Einar,
I've sung the dark lay
That the weird sisters runed, and
Which thou must obey.
So fondly Jarl Egill loved Einar's proud daughter.

The curl of that proud lip,
The flash of that eye,
The swell of that bosom,
So full and so high,
Like foam of sea-billow,
Thy white bosom shows,
Like flash of red levin* lightning
Thine eagle eye glows.
Ha! firmly and boldly,
So stately and free,
Thy foot treads this chamber,
As bark rides the sea.
This likes me—this likes me,
Stout maiden of mold*, (earth)
Thou wooest to purpose;
Bold hearts love the bold.
So shouted Jarl Egill, and clutched the proud maiden.

Away and away then,
I have thy small hand;
Joy with me—our tall bark
Now bears toward the strand.
I call it The Raven,
The wing of black night,
That shadows forth ruin
O'er islands of light.
Once more on its long deck,
Behind us the gale,
Thou shalt see how before it
Great kingdoms do quail.
Thou shalt see then how truly
My noble-souled maid,
The ransom of kings can
Be won by this blade.
So bravely Jarl Egill did soothe the pale trembler.

Ay, gaze on its large hilt,
One wedge of red gold;
But doat on its blade, gilt
With blood of the bold.
The hilt is right seemly,
But nobler the blade,
That swart Velint's hammer
With cunning spells made.
I call it the Adder,

Death lurks in its bite,
Through bone and proof-harness
It scatters pale light.
Fair daughter of Einar,
Deem high of the fate
That makes thee, like this blade
Proud Egill's loved mate.
So Jarl Egill bore off Torf Einar's bright daughter.

## They Come, the Merry Summer Months

They come, the merry summer months of beauty, song, and flowers;
They come, the gladsome months that bring thick leafiness to bowers.
Up, up, my heart, and walk abroad; fling cark and care aside;
Seek silent hills, or rest thyself where peaceful waters glide;
Or, underneath the shadow vast of patriarchal tree,
Scan through its leaves the cloudless sky in rapt tranquillity.

The grass is soft, its velvet touch is grateful to the hand;
And, like the kiss of maiden love, the breeze is sweet and bland;
The daisy and the buttercup are nodding courteously;
It stirs their blood with kindest love, to bless and welcome thee;
And mark how with thine own thin locks—they now are silvery gray—
That blissful breeze is wantoning, and whispering, "Be gay."

There is no cloud that sails along the ocean of yon sky
But hath its own winged mariners to give it melody;
Thou seest their glittering fans outspread, all gleaming like red gold;
And hark, with shrill pipe musical, their merry course they hold.
God bless them all, those little ones, who, far above this earth,
Can make a scoff of its mean joys, and vent a nobler mirth.

But soft, mine ear upcaught a sound—from yonder wood it came.
The spirit of the dim green glade did breathe his own glad name.
Yes, it is he, the hermit bird, that, apart from all his kind,
Slow spells his beads monotonous to the soft western wind.
Cuckoo! Cuckoo! he sings again—his notes are void of art;
But simplest strains do soonest sound the deep founts of the heart.

Good Lord! it is a gracious boon for thought-crazed wight like me,
To smell again these summer flowers beneath this summer tree.
To suck once more in every breath their little souls away,
And feed my fancy with fond dreams of youth's bright summer day,
When, rushing forth like untamed colt, the reckless, truant boy
Wandered through greenwoods all day long, a mighty heart of joy.

I'm sadder now—I have had cause—but O, I'm proud to think
That each pure joy-fount, loved of yore, I yet delight to drink;
Leaf, blossom, blade, hill, valley, stream, the calm, unclouded sky,
Still mingle music with my dreams, as in the days gone by.
When summer's loveliness and light fall round me dark and cold,
I'll bear indeed life's heaviest curse—a heart that hath waxed old.

## The Mermaiden

"The night is mirk, and the wind blaws shill,
And the white faem weets my bree,
And my mind misgi'es me, gay maiden,
That the land we sall never see."
Then up and spak the mermaiden,
And she spak blithe and free,
"I never said to my bonny bridegroom,
That on land we sud weddit be.

"Oh I never said that ane earthly priest
Our bridal blessing should gie,
And I never said that a landwart bouer
Should hald my luve and me."
"And whare is that priest, my bonny maiden,
If ane earthly wicht is na he?"
"Oh, the wind will sough*, and the sea will rair, swoosh
When weddit we twa sall be."

"And where is that bouer, my bonnie maiden,
If on land it sudna be?"
"Oh, my blithe bouer is low," said the mermaiden,
"In the bonny green howes* o' the sea. depths
My gay bouer is bigit* o' the gude ships' keels, built
And the banes o' the drowned at sea.
The fish are the deer that fill my parks,
And the water waste my dowry.

"And my bouer is sklaitit* wi' the big blue waves, sprinkled
And paved wi' the yellow sand;
And in my chaumers* grow bonnie white flowers "chambers"
That never grew on land.
And have ye e'er seen, my bonnie bridegroom,
A leman* on earth that wud gie mistress
Acre for acre o' the red plowed land,
As I'll gie to thee o' the sea?

"The moon will rise in half ane hour,
And the wee bricht sternes will shine;
Then we'll sink to my bouer neath the wan water
Full fifty fathom and nine."
A wild, wild screech gied the fey bridegroom,
And a loud, loud laugh the bride;
For the moon raise up, and the twa sank down
Under the silvered tide.

## The Ettin o' Sillarwood

"O Sillarwood, sweet Sillarwood,
Gin Sillarwood were mine,
I'd big* a bouir in Sillarwood build
And theik* it ower wi' thyme. thatch

At ilka door and ilka bore* hole, window
The red red rose wud shine."

It's up and sang the bonnie bird
Upon her milk-white hand:
"I wudna lig in Sillarwood,
For all a gude Earl's land.
I wudna sing in Sillarwood,
Though gowden glist* ilk wand. glittered

"The wild boar rakes* in Sillarwood, roams
The buck drives through the shaw*, wood
And simmer woos the Southern wind
Through Sillarwood to blaw:

Through Sillarwood, sweet Sillarwood,
The deer-hounds run so free;
But the hunter stark of Sillarwood
An Ettin* lang is he." evil spirit

"O, Sillarwood, sweet Sillarwood,"
Fair Marjorie did sing,
"On the tallest tree in Sillarwood
That Ettin lang will hing."

The Southern wind it blaws fu' saft,
And Sillarwood is near;
Fair Marjorie's sang in Sillarwood
The stark hunter did hear.

He band his deer-hounds in their leash,
Set his bow against a tree,
And three blasts on his horn has brocbt
The wood-elf to his knee.

"Gae bring to me a shapely weed
Of silver and of gold,
Gae bring to me as stark a steed
As ever stept on mold;
For I maun ride frae Sillarwood
This fair maid to behold."

The wood-elf twisted sunbeams red
Into a shapely weed;
And the tallest birk in Sillarwood
He hewed into a steed,—
And shod it wi' the burning gold
To glance like ony glede*. spark

The Ettin shook his bridle-reins
And merrily they rung,
For four-and-twenty sillar bells
On ilka side were hung.

The Ettin rade, and better rade,
Some thretty miles and three;
A bugle-horn hung at his breast,
A lang sword at his knee:
"I wud I met," said the Ettin lang,
"The maiden Marjorie."

The Ettin rade and better rade
Till he has reached her bouir;
And there he saw fair Marjorie
As bricht as lily flouir.

"O Sillarwood, Sweet Sillarwood,
Gin Sillarwood were mine,
The sleuthest* hawk o' Sillarwood    laziest
On dainty flesh wud dine."

"Weel met, weel met," the Ettin said,
"For ae kiss o' thy chin,
I'll welcome thee to Sillarwood
And a' that grows therein."

"If ye may leese* me Sillarwood,    (allow)
Wi' a' that grows therein,
Ye're free to kiss my cheek," she said,
"Ye're free to kiss my chin:
The Knicht that hechts* me Sillarwood    promises
My maiden thocht sal win.

"My luve I've laid on Sillarwood,
Its bonnie aiken* tree;    "oaken"
And gin that I hae Sillarwood
I'll link* alang wi' thee."    walk arm in arm

Then on she put her green mantel
Weel furred wi' minivere;
Then on she put her velvet shoon,
The silver shining clear:

She proudly vaulted on the black,
He bounded on the bay—
The stateliest pair that ever took
To Sillarwood their way.

It's up and sang the gentle bird
On Marjorie's fair hand,
"I wudna wend to Sillarwood
For a' its timbered land;
Nor wud I lig* in Sillarwood    lie
Though gowden glist ilk wand!

"The Hunters chase through Sillarwood
The playfu' herte and rae*:    "roe"

Nae maiden that socht Sillarwood
Ere back was seen to gae!"

The Ettin leuch, the Ettin sang,
He whistled merrily:
"If sic a bird," he said, "were mine,
I'd hing it on a tree."

"Were I the Lady Marjorie,
Thou hunter fair but free,
My horse's head I'd turn about
And think nae mair o' thee."

It's on they rade, and better rade—
They shimmered in the sun;
Twas sick and sair grew Marjorie
Lang ere that ride was done.

Yet on they rade and better rade—
They neared the Cross o' stane;
The tall Knicht when he passed it by
Felt cauld in every bane.

But on they rade and better rade:—
It ever grew mair mirk:
O loud, loud nichered the bay steed
As they passed Mary's Kirk.

"I'm weary o' this eerie road,"
Maid Marjorie did say,
"We canna weel get Sillarwood
Afore the set o' day!"

"It's no the sinkin' o' the sun
That gloamin's sae the ground;
The heicht it is o' Sillarwood
That shadows a' around."

"Methocht Sir Knicht, broad Sillarwood
A pleasant bield* wud be, shelter
Wi' nuts on ilka hazel bush,
And birds on ilka tree;
But oh, the dimness o' this wood
Is terrible to me."

"The trees ye see seem wondrous big,
The branches wondrous braid;
Then marvel nae if sad suld be
The path we hae to tread."

Thick grew the air, thick grew the trees,
Thick hung the leaves around;
And deeper did the Ettin's voice

In the dread dimness sound.
"I think," said Maiden Marjorie,
"I hear a horn and hound."

"Ye weel may hear the hound," he said,
"Ye weel may hear the horn;
For I can hear the wild halloo
That freichts the face o' morn.

"The Hunters fell o' Sillarwood
Hae packs full fifty-three:
They hunt all day, they hung all nicht—
They never bow* an ee. (close)

"The Hunters fell o' Sillarwood,
Hae steeds but* blude or bane. without
They bear fiert* maidens to a weird* proud/fate
Where mercy there is nane.

"And I, the Laird o' Sillarwood
Hae beds baith deep and wide,
(Of clay-cauld earth) where to streik* stretch
A proud and dainty bride.

"Ho! look beside yon bonny birk,
The latest blink o' day
Is gleamin' on a comely heap
Of freshly dug red clay.

"Riecht cunning hands they were that digged
Forenent the birken tree,
Where every leaf that draps, frore maid
Will piece a shroud for thee:
It's they can lie on lily breast
As they can lie on lea.

"And they will hap thy lily breist
Till flesh fa's aff the bane,
Nor tell thy feres how Marjorie
To Sillarwood hath gane.

"Thy bed is strewed, Maid Marjorie,
Wi' bracken and wi' brier;
And ne'er will gray cock clarion wind
For ane that slumbers here.
Ye wedded hae the Ettin stark,—
He rules the Realms of Fear."

## The Fit Shaking

Sober thoughts on men and things by me, Peter Pirnie, Esq., late manufacturer (now retired from public life on a sma competency) umquhyle a bailie, &c., &c., of Paisley.

[This is an anecdote from Motherwell's Galt-like sketch, *Memoirs of a Paisley Bailie*, which was itself printed in a Scottish miscellany entitled *The Laird of Logan*, edited in 1868 by John Carrick.]

### Chapter I: Me and the public.

There will, no doubt, be an uncommon clatter amang the Corks of the Causeyside, as weel as upon the plainstanes at the Corse, and amang all the members of the pap-in clubs that forgether in the Water-Wynd, now called St. Mirren Street, or in the Town's House, where the bailies and other ostensible and 'sponsible persons meet at orra[1] times to weet their whistle, when it is known and understood that I have taen pen in hand to write my ain life, and to enlichten all and sindry anent my manifold experiences of men and things, seasoned with suitable reflections on passing occurrents.

### Chapter II: The Fashes,[2] Fykes, and Downdraughts o' Office.

When I was in the Magistracy at a very troublesome time, I was sair fashit with the dounricht lies that were told against me, but I had just to put a stout heart to a stey[3] brae, and do my duty, in spite of man or deevil. Hech, Sirs, what an awsum weight of duty and dignity is sometimes laid upon the head and shouthers of ane efficient magistrate in perilous times! But on this point I have a word or twa to say when in due course of time and of nature I was eleckit a Bailie, and took upon me the discharge of the duties thereunto effeiring, as the Town Clerk said when he clapt a cocked hat for the first time on my beld pow,[4] and shaking me by the nieve[5] added, that I was the fountain of all justice and a ruler in the land, which was naething mair than a simple condescendence of facks.

I am obligated further to remark, that naebody, man, woman, or wean, can say, or allege, that I ever socht, in the lang course of my useful and busy life, to rooze[6] mysel and my actions at the expense of my neibors. Backbiters and siclike garbage of humanity, I hold in great detestation. They think, puir born fools that they are, that, by pulling anither doun, they will rise themsels. They may be as illdeedy as a twa hornit deel, and yet, after all, they are but sumphs and gomerils. A backbiter or cat-witted creature, that spends his time in picking out and railing against the faults and frailties of others, may jalouse[7] that, by spitting upon their character, he is bigging up a bonny bield[8] of goodly thochts for himsel in the minds of his hearers, but he is out of his reckoning as far as ever Captain Parry was, when he thocht to tumble the wulcat at the North Pole. He'll aye be suspeckit and keepit at arms length. Sweet is the treason, but foul is the traitor. The backbiter is like a leper: he has aye a clapper

---

[1] Odd.

[2] Troubles.

[3] Steep.

[4] Head.

[5] Hand.

[6] Praise.

[7] Suspect.

[8] Shelter.

to warn others of his infection, and that is, his ain ill scrapit and venomous tongue.

It has been my constant endeavor to sook the marrow of reflection out of every circumstance and accident of life; and, as weel as I could, to preserve, above all, an even mind and a resigned speerit. Fiery tempered bodies aye get into a carfuffle about trifles; but I never saw ony good come of losing temper about what it was out of the power of man to mend or prevent. "To jouk[1] and let the jaw gang by," is an auld proverb, though it may not be in Davie Lindsay; and, "what cannot be mendit suld be soon endit," is anither. My puir faither, that's deid and gane, and laid in the mools[2] mony a year syne, was a deacon at proverbs, and, saving some pickles[3] of warldly wisdom of that sort, education I never had till I wrocht to put mysel to the schule, when I got on like a house in fire, and ran through the wee spell like a lamplichter, which was an uncommon thing for a bairn o' my years.

Chapter III: Observes, mair particular on book inditing.

When Solomon delivered his opingyon anent book-manufacturing, with some thing mair of bitterness than a body could expeck from ane that has written meikle and no leetle himsel, has not stated his balance-sheet fairly; for ye see he has lost sicht of the credit-side of the account a'thegither. He has forgot to balance the weariness of the flesh, with the pleasour whilk every sensible mind feels when, day by day, and page by page, it beholds the works of its individual hands prospering and increasing; and the images, and creations, and visions of the brain assuming a tangible shape, whereby they can influence and direck other minds, and be as eternal finger-posts in the paths of learning and virtue for generations after generations, to guide them in their search after the wells of divine truth and universal benevolence. It does not come weel aff ane like me to differ with a greater and a better man than mysel—ane that was a crownit king, and ruled over a powerful and singular people; and ane whase name rang frae the outermost end of Ethiopia to the far'est bounds of Assyria (marching as I would jalouse, with the Chinese dyke), as renowned for natural wisdom and acquired knowledge; while I, at the heichest pitch of my earthly dignity, was naething mair than the first Bailie of a great manufacturing and intelligent town, and wauked and sleeped for full twa years with a gowd chain, significant of authority, about my neck, and my name and reputation was soundit nae far'er nor Glasgow or Embro, Manchester, or, aiblins,[4] Lunnun.

I will confess that my ain gratification has had no inconsiderable weight with me in becoming an author. Books are a sort of passport to worldly immortality. Bairns may keep up a name, but they cannot maintain the fame of ane that has actit his part like a man in this theater of the world. I have liked weel to hear poets and sang-writers express themsels feelingly, on this natural passion of man's heart. Really, without a sark to their back, a bite in their belly, or a saxpence in their pouch, I have heard, in my time, some of them speak like Emperors about the way they wud be idoleezed by after ages.

Puir creatures! my heart bled for them and their dreams, and aften hae I stappit a sma' trifle intil their loof,[5] just that they micht not die of downright starvation. They aye received it as a lend, and looked as proud as gin they had obleegit me by taking it; however, their term-day never cam roun', and I didna mind, as the siller was never posted in ony ither way in my books, than as "incidents disbursed." But some of the

---

[1]Duck, take evasive action.

[2]"Molds" (earth).

[3]Bits.

[4]Perhaps.

[5]Palm.

words of these flichty creatures stuck to my memory; for, fou or sober, they had aye some glimpses of a deep-searching wisdom into human nature and feelings, very profitable for a man of my understanding to ponder upon, after warehouse hours and the cares of the day were bye.

Chapter IV: Just before I hae done wi' mysel.

There is anither observe which I think I am enteetlit to mak, and that is that it is an uncommon fine thing in itsel, for a man, in the fall of his days, to meditate upon his bypast life, and the uncos[1] thereof, its lichts and its shadows, and all its turnings and windings. For my ain individual part, I may well repeat, as I have before observed, that meikle have I seen, and meikle have I learned, in this idle stramash, and that, being of an observing turn, my hope is, that every change in the crook of my lot has not owerslided without improvement.

I will not say I would be living and life-like at this moment of time, presently occupied in endyting my ain life, in my cozy back parlor, whilk looks into a pleesant bit garden weel plenished wi' vegetables, sic as leeks, cabbage, green kail, turnips and carrots, forbye pinks, sweet-williams, roses and lilies, and other savory herbs, and sax grosset-busses as round as a bee's skep, and, without leeing, ilka ane the bouk of a rick of hay, wi' twa apple trees, a pear tree, a geen tree, and some ither bonny things that needna be named, over and above a fine sundial, standing in the center of the middle walk, the whilk is nicely laid wi gravel and white chuckey stanes, and bordered with bachelors buttons, daisies, boxwood, spearmint and rosemary, the smell whereof is very pleesant and refreshing in the callerness[2] of morning, or the saftness of the gloamin.

Such are a few of the digested reasons which have promuved me to turn author in my auld days; and, having told the public who I am and what I mean to do, I shall cease my labors for the present, and, in my second chapter, enter at ance into particulars, like a man of business habits.

Chapter V: Amang my first public concernments in a magisterial capacity.

A shaking o' the feet was proposed at a county meeting, to relieve thae puir bodies that are thrown on their ain shifts, and can neither work nor want; and also to afford a mouthfu', in the mean time, to creatures flesh and bluid, like oursels, wha are willing to work, but canna find a maister. This grand fit-shaking, or ball, as it was phrased, was proposed, at a County Meeting, and was patroneesed by all the principal folks in the town, and there was an unco talk about this lord and that lady being sure to be there, till the hail place was in a perfect fizz, frae the east till the west toll—frae the head of the Causeyside till the Score. It's impossible to tell you the forenoon visits amang the leddies, and the bit quiet cracks[3] amang the gentlemen ower an afternoon's glass anent it.

As for me, I keepit a gayen quiet sough for a while, no wantin to take a lead in the matter; and, indeed, sic sichts were, in comparison, neathing to me, that had rubbed shouthers with the first nobility in the land, forbye seen the king, as is written in my life; but it was quite different with my wife, that hadna seen ony sic grand ado's; and as for our son, Tummas, and my oldest dochter, Miss Jean, that had just got a finishing touch at a fashionable schule in Embro, and could sing like a linty, loup like a maukin,[4] and play on the piano to the bargain, they were neither to hand

---

[1] Strange events.

[2] Freshness.

[3] Chats.

[4] Hare.

nor bind. They insisted that they should be allowit to show aff their new steps, and they said it was expeckit by the hail respectable inhabitants of the toun, that Bailie Pirnie should countenance the assembly, seeing that the magistrates had sic a lang finger in the pie.

Of coorse it was out of the power of flesh to stand against their chaunering, mair especially as afore they spoke I had coft[1] four tickets, just for the credit of the thing, but no intending to gane—nor would I hae set mysel forrit on the occasion, had it no been looked for by the public—this is a positive fack, and my being there was no piece of ostentation; for sic a thing is no in my hail corporation, as ye may have observed frae first to last in my written buke.

To me, as the faither of a family and the head of a house, it was the soorce of no small contentment to be the means, in an honest way, of adding to the innocent pleasures of my wife and bairns; and really, when I tauld them it was my final determination that the gudewife should hae her ain say in the matter, and that the family should appear in sic state and grandeur at the ball, as effeired to their station in society, I was downright worried with kindness. The young things danced round me as gin they were clean gaen gyte, and nearly grat[2] for fainness, and the worthy and virtuous partner of my bosom and bedfellow said no a word, but just gave me ane o' the auld langsyne blinks[3] of affection, when we first forgathered as lad and lass, and used to take a bit daiker to the country, to see how the gowans and the gerss were growing, and the birds singing in the woods. In a simmer Saturday's afternoon. Hech, sirs, it's mony a year sinsyne; but the memories of these sweet days of youth never die in the heart, that has truly and purely luved, as me and my wife have done.

### Chapter VI: Doings about the family braws.

Kenning fu' weel that our house would, as a matter of needcessity, be turned upside doun, for a day or twa, with mantua-makers, tailors, milliners, shoemakers, bonnet-makers, and siclike clamjamfry, making new dresses and ither necessars for our domestic establishment, I thocht it behooved me to give mysel a day's recreation or twa by visiting a freend either in Greenock or Glasgow, til the house calmed again. Accordingly, I just daunered doun to the Bank and drew a bit five-pund note, and with that in my pouch I thocht I need neither fear cauld nor hunger, for the short time I was to be awa frae hame.

Having spent a day or twa with my auld friend Mungo McWattie—ye'll aiblins ken him, a retired bachelor in the Stockwall; he was ance in the fleecy-hosiery line, and very bien[4] in his circumstances,—I returned hame, just in time to see my wife's and my lassie's braws come hame, forbye a braw new blue coat with yellow buttons, a silk vest bonnily spraingit with various colors, and tight pataloons, made to fit like a glove, for Tummas. Sic an unco wastrie in the way of claiths, great feck o' whulk couldna look decent a second day, made me a thocht donsy, I must confess; but, when I began to reflect on the matter with a mair philosophical speerit, I saw there was even in this prodigality and vanity, the workings out of a beautiful Providence. For ye'll observe that this was a Charity Ball, and operated as such in a twafald sense or degree. First, the sale of the tickets created a fund for real sufferers under the sair pinch of want and starvation; and, second, a lively impulse was given to the industry of ithers, wha were necessarily employed in the decorement and garnishing furth of them that bocht the tickets. Manufacturers of broad cloth, muslin, shawls.

---

[1]Bought.

[2]Wept.

[3]Looks.

[4]Comfortable.

tailors, mantua-makers, milliners, bonnet-makers, hatmakers, shoe-makers, glove makers, haberdashers and shopkeepers—even the sellers o' needles and preens, and sic sma wares, had either frae this soorce a direck or indireck gude. And when I saw that the Ball was devised, not for the mere bodily recreation of them that attended it, but to supply food and raiment to the necessitous and hungry, and that when it did this to a certain extent, it moreover added a spur to the industry of mony a hard-working, weelmeaning, and industrious body, that lives by the labor and skill of their ten fingers, I could not but admire the twa-handed way in whilk the milk of charity was squeezed frae the human heart, and made, like a refreshing shower, to fall ower a far wider surface than the wee clud in the sky would at first betoken.

### Chapter VII: I may say "Lang lookit for come at last."

The eventful day of the ball at last came round in due order of nature, and an unco ganging up stairs and doun stairs there was in our bit self-conteened house. Wife and dochter were putting on and putting aff this and the other thing. Tummas was like to drive down the roof of the parlor trying his new steps in the toom[1] garret aboon, and, when unwittingly I turned up my face to consider whar the din could come frae, a lump of plaister, as big as the croon of my hat, fell right in my face, and dung[2] the fire frae my een like sparks in a smiddy.

Sic things in a weel regulated family canna be tolerated in ordinar cases, but as this was a day expressly set apairt for enjoyment, I owerlooked the fault and took a turn twice round my garden, to cool my blude, and see gif ony robin red-breasts were hirplin'[3] and chitterin' aboot; for ever since the melancholy death of the babes in the wood, one has an uncommon sympathy for thae wee considerate creatures, on account of them theeking[4] the perishing innocents with leaves, as is set furth at length in the auld ballat.

As ye may jalouse, there were few in our house could tak ony denner that day; but for my pairt, I may say I took my ordinary pick;—mair be token, we had singed sheep's head, trotters conform, and a very 'sponsible looking chuckie, as could be, the whilk fare is no to be despised as times gang.

After denner, I comforted my stamach with a leetle brandy toddy, and sooked it aff hooly and fairly, being nowise concerned like the rest of the household, anent either dress or looks, on the approaching grand occasion. The fack is, I had made up my mind frae the first, to appear in the samen dress as that in whilk I had the honor to visit his late gracious Majesty, at his palace of Holyrood, where I can assure you I was as civilly entreated as the first of the land, no excluding the Lord Provost of Glasgow, though he and his tounsfolk tried to put themselves desperately far forrit; but the King saw through them brawly, and kent a spoon frae a stot's horn as weel as the maist of his liege subjects.

### Chapter VIII: Conteens our out-ganging.

Preceesely as the clock chappit ten, a noddy and a pair of horses drew up at our door, and out cam the hale byke[5] of us as clean and trig as gin we had been faulded by in a bandbox. It's a fack, my heart lap to my mouth when I saw our gude-wife buskit and bedinkt in a real fashionable new silk goun, and with a beautiful spreading umbrella-shaped cap, transparent as a butterfly's wings, and ornamented with

---

[1]Empty.
[2]Struck.
[3]Hopping.
[4]Covering.
[5]Swarm.

gumflowers and other conceits, as natural as the life.

I was just about to take her all up in my arms and gie her a bit smack on the cheek, she looked sae bonny, but na away sho spouted into the noddy, with her good-natured "hout awa' Gudeman, behave yoursel before folk," as the sang says, "Do you ken that you woud birze my balloon sleeves out of a' shape?"

Dochter Jess was very modestly attired in a nice pink-colored robe, the fashion of which I cannot weel describe, and her hair was done up in the most approved London style, by Mr. Moore the perfumer, whose fingers, no to mention his legs, running about frae morn till e'en, I'm guessing were gayen sair. It did me good to look on Tummas, he was sae straucht, slim, and perjink,[1] though I thocht quietly to mysel the lad was looking mair like a sodger than a saint—but let that flea stick to the wa', seeing that his auld faither was in fack drum-major at this march to Vanity Fair.

Into the noddy we got at last, bag and baggage, and up streets and doun streets, dunting, and jingling we brattled like mad. Shooting out my neb[2] at the window, I could see chaises and noddies fleeing about in a' directions like sae mony fiery comets, which was a very enterteening and enlivening, sicht; howsumer, some wandeidy weans cried "whip behind! whip behind!" and quick as thocht, scringe cam the drivers whip alangside the noddy, and in its waganging gave me a skelp athort the chaftblade,[3] that was smarter than it was welcome, and keepit me from poking out my head again, till the steps were let doun.

Without farther misadventure we drave up in graund style to the Inn's door, and, lang or we cam there, we could hear distinctly the sounds of music, dancing, and gilravitching of all kinds; and baith my bairns were just beside themsels for fear they had lost all the fun. But I quieted their apprehensions on that score, by remarking that it was not likely that anything very partecklar would take place till we arrived, seeing that the stewards had expressly sent a carriage for the accommodation of our party. And though I wasna eleckit a steward, they kent fu' weel that it couldna be in my nature to tak umbrage at unintentional neglect, and bide awa frae the ploy like some conceity bodies, that bizz and fizz, and spit fire like a peeoy, in spite and vexation whenever they are no made the tongue o' the trump, and happen in ony way to be owerlookit in the making up of the lists.

About the door there was an uncommon crowd of men, women, and weans, curious to see us alicht; and for a time, I could not see a spot where to pit a foot, unless I made a straucht step forrit, and made a virtue of necessity by using the first head in my way for a stepping-stane. Seeing our dilemma, a police-offisher at the outer door, wha had recognized me, immediately cleared the road, right and left, in a twinkling, with his baton, crying all the time, "Mak way for the Bailie, ye born deevils ye!—mak way, can ye no, for the Bailie?" and by his exertions we all got safe and soun within the porch, and without any of the women-folk getting their braws the least soiled or crumpled.

It's needless to tell you ony mair about Willie Tamson the town-offisher, standing at the ballroom door, in his new stand of scarlet claes with halbert in hand. Whenever he got wit of me, wide open flees the muckle door as if by magic, and in I gangs gallantly supporting my wife on my arm, while Tummas cleekit with his sister. No having been in the room for this many a year—in fack, to be plain, no since the Pitt dinners and Waterloo dinners were given up—there cam a stound to my heart, to be shooled in as it were all of a sudden into a most spacious hall, and amang a

---

[1]Neat.

[2]Beak, nose.

[3]Cheek-bone, or jaw-bone.

perfect hatter of unkent faces. But just as I was in a kind of swither whether to march forrit to the head of the room or slip quietly doun upon an empty firm near the door, up comes ane of the stewards, and taking my loof in baith his, shook me heartily, saying with a very kindly laugh,

"Oh, but ye're lang o' coming,
Lang, lang, lang o' coming.
Oh, but ye're lang o' coming—
Right welcome Bailie Pirnie!"

And then the Lord Provost and other gentlemen gathered round me, and in the twinkling of a bed-post, I seeing mysel amang kent friends and no frem[1] faces, crackit as crouse[2] as if I had been in my ain hoose laying doun the law anent domistic obedience, ower my third tumbler of double nappy.

## Chapter IX: The ball itsel.

A scene of greater splendor, beauty, and magnificence, saving and excepting, always, the royal doings at Embro, I never witnessed in my life. I am sure there was full twa hundred gentlemen and leddies, and every ane seemed happier than anither. Then there was a perfect sea of waving plumes, and sashes, and ribands, and artificial flowers and sic a variety and tasty combination of brilliant colors I'll be bound to say, I never saw equaled in the best India shawl-pattern that ever came through my hands, and that's no few, as the feck of my friends ken.

When I was in a bewilderment of delight, looking at the fine swanlike shapes of the young leddies that were gliding up and doun the room, like sae many beautifu' intelligences, or speerits from a higher world, with een glancing like diamonds, and feet sae wee and genty, that when they touched the floor the sound of them was nae mair heard than if it had been a feather lighting in the water, all at once there burst forth just abune my individual head, a particular fine concert of big fiddles and wee fiddles, horns, trumble-bumbles, trumpets, and what not, which was quite soul stirring to hear. At first I thocht this might be out of compliment to me, and not to be unceevil, I graciously bowed to the company; but I fand I was mistane, for it was naething mair than the music striking up for a quadrille, and, as I live, wha did I see standing up in a set, but baith my childer, son and dochter, as prejink and genteel, or I'm far out of my reckoning, as the best born that was there. The pride of a faither's heart on sic an occasion, naebody but a paurent that likes his offspring weel can possibly conceive.

Fashions in music and dancing have suffered great changes since my young days. I cannot say that I understood either the figure of the dance or its music; but they were pleasant eneuch. The quadrilles are graceful and dreamy-like motions, but they dinna bring the color to ane's cheek, and gar the heart-blood rush, like a milldam, frae head till heel, like the Scotch reel or Strathspey. And then there's nae clapping of hands, and whirling round, and crying "heuch, heuch" when the dance warms, and the fiddler's arms are fleeing faster than a weaver's shuttle, and they themselves lay down their lugs to their wark in dead earnest.

Being a gae noticing kind of a body, I may observe, that, in general, the leddies had the heels of the beaux, in the matter of dancing. A good wheen of the latter, though they might slide backwards and forwards, and jee awa to this side and that side, with a bit trintle and a step weel eneuch, seemed often in a kippage[3] to ken what to do with their shouthors and their arms and their heads. The upper and the

---

[1]Strange.

[2]Bravely.

[3]Confusion.

douner man did not move in accordance, something like a bad rider that gangs wigglety-wagglety, clean contrary to the motion of the beast he is on the back of.

But the feck of the leddies carried themselves like queens; frae head to heel they moved as a graceful and complete unity; and had ye seen, as I saw, their bonny modest faces glancing past ye, radiant with the sweetest natured smiles, and their countenances presenting every variety of fine outline and expression, ye wuld have exclaimed with me and Burns the poet:

"All nature swears the lovely dears,
Her noblest work she classes, O;
Her prentice haund she tried on man,
And then she made the lasses."

After the quadrilles we had country dances; but, so far as I observed, neither the Haymakers nor the Soldiers Joy formed a part of the entertainment, though there were a gude number of gentleman conneckit with the agricultural interests of the country present, and a fine show of strapping offishers frae the barracks. The scarlet coats of the offishers, with the great bobs of gowd on their shouthers, had a fine effeck, and contrasted nicely with the silk, and satins, and muslins of the leddies, and the blue and black coats of the gentlemen civilians.

It is out of the power of language to describe the liveliness that a sprinkling of red coats gives to a dance. Some of the offishers danced with their lang swurds at their side, and I was looking every minute for ane or twa couping heels ower head, but they keepit their feet uncoweel considering all things; nevertheless I shall be bauld to mak this observe, that it is desperate difficult to gang let abee dance, with an iron spit hinging at ane's side. But, abune a', I thocht I could see the swurds sometimes come deg against the tender shanks of the leddies, and a lick across the shins frae cauld iron is sair to bide. Our yeomanry cavalry never dance with their swurds on, and the foot soldiers should tak a pattern and example from them thereanent, from this time henceforward and forever.

The country dances blawn by, then cam waltzes, and the leddies and their partners gaed round and round about like tee-totums, at sic a frichtsom rate, that really I lost my presence of mind for a time, on seeing our Miss Jess as forward as the lave,[1] and twirling and sooming aboot like a balloon on fire. She was driving doun the room with a tall grenadier offisher, and, seeing her whirling round him and better round him, I cried, at the highest pitch of my voice, "For Gudesake, Jess, haud fast by the sash or shouther, else ye'll for a certainty flee out at the winnock-bole like a witch, and break your harn-pan on the hard causey!" There was an unco titter among the leddies, and my wife sidling up to me, telt me to hauld my whisht and no to mak a fule o the lassie, for she was just under the protection of a mercifu' Providence like the lave. Be that as it may, I confess I was glad to see the waltzing at an end, and our Jess again anchored on a furm, peching[2] and blawing, but safe and sound, lith and limb, and as red in the cheek as a peony rose.

Aboot this time some of the principal gentry made up parties for playing at cards, and ithers gaed to the adjacent, to weet their thrapples,[3] for the stour[4] kicked up by the dancers was like to mak the maist of us on-lookers, a wee hue hearse. Some of us had brandy toddy, ithers scaudit wine—while anither class contented themsels with sma-stell whisky, made intil toddy. When I appeared in the adjacent every ane was looder than anither in praise of my fine family; and, with faitherly

---

[1]Rest.

[2]Breathing hard.

[3]Throats.

[4]Dust.

pride, I telt my freends that I spared nae expense in giving my bairns a gude education, for which I received an approving nod from some gayen influential quarters that shall be nameless.

No having served an apprenticeship either to the tayloring or millinery line, I'll no pretend to give an account of the leddies' dresses, or the gentlemen's costume. In general, I may say, baith were very becoming. Some leddies were tastily, but plainly put on, others were gorgeously bedecked, looking like Indian empresses, or princesses of the blood royal at least; some had caps, and ithers had naething but their bare heads with a bit simple flower, or sic like chaste ornament stuck among their clustering ringlets.

The newspapers gave but a faint idea of the Toutin Assembly but, tak my word for it, it was in every respeck uncommon pretty and creditable to the toun, beating, by far and awa ony thing, seen in the kingdom since the King's ball at Embro. Anent the music, I shall say, Kinnikame played his pairt with great bir. In fack, I fand my auld timmers like to dance in despite of my sell, and noos and tans I crackit my thooms like a whip, for a gash of pleesant remembrances conneckit with the scenes of early life, whan I mysel figured at "penny reels, bottlings," and "washing o' aprons," cam ower my heart with a fullness that even amounted to pain.

I wasna then as I am now, but circumstances have naething altered the naturality of my heart, or gart me feel ashamed of the poortith of my younger days, or turn up my neb in scorn at the innocent recreations and pastimes, whilk were then within my reach. It would be weel for the hale tot of our prosperous men of the world, did they think and feel like me, on this and mony ither important subjects.

Chapter X: Conteens the hame-coming and particulars thereanent.

But I'm spinning out the thread of my discourse, I fear ower sma, and least it should break, I'll just wind up my pirn, and hae done with a remark or sae. And first, I will say, that frae beginning till end, frae the A to the Zed of this uncommon splendid concern, it was everything that a good charitable heart desired. Gaiety, elegance, good humor, and unsophisticated taste, went hand in hand throughout the nicht. Every one seemed anxious to please, and bent upon being pleased. There was nae upsetting, nae unpleasing distinctions keepit up, farder than what correck feeling and a due regard to the conventionalities of gude society required. We were in short, as it were, all chicks of ae cleckin, cudlin close and cozily under the expansive wings of kindliest sympathy and godlike charity.

All human enjoyments have an end, and sae had oor assembly. Aboot three o'-clock in the morning, the company began to lift, and the room to get thinner and thinner. In a wee while afterwards, a flunkey cam up to me and my wife, and telt us that our carriage was waiting, at the door; whereupon we bundled up our things like douce sober folks, and gaed our ways doun the stairs, through the lobby, and intil the chaise; but there being only three insides, Tummas had to tak an outside, on the box alang with the driver; but he was weel wrappit up in a camlet cloak, with a red comforter aboot his neck, besides, his mother insisted that he should row her shawl ower his head, just to keep his teeth frae chitterin', but whether he did sae or not I cannot say.

Home we got at last without any misshanter. My wife was quite delightit with the entertainment—she is a real feeling and sensible woman; and when we were in the coach and began talking about our twa bairns, their first appearance in public, she could scarcely speak, for her motherly affection and pride were gratified to the full, but just tenderly squeezing my hand, she said, "O Peter, this was a nicht!" and I had just time to reply "Deeds I, my doo," when the coach drew up, and the hail lot of us alichtit at our ain bourock.

## ERSKINE CONOLLY (1798–1843)

### Mary Macneil

The last gleam o' sunset in ocean was sinkin,
Owre mountain an' meadowland glintin fareweel;
An' thousands o' stars in the heavens were blinkin,
As bright as the een o' sweet Mary Macneil.
A' glowin wi' gladness she leaned on her lover,
Her een tellin secrets she thought to conceal;
And fondly they wandered whar nane might discover
The tryst o' young Ronald an' Mary Macneil.

Oh, Mary was modest, an' pure as the lily,
That dew-draps o' mornin' in fragrance reveal;
Nae fresh bloomin' flow'ret in hill or in valley
Could rival the beauty of Mary Macneil.
She moved, and the graces played sportive around her;
She smiled, and the hearts o' the cauldest wad thrill;
She sang, and the mavis cam' listenin in wonder,
To claim a sweet sister in Mary Macneil.

But ae bitter blast on its fair promise blawin,
Frae spring a' its beauty an' blossoms will steal;
An' ae sudden blight on the gentle heart fa'in,
Inflicts the deep wound nothing earthly can heal.
The simmer saw Ronald on glory's path hiein;
The autumn, his corse on the red battlefiel;
The winter the maiden found heartbroken, dyin;
An' spring spread the green turf ower Mary Macneil.

## ROBERT GILFILLAN (1798–1850)

### Tis Sair to Dream

Tis sair to dream o' them we like,
That waking we sall never see;
Yet, oh how kindly was the smile
My laddie in my sleep gave me.
I thought we sat beside the burn
That wimples down the flowery glen,
Where, in our early days o' love,
We met that ne'er sall meet again.

The simmer sun sank neath the wave,
And gladdened, wi' his parting ray,
The woodland wild and valley green,
Fast fading into gloamin' gray.
He talked of days o' future joy,
And yet my heart was haflins sair,
For when his eye it beamed on me,
A withering death-like glance was there.

I thought him dead, and then I thought
That life was young and love was free,
For oer our heads the mavis sang,
And hameward hied the janty bee.
We pledged our love and plighted troth,
But cauld, cauld was the kiss he gave,
When starting from my dream, I found
His troth was plighted to the grave.

I canna weep, for hope is fled,
And nought would do but silent mourn,
Were't no for dreams that should na come,
To whisper back my love's return;
Tis sair to dream o' them we like,
That waking we sall never see;
Yet, oh how kindly was the smile
My laddie in my sleep gave me.

## The Exile's Song

Oh, why left I my hame?
Why did I cross the deep?
Oh, why left I the land
Where my forefathers sleep?
I sigh for Scotia's shore,
And I gaze across the sea,
But I canna get a blink* glimpse
O' my ain country.

The palm-tree waveth high,
And fair the myrtle springs:
And, to the Indian maid,
The bulbul sweetly sings.
But I dinna see the broom
Wi' its tassels on the lee,
Nor hear the lintie's sang
O' my ain country.

Oh, here no Sabbath bell
Awakes the Sabbath morn,
Nor song of reapers heard
Amang the yellow corn:
For the tyrant's voice is here,
And the wail of slavery;
But the sun of freedom shines
In my ain country.

There's a hope for every woe,
And a balm for every pain,
But the first joys o' our youth
Come never back again.
There's a track upon the deep,

And a path across the sea;
But the weary ne'er return
To their ain country.

## Manor Braes

Where Manor stream rins blithe an' clear,
And Castlehill's white wa's appear,
I spent ae day, aboon a' days,
By Manor stream, mang Manor braes.
The purple heath was just in bloom,
And bonnie waved the upland broom,
The flocks on flowery braes lay still,
Or, heedless, wandered at their will.

Twas there, mid nature's calm repose,
Where Manor clearest, saftest flows,
I met a maiden fair to see,
Wi' modest look and bashfu' ee.
Her beauty to the mind did bring
A morn where summer blends wi' spring,
So bright, so pure, so calm, so fair,
Twas bliss to look—to linger there.

Ilk word cam' frae her bosom warm,
Wi' love to win and sense to charm,
So much of nature, nought of art,
She'll live enthroned within my heart.
Aboon her head the laverock sang,
And neath her feet the wild-flowers sprang.
Oh, let me dwell, where beauty strays,
By Manor stream an' Manor braes.

I speired* gif ane sae young an' fair — asked
Knew aught of love, wi' a' its care?
She said her heart frae love was free,
But aye she blushed wi' downcast ee.
The parting cam' as partings come,
Wi' looks that speak, though tongues be dumb;
Yet I'll return, ere many days,
To live an' love mang Manor braes.

## The Bonnie Braes of Scotland

O, the bonnie braes of Scotland,
My blessings on them a',
May peace be found in ilka* cot — every
And joy in ilka ha*. — "hall"
Whaure'er a beild*, however laigh*, — shelter/low
By burn or brae appears,
Be there the gladsome smile o' youth,
And dignity of years.

O, the bonnie braes of Scotland
Sae blooming and sae fair,
There's mony a hame o' kindness
And couthie* dwallin' there; snug
And mair o' warldly happiness
Than folk wad seem to ken,
For the leal* and happy heart "loyal"
Mak's the canty* but and ben.[1] pleasant

O, wha wad grasp at fame or power,
Or walth seek to obtain,
Be't mang the busy scenes o' life,
Or on the stormy main;
When the shepherd on his hill,
Or the peasant at his plew,
Find sic a share o' happiness
Wi' unco* sma' ado? very

The wind may whistle loud and cauld,
And sleety blasts may blaw,
Or swirlin' round in whitening wreathes,
May drift the wintry snaw:
But the gloamin' star comes blinkin'
Afore he maist does ken,
And his wifie's cheerfu' smile
Maks the canty but and ben.

O, the bonnie braes of Scotland
To my remembrance bring
The lang, lang simmer sunny day,
When life was in its spring;
When, mang the wild flowers wandering,
The happy hours went by,
The future wakening no a fear,
Nor yet the past a sigh.

O, the bonnie braes of Scotland,
Hame o' the fair and free,
And hame it is a kindly word,
Whaure'er that hame may be.
My weary steps I'd fain retrace
Back to the sunny days,
When youthfu' hearts together joyed
Mang Scotland's bonnie braes.

## In the Days o' Langsyne

In the days o' langsyne when we carles* were young, fellows
An' nae foreign fashions amang us had sprung;
When we made our ain bannocks*, and brewed our ain yill, cakes

[1]"But and ben" —outer and inner rooms (i.e. a two-room cottage).

An' were clad frae the sheep that gaed white on the hill;
O' the thocht o' thae days gars my auld heart aye fill.

In the days o' langsyne we were happy and free,
Proud lords on the land, and kings on the sea.
To our foes we were fierce, to our friends we were kind,
An' where battle raged loudest, you ever did find
The banner of Scotland float high in the wind.

In the days o' langsyne we aye ranted and sang
By the warm ingle-side, or the wild braes amang.
Our lads busked* braw, and our lasses looked fine, dressed
An' the sun on our mountains seemed ever to shine.
O, where is the Scotland o' bonnie langsyne?

In the days o' langsyne ilka glen had its tale.
Sweet voices were heard in ilk breath o' the gale;
An' ilka wee burn had a sang o' its ain,
As it trotted alang through the valley or plain.
Shall we e'er hear the music o' streamlets again?

In the days o' langsyne there were feasting and glee,
Wi' pride in ilk heart, and joy in ilk e'e;
And the auld, mang the nappy, their eild seemed to tyne*. lose
It was your stoup* the nicht, and the morn twas mine; cup
O, the days o' langsyne—oh, the days o' langsyne.

## JAMES HYSLOP (1798–1827)

### A Love Song

How sweet the dewy bell is spread,
Where Spango's mossy streams are lavin',
The heathery locks o' deepenin' red
Around the mountain brow aye wavin'.
Here, on the sunny mountain side,
Dear lassie, we'll lie down thegither,
Where nature spreads luve's crimson bed,
Among the bonnie bloomin' heather.

Lang hae I wished, my lovely maid,
Amang thae fragrant wilds to lead ye;
And now, aneath my tartan plaid,
How blest I lie wi' you aside me.
And art thou happy, dearest, speak,
Wi' me aneath the tartan plaidie?
Yes, that dear glance, sae saft and meek,
Resigns thee to thy shepherd laddie.

The saftness o' the gentle dove,
Its eyes in dying sweetness closin',
Is like thae langid eyes o' love,

Sae fondly on my heart reposin'.
When simmer suns the flowers expand,
In a' their silken beauties shinin',
They're no sae saft as thy white hand,
Upon my love-warm cheek reclinin'.

While thus aneath my tartan plaid
Sae warmly to my lips I press ye,
That hinnied bloom o' dewy red
Is nocht like thy sweet lips, dear lassie.
Reclined on luve's soft crimson bed,
Our hearts sae fondly locked thegither,
Thus oer my cheek thy ringlets spread,
How happy, happy mang the heather.

## DAVID MOIR (1798–1851)

[Moir is remembered as the author of *The Life of Mansie Wauch, Tailor of Dalkeith* (1828), a comic novel of small-town Scottish life which, along with the works of John Galt, helped to create the taste for sentimental rusticity which the "Kailyard" novelists of the later century were able to satisfy. He was, as well, a poet.]

### The Rustic Lad's Lament in the Town

O, wad that my time were owre but,
Wi' this wintry sleet and snaw,
That I might see our house again,
I' the bonnie birken shaw*. wood
For this is no my ain life,
And I peak and pine away
Wi' the thochts o' hame and the young flowers,
In the glad green month of May.

I used to wauk in the morning
Wi' the loud sang o' the lark,
And the whistling o' the plowman lads,
As they gaed to their wark.
I used to wear the bit young lambs
Frae the tod* and the roaring stream; fox
But the warld is changed, and a' thing now
To me seems like a dream.

There are busy crowds around me,
On ilka* lang dull street; every
Yet, though sae mony surround me,
I ken na ane I meet;
And I think o' kind kent faces,
And o' blithe an' cheery days,
When I wandered out wi' our ain folk,
Out owre the simmer braes.

Waes me, for my heart is breaking.
I think o' my brither sma',
And on my sister greeting*, weeping
When I cam frae hame awa.
And O, how my mither sobbit,
As she shook me by the hand,
When I left the door o' our auld house,
To come to this stranger land.

There's nae hame like our ain hame—
O, I wush that I were there.
There's nae hame like our ain hame
To be met wi' onywhere.
And O that I were back again,
To our farm and fields sae green;
And heard the tongues o' my ain folk,
And were what I hae been.

## Casa's Dirge

Vainly for us the sunbeams shine,
Dimmed is our joyous hearth.
O Casa, dearer dust than thine
Ne'er mixed with mother earth.
Thou wert the cornerstone of love,
The keystone of our fate.
Thou art not. Heaven scowls dark above,
And earth is desolate.

Ocean may rave with billows curled
And moons may wax and wane,
And fresh flowers blossom; but this world
Shall claim not thee again.
Closed are the eyes which bade rejoice
Our hearts till love ran oer.
Thy smile is vanished and thy voice
Silent for evermore.

Yes, thou art gone—our hearth's delight,
Our boy so fond and dear.
No more thy smiles to glad our sight,
No more thy songs to cheer.
No more thy presence, like the sun,
To fill our home with joy.
Like lightning hath thy race been run,
As bright as swift, fair boy.

Now winter with its snow departs,
The green leaves clothe the tree;
But summer smiles not on the hearts
That bleed and break for thee.
The young May weaves her flowery crown,

Her boughs in beauty wave.
They only shake their blossoms down
Upon thy silent grave.

Dear to our souls is every spot
Where thy small feet have trod.
There odors, breathed from Eden, float,
And sainted is the sod.
The wild bee with its buglet fine,
The blackbird singing free,
Melt both thy mother's heart and mine.
They speak to us of thee.

Only in dreams thou comest now
From heaven's immortal shore,
A glory round that infant brow,
Which death's pale signet bore.
Twas thy fond looks, twas thy fond lips,
That lent our joys their tone.
And life is shaded with eclipse,
Since thou from earth art gone.

Thine were the fond, endearing ways,
That tenderest feeling prove.
A thousand wiles to win our praise,
To claim and keep our love.
Fondness for us thrilled all thy veins;
And, Casa, can it be
That nought of all the past remains
Except vain tears for thee?

Idly we watch thy form to trace
In children on the street.
Vainly, in each familiar place,
We list thy pattering feet.
Then, sudden, oer these fancies crushed,
Despair's black pinions wave.
We know that sound for ever hushed.
We look upon thy grave.

O heavenly child of mortal birth,
Our thoughts of thee arise,
Not as a denizen of earth,
But inmate of the skies.
To feel that life renewed is thine
A soothing balm imparts,
We quaff from out Faith's cup divine,
And Sabbath fills our hearts.

Thou leanest where the fadeless wands
Of amaranth bend oer.
Thy white wings brush the golden sands
Of heaven's refulgent shore.

Thy home is where the psalm and song
Of angels choir abroad,
And blessed spirits, all day long,
Bask round the throne of God.

There change and change are not. The soul
Quaffs bliss as from a sea,
And years, through endless ages, roll,
From sin and sorrow free.
There gush for aye fresh founts of joy,
New raptures to impart.
Oh, dare we call thee still *our* boy,
Who now a seraph art?

A little while—a little while—
Ah, long it cannot be.
And thou again on us wilt smile,
Where angels smile on thee.
How selfish is the worldly heart,
How sinful to deplore.
Oh, that we were where now thou art,
Not lost, but gone before.

## JOANNA PICKEN (1798–1859)

### An Auld Friend wi' a New Face

A queer kind o' lott'ry is marriage—
Ye never ken what ye may draw.
Ye may get a braw* hoose an' a carriage, — fine
Or maybe get nae hoose ava*. — at all
I say na tis best to be single,
But ae thing's to me unco* clear: — very
Far better sit lane by the ingle* — fire
Than thole* what some wives hae to bear. — suffer
   It's braw to be dancin' and gaffin'* — chatting
   As lang as nae trouble befa'—
   But hech! she is soon ower wi' daffin'* — fooling
   That's wooed, an' married, an' a'.

She maun labor frae sunrise till dark,
An' aft though her means be but sma,
She gets little thanks for her wark—
Or as aften gets nae thanks ava.
She maun tak just whate'er may come,
An' say nocht o' her fear or her hope.
There's nae use o' lievin' in Rome,
An' trying' to fecht wi' the Pope.
   Hectored an' lectured an' a,
   Snubbed for whate'er may befa',
   Than this, she is far better aff
   That never gets married ava'.

Oh, then come the bairns without number,
An' there's naething but kisses an' licks—
Adieu then to sleep an' to slumber,
An the Pa is as cross as twa sticks.
A' the week she is makin' their parritch,
An' turnin' auld frocks into new;
An' on Sunday she learns them their carritch,
Puir wife, there's nae rest-day for you.
  Warkin' an' fechtin' awa,
  Saturday, Sunday, an' a'.
  In troth she is no that ill aff
  That never gets married ava.

In nae time the cauld an' the wheesles
Get into your family sae sma,
An' the chincough, the croup, or the measles
Is sure to tak aff ane or twa.
An' wi' them gang the puir mither's joys.
Nae comfort seems left her ava—
As she pits by the claes and the toys
That belanged to the wee things awa.
  Doctors an' drugs an' a',
  Bills an' buryin's an' a',
  Oh surely her heart may be lichter
  That never was married ava.

The married maun aft bear man's scornin',
An' humor his capers an' fykes;
But the single can rise in the mornin',
An' gang to her bed when she likes;
An' when ye're in sickness and trouble,
Just tell me at wha's door ye ca';
It's no whar ten bairns mak a hubble,
But at hers that has nae bairns ava.
  Usefu', an' peacefu', an' canty,
  Quiet, an' canny, an' a',
  It's gude to hae sister or auntie
  That never was married ava.

A wife maun be humble an' hamely,
Aye ready to rise, or to rin;
An' oh, when she's brocht up a family,
It's then her warst sorrows begin;
For the son, he maun e'en hae a wife;
A' the dochter a hoose o' her ain;
An' then, through the battle o' life,
They ne'er may forgather again.
  Canty, and quiet, an' a',
  Although her bit mailin* be sma, homestead
  In truth she is no that ill aff
  That never gets married ava.

It's far better still to keep single
Than sit wi' yer face at the wa',
An' greet* ower the sons and the dochters weep
Ye've buried and married awa.
I fain wad deny, but I canna,
Although to confess it I grieve,
Folks seldom care muckle for granny,
Unless she has something to leave.
It's nae that I seek to prevent ye,
For that wad be rhyme thrown awa';
But, lassies, I pray, just content ye,
Although ye're ne'er married ava.

## ROBERT POLLOK (1798–1827)

### Helen's Tomb

At morn a dew-bathed rose I past,
All lovely on its native stalk,
Unmindful of the noonday blast,
That strewed it on my evening's walk.

So, when the morn of life awoke,
My hopes sat bright on fancy's bloom,
Forgetful of the death-aimed stroke
That laid them in my Helen's tomb.

Watch there my hopes, watch Helen sleep,
Nor more with sweet-lipped fancy rave,
But with the long grass sigh and weep
At dewy eve by Helen's grave.

## HENRY SCOTT RIDDELL (1798–1870)

### Ours Is the Land

Ours is the land of gallant hearts,
The land of lovely forms;
The island of the mountain harp,
The torrents, and the storms:
The land that bears the freemen's tread,
And never bore the slave's;
Where far and deep the green-woods spread,
And wild the thistle waves.

Ere ever Ossian's lofty voice
Had told of Fingal's fame,
Ere ever from their native clime
The Roman eagles came,
Our land had given heroes birth
That durst the boldest brave,

And taught above tyrannic dust
The thistle tufts to wave.

What need we say how Wallace fought,
And how his foemen fell?
Or how on glorious Bannockburn
The freeborn bore them well?
Ours is the land of gallant hearts,
The land of honored graves,
Whose wreath of fame shall ne'er depart,
While yet the thistle waves.

## Would That I Were Where Wild Woods Wave

Would that I were where wild woods wave,
Aboon the beds where sleep the brave;
And where the streams o' Scotia lave
Her hills and glens o' grandeur.

Where freedom reigns and friendship dwells,
Bright as the sun upon the fells*, hills
When autumn brings the heather-bells
In all their native splendor.
The thistle wi' the hawthorn joins,
The birks mix wi' the mountain pines,
And heart with dauntless heart combines
For ever to defend her.

There roam the kind, and live the leal,
By lofty ha' and lowly shiel*; cottage
And she for whom the heart must feel
A kindness still mair tender.
Fair, where the light hill breezes blaw,
The wild flowers bloom by glen and shaw*; wood
But she is fairer than them a',
Wherever she may wander.

Still, far or near, by wild or wood,
I'll love the generous, wise, and good;
But she shall share the dearest mood
That heaven to life may render.
What boots it then thus on to stir,
And still from love's enjoyment err,
When I to Scotland and to her
Must all this heart surrender.

## Scotland Yet

Gae bring my guid auld harp ance mair,
Gae bring it free and fast,
For I maun sing anither sang,
Ere a' my glee be past.

And trow ye as I sing, my lads,
The burden o't shall be,
Auld Scotland's howes* and Scotland's knowes*, lowlands/"knolls"
And Scotland's hills for me.
We'll drink a cup to Scotland yet,
Wi' a' the honors three.

The heath waves wild upon her hills,
And, foaming frae the fells,
Her fountains sing o' freedom still,
As they dance down the dells.
And weel I lo'e the land, my lads,
That's girded by the sea.
Then Scotland's vales and Scotland's dales,
And Scotland's hills for me.
We'll drink a cup to Scotland yet,
Wi' a' the honors three.

The thistle wags upon the fields,
Where Wallace bore his blade,
That gave her foemen's dearest bluid
To dye her auld gray plaid.
And looking to the lift*, my lads, sky
He sang this doughty glee,
Auld Scotland's right and Scotland's might,
And Scotland's hills for me;
We'll drink a cup to Scotland yet,
Wi' a' the honors three.

They tell o' lands wi' brighter skies,
Where freedom's voice ne'er rang.
Gie me the hills where Ossian lies,
And Coila's minstrel sang.
For I've nae skill o' lands, my lads,
That kenna to be free.
Then Scotland's right and Scotland's might,
And Scotland's hills for me.
We'll drink a cup to Scotland yet,
Wi' a' the honors three.

## The Dowie Dens o' Yarrow

Oh, sister, there are midnight dreams
That pass not with the morning,
Then ask not why my reason swims
In a brain sae wildly burning;
And ask not why I fancy how
Yon wee birds sing wi' sorrow,
For bluid lies mingled wi' the dew
In the dowie* dens o' Yarrow. sad, gloomy

My dream's wild light was not o' night,
Nor o' the doolfu' morning,
Thrice on the stream was seen the gleam
That seemed his sprite returning;
For sword-girt men came down the glen,
An hour before the morrow,
And pierced the heart aye true to mine,
In the dowie dens o' Yarrow.

Oh, there are red, red drops o' dew
Upon the wild flower's blossom,
But they couldna cool my burning brow,
And shall not stain my bosom;
But from the clouds o' yon dark sky
A cold, cold shroud I'll borrow,
And long and deep shall be my sleep
In the dowie dens o' Yarrow.

This form the bluid-dyed flower shall press
By the heart o' him that lo'ed me;
And I'll steal frae his lips a long, long kiss,
In the bower where oft he wooed me;
For my arm shall fold and my tresses shield
The form o' my death-cold marrow*, mate
When the breeze shall bring the raven's wing
O'er the dowie dens o' Yarrow.

## Flora's Lament

More dark is my soul than the scenes of yon islands,
Dismantled of all the gay hues that they wore;
For lost is my hope since the Prince of the Highlands
Mong these, his wild mountains, can meet me no more.
Ah, Charlie, how wrung was this heart when it found thee
Forlorn, and the die of thy destiny cast.
Thy Flora was firm mid the perils around thee,
But where were the brave of the land that had owned thee,
That she—only she—should be true to the last?

The step's in the bark on the dark heaving waters,
That now should have been on the floor of a throne;
And, alas for auld Scotland, her sons and her daughters,
Thy wish was their welfare, thy cause was their own.
But 'lorn may we sigh where the hill-winds awaken,
And weep in the glen where the cataracts foam,
And sleep where the dew-drops are deep on the bracken;
Thy foot has the land of thy fathers forsaken,
And more—never more will it yield thee a home.

Oh, yet when afar, in the land of the stranger,
If e'er on thy spirit remembrance may be
Of her who was true in these moments of danger,

Reprove not the heart that still lives but for thee.
The night-shrouded flower from the dawning shall borrow
A ray, all the glow of its charms to renew,
But Charlie, ah Charlie, no ray to thy Flora
Can dawn from thy coming to chase the dark sorrow
Which death, in thine absence, alone can subdue.

## The Minstrel's Grave

I sat in the vale, neath the hawthorns so hoary,
And the gloom of my bosom seemed deep as their shade,
For remembrance was fraught with the far-traveled story,
That told where the dust of the minstrel was laid.
I saw not his harp on the wild boughs above me,
I heard not its anthems the mountains among;
But the flow'rets that bloomed on his grave were more lovely
Than others would seem to that earth that belong.

"Sleep on," said my soul, "in the depths of thy slumber;
Sleep on, gentle bard, till the shades pass away;
For the lips of the living the ages shall number
That steal oer thy heart in its couch of decay.
Oh, thou wert beloved from the dawn of thy childhood,
Beloved till the last of thy suffering was seen,
Beloved now that oer thee is waving the wild-wood,
And the worm only living where rapture hath been.

"Till the footsteps of time are their travel forsaking,
No form shall descend, and no dawning shall come,
To break the repose that thy ashes are taking,
And call them to life from their chamber of gloom.
Yet sleep, gentle bard, for, though silent for ever,
Thy harp in the hall of the chieftain is hung.
No time from the mem'ry of mankind shall sever
The tales that it told, and the strains that it sung."

## The Minstrel's Bower

Oh, lassie, if thou'lt gang to yonder glen wi' me,
I'll weave the wilds amang a bonnie bower for thee.
I'll weave a bonnie bower o' the birks and willows green,
And to my heart thou'lt be what nae other e'er has been.
When the dew is on the flower, and the starlight on the lea,
In the bonnie greenwood bower I'll wake my harp to thee.
I'll wake my hill-harp's strain, and the echoes o' the dell
Shall restore the tales again that its notes o' love shall tell.

Oh, lassie, thou art fair as the morning's early beam,
As the image of a flower reflected frae the stream.
There's kindness in thy heart, and there's language in thine ee,
But ah, its looks impart nae sweet tale o' love to me.
Oh lassie, wert thou mine I wad love thee wi' such love

As the lips can ne'er define, and the cold can never prove.
In the bower by yonder stream our happy home should be,
And our life a blissful dream, while I lived alone for thee.

When I am far away my thoughts on thee shall rest,
Allured, as by a ray, frae the dwellings o' the blest;
For beneath the clouds o' dew, where'er my path may be,
Oh, a maiden fair as thou, I again shall never see.

## ALEXANDER SMART (1798–1866)

### The Herd Laddie

It's a lang time yet till the kye gae hame;
It's a weary time yet till the kye gae hame;
Till the lang shadows fa' in the sun's yellow flame,
And the birds sing gude-night, as the kye gae hame.

Sair langs the herd laddie for gloamin's sweet fa',
But slow moves the sun to the hills far awa'.
In the shade o' the broom-bush how fain would he lie,
But there's nae rest for him when he's herding the kye.

They'll no be content wi' the grass on the lea,
For do what he will to the corn aye they'll be.
The weary wee herd laddie to pity there is nane,
Sae tired and sae hungry wi' herding his lane*. (alone)

When the bee's in its byke, and the bird in its nest,
And the kye in the byre*, that's the hour he lo'es best. cattle barn
Wi' a fu' cog o' brose he sleeps like a stane,
But it scarce seems a blink till he's waukened again.

### Spring Time

The cauld north wind has soughed* awa', swooshed
The snaw has left the hill,
And briskly to the wastlin' breeze
Reels round yon bonny mill.
The cheery spring, in robes o' green,
Comes laughin' ower the lea,
While burnies by their flowery banks
Rin singin' to the sea.

The lintie whids amang the whins,
Or whistles on the thorn.
The bee comes hummin' frae his byke*, hive
And tunes his bugle-horn.
The craik rins rispin' through the corn,
The hare sends down the furrow;
The merry lav'rock frae the lift* sky
Pipes out his blithe gude-morrow.

Now springs the docken by the dyke,
The nettle on the knowe*. "knoll"
The puddock's* croakin' in the pool, frog's
Where green the rushes grow.
The primrose nods its yellow head,
The gowan* sports its charms. daisy
The burrie-thistle to the breeze
Flings out its prickly arms.

Now moudiewarts* begin to howk moles
And bore the tender fallow;
And deuks are paidlin' in the pool,
Where skims the gapin' swallow.
The clockin' hen, wi' clamorous din,
The midden* scarts an' scrubs; trash heap
The goose brings a' her gaislins out,
To daidle through the dubs.

New bairns get aff their hose an' shoon,
And rin ther'out a' barefit;
But rantin through the bloomin' whins,
The rogues get mony a sair fit.
Ill fares it then, by bush or brake,
If on the nest they light,
Of buntlin' wi' the tuneless beak,
Or ill-starred yellow-yite.

The gowk's* heard in the leafy wood, cuckoo's
The lambs frisk oer the field;
The wee bird gathers taits o' woo,
To busk its cozy bield*; shelter
The corbie croaks upon the tree,
His auld paternal tower;
While the sentimental cushie doo* "dove"
Croods in her greenwood bower.

The kye gae lowin' oer the loan,
As cheery daylight fades;
And bats come flaffin' through the fauld,
And birds gae to their beds;
Then jinkin' out by bent* an' brae, field
When they are seen by no man,
The lads and lasses blithely meet,
And cuddle in the gloamin'.

The cauld north wind has soughed awa,
The snaw has left the hill,
And briskly to the wastlin' breeze
Reels round yon bonny mill;
The cheery spring, in robes o' green,
Comes laughin' ower the lea,
While burnies by their flowery banks
Rin singin' to the sea.

## WILLIAM THOM (1798–1848)

### The Blind Boy's Pranks

Men grew sae cauld, maids sae unkind,
Love kent na whaur to stay;
Wi' fient* an arrow, bow, or string— scarcely
Wi' droopin' heart an' drizzled wing,
He fought his lonely way.

Is there nae mair, in Gairloch fair,
Ae spotless home for me?
Have politics, an' corn, an' kye,
Ilk bosom stappit? Fie, O fie!
I'll swithe me oer the sea.

He launched a leaf o' jessamine,
On whilk he dared to swim,
An' pillowed his head on a wee rose-bud;
Syne slighted Love awa' did scud
Down Ury's waefu' stream.

The birds sang bonnie as Love drew near,
But dowie* when he gaed by; sad
Till lulled wi' the sough o' monie a sang,
He slept fu' soun' as he sailed alang
Neath heaven's gowden sky.

Twas just when creepin' Ury greets
Its mountain cousin Don,
There wandered forth a weel-faured dame,
Wha listless gazed on the bonnie stream,
As it flirted an' played wi' a sunny beam
That flickered its bosom upon.

Love happit his head, I trow, that time,
When the jessamine bark drew nigh,
An' the lassie espied the wee rose-bud,
An' aye her heart gae thud for thud,
An' quiet it wadna lie.

"O gin I but had yon wearied wee flower
That floats on the Ury so fair."
She lootit her hand for the silly rose-leaf,
But little kent she o' the paukie* thief, sly
That was lurkin' an' laughin' there.

Love glowered when he saw her bonnie dark e'e,
An' swore by heaven's grace
He ne'er had seen nor thought to see,
Since e'er he left the Paphian lea,
Mair lovely a dwallin'-place.

Syne first of a', in her blythesome breast,
He built a bower, I ween;
An' what did the waefu' devilick neist:
But kindled a gleam like the rosy east,
That sparkled frae baith her e'en.

An' O beneath ilk high e'e-bree
He placed a quiver there;
His bow? what but her shinin' brow?
An' O sic deadly strings he drew
Frae out her silken hair.

Guid be our guard! sic deeds waur dune
Roun' a' our country then;
An' mony a hangin' lug* was seen — ear, flap
Mang farmers fat an' lawyers lean,
An' herds o' common men.

## They Speak o' Wyles

They speak o' whyles in woman's smiles,
An' ruin in her e'e—
I ken they bring a pang at whiles
That's unco* sair to dree*; — very/endure
But mind ye this, the half-ta'en kiss,
The first fond fa'in' tear,
Is, heaven kens, fu' sweet amends
An' tints o' heaven here.

When twa leal* hearts in fondness meet, — "loyal"
Life's tempests howl in vain—
The very tears o' love are sweet
When paid with tears again.
Shall sapless prudence shake its pow*, — head
Shall cauldrife caution fear?
Oh, dinna, dinna droun the lowe* — flame
That lichts a heaven here.

What though we're ca'd a wee before
The stale "three score an' ten,"
When Joy keeks* kindly at your door, — peeks
Aye bid her welcome ben*. — in
About yon blissfu' bowers above
Let doubtfu' mortals speir*, — ask
Sae weel ken we that "Heaven is love"
Since love makes heaven here.

## Ye Dinna Ken Yon Bower

Ye dinna ken yon bower,
Frae the glow'rin warl' hidden,
Ye maunna ken yon bower

Bonnie in the gloamin'.
Nae woodbine sheds a fragrance there,
Nae rose, nae daffodillie fair;
But, oh, yon flow'r beyond compare
That blossoms in the gloamin.

There's little licht in yon bower,
Day and darkness elbow ither,
That's the licht in yon bower,
Bonnie in the gloamin.
Awa ye sun, wi' lavish licht,
And bid brown Benachie guid nicht.
To me a star mair dearly bricht
Aye glimmers in the gloamin.

There's nae a sound in yon bower,
Merl's sough nor mavis singin';
Whispers saft in yon bower,
Mingle in the gloamin.
What though drowsy lav'rocks rest,
Cow'rin' in their sangless nest?
When, oh, the voice that I like best
Cheers me in the gloamin.

There's artless truth in yon bower,
Sweeter than the scented blossom;
Bindin' hearts in yon bower,
Glowin' in the gloamin.
The freshness o' the upland lea,
The fragrance o' the blossomed pea,
A' mingle in her breath to me,
Sichin'* in the gloamin. "sighing"

Then haud awa' frae yon bower,
Cauldrife breast or loveless bosom;
True love dwells in yon bower,
Gladdest in the gloamin.

## My Hameless Ha'

Oh, how can I be cheerie in this hameless ha'?
The very sun glints eerie on the gilded wa';
An' aye the nicht sae dreary,
Ere the dowie* morn daw, sad
Whan I canna win to see you
My Jamie ava.

Though monie miles between us, an' far, far frae me,
The bush that wont to screen us frae the cauld warl's e'e,
Its leaves may waste and wither,
But its branches winna fa';

An' hearts may haud thegither,
Though frien's drap awa'.

Ye promised to speak o' me to the lanesome moon,
An' weird kind wishes to me, in the lark's saft soun';
I doat upon that moon,
Till my very heart fills fu';
An' aye yon birdie's tune
Gars* me greet* for you. makes/weep

Then how can I be cheerie in the stranger's ha'?
A gowden prison dreary, my luckless fa'.
Tween leavin' o' you, Jamie,
An' ills that sorrow me
I'm weary o' the warl'
An' carena though I dee.

## ROBERT HOGG (1799–1834)

### When Autumn Comes

When autumn comes, an' heather bells
Bloom bonnie ower yon moorland fells*, hills
An' corn that waves on lowland dales
Is yellow ripe appearing;

Bonnie lassie, will ye gang
Shear wi' me the hale day lang;
An' love will mak us eithly* bang easily
The weary toil o' shearing?

An' if the lasses should envy,
Or say we love, then you an' I
Will pass ilk ither slyly by,
As if we werna caring.

But aye I wi' my heuk will whang
The thistles, if in prickles strang
Your bonnie milk white hands they wrang,
When we gang to the shearing.

An' aye we'll haud our rig afore,
An' ply to hae the shearing oer,
Syne you will soon forget you bore
Your neighbors' jibes and jeering.

For then, my lassie, we'll be wed,
When we hae proof o' ither had,
An' nae mair need to mind what's said
When we're thegither shearing.

## JOHN IMLAH (1799–1846)

### Luckie Nanse Norrie
Portrait of a Dame Who Fell in the Midden Looking at the Moon

Lucky Nanse Norrie was puir as a kirk-mouse,
Little to look to, but want, or the wark-house,
Humble her bidin', and hamely her breedin',
Clootit* and scant was the hail o' her cleedin'; patched
But Lucky was wily, and Lucky was war'ly,
She ettled* to cleck in a wealthy auld carlie*; determined/fellow
The Laird o' some land ayont Elgin o' Moray,
Wi' mair gear* than gumption—and did it—Nanse Norrie. money

Weel buiket* and buck'lt she cam' by her marriage "booked" (registered)
To sit in a sofa and hurl in a carriage;
Sair, sair, she socht to get grit wi' the gentry;
Lucky was gloomed* on, sae quat her ain kintry, frowned
Awa south about went to be residenter,
To be big amang sma folk, whaur naebody kent her.
Sow lugs* makna silk purses—truth trite and hoary, ears
Nor walth mak a leddy o' Lucky Nanse Norrie.

She had lackeys in livery to tend to her callin',
She'd servants o' a' kin's, but weet nurse in her dwallin'.
Now woman grown wife looks for mair than a marrow*, mate
For feckless the quiver without'n ae arrow;
And honor'd's the briest to the barnie-lip teemin',
Wi' what taks awa the reproach amang women.
The Laird had nae heir, and his pow* now was hoary— head
He was childish—and childless was Lucky Nanse Norrie.

She cut auld frien's for strangers—to see them twas shamefu',
How they'd cringe for a crumb—kiss her fit* for a wamefu'*; "foot"/bellyful
For though she took care o' her cash, to the cuppers
She crammed them wi' dainty het dinners and suppers.
But och siccan kyte-hungry frien's! the deil speed them—
Will fawn to the face and back-bite them wha feed them;
Get drunk like a lord, wi' the laird in his glory,
And laugh in their sleeves at puir Lucky Nanse Norrie.

Lucky, though walthy, was siccar* and selfish, tight-fisted
Mean as a muc-worm, close as a shell-fish;
Drivin' hard bargains, for cash wi' the needy,
O' gifts come frae wham they may, grippy and greedy,
Even frae folks wha were scarce worth the price o' a sneeshin'*, snuff
And aye foun' that the fat sow's hind quarter's maist creesh* on; grease
Gif she e'er did sma kindness, we a' heard the story,
For she tootit her ain trumpit, Lucky Nanse Norrie.

The bachels* forgot in the slipper o' satin, old shoes
And shanks mair at ease in the saft-cushioned phaeton,

And cordial companions of opposite gender,
Wi' consciences teugh, if wi' characters tender.
And broken-down gentles on broken-up incomes,
And nae over nice now in what way the tin comes;
But tell't na in Gath, for a breath o' the story
Wad dim her gentility, Lucky Nanse Norrie.

O dinna envy her, thou fair peasant maiden,
Though thy fare be but scant, thy frock but coarse plaiden;
Tak the lad that your ee likes, your heart's secret idol,
Though a shake-down o' peas strae, the bed o' your bridal.
Though vice feast in state, in fine laces and linen,
Wear the cloak o' thy wark, eat the cake o' thy winnin',
And lilt at thy wheel oer this sang that's nae story:
Tak the cap if it fit you weel—Lucky Nanse Norrie.

## Hielan' Heather

Hey for the Hielan' heather!
Hey for the Hielan' heather!
Dear to me, an' aye shall be,
The bonnie braes o' Hielan' heather.

The moss-muir black an' mountain blue,
Whare mists at morn an' gloamin' gather;
The craigs an' cairns o' hoary hue,
Whare blooms the bonnie Hielan' heather.

Whare mony a wild bird wags its wing,
Baith sweet o' sang an' fair o' feather;
While caverned cliffs wi' echo ring
Amang the hills o' Hielan' heather.

Whare, light o' heart an' light o' heel,
Young lads and lasses trip thegither
The native Norlan' rant and reel
Amang the halesome Hielan' heather.

The broom an whin, by loch an' linn*, waterfall
Are tipped wi' gowd in simmer weather.
How sweet an' fair! but meikle mair
The purple bells o' Hielan' heather.

Whare'er I rest, whare'er I range,
My fancy fondly travels thither.
Nae country charms, nae customs change
My feelings frae the Hielan' heather.

## The Gathering

Rise, rise! Lowland and Highlandmen,
Bald sire to beardless son, each come and early;

Rise, rise, mainland and islandmen,
Belt on your broad claymores—fight for Prince Charlie.
Down from the mountain steep,
Up from the valley deep,
Out from the clachan*, the bothie*, and shieling*, village/worker's hut/cottage
Bugle and battle-drum,
Bid chief and vassal come,
Bravely our bagpipes the pibroch is pealing.

Men of the mountains—descendants of heroes,
Heirs of the fame as the hills of your fathers;
Say, shall the Southern—the Sassenach* fear us (English)
When to the war-peal each plaided clan gathers?
Too long on the trophied walls
Of your ancestral halls,
Red rust hath blunted the armor of Albin.
Seize, then, ye mountain Macs,
Buckler and battle-ax,
Lads of Lochaber, Braemar, and Breadablin.

When hath the tartan plaid mantled a coward?
When did the blue bonnet crest the disloyal?
Up, then, and crowd to the standard of Stuart,
Follow your leader—the rightful—the royal,
Chief of Clanronald,
Donald Macdonald,
Lovat, Lochiel, with the Grant and the Gordon,
Rouse every kilted clan,
Rouse every loyal man,
Gun on the shoulder, and thigh the good sword on.

## JAMES MAYNE ( ? –1842)

### Maggy Maclane

Doon i' the glen by the lown* o' the trees, shelter
Lies a wee thecket bield*, like a bike* for the bees; shelter/hive
But the hinnie there skepped—gin ye're no dour to please—
It's virgin Miss Maggy Maclane.
There's few seek Meg's shed noo, the simmer sun jookin;
It's aye the dry floor, Meg's—the day e'er sae drookin*. drenched
But the heather-blabs hing whare the red blude's been shooken
I' bruilzies* for Maggy Maclane. brawls

Doon by Meg's howf-tree the gowk* comes to woo; cuckoo
But the corncraik's aye fleyed at her hallan-door joo.
An' the redbreast ne'er cheeps but the weird's at his mou,
For the last o' the roses that's gane.
Nae trystin at Meg's noo—nae Halloween rockins.
Nae howtowdie guttlens—nae mart-puddin' yockins*. "yokings"
Nae bane i' the blast's teeth blaws snell* up Glendockens, fierce
Clean bickers wi' Maggy Maclane.

Meg's auld lyart* gutcher swarfed* dead i' the shaw; — gray/swooned
Her bein*, fouthy minnie,—she's aff an' awa. — snug
The gray on her pow* but a simmerly snaw— — head
The couthy*, cosh* Widow Maclane. — spirited/friendly
O titties be tentie*, though air i' the day wi' ye, — careful
Think that the green grass may ae day be hay wi' ye.
Think of the leal minnie—mayna be aye wi' ye,
When sabbin for Maggy Maclane.

Lallan joes*—Hielan joes—Meg ance had wale; — sweethearts
Folk wi' the siller, and chiefs wi' the tail.
The yaud* left the burn to drink out o' Meg's pail. — old horse
The sheltie braw kent "the Maclane;"
Awa owre the muir they cam stottin an' stoicherin,
Tramper an' traveler, a' beakin an' broicherin,
Cadgers* an' cuddy-creels, oigherin—hoigherin. — peddlers
"The lanlowpers!" quo Maggy Maclane.

Cowtes* were to fother: Meg owre the burn flang. — "colts"
Nowte* were to tether:—Meg through the wood rang. — cattle
The widow she kenned-na to bless or to bann*. — curse
Sic waste o' gude wooers to hain.
Yet, aye at the souter*, Meg grumphed her, an' grumphed her. — cobbler
The loot-shouthered wabster*, she humphed her, and humphed her. — weaver
The lamiter* tailor, she stumped her, and stumped her. — lame
Her minnie might groo* or grane. — shiver

The tailor he likit cockleekie broo;
An' doon he cam wi' a beck an' a boo:—
Quo Meg—"We'se soon tak the clecken aff you,"
An' plump i' the burn he's gane!
The widow's cheek reddened; her heart it played thud, aye;
Her garters she cuist roun' his neck like a wuddie*. — noose
She linkit him oot; but wi' wringin his duddies,
Her wood-ring it's burst in twain.

Wowf was the widow—to haud nor to bing.
The tailor he's aff, an' he's coft* a new ring. — bought
The deil squeeze his craig's* no wordy the string. — gullet's
He's waddet auld Widow Maclane!
Auld?—and a bride! Na, ye'd pitied the tea-pat.
O saut were the skadyens*, but balm's in Glenlivat. — herring
The haggis was bockin oot bluters o' bree-fat,
An' hotched* to the piper its lane. — bobbed

Doon the burnside, i' the lown o' the glen,
Meg reists her bird-lane, i' a but-an'-a-ben;
Steal doon when ye dow*,—i' the dearth, gentlemen,— — can
Ye'se be awmous* to Maggy Maclane. — alms
Lane bauks the virgin—nae white pows now keekin* — peeking
Through key-hole an' cranny; nae cash blade stan's sleekin
His nicherin' naigie, his gaudamous* seekin, — a feast
Alack for the days that are gane.

Lame's fa'n the souter—some steek i' his thie.
The cooper's clean gyte*, wi' a hoopin coughee. crazed
The smith's got sae blin—wi' a spunk i' is e'e—
He's tined* glint o' Maggy Maclane. lost
Meg brake the kirk pew-door—Auld Beukie leuked near-na her.
She dunkled her pattie—Young Sneekie ne'er speired* for her. asked
But the warst's when the wee mouse leuks out, wi' a tear to her,
Frae the meal-kist* o' Maggy Maclane. "chest"

## CHARLES, LORD NEAVES (1800–1876)

### Let Us All Be Unhappy on Sunday
(A Lyric for Saturday Night)

We zealots made up of stiff clay,
The sour-looking children of sorrow,
While not over jolly today,
Resolve to be wretched tomorrow.
We can't for a certainty tell
What mirth may molest us on Monday;
But, at least, to begin the week well,
Let us all be unhappy on Sunday.

That day, the calm season of rest,
Shall come to us freezing and frigid.
A gloom all our thoughts shall invest,
Such as Calvin would call over-rigid,
With sermons from morning to night,
We'll strive to be decent and dreary:
To preachers a praise and delight,
Who ne'er think that sermons can weary.

All tradesmen cry up their own wares.
In this they agree well together.
The mason by stone and lime swears.
The tanner is always for leather.
The smith still for iron would go.
The schoolmaster stands up for teaching;
And the parson would have you to know,
There's nothing on earth like his preaching.

The face of kind nature is fair;
But our system obscures its effulgence:
How sweet is a breath of fresh air!
But our rules don't allow the indulgence.
These gardens, their walks and green bowers,
Might be free to the poor man for one day;
But no, the glad plants and gay flowers
Mustn't bloom or smell sweetly on Sunday.

What though a good precept we strain
Till hateful and hurtful we make it.
What though in thus pulling the rein,
We may draw it as tight as to break it.
Abroad we forbid folks to roam,
For fear they get social or frisky;
But of course they can sit still at home,
And get dismally drunk upon whisky.

Then, though we can't certainly tell
How mirth may molest us on Monday;
At least, to begin the week well,
Let us all be unhappy on Sunday.

## JAMES TELFER (1800–1862)

### The Gloamin Buchte

The sun was reid as a furnace mouth,
As he sank on the Ettrick hill;
And gloamin gatherit from the east,
The dowy* world to fill. sad

When bonnie Jean Rool she milkit the yowes,
I' the buchte* aboon the linn; sheepfold
And they were wild and ill to wear,
But the hindmost buchtfu' was in.

O milk them weil, my bonnie Jean Rool,
The wily shepherd could say,
And sing to me "The Keach i' the Creel,"
To put the time away.

It's fer owre late at e'en, shepherd,
Replied the maiden fair;
The fairies wad hear, quo bonnie Jean Rool,
And wi' louting* my back is sair. bending

He's taen her round the middle sae sma,
While the yowes ran by between,
And out o' the buchte he's laid her down,
And all on the dewy green.

The star o' love i' the eastern lift* sky
Was the only e'e they saw.
The only tongue that they might hear
Was the linn's* deep murmuring fa'. waterfall's

O who can tell of youthfu' love?
O who can sing or say?
It is a theme for minstrel meet,
And yet transcends his lay.

It is a thraldom, well I ween,
To hold the heart in silk;
It is a draught to craze the brain,
Yet milder than the milk.

O sing me the sang, my bonnie Jean Rool,
Now, dearest, sing to me.
The angels will listen at yon little holes,
And witness my vows to thee.

I mayna refuse, quo bonnie Jean Rool,
Sae weel ye can me win.
And she sat in his arms, and sweetly she sang,
And her voice rang frae the linn.

The liltings o' that silver voice,
Might weel the wits beguile.
They clearer were than shepherd's pipe
Heard oer the hills a mile.

The liltings o' that silver voice,
That rose an' fell so free,
They softer were than lover's lute,
Herd oer a sleeping sea.

The liltings o' that silver voice
Were melody sae true;
They sprang up through the welkin wide
To the heaven's keystane blue.

Sing on, sing on, my bonnie Jean Rool,
Sing on your sang sae sweet.
Now Christ me save, quo the bonnie lass,
Whence comes that waesome greet*? weeping

They turned their gaze to the Mourning Cleuch,
Where the greeting seemed to be,
And there beheld a little green bairn
Come oer the darksome lea.

And aye it raised a waesome greet,
But and an eerie cry,
Until it came to the buchte fauld end,
Where the winsome pair did lie.

It lookit around with it snail-cap eyne,
That made their hearts to grou*; shiver
Then turned upright its grass-green face,
And opened its goblin mou';

Then raised a yule, sae loud and lang—
Sae yerlish and sae shrill,

As dirled up through the twinkling holes
The second lift until.

I tell the tale as told to me,
I swear so by my fay*; "faith"
And whether or not of glamoury*, witchcraft
In sooth I cannot say.

That youling yowte sae yerlish was,
But and sae lang and loud,
The rising moon like saffron grew,
And holed ahint a cloud.

And round the boddom o' the lift,
It rang the world through,
And boomed against the milky way,
Afore it closed its mou'.

Then neist* it raised its note and sang next
Sae witchingly and sweet,
The moudies*, powtelit out o' the yirth, moles
And kissed the singer's feet.

The waizle dun frae the auld gray cairn,
The thief foulmart* came nigh; polecat
The hurcheon* raxed his scory chafts, hedgehog
And gepit wi' girning joy.

The tod* he came frae the Screthy holes, fox
And courit fou cunningly;
The stinkin brock* wi' his lang lank lysk, badger
Shot up his gruntle to see.

The kid and martin ran a race
Amang the dewy fern;
The mawkin* gogglet i' the singer's face, hare
Th' enchanting notes to learn.

The pert little esks* they curlit their tails, newts
And danced a mirthsome reel;
The tad held up her auld dun lufes,
She likit the sang sae weel.

The heron came frae the witch-pule tree,
The houlet frae Deadwood howe;
The auld gray corbie hoverit aboon,
While tears down his cheeks did flow.

The yowes they lap out oer the buchte,
And skippit it up and doon;
And bonnie Jean Rool i' the shepherd's arms,
Fell back out-owre in a swoon.

It might be glamourie or not,
In sooth I cannot say,
It was the witching time of night—
The hour o' gloamin gray,
And she that lay in her lover's arms
I wis was a weel-faured may*. maid

Her pulses all were beating true,
Her heart was louping light,
Unto that wondrous melody—
That simple song of might.

The Song

O where is tiny Hew?
O where is little Len?
And where is bonnie Lu?
And Menie o' the glen?
And where's the place o' rest?
The ever changing hame—
Is it the gowan's* breast, daisy's
Or neath the bell o' faem?
Chorus.—ay lu lan, lan dil y'u, &c.

The fairest rose you find
May have a taint within.
The flower o' womankind,
May ope her breast to sin.
The foxglove cup you'll bring,
The tail of shooting sterne,
And at the grassy ring,
We'll pledge the pith o' fern.
Chorus.—ay lu lan, lan dil y'u, &c.

And when the blushing moon
Glides down the western sky,
By streamer's wing we soon
Upon her top will lie:-
Her hichest horn we'll ride;
And quaff her yellow dew,
And frae her skaddowy side,
The burning day we'll view.
Chorus.—ay lu lan, lan dil y'u, &c.

The strain raise high, the strain fell low,
Then fainted fitfully;
And bonnie Jean Rool she lookit up,
To see what she might see.

She lookit hich to the boding hill,
And laigh to the darkling dean;
She heard the sounds still ringin' i' the lift,
But naething could be seen.

She held her breath with anxious care,
And thought it all a dream:—
But an eerie nicher she heard i' the linn,
And a plitch-platch in the stream.

Never a word said bonny Jeany Rool,
But, shepherd, let us gang;
And never mair, at a gloamin buchte,
Wald she sing another sang.

## JANE WELSH CARLYLE (1801–1866)

[Jane Welsh Carlyle was the wife of the great Victorian essayist and historian, Thomas Carlyle, and a fine prose stylist in her own right. She is primarily known for the great number of fine letters she wrote to her husband, whose travels took him often from her side. The following, however, is apparently a journal entry. Carlyle found it after her death. For reasons which she implies in the story itself, she had apparently never shown it to him. This is a touching account of her visit, after an absence of many years, to Haddington, Scotland, the town of her upbringing.]

### A Visit to Haddington

On Tuesday, 24th July 1849, I left Rawdon, after breakfast, and at five of the afternoon reached Morpeth; where I had decided to pass the night. William Forster escorted me thus far, and stayed to start me by the 2 o'clock train next day; — out of pure charity, having adopted Donovan's theory of me, that I am wholly without observing Faculty, with large reflectiveness turned inward; — a sort of woman, that, ill-adapted for traveling by railway, alone, with two boxes, a writing-case, and carpet-bag. Anyhow, I was much the better of such a cheerful companion; to stave off the nervousness about Haddington; not to speak of the material comforts, — a rousing fire, brandynegus, &c. — which he ordered for me at the Inn, and which I should not have had the audacity to order, on my own basis.

After a modest dinner of chops and cherry tart; we walked by the River-side in a drizzling rain (that was at my suggestion); then back to the Phoenix for tea, chess, and speculative talk till midnight; when I went to bed expecting no sleep to speak of, and of course slept unusually well; for the surest way to get a thing in this life is to be prepared for doing without it, — to the exclusion even of hope.

Next morning was bright as diamonds, and we walked all about the Town and neighboring Heights; where, rendered unusually communicative by our isolated position, I informed William Edward that my maternal grandmother was "descended from a gang of Gypsies"; was in fact grandniece to Matthew Baillie who "suffered at Lanark", — that is to say, was hanged there, — a genealogical fact Forster said which made me at last intelligible for him, — "a cross betwixt John Knox and a Gypsy how that explained all". — By the way, my uncle has told me since I came here, that the wife of that Matthew Baillie, Margaret Euston by name, was the original of Sir W. Scott's Meg Merrilies. Matthew himself was the last of the Gypsies,—could steal a horse from under the owner if he liked, but left always the saddle and bridle; a thorough gentleman in his way, and six feet four in stature!

But to go back to Morpeth, we again dined at the Phoenix; then Forster put me into my carriage, and my luggage in the van and I was shot off towards Scotland; — while himself took train for Ireland!

From Morpeth to Haddington is a journey of only four hours; again "the wished for come too late"! rapidest traveling to Scotland now, and no home there any more!

The first locality I recognized was the Peer Bridge: I had been there once before, a little child, in a postchaise with my Father; he had held his arm round me while I looked down the ravine; it was my first sight of the Picturesque, that. I recognized the place even in passing it at railway speed, after all these long long years.

At the Dunbar station an old lady in widow's dress, and a young one, her daughter, got into the carriage which I had had so far all to myself; a man in yeomanry uniform waiting to see them off. "Ye'll maybe come and see us the morn'snicht?" said the younger lady from the carriage. "What for did ye no come to the Ball?" answered the yeoman, with a look "to split a pitcher"? The young lady tchicktchicked and looked deprecatingly, and tried again and again to enchain conversation; but, to everything she said, came the same answer; "What for did ye no come to the Ball?"— The poor young lady then tried holding her tongue; her lover (only her lover would have used her so brutally) did the same; but rested his chin on the carriage window to scowl at her with more convenience. The interest was rising; but one could see who of them would speak first.

"Oh!" broke out the young lady, "I'm just mourning!" "What for?" — "Oh, just that ball!" — "What for then did ye no come?" growled the repeating decimal; "I waited an oor for ye!" and he got his upper lip over the strap of his cap and champed it — like a horse! — Squeal went the engine; we were off; the young lady "just mourned" for a minute or two, then fell to talking with her Mother; for me, I reflected how "the feelings were just the same there as here," and the Devil everywhere busy!

Before these ladies got out at Drem I had identified the pale, old, shriveled widow with a buxom bright-eyed rosy Mrs. Frank Sheriff of my time. The Daughter had not only grown up but got herself born in the interval. What chiefly struck me, however, indeed confounded me, was to be stared at by Mrs. Sheriff as a stranger, or even foreigner! for, when I asked her some questions about the road, she answered with that compassionate distinctness which one puts on with only foreigners — or idiots. I began to think my precautions for keeping Incognita in my native place might turn out to have been superfluous.

One of these precautions had the foolishest little consequence. In leaving London, I had written the addresses for my luggage on the backs of other people's visiting-cards, "without respect of persons"; a stupid practice when one thinks of it! — but at Morpeth I removed three of the cards, leaving one to the carpet-bag, carpet-bags being so confoundable; I was at the pains however to rub off my own name from that card, which, for the rest, happened to be Mrs. Humphrey St John Mildmay's. Well! at Longniddry, where I had to wait some fifteen minutes for the cross-train to Haddington, "there came to pass" a Porter! who helped me with my things, and would not leave off helping me — quite teased me in fact with delicate attentions. At last he made me a low bow and said he was "not aware that any of the family were in this quarter". I believe I answered; "quite well I thank you"; for I was getting every instant more excited with my circumstances. He shut the carriage-door on me, then opened it again and said with another low bow; "Excuse me, Ma'm but I was in the service of the brother of Mr. Humphrey St John Mildmay." I am positive as to my answer this time that it was; "Oh thank you no! I am quite another person!"

A few minutes more and I was at the Haddington Station; where I looked out timidly, then more boldly, as my senses took in the utter strangeness of the scene; and luckily I had "the cares of luggage" to keep down sentiment for the moment. No vehicle was in waiting but a dusty little omnibus licensed to carry — any number, it seemed! for on remarking there was no seat for me I was told by all the insides in a breath; "never heed! come in! that makes no difference!" And so I was trundled to the George Inn, where a Landlord and Waiter, both strangers to me, and looking half-asleep showed me to the best room on the first floor, — a large old-fashioned, three-windowed room, looking out on the Fore Street, — and, without having spoken one word, shut the door on me, and there I was at the end of it! Actually in the George Inn, Haddington, alone, amidst the silence of death!

I sat down quite composedly at a window, and looked up the street, — towards our old house; it was the same street, the same houses; but so silent, dead, petrified! it looked, the old place, just as I had seen it at Chelsea in my dreams — only more dreamlike! Having exhausted that outlook, I rung my bell, and told the silent Landlord to bring tea, and took order about my bedroom. The tea swallowed down; I notified my wish to view "the old Church there," and the keeper of the keys was immediately fetched me. In my part of stranger-in-search-of-the-Picturesque, I let myself be shown the way which I knew every inch of, — shown the "the school-houses" where myself had been Dux,— "the play-ground," "the Boolin green," and so on to the church-gate, which so soon as my guide had unlocked for me, I told him he might wait— that I needed him no further.

The Church-yard had become very full of graves. Within the Ruin were two new smartly got up tombs; His[1] looked old, old; was surrounded by nettles; the inscription all over moss; except two lines which had been quite recently cleared — by whom? Who had been there, before me, still caring for his tomb after 29 years? The old Ruin knew, and could not tell me! that place felt the very center of eternal silence — silence and sadness world without end!

When I returned to the sexton, or whatever he was, he asked would I not walk through the church; I said yes, and he led the way, but without playing the Cicerone any more; he had become pretty sure there was no need. Our pew looked to have never been new-lined since we occupied it; the green cloth was become all but white from age! I looked at it in the dim twilight till I almost fancied I saw my beautiful Mother in her old corner, and myself a bright-looking girl in the other! It was time to "come out of that"!

Meaning to return to the Churchyard next morning, to clear the moss from the inscription; I asked my conductor where he lived — with the key. "Next door to the house that was Dr. Welsh's," he answered, with a sharp glance at my face; then added gently; "excuse me mem for mentioning that, but the minute I set eyes on ye at the George, I jaloosed it was her we all looked after whenever she went up or down."

"You won't tell of me?" I said, crying, like a child caught stealing apples; and gave him half a crown to keep my secret, and open the gate for me at eight next morning. Then turning, up the waterside by myself, I made the circuit of the Haugh, Dodd's Gardens and Babbies Butts, — the customary evening walk in my teens; and except that it was perfectly solitary (in the whole round I met just two little children walking hand in hand, like the Babes of the Wood) the whole thing looked exactly as I left it 22 years back! the very puddles made by the last rain I felt to have stepped over before. — But where were all the living beings one used to meet? What could have come to the place to strike it so dead? I have been since answered; the railway had come to it, and ruined it. At all rates "it must have taken a great deal to make a place so dull as that"! —

Leaving the lanes I now went boldly through the streets, the thick black veil, put on for the occasion, thrown back; I was getting confident that I might have ridden like the Lady Godiva through Haddington, with impunity, — so far as recognition went. — I looked through the sparred door of our old coachhouse, which seemed to be vacant; the House itself I left over till morning, when its occupants should be asleep.

---

[1] Her father's.

Passing a Cooper's shop which I had once had the run of, I stept in and bought two little quaighs; then in the character of traveling Englishwoman, suddenly seized with an unaccountable passion for wooden dishes, I questioned the Cooper as to the Past and Present of his town. He was the very man for me, being ready to talk the tongue small in his head about his town'sfolks, men, women, and children of them.

He told me amongst other interesting things, that "Doctor Welsh's death was the sorest loss ever came to the Place"; — that myself "went away into England and — died there"! adding a handsome enough tribute to my memory. "Yes! Miss Welsh!— he remembered her famously, — used to think her the tastiest young lady in the whole Place — but she was very — not just to call proud, — very reserved in her company." — In leaving this man I felt more than ever like my own ghost; if I had really been walking after my death and burial, there could not I think have been any material difference in my sensations.

My next visit was to the front gate of Sunny Bank, where I stood some minutes, looking up at the beautifully quiet House; not unlike the "outcast Peri" done into prose. How would my old godmother and the others have looked, I wondered, had they known who was there, so near them! I longed to go in and kiss them once more, but positively dared not; I felt that their demonstrations of affection would break me down into a torrent of tears, which there was no time for; so I contented myself with kissing — the gate (!) and returned to my Inn, it being now near Dark. Surely it was the silentest Inn on the Planet! not a living being male or female to be seen in it except when I rung my bell, and then the Landlord or Waiter (both old men) did my bidding promptly and silently and vanished again into space. On my reentrance I rung for candles, and for a glass of sherry and hot water; my feet had been wetted amongst the long grass of the churchyard, and I felt to be taking cold; so I made myself negus as an antidote, and they say I am not a practical woman!

Then it struck me; I would write to Mr. Carlyle, — one more letter from the old place, after so much come and gone. Accordingly I wrote till the Town clock (the first familiar voice I had heard) struck eleven, then twelve, and near one I wrote the Irish address on my letter and finally put myself to bed — in the George Inn of Haddington, good God! — I thought it too strange and mournful a position for ever falling asleep in; nevertheless I slept in the first instance; for I was "a-weary a-weary," body and soul of me! But, alas! the only noise I was to hear in Haddington "transpired" exactly at the wrong moment; before I had slept one hour I was awoke by — an explosion of cats! The rest of that night I spent betwixt sleeping and waking, in night-mare efforts to "sort up my thoughts." At half after five I put my clothes on, and began the business of the day by destroying in a moment of enthusiasm — for silence — the long letter "all about feelings" which I had written the night before. Soon after six I was haunting our old house, while the present occupants still slept. I found the garden door locked, and iron stanchions, — my Heavens! — on the porch and cellar windows, "significative of much"! for the rest, there was a general need of paint and whitewash: in fact the whole premises had a bedimmed melancholy look as of having "seen better days".

It was difficult for me to realize to myself that the people inside were only asleep — and not dead — dead since many years. Ah! one breathed freer in the churchyard, with the bright morning sunshine streaming down on it than near that (so-called) habitation of the living! I went straight from the one to the other. The gate was still locked; for I was an hour before my time; so I made a dash at the wall, some seven feet high I should think, and dropt safe on the inside — a feat I should never have imagined to try in my actual phase, not even with a mad bull at my heels; if I had not trained myself to it at a more elastic age. Godefroi Cavaignac's "Quoi donc je ne suis pas mort?" crossed my mind but I had none of that feeling — moi, — was morte enough, I knew, whatever face I might put on it! only, what one has well learnt one never forgets.

When I had scraped the moss out of the inscription, as well as I could with the only thing in my dressing case at all suited to the purpose, namely his own button hook with the mother-of-pearl handle; I made a deliberate survey of the whole churchyard; and most of the names I had missed out of the signboards turned up for me once more on the tombstones. It was strange the feeling of almost glad recognition that came over me, in finding so many familiar figures out of my childhood and youth all gathered together in one place; But still more interesting for me than these later graves were two that I remembered to have weeped little innocent tears over before I had a conception what real weeping meant, — the grave of the little girl who was burnt to death, through drying her white muslin frock at the fire, and that of the young officer (Rutherford) who was shot in a duel. The oval tablet of white marble over the little girl's grave looked as bright and spotless as on the first day — as emblematic of the child existence it commemorated; it seemed to my somewhat excited imagination that the youthfulness and innocence there buried had impregnated the marble to keep it snow-white for ever!

When the sexton came at eight to let me in; he found me ready to be let out. "How in the world had I got in?" — "over the wall." "No! surely I couldn't mean that?" — "Why not?" — "Lordsake then," cried the man in real admiration, "there is no end to you!"

He told me at parting; "there is one man in this Town, Mem, you might like to see —James Robertson, your Father's old servant." Our own old Jamie! he was waiter at the Star good gracious! had returned to Haddington within the last year. "Yes indeed" — I said, "he must be sent to me at The George an hour hence; and told only that a Lady wanted him."

It was still but eight o'clock, so I should have time to look at Sunny Bank from the back gate, and streamed off in that direction; but passing my dear old schoolhouse I observed the door a little ajar, walked in and sat down in my old seat; to the manifest astonishment of a decent woman who was sweeping the floor. Ach Gott! our maps and Geometrical Figures had given place to texts from Scripture and the foolishest half-penny pictures! it was become an Infant School, Good God! and a Miss Alexander was now teacher where Edward Irving and James Brown had taught! — Miss A. — and her Infants were not, it seemed early risers; their schoolroom after eight o'clock was only being swept; it was at seven of the morning that James Brown once found me asleep there — after two hours hard study — asleep betwixt the leaves of the great atlas, like a keep lesson! but "things have been all gone to the Devil ever since the reform bill"; as my Uncle is always telling us. The woman interrupted her sweeping to inform me amongst other things that it "was a most terrible place for dust"; that "a deal was put into Bairns now, which she dooted was waste wark"; that "it was little one got by cleaning after them," and "if her Husband had his legs, they might have the school that liked".

Not the vestige of a Boy or even of a girl was to be seen about the Grammar School either; that school, I afterwards heard from Jamie "had gone to just perfect nonsense" — "There was a Master (one White) but no scholars." "How is that," I asked; "are there no children here any longer?" "Why, its not altogether the want o' children," said Jamie, with his queer old smudge of inarticulate fun; "but the new Master is rather severe, — broke the jawbone of a wee Boy — they tell me; but indeed the whole place is sore gone down." I should think so! But I am not got to Jamie yet; another meeting came off before that one.

Sunny Bank looked even lovelier "in the light of a new morning" than it had done in the evening dusk. A hedge of red roses in full blow extended now from the House to the gate; and I thought I might go in and gather one without evoking any — Beast.

Once inside the gate I passed easily to the idea of proceeding as far as the back-door, just to ask the servant how they all were, and leave compliments without naming myself; the servants only would be a-stir so early. Well! when I had knocked at the door with my finger "sharp but mannerly"; it was opened by a tidy maidservant exhibiting no more surprise than if I had been the Baker's boy! Strange, was it not, that anybody should be in a calm state of mind, while I was so full of emotions? strange that the universe should pursue its own course without reference to my presence in Haddington!!

"Are your Ladies quite well"; I asked nevertheless. "Miss Jess and Miss Catherine are quite well, Miss Donaldson rather complaining; you are aware Mem that Mr. Donaldson is dead?" "Oh dear yes!" I said, thinking she meant Alexander. "At what hour do your Ladies get up?" "They are up Mem and done breakfast. Will you walk round to the front door?" — Goodness gracious! should I "walk round" or not? — My own nerves had got braced somewhat by the morning air; but their nerves — how would the sight of me thus "promiscuously" operate on them?

"You had better go round and let me tell the Ladies," put in the servant, as if in reply to my cogitations; "what name shall I say?" — "None, I think, perhaps my name would startle them more than myself; tell them; someone they will be glad to see." And so, flinging the responsibility on Providence, who is made for being fallen back upon in such dilemmas, ("Providence must have meant me to see them in raising them out of bed so betimes!"), I did "go round," with my heart thumping, "like, — like, — like — anything".

The maidservant met me at the front-door and conducted me to the Drawingroom, where was — nobody; but on a table lay a pile of black-bordered note-paper which explained to me, that it was Mr. Donaldson of London who was dead; the last Brother — dead in these very days! I wished I had not come in; but it was out of time now. The door opened and showed me Miss Catherine changed into an old woman, and showed Miss Catherine me, changed into one of— a certain age! She remained at the door, motionless, speechless, and I couldn't rise off my chair, at least I didn't; but when I saw her eyes staring "like watch-faces," I said, "Oh Miss Catherine don't be frightened at me!" — and then she quite shrieked "Jeannie! Jeannie! Jeannie Welsh! my Jeannie! my Jeannie!" — Oh mercy I shan't forget that scene in a hurry! I got her in my arms and kissed her into her wits again; and then we both cried a little — naturally —; both of us had had enough since we last met to cry for. I explained to her "how I was situated," as Mr. C. would say, and that I was meaning to visit them after — like a Christian; and she found it all "most wisely done, done like my own self". — Humph! — Poor Miss Catherine! it's little she knows of my own self's and perhaps the less the better!

She told me about their Brother's death, which had been sudden at the last. Supposing me still in London as usual, and that in London we hear of one another's deaths; they had been saying it was strange I did not write to them and my godmother had remarked, "it is not like her!" just while I was standing at their gate most likely; for it was "the evening before, about dark," they had been speaking of me.

But again the door opened and showed Miss Jess — Ach! — she had to be told who I was, and pretty loudly too; but when she did take in the immense fact, oh my! it she didn't "show feeling enough" (her own favorite expression of old)! — Poor Jess after all! We used to think she showed even more feeling than she felt, and nothing came out on the present emergence to alter our opinion of her. But enough — the very old, it seems to me, should be admitted, by favor, to the privilege of the Dead, — have "no ill" spoken of them, that can possibly be helped.

My "Godmother" was keeping her bed "with rheumatism" and grief; as I "would really come back soon," it was settled to leave her quiet. They offered me breakfast, — it was still on the table: but "horrible was the thought" to me! It was all so solemn and doleful there that I should have heard every morsel going down my throat! besides I was engaged to breakfast with myself at the George. So, with blessings for many days, I slipt away from them like a knotless thread. My friend the Cooper, espying me from his doorway, on the road back, planted himself firmly in my path: "if I would just compliment him with my name, he would be terribly obliged; we had been uncommon comfortable together, and he must know what they called me"! I told him, and he neither died on the spot nor went mad; he looked pleased and asked how many children I had had. None, I told him. "None!" (in a tone of astonishment, verging on horror.) "None at all! then what on the Earth had I been doing all this time?" "Amusing myself," I told him. He ran after me, to beg I would give him a call on my return (I had spoken of returning) "as he might be making something, belike, to send south with me, something small and of a fancy sort, liker myself than them I had bought".

Breakfast stood ready for me at the Inn, and was discussed in five minutes. Then I wrote a note to Mr. C., a compromise betwixt "all about feelings" and "the new silent system" — of the Prisons. Then I went to my bedroom to pack up. The chambermaid came to say a gentleman was asking for me. "For me?" "Yes! he asked for the lady stopping here" (no influx of company at the George it seemed) "Did you see him" I asked, divining Jamie, "are you sure it is a gentleman?" "I am sure of his being put on like one." I flew down to my parlor, and there was Jamie sure enough! Jamie to the Life! and I threw my arms round his neck, that did I! — He stood quite passive and quite pale with great tears rolling down; it was minutes before he spoke, and then he said only, low under his breath; "Mrs. — Carlyle!" So nice he looked, and hardly a day older, and really as like "a gentleman" as some Lords; he had dressed himself in his Sunday clothes for the occasion, and they were capital good ones.

"And you knew me, Jamie, at first sight?" I asked.

"Toot! we knew ye afore we seed ye."

— "Then you were told it was me?"

— "No! they told us just we was to speak to a Lady at the George, and I knew it was Mrs. Carlyle."

— "But how could you tell, dear Jamie?"

"Hoots! who else could it be?"

Dear funniest of created Jamies! — While he was ostler at the Black Bull, Edinburgh; "one of them what-ye-call Bagmen furgottet his patterns" at Haddington, and he (Jamie) was "sent to take them up; and falling in talk with Him of the Star, it came out there was no waiter, and so in that way, said Jamie, "we came back to the old place." He told me all sorts of particulars "more profitable to the soul of man" than anything I should have got out of Mr. Charteris in three years, never to say "three weeks". But "a wagon came in atween ten and eleven and he must be stepping west". "He was glad to have seen me looking so (dropping his voice) — stootish!" (I saw him, from the omnibus, after, unloading the wagon, in his workday clothes, almost on the very spot where, for a dozen years, he had helped me in and out of our carriage!)

And now there only remained to pay my bill and await the omnibus. I have that bill of 6/6 in my writing-case; and shall keep it all my days; not only as an eloquent memorial of human change — like grass from graves and all that sort of thing; but as the first Inn bill I ever in my life contracted and paid on my own basis.

Another long look from the George Inn window, — and then into the shabby little omnibus again; where the faces of a Lady next me and a gentleman opposite me tormented my memory without result.

In the railway carriage which I selected, an old gentleman had taken his seat, and I recognized him at once as Mr. Lea — the same who made the little obelisk which hangs in my bedroom at Chelsea. He had grown old like a golden pippin, merely crined[1] with the bloom upon him. I laid my hand on his arm, turning away my face, and said, "Thank God here is one person I feel no difficulty about." "I don't know you," he said in his old blunt way, "who are you?" — "Guess!" — "Was it you who got over the churchyard wall this morning? I saw a stranger-lady climb the wall and I said to myself that's Jeannie Welsh! — no other woman would climb the wall instead of going in at the gate — are you Jeannie Welsh?" I owned the soft impeachment; then such shaking of hands! embracing even! But so soon as things had calmed down a little between us; Mr. Lea laid his hand on my shoulder and said as if pursuing knowledge under difficulties; "Now tell me, my Dear, why did you get over the wall instead of just asking for the key?"

He spoke of William Ainsley's death; I said I had never known him, that he went to India before I could remember. "Nonsense," said Mr. Lea; "not remember William Ainsley? — never knew William Ainsley? What are you thinking of? Why, didn't he wrap you in a shawl and run away with you to our house the very day you were born, I believe?"

— I said it might he very true but that the circumstance had escaped my recollection. Mr. Lea was left at Longniddry where he came daily, he said, to bathe in the sea. What energy!

While waiting there for the train from London, I saw again my Lady and Gentleman of the omnibus, and got their names from Mr. Lea; they were not people I had ever visited with, but I had been at school with them both. We passed and repassed one another without the slightest sign of recognition on their side.

George Cunningham too was pacing the Longniddry-platform, the Boy of our school who never got into trouble and never helped others out of it, — a slow bullet-headed boy who said his lessons like an eight-day clock and never looked young; now, on the wrong side of forty it might be doubted if he ever would look old. He came up to me and shook hands, and asked me by name how I did, exactly as though we met on change every day of our lives! To be sure I had seen him once since we were at school together, had met him at Craik's some twelve years ago. — Such as he was; we stood together till the train came up, and "talked of geography, politics, and nature".

At Edinburgh Jeannie's sweet little face looked wildly into the carriage for me, and next minute we were chirping and twittering together on the platform whilst the eternal two boxes writing-case and carpet-bag were being once more brought into one focus. "Look, look, cousin" said Jeannie, "there are people who know you!" and looking as I was bid; who but the pair who had accompanied me from Haddington were standing, with their heads laid together, and the eyes starting out of them me-ward! The Lady the instant she saw I noticed them sprang forward extending her hand; the husband "emboldened by her excellent example" did the same; they were "surprised," "delighted," everything that could be wished; "had not had a conception of its being me till they saw me smiling" — "Eh, sirs!" said my Mother's old nurse to her arter a separation of twenty years, "there's no a featur o' ye left, but just the bit smile!"

I will call for these Richardsons when I go back to Haddington; I liked their hop-skip-and-jump over ceremony — their oblivion in the enthusiasm of the moment that we had "belonged to different circles" (Haddingtonly speaking).

And now having brought myself to Edinburgh and under the little protecting wing of Jeannie, I bid myself adieu and "wave my lily hand" — I was back into the Present! and it is only in connection with the Past that I can get up a sentiment for

[1] Shrunk.

myself. The Present Mrs. Carlyle is what shall I say? — detestable — upon my honor.

## To a Swallow

Thou too hast traveled, little fluttering thing—
Hast seen the world, and now thy weary wing
Thou too must rest.
But much, my little bird, couldst thou but tell,
I'd give to know why here thou lik'st so well
To build thy nest.

For thou has passed fair places in thy flight:
A world lay all beneath thee where to light;
And, strange thy taste,
Of all the varied scenes that met thine eye—
Of all the spots for building neath the sky—
To choose this waste.

Did fortune try thee? was thy little purse
Perchance run low, and thou, afraid of worse,
Felt here secure?
Ah, no, thou need'st not gold, thou happy one.
Thou know'st it not. Of all God's creatures, man
Alone is poor.

What was it, then? some mystic turn of thought,
Caught under German eaves, and hither brought,
Marring thine eye
For the world's loveliness, till thou art grown
A sober thing that dost but mope and moan
Not knowing why?

Nay, if thy mind be sound, I need not ask,
Since here I see thee working at thy task
With wing and beak.
A well-laid scheme doth that small head contain,
At which thou work'st, brave bird, with might and main,
Nor more need'st seek.

In truth, I rather take it thou hast got
By instinct wise much sense about thy lot,
And hast small care
Whether an Eden or a desert be
Thy home so thou remain'st alive and free
To skim the air.

God speed thee, pretty bird; may thy small nest
With little ones all in good time be blest.
I love thee much:
For well thou managest that life of thine,
While I! Oh, ask not what I do with mine.
Would I were such.

## William Foster (1801–1864)

### The Bonny Tweed for Me

The hunter's e'e grows bright as the fox frae covert steals,
The fowler lo'es the gun, wi' the pointer at his heels,
But of a' the sports I ken, that can stir the heart wi' glee,
The troutin' stream, the fishin' gad*, the bonny Tweed for me. "good"

Wi' the gowan at the waterside, the primrose on the brae,
When sheets o' snawy blossom cleed the cherry and the slae,
When sun and wind are wooin' baith, the leaflet on the tree;
Then the troutin' stream, the fishin' gad, the bonny Tweed for me.

When the fresh green sward is yieldin' wi' a spring aneath the fit*, "foot"
And swallows thrang on either wing out owre the waters flit;
While the joyous laverocks*, toorin' high, shoor out their concert free— larks
Then the troutin' stream, the fishin' gad, the bonny Tweed for me.

Cheered wi' the honest plowman's sang, that maks his wark nae toil—
The flocks o' seagulls round him as his coulter tears the soil;
When the craw-schule* meets in council grave upon the furrowed lea— "school"
Then the troutin' stream, the fishin' gad, the bonny Tweed for me.

The modest wagtail joukin' past, wi' saft and buoyant flight,
And gurglin' streams are glancin' by, pure as the crystal bright,
When fish rise thick and threefauld, at the drake or woodcock flee—
Then the troutin' stream, the fishin' gad, the bonny Tweed for me.

I like the merry spring, wi' the bluid in nature's veins,
The dancin' streamlet's music, as it trinkles through the stanes,
The silver white upon the hook my light gad bending free—
Wha wadna visit bonny Tweed and share sic sport wi' me?

While there, time wings wi' speed o' thought, the day flees past sae soon,
That wha wad dream o' weariness till a' the sport is dune?
We hanker till the latest blink* is shed frae gloamin's e'e, glance
Laith, laith to quit the troutin' stream, the fishin' gad, and flee.

## James Stewart (1801–1843)

### The Tailor o' Monzie

Our gudeman's breeks were riven sair;
The tailor cam' to mak' a pair;
When gloamin' fell assembled were
O's a' bout thretty-three, man.
On stools an' auld tree-roots we sat,
An' O, sae muckle fun's we gat
Frae funny Patie Whip-the-cat,[1]
The tailor o' Monzie, man.

---

[1] A common name for tailors.

O, he's a curiosity,
A curious curiosity,
A perfect curiosity,
The Tailor o' Monzie, man.

The lasses' spindles hadna space
To whirl an' bob their circlin' race,
For, head an' thrawart, back an' face,
We sat promiscuously, man,
"Like midges i' the motty sun,
Or corbie craws on tattie grun',"
Sae thick were we to hear the fun
Frae Patie o' Monzie, man.

A lang dispute anent* the State — about
Gleyed* Andro Toshack held wi' Pate, — squinty
Wha, drawin' a steek wi' nettled heat,
Drobbed Andro's ringle* ee, man — wall
Andro roared, grew pale and faint:
"My feth," quo the gudeman, "I kent
He'd gie ye piercing argument,
Our Tailor o' Monzie."

Wee Gibbie Bryce was greetin', vext
That he had made the Kirk his text;
For Patie gat him jammed an' fixt
In Patronage's plea, man:
He rave poor Gibbie's sense to rags,
Made him a lauchin' stock to wags:—
The hale house waved their arms like flags:
"Hurrah for Patie Monzie, man!"

Wi' canty* tale an' funny joke, — lively
Wi' lauchin' when the tailor spoke,
The nicht wore on till twal' o'clock
In loud guffaw an' glee, man.
The gudewife reavilt a' her yarn;
She tint* the thread-end o' her pirn, — lost
Lauchin' like her youngest bairn
At Patie o' Monzie, man.

Twad tak a tale as lang's an ell,
Twad tak an hour that tale to tell
O' what I heard an' saw mysel'
That nicht o' nichts to me, man.
If there's a man that we should dawt*, — pet
Whom nature made without a faut,
He's surely Patie Whip-the-ca,
The Tailor o' Monzie, man.

## WILLIAM WILSON (1801–1860)

### Auld Johnny Graham

Dear aunty, what think ye o' auld Johnny Graham?
The carle* sae pawkie and slee. churl
He wants a bit wifie to tend his bein* hame, snug
And the body has ettled* at me. aimed

Wi' bonnet sae vaunty, an' owerlay* sae clean, collar, necktie
An' ribbon that waved boon* his bree, (above)
He cam, doun the cleugh at the gloamin' yestreen,
An' rappit, an soon speert* for me. asked

I bade him come ben* whare my minnie sae thrang* in/busy
Was birlin her wheel eidently*, industriously
An', foul fa' the carle, he was na' that lang
Ee he tauld out his errand o me.

"Hech, Tibby, lass, a' yon braid acres o' land,
Wi' ripe craps that wave bonnily,
An' meikle mair gear shall be at yer command,
Gin ye will look kindly on me.

"Yon herd o' fat owsen that rout i' the glen,
Sax naigies that nibble the lea;
The kye i' the sheugh, and the sheep i' the pen,
I'se gie a', dear Tibby, to thee.

"An' lassie, I've goupins o' gowd in a stockin,
An' pearlin's wad dazzle yer e'e;
A mettled, but canny young yaud* for the yokin' horse, nag
When ye wad gae jauntin' wi' me.

"I'll hap* ye and fend ye, and busk ye and tend ye, clothe
And mak ye the licht o' my e'e.
I'll comfort and cheer ye, and daut* ye and dear ye, pet
As couthy as couthy can be.

"I've loed ye, dear lassie, since first, a bit bairn,
Ye ran up the knowe to meet me;
An' deckit my bonnet wi' blue bells an' fern,
Wi' meikle glad laughin' an' glee.

"An' noo woman grown, an' mensefu'* an' fair, proper
An' gracefu' as gracefu' can be—
Will ye tak an auld carle wha ne'er had a care
For woman, dear Tibby, but thee?"

Sae, aunty, ye see I'm a' in a swither,
What answer the body to gie—
But aften I wish he wad tak my auld mither,
And let puir young Tibby abee.

## ROBERT CHAMBERS (1802–1871)

### Scotland

Scotland, the land of all I love,
The land of all that love me;
Land whose green sod my youth has trod,
Whose sod shall lie above me.
Hail, country of the brave and good;
Hail, land of song and story;
Land of the uncorrupted heart,
Of ancient faith and glory.

Like mother's bosom oer her child,
The sky is glowing oer me;
Like mother's ever smiling face,
The land lies bright before me.
Land of my home, my father's land:
Land where my soul was nourished;
Land of anticipated joy,
And all by memory cherished.

Oh Scotland, through thy wide domain
What hill, or vale, or river,
But in this fond enthusiast heart
Has found a place for ever?
Nay, hast thou but a glen or shaw*, wood
To shelter farm or sheiling*, cottage
That is not fondly garnered up
Within its depths of feeling?

Adown thy hills run countless rills,
With noisy, ceaseless motion;
Their waters join the rivers broad,
Those rivers join the ocean;
And many a sunny, flowery brae,
Where childhood plays and ponders,
Is freshened by the lightsome flood,
As wimpling on it wanders.

Within thy long-descending vales,
And on the lonely mountain,
How many wild spontaneous flowers
Hang oer each flood and fountain.
The glowing furze, the "bonnie broom,"
The thistle and the heather;
The bluebell and the gowan* fair, daisy
Which childhood likes to gather.

Oh for that pipe of silver sound,
On which the shepherd lover,
In ancient days, breathed out his soul,
Beneath the mountain's cover.

Oh for that Great Lost Power of Song,
So soft and melancholy,
To make thy every hill and dale
Poetically holy.

And not alone each hill and dale,
Fair as they are by nature,
But every town and tower of thine,
And every lesser feature;
For where is there the spot of earth
Within my contemplation,
But from some noble deed or thing
Has taken consecration.

Scotland, the land of all I love,
The land of all that love me;
Land whose green sod my youth has trod,
Whose sod shall lie above me.
Hail, country of the brave and good;
Hail, land of song and story;
Land of the uncorrupted heart,
Of ancient faith and glory.

## Lament for the Old Highland Warriors

Oh, where are the pretty men of yore?
Oh, where are the brave men gone?
Oh, where are the heroes of the north?
Each under his own gray stone.
Oh, where now the broad bright claymore?
Oh, where are the trews and plaid?
Oh, where now the merry Highland heart?
In silence for ever laid

Och on a rie, och on a rie,
Och on a rie, all are gone.
Och on a rie, the heroes of yore,
Each under his own gray stone.

The chiefs that were foremost of old,
Macdonald and brave Lochiel,
The Gordon, the Murray, and the Graham,
With their clansmen true as steel;
Who followed and fought with Montrose,
Glencairn, and bold Dundee;
Who to Charlie gave their swords and their all,
And would aye rather fa' than flee.

The hills that our brave fathers trod
Are now to the stranger a store.
The voice of the pipe and the bard
Shall awaken never more.

Such things it is sad to think on—
They come like the mist by day—
And I wish I had less in this world to leave,
And be with them that are away.

## Young Randal

Young Randal was a bonnie lad when he gaed awa,
Young Randal was a bonnie lad when he gaed awa,
Twas in the sixteen hundred year o' grace and thritty-twa
That Randal, the laird's youngest son, gaed awa.

It was to seek his fortune in the High Germanie—
To fecht the foreign loons* in the High Germanie — rascals
That he left his father's tower o' sweet Willanslee
And mony mae friends in the North Countie.

He left his mother in her bower, his father in the ha',
His brother at the outer yett* but and his sisters twa, — gate
And his bonnie cousin Jean, that looked owre the castle wa',
And, mair than a' the lave*, loot the tears down fa'. — rest

"Oh, whan will ye come back?" sae kindly did she speir,
"Oh, whan will ye come back, my hinny and my dear?"
"Whenever I can win eneuch o' Spanish gear
To dress ye out in pearlins* and silks, my dear." — lace

Oh, Randal's hair was coal-black when he gaed awa;
Oh, Randal's cheeks were roses red when he gaed awa;
And in his bonnie e'e a spark glintit high,
Like the merry, merry look in the morning sky.

Oh, Randal was an altert man when he came hame—
A sair altert man was he whan he came hame;—
Wi' a ribbon at his breast, and a Sir at his name,
And gray, gray cheeks did Randal come hame.

He lichtit at the outer yett and rispit wi' the ring,
And down came a lady to see him come in;
And after the lady came bairns fifteen:
"Can this muckle wife be my true love Jean?"

"Whatna stoure* carle is this," quo the dame, — rough
"Sae gruff and sae grand, and sae feckless and lame?"
"Oh, tell me, fair madame, are ye bonnie Jeanie Graham?"
"In troth," quo the lady, "sweet sir, the very same."

He turned him about wi' a waefu' e'e,
And a heart as sair as sair could be.
He lap on his horse, and awa did wildly flee,
And never mair came back to sweet Willanslee.

Oh, dule on the poortith* o' this countrie, poverty
And dule on the wars o' the High Germanie,
And dule on the love that forgetfu' can be:
For they've wrecked the bravest heart in this hale countrie!

## HUGH MILLER (1802–1856)

### Ode to My Mither Tongue

I loe the tones in mine ear that rung
In the days when care was unkind to me;
Ay, I loe thee weel, my mither tongue,
Though gloom the sons o' lear* at thee. learning
Ev'n now, though little skilled to sing,
I've raxed* me doun my simple lyre; reached
O, while I sweep ilk sounding string,
Nymph o' my mither tongue, inspire.

I loe thee weel, my mither tongue,
An' a' thy tales, or sad or wild;
Right early to my heart they clung,
Right soon my darkening thoughts beguiled—
Ay, aft to thy sangs o' a langsyne day,
That tell o' the bluidy fight sublime,
I've listened, till died the present away,
An' returned the deeds o' departed time.

An' gloom the sons o' lear at thee?
An' art thou reckoned poor an' mean?
Ah, could I tell as weel's I see,
Of a' thou art, an' a' thou'st been.
In thee has sung the enraptured bard
His triumphs over pain and care;
In courts and camps thy voice was heard—
Aft heard within the house o' prayer.

In thee, whan came proud England's might,
Wi' its steel to dismay and its gold to seduce,
Blazed the bright soul o' the Wallace wight,
And the patriot thoughts o' the noble Bruce.
Thine were the rousing strains that breathed
Frae the warrior bard ere closed the fray;
Thine, whan victory his temples wreathed,
The sang that arose oer the prostrate fae.

An' loftier still, the enraptured saint,
When the life o' time was glimmering awa',
Joyful o' heart, though feeble and faint,
Tauld in thee o' the glories he saw—
O' the visions bright o' a coming life,
O' angels that joy oer the closing grave,

An' o' Him that bore turmoil an' strife,
The children o' death to succor and save.

An' aft, whan the bluid hounds tracked the heath,
Whan followed the bands o' the bluidy Dundee,
The sang o' praise, an' the prayer o' death,
Arose to Heaven in thee.
In thee, whan Heaven's ain sons were called
To sever ilk link o' the papal chain,
Thundered the ire o' that champion bauld
Whom threat'nins and dangers assailed in vain.

Ah, mither tongue, in days o' yore,
Fu' mony a noble bard was thine;
The clerk o' Dunkeld, and the coothy* Dunbar, pleasant
An' the best o' the Stuart line;
An' him wha tauld o' Southron wrang
Cowed by the might o' Scottish men;
Him o' the Mount and the gleesome sang,
And him the pride o' the Hawthornden.

Of bards were thine in latter days
Sma need to tell, my mither tongue.
Right bauld and slee were Fergie's lays,
An' roared the laugh when Ramsay sung;
But wha without a tear can name
The swain this warl' shall ne'er forget?
Thine, mither tongue, his sangs o' fame,
Twill learning be to ken thee yet.

## JOHN PARK (1804–1865)

### Where Gadie Rins

Oh, an I were where Gadie rins,
Where Gadie rins, where Gadie rins,
Oh, an I were where Gadie rins,
At the back o' Benochie.

I wish I were where Gadie rins,
Mang fragrant heath and yellow whins,
Or, brawlin' doun the bosky linns*, waterfalls
At the back o' Benochie.

To hear ance mair the blackbird's sang,
To wander birks* and braes amang, birches
Wi' frien's and fav'rites, left sae lang,
At the back o' Benochie.

How mony a day, in blithe spring time,
How mony a day, in summer's prime,

I wiled awa' my careless time
On the heights o' Benochie.

Ah, fortune's flowers wi' thorns are rife,
And walth is won wi' grief and strife—
Ae day gi'e me o' youthfu' life
At the back o' Benochie.

O, Mary, there on ilka nicht,
When baith our hearts were young and licht,
We've wandered, when the moon was bricht,
Wi' speeches fond and free.

O, ance, ance mair, where Gadie rins,
Where Gadie rins, where Gadie rins—
Oh, micht I die where Gadie rins
At the back o' Benochie.

## WILLIAM ANDERSON (1805–1866)

### At E'ening Whan the Kye

At e'ening whan the kye war in,
An' lasses milking thrang,
A neebour laird cam' ben* the byre*, — in/barn
The busy maids amang.
He stood ahint the routin' kye
An' round him glowered a wee,
Then stole to whar young Peggy sat,
The milk pail at her knee.

"Sweet Peggy, lass," thus spake the laird,
"Wilt listen to my tale?"
"Stan' out the gate, laird," Peggy cried,
"Or you will coup the pail.
Mind, Hawkie here's a timorous beast,
An' no acquent wi' you."
"Ne'er fash*," quo he, "the milking time's — trouble
The sweetest time to woo.

"Ye ken, I've aften tauld ye that
I've thretty kye and mair,
An' ye'd be better owning them
Than sittin milkin there.
My house is bein*, and stocket weel — snug
In hadden* and in ha', — holding
An' ye've but just to say the word
Tae leddy be o' a'."

"Wheest*, laird," quo Peggy, "dinna mak — shush
Yersel a fool an' me,
I thank ye, for your offer kind,

But sae it canna be.
Maybe yer weel stocked house and farm,
An' thretty lowing kine,
May win some ither lassie's heart,
They hae nae charms for mine.

"For in the kirk I hae been cried,
My troth is pledged and sworn,
An' tae the man I like mysel'
I'll married be the morn."
The laird, dumfoundered at her words,
Had nae mair will to try'r;
But turned, and gaed far faster out,
Than he'd come in the byre.

## I'm Naebody Noo

I'm naebody noo, though in days that are gane,
Whan I'd hooses, and lands, and gear* o' my ain, money
There war mony to flatter, and mony to praise,
And wha but myself was sae prood in those days.

An' then roun' my table wad visitors thrang,
Wha laughed at my joke, and applauded my sang,
Though the tane had nae point, and the tither nae glee;
But of course they war grand when comin frae me.

Whan I'd plenty to gie, o' my cheer and my crack*, chat
There war plenty to come, and wi' joy to partak;
But whenever the water grew scant at the well,
I was welcome to drink all alane by mysel.

Whan I'd nae need o' aid, there were plenty to proffer,
And noo whan I want it, I ne'er get the offer;
I could greet* whan I think hoo my siller decreast, weep
In the feasting o' those who came only to feast.

The fulsome respec' to my gowd they did gie
I thought a' the time was intended for me,
But whanever the end o' my money they saw,
Their friendship, like it, also flickered awa.

My advice ance was sought for by folk far and near,
Sic great wisdom I had ere I tint* a' my gear, lost
I'm as weel able yet to gie counsel, that's true,
But I may just haud my wheest, for I'm naebody noo.

## HENRY BELL (1805–1874)

### My Vis-a-Vis

That olden lady—can it be?
Well, well, how seasons slip away.
Do let me hand her cup of tea
That I may gently to her say—
"Dear madam, thirty years ago,
When both our hearts were full of glee,
In many a dance and courtly show
I had you for my vis-a-vis.

"That pale blue robe, those chestnut curls,
That Eastern jewel on your wrist,
That neck-encircling string of pearls
Whence hung a cross of amethyst,
I see them all,—I see the tulle
Looped up with roses at the knee.
Good Lord, how fresh and beautiful
Was then your cheek, my vis-a-vis.

"I hear the whispered praises yet,
The buzz of pleasure when you came,
The rushing eagerness to get
Like moths within the fatal flame:
As April blossoms, faint and sweet,
As apples when you shake the tree,
So hearts fell showering at your feet
In those glad days, my vis-a-vis.

"And as for me, my breast was filled
With silvery light in every cell.
My blood was some rich juice distilled
From amaranth and asphodel.
My thoughts were airier than the lark
That carols oer the flowery lea.
They well might breathlessly remark:
'By Jove, that *is* a vis-a-vis.'

"O time and change, what is't you mean?
Ye gods, can I believe my ears?
Has that bald portly person been
Your husband, ma'am, for twenty years?
That six-foot officer your son,
Who looks oer his mustache at me?
Why did not Joshua stop *our* sun
When I was first your vis-a-vis?

"Forgive me, if I've been too bold,
Permit me to return your cup.
My heart was beating as of old,
One drop of youth still bubbled up."

So spoke I. Then, like cold December,
Only these brief words said she:
"I do not in the least remember
I ever was your vis-a-vis."

## GEORGE OUTRAM (1805–1856)

### The Annuity

I gaed to spend a week in Fife—
An unco* week it proved to be— strange
For there I met a waesome wife
Lamentin' her viduity.
Her grief brak out sae fierce and fell,
I thought her heart wad burst the shell;
And—I was sae left tae mysel—
I sell't her an annuity.

The bargain lookit fair eneugh—
She just was turned o' saxty-three:
I couldna guessed she'd prove sae teugh,
By human ingenuity.
But years have come, and years have gane,
And there she's yet as stiev's* a stane— stout as
The limmer's* growin' young again, creature is
Since she got her annuity.

She's crined* awa' to bane and skin, shriveled
But that it seems is nought to me;
She's like to live—although she's in
The last stage o' tenuity.
She munches wi' her wizened gums,
An' stumps about on legs o' thrums* threadpaper
But comes—as sure as Christmas comes—
To ca' for her annuity.

She jokes her joke, an' cracks her crack*, chatter
As spunkie as a growin' flea—
An' there she sits upon my back,
A livin' perpetuity.
She hurkles* by her ingle* side, crouches/fire
An' toasts an' tans her wrunkled hide—
Lord kens how lang she yet may bide
To ca' for her annuity.

I read the tables drawn wi' care
For an Insurance Company.
Her chance o' life was stated there,
Wi' perfect perspicuity.
But tables here or tables there,
She's lived ten years beyond her share,

An's like to live a dizzen mair,
To ca' for her annuity.

I gat the loun* that drew the deed— fellow, rascal
We spelled it oer right carefully;—
In vain he yerked his souple head,
To find an ambiguity.
It's dated—tested—a' complete—
The proper stamp—nae word delete—
And deligence, as on decreet,
May pass for her annuity.

Last Yule she had a fearfu' hoast*— cough
I thought a kink* might set me free; fit
I led her out, mang snaw and frost,
Wi' constant assiduity.
But Deil ma' care—the blast gaed by,
And missed the auld anatomy;
It just cost me a tooth, forbye
Discharging her annuity.

I thought that grief might gar* her quit— make
Her only son was lost at sea—
But aff her wits behoved to flit,
An' leave her in fatuity.
She threeps*, and threeps, he's livin' yet, swears
For a' the tellin' she can get;
But catch the doited runt forget
To ca' for her annuity.

If there's a sough o' cholera
Or thyphus—wha sae gleg* as she? spry
She buys up baths, an' drugs, an' a',
In siccan* superfluity. such
She doesna need—she's fever proof—
The pest gaed owre her very roof;
She tauld me sae—an' then her loof* hand
Held out for her annuity.

Ae day she fell—her arm she brak,—
A compound fracture as could be;
Nae leech the cure wad undertak,
Whate'er was the gratuity.
It's cured! She handles't like a flail—
It does as weel in bits as hale;
But I'm a broken man mysel
Wi' her and her annuity.

Her broozled* flesh and broken banes, bruised
Are weel as flesh an' banes can be,
She beats the tades* that live in stanes, "toads"
An' fatten in vacuity.
They die when they're exposed to air—

They canna thole* the atmosphere; endure
But her! expose her onywhere—
She lives for her annuity.

If mortal means could nick her thread,
Sma' crime it wad appear to me:
Ca't murder—or ca't homicide—
I'd justify't—and do it tae.
But how to fell a withered wife
That's carved out o' the tree o' life—
The timmer* limmer daurs the knife hale
To settle her annuity.

I'd try a shot.—But whar's the mark?—
Her vital parts are hid frae me;
Her back-bane wanders through her sark
In an unkenned corkscrewity.
She's palsified—an' shakes her head
Sae fast about, ye scarce can see't;
It's past the power o' steel or lead
To settle her annuity.

She might be drowned;—but go she'll not
Within a mile o' loch or sea;—
Or hanged—if cord could grip a throat
O' siccan exiguity.
It's fitter far to hang the rope—
It draws out like a telescope:
Twad tak a dreadfu' length o' drop
To settle her annuity.

Will pushion* do't?—It has been tried; poison
But, be't in hash or fricassee,
That's just the dish she can't abide,
Whatever kind o' *gout* it hae.
It's needless to assail her doubts,—
She gangs by instinct—like the brutes—
An' only eats an' drinks what suits
Hersel an' her annuity.

The Bible says the age o' man
Threescore an' ten perchance may be;
She's ninety-four;—let them wha can
Explain the incongruity.
She suld hae lived afore the Flood—
She's come o' Patriarchal blood—
She's some auld Pagan, mummified
Alive for her annuity.

She's been embalmed inside and out—
She's sauted to the last degree—
There's pickle in her very snout
Sae caper-like an' cruety*; like vinegar

Lot's wife was fresh compared to her;
They've kyanised the useless knir*— dwarf
She canna decompose—nae mair
Than her accursed annuity.

The water-drap wears out the rock
As this eternal jad wears me;
I could withstand the single shock,
But no the continuity.
It's pay me here—an' pay me there—
An' pay me, pay me, evermair;
I'll gang demented wi' despair—
I'm *charged* for her annuity!

## Cessio Bonorum

Air—"Tullochgorum"

Come ben* ta house, an' steek* ta door, in/shut
An' bring her usquebaugh* galore, whiskey
An' piper plo' wi' a' your pow'r
To reel o' Tullochgorum.
For we'se be crosse* an' canty* yet— bold/pleasant
Crosse an' canty,
Crosse an' canty—
We'se be crosse an' canty yet
Around a Hieland jorum.
We'se be crosse an' canty yet,
For better luck she never met—
She's gotten out an' paid her debt
Wi' a Cessio Ponorum!
Huch! tirrum, tirrum, etc.

She meant ta pargain to dispute,
An' pay ta price she wadna do't,
But on a bill her mark she put,
An' hoped to hear no more o'm.
Blithe an' merry was she then—
Blithe an' merry,
Blithe an' merry—
Blithe an' merry was she then
She thought she had come oer 'm.
Blithe an' merry was she then—
But unco little did she ken
O' Shirra's laws, an Shirra's men,
Or Cessio Ponorum!
Huch! tirrum, tirrum, etc.

Cot tamn!—but it was pad indeed.
They took her up wi' meikle speed—
To jail they bore her—feet an' head—
An' flung her on ta floor o'm.

Wae an' weary has she been—
Wae an' weary,
Wae an' weary—
Wae an' weary has she been
Amang ta debitorum.
Wae an' weary has she been,
An' most uncivil people seen—
She's much peholden to her frien'
Ta Cessio Ponorum!
Huch! tirrum, tirrum, etc.

She took an oath she couldna hear—
Twas something about goods an' gear*— money
She thought it proper no to spier* ask
Afore ta dominorum.
She kent an' cardna if twas true—
Kent an' cardna,
Kent an' cardna—
Kent an' cardna if twas true,
But easily she swore 'm.
She kent an' cardna if twas true,
But scrap't her foot, an' made her poo,
Then, oich!—as to ta door she flew
Wi' her Cessio Ponorum!
Huch! tirrum, tirrum, etc.

She owed some bits o' odds an' ends,
An' twa three debts to twa three friend—
She kent fu' weel her dividends
Could paid anither score o'm.
Ta fees an' charges were but sma'—
Fees an' charges,
Fees an' charges—
Ta fees an' charges were but sma',
Huch! tat for fifty more o'm!
Ta fees an' charges were but sma'—
But little kent she o' the law.
Tamn!—if she hasn't paid then a'
Wi' her Cessio Ponorum!
Huch! tirrum, tirrum, etc.

But just let that cursed loon* come here rascal
That took her bill!—she winna swear,—
But, ooghh!—if she could catch him near
Ta crags o' Cairngorum!
If belt an' buckle can keep fast—
Belt an' buckle,
Belt an' buckle—
If belt an' buckle can keep fast,
She'd mak' him a' terrorem.
If belt an' buckle can keep fast,
Her caption would be like to last,
Py Cot!—but she would poot him past

A Cessio Ponorum!
Huch! tirrum, tirrum, etc.

## GEORGE ALLAN (1806–1835)

### Old Scotland

The breeze blows fresh, my gallant mates,
Our vessel cleaves her way,
Down ocean's depths, oer heaven's heights,
Through darkness and through spray.
No loving moon shines out for us,
No star our course to tell.
And must we leave old Scotland thus?
My native land, farewell.

Then fast spread out the flowing sheet,
Give welcome to the wind.
Is there a gale we'd shrink to meet
When treachery's behind?
The foaming deep our couch will be,
The storm our vesper bell,
The low'ring heaven our canopy,
My native land, farewell.

Away, away across the main,
We'll seek some happier clime,
Where daring is not deemed a stain,
Nor loyalty a crime.
Our hearts are wrung, our minds are tossed,
Wild as the ocean's swell;
A kingdom and a birthright lost!
Old Scotland, fare thee well.

## JOHN STERLING (1806–1844)

### The Spice Tree

The spice tree lives in the garden green;
Beside it the fountain flows;
And a fair bird sits the boughs between,
And sings his melodious woes.

No greener garden e'er was known
Within the bounds of an earthly king;
No lovelier skies have ever shone
Than those that illumine its constant spring.

That coil-bound stem has branches three;
On each a thousand blossoms grow;
And, old as aught of time can be,
The root stands fast in the rocks below.

In the spicy shade ne'er seems to tire
The fount that builds a silvery dome;
And flakes of purple and ruby fire
Gush out, and sparkle amid the foam.

The fair white bird of flaming crest,
And azure wings bedropt with gold,
Ne'er has he known a pause of rest,
But sings the lament that he framed of old:

"O princess bright, how long the night
Since thou art sunk in the waters clear.
How sadly they flow from the depth below—
How long must I sing and thou wilt not hear?

"The waters play, and the flowers are gay,
And the skies are sunny above;
I would that all could fade and fall,
And I, too, cease to mourn my love.

"O, many a year, so wakeful and drear,
I have sorrowed and watched, beloved, for thee.
But there comes no breath from the chambers of death,
While the lifeless fount gushes under the tree."

The skies grow dark, and they glare with red;
The tree shakes off its spicy bloom;
The waves of the fount in a black pool spread;
And in thunder sounds the garden's doom.

Down springs the bird with a long shrill cry,
Into the sable and angry flood;
And the face of the pool, as he falls from high,
Curdles in circling stains of blood.

But sudden again upswells the fount;
Higher and higher the waters flow;
In a glittering diamond arch they mount,
And round it the colors of morning glow.

Finer and finer the watery mound
Softens and melts to a thin-spun veil,
And tones of music circle around,
And bear to the stars the fountain's tale.

And swift the eddying rainbow screen
Falls in dew on the grassy floor;
Under the spice tree the garden's queen
Sits by her lover, who wails no more.

## Louis XV

The king with all his kingly train
Had left his Pompadour behind,
And forth he rode in Senart's wood
The royal beasts of chase to find.
That day by chance the monarch mused,
And turning suddenly away,
He struck alone into a path
That far from crowds and courtiers lay.

He saw the pale green shadows play
Upon the brown untrodden earth.
He saw the birds around him flit
As if he were of peasant birth.
He saw the trees that know no king
But him who bears a woodland ax.
He thought not, but he looked about
Like one who skill in thinking lacks.

Then close to him a footstep fell,
And glad of human sound was he,
For truth to say he found himself
A weight from which he fain would flee.
But that which he would ne'er have guessed
Before him now most plainly came.
The man upon his weary back
A coffin bore of rudest frame.

"Why, who art thou?" exclaimed the king,
"And what is that I see thee bear?"
"I am a laborer in the wood,
And tis a coffin for Pierre.
Close by the royal hunting lodge
You may have often seen him toil;
But he will never work again,
And I for him must dig the soil."

The laborer ne'er had seen the king,
And this he thought was but a man,
Who made at first a moment's pause,
And then anew his talk began:
"I think I do remember now,—
He had a dark and glancing eye,
And I have seen his slender arm
With wondrous blows the pick-ax ply.

"Pray tell me, friend, what accident
Can thus have killed our good Pierre?"
"Oh, nothing more than usual, Sir,
He died of living upon air.
Twas hunger killed the poor good man,
Who long on empty hopes relied.

He could not pay gabell and tax,
And feed his children, so he died."

The man stopped short, and then went on,—
"It is, you know, a common thing.
Our children's bread is eaten up
By courtiers, mistresses, and king."
The king looked hard upon the man,
And afterwards the coffin eyed,
Then spurred to ask of Pompadour,
How came it that the peasants died.

## The Rose and the Gauntlet

Low spake the knight to the peasant-girl,—
"I tell thee sooth, I am belted earl.
Fly with me from this garden small,
And thou shalt sit in my castle's hall.

"Thou shalt have pomp, and wealth, and pleasure,
Joys beyond thy fancy's measure.
Here with my sword and horse I stand,
To bear thee away to my distant land.

"Take, thou fairest, this full-blown rose,
A token of love that as ripely blows."
With his glove of steel he plucked the token,
But it fell from his gauntlet crushed and broken.

The maiden exclaimed,—"Thou seest, Sir Knight,
Thy fingers of iron can only smite;
And, like the rose thou hast torn and scattered,
I in thy grasp should be wrecked and shattered."

She trembled and blushed, and her glances fell;
But she turned from the knight, and said, "Farewell."
"Not so," he cried, "will I lose my prize;
I heed not thy words, but I read thine eyes."

He lifted her up in his grasp of steel,
And he mounted and spurred with furious heel;
But her cry drew forth her hoary sire,
Who snatched his bow from above the fire.

Swift from the valley the warrior fled,
Swifter the bolt of the cross-bow sped;
And the weight that pressed on the fleet-foot horse
Was the living man, and the woman's corse.

That morning the rose was bright of hue;
That morning the maiden was fair to view;
But the evening sun its beauty shed
On the withered leaves, and the maiden dead.

## CAROLINE OLIPHANT (1807–1831)

### Oh Never, No Never

Oh, never, no, never,
Thou'lt meet me again.
Thy spirit for ever
Has burst from its chain;
The links thou hast broken
Are all that remain,
For never, oh never,
Thou'lt meet me again.

Like the sound of the viol,
That dies on the blast;
Like the shade on the dial,
Thy spirit has passed.
The breezes blow round me,
But give back no strain.
The shade on the dial
Returns not again.

When roses enshrined thee,
In light trellised shade,
Still hoping to find thee,
How oft have I strayed.
Thy desolate dwelling
I traverse in vain;—
The stillness has whispered,
Thou'lt ne'er come again.

I still haste to meet thee,
When footsteps I hear;
And start, when to greet me
Thou dost not appear;
Then afresh oer my spirit
Steals mem'ry of pain;—
For never, oh never,
Thou'lt meet me again.

## JAMES BALLANTINE (1808–1877)

### Muckle-Mou'd Meg

"Oh, wha hae ye brought us hame now, my brave lord,
Strappit flaught ower his braid saddle-bow?
Some bauld Border reiver* to feast at our board, raider, thief

An' herry our pantry, I trow.
He's buirdly* an' stalwart in lith an' in limb; well-made
Gin ye were his master in war
The field was a saft eneugh litter for him,
Ye needna hae brought him sae far.
Then saddle an' munt again, harness an' dunt* again, strike
An' when ye gae hunt again, strike higher game."

"Hoot, whisht* ye, my dame, for he comes o' gude kin, quiet
An' boasts o' a lang pedigree;
This night he maun share o' our gude cheer within,
At morning's gray dawn he maun dee.
He's gallant Wat Scott, heir o' proud Harden Ha',
Wha ettled* our lands clear to sweep; determined
But now he is snug in Auld Elibank's paw,
An' shall swing frae our dungeon-keep.
Though saddle an' munt again, harness an' dunt again,
I'll ne'er when I hunt again strike higher game."

"Is this young Wat Scott? an' wad ye rax* his craig*, stretch/throat
When our daughter is fey for a man?
Gae, gaur* the loun* marry our muckle-mou'd Meg, make/man, rascal
Or we'll ne'er get the jaud aff our han'."
"Od, hear our gudewife, she wad fain save your life;
Wat Scott, will ye marry or hang?"
But Meg's muckle mou set young Wat's heart agrue,
Wha swore to the woodie* he'd gang. (scaffold)
Ne'er saddle nor munt again, harness nor dunt again,
Wat ne'er shall hunt again, ne'er see his hame.

Syne muckle-mou'd Meg pressed in close to his side,
An' blinkit fu' sleely and kind,
But aye as Wat glowered at his braw proffered bride,
He shook like a leaf in the wind.
"A bride or a gallows, a rope or a wife!"
The morning dawned sunny and clear—
Wat boldly strode forward to part wi' his life,
Till he saw Meggy shedding a tear;
Then saddle an' munt again, harness an' dunt again,
Fain wad Wat hunt again, fain wad be hame.

Meg's tear touched his bosom, the gibbet frowned high,
An' slowly Wat strode to his doom;
He gae a glance round wi' a tear in his eye,
Meg shone like a star through the gloom.
She rushed to his arms, they were wed on the spot,
An' lo'ed ither muckle and lang;
Nae bauld border laird had a wife like Wat Scott;
Twas better to marry than hang.
So saddle an' munt again, harness an' dunt again,
Elibank hunt again, Wat's snug at hame.

## The Last Laird o' the Auld Mint

A Canongate Croon, To Be Chaunted—Not Sung

Auld Willie Nairn, the last Laird o' the Mint,
Had an auld farrant* pow*, an' auld farrant thoughts in't; fashioned/head
There ne'er was before sic a body in print,
As auld Willie Nairn, the last Laird o' the Mint.
So list and ye'll find ye hae muckle to learn,
An' ye'll still be but childer to auld Willie Nairn.

Auld Nanse, an auld maid, kept his house clean an' happy,
For the body was tidy, though fond o' a drappy;
An' aye when the Laird charged the siller-taed cappy,
That on great occasions made caaers aye nappy*. intoxicated
While the bicker* gaed round, Nanny aye got a sharin'— "beaker"
There are few sic-like masters as auld Willie Nairn.

He'd twa muckle tabbies, ane black an' ane white,
That purred by his side, at the fire, ilka night,
And gazed in the embers wi' sage-like delight,
While he ne'er took a meal, but they bath gat a bite;
For baith beast an' body aye gat their full sairin—
He could ne'er feed alane, couthy* auld Willie Nairn. good-natured

He had mony auld queer things, frae queer places brought—
He had rusty auld swords, whilk Ferrara had wrought—
He had axes, wi' whilk Bruce an' Wallace had fought—
An' auld Roman bauchles, wi' auld baubees* bought; small coins
For aye in the Cowgate, for auld nick-nacks stairin',
Day after day, daundered* auld, sage Willie Nairn. strolled

There are gross gadding gluttons, and pimping wine-bibbers,
That are fed for their scandal, and called pleasant fibbers;
But the only thanks Willie gae them for their labors,
Were, "We cam nae here to speak ill o' our neighbors."
O, truth wad be bolder, an' falsehood less darin',
Gin* ilk ane wad treat them like auld Willie Nairn. if

His snaw-flaikit locks, an' his lang pouthered queue,
Commanded assent to ilk word frae his mou';
Though a leer in his e'e, an' a lurk in his brow,
Made ye ferlie*, gin he thought his ain stories true; wonder
But he minded o' Charlie when he'd been a bairn,
An' wha, but Bob Chambers, could thraw* Willie Nairn. twist, throw

Gin ye speered* him anent ony auld hoary house, asked
He cocked his head heigh, an' he set his staff crouse*, bold
Syne gazed through his specks, till his heart-springs brak loose,
Then mid tears in saft whispers, wad scarce wauk a mouse;
He told ye some tale o't, wad mak your heart yearn,
To heard mair auld stories frae auld Willie Nairn.

E'en wee snarling dogs gae a kind yowffin bark,
As he daundered doun closes*, baith ourie and dark; lanes
For he kend ilka doorstane and ald warld mark,
An' even amid darkness his love lit a spark;
For mony sad scene that wad melt a cauld airn,
Was relieved by the kind heart o' auld Willie Nairn.

The laddies ran to him to redd* ilka quarrel, separate, amend
An' he southered a' up wi' a snap or a farl*; scone, cookie
While vice that had daured to stain virtue's pure laurel,
Shrunk cowed, frae the glance o' the stalwart auld carl*: fellow
Wi' the weak he was wae, wi' the strong he was stern—
For dear, dear was virtue to auld Willie Nairn.

To spend his last shilling auld Willie had vowed;—
But ae stormy night, in a coarse rauchan* rowed, plaid, cloak
At his door a wee wean skirled lusty an' loud,
An' the Laird left him heir to his lands an' his gowd!
Some are fond o' a name, some are fond o' a cairn,
But auld Will was fonder o' young Willie Nairn.

O, we'll ne'er see his like again, now he's awa.
There are hunders mair rich, there are thousands mair braw*, handsome
But he gae a' his gifts, an' they whites werena sma',
Wi' a grace made them lightly on puir shouthers fa':
An' he gae in the dark, when nae rude e'e was glarin',
There was deep hidden pathos in auld Willie Nairn.

## The Feeding Shower

The feeding shower comes brattlin' doun,
The south wind sughs wi' kindly soun',
The auld trees shake their leafy pows*, heads
Young glossy locks dance round their brows,
And leaf and blade, and weed and flower,
A' joyous drink the feeding shower.

The misty clud creeps ower the hill,
And maks each rut a gurglin' rill,
And tips wi' gowd each auld whin cowe*, sprig
And gaurs* the heath wi' purple glow, makes
And sterile rocks, gray, bleak, and dour,
Grow verdant wi' the feeding shower.

The ewes and lambs a' bleat and brouse,
The kye and couts* a' dream and drouse, "colts"
Mang grass wha's deep rich velvet green
Is glist a' owre wi' silver sheen,
And birdies churm in ilka bower,
A welcome to the feeding shower.

The soil, a' gizened sair before,
Is filled wi' moisture to the core;
Ducks daidlin' in the dubs* are seen, ponds
The cawin' corbies crowd the green;
Their beaks are sharp when rain cluds lower—
They batten in the feeding shower.

Furth frae their stalks the ears o' grain
Peep sleely, lapping up the rain,
Ilk gowan* opes its crimson mou', daisy
And nods, and winks, till droukit* fou, drenched
And buttercups are whomled* ower, tipped
Brim laden wi' the feeding shower.

The drowsy sun, as dozed wi' sleep,
Doun through the lift begins to peep,
And, slantin' wide in glist'nin' streams,
The light on bright new verdure gleams,
And nature, grateful, owns His power
Wha sends the genial feeding shower.

## Lament for Ancient Edinburgh

Come listen, cronies, ane an' a',
While on my dowie* reed I blaw; sad
And mourn the sad untimely fa'
O' our auld toun,
Whilk, spite o' justice, sense, an' law,
They're dingin'* down. knocking

Auld streets and closes, wynds and houses,
The scenes o' mony genial bouzes,
Whaur Burns an' Ramsay wooed the Muses
In days lang past,
Wi' sacrilegious dunts* an' bruises blows
Are fa'ing fast.

Our city wa's, wi' yetts* sae stout, gates
That keepit midnight reivers* out, thieves
And saved our sires frae mony a bout
O' southern foe,
To hain* us twa three staps about save
Are now laid low.

The ancient Krames whaur weanies tottit,
Whaur a' wee wairdless callants* trottit, fellows
Though scantly fed, an' scrimply coatit,
To spend their a'
On dirlin' drums or ba's that stottit
Against the wa'.

Whaur wee lead penny watches glanced,
Whaur wee pig penny horses pranced,
Whaur crowds o' bairnies gazed entranced
A' round in rings,
While timmer* tumblers swung an' danced — wooden
On horse-hair strings.

An' bawbee* Dalls the fashions apit, — (small coin)
Sae rosy cheekit, jimpy* shapit, — slender
An' wee bit lassies gazed an' gapit
Wi' mouth an' ee,
Till frae their mithers they had scrapit
The prized bawbee.

The City Guard sae proud an' dorty*, — ill-tempered
Brave remnant o' the twa-and-forty,
Wad gie their Highland beaks a snortie
And ban* in Earse, — curse
Then sally forth in warlike sortie
Right bauld an' fierce.

Rogues aye gat aff for draps o' liquor,
But callants aye were keepit sicker;
Wae fa' them puir things at a bicker*, — beaker
Unless they watched it,
And reckless bolted a' the quicker,
I trow they catched it.

Wow, but "ta guard," were brisk an' braw,
Their begnets glancing in a raw,
But now, puir bodies, they're awa,
Let's drap a tear;
Death's gi'en our teugh auld friends a ca'—
He'll soon come here.

The auld Wast Bow sae steep an' crookit,
Whaur mony cozy dens were coukit,
Whaur beggars hoosed, an' blackguards joukit* — ducked
Frae law's keen grup,
Whaur daidlin bodies sat an' souket
Hale puncheons* up. — casks

Whaur bawbee pies wee callants moupit,
Whaur drucken dumbies skirled an' whoopit,
Whaur ballant singers, hoarse and roopit*, — creaking
Proclaimed dread war
Wi' preachers, wha, without a poopit,
Held furth mang glaur.

Whaur tinklers rang their earthen muggies,
Whaur stands were crammed wi' wudden luggies*, — bowls
Whaur scarlet cats and sky blue doggies
Stood brawly spattit,

Whaur callants wi white mice an puggies
Like hares lay squattit.

An there were frail auld men, knee-breekit,
Wi' mumlin' tongues an' een half steekit*, — shut
Wha daunnerit on thegither cleekit
To some lown beild*, — shelter
And in the sunshine sat an' beekit
Their healthy eild.

A wean, I striddled on their backs,
A callant, joined their forenoon walks,
An' humored a' their auld knick-knacks
Right leal an' kind,
While wi' Auld Reekie's choicest cracks* — stories, chatter
They stored my mind.

The howffs* whaur a' thae arts grew great in, — haunts, pubs
Whaur a' thae worthies held their state in,
Whaur worn-out wights fand snug retreat in,
Frae wranglin' spouse,
Hae felt the heavy hand o' fate on
Their hoary pows*. — heads

Nae ferlie* though I mak my mane — wonder
For thae black smeekit wa's now gane;
Linkit an' twined round every stane,
Is some auld notion,
That drives my bluid through ilka vein,
Wi' wild emotion.

## The Rainy Harvest Day

Gray-bearded Day nods drowsily,
Cauld hazy cluds hang ower the plain,
And Nature looks wi' pensive ee
On rich ripe fields o' gowden grain;
A' droukit* heavy louting low, — wet
Like mourners shedding tears o' woe.

The craws in conclave crowd the dyke,
The sparrows cluster round the barn,
Aneath the cart-shed cowers the tyke*, — dog
Ahint the stooks the poultry dern*; — hide
Nor leaf, nor stem, nor bough is stirred,
Nor sound is heard o' beast or bird.

Thick vapors gather ower the glens,
The shaggy hills are veiled in gray,
The sheep are gathered in their pens,
Nae shepherd climbs thae heights today;

And browsing neath the drowsy trees,
Are cattle clovered to the knees.

Doun fa's the thick an' grizzly weet,
Plout, ploutin', on our auld trough-stane,
The bairnies wi' their raw red feet,
Dance through the drumlie* dubs o' rain; muddy
While loaded leaf, an' steekit* flower, shut
Keep joukin'* frae the peltin' shower. ducking

Doun pours the rain, doun fa's the grain,
Its gowden tresses press the earth,
Oh, dool and wae, sic harvest day
Gies cause to fear for coming dearth;
And maks us doubt His high behest,
As if He kenned nae what was best.

The shearers listless lounge about
In shed an' stable, barn an' byre;
The anxious farmer gins to doubt
Gin e'er the weather will be dryer,
And shakin' slow his touzy head,
Growls, "This is sair to thole* indeed." endure

But noo he taps the weather-glass,
His brow is flushed—he sees it rise;
Th' excited reapers round him press
Wi' ruddy cheeks an' sparklin' eyes;
And in each strong right hand is seen
A sickle gleaming sharp and keen.

And, lo, the sun streams brichtly doun,
The hazy cluds dissolve in air,
While Nature wears a shining crown
Of glory on her forehead fair;
Hymning anew oer hill and dale,
"Seed-time and harvest ne'er shall fail."

## Coal Jock

King o' the coal mine, dingy Knicht,
Wi' phiz sae grim, an' ee sae bricht,
Stand still, ye black an' coomy* fricht, sooty
I'll jot ye doun;
Syne bawl awa' wi' a' your micht,
An' wauk the toun.

When was there e'er a word o' truth
Cam frae that muckle, thick-lipped mouth,
That, burning wi' a stounding tooth,
Dries up your craigie*, throat

An' gapes wi' a perpetual drouth* thirst
For dear Kilbagie?

Drink less, an' feed your naigie better,
For mony corn-bing ye're its debtor;
Poor brute, it needs nae rape or fetter
To tie it up,
At yillhouse* doors a patient waiter ale-house
On your gee-hup!

The puir auld brute's bow-houghed an' blin',
Sharp-pointed banes shine through its skin;
Its mar'less shoon are worn as thin
As Queen Anne coins;
An' oh, its scant o' pith an' win'
To climb steep wyn's.

Your sair patched cart sae jolts and reels,
Wi' squeakin' trams an' creakin' wheels,
An' whomles aft your horse's heels
Sae hie in air,
That no a passer by but feels
Baith grieved an' sair.

I kenna how ye pass the tolls,
Or get bawbees to pay your coals,
Amang the needy, naked shoals
That winter cruel
Sends crawlin' forth, frae cauld bleak holes,
To grawl for fuel.

Ah, what a crowd o' shiverin' wretches
Here cower in rags, or limp on crutches;
Ane wha wad fain hae been a duchess,
Now sair disjaskit,
Gathers sma' coals, and vends braw mutches*, caps, kerchiefs
A' in ae basket.

Anither shows some glitterin' toys,
Wi' dalls for lassies—ba's for boys,
Plays on a trump, whase pleasin' noise
Delights Jock's ear.
An' aff he bears his penny prize
His naig to cheer.

Ane o' the street-musician crew
Is busy priggin' wi' him now,
An' twa auld sangs he swears are new,
He pawns on Jock,
For an auld hod o' coals half-fou,—
A weel-matched troke*. bargain

Here comes a genty cleanly granny,
Wi' sma' coal-tub an' wee meal-cannie;
Ye canna weel refuse her peeny,
It's e'en her a';
Yes, fegs, ye'll fill her tub, an' winna
Tak aught ava.

Let him wha scowls on sic as thee,
But come an' watch thy tricks like me,
He'll aye find some redeeming plea,
Some kindly feature,
To gaur him gaze wi' brighter ee,
On human nature.

Puir, wairdless wretch, ye'd need anither
Wi' stern rebuke your heart to wither;
For me, I'm blithe to halt an' swither
Afore I fyke* ye; vex
I feel I'm e'en a failin' brither,
An' far ower like ye.

Alack, alack, crime's never scant
Amang the pale-faced sons o' want;
Yet grit folk shouldna gape an' gaunt,
An' shake their pows*, heads
But something frae their pantries grant
To feed toom* mou's. empty

Tis poortith's* keen an' witherin' blight, poverty's
That gi'es to crime its greatest might;
Gif want's awa, temptation's light
To beg or steal;
Then pity poortith's wretched plight
An' help, an' feel.

## Ye're Ower Bonnie

Oh, will thae pawky een o' thine
Never tire o' killin'?
Gudesake, mind this heart o' mine
Canna aye be thrillin'.
Although ane's heart might thole* ae wound, endure
An' time might close the hole in't,
Ilk piercing glance sae gars it stound,
That there's nae langer tholin't.
Ye're ower bonnie, ye're ower bonnie,
Sae steek* that witchin' ee; shut
Its light flees gleamin' through my brain,
An' dings* me a' ajee. knocks

A hunder times ye've dang me daft
Wi' your light-hearted daffin'*, teasing

Aye echoin' back my words sae saft,
Wi' noisy merry laughin'.
Yet ye're sae sweet, ye maun be kind;
I vow I'll leave thee never;
Shine like the sun, I'll gaze till blind,
Adorin' thee for ever.
Ye're ower bonnie, ye're ower bonnie,
Yet oh that witchin' ee,
Whase light flees gleamin' through my brain,
Is love an' life to me.

### Jamie and Phemie

Auld Johnnie comes over and he cracks* wi' my mither, — chats
The auld warld carle is pawky* an' slee; — clever
Lang Sandy gangs out an' gets fu' wi' my brither,
And bribes the poor coof* to be blackfoot to me. — fool
Bot my manly Jamie, wi' forehead sae hie,
Has a lowe* in his cheek, an' a star in his ee; — hollow
I wotna gin Jamie e'er cracks o' puir Phemie,
But weel do I wot a' his thoughts are wi' me.

I wotna how worth is sae bashfu' and backward,
I wotna how fools are sae forward an' free,
I wotna how Jamie's sae blate* and sae awkward, — shy
I wotna what gaurs my heart wander ajee;
But ah, there's a flame that the world canna see,
In the slee keekin'* glance o' a love-lichted ee; — peeking
An' Jamie's aye keekin', while others are speakin',
An' I wad keek too, but he's keekin' on me.

### The Highland Widow's Lament

Och-on och-rie, Och-on och-rie!
I'm weary, sad, and lone;
And who can cheer the desolate,
When all their friends are gone?
The midnight wind that stirs the heath,
And wails with hollow moan,
Is laden with the voice of death,
And I am left alone.

Och-on och-rie, Och-on och-rie!
That ancient mournful strain,
Which echoes through each Highland glen,
Hath rent my heart in twain.
I gaze upon my roofless cot,
And on my cold hearth stone,
I murmur, am I God-forgot,
That I am left alone?

Och-on och-rie, Och-on och-rie!
Still swells that melting air,
Blest spirits of my gallant boys,
I hear your voices there.
Ye fought—a Scottish Prince to place
Upon a Scottish throne;
Ye died—the last of all your race,
And I am left alone.

## HORATIUS BONAR (1808–1889)

### Abide With Us

Tis evening now.
O Savior, wilt not thou
Enter my home and heart,
Nor ever hence depart,
Even when the morning breaks,
And earth again awakes?
Thou wilt abide with me,
And I with thee.

The world is old.
Its air grows dull and cold.
Upon its aged face
The wrinkles come apace.
Its western sky is wan,
Its youth and joy are gone.
O Master, be our light,
When oer us falls the night.

Evil is round.
Iniquities abound.
Our cottage will be lone
When the great Sun is gone.
O Savior, come and bless,
Come share our loneliness.
We need a comforter.
Take up thy dwelling here.

### The Martyrs of Scotland

There was gladness in Zion, her standard was flying,
Free oer her battlements glorious and gay.
All fair as the morning shone forth her adorning,
And fearful to foes was her godly array.

There is mourning in Zion, her standard is lying
Defiled in the dust, to the spoiler a prey;
And now there is wailing, and sorrow prevailing,
For the best of her children are weeded away.

The good have been taken, their place is forsaken—
The man and the maiden, the green and the gray;
The voice of the weepers wails over the sleepers—
The martyrs of Scotland that now are away.

The hue of her waters is crimsoned with slaughters,
And the blood of the martyrs has reddened the clay;
And dark desolation broods over the nation,
For the faithful are perished, the good are away.

On the mountains of heather they slumber together.
On the wastes of the moorland their bodies decay.
How sound is their sleeping, how safe is their keeping,
Though far from their kindred they molder away.

Their blessing shall hover, their children to cover,
Like the cloud of the desert, by night and by day.
Oh, never to perish, their names let us cherish,
The martyrs of Scotland that now are away.

## JOHN STUART BLACKIE (1809–1895)

### Dora

I can like a hundred women,
I can love a score,
Only one with heart's devotion
Worship and adore.
Mary, Jessie, Lucy, Nancy,
With a fine control
Hold my eye or stir my fancy;
Dora fills my soul.

Dainty doves are doves of Venus,
(Plumy, soft delight),
But my dove (O wonder!), Dora,
Hath an eagle's might.
Doves are pretty, doves are stupid,
But who Dora loves
Finds Minerva masqued in Cupid,
Strength in downy doves.

Like the sun's face brightly dancing
On the shimmering sea,
But, like Ocean, deep is Dora,
Strong, and fair, and free.
Chirping like a gay Cicala
In a sunny bower,
But a Muse is that Cicala
Sings with thoughtful power.

Like a beck that bickers blithely
Down the daisied lea,
So her bright soul bursts and blossoms
In spontaneous glee.
Full of gamesome show is Dora;
But behind the scene
Sits the lofty will of Dora,
Thronèd like a queen.

Lovely marvel; oak and lily
From one root came forth,
Twined in leafy grace together
At my Dora's birth.
Mellow Eve, and bright Aurora,
Sober Night and Noon,
Dwell, divinely blent, in Dora,
To a jarless tune.

I can like a hundred women,
I can love a score,
Only one with heart's devotion
Worship and adore.
Mary, Jessie, Lucy, Nancy,
With a fine control
Hold my eye or stir my fancy;
Dora fills my soul.

## My Loves

Name the leaves on all the trees,
Name the waves on all the seas,
Name the notes of all the groves,
Thus thou namest all my loves.

I do love the dark, the fair,
Golden ringlets, raven hair,
Eye that swims in sunny light,
Glance that shoots like lightning bright.

I do love the stately dame
And the sportive girl the same;
Every changeful phase between
Blooming cheek and brow serene.

I do love the young, the old,
Maiden modest, virgin bold,
Tiny beauties, and the tall;
Earth has room enough for all.

Which is better, who can say,
Lucy grave, or Mary gay?

She who half her charms conceals,
She who flashes while she feels?

Why should I my love confine?
Why should fair be mine or thine?
If I praise a tulip, why
Should I pass the primrose by?

Paris was a pedant fool
Meting beauty by the rule,
Pallas? Juno? Venus?—he
Should have chosen all the three.

I am wise, life's every bliss
Thankful tasting; and a kiss
Is a sweet thing, I declare,
From a dark maid or a fair!

## My Bath

(Scene—Kinnaird Burn, near Pitlochrie)

Come here, good people great and small, that wander far abroad,
To drink of drumly* German wells, and make a weary road — dirty
To Baden and to Wiesbaden, and how they all are named,
To Calsbad and to Kissingen, for healing virtue famed;
Come stay at home, and keep your feet from dusty travel free,
And I will show you what rare bath a good God gave to me.
Tis hid among the Highland hills beneath the purple brae,
With cooling freshness free to all, nor doctor's fee to pay.

No craft of mason made it here, nor carpenter, I wot;
Nor tinkering fool with hammering tool to shape the charmed spot;
But down the rocky-breasted glen the foamy torrent falls
Into the amber caldron deep, fenced round with granite walls.
Nor gilded beam, nor pictured dome, nor curtain, roofs it in,
But the blue sky rests, and white clouds float, above the bubbling linn*, — waterfall
Where God's own hand hath scooped it out in nature's Titan hall,
And from her cloud-fed fountains drew its waters free to all.

Oh come and see my Highland bath, and prove its freshening flood,
And spare to taint your skin with swathes of drumly German mud.
Come plunge with me into the wave like liquid topaz fair,
And to the waters give your back that spout down bravely there;
Then float upon the swirling flood, and, like a glancing trout,
Plash about, and dash about, and make a lively rout,
And to the gracious sun display the glory of your skin,
As you dash about and splash about in the foamy-bubbling linn.

Oh come and prove my bonnie bath; in sooth tis furnished well
With trees, and shrubs, and spreading ferns, all in the rocky dell,
And roses hanging from the cliff in grace of white and red,

And little tiny birches nodding lightly overhead,
And spiry larch with purple cones, and tips of virgin green,
And leafy shade of hazel copse with sunny glints between.
Oh might the Roman wight be here who praised Bandusia's well,
He'd find a bath to nymphs more dear in my sweet Highland dell.

Some folks will pile proud palaces, and some will wander far
To scan the blinding of a sun, or the blinking of a star;
Some sweat through Afric's burning sands; and some will vex their soul
To find heaven knows what frosty prize beneath the Arctic pole.
God bless them all; and may they find what thing delights them well
In east or west, or north or south,—but I at home will dwell.
Where fragrant ferns their fronds uncurl, and healthful breezes play,
And clear brown waters grandly swirl beneath the purple brae.

Oh come and prove my Highland bath, the burn, and all the glen,
Hard-toiling wights in dingy nooks, and scribes with inky pen,
Strange thoughtful men with curious quests that vex your fretful brains,
And scheming sons of trade who fear to count your slippery gains;
Come wander up the burn with me, and thread the winding glen,
And breathe the healthful power that flows down from the breezy Ben,
And plunge you in the deep brown pool; and from beneath the spray
You'll come forth like a flower that blooms neath freshening showers in May.

## The Two Meek Margarets

It fell on a day in the blooming month of May,
When the trees were greenly growing,
That a captain grim went down to the brim
O' the sea, when the tide was flowing.

Twa maidens he led, that captain grim,
Wi' his redcoat loons* behind him, rascals
Twa meek-faced maids, and he sware that he
In the salt sea-swell should bind them.

And a' the burghers o' Wigton town
Came down, full sad and cheerless,
To see that ruthless captain drown
These maidens meek but fearless.

O what had they done, these maidens meek,
What crime all crimes excelling,
That they should be staked on the ribbed sea-sand,
And drowned, where the tide was swelling?

O waes me, wae, but the truth I maun say,
Their crime was the crime of believing
Not man, but God, when the last false Stuart
His Popish plot was weaving.

O spare them, spare them, thou captain grim!
No, no—to a stake he hath bound them,
Where the floods as they flow, and the waves as they grow,
Shall soon be deepening round them.

The one had threescore years and three;
Far out on the sand they bound her,
Where the first dark flow of the waves as they grow,
Is quickly swirling round her.

The other was a maiden fresh and fair;
More near to the land they bound her,
That she might see by slow degree
The grim waves creeping round her.

O captain, spare that maiden gray,
She's deep in the deepening water!
No, no, she's lifted her hands to pray,
And the choking billow caught her.

See, see, young maid, cried the captain grim,
The wave shall soon ride oer thee.
She's swamped in the brine whose sin was like thine.
See that same fate before thee.

I see the Christ who hung on a tree
When his life for sins he offered.
In one of his members, even he
With that meek maid hath suffered.

O captain, save that meek young maid.
She's a loyal farmer's daughter.
Well, well, let her swear to good King James,
And I'll hale her out from the water.

I will not swear to Popish James,
But I pray for the head of the nation,
That he and all, both great and small,
May know God's great salvation.

She spoke, and lifted her hands to pray,
And felt the greedy water,
Deep and more deep around her creep,
Till the choking billow caught her.

O Wigton, Wigton, I'm wae to sing
The truth o' this waesome story;

But God will sinners to judgment bring,
And his saints shall reign in glory.

## ALEXANDER HUME (1809–1851)

### Sandy Allan

Wha is he I hear sae crouse*, brave
There ahint the hallan*? partition, fire-screen
Whase skirling rings through a' the house,
Ilk corner o' the dwallin'.
O, it is ane, a weel kent chiel*, fellow
As mirth e'er set a bawlin'.
Or filled a neuk in drouthy* biel,— thirsty
It's canty* Sandy Allan. lively

He has a gaucy* kind gudewife, handsome
This blithesome Sandy Allan,
Who loes him mickle mair than life,
An' glories in her callan*. fellow
As sense an' sound are ane in song,
Sae's Jean an' Sandy Allan:
Twa hearts, yet but ae pulse an' tongue,
Hae Luckie an' her callan.

To gie to a', it's aye his rule,
Their proper name an' callin'.
A knave's a knave, a fool's a fool,
Wi' honest Sandy Allan.
For ilka vice he has a dart,
An' heavy is its fallin';
But aye for worth a kindred heart
Has ever Sandy Allan.

To kings his knee he winna bring,
Sae proud is Sandy Allan,
The man wha richtly feels is king,
Ower rank wi' Sandy Allan.
Auld nature, just to show the warl'
Ae truly honest callan,
E'en strippit till't, and made a carle*, fellow
An' ca'd him Sandy Allan.

### Oh, Years Hae Come

Oh, years hae come, an' years hae gane,
Sin' first I sought the warld alane,

Sin' first I mused wi' heart sae fain
   On the hills o' Caledonia.
But oh, behold the present gloom,
My early friends are in the tomb,
And nourish now the heather bloom
   On the hills o' Caledonia.

My father's name, my father's lot,
Is now a tale that's heeded not,
Or sang unsung, if no forgot,
   On the hills o' Caledonia.
O' our great ha' there's left nae stane—
A' swept away, like snaw lang gane;
Weeds flourish oer the auld domain
   On the hills o' Caledonia.

The Ti'ot's banks are bare and high,
The stream rins sma and mournfu' by,
Like some sad heart maist grutten* dry,     wept
   On the hills o' Caledonia.
The wee birds sing no frae the tree,
The wild-flowers bloom no on the lea,
As if the kind things pitied me
   On the hills o' Caledonia.

But friends can live, though cold they lie,
An' mock the mourner's tear an' sigh;
When we forget them, then they die
   On the hills o' Caledonia.
An' howsoever changed the scene,
While memory an' my feeling's green,
Still green to my auld heart an' een
   Are the hills o' Caledonia.

## JOHN BROWN (1810–1882)

[Brown was a practicing physician in Edinburgh, and a writer of charming and witty informal essays, rather after the fashion of Charles Lamb. He produced works on a wide variety of subjects, but is especially known for his treatment of dogs. Perhaps his best known canine essay is the famous "Rab and his Friends" (1859), printed here.]

### Rab and His Friends

Four and thirty years ago, Bob Ainslie and I were coming up Infirmary Street from the Edinburgh High School, our heads together, and our arms intertwisted, as only lovers and boys know how, or why.

When we got to the top of the street, and turned north, we espied a crowd at the Tron Church. "A dog-fight!" shouted Bob, and was off; and so was I, both of us all but praying that it might not be over before we got up. And is not this boy-nature? and human nature too? and don't we all wish a house on fire not to be out before we see it? Dogs like fighting; old Isaac says they "delight" in it, and for the best of all reasons; and boys are not cruel because they like to see the fight. They see three of the great cardinal virtues of dog or man—courage, endurance, and skill—in intense action. This is very different from a love of making dogs fight, and enjoying, and aggravating, and making gain by their pluck. A boy—be he ever so fond himself of fighting, if he be a good boy, hates and despises all this, but he would have run off with Bob and me fast enough: it is a natural, and a not wicked interest, that all boys and men have in witnessing intense energy in action.

Does any curious and finely-ignorant woman wish to know how Bob's eye at a glance announced a dog-fight to his brain? He did not, he could not see the dogs fighting; it was a flash of an inference, a rapid induction. The crowd round a couple of dogs fighting is a crowd masculine mainly, with an occasional active, compassionate woman, fluttering wildly round the outside, and using her tongue and her hands freely upon the men, as so many "brutes"; it is a crowd annular, compact, and mobile; a crowd centripetal, having its eyes and its heads all bent downwards and inwards to one common focus.

Well, Bob and I are up, and find it is not over: a small thoroughbred, white Bull Terrier, is busy throttling a large Shepherd's dog, unaccustomed to war, but not to be trifled with. They are hard at it; the scientific little fellow doing his work in great style, his pastoral enemy fighting wildly, but with the sharpest of teeth and a great courage. Science and breeding, however, soon had their own; the Game Chicken, as the premature Bob called him, working his way up, took his final grip of poor Yarrow's throat,—and he lay gasping and done for. His master, a brown, handsome, big young shepherd from Tweedsmuir, would have liked to have knocked down any man, would "drink up Esil, or eat a crocodile," for that part, if he had a chance. It was no use kicking the little dog; that would only make him hold the closer. Many were the means shouted out in mouthfuls, of the best possible ways of ending it. "Water!" but there was none near, and many cried for it who might have got it from the well at Blackfriars Wynd.

"Bite the tail!" and a large, vague, benevolent, middle-aged man, more desirous than wise, with some struggle got the bushy end of Yarrow's tail into his ample mouth, and bit it with all his might. This was more than enough for the much-enduring, much-perspiring shepherd, who, with a gleam of joy over his broad visage, delivered a terrific facer upon our large, vague, benevolent, middle-aged friend,—who went down like a shot.

Still the Chicken holds; death not far off.

"Snuff! a pitch of snuff!" observed a calm, highly-dressed young buck, with an eye-glass in his eye.

"Snuff, indeed!" growled the angry crowd, affronted and glaring.

"Snuff! a pinch of snuff!" again observed the buck, but with more urgency; whereon were produced several open boxes, and from a mull which may have been at Culloden, he took a pinch, knelt down, and presented it to the nose of the Chicken. The laws of physiology and of snuff take their course; the Chicken sneezes, and Yarrow is free!

The young pastoral giant stalks off with Yarrow in his arms,—comforting him. But the Bull Terrier's blood is up, and his soul unsatisfied; he grips the first dog he meets, and discovering she is not a dog, in Homeric phrase, he makes a brief sort of *amende,* and is off. The boys, with Bob and me at their head, are after him: down Niddry Street he goes, bent on mischief; up the Cowgate like an arrow—Bob and I, and our small men, panting behind.

There, under the single arch of the South Bridge, is a huge mastiff, sauntering down the middle of the causeway, as if with his hands in his pockets: he is old, gray, brindled, as big as a little highland bull, and has the Shakespearean dewlaps shaking as he goes.

The Chicken makes straight at him, and fastens on his throat. To our astonishment, the great creature does nothing but stand still, hold himself up, and roar—yes, roar; a long, serious, remonstrative roar. How is this? Bob and I are up to them. *He is muzzled*! The bailies had proclaimed a general muzzling, and his master, studying strength and economy mainly, had encompassed his huge jaws in a home-made apparatus, constructed out of the leather of some ancient *breechin*. His mouth was open as far as it could; his lips curled up in rage—a sort of terrible grin; his teeth gleaming, ready, from out the darkness; the strap across his mouth tense as a bowstring; his whole frame stiff with indignation and surprise; his roar asking us all round, "Did you ever see the like of this?" He looked a statue of anger and astonishment done in Aberdeen granite.

We soon had a crowd: the Chicken held on.

"A knife!" cried Bob; and a cobbler gave him his knife: you know the kind of knife, worn away obliquely to a point, and always keen. I put its edge to the tense leather; it ran before it; and then! —one sudden jerk of that enormous head, a sort of dirty mist about his mouth, no noise,—and the bright and fierce little fellow is dropped, limp, and dead. A solemn pause: this was more than any of us had bargained for. I turned the little fellow over, and saw he was quite dead; the mastiff had taken him by the small of the back like a rat, and broken it.

He looked down at his victim appeased, ashamed, and amazed; snuffed him all over, stared at him, and taking a sudden thought, turned round and trotted off. Bob took the dead dog up, and said, "John, we'll bury him after tea."

"Yes," said I, and was off after the mastiff. He made up the Cowgate at a rapid swing; he had forgotten some engagement. He turned up the Candlemaker Row, and stopped at the Harrow Inn.

There was a carrier's cart ready to start, and a keen, thin, impatient, black-a-vised little man, his hand at his gray horse's head, looking about angrily for something. "Rab, ye thief!" said he, aiming a kick at my great friend, who drew cringing up, and avoiding the heavy shoe with more agility than dignity, and watching his master's eye, slunk dismayed under the cart, his ears down, and as much as he had of tail down too.

What a man this must be—thought I—to whom my tremendous hero turns tail! The carrier saw the muzzle hanging, cut and useless, from his neck, and I eagerly told him the story, which Bob and I always thought, and still think, Homer, or King David, or Sir Walter alone were worthy to rehearse. The severe little man was mitigated, and condescended to say, "Rab, my man, puir Rabbie,"—whereupon the stump of a tail rose up, the ears were cocked, the eyes filled, and were comforted; the two friends were reconciled.

"Hupp!" and a stroke of the whip were given to Jess; and off went the three.

Bob and I buried the Game Chicken that night (we had not much of a tea) in the back-green of his house in Melville Street, No. 17, with considerable gravity and silence; and being at the time in the Iliad, and, like all boys, Trojans, we called him Hector of course.

Six years have passed,—a long time for a boy and a dog: Bob Ainslie is off to the wars; I am a medical student and clerk at Minto House Hospital.

Rab I saw almost every week, on the Wednesday, and we had much pleasant intimacy. I found the way to his heart by frequent scratching of his huge head, and an occasional bone. When I did not notice him he would plant himself straight before me, and stand wagging that bud of a tail, and looking up, with his head a little to the one side. His master I occasionally saw; he used to call me "Maister John," but was laconic as any Spartan.

One fine October afternoon, I was leaving the hospital, when I saw the large gate open, and in walked Rab, with that great and easy saunter of his. He looked as if taking general possession of the place; like the Duke of Wellington entering a subdued city, satiated with victory and peace. After him came Jess, now white from age, with her cart; and in it a woman, carefully wrapped up,—the carrier leading the horse anxiously, and looking back. When he saw me, James (for his name was James Noble) made a curt and grotesque "boo," and said, "Maister John, this is the mistress; she's got a trouble in her breest—some kind o' an income we're thinking."

By this time I saw the woman's face; she was sitting on a sack filled with straw, her husband's plaid round her, and his big-coat with its large white metal buttons, over her feet.

I never saw a more unforgettable face—pale, serious, *lonely,* delicate, sweet, without being at all what we call fine. She looked sixty, and had on a mutch, white as snow, with its black ribbon; her silvery, smooth hair setting off her dark-gray eyes—eyes such as one sees only twice or thrice in a lifetime, full of suffering, full also of the overcoming of it: her eyebrows black and delicate, and her mouth firm, patient, and contented, which few mouths ever are.

As I have said, I never saw a more beautiful countenance, or one more subdued to settled quiet.

"Ailie," said James, "this is Maister John, the young Doctor; Rab's freend, ye ken. We often speak aboot you, doctor."

She smiled, and made a movement, but said nothing; and prepared to come down, putting her plaid aside and rising. Had Solomon, in all his glory, been handing down the Queen of Sheba at his palace gate he could not have done it more daintily, more tenderly, more like a gentleman, than did James the Howgate carrier, when he lifted down Ailie his wife. The contrast of his small, swarthy, weather-beaten, keen, worldly face to hers—pale, subdued, and beautiful—was something wonderful. Rab looked on concerned and puzzled, but ready for anything that might turn up,—were it to strangle the nurse, the porter, or even me. Ailie and he seemed great friends.

"As I was sayin', she's got a kind o' trouble in her breest, doctor; wull ye tak a look at it?"

We walked into the consulting-room, all four; Rab grim and comic, willing to be happy and confidential if cause could be shown, willing also to be the reverse, on the same terms. Ailie sat down, undid her open gown and her lawn handkerchief round her neck, and without a word, showed me her right breast. I looked at and examined it carefully,—she and James watching me, and Rab eyeing all three. What could I say? There it was, that had once been so soft, so shapely, so white, so gracious and bountiful, so "full of all blessed conditions,"—hard as a stone, a center of horrid pain, making that pale face, with its gray, lucid, reasonable eyes, and its sweet resolved month, express the full measure of suffering overcome. Why was that gentle, modest, sweet woman, clean and lovable, condemned by God to bear such a burden?

I got her away to bed.

"May Rab and me bide?" said James.

"You may; and Rab, if he will behave himself."

"I'se warrant he's do that, doctor"; and in slank the faithful beast. I wish you could have seen him. There are no such dogs now. He belonged to a lost tribe. As I have said, he was brindled and gray like Rubislaw granite; his hair short, hard, and close, like a lion's; his body thick set, like a little bull—a sort of compressed Hercules of a dog. He must have been ninety pounds' weight, at the least; he had a large blunt head; his muzzle black as night, his mouth blacker than any night, a tooth or two—being all he had—gleaming out of his jaws of darkness. His head was scarred with the records of old wounds, a sort of series of fields of battle all over it; one eye out, one ear cropped as close as was Archbishop Leighton's father's; the remaining eye had the power of two; and above it, and in constant communication with it, was a tattered rag of an ear, which was forever unfurling itself, like an old flag; and then that bud of a tail, about one inch long, if it could in any sense be said to be long, being as broad as long—the mobility, the instantaneousness of that bud were very funny and surprising, and its expressive twinklings and winkings, the intercommunications between the eye, the ear, and it, were of the oddest and swiftest.

Rab had the dignity and simplicity of great size; and having fought his way all along the road to absolute supremacy, he was as mighty in his own line as Julius Caesar or the Duke of Wellington, and had the gravity of all great fighters.

You must have often observed the likeness of certain men to certain animals, and of certain dogs to men. Now, I never looked at Rab without thinking of the great Baptist preacher, Andrew Fuller. The same large, heavy, menacing, combative, somber, honest countenance, the same deep inevitable eye, the same look,—as of thunder asleep, but ready,— neither a dog nor a man to be trifled with.

Next day, my master, the surgeon, examined Ailie. There was no doubt it must kill her, and soon. It could be removed—it might never return—it would give her speedy relief—she should have it done.

She curtsied, looked at James, and said, "When?"

"To-morrow," said the kind surgeon—a man of few words. She and James and Rab and I retired. I noticed that he and she spoke little, but seemed to anticipate everything in each other.

The following day, at noon, the students came in, hurrying up the great stair. At the first landing-place, on a small well-known blackboard, was a bit of paper fastened by wafers and many remains of old wafers beside it. On the paper were the words, "An operation today. J.B. Clerk."

Up ran the youths, eager to secure good places; in they crowded, full of interest and talk. "What's the case?" "Which side is it?"

Don't think them heartless; they are neither better nor worse than you or I; they get over their professional horrors, and into their proper work—and in them pity—as an emotion, ending in itself or at best in tears and a long-drawn breath—lessens. while pity as a motive is quickened, and gains power and purpose. It is well for poor human nature that it is so.

The operating theater is crowded; much talk and fun, and all the cordiality and stir of youth. The surgeon with his staff of assistants is there. In comes Ailie: one look at her quiets and abates the eager students. That beautiful old woman is too much for them; they sit down, and are dumb, and gaze at her. These rough boys feel the power of her presence. She walks in quickly, but without haste; dressed in her mutch, her neckerchief, her white dimity short gown, her black bombazine petticoat, snowing her white worsted stockings and her carpet-shoes. Behind her was James with Rab. James sat down in the distance, and took that huge and noble head between his knees. Rab looked perplexed and dangerous, forever cocking his ear and dropping it as fast. Ailie stepped up on a seat, and laid herself on the table, as her friend the surgeon told her; arranged herself, gave a rapid look at James, shut her eyes, rested herself on me, and took my hand.

The operation was at once begun; it was necessarily slow; and chloroform —one of God's best gifts to his suffering children— was then unknown.

The surgeon did his work.

The pale face showed its pain, but was still and silent.

Rab's soul was working within him; he saw that something strange was going on, — blood flowing from his mistress, and she suffering; his ragged ear was up, and importunate; he growled and gave now and then a sharp impatient yelp; he would have liked to have done something to that man. But James had him firm, and gave him a *glower* from time to time, and an intimation of a possible kick;—all the better for James, it kept his eye and his mind off Ailie.

It is over: she is dressed, steps gently and decently down from the table, looks for James; then, turning to the surgeon and the students, she curtsies,—and in a low, clear voice, begs their pardon if she has behaved ill. The students—all of us—wept like children; the surgeon happed her up carefully, and, resting on James and me, Ailie went to her room, Rab following. We put her to bed. James took off his heavy shoes, crammed with tackets, heel-capt, and toe-capt and put them carefully under the table, saying, "Maister John, I'm for nane o' yer strynge nurse bodies for Ailie. I'll be her nurse, and I'll gang aboot on my stockin' soles as canny as pussy." And so he did; and handy and clever, and swift and tender as any woman, was that horny-handed, snell, peremptory little man. Everything she got he gave her: he seldom slept; and often I saw his small shrewd eyes out of the darkness, fixed on her. As before, they spoke little.

Rab behaved well, never moving, showing us how meek and gentle he could be, and occasionally, in his sleep, letting us know that he was demolishing some adversary. He took a walk with me every day, generally to the Candlemaker Row; but he was somber and mild; declined doing battle, though some fit cases offered, and indeed submitted to sundry indignities; and was always very ready to turn, and came faster back, and trotted up the stair with much lightness, and went straight to that door.

Jess, the mare, had been sent, with her weather worn cart, to Howgate, and had doubtless her own dim and placid meditations and confusions, on the absence of her master and Rab, and her unnatural freedom from the road and her cart.

For some days Ailie did well. The wound healed "by the first intention"; for as James said, "Our Ailie's skin's ower clean to beil." The students came in quiet and anxious, and surrounded her bed. She said she liked to see their young, honest faces. The surgeon dressed her, and spoke to her in his own short kind way, pitying her through his eyes, Rab and James outside the circle,—Rab being now reconciled, and even cordial, and having made up his mind that as yet nobody required worrying, but, as you may suppose, semper *paratus*.

So far well: but, four days after the operation, my patient had a sudden and long shivering, a "groosin'," as she called it. I saw her soon after; her eyes were too bright, her cheek colored; she was restless, and shamed of being so; the balance was lost; mischief had begun. On looking at the wound, a blush of red told the secret: her pulse was rapid, her breathing anxious and quick, she wasn't herself, as she said, and was vexed at her restlessness.

We tried what we could; James did everything, was everywhere; never in the way, never out of it; Rab subsided under the table into a dark place, and was motionless, all but his eye, which followed every one. Ailie got worse; began to wander in her mind, gently; was more demonstrative in her ways to James, rapid in her questions, and sharp at times.

He was vexed, and said, "She was never that way afore; no, never."

For a time she knew her head was wrong, and was always asking our pardon—the dear, gentle old woman: then delirium set in strong, without pause. Her brain gave way, and then came that terrible spectacle,—

"The intellectual power, through words and things,
Went sounding on its dim and perilous way,"

She sang bits of old songs and Psalms, stopping suddenly, mingling the Psalms of David and the diviner words of his Son and Lord, with homely odds and ends and scraps of ballads.

Nothing more touching, or in a sense more strangely beautiful, did I ever witness. Her tremulous, rapid, affectionate, eager, Scotch voice,—the swift, aimless, bewildered mind, the baffled utterance, the bright and perilous eye; some wild words, some household cares, something for James, the names of the dead, Rab called rapidly and in a "fremyt"[1] voice, and he starting up surprised, and slinking off as if he were to blame somehow, or had been dreaming he heard; many eager questions and beseechings which James and I could make nothing of, and on which she seemed to set her all, and then sink back ununderstood. It was very sad, but better than many things that are not called sad. James hovered about, put out and miserable, but active and exact as ever; read to her when there was a lull, short bits from the Psalms, prose and meter, chanting the latter in his own rude and serious way, showing great knowledge of the fit words, bearing up like a man, and doting over her as his "ain Ailie." "Ailie, ma woman!" "Ma ain bonnie wee dawtie!"

The end was drawing on; the golden bowl was breaking; the silver cord was fast being loosed— that *animula blandula, vagula, hospes, comesque,* was about to flee. The body and the soul—companions for sixty years—were being sundered, and taking leave. She was walking alone, through the valley of that shadow, into which one day we must all enter, —and yet she was not alone, for we know whose rod and staff were comforting her.

One night she had fallen quiet, and as we hoped, asleep; her eyes were shut. We put down the gas, and sat watching her. Suddenly she sat up in bed, and taking a bed-gown which was lying on it rolled up, she held it eagerly to her breast,—to the right side. We could see her eyes bright with a surprising tenderness and joy, bending over this bundle of clothes. She held it as a woman holds her sucking child; opening out her night-gown impatiently, and holding it close, and brooding over it, and murmuring foolish little words, as over one whom his mother comforteth, and who sucks and is satisfied. It was pitiful and strange to see her wasted dying look, keen and yet vague—her immense love.

"Preserve me!" groaned James, giving way. And then she rocked back and forward, as if to make it sleep, hushing it, and wasting on it her infinite fondness.

"Wae's me, doctor; I declare she's thinkin' it's that bairn."

"What bairn?"

"The only bairn we ever had; our wee Mysie, and she's in the kingdom, forty years and mair."

It was plainly true: the pain in the breast, telling its urgent story to a bewildered, ruined brain, was misread and mistaken; it suggested to her the uneasiness of a breast full of milk, and then the child; and so again once more they were together, and she had her ain wee Mysie in her bosom.

This was the close. She sank rapidly: the delirium left her; but, as she whispered, she was "clean silly"; it was the lightening before the final darkness. After having for some time lain still—her eyes shut, she said "James!"

He came close to her, and lifting up her calm, clear, beautiful eyes, she gave him a long look, turned to me kindly but shortly, looked for Rab but could not see him, then turned to her husband again, as if she would never leave off looking, shut her eyes, and composed herself. She lay for some time breathing quick, and passed away so gently, that when we thought she was gone, James, in his old-fashioned way, held the mirror to her face. After a long pause, one small spot of dimness was breathed out; it vanished away, and never returned, leaving the blank clear darkness of the mirror without a stain.

"What is our life? it is even a vapor, which appeareth for a little time, and then

---

[1] Strange.

vanisheth away."

Rab all this time had been full awake and motionless; he came forward beside us: Ailie's hand, which James had held, was hanging down; it was soaked with his tears; Rab licked it all over carefully, looked at her, and returned to his place under the table.

James and I sat, I don't know how long, but for some time,—saying nothing: he started up abruptly and with some noise went to the table, and putting his right fore and middle fingers each into a shoe, pulled them out, and put them on, breaking one of the leather latchets, and muttering in anger, "I never did the like o' that afore!"

I believe he never did; nor after either.

"Rab!" he said roughly, and pointing with his thumb to the bottom of the bed. Rab leapt up, and settled himself; his head and eye to the dead face. "Maister John, ye'll wait for me," said the carrier; and disappeared in the darkness, thundering down-stairs in his heavy shoes. I ran to a front window; there he was, already round the house, and out at the gate, fleeing like a shadow.

I was afraid about him, and yet not afraid; so I sat down beside Rab, and being wearied, fell asleep. I awoke from a sudden noise outside. It was November, and there had been a heavy fall of snow. Rab was in *statu quo;* he heard the noise too, and plainly knew it, but never moved. I looked out; and there, at the gate, in the dim morning—for the sun was not up—was Jess and the cart,—a cloud of steam rising from the old mare. I did not see James; he was already at the door, and came up the stairs, and met me. It was less than three hours since he left, and he must have posted out—who knows how?—to Howgate, full nine miles off; yoked Jess, and driven her astonished into town. He had an armful of blankets, and was streaming with perspiration. He nodded to me, spread out on the floor two pairs of clean old blankets having at their corners, "A. G., 1794," in large letters, in red worsted. These were the initials of Alison Graeme, and James may have looked in at her from without—himself unseen but not unthought of—when he was "wat, wat, and weary," and after having walked many a mile over the hills, may have seen her sitting, while "a' the lave were sleepin'"; and by the firelight working her name on the blankets, for her ain James's bed.

He motioned Rab down, and taking his wife in his arms, laid her in the blankets, and happed her carefully and firmly up, leaving the face uncovered; and then lifting her, he nodded again shortly to me, and with a resolved but utterly miserable face, strode along the passage, and down-stairs, followed by Rab. I followed with a light; but he didn't need it. I went out, holding stupidly the candle in my hand in the calm frosty air; we were soon at the gate. I could have helped him, but I saw he was not to be meddled with, and he was strong, and did not need it.

He laid her down as tenderly, as safely, as he had lifted her out ten days before—as tenderly as when he held her first in his arms when she was only "A. G.,"—sorted her, leaving that beautiful sealed face open to the heavens; and then taking Jess by the head, he moved away. He did not notice me, neither did Rab, who presided behind the cart.

I stood till they passed through the long shadow of the College, and turned up Nicolson Street. I heard the solitary cart sound through the streets, and die away and come again; and I returned, thinking of that company going up Libberton Brae, then along Roslin Muir, the morning light touching the Pentlands and making them like onlooking ghosts, then down the hill through Anchindinlly woods, past "haunted Woodhouselee"; and as daybreak came weeping up the bleak Lammermuirs, and fell on his own door, the company would stop, and James would take the key, and lift Ailie up again, laying her on her own bed, and, having put Jess up, would return with Rab and shut the door.

James buried his wife, with his neighbors mourning, Rab inspecting the solemnity from a distance. It was snow, and that black ragged hole would look strange in the midst of the swelling spotless cushion of white. James looked after everything; then rather suddenly fell ill, and took to bed; was insensible when the doctor came, and soon died. A sort of low fever was prevailing in the village, and his want of sleep, his exhaustion, and his misery, made him apt to take it. The grave was not difficult to reopen. A fresh fall of snow had again made all things white and smooth; Rab once more looked on, and slunk home to the stable.

And what of Rab? I asked for him next week of the new carrier who got the goodwill of James's business, and was now master of Jess and her cart.

"How's Rab?"

He put me off, and said rather rudely, "What's *your* business wi' the dowg?" I was not to be so put off.

"Where's Rab?"

He, getting confused and red, and intermeddling with his hair, said, "'Deed, sir, Rab's deid."

"Dead! What did he die of?"

"Weel, sir," said he, getting redder, "he didna exactly dee; he was killed. I had to brain him wi' a rack-pin; there was nae doin' wi' him. He lay in the treviss wi' the mear, and wad na come oot. I tempit him wi' kail and meat, but he wad tak naething, and keepit me frae feedin' the beast, and he was aye gur gurrin,' and grup gruppin' me by the legs. I was laith to make awa wi' the auld dowg, his like was na atween this and Thornhill,—but, 'deed, sir, I could do naething else."

I believed him. Fit end for Rab, quick and complete. His teeth and his friends gone, why should he keep the peace, and be civil?

## WILLIAM MILLER (1810–1872)

[David Robertson, a Glasgow publisher, printed a series of poetry collections which have become known as "Whistle-binkie" poems, after their title, *Whistle-Binkie, or The Paper of the Party, Being a Collection of Songs for the Social Circle.* The poems were relatively simple, strongly rhymed, and in the sentimental and sometimes gnomic style of popular songs of the day. William Miller was one of the most successful—perhaps notorious—of the Whistle-binkie poets, and "Wee Willie Winkie," is one of the most famous such works. Other Whistle-binkie poets represented in this anthology would include James Ballantine, Alexander Rodger and William Thom. The inclusion of "Wee Willie Winkle" in this anthology is based partly upon the Victorian practice of "mainstreaming" such poetry in their own collections. The charming "Auld Daddy Darkness," which follows Miller's, is another example of a fine children's poem, which appeared in popular anthologies alongside the more usual categories. Many nineteenth century poets—Louis Stevenson is a notable example—tried their hand at poems for young people. In Stevenson's case, it is sometimes difficult to decide in which age category to put them. The same might be said for some modern poets, for example the American, Robert Frost, or the fine Scots poet, William Soutar.]

### Wee Willie Winkie

Wee Willie Winkie rins through the town,  
Up stairs and doon stairs, in his nicht-gown,  
Tirlin'* at the window, cryin' at the lock, *sounding*  
"Are the weans in their bed?—for it's now ten o'clock."

Hey, Willie Winkie, are ye comin' ben*? in
The cat's singin' gay thrums to the sleepin' hen,
The dog's speldered on the floor, and disna gie a cheep;
But here's a waukrife* laddie, that winna fa' asleep.. wakeful

Ony thing but sleep, ye rogue:—glow'rin' like the moon,
Rattlin' in an airn jug wi' an airn spoon,
Rumblin', tumblin' round' about, crawin' like a cock,
Skirlin' like a kenna what—wauknin' sleepin' folk.

Hey, Willie Winkie, the wean's in a creel,
Waumblim' aff a body's knee like a vera eel,
Ruggin' at the cat's lug*, and ravellin' a' her thrums: ear
Hey, Willie Winkie,—See, there he comes!

Weary is the mither that has a storie wean,
A wee stumpie stousie, that canna rin his lane*, by himself
That has a battle aye wi' sleep, before he'll close an ee:
But a kiss frae aff his rosy lips gies strength anew to me!

## Cockie-Leerie-La

There is a country gentleman,
Who leads a thrifty life,
Ilk morning scraping orra* things odd
Thegither for his wife—
His coat o' glowing ruddy brown,
And wavelet wi' gold—
A crimson crown upon his head,
Well fitting one so bold.

If ithers pick where he did scrape,
He brings them to disgrace,
For, like a man o' metal, he
Siclike meets face to face.
He gies the loons* a lethering, rascals
A crackit croon* to claw— "crown"
There is nae gaun about the bush
Wi' Cockie-leerie-la.

His step is firm and evenly,
His look both sage and grave—
His bearing bold, as if he said,
"I'll never be a slave."
And though he hauds his head fu' high,
He glinteth to the grun,
Nor fyles* his silver spurs in dubs "defiles"
Wi' glowerin' at the sun.

And whiles I've thocht had he a hand
Wharwi' to grip a stickie,
A pair o' specks across his neb*, beak
And round his neck a dickie,
That weans wad laughing haud their sides,
And cry, "Preserve us a'.
Ye're some frien' to Doctor Drawbluid,
Douce Cockie-leerie-la."

So learn frae him to think nae shame
To work for what ye need,
For he that gapes till he be fed,
May gape till he be dead.
And if ye live in idleness,
Ye'll find unto your cost,
That they wha winna work in heat,
Maun hunger in the frost.

And hain* wi' care ilk sair-won plack*, guard/(small coin)
And honest pride will fill
Your purse wi' gear—e'en far-off frien's
Will bring grist to your mill;
And if, when grown to be a man,
Your name's without a flaw,
Then rax* your neck, and tune your pipes stretch
To Cockie-leerie-la.

## JAMES FERGUSON (DATES UNKNOWN)

### Auld Daddy Darkness

Auld Daddy Darkness creeps frae his hole,
Black as a blackamoor, blin' as a mole:
Stir the fire till it lowes*, let the bairnie sit, flames
Auld Daddy Darkness is no wantit yit.

See him in the corners hidin' frae the licht,
See him at the window gloomin' at the nicht;
Turn up the gas licht, close the shutters a',
An' Auld Daddy Darkness will flee far awa'.

Awa' to hide the birdie within its cozy nest,
Awa' to lap the wee flooers on their mither's breast,
Awa' to loosen Gaffer Toil frae his daily ca',
For Auld Daddy Darkness is kindly to a'.

He comes when we're weary to wean's frae oor waes,
He comes when the bairnies are getting aff their claes;
To cover them sae cozy, an' bring bonnie dreams,
So Auld Daddy Darkness is better than he seems.

Steek* yer een, my wee tot, ye'll see Daddy then; shut
He's in below the bed claes, to cuddle ye he's fain;
Noo nestle to his bosie, sleep and dream yer fill,
Till Wee Davie Daylicht comes keekin'* owre the hill. peeping

## THOMAS SMIBERT (1810–1854)

### The Scottish Widow's Lament

Afore the Lammas tide
Had dunned the birken* tree, birch
In a' our water-side
Nae wife was blest like me.
A kind gudeman, and twa
Sweet bairns were round me here,
But they're a' ta'en awa'
Sin' the fa' o' the year.

Sair trouble cam our gate*, way
And made me, when it cam,
A bird without a mate,
A ewe without a lamb.
Our hay was yet to maw,
And our corn was to shear,
When they a' dwined awa'
In the fa' o' the year.

I downa* look a field, cannot
For aye I trow I see
The form that was a bield* shelter
To my wee bairns and me.
But wind, and weet, and snaw,
They never mair can fear,
Sin' they a' got the ca'
In the fa' o' the year.

Aft on the hill at e'ens
I see him mang the ferns,
The lover o' my teens,
The father o' my bairns:
For there his plaid I saw
As gloamin' aye drew near—
But my a's now awa'
Sin' the fa' o' the year.

Our bonnie rigs* theirsel', (fields)
Reca' my waes to mind,
Our puir dumb beasties tell
O' a' that I hae tined*; lost
For wha our wheat will saw,
And wha our sheep will shear,

Sin' my a' gaed awa'
In the fa' o' the year?

My hearth is growing cauld,
And will be caulder still;
And sair, sair in the fauld
Will be the winter's chill;
For peats were yet to ca,
Our sheep they were to smear,
When my a' passed awa'
In the fa' o' the year.

I ettle* whiles to spin, struggle, aim
But wee, wee patterin' feet
Come rinnin' out and in,
And then I just maun greet*: weep
I ken it's fancy a',
And faster rowes the tear,
That my a' dwined awa'
In the fa' o' the year.

Be kind, O heaven abune,
To ane sae wae and lane*, alone
An' tak her hamewards soon,
In pity o' her maen.
Long ere the March winds blaw,
May she, far far frae here,
Meet them a' that's awa'
Sin' the fa' o' the year.

## ALICIA SPOTTISWOOD, LADY SCOTT (1810–1900)

### Ettrick

When we first rade down Ettrick,
Our bridles were ringing, our hearts were dancing,
The waters were singing, the sun was glancing,
An' blithely our voices rang out thegither,
As we brushed the dew frae the blooming heather,
When we first rade down Ettrick.

When we next rade down Ettrick,
The day was dying, the wild birds calling,
The wind was sighing, the leaves were falling,
An' silent an' weary, but closer thegither,
We urged our steeds through the faded heather,
When we next rade down Ettrick.

When I last rade down Ettrick,
The winds were shifting, the storm was waking,
The snow was drifting, my heart was breaking,
For we never again were to ride thegither,

In sun or storm on the mountain heather,
When I last rade down Ettrick.

## Durisdeer

We'll meet nae mair at sunset, when the weary day is dune,
Nor wander hame thegither, by the lee licht o' the moon.
I'll hear your step nae longer amang the dewy corn,
For we'll meet nae mair, my bonniest, either at eve or morn.

The yellow broom is waving, abune the sunny brae,
And the rowan berries dancing, where the sparkling waters play.
Though a' is bright and bonnie, it's an eerie place to me,
For we'll meet nae mair, my dearest, either by burn or tree.

Far up into the wild hills, there's a kirkyard auld and still,
Where the frosts lie ilka morning, and the mists hang low and chill,
And there ye sleep in silence, while I wander here my lane,[1]
Till we meet ance mair in Heaven, never to part again.

## The Comin' o' the Spring

There's no a muir in my ain land but's fu' o' sang the day,
Wi' the whaup, and the gowden plover, and the lintie upon the brae.
The birk* in the glen is springin', the rowan-tree in the shaw*, "birch"/wood
And every burn is rinnin' wild wi' the meltin' o' the snaw.

The wee white cluds in the blue lift* are hurryin' light and free, sky
Their shadows fleein' on the hills, where I, too, fain wad be;
The wind frae the west is blawin', and wi' it seems to bear
The scent o' the thyme and gowan* through a' the caller* air. daisy/fresh

The herd doon the hillside's linkin'. O licht his heart may be
Whose step is on the heather, his glance ower muir and lea.
On the Moss are the wild ducks gatherin' whar the pules* puffs, traces
like diamonds lie,
And far up soar the wild geese, wi' weird, unyirdly* cry. unearthly

In mony a neuk the primrose lies hid frae stranger een,
An' the broom on the knowes* is wavin' wi' its cludin o' gowd and "knolls"
green;
Ower the first green springs o' heather, the muir-fowl faulds his wing,
And there's nought but joy in my ain land at the comin' o' the Spring.

## Lammermoor

Oh, wild and stormy Lammermoor!
Would I could feel once more
The cold north wind, the wintry blast,

[1]My lane: alone.

That sweeps thy mountains oer.
Would I could see thy drifted snow
Deep, deep in cleuch* and glen, ravine
And hear the scream of the wild birds,
And was free on thy hills again.

I hate this dreary southern land,
I weary day by day
For the music of thy many streams
In the birchwoods far away.
From all I love they banish me,
But my thoughts they cannot chain;
And they bear me back, wild Lammermoor,
To thy distant hills again.

## Shame on Ye, Gallants

Shame on ye, gallants, that rise not readily;
Rouse ye and march at your Prince's call.
Wha sae base but would arm him speedily
For the noblest Stuart amang them all?
He comes like the dawn on our lang night of slavery,
Hope in his smile, and light in his ee;
He sought us alone in his youth and his bravery
Frae the tyrant usurper to set us free.

Shame on ye, gallants, the sun shineth fairly
To brighten each step of the conqueror's way.
The winds are singing a welcome to Charlie,
And the rebels are running before him the day.
Weel may we trust him to bear himsel' dauntlessly.
Scotland can witness frae heroes he springs;
Noble his spirit, untainted his gallantry,
Worthy the son of a hundred kings.

# THOMAS STODDART (1810–1880)

## The Angler's Invitation

Come when the leaf comes, angle with me,
Come when the bee hums over the lea,
Come with the wild flowers—
Come with the wild showers—
Come when the singing bird calleth for thee.

Then to the stream side, gladly we'll hie,
Where the gray trout glide silently by,
Or in some still place

Over the hill face
Hurrying onward, drop the light fly.

Then, when the dew falls, homeward we'll speed
To our own loved walls down on the mead,
There, by the bright hearth,
Holding our night mirth,
We'll drink to sweet friendship in need and in deed.

## The River

Through sun-bright lakes,
Round islets gay,
The river takes
Its western way,
And the water-chime
Soft zephyrs time
Each gladsome summer day.

The starry trout,
Fair to behold,
Roameth about
On fin of gold;
At root of tree
His haunt you see,
Rude rock or crevice old.

And hither dart
The salmon gray,
From the deep heart
Of some sea bay;
And harling wild
Is here beguiled
To hold autumnal play.

Oh, tis a stream
Most fair to see,
As in a dream
Flows pleasantly;
And our hearts are wooed
To a kind sweet mood
By its wondrous witchery.

## Her, a Statue

Her life is in the marble, yet a fall
Of sleep lies on the heart's fair arsenal,
Like new showered snow. You hear no whisper through
Those love-divided lips; no pearly dew
Trembles on her pale orbs, that seem to be
Bent on a dream of immortality.

She sleeps: her life is sleep—a holy rest,
Like that of wing-borne cloud, that, in the west,
Laves his aerial image, till afar
The sunlight leaves him, melting into star.
Did Phidias from her brow the veil remove,
Uncurtaining the peerless queen of love?
The fluent stone in marble waves recoiled,
Touched by his hand, and left the wondrous child,
A Venus of the foam. How softly fair
The dove-like passion on the sacred air
Floats round her, nesting in her wreathed hair,
That tells, though shadeless, of its auburn hue,
Bathed in a hoar of diamond-dropping dew.

How beautiful!—Was this not one of eld,
That Chaos on his boundless bosom held,
Till Earth came forward in a rush of storm,
Closing his ribs upon her wingless form?
How beautiful!—The very lips do speak
Of love, and bid us worship: the pale cheek
Seems blushing through the marble—through the snow.
And the undrap'ried bosom feels a flow
Of fever on its brightness; every vein
At the blue pulse swells softly, like a chain
Of gentle hills. I would not fling a wreath
Of jewels on the brow, to flash beneath
Those queenly tresses; for itself is more
Than sea-born pearl of some Elysian shore.

Such, with a heart like woman! I would cast
Life at her foot, and, as she glided past,
Would bid her trample on the slavish thing—
Tell her, I'd rather feel me withering
Under her step, than be unknown for aye.
And, when her pride had crushed me, she might see
A love-winged spirit glide in glory by,
Striking the tent of its mortality.

## JAMES GUTHRIE (?1811–1893)

### The Unseen

Twas on a wild and gusty night, in winter's dreary gloom,
I sat in meditation rapt, within my lonesome room,
While like a panorama passed the days of love's sweet joy,
And all youth's blissful visions bright which cheered me when a boy.

The winds let loose, mad shrieking howled, among the leafless trees,
Sad from the distance hollow came the murmur of the seas,
While on the trembling window panes wild dashed the sobbing rain,
Like a maiden by her lover left in sorrow and in pain.

Clear high above the blast arose, like an ancient melody,
The silver tones of a well known voice— "I come, my love, to thee.
My broken vows forgive, fain I would come to thee for rest,
And pillow soft my weary head upon thy faithful breast."

Like summer cloud across the blue, a shadow on my soul
Fell dark and heavily, but quick it vanished like a scroll.
Yes, freely I forgave, forgot the change she'd wrought in me,
And seizing quick the lamp, I cried, "I come, my love, to thee."

The door I opened wide, and blushed to welcome to my hearth,
Her to my heart the dearest jewel, most precious gem of earth.
Alas, the flickering taper frail, it went out like a spark,
And lo, all weeping, left me lone, faint crying in the dark.

"Beloved, O beloved, come, I wait to welcome thee."
But no refrain came answering back, save the wailing of the sea.
Yet still I cried—"Beloved, come"—as if I'd cry my last,
Heard only by the rushing wind mocked by the stormy blast.

Deserted, sad, woe's me, returned into my widowed room,
The chambers of my soul hung round with dark funereal gloom,
Loud on the shivering window-panes wild beats the sobbing rain,
Like a lover by his false one left in sorrow and in pain.

## Forget Her?

Forget her? mock me not; behold
The everlasting hills,
Adown whose rugged fissures dash
A thousand flashing rills.
E'en they, inheriting decay,
Slow molder, though unseen;
But love, celestial sacred flower,
Is ever fresh and green.

Forget her? gaze on that bright stream,
E'er deepening as it runs
Its rocky channel, leaping free,
In storms and summer suns.
So in my heart of hearts do years,
As onward swift they roll,
The deeper grave in diamond lines
Her name upon my soul.

Forget her! hast thou ever loved?
Know then love cannot die.
Eternal as the eternal God,

Twill ripen in the sky.
Oh yes, sad, drenched in tears on earth,
By storms and tempests riven,
Twill only blossom in its prime
In the golden air of heaven.

## Wills' Bonnie Braes

We love but once; in after life,
Midst sorrows, hopes, and waes,
How fondly turns my yearning heart
To Wills' bonnie braes.

Upon a flower enameled bank
We sat in golden joy,
Within our inmost heart of hearts
What bliss without alloy.

The glad birds sang their even-song
Above each guarded nest,
Then folding soft their dewy wings,
Sank lovingly to rest.

Coy with her sunny ringlets fair
Did arch the zephyr's play,
While murmured fondly at our feet
The wavelets of the Tay.

Expressive silence reigned around,
I clasped her hand in mine—
She raised her eyes—I read it there—
Her answer— "I am thine."

Alas, cruel Mammon with his wand
Hath cleft the rocks in twain,
And all our favorite pathways sweet
Have crumbled in the main.

All, all is changed, yet not more changed,
Woe's me, alas, than she;
Yet no reproach escapes my lips,
Though ever lost to me.

No turning love to scornful hate.
No wailing oer my waes.
I only dream of early joys,
On Wills' bonnie braes.

### The Bonnie Braes o' Airlie

Bonnie sing the birds in the bright English valleys,
Bonnie bloom the flowers in the lime sheltered alleys,
Golden rich the air, with perfume laden rarely,
But dearer far to me the bonnie braes o' Airlie.

Winding flows the Cam, but it's no my ain loved Isla;
Rosy decked the meads, but they're no like dear Glenisla;
Cloudless shines the sun, but I wish I saw it fairly
Sweet blinkin' through the mist on the bonnie braes o' Airlie.

Thirsting for a name, I left my native mountains,
Drinking here my fill at the pure classic fountains;
Striving hard for fame, I've wrestled late and early,
An' a' that I might rest on the bonnie braes o' Airlie.

Yonder gleams the prize for which I've aye been longing—
Darkness comes atween, my struggles sad prolonging,
Dimly grow my een, and my heart is breaking sairly,
Waes me, I'll never see the bonnie braes o' Airlie.

## WILLIAM SCOTT (1811–1890)

[An artist as well as a poet, Scott was born and raised in Edinburgh. At twenty-nine, he moved to London, where he spent much of his life, supporting himself as an artist, or art educator. He was considered one of the Pre-Raphaelites, and that group's use of folk elements and a kind of dreamy medievalism can be seen in his own work.]

### The Witch's Ballad

O I hae come from far away,
From a warm land far away,
A southern land across the sea,
With sailor-lads about the mast,
Merry and canny, and kind to me.

And I hae been to yon town
To try my luck in yon town;
Nort, and Mysie, Elspie too.
Right braw* we were to pass the gate, — handsome
Wi' gowden clasps on girdles blue.

Mysie smiled wi' miminy* mouth, — demure
Innocent mouth, miminy mouth;
Elspie wore a scarlet gown,
Nort's gray eyes were unco* gleg*, — very/sharp
My Castile comb was like a crown.

We walked abreast all up the street,
Into the market up the street;
Our hair with marigolds was wound,
Our bodices with love-knots laced,
Our merchandise with tansy bound.

Nort had chickens. I had cocks,
Gamesome cocks, loud-crowing cocks;
Mysie ducks, and Elspie drakes,
—For a wee groat or a pound;
We lost nae time wi' gives and takes.

—Lost nae time, for well we knew,
In our sleeves full well we knew,
When the gloaming came that night,
Duck nor drake, nor hen nor cock
Would be found by candle-light.

And when our chaffering all was done,
All was paid for, sold and done,
We drew a glove on ilka* hand, each
We sweetly curtsied, each to each,
And deftly danced a saraband.

The market-lassies looked and laughed.
Left their gear, and looked and laughed;
They made as they would join the game,
But soon their mithers, wild and wud*, mad
With whack and screech they stopped the same.

Sae loud the tongues o' randies* grew, viragoes
The flytin'* and the skirlin' grew, scolding
At all the windows in the place,
Wi' spoons or knives, wi' needle or awl,
Was thrust out every hand and face.

And down each stair they thronged anon,
Gentle, semple, thronged anon:
Souter* and tailor, frowsy Nan, cobbler
The ancient widow young again,
Simpering behind her fan.

Without a choice, against their will,
Doited, dazed, against their will,
The market lassie and her mither,
The farmer and his husbandman,
Hand in hand dance a' thegither.

Slow at first, but faster soon,
Still increasing, wild an fast,
Hoods and mantles, hats and hose,
Blindly doffed and cast away,
Left them naked, heads and toes.

They would have torn us limb from limb,
Dainty limb from dainty limb;
But never one of them could win
Across the line that I had drawn
With bleeding thumb a-widdershin.[1]

But there was Jeff the provost's son,
Jeff the provost's only son;
There was Father Auld himsel',
The Lombard frae the hostelry,
And the lawyer Peter Fell.

All goodly men we singled out,
Waled* them well, and singled out, chose
And drew them by the left hand in;
Mysie the priest, and Elspie won
The Lombard, Nort the lawyer carle,
I mysel' the provost's son.

Then, with cantrip* kisses seven, magic
Three times round with kisses seven,
Warped and woven there spun we
Arms and legs and flaming hair,
Like a whirlwind on the sea.

Like a wind that sucks the sea,
Over and in and on the sea,
Good sooth it was a mad delight;
And every man of all the four
Shut his eyes and laughed outright.

Laughed as long as they had breath,
Laughed while they had sense or breath;
And close about us coiled a mist
Of gnats and midges, wasps and flies,
Like the whirlwind shaft it rist.

Drawn up I was right off my feet,
Into the mist and off my feet;
And, dancing on each chimney-top,
I saw a thousand darling imps
Keeping time with skip and hop.

And on the provost's brave ridge-tile,
On the provost's grand ridge-tile,
The Blackamoor first to master me I saw,
I saw that winsome smile,
The mouth that did my heart beguile,
And spoke the great Word over me,
In the land beyond the sea.

---

[1] At an angle oblique to the sun (part of a magic ritual).

I called his name, I called aloud,
Alas! I called on him aloud;
And then he filled his hand with stour*, dust
And threw it towards me in the air,
My mouse flew out, I lost my power.

My lusty strength, my power, were gone;
Power was gone, and all was gone.
He will not let me love him more.
Of bell and whip and horse's tail
He cares not if I find a store.

But I am proud if he is fierce.
I am as proud as he is fierce;
I'll turn about and backward go,
If I meet again that Blackamoor,
And he'll help us then, for he shall know
I seek another paramour.

And we'll gang once more to yon town,
Wi' better luck to yon town;
We'll walk in silk and cramoisie*, "crimson"
And I shall wed the provost's son:
My lady of the town I'll be.

For I was born a crowned king's child,
Born and nursed a king's child,
King o' a land ayont* the sea, beyond
Where the Blackamoor kissed me first,
And taught me art and glamourie.

Each one in her wame* shall hide stomach
Her hairy mouse, her wary mouse,
Fed on madwort and agramie,—
Wear amber beads between her breasts,
And blind-worm's skin about her knee.

The Lombard shall be Elspie's man,
Elspie's gowden husband-man;
Nort shall take the lawyer's hand;
The priest shall swear another vow:
We'll dance again the saraband.

## A Spring Morning

Vaguely at dawn within the temperate clime
Of glimmering half-sleep, in this chamber high,
I heard the jackdaws in their loopholes nigh,
Fitfully stir: as yet it scarce was time
Of dawning, but the nestlings' hungry chime
Awoke me, and the old birds soon had flown;

Then was a perfect lull, and I went down
Into deep slumber beneath dreams or rhyme.

But, suddenly renewed, the clamoring grows,
The callow beaklings clamoring every one,
The gray-heads had returned with worm and fly;
I looked up and the room was like a rose,
Above the hill-top was the brave young sun,
The world was still as in an ecstasy.

## Winter Coming

The strong wind blows from oer the sea,
Foam-freckled far and near;
Within the casement closed we say,
Winter at last is here.

The long boughs of the old trees creak,
And strike against the rain;
The dead leaves and the little birds
Are thrown on the window pane.

From room to room the careful dame
Each bolt and latch doth try;
The storm-sprite on the winding stair
Sings to her mournfully.

The sound of fast-running waters fills
The air both night and day,
And mists like ghosts from all the glens
Rise and are driven away.

Sad is the rushing of railing rain,
And swollen streams wailing low;
And the fitful wind, like a slave pursued
By the fast gathering snow.

From the flower-beds the rank heaps fall
Across the bordered walk;
The sunflower props like beggars slant
In rags of leaves and stalk.

The farmer drives his horses home,
The cows are in the byre;
The frost is come, and the plowman sits
Idle beside the fire.

Away to the South like the swallows
We turn our eyes again,
To be lost once more in the labyrinths
And multitudes of men.

## Youth and Age

Our night repast was ended; quietness
Returned again: the boys were in their books;
The old man slept, and by him slept his dog:
My thoughts were in the dream-land of tomorrow:
A knock is heard; anon the maid brings in
A black-sealed letter that some over-worked
Late messenger leaves. Each one looks round and scans,
But lifts it not, and I at last am told
To read it. "Died here at his house this day"—
Some well-known name not needful here to print,
Follows at length. Soon all return again
To their first stillness, but the old man coughs,
And cries, "Ah, he was always like the grave,
And still he was but young!" while those who stand
On life's green threshold smile within themselves,
Thinking how very old he was to them,
And what long years, what memorable deeds,
Are theirs in prospect. Little care have they
What old man dies, what child is born, indeed;
Their day is coming, and their sun shall shine!

## Hero-Worship

How would the centuries long asunder
Look on their sires with angry wonder,
Could some strong necromantic power
Revive them for one spectral hour.
Bondsmen of the past are we,—
Predestined bondsmen: could we see
The dead now deified, again
Peering among environing men,
We might be free.

## Glenkindie

About Glenkindie and his man,
A false ballant hath long been writ.
Some bootless loon* had written it, rascal
Upon a bootless plan.

But I have found the true at last,
And here it is—so hold it fast.
Twas made by a kind damosel
Who loved him and his man right well:

Glenkindie, best of harpers, came
Unbidden to our town;
And he was sad, and sad to see,
For love had worn him down.

It was love, as all men know,
The love that brought him down,
The hopeless love for the King's daughter,
The dove that heired a crown.

Now he wore not that collar of gold,
His dress was forest green,
His wondrous fair and rich mantle
Had lost its silvery sheen.

But still by his side walked Rafe, his boy,
In goodly cramosie*. crimson
Of all the boys that ever I saw,
The goodliest boy was he.

O Rafe the page, Oh Rafe the page—
Ye stole the heart frae me.
O Rafe the page, O Rafe the page,
I wonder where ye be.
We ne'er may see Glenkindie more,
But may we never see thee?

Glenkindie came within the hall,
We set him on the dais,
And gave him bread, and gave him wine,
The best in all the place.

We set for him the guest's high chair,
And spread the naperie.
Our Dame herself would serve for him,
And I for Rafe, perdie!

But down he sat on a low, low stool,
And thrust his long legs out,
And leaned his back to the high chair,
And turned his harp about.

He turned it round, he stroked the strings,
He touched each tirling-pin,
He put his mouth to the sounding-board
And breathed his breath therein.

And Rafe sat over against his face,
And looked at him wistfully.
I almost grat* ere he began, wept
They were so sad to see.

The very first stroke he strack that day,
We all came crowding near;
And the second stroke he strack that day,
We all were smit with fear.

The third stroke that he strack that day,
Full fain we were to cry;
The fourth stroke that he strack that day,
We thought that we would die.

No tongue can tell how sweet it was,
How far, and yet now near,
We saw the saints in Paradise,
And bairnies on their bier.

And our sweet Dame saw her good lord—
She told me privilie—
She saw him as she saw him last,
On his ship upon the sea.

Anon he laid his little harp by,
He shut his wondrous eyes.
We stood a long time like dumb things,
Stood in a dumb surprise.

Then all at once we left that trance,
And shouted where we stood.
We clasped each other's hands and vowed
We would be wise and good.

Soon he rose up and Rafe rose too,
He drank wine and broke bread.
He clasped his hands with our trembling Dame,
But never a word he said.
They went—alack and lack-a-day!
They went the way they came.

I followed them all down the floor,
And oh but I had drouth* — thirst
To touch his cheek, to touch his hand,
To kiss Rafe's velvet mouth.

But I know such was not for me.
They went straight from the door.
We saw them fade within the mist,
And never saw them more.

## Love's Calendar

That gusty spring, each afternoon
By the ivied cot I passed,
And noted at that lattice soon
Her fair face downward cast;
Still in the same place seated there,
So diligent, so very fair.

Oft-times I said I knew her not,
Yet that way round would go,
Until, when evenings lengthened out,
And bloomed the may-hedge row,
I met her by the wayside well,
Whose waters, maybe, broke the spell.

For, leaning on her pail, she prayed,
I'd lift it to her head.
So did I; but I'm much afraid
Some wasteful drops were shed,
And that we blushed, as face to face
Needs must we stand the shortest space.

Then when the sunset mellowed through
The ears of rustling grain,
When lattices wide open flew,
When ash-leaves fell like rain,
As well as I she knew the hour
At morn or eve I neared her bower.

And now that snow oerlays the thatch,
Each starlit eve within
The door she waits, I raise the latch,
And kiss her lifted chin;
Nor do I think we've blushed again,
For Love hath made but one of twain.

## WILLIAM AYTOUN (1813–1865)

[Aytoun's four works below express his wide range as a writer, which included serious poetry, burlesque ballads, and short stories. *Lays of the Scottish Cavaliers* (1849), a series of ballad romances from Scottish history, made him famous. "The Execution of Montrose" is a fine example.

"How We Got Up the Glenmutchkin Railway" is primarily a satire, and it is as a satirist Aytoun is most likely to be remembered. Especially successful in this line were the well-known "Bon Gaultier Ballads" (1845, 1857), which he wrote with Theodore Martin, a fellow Scot.]

### The Old Scottish Cavalier[1]

Come listen to another song,
Should make your heart beat high,
Bring crimson to your forehead,
And the luster to your eye;
It is a song of olden time,
Of days long since gone by,

[1] Alexander Forbes, Lord Pitsligo (1677-1762), an enthusiastic Jacobite, shown here in support of Bonnie Prince Charlie in the campaigns of 1745-1746. The white rose was the Jacobite emblem. "His father" is described as fighting in the original Jacobite actions following the Revolution of 1688.

And of a baron stout and bold
As e'er wore sword on thigh.
Like a brave old Scottish cavalier,
All of the olden time.

He kept his castle in the north,
Hard by the thundering Spey;
And a thousand vassals dwelt around,
All of his kindred they.
And not a man of all that clan
Had ever ceased to pray
For the royal race they loved so well,
Though exiled far away
From the steadfast Scottish cavaliers,
All of the olden time.

His father drew the righteous sword
For Scotland and her claims,
Among the loyal gentlemen
And chiefs of ancient names
Who swore to fight or fall beneath
The standard of King James,
And died at Killiecrankie Pass
With the glory of the Graemes;
Like a true old Scottish cavalier
All of the olden time.

He never owned the foreign rule,
No master he obeyed,
But kept his clan in peace at home,
From foray and from raid;
And when they asked him for his oath,
He touched his glittering blade,
And pointed to his bonnet blue,
That bore the white cockade;
Like a leal* old Scottish cavalier, loyal
All of the olden time.

At length the news ran through the land—
The Prince had come again.
That night the fiery cross[1] was sped
Oer mountain and through glen;
And our old baron rose in might,
Like a lion from his den,
And rode away across the hills
To Charlie and his men,
With the valiant Scottish cavaliers,
All of the olden time.

[1] The sign for the clans to gather.

He was the first that bent the knee
When the standard waved abroad,
He was the first that charged the foe
On Preston's bloody sod;
And ever, in the van of fight,
The foremost still he trod,
Until on bleak Culloden's heath,
He gave his soul to God,
Like a good old Scottish cavalier,
All of the olden time.

Oh! never shall we know again
A heart so stout and true—
The olden times have passed away,
And weary are the new;
The fair White Rose has faded
From the garden where it grew,
And no fond tears, save those of heaven,
The glorious bed bedew
Of the last old Scottish cavalier,
All of the olden time.

## The Execution of Montrose

Come hither, Evan Cameron!
Come, stand beside my knee:
I hear the river roaring down
Towards the wintry sea.
There's shouting on the mountain-side,
There's war within the blast;
Old faces look upon me,
Old forms go trooping past:
I hear the pibroch* wailing (bagpipes)
Amidst the din of fight,
And my dim spirit wakes again
Upon the verge of night.

Twas I that led the Highland host
Through wild Lochaber's snows,
What time the plaided clans came down
To battle with Montrose.
I've told thee how the Southrons* fell (English)
Beneath the broad claymore,
And how we smote the Campbell clan
By Inverlochy's shore.
I've told thee how we swept Dundee,
And tamed the Lindsays' pride;
But never have I told thee yet
How the great Marquis died.

A traitor sold him to his foes;
O deed of deathless shame!

I charge thee, boy, if e'er thou meet
With one of Assynt's name—
Be it upon the mountain's side,
Or yet within the glen,
Stand he in martial gear alone,
Or backed by armed men—
Face him, as thou wouldst face the man
Who wronged thy sire's renown;
Remember of what blood thou art,
And strike the caitiff down.

They brought him to the Watergate,
Hard bound with hempen span,
As though they held a lion there,
And not a fenceless man.
They set him high upon a cart,
The hangman rode below,
They drew his hands behind his back
And bared his noble brow.
Then, as a hound is slipped from leash,
They cheered the common throng,
And blew the note with yell and shout
And bade him pass along.

It would have made a brave man's heart
Grow sad and sick that day,
To watch the keen malignant eyes
Bent down on that array.
There stood the Whig west-country lords,
In balcony and bow;
There sat their gaunt and withered dames,
And their daughters all a-row.
And every open window
Was full as full might be
With black-robed Covenanting carles*, men, rascals,
That goodly sport to see.

But when he came, though pale and wan,
He looked so great and high,
So noble was his manly front,
So calm his steadfast eye,
The rabble rout forbore to shout,
And each man held his breath,
For well they knew the hero's soul
Was face to face with death.
And then a mournful shudder
Through all the people crept,
And some that came to scoff at him
Now turned aside and wept.

But onwards—always onwards,
In silence and in gloom,
The dreary pageant labored,

Till it reached the house of doom.
Then first a woman's voice was heard
In jeer and laughter loud,
And an angry cry and a hiss arose
From the heart of the tossing crowd:
Then as the Graeme looked upwards,
He saw the ugly smile
Of him who sold his king for gold,
The master-fiend Argyle.

The Marquis gazed a moment,
And nothing did he say,
But the cheek of Argyle grew ghastly pale
And he turned his eyes away.
The painted harlot by his side,
She shook through every limb,
For a roar like thunder swept the street,
And hands were clenched at him;
And a Saxon soldier cried aloud,
"Back, coward, from thy place!
For seven long years thou hast not dared
To look him in the face."

Had I been there with sword in hand,
And fifty Camerons by,
That day through high Dunedin's streets
Had pealed the slogan-cry.
Not all their troops of trampling horse,
Nor might of mailed men,
Not all the rebels in the south
Had borne us backwards then.
Once more his foot on Highland heath
Had trod as free as air,
Or I, and all who bore my name,
Been laid around him there.

It might not be. They placed him next
Within the solemn hall,
Where once the Scottish kings were throned
Amidst their nobles all.
But there was dust of vulgar feet
On that polluted floor,
And perjured traitors filled the place
When good men sate before.
With savage glee came Warristoun
To read the murderous doom;
And then uprose the great Montrose
In the middle of the room.

"Now, by my faith as belted knight,
And by the name I bear,
And by the bright Saint Andrew's cross
That waves above us there,

Yea, by a greater, mightier oath—
And oh, that such should be—
By that dark stream of royal blood
That lies twixt you and me,
I have not sought in battle-field
A wreath of such renown,
Nor dared I hope on my dying day
To win the martyr's crown.

"There is a chamber far away
Where sleep the good and brave,
But a better place ye have named for me
Than by my father's grave.
For truth and right, gainst treason's might,
This hand hath always striven,
And ye raise it up for a witness still
In the eye of earth and heaven.
Then nail my head on yonder tower,
Give every town a limb,
And God who made shall gather them:
I go from you to Him."

The morning dawned full darkly,
The rain came flashing down,
And the jagged streak of the levin-bolt* lightning
Lit up the gloomy town:
The thunder crashed across the heaven,
The fatal hour was come;
Yet aye broke in with muffled beat
The 'larum of the drum.
There was madness on the earth below
And anger in the sky,
And young and old, and rich and poor,
Came forth to see him die.

Ah, God, that ghastly gibbet.
How dismal tis to see
The great tall spectral skeleton,
The ladder and the tree.
Hark, hark, it is the clash of arms—
The bells begin to toll—
"He is coming, he is coming,
God's mercy on his soul."
One last long peal of thunder:
The clouds are cleared away,
And the glorious sun once more looks down
Amidst the dazzling day.

"He is coming, he is coming!"
Like a bridegroom from his room,
Came the hero from his prison
To the scaffold and the doom.
There was glory on his forehead,

There was luster in his eye,
And he never walked to battle
More proudly than to die:
There was color in his visage,
Though the cheeks of all were wan,
And they marveled as they saw him pass,
That great and goodly man.

He mounted up the scaffold,
And he turned him to the crowd;
But they dared not trust the people,
So he might not speak aloud.
But he looked upon the heavens,
And they were clear and blue,
And in the liquid ether
The eye of God shone through;
Yet a black and murky battlement
Lay resting on the hill,
As though the thunder slept within—
All else was calm and still.

The grim Geneva ministers
With anxious scowl drew near,
As you have seen the ravens flock
Around the dying deer.
He would not deign them word nor sign,
But alone be bent the knee,
And veiled his face for Christ's dear grace
Beneath the gallows-tree.
Then radiant and serene he rose,
And cast his cloak away:
For he had ta'en his latest look
Of earth and sun and day.

A beam of light fell oer him,
Like a glory round the shriven,
And he climbed the lofty ladder
As it were the path to heaven.
Then came a flash from out the cloud,
And a stunning thunder-roll;
And no man dared to look aloft,
For fear was on every soul.
There was another heavy sound,
A hush and then a groan;
And darkness swept across the sky—
The work of death was done.

## How We Got Up the Glenmutchkin Railway and How We Got Out of It

I was confoundedly hard up.

My patrimony, never of the largest, had been for the last year on the decrease—a herald would have emblazoned it, "ARGENT, a moneybag improper, in detriment"— and though the attenuating process was not excessively rapid, it was, nevertheless, proceeding at a steady ratio.

As for the ordinary means and appliances by which men contrive to recruit their exhausted exchequers, I knew none of them. Work I abhorred with a detestation worthy of a scion of nobility; and, I believe, you could just as soon have persuaded the lineal representative of the Howards or Percys to exhibit himself in the character of a mountebank, as have got me to trust my person on the pinnacle of a three-legged stool. The rule of three is all very well for base mechanical souls; but I flatter myself I have an intellect too large to be limited to a ledger.

"Augustus," said my poor mother to me, while stroking my hyacinthine tresses, one fine morning, in the very dawn and budding-time of my existence—"Augustus, my dear boy, whatever you do, never forget that you are a gentleman."

The maternal maxim sunk deeply into my heart, and I never for a moment have forgotten it.

Notwithstanding this aristocratical resolution, the great practical question "How am I to live!" began to thrust itself unpleasantly before me.

I am one of that unfortunate class who have neither uncles nor aunts. For me, no yellow liverless individuals, with characteristic bamboo and pigtail—emblems of half-a-million— returned to his native shores from Ceylon or remote Penang. For me, no venerable spinster hoarded in the Trongate, permitting herself few luxuries during a long-protracted life, save a lass and a lanthorn, a parrot, and the invariable baudrons[1] of antiquity. No such luck was mine. Had all Glasgow perished by some vast epidemic, I should not have found myself one farthing the richer. There would have been no golden balsam for me in the accumulated woes of Tradestown, Shettleston, and Camlachie.

The time has been when—according to Washington Irving and other veracious historians—a young man had no sooner got into difficulties than a guardian angel appeared to him in a dream, with the information that at such and such a bridge, or under such and such a tree, he might find, at a slight expenditure of labor, a gallipot secured with bladder, and filled with glittering tomauns;[2] or in the extremity of despair, the youth had only to append himself to a cord, and straightaway the other end thereof, forsaking its staple in the roof, would disclose amidst the fractured ceiling the glories of a profitable pose.

These blessed days have long since gone by—at any rate, no such luck was mine. My guardian angel was either woefully ignorant of metallurgy or the stores had been surreptitiously ransacked; and as to the other expedient, I frankly confess I should have liked some better security for its result, than the precedent of the "Heir of Lynn."

It is a great consolation amidst all the evils of life, to know that, however bad your circumstances may be, there is always somebody else in nearly the same predicament. My chosen friend and ally, Bob M'Corkindale, was equally hard up with myself, and, if possible, more averse to exertion. Bob was essentially a speculative man—that is, in a philosophical sense. He had once got hold of a stray volume of Adam Smith, and muddled his brains for a whole week over the intricacies of the *Wealth of Nations.* The result was a crude farrago of notions regarding the true nature of money, the soundness of currency, and relative value of capital, with which he nightly favored an admiring audience at "The Crow"; for Bob was by no means— in the literal acceptation of the word—a dry philosopher.

On the contrary, he perfectly appreciated the merits of each distinct distillery;

---

[1]Domestic cats.

[2]Fairy mounds.

and was understood to be the compiler of a statistical work entitled, *A Tour Through The Alcoholic Districts of Scotland.* It had very early occurred to me, who knew as much of political economy as of the bagpipes, that a gentleman so well versed in the art of accumulating national wealth, must have some remote ideas of applying his principles profitably on a smaller scale. Accordingly, I gave M'Corkindale an unlimited invitation to my lodgings; and, like a good hearty fellow as he was, he availed himself every evening of the license; for I had laid in a fourteen-gallon cask of Oban whisky, and the quality of the malt was undeniable.

These were the first glorious days of general speculation. Rail roads were emerging from the hands of the greater into the fingers of the lesser capitalists. Two successful harvests had given a fearful stimulus to the national energy; and it appeared perfectly certain that all the populous towns would be united, and the rich agricultural districts intersected, by the magical bands of iron. The columns of the newspapers teemed every week with the parturition of novel schemes; and the shares were no sooner announced than they were rapidly subscribed for.

But what is the use of my saying anything more about the history of last year? Every one of us remembers it perfectly well. It was a capital year on the whole, and put money into many a pocket. About that time,

Bob and I commenced operations. Our available capital, or negotiable bullion, in the language of my friend, amounted to about three hundred pounds, which we set aside as a joint fund for speculation. Bob, in a series of learned discourses, had convinced me that it was not only folly, but a positive sin, to leave this sum lying in the bank at a pitiful rate of interest, and otherwise unemployed, whilst every one else in the kingdom was having a pluck at the public pigeon.

Somehow or other, we were unlucky in our first attempts. Speculators are like wasps; for when they have once got hold of a ripening and peach-like project, they keep it rigidly for their own swarm, and repel the approach of interlopers. Notwithstanding all our efforts, and very ingenious ones they were, we never, in a single instance, succeeded in procuring an allocation of original shares; and though we did now and then make a hit by purchase, we more frequently bought at a premium, and parted with our scrip at a discount. At the end of six months, we were not twenty pounds richer than before.

"This will never do," said Bob, as he sat one evening in my rooms compounding his second tumbler. "I thought we were living in an enlightened age; but I find I was mistaken. That brutal spirit of monopoly is still abroad and uncurbed. The principles of free-trade are utterly forgotten, or misunderstood. Else how comes it that David Spreul received but yesterday an allocation of two hundred shares in the Westermidden Junction; whilst your application and mine, for a thousand each, were overlooked? Is this a state of things to be tolerated? Why should he, with his fifty thousand pounds, receive a slapping premium, whilst our three hundred of available capital remains unrepresented? The fact is monstrous, and demands the immediate and serious interference of the legislature."

"It is a bloody shame," I said, fully alive to the manifold advantages of a premium.

"I'll tell you what, Dunshunner," rejoined M'Corkindale. "It's no use going on in this way. We haven't shown half pluck enough. These fellows consider us as snobs, because we don't take the bull by the horns. Now's the time for a bold stroke. The public are quite ready to subscribe for anything—and we'll start a railway for ourselves."

"Start a railway with three hundred pounds of capital!"

"Pshaw, man! you don't know what you're talking about—we've a great deal more capital than that. Have not I told you seventy times over, that everything a man has—his coat, his hat, the tumblers he drinks from, nay, his very corporeal existence—is absolute marketable capital? What do you call that fourteen-gallon cask, I should like to know?"

"A compound of hoops and staves, containing about a quart and a half of spirits—you have effectually accounted for the rest."

"Then it has gone to the fund of profit and loss, that's all. Never let me hear you sport those old theories again. Capital is indestructible, as I am ready to prove to you any day, in half an hour. But let us sit down seriously to business. We are rich enough to pay for the advertisements, and that is all we need care for in the mean time. The public is sure to step in, and bear us out handsomely with the rest."

"But where in the face of the habitable globe shall the railway be? England is out of the question, and I hardly know of a spot in the Lowlands that is not occupied already."

"What do you say to a Spanish scheme—the Alcantara Union? Hang me if I know whether Alcantara is in Spain or Portugal; but nobody else does, and the one is quite as good as the other. Or what would you think of the Palermo Railway, with a branch to the sulfur mines?—that would be popular in the North—or the Pyrenees Direct? They would all go to a premium."

"I must confess I should prefer a line at home."

"Well, then, why not try the Highlands? There must be lots of traffic there in the shape of sheep, grouse, and Cockney tourists, not to mention salmon and other etceteras. Couldn't we tip them a railway somewhere in the west?"

"There's Glenmutchkin, for instance—"

"Capital, my dear fellow! Glorious? By Jove, first-rate!" shouted Bob in an ecstasy of delight. "There's a distillery there, you know, and a fishing-village at the foot—at least there used to be six years ago, when I was living with the exciseman. There may be some bother about the population, though. The last laird shipped every mother's son of the aboriginal Celts to America; but, after all, that's not of much consequence. I see the whole thing! Unrivaled scenery—stupendous waterfalls—herds of black cattle—spot where Prince Charles Edward met Macgrugar of Glengrugar and his clan. We could not possibly have lighted on a more promising place. Hand us over that sheet of paper, like a good fellow, and a pen. There is no time to be lost, and the sooner we get out the prospectus the better."

"But, heaven bless you, Bob, there's a great deal to be thought of first. Who are we to get for a provisional committee?"

"That's very true," said Bob, musingly. "We must treat them to some respectable names, that is, good sounding ones. I'm afraid there is little chance of our producing a Peer to begin with?"

"None whatever—unless we could invent one, and that's hardly safe—*Burke's Peerage* has gone through too many editions. Couldn't we try the Dormants?"

"That would be rather dangerous in the teeth of the standing orders. But what do you say to a baronet? There's Sir Polloxfen Tremens. He got himself served the other day to a Nova Scotia baronetcy, with just as much title as you or I have; and he has sported the riband, and dined out on the strength of it ever since. He'll join us at once, for he has not a sixpence to lose."

"Down with him, then," and we headed the Provisional list with the pseudo Orange-tawny.

"Now," said Bob, "it's quite indispensable, as this is a Highland line, that we should put forward a Chief or two. That has always a great effect upon the English, whose feudal notions are rather of the mistiest, and principally derived from Waverley."

"Why not write yourself down as the Laird of M'Corkindale?" said I. "I dare say you would not be negatived by a counter-claim."

"That would hardly do," replied Bob," as I intend to be Secretary. After all, what's the use of thinking about it? Here goes for an extempore Chief"; and the villain wrote down the name of Tavish M'Tavish of Invertavish.

"I say, though," said I, "we must have a real Highlander on the list. If we go on this way, it will become a Justiciary matter."

"You're devilish scrupulous, Gus," said Bob, who, if left to himself, would have stuck in the names of the heathen gods and goddesses, or borrowed his directors from the Ossianic chronicles, rather than have delayed the prospectus. "Where the mischief are we to find the men? I can think of no others likely to go the whole hog, can you?"

"I don't know a single Celt in Glasgow except old M'Closkie, the drunken porter at the corner of Jamaica Street."

"He's the very man! I suppose, after the manner of his tribe, he will do anything for a pint of whisky. But what shall we call him? Jamaica Street, I fear, will hardly do for a designation."

"Call him THE M'CLOSKIE. It will be sonorous in the ears of the Saxon."

"Bravo!" and another Chief was added to the roll of the clans.

"Now," said Bob, "we must put you down. Recollect, all the management—that is, the allocation—will be intrusted to you. Augustus—you haven't a middle name, I think?—well, then, suppose we interpolate 'Reginald', it has a smack of the Crusades. Augustus Reginald Dunshunner, Esq. of—where, in the name of Munchausen?"

"I'm sure I don't know. I never had any land beyond the contents of a flower-pot. Stay—I rather think I have a superiority somewhere about Paisley."

"Just the thing," cried Bob. "It's heritable property, and therefore titular. What's the denomination?"

"St. Mirrens."

"Beautiful! Dunshunner of St. Mirrens, I give you joy! Had you discovered that a little sooner—and I wonder you did not think of it—we might both of us have had lots of allocations. These are not the times to conceal hereditary distinctions. But now comes the serious work. We must have one or two men of known wealth upon the list. The chaff is nothing without a decoy-bird. Now, can't you help me with a name?"

"In that case," said I, "the game is up, and the whole scheme exploded. I would as soon undertake to evoke the ghost of Croesus."

"Dunshunner," said Bob very seriously, "to be a man of information, you are possessed of marvelous few resources. I am quite ashamed of you. Now listen to me. I have thought deeply upon this subject, and am quite convinced that, with some little trouble, we may secure the co-operation of a most wealthy and influential body—one, too, that is generally supposed to have stood aloof from all speculation of the kind, and whose name would be a tower of strength in the moneyed quarters. I allude," continued Bob, reaching across for the kettle, "to the great Dissenting Interest."

"The what?" cried I, aghast.

"The great Dissenting Interest. You can't have failed to observe the row they have lately been making about Sunday traveling and education. Old Sam Sawley, the coffin-maker, is their principal spokesman here; and wherever he goes the rest will follow, like a flock of sheep bounding after a patriarchal ram. I propose, therefore, to wait upon him to-morrow, and request his co-operation in a scheme which is not only to prove profitable, but to make head against the lax principles of the present age. Leave me alone to tickle him. I consider his name, and those of one or two others belonging to the same meeting-house—fellows with bank-stock, and all sorts of tin—as perfectly secure. These dissenters smell a premium from an almost incredible distance. We can fill up the rest of the committee with ciphers, and the whole thing is done."

"But the engineer—we must announce such an officer as a matter of course."

"I never thought of that," said Bob. "Couldn't we hire a fellow from one of the steamboats?"

"I fear that might get us into trouble. You know there are such things as gradients and sections to be prepared. But there's Watty Solder, the gas-fitter, who failed the other day. He's a sort of civil engineer by trade, and will jump at the proposal like a trout at the tail of a May fly."

"Agreed. Now, then, let's fix the number of shares. This is our first experiment, and I thing we ought to be moderate. No sound political economist is avaricious. Let us say twelve thousand, at twenty pounds apiece."

"So be it."

"Well, then, that's arranged. I'll see Sawley and the rest to-morrow; settle with Solder, and then write out the prospectus. You look in upon me in the evening, and we'll revise it together. Now, by your leave, let's have in the Welsh rabbit and another tumbler to drink success and prosperity to the Glenmutchkin Railway."

I confess that, when I rose on the morrow, with a slight headache and a tongue indifferently parched, I recalled to memory, not without perturbation of conscience, and some internal qualms, the conversation of the previous evening. I felt relieved, however, after two spoonfuls of carbonate of soda, and a glance at the newspaper, wherein I perceived the announcement of no less than four other schemes equally preposterous with our own. But, after all, what right had I to assume that the Glenmutchkin project would prove an ultimate failure? I had not a scrap of statistical information that might entitle me to form such an opinion. At any rate, Parliament, by substituting the Board of Trade as an initiating body of inquiry, had created a responsible tribunal, and freed us from the chance of obloquy. I saw before me a vision of six months' steady gambling, at manifest advantage, in the shares, before a report could possibly be pronounced, or our proceedings be in any way overhauled.

Of course I attended that evening punctually at my friend M'Corkindale's. Bob was in high feather; for Sawley no sooner heard of the principles upon which the railway was to be conducted, and his own nomination as a director, than he gave in his adhesion, and promised his unflinching support to the uttermost. The Prospectus ran as follows:

DIRECT GLENMUTCHKIN RAILWAY
In 12,000 Shares of £20 each. Deposit £I per Share.
Provisional Committee

SIR POLLOXFEN TREMENS, Bart. of Toddymains.
TAVISH M'TAVISH of Invertavish.
THE M'CLOSKIE.
AUGUSTUS REGINALD DUNSHUNNER, Esq., of St. Mirrens.
SAMUEL SAWLEY, Esq., Merchant.
MHIC-MHAC-VICH-INDUIBH.
PHELIM O'FINLAN, Esq., of Castle-rook, Ireland.
THE CAPTAIN of M'ALCOHOL.
FACTOR for GLENTUMBLERS.
JOHN JOB JOBSON, Esq., Manufacturer.
EVAN M'CLAW of Glenscart and Inveryewky.
JOSEPH HECKLES, Esq.
HABBAKUK GRABBIE, Portioner in Ramoth-Drumclog.
Engineer—WALTER SOLDER, Esq.
Interim-Secretary—ROBERT M'CORKINDALE, Esq.

"The necessity of a direct line of Railway communication through the fertile and populous district known as the VALLEY of GLENMUTCHKIN, has been long felt and universally acknowledged. Independently of the surpassing grandeur of its mountain scenery, which shall immediately be referred to, and other considerations of even greater importance, GLENMUTCHKIN is known to the capitalist as the most important BREEDING STATION in the Highlands of Scotland, and indeed as the great emporium from which the southern markets are supplied.

"It has been calculated by a most eminent authority, that every acre in the strath is capable of rearing twenty head of cattle; and, as has been ascertained after a careful admeasurement, that there are not less than TWO HUNDRED THOUSAND improvable acres immediately contiguous to the proposed line of Railway, it may confidently be assumed that the number of cattle to be conveyed along the line will amount to FOUR MILLIONS annually, which, at the lowest estimate, would yield a revenue larger, in proportion to the capital subscribed, than that of any Railway as yet completed within the United Kingdom.

"From this estimate the traffic in Sheep and Goats, with which the mountains are literally covered, has been carefully excluded, it having been found quite impossible (from its extent) to compute the actual revenue to be drawn from that most important branch. It may, however, be roughly assumed as from seventeen to nineteen *per cent* upon the whole, after deduction of the working expenses.

"The population of Glenmutchkin is extremely dense. Its situation on the west coast has afforded it the means of direct communication with America, of which for many years the inhabitants have actively availed themselves. Indeed, the amount of exportation of live stock from this part of the Highlands to the Western continent has more than once attracted the attention of Parliament. The Manufacturers are large and comprehensive, and include the most famous distilleries in the world. The Minerals are most abundant, and amongst these may be reckoned quartz, porphyry, feldspar, malachite, manganese, and basalt.

"At the foot of the valley, and close to the sea, lies the important village known as the CLACHAN of INVERSTARVE. It is supposed by various eminent antiquaries to have been the capital of the Picts, and, amongst the busy inroads of commercial prosperity, it still retains some interesting traces of its former grandeur. There is a large fishing station here, to which vessels from every nation resort, and the demand for foreign produce is daily and steadily increasing.

"As a sporting country Glenmutchkin is unrivaled; but it is by the tourists that its beauties will most greedily be sought. These consist of every combination which plastic nature can afford—cliffs of unusual magnitude and grandeur—waterfalls only second to the sublime cascades of Norway—woods, of which the bark is a remarkably valuable commodity. It need scarcely be added, to rouse the enthusiasm inseparable from this glorious glen, that here, in 1745, Prince Charles Edward Stuart, then in the zenith of his hopes, was joined by the brave Sir Grugar M'Grugar at the head of his devoted clan.

"The Railway will be twelve miles long, and can be completed within six months after the Act of Parliament is obtained. The gradients are easy, and the curves obtuse. There are no viaducts of any importance, and only four tunnels along the whole length of the line. The shortest of these does not exceed a mile and a half.

"In conclusion, the projectors of this Railway beg to state that they have determined, as a principle, to set their face AGAINST ALL SUNDAY TRAVELING WHATSOEVER, and to oppose EVERY BILL which may hereafter be brought into Parliament, unless it shall contain a clause to that effect. It is also their intention to take up the cause of the poor and neglected STOKER, for whose accommodation, and social, moral, religious, and intellectual improvement, a large stock of evangelical tracts will speedily be required. Tenders of these, in quantities of not less than 12,000 may be sent in to the Interim Secretary. Shares must be applied for within ten days from the present date.

By order of the Provisional Committee, ROBT. M'CORKINDALE, *Secretary.*

"There!" said Bob, slapping down the prospectus on the table, with the jauntiness of a Cockney vouchsafing a Pint of Hermitage to his guests—"What do you think of that? If it doesn't do the business effectually, I shall submit to be called a Dutchman. That last touch about the stoker will bring us in the subscriptions of the old ladies by the score."

"Very masterly, indeed," said I. "But who the deuce is Mhic-Mhac-vich-Induibh?"

*"A bona fide* chief, I assure you, though a little reduced: I picked him up upon the Broomielaw. His grandfather had an island somewhere to the west of the Hebrides; but it is not laid down in the maps."

"And the Captain of M'Alcohol?"

"A crack distiller."

"And the Factor for Glentumblers?"

"His principal customer. But, bless you, my dear St. Mirrens, don't bother yourself any more about the committee. They are as respectable a set—on paper at least—as you would wish to see of a summer's morning, and the beauty of it is that they will give us no manner of trouble. Now about the allocation. You and I must restrict ourselves to a couple of thousand shares apiece. That's only a third of the whole, but it won't do to be greedy."

"But, Bob, consider! Where on earth are we to find the money to pay up the deposits?"

"Can you, the principal director of the Glenmutchkin Railway, ask me, the secretary, such a question? Don't you know that any of the banks will give us tick to the amount 'of half the deposits.' All that is settled already, and you can get your two thousand pounds whenever you please merely for the signing of a bill. Sawley must get a thousand according to stipulation—Jobson, Heckles, and Grabbie, at least five hundred a-piece, and another five hundred, I should think, will exhaust the remaining means of the committee. So that, out of our whole stock, there remain just five thousand shares to be allocated to the speculative and evangelical public. My eyes! won't there be a scramble for them!"

Next day our prospectus appeared in the newspapers. It was read, canvassed, and generally approved of. During the afternoon, I took an opportunity of looking into the Tontine, and whilst under shelter of the *Glasgow Herald,* my ears were solaced with such ejaculations as the following:—

"I say, Jimsy, hae ye seen this grand new prospectus for a railway tae Glenmutchkin?"

"Ay—it looks no that ill. The Hieland lairds are pitting their best fit foremost. Will ye apply for shares?"

"I think I'll tak' twa hundred. Wha's Sir Polloxfen Tremens?"

"He'll be yin o' the Ayrshire folk. He used to rin horses at the Paisley races."

("The devil he did!" thought I.)

"D'ye ken ony o' the directors, Jimsy?"

"I ken Sawley fine. Ye may depend on't, it's a gude thing, if he's in't, for he's a howkin'[1] body."

"Then it's sure to gae up. What prem. d'ye think it will bring?"

---

[1]Digging, investigating.

"Twa pund a share, and maybe mair." —"'Od, I'll apply for three hundred!"

"Heaven bless you, my dear countrymen!" thought I as I sallied forth to refresh myself with a basin of soup, "do but maintain this liberal and patriotic feeling—this thirst for national improvement, internal communication, and premiums—a short while longer, and I know whose fortune will be made."

On the following morning my breakfast-table was covered with shoals of letters, from fellows whom I scarcely ever had spoken to—or who, to use a franker phraseology, had scarcely ever condescended to speak to me—entreating my influence as a director to obtain them shares in the new undertaking. I never bore malice in my life, so I chalked them down, without favoritism, for a certain proportion. Whilst engaged in this charitable work, the door flew open, and M'Corkindale, looking utterly haggard with excitement, rushed in.

"You may buy an estate whenever you please, Dunshunner," cried he, "the world's gone perfectly mad! I have been to Blazes the broker, and he tells me that the whole amount of the stock has been subscribed for four times over already, and he has not yet got in the returns from Edinburgh and Liverpool!"

"Are they good names though, Bob—sure cards—none of your M'Closkies, and M'Alcohols?"

"The first names in the city, I assure you, and most of them holders for investment. I wouldn't take ten millions for their capital."

"Then the sooner we close the list the better."

"I think so too. I suspect a rival company will be out before long. Blazes says the shares are selling already conditionally on allotment, at seven-and-sixpence premium."

"The deuce they are! I say, Bob, since we have the cards in our hands, would it not be wise to favor them with a few hundred at that rate? A bird in the hand, you know, is worth two in the bush, eh?"

"I know no such maxim in political economy," replied the secretary. "Are you mad, Dunshunner? How are the shares ever to go up, if it gets wind that the directors are selling already? Our business just now, is to *bull* the line, not to *bear* it; and if you will trust me, I shall show them such an operation on the ascending scale, as the Stock Exchange has not witnessed for this long and many a day. Then, to-morrow, I shall advertise in the papers that the committee, having received applications for ten times the amount of stock, have been compelled, unwillingly, to close the lists. That will be a slap in the face to the dilatory gentlemen, and send up the shares like wildfire."

Bob was right. No sooner did the advertisement appear, than a simultaneous groan was uttered by some hundreds of disappointed speculators, who with unwonted and unnecessary caution had been anxious to see their way a little before committing themselves to our splendid enterprise.

In consequence, they rushed into the market, with intense anxiety to make what terms they could at the earliest stage, and the seven-and-sixpence of premium was doubled in the course of a forenoon. The allocation passed over very peaceably. Sawley, Heckles, Jobson, Grabbie, and the Captain of M'Alcohol, besides myself, attended, and took part in the business. We were also threatened with the presence of the M'Closkie and Vich-Induibh; but M'Corkindale, entertaining some reasonable doubts as the effect which their corporeal appearance might have upon the representatives of the dissenting interest, had taken the precaution to get them snugly housed in a tavern, where an unbounded supply of gratuitous Ferintosh deprived us of the benefit of their experience. We, however, allotted them twenty shares apiece.

Sir Polloxfen Tremens sent a handsome, though rather illegible letter of apology dated from an island in Loch Lomond, where he was said to be detained on particular business.

Mr. Sawley, who officiated as our chairman, was kind enough, before parting, to pass a very flattering eulogium upon the excellence and candor of all the preliminary arrangements. It would now, he said, go forth to the public that this line was not, like some others he could mention, a mere bubble, emanating from the stank of private interest, but a solid, lasting superstructure, based upon the principles of sound return for capital, and serious evangelical truth (hear, hear). The time was fast approaching, when the gravestone, with the words "HIC OBIIT" chiseled upon it, would be placed at the head of all the other lines which rejected the grand opportunity of conveying education to the stoker. The stoker, in his (Mr. Sawley's) opinion, had a right to ask the all-important question, "Am I not a man and a brother?" (Cheers).

Much had been said and written lately about a work called *Tracts for the Times.* With the opinions contained in that publication he was not conversant, as it was conducted by persons of another community from that to which he (Mr. Sawley) had the privilege to belong. But he hoped very soon, under the auspices of the Glenmutchkin Railway Company, to see a new periodical established, under the title of *Tracts for the Trains.* He never for a moment would relax his efforts to knock a nail into the coffin, which, he might say, was already made, and measured, and cloth-covered for the reception of all establishments; and with these sentiments, and the conviction that the shares must rise, could it be doubted that he would remain a fast friend to the interests of this Company for ever? (much cheering).

After having delivered this address, Mr. Sawley affectionately squeezed the hands of his brother directors, leaving several of us much overcome. As, however, M'Corkindale had told me that every one of Sawley's shares had been disposed of in the market the day before, I felt less compunction at having refused to allow that excellent man an extra thousand beyond the amount he had applied for, not withstanding of his broadest hints, and even private entreaties.

"Confound the greedy hypocrite" said Bob; "does he think we shall let him Burke the line for nothing? No—no! let him go to the brokers and buy his shares back, if he thinks they are likely to rise. I'll be bound he has made a cool five hundred out of them already."

On the day which succeeded the allocation, the following entry appeared in the Glasgow share-lists. "Direct Glenmutchkin Railway 15s. 15s. 6d. 15s. 6d. 16s. 15s. 6d. 16s. 16s. 6d. 16s. 6d. 16s. 17s. 18s. 18s. 19s. 6d. 21s. 21s. 22s. 6d. 24s. 25s. 6d. 27s. 29s 29s. 6d. 30s. 31s. pm."

"They might go higher, and they ought to go higher," said Bob, musingly; "but there's not much more stock to come and go upon, and these two share-sharks, Jobson and Grabbie, I know, will be in the market to-morrow. We must not let them have the whip hand of us. I think upon the whole, Dunshunner, though it's letting them go dog cheap, that we ought to sell half our shares at the present premium, whilst there is a certainty of getting it."

"Why not sell the whole? I'm sure I have no objections to part with every stiver of the scrip on such terms."

"Perhaps," said Bob, "upon general principles you might be right; but then remember that we have a vested interest in the line."

"Vested interest be hanged!"

"That's very well—at the same time it is no use to kill your salmon in a hurry. The bulls have done their work pretty well for us, and we ought to keep something on hand for the bears; they are snuffing at it already. I could almost swear that some of those fellows who have sold to-day are working for a time-bargain."

We accordingly got rid of a couple of thousand shares, the proceeds of which not only enabled us to discharge the deposit loan, but left us a material surplus. Under these circumstances, a two-hand banquet was proposed and unanimously carried, the commencement of which I distinctly remember, but am rather dubious as to the end.

So many stories have lately been circulated to the prejudice of railway directors, that I think it my duty to state that this entertainment was scrupulously defrayed by ourselves, and not carried to account, either of the preliminary survey, or the expense of the provisional committee.

Nothing effects so great a metamorphosis in the bearing of outer man as a sudden change of fortune. The anemone of garden differs scarcely more from its unpretending prototype of the woods, than Robert M'Corkindale, Esq., Secretary and Projector of the Glenmutchkin Railway, differed from Bob M'Corkindale, the seedy frequenter of "The Crow." In the days of yore, men eyed the surtout—napless at the velvet collar, and preternaturally white at the seams—which Bob vouchsafed to wear, with looks of dim suspicion, as if some faint reminiscence, similar to that which is said to recall the memory of a former state of existence, suggested to them a notion that the garment had once been their own. Indeed, his whole appearance was then wonderfully second-hand.

Now he had cast his slough. A most undeniable Taglioni, with trimmings just bordering upon frogs, gave dignity to his demeanor and twofold amplitude to his chest. The horn eyeglass was exchanged for one of purest gold, the dingy high-lows for well-waxed Wellingtons, the Paisley fogle for the fabric of the China loom. Moreover, he walked with a swagger, and affected in common conversation a peculiar dialect which he opined to be the purest English, but which no one—except a bagman—could be reasonably expected to understand. His pockets were invariably crammed with share-lists; and he quoted, if he did not comprehend, the money article from the Times.

This sort of assumption, though very ludicrous in itself, goes down wonderfully. Bob gradually became a sort of authority, and his opinions got quoted on Change. He was no ass, notwithstanding his peculiarities, and made good use of his opportunity.

For myself, I bore my new dignities with an air of modest meekness. A certain degree of starchness is indispensable for a railway director, if he means to go forward in his high calling and prosper; he must abandon all juvenile eccentricities, and aim at the appearance of a decided enemy to free trade in the article of Wild Oats. Accordingly, as the first step towards respectability, I eschewed colored waistcoats, and gave out that I was a marrying man.

No man under forty, unless he is a positive idiot, will stand forth as a theoretical bachelor. It is all nonsense to say that there is anything unpleasant in being courted. Attention, whether from male or female, tickles the vanity; and although I have a reasonable, and I hope, not unwholesome regard for the gratification of my other appetites, I confess that this same vanity is by far the most poignant of the whole.

I therefore surrendered myself freely to the soft allurements thrown in my way by such matronly denizens of Glasgow as were possessed of stock in the shape of marriageable daughters; and walked the more readily into their toils, because every party, though nominally for the purposes of tea, wound up with a hot supper, and something hotter still by way of assisting the digestion.

I don't know whether it was my determined conduct at the allocation, my territorial title, or a most exaggerated idea of my circumstances, that worked upon the mind of Mr. Sawley. Possibly it was a combination of the three; but sure enough few days had elapsed before I received a formal card of invitation to a tea and serious conversation.

Now serious conversation is a sort of thing that I never shone in, possibly because my early studies were framed in a different direction; but as I really was unwilling to offend the respectable coffin-maker, and as I found that the Captain of M'Alcohol—a decided trump in his way—had also received a summons, I notified my acceptance.

M'Alcohol and I went together. The Captain, an enormous browny Celt, with superhuman whiskers, and a shock of the fieriest hair, had figged himself out, *more majorum,* in the full Highland costume. I never saw Rob Roy on the stage look half so dignified or ferocious. He glittered from head to foot, with dirk, pistol, and skean-dhu,[1] and at least a hundredweight of cairngorms cast a prismatic glory around his person. I felt quite abashed beside him.

We were ushered into Mr. Sawley's drawing-room. Round the walls, and at considerable distances from each other, were seated about a dozen characters, male and female, all of them dressed in sable, and wearing countenances of woe. Sawley advanced, and wrung me by the hand with so piteous an expression of visage, that I could not help thinking some awful catastrophe had just befallen his family.

"You are welcome, Mr. Dunshunner—welcome to my humble tabernacle. Let me present you to Mrs. Sawley"—and a lady, who seemed to have bathed in the Yellow Sea, rose from her seat, and favored me with a profound curtsy.

"My daughter—Miss Selina Sawley."

I felt in my brain the scorching glance of the two darkest eyes it ever was my fortune to behold, as the beauteous Selina looked up from the perusal of her handkerchief hem. It was a pity that the other features were not corresponding; for the nose was flat, and the mouth of such dimensions, that Harlequin might have jumped down it with impunity—but the eyes *were* splendid.

In obedience to a sign from the hostess, I sank into a chair beside Selina; and not knowing exactly what to say, hazarded some observation about the weather.

"Yes, it is indeed a suggestive season. How deeply, Mr. Dunshunner, we ought to feel the pensive progress of autumn towards a soft and premature decay. I always think, about this time of the year, that nature is falling into a consumption!"

"To be sure, ma'am," said I, rather taken aback by this style of colloquy, "the trees are looking devilishly hectic."

"Ah, you have remarked that too. Strange, it was but yesterday that I was wandering through Kelvin Grove, and as the phantom breeze brought down the withered foliage from the spray, I thought how probable it was that they might ere long rustle over young and glowing hearts deposited prematurely in the tomb."

This, which struck me as a very passable imitation of Dickens's pathetic writings, was a poser. In default of language, I looked Miss Sawley straight in the face, and attempted a substitute for a sigh. I was rewarded with a tender glance.

"Ah!" said she, "I see you are a congenial spirit. How delightful, and yet how rare it is to meet with any one who thinks in unison with yourself. Do you ever walk in the Necropolis, Mr. Dunshunner? It is my favorite haunt of a morning. There we can wean ourselves, as it were, from life, and, beneath the melancholy yew and cypress, anticipate the setting star. How often there have I seen the procession—the funeral of some very, *very* little child"—

"Selina, my love," said Mrs. Sawley, "have the kindness to ring for the cookies."

I, as in duty bound, started up to save the fair enthusiast the trouble, and was not sorry to observe my seat immediately occupied by a very cadaverous gentleman, who was evidently jealous of the progress I was rapidly making. Sawley, with an air of great mystery, informed me that this was a Mr. Dalgleish of Raxmathrapple, the representative of an ancient Scottish family who claimed an important heritable office. The name, I thought, was familiar to me, but there was something in the appearance of Mr. Dalgleish which, notwithstanding the smiles of Miss Selina, rendered a rivalship in that quarter utterly out of the question.

---

[1]Stocking-dirk.

I hate injustice, so let me do due honor in description to the Sawley banquet. The tea-urn most literally corresponded to its name. The table was decked out with divers platters, containing seed-cakes cut into rhomboids, almond biscuits, and ratafia drops. Also, on the sideboard, there were two salvers, each of which contained a congregation of glasses, filled with port and sherry. The former fluid, as I afterwards ascertained, was of the kind advertised as "curious," and proffered for sale at the reasonable rate of sixteen shillings per dozen. The banquet, on the whole, was rather peculiar than enticing; and, for the life of me, I could not divest myself of the idea that the selfsame viands had figured, not long before, as funeral refreshments at a dirge.

No such suspicion seemed to cross the mind of M'Alcohol, who hitherto had remained uneasily surveying his nails in a corner, but at the first symptom of food started forwards, and was in the act of making a clean sweep of the china, when Sawley proposed the singular preliminary of a hymn. The hymn was accordingly sung. I am thankful to say it was such a one as I never heard before, or expect to hear again; and unless it was composed by the Reverend Saunders Peden in an hour of paroxysm on the moors, I cannot conjecture the author.

After this original symphony, tea was discussed, and after tea, to my amazement, more hot brandy-and-water that I ever remember to have seen circulated at the most convivial party. Of course this effected a radical change in the spirits and conversation of the circle. It was again my lot to be placed by the side of the fascinating Selina, whose sentimentality gradually thawed away beneath the influence of sundry sips, which she accepted with a delicate reluctance.

This time Dalgleish of Raxmathrapple had not the remotest chance. M'Alcohol got furious, sang Gaelic songs, and even delivered a sermon in genuine Erse, without incurring a rebuke; whilst, for my own part, I must needs confess that I waxed unnecessarily amorous, and the last thing I recollect was the pressure of Mr. Sawley's hand at the door, as he denominated me his dear boy, and hoped I would soon come back and visit Mrs. Sawley and Selina.

The recollection of these passages next morning was the surest antidote to my return.

Three weeks had elapsed, and still the Glenmutchkin Railway shares were at a premium, though rather lower than when we sold. Our engineer, Watty Solder, returned from his first survey of the line, along with an assistant who really appeared to have some remote glimmerings of the science and practice of mensuration. It seemed, from a verbal report, that the line was actually practicable; and the survey would have been completed in a very short time— "If," according to the account of Solder, "there had been ae hoos in the glen. But ever sin' the distillery stoppit—and that was twa year last Martinmas—there wasna a hole whaur a Christian could lay his head, muckle less get white sugar to his toddy, forbye the change-house at the clachan;[1] and the auld luckie that keepit it was sair forfochten wi' the palsy, and maist in the dead-thraws. There was naebody else living within twal miles o' the line, barring a tacksman, a lamiter,[2] and a bauldie."

We had some difficulty in preventing Mr. Solder from making this report open and patent to the public, which premature disclosure might have interfered materially with the preparation of our traffic tables, not to mention the marketable value of the shares. We therefore kept him steadily at work out of Glasgow, upon a very liberal allowance, to which, apparently, he did not object.

"Dunshunner," said M'Corkindale to me one day, "I suspect that there is some-

---

[1]Village.

[2]Cripple.

thing going on about our railway more than we are aware of. Have you observed that the shares are preternaturally high just now?"

"So much the better. Let's sell."

"I did this morning—both yours and mine, at two pounds ten shillings premium."

"The deuce you did! Then we're out of the whole concern."

"Not quite. If my suspicions are correct, there's a good deal more money yet to be got from the speculation. Somebody has been bulling the stock without orders; and, as they can have no information which we are not perfectly up to, depend upon it, it is done for a purpose. I suspect Sawley and his friends. They have never been quite happy since the allocation; and I caught him yesterday pumping our broker in the back shop. We'll see in a day or two. If they are beginning a bearing operation, I know how to catch them."

And, in effect, the bearing operation commenced.

Next day, heavy sales were affected for delivery in three weeks; and the stock, as if waterlogged, began to sink.

The same thing continued for the following two days, until the premium became nearly nominal. In the mean time, Bob and I, in conjunction with two leading capitalists whom we let into the secret, bought up steadily every share that was offered; and at the end of a fortnight we found that we had purchased rather more than double the amount of the whole original stock. Sawley and his disciples, who, as M'Corkindale suspected, were at the bottom of the whole transaction, having beared to their heart's content, now came into the market to purchase, in order to redeem their engagements.

The following extracts from the weekly share-lists will show the results of their endeavors to regain their lost position:—

GLENMUTCHKIN RAIL, £ 1 paid

| Sat. | Mon. | Tues. | Wed. | Thurs. | Frid. | Sat. |
|---|---|---|---|---|---|---|
| 1 1/8 | 2 1/4 | 4 3/8 | 7 1/2 | 10 3/4 | 15 3/8 | 17 |

and Monday was the day of delivery.

I have no means of knowing in what frame of mind Mr. Sawley spent the Sunday, or whether he had recourse for mental consolation to Peden; but on Monday morning he presented himself at my door in full funeral costume, with about a quarter of a mile of crape swathed round his hat, black gloves, and a countenance infinitely more doleful than if he had been attending the internment of his beloved wife.

"Walk in, Mr. Sawley," said I cheerfully. "What a long time it is since I have had the pleasure of seeing you—too long indeed for brother directors. How are Mrs. Sawley and Miss Selina—won't you take a cup of coffee?"

"Grass, sir, grass!" said Mr. Sawley, with a sigh like the groan of a furnace-bellows. "We are all flowers of the oven—weak, erring creatures, every one of us. Ah Mr. Dunshunner, you have been a great stranger at Lykewake Terrace!"

"Take a muffin, Mr. Sawley. Anything new in the railway world?"

"Ah, my dear sir—my good Mr. Augustus Reginald—I wanted to have some serious conversation with you on that very point. I am afraid there is something far wrong indeed in the present state of our stock."

"Why, to be sure it is high; but that, you know, is a token of the public confidence in the line. After all, the rise is nothing compared to that of several English railways; and individually, I suppose, neither of us have any reason to complain."

"I don't like it," said Sawley, watching me over the margin of his coffee-cup. "I don't like it. It savors too much of gambling for a man of my habits. Selina, who is a sensible girl, has serious qualms on the subject."

"Then why not get out of it? I have no objection to run the risk, and if you like to transact with me, I will pay you ready money for every share you have at the present market price."

Sawley writhed uneasily in his chair.

"Will you sell me five hundred, Mr. Sawley? Say the word and it is a bargain."

"A time bargain?" quavered the coffin-maker.

"No. Money down, and scrip handed over."

"I—I can't. The fact is, my dear friend, I have sold all my stock already!"

"Then permit me to ask, Mr. Sawley, what possible objection you can have to the present aspect of affairs? You do not surely suppose that we are going to issue new shares and bring down the market, simply because you have realized at a handsome premium?"

"A handsome premium! O Lord!" moaned Sawley.

"Why, what did you get for them?"

"Four, three, and two and a half."

"A very considerable profit indeed," said I; "and you ought to be abundantly thankful. We shall talk this matter over at another time, Mr. Sawley, but just now I must beg you to excuse me. I have a particular engagement this morning with my broker—rather a heavy transaction to settle—and so—"

"It's no use beating about the bush, any longer," said Mr. Sawley in an excited tone, at the same time dashing down his crape-covered castor on the floor. "Did you ever see a ruined man with a large family? Look at me, Mr. Dunshunner—I'm one, and you've done it."

"Mr. Sawley, are you in your senses?"

"That depends on circumstances. Haven't you been buying stock lately?"

"I am glad to say I have—two thousand Glenmutchkins, I think, and this is the day of delivery."

"Well, then—can't you see how the matter stands? It was I who sold them."

"Well!"

"Mother of Moses, sir! don't you see I'm ruined?"

"By no means—but you must not swear. I pay over the money for your scrip, and you pocket a premium. It seems to me a very simple transaction."

"But I tell you I haven't got the scrip!" cried Sawley, gnashing his teeth, whilst the cold beads of perspiration gathered largely on his brow.

"This is very unfortunate! Have you lost it?"

"No!—the devil tempted me, and I oversold!"

There was a very long pause, during which I assumed an aspect of serious and dignified rebuke.

"Is it possible?" said I in a low tone, after the manner of Kean's offended fathers. "What! you, Mr. Sawley—the stoker's friend—the enemy of gambling—the father of Selina—condescend to so equivocal a transaction? You amaze me. But I never was the man to press heavily on a friend"—here Sawley brightened up—"your secret is safe with me, and it shall be your own fault if it reaches the ears of the Session. Pay me over the difference at the present full market price, and I release you of your obligation."

"Then I'm in the Gazette, that's all," said Sawley doggedly, "and a wife and nine beautiful babes upon the parish. I had hoped other things from you, Mr. Dunshunner—I thought you and Selina—"

"Nonsense, man! Nobody goes into the Gazette just now—it will be time enough when the general crash comes. Out with your cheque-book, and write me an order for four-and-twenty thousand. Confound fractions! in these days one can afford to be liberal."

"I haven't got it," said Sawley. "You have no idea how bad our trade has been of late, for nobody seems to think of dying. I have not sold a gross of coffins this fortnight. But I'll tell you what—I'll give you five thousand down in cash, and ten thousand in shares—further I can't go."

"Now, Mr. Sawley," said I, "I may be blamed by worldly-minded persons for what I am going to do; but I am a man of principle, and feel deeply for the situation of your amiable wife and family. I bear no malice, though it is quite clear that you intended to make me the sufferer. Pay me fifteen thousand over the counter and we cry quits for ever."

"Won't you take Camlachie Cemetery shares? They are sure to go up."

"No!"

"Twelve Hundred Cowcaddens' Water, with an issue of new stock next week?"

"Not if they disseminated the Ganges!"

"A thousand Ramshorn Gas—four per guaranteed until the act?"

"Not if they promised twenty, and melted down the sun in their retort!"

"Blawweary Iron? Best spec. going."

"No, I tell you once for all! If you don't like the offer—and it is an uncommonly liberal one—say so, and I'll expose you this afternoon upon Change."

"Well then, there's a cheque, But may the—"

"Stop, sir! Any such profane expressions, and I shall insist upon the original bargain. So, then—now we're quits. I wish you a very good-morning, Mr. Sawley, and better luck next time. Pray remember me to your amiable family."

The door had hardly closed upon the discomfited coffin-maker, and I was still in the preliminary steps of an extempore *pas seul,* intended as the outward demonstration of exceedingly inward joy, when Bob M'Corkindale entered. I told him the result of the morning's conference.

"You have let him off too easily," said the Political Economist. "Had I been his creditor, I certainly should have sacked the shares into the bargain. There is nothing like rigid dealing between man and man."

"I am contented with moderate profits," said I; "besides, the image of Selina overcame me. How goes it with Jobson and Grabbie?"

"Jobson has paid, and Grabbie compounded. Heckles—may he die an evil death!—has repudiated, become a lame duck, and waddled; but no doubt his estate will pay a dividend."

"So, then, we are clear of the whole Glenmutchkin business, and at a handsome profit."

"A fair interest for the outlay of capital—nothing more. But, I'm not quite done with the concern yet."

"How so? not another bearing operation?"

"No; that cock would hardly fight. But you forget that I am secretary of the company, and have a small account against them for services already rendered. I must do what I can to carry the bill through Parliament; and, as you have now sold your whole shares, I advise you to resign from the direction, go down straight to Glenmutchkin, and qualify yourself for a witness. We shall give you five guineas a day, and pay all your expenses."

"Not a bad notion. But what has become of M'Closkie, and the other fellow with the jaw-breaking name?"

"Vich-Induibh? I have looked after their interests, and in duty bound, sold their shares at a large premium, and despatched them to their native hills on annuities."

"And Sir Polloxfen?"

"Died yesterday of spontaneous combustion."

As the company seemed breaking up, I thought I could not do better than take M'Corkindale's hint, and accordingly betook myself to Glenmutchkin, along with the Captain of M'Alcohol, and we quartered ourselves upon the Factor for Glentumblers.

We found Watty Solder very shaky, and his assistant also lapsing into habits of painful inebriety. We saw little of them except of an evening, for we shot and fished the whole day, and made ourselves remarkably comfortable.

By singular good-luck, the plans and sections were lodged in time, and the Board of Trade very handsomely reported in our favor, with a recommendation of what they were pleased to call "the Glenmutchkin system," and a hope that it might generally be carried out. What this system was, I never clearly understood; but, of course, none of us had any objections. This circumstance gave an additional impetus to the shares, and they once more went up. I was, however too cautious to plunge a second time into Charybdis, but M'Corkindale did, and again emerged with plunder.

When the time came for the parliamentary contest, we all emigrated to London. I still recollect, with lively satisfaction, the many pleasant days we spent in the metropolis at the company's expense. There were just a neat fifty of us, and we occupied the whole of an hotel. The discussion before the committee was long and formidable. We were opposed by four other companies who patronized lines, of which the nearest was at least a hundred miles distant from Glenmutchkin; but as they founded their opposition upon dissent from "the Glenmutchkin system" generally, the committee allowed them to be heard. We fought for three weeks a most desperate battle, and might in the end have been victorious, had not our last antagonist, at the very close of his case, pointed out no less than seventy-three fatal errors in the parliamentary plan deposited by the unfortunate Solder. Why this was not done earlier, I never exactly understood; it may be, that our opponents, with gentlemanly consideration, were unwilling to curtail our sojourn in London—and their own. The drama was now finally closed, and after all preliminary expenses were paid, sixpence per share was returned to the holders upon surrender of their scrip.

Such is an accurate history of the Origin, Rise, Progress and Fall of the Direct Glenmutchkin Railway. It contains a deep moral, if anybody has sense enough to see it; if not, I have a new project in my eye for next session, of which timely notice shall be given.

## CHARLES MACKAY (1814–1889)

[Mackay's style, turgid and sentimental, resembles that of the melodrama—the popular entertainment of the day. Verse such as his is completely out of fashion in our own time, but it has power, and represents a major aspect of Victorian taste.]

### The Mowers

An Anticipation of the Cholera, 1848

Dense on the stream the vapors lay,
Thick as wool on the cold highway;
Spongy and dim each lonely lamp
Shone oer the streets so dull and damp;
The moonbeam could not pierce the cloud
That swathed the city like a shroud.
There stood three shapes on the bridge alone,
Three figures by the coping stone;
Gaunt, and tall, and undefined,
Specters built of mist and wind;
Changing ever in form and height,
But black and palpable to sight.
"This is a city fair to see,"

Whispered one of the fearful three;
"A mighty tribute it pays to me.
Into its river, winding slow,
Thick and foul from shore to shore,
The vessels come, the vessels go,
And teeming lands their riches pour.
It spreads beneath the murky sky
A wilderness of masonry;
Huge, unshapely, overgrown,
Dingy brick and blackened stone.
Mammon is its chief and lord,
Monarch slavishly adored;
Mammon sitting side by side
With pomp, and luxury, and pride;
Who call his large dominions theirs,
Nor dream a portion is despair's.
Countless thousands bend to me
In rags and purple, in hovel and hall,
And pay the tax of misery
With tears, and blood, and spoken gall.
Whenever they cry
For aid to die,
I give them courage to dare the worst,
And leave their ban on a world accurst.
I show them the river so black and deep,
They take the plunge, they sink to sleep.
I show them poison, I show them rope,
They rush to death without a hope.
Poison, and rope, and pistol ball,
Welcome either, welcome all.
I am the lord of the teeming town—
*I mow them down, I mow them down."*
"Aye thou art great, but greater I,"
The second specter made reply.
"Thou rulest with a frown austere,
Thy name is synonym of fear.
But I, despotic and hard as thou,
Have a laughing lip, an open brow.
I build a temple in every lane,
I have a palace in every street;
And the victims throng to the doors amain,
And wallow like swine beneath my feet.
To me the strong man gives his health,
The wise man reason, the rich man wealth,
Maids their virtue, youth its charms,
And mothers the children in their arms.
Thou art a slayer of mortal men—
Thou of the unit, I of the ten.
Great thou art, but greater I,
To decimate humanity.
Tis I am the lord of the teeming town—
*I mow them down, I mow them down."*
"Vain boasters to exult at death,"

The third replied, "so feebly done;
I ope my jaws, and with a breath
Slay thousands while you think of one.
All the blood that Caesar spilled,
All that Alexander drew,
All the hosts by 'glory' killed,
From Agincourt to Waterloo,
Compared with those whom I have slain,
Are but a river to the main.
I brew disease in stagnant pools,
And wandering here, disporting there,
Favored much by knaves and fools,
I poison streams, I taint the air;
I shake from my locks the spreading pest,
I keep the typhus at my behest;
In filth and slime
I crawl, I climb,
I find the workman at his trade,
I blow on his lips, and down he lies.
I look in the face of the ruddiest maid,
And straight the fire forsakes her eyes—
She droops, she sickens, and she dies;
I stint the growth of babes new born,
Or shear them off like standing corn.
I rob the sunshine of its glow.
I poison all the winds that blow.
Whenever they pass they suck my breath,
And freight their wings with certain death.
Tis *I* am the lord of the crowded town—
*I mow them down, I mow them down.*

"But great as we are, there cometh one
Greater than you—greater than I,
To aid the deeds that shall be done,
To end the work that we've begun,
And thin this thick humanity.
I see his footmarks east and west;
I hear his tread in the silence fall.
He shall not sleep, he shall not rest—
He comes to aid us one and all.
Were men as wise as men might be,
They would not work for you, for me,
For him that cometh over the sea;
But they will not heed the warning voice.
The Cholera comes, rejoice! rejoice!
*He* shall be lord of the swarming town,
*And mow them down, and mow them down."*

## Louise on the Door-Step

Half past three in the morning,
And no one in the street

But me, on the sheltering door-step
Resting my weary feet,
Watching the rain drops patter
And dance where the puddles run,
As bright in the flaring gaslight
As dewdrops in the sun.

There's a light upon the pavement—
It shines like a magic glass,
And there are faces in it
That look at me and pass.
Faces—ah, well remembered
In the happy long ago,
When my garb was white as lilies,
And my thoughts as pure as snow.

Faces, ah, yes, I see them—
One, two, and three—and four—
That come in the gust of tempests,
And go on the winds that bore.
Changeful and evanescent,
They shine mid storm and rain,
Till the terror of their beauty
Lies deep upon my brain.

One of them frowns: I know him,
With his thin long snow-white hair—
Cursing his wretched daughter
That drove him to despair.
And the other, with wakening pity
In her large tear-streaming eyes,
Seems as she yearned toward me,
And whispered "Paradise."

They pass—they melt in the ripples—
And I shut mine eyes, that burn,
To escape another vision
That follows where're I turn—
The face of a false deceiver
That lives and lies; ah, me,
Though I see it in the pavement,
Mocking my misery.

They are gone—all three—quite vanished.
Let nothing call them back,
For I've had enough of phantoms,
And my heart is on the rack.
God help me in my sorrow;
But there, in the wet, cold stone,
Smiling in heavenly beauty,
I see my lost, mine own.

There, on the glimmering pavement,
With eyes as blue as morn,
Floats by the fair-haired darling
Too soon from my bosom torn.
She clasps her tiny fingers—
She calls me sweet and mild,
And says that my God forgives me
For the sake of my little child.

I will go to her grave to-morrow,
And pray that I may die;
And I hope that my God will take me
Ere the days of my youth go by.
For I am old in anguish,
And long to be at rest,
With my little babe beside me,
And the daisies on my breast.

## The Two Houses

"Twill overtask a thousand men,
With all their strength and skill,
To build my lord ere New Year's eve
His castle on the hill."
"Then take two thousand," said my lord,
"And labor with a will."

They wrought, these glad two thousand men,
But long ere winter gloom,
My lord had found a smaller house,
And dwelt in one dark room;
And one man built it in one day,
While the bells rang "ding, dong, boom;
Shut up the door, shut up the door,
Shut up the door till doom."

## ROBERT NICOLL (1814–1837)

### We'll A' Go Pu' the Heather

We'll a' go pu' the heather,
Our byres* are a' to theek*: barns/thatch
Unless the peat-stack get a hap,
We'll a' be smoored* wi' reek. smothered
Wi' rantin' sang awa we'll gang,
While summer skies are blue,
To fend against the winter cauld
The heather we will pu'.

I like to pu' the heather,
We're aye sae mirthfu' where
The sunshine creeps atour the crags,

Like reveled golden hair.
Where on the hill-tap we can stand
Wi' joyfu' heart I trow,
And mark ilk grassy bank and holm,
As we the heather pu'.

I like to pu' the heather,
Where harmless lambkins run,
Or lay them down beside the burn
Like gowans* in the sun; daisies
Where ilka foot can tread upon
The heath-flower wet wi' dew,
When comes the starnie ower the hill,
While we the heather pu'.

I like to pu' the heather,
For ane can gang awa,
But no before a glint o' love
On some ane's e'e doth fa'.
Sweet words we dare to whisper there,
"My hinny and my doo*," dove
Till maistly we wi' joy could greet* weep
As we the heather pu'.

We'll a' go pu' the heather,
For at yon mountain fit* "foot"
There stands a broom bush by a burn,
Where twa young folk can sit.
He meets me there at morning's rise,
My beautiful and true.
My father said the word—the morn
The heather we will pu'.

## Bonnie Bessie Lee

Bonnie Bessie Lee had a face fu' o' smiles,
And mirth round her ripe lip was aye dancing slee;
And light was the footfa', and winsome the wiles,
O' the flower o' the parochin—our ain Bessie Lee.

Wi' the bairns she would rin, and the school laddies paik*, frolic
And oer the broomy braes like a fairy would flee,
Till auld hearts grew young again wi' love for her sake.
There was life in the blithe blink* o' Bonnie Bessie Lee. glance

She grat* wi' the waefu', and laughed wi' the glad, wept
And light as the wind mang the dancers was she;
And a tongue that could jeer, too, the little limmer* had, rascal
Whilk keepit aye her ain side for Bonnie Bessie Lee.

And she whiles had a sweetheart, and sometimes had twa—
A limmer o' a lassie—but, atween you and me,

Her warm wee bit hearty she ne'er threw awa,
Though mony a ane had sought it frae Bonnie Bessie Lee.

But ten years had gane since I gazed on her last,
For ten years had parted my auld hame and me;
And I said to mysel, as her mither's door I past,
"Will I ever get anither kiss frae Bonnie Bessie Lee?"

But time changes a' thing—the ill-natured loon*. lout
Were it ever sae rightly he'll no let it be;
But I rubbit at my een, and I thought I would swoon,
How the carle* had come roun' about our ain Bessie Lee. low fellow

The wee laughing lassie was a gudewife grown auld,
Twa weans at her apron and ane on her knee.
She was douce*, too, and wiselike—and wisdom's sae could. respectable
I would rather hae the ither ane than this Bessie Lee.

## Ordé Braes

There's nae hame like the hame o' youth,
Nae ither spot sae fair;
Nae ither faces look sae kind
As the smilin' faces there.
An' I hae sat by mony streams,
Hae traveled mony ways;
But the fairest spot on the earth to me
Is on bonnie Ordé Braes.

An ell-lang wee thing then I ran
Wi' the ither neebor bairns,
To pu' the hazel's shining nuts,
An' to wander mang the ferns;
An' to feast on the bramble-berries brown,
An' gather the glossy slaes*, sloe-berries
By the burnie's side, an' aye sinsyne
I hae loved sweet Ordé braes.

The memories o' my father's hame,
An' its kindly dwellers a',
O' the friends I loved wi' a young heart's love
Ere care that heart could thraw*, twist
Are twined wi' the stanes o' the silver burn,
An' its fairy crooks an' bays,
That onward sang' neath the gowden broom
Upon bonnie Ordé Braes.

Aince in a day there were happy hames
By the bonnie Ordé's side.

Nane ken how meikle peace an' love
In a straw roofed cot can bide.
But the hames are gane, an' the hand o' time
The roofless wa's doth raze.
Laneness an' sweetness hand in hand
Gang ower the Ordé Braes.

Oh, an'* the sun were shinin' now, (if)
An' oh, an' I were there,
Wi' twa three friends o' auld langsyne,
My wanderin' joy to share.
For though on the hearth o' my bairnhood's hame
The flock o' the hills doth graze,
Some kind hearts live to love me yet
Upon bonnie Ordé Braes.

## The Muir o' Gorse an' Broom

I winna bide in your castle ha's,
Nor yet in your lofty towers.
My heart is sick o' your gloomy hame,
An' sick o' your darksome bowers;
An' oh, I wish I were far awa'
Frae their grandeur an' their gloom,
Where the freeborn lintie sings its sang
On the Muir o' Gorse an' Broom.

Sae weel as I like the healthfu' gale
That blaws fu' kindly there,
An' the heather brown, an' the wild blue-bell
That wave on the muirland bare;
An' the singing birds, an' the humming bees,
An' the little lochs that toom* empty
Their gushing burns to the distant sea
Oer the Muir o' Gorse an' Broom.

Oh, if I had a dwallin' there,
Biggit laigh* by a burnie's side, "low"
Where ae aik tree, in the summer time,
Wi' its leaves that hame might hide;
Oh, I wad rejoice frae day to day,
As blithe as a young bridegroom;
For dearer than palaces to me
Is the Muir o' Gorse an' Broom.

In a lanely cot on a muirland wild,
My mither nurtured me.
O' the meek wild flowers I playmates made,

An' my hame wi' the wandering bee.
An' oh, if I were far awa
Frae your grandeur an' your gloom,
Wi' them again, an' the bladden* gale, pounding
On the Muir o' Gorse an' Broom.

## A Maiden's Meditation

Nae sweetheart hae I,
Yet I'm no that ill-faured;
But there's ower mony lasses,
An' wooers are scared.
This night I the hale
O' my tocher* wad gie, dowry
If a' ither body
Were married but me.

Syne I wad get plenty
About me to speer*, ask
Folk wadna be fashious* fussy
Bout beauty or gear*. money
Hearts broken in dozens
Around I wad see,
If a' ither body
Were married but me.

Ae lover would hae
A' my errands to rin.
Anither should tend me
Baith outby an' in;
And to keep me gude-humored
Would tak twa or three,
If a' ither body
Were married but me.

Fond wooers in dozens,
Where I hae na ane,
An' worshippin' hearts
Where I'm langin' alane:
Frae morning to e'enin',
How blessed I wad be,
If a' ither body
Were married but me.

A daft dream was yon—
It has faded awa.
Nae body in passin'
E'er gies me a ca'—

Nae sweetheart adorin'
I ever shall see,
Till a' ither body
Be married but me.

## MARION AIRD (1815–1888)

### A Memory Dear

O sing me the song
Of years long agone,
When we met in gloamins
So cheery,

For my heart oft is sore
For the loved ones of yore,
Who come nae mair back,
When I am eerie.

Wherever ye be,
By shore or by sea,
Ye still sing to me
When aweary.

There's a throne wi' nae sea,
Though friends parted be,
Where we'll rest in the lea
When life-weary.

## JOHN CRAWFORD (1816–1873)

### The Land o' the Bonnet and Plaid

Hurra for the land o' the broom-covered brae,
The land o' the rowan, the haw, and the slae;
Where waves the blue harebell in dingle and glade—
The land o' the pibroch, the bonnet, and plaid.

Hurra, for the hills o' the cromlech and cairn,
Where blossoms the thistle by hillocks o' fern;
There freedom in triumph an altar has made
For holiest rites in the land o' the plaid.

A coronal wreath, where the wild flowers bloom,
To garnish the martyr and patriot's tomb:
Shall their names ever perish—their fame ever fade,
Who ennobled the land o' the bonnet and plaid?

Oh, hame o' my bairnhood, ye hills o' my love,
The haunt o' the freeman for aye may ye prove;
And honored for ever be matron and maid
In the land o' the heather, the bonnet, and plaid.

Hurra, for the land o' the deer and the rae,
O' the gowany* glen and the bracken-clad brae, daisy-filled
Where blooms our ain thistle, in sunshine and shade—
Dear badge o' the land o' the bonnet and plaid.

## THEODORE MARTIN (1816–1909) AND WILLIAM AYTOUN

[Martin and Aytoun collaborated in a number of verse parodies which were published in 1845 as *The Book of Ballads Edited by Bon Gaultier*, thereafter known simply as the Bon Gaultier ballads. The following two poems are good examples of their work.]

### The Massacre of the Macpherson

Fhairshon swore a feud
Against the clan M'Tavish;
Marched into their land
To murder and to rafish;
For he did resolve
To extirpate the vipers,
With four-and-twenty men
And five-and-thirty pipers.

But when he had gone
Half-way down Strath Canaan,
Of his fighting tail
Just three were remainin'.
They were all he had,
To back him in ta battle,
All the rest had gone
Off, to drive ta cattle.

"Fery coot!" cried Fhairshon.
"So my clan disgraced is;
Lads, we'll need to fight,
Before we touch the peasties.
Here's Mhic-Mac-Methusaleh
Coming wi' his fassals,
Gillies* seventy-three, retainers
And sixty Dhuinewassails!"

"Coot tay to you, sir;
Are you not ta Fhairshon?
Was you coming here
To fisit any person?
You are a plackguard, sir!

It is now six hundred
Coot long years, and more,
Since my glen was plundered."

"Fat is tat you say?
Dare you cock your peaver?
I will teach you, sir,
Fat is coot pehafiour!
You shall not exist
For another day more;
I will shot you, sir,
Or stap you with my claymore!"

"I am fery glad,
To learn what you mention,
Since I can prevent
Any such intention."
So Mhic-Mac-Methusaleh
Gave some warlike howls,
Trew his skian-dhu,
An' stuck it in his powels.

In this fery way
Tied ta failiant Fhairshon,
Who was always thought
A superior person.
Fhairshon had a son,
Who married Noah's daughter;
And nearly spoiled ta Flood,
By trinking up ta water:

Which he would have done,
I at least pelieve it,
Had ta mixture peen
Only half Glenlivet.
This is all my tale:
Sirs, I hope tis new t' ye!
Here's your fery good healths,
And tamn ta whusky tuty!

## The Queen in France
### An Ancient Scottish Ballad

#### Part I

It fell upon the August month,
When landsmen bide at hame,
That our gude Queen went out to sail
Upon the saut-sea faem.

And she has ta'en the silk and gowd,
The like was never seen;

And she has ta'en the Prince Albert,
And the bauld Lord Aberdeen.

"Ye'se bide at hame, Lord Wellington:
Ye daurna gang wi' me:
For ye hae been ance in the land o' France,
And that's eneuch for ye.

"Ye'se bide at hame, Sir Robert Peel,
To gather the red and the white monie;
And see that my men do not eat me up
At Windsor wi' their gluttony."

They hadna sailed a league, a league,—
A league, but barely twa,
When the lift* grew dark, and the waves grew wan, sky
And the wind began to blaw.

"O weel, weel may the waters rise,
In welcome o' their Queen;
What gars* ye look sae white, Albert? makes
What makes your ee sae green?"

"My heart is sick, my heid is sair:
Gie me a glass o' the gude brandy:
To set my foot on the braid green sward,
I'd gie the half o' my yearly fee.

"It's sweet to hunt the sprightly hare
On the bonny slopes o' Windsor lea,
But O, it's ill to bear the thud
And pitching o' the saut, saut sea!"

And aye they sailed, and aye they sailed,
Till England sank behind,
And over to the coast of France
They drave before the wind.

Then up and spak the King o' France,
Was birling at the wine:
"O wha may be the gay lady,
That owns that ship sae fine?

"And wha may be that bonny lad,
That looks sae pale and wan?
I'll wad my lands o' Picardie,
That he's nae Englishman."

Then up and spak an auld French lord,
Was sitting beneath his knee,
"It is the Queen o' braid England
That's come across the sea."

"And O an it be England's Queen,
She's welcome here the day;
I'd rather hae her for a friend
Than for a deadly fae.

"Gae, kill the eerock in the yard,
The auld sow in the sty,
And bake for her the brockit calf,
But and the puddock-pie!"

And he has gane until the ship,
As soon as it drew near,
And he has ta'en her by the hand—
"Ye're kindly welcome here!"

And syne he kissed her on ae cheek,
And syne upon the ither;
And he ca'd her his sister dear,
And she ca'd him her brither.

"Light doun, light doun now, lady mine,
Light doun upon the shore;
Nae English king has trodden here
This thousand years and more."

"And gin I lighted on your land,
As light fu' weel I may,
O, am I free to feast wi' you,
And free to come and gae?"

And he has sworn by the Haly Rood,
And the black stane o' Dumblane,
That she is free to come and gae
Till twenty days are gane.

"I've lippened to a Frenchman's aith,"
Said gude Lord Aberdeen;
"But I'll never lippen to it again
Sae lang's the grass is green.

"Yet gae your ways, my sovereign liege,
Sin' better mayna be;
The wee bit bairns are safe at hame,
By the blessing o' Marie!"

Then doun she lighted frae the ship,
She lighted safe and sound;
And glad was our good Prince Albert
To step upon the ground.

"Is that your Queen, my Lord?" she said,
"That auld and buirdly dame?

I see the crown upon her head;
But I dinna ken her name."

And she has kissed the Frenchman's Queen,
And eke her daughters three,
And gien her hand to the young Princess,
That louted* upon the knee. bowed

And she has gane to the proud castel,
That's biggit* beside the sea: built
But aye, when she thought o' the bairns at hame,
The tear was in her ee.

She gied the King the Cheshire cheese,
But and the porter fine;
And he gied her the puddock-pies,
But and the blude-red wine.

Then up and spak the dourest prince,
An admiral was he;
"Let's keep the Queen o' England here,
Sin' better mayna be!

"O mony is the dainty king
That we hae trappit here;
And mony is the English yerl
That's in our dungeons drear!"

"You lee, you lee, ye graceless loon*, rascal
Sae loud's I hear ye lee!
There never yet was Englishman
That came to skaith* by me. harm

"Gae oot, gae oot, ye fause traitor!
Gae oot until the street;
It's shame that Kings and Queens should sit
Wi' sic a knave at meat!"

Then up and raise the young French lord,
In wrath and hie disdain—
"O ye may sit, and ye may eat
Your puddock-pies alane!

"But were I in my ain gude ship,
And sailing wi' the wind,
And did I meet wi' auld Napier,
I'd tell him o' my mind."

O then the Queen leuch* loud and lang, "laughed"
And her color went and came:
"Gin ye meet wi' Charlie on the sea,
Ye'll wish yersel at hame!"

And aye they birlit at the wine,
And drank richt merrily,
Till the auld cock crawed in the castle-yard,
And the Abbey bell struck three.

The Queen she gaed until her bed,
And Prince Albert likewise;
And the last word that gay lady said
Was—"O thae puddock -pies!"

Part II

The sun was high within the lift
Afore the French King raise;
And syne he louped intil his sark*, shirt
And warslit on his claes.

"Gae up, gae up, my little foot-page,
Gae up until the toun;
And gin* ye meet wi' the auld harper, if
Be sure ye bring him doun."

And he has met wi' the auld harper;
O but his een were reid;
And the bizzing o' a swarm of bees
Was singing in his heid.

"Alack! alack!" the harper said,
"That this should e'er hae been!
I daurna gang before my liege,
For I was fou* yestreen." (drunk)

"It's ye maun come, ye auld harper;
Ye daurna tarry lang;
The King is just dementit-like
For wanting o' a sang."

And when he came to the King's chamber,
He loutit on his knee,
"O what may be your gracious will
Wi' an auld frail man like me?"

"I want a sang, harper," he said,
"I want a sang richt speedily;
And gin ye dinna make a sang,
I'll hang ye up on the gallows tree."

"I canna do't, my liege," he said,
"Hae mercy on my auld gray hair!
But gin that I had got the words,
I think that I might mak the air."

"And wha's to mak the words, fause loon,
When minstrels we have barely twa;

And Lamartine is in Paris toun,
And Victor Hugo far awa'!"

"The deil may gang for Lamartine,
And flee awa' wi' auld Hugo,
For a better minstrel than them baith
Within this very toun I know.

"O kens my liege the gude Walter,
At hame they ca' him BON GAULTIER.
He'll rhyme ony day wi' True Thomas,
And he is in the castle here."

The French King first he lauchit loud,
And syne did he begin to sing;
"My e'en are auld, and my heart is cauld,
Or I suld ha'e known the minstrels' King.

"Gae take to him this ring o' gowd,
And this mantle o' the silk sae fine,
And bid him mak a maister sang
For his sovereign lady's sake and mine."

"I winna take the gowden ring,
Nor yet the mantle fine:
But I'll mak the sang for my lady's sake,
And for a cup of wine."

The Queen was sitting at the cards,
The King ahint her back;
And aye she dealed the red honors,
And aye she dealed the black;

And syne unto the dourest Prince
She spak richt courteously;—
"Now will ye play, Lord Admiral,
Now will ye play wi' me?"

The dourest Prince he bit his lip,
And his brow was black as glaur;
"The only game that e'er I play
Is the bluidy game o' war!"

"And gin ye play at that, young man,
It weel may cost ye sair:
Ye'd better stick to the game at cards,
For you'll win nae honors there!"

The King he leuch, and the Queen she leuch,
Till the tears ran blithely doun;
But the admiral he raved and swore,
Til they kicked him frae the room.

The Harper came, and the Harper sang,
And O but they were fain*: pleased
For when he had sung the gude sang twice,
They called for it again.

It was the sang o' the Field o' Gowd,
In the days of auld langsyne;
When bauld King Henry crossed the seas,
Wi' his brither King to dine.

And aye he harped, and aye he carped,
Till up the Queen she sprang—
"I'll wad* a County Palatine, wager
Gude Walter made that sang."

Three days had come, three days had gane,
The fourth began to fa',
When our gude Queen to the Frenchman said,
"It's time I was awa!

"O, bonny are the fields o' France,
And saftly draps the rain;
But my bairnies are in Windsor Tower,
And greeting* a' their lane. weeping

"Now ye maun come to me, Sir King,
As I have come to ye;
And a benison upon your heid
For a' your courtesy!

"Ye maun come, and bring your lady fere;
Ye sall na say me no;
And ye'se mind, we have aye a bed to spare
For that gawsy chield Guizot."

Now he has ta'en her lily-white hand,
And put it to his lip,
And he has ta'en her to the strand,
And left her in her ship.

"Will ye come back, sweet bird? he cried,
"Will ye come kindly here,
When the lift is blue, and the laverocks* sing, larks
In the spring-time o' the year?"

"It's I would blithely come, my Lord,
To see ye in the spring:
It's I would blithely venture back,
But for ae little thing.

"It isna that the winds are rude,
Or that the waters rise,

But I loe the roasted beef at hame,
And no thae puddock-pies!"

## THOMAS LATTO (1818– ? )

### When We Were at the Schule

The laddies plague me for a sang,
I e'en maun play the fool.
I'll sing them ane about the days
When we were at the schule—
Though now the frosty pow* is seen head
Whaur waved the curly hair,
And many a blithesome heart is cauld,
Sin' first we sported there.

When we were at the schule, my frien,
When we were at the schule;
Nae after days are like the days
When we were at the schule.

Yet muckle Jock is to the fore,
And canny, creepin' Hugh,
And Bob the pest, an' Sugar-pouch,
The best o' a' the crew;
And raggit Willie is the laird
O' twa-three landart* farms; country
And Katie Spence, the pridefu' thing,
Now cuddles in his arms.

O do ye mind the maister's hat,
Sae auld, sae bare an' brown,
We carried to the burnie's side,
An' sent it soomin'* down? "swimming"
We thought how clever a' was planned,
When—whatna voice was that?
A head is raised aboon the hedge—
"I'll thank ye for *my* hat!"

O weel I mind our hingin' lugs*, ears
Our het an' tinglin' paws;
O weel I mind his solemn look,
An' weel I mind the tawse*. strap
What awfu' snuffs that day he took,
An' panged* them up his nose. stuffed
An' rapped the box as if to strike
A terror to his foes.

An' do ye mind, at countin' time,
How watchfu' he has lain,
To catch us steal frae ithers' slates,
A' jot it on our ain;
An' how we feared, at writin' hour,
His glunches* and his glooms— scowls
How many times a day he said
Our fingers a' were thooms.

An' weel I min' that afternoon,
Twas manfu' like yersel',
Ye took the pawmies an' the shame,
To save wee Johnnie Bell.
The maister found it out belive*; right away
He took ye on his knee;
And as he looked into your face,
The tear was in his e'e.

But mind ye, lad, yon afternoon,
How fleet ye skipped awa,
For ye had cracked auld Jenny's pane,
When playin' at the ba'?
Nae pennies had we—Jenny grat*; wept
It cut us to the core.
Ye took your mither's hen at nicht,
An' left it at her door.

And sic a steer his granny made,
When talepyet* Jamie Rae tell-tale
We dookit roarin' at the pump,
Syne rowed him down the brae.
But how the very maister leugh,
When leein' Saddler Wat
Cam' in an' threept* that cripple Tam insisted
Had chased an' killed his cat.

Aye, laddies, ye may wink awa'—
Truth shouldna a' be tauld.
I fear the schules o' modern days
Are no unlike tha auld.
And are nae we but laddies yet,
Wha get the name o' men,
And living by the ingle*-side fire
Thae happy days again.

When we were at the schule, my frien',
When we were at the schule?

We're no sae wise—we're learning aye—
We never leave the schule.

## The Kiss Ahint the Door

There's meikle bliss in ae fond kiss,
Whyles mair than in a score;
But wae betak the stouin smack
I took ahint* the door. behind

"O laddie, wheesht*, for sic a fricht silence
I ne'er was in afore,
Fu' brawly* did my mither hear (well)
The kiss ahint the door."
The wa's are thick—ye needna fear;
But gin they jeer an' mock,
I'll swear it was a startit cork,
Or wyte* the rusty lock. blame

We stappit ben*, while Maggie's face in
Was like a lowin'* coal; blazing
And as for me, I could hae crept
Into a rabbit's hole.
The mither looked—saff's how she look't.
Thae mithers are a bore,
An' gleg* as ony cat to hear sharp
A kiss ahint the door.

The douce* gudeman, though he was there, sober
As weel micht been in Rome,
For by the fire he puffed his pipe,
An' never fashed* his thoom. bothered
But tittrin' in a corner stood
The gawky sisters four—
A winter's nicht for me they micht
Hae stood ahint the door.

"How daur ye tak sic freedoms here?"
The bauld gudewife began;
Wi' that a foursome yell gat up—
I to my heels an' ran;
A besom* whiskit by my lug*, broom/ear
And dishclouts half a score.
Catch me again, though fidgin' fain,
At kissin' hint the door.

## Sly Widow Skinner

O the days when I strutted (to think o't I'm sad)
The heir to a cozy bit mailen*, farm
When sly Widow Skinner gat round me, the jaud!
For she thocht my auld daddy was failin', was failin',
For she thocht my auld daddy was failin'.

I promised to tak her for better for worse,
Though sma was my chance to be happy,
For I found she had courted na me, but my purse,
What's waur—that she liket a drappy, a drappy,
What's waur, that she liket a drappy.

Then ae nicht at a kirn I saw Maggy Hay,
To see her was straight to adore her.
The widow looked blue when I passed her neist day,
An' waited na e'en to speer* for her, speer for her, ask
An' waited na e'en to speer for her.

O pity my case, I was terribly raw,
And she was a terrible Tartar.
She spak about "measures" and "takin' the law,"
And I set mysel' down for a martyr, a martyr,
And I set mysel' down for a martyr.

Weel, I buckled wi' Meg, an the blithe honeymoon
Scarce was ower when the widow I met her,
She girningly* whispered, "Hech, weel hae ye dune, grimacing
But tent* me, lad, I can do better, do better, watch
But tent me, lad, I can do better:—

"Gin ye canna get berries, put up wi' the hools*." "hulls"
Her proverb I counted a' blether,
But,—widows for ever for hookin' auld fools,—
Neist week she was cried wi' my feyther, my feyther.
Neist week she was cried wi' my feyther.

# GEORGE MURRAY (1819–1868)

## The Auld Kirk o' Scotland

The gude auld Kirk o' Scotland,
The wild winds round her blaw,
And when her foemen hear her sough,
They prophecy her fa';
But what although her fate has been
Amang the floods to sit—
The gude auld Kirk o' Scotland,
She's nae in ruins yet.

There may be wrath within her wa's,
What reck? her wa's are wide.
It's but the beating of a heart,
The rushing of a tide.
Whose motion keeps its waters pure.
Then let them foam or fret;
The gude auld Kirk o' Scotland,
She's nae in ruins yet.

She was a lithe, she was a licht,
When a'thing else was mirk,
An' mony a trembling heart has found
Its bield* behind the Kirk; shelter
She bore the brunt, and did her due,
When Scotland's sword was wet;
The gude auld Kirk o' Scotland,
She's nae in ruins yet.

The clouds that overcast her sky
Maun shortly flit awa',
A bonnie, blue and peaceful heaven
Smiles sweetly through them a'.
Her country's life-blood's in her veins,
The wide warld's in her debt.
The gude auld Kirk o' Scotland,
She's nae in ruins yet.

## JOHN SHAIRP (1819–1885)

### Cailleach Bein-Y-Vreich

Weird wife* of Bein-y-Vreich, horo, horo! (woman)
Aloft in the mist she dwells;
Vreich horo! Vreich horo! Vreich horo!
All alone by the lofty wells.

Weird, weird wife, with the long gray locks,
She follows her fleet-foot stags,
Noisily moving through splintered rocks,
And crashing the grisly crags.

Tall wife, with the long gray hose, in haste
The rough stony beach she walks;
But dulse or seaweed she will not taste,
Nor yet the green kail stalks.

"And I will not let my herds of deer,
My bonny red deer go down;
I will not let them down to the shore,
To feed on the sea shells brown.

"Oh, better they love in the corrie's recess,
Or on mountain top to dwell,
And feed by my side on the green, green cress,
That grows by the lofty well.

"Broad Bein-y-Vreich is grisly and drear,
But wherever my feet have been
The well-springs start for my darling deer,
And the grass grows tender and green.

"And there high up on the calm nights clear,
Beside the lofty spring,
They come to my call, and I milk them there,
And a weird wild song I sing.

"But when hunter men round my dun deer prowl,
I will not let them nigh;
Through the rended cloud I cast one scowl,
They faint on the heath and die.

"And when the north wind oer the desert bare
Drives loud, to the corries below
I drive my herds down, and bield* them there — shelter
From the drifts of the blinding snow.

"Then I mount the blast, and we ride full fast,
And laugh as we stride the storm,
I, and the witch of the Cruachan Ben,
And the scowling-eyed Seul-Gorm."

## The Bush Aboon Traquair

[Like Skinner's "Tullochgorum," this poem is a song about a song. "The Bush Aboon Traquair" was an old air, as Shairp says in the third stanza. The reader may consult Robert Crawford's version (in Volume I), with the identical title. It was written about 1730.]

Will ye gang wi' me and fare
To the bush aboon Traquair?
Owre the high Minchmuir we'll up and awa',
This bonnie summer noon,
While the sun shines fair aboon,
And the licht sklents* saftly doun on holm and ha'. — slants

And what wad ye do there,
At the bush aboon Traquair?
A long dreich* road, ye had better let it be: — tiring
Save some auld skrunts* o' birk — stumps
I' the hill-side lirk*, — low spot
There's nocht i' the warld for man to see.

But the blithe lilt o' yon air,
"The Bush aboon Traquair"—
I need nae mair, it's eneuch for me.
Owre my cradle its sweet chime
Cam soughin' frae auld time.
Sae tide what may, I'll awa' and see.

At what saw ye there,
At the bush aboon Traquair?
Or what did ye hear that was worth your heed?
I heard the cushies* croon — wood pigeons
Through the gowden afternoon,
And the Quair burn singing doun to the vale o' Tweed.

And birks saw I, three or four,
Wi' gray moss bearded owre,
The last that are left o' the birken shaw*; — wood
Whar mony a simmer e'en
Fond lovers did convene,
Thae bonnie, bonnie gloamins that are lang awa'.

Frae mony a butt and ben*, — (two-room house)
By muirland, holm, and glen,
They cam ane hour to spen' on the green-wood sward;
But lang ha'e lad an' lass
Been lying neath the grass,
The green, green grass o' Traquair kirkyard.

They were blest beyond compare
When they held their trysting there,
Amang thae greenest hills shone on by the sun;
And then they wan a rest,
The lownest* and the best, — quietest
I' Traquair kirkyard when a' was dune.

Now the birks to dust may rot,
Names o' luvers be forgot,
Nae lads and lasses there ony mair convene;
But the blithe lilt o' yon air
Keeps the bush aboon Traquair
And the luve that ance was there aye fresh and green.

## The Clearance Song

From Lochourn to Glenfinnan the gray mountains ranging,
Naught falls on the eye but the changed and the changing;
From the hut by the lochside, the farm by the river,
Macdonalds and Cameron pass—and for ever.

The flocks of one stranger the long glens are roaming,
Where a hundred bien* homesteads smoked bonny at gloaming, — snug

Our wee crofts run wild wi' the bracken and heather,
And our gables stand ruinous, bare to the weather.

To the green mountain shealings* went up in old summers — huts
From farm town and clachan* how mony blithe comers. — village
Though green the hill pastures lie, cloudless the heaven,
No milker is singing there, morning or even.

Where high Mam-clach-ard by the ballach* is breasted, — pass
Ye may see the gray cairns where old funerals rested;
They who built them have long in their green graves been sleeping,
And their sons gone to exile, or willing or weeping.

The chiefs, whom for ages our claymores defended,
Whom landless and exiled our fathers befriended,
From their homes drive their clansmen, when famine is sorest,
Cast out to make room for the deer of the forest.

Yet on far fields of fame, when the red ranks were reeling,
Who prest to the van like the men from the shealing?
Ye were fain in your need Highland broadswords to borrow,
Where, where are they now, should the foe come tomorrow?

Alas for the day of the mournful Culloden.
The clans from that hour down to dust have been trodden;
They were leal to their Prince, when red wrath was pursuing,
And have reaped in return but oppression and ruin.

It's plaintive in harvest, when lambs are a-spaining*, — weaning
To hear the hills loud with ewe-mothers complaining—
Ah, sadder that cry comes from mainland and islands,
The sons of the Gael have no home in the Highlands.

## JOSEPH PATON (1821–1901)

### Timor Mortis Conturbat Me[1]

Could I have sung one song that should survive
The singer's voice, and in my country's heart
Find loving echo—evermore a part
Of all her sweetest memories; could I give
One great thought to the people, that should prove
The spring of noble action in their hour
Of darkness, or control their headlong power
With the firm reins of justice and of love;
Could I have traced one form that should express

---

[1] "The fear of death disturbs me." This is the refrain of Dunbar's "Lament for the Makars," which, of course, also treats the death of poets.

The sacred mystery that underlies
All beauty, and through man's enraptured eyes
Teach him how beautiful is holiness—
I had not feared thee. But to yield my breath,
Life's purpose unfulfilled—this is thy sting, O Death.

### There Is a Wail in the Wind Tonight

There is a wail in the wind tonight,
A dirge in the plashing rain,
That brings old yearnings round my heart,
Old dreams into my brain,
As I gaze into the wintry dark
Through the blurred and blackened pane:
Far memories of golden hours
That will not come again,—
Alas,
That never will come again.

Wild woodland odors wander by—
Warm breath of new-mown hay—
I hear the broad, brown river flow,
Half-hid in bowering May;
While eyes of love look through my soul,
As on that last sweet day;
But a chilly shadow floats between
That will not pass away—
Ah, no,
That never will pass away.

## ROBERT LEIGHTON (1822–1869)

### The Dried-Up Fountain

Outside the village, by the public road,
I know a dried-up fountain, overgrown
With herbs, the haunt of legendary toad,
And grass, by nature sown.

I know not where its trickling life was stilled;
No living ears its babbling tongue has caught;
But often, as I pass, I see it filled
And running oer with thought.

I see it as it was in days of old,
The blue-eyed maiden stooping oer its brim,
And smoothing in its glass her locks of gold,
Lest she should meet with him.

She knows that he is near, yet I can see
Her sweet confusion when she hears him come.

No tryst had they, though every evening he
Carries her pitchers home.

The ancient beggar limps along the road
At thirsty noon, and rests him by its brink.
The dusty peddler lays aside his load,
And pauses there to drink.

And there the village children come to play,
When busy parents work in shop and field.
The swallows, too, find there the loamy clay
When neath the eaves they build.

When cows at eve come crooning home, the boy
Leaves them to drink, while his mechanic skill
Within the brook sets up, with inward joy,
His tiny water mill.

And when the night is hushed in summer sleep,
And rest has come to laborer and team,
I hear the runnel through the long grass creep,
As twere a whispering dream.

Alas, tis all a dream. Lover and lass,
Children and wanderers, are in their graves;
And where the fountain flowed a greener grass—
Its *In Memoriam* —waves.

## Scotch Words

They speak in riddles north beyond the Tweed.
The plain, pure English they can deftly read;
Yet when without the book they come to speak,
Their lingo seems half English and half Greek.

Their jaws are *chafts*; their hands, when closed, are *neives*;
Their bread's not cut in slices, but in *sheives*;
Their armpits are their *oxters*; palms are *luifs*;
Their men are *cheilds*; their timid fools are *cuiffs*;
Their lads are *callants*, and their women *kimmers*;
Good lasses *denty queans*, and bad ones *limmers*.
They *thole* when they endure, *scart* when they scratch;
And when they give a sample it's a *swatch*.
Scolding is *flytin'*, and a long palaver
Is nothing but a *blether* or a *haver*.
This room they call the *but*, and that the *ben*;[1]
And what they do not know they *dinna ken*.
On keen cold days they say the *wind blaws snell*.
And when they wipe their nose they *dicht their byke*;
And they have words that Johnson could not spell,

[1] Outer and inner rooms (of a two-room cottage).

As *umph'm*, which means—anything you like;
While some, though purely English, and well known,
Have yet a Scottish meaning of their own:—
To *prig's* to plead, beat down a thing in cost;
To *coff's* to purchase, and a cough's a *host*;
To *crack* is to converse; the *lift's* the sky;
And *bairns* are said to *greet* when children cry.
When lost, folk never ask the way they want—
They *speir the gate*; and when they yawn they *gaunt*.
Beetle with them is *clock*; a flame's a *lowe*;
Their straw is *strae*, chaff *cauff*, and hollow *howe*;
A *pickle* means a few; *muckle* is big,
And a piece of crockeryware is called a *pig*.

Speaking of pigs—when Lady Delacour
Was on her celebrated Scottish tour,
One night she made her quarters at the "Crown,"
The head inn of a well known county town,
The chambermaid, on lighting her to bed,
Before withdrawing curtsied low, and said—
"This nicht is cauld, my leddy, wad ye please,
To hae a pig i' the bed to warm your taes?"
"A pig in bed to tease! What's that you say?
You are impertinent—away, away!"
"Me impudent! no, mem—I meant nae harm,
But just the greybeard pig to keep ye warm."
"Insolent Hussy, to confront me so!
This very instant shall your mistress know.
The bell—there's none, of course—go, send her here."
"My mistress, mem, I dinna need to fear;
In sooth, it was hersel' that bade me speir.
Nae insult, mem; we thocht ye wad be gled,
On this cauld nicht, to hae a pig i' the bed."
"Stay, girl; your words are strangely out of place,
And yet I see no insult in your face.
Is it a custom in your country, then,
For ladies to have pigs in bed wi' them?"
"Oh, quite a custom wi' the gentles, mem—
Wi' gentle ladies, ay, and gentle men;
And, troth, if single, they wad sairly miss
Their het pig on a cauldrife nicht like this."
"I've seen strange countries—but this surely beats
Their rudest makeshift for a warming pan.
Suppose, my girl, I should adopt your plan,
You would not put the pig between the sheets?"
"Surely, my leddy, and nae itherwhere:
Please, mem, ye'll find it do the maist guid there."
"Fie, fie, twould dirty them, and if I keep
In fear of that, you know, I shall not sleep."
"Ye'll sleep far better, mem. Tak my advice;
The nicht blaws snell—the sheets are cauld as ice;
I'll fetch ye up a fine, warm, cozy pig;
I'll mak ye sae comfortable and trig*, snug

Wi' coortains, blankets, every kind o' hap,
And warrant ye to sleep as soond's a tap.
As for the fylin* o' the sheets—dear me, "defiling"
The pig's as clean outside as pig can be,
A weel-closed mooth's eneuch for ither folk,
But if ye like, I'll put it in a poke."
"But, Effie—that's your name, I think you said—
Do you, yourself, now, take a pig to bed?"
"Na, na mem, pigs are only for the great,
Wha lie on feather beds, and sit up late.
Feathers and pigs are no for puir riff-raff—
Me and my neibour lassie lies on cauff."
"What's that—a calf! If I your sense can gather,
You and the other lassie sleep together,
Two in a bed, and with the calf between:
That, I suppose, my girl, is what you mean?"
"Na, na, my leddy—'od ye're jokin noo—
We sleep thegither, that is very true—
But nocht between us: wi' our claes all aff,
Except our sarks, we lie upon the cauff."
"Well, well, girl, I am surprised to hear
That we of English habits live so near
Such barbarous customs.—Effie, you may go:
As for the pig, I thank you, but—no, no—
Ha, ha, good night—excuse me if I laugh—
I'd rather be without both pig and calf."

On the return of Lady Delacour,
She wrote a book about her northern tour,
Wherein the facts are graphically told,
That Scottish gentlefolks, when nights are cold,
Take into bed fat pigs to keep them warm;
While common folk, who share their beds in halves—
Denied the richer comforts of the farm—
Can only warm their sheets with lean, cheap calves.

## WILLIAM MURDOCH (1823- ? )

### The Bagpipes

Let ither poets rave and rant,
How fiddles can the saul enchant,
How harps and organs lift the sant
To heaven aboon;
For me, my lugs* I winna grant ears
To siclike din.

The swelling horn, and sounding drum,
Yield pleasing notes nae doubt to some,
And chields* wha at pianos thrum, fellows
Think nought's sae braw*; fine

But Scotland's skirling bagpipes' bum
Is worth them a'.

O, weel I loe the martial strains,
That swelled our forbears' hearts and veins,
And led them on through reeking plains
O' death and gore,
To drive oppression, and its chains,
Frae Scotia's shore.

Foul fa' the Scot o' modern days,
Wha kens o' Scotland's former waes,
Can tamely sit, while Donald plays
A pibroch[1] peal;
Nor feels his bosom in a blaze
O' patriot zeal.

In yore, when Roman lads were boun'
To rieve* us o' our royal crown, rob
Frae Highland hills our sires came doun
To deadly gripes;
Fired by the bauld inspiring soun'
O' Scotland's pipes,

And weel the Dane and Roman chiels
Kenned when they heard the bagpipe's peals,
That Donald was upon their heels
In martial raw*; "row"
Sae faith they took to southern fiel's
And were na slaw.

The Saxon thocht he micht afford
To reign supreme, as Scotland's lord;
Sae poured his troops, horde after horde,
On Scottish plains;
And claimed dominion by the sword,
Oer our domains.

His flags were waving on ilk height,
When stern, undaunted, Wallace wight,
His claymore waved for freedom's right
And Scotland's weal;
And dared proud Edward's vaunted might
In mony a fiel'.

---

[1]The classic bagpipe music.

He led his men to battle's brunt,
The pipers marching at the front,
Wi' stirring peal and solemn grunt
They cheered the way,
Nor tarried, be't for brose* or strunt*, whisky
Till banged the fae.

And syne, when Bruce displayed his ranks
For battle on red Bannock's banks,
He placed the pipers at the flanks,
Wha blew sae weel,
That trembling seized the southron shanks,
And played the deil.

They couldna bide the clours*, and paicks, blows
That showered frae our Lochaber aix;
They shook, as coward only shakes
When touched by steel.
Then cursed our land o' hills and cakes,
And fled the fiel'.

And when that shout o' victory rose,
Which rent the veil o' Scottish woes,
The swelling pibroch spurred our foes
To quicker bound,
And stamped the land where Bannock flows
As sacred ground.

Thy bagpipes, Scotland, lang hae been
Thy vera best and truest frien',
On bluidy field or dewy green,
At gloamings gray,
When lads and lasses wad convene
To dance and play.

When charmed by our dear bagpipes' din,
What ither race beneath the sun
Can match our hardy Highland kin
At reel or jig?
They loup, and fling, and jink, and rin,
Nor ever lig.

But change the tune to martial air,
Their shouts will mak the mountains rair;
Their courage danger ne'er could scare,
When Scotland's guid
Required their helps, or aiblins* mair, perhaps
Their very bluid.

Just sound one swelling pibroch peal,
And say Victoria needs their steel,
Nae twa ways then; ilk hardy chiel
His kilt puts on,
And bids his native hills fareweel
Without a groan.

And when they meet their country's faes,
Their courage kindles to a blaze;
See Scotland's gallant, daring "Grays"
And Forty-twa,
Lead on the charge, that winged the days
O' Bonna's fa'.

"These kilted savages," he swore,
"That came from Scotland's rocky shore—
Stern, as their fathers were in yore,
With dirk and plaid—
Have grieved my gallant heroes more
Than ought beside."

And see them on the Crimean plains,
Where slavery still eternal reigns;
Nae odds could cool their boiling veins,
Nor quench their zeal;
The rust of cowardice ne'er stains
The Scottish steel.

My country's pipes! while life is mine
I'll love thy strains, as air divine;
Linked as ye are wi' auld langsyne,
My Scottish heart,
Though frae you sundered by the brine,
Will never part.

And when on death's cold beir I'm laid,
Let pipers round me serenade;
And wrap me in a Scottish plaid
For sheet and shroud;
And oer my grave be tribute paid
*One pibroch, loud.*

## Address to My Auld Blue Bonnet

Let fools wi' muckle purses haver* blather
Bout hats o' silk, or costly beaver,
And flirts o' beaux and menseless* chaps foolish
Brag oer their one-pound-four light naps;

But nane o' them deserves a sonnet
Sae much as you, my auld blue bonnet.
For mony years noo past and gane
Ye've happed my pow* frae wind and rain; head
The equinoxial gales micht blaw,
The lammas tide in torrents fa';
Auld winter too micht show his form,
Deep wrapped in clouds, and clothed in storm,
Wi' frost, hail, snaw, and blashy sleet,
Shroud nature like a winding sheet,
But capped by thee, my bonnet blue,
His storms as yet I've wuddled through,
Nor cared I for his wrath a bodle*, (small coin)
Ye lent sic comfort to my noddle.
Since first ye left thy native toon,
Sae famed for nicht-caps and for shoon,
Richt mony ups and downs I've seen,
Wi' pleasant blinks* at times between; glances
I've tasted bliss, I've shed saut tears,
I've sprung frae youth to manhood's years,
I've wandered far, I've wandered wide,
Frae hame, and a' I loved beside;
But thanks to fate, I'm here again,
Snug seated by my ain hearthstane.
Dear comrade of my youthful glee,
What memories fond are linked wi' thee.
What joyous transports have I felt
When at the shrine of love I knelt,
And sued, nor did I sue in vain,
For Meg's love in return again.
O happy, mair than happy days,
When mang fair Cart's green banks and braes,
On gloamings gray I wont to stroll,
Wi' her whose love enwrapt my soul.
I sighed a' day, and dreamed a' nicht,
And she, poor thing, was never richt,
Till baith grew tired o' living single,
And bairns noo ramp around our ingle*. fireside
An' still I bless the page o' life
That gied me Peggy for a wife.

My guid auld frien', it maks me wae,
That fashions should be changing sae;
In youth ye was my very pride,
Ye was sae braw, sae blue, and wide;
Gang whar I micht, be't up, be't down,
Ye was my comforter an' crown.
Ilk height and howe*, ilk moss and moor, low

Tween this and Scotland's southern shore,
And far awa mong Highland shiels*, cottages
I've trod wi' thee and blistered heels;
But noo, alake, my guid auld frien',
Nae gate* wi' thee daur I be seen. way
Or modern folks will jibe and joke,
And ca' thee beggar's aumos* pock. alms
Ochon-a-nee, and lack-a-day,
That e'er we should grow auld or gray.
Poor worn-out men, and threadbare claes,
Are no the things for noo-a-days.
When young, and strong, and fit for use,
They're aye made welcome in the house,
But ance turn auld, be't man or bonnet,
The fire or hook they're taught to shun it,
By youthful pomp, and youthful pride,
Like auld worn boots they're cast aside,
Or aiblins* sent, for guid or ill, perhaps
To almshouse or the carding mill.
Sae gae your wa's, ye're out o' date,
And e'en maun just submit to fate.
My conscience winna let me steer ye,
And fashion says I maunna wear ye,
Sae we maun part, and nae remeid*, "remedy"
But buy a beaver in your stead,
And swap you wi' some gangrel* body, vagabond
For tea-cup, or a dish for crowdy*; (oatmeal)
But aye whene'er I glance upon it,
I'll mind o' you—my auld blue bonnet.

## GEORGE MACDONALD (1824–1905)

[The writings of George MacDonald are dominated by Christian mysticism. MacDonald, unable to accept the limitations required for belief in a specific church, resigned his position as a Congregationalist minister, and supported his wife and eleven children by his writing, lectures and free-lance preaching. His books are a bizarre combination of realistic observation—especially of the Scottish scene—of conventional melodrama, and of religious fervor. Virtually all of his many novels contain scenes of exceptional insight and power, though their clumsy structures and religious intensity have attracted few readers in our time. His children's books and fantasies have worn better. In each category he is a major figure. "The Golden Key" has won a place as a classic of fantasy. Clearly it is an allegory. There is a general critical agreement that the "key" itself represents faith. Beyond that—every man for himself. As the following attest, MacDonald is also a poet of real charm.]

### What the Auld Fowk Are Thinkin

The bairns i' their beds, worn oot wi' nae wark,
Are sleepin, nor ever an eelid winkin;

The auld fowk lie still wi' their een starin stark,
An' the mirk pang-fou* o' the things they are thinkin. stuffed full

Whan oot o' ilk corner the bairnies they keek*, peep
Lauchin an' daffin*, airms loosin an' linkin, fooling
The auld fowk they watch frae the warm ingle*-cheek, fireside
But the bairns little think what the auld fowk are thinkin.

Whan the auld fowk sit quaiet at the reet* o' a stook*, (foot)/ "stalk"
I' the sunlicht their washt een blinterin an' blinkin,
Fowk scythin, or bin'in, or shearin wi' heuk
Carena a strae what the auld fowk are thinkin.

At the kirk, whan the minister's dreich* an' dry, dreary
His fardens as gien* they were gowd guineas chinkin, "gin" (if)
An' the young fowk are noddin, or fidgetin sly,
Naebody kens what the auld fowk are thinkin.

When the young fowk are greitin* about the bed weeping
Whaur like water through san' the auld life is sinkin,
An' some wud say the last word was said,
The auld fowk smile, an' ken what they're thinkin.

## Song of the Summer Days

A morn of winds and swaying trees—
Earth's jubilance rushing out!
The birds are fighting with the breeze;
The waters heave about.

White clouds are swept across the sky,
Their shadows oer the graves;
Purpling the green, they float and fly
Athwart the sunny waves.

The long grass—an earth-rooted sea—
Mimics the watery strife.
To boat or horse? Wild motion we
Shall find harmonious life.

But whither? Roll and sweep and bend
Suffice for Nature's part;
But motion to an endless end
Is needful for our heart.

## Songs of the Autumn Night

O Night, send up the harvest moon
To walk about the corn;
To make of midnight magic noon,
And ripen on till morn.

In golden ranks, with golden crowns,
All in the yellow land,
Old solemn kings in rustling gowns,
The sheaves moon-charmed stand.

Sky-mirror she, afloat in space,
Beholds our coming morn.
Her heavenly joy hath such a grace,
It ripens earthly corn.

Like some lone saint with upward eyes,
Lost in the deeps of prayer;
The people still their prayers and sighs,
And gazing ripen there.

So, like the corn, moon-ripened last,
Would I weary and gray,
On golden memories ripen fast,
And ripening pass away.

In an old night so let me die;
A slow wind out of doors;
A waning moon low in the sky;
A vapor on the moors;

A fire just dying in the gloom
Earth haunted all with dreams;
A sound of waters in the room;
A mirror's moony gleams;

And near me, in the sinking night,
More thoughts than move in me,
Forgiving wrong, and loving right,
And waiting till I see.

## Song of the Spring Days

Blow on me, wind, from west and south;
Sweet summer-spirit, blow.
Come like a kiss from dear child's mouth,
Who knows not what I know.

The earth's perfection dawneth soon;
Ours lingereth alway.
We have a morning, not a noon;
Spring, but no summer gay.

Rose-blotted eve, gold-branded morn
Crown soon the swift year's life.
In us a higher hope is born,
And claims a longer strife.

Will heaven be an eternal spring
With summer at the door?
Or shall we one day tell its king
That we desire no more?

## Gaein' and Comin'

Whan Andrew frae Strathbogie gaed,
The lift* was lowerin' dreary, sky
The sun he wadna raise his heid,
The wind was laigh* and eerie. low
In's pooch he had a plack* or twa, (small coin)
I vow he hadna mony;
Yet Andrew likes a hearty sang,
For Lizzy was sae bonnie.
O Lizzie, Lizzie, bonnie lassie,
Bonnie gaucy* hizzie. handsome
What richt had ye to luik at me,
And drive me daft and dizzy?

When Andrew to Strathbogie cam',
The sun was shinin' rarely;
He rode a horse that pranced and sprang—
I vow he sat him fairly.
And he had gowd to spend and spare,
And a heart as true as ony;
But's luik was doon, and his sigh was sair,
For Lizzie was sae bonny.
O Lizzie, Lizzie, bonny hizzie,
You've turned the daylicht dreary,
Ye're straught and rare, ye're fause and fair,
Hech! auld John Armstrong's deary.

## Ane by Ane

Ane by ane they gang awa',
The Gatherer gathers great an' sma,
Ane by ane maks ane an' a'.

Aye when ane sets doun the cup,
Ane ahint* maun tak it up, behind
Yet thegither they will sup.

Golden-heided, ripe an' strang,
Shorn will be the hairst* ere lang, harvest
Syne begins a better sang.

## Mammon Marriage

The croak of a raven hoar,
A dog's howl, kennel-tied.
Loud shuts the carriage-door.

The two are away on their ghastly ride
To Death's salt shore.

Where are the love and the grace?
The bridegroom is thirsty and cold.
The bride's skull sharpens her face.
But the coachman is driving, jubilant, bold,
The devil's pace.

The horses shivered and shook
Waiting gaunt and haggard
With sorry and evil look;
But swift as a drunken wind they staggered
'Longst Lethe brook.

Long since, they ran no more;
Heavily pulling they died
On the sand of the hopeless shore
Where never swelled or sank a tide,
And the salt burns sore.

Flat their skeletons lie,
White shadows on shining sand.
The crusted reins go high
To the crumbling coachman's bony hand
On his knees awry.

Side by side, jarring no more,
Day and night side by side,
Each by a doorless door,
Motionless sit the bridegroom and bride
On the Dead-Sea shore.

## Why Do the Houses Stand

Why do the houses stand
When they that built them are gone;
When remaineth even of one
That lived there and loved and planned
Not a face, not an eye, not a hand,
Only here and there a bone?
Why do the houses stand
When they who built them are gone?
Oft in the moonlighted land
When the day is overblown,
With happy memorial moan
Sweet ghosts in a loving band
Roam through the houses that stand—
For the builders are not gone.

## The Earl o' Quarterdeck
### A New Old Ballad

The wind it blew, and the ship it flew;
And it was "Hey for hame!
And ho for hame!" But the skipper cried,
"Haud her oot oer the saut sea faem."

Then up and spoke the king himsel':
"Haud on for Dumferline!"
Quo the skipper, "Ye're king upo' the land—
I'm king upo' the brine."

And he took the helm intil his hand,
And he steered the ship sae free;
Wi' the wind astarn, he crowded sail,
And stood right out to sea.

Quo the king, "There's treason in this, I vow;
This is something underhand!
'Bout ship." Quo the skipper, "Yer grace forgets
Ye are king but o' the land!"

And still he held to the open sea;
And the east-wind sank behind;
And the west had a bitter word to say,
Wi' a white-sea roarin' wind.

And he turned her head into the north.
Said the king: "Gar fling him oer."
Quo the fearless skipper: "It's a' ye're worth!
Ye'll ne'er see Scotland more."

The king crept down the cabin-stair,
To drink the gude French wine.
And up she came, his daughter fair,
And luikit ower the brine.

She turned her face to the drivin' hail,
To the hail but and the weet;
Her snood* it brak, and, as lang's hersel', kerchief
Her hair drave out i' the sleet.

She turned her face frae the drivin' win'—
"What's that ahead?" quo she.
The skipper he threw himsel' frae the win',
And he drove the helm a-lee.

"Put to yer hand, my lady fair!
Put to yer hand," quo he;
"Gin she dinna face the win' the mair,
It's the waur for you and me."

For the skipper kenned that strength is strength,
Whether woman's or man's at last.
To the tiller the lady she laid her han',
And the ship laid her cheek to the blast.

For that slender body was full o' soul,
And the will is mair than shape;
As the skipper saw when they cleared the berg,
And he heard her quarter scrape.

Quo the skipper: "Ye are a lady fair,
And a princess grand to see;
But ye are a woman, and a man wad sail
To hell in yer company."

She liftit a pale and queenly face;
Her een flashed, and syne they swim.
"And what for no to heaven?" she says,
And she turned awa' frae him.

But she took na her han' frae the good ship's helm,
Until the day did daw;
And the skipper he spak, but what he said
It was said atween them twa.

And then the good ship she lay to,
With the land far on the lee;
And up came the king upo' the deck,
Wi' wan face and bluidshot ee.

The skipper he louted* to the king: bowed
"Gae wa', gae wa'," said the king.
Said the king, like a prince, "I was a' wrang,
Put on this ruby ring."

Then the wind blew lowne*, and the stars cam' oot, softly
And the ship turned to the shore:
And, afore the sun was up again,
They saw Scotland ance more.

That day the ship hung at the pier-heid,
And the king he stept on the land.
"Skipper, kneel down," the king he said,
"Hoo daur ye afore me stand?"

The skipper he louted on his knee,
The king his blade he drew.
Said the king, "Haw daured ye contre me?
I'm aboard my ain ship noo.

"I canna mak ye a king," said he,
"For the Lord alone can do that;

And besides ye took it intil yer ain han'
And crooned yersel' sae pat!

"But wi' what ye will I redeem my ring;
For ance I am at your beck.
And first, as ye loutit Skipper o' Doon,
Rise up Yerl o' Quarterdeck."

The skipper he rose and looked at the king
In his een for all his croon;
Said the skipper, "Here is yer grace's ring,
And yer daughter is my boon."

The reid blude sprang into the king's face,—
A wrathful man to see.
"The rascal loon abuses our grace;
Gae hang him upon yon tree."

But the skipper he sprang aboard his ship,
And he drew his biting blade;
And he struck the chain that held her fast,
But the iron was ower weel made.

And the king he blew a whistle loud;
And tramp, tramp, down the pier,
Cam' twenty riders on twenty steeds,
Clankin' wi' spur and spear.

"He saved your life!" cried the lady fair;
"His life ye daurna spill!"
"Will ye come atween me and my hate?"
Quo the lady, "And that I will!"

And on cam' the knights wi' spur and spear,
For they heard the iron ring.
"Gin ye care na for yer father's grace,
Mind ye that I am the king."

"I kneel to my father for his grace,
Right lowly on my knee;
But I stand and look the king in the face,
For the skipper is king o' me."

She turned and she sprang upo' the deck,
And the cable splashed in the sea.
The good ship spread her wings sae white,
And away with the skipper goes she.

Now was not this a king's daughter,
And a brave lady beside?
And a woman with whom a man might sail
Into the heaven wi' pride?

## A Prayer

When I look back upon my life nigh spent,
Nigh spent, although the stream as yet flows on,
I more of follies than of sins repent,
Less for offense than love's shortcomings moan.
With self, O Father, leave me not alone—
Leave not with the beguiler the beguiled.
Besmirched and ragged, Lord, take back thine own.
A fool I bring thee to be made a child.

## Travelers' Song

Bands of dark and bands of light
Lie athwart the homeward way.
Now we cross a belt of night,
Now a strip of shining day.

Now it is a month of June,
Now December's shivering hour.
Now rides high loved memories' moon,
Now the dark is dense with power.

Summers, winters, days, and nights,
Moons, and clouds, they come and go;
Joys and sorrows, pains, delights,
Hope and fear, and yes and no.

All is well: come, girls and boys,
Not a weary mile is vain.
Hark—dim laughter's radiant noise!
See the windows through the rain.

## Light

Thou art the joy of age.
Thy sun is dear when long the shadow falls.
Forth to its friendliness the old man crawls,
And, like the bird hung out in his poor cage
To gather song from radiance, in his chair
Sits by the door; and sitteth there
His soul within him, like a child that lies
Half dreaming, with half-open eyes,
At close of a long afternoon in summer—
High ruins round him, ancient ruins, where
The raven is almost the only comer;
Half dreams, half broods, in wonderment
At thy celestial descent,
Through rifted loops alighting on the gold
That waves its bloom in many an airy rent.
So dreams the old man's soul, that is not old,
But sleepy mid the ruins that enfold.
  What soul-like changes, evanescent moods,

Upon the face of the still passive earth,
Its hills, and fields, and woods,
Thou with thy seasons and thy hours art ever calling forth.
Even like a lord of music bent
Over his instrument,
Who gives to tears and smiles an equal birth.
When clear as holiness the morning ray
Casts the rock's dewy darkness at its feet,
Mottling with shadows all the mountain gray;
When, at the hour of sovereign noon,
Infinite silent cataracts sheet
Shadowless through the air of thunder-breeding June;
And when a yellower glory slanting passes
Twixt longer shadows oer the meadow grasses;
When now the moon lifts up her shining shield,
High on the peak of a cloud-hill revealed;
Now crescent, low, wandering sun-dazed away,
Unconscious of her own star-mingled ray,
Her still face seeming more to think than see,
Makes the pale world lie dreaming dreams of thee.
No mood of mind, no melody of soul,
But lies within thy silent soft control
Of operative single power,
And simple unity the one emblem,

Yet all the colors that our passionate eyes devour,
In rainbow, moonbow, or in opal gem,
Are the melodious descant of divided thee.
Lo thee in yellow sands, lo thee
In the blue air and sea,
In the green corn, with scarlet poppies lit.
Thy half souls parted, patient thou dost sit.
Lo thee in speechless glories of the west;
Lo thee in dewdrop's tiny breast.
Thee on the vast white cloud that floats away,
Bearing upon its skirt a brown moon ray.
Regent of color, thou dost fling
Thy over flowing skill on everything.
The thousand hues and shades upon the flowers
Are all the pastime of thy leisure hours;
And all the jeweled ores in mines that hidden be
Are dead till touched by thee.

## I Dreamed That I Woke From a Dream

I dreamed that I woke from a dream,
And the house was full of light.
At the window two angel sorrows
Held back the curtains of night.

The door was wide, and the house
Was full of the morning wind.

At the door two armed warders
Stood silent, with faces blind.

I ran to the open door,
For the wind of the world was sweet.
The warders with crossing weapons
Turned back my issuing feet.

I ran to the shining windows—
There the winged sorrows stood.
Silent they held the curtains,
And the light fell through in a flood.

I clomb to the highest window—
Ah, there, with shadowed brow,
Stood one lonely, radiant sorrow,
And that, my love, was thou.

## O Lassie Ayont the Hill

O lassie ayont* the hill, beyond
Come ower the tap o' the hill,
Or roun' the neuk o' the hill,
For I want ye sair the nicht,
I'm needin' ye sair the nicht,
For I'm tired and sick o' mysel',
A body's sel' 's the sairest weicht—
O lassie come owre the hill.

Gin a body could be a thocht o' grace,
And no a sel' ava!
I'm sick o my heid, and my han's, and my face,
An' my thochts and mysel' and a'.
I'm sick o' the warl' and a';
The licht gangs by wi' a hiss;
For through my een the sunbeams fa';
But my weary heart they miss.

O lassie ayont the hill,
Come owre the tap o' the hill,
Or roun' the neuk o' the hill;
Bidena ayont the hill.

For gin* ance I saw yer bonnie heid, if
And the sunlicht o' yer hair,
The ghaist o' mysel' wad fa' doun deid;
I wad be mysel' nae mair,
I wad be mysel' nae mair,
Filled o' the sole remeid*; remedy

Slain by the arrows o' licht frae yer hair,
Killed by yer body and heid.

But gin ye lo'ed me ever sae sma,
For the sake o' my bonnie dame,
Whan I cam' to life, as she gaed awa,
I could bide my body and name,
I micht bide by mysel' the weary same;
Aye setting up its heid
Till I turn frae the claes that cover my frame,
As gin they war roun' the deid.

But gin ye lo'ed me as I loe you,
I wad ring my ain deid knell;
Mysel' wad vanish, shot through and through
Wi' the shine o' yer sunny sel',
By the licht aneath yer broo,
I wad dee to mysel', and ring my bell,
And only live in you.

O lassie ayont the hill,
Come ower the tap o' the hill,
Or roun' the neuk o' the hill,
For I want ye sair the nicht,
I'm needin' ye sair the nicht,
For I'm tired and sick o' mysel',
A body's sel' 's the sairest weicht—
O lassie come owre the hill.

## The Sheep and the Goat

The thousand streets of London gray
Repel all country sights;
But bar not winds upon their way,
Nor quench the scent of new-mown hay
In depth of summer nights.

And here and there an open spot,
Still bare to light and dark,
With grass receives the wanderer hot;
There trees are growing, houses not—
They call the place a park.

Soft creatures, with ungentle guides,
God's sheep from hill and plain,
Flow thitherward in fitful tides,
There weary lie on woolly sides,
Or crop the grass amain.

And from dark alley, yard, and den,
In ragged skirts and coats,
Troop hither tiny sons of men,
Wild things, untaught of word or pen—
The little human goats.

In Regent's Park one cloudless day,
An overdriven sheep,
Arrived from long and dusty way,
Throbbing with thirst and hotness lay,
A panting woolen heap.

But help is nearer than we know
For ills of every name:
Ragged enough to scare the crow,
But with a heart to pity woe,
A quick-eyed urchin came.

Little he knew of field or fold,
Yet knew what ailed; his cap
Was ready cup for water cold;
Though rumpled, stained, and very old,
Its rents were small—good hap!

Shaping the rim and crown he went,
Till crown from rim was deep.
The water gushed from pore and rent.
Before he came one half was spent—
The other saved the sheep.

O little goat, born, bred in ill,
Unwashed, half-fed, unshorn,
Thou to the sheep from breezy hill
Wast bishop, pastor, what you will,
In London dry and lorn.

And let priests say the thing they please,
My hope, though very dim,
Thinks he will say who always sees,
In doing it to one of these
Thou didst it unto him.

## The Waesome Carl

There cam a man to our toon-en',
An' a waesome carl* was he; churl
Snipie-nebbit*, and crookit-mou'd, beaked
And gleyt o' ae blinterin ee.

Muckle he spied, and muckle he spak,
But the owercome o' his sang,
Whatever the tune, was aye the same:—
There's nane o' ye a' but's wrang.

Ye're a' wrang, and a' wrang,
And a'thegither a' wrang;
There's no a man aboot the toon
But's a'thegither a' wrang.

That's no the gait* to fire the breid, — way
Nor yet to brew the yill*; — ale
That's no the gait to hand the pleuch,
Nor yet to ca' the mill;
That's no the gait to milk the coo,
Nor yet to spean* the calf; — wean
Nor yet to tramp the girnel-meal—
Ye kenna yer wark by half!

The minister wasna fit to pray,
And lat alane to preach.
Ne nowther had the gift o' grace,
Nor yet the gift o' speech.
He mind't him o' Balaam's ass,
Wi' a differ ye may ken.
The Lord he opened the ass's mou',
The minister opened's ain.

The puir precentor cudna sing,
He gruntit like a swine.
The verra elders cudna pass
The ladles till* his min'. — to
And for the rulin'-elder's grace,
It wasna worth a horn.
He didna half uncurse the meat,
Nor pray for mair the morn.

And aye he gied his nose a thraw*, — twist
And aye he crook't his mou';
And aye he cockit up his ee,
And said—Tak tent* the noo. — care
We snichert hint* oor loof*, man, — behind/hand
But never said him nay;
As gin* he had been a prophet, man, — if
We loot him say his say.

Quo oor gudeman: The crater's daft—
Heard ye ever sic a claik*? — (bird-cry)

Lat's see gin he can turn a han',
Or only luik and craik*. "croak"
It's true we maunna lippen* till him— trust
He's fairly crack wi' pride;
But he maun live—we canna kill him—
Gin he can work, he's bide.

It's true it's but a laddie's turn,
But we'll begin wi' a sma thing:
There's a' thae weyds to gaither and burn—
And he's the man for a' thing!
We yokit for yon heich peat-moss—
There was peats to cast and ca'—
Weel rid, we reckon, o' him and his
Lang tongue till gloamin'-fa'.

For, losh, or* it was denner time, "ere"
The toon was in a low*! blaze
The reek rase up as it had been
Frae Sodom-flames, I vow.
We lowst* and rade like mad, for byre let go
And ruck war blazin' fell,
As gin the deil had brocht the fire
To mak anither hell.

And there, on-luikin', the carl stude,
Wi' 's han's aneath his tails.
To see him maisthan' drave us wud*, mad
We ill could haud oorsels.
It's a' your wit*; I tauld ye sae. fault
Ye're a' wrang to the last.
What gart ye burn thae deevilich weyds
Whan the win' blew frae the wast?

Ye're a' wrang, and a' wrang,
And a'thegither a' wrang;
There's no a man in a' the warl'
But's a'thegither a' wrang.

## Annie She's Dowie

Annie she's dowie*, and Willie he's wae. sad
What can be the maitter wi' siccan a twae—
For Annie she's fair as the first o' the day,
And Willie he's honest and stalwart and gay?

Oh, the tane has a daddy is poor and is proud,
And the tither a minnie that cleiks at the goud.

They lo'ed ane anither, and said their say—
But the daddy and minnie they pairtit the twae.

## The Golden Key

There was a boy who used to sit in the twilight and listen to his great-aunt's stories.

She told him that if he could reach the place where the end of the rainbow stands, he would find there a golden key.

"And what is the key for?" the boy would ask. "What is it the key of? What will it open?"

"That nobody knows," his aunt would reply. "He has to find that out."

"I suppose, being gold," the boy once said, thoughtfully, "that I could get a good deal of money for it if I sold it."

"Better never find it than sell it," returned his aunt.

And then the boy went to bed and dreamed about the golden key.

Now all that his great-aunt told the boy about the golden key would have been nonsense, had it not been that their little house stood on the borders of Fairyland. For it is perfectly well known that out of Fairyland nobody ever can find where the rainbow stands. The creature takes such good care of its golden key, always flitting from place to place, lest any one should find it! But in Fairyland it is quite different. Things that look real in this country look very thin indeed in Fairyland, while some of the things that here cannot stand still for a moment, will not move there. So it was not in the least absurd of the old lady to tell her nephew such things about the golden key.

"Did you ever know anybody find it?" he asked, one evening.

"Yes. Your father, I believe, found it."

"And what did he do with it, can you tell me?"

"He never told me."

"What was it like?"

"He never showed it to me."

"How does a new key come there always?"

"I don't know. There it is."

"Perhaps it is the rainbow's egg."

"Perhaps it is. You will be a happy boy if you find the nest."

"Perhaps it comes tumbling down the rainbow from the sky."

"Perhaps it does."

One evening, in summer, he went into his own room, and stood at the lattice-window, and gazed into the forest which fringed the outskirts of Fairyland. It came close up to his great-aunt's garden, and, indeed, sent some straggling trees into it. The forest lay to the east, and the sun, which was setting behind the cottage, looked straight into the dark wood with his level red eye. The trees were all old, and had few branches below, so that the sun could see a great way into the forest and the boy, being keen-sighted, could see almost as far as the sun. The trunks stood like rows of red columns in the shine of the red sun, and he could see down aisle after aisle in the vanishing distance. And as he gazed into the forest he began to feel as if the trees were all waiting for him, and had something they could not go on with till he came to them. But he was hungry, and wanted his supper. So he lingered.

Suddenly, far among the trees, as far as the sun could shine, he saw a glorious thing. It was the end of a rainbow, large and brilliant. He could count all the seven colors, and could see shade after shade beyond the violet; while before the red stood a color more gorgeous and mysterious still. It was a color he had never seen before.

Only the spring of the rainbow-arch was visible. He could see nothing of it above the trees.

"The golden key!" he said to himself, and darted out of the house, and into the wood.

He had not gone far before the sun set. But the rainbow only glowed the brighter. For the rainbow of Fairyland is not dependent upon the sun, as ours is. The trees welcomed him. The bushes made way for him. The rainbow grew larger and brighter; and at length he found himself within two trees of it.

It was a grand sight, burning away there in silence, with its gorgeous, its lovely, its delicate colors, each distinct, all combining. He could now see a great deal more of it. It rose high into the blue heavens, but bent so little that he could not tell how high the crown of the arch must reach. It was still only a small portion of a huge bow.

He stood gazing at it till he forgot himself with delight—even forgot the key which he had come to seek. And as he stood it grew more wonderful still. For in each of the colors, which was as large as the column of a church, he could faintly see beautiful forms slowly ascending as if by the steps of a winding stair. The forms appeared irregularly—now one, now many, now several, now none—men and women and children—all different, all beautiful.

He drew nearer to the rainbow. It vanished. He started back a step in dismay. It was there again, as beautiful as ever. So he contented himself with standing as near it as he might, and watching the forms that ascended the glorious colors towards the unknown height of the arch, which did not end abruptly, but faded away in the blue air; so gradually that he could not say where it ceased.

When the thought of the golden key returned, the boy very wisely proceeded to mark out in his mind the space covered by the foundation of the rainbow, in order that he might know where to search, should the rainbow disappear. It was based chiefly upon a bed of moss.

Meantime it had grown quite dark in the wood. The rainbow alone was visible by its own light. But the moment the moon rose the rainbow vanished. Nor could any change of place restore the vision to the boy's eyes. So he threw himself down upon the mossy bed, to wait till the sunlight would give him a chance of finding the key. There he fell fast asleep.

When he woke in the morning the sun was looking straight into his eyes. He turned away from it, and the same moment saw a brilliant little thing lying on the moss within a foot of his face. It was the golden key. The pipe of it was of plain gold, as bright as gold could be. The handle was curiously wrought and set with sapphires. In a terror of delight he put out his hand and took it, and had it.

He lay for a while, turning it over and over, and feeding his eyes upon its beauty. Then he jumped to his feet, remembering that the pretty thing was of no use to him yet. Where was the lock to which the key belonged? It must be somewhere, for how could anybody be so silly as make a key for which there was no lock? Where should he go to look for it? He gazed about him, up into the air, down to the earth, but saw no keyhole in the clouds, in the grass, or in the trees.

Just as he began to grow disconsolate, however, he saw something glimmering in the wood. It was a mere glimmer that he saw, but he took it for a glimmer of rainbow, and went towards it.—And now I will go back to the borders of the forest.

Not far from the house where the boy had lived, there was another house, the owner of which was a merchant, who was much away from home. He had lost his wife some years before, and had only one child, a little girl, whom he left to the charge of two servants, who were very idle and careless. So she was neglected and left untidy, and was sometimes ill-used besides.

Now it is well known that the little creatures commonly called fairies, though there are many different kinds of fairies in Fairyland, have an exceeding dislike to untidiness. Indeed, they are quite spiteful to slovenly people. Being used to all the lovely ways of the trees and flowers, and to the neatness of the birds and all woodland creatures, it makes them feel miserable, even in their deep woods and on their grassy carpets, to think that within the same moonlight lies a dirty, uncomfortable, slovenly house. And this makes them angry with the people that live in it, and they would gladly drive them out of the world if they could. They want the whole earth nice and clean. So they pinch the maids black and blue, and play them all manner of uncomfortable tricks.

But this house was quite a shame, and the fairies in the forest could not endure it. They tried everything on the maids without effect, and at last resolved upon making a clean riddance, beginning with the child. They ought to have known that it was not her fault, but they have little principle and much mischief in them, and they thought that if they got rid of her the maids would be sure to be turned away.

So one evening, the poor little girl having been put to bed early, before the sun was down, the servants went off to the village, locking the door behind them. The child did not know she was alone, and lay contentedly looking out of her window towards the forest, of which, however, she could not see much, because of the ivy and other creeping plants which had straggled across her window.

All at once she saw an ape making faces at her out of the mirror, and the heads carved upon a great old wardrobe grinning fearfully. Then two old spider-legged chairs came forward into the middle of the room, and began to dance a queer, old-fashioned dance. This set her laughing, and she forgot the ape and the grinning heads. So the fairies saw they had made a mistake, and sent the chairs back to their places.

But they knew that she had been reading the story of Silverhair all day. So the next moment she heard the voices of three bears upon the stairs, big voice, middle voice, and little voice, and she heard their soft, heavy tread, as if they had stockings over their boots, coming nearer and nearer to the door of her room, till she could bear it no longer. She did just as Silverhair did, and as the fairies wanted her to do: she darted to the window, pulled it open, got up on the ivy, and so scrambled to the ground. She then fled to the forest as fast as she could run.

Now, although she did not know it, this was the very best way she could have gone; for nothing is ever so mischievous in its own place as it is out of it; and, besides, these mischievous creatures were only the children of Fairyland, as it were, and there are many other beings there as well; and if a wanderer gets in among them, the good ones will always help him more than the evil ones will be able to hurt him.

The sun was now set, and the darkness coming on, but the child thought of no danger but the bears behind her. If she had looked round, however, she would have seen that she was followed by a very different creature from a bear. It was a curious creature, made like a fish, but covered, instead of scales, with feathers of all colors, sparkling like those of a humming-bird. It had fins, not wings, and swam through the air as a fish does through the water. Its head was like the head of a small owl.

After running a long way, and as the last of the light was disappearing, she passed under a tree with drooping branches. It dropped its branches to the ground all about her, and caught her as in a trap. She struggled to get out, but the branches pressed her closer and closer to the trunk. She was in great terror and distress, when the air-fish, swimming into the thicket of branches, began tearing them with its beak. They loosened their hold at once, and the creature went on attacking them, till at length they let the child go. Then the air-fish came from behind her, and swam on in front, glittering and sparkling all lovely colors; and she followed.

It led her gently along till all at once it swam in at a cottage-door. The child followed still. There was a bright fire in the middle of the floor, upon which stood a pot without a lid, full of water that boiled and bubbled furiously. The air-fish swam straight to the pot and into the boiling water, where it lay quiet. A beautiful woman rose from the opposite side of the fire and came to meet the girl. She took her up in her arms, and said,—

"Ah, you are come at last! I have been looking for you a long time."

She sat down with her on her lap, and there the girl sat staring at her. She had never seen anything so beautiful. She was tall and strong, with white arms and neck, and a delicate flush on her face. The child could not tell what was the color of her hair, but could not help thinking it had a tinge of dark green. She had not one ornament upon her, but she looked as if she had just put off quantities of diamonds and emeralds. Yet here she was in the simplest, poorest little cottage, where she was evidently at home. She was dressed in shining green.

The girl looked at the lady, and the lady looked at the girl.

"What is your name?" asked the lady.

"The servants always called me Tangle."

"Ah, that was because your hair was so untidy. But that was their fault, the naughty women! Still it is a pretty name, and I will call you Tangle too. You must not mind my asking you questions, for you may ask me the same questions, every one of them, and any others that you like. How old are you?"

"Ten," answered Tangle.

"You don't look like it," said the lady.

"How old are you, please?" returned Tangle.

"Thousands of years old," answered the lady.

"You don't look like it," said Tangle.

"Don't I? I think I do. Don't you see how beautiful I am?"

And her great blue eyes looked down on the little Tangle, as if all the stars in the sky were melted in them to make their brightness.

"Ah, but," said Tangle, "when people live long they grow old. At least I always thought so."

"I have no time to grow old," said the lady. "I am too busy for that. It is very idle to grow old.—But I cannot have my little girl so untidy. Do you know I can't find a clean spot on your face to kiss?"

"Perhaps," suggested Tangle, feeling ashamed, but not too much so to say a word for herself—"perhaps that is because the tree made me cry so."

"My poor darling!" said the lady, looking now as if the moon were melted in her eyes, and kissing her little face, dirty as it was, "the naughty tree must suffer for making a girl cry."

"And what is your name, please?" asked Tangle.

"Grandmother," answered the lady.

"Is it really?"

"Yes, indeed. I never tell stories, even in fun."

"How good of you!"

"I couldn't if I tried. It would come true if I said it, and then I should be punished enough."

And she smiled like the sun through a summer-shower.

"But now," she went on, "I must get you washed and dressed, and then we shall have some supper."

"Oh, I had supper long ago," said Tangle.

"Yes, indeed you had," answered the lady—"three years since you ran away from the bears. You don't know that it is three years since you ran away from the bears. You are thirteen and more now."

Tangle could only stare. She felt quite sure it was true.

"You will not be afraid of anything I do with you—will you?" said the lady.

"I will try very hard not to be; but I can't be certain, you know," replied Tangle.

"I like your saying so, and I shall be quite satisfied," answered the lady.

She took off the girl's night-gown, rose with her in her arms, and going to the wall of the cottage, opened a door. Then Tangle saw a deep tank, the sides of which were filled with green plants, which had flowers of all colors. There was a roof over it like the roof of the cottage. It was filled with beautiful clear water, in which swam a multitude of such fishes as the one that had led her to the cottage. It was the light their colors gave that showed the place in which they were.

The lady spoke some words Tangle could not understand, and threw her into the tank.

The fishes came crowding about her. Two or three of them got under her head and kept it up. The rest of them rubbed themselves all over her, and with their wet feathers washed her quite clean. Then the lady, who had been looking on all the time, spoke again; whereupon some thirty or forty of the fishes rose out of the water underneath Tangle, and so bore her up to the arms the lady held out to take her. She carried her back to the fire, and, having dried her well, opened a chest, and taking out the finest linen garments, smelling of grass and lavender, put them upon her, and over all a green dress, just like her own, shining like hers, and soft like hers, going into just such lovely folds from the waist, where it was tied with a brown cord, to her bare feet.

"Won't you give me a pair of shoes too, grandmother?" said Tangle.

"No, my dear; no shoes. Look here. I wear no shoes."

So saying, she lifted her dress a little, and there were the loveliest white feet, but no shoes. Then Tangle was content to go without shoes too. And the lady sat down with her again, and combed her hair, and brushed it, and then left it to dry while she got the supper.

First she got bread out of one hole in the wall; then milk out of another; then several kinds of fruit out of a third; and then she went to the pot on the fire, and took out the fish now nicely cooked, and, as soon as she had pulled off its feathered skin, it was ready to be eaten.

"But," exclaimed Tangle. And she stared at the fish, and could say no more.

"I know what you mean," returned the lady. "You do not like to eat the messenger that brought you home. But it is the kindest return you can make. The creature was afraid to go until it saw me put the pot on, and heard me promise it should be boiled the moment it returned with you. Then it darted out of the door at once. You saw it go into the pot of itself the moment it entered, did you not?"

"I did," answered Tangle, "and I thought it very strange; but then I saw you, and forgot all about the fish."

"In Fairyland," resumed the lady, as they sat down to the table, "the ambition of the animals is to be eaten by the people; for that is their highest end in that condition. But they are not therefore destroyed. Out of that pot comes something more than the dead fish, you will see."

Tangle now remarked that the lid was on the pot. But the lady took no further notice of it till they had eaten the fish, which Tangle found nicer than any fish she had ever tasted before. It was as white as snow, and as delicate as cream. And the moment she had swallowed a mouthful of it, a change she could not describe began to take place in her. She heard a murmuring all about her, which became more and more articulate, and at length, as she went on eating, grew intelligible. By the time she had finished her share, the sounds of all the animals in the forest came crowding through the door to her ears; for the door still stood wide open, though it was pitch dark outside; and they were no longer sounds only; they were speech, and speech that she could understand. She could tell what the insects in the cottage were saying to each other too. She had even a suspicion that the trees and flowers all about the cottage were holding midnight communications with each other; but what they said she could not hear.

As soon as the fish was eaten, the lady went to the fire and took the lid off the pot. A lovely little creature in human shape, with large white wings, rose out of it, and flew round and round the roof of the cottage; then dropped, fluttering, and nestled in the lap of the lady. She spoke to it some strange words, carried it to the door, and threw it out into the darkness. Tangle heard the flapping of its wings die away in the distance.

"Now have we done the fish any harm?" she said, returning.

"No," answered Tangle, "I do not think we have. I should not mind eating one every day."

"They must wait their time, like you and me too, my little Tangle."

And she smiled a smile which the sadness in it made more lovely.

"But," she continued, "I think we may have one for supper to-morrow."

So saying she went to the door of the tank, and spoke; and now Tangle understood her perfectly.

"I want one of you," she said,—"the wisest."

Thereupon the fishes got together in the middle of the tank, with their heads forming a circle above the water, and their tails a larger circle beneath it. They were holding a council, in which their relative wisdom should be determined. At length one of them flew up into the lady's hand, looking lively and ready.

"You know where the rainbow stands?" she asked.

"Yes, mother, quite well," answered the fish.

"Bring home a young man you will find there, who does not know where to go."

The fish was out of the door in a moment. Then the lady told Tangle it was time to go to bed; and, opening another door in the side of the cottage, showed her a little arbor, cool and green, with a bed of purple heath growing in it, upon which she threw a large wrapper made of the feathered skins of the wise fishes, shining gorgeous in the firelight. Tangle was soon lost in the strangest, loveliest dreams. And the beautiful lady was in every one of her dreams.

In the morning she woke to the rustling of leaves over her head, and the sound of running water. But, to her surprise, she could find no door—nothing but the moss-grown wall of the cottage. So she crept through an opening in the arbor, and stood in the forest. Then she bathed in a stream that ran merrily through the trees, and felt happier; for having once been in her grandmother's pond, she must be clean and tidy ever after; and, having put on her green dress, felt like a lady.

She spent that day in the wood, listening to the birds and beasts and creeping things. She understood all that they said, though she could not repeat a word of it; and every kind had a different language, while there was a common though more limited understanding between all the inhabitants of the forest.

She saw nothing of the beautiful lady, but she felt that she was near all the time; and she took care not to go out of sight of the cottage. It was round, like a snow-hut or a wigwam; and she could see neither door nor window in it. The fact was, it had no windows, and though it was full of doors, they all opened from the inside, and could not even be seen from the outside.

She was standing at the foot of a tree in the twilight, listening to a quarrel between a mole and a squirrel, in which the mole told the squirrel that the tail was the best of him, and the squirrel called the mole Spade-fists, when, the darkness having deepened around her, she became aware of something shining in her face, and looking round, saw that the door of the cottage was open, and the red light of the fire flowing from it like a river through the darkness. She left Mole and Squirrel to settle matters as they might, and darted off to the cottage. Entering, she found the pot boiling on the fire, and the grand, lovely lady sitting on the other side of it.

"I've been watching you all day," said the lady. "You shall have something to eat by-and-by, but we must wait till our supper comes home."

She took Tangle on her knee, and began to sing to her—such songs as made her wish she could listen to them for ever. But at length in rushed the shining fish, and snuggled down in the pot. It was followed by a youth who had outgrown his worn garments. His face was ruddy with health, and in his hand he carried a little jewel, which sparkled in the firelight.

The first words the lady said were,—

"What is that in your hand, Mossy?"

Now Mossy was the name his companions had given him, because he had a favorite stone covered with moss, on which he used to sit whole days reading; and they said the moss had begun to grow upon him too.

Mossy held out his hand. The moment the lady saw that it was the golden key, she rose from her chair, kissed Mossy on the forehead, made him sit down on her seat, and stood before him like a servant. Mossy could not bear this, and rose at once. But the lady begged him, with tears in her beautiful eyes, to sit, and let her wait on him.

"But you are a great, splendid, beautiful lady," said Mossy.

"Yes, I am. But I work all day long—that is my pleasure; and you will have to leave me so soon!"

"How do you know that, if you please, madam?" asked Mossy.

"Because you have got the golden key."

"But I don't know what it is for. I can't find the key-hole. Will you tell me what to do?"

"You must look for the key-hole. That is your work. I cannot help you. I can only tell you that if you look for it you will find it."

"What kind of box will it open? What is there inside?"

"I do not know. I dream about it, but I know nothing."

"Must I go at once?"

"You may stop here to-night, and have some of my supper. But you must go in the morning. All I can do for you is to give you clothes. Here is a girl called Tangle, whom you must take with you."

"That *will* be nice," said Mossy.

"No, no!" said Tangle. "I don't want to leave you, please, grandmother."

"You must go with him, Tangle. I am sorry to lose you but it will be the best thing for you. Even the fishes, you see, have to go into the pot, and then out into the dark. If you fall in with the Old Man of the Sea, mind you ask whether he has not got some more fishes ready for me. My tank is getting thin."

So saying, she took the fish from the pot, and put the lid on as before. They sat down and ate the fish, and then the winged creature rose from the pot, circled the roof, and settled on the lady's lap. She talked to it, carried it to the door, and threw it out into the dark. They heard the flap of its wings die away in the distance.

The lady then showed Mossy into just such another chamber as that of Tangle; and in the morning he found a suit of clothes laid beside him. He looked very handsome in them. But the wearer of Grandmother's clothes never thinks about how he or she looks, but thinks always how handsome other people are.

Tangle was very unwilling to go.

"Why should I leave you? I don't know the young man," she said to the lady.

"I am never allowed to keep my children long. You need not go with him except you please, but you must go some day; and I should like you to go with him, for he has the golden key. No girl need be afraid to go with a youth that has the golden key. You will take care of her, Mossy, will you not?"

"That I will," said Mossy.

And Tangle cast a glance at him and thought she should like to go with him.

"And," said the lady, "if you should lose each other as you go through the—

the—I never can remember the name of that country,—do not be afraid, but go on and on."

She kissed Tangle on the mouth and Mossy on the forehead, led them to the door, and waved her hand eastward. Mossy and Tangle took each other's hand and walked away into the depth of the forest. In his right hand Mossy held the golden key.

They wandered thus a long way, with endless amusement from the talk of the animals. They soon learned enough of their language to ask them necessary questions. The squirrels were always friendly, and gave them nuts out of their own hoards; but the bees were selfish and rude, justifying themselves on the ground that Tangle and Mossy were not subjects of their queen, and charity must begin at home, though indeed they had not one drone in their poorhouse at the time. Even the blinking moles would fetch them an earth-nut or a truffle now and then, talking as if their mouths, as well as their eyes and ears, were full of cotton wool, or their own velvety fur. By the time they got out of the forest they were very fond of each other, and Tangle was not in the least sorry that her grandmother had sent her away with Mossy.

At length the trees grew smaller, and stood farther apart, and the ground began to rise, and it got more and more steep, till the trees were all left behind, and the two were climbing a narrow path with rocks on each side. Suddenly they came upon a rude doorway, by which they entered a narrow gallery cut in the rock. It grew darker and darker, till it was pitch-dark, and they had to feel their way. At length the light began to return, and at last they came out upon a narrow path on the face of a lofty precipice. This path went winding down the rock to a wide plain, circular in shape, and surrounded on all sides by mountains. Those opposite to them were a great way off, and towered to an awful height, shooting up sharp, blue, ice-enameled pinnacles. An utter silence reigned where they stood. Not even the sound of water reached them.

Looking down, they could not tell whether the valley below was a grassy plain or a great still lake. They had never seen any space look like it. The way to it was difficult and dangerous, but down the narrow path they went, and reached the bottom in safety. They found it composed of smooth, light-colored sandstone, undulating in parts, but mostly level. It was no wonder to them now that they had not been able to tell what it was, for this surface was everywhere crowded with shadows.

It was a sea of shadows. The mass was chiefly made up of the shadows of leaves innumerable, of all lovely and imaginative forms, waving to and fro, floating and quivering in the breath of a breeze whose motion was unfelt, whose sound was unheard. No forests clothed the mountain-sides, no trees were anywhere to be seen, and yet the shadows of the leaves, branches, and stems of all various trees covered the valley as far as their eyes could reach. They soon spied the shadows of flowers mingled with those of the leaves, and now and then the shadow of a bird with open beak, and throat distended with song. At times would appear the forms of strange, graceful creatures, running up and down the shadow-boles and along the branches, to disappear in the wind-tossed foliage.

As they walked they waded knee-deep in the lovely lake. For the shadows were not merely lying on the surface of the ground, but heaped up above it like substantial forms of darkness, as if they had been cast upon a thousand different planes of the air. Tangle and Mossy often lifted their heads and gazed upwards to descry whence the shadows came; but they could see nothing more than a bright mist spread above them, higher than the tops of the mountains, which stood clear against it. No forests, no leaves, no birds were visible.

After a while, they reached more open spaces, where the shadows were thinner; and came even to portions over which shadows only flitted, leaving them clear for such as might follow. Now a wonderful form, half bird-like half human, would float across on outspread sailing pinions. Anon an exquisite shadow group of gamboling children would be followed by the loveliest female form, and that again by the grand stride of a Titanic shape, each disappearing in the surrounding press of shadowy foliage. Sometimes a profile of unspeakable beauty or grandeur would appear for a moment and vanish. Sometimes they seemed lovers that passed linked arm in arm, sometimes father and son, sometimes brothers in loving contest, sometimes sisters entwined in gracefullest community of complex form. Sometimes wild horses would tear across, free, or bestrode by noble shadows of ruling men. But some of the things which pleased them most they never knew how to describe.

About the middle of the plain they sat down to rest in the heart of a heap of shadows. After sitting for a while, each, looking up, saw the other in tears: they were each longing after the country whence the shadows fell.

"We must find the country from which the shadows come," said Mossy.

"We must, dear Mossy," responded Tangle. "What if your golden key should be the key to it?"

"Ah, that would be grand," returned Mossy. "But we must rest here for a little, and then we shall be able to cross the plain before night."

So he lay down on the ground, and about him on every side, and over his head, was the constant play of wonderful shadows. He could look through them, and see the one behind the other, till they mixed in a mass of darkness. Tangle, too, lay admiring, and wondering, and longing for the country whence the shadows came. When they were rested they rose and pursued their journey.

How long they were in crossing this plain I cannot tell; but before night Mossy's hair was streaked with gray, and Tangle had got wrinkles on her forehead.

As evening drew on, the shadows fell deeper and rose higher. At length they reached a place where they rose above their heads, and made all dark around them. Then they took hold of each other's hand, and walked on in silence and in some dismay. They felt the gathering darkness, and something strangely solemn besides, and the beauty of the shadows ceased to delight them. All at once Tangle found that she had not a hold of Mossy's hand, though when she lost it she could not tell.

"Mossy, Mossy!" she cried aloud in terror.

But no Mossy replied.

A moment after, the shadows sank to her feet, and down under her feet, and the mountains rose before her. She turned towards the gloomy region she had left, and called once more upon Mossy. There the gloom lay tossing and heaving, a dark, stormy, foamless sea of shadows, but no Mossy rose out of it, or came climbing up the hill on which she stood. She threw herself down and wept in despair.

Suddenly she remembered that the beautiful lady had told them, if they lost each other in a country of which she could not remember the name, they were not to be afraid, but to go straight on.

"And besides," she said to herself, "Mossy has the golden key, and so no harm will come to him, I do believe."

She rose from the ground, and went on.

Before long she arrived at a precipice, in the face of which a stair was cut. When she had ascended half-way, the stair ceased, and the path led straight into the mountain. She was afraid to enter, and turning again towards the stair, grew giddy at sight of the depth beneath her, and was forced to throw herself down in the mouth of the cave.

When she opened her eyes, she saw a beautiful little creature with wings standing beside her, waiting.

"I know you," said Tangle. "You are my fish."

"Yes. But I am a fish no longer. I am an aeranth now."

"What is that?" asked Tangle.

"What you see I am," answered the shape. "And I am come to lead you through the mountain."

"Oh, thank you, dear fish—aeranth I mean," returned Tangle, rising.

Thereupon the aeranth took to his wings, and flew on through the long narrow passage, reminding Tangle very much of the way he had swum on before when he was a fish. And the moment his white wings moved, they began to throw off a continuous shower of sparks of all colors, which lighted up the passage before them.—All at once he vanished, and Tangle heard a low, sweet sound, quite different from the rush and crackle of his wings. Before her was an open arch, and through it came light, mixed with the sound of sea-waves.

She hurried out, and fell, tired and happy, upon the yellow sand of the shore. There she lay, half asleep with weariness and rest, listening to the low plash and retreat of the tiny waves, which seemed ever enticing the land to leave off being land, and become sea. And as she lay, her eyes were fixed upon the foot of a great rainbow standing far away against the sky on the other side of the sea. At length she fell fast asleep.

When she awoke, she saw an old man with long white hair down to his shoulders, leaning upon a stick covered with green buds, and so bending over her.

"What do you want here, beautiful woman?" he said.

"Am I beautiful? I am so glad!" answered Tangle, rising. "My grandmother is beautiful."

"Yes. But what do you want?" he repeated, kindly.

"I think I want you. Are not you the Old Man of the Sea?"

"I am."

"Then grandmother says, have you any more fishes ready for her?"

"We will go and see, my dear," answered the old man, speaking yet more kindly than before. "And I can do something for you, can I not?"

"Yes—show me the way up to the country from which the shadows fall," said Tangle.

For there she hoped to find Mossy again.

"Ah, indeed, that would be worth doing," said the old man. "But I cannot, for I do not know the way myself. But, I will send you to the Old Man of the Earth. Perhaps he can tell you. He is much older than I am."

Leaning on his staff, he conducted her along the shore to a steep rock, that looked like a petrified ship turned upside down. The door of it was the rudder of a great vessel, ages ago at the bottom of the sea. Immediately within the door was a stair in the rock, down which the old man went, and Tangle followed. At the bottom the old man had his house, and there he lived.

As soon as she entered it, Tangle heard a strange noise, unlike anything she had ever heard before. She soon found that it was the fishes talking. She tried to understand what they said; but their speech was so old-fashioned, and rude, and undefined, that she could not make much of it.

"I will go and see about those fishes for my daughter," said the Old Man of the Sea.

And moving a slide in the wall of his house, he first looked out, and then tapped upon a thick piece of crystal that filled the round opening. Tangle came up behind him, and peeping through the window into the heart of the great deep green ocean, saw the most curious creatures, some very ugly, all very odd, and with especially queer mouths, swimming about everywhere, above and below, but all coming towards the window in answer to the tap of the Old Man of the Sea. Only a few could get their mouths against the glass; but those who were floating miles away yet turned their heads towards it. The Old Man looked through the whole flock carefully for some minutes, and then turning to Tangle, said,—

"I am sorry I have not got one ready yet. I want more time than she does. But I will send some as soon as I can."

He then shut the slide.

Presently a great noise arose in the sea. The Old Man opened the slide again, and tapped on the glass, whereupon the fishes were all as still as sleep.

"They were only talking about you," he said. "And they do speak such nonsense!—To-morrow," he continued, "I must show you the way to the Old Man of the Earth. He lives a long way from here."

"Do let me go at once," said Tangle.

"No. That is not possible. You must come this way first."

He led her to a hole in the wall, which she had not observed before. It was covered with the green leaves and white blossoms of a creeping plant.

"Only white-blossoming plants can grow under the sea," said the Old Man. "In there you will find a bath, in which you must lie till I call you."

Tangle went in, and found a smaller room or cave, in the further corner of which was a great basin hollowed out of a rock, and half-full of the clearest sea-water. Little streams were constantly running into it from cracks in the wall of the cavern. It was polished quite smooth inside, and had a carpet of yellow sand in the bottom of it. Large green leaves and white flowers of various plants crowded up and over it, draping and covering it almost entirely.

No sooner was she undressed and lying in the bath, than she began to feel as if the water were sinking into her, and she were receiving all the good of sleep without undergoing its forgetfulness. She felt the good coming all the time. And she grew happier and more hopeful than she had been since she lost Mossy. But she could not help thinking how very sad it was for a poor old man to live there all alone, and have to take care of a whole seaful of stupid and riotous fishes.

After about an hour, as she thought, she heard his voice calling her, and rose out of the bath. All the fatigue and aching of her long journey had vanished. She was as whole, and strong, and well as if she had slept for seven days.

Returning to the opening that led into the other part of the house, she started back with amazement, for through it she saw the form of a grand man, with a majestic and beautiful face, waiting for her.

"Come," he said; "I see you are ready."

She entered with reverence.

"Where is the Old Man of the Sea?" she asked, humbly.

"There is no one here but me," he answered smiling. "Some people call me the Old Man of the Sea. Others have another name for me, and are terribly frightened when they meet me taking a walk by the shore. Therefore I avoid being seen by them, for they are so afraid, that they never see what I really am. You see me now.—But I must show you the way to the Old Man of the Earth."

He led her into the cave where the bath was, and there she saw, in the opposite corner a second opening in the rock.

"Go down that stair, and it will bring you to him," said the Old Man of the Sea.

With humble thanks Tangle took her leave. She went down the winding-stair, till she began to fear there was no end to it. Still down and down it went, rough and broken, with springs of water bursting out of the rocks and running down the steps beside her. It was quite dark about her, and yet she could see. For after being in that bath, people's eyes always give out a light they can see by. There were no creeping things in the way. All was safe and pleasant, though so dark and damp and deep.

At last there was not one step more, and she found herself in a glimmering cave. On a stone in the middle of it sat a figure with its back towards her—the figure of an old man bent double with age. From behind she could see his white beard spread out on the rocky floor in front of him. He did not move as she entered, so she passed round that she might stand before him and speak to him. The moment she looked in his face, she saw that he was a youth of marvelous beauty. He sat entranced with the delight of what he beheld in a mirror of something like silver, which lay on the floor at his feet. and which from behind she had taken for his white beard. He sat on, heedless of her presence, pale with the joy of his vision. She stood and watched him. At length, all trembling, she spoke. But her voice made no sound. Yet the youth lifted up his head. He showed no surprise, however, at seeing her—only smiled a welcome.

"Are you the Old Man of the Earth?" Tangle had said.

And the youth answered, and Tangle heard him, though not with her ears.

"I am. What can I do for you?"

"Tell me the way to the country whence the shadows fall."

"Ah, that I do not know. I only dream about it myself. I see its shadows sometimes in my mirror: the way to it I do not know. But I think the Old Man of the Fire must know. He is much older than I am. He is the oldest of all."

"Where does he live?"

"I will show you the way to his place. I never saw him myself."

So saying, the young man rose, and then stood for a while gazing at Tangle.

"I wish I could see that country too," he said. "But I must mind my work."

He led her to the side of the cave, and told her to lay her ear against the wall.

"What do you hear?" he asked.

"I hear," answered Tangle, "the sound of a great water running inside the rock."

"That river runs down to the dwelling of the oldest man of all—the Old Man of the Fire. I wish I could go to see him. But I must mind my work. The river is the only way to him."

Then the Old Man of the Earth stooped over the floor of the cave, raised a huge stone from it, and left it leaning. It disclosed a great hole that went plumb-down.

"That is the way," he said.

"But there are no stairs."

"You must throw yourself in. There is no other way."

She turned and looked him full in the face—stood so for a whole minute, as she thought: it was a whole year—then threw herself headlong into the hole.

When she came to herself, she found herself gliding down fast and deep. Her head was underwater, but that did not signify, for, when she thought about it, she could not remember that she had breathed once since her bath in the cave of the Old Man of the Sea. When she lifted up her head a sudden and fierce heat struck her, and she sank it again instantly, and went sweeping on.

Gradually the stream grew shallower. At length she could hardly keep her head under. Then the water could carry her no farther. She rose from the channel, and went step for step down the burning descent. The water ceased altogether. The heat was terrible. She felt scorched to the bone, but it did not touch her strength. It grew hotter and hotter. She said, "I can bear it no longer." Yet she went on.

At the long last, the stair ended at a rude archway in an all but glowing rock. Through this archway Tangle fell exhausted into a cool mossy cave. The floor and walls were covered with moss—green, soft, and damp. A little stream spouted from a rent in the rock and fell into a basin of moss. She plunged her face into it and drank. Then she lifted her head and looked around. Then she rose and looked again. She saw no one in the cave. But the moment she stood upright she had a marvelous sense that she was in the secret of the earth and all its ways. Everything she had seen, or learned from books; all that her grandmother had said or sung to her; all the talk of the beasts, birds, and fishes; all that had happened to her on her journey with Mossy, and since then in the heart of the earth with the Old man and the Older man—all was plain: she understood it all, and saw that everything meant the same thing though she could not have put it into words again.

The next moment she descried, in a corner of the cave, a little naked child, sitting on the moss. He was playing with balls of various colors and sizes, which he disposed in strange figures upon the floor beside him. And now Tangle felt that there was something in her knowledge which was not in her understanding. For she knew there must be an infinite meaning in the change and sequence and individual forms of the figures into which the child arranged the balls, as well as in the varied harmonies of their colors, but what it all meant she could not tell. He went on busily, tirelessly, playing his solitary game, without looking up, or seeming to know that there was a stranger in his deep-withdrawn cell. Diligently as a lace-maker shifts her bobbins, he shifted and arranged his balls. Flashes of meaning would now pass from them to Tangle, and now again all would be not merely obscure, but utterly dark. She stood looking for a long time, for there was fascination in the sight; and the longer she looked the more an indescribable vague intelligence went on rousing itself in her mind.

For seven years she had stood there watching the naked child with his colored balls, and it seemed to her like seven hours, when all at once the shape the balls took, she knew not why, reminded her of the Valley of Shadows, and she spoke:—

"Where is the Old Man of the Fire?" she said.

"Here I am," answered the child, rising and leaving his balls on the moss. "What can I do for you?"

There was such an awfulness of absolute repose on the face of the child that Tangle stood dumb before him. He had no smile, but the love in his large gray eyes was deep as the center. And with the repose there lay on his face a shimmer as of moonlight, which seemed as if any moment it might break into such a ravishing smile as would cause the beholder to weep himself to death. But the smile never came, and the moonlight lay there unbroken. For the heart of the child was too deep for any smile to reach from it to his face.

"Are you the oldest man of all?" Tangle at length, although filled with awe, ventured to ask.

"Yes, I am. I am very, very old. I am able to help you, I know. I can help everybody."

And the child drew near and looked up in her face so that she burst into tears.

"Can you tell me the way to the country the shadows fall from?" she sobbed.

"Yes. I know the way quite well. I go there myself sometimes. But you could not go my way; you are not old enough. I will show you how you can go."

"Do not send me out into the great heat again," prayed Tangle.

"I will not," answered the child.

And he reached up and put his little cool hand on her heart.

"Now," he said, "you can go. The fire will not burn you. Come."

He led her from the cave, and following him through another archway, she found herself in a vast desert of sand and rock. The sky of it was of rock, lowering over them like solid thunderclouds; and the whole place was so hot that she saw, in bright rivulets, the yellow gold and white silver and red copper trickling molten from the rocks. But the heat never came near her.

When they had gone some distance, the child turned up a great stone, and took something like a egg from under it. He next drew a long curved line in the sand with his finger, and laid the egg on it. He then spoke something Tangle could not understand. The egg broke, a small snake came out, and, lying in the line in the sand, grew and grew till he filled it. The moment he was thus full grown, he began to glide away, undulating like a sea-wave.

"Follow that serpent," said the child. "He will lead you the right way."

Tangle followed the serpent. But she could not go far without looking back at the marvelous Child. He stood alone in the midst of the glowing desert, beside a fountain of red flame that had burst forth at his feet, his naked whiteness glimmering a pale rosy red in the torrid fire. There he stood, looking after her, till, from the lengthening distance, she could see him no more. The serpent went straight on, turning neither to the right nor left.

Meantime Mossy had got out of the lake of shadows, and, following his mournful, lonely way, had reached the sea-shore. It was a dark, stormy evening. The sun had set. The wind was blowing from the sea. The waves had surrounded the rock within which lay the Old Man's House. A deep water rolled between it and the shore, upon which a majestic figure was walking alone.

Mossy went up to him and said,—

"Will you tell me where to find the Old Man of the Sea?"

"I am the Old Man of the Sea," the figure answered.

"I see a strong kingly man of middle age," returned Mossy.

Then the Old Man looked at him more intently, and said, "Your sight, young man, is better than that of most who take this way. The night is stormy: come to my house—and tell me what I can do for you."

Mossy followed him. The waves flew from before the footsteps of the Old Man of the Sea, and Mossy followed upon dry sand.

When they had reached the cave, they sat down and gazed at each other.

Now Mossy was an old man by this time. He looked much older than the Old Man of the Sea, and his feet were very weary.

After looking at him for a moment, the Old Man took him by the hand and led him into his inner cave. There he helped him to undress, and laid him in the bath. And he saw that one of his hands Mossy did not open. "What have you in that hand?" he asked.

Mossy opened his hand, and there lay the golden key.

"Ah," said the Old Man, "that accounts for your knowing me. And I know the way you have to go."

"I want to find the country whence the shadows fall," said Mossy.

"I dare say you do. So do I. But meantime, one thing is certain—What is that key for, do you think?"

"For a keyhole somewhere. But I don't know why I keep it. I never could find the keyhole. And I have lived a good while, I believe," said Mossy, sadly. "I'm not sure that I'm not old. I know my feet ache."

"Do they?" said the Old Man, as if he really meant to ask the question; and Mossy, who was still lying in the bath, watched his feet for a moment before he replied.

"No, they do not," he answered. "Perhaps I am not old either."

"Get up and look at yourself in the water."

He rose and looked at himself in the water, and there was not a gray hair on his head or a wrinkle on his skin.

"You have tasted of death now," said the Old Man. "It is good?"

"It is good," said Mossy. "It is better than life."

"No," said the Old Man: "it is only more life.—Your feet will make no holes in the water now."

"What do you mean?"

"I will show you that presently."

They returned to the outer cave, and sat and talked together for a long time. At length the Old Man of the Sea rose, and said to Mossy, "Follow me."

He led him up the stair again, and opened another door. They stood on the level of the raging sea, looking towards the east. Across the waste of waters, against the bosom of a fierce black cloud, stood the foot of a rainbow, glowing in the dark.

"This indeed is my way," said Mossy, as soon as he saw the rainbow, and stepped out upon the sea. His feet made no holes in the water. He fought the wind, and clomb the waves, and went on towards the rainbow.

The storm died away. A lovely day and a lovelier night followed. A cool wind blew over the wide plain of the quiet ocean. And still Mossy journeyed eastward. But the rainbow had vanished with the storm.

Day after day he held on, and he thought he had no guide. He did not see how a shining fish under the waters directed his steps. He crossed the sea, and came to a great precipice of rock, up which he could discover but one path. Nor did this lead him farther than half-way up the rock, where it ended on a platform. Here he stood and pondered.—It could not be that the way stopped here, else what was the path for? It was a rough path, not very plain, yet certainly a path.—He examined the face of the rock. It was smooth as glass. But as his eyes kept roving hopelessly over it, something glittered, and he caught sight of a row of small sapphires. They bordered a little hole in the rock.

"The keyhole!" he cried.

He tried the key. It fitted. It turned. A great clang and clash, as of iron bolts on huge brazen caldrons, echoed thunderously within. He drew out the key. The rock in front of him began to fall. He retreated from it as far as the breadth of the platform would allow. A great slab fell at his feet. In front was still the solid rock, with this one slab fallen forward out of it. But the moment he stepped upon it, a second fell, just short of the edge of the first, making the next step of a stair, which thus kept dropping itself before him as he ascended into the heart of the precipice. It led him into a hall fit for such an approach—irregular and rude in formation, but floor, sides, pillars, and vaulted roof, all of one mass of shining stones of every color that light can show. In the center stood seven columns, ranged from red to violet. And on the pedestal of one of them sat a woman, motionless, with her face bowed upon her knees. Seven years had she sat there waiting. She lifted her head as Mossy drew near. It was Tangle. Her hair had grown to her feet, and was rippled like the windless sea on broad sands. Her face was beautiful, like her grandmother's and as still and peaceful as that of the Old Man of the Fire. Her form was tall and noble. Yet Mossy knew her at once.

"How beautiful you are, Tangle!" he said, in delight and astonishment.

"Am I?" she returned. "Oh, I have waited for you so long! But you, you are like the Old Man of the Sea. No. You are like the Old Man of the Earth. No, no. You are like the oldest man of all. You are like them all. And yet you are my own old Mossy. How did you come here? What did you do after I lost you? Did you find the keyhole? Have you got the key still?"

She had a hundred questions to ask him, and he a hundred more to ask her. They told each other all their adventures, and were as happy as man and woman could be. For they were younger and better, and stronger and wiser, than they had ever been before.

It began to grow dark. And they wanted more than ever to reach the country whence the shadows fall. So they looked about them for a way out of the cave. The door by which Mossy entered had closed again, and there was half a mile of rock between them and the sea. Neither could Tangle find the opening in the floor by which the serpent had led her thither. They searched till it grew so dark that they could see nothing, and gave it up.

After a while, however, the cave began to glimmer again. The light came from the moon, but it did not look like moonlight, for it gleamed through those seven pillars in the middle, and filled the place with all colors. And now Mossy saw that there was a pillar beside the red one, which he had not observed before. And it was of the same new color that he had seen in the rainbow when he saw it first in the fairy forest. And on it he saw a sparkle of blue. It was the sapphires round the keyhole.

He took his key. It turned in the lock to the sounds of Aeolian music. A door opened upon slow hinges, and disclosed a winding stair within. The key vanished from his fingers. Tangle went up. Mossy followed. The door closed behind them. They climbed out of the earth; and, still climbing, rose above it. They were in the rainbow. Far abroad, over ocean and land, they could see through its transparent walls the earth beneath their feet. Stairs beside stairs wound up together, and beautiful beings of all ages climbed along with them. They knew that they were going up to the country whence the shadows fall.

And by this time I think they must have got there.

## JAMES SMITH (1824–1887)

### Burd Ailie

Burd Ailie sat doun by the wimplin burn,
Wi' the red, red rose in her hair;
An' bricht was the glance o' her bonnie black e'e,
As her heart throbbed fast and sair.
An' aye as she looked on ilk clear wee wave,
She murmured her true love's name,
An' sighed when she thocht on the distant sea,
An' the ship sae far frae hame.

The robin flew hie owre the gowden broom,
An' he warbled fu' cheerily.
"Oh, tell me—oh tell me, thou bonnie wee bird,
Will I ever my true luve see?"
Then saftly an' sweetly the robin sang:
"Puir Ailie, I'm laith to tell;
For the ship's i' the howe* o' a roaring wave, *trough*
An' thy luve's i' the merlin's cell."

"Oh, tell me—oh tell me, thou bonnie wee bird,
Did he mind on the nicht langsyne
When we plichted our troth by the trystin tree?
Was his heart aye true to mine?"
"Oh, fond an' true," the sweet robin sang;
"But the merlin he noo maun wed;
For the sea-weed's twined in his yellow hair,
An' the coral's his bridal bed."

Burd Ailie lay low by the wimplin' burn,
Wi' the red, red rose in her hair;
But gane was the glance o' her bonnie black e'e,
An' the robin sang nae mair.
For an angel cam' doun at the fa' o' the nicht,
As she murmured her true luve's name;
An' took her awa' frae a broken heart,
And the ship that wad ne'er come hame.

## Doun Fair Dalmeny's Rosy Dells

Doun fair Dalmeny's rosy dells,
Sweet Mary wandered, sad an' wae;
The sunlicht faded owre the lea,
An' cheerless fell the simmer day.
The warblin' mavis sang nae mair,
As aft she sighed, in heavy sorrow.
"O lanely, lanely lies my luve;
An' cauld's the nicht that brings nae morrow.

"By yonder hoary castle wa',
Where murmurs deep the dark blue sea,
I wearied sair the langsome nicht,
Till tears bedimmed my sleepless e'e.
The boat gaed doun by Cramond's isle—
O weary fa' that nicht o' sorrow,
For lanely, lanely lies my luve,
An' cauld's the nicht that brings nae morrow.

"O foaming waves, that took my luve—
My ain true luve, beyond compare.
O will I see his winsome form,
And hear his dear lo'ed voice nae mair?"
Fu' deep the snaw-white surges moaned:
"O sair's the burden o' thy sorrow,
For lanely, lanely lies thy luve,
An' cauld's the nicht that brings nae morrow."

She wandered weary by the shore,
An' murmured aft his name sae dear;
Till owre Dalmeny's dewy dells
The silver moon shone sweet an' clear.
An' saft the trembling breezes sighed,
As far she strayed, in hopeless sorrow:
"O lanely, lanely lies thy luve:
An' cauld's the nicht that brings nae morrow."

## The Lintwhite

A lintwhite sat in her mossy nest,
Ae eerie morn in spring,
An' lang she looked at the cauld gray lift*, sky
Wi' the wee birds under her wing.
An' aye as she lookit, wi' shiverin' breist,
Sae waesomely she sang:
"O tell me true, ye winds that blaw,
Why tarries my luve sae lang?

"I've socht him doun i' the fairy glen,
An' far owre the lanely lea—
I've socht him doun i' yon saft green yird,
An' high on the birken tree;—
I've socht till the wee things cried me hame,
Wi' mony a heavy pang.
O tell me true, ye winds that blaw,
Why tarries my luve sae lang?"

"O waly," the norland breezes moaned;
"Sae weel may thy heart be sair;
For the hawk's awa' wi' thy ain true luve,
An' he'll sing thee a sang nae mair.
Fu wae was his fate on yon auld aik tree,
That aft wi' his warblin' rang.
Noo speir* nae mair, wee shiverin' bird, ask
Why tarries thy luve sae lang?"

The lintwhite flew frae her mossy nest,
For she couldna thole* the sting; endure
An' she flichtered east, an' she flichtered west,
Til she droukit* her downy wing; drenched
An' aye as she fluttered the lee-lang day,
Sae wild an' sae shrill she sang:
"O tell me—tell me true, ye winds,
Why tarries my luve sae lang?"

## WALTER SMITH (1824–1908)

### Miss Penelope Leith

Last heiress she of many a rood,
Where Ugie winds through Buchan braes—
A treeless land, where beeves are good,
And men have quaint old-fashioned ways,
And every burn has ballad lore,
And every hamlet has its song,
And on its surf-beat rocky shore
The eerie legend lingers long.
Old customs live there, unaware
That they are garments cast away,
And what of light is shining there
Is lingering light of yesterday.

Never to her the new day came,
Or if it came she would not see;
This world of change was still the same
To our old-world Penelope.
New fashions rose, old fashions went,
But still she wore the same brocade,

With lace of Valenciennes or Ghent
More dainty by her darning made,
A little patch upon her face,
A tinge of color on her cheek,
A frost of powder, just to grace
The locks that time began to streak.

A stately lady; to the poor
Her manner was without reproach;
But from the causeway she was sure
To snub the Provost in his coach.
In pride of birth she did not seek
Her scorn of upstarts to conceal,
But of a bailie's wife would speak
As if she bore the fisher's creel.
She said it kept them in their place,
Their fathers were of low degree;
She said the only saving grace
Of upstarts was humility.

The quaint old Doric still she used,
And it came kindly from her tongue;
And oft the "mim*-folk" she abused, prim
Who mincing English said or sung.
She took her claret, nothing loath,
Her snuff that one small nostril curled.
She might rap out a good round oath,
But would not mince it for the world.
And yet the wild word sounded less
In that Scotch tongue of other days.
Twas just like her old-fashioned dress,
And part of her old-fashioned ways.

At every fair her face was known,
Well-skilled in kyloes* and in queys*; cattle/heifers
And well she led the fiddler on
To "wale*" the best of his strathspeys. choose
Lightly she held the man who rose
While the toast-hammer still could rap,
And brought her gossip to a close,
Or spoilt her after-dinner nap.
Tea was for women, wine for men,
And if they quarreled oer their cups,
They might go to the peat-moss then,
And fight it out like stags or tups*. rams

She loved a bishop or a dean,
A surplice or a rocket well,
At all the church's feasts was seen,
And called the kirk, conventicle;
Was civil to the minister,
But stiff and frigid to his wife,
And looked askance, and sniffed at her,

As if she lived a dubious life.
But yet his sick her cellars knew,
Well stored from Portugal or France,
And many a savory soup and stew
Her game-bags furnished to the manse.

But if there was a choicer boon
Above all else she would have missed,
It was on Sunday afternoon
To have her quiet game at whist
Close to the window, when the Whigs
Were gravely passing from the kirk,
And some on foot, and some in gigs,
Would stare at her unhallowed work.
She gloried in her "devil's books"
That cut their sour hearts to the quick.
Rather than miss their wrathful looks
She would have almost lost the trick.

Her politics were of the age
Of Claverhouse or Bolingbroke.
Still at the Dutchman she would rage,
And still of gallant Grahame she spoke.
She swore twas right that Whigs should die
Psalm-sniveling in the wind and rain,
Though she would ne'er have harmed a fly
For buzzing on the window-pane.
And she had many a plaintive rhyme
Of noble Charlie and his men.
For her there was no later time—
All history had ended then.

The dear old sinner. Yet she had
A kindly human heart, I wot,
And many a sorrow she made glad,
And many a tender mercy wrought.
And though her way was somewhat odd,
Yet in her way she feared the Lord,
And thought she best could worship God
By holding Pharisees abhorred,
By being honest, fearless, true,
And thorough both in word and deed,
And by despising what is new,
And clinging to her old-world creed.

## Glenaradale

There is no fire of the crackling boughs
On the hearth of our fathers,
There is no lowing of brown-eyed cows
On the green meadows,
Nor do the maidens whisper vows

In the still gloaming,
Glenaradale.

There is no bleating of sheep on the hill
Where the mists linger,
There is no sound of the low hand-mill
Ground by the women,
And the smith's hammer is lying still
By the brown anvil,
Glenaradale.

Ah, we must leave thee, and go away
Far from Ben Luibh,
Far from the graves where we hoped to lay
Our bones with our fathers',
Far from the kirk where we used to pray
Lowly together,
Glenaradale.

We are not going for hunger of wealth,
For the gold and silver,
We are not going to seek for health
On the flat prairies,
Nor yet for the lack of fruitful tilth
On thy green pastures,
Glenaradale.

Content with the croft and the hill were we,
As all our fathers,
Content with the fish in the lake to be
Carefully netted,
And garments spun of the wool from thee,
O black-faced wether
Of Glenaradale.

No father here but would give a son
For the old country,
And his mother the sword would have girded on
To fight her battles:
Many's the battle that has been won
By the brave tartans,
Glenaradale.

But the big-horned stag and his hinds, we know,
In the high corries*, mountain hollows
And the salmon that swirls the pool below
Where the stream rushes,
Are more than the hearts of men, and so
We leave thy green valley,
Glenaradale.

## The Self-Exiled

There came a soul to the gate of Heaven
Gliding slow—
A soul that was ransomed and forgiven,
And white as snow.
And the angels all were silent.

A mystic light beamed from the face
Of the radiant maid,
But there also lay on its tender grace
A mystic shade.
And the angels all were silent.

As sunlit clouds by a zephyr borne
Seem not to stir,
So to the golden gates of morn
They carried her.
And the angels all were silent.

"Now open the gate, and let her in,
And fling it wide,
For she has been cleansed from stain of sin,"
St. Peter cried.
And the angels all were silent.

"Though I am cleansed from stain of sin,"
She answered low,
"I came not hither to enter in,
Nor may I go."
And the angels all were silent.

"I come," she said, "to the pearly door,
To see the throne
Where sits the Lamb on the sapphire floor,
With God alone."
And the angels all were silent.

"I come to hear the new song they sing
To Him that died,
And note where the healing waters spring
From His pierced side."
And the angels all were silent.

"But I may not enter there," she said,
"For I must go
Across the gulf where the guilty dead
Lie in their woe."
And the angels all were silent.

"If I enter heaven I may not pass
To where they be,
Though the wail of their bitter pain, alas,

Tormenteth me."
And the angels all were silent.

"If I enter heaven I may not speak
My soul's desire
For them that are lying distraught and weak
In flaming fire."
And the angels all were silent.

"I had a brother, and also another
Whom I loved well.
What if, in anguish, they curse each other
In the depths of hell?"
And the angels all were silent.

"How could I touch the golden harps,
When all my praise
Would be so wrought with grief-full warps
Of their sad days?"
And the angels all were silent.

"How love the loved who are sorrowing,
And yet be glad?
How sing the songs ye are fain to sing,
While I am sad?"
And the angels all were silent.

"Oh, clear as glass is the golden street
Of the city fair,
And the tree of life it maketh sweet
The lightsome air."
And the angels all were silent.

"And the white-robed saints with their crowns and palms
Are good to see,
And oh, so grand are the sounding psalms,
But not for me."
And the angels all were silent.

"I come where there is no night," she said,
"To go away,
And help, if I yet may help, the dead
That have no day."
And the angels all were silent.

St. Peter he turned the keys about,
And answered grim,
"Can you love the Lord, and abide without,
Afar from Him?"
And the angels all were silent.

"Can you love the Lord who died for you
And leave the place

Where His glory is all disclosed to view,
And tender grace?"
And the angels all were silent.

"They go not out who come in here;
It were not meet.
Nothing they lack, for He is here,
And bliss complete."
And the angels all were silent.

"Should I be nearer Christ," she said,
"By pitying less
The sinful living or woeful dead
In their helplessness?"
And the angels all were silent.

"Should I be liker Christ were I
To love no more
The loved, who in their anguish lie
Outside the door?"
And the angels all were silent.

"Did He not hang on the cursed tree,
And bear its shame,
And clasp to His heart, for love of me,
My guilt and blame?"
And the angels all were silent.

"Should I be liker, nearer Him,
Forgetting this,
Singing all day with the seraphim,
In selfish bliss?"
And the angels all were silent.

The Lord Himself stood by the gate,
And heard her speak
Those tender words compassionate,
Gentle and meek.
And the angels all were silent.

Now, pity is the touch of God
In human hearts,
And from that way He ever trod
He ne'er departs.
And the angels all were silent.

And He said, "Now will I go with you,
Dear child of love,
I am weary of all this glory, too,
In heaven above."
And the angels all were silent.

"We will go seek and save the lost,
If they will hear,
They who are worst but need me most,
And all are dear."
And the angels were not silent.

## WILLIAM MACGONAGALL (1825–1902)

[MacGonagall, son of Irish immigrants, was a weaver for many years, before he turned to poetry, after which he made a living by giving readings. A true primitive, MacGonagall seems to have taken his poetry quite seriously. Many of his audience were no doubt pleased by his vigorous lines; others laughed at him. He is today regarded as a wildly funny artist (if unconsciously so), and a true satire upon popular taste. The following is one of his best known works.]

### Railway Bridge of the Silvery Tay

Beautiful new railway bridge of the silvery Tay,
With your strong brick piers and buttresses in so grand array;
And your thirteen central girders, which seems to my eye,
Strong enough all windy storms to defy.

And as I gaze upon thee my heart feels gay,
Because thou art the greatest railway bridge of the present day;
And can be seen for miles away,
From north, south, east, or west, of the Tay,
On a beautiful and clear sunshiny day,
And ought to make the hearts of the Mars boys feel gay;
Because thine equal nowhere can be seen,
Only near by Dundee and the bonnie Magdalen Green.

Beautiful new railway bridge of the silvery Tay,
With your beautiful side screens along your railway;
Which will be a great protection on a windy day,
So as the railway carriages won't be blown away;
And ought to cheer the hearts of the passengers night and day,
As they are conveyed along thy beautiful railway.
And towering above the silvery Tay,
Spanning the beautiful river from shore to shore;
Upwards of two miles and more,
Which is most wonderful to be seen—
Near by Dundee and the bonnie Magdalen Green.

Thy structure, to my eye, seems strong and grand,
And the workmanship most skillfully planned;
And I hope the designers, Messrs. Barlow & Arrol, will prosper for many a day,
For erecting thee across the beautiful Tay.
And I think nobody need have the least dismay,
To cross oer thee by night or day;
Because thy strength is visible to be seen—
Near by Dundee and the bonnie Magdalen Green.

Beautiful new railway bridge of the silvery Tay,
I wish you success for many a year and day,
And I hope thousands of people will come from far and away,
Both high and low, without delay,
From the north, south, east and the west,
Because as a railway bridge thou art the best;
Thou standest unequaled to be seen—
Near by Dundee and the bonnie Magdalen Green.

And for beauty thou art most lovely to be seen,
As the train crosses oer thee with her cloud of steam
And you look well painted with the color of marone,
And to find thy equal there is none;
Which, without fear of contradiction, I venture to say,
Because you are the longest railway bridge of the present day;
That now crosses oer a tidal river stream,
And the most handsome to be seen—
Near by Dundee and the bonnie Magdalen Green.

The New Yorkers boast about their Brooklyn Bridge,
But in comparison to thee it seems like a midge,
Because thou spannest the silvery Tay,
A mile and more longer I venture to say;
Besides the railways carriages are pulled across by a rope,
Therefore Brooklyn Bridge cannot with thee cope;
And as you have been opened on the 20th day of June,
I hope Her Majesty Queen Victoria will visit thee very soon;
Because thou art worthy of a visit from Duke, Lord, or Queen,
And strong and securely built, which is most worthy to be seen—
Near by Dundee and the bonnie Magdalen Green.

## WILLIAM ALEXANDER (1826–1894)

[A farmer, journalist and finally writer of fiction, Alexander is best known for the 1870 novel, *Johnny Gibb of Gushetneuk*. That book is in turn celebrated for its vigorous, earthy scenes of Aberdeenshire country life. A good sense of Alexander's forthright style, careful attention to historic detail and insight into rural mores is given in the three following works. The first is a short story, and the others are taken from *Notes and Sketches: Illustrations of Northern Rural Life in the Eighteenth Century* (1876).]

### Baubie Huie's Bastard Geet

#### Jock Huie's Household—Baubie Enters Life

I am not prepared to say how far Baubie Huie's own upbringing had been a model of judicious parental nurture. There was ground to fear that it had not been at all times regulated by an enlightened regard to the principle laid down by King Solomon, concerning the training of children. Jock Huie had a muckle sma' faimily, crammed into limited space, in so far as the matter of house accommodation was concerned. It was a little, clay-built, "rape-thackit" cot in which Jock, with Eppie, his wife, and their family dwelt; and the "creaturs" came so thickly, and in such multitude, that Jock, who was a "darger," and did "days' warks" here and there, as he could find them, experienced rather queer sensations when an unusually "coorse" day happened to coop him up at home among the "smatterie" of youngsters.

"Saul o' me, 'oman," would Jock exclaim, when patience had reached its limit; "the din o' that bairns o' yours wud rive a heid o' steen—-gar them be quaet, aw'm sayin', or I'll hae to tak' a horse fup[1] to them."

"Haud yer tongue, man; gin ye war amo' them fae screek o' day till gloamin' licht's I am, ye mith speak. Fat can the creaturs dee fan they canna get leuket owre a door?" Eppie would reply.

Notwithstanding his formidable threat, Jock Huie rarely lifted his hand in the way of active correction of his offspring. His wife. who was not indisposed to govern a little more sharply if she could, knew of only one way of enforcing obedience, or some approach thereto, when matters had come to a decided pass of the character indicated, and which may be best described in plain English as indiscriminate chastisement, applied with sufficient heartiness though it might be quite as much in accordance with the dictates of temper as of calm reason. And so it came to pass that, as most of the youthful Huies were gifted with pretty definite wills of their own, the progress of physical development on their part might be taken, in a general way, as indicative, in inverse proportion, of the measure of moral and mental sway which the parental will was able to exercise over them.

All that by the way, however. Jock Huie got his family brought up as he best could, and off his hands mainly; and he, personally, continued his dargin' with perhaps a little less vir than aforetime. Jock was a man of large bones and strong bodily frame; when thirty he had physical strength that seemed equal to any task, and endurance against which no amount of rough usage appeared to tell with evil effect. But after all, men of Jock Huie's class do not wear long. Jock was now a man only a few years past fifty; yet digging in wet drains and ditches, and eating a bit of oat cake, washed down with "treacle ale," to his dinner, day by day, had procured for him a very appreciable touch of "rheumatics," and other indications that he had fairly passed his prime.

And Baubie, his eldest daughter, though not the eldest member of his family, for Jock had various sons older than she—Baubie had grown up—a buxom, ruddy-cheeked "quine" of nineteen. She was servan' lass to the farmer of Brigfit—Briggies in short.

I remember very distinctly a bonnie summer gloamin at that time. It was gey[2] late owre i' the evenin'. Baubie had milket the kye, seyt the milk, and wash'n up her dishes. Her day's work was at last fairly done, and why should not Baubie go out to the Toon Loan to enjoy the quiet scene as the cool dews of evening began to fall upon the landscape around the cozy, old-fashioned farm "steading" of Brigfit.

It matters nothing in this narration where I had been that evening, further than to say that, as I pursued my journey homeward, the road took me past the corner of Briggies' stable, where, altogether unexpectedly to me, I encountered Baubie Huie "in maiden mediation fancy free." Though Baubie's junior by a twelvemonth or so, I had developed since we two had last met from a mere herd loon[3] into a sort of rawish second or third horseman. We had known each other more or less from infancy, Baubie and I, and our talk during the short parley that now ensued had a tinge of the bygone time in it; though, of course, we could not help giving fulfillment, in our own way, to the saying that out of the abundance of the heart, the mouth speaketh; and, naturally of life, that which most occupied our hearts was the present as it bore on

---

[1]In this dialect the "f" is often a substitute for "wh."

[2]Very, quite.

[3]Boy, worker.

our respective positions and prospects.

My own notion (it may be said in confidence) was that I was climbing up the pathway to maturity of life and definiteness of position with creditable alacrity; but in this direction I speedily found that Baubie Huie had fairly out-distanced me. Why, here was the very same "quine" who, almost the last time I saw her, was lugging along a big, sulky bairn, half her own size, wrapped in an old tartan plaid, and her weather-bleached hair hanging loosely about her shoulders—and that bairn her own younger brother—that very quine, giggling and tossing her head knowingly as she spoke, in what seemed a tone of half masculine license, about the "chiels" that were more or less familiarly known as sweethearts among young women in the neighborhood of Brigfit. In matters of love and courtship, I was, it must be confessed, an entire novice; whereas in such affairs, it was obvious, Baubie had become an adept; and if I had been somewhat put out by the ready candor with which she criticized the physical appearance and general bearing of this and the other young man—hangers on after Baubie, I was given to understand—I was nothing short of completely "flabbergasted" when, just as we were parting, she said—

"Dinna ye never gae fae hame at even, min? Ye mith come owre the gate some nicht an' see's."

What my confused and stuttering reply amounted to I cannot really say—something grotesquely stupid, no doubt. What it called forth on Baubie's part, at any rate, was another round of giggling and the exclamation, as she turned off toward the dwelling-house of Brigfit—

"Weel, weel, Robbie, a' nicht wi' you; an' a file o' the morn's mornin'."—This was simply the slang form of saying "good night" among persons of Baubie's class. And she added—"I'll need awa' in; for there's Briggies, the aul' snot, at the ga'le o' the hoose— he'll be barrin' 's oot again, eenoo."

Now, far be it from me to say that Baubie was a vicious or immodest young woman. I really am not prepared to say that she was anything of the sort. She had simply got the training that hundreds in her station of life in these northern shires do—home training that is. And after she left the parental roof, her experiences had been the common experiences of her class—that is to associate freely with promiscuous assemblages of farm-servants, male and female; mainly older than herself, without any supervision worth mentioning, as she moved from one situation to another. And how could Baubie, as an apt enough scholar, do other than imbibe the spirit and habits of those in whose companionship she lived day by day? Baubie was simply the natural product of the system under which she had been reared. Her moral tone, as indexed by her speech, might not be very high; and yet, after all, it is very possible to have the mere verbal proprieties fully attended to, where the innate morality is no whit better. Coarseness in the outer form, which is thrust on the view of all, is bad enough; depravity in the inner spirit, which is frequently concealed from many, may be a good deal worse.

Brigfit was a decent man; a very decent man, for he was an elder in the parish kirk, and a bachelor of good repute. He was a careful, industrious farmer, the extent of whose haudin enabled him; to "ca' twa pair." Briggies was none of your stylish gentlemen farmers; he needed neither gig nor "shalt" to meet his personal convenience, but did his ordinary business journeys regularly on foot. And he stood on reasonably amicable terms with his servants; but he sought little of their confidence, and as little did he give to them of his own. Only Briggies had certain inflexible rules, and one was that his household should be in bed every night by nine o'clock in winter, and an hour later in summer; when he would himself solemnly put the bar on the door, and then walk as solemnly along to the "horn en'" to seek repose.

Briggies was a very early riser, and as it was his hand that usually put the bar on the door at night, so, honest man, was it his hand that ordinarily took it off in the morning in time to see that the household proper and the occupants of the outside "chaum'er," consisting of the male servants, were stirring to begin the labors of the day in due season. According to Baubie Huie's account, the bar was sometimes tampered with during the interval by the "deems"; only if matters were gone about quietly enough, Briggies, whether or not he might suspect aught in that way, usually said nothing.

"Augh, Robbie, man! Fear't for Briggies kennin? Peer body! fan onything comes in's noddle aboot's nowte beasts he canna get rest, but 'll be up an' paumerin aboot the toon' o' the seelence o' the nicht, fan it's as mark 's pick in winter, forbye o' the simmer evenin's. So ae nicht i' the spring time that me an' my neebour hedna been wuntin to gae to oor beds, we pits oot the lamp in gweed time, an' sits still, as quaet 's pussy, till Briggies hed on the bar an' away till 's bed. I'm nae sayin' gin onybody was in ahin that or no, but lang aifter the wee oor hed struck'n, me an' Jinse was thereoot. I suppose the chiels hed made mair noise nor they sud 'a deen, caperin' owre the causeway wi' their muckle tacketie beets. At ony rate in a blink there was Briggies oot an' roon to the byres wi' the booet in 's han'. Fan he hed glampit aboot amo' the beasts till he was satisfeet, he gaes awa' to the hoose again; an' we wusna lang o' bein' aifter 'im. But fudder or no he had leuket ben to the kitchie to see gin we wus there, he hed pitten the bar siccar aneuch on upo' the door this time, I can tell ye; an' nae an in cud we win for near an oor, till we got an aul' ledder an' pat it up to the en' o' the hoose, an' syne I made oot to creep in at the ga'le winnochie— Fat did he say aifterhin? Feint[1] a thing. Briggies never loot on, though he cudna but 'a hed 's ain think, 'cause gin he didna hear huz, he be 't till 'a kent gyaun oot' that the bar sudna 'a been aff o the door at that time o' nicht."

In this wise did Baubie Huie keep up the colloquy, my side of which, candor compels me to say, was very badly sustained; for had I been ever so willing to take my part, the requisite fluency and *abandon* had not been attained, to say nothing of the utter absence of knowledge germane to the subject in hand, and personally acquired.

As a matter of course, I did not accept Baubie Huie's invitation to visit Brigfit. If the truth were to be told, I was too much of a greenhorn; one who would have been accurately described by Baubie and her associates as utterly destitute of "spunk." My Mentor of that date, a vigorous fellow of some eight and twenty years, whose habits might be not incorrectly described by the word "haiveless," whose speech was at least as free, as refined, and who occupied the responsible position of first horseman, did not indeed hesitate to characterize my behavior in relation to such matters, generally, in almost those very words. He knew Baubie Huie, moreover, and his estimate of Baubie was expressed in the words— "Sang, she's a richt quine yon, min; there's nae a deem i' the pairt'll haud 'er nain wi' ye better nor she'll dee; an' she's a fell ticht gweed-leukin hizzie tee," which, no doubt, was a perfectly accurate description according to the notions entertained by the speaker of the qualities desirable in the female sex.

However these things may be, Baubie Huie continued to perform her covenanted duties to the farmer of Brigfit; and, so far as known, yielding the elder average satisfaction as a servant during the summer "half-year."

## II
### Baubie Returns Home

It was nearing the term of Martinmas, and Jock Huie, who had been laid off work for several days by a "beel't thoom," was discussing his winter prospect with

---

[1] Scarcely.

Eppie, his wife. Meal was "fell chape," and the potato crop untouched by disease; but Jock's opinion was that, as prices were low for the farmer, feein' would be slack. Cattle were down too, and though the price of beef and mutton was a purely abstract question for him personally—he being a strict vegetarian in practice, not by choice but of necessity —Jock was economist enough to know that the fact bore adversely on the farmer's ability to employ labor; so that, altogether, with a superfluity of regular servants unengaged, and a paucity of work for the common "darger" in the shape of current farming improvements going on, he did not regard the aspect of things as cheering for his class.

"Aw howp neen o' that loons o' ours 'll throw themsel's oot o' a place," said Jock. "Wud ye think ony o' them wud be bidin'?"

"That wud be hard to say, man," replied Eppie.

"That widdifus[1] o' young chiels 's aye sae saucy to speak till," said Jock; whether he meant that the sauciness would be exhibited in the concrete from his own sons toward himself, or if the remark applied to the bearing of servant chiels generally on the point under consideration, was not clear. "But better to them tak' a sma' waage nor lippen[2] to orra[3] wark; an' hae to lie aboot idle the half o' the winter."

"Weel ken we that," said Eppie, with a tolerably lively recollection of her experiences in having previously had one or two of her sons "at hame" during the winter season. "Mere ate-meats till Can'lesmas; I'm seer fowk hae's little need o' that; but creaturs'll tak' their nain gate for a' that."

"Aw howp Baubie's bidin' wi' Briggies, ony wye," added Jock.

"I ken naething aboot it," said Eppie, in a tone that might be described as dry; "Baubie's gey an' gweed at keepin' 'er coonsel till 'ersel." It was only a fortnight to the term, and Jock would not be kept long in suspense regarding those questions affecting the family arrangements on which he had thus incidentally touched. In point of fact, his mind was set at rest so far when only half the fortnight had run. For the feeing market came in during that period, and as Jock's thumb had not yet allowed him to resume work, he "took a step doon" to the market, where he had the satisfaction of finding that his sons had all formed engagements as regular farm servants. As for Baubie, though Jock learned on sufficient authority that she was present in the market, he failed to "meet in" with her. Concerning Baubie's intended movements, he learnt, too, that she was *not* staying with Briggies; Briggies himself had indeed told him so; but beyond that, Jock's enquiries on the subject did not produce any enlightenment for him.

Subsequently to the feeing market, Jock Huie had once and again reverted to the subject of Baubie's strange behavior in keeping the family in ignorance of her movements and intentions, but without drawing forth much in the way of response from his wife beyond what she had generally expressed in her previous remark.

The afternoon of the term day had come, and servants who were flittin' were moving here and there. I cannot state the nature of the ruminations that had passed, or were passing, through the mind of either Jock Huie or his wife Eppie concerning their daughter Baubie; but Jock, honest man, had just left his cottage in the gray gloamin to go to the smiddy and get his tramp-pick sharpened with the view of resuming work next day in full vigor, when Baubie, dressed in her Sunday garments, and carrying a small bundle, entered. There was a brief pause; and then Baubie's mother, in a distinct and very deliberate tone, said—

"Weel, Baubie, 'oman; an' *ye're* here neist."

---

[1]Scoundrel ("gallows—full").

[2]Trust.

[3]Odd, occasional.

At these words, Baubie, who had just laid aside her bundle, threw herself down beside it, on the top of the family "deece,"[1] with the remark,

"Aye; faur ither wud aw gae?"

And then she proceeded silently to untie the strings of her bonnet. Neither Baubie nor her mother was extremely agitated, but there was a certain measure of restrained feeling operating upon both the one and the other. The mother felt that a faithful discharge of the maternal duty demanded that she should give utterance to a reproof as severe as she could properly frame, accompanied by reproaches, bearing on the special wickedness and ingratitude of the daughter; and, on the part of the daughter along with a vague sense of the fitness of all this, in a general way, there were indications of a volcanic state of temper, which might burst out with considerable, if misplaced fierceness, on comparatively slight provocation. And wherefore create a scene of verbal violence? for deep down, below those irascible feelings, did there not lurk in Eppie Huie's bosom a kind of latent sense that if such crises as that which had now emerged were not to be regarded as absolutely certain, they were assuredly to be looked upon as very much in the nature of events inevitable in the ordinary history of the family? And thus it was that Eppie Huie, virtually accepting the situation as part of the common lot, went no further than a general rasping away at details, and the consequences arising out of the main fact.

"Weel, weel, Baubie, 'oman, ye've begun to gae the aul' gate[2] in braw time—ye'll fin't a hard road to yersel', as weel's to them 't 's near conneckit wi' you. Fat gar't ye keep oot o' yer fader's sicht at the market—haudin 'im gyaun like a wull stirk seekin' ye, an' makin' a feel o' 'im?"

"Aw'm seer ye needna speer that—'s gin ye hedna kent to tell 'im yersel'."

"That's a bonnie story to set up noo, ye limmer[3]—that I sud say the like," said Eppie with some heat. "Didnin ye deny't i' my face the vera last time that ye was here?"

"H-mph! an' aw daursay ye believ't 's!"

"Weel, Baubie, 'oman, it's a sair say 't we sud be forc't to tak' for a muckle black lee fat 's been threepit,[4] an' yea-threepit i' oor witters be' them that's sibbest til 's."

To this observation Baubie made no reply: and after a short silence Eppie Huie continued in a dreary monotone—

"Ay, ay. An' this is fat folk get for toilin' themsel's to deith feshin up a faimily! There's little aneuch o' peace or rest for's till oor heid be aneth the green sod—jist oot o' ae tribble in till anither. Little did I or yer peer fader think short syne that ye was to be hame to be a burden till 's."

"Aw ha'ena been a burden yet ony wye," said Baubie with some sharpness, "ye needna be sae ready speakin' that gate."

To this retort Eppie Huie made some reply to the effect that others similarly circumstanced had uttered such brave words, and that time would tell in Baubie's case as it had told in theirs. She then rose and put some water in a small pot, which she hung upon the "crook" over the turf fire, in the light of which Baubie and she had hitherto sat.

"Fa 's the fader o' 't than?" said Eppie Huie, as she turned about from completing the operation just mentioned; but though the words were uttered in a very distinct as well as abrupt tone, there was no answer till she repeated her question in

---

[1]Wooden seat (table, bed).

[2]Way, path.

[3]Tramp, no-good.

[4]Rumored.

the form of a sharp "Aw'm sayin'?"

"Ye'll ken that a-time aneuch," answered Baubie.

"Ken 't a-time aneuch!—an' you here"—

"Ay, an' me here—an' fat aboot it? It winna be here the morn, nor yet the morn's morn," said Baubie in a harder and more reckless tone than she had yet assumed.

Eppie Huie had, no doubt, a sense of being baffled, more or less. She resumed her seat, uttering as she did so, something between a sigh and a groan.

There was nothing more said until the water in the little pot having now got to "the boil," Eppie rose, and lighting the rush wick in the little black lamp that hung on the shoulder of the "swye" from which the crook depended, proceeded to "mak the sowens."[1] When the lamp had been lighted, Baubie rose from her place on the deece, and lifting her bonnet, which now lay beside her, and her bundle, said,

"A'm gyaun awa' to my bed."

"Ye better wyte an' get yer sipper —the sowens'll be ready eenoo."

"Aw'm nae wuntin' nae sipper," said Baubie, turning to go as she spoke. "There's nae things lyin' i' the mid-hoose bed, is there?"

"Naething; oonless it be the muckle basket, wi' some o' yer breeders' half-dry't claes. Tak' that bit fir i' yer han'—ye'll need it, ony wye, to lat ye see to haud aff o' the tubs an' the basket."

And Baubie went off to bed forthwith, notwithstanding a sort of second invitation, as she was lighting the fir, to wait for some supper. I rather think that after all she did not relish the comparative light so much as the comparative darkness. And then if she stayed to get even the first practicable mouthful of "sowens," was there not considerable risk that Jock Huie, her father, might drop in upon her on his return from the smiddy? Not that Baubie had an unreasonable sensitive dread of facing her father. But having now got over what she would have called "the warst o' 't" with her mother, she felt that her mother, being on the whole so well "posted up," might be left with advantage to break the ice, at least, to the old man.

When Jock Huie returned from the smiddy that evening, an event that happened in about half an hour after his daughter Baubie had gone to hed, he seemed to be moody, and in a measure out of temper. He put aside his bonnet, and sat down in his usual corner, while Eppie set the small table for his supper, only one or two remarks of a very commonplace sort having been made up to that point.

"Ye'll better saw awa', man; they've been made this file," said Eppie, as she lifted the dish with the "sowens" to the table from the hearthstone, where it had been placed in order to retain warmth in the mess.

"Aw'm sayin', 'oman," quoth Jock, apparently oblivious to his wife's invitation, "div ye ken onything about that jaud Baubie— there's something or anither nae richt, ere she wud haud oot o' fowk's road this gate?"

"Baubie's here, man," said Eppie Huie; and the brevity of her speech was more than made up by the significance of the words and the tone in which they were uttered.

"Here?" exclaimed Jock in a tone of inquiry, and looking towards his wife as he spoke.

"She's till 'er bed i' the mid-hoose," said Eppie in reply; and, perceiving that Jock's look was only half answered, she added, "Aw daursay she wasna owre fain to see you."

"Fat!" cried Jock, "she'll be wi' a geet to some chiel, is she?"

---

[1] An oatmeal dish.

"Ou ye needna speer,"[1] said Eppie in a tone of "dowie"[2] resignation.

"Weel, that does cowe the gowan—a quine o' little mair nor nineteen. But aw mith 'a been seer o' 't. It wasna for naething that she was playin' hide-an'-seek wi' me yon gate. Brawlie kent I that she was i' the market wi' a set o' them. Deil speed them a', weela-wat."

Jock Huie was not a model man exactly in point of moral sentiment; neither was he a man of keen sensibility. But he did nevertheless possess a certain capability of sincere, if it might be uncultured feeling; and he now placed his rough, weather-beaten face against the horny palms of his two hands, and, resting his two elbows on his knees, gave utterance to a prolonged "Hoch-hey!" Jock maintained this attitude for sometime, and probably would have maintained it good deal longer, but for the practical view of matters taken by his wife, and the practical advice urgently pressed upon him by her when her patience had got exhausted:—

"Aw'm sayin', man, ye needna connach yer sipper; that'll dee nae gweed to nae-body.—Tak' your sowens! Ye're lattin them grow stiff wi' caul', for a' the tribble 't aw was at keepin' them het to you."

Thus admonished, Jock Huie took his supper in silence; and, thereafter, with little more talk beyond one or two questions from Jock of a like nature with those which had been so ineffectually addressed to Baubie by her mother, the husband and wife retired to bed.

## III

### The Geet's Advent—Initial Difficulties in Acquiring An Ecclesiastical Status

That Jock Huie's daughter, Baubie, had returned home to her father and mother was a fact about which there could be no manner of doubt or equivocation; as to the cause of Baubie's return, there was a general concurrence of opinion in the neighborhood; indeed, it had been a point settled long before, among elderly and sagacious females who knew her, that Baubie would speedily appear in her true colors. Yet there were a few of this same class of people in whose sides Baubie was still somewhat of a thorn. For when the first few days were over after her return, so far from shrinking out of their sight, Baubie flung herself across their path at the most unexpected times, and exhibited an unmistakable readiness to meet their friendly criticisms with a prompt retort. Or was it a staring personal scrutiny—well, Baubie was almost ostentatiously ready to stand that ordeal, and stare with the best of her starers in return. Baubie was perfectly able to take care of herself, and if a young woman of her spirit chose to remain six months out of the "hire house," whose business was that but her own? Baubie would like to know that.

It is not to be supposed that this bravado went far in the way of deceiving any but very inexperienced people, if it deceived even them, which is more than doubtful. And in the nature of the case, it would at any rate deceive no one very long.

It was just at Candlemas when it was reported that Jock Huie had become a grandfather; a genealogical dignity the attainment of which did not seem to excite in Jock's breast any particular feeling of elation. Such an idea as that of apprehension lest the line of Huies in his branch should become extinct had certainly never troubled Jock to the extent that would have made him anxious to welcome a grandchild, legitimate or illegitimate; and the belief that this particular bairn was born to be a direct and positive burden upon him hardly tended to make its advent either auspicious or cheering. Jock knew full well the "tyauve" he had had in

---

[1] Ask.

[2] Sad.

bringing up his own family proper; and now, ere the obstreperous squalling of the younger of them was well out of his ears, why here was another sample of the race, ready to renew and continue all that turmoil and uproar, by night and by day, from which his small hut had never been free for a good twenty years of his lifetime.

"An' it's a laddie, ye say, that the quine Huie's gotten?"

"A laddie; an' a-wat a richt protty gate-farrin bairnie 's ever ye saw wi' yer twa een."

"Fan cam' 't hame no?"

"It was jist the streen,[1] nae langer gane. Aifter 't was weel gloam't, I hears a chap at the window, an' fa sud this be but Eppie 'ersel', peer creatur. I pat my tartan shawl aboot my heid immedantly, an' aifter tellin' the littleans to keep weel ootbye fae the fire, an' biddin' their sister pit them to their beds shortly, I crap my wa's roun' as fest 's aw cud. Jock was nae lang come hame fae 's day's wark, an' was sittin' i' the neuk at 's bit sipper. 'He's jist makin' ready to gae for Mrs. Slorach,' says she. 'Awat I was rael ill-pay't for 'im, peer stock, tir't aneuch nae doot, jist aff o' a sair day's wark. It was a freely immas nicht, wi' byous coorse ploiterie road; an' it's three mile gweed, but I can asseer ye Jock hed gnae weel, for it wasna muckle passin' twa oors fan he's back an' Mrs. Slorach wi' 'im."

"Weel, weel, Jock'll get's nain o' 't lickly, honest man. It'll be a won'er an' they hinna the tsil' to fesh up."

"Ou weel-a-wat that's true aneuch; but there's never a hicht but there's a howe[2] at the boddom o' 't, as I said to Eppie fan she first taul' me o' Baubie's misfortune; an' there's never a mou'[3] sen' but the maet's sen' wi' 't."

"Div they ken yet fa's the fader o' the creatur?"

"Weel, she hed been unco stubborn aboot it no; but aw'm thinkin' she hed taul' 'er mither at the lang len'th. At a roch guess, a body mith gae farrer agley,[4] aw daursay, nor licken 't to ane o' yon chiels 't was aboot the toon wi' 'er at Briggies'—yon skyeow-fittet breet."

The foregoing brief extract from the conversation of a couple of those kindly gossips who had all along taken a special interest in her case will indicate with sufficient distinctness the facts surrounding the birth of Baubie Huie's Geet.

The reputed father of the geet was a sort of nondescript chap, whose habit it was to figure at one time as an indifferent second or third "horseman," and next time as an "orra man";[5] a bulletheaded bumpkin, with big unshapely feet, spreading considerably outward as he walked; a decided taste for smoking tobacco; of somewhat more than average capability in talking bucolic slang of a gross sort; yet possessing withal a comfortable estimate of his own graces of person and manner in the eyes of the fair sex. Such was the—sweetheart, shall we say?—of Baubie Huie.

How one might best define the precise relationship existing between the nondescript chiel and Baubie, it would not be easy to say. It was believed that on the feeing market night he had taken Baubie home to Briggies', he being not greatly the worse of drink, and that on the term night he had accompanied her part of the way toward her father's house. There was also a sort of vague impression that he had since then come once or twice to visit Baubie, keeping as well out of sight and ken of Jock Huie and his wife as might be. Be that as it may, now that the child was born, Jock,

---

[1] Streen = "last evening."

[2] Low spot, hollow.

[3] "Mouth."

[4] Awry.

[5] Odd-job man.

who was very much of a practical man, desired to know articulately from the man himself whether he was to "tak wi' 't an' pay for't." The idea of asking whether the fellow had any intention of doing the one thing which a man with a shred of honor about him would have felt bound to do in the circumstances—viz., marrying his daughter—had really not occurred to Jock Huie.

And so it came to pass, that after a certain amount of rather irritating discussion between himself and the female members of his family, and as the nondescript took very good care not to come to him, Jock "took road" to hunt up the nondescript, who, as he discovered after some trouble, was now serving on a farm some five or six miles off. He found him as third horseman at the plow in a field of "neep-reet," along with his two fellow plowmen. The nondescript had a sufficient aspect of embarrassment when Jock Huie caught him up at the end rig, where he had been waiting till the plows should come out, to indicate that he would not have been disappointed had the visit been omitted; and it seemed not improbable that his two companions might thereafter offer one or two interrogatory remarks on the subject, which would not be a great deal more welcome. At any rate, Jock Huie had the satisfaction of finding that the nondescript "wasna seekin' to deny't"; nay, that he did not refuse to "pay for't," any backwardness on his part in that respect up to the date of visit, being readily accounted for by the fact that it was the middle of the half-year, when a man was naturally run of cash. Threats about "'reestin' waages," therefore, were perfectly uncalled-for; and, indeed, a sort of unjust aspersion on the general character of the nondescript. It was right that Jock Huie should know that.

"Ye sud hae the civeelity to lat fowk ken faur ye are than; an' ye think ony ill o' that. Bonnie story to haud me trailin' here, lossin' half a day seekin' ye," retorted Jock with some roughness of tone.

Between the date of Jock Huie's visit just mentioned and the term of Whitsunday, the father of Baubie Huie's geet visited the abode of the Huies once at any rate; and in course of the conference that ensued, it so happened that the subject of getting the geet christened came up—the needful preliminary to that being, as Jock explained, to appear and give satisfaction to that grave Church Court, the Kirk-Session. This was a point which both the paternal and maternal Huie were a good deal more eager to discuss and settle about than either of the immediate parents of the geet. Indeed, the nondescript seemed penetrated with a sort of feeling that that was a part of the business hardly in his line. Not that he objected on principle to the geet being christened; far from it; for when Eppie Huie had stated the necessity of getting themselves "clear't," and having that rite performed, and Jock Huie had vigorously backed up her statement, the nondescript assented with a perfectly explicit "Ou ay"; only he showed a decided tendency always to let the matter drop again. This did not suit Jock Huie's book in the least, however, and he manifested a determination to have the business followed out that was not at all comfortable to the nondescript.

When the nondescript had pondered over the situation for a few days, and all along with the feeling that something must really be done, for he did not in the least relish the idea of further calls from Jock Huie, the happy thought occurred to him of calling on his old master, Briggies, who was one of the elders of the Kirk, and, being after all a humane man, would no doubt be prevailed upon to pave the way for him and Baubie making penitential appearance before the session, and receiving censure and "absolution." So he called on Briggies, and was rather dryly told that, neither Baubie nor he being "commeenicants," apart from the censure of the session, which had to be encountered in the first place, he, at any rate, "as the engaging parent" (and perhaps Baubie too), would have to undergo an examination, at the hands of the minister, as to his knowledge of the cardinal doctrines of the Christian faith, and the significance of the rite of baptism in particular.

"Fat wye cud ye expeck to win throw itherweese, min?" Briggies felt bound to speak as an elder in this case—"Gin fowk winna leern to behave themsel's they maun jist stan' the consequences. The vera Kirk-Session itsel' cudna relieve ye, man, upo' nae ither precunnance."

The nondescript returned much pondering on this disheartening information, which he got opportunity, by and bye, of communicating to Baubie. In private conference, the two agreed that "a scaulin' fae the session," by itself—a thing they had been both accustomed to hear spoken of with extreme jocularity, not less than they had seen those who had undergone the same, regarded as possessing something of the heroism that is rather to be envied—a scaulin' fae the session might well be borne; but to stand a formal examination before the minister in cold blood was another affair. The dilemma having occurred, the two horns were presented to Jock Huie, who was so relentlessly forcing them on to impalement, in the hope of softening his heart, or at any rate awakening his sympathy; but Jock was just as determined as ever that they must go forward in the performance of their Christian duty, and his one reply was, "Ou, deil care; ye maun jist haud at the Catechis."

## IV

### The Geet's Status, Ecclesiastical and Social, Defined

"Aw'm sayin', 'oman, that geet maun be kirsen't some wye or anither; we canna lat the creatur grow up like a haethen."

The speaker in this case was Jock Huie, and the person addressed his wife Eppie. It was a fine Saturday evening toward the latter end of June, and Jock, who had got home from his work at the close of the week, was now in a deliberative mood.

"Weel, man, ye'll need to see fat wye 't's to be manag't," was Eppie's reply.

"They'll jist need 'o tak' her 'er leen; that's a' that I can say aboot it," said Jock.

"Ah-wa, man; wa won'er to her ye speak."

"Weel fat else can ye dee? Aw tell ye the littlean 'll be made a moniment o' i' the kwintra side."

"Ou, weel, ye maun jist gae to the minaister yersel', man, an' tell 'im fat gate her an' huz tee 's been guidet; he's a rael sympatheesin person, an' there's nae doot he'll owreleuk onything as far's he can."

"Sorra set 'im, weel-a-wat!" said Jock Huie emphatically, as he knocked the half-burnt "dottal" of tobacco out of his pipe into the palm of his hand, with a sort of savage thump.

Whether Jock Huie's portentous objurgation on the subject of the Catechism had much or anything to do with the result it would perhaps be difficult to say, but it was a simple matter of fact that after it had been uttered, the father of Baubie's geet exhibited even more than previously a disposition to fight shy of the path of duty on which Jock sought to impel him. The Whitsunday term was drawing on; the Whitsunday term had arrived and the geet still unchristened. Then it was found that the father of the geet had deemed it an expedient thing to seek an appreciable change of air by "flittin'" entirely beyond "kent bounds." True it was, that on the very eve of his departure he had by the hands of a third party transmitted to Baubie for the maintenance of her geet a "paper note" of the value of one pound, and along with it a verbal message to the effect that he was "gyaun to the pairis' o' Birse"; but as it had been a not infrequent practice among the witty to mention the parish named as a sort of mythical region to which one might be condemned to go, for whom no other sublunary use was apparent, Baubie herself was far from assured that the literal

Birse was meant; and we may add was equally at a loss as to whether she had further remittances to look for, or if the note was a once and single payment, in full discharge of the nondescript's obligations in respect to the present maintenance, and prospective upbringing of his son—the Bastard Geet.

Baubie Huie's Bastard Geet had now reached the age of fully four months; no wonder if the grand-paternal anxieties should be aroused as to the danger of the "peer innocent" merging into heathenism and becoming a bye-word to the parish. And as Jock Huie had expressed his sense of the importance of kirsenin' as a preventative, so after all, it fell to Jock's lot to take the responsible part in getting the rite performed. The name was a matter of difficulty; had there been an available father, it would have been his duty to confer with the mother on the point, and be fully instructed what name to bestow on the infant; and in the case of his own children, the male part of them at any rate, Jock Huie had never been much at a loss about the names. Among his sons, Tam, Sawney, and Jock, came in, in orderly succession; but, ponder as he would, the naming of Baubie's geet puzzled him long. Its reputed father bore the name of Samuel—cut down to Samie—Caie, and Jock rejected promptly and with scorn the suggestion, coming from its mother, to inflict upon the bairn any such name, which he, in strong language, declared to be nauseous enough to serve as an emetic to a dog. Indeed, Jock's honest hatred of the nondescript had now reached a pitch that made him resolutely decline to pronounce his name at all; a practice in which, as a rule, he was tacitly imitated by his wife and daughter.

Partly from this cause, and partly by reason of the still further delay that occurred in getting the christening over, it came to pass that the poor youngster began to have attached to it, with a sort of permanency, the title of Baubie Huie's Bastard Geet; and when at last the parson had done the official duty in question, and Jock Huie, with a just sense of his position in the matter, had boldly named the bairn after himself, it only led to the idle youth of the neighborhood ringing the changes on the geet in this fashion—

Aul' Jock, an' young Jock, an' Jock comin' tee;
There'll never be a gweed Jock till aul' Jock dee.

But notwithstanding of all these things the geet throve and grew as only a sturdy scion of humanity could be expected to do.

To say that Baubie Huie was passionately attached to her child, would perhaps be rather an over-statement, yet was she pleased to nurse the poor geet with a fair amount of kindness; and physically the geet seemed to make no ungrateful return. It was edifying to note the bearing of the different members of the family towards the geet. The practical interest taken in its spiritual welfare by old Jock Huie has been mentioned; and despite the trouble it had caused him, Jock was equally prepared now to let the geet have the first and tenderest "bite" from his hard-won daily crust to meet its temporal wants; a measure of self-denial such as many a philanthropist of higher station and greater pretensions has never set before himself.

The nature of Eppie Huie's feelings toward the geet was sufficiently indicated by the skilled and careful nursing she would expend upon it at those times when Baubie, tired of her charge, with an unceremonious—"Hae, tak' 'im a file, mither" —would hand over the geet "body bulk" to the charge of its granny.

When any of Jock Huie's grown-up sons happened to visit home, their cue was simply to ignore the geet altogether. Even when it squalled the loudest they would endeavor to retain the appearance of stolid obliviousness of its presence; just as they did when the hapless geet crowed and "walloped" its small limbs in the superabundance of its joy at being allowed the novel pleasure of gazing at them. The members of the family who were Baubie's juniors, did not profess indifference; only their feeling toward the geet, when it came under their notice on these temporary visits home, was in the main the reverse of amicable. Her younger sister, indeed, in Baubie's hearing, designated the unoffending geet a "nasty brat," whereat Baubie flared up hotly and reminded her that it was not so very long since she, the sister, was an equally "nasty brat," to say the very least of it; as she, Baubie, could very well testify from ample experience of the degrading office of nurse to her. "Fat ever 't be, ye may haud yer chat ony wye," said Baubie, and the sister stood rebuked.

When harvest came, the geet being now six months old, was "spean't,"[1] and Baubie "took a hairst." Handed over to the exclusive custody of its granny for the time being, the geet was destined thenceforth to share both bed and board, literally, with Eppie and Jock her husband. The tail of the speaning process when the geet got "fretty," and especially overnight, brought back to Jock Huie a lively remembrance of by-gone experiences of a like nature; and he once or twice rather strongly protested against the conduct of "that ablich" in "brakin' 's nicht's rest" with its outcries. But, on the whole, Jock bore with the geet wonderfully.

When her hairst was finished, it was Baubie's luck to get continuous employment from the same master till Martinmas. When that period had arrived, Baubie, of her own free will and choice, again stood the feeing market, and found what she deemed a suitable engagement at a large farm several miles off, whither she went in due time; and where, as was to be expected, she found the domestic supervision of the male and female servants less stringent on the whole than it had been at the elder's at Brigfit. In so far as her very moderate wages allowed, after meeting her own needs in the matter of dress, Baubie Huie was not altogether disinclined to contribute toward the support of her bastard geet.

As a matter of course, nothing further was heard of or from the nondescript father of the geet. He had moved sufficiently far off to be well out of sight at any rate, and Jock Huie had no means of finding him out and pressing the claim against him in respect of the child's maintenance, except by means of the Poor Law Inspector; and Jock, being a man of independent spirit, had not yet thought of calling in the services of the "Boord." As time went on, Baubie's maternal care did not manifest itself in an increasing measure in this particular of furnishing the means to support the geet more than it did in any other respect affecting her offspring.

After one or two more flittings from one situation to another, it became known that Baubie Huie was about to be married. At another Martinmas term there had been an interval of two years—Baubie once more returned home; but this time frankly to announce to Jock and Eppie Huie that she was "gyaun to be mairriet" to one Peter Ga', who had been a fellow-servant with her during a recent half-year. From considerate regard for the convenience of her parents, and other causes, the happy day would not be delayed beyond a fortnight; and there would be no extensive "splore" on the occasion, to disturb materially the domestic arrangements of the Huies.

On this latter point certain of the neighbors were keenly disappointed. Because there were no marriage rejoicings to speak of, they missed an invitation to join in the same, and they spoke in this wise:—

"An' there's to be nae mairriage ava, ye was sayin'?"

"Hoot—fat wye cud there? The bridegreem an aul' widow man 't mith be 'er fader, wi' three-four o' a faimily."

"Na, sirs; a bonny bargaine she'll be to the like o' 'im—three or four o' a faimily, ye say?"

"So aw b'lieve; an' aw doot it winna be lang ere Baubie gi'e 'im ane mair to haud it haill wi'."

"Wee, weell. Only fat ither cud ye expeck; but the man maun hae been sair mis-

---

[1] Weaned.

guidet 't loot 's een see the like o' 'er."

"An' ye may say 't."

"Fat siclike o' a creatur is he, ken ye?"

"Ou weel, he's a byous quate man it wud appear, an' a gweed aneuch servan', but sair haud'n doon naitrally. Only the peer stock maun be willin' to dee the richt gate in a menner, or he wud a never propos't mairryin Baubie."

"Gweed pit 'im wi' the like o' 'er, weel-a-wat—senseless cuttie."

Naturally, and by right, when Baubie had got a home of her own, she ought to have resumed the custody of her Bastard Geet, now a "gangrel bairn" of fully two years; but on the one hand, it was evident that Mr. and Mrs. Ga' had the prospect of finding the available accommodation in a hut, whose dimensions afforded scope for only a very limited but and ben, sufficiently occupied by and bye without the geet; and on the other, Eppie Huie, though abundantly forfough'en[1] for a woman of her years in keeping her house, attending to the wants of her husband, Jock, and meeting such demands as her own family made upon her exertions as general washerwoman, would have rather demurred to parting with the geet, to whom she had become, as far as the adverse circumstances of the case allowed, attached. And thus the geet was left in the undisputed possession of Jock and Eppie Huie, to be trained by them as they saw meet.

Unlucky geet, say you? Well, one is not altogether disposed to admit that without some qualification. Sure enough, Jock Huie, senior, would and did permit Baubie's geet to grow up an uncouth, unkempt, and, in the main, untaught bairn; yet was there from him, even, a sort of genuine, if somewhat rugged affection, flowing out toward little Jock Huie (as the geet was alternatively styled); as when he would dab the shaving brush playfully against the geet's unwhiskered cheek, while sternly refusing him a grip of the gleaming razor, as he lifted the instrument upward for service on his own face; or, at another time, would quench the geet's aspiration after the garments of adult life, manifested in its having managed to thrust its puny arms into a huge sleeved moleskin vest belonging to Jock himself, by dropping his big "wyv'n bonnet" over the toddling creature's head, and down to his shoulders. Bitter memories of Samie Caie had faded into indistinctness more or less. And when the neighbor wives, as they saw the geet with an old black "cutty" in his hand, gravely attempting to set the contents of the same alight with a fiery sod in imitation of its grandfather, would exclaim, admiringly, "Na, but that laddie is a bricht Huie, Jock, man," Jock would feel a sort of positive pride in the youngster, who bade so fairly to do credit to his upbringing.

No; it might be that meager fare—meager even to pinching at times—was what the inmates of Jock Huie's cot had to expect; it might be that in a moral and intellectual point of view the nourishment going was correspondingly scanty and insufficient, to say the least of it; but in being merely left to grow up under these negatively unfavorable conditions, a grotesque miniature copy of the old man at whose heels he had learnt to toddle about with such assiduity, I can by no means admit that, as compared with many and many a geet whose destiny it is to come into the world in the like irregular fashion, the lot of Baubie Huie's Bastard Geet could be justly termed unlucky.

## The Kirk Session

The oversight exercised by the Kirk Session, and the extent to which it felt bound to interfere for the regulation of morals and promotion of the material interests

[1] Tired, worn down.

of the parishioners, were not a little remarkable. If the Session might not still go the length of "dealing" with women of rank and position, as had been done a century earlier, worrying them effectually because they failed to appear duly at church, and were "suspect" of being "obstinate papists" and the like, they had, at any rate, little difficulty in getting an ordinary laird to submit to discipline; to pay the wonted fine for his incontinence, and probably a good round sum in addition for behoof of the poor—if on that footing he might obtain the privilege of taking his rebuke in private, and not in presence of the congregation, a concession not very infrequently made latterly.

There were not wanting instances, moreover, of persons of the Episcopal persuasion coming voluntarily forward, and, for the quieting of their own consciences, presumably, entreating discipline to be exercised upon them. And while the sway of the Session received something like universal acknowledgment the variety of things in which it intermeddled was great. Censure would be threatened, or, if need were, passed upon "dishaunters of ordinances," upon women who indulged in idle "claik" about the kirk door on Sunday, or used their tongues in vulgar and scandalous "flyting"[1] at other seasons, and so on.

Special Acts were formulated to meet special evils; as that of vagrancy, when warning would be given that "contraveners" who chose to entertain improper people, who could not produce satisfactory "testificats" would be dealt with as "scandalous persons" themselves; and such occasions as penny bridals had to be legislated upon by Synod, Presbytery, and Session, with a view to restrain the undue jollities to which they led; or otherwise suppress the institution altogether.

When moral lapses of the kind with which Kirk Sessions have all along been but too familiar had to be dealt with, the discipline was proportioned to the gravity of the offense. A money penalty of four to six pounds Scots, equal to as many shillings sterling, was the current pecuniary mulct, and the "public appearances" of the defaulters for rebuke might be few or many, according to circumstances. For single offenses that bore no special aggravation once or twice was deemed sufficient, if the parties "carried" themselves properly. In more complicated cases the Session studied the effects; and where due tokens of penitence seemed wanting, or merely in the incipient stage, they, like faithful men, could only exhort the defaulters to "continue the profession of their repentance" in a becoming spirit, they freely according them ample opportunity for so doing.

And the end desired was often not attained very soon. Concerning a woman who was a "trelapser" in a country parish in 1720, we find this brief entry in the Session minute: "Compeared in sacco. *pro* 7 mo., and was rebuked"; that is, she appeared for the seventh Sunday in sackcloth. On her eighth appearance she is "examined *coram,* and, appearing to be weighted with a sense of her sin," the Session "gave it as their advice that absolution should be allowed her upon her next appearance. She paid four lib. penalty," and was then handed over to the Presbytery for final absolution. The case is an illustrative one, and such cases were by no means of exceptional occurrence.

In some instances the boundary line between the ecclesiastical and civil jurisdictions was curiously traversed. When a case of infanticide had occurred, and the deed had been discovered by the dead body of the murdered bairn being got, the Kirk-Session would occasionally set itself to find out who the unnatural mother was. The mode adopted was to order all the "free" or unmarried women to "compear" at the kirk; and there, for the honor of the parish, individually to satisfy a jury of midwives that none of them had given birth to the defunct infant, with certification

---

[1]Scolding.

that any "free woman" who chose to disobey the order would be held as taking guilt to herself. Reversing the maxim of law which says that every person shall be held innocent till proved guilty, the Session boldly announced the principle of holding those guilty who did not adopt the prescribed means to prove their innocence.

And then in return for the Session thus, in its own way, taking up what was clearly the duty of the Civil Court, the Civil Court reciprocated at times by recognizing the function of the Session in what would seem a rather odd fashion. At the Aberdeen Quarter Sessions in May, 1760, Adam Lind, in Tarves, pleads guilty to giving insulting and abusive language to a county Justice of the Peace at a private Session. He is sent to jail for fourteen days, and fined £5; and also "to appear first Sunday after his liberation within the Kirk of Tarves immediately after divine service, and in presence of the congregation convened for the time, make acknowledgment of his insulting the said Justice, and to procure a report and certificate under the hand of the Session-clerk and two elders, of his having made such acknowledgment." Expenses were given against him too, and £10 demanded in security of performance.

The Session interested itself in such matters as the building of bridges, which, properly enough, it recognized as "a pious work," and would readily order a collection to be made to help on an undertaking of that kind. And if a farmer got his "steading" burnt down, not only the Session of his own parish, but those of other surrounding parishes would agree to render him aid in the same way.

But indeed there was no interest, temporal or spiritual, in which the Session might not intermeddle. An illustration of this of a rather peculiar sort is found in the records of the Kirk-Session of Chapel of Garioch. It was in the autumn of 1737, about the time when John Skinner, as a youthful tutor at Monymusk House, in the neighboring parish of that name, was inditing his "Christmas Ba'in." The well-to-do tenant in the pleasant farm of Bridgend, on the banks of the Ury, who had been among the first to build a pew for himself in the parish kirk in 1718, had died leaving a family of seven sons, still alive, for two of whom he had been able to provide separate farms, leaving the rest together in family at Bridgend. His widow had followed him to the grave in the bygone spring, and now it was noised through the parish that her ghost had been seen; and indeed was causing no little terror about Bridgend.

The Session being convened on a certain date, the minister, Mr. Gilbert Gerard, reported that he had something to lay before them concerning the "said pretended spirit." His statement, in substance, was that he, as minister of the parish, had been asked by George Watt from Bridgend, to come and "converse with the spirit, who, ever since about three or four weeks after the death of his mother in the preceding February, had frequently appeared and spoken to him and his brothers without the windows of the rooms where they lay, to their great terror and amazement."

On being "posed" as to its identity by George Watt and his brothers, the ghost, with a superabundance of sanctions, "solemnly averred and swore" that "it was a good spirit; yea, the very spirit of their glorified mother," sent from heaven to "reveal several things to them for their temporal and eternal good, which they were to behove and do at their highest peril." But while the spirit—"which spoke always with a shrill and heavenly voice," making the beds and house where they lay to "shake and tremble again"—"gave them very good instructions and counsels," and even told them "the very secrets of their hearts," the main burden it had been charged to deliver was "that it was the will of the great God that Geordie Watt should marry Tibbie Mortimer (who then was the only woman-servant in that family), because that Tibbie was now in a gracious state, and had been predestinated to glory from all eternity."

This somewhat incongruous revelation had first been made to George Watt when he was lying in bed all alone; whereupon George, like a prudent man, objected, as he alleged, to a marriage so unequal in point of worldly circumstances, and so contrary to his inclination, until it should be made clear to him and others that what he was desired to do really was the will of God. The accommodating spirit undertook to satisfy him on that point; and the seven brothers having, according to compact settled beforehand, duly assembled in the same room, the ghost appeared at the window and repeated its commission, with the portentous threat that "unless Geordie Watt should marry Tibbie Mortimer, he and all his brothers, and all things belonging to them, should certainly be consumed with fire from heaven!" Geordie himself at least having, in addition, nothing to look for thereafter but everlasting punishment. By all this, and similar revelations and threats oft repeated, George Watt had as he averred, got so "frightened and straitened" that he felt impelled to come to the minister, who, in following out George's request, had gone to Bridgend on the previous Thursday evening, taking with him a member of the Session and his own servant. His first care was to pray with the family of seven sons, and the next to take what precautions he could with a view to prevent being imposed upon, and, if possible, to unravel the matter.

After some hours waiting, a voice was heard at a little window of the bedroom in which Geordie Watt slept, "pronouncing with a very wild and vehement tone" that its owner was come in the name of the Trinity to speak to them all—" to men, minister, and all, "Speak, George Watt, speak, men and minister! Come here and I will discourse you all," said the irrepressible ghost. On hearing the "bold and blasphemous expressions" used, the company were in "the greatest consternation"; all but the wide-awake parson, who started to his feet and ran outside, making his way to the corner of the house nearest to where the ghost seemed to be. "The appearance which first presented to his view," says the Session minute, "was about the bulk of ane ordinary woman, covered with white clean linen head and arms down to the middle of the body before, and somewhat farther behind. Then, willing to unravel the matter whatever the event should be, he made such a trial of the apparition as he thought agreeable to the principles of the Christian revelation and true philosophy; and by its resistance to the end of a small rod which he had in his hand, he soon found it to be a material substance. And immediately the pretended spirit took itself to its heels, and he running after it a few paces, caught it by the neck, and his servant coming up at the same time on the other side, caught it by the arm. The apparition was brought flat to the ground, and then, being charged as a base impostor to speak, it was silent till he pulled the white veil from its face, whereupon (it being a bright moonshine) he clearly saw that it was the above-named Isobel Mortimer."

Alas, poor Tibbie. What a collapse of her skillfully-devised plot. She was remorselessly led into the "firehouse" in presence of the seven brothers Watt, where the minister hold forth to her "at some length" on "the blasphemy, devilish tricks, and mischievous pranks" of which she had been guilty; when, sad to say in place of becoming penitence, Tibbie "discovered" such a "surprising boldness and impudence, obdurateness, and obstinacy," that the minister was restrained from handing her over to the civil magistrate only by the entreaty of the family, whose servant she had been for a considerable time. He contented himself, however, with seeing her "march off, bag and baggage, before he left that place."

What the Session did was to pass a set of formal resolutions, wherein they found that "this vile, base, and impudent woman" had gone on "in a course of horrid blasphemy"; had "prescribed charms and suspicious things," disturbing that "sober and orderly family" by her imposture, frightening them "to the great prejudice of their health, yea, to the endangering of their lives"; doing what she could to set the brothers by the ears, and moreover, venting as revelations from God "most false, malicious, and black calumnies against several persons of an untainted character and reputation." In regard the case of "this wicked wretch" was "altogether very complex and of a singular nature," the Session reserved it as it stood for the advice of the Presbytery.

The lapse of a little time seems to have shed new light on the matter, and brought the demure Geordie Watt into the foreground in another guise. Some ten months thereafter it was recorded that Isobel Mortimer had been before the Presbytery, and by them convicted "of the sin and scandal of fornication with George Watt in Bridgend, as also of acting the part of a ghost and blaspheming the holy name of God." She was ordered to appear in sackcloth before the congregation; and threatened at first to be contumacious; but by and by promised to satisfy discipline, and entered on the profession of her repentance by appearing "in sacco" for the first time on 3rd December, 1738.

Meanwhile there had been strenuous dealing with Geordie Watt. On account of "the several presumptions that lay against him of his being in less or more conscious of, or having a hand in ye abominable part yt Isa. Mortimer acted," Geordie had also been ordered to appear before the congregation in sackcloth; but he protested against the award, vowing that "he would never satisfy in sackcloth for yt which he knew nothing about." He was willing to "satisfy" in the ordinary way for what we suppose we may, in his case at least, call the major charge.

Geordie, who had not been altogether a simpleton evidently, offered to pay 100 merks for behoof of the poor on condition of being liberated from the sackcloth, and as the Session had got into the way of listening favorably to such proposals by defaulters of substance, his bribe obtained him that indulgence. He simply appeared three Sundays "in his own seat," and paid the statutory penalty of four pounds Scots.

As for poor Tibbie Mortimer, she, in fulfillment of the Presbyterial order, had no choice but don the sackcloth and sit in public four Sundays at Chapel of Garioch. She was then called in "and exhorted to continue the profession of her repentance" at Monymusk, which probably had been her native parish. So long after as March, 1740, she is again remitted to the Chapel Session "to do with her as they shall see cause," and "as they were of opinion yt her oftener appearing there could be of little edification," they agreed that she should be dismissed "after sitting one Sabbath more in sackcloth and paying one guinea for the use of the poor." Next month she appeared and paid 12 lb. 12 sh. penalty, and was absolved.

## The State of the People

An impartial survey of the life to which those illustrations refer, is fitted to suggest various reflections more or less to the purpose. On its material side, as compared with the life of the present day, it was poor; and that poverty permeated the "commonality" more or less in all its sections. In the measure of absolute wealth owned by the comparatively well-to-do amongst the rural population, the thousands of to-day may almost literally be said to have been represented by hundreds in the time at which we have glanced; and the hundreds by tens. And though the relative value of money has very much decreased, the social conveniences and comforts enjoyed, or that could be commanded, by even the "bein"[1] householder of the eighteenth century, were meager indeed in comparison with those in which a large part of the population now participate without difficulty, and as a matter of course.

The condition of the laboring population at any given period affords a reliable index to the general civilization and social well-being of the community of which they form an indispensable part. And although the separation of classes was not by any means so distinctly marked seventy or a hundred years ago as now— the farmer

---

[1] Snug.

and his helps, male and female, ordinarily eating their meals at the same table, while the weaver, the smith, and the tailor, could meet either class on a common footing—yet was it the case that those whose lot it was to earn a livelihood by the labor of their hands were alike indifferently housed, and meagerly fed at all times. Before the progress of agricultural improvement had so far mended matters, they also suffered severely from unsanitary natural conditions, such as the abounding march vapors that rose from stagnant undrained swamps, and crept about many of their habitations.

Ague was a common complaint in many parts of Scotland during a considerable portion of the past century; indeed, it was so common in some districts among the peasantry, in spring and autumn particularly, that farmers occasionally found it difficult to get through the ordinary operations of the season for want of laborers. And when a special piece of work had to be executed it was not unusual, we are told, "to order six laborers instead of four, from the probability that some of them, before the work could be finished, would be rendered unfit for labor by an attack of this disorder. Indeed, in several parishes," it is added, "the inhabitants, with very few exceptions, had an annual attack."

And when Sir John Sinclair wrote one of his later papers early in the present century, he deemed the fact that ague had become less common, and had been entirely banished from a number of districts, "So highly honorable to agriculture," that he says he could not mention it without "a high degree of pride and pleasure." Malignant fevers too ravaged country localities now and again, with a severity unknown to the living generation, elder or younger, at times almost literally decimating the population of a parish. And of course small-pox, when it came, had its way unchecked; killing not a few, leaving its indelible impress on many a countenance, and often producing blindness, where the attack was not fatal.

Touching the religious and moral aspects of the question, it were perhaps easier than it is desirable, or quite wise, to make sweeping statements on the one side or the other. Where the sense of religious obligation was really felt the theological opinions of the time were no doubt severe, and the prevailing notions concerning Christian liberty narrow and restricted. It does not, however, betoken any great depth of insight, nor is it indicative of a true and adequate comprehension of facts in their due relations or a really cosmopolitan philosophy, to misapprehend totally the distinction between earnest piety of even the gloomier sort, and simple fanaticism or pure hypocrisy.

In the regions to which we have had reference, and during the time under notice, an actively religious spirit was certainly not a prominent feature. With considerable show of reason it might be said the very reverse was the case. The dominant Presbyterianism managed parish affairs creditably; supplied a reasonable proportion of passable sermons, prevailingly of the type of theology known as "Moderate," as contra-distinguished from "Evangelical," weekly; carried on the stated diets of catechizing, yearly, and took oversight of the schools; its ministry yielding a man here and there destined to eminence more or less, as occasionally too, a brother with pronouncedly erratic tendencies, who ruled his diocese after his own queer fashion, and left his corresponding moral impress upon a generation of parishioners when be had disappeared from the scene.

Episcopalians, who in due course "suffered" for their nonjurant principles, did not bulk largely; neither did the followers of the first or second Secession. The feelings of contempt and aversion with which seceders were regarded were very general; as one can readily understand from occasional references made to them by contemporary writers.

A sufficiently pointed example of the estimation in which they were held by the land-owning class is furnished by the articles and conditions of tack[1] for his lands, registered in the Sheriff Court books of Aberdeenshire, in February, 1781, by Alexander Fraser, of Strichen. In the second Article, in which are specified the various offenses for which tenants shall be held to have forfeited their tacks, such as their becoming bankrupt or the like, it is *inter alia* specified—"or, *eighthly* shall knowingly or willfully take into their service, or harbor, or set ground to any Seceders or thieves, vagabonds or beggars, or any other person who has not sufficient testimonials of their former good and honest behavior, to the satisfaction of the said Alexander Fraser, or his foresaids, or to such as are suspected to harbor any of the above-mentioned."

We may possibly look upon the laird of Strichen, himself a Roman Catholic, as somewhat extreme in his intolerance, yet putting it in a mildly negative form, one cannot, at any rate, regard such facts as that Seceders were very limited in number, and that they were held in general contempt, as furnishing evidence of any deep or wide-spread interest in religious questions. Thus far, at least, we may safely go.

The question of the comparative morality of the people may be handled with all requisite freedom, even should it be at the risk of challenge on some points. The idea that degeneracy, in point of morals, has crept in amongst our rural population within the past half century or so and that if a greatly higher standard was not uniformly maintained in the time immediately preceding, a sort of Arcadian innocence and simplicity prevailed very generally at least, finds acceptance with some who profess to have knowledge of the subject.

Unhappily the records of the time do not seem to bear out such ideas in the very least. In their everyday life, rude roistering, drinking, quarreling, and fighting were the too frequent recreations of the common people a hundred years ago. Even then there were complaints that the people were not what they had been in the previous times of fancied guilelessness and primitive virtue. Only they did not gather up and tabulate the details of crime as is now done, and in so far as mere personal outbreaks went, if the offenders escaped the notice of the Kirk session, the Civil Court would hardly interfere unless the fray had been so savage as to involve actual loss of life or very serious damage "to lith or limb."

The character of those whose position placed them above the common people was not always indeed regarded as entitling them to be spoken of with unqualified respect. The writer of a letter of date 1750, discussing the agriculture of the time, gives his opinion of Aberdeenshire landlords, and the relations between them and their tenants in these words—"The landed gentlemen, many of them, look upon religion as below them, morality as an unnecessary incumbrance, economy as sordid, and their tenants as a species of animals, made to be abused and oppressed—to labor and spend their strength to maintain their luxury and riot." Like enough the writer desired to put in his tints strongly, but what nineteenth century Radical has ever denounced the territorial shortcomings of his time in more unsparing terms!

Nor even in relation to the sore subject of bastardy did the people of last century in the north-east of Scotland hold a greatly more favorable position than their descendants do. Possibly the actual percentage of illegitimate births may have been somewhat less. We have no available statistics of a comprehensive sort to compare with the Registrar's figures of the present time. But the Kirk-Session records serve the end in a rough, yet reasonably reliable way. And a careful scrutiny of some of these records does not encourage the belief that even the proportional number of bastards to population was always very appreciably less—the number of aggravated and spe-

[1]Lease.

cially bad cases that needed severe dealing, and where the Session had to call in the aid of the Presbytery, was certainly as great or greater than now.

Any inquiry bearing on the causes of a high rate of bastardy in these districts would lead us into irrelevant and probably fruitless discussion of a vexed question. But of one thing we may hold ourselves assured—that at no period known to history was the proportion of bastard births other than considerable. Starting on that basis and keeping clearly in view that so it has been all through, we can at least more readily understand how the result of a traditional and inherited moral sentiment all too deadened and dormant, should serve to take the edge off the feeling of shame and blunt the sense of honor in the sex amongst whom chastity is properly deemed the crown of all the virtues. Born into and nurtured from childhood in a pervasive social atmosphere of this sort it becomes readily intelligible how women whose characters otherwise one would be sorry to impugn in the least barely realize it as any permanent stain on their womanhood to have been the mother of n bastard.

And here, doubtless, we touch the most formidable phase of a species of immorality that has gained for the common people of these regions an unenviable notoriety. We need not contrast it with the measure of the like vice as it exists among the classes where purity in one sex is demanded and valued; and, indeed, such contrast or comparison cannot be made. Only this much may be said with truth: that while the women who sadly fail in virgin modesty ordinarily prove true and faithful wives when married, even the men who join with them in wedlock do also as a rule act with conjugal fidelity thereafter. With them the vice as it exists is gross and open; we see it in its full extent, and may know its limits; and in this way the common people of the rural community probably suffer some considerable injustice when their sins in this respect are sought to be contrasted with those of certain other classes more highly civilized it may be, and enjoying far greater social advantages.

Generally viewed then, the life of last century, in so far as it has come under our notice, cannot be regarded as strongly typical of the "good old times." Confining our retrospect to that period we should certainly be compelled to say—

> Those times were never
> Airy visions sat for the picture.

Along with abounding poverty of means and resources, we find that industry was stagnant, and unprogressive, and that the ordinary rural life of the time was strongly tinctured with superstition, or simply in the state of uninquiring indifference as regards its spiritual beliefs. It had nevertheless its own features of attraction, as contrasted with the life that has followed it. There was a sense of quiet leisureliness about the manner in which each man held his position and transacted the business of his daily life; an absence of hurry and headlong competition, and a feeling of neighborliness and hospitality amongst the constituent membership of each small community that did much to make life not merely tolerable, but rationally enjoyable. The changes that have occurred in these respects, we may warrantably say, have not all been in the nature of an unqualified social gain.

## JAMES CARNEGIE, EARL OF SOUTHESK (1827–1905)

### November's Cadence

The bees about the Linden-tree,
When blithely summer blooms were springing,
Would hum a heartsome melody,
The simple baby-soul of singing;
And thus my spirit sang to me
When youth its wanton way was winging:

"Be glad, be sad—thou hast the choice—
But mingle music with thy voice."

The linnets on the Linden-tree,
Among the leaves in autumn dying,
Are making gentle melody,
A mild, mysterious, mournful sighing;
And thus my spirit sings to me
While years are flying, flying, flying:
"Be sad, be sad, thou hast no choice,
But mourn with music in thy voice."

## Pigworm and Dixie

Well, if ever a man is in want of a wife
To poison his pleasure and pester his life,
First place let him go to Ben Dixie's, you know,
And see what that awful example will show.

Oh, such a good fellow was rollicking Ben,
Beloved by the girls and the right sort of men.
You may call me a lie, but—'pon honor tis said—
For a twelvemonth he never went sober to bed.

Yes; rollicking Ben was a fellow of sense,
Who hated all stick-me-up humbug pretense;
As to that I can swear, for no hogs in the sty
Were more thick with each other than Dixie and I.

What a jolly old crib was his house in the dale,
A Garden of Eden of baccy and ale:
Any hour of the day you could eat at your ease,
There were always some ends of cold bacon or cheese.

Lawk! now if you enter his prig of a house,
Not a scrap can you find that would serve for a mouse;
And you wait and you wait till the dinner comes in,
Though perhaps you're as hungry and thirsty as sin.

But at last there's a row,—jingle-jing goes a bell,
And you sit yourself down, and you feed like a swell!
Oh, that shiny new tablecloth!—give me the cheer
Of the old one, all gravy and mustard and beer.

Ah yes, Mrs. Dixie, you're awfully neat,
With your fat little hands and your smart little feet;
And you trot up and down, and you perk up your head,
And you smell like a rose in a lavender bed.

And you smirk and you smile and you puff out your breast
Like a pigeon a-pouting and walking its best;

And so mighty polite—why—why, a fellow can't dare
To chaff when he wants to, and swagger and swear.

Lawk! I'd like to yell out, like a throttle-choked hen,
When I think of the days of good *bachelor* Ben;
No wife to torment one, dressed up like a doll,—
But that jolly kind creature, young housekeeper Moll.

She was something to see, as you smoked in your chair,
With her rolling black eyes and the kink in her hair;
With her shoes down at heel, and her cheeks pink as paint,
And holes in her stockings—no beastly constraint!

And her ringlets they smelt like a hairdresser's shop;
And her dress was green stuff, spattered over with slop;
And her hands were good large ones, her ankles were thick,
And her nails they were bitten clean down to the quick.

She'd a taste of a temper, but nothing like vice—
It is downright unchristian to be too precise;
For a shy with a bottle I don't know her match;
But good lawk! what is that when a fellow can catch?

Oh, wasn't it prime! you could drink, you could smoke,
You could chuck out a curse, you could sing, you could joke;
Things are changed now, alas,—all is bother and bore,—
Why, the Missus looks wild if you spit on the floor!

Faugh! to hear how they jaw, it quite gives one a turn,—
As if words were hot mealy potatoes that burn.
"A little more beef please,"—then faces they pull;
Can't he say,—"Shove us over some more of that bull"?

Yes, I hate the whole set with their finikin ways.
It was "live and let live" in the jolly old days.
The hens in the kitchen took all that they chose,
And the pups in the parlor rolled over your toes.

But now (set us up!) they've a precious fine lot
Of young-uns who gobble the pick of the pot;
And they sit up so pert, each small brat in its place,
And when stuffed nigh to bursting they squeak out a grace!

Well, perhaps I'm not perfect though fairly so-so;
But thank Heav'n, I'm no hypocrite—hang it all, no!
Before I'd go in for that sanctified bosh,
I'd as soon send a red flannel shirt to the wash.

Jolly Ben—bless his soul! when he used to begin,
He would swear till you thought the old deuce had come in:
Now see him with Missus, as prim as a pea,
Trudging slowly to church, with the brats in their lee.

Mrs. Dixie got up in her lavender dress,
And poor Ben such a swell as no words can express,
With white pants, and a rose, and a tile with a twist,
And a pair of small girls hanging on to his fist.

So they toddle along to the jole of the bell,
And they go to a pew, and get blest with a spell
Of singing and preaching and things in that style—
Ben sleeps, I'll be bound, for the most of the while!

But humbug for ever! hypocrisy pays,
Like the bills on the walls about pickles and plays;
Yes, it's worth heaps of cash to be called "honest Ben,"
And be toadied and praised by all manner of men.

Who but he! they can't meet to be jolly and dine,
After judging the horses and cattle and swine,
But up starts Squire Blount—"Fill a bumper," says he
"For a toast in which no one can fail to agree,—

"The health of that pattern to farmers and all,
Mr. Benjamin Dixie of Rosemary Hall!"
Then they clap their fat paws, they roar and they swill—
Euch! bring me a basin, I'm going to be ill.

If there's one thing I hate it's that bumtious conceit—
To set up to be tidy and pretty and neat:
It's as much as to say to a fellow, you see,
"What does nicely for you is not fit for big me!"

Instead of the grass and the puddles of muck,
And the sow with her piggies and goosey and duck
And a midden,[1] and plenty old kettles and tubs,
They've got gardens and roses, and things they call shrubs.

Just you walk through the garden and tear off a flow'r
For a shy at the hens—don't the Missus look sour!
Or go near those cantankerous buffers of bees—
"After you, sir," is manners; "you first, if you please."

Why those brutes won't abide me I really can't say,
For whenever they see me they hunt me away:
They object to bad smells, but that isn't my case,
Few days but I souse both my hands and my face.

Now Ben Dixie he scrubs in a terrible way,
Till he shines like a sixpence and smells of new hay;
I liked him far better all mire, muck, and grease,
When the man and his midden were quite of a piece.

---

[1]Trashheap or dungheap.

What nonsense they talk about scrubbing off dirt,
As if things that come natural ever could hurt;
But Ben, the big booby, has grown like the eels,
The more he is skinned, the more lively he feels.

If you stay for the night at that Rosemary Hall,
You're a mighty queer chap, if you like it at all.
"Fresh air," quoth the blockhead! I say it's a chouse
To hang out in a windmill and call it a house.

And there's lots of oak panels as bright as the stars,
And the place stinks of roses and blue and white jars;
And your bed's got white curtains that can't be drawn round,
And you tumble and grunt like a pig in a pound.

And you're nearly sent mad with the peppery smell
Of dead flow'rs dry in bowls, and of live ones as well;
And the nightingales sing till you wish em in Spain,
And at dawn you've the thrushes and blackbirds again.

And your nice morning sleep is disturbed by the noise
Of dear Ben's blessed darlings, his girls and his boys,
A-feeding the turkeys with stuff from a pail,
And screechy pea-devils with eyes in the tail.

And there's booing of oxen and mooing of cows;
And the hogs and the horses, confound em for rows.
And the sheep, and the cur-dog bow-wowing the flock:
Oh, of course, Master Dixie keeps excellent stock.

Poor wretch, I don't fancy that anything pays
For toiling and moiling—I live all *my* days:
A sort of a god, with my baccy and bowl,
As jolly and snug as a toad in a hole.

No, it ain't mighty grand, but it suits to a T,
It's a capital den for a fellow like me;
No draughts and dry roses to keep you a-snort,
But a sensible place looking into a court.

On the ground-floor of course,—I object to a stair
For the higher you go you get more of the air;
The grate's pretty big, but the window's quite small—
Such a fit, sir. in fact it won't open at all.

There ain't neither shutter nor bothersome blind,
But there's dust on the glass, and the sun keeps behind;
And I snooze on my bed for the most of the day,
And the best of the night I am up and away.

Oh, it's jolly to lie on your back half a-doze,
And to kick off the quilt with your lazy old toes;

And you stare at your stockings as long as you please,
And you wriggle your trousers right over your knees.

Then you stretch and get hold of your pipe for a whiff,
And make matters serene with a drop of the "stiff";
If you're peckish inclined, there is nothing to do
More easy than fry a red herring or two.

As Bill Shakespeare remarks, "There is no place like home,"
I'm as proud of my crib as a cock of his comb.
Life's sweet there—though once, I must really confess,
I had nearly dropped in for a bit of a mess.

A young cove he came canting with tracts on the sly,
"Converting" he called it. "Now, Mister," said I,
"Unless your name's 'Walker' this instant, d'ye see,
We'll 'convert' you to sausage, will Towzer and me.

So he turned—did this cove—pretty white in the gill:
"Good-day, sir," says he; "as you like me so ill,
I'll never come in to annoy you no more,—
Though I'm bound to be sometimes a-passing your door."

Well, before it got dark on that very same day,
I was taken all no-how, a queer kind of way:
All my bones and my gizzards were aching like fun,
And my brains were like boots hanging out in the sun.

Oh, I felt monstrous bad, and I soon got so weak
I could scarce raise my head, and I hardly could speak;
And no creature came near me, I thought I should die,—
When at length sounds the step of a man passing by.

And old Towzer he kicks up a deuce of a din,
The door opens slow, and a fellow peeps in—
Nick Chousem, my partner;—says he, "Here's a go!
Bye-bye, Joey Pigworm,—it's small-pox, you know."

And I lay and I blubbered. The rest I forget.
When I opened my peepers, the first thing I met
Was the mission-cove, watching me anxious and fond,
Like a hen whose small ducks are a-swim in a pond.

Well, of course I recovered—that's middling clear,
For if I'd skedaddled I shouldn't be here:
That good cove pulled me out of Old Gooseberry's gripe,—
And his tracts came quite useful for lighting one's pipe.

Not ungrateful, sir, no! he declined my advice,
But I showed him neat things with the cards and the dice;
And my dog runs to meet him a-wagging its tail,
And it grins, "How d'ye do" like a shark in a gale.

No, it don't pay a bit to be seedy, you see,—
Not, at least, for mere common-sense snobbies like me:
But Ben—let his thumb ache, they rush to inquire,—
Town, village, and country, lord, parson, and squire.

Lawk, when Ben comes to die, bless their heads and their eyes,
How the crape and the white pocket-wipers will rise.
And the funeral cards will be scattered like peas,
And the folks will come swarming like mites on a cheese.

And they'll drive up a gimcracky hypocrite hearse;
And they'll shove him inside, like a pig in a purse;
And they'll carry him off to the burial crib;
And the parson will come, like a rook in a bib.

Then they'll earth up his corpse in a daisy-bank hole;
And the boom of the organ will sweep off his soul,
As you blow off the froth from a buzzy brown bowl:
And the bloodhound bell will jole—jole—jole.

O lawk! can't I see it? and afterwards too,
The Missus and children all making boohoo;
And creeping like blackbirds down Sweetbriar Lane
A-weeping, and wishing him with them again.

And the little pale girls in their bombazine stuff,
With their hair running loose like a parcel of fluff,
And nice flow'rs in their hands for the grave of "Papa."
Such a comfort to Ben in his coffin, ha ha!

Rum business is life! but it ends all a-piece
For the easy good chaps and the hard-working geese:
And why should they grudge a poor beast of a man
To be happy and jolly the best way he can?

Says the mission-cove once,—"You've no sort of excuse
For to cumber the earth, if you're no sort of use."
"How," says I, "could the beggarsome planet be filled,
If the coves that do nothing were taken and killed?"

Some fine day, by and by, I shall likely expire—
They'll not take up Joe Pigworm in char'ots of fire;—
Well! when Gooseberry wants me I'll meet him quite brave:
I wonder what folk will strew over my grave!

Nick Chousem, I daresay, will miss me a bit,
And he'll sit on my grave, and he'll smoke there and spit;
And perhaps I'll be missed by my brute of a dog
For I lick him and kick him, and give him his prog.

Lawk, what do I care! My blest body will rot,
My blest soul (if I've got one) will toddle to pot,

And I'll treat the poor worms to a famous repast—
Oh yes, I'll be useful to something at last!

## ALEXANDER NICOLSON (1827–1893)

### Skye

[A reference to the Highland Clearances, in which landlords evicted tenants from hereditary farm holdings in order to raise sheep, or in some instances game.]

My heart is yearning to thee, O Skye,
Dearest of islands.
There first the sunshine gladdened my eye,
On the sea sparkling.
There doth the dust of my dear ones lie,
In the old graveyard.

Bright are the golden green fields to me,
Here in the Lowlands;
Sweet sings the mavis in the thorn tree,
Snowy with fragrance;
But, oh, for a breath of the great North Sea,
Girdling the mountains.

Good is the smell of the brine that laves
Black rock and skerry,
Where the great palm-leaved tangle waves
Down in the green depths,
And round the craggy bluff, pierced with caves,
Seagulls are screaming.

When the sun sinks beyond Hunish Head,
Swimming in glory,
As he goes down to his ocean bed
Studded with islands,
Flushing the Coolin with royal red,
Would I were sailing.

Many a hearth round that friendly shore
Giveth warm welcome.
Charms still are there, as in days of yore
More than of mountains;
But hearths and faces are seen no more,
Once of the brightest.

Many a poor black cottage is there,
Grimy with peat smoke,
Sending up in the soft evening air
Purest blue incense,
While the low music of psalm and prayer
Rises to heaven.

Kind were the voices I used to hear
Round such a fireside,
Speaking the mother-tongue old and dear,
Making the heart beat
With endless tales of wonder and fear,
Or plaintive singing.

Great were the marvelous stories told
Of Ossian's heroes,
Giants and witches, and young men bold,
Seeking adventures,
Winning king's daughters and guarded gold
Only with valor.

Reared in those dwellings have brave ones been.
Brave ones are still there.
Forth from their darkness on Sundays I've seen
Coming pure linen,
And like the linen the souls were clean
Of them that wore it.

See that thou kindly use them, O man,
To whom God giveth
Stewardship over them, in thy short span,
Not for thy pleasure.
Woe be to them who choose for a clan
Four-footed people.

Blessings be with ye, both now and aye,
Dear human creatures.
Yours is the love that no gold can buy
Nor time can wither.
Peace be to thee and thy children, O Skye,
Dearest of islands.

## JAMES THOMSON, OF HAWICK (1827–1888)

### Hogmanay

Up frae their cozy beds
Afore the peep o' day,
Skippin' round the corner,
Brattlin'* down the brae, clattering
Hearts a' sae happy,
Faces blithe and gay,
A merry band o' bairnies
Seek their Hogmanay.[1]

Careless o' the blast sae bleak,
Snawy drift or shower,

[1] The holiday of December 31.

Though the roses on their cheek
Turn like the blaewart flower,—
Frae ilka door they're jinkin'* rushing out
To hail the happy day;
And they a' gang a-linkin'* arm in arm
To seek their Hogmanay.

Bonnie bairnies, come awa';
It's little I've to gi'e,
But ye shall hae my blessing a',
An' ae bawbee.
When manhood's care comes oer ye,
Ye'll mind the merry day
When, happy-hearted bairnies,
Ye sought your Hogmanay.

## Hairst

The yellow corn waves in the field,
The merry hairst's* begun; harvest's
And steel-plate sickles, sharp and keen,
Are glintin' in the sun,
While strappin' lads, and lassies braw,
A' kiltit to the knee,
Bring to my mind a hairst langsyne,
When Robin shuire wi' me.

Light lie the mools* upon his breast; "molds" (dirt)
He was a strappin' chield*,— fellow
A better shearer ne'er drew huik
Upon a harvest field.
And didna joy loup in my heart,
And sparkle frae my e'e,
Sae proud was I, when Robin said
He'd shear alang wi' me.

That was a lightsome hairst to me,—
For love maks light o' toil,—
The kindly blink o' Robin's e'e
Could a' my care beguile.
At restin' time amang the stooks
I sat upon his knee,
And wondered if the warld could haud
A blither lass than me.

Lang Sandy and his sister Jean
Thocht nane wi' them could shear,
And a' the hairst at Rab an' me
Threw mony a taunt an' jeer.
Rab ga'e them aye as guid's they brought,
And took it a' in fun:
But inly vowed to heat their skin
Afore the hairst was done.

The kirn-day cam', a kemp* began, contest
And hald and fast it grew;
Across the rig* wi' lightnin' speed row
The glintin' sickles flew.
Lang Sandy wam'let* like an eel, moved side to side
But soon fell in the rear;
For no a pair in a' the boon* band
Wi' Rab an' me could shear.

We cleared our rig baith tight and clean,
And thought the day our ain,
When wae's my heart! I brak' my huik
Upon a meikle stane.
"Mak' bands," quo' Robin—while the sweat
Like raindrops trickled doon;—
But Robin reached the land-end first
And foremost o' the boon.

I thought that I wad swoon wi' joy
When dightin' Robin's brow,
He says, "Meg, gin ye'll buckle to,
I'll shear through life wi' you."
What could I do but buckle to—
He was sae frank an' free?
And often did I bless the day
That Robin shuire wi' me.

## MARGARET OLIPHANT (1828–1897)

[Margaret Oliphant is one of Scotland's finest novelists, though today rather neglected. Her husband's death at an early age forced her into a career as a writer, by which efforts she supported her own three children plus her brother and his family. She was astonishingly fertile, producing over ninety novels as well as volumes of essays, guidebooks, histories, biographies. She wrote many novels with Scottish backgrounds, but living much of her time in England and writing for a largely English public, she devoted most of her works to English life, especially a series of gently realistic comedies of manners about a mythical English town which she called Carlingford (1863–1876). *The Chronicles of Carlingford* much resemble Anthony Trollope's Barsetshire novels, and are not unworthy of comparison therewith in terms of quality as well as style and theme. Perhaps the most notable works in the Carlingford volumes are *Salem Chapel* and *Miss Marjoribanks*. The series is represented here by "The Rector."

Margaret Oliphant also wrote a number of tales of the supernatural, marred to modern taste by a dose of moralizing. "The Library Window" is a nice combination of her talents—a fine eye for character depiction (especially female), middle-class social interaction, and insight into the "other world." The young narrator of "The Library Window" is just coming of age, and discovering her femininity and the special vision which is both her gift and her curse.]

# The Rector

## CHAPTER I.

It is natural to suppose that the arrival of the new Rector was a rather exciting event for Carlingford. It is a considerable town, it is true, nowadays, but then there are no alien activities to disturb the place—no manufactures, and not much trade. And there is a very respectable amount of very good society at Carlingford. To begin with, it is a pretty place—mild, sheltered, not far from town; and naturally its very reputation for good society increases the amount of that much-prized article. The advantages of the town in this respect have already put five per cent upon the house-rents; but this, of course, only refers to the *real* town, where you can go through an entire street of high garden-walls, with houses inside full of the retired exclusive comforts, the dainty economical refinement peculiar to such places; and where the good people consider their own society as a warrant of gentility less splendid, but not less assured, than the favor of Majesty itself. Naturally there are no Dissenters in Carlingford—that is to say, none above the rank of a greengrocer or milkman; and in bosoms devoted to the Church it may be well imagined that the advent of the new Rector was an event full of importance, and even of excitement.

He was highly spoken of, everybody knew; but nobody knew who had spoken highly of him, nor had been able to find out, even by inference, what were his views. The Church had been Low during the last Rector's reign—profoundly Low—lost in the deepest abysses of Evangelicalism. A determined inclination to preach to everybody had seized upon that good man's brain; he had half emptied Salem Chapel, there could be no doubt; but, on the other hand, he had more than half filled the Chapel of St Roque, half a mile out of Carlingford, where the perpetual curate, young, handsome, and fervid, was on the very topmost pinnacle of Anglicanism. St Roque's was not more than a pleasant walk from the best quarter of Carlingford, on the north side of the town, thank heaven! which one could get at without the dread passage of that new horrid suburb, to which young Mr. Rider, the young doctor, was devoting himself. But the Evangelical Rector was dead, and his reign was over, and nobody could predict what the character of the new administration was to be. The obscurity in which the new Rector had buried his views was the most extraordinary thing about him. He had taken high honors at college, and was "highly spoken of"; but whether he was High, or Low, or Broad, muscular or sentimental, sermonizing or decorative, nobody in the world seemed able to tell.

"Fancy if he were just to be a Mr. Bury over again! Fancy him going to the canal, and having sermons to the bargemen, and attending to all sorts of people except to us, whom it is his duty to attend to!" cried one of this much-canvassed clergyman's curious parishioners. "Indeed I do believe he must be one of these people. If he were in society at all, somebody would be sure to know."

"Lucy dear, Mr. Bury christened you," said another not less curious but more tolerant inquirer.

"Then he did you the greatest of all services," cried the third member of the little group which discussed the new Rector under Mr. Wodehouse's blossomed apple-trees. "He conferred such a benefit upon you that he deserves all reverence at your hand. Wonderful idea! a man confers this greatest of Christian blessings on multitudes, and does not himself appreciate the boon he conveys!"

"Well, for that matter, Mr. Wentworth, you know—" said the elder lady: but she got no farther. Though she was verging upon forty, leisurely, pious, and unmarried, that good Miss Wodehouse was not polemical. She had "her own opinions," but few people knew much about them. She was seated on a green garden-bench which surrounded the great May-tree in that large, warm, well-furnished garden. The high brick walls, all clothed with fruit-trees, shut in an enclosure of which not a morsel except this velvet grass, with its nests of daisies, was not under the highest and most careful cultivation. It was such a scene as is only to be found in an old country town; the walls jealous of intrusion, yet thrusting tall plumes of lilac and stray branches of apple-blossom, like friendly salutations to the world without; within, the blossoms drooping over the light bright head of Lucy Wodehouse underneath the apple-trees, and impertinently flecking the Rev. Frank Wentworth's Anglican coat.

These two last were young people, with that indefinable harmony in their looks which prompts the suggestion of "a handsome couple" to the bystander. It had not even occurred to them to be in love with each other, so far as anybody knew, yet few were the undiscerning persons who saw them together without instinctively placing the young curate of St Roque's in permanence by Lucy's side. She was twenty, pretty, blue-eyed, and full of dimples, with a broad Leghorn hat thrown carelessly on her head, untied, with broad strings of blue ribbon falling among her fair curls—a blue which was "repeated," according to painter jargon, in ribbons at her throat and waist. She had great gardening gloves on, and a basket and huge pair of scissors on the grass at her feet, which grass, besides, was strewed with a profusion of all the sweetest spring blossoms—the sweet narcissus, most exquisite of flowers, lilies of the valley, white and blue hyacinths, golden ranunculus globes—worlds of sober, deep-breathing wallflower.

If Lucy had been doing what her kind elder sister called her "duty," she would have been at this moment arranging her flowers in the drawing-room; but the times were rare when Lucy did her duty according to Miss Wodehouse's estimate; so instead of arranging those clusters of narcissus, she clubbed them together in her hands into a fragrant dazzling sheaf, and discussed the new Rector—not unaware, perhaps, in her secret heart, that the sweet morning, the sunshine and flowers, and exhilarating air were somehow secretly enhanced by the presence of that black Anglican figure under the apple-trees.

"But I suppose," said Lucy, with a sigh, "we must wait till we see him; and if I must be very respectful of Mr. Bury because he christened me, I am heartily glad the new Rector has no claim upon my reverence. I have been christened, I have been confirmed—"

"But, Lucy, my dear, the chances are he will marry you," said Miss Wodehouse, calmly; "indeed, there can be no doubt that it is only natural he should, for he *is* the Rector, you know; and though we go so often to St Roque's, Mr. Wentworth will excuse me saying that he is a very young man."

Miss Wodehouse was knitting; she did not see the sudden look of dismay and amazement which the curate of St Roque's darted down upon her, nor the violent sympathetic blush which blazed over both the young faces. How shocking that elderly quiet people should have such a faculty for suggestions! You may be sure Lucy Wodehouse and young Wentworth, had it not been "put into their heads" in such an absurd fashion, would never, all their virtuous lives, have dreamt of anything but friendship.

Deep silence ensued after this simple but startling speech. Miss Wodehouse knitted on, and took no notice; Lucy began to gather up the flowers into the basket, unable for her life to think of anything to say. For his part, Mr. Wentworth gravely picked the apple-blossoms off his coat, and counted them in his hand. That sweet summer snow kept dropping, dropping, falling here and there as the wind carried it, and with a special attraction to Lucy and her blue ribbons: while behind, Miss Wodehouse sat calmly on the green bench, under the May-tree just beginning to bloom, without lifting her eyes from her knitting. Not far off, the bright English house, all beaming with open doors and windows, shone in the sunshine. With the white May peeping out among the green overhead, and the sweet narcissus in a great dazzling sheaf upon the grass, making all the air fragrant around them, can anybody fancy a sweeter domestic out-of-door scene? or else it seemed so to the perpetual curate of St Roque's.

Ah me! and if he was to be perpetual curate, and none of his great friends thought upon him, or had preferment to bestow, how do you suppose he could ever, ever marry Lucy Wodehouse, if they were to wait a hundred years?

Just then the garden-gate—the green gate in the wall—opened to the creaking murmur of Mr. Wodehouse's own key. Mr. Wodehouse was a man who creaked universally. His boots were a heavy infliction upon the good-humor of his household; and like every other invariable quality of dress, the peculiarity became identified with him in every particular of his life. Everything belonging to him moved with a certain jar, except, indeed, his household, which went on noiseless wheels, thanks to Lucy and love.

As he came along the garden path, the gravel started all round his unmusical foot. Miss Wodehouse alone turned round to hail her father's approach, but both the young people looked up at her instinctively, and saw her little start, the falling of her knitting-needles, the little flutter of color which surprise brought to her maidenly, middle-aged cheek. How they both divined it I cannot tell, but it certainly was no surprise to either of them when a tall embarrassed figure, following the portly one of Mr. Wodehouse, stepped suddenly from the noisy gravel to the quiet grass, and stood gravely awkward behind the father of the house.

"My dear children, here's the Rector—delighted to see him! we're all delighted to see him!" cried Mr. Wodehouse. "This is my little girl Lucy, and this is my eldest daughter. They're both as good as curates, though I say it, you know, as shouldn't. I suppose you've got something tidy for lunch, Lucy, eh? To be sure you ought to know—how can I tell? She might have had only cold mutton, for anything I knew—and that won't do, you know, after college fare. Hollo, Wentworth! I beg your pardon—who thought of seeing you here? I thought you had morning service, and all that sort of thing. Delighted to make you known to the Rector so soon. Mr. Proctor—Mr. Wentworth of St Roque's."

The Rector bowed. He had no time to say anything, fortunately for him; but a vague sort of color fluttered over his face. It was his first living; and cloistered in All-Souls for fifteen years of his life, how is a man to know all at once how to accost his parishioners? especially when these curious unknown specimens of natural life happen to be female creatures, doubtless accustomed to compliment and civility. If ever any one was thankful to hear the sound of another man's voice, that person was the new Rector of Carlingford, standing in the bewildering garden-scene into which the green door had so suddenly admitted him, all but treading on the dazzling bundle of narcissus, and turning with embarrassed politeness from the perpetual curate, whose salutation was less cordial than it might have been, to those indefinite flutters of blue ribbon from which Mr. Proctor's tall figure divided the ungracious young man.

"But come along to lunch. Bless me! don't let us be too ceremonious," cried Mr. Wodehouse. "Take Lucy, my dear sir—take Lucy. Though she has her garden-gloves on, she's manager indoors for all that. Molly here is the one we coddle up and take care of. Put down your knitting, child, and don't make an old woman of yourself. To be sure, it's your own concern—you should know best; but that's my opinion. Why, Wentworth, where are you off to? 'Tisn't a fast, surely—is it, Mary?—nothing of the sort; it's Thursday—*Thursday,* do you hear? and the Rector newly arrived. Come along."

"I am much obliged, but I have an appointment," began the curate, with restraint.

"Why didn't you keep it, then, before *we* came in," cried Mr. Wodehouse, "chatting with a couple of girls like Lucy and Mary? Come along, come along—an appointment with some old woman or other, who wants to screw flannels and things out of you—well, I suppose so! I don't know anything else you could have to say to them. Come along."

"Thank you. I shall hope to wait on the Rector shortly," said young Wentworth, more and more stiffly; "but at present I am sorry it is not in my power. Good morning, Miss Wodehouse—good morning; I am happy to have had the opportunity—" and the voice of the perpetual curate died off into vague murmurs of politeness as he made his way towards the green door.

That green door! what a slight, paltry barrier one plank and no more; but outside a dusty dry road, nothing to be seen but other high brick walls, with here and there an apple-tree or a lilac, or the half developed flower-turrets of a chestnut looking over nothing to be seen but a mean little costermonger's cart, with a hapless donkey, and, down in the direction of St Roque's, the long road winding, still drier and dustier. Ah me! was it paradise inside? or was it only a merely mortal lawn dropped over with apple-blossoms, blue ribbons, and other vanities? Who could tell? The perpetual curate wended sulky on his way. I fear the old woman would have made neither flannel nor tea and sugar out of him in that inhuman frame of mind.

"Dreadful young prig that young Wentworth," said Mr. Wodehouse, "but comes of a great family, you know, and gets greatly taken notice of—to be sure he does, child. I suppose it's for his family's sake: I can't see into people's hearts. It may be higher motives, to be sure, and all that. He's gone off in a huff about something; never mind, luncheon comes up all the same. Now, let's address ourselves to the business of life."

For when Mr. Wodehouse took knife and fork in hand a singular result followed. He was silent—at least he talked no longer: the mystery of carving, of eating, of drinking—all the serious business of the table—engrossed the good man. He had nothing more to say for the moment; and then a dread unbroken silence fell upon the little company. The Rector colored, faltered, cleared his throat—he had not an idea how to get into conversation with such unknown entities. He looked hard at Lucy, with a bold intention of addressing her; but, having the bad fortune to meet her eye, shrank back, and withdrew the venture. Then the good man inclined his profile towards Miss Wodehouse. His eyes wandered wildly round the room in search of a suggestion; but, alas! it was a mere dining-room, very comfortable, but not imaginative. In his dreadful dilemma he was infinitely relieved by the sound of somebody's voice.

"I trust you will like Carlingford, Mr. Proctor," said Miss Wodehouse, mildly.

"Yes—oh yes; I trust so," answered the confused but grateful man; "that is, it will depend very much, of course, on the kind of people I find here."

"Well, we are a little vain. To tell the truth, indeed, we rather pride ourselves a little on the good society in Carlingford," said his gentle and charitable interlocutor.

"Ah, yes—ladies?" said the Rector: "hum—that was not what I was thinking of."

"But, oh, Mr. Proctor," cried Lucy, with a sudden access of fun, "you don't mean to say that you dislike ladies' society, I hope?"

The Rector gave an uneasy half-frightened glance at her. The creature was dangerous even to a Fellow of All Souls.

"I may say I know very little about them," said the bewildered clergyman. As soon as he had said the words he thought they sounded rude; but how could he help it—the truth of his speech was indisputable.

"Come here, and we'll initiate you—come here as often as you can spare us a little of your time," cried Mr. Wodehouse, who had come to a pause in his operations. "You couldn't have a better chance. They're head people in Carlingford, though I say it. There's Mary, she's a learned woman; take you up in a false quantity, sir, a deal sooner than I should. And Lucy, she's in another line altogether; but there's quantities of people swear by her. What's the matter, children, eh? I suppose so—

people tell me so. If people tell me so all day long, I'm entitled to believe it, I presume?"

Lucy answered this by a burst of laughter, not loud but cordial, which rang sweet and strange upon the Rector's ears. Miss Wodehouse, on the contrary, looked a little ashamed, blushed a pretty pink old-maidenly blush, and mildly remonstrated with papa. The whole scene was astonishing to the stranger. He had been living out of nature so long that he wondered within himself whether it was common to retain the habits and words of childhood to such an age as that which good Miss Wodehouse put no disguise upon, or if sisters with twenty years of difference between them were usual in ordinary households. He looked at them with looks which to Miss Wodehouse appeared disapproving, but which in reality meant only surprise and discomfort.

He was exceedingly glad when lunch was over, and he was at liberty to take his leave. With very different feelings from those of young Wentworth the Rector crossed the boundary of that green door. When he saw it closed behind him he drew a long breath of relief, and looked up and down the dusty road, and through those lines of garden walls, where the loads of blossom burst over everywhere, with a sensation of having escaped and got at liberty. After a momentary pause and gaze round him in enjoyment of that liberty, the Rector gave a start and went on again rapidly. A dismayed, discomfited, helpless sensation came over him. These parishioners!—these female parishioners! From out of another of those green doors had just emerged a brilliant group of ladies, the rustle of whose dress and murmur of whose voices he could hear in the genteel half-rural silence. The Rector bolted: he never slackened pace nor drew breath till he was safe in the vacant library of the Rectory, among old Mr. Bury's book-shelves. It seemed the only safe place in Carlingford to the languishing transplanted Fellow of All-Souls.

## CHAPTER II.

A month later, Mr. Proctor had got fairly settled in his new Rectory, with a complete modest establishment becoming his means—for Carlingford was a tolerable living. And in the newly-furnished sober drawing-room sat a very old lady, lively but infirm, who was the Rector's mother. Nobody knew that this old woman kept the Fellow of All-Souls still a boy at heart, nor that the reserved and inappropriate man forgot his awkwardness in his mother's presence. He was not only a very affectionate son, but a dutiful good child to her. It had been his pet scheme for years to bring her from her Devonshire cottage, and make her mistress of his house. That had been the chief attraction, indeed, which drew him to Carlingford; for had he consulted his own tastes, and kept to his college, who would insure him that at seventy-five his old mother might not glide away out of life without that last gleam of sunshine long intended for her by her grateful son?

This scene, accordingly, was almost the only one which reconciled him to the extraordinary change in his life. There she sat, the lively old lady; very deaf, as you could almost divine by that vivid inquiring twinkle in her eyes; feeble too, for she had a silver-headed cane beside her chair, and even with that assistance seldom moved across the room when she could help it. Feeble in body, but alert in mind, ready to read anything, to hear anything, to deliver her opinions freely; resting in her big chair in the complete repose of age, gratified with her son's attentions, and overjoyed in his company; interested about everything, and as ready to enter into all the domestic concerns of the new people as if she had lived all her life among them.

The Rector sighed and smiled as he listened to his mother's questions, and did his best, at the top of his voice, to enlighten her. His mother was, let us say, a hundred years or so younger than the Rector. If she had been his bride, and at the blithe commencement of life, she could not have shown more inclination to know all about Carlingford. Mr. Proctor was middle-aged, and preoccupied by right of his years; but his mother had long ago got over that stage of life. She was at that point when some energetic natures, having got to the bottom of the hill, seem to make a fresh start and reascend. Five years ago, old Mrs. Proctor had completed the human term; now she had recommenced her life.

But, to tell the very truth, the Rector would very fain, had that been possible, have confined her inquiries to books and public affairs. For to make confidential disclosures, either concerning one's self or other people, in a tone of voice perfectly audible in the kitchen, is somewhat trying. He had become acquainted with those dread parishioners of his during this interval. Already they had worn him to death with dinner-parties—dinner-parties very pleasant and friendly, when one got used to them; but to a stranger frightful reproductions of each other, with the same dishes, the same dresses, the same stories, in which the Rector communicated gravely with his next neighbor, and eluded as long as he could those concluding moments in the drawing-room which were worst of all.

It cannot be said that his parishioners made much progress in their knowledge of the Rector. What his "views" were, nobody could divine any more than they could before his arrival. He made no innovations whatever; but he did not pursue Mr. Bury's Evangelical ways, and never preached a sermon or a word more than was absolutely necessary. When zealous Churchmen discussed the progress of Dissent, the Rector scarcely looked interested; and nobody could move him to express an opinion concerning all that lovely upholstery with which Mr. Wentworth had decorated St Roque's. People asked in vain, what was he? He was neither High nor Low, enlightened nor narrow-minded; he was a Fellow of All-Souls.

"But now tell me, my dear," said old Mrs. Proctor, "who's Mr. Wodehouse?"

With despairing calmness, the Rector approached his voice to her ear. "He's a churchwarden!" cried the unfortunate man, in a shrill whisper.

"He's what?—you forget I don't hear very well. I'm a great deal deafer, Morley, my dear, than I was the last time you were in Devonshire. What did you say Mr. Wodehouse was?"

"He's an ass!" exclaimed the baited Rector.

Mrs. Proctor nodded her head with a great many little satisfied assenting nods.

"Exactly my own opinion, my dear. What I like in your manner of expressing yourself, Morley, is its conciseness," said the laughing old lady. "Just so—exactly what I imagined; but being an ass, you know, doesn't account for him coming here so often. What is he besides, my dear?"

The Rector made spasmodic gestures towards the door, to the great amusement of his lively mother; and then produced, with much confusion and after a long search, his pocket-book, on a leaf of paper in which he wrote loudly, in big characters—"He's a churchwarden—they'll hear in the kitchen."

"He's a churchwarden! And what if they do hear in the kitchen?" cried the old lady, greatly amused; "it isn't a sin. Well, now, let me hear: has he a family, Morley?"

Again Mr. Proctor showed a little discomposure. After a troubled look at the door, and pause, as if he meditated a remonstrance, he changed his mind, and answered, "Two daughters!" shouting sepulchrally into his mother's ear.

"Oh so!" cried the old lady—"two *daughters—so, so* that explains it all at once. I know now why he comes to the Rectory so often. And, I declare, I never thought of it before. Why, you're always there!—so, so—and he's got *two daughters,* has he? To be sure; now I understand it all."

The Rector looked helpless and puzzled. It was difficult to take the initiative and ask why—but the poor man looked so perplexed and ignorant, and so clearly unaware what the solution was, that the old lady burst into shrill, gay laughter as she looked at him.

"I don't believe you know anything about it," she said. "Are they old or young? are they pretty or ugly? Tell me all about them, Morley."

Now Mr. Proctor had not the excuse of having forgotten the appearance of the two Miss Wodehouses: on the contrary, though not an imaginative man, he could have fancied he saw them both before him—Lucy lost in noiseless laughter, and her good elder sister deprecating and gentle as usual. We will not even undertake to say that a gleam of something blue did not flash across the mind of the good man, who did not know what ribbons were. He was so much bewildered that Mrs. Proctor repeated her question, and, as she did so, tapped him pretty smartly on the arm to recall his wandering thoughts.

"One's one thing," at last shouted the confused man, "and t'other's another!" An oracular deliverance which surely must have been entirely unintelligible in the kitchen, where we will not deny that an utterance so incomprehensible awoke a laudable curiosity.

"My dear, you're lucid!" cried the old lady. "I hope you don't preach like that. T'other's another!—is she so? and I suppose that's the one you're wanted to marry—eh? For shame, Morley, not to tell your mother!"

The Rector jumped to his feet, thunderstruck. Wanted to marry!—the idea was too overwhelming and dreadful—his mind could not receive it. The air of alarm which immediately diffused itself all over him—his unfeigned horror at the suggestion—captivated his mother. She was amused, but she was pleased at the same time. Just making her cheery outset on this second lifetime, you can't suppose she would have been glad to hear that her son was going to jilt her, and appoint another queen in her stead.

"Sit down and tell me about them," said Mrs. Proctor, "my dear, you're wonderfully afraid of the servants hearing. They don't know who we're speaking of. Aha! and so you didn't know what they meant—didn't you? I don't say you shouldn't marry, my dear—quite the reverse. A man *ought* to marry, one time or another. Only it's rather soon to lay their plans. I don't doubt there's a great many unmarried ladies in your church, Morley. There always is in a country place."

To this the alarmed Rector answered only by a groan—a groan so expressive that his quick-witted mother heard it with her eyes.

"They will come to call on me," said Mrs. Proctor, with fun dancing in her bright old eyes. "I'll tell you all about them, and you needn't be afraid of the servants. Trust to me, my dear—I'll find them out. And now, if you wish to take a walk, or go out visiting, don't let me detain you, Morley. I shouldn't wonder but there's something in the papers I would like to see—or I even might close my eyes for a few minutes: the afternoon is always a drowsy time with me. When I was in Devonshire, you know, no one minded what I did. You had better refresh yourself with a nice walk, my dear boy."

The Rector got up well pleased. The alacrity with which he left the room, however, did not correspond with the horror-stricken and helpless expression of his face, when, after walking very smartly all-round the Rectory garden, he paused with his hand on the gate, doubtful whether to retreat into his study, or boldly to face that world which was plotting against him The question was a profoundly serious one to Mr. Proctor. He did not feel by any means sure that he was a free agent, or could assert the ordinary rights of an Englishman, in this most unexpected dilemma.

How could he tell how much or how little was necessary to prove that a man had "committed himself"? For anything he could tell, somebody might be calculating upon him as her lover, and settling his future life for him. The Rector was not vain—he did not think himself an Adonis; he did not understand anything about the matter, which indeed was beneath the consideration of a Fellow of All-Souls. But have not women been incomprehensible since ever there was in this world a pen with sufficient command of words to call them so? And is it not certain that, whether it may be to their advantage or disadvantage, every soul of them is plotting to marry somebody?

Mr. Proctor recalled in dim but frightful reminiscences stories which had dropped upon his ear at various times of his life. Never was there a man, however ugly, disagreeable, or penniless, but he could tell of a narrow escape he had, some time or other. The Rector recollected and trembled. No woman was ever so dismayed by the persecutions of a lover, as was this helpless middle-aged gentleman under the conviction that Lucy Wodehouse meant to marry him. The remembrance of the curate of St Roque's gave him no comfort: her sweet youth, so totally unlike his sober age, did not strike him as unfavorable to her pursuit of him. Who could fathom the motives of a woman? His mother was wise, and knew the world, and understood what such creatures meant. No doubt it was entirely the case—a dreadful certainty—and what was he to do?

At the bottom of all this fright and perplexity must it be owned that the Rector had a guilty consciousness within himself, that if Lucy drove the matter to extremities, he was not so sure of his own powers of resistance as he ought to be? She might marry him before he knew what he was about; and in such a case the Rector could not have taken his oath at his own private confessional that he would have been so deeply miserable as the circumstances might infer. No wonder he was alarmed at the position in which he found himself; nobody could predict how it might end.

When Mr. Proctor saw his mother again at dinner, she was evidently full of some subject which would not bear talking of before the servants. The old lady looked at her son's troubled apprehensive face with smiles and nods and gay hints, which he was much too preoccupied to understand, and which only increased his bewilderment. When the good man was left alone over his glass of wine, he drank it slowly, in funereal silence, with profoundly serious looks; and what between eagerness to understand what the old lady meant, and reluctance to show the extent of his curiosity, had a very heavy half-hour of it in that grave solitary dining-room.

He roused himself with an effort from this dismal state into which he was falling. He recalled with a sigh the classic board of All-Souls. Woe for the day when he was seduced to forsake that dear retirement! Really, to suffer himself to fall into a condition so melancholy, was far from being right. He must rouse himself—he must find some other society than parishioners; and with a glimpse of a series of snug little dinner-parties, undisturbed by the presence of women, Mr. Proctor rose and hurried after his mother, to hear what new thing she might have to say.

Nor was he disappointed. The old lady was snugly posted, ready for a conference. She made lively gestures to hasten him when he appeared at the door, and could scarcely delay the utterance of her news till he had taken his seat beside her. She had taken off her spectacles, and laid aside her paper, and cleared off her work into her work-basket. All was ready for the talk in which she delighted .

"My dear, they've been here," said old Mrs. Proctor rubbing her hands—"both together, and as kind as could be—exactly as I expected. An old woman gets double the attention when she's got an unmarried son. I've always observed that; though in Devonshire, what with your fellowship and seeing you so seldom, nobody took much notice. Yes, they've been here; and I like them a great deal better than I expected, Morley, my dear."

The Rector, not knowing what else to say, shouted "Indeed, mother!" into the old lady's ear.

"Quite so," continued that lively observer—"nice young women—not at all like their father, which is a great consolation. That elder one is a very sensible person, I am sure. She would make a nice wife for somebody, especially for a clergyman. She is not in her first youth, but neither are some other people. A very nice creature indeed, I am quite sure."

During all this speech the Rector's countenance had been falling, falling. If he was helpless before, the utter woe of his expression now was a spectacle to behold. The danger of being married by proxy was appalling certainly, yet was not entirely without alleviations; but Miss Wodehouse! who ever thought of Miss Wodehouse? To see the last remains of color fade out of his cheek, and his very lip fall with disappointment, was deeply edifying to his lively old mother. She perceived it all, but made no sign.

"And the other is a pretty creature—certainly pretty: shouldn't you say she was pretty, Morley?" said his heartless mother.

Mr. Proctor hesitated, hemmed—felt himself growing red—tried to intimate his sentiments by a nod of assent; but that would not do, for the old lady had presented her ear to him, and was blind to all his gestures.

"I don't know much about it, mother," he made answer at last.

"Much about it! it's to be hoped not. I never supposed you did; but you don't mean to say you don't think her pretty?" said Mrs. Proctor—"but, I don't doubt in the least, a sad flirt. Her sister is a very superior person, my dear."

The Rector's face lengthened at every word—a vision of these two Miss Wodehouses rose upon him every moment clearer and more distinct as his mother spoke. Considering how ignorant he was of all such female paraphernalia, it is extraordinary how correct his recollection was of all the details of their habitual dress and appearance. With a certain dreadful consciousness of the justice of what his mother said, he saw in imagination the mild elder sister in her comely old-maidenhood. Nobody could doubt her good qualities, and could it be questioned that for a man of fifty, if he was to do anything so foolish, a woman not quite forty was a thousand times more eligible than a creature in blue ribbons?

Still the unfortunate Rector did not seem to see it: his face grew longer and longer—he made no answer whatever to his mother's address; while she, with a spice of natural female malice against the common enemy triumphing for the moment over the mother's admiration of her son, sat wickedly enjoying his distress, and aggravating it. His dismay and perplexity amused this wicked old woman beyond measure.

"I have no doubt that younger girl takes a pleasure in deluding her admirers," said Mrs. Proctor; "she's a wicked little flirt, and likes nothing better than to see her power. I know very well how such people do; but, my dear," continued this false old lady, scarcely able to restrain her laughter, "if I were you, I would be very civil to Miss Wodehouse. You may depend upon it, Morley, that's a very superior person. She is not very young, to be sure, but you are not very young yourself. She would make a nice wife—not too foolish, you know, nor fanciful. Ah! I like Miss Wodehouse, my dear."

The Rector stumbled up to his feet hastily, and pointed to a table at a little distance, on which some books were lying. Then he went and brought them to her table. "I've brought you some new books," he shouted into her ear. It was the only way his clumsy ingenuity could fall upon for bringing this most distasteful conversation to an end.

The old lady's eyes were dancing with fun and a little mischief, but, notwithstanding, she could not be so false to her nature as to show no interest in the books. She turned them over with lively remarks and comment. "But for all that, Morley, I would not have you forget Miss Wodehouse," she said, when her early bedtime came. "Give it a thought now and then, and consider the whole matter. It is not a thing to be done rashly; but still you know you are settled now, and you ought to be thinking of settling for life."

With this parting shaft she left him. The troubled Rector, instead of sitting up to his beloved studies, went early to bed that night, and was pursued by nightmares through his unquiet slumbers. Settling for life! Alas! there floated before him vain visions of that halcyon world he had left—that sacred soil at All-Souls, where there were no parishioners to break the sweet repose. How different was this discomposing real world!

## CHAPTER III.

Matters went on quietly for some time without any catastrophe occurring to the Rector. He had shut himself up from all society, and declined the invitations of the parishioners for ten long days at least; but finding that the kind people were only kinder than ever when they understood he was "indisposed," poor Mr. Proctor resumed his ordinary life, confiding timidly in some extra precautions which his own ingenuity had invented. He was shyer than ever of addressing the ladies in those parties he was obliged to attend.

He was especially embarrassed and uncomfortable in the presence of the two Miss Wodehouses, who, unfortunately, were very popular in Carlingford, and whom he could not help meeting everywhere. Notwithstanding this embarrassment, it is curious how well he knew how they looked, and what they were doing, and all about them. Though he could not for his life have told what these things were called, he knew Miss Wodehouse's dove-colored dress and her French gray; and all those gleams of blue which set off Lucy's fair curls, and floated about her pretty person under various pretenses, had a distinct though inarticulate place in the good man's confused remembrance. But neither Lucy nor Miss Wodehouse had brought matters to extremity. He even ventured to go to their house occasionally without any harm coming of it, and lingered in that blooming fragrant garden, where the blossoms had given place to fruit, and ruddy apples hung heavy on the branches which had once scattered their petals, rosy-white, on Frank Wentworth's Anglican coat. Yet Mr. Proctor was not lulled into incaution by this seeming calm. Other people besides his mother had intimated to him that there were expectations current of his "settling in life." He lived not in false security, but wise trembling, never knowing what hour the thunderbolt might fall upon his head.

It happened one day, while still in this condition of mind, that the Rector was passing through Grove Street on his way home. He was walking on the humbler side of the street, where there is a row of cottages with little gardens in front of them—cheap houses, which are contented to be haughtily overlooked by the staircase windows and blank walls of their richer neighbors on the other side of the road. The Rector thought. but could not be sure, that he had seen two figures like those of the Miss Wodehouses going into one of these houses, and was making a little haste to escape meeting those enemies of his peace. But as he went hastily on, he heard sobs and screams—sounds which a man who hid a good heart under a shy exterior could not willingly pass by. He made a troubled pause before the door from which these outcries proceeded, and while he stood thus irresolute whether to pass on or to stop and inquire the cause, some one came rushing out and took hold of his arm. "Please, sir, she's dying—oh, please, sir, she thought a deal o' you. Please, will you come in and speak to her?" cried the little servant-girl who had pounced upon him so.

The Rector stared at her in amazement. He had not his prayer-book—he was not prepared; he had no idea of being called upon in such an emergency. In the mean time the commotion rather increased in the house, and he could hear in the distance a voice adjuring some one to go for the clergyman. The Rector stood uncertain and perplexed, perhaps in a more serious personal difficulty than had ever happened to him all his life before. For what did he know about deathbeds? or what had he to say to any one on that dread verge? He grew pale with real vexation and distress.

"Have they gone for a doctor? that would be more to the purpose," he said, unconsciously, aloud.

"Please, sir, it's no good," said the little maid-servant. "Please, the doctor's been, but he's no good—and she's unhappy in her mind, though she's quite resigned to go: and oh, please, if you would say a word to her, it might do her a deal of good."

Thus adjured, the Rector had no choice. He went gloomily into the house and up the stair after his little guide. Why did not they send for the minister of Salem Chapel close by? or for Mr. Wentworth, who was accustomed to that sort of thing? Why did they resort to him in such an emergency? He would have made his appearance before the highest magnates of the land—before the Queen herself—before the bench of bishops or the Privy Council with less trepidation than he entered that poor little room.

The sufferer lay breathing heavily in the poor apartment. She did not look very ill to Mr. Proctor's inexperienced eyes. Her color was bright, and her face full of eagerness. Near the door stood Miss Wodehouse, looking compassionate but helpless, casting wistful glances at the bed, but standing back in a corner as confused and embarrassed as the Rector himself. Lucy was standing by the pillow of the sick woman with a watchful readiness visible to the most unskilled eye—ready to raise her, to change her position, to attend to her wants almost before they were expressed. The contrast was wonderful. She had thrown off her bonnet and shawl, and appeared, not like a stranger, but somehow in her natural place, despite the sweet youthful beauty of her looks, and the gay girlish dress with its floating ribbons. These singular adjuncts notwithstanding, no homely nurse in a cotton gown could have looked more alert or serviceable, or more natural to the position, than Lucy did. The poor Rector, taking the seat which the little maid placed for him directly in the center of the room, looked at the nurse and the patient with a gasp of perplexity and embarrassment. A deathbed, alas! was an unknown region to him.

"Oh, sir, I'm obliged to you for coming—oh, sir, I'm grateful to you," cried the poor woman in the bed. "I've been ill, off and on, for years, but never took thought to it as I ought. I've put off and put off, waiting for a better time—and now, God help me, it's perhaps too late. Oh, sir, tell me, when a person's ill and dying, is it too late?"

Before the Rector could even imagine what he could answer, the sick woman took up the broken thread of her own words, and continued—

"I don't feel to trust as I ought to—I don't feel no confidence," she said, in anxious confession. "Oh, sir, do you think it matters if one feels it?—don't you think things might be right all the same though we *were* uneasy in our minds? My thinking can't change it one way or another. Ask the good gentleman to speak to me, Miss Lucy dear—he'll mind what you say."

A look from Lucy quickened the Rector's speech, but increased his embarrassments. "It—it isn't her doctor she has no confidence in?" he said, eagerly.

The poor woman gave a little cry. "The doctor—the doctor! what can he do to a poor dying creature? Oh, Lord bless you, it's none of them things I'm thinking of; it's my soul—my soul!"

"But my poor good woman," said Mr. Proctor, "though it is very good and praiseworthy of you to be anxious about your soul, let us hope that there is no such—no such *haste* as you seem to suppose."

The patient opened her eyes wide, and stared, with the anxious look of disease, in his face.

"I mean," said the good man, faltering under that gaze "that I see no reason for your making yourself so very anxious. Let us hope it is not so bad as that. You are very ill, but not *so* ill—I suppose."

Here the Rector was interrupted by a groan from the patient, and by a troubled, disapproving, disappointed look from Lucy Wodehouse. This brought him to a sudden standstill. He gazed for a moment helplessly at the poor woman in the bed. If he had known anything in the world which would have given her consolation, he was ready to have made any exertion for it; but he knew nothing to say—no medicine for a mind diseased was in his repositories. He was deeply distressed to see the disappointment which followed his words, but his distress only made him more silent, more helpless, more inefficient than before.

After an interval which was disturbed only by the groans of the patient and the uneasy fidgeting of good Miss Wodehouse in her corner, the Rector again broke silence. The sick woman had turned to the wall, and closed her eyes in dismay and disappointment—evidently she had ceased to expect anything from him.

"If there is anything I can do," said poor Mr. Proctor, "I am afraid I have spoken hastily. I meant to try to calm her mind a little; if I can be of any use?"

"Ah, maybe I'm hasty," said the dying woman, turning round again with a sudden effort— "but, oh, to speak to me of having time when I've one foot in the grave already!"

"Not so bad as that—not so bad as that," said the Rector, soothingly.

"But I tell you it is as bad as that," she cried, with the brief blaze of anger common to great weakness. "I'm not a child to be persuaded different from what I know. If you'd tell me—if you'd say a prayer—ah, Miss Lucy, it's coming on again."

In a moment Lucy had raised the poor creature in her arms, and in default of the pillows which were not at hand, had risen herself into their place, and supported the gasping woman against her own breast. It was a paroxysm dreadful to behold, in which every laboring breath seemed the last. The Rector sat like one struck dumb, looking on at that mortal struggle. Miss Wodehouse approached nervously from behind, and went up to the bedside, faltering forth questions as to what she could do. Lucy only waved her hand, as her own light figure swayed and changed, always seeking the easiest attitude for the sufferer. As the elder sister drew back, the Rector and she glanced at each other with wistful mutual looks of sympathy. Both were equally well-disposed, equally helpless and embarrassed. How to be of any use in that dreadful agony of nature was denied to both. They stood looking on, awed and self-reproaching. Such scenes have doubtless happened in sick-rooms before now.

When the fit was over, a hasty step came up the stair, and Mr. Wentworth entered the room. He explained in a whisper that he had not been at home when the messenger came, but had followed whenever he heard of the message. Seeing the Rector, he hesitated, and drew back with some surprise, and, even (for he was far from perfect) in that chamber, a little flush of offense. The Rector rose abruptly, waving his hand, and went to join Miss Wodehouse in her corner. There the two elderly spectators looked on silent at ministrations of which both were incapable; one watching with wondering yet affectionate envy how Lucy laid down the weakened but relieved patient upon her pillows; and one beholding with a surprise he could not conceal, how a young man, not half his own age, went softly, with all the confidence yet awe of nature, into those mysteries which he dared not touch upon.

The two young creatures by the deathbed acknowledged that their patient was dying; the woman stood by her watchful and affectionate—the man held up before her that cross, not of wood or metal, but of truth and everlasting verity, which is the only hope of man. The spectators looked on, and did not interrupt—looked on, awed and wondering—unaware of how it was, but watching, as if it were a miracle wrought before their eyes. Perhaps all the years of his life had not taught the Rector so much as did that half-hour in an unknown poor bedchamber, where, honest and humble, he stood aside, and, kneeling down, responded to his young brother's prayer. His young brother—young enough to have been his son—not half nor a quarter part so learned as he; but a world further on in that profession which they shared—the art of winning souls.

When those prayers were over, the Rector, without a word to anybody, stole quietly away. When he got into the street, however, he found himself closely followed by Miss Wodehouse, of whom he was not at this moment afraid. That good creature was crying softly under her veil. She was eager to make up to him, to open out her full heart; and indeed the Rector, like herself, in that wonderful sensation of surprised and unenvying discomfiture, was glad at that moment of sympathy too.

"Oh, Mr. Proctor, isn't it wonderful?" sighed good Miss Wodehouse.

The Rector did not speak but he answered by a very emphatic nod of his head.

"It did not use to be so when you and I were young," said his companion in failure. "I sometimes take a little comfort from that; but no doubt, if it had been in me, it would have shown itself somehow. Ah, I fear, I fear, I was not well brought up; but, to be sure, that dear child has not been brought up at all, if one may say so. Her poor mother died when she was born. And oh, I'm afraid I never was kind to Lucy's mother, Mr. Proctor. You know she was only a year or two older than I was; and to think of that child, that baby! What a world she is, and always was, before me, that might have been her mother, Mr. Proctor!" said Miss Wodehouse, with a little sob.

"But things were different in our young days," said the Rector, repeating her sentiment, without inquiring whether it were true or not, and finding a certain vague consolation in it.

"Ah, that is true," said Miss Wodehouse—"that is true; what a blessing things are so changed; and these blessed young creatures," she added softly, with tears falling out of her gentle old eyes—"these blessed young creatures are near the Fountainhead."

With this speech Miss Wodehouse held out her hand to the Rector, and they parted with a warm mutual grasp. The Rector went straight home—straight to his study, where he shut himself in, and was not to be disturbed; that night was one long to be remembered in the good man's history. For the first time in his life he set himself to inquire what was his supposed business in this world. His treatise on the Greek verb, and his new edition of Sophocles, were highly creditable to the Fellow of All-Souls; but how about the Rector of Carlingford?

What was he doing here, among that little world of human creatures who were dying, being born, perishing, suffering, falling into misfortune and anguish, and all manner of human vicissitudes, every day? Young Wentworth knew what to say to that woman in her distress; and so might the Rector, had her distress concerned a disputed translation, or a disused idiom. The good man was startled in his composure and calm. Today he had visibly failed in a duty which even in All-Souls was certainly known to be one of the duties of a Christian priest. Was he a Christian priest or what was he? He was troubled to the very depths of his soul. To hold an office the duties of which he could not perform was clearly impossible. The only question, and that a hard one, was, whether he could learn to discharge those duties, or whether he must cease to be Rector of Carlingford. He labored over this problem in his solitude, and could find no answer. "Things were different when we were young," was the only thought that was any comfort to him, and that was poor consolation.

For one thing, it is hard upon the most magnanimous of men to confess that he has undertaken an office for which he has not found himself capable. Magnanimity was perhaps too lofty a word to apply to the Rector; but he was honest to the bottom of his soul. As soon as he became aware of what was included in the duties of his office, he must perform them, or quit his post. But how to perform them? Can one learn to convey consolation to the dying, to teach the ignorant, to comfort the sorrowful? Are these matters to be acquired by study, like Greek verbs or intricate measures?

The Rector's heart said No. The Rector's imagination unfolded before him, in all its halcyon blessedness, that ancient paradise of All-Souls, where no such confounding demands ever disturbed his beatitude The good man groaned within himself over the mortification, the labor, the sorrow, which this living was bringing upon him. "If I had but let it pass to Morgan, who wanted to marry," he said with self-reproach; and then suddenly bethought himself of his own most innocent filial romance, and the pleasure his mother had taken in her new house and new beginning of life. At that touch the tide flowed back again. Could he dismiss her now to another solitary cottage in Devonshire, her old home there being all dispersed and broken up, while the house she had hoped to die in cast her out from its long-hoped-for shelter? The Rector was quite overwhelmed by this new aggravation. If by any effort of his own, any sacrifice to himself, he could preserve this bright new home to his mother, would he shrink from that labor of love?

## CHAPTER IV.

Such a blessed exemption, however, was not to be hoped for. When the Rector was solemnly sent for from his very study to visit a poor man who was not expected to live many days, he put his prayer-book under his arm, and went off doggedly, feeling that now was the crisis. He went through it in as exemplary a manner as could have been desired, but it was dreadful work to the Rector. If nobody else suspected him, he suspected himself. He had no spontaneous word of encouragement or consolation to offer; he went through it as his duty with a horrible abstractness. That night he went home disgusted beyond all possible power of self reconciliation. He could not continue this. Good Evangelical Mr. Bury, who went before him, and by nature loved preaching, had accustomed the people to much of such visitations. It was murder to the Fellow of All-Souls.

That night Mr. Proctor wrote a long letter to his dear cheery old mother, disclosing all his heart to her. It was written with a pathos of which the good man was wholly unconscious, and finished by asking her advice and her prayers. He sent it up to her next morning on her breakfast tray, which he always furnished with his own hands, and went out to occupy himself in paying visits till it should be time to see her, and ascertain her opinion.

At Mr. Wodehouse's there was nobody at home but Lucy, who was very friendly, and took no notice of that sad encounter which had changed his views so entirely. The Rector found, on inquiry, that the woman was dead, but not until Mr. Wentworth had administered to her fully the consolations of the Church. Lucy did not look superior, or say anything in admiration of Mr. Wentworth, but the Rector's conscience supplied all that was wanting. If good Miss Wodehouse had been there with her charitable looks, and her disefficiency so like his own, it would have been a consolation to the good man. He would have turned joyfully from Lucy and her blue ribbons to that distressed dove-colored woman, so greatly had recent events changed him. But the truth was, he cared nothing for either of them nowadays. He was delivered from those whimsical distressing fears. Something more serious had obliterated those lighter apprehensions. He had no leisure now to think that somebody had planned to marry him; all his thoughts were fixed on matters so much more important that this was entirely forgotten.

Mrs. Proctor was seated as usual in the place she loved, with her newspapers, her books, her work-basket, and silver headed cane at the side of her chair. The old lady, like her son, looked serious. She beckoned him to quicken his step when she saw him appear at the drawing-room door, and pointed to the chair placed beside her, all ready for this solemn conference. He came in with a troubled face, scarcely venturing to look at her, afraid to see the disappointment which he had brought upon his dearest friend. The old lady divined why it was he did not lift his eyes. She took his hand and addressed him with all her characteristic vivacity.

"Morley, what is this you mean, my dear? When did I ever give my son reason to distrust me? Do you think I would suffer you to continue in a position painful to yourself for my sake? How dare you think such a thing of me, Morley? Don't say so? you didn't mean it; I can see it in your eyes."

The Rector shook his head, and dropped into the chair placed ready for him. He might have had a great deal to say for himself could she have heard him. But as it was, he could not shout all his reasons and apologies into her deaf ear. "As for the change to me," said the old lady, instinctively seizing upon the heart of the difficulty, "that's nothing—simply nothing. I've not had time to get attached to Carlingford. I've no associations with the place. Of course I shall be very glad to go back to all my old friends. Put that out of the question, Morley."

But the Rector only shook his head once more. The more she made light of it, the more he perceived all the painful, circumstances involved. Could his mother go back to Devonshire and tell all her old ladies that her son had made a failure in Carlingford? He grieved within himself at the thought. His brethren at All-Souls might understand *him;* but what could console the brave old woman for all the condolence and commiseration to which she would be subject? "It goes to my heart, mother," he cried in her ear.

"Well, Morley, I am very sorry you find it so," said the old lady; "very sorry you can't see your way to all your duties. They tell me the late Rector was very Low Church, and visited about like a Dissenter, so it is not much wonder you with your different habits, find yourself a good deal put out; but, my dear, don't you think it's only at first? Don't you think after a while the people would get into your ways, and you into theirs? Miss Wodehouse was here this morning, and was telling me a good deal about the late Rector. It's to be expected you should find the difference; but by-and-by, to be sure, you might get used to it, and the people would not expect so much."

"Did she tell you where we met the other day?" asked the Rector, with a brevity rendered necessary by Mrs. Proctor's infirmity.

"She told me—she's a dear confused good soul," said the old lady—"about the difference between Lucy and herself, and how the young creature was twenty times handier than she, and something about young Mr. Wentworth of St Roque's. Really, by all I hear, that must be a very presuming young man," cried Mrs. Proctor, with a lively air of offense. "His interference among your parishioners, Morley, is really more than I should be inclined to bear."

Once more the good Rector shook his head. He had not thought of that aspect of the subject. He was indeed so free from vanity or self-importance, that his only feeling in regard to the sudden appearance of the perpetual curate was respect and surprise. He would not be convince otherwise even now. "He can do his duty, mother," he answered, sadly.

"Stuff and nonsense!" cried the old lady. "Do you mean to tell me a boy like that can do his duty better than my son could do it, if he put his mind to it? And if it is your duty, Morley, dear," continued his mother, melting a little, and in a coaxing persuasive tone, "of course I know you will do it, however hard it may be."

"That's just the difficulty," cried the Rector, venturing on a longer speech than usual, and roused to a point at which he had no fear of the listeners in the kitchen; "such duties require other training than mine has been. I can't!—do you hear me, mother?—I must not hold a false position; that's impossible."

"You shan't hold a false position," cried the old lady; "that's the only thing that *is* impossible—but, Morley, let us consider, dear. You are a clergyman, you know; you ought to understand all that's required of you a great deal better than these people do. My dear, your poor father and I trained you up to be a clergyman," said Mrs. Proctor, rather pathetically, "and not to be a Fellow of All-Souls."

The Rector groaned. Had it not been advancement, progress, unhoped-for good fortune, that made him a member of that learned corporation? He shook his head. Nothing could change the fact now. After fifteen years' experience of that Elysium, he could not put on the cassock and surplice with all his youthful fervor. He had settled into his life-habits long ago. With the quick perception which made up for her deficiency, his mother read his face, and saw the cause was hopeless; yet with female courage and pertinacity made one effort more.

"And with an excellent hard-working curate," said the old lady—"a curate whom, of course, we'd do our duty by, Morley, and who could take a great deal of the responsibility off your hands; for Mr. Leigh, though a nice young man, is not, I know, the man you would have chosen for such a post; and still more, my dear son—we were talking of it in jest not long ago, but it is perfect earnest, and a most important matter—with a good wife, Morley; a wife who would enter into all the parish work, and give you useful hints, and conduct herself as a clergyman's wife should—with such a wife—"

"Lucy Wodehouse!" cried the Rector, starting to his feet, and forgetting all his proprieties; "I tell you the thing is impossible. I'll go back to All-Souls."

He sat down again doggedly, having said it. His mother sat looking at him in silence, with tears in her lively old eyes. She was saying within herself that she had seen his father take just such a "turn," and that it was no use arguing with them under such circumstances. She watched him as women often do watch men, waiting till the creature should come to itself again and might be spoken to. The incomprehensibleness of women is an old theory, but what is that to the curious wondering observation with which wives, mothers, and sisters watch the other unreasoning animal in those moments when he has snatched the reins out of their hands, and is not to be spoken to! What he will make of it in those unassisted moments, afflicts the compassionate female understanding. It is best to let him come to, and feel his own helplessness. Such was Mrs. Proctor's conclusion, as, vexed, distressed, and helpless, she leant back in her chair, and wiped a few tears of disappointment and vexation out of her bright old eyes.

The Rector saw this movement, and it once more excited him to speech. "But you shall have a house in Oxford, mother," he cried—"you shan't go back to Devonshire—where I can see you every day, and you can hear all that is going on. Bravo! that will be a thousand times better than Carlingford."

It was now Mrs. Proctor's turn to jump up, startled, and put her hand on his mouth and point to the door. The Rector did not care for the door; he had disclosed his sentiments, he had taken his resolution, and now the sooner it was all over the better for the emancipated man.

Thus concluded the brief incumbency of the Reverend Morley Proctor. He returned to Oxford before his year of grace was over, and found everybody very glad to see him; and he left Carlingford with universal good wishes. The living fell to Morgan, who wanted to be married, and whose turn was much more to be a working clergyman than a classical commentator. Old Mrs. Proctor got a pretty house under shelter of the trees of St Giles's, and half the undergraduates fell in love with the old lady in the freshness of her second lifetime. Carlingford passed away like a dream from the lively old mother's memory, and how could any reminiscences of that uncongenial locality disturb the recovered beatitude of the Fellow of All-Souls?

Yet all was not so satisfactory as it appeared. Mr. Proctor paid for his temporary absence. All-Souls was not the Elysium it had been before that brief disastrous voyage into the world. The good man felt the stings of failure; he felt the mild jokes of his brethren in those Elysian fields. He could not help conjuring up to himself visions of Morgan with his new wife in that pretty Rectory. Life, after all, did not consist of books, nor were Greek verbs essential to happiness. The strong emotion into which his own failure had roused him; the wondering silence in which he stood looking at the ministrations of Lucy Wodehouse and the young curate; the tearful sympathetic woman as helpless as himself, who had stood beside him in that sick chamber, came back upon his recollection strangely, amidst the repose, not so blessed as heretofore, of All-Souls.

The good man had found out that secret of discontent which most men find out a great deal earlier than he. Something better, though it might be sadder, harder, more calamitous, was in this world. Was there ever human creature yet that had not something in him more congenial to the thorns and briars outside to be conquered, than to that mild paradise for which our primeval mother disqualified all her children? When he went back to his dear cloisters, good Mr. Proctor felt that sting: a longing for the work he had rejected stirred in him—a wistful recollection of the sympathy he had not sought.

And if in future years any traveler, if travelers still fall upon adventures, should light upon a remote parsonage in which an elderly embarrassed Rector, with a mild wife in dove-colored dresses, toils painfully after his duty, more and more giving his heart to it, more and more finding difficult expression for the unused faculty, let him be sure that it is the late Rector of Carlingford, self-expelled out of the uneasy paradise, setting forth untimely, yet not too late. into the laborious world.

## The Library Window
### A Story of the Seen and Unseen

#### ONE

I was not aware at first of the many discussions which had gone on about that window. It was almost opposite one of the windows of the large old-fashioned drawing-room of the house in which I spent that summer, which was of so much importance in my life. Our house and the library were on opposite sides of the broad High Street of St Rule's, which is a fine street, wide and ample, and very quiet, as strangers think who come from noisier places; but in a summer evening there is much coming and going, and the stillness is full of sound—the sound of footsteps and pleasant voices, softened by the summer air.

There are even exceptional moments when it is noisy: the time of the fair, and on Saturday nights sometimes, and when there are excursion trains. Then even the softest sunny air of the evening will not smooth the harsh tones and the stumbling steps; but at these unlovely moments we shut the windows, and even I, who am so fond of that deep recess where I can take refuge from all that is going on inside, and make myself a spectator of all the varied story out of doors, withdraw from my watch-tower.

To tell the truth, there never was very much going on inside. The house belonged to my aunt, to whom (she says, Thank God!) nothing ever happens. I believe that many things have happened to her in her time; but that was all over at the period of which I am speaking, and she was old, and very quiet. Her life went on in a routine never broken. She got up at the same hour every day, and did the same things in the same rotation, day by day the same. She said that this was the greatest support in the world, and that routine is a kind of salvation. It may be so; but it is a very dull salvation, and I used to feel that I would rather have incident, whatever kind of incident it might be. But then at that time I was not old, which makes all the difference.

At the time of which I speak the deep recess of the drawing-room window was a great comfort to me. Though she was an old lady (perhaps because she was so old) she was very tolerant, and had a kind of feeling for me. She never said a word, but often gave me a smile when she saw how I had built myself up, with my books and my basket of work. I did very little work, I fear—now and then a few stitches when the spirit moved me, or when I had got well afloat in a dream, and was more tempted to follow it out than to read my book, as sometimes happened.

At other times, and if the book were interesting, I used to get through volume after volume sitting there, paying no attention to anybody. And yet I did pay a kind of attention. Aunt Mary's old ladies came in to call, and I heard them talk, though I very seldom listened; but for all that, if they had anything to say that was interesting, it is curious how I found it in my mind afterwards, as if the air had blown it to me.

They came and went, and I had the sensation of their old bonnets gliding out and in, and their dresses rustling; and now and then had to jump up and shake hands with some one who knew me, and asked after my papa and mamma. Then Aunt Mary would give me a little smile again, and I slipped back to my window. She never seemed to mind.

My mother would not have let me do it, I know. She would have remembered dozens of things there were to do. She would have sent me upstairs to fetch something which I was quite sure she did not want, or downstairs to carry some quite unnecessary message to the housemaid. She liked to keep me running about. Perhaps that was one reason why I was so fond of Aunt Mary's drawing-room, and the deep recess of the window, and the curtain that fell half over it, and the broad window-seat, where one could collect so many things without being found fault with for untidiness. Whenever we had anything the matter with us in these days, we were sent to St Rule's to get up our strength. And this was my case at the time of which I am going to speak.

Everybody had said, since ever I learned to speak, that I was fantastic and fanciful and dreamy, and all the other words with which a girl who may happen to like poetry, and to be fond of thinking, is so often made uncomfortable. People don't know what they mean when they say fantastic. It sounds like Madge Wildfire or something of that sort. My mother thought I should always be busy, to keep nonsense out of my head. But really I was not at all fond of nonsense. I was rather serious than otherwise. I would have been no trouble to anybody if I had been left to myself. It was only that I had a sort of second-sight, and was conscious of things to which I paid no attention. Even when reading the most interesting book, the things that were being talked about blew in to me; and I heard what the people were saying in the streets as they passed under the window. Aunt Mary always said I could do two or indeed three things at once—both read and listen, and see. I am sure that I did not listen much, and seldom looked out, of set purpose—as some people do who notice what bonnets the ladies in the street have on; but I did hear what I couldn't help hearing, even when I was reading my book, and I did see all sorts of things, though often for a whole half-hour I might never lift my eyes.

This does not explain what I said at the beginning, that there were many discussions about that window. It was, and still is, the last window in the row, of the college library, which is opposite my aunt's house in High Street. Yet it is not exactly opposite, but a little to the west, so that I could see it best from the left side of my recess. I took it calmly for granted that it was a window like any other till I first heard the talk about it which was going on in the drawing-room.

"Have you never made up your mind, Mrs. Balcarres," said old Mr. Pitmilly, "whether that window opposite is a window or no?" He said Mistress Balcarres—and he was always called Mr. Pitmilly, Morton: which was the name of his place.

"I am never sure of it, to tell the truth," said Aunt Mary, "all these years."

"Bless me!" said one of the old ladies, "and what window may that be?"

Mr. Pitmilly had a way of laughing as he spoke, which did not please me; but it was true that he was not perhaps desirous of pleasing me. He said, "Oh, just the window opposite," with his laugh running through his words; "our friend can never make up her mind about it, though she has been living opposite it since—"

"You need never mind the date," said another, "the Leebrary window! Dear me, what should it be but a window? up at that height it could not be a door."

"The question is," said my aunt, "if it is a real window with glass in it, or if it is merely painted, or if it once was a window, and has been built up. And the oftener people look at it, the less they are able to say."

"Let me see this window," said old Lady Carnbee, who was very active and strong-minded; and then they all came crowding upon me—three or four old ladies, very eager, and Mr. Pitmilly's white hair appearing over their heads, and my aunt sitting quiet and smiling behind.

"I mind the window very well," said Lady Carnbee; "ay; and so do more than me. But in its present appearance it is just like any other window; but has not been cleaned, I should say, in the memory of man."

"I see what ye mean," said one of the others. "It is just a very dead thing without any reflection in it; but I've seen as bad before."

"Ay, it's dead enough," said another, "but that's no rule; for these hizzies of women-servants in this ill age—"

"Nay, the women are well enough," said the softest voice of all, which was Aunt Mary's. "I will never let them this risk their lives cleaning the outside of mine. And there are no women-servants in the Old Library; there is maybe something more in it than that."

They were all pressing into my recess, pressing upon me, a row of old faces, peering into something they could not understand. I had a sense in my mind how curious it was, the wall of old ladies in their old satin gowns all glazed with age. Lady Carnbee with her lace about her head. Nobody was looking at me or thinking of me; but I felt unconsciously the contrast of my youngness to their oldness, and stared at them as they stared over my head at the Library window. I had given it no attention up to this time. I was more taken up with the old ladies than with the thing they were looking at.

"The framework is all right at least, I can see that, and pented black—"

"And the panes are pented black too. It's no window, Mrs. Balcarres. It has been filled in, in the days of the window duties you will mind, Leddy Carnbee."

"Mind!" said that oldest lady. "I mind when your mother was marriet, Jeanie; and that's neither the day nor yesterday. But as for the window, it's just a delusion: and that is my opinion of the matter, if you ask me."

"There's a great want of light in that muckle room at the college," said another. "If it was a window, the Leebrary would have more light."

"One thing is clear," said one of the younger ones, "it cannot be a window to see through. It may be filled in or it may be built up, but it is not a window to give light."

"And whoever heard of a window that was no to see through?" Lady Carnbee said. I was fascinated by the look on her face, which was a curious scornful look as of one who knew more than she chose to say: and then my wandering fancy was caught by her hand as she held it up, throwing back the lace that drooped over it. Lady Carnbee's lace was the chief thing about her—heavy black Spanish lace with large flowers. Everything she wore was trimmed with it. A large veil of it hung over her old bonnet.

But her hand coming out of this heavy lace was a curious thing to see. She had very long fingers, very taper, which had been much admired in her youth; and her hand was very white, or rather more than white, pale, bleached, and bloodless, with large blue veins standing up upon the back; and she wore some fine rings, among others a big diamond in an ugly old claw setting. They were too big for her, and were wound round and round with yellow silk to make them keep on: and this little cushion of silk, turned brown with long wearing, had twisted round so that it was more conspicuous than the jewels; while the big diamond blazed underneath in the hollow of her hand, like some dangerous thing hiding and sending out darts of light. The hand, which seemed to come almost to a point, with this strange ornament underneath, clutched at my half-terrified imagination. It too seemed to mean far more than was said. I felt as if it might clutch me with sharp claws, and the lurking, dazzling creature bite—with a sting that would go to the heart.

Presently, however, the circle of the old faces broke up, the old ladies returned to their seats, and Mr. Pitmilly, small but very erect, stood up in the midst of them, talking with mild authority like a little oracle among the ladies. Only Lady Carnbee always contradicted the neat, little, old gentleman. She gesticulated, when she talked, like a Frenchwoman, and darted forth that hand of hers with the lace hanging over it, so that I always caught a glimpse of the lurking diamond. I thought she looked like a witch among the comfortable little group which gave such attention to everything Mr. Pitmilly said.

"For my part, it is my opinion there is no window there at all," he said. "It's very like the thing that's called in scientific language an optical illusion. It arises generally, if I may use such a word in the presence of ladies, from a liver that is not just in the perfitt order and balance that organ demands—and then you will see things—a blue dog, I remember, was the thing in one case, and in another—"

"The man has gane gyte," said Lady Carnbee; "I mind the windows in the Auld Leebrary as long as I mind anything. Is the Leebrary itself an optical illusion too?"

"Na, na," and "No, no," said the old ladies; "a blue dogue would be a strange vagary: but the Library we have all kent from our youth," said one. "And I mind when the Assemblies were held there one year when the Town Hall was building," another said.

"It is just a great divert to me," said Aunt Mary: but what was strange was that she paused there, and said in a low tone, "now": and then went on again, "for whoever comes to my house, there are aye discussions about that window. I have never just made up my mind about it myself. Sometimes I think it's a case of these wicked window duties, as you said, Miss Jeanie, when half the windows in our houses were blocked up to save the tax. And then, I think, it may be due to that blank kind of building like the great new buildings on the Earthen Mound in Edinburgh, where the windows are just ornaments. And then whiles I am sure I can see the glass shining when the sun catches it in the afternoon."

"You could so easily satisfy yourself, Mrs. Balcarres, if you were to—"

"Give a laddie a penny to cast a stone, and see what happens," said Lady Carnbee.

"But I am not sure that I have any desire to satisfy myself," Aunt Mary said. And then there was a stir in the room, and I had to come out from my recess and open the door for the old ladies and see them downstairs, as they all went away following one another. Mr. Pitmilly gave his arm to Lady Carnbee, though she was always contradicting him; and so the tea-party dispersed. Aunt Mary came to the head of the stairs with her guests in an old-fashioned gracious way, while I went down with them to see that the maid was ready at the door. When I came back Aunt Mary was still standing in the recess looking out. Returning to my seat she said, with a kind of wistful look, "Well, honey: and what is your opinion?"

"I have no opinion. I was reading my book all the time," I said.

"And so you were, honey, and no' very civil; but all the same I ken well you heard every word we said."

## TWO

It was a night in June; dinner was long over and had it been winter the maids would have been shutting up the house, and my Aunt Mary preparing to go upstairs to her room. But it was still clear daylight, that daylight out of which the sun has been long gone, and which has no longer any rose reflections, but all has sunk into a pearly neutral tint—a light which is daylight yet is not day.

We had taken a turn in the garden after dinner, and now we had returned to what we called our usual occupations. My aunt was reading. The English post had come in, and she had got her "Times," which was her great diversion. The "Scotsman" was her morning reading, but she liked her "Times" at night.

As for me, I too was at my usual occupation, which at that time was doing nothing. I had a book as usual, and was absorbed in it: but I was conscious of all that was going on all the same. The people strolled along the broad pavement, making remarks as they passed under the open window which came up into my story or my dream, and sometimes made me laugh. The tone and the faint sing-song, or rather chant, of the accent, which was "a wee Fifish," was novel to me, and associated with holiday, and pleasant; and sometimes they said to each other something that was amusing, and often something that suggested a whole story; but presently they began to drop off, the footsteps slackened, the voices died away.

It was getting late, though the clear soft daylight went on and on.

All through the lingering evening, which seemed to consist of interminable hours, long but not weary, drawn out as if the spell of the light and the outdoor life might never end, I had now and then, quite unawares, cast a glance at the mysterious window which my aunt and her friends had discussed, as I felt, though I dared not say it even to myself, rather foolishly. It caught my eye without any intention on my part, as I paused, as it were, to take breath, in the flowing and current of undistinguishable thoughts and things from within which carried me along.

First it occurred to me with a little sensation of discovery, how absurd to say it was not a window, a living window, one to see through! Why, then, had they never *seen* it, these old folk?

I saw as I looked up suddenly the faint grayness as of visible space within—a room behind, certainly—dim, as it was natural a room should be on the other side of the street—quite indefinite: yet so clear that if some one were to come to the window there would be nothing surprising in it. For certainly there was a feeling of space behind the panes which these old half-blind ladies had disputed about whether they were glass or only fictitious panes marked on the wall.

How silly! when eyes that could see could make it out in a minute. It was only a grayness at present, but it was unmistakable, a space that went back into gloom, as every room does when you look into it across a street.

There were no curtains to show whether it was inhabited or not; but a room—oh, as distinctly as ever room was! I was pleased with myself, but said nothing, while Aunt Mary rustled her paper, waiting for a favorable moment to announce a discovery which settled her problem at once. Then I was carried away upon the stream again, and forgot the window, till something threw unawares a word from the outer world, "I'm goin' hame; it'll soon be dark."

Dark! what was the fool thinking of? it never would be dark if one waited out, wandering in the soft air for hours longer; and then my eyes, acquiring easily that new habit, looked across the way again.

Ah, now! nobody indeed had come to the window; and no light had been lighted, seeing it was still beautiful to read by—a still, clear, colorless light; but the room inside had certainly widened. I could see the gray space and air a little deeper, and a sort of vision, very dim, of a wall, and something against it; something dark, with the blackness that a solid article, however indistinctly seen, takes in the lighter darkness that is only space—a large, black, dark thing coming out into the gray.

I looked more intently, and made sure it was a piece of furniture, either a writing-table or perhaps a large bookcase. No doubt it must be the last, since this was part of the old library. I never visited the old College Library, but I had seen such places before, and I could well imagine it to myself. How curious that for all the time these old people had looked at it, they had never seen this before!

It was more silent now, and my eyes, I suppose, had grown dim with gazing, doing my best to make it out, when suddenly Aunt Mary said, "Will you ring the bell, my dear? I must have my lamp."

"Your lamp?" I cried, "when it is still daylight." But then I gave another look at my window, and perceived with a start that the light had indeed changed: for now I saw nothing. It was still light, but there was so much change in the light that my room, with the gray space and the large shadowy bookcase, had gone out, and I saw them no more: for even a Scotch night in June, though it looks as if it would never end, does darken at the last. I had almost cried out, but checked myself, and rang the bell for Aunt Mary, and made up my mind I would say nothing till next morning, when to be sure naturally it would be more clear.

Next morning I rather think I forgot all about it—or was busy: or was more idle than usual: the two things meant nearly the same. At all events I thought no more of the window, though I still sat in my own, opposite to it, but occupied with some other fancy. Aunt Mary's visitors came as usual in the afternoon; but their talk was of other things, and for a day or two nothing at all happened to bring back my thoughts into this channel. It might be nearly a week before the subject came back, and once more it was old Lady Carnbee who set me thinking; not that she said anything upon that particular theme. But she was the last of my aunt's afternoon guests to go away, and when she rose to leave she threw up her hands, with those lively gesticulations which so many old Scotch ladies have.

"My faith!" said she, "there is that bairn there still like a dream. Is the creature bewitched, Mary Balcarres? and is she bound to sit there by night and by day for the rest of her days? You should mind that there's things about, uncanny for women of our blood."

I was too much startled at first to recognize that it was of me she was speaking. She was like a figure in a picture, with her pale face the color of ashes, and the big pattern of the Spanish lace hanging half over it, and her hand held up, with the big diamond blazing at me from the inside of her uplifted palm. It was held up in surprise, but it looked as if it were raised in malediction; and the diamond threw out darts of light and glared and twinkled at me. If it had been in its right place it would not have mattered; but there, in the open of the hand! I started up, half in terror, half in wrath. And then the old lady laughed, and her hand dropped.

"I've wakened you to life, and broke the spell," she said, nodding her old head at me, while the large black silk flowers of the lace waved and threatened. And she took my arm to go down-stairs, laughing and bidding me be steady, and no' tremble and shake like a broken reed. "You should be as steady as a rock at your age. I was like a young tree," she said, leaning so heavily that my willowy girlish frame quivered—"I was a support to virtue, like Pamela, in my time."

"Aunt Mary, Lady Carnbee is a witch!" I cried, when I came back.

"Is that what you think, honey? well: maybe she once was," said Aunt Mary, whom nothing surprised.

And it was that night once more after dinner, and after the post came in, and the "Times," that I suddenly saw the Library window again. I had seen it every day—and noticed nothing; but tonight, still in a little tumult of mind over Lady Carnbee and her wicked diamond which wished me harm, and her lace which waved threats and warnings at me, I looked across the street, and there I saw quite plainly the room opposite, far more clear than before.

I saw dimly that it must be a large room, and that the big piece of furniture against the wall was a writing-desk. That in a moment, when first my eyes rested upon it, was quite clear: a large old-fashioned escritoire, standing out into the room: and I knew by the shape of it that it had a great many pigeon-holes and little drawers in the back, and a large table for writing. There was one just like it in my father's library at home.

It was such a surprise to see it all so clearly that I closed my eyes, for the moment almost giddy, wondering how papa's desk could have come here—and then when I reminded myself that this was nonsense, and that there were many such writing-tables besides papa's, and looked again—lo! it had all become quite vague and indistinct as it was at first; and I saw nothing but the blank window, of which the old ladies could never be certain whether it was filled up to avoid the window-tax, or whether it had ever been a window at all.

This occupied my mind very much, and yet I did not say anything to Aunt Mary. For one thing, I rarely saw anything at all in the early part of the day; but then that is natural: you can never see into a place from the outside, whether it is an empty room or a looking-glass, or people's eyes, or anything else that is mysterious, in the day. It has, I suppose, something to do with the light. But in the evening in June in Scotland—then is the time to see. For it is daylight, yet it is not day, and there is a quality in it which I cannot describe, it is so clear, as if every object was a reflection of itself.

I used to see more and more of the room as the days went on. The large escritoire stood out more and more into the space: with sometimes white glimmering things, which looked like papers, lying on it: and once or twice I was sure I saw a pile of books on the floor close to the writing-table, as if they had gilding upon them in broken specks, like old books. It was always about the time when the lads in the street began to call to each other that they were going home, and sometimes a shriller voice would come from one of the doors, bidding somebody to "cry upon the laddies" to come back to their suppers. That was always the time I saw best, though it was close upon the moment when the veil seemed to fall and the clear radiance became less living, and all the sounds died out of the street, and Aunt Mary said in her soft voice, "Honey, will you ring for the lamp?" She said honey as people say darling: and I think it is a prettier word.

Then finally, while I sat one evening with my book in my hand, looking straight across the street, not distracted by anything, I saw a little movement within. It was not any one visible—but everybody must know what it is to see the stir in the air the little disturbance—you cannot tell what it is, but that it indicates some one there, even though you can see no one. Perhaps it is a shadow making just one flicker in the still place. You may look at an empty room and the furniture in it for hours, and then suddenly there will be the flicker, and you know that something has come into it. It might only be a dog or a cat; it might be, if that were possible, a bird flying across; but it is some one, something living, which is so different, so completely different, in a moment from the things that are not living.

It seemed to strike right through me, and I gave a little cry. Then Aunt Mary stirred a little, and put down the huge newspaper that almost covered her from sight, and said, "What is it, honey?" I cried "Nothing," with a little gasp, quickly, for I did not want to be disturbed just at this moment when somebody was coming. But I suppose she was not satisfied, for she got up and stood behind to see what it was, putting her hand on my shoulder. It was the softest touch in the world, but I could have flung it off angrily: for that moment everything was still again, and the place grew gray and I saw no more.

"Nothing," I repeated, but I was so vexed I could have cried. "I told you it was nothing, Aunt Mary. Don't you believe me, that you come to look—and spoil it all!"

I did not mean of course to say these last words; they were forced out of me. I was so much annoyed to see it all melt away like a dream: for it was no dream, but as real as—as real as—myself or anything I ever saw.

She gave my shoulder a little pat with her hand. "Honey," she said, "were you looking at something? Is't that? is't that?"

"Is it what?" I wanted to say, shaking off her hand, but something in me stopped me: for I said nothing at all, and she went quietly back to her place. I suppose she must have rung the bell herself, for immediately I felt the soft flood of the light behind me, and the evening outside dimmed down, as it did every night, and I saw nothing more.

It was next day, I think, in the afternoon that I spoke. It was brought on by something she said about her fine work. "I get a mist before my eyes," she said; "you will have to learn my old lace stitches, honey—for I soon will not see to draw the threads."

"Oh, I hope you will keep your sight," I cried, without thinking what I was saying. I was then young and very matter-of-fact. I had not found out that one may mean something, yet not half or a hundredth part of what one seems to mean: and even then probably hoping to be contradicted if it is anyhow against one's self.

"My sight!" she said, looking up at me with a look that was almost angry; "there is no question of losing my sight—on the contrary, my eyes are very strong. I may not see to draw fine threads, but I see at a distance as well as ever I did—as well as you do."

"I did not mean any harm, Aunt Mary," I said. "I thought you said— But how can your sight be as good as ever when you are in doubt about that window? I can see into the room as clear as—" My voice wavered, for I had just looked up and across the street, and I could have sworn that there was no window at all, but only a false image of one painted on the wall.

"Ah!" she said, with a little tone of keenness and of surprise: and she half rose up, throwing down her work hastily, as if she meant to come to me: then, perhaps seeing the bewildered look on my face, she paused and hesitated— "Ay, honey," she said, "have you got so far ben[1] as that?"

What did she mean? Of course I knew all the old Scotch phrases as well as I knew myself; but it is a comfort to take refuge in a little ignorance, and I know I pretended not to understand whenever I was put out. "I don't know what you mean by 'far ben'," I cried out, very impatient. I don't know what might have followed, but some one just then came to call, and she could only give me a look before she went forward, putting out her hand to her visitor. It was a very soft look, but anxious, and as if she did not know what to do: and she shook her head a very little, and I thought, though there was a smile on her face, there was something wet about her eyes. I retired into my recess, and nothing more was said.

But it was very tantalizing that it should fluctuate so; for sometimes I saw that room quite plain and clear—quite as clear as I could see papa's library, for example, when I shut my eyes. I compared it naturally to my father's study, because of the shape of the writing-table, which, as I tell you, was the same as his. At times I saw the papers on the table quite plain, just as I had seen his papers many a day. And the little pile of books on the floor at the foot—not ranged regularly in order, but put down one above the other, with all their angles going different ways, and a speck of the old gilding shining here and there. And then again at other times I saw nothing, absolutely nothing, and was no better than the old ladies who had peered over my head, drawing their eyelids together, and arguing that the window had been shut up because of the old long-abolished window tax, or else that it had never been a window at all. It annoyed me very much at those dull moments to feel that I too

---

[1]In.

puckered up my eyelids and saw no better than they.

Aunt Mary's old ladies came and went day after day while June went on. I was to go back in July, and I felt that I should be very unwilling indeed to leave until I had quite cleared up—as I was indeed in the way of doing—the mystery of that window which changed so strangely and appeared quite a different thing, not only to different people, but to the same eyes at different times. Of course I said to myself it must simply be an effect of the light. And yet I did not quite like that explanation either, but would have been better pleased to make out to myself that it was some superiority in me which made it so clear to me, if it were only the great superiority of young eyes over old—though that was not quite enough to satisfy me, seeing it was a superiority which I shared with every little lass and lad in the street.

I rather wanted, I believe, to think that there was some particular insight in me which gave clearness to my sight—which was a most impertinent assumption, but really did not mean half the harm it seems to mean when it is put down here in black and white. I had several times again, however, seen the room quite plain, and made out that it was a large room, with a great picture in a dim gilded frame hanging on the farther wall, and many other pieces of solid furniture making a blackness here and there, besides the great escritoire against the wall, which had evidently been placed near the window for the sake of the light. One thing became visible to me after another, till I almost thought I should end by being able to read the old lettering on one of the big volumes which projected from the others and caught the light; but this was all preliminary to the great event which happened about Midsummer Day—the day of St John, which was once so much thought of as a festival, but now means nothing at all in Scotland any more than any other of the saints' days: which I shall always think a great pity and loss to Scotland, whatever Aunt Mary may say.

## THREE

It was about midsummer, I cannot say exactly to a day when, but near that time, when the great event happened. I had grown very well acquainted by this time with that large dim room. Not only the escritoire, which was very plain to me now, with the papers upon it, and the books at its foot, but the great picture that hung against the farther wall, and various other shadowy pieces of furniture, especially a chair which one evening I saw had been moved into the space before the escritoire,—a little change which made my heart beat, for it spoke so distinctly of some one who must have been there, the some one who had already made me start, two or three times before, by some vague shadow of him or thrill of him which made a sort of movement in the silent space: a movement which made me sure that next minute I must see something or hear something which would explain the whole—if it were not that something always happened outside to stop it, at the very moment of its accomplishment.

I had no warning this time of movement or shadow. I had been looking into the room very attentively a little while before, and had made out everything almost clearer than ever; and then had bent my attention again on my book, and read a chapter or two at a most exciting period of the story: and consequently had quite left St Rule's, and the High Street, and the College Library, and was really in a South American forest, almost throttled by the flowery creepers, and treading softly lest I should put my foot on a scorpion or a dangerous snake.

At this moment something suddenly calling my attention to the outside, I looked across, and then, with a start, sprang up, for I could not contain myself. I don't know what I said, but enough to startle the people in the room, one of whom was old Mr. Pitmilly. They all looked round upon me to ask what was the matter. And when I gave my usual answer of "Nothing," sitting down again shamefaced but very much excited, Mr. Pitmilly got up and came forward, and looked out, apparently to see what was the cause. He saw nothing, for he went back again, and I could hear him telling Aunt Mary not to be alarmed, for Missy had fallen into a doze with the heat, and had startled herself waking up, at which they all laughed: another time I could have killed him for his impertinence, but my mind was too much taken up now to pay any attention. My head was throbbing and my heart beating. I was in such high excitement, however, that to restrain myself completely, to be perfectly silent, was more easy to me then than at any other time of my life.

I waited until the old gentleman had taken his seat again, and then I looked back. Yes, there he was! I had not been deceived. I knew then, when I looked across, that this was what I had been looking for all the time—that I had known he was there, and had been waiting for him, every time there was that flicker of movement in the room—him and no one else. And there at last, just as I had expected, he was. I don't know that in reality I ever had expected him, or any one: but this was what I felt when, suddenly looking into that curious dim room, I saw him there.

He was sitting in the chair, which he must have placed for himself, or which some one else in the dead of night when nobody was looking must have set for him, in front of the escritoire—with the back of his head towards me, writing. The light fell upon him from the left hand and therefore upon his shoulders and the side of his head, which, however, was too much turned away to show anything of his face. Oh, how strange that there should be some one staring at him as I was doing, and he never to turn his head, to make a movement! If any one stood and looked at me, were I in the soundest sleep that ever was, I would wake, I would jump up, I would feel it through everything. But there he sat and never moved.

You are not to suppose, though I said the light fell upon him from the left hand, that there was very much light. There never is in a room you are looking into like that across the street; but there was enough to see him by—the outline of his figure dark and solid, seated in the chair, and the fairness of his head visible faintly, a clear spot against the dimness. I saw this outline against the dim gilding of the frame of the large picture which hung on the farther wall.

I sat all the time the visitors were there, in a sort of rapture, gazing at this figure. I knew no reason why I should be so much moved. In an ordinary way, to see a student at an opposite window quietly doing his work might have interested me a little, but certainly it would not have moved me in any such way. It is always interesting to have a glimpse like this of an unknown life—to see so much and yet know so little, and to wonder, perhaps, what the man is doing, and why he never turns his head. One would go to the window—but not too close, lest he should see you and think you were spying upon him—and one would ask, Is he still there? is he writing, writing always? I wonder what he is writing! And it would be a great amusement: but no more.

This was not my feeling at all in the present case. It was a sort of breathless watch, an absorption. I did not feel that I had eyes for anything else, or any room in my mind for another thought. I no longer heard, as I generally did, the stories and the wise remarks (or foolish) of Aunt Mary's old ladies or Mr. Pitmilly. I heard only a murmur behind me, the interchange of voices, one softer, one sharper; but it was not as in the time when I sat reading and heard every word, till the story in my book, and the stories they were telling (what they said almost always shaped into stories), were all mingled into each other, and the hero in the novel became somehow the hero (or more likely heroine) of them all. But I took no notice of what they were saying now. And it was not that there was anything very interesting to look at, except the fact that he was there.

He did nothing to keep up the absorption of my thoughts. He moved just so much as a man will do when he is very busily writing, thinking of nothing else. There was a faint turn of his head as he went from one side to another of the page he was writing;

but it appeared to be a long long page which never wanted turning. Just a little inclination when he was at the end of the line, outward, and then a little inclination inward when he began the next. That was little enough to keep one gazing. But I suppose it was the gradual course of events leading up to this, the finding out of one thing after another as the eyes got accustomed to the vague light: first the room itself, and then the writing-table, and then the other furniture, and last of all the human inhabitant who gave it all meaning.

This was all so interesting that it was like a country which one had discovered. And then the extraordinary blindness of the other people who disputed among themselves whether it was a window at all! I did not, I am sure, wish to be disrespectful, and I was very fond of my Aunt Mary, and I liked Mr. Pitmilly well enough, and I was afraid of Lady Carnbee. But yet to think of the—I know I ought not to say stupidity—the blindness of them, the foolishness, the insensibility! discussing it as if a thing that your eyes could see was a thing to discuss! It would have been unkind to think it was because they were old and their faculties dimmed. It is so sad to think that the faculties grow dim, that such a woman as my Aunt Mary should fail in seeing, or hearing, or feeling, that I would not have dwelt on it for a moment, it would have seemed so cruel! And then such a clever old lady as Lady Carnbee, who could see through a millstone, people said—and Mr. Pitmilly, such an old man of the world. It did indeed bring tears to my eyes to think that all those clever people, solely by reason of being no longer young as I was, should have the simplest things shut out from them; and for all their wisdom and their knowledge be unable to see what a girl like me could see so easily. I was too much grieved for them to dwell upon that thought, and half ashamed, though perhaps half proud too, to be so much better off than they.

All those thoughts flitted through my mind as I sat and gazed across the street. And I felt there was so much going on in that room across the street! He was so absorbed in his writing, never looked up, never paused for a word, never turned round in his chair, or got up and walked about the room as my father did. Papa is a great writer, everybody says: but he would have come to the window and looked out, he would have drummed with his fingers on the pane, he would have watched a fly and helped it over a difficulty, and played with the fringe of the curtain, and done a dozen other nice, pleasant, foolish things, till the next sentence took shape. "My dear, I am waiting for a word," he would say to my mother when she looked at him, with a question why he was so idle, in her eyes; and then he would laugh, and go back again to his writing-table.

But He over there never stopped at all. It was like a fascination. I could not take my eyes from him and that little scarcely perceptible movement he made, turning his head. I trembled with impatience to see him turn the page, or perhaps throw down his finished sheet on the floor, as somebody looking into a window like me once saw Sir Walter do, sheet after sheet. I should have cried out if this Unknown had done that. I should not have been able to help myself, whoever had been present; and gradually I got into such a state of suspense waiting for it to be done that my head grew hot and my hands cold.

And then, just when there was a little movement of his elbow, as if he were about to do this, to be called away by Aunt Mary to see Lady Carnbee to the door! I believe I did not hear her till she had called me three times, and then I stumbled up, all flushed and hot, and nearly crying. When I came out from the recess to give the old lady my arm (Mr. Pitmilly had gone away some time before), she put up her hand and stroked my cheek. "What ails the bairn?" she said; "she's fevered. You must not let her sit her lane in the window, Mary Balcarres. You and me know what comes of that." Her old fingers had a strange touch, cold like something not living, and I felt that dreadful diamond sting me on the cheek.

I do not say that this was not just a part of my excitement and suspense; and I know it is enough to make any one laugh when the excitement was all about an unknown man writing in a room on the other side of the way, and my impatience because he never came to an end of the page. If you think I was not quite as well aware of this as any one could be! but the worst was that this dreadful old lady felt my heart beating against her arm that was within mine. "You are just in a dream," she said to me, with her old voice close at my ear as we went down-stairs. "I don't know who it is about, but it's bound to be some man that is not worth it. If you were wise you would think of him no more."

"I am thinking of no man!" I said, half crying. "It is very unkind and dreadful of you to say so, Lady Carnbee. I never thought of—any man, in all my life!" I cried in a passion of indignation. The old lady clung tighter to my arm, and pressed it to her, not unkindly.

"Poor little bird," she said, "how it's strugglin' and flutterin'! I'm not saying but what it's more dangerous when it's all for a dream."

She was not at all unkind; but I was very angry and excited, and would scarcely shake that old pale hand which she put out to me from her carriage window when I had helped her in. I was angry with her, and I was afraid of the diamond, which looked up from under her finger as if it saw through and through me; and whether you believe me or not, I am certain that it stung me again—a sharp malignant prick, oh full of meaning! She never wore gloves, but only black lace mittens, through which that horrible diamond gleamed.

I ran upstairs—she had been the last to go—and Aunt Mary too had gone to get ready for dinner, for it was late. I hurried to my place, and looked across, with my heart beating more than ever. I made quite sure I should see the finished sheet lying white upon the floor. But what I gazed at was only the dim blank of that window which they said was no window. The light had changed in some wonderful way during that five minutes I had been gone, and there was nothing, nothing, not a reflection, not a glimmer. It looked exactly as they all said, the blank form of a window painted on the wall.

It was too much: I sat down in my excitement and cried as if my heart would break. I felt that they had done something to it, that it was not natural, that I could not bear their unkindness—even Aunt Mary. They thought it not good for me! not good for me! and they had done something—even Aunt Mary herself—and that wicked diamond that hid itself in Lady Carnbee's hand. Of course I knew all this was ridiculous as well as you could tell me; and I was exasperated by the disappointment and the sudden stop to all my excited feelings, and I could not bear it. It was more strong than I.

I was late for dinner, and naturally there were some traces in my eyes that I had been crying when I came into the full light in the dining-room, where Aunt Mary could look at me at her pleasure, and I could not run away. She said, "Honey, you have been shedding tears. I'm loth, loth that a bairn of your mother's should be made to shed tears in my house."

"I have not been made to shed tears," cried I; and then, to save myself another fit of crying, I burst out laughing and said, "I am afraid of that dreadful diamond on old Lady Carnbee's hand. It bites—I am sure it bites! Aunt Mary, look here."

"You foolish lassie," Aunt Mary said; but she looked at my cheek under the light of the lamp, and then she gave it a little pat with her soft hand. "Go away with you, you silly bairn. There is no bite; but a flushed cheek, my honey, and a wet eye. You must just read out my paper to me after dinner when the post is in: and we'll have no more thinking and no more dreaming for tonight."

"Yes, Aunt Mary," said I. But I knew what would happen; for when she opens up her "Times," all full of the news of the world, and the speeches and things which she takes an interest in, though I cannot tell why—she forgets. And as I kept very quiet and made not a sound, she forgot to-night what she had said, and the curtain hung a little more over me than usual, and I sat down in my recess as if I had been a hundred miles away.

And my heart gave a great jump, as if it would have come out of my breast; for he was there. But not as he had been in the morning—I suppose the light, perhaps, was not good enough to go on with his work without a lamp or candles—for he had turned away from the table and was fronting the window, sitting leaning back in his chair, and turning his head to me. Not to me—he knew nothing about me. I thought he was not looking at anything; but with his face turned my way.

My heart was in my mouth: it was so unexpected, so strange! though why it should have seemed strange I know not, for there was no communication between him and me that it should have moved me; and what could be more natural than that a man, wearied of his work, and feeling the want perhaps of more light, and yet that it was not dark enough to light a lamp, should turn round in his own chair, and rest a little, and think—perhaps of nothing at all?

Papa always says he is thinking of nothing at all. He says things blow through his mind as if the doors were open, and he has no responsibility. What sort of things were blowing through this man's mind? or was he thinking, still thinking, of what he had been writing and going on with it still?

The thing that troubled me most was that I could not make out his face. It is very difficult to do so when you see a person only through two windows, your own and his. I wanted very much to recognize him afterwards if I should chance to meet him in the street. If he had only stood up and moved about the room, I should have made out the rest of his figure, and then I should have known him again; or if he had only come to the window (as papa always did), then I should have seen his face clearly enough to have recognized him. But, to be sure, he did not see any need to do anything in order that I might recognize him, for he did not know I existed; and probably if he had known I was watching him, he would have been annoyed and gone away.

But he was as immovable there facing the window as he had been seated at the desk. Sometimes he made a little stir with a hand or a foot, and I held my breath, hoping he was about to rise from his chair—but he never did it. And with all the efforts I made I could not be sure of his face. I puckered my eyelids together as old Miss Jeanie did who was shortsighted, and I put my hands on each side of my face to concentrate the light on him: but it was all in vain. Either the face changed as I sat staring, or else it was the light that was not good enough, or I don't know what it was. His hair seemed to me light—certainly there was no dark line about his head, as there would have been had it been very dark—and I saw, where it came across the old gilt frame on the wall behind, that it must be fair: and I am almost sure he had no beard. Indeed I am sure that he had no beard, for the outline of his face was distinct enough; and the daylight was still quite clear out of doors, so that I recognized perfectly a baker's boy who was on the pavement opposite, and whom I should have known again whenever I had met him: as if it was of the least importance to recognize a baker's boy!

There was one thing however, rather curious about this boy. He had been throwing stones at something or somebody. In St Rule's they have a great way of throwing stones at each other, and I suppose there had been a battle. I suppose also that he had one stone in his hand left over from the battle, and his roving eye took in all the incidents of the street to judge where he could throw it with most effect and mischief. But apparently he found nothing worthy of it in the street, for he suddenly turned round with a flick under his leg to show his cleverness, and aimed it straight at the window. I remarked without remarking that it struck with a hard sound and without any breaking glass, and fell straight down on the pavement. But I took no notice of this even in my mind, so intently was I watching the figure within, which moved not nor took the slightest notice, and remained just as dimly clear, as perfectly seen, yet as indistinguishable, as before. And then the light began to fail a little, not diminishing the prospect within, but making it still less distinct than it had been. Then I jumped up, feeling Aunt Mary's hand upon my shoulder. "Honey," she said, "I asked you twice to ring the bell; but you did not hear me."

"Oh, Aunt Mary!" I cried in great penitence, but turning again to the window in spite of myself.

"You must come away from there: you must come away from there," she said, almost as if she were angry: and then her soft voice grew softer, and she gave me a kiss: "never mind about the lamp, honey: I have rung myself, and it is coming; but, silly bairn, you must not aye be dreaming—your little head will turn."

All the answer I made, for I could scarcely speak, was to give a little wave with my hand to the window on the other side of the street.

She stood there patting me softly on the shoulder for a whole minute or more, murmuring something that sounded like, "She must go away, she must go away." Then she said, always with her hand soft on my shoulder, "Like a dream when one awaketh." And when I looked again, I saw the blank of an opaque surface and nothing more.

Aunt Mary asked me no more questions. She made me come into the room and sit in the light and read something to her. But I did not know what I was reading, for there suddenly came into my mind and took possession of it, the thud of the stone upon the window, and its descent straight down, as if from some hard substance that threw it off: though I had myself seen it strike upon the glass of the panes across the way.

FOUR

I am afraid I continued in a state of great exaltation and commotion of mind for some time. I used to hurry through the day till the evening came, when I could watch my neighbor through the window opposite. I did not talk much to any one, and I never said a word about my own questions and wonderings. I wondered who he was, what he was doing, and why he never came till the evening (or very rarely); and I also wondered much to what house the room belonged in which he sat. It seemed to form a portion of the old College Library, as I have often said. The window was one of the line of windows which I understood lighted the large hall; but whether this room belonged to the library itself, or how its occupant gained access to it, I could not tell. I made up my mind that it must open out of the hall, and that the gentleman must be the Librarian or one of his assistants, perhaps kept busy all the day in his official duties, and only able to get to his desk and do his own private work in the evening. One has heard of so many things like that—a man who had to take up some other kind of work for his living, and then when his leisure-time came, gave it all up to something he really loved—some study or some book he was writing.

My father himself at one time had been like that. He had been in the Treasury all day, and then in the evening wrote his books, which made him famous. His daughter, however little she might know of other things, could not but know that! But it discouraged me very much when somebody pointed out to me one day in the street an old gentleman who wore a wig and took a great deal of snuff, and said, That's the Librarian of the old College. It gave me a great shock for a moment; but then I remembered that an old gentleman has generally assistants, and that it must be one of them.

Gradually I became quite sure of this. There was another small window above, which twinkled very much when the sun shone, and looked a very kindly bright little window, above that dullness of the other which hid so much. I made up my mind this was the window of his other room, and that these two chambers at the end of the beautiful hall were really beautiful for him to live in, so near all the books, and so retired and quiet, that nobody knew of them. What a fine thing for him! and you could see what use he made of his good fortune as he sat there, so constant at his writing for hours together.

Was it a book he was writing, or could it be perhaps poems? This was a thought which made my heart beat; but I concluded with much regret that it could not be poems, because no one could possibly write poems like that, straight off, without pausing for a word or a rhyme. Had they been poems he must have risen up, he must have paced about the room or come to the window as papa did—not that papa wrote poems: he always said, "I am not worthy even to speak of such prevailing mysteries," shaking his head—which gave me a wonderful admiration and almost awe of a poet, who was thus much greater even than papa. But I could not believe that a poet could have kept still for hours and hours like that. What could it be then? perhaps it was history; that is a great thing to work at, but you would not perhaps need to move nor to stride up and down, or look out upon the sky and the wonderful light.

He did move now and then, however, though he never came to the window. Sometimes, as I have said, he would turn round in his chair and turn his face towards it, and sit there for a long time musing when the light had begun to fail, and the world was full of that strange day which was night, that light without color, in which everything was so clearly visible, and there were no shadows. "It was between the night and the day, when the fairy folk have power." This was the after-light of the wonderful, long, long summer evening, the light without shadows.

It had a spell in it, and sometimes it made me afraid: and all manner of strange thoughts seemed to come in, and I always felt that if only we had a little more vision in our eyes we might see beautiful folk walking about in it, who were not of our world. I thought most likely he saw them from the way he sat there looking out: and this made my heart expand with the most curious sensation, as if of pride that, though I could not see, he did, and did not even require to come to the window, as I did, sitting close in the depth of the recess, with my eyes upon him, and almost seeing things through his eyes.

I was so much absorbed in these thoughts and in watching him every evening—for now he never missed an evening, but was always there—that people began to remark that I was looking pale and that I could not be well, for I paid no attention when they talked to me, and did not care to go out, nor to join the other girls for their tennis, nor to do anything that others did; and some said to Aunt Mary that I was quickly losing all the ground I had gained, and that she could never send me back to my mother with a white face like that.

Aunt Mary had begun to look at me anxiously for some time before that, and, I am sure, held secret consultations over me, sometimes with the doctor, and sometimes with her old ladies, who thought they knew more about young girls than even the doctors. And I could hear them saying to her that I wanted diversion, that I must be diverted, and that she must take me out more, and give a party, and that when the summer visitors began to come there would perhaps be a ball or two, or Lady Carnbee would get up a picnic.

"And there's my young lord coming home," said the old lady whom they called Miss Jeanie, "and I never knew the young lassie yet that would not cock up her bonnet at the sight of a young lord."

But Aunt Mary shook her head. "I would not lippen[1] much to the young lord,"

---

[1] Trust.

she said. "His mother is sore set upon siller for him; and my poor bit honey has no fortune to speak of. No, we must not fly so high as the young lord; but I will gladly take her about the country to see the old castles and towers. It will perhaps rouse her up a little."

"And if that does not answer we must think of something else," the old lady said.

I heard them perhaps that day because they were talking of me, which is always so effective a way of making you hear—for latterly I had not been paying any attention to what they were saying; and I thought to myself how little they knew, and how little I cared about even the old castles and curious houses, having something else in my mind. But just about that time Mr. Pitmilly came in, who was always a friend to me, and, when he heard them talking, he managed to stop them and turn the conversation into another channel. And after a while, when the ladies were gone away, he came up to my recess, and gave a glance right over my head. And then he asked my Aunt Mary if ever she had settled her question about the window opposite, "that you thought was a window sometimes, and then not a window, and many curious things," the old gentleman said.

My Aunt Mary gave me another very wistful look; and then she said, "Indeed, Mr. Pitmilly, we are just where we were, and I am quite as unsettled as ever; and I think my niece she has taken up my views, for I see her many a time looking and wondering, and I am not clear now what her opinion is."

"My opinion!" I said, "Aunt Mary." I could not help being a little scornful, as one is when one is very young. "I have no opinion. There is not only a window but there is a room, and I could show you—" I was going to say, "show you the gentleman who sits and writes in it," but I stopped, not knowing what they might say, and looked from one to another. "I could tell you—all the furniture that is in it," I said. And then I felt something like a flame that went over my face, and that all at once my cheeks were burning. I thought they gave a little glance at each other, but that may have been folly. "There is a great picture, in a big dim frame," I said, feeling a little breathless, "on the wall opposite the window—"

"Is there so?" said Mr. Pitmilly, with a little laugh. And he said, "Now I will tell you what we'll do. You know that there is a conversation party, or whatever they call it, in the big room to-night, and it will be all open and lighted up. And it is a handsome room, and two-three things well worth looking at. I will just step along after we have all got our dinner, and take you over to the pairty, madam—Missy and you—"

"Dear me!" said Aunt Mary. "I have not gone to a pairty for more years than I would like to say—and never once to the Library Hall." Then she gave a little shiver, and said quite low, "I could not go there."

"Then you will just begin again to-night, madam," said Mr. Pitmilly, taking no notice of this, "and a proud man will I be leading in Mistress Balcarres that was once the pride of the ball!"

"Ah, once!" said Aunt Mary, with a low laugh and then a sigh. "And we'll not say how long ago"; and after that she made a pause, looking always at me: and then she said, "I accept your offer, and we'll put on our braws; and I hope you will have no occasion to think shame of us. But why not take your dinner here?"

That was how it was settled, and the old gentleman went away to dress, looking quite pleased. But I came to Aunt Mary as soon as he was gone, and besought her not to make me go. "I like the long bonnie night and the light that lasts so long. And I cannot bear to dress up and go out, wasting it all in a stupid party. I hate parties, Aunt Mary!" I cried, "and I would far rather stay here."

"My honey," she said, taking both my hands, "I know it will maybe be a blow to you,—but it's better so."

"How could it be a blow to me?" I cried; "but I would far rather not go."

"You'll just go with me, honey, just this once: it is not often I go out. You will go with me this one night, just this one night, my honey sweet."

I am sure there were tears in Aunt Mary's eyes, and she kissed me between the words. There was nothing more that I could say; but how I grudged the evening! A mere party, a conversazione (when all the College was away, too, and nobody to make conversation!), instead of my enchanted hour at my window and the soft strange light, and the dim face looking out, which kept me wondering and wondering what was he thinking of, what was he looking for, who was he? all one wonder and mystery and question, through the long, long, slowly fading night!

It occurred to me, however, when I was dressing—though I was so sure that he would prefer his solitude to everything—that he might perhaps, it was just possible, be there. And when I thought of that, I took out my white frock—though Janet had laid out my blue one—and my little pearl necklace which I had thought was too good to wear. They were not very large pearls, but they were real pearls, and very even and lustrous though they were small; and though I did not think much of my appearance then, there must have been something about me—pale as I was but apt to color in a moment, with my dress so white, and my pearls so white, and my hair all shadowy—perhaps, that was pleasant to look at: for even old Mr. Pitmilly had a strange look in his eyes, as if he was not only pleased but sorry too, perhaps thinking me a creature that would have troubles in this life, though I was so young and knew them not.

And when Aunt Mary looked at me, there was a little quiver about her mouth. She herself had on her pretty lace and her white hair very nicely done, and looked her best. As for Mr. Pitmilly, he had a beautiful fine French cambric frill to his shirt, plaited in the most minute plaits, and with a diamond pin in it which sparkled as much as Lady Carnbee's ring; but this was a fine frank kindly stone, that looked you straight in the face and sparkled, with the light dancing in it as if it were pleased to see you, and to be shining on that old gentleman's honest and faithful breast: for he had been one of Aunt Mary's lovers in their early days, and still thought there was nobody like her in the world.

I had got into quite a happy commotion of mind by the time we set out across the street in the soft light of the evening to the Library Hall. Perhaps, after all, I should see him, and see the room which I was so well acquainted with, and find out why he sat there so constantly and never was seen abroad. I thought I might even hear what he was working at, which would be such a pleasant thing to tell papa when I went home. A friend of mine at St Rule's—oh, far, far more busy than you ever were, papa!—and then my father would laugh as he always did, and say he was but an idler and never busy at all.

The room was all light and bright, flowers wherever flowers could be, and the long lines of the books that went along the walls on each side, lighting up wherever there was a line of gilding or an ornament, with a little response. It dazzled me at first all that light: but I was very eager, though I kept very quiet, looking round to see if perhaps in any corner, in the middle of any group, he would be there. I did not expect to see him among the ladies. He would not be with them,—he was too studious, too silent: but, perhaps among that circle of gray heads at the upper end of the room—perhaps—

No: I am not sure that it was not half a pleasure to me to make quite sure that there was not one whom I could take for him, who was at all like my vague image of him. No: it was absurd to think that he would be here, amid all that sound of voices, under the glare of that light. I felt a little proud to think that he was in his room as usual, doing his work, or thinking so deeply over it, as when he turned round in his chair with his face to the light.

I was thus getting a little composed and quiet in my mind, for now that the expectation of seeing him was over, though it was a disappointment, it was a satisfaction too—when Mr. Pitmilly came up to me, holding out his arm. "Now," he said, "I am going to take you to see the curiosities." I thought to myself that after I had seen them and spoken to everybody I knew, Aunt Mary would let me go home, so I went very willingly, though I did not care for the curiosities. Something, however, struck me strangely as we walked up the room. It was the air, rather fresh and strong, from an open window at the east end of the hall. How should there be a window there? I hardly saw what it meant for the first moment, but it blew in my face as if there was some meaning in it, and I felt very uneasy without seeing why.

Then there was another thing that startled me. On that side of the wall which was to the street there seemed no windows at all. A long line of bookcases filled it from end to end. I could not see what that meant either, but it confused me. I was altogether confused. I felt as if I was in a strange country, not knowing where I was going, not knowing what I might find out next. If there were no windows on the wall to the street, where was my window? My heart, which had been jumping up and calming down again all the time, gave a great leap at this, as if it would have come out of me—but I did not know what it could mean.

Then we stopped before a glass case, and Mr. Pitmilly showed me some things in it. I could not pay much attention to them. My head was going round and round. I heard his voice going on, and then myself speaking with a queer sound that was hollow in my ears; but I did not know what I was saying or what he was saying. Then he took me to the very end of the room, the east end, saying something that I caught—that I was pale, that the air would do me good. The air was blowing full on me, lifting the lace of my dress, lifting my hair, almost chilly. The window opened into the pale daylight, into the little lane that ran by the end of the building.

Mr. Pitmilly went on talking, but I could not make out a word he said. Then I heard my own voice, speaking through it, though I did not seem to be aware that I was speaking. "Where is my window?—where, then, is my window?" I seemed to be saying, and I turned right round, dragging him with me, still holding his arm. As I did this my eye fell upon something at last which I knew. It was a large picture in a broad frame, hanging against the farther wall.

What did it mean? Oh, what did it mean? I turned round again to the open window at the east end, and to the daylight, the strange light without any shadow, that was all round about this lighted hall, holding it like a bubble that would burst, like something that was not real. The real place was the room I knew, in which that picture was hanging, where the writing-table was, and where he sat with his face to the light. But where was the light and the window through which it came?

I think my senses must have left me. I went up to the picture which I knew, and then I walked straight across the room, always dragging Mr. Pitmilly, whose face was pale, but who did not struggle but allowed me to lead him, straight across to where the window was—where the window was not;—where there was no sign of it. "Where is my window?—where is my window?" I said. And all the time I was sure that I was in a dream, and these lights were all some theatrical illusion, and the people talking; and nothing real but the pale, pale, watching, lingering day standing by to wait until that foolish bubble should burst.

"My dear," said Mr. Pitmilly, "my dear! Mind that you are in public. Mind where you are. You must not make an outcry and frighten your Aunt Mary. Come away with me. Come away, my dear young lady! and you'll take a seat for a minute or two and compose yourself; and I'll get you an ice or a little wine." He kept patting my hand, which was on his arm, and looking at me very anxiously. "Bless me! bless me! I never thought it would have this effect," he said.

But I would not allow him to take me away in that direction. I went to the picture again and looked at it without seeing it: and then I went across the room again, with some kind of wild thought that if I insisted I should find it. "My window—my window!" I said.

There was one of the professors standing there, and he heard me. "The window!" said he. "Ah, you've been taken in with what appears outside. It was put there to be in uniformity with the window on the stair. But it never was a real window. It is just behind that bookcase. Many people are taken in by it," he said.

His voice seemed to sound from somewhere far away, and as if it would go on for ever; and the hall swam in a dazzle of shining and of noises round me; and the daylight through the open window grew grayer, waiting till it should be over, and the bubble burst.

FIVE

It was Mr. Pitmilly who took me home; or rather it was I who took him, pushing him on a little in front of me, holding fast by his arm, not waiting for Aunt Mary or any one. We came out into the daylight again outside, I, without even a cloak or a shawl, with my bare arms, and uncovered head, and the pearls round my neck. There was a rush of the people about, and a baker's boy, that baker's boy, stood right in my way and cried, "Here's a braw ane!" shouting to the others: the words struck me somehow, as his stone had struck the window, without any reason. But I did not mind the people staring, and hurried across the street, with Mr. Pitmilly half a step in advance.

The door was open, and Janet standing at it, looking out to see what she could see of the ladies in their grand dresses. She gave a shriek when she saw me hurrying across the street; but I brushed past her, and pushed Mr. Pitmilly up the stairs, and took him breathless to the recess, where I threw myself down on the seat, feeling as if I could not have gone another step farther, and waved my hand across to the window. "There! There!" I cried. Ah! there it was—not that senseless mob—not the theater and the gas, and the people all in a murmur and clang of talking. Never in all these days had I seen that room so clearly. There was a faint tone of light behind, as if it might have been a reflection from some of those vulgar lights in the hall, and he sat against it, calm, wrapped in his thought, with his face turned to the window. Nobody but must have seen him. Janet could have seen him had I called her upstairs. It was like a picture, all the things I knew, and the same attitude, and the atmosphere, full of quietness, not disturbed by anything. I pulled Mr. Pitmilly's arm before I let him go,—"You see, you see!" I cried. He gave me the most bewildered look, as if he would have liked to cry. He saw nothing! I was sure of that from his eyes. He was an old man, and there was no vision in him. If I had called up Janet, she would have seen it all. "My dear!" he said. "My dear!" waving his hands in a helpless way.

"He has been there all these nights," I cried, "and I thought you could tell me who he was and what he was doing; and that he might have taken me in to that room, and showed me, that I might tell papa. Papa would understand, he would like to hear. Oh, can't you tell me what work he is doing, Mr. Pitmilly? He never lifts his head as long as the light throws a shadow, and then when it is like this he turns round and thinks, and takes a rest!"

Mr. Pitmilly was trembling, whether it was with cold or I know not what. He said, with a shake in his voice, "My dear young lady—my dear—" and then stopped and looked at me as if he were going to cry. "It's peetiful, it's peetiful," he said; and then in another voice, "I am going across there again to bring your Aunt Mary home; do you understand, my poor little thing, my—I am going to bring her home—you will be better when she is here."

I was glad when he went away, as he could not see anything: and I sat alone in the dark which was not dark, but quite clear light—a light like nothing I ever saw. How clear it was in that room! not glaring like the gas and the voices, but so quiet, everything so visible, as if it were in another world. I heard a little rustle behind me, and there was Janet, standing staring at me with two big eyes wide open. She was only a little older than I was. I called to her, "Janet, come here, come here, and you will see him,—come here and see him!" impatient that she should be shy and keep behind.

"Oh, my bonnie young leddy!" she said, and burst out crying. I stamped my foot at her, in my indignation that she would not come, and she fled before me with a rustle and swing of haste, as if she were afraid. None of them, none of them! not even a girl like myself, with the sight in her eyes, would understand. I turned back again, and held out my hands to him sitting there, who was the only one that knew.

"Oh," I said, "say something to me! I don't know who you are, or what you are: but you're lonely and so am I; and I only—feel for you. Say something to me!" I neither hoped that he would hear, nor expected any answer. How could he hear, with the street between us, and his window shut, and all the murmuring of the voices and the people standing about? But for one moment it seemed to me that there was only him and me in the whole world.

But I gasped with my breath, that had almost gone from me, when I saw him move in his chair! He had heard me, though I knew not how. He rose up, and I rose too, speechless, incapable of anything but this mechanical movement. He seemed to draw me as if I were a puppet moved by his will. He came forward to the window, and stood looking across at me. I was sure that he looked at me. At last he had seen me: at last he had found out that somebody, though only a girl, was watching him, looking for him, believing in him.

I was in such trouble and commotion of mind and trembling, that I could not keep on my feet, but dropped kneeling on the window-seat, supporting myself against the window, feeling as if my heart were being drawn out of me. I cannot describe his face. It was all dim, yet there was a light on it: I think it must have been a smile; and as closely as I looked at him he looked at me. His hair was fair, and there was a little quiver about his lips. Then he put his hands upon the window to open it. It was stiff and hard to move; but at last he forced it open with a sound that echoed all along the street. I saw that the people heard it, and several looked up. As for me, I put my hands together, leaning with my face against the glass, drawn to him as if I could have gone out of myself, my heart out of my bosom, my eyes out of my head. He opened the window with a noise that was heard from the West Port to the Abbey. Could any one doubt that?

And then he leaned forward out of the window, looking out. There was not one in the street but must have seen him. He looked at me first, with a little wave of his hand, as if it were a salutation—yet not exactly that either, for I thought he waved me away; and then he looked up and down in the dim shining of the ending day, first to the east, to the old Abbey towers, and then to the west, along the broad line of the street where so many people were coming and going, but so little noise, all like enchanted folk in an enchanted place.

I watched him with such a melting heart, with such a deep satisfaction as words could not say; for nobody could tell me now that he was not there,—nobody could say I was dreaming any more. I watched him as if I could not breathe—my heart in my throat, my eyes upon him. He looked up and down, and then he looked back at me. I was the first, and I was the last, though it was not for long: he did know, he did see, who it was that had recognized him and sympathized with him all the time. I was in a kind of rapture, yet stupor too; my look went with his look, following it as if I were his shadow; and then suddenly he was gone and I saw him no more.

I dropped back again upon my seat, seeking something to support me, something to lean upon. He had lifted his hand and waved it once again to me. How he went I cannot tell, nor where he went I cannot tell; but in a moment he was away, and the window standing open, and the room fading into stillness and dimness, yet so clear, with all its space, and the great picture in its gilded frame upon the wall.

It gave me no pain to see him go away. My heart was so content, and I was so worn out and satisfied—for what doubt or question could there be about him now? As I was lying back as weak as water, Aunt Mary came in behind me, and flew to me with a little rustle as if she had come on wings, and put her arms round me, and drew my head on to her breast. I had begun to cry a little, with sobs like a child. "You saw him, you saw him!" I said. To lean upon her, and feel her so soft, so kind, gave me a pleasure I cannot describe, and her arms round me, and her voice saying "Honey, my honey!"—as if she were nearly crying too.

Lying there I came back to myself, quite sweetly, glad of everything. But I wanted some assurance from them that they had seen him too. I waved my hand to the window that was still standing open, and the room that was stealing away into the faint dark. "This time you saw it all?" I said, getting more eager. "My honey!" said Aunt Mary, giving me a kiss: and Mr. Pitmilly began to walk about the room with short little steps behind, as if he were out of patience. I sat straight up and put away Aunt Mary's arms. "You cannot be so blind, so blind!" I cried. "Oh, not to-night, at least not to-night!"

But neither the one nor the other made any reply. I shook myself quite free, and raised myself up. And there, in the middle of the street, stood the baker's boy like a statue, staring up at the open window, with his mouth open and his face full of wonder—breathless, as if he could not believe what he saw. I darted forward, calling to him, and beckoned him to come to me. "Oh, bring him up! bring him, bring him to me!" I cried.

Mr. Pitmilly went out directly, and got the boy by the shoulder. He did not want to come. It was strange to see the little old gentleman, with his beautiful frill and his diamond pin, standing out in the street, with his hand upon the boy's shoulder, and the other boys round, all in a little crowd. And presently they came towards the house, the others all following, gaping and wondering. He came in unwilling, almost resisting, looking as if we meant him some harm. "Come away, my laddie, come and speak to the young lady," Mr. Pitmilly was saying. And Aunt Mary took my hands to keep me back. But I would not be kept back.

"Boy," I cried, "you saw it too: you saw it: tell them you saw it! It is that I want, and no more."

He looked at me as they all did, as if he thought I was mad. "What's she wantin' wi' me?" he said; and then, "I did nae harm, even if I did throw a bit stane at it—and it's nae sin to throw a stane."

"You rascal!" said Mr. Pitmilly, giving him a shake; "have you been throwing stones? You'll kill somebody some of these days with your stones." The old gentleman was confused and troubled, for he did not understand what I wanted, nor anything that had happened. And then Aunt Mary, holding my hands and drawing me close to her, spoke. "Laddie," she said, "answer the young lady, like a good lad. There's no intention of finding fault with you. Answer her, my man, and then Janet will give ye your supper before you go."

"Oh speak, speak!" I cried; "answer them and tell them! you saw that window opened, and the gentleman look out and wave his hand?"

"I saw nae gentleman," he said, with his head down, "except this wee gentleman here."

"Listen, laddie," said Aunt Mary. "I saw ye standing in the middle of the street staring. What were ye looking at?"

"It was naething to make a wark about. It was just yon windy yonder in the library that is nae windy. And it was open—as sure's death. You may laugh if you like. Is that a' she's wantin' wi' me?"

"You are telling a pack of lies, laddie," Mr. Pitmilly said.

"I'm tellin' nae lees—it was standin' open just like ony ither windy. It's as sure's death. I couldna believe it mysel'; but it's true."

"And there it is," I cried, turning round and pointing it out to them with great triumph in my heart. But the light was all gray, it had faded, it had changed. The window was just as it had always been, a somber break upon the wall.

I was treated like an invalid all that evening, and taken upstairs to bed, and Aunt Mary sat up in my room the whole night through. Whenever I opened my eyes she was always sitting there close to me, watching. And there never was in all my life so strange a night. When I would talk in my excitement, she kissed me and hushed me like a child. "Oh, honey, you are not the only one!" she said. "Oh whisht, whisht, bairn! I should never have let you be there!"

"Aunt Mary, Aunt Mary, you have seen him too?"

"Oh whisht, whisht, honey!" Aunt Mary said: her eyes were shining—there were tears in them. "Oh whisht, whisht! Put it out of your mind, and try to sleep. I will not speak another word," she cried.

But I had my arms round her, and my mouth at her ear. "Who is he there?—tell me that and I will ask no more—"

"Oh honey, rest, and try to sleep! It is just—how can I tell you?—a dream! Did you not hear what Lady Carnbee said?—the women of our blood—"

"What? what? Aunt Mary, oh Aunt Mary—"

"I canna tell you," she cried in her agitation, "I canna tell you! How can I tell you, when I know just what you know and no more? It is a longing all your life after—it is a looking—for what never comes."

"He will come," I cried. "I shall see him tomorrow—that I know!"

She kissed me and cried over me, her cheek hot and wet like mine. "My honey, try if you can sleep—try if you can sleep: and we'll wait to see what to-morrow brings."

"I have no fear," said I; and then I suppose, though it is strange to think of, I must have fallen asleep—I was so worn-out, and young, and not used to lying in my bed awake. From time to time I opened my eyes, and sometimes jumped up remembering everything: but Aunt Mary was always there to soothe me, and I lay down again in her shelter like a bird in its nest.

But I would not let them keep me in bed next day. I was in a kind of fever, not knowing what I did. The window was quite opaque, without the least glimmer in it, flat and blank like a piece of wood. Never from the first day had I seen it so little like a window. "It cannot be wondered at," I said to myself, "that seeing it like that, and with eyes that are old, not so clear as mine, they should think what they do." And then I smiled to myself to think of the evening and the long light, and whether he would look out again, or only give me a signal with his hand. I decided I would like that best: not that he should take the trouble to come forward and open it again, but just a turn of his head and a wave of his hand. It would be more friendly and show more confidence,—not as if I wanted that kind of demonstration every night.

I did not come down in the afternoon, but kept at my own window upstairs alone, till the tea-party should be over. I could hear them making a great talk; and I was sure they were all in the recess staring at the window, and laughing at the silly lassie. Let them laugh! I felt above all that now. At dinner I was very restless, hurrying to get it over; and I think Aunt Mary was restless too. I doubt whether she read her "Times" when it came; she opened it up so as to shield her, and watched from a corner.

And I settled myself in the recess, with my heart full of expectation. I wanted nothing more than to see him writing at his table, and to turn his head and give me a little wave of his hand, just to show that he knew I was there. I sat from half-past seven o'clock to ten o'clock: and the daylight grew softer and softer, till at last it was as if it was shining through a pearl, and not a shadow to be seen. But the window all the time was as black as night, and there was nothing, nothing there.

Well: but other nights it had been like that; he would not be there every night only to please me. There are other things in a man's life, a great learned man like that. I said to myself I was not disappointed. Why should I be disappointed? There had been other nights when he was not there. Aunt Mary watched me, every movement I made, her eyes shining, often wet, with a pity in them that almost made me cry: but I felt as if I were more sorry for her than for myself.

And then I flung myself upon her, and asked her, again and again, what it was, and who it was, imploring her to tell me if she knew? and when she had seen him, and what had happened? and what it meant about the women of our blood? She told me that how it was she could not tell, nor when: it was just at the time it had to be; and that we all saw him in our time—"that is," she said, "the ones that are like you and me." What was it that made her and me different from the rest? but she only shook her head and would not tell me. "They say," she said, and then stopped short. "Oh, honey, try and forget all about it—if I had but known you were of that kind! They say—that once there was one that was a Scholar, and liked his books more than any lady's love. Honey, do not look at me like that. To think I should have brought all this on you!"

"He was a Scholar?" I cried.

"And one of us, that must have been a light woman, not like you and me—But maybe it was just in innocence; for who can tell? She waved to him and waved to him to come over: and yon ring was the token: but he would not come. But still she sat at her window and waved and waved—till at last her brothers heard of it, that were stirring men; and then—oh, my honey, let us speak of it no more!"

"They killed him!" I cried, carried away. And then I grasped her with my hands, and gave her a shake, and flung away from her. "You tell me that to throw dust in my eyes—when I saw him only last night: and he as living as I am, and as young!"

"My honey, my honey!" Aunt Mary said.

After that I would not speak to her for a long time; but she kept close to me, never leaving me when she could help it, and always with that pity in her eyes. For the next night it was the same; and the third night. That third night I thought I could not bear it any longer. I would have to do something—if only I knew what to do! If it would ever get dark, quite dark, there might be something to be done. I had wild dreams of stealing out of the house and getting a ladder, and mounting up to try if I could not open that window, in the middle of the night—if perhaps I could get the baker's boy to help me; and then my mind got into a whirl, and it was as if I had done it; and I could almost see the boy put the ladder to the window, and hear him cry out that there was nothing there. Oh, how slow it was, the night! and how light it was, and everything so clear—no darkness to cover you, no shadow, whether on one side of the street or on the other side!

I could not sleep, though I was forced to go to bed. And in the deep midnight, when it is dark dark in every other place, I slipped very softly downstairs, though there was one board on the landing-place that creaked—and opened the door and stepped out. There was not a soul to be seen, up or down, from the Abbey to the West Port: and the trees stood like ghosts, and the silence was terrible, and everything as clear as day. You don't know what silence is till you find it in the light like that, not morning but night, no sun rising, no shadow, but everything as clear as the day.

It did not make any difference as the slow minutes went on: one o'clock, two o'-clock. How strange it was to hear the clocks striking in that dead light when there was nobody to hear them! But it made no difference. The window was quite blank; even the marking of the panes seemed to have melted away. I stole up again after a long time, through the silent house, in the clear light, cold and trembling, with despair in my heart.

I am sure Aunt Mary must have watched and seen me coming back, for after a while I heard faint sounds in the house; and very early, when there had come a little sunshine into the air, she came to my bedside with a cup of tea in her hand; and she, too, was looking like a ghost. "Are you warm, honey—are you comfortable?" she said. "It doesn't matter," said I. I did not feel as if anything mattered; unless if one could get into the dark somewhere—the soft, deep dark that would cover you over and hide you—but I could not tell from what. The dreadful thing was that there was nothing, nothing to look for, nothing to hide from—only the silence and the light.

That day my mother came and took me home. I had not heard she was coming; she arrived quite unexpectedly, and said she had no time to stay, but must start the same evening so as to be in London next day, papa having settled to go abroad. At first I had a wild thought I would not go. But how can a girl say I will not, when her mother has come for her, and there is no reason, no reason in the world, to resist, and not right! I had to go, whatever I might wish or any one might say.

Aunt Mary's dear eyes were wet; she went about the house drying them quietly with her handkerchief, but she always said, "It is the best thing for you, honey—the best thing for you!" Oh, how I hated to hear it said that it was the best thing, as if anything mattered, one more than another! The old ladies were all there in the afternoon, Lady Carnbee looking at me from under her black lace, and the diamond lurking, sending out darts from under her finger. She patted me on the shoulder, and told me to be a good bairn. "And never lippen to what you see from the window," she said. "The eye is deceitful as well as the heart." She kept patting me on the shoulder, and I felt again as if that sharp wicked stone stung me. Was that what Aunt Mary meant when she said yon ring was the token? I thought afterwards I saw the mark on my shoulder. You will say why? How can I tell why? If I had known, I should have been contented, and it would not have mattered any more.

I never went back to St Rule's, and for years of my life I never again looked out of a window when any other window was in sight. You ask me did I ever see him again? I cannot tell: the imagination is a great deceiver, as Lady Carnbee said: and if he stayed there so long, only to punish the race that had wronged him, why should I ever have seen him again? for I had received my share.

But who can tell what happens in a heart that often, often, and so long as that, comes back to do its errand? If it was he whom I have seen again, the anger is gone from him, and he means good and no longer harm to the house of the woman that loved him. I have seen his face looking at me from a crowd. There was one time when I came home a widow from India, very sad, with my little children: I am certain I saw him there among all the people coming to welcome their friends. There was nobody to welcome me,—for I was not expected: and very sad was I, without a face I knew: when all at once I saw him, and he waved his hand to me. My heart leaped up again: I had forgotten who he was, but only that it was a face I knew, and I landed almost cheerfully, thinking here was some one who would help me. But he had disappeared, as he did from the window, with that one wave of his hand.

And again I was reminded of it all when old Lady Carnbee died—an old, old woman—and it was found in her will that she had left me that diamond ring. I am afraid of it still. It is locked up in an old sandal-wood box in the lumber-room in the little old country-house which belongs to me, but where I never live. If any one would steal it, it would be a relief to my mind. Yet I never knew what Aunt Mary meant when she said, "Yon ring was the token," nor what it could have to do with that strange window in the old College Library of St Rule's.

## THOMAS PATTISON (1828–1865)

### The Islesman's Home

Know'st thou the land where the herd houseless strayed,
When Summer's night was but one gloaming shade—
Where still the billows roll in sunny gold,
And thousand moors their thousand waters hold—
Know'st thou that land? The hardy Islesman's home,
Whence oft, alas, an exile he must roam.

Know'st thou its hills, where wandering mists repose,
And bleach the rocks oer which the heather grows;
Whose warmest couch the grouse and blackcock share—
Those chartered denizens of earth and air—
Know'st thou its hills whence the eye glances free
Over the measureless and western sea?

Know'st thou its lochs, on which, when sunset's oer,
The boat glides softly to the fragrant shore;
While cattle bellow and the house-dogs bay,
And hamlet noises pass with light away—
Know'st thou its lochs? On them night's sky-born beam
Welcomes in peace the poorest taper's gleam.

## JOHN VEITCH (1829–1894)

### The Laird of Schelynlaw

Schelynlaw Tower is fair on the brae,
Its muirs are green and wide,
And Schelynlaw's ewes are the brawest ewes
In a' the country-side.

The birk* grows there and the rowan red, "birch"
And the burnie brattles down,
And there are nae sic knowes* as Schelynlaw's, "knolls"
With the heather and bent* sae brown. grass

But wife, three bairns are a' frae him gane,
Twa sons in a deidly raid;
And but yestreen his bonnie lass Jean
In Traquair kirkyard was laid.

A lane auld man in his ain auld keep,—
What ane could wish him ill?
Not e'en Traquair wi' his black fause heart
And his loons* that range the hill. men, rascals

Out in the morn to the muirland dun
Rode ane frae Schelynlaw's gate,
Into the mist of the hill he rode,
His errand might not wait.

The opening arms of the gray hill haur* "hoar"
Folded the rider dim;
Oh, cloud of the muir, tis a gruesome deed
Ye hide in your misty rim.

Up he made for the Black Syke Rig,
And round by the Fingland glen,
But he turned and turned him aye in the mist;
Its glower was as faces of men!

And oft a voice sounded low in his ear,
"The sun is no' gaun to daw—
For that straik o' blude and that clot o' blude,
On the breist o' auld Schelynlaw."

Twas late o' night—to the House of Traquair
A horseman came jaded and rude,
None asked him whence or why he came,
Nor whose on his hands was the blude.

"But hae ye the Bond?" said hard Traquair.
"The Bond i' faith I hae;
The deid sign nae mair, the lands are thine,
But foul was the stroke I gae.

"I've ridden wi' you ower moss and fell,
In moonlight and in mirk,
And monie a stalwart man I've hewn,—
So shrive me, Haly Kirk.

"Lewinshope Tam and Wulrus Will
I slew, and Jock o' the Ha';
But there's my richt hand to burn in flame,
Could I bring back auld Schelynlaw."

Schelynlaw's lands were ne'er bought or sold,
Yet they fell to the house of Traquair;
But Jock o' Grieston that rode that morn
Was ne'er seen to ride ony mair.

High in state rose the noble Earl,
Well did he please the King;
He could tell any lie to the States or the Kirk,
His warrant the signet-ring.

Many a year has come and gone,
His pride and his power are away;
A graceless son has the old lord's lands,
And the father's hairs are gray.

The Court is back to Edinburgh town,
Lairds and braw leddies ride there;

A dole some give to a bowed-down man,
In pity,—'tis auld Traquair.

## The Death of Lord Maxwell

[The Battle of Dryfe Sands was fought in December, 1593, between the Johnstons and the Maxwells. Each commander had offered a bounty for "the head or the hand" of the other. Veitch refers to the following ballad as based upon a "tradition" associated with the battle.]

The leddy sat alane i' the Peel,
A' through the weary noon;
For the fray was struck at early morn,
And now the sun was doon.

Nocht she saw of the fecht that swung
In deid grips frae the tower;
But distant soughs would rise and fall
Of mortal strife and stour*. dust, struggle

And hurrying birds, ane after ane,
Fled seawards frae the land,
And every shriek that crossed the roof
Was a wail from far Dryfe's strand.

"I'll oot and see how fare my sons,
I can thole* na' this unrest"— endure
She locked the door o' the auld gray keep,—
Wi' the airn key hied her west.

She hadna gaen a mile, a mile,
A mile but barely one,
When there she saw a deid man's face,
I wot, twas her son John.

Nae stop she made but further sped,
And by the Red Syke fa',
There streakit lay her lad Willie,
The flower among them a'.

"A curse upon the Lord Maxwell,
An' a curse upon his name,—
Tis he has wrought me a' this dule,—
God wyte* him wi' the blame!" stigmatize

The evening tide was warstling sair,
Sair warstling wi' the faem*, "foam"
Aye bearing straight upon the sands,
Deep moaning as it came.

But whatna wounded man is this,
That lies upon the strand?
I wot it is the Lord Maxwell,
And they've hacked off his hand!

"Oh, Leddy Johnston gie to me
Ae cup o' water clear,
Unhook the basnet frae my heid,
I'm faint for want o' air."

"Now by my sooth ye fause fell loon*, rascal
Sair Lord ye've been to me,
'To set her hood' ye brunt Lochwood,
My sons lie deid by thee!

"Nae cup o' water shall ye get,
Nor yet a breath o' air,
But a reft mother's hate ye'll ken,
Ere lang as ye lie there."

She gae ae look to the western sky,
It frowned a lurid red;
She didna turn that way again,
For a fear was overhead.

Ae moment's grip o' the tower door key,
She swung it ower his bree*; brow
They fand the great Lord Maxwell cauld,
Next morning by the sea!

## The Lady Fleming's Dream

[The deed referred to in this ballad took place in November, 1524.]

"Fare ye not with the hawk this morn,
Fare not, my lord, my life,
I've striven last night with a fearsome dream
Long hours of eerie strife.

"I saw oer the ridge of the Culter Fell
From the south a darkness creep,
Shapeless and slow it moved in the air,
Some purpose dread in its keep.

"Down the Culter Hope it moved and swung
Till it wreathed itself to form,
And there it grew to a black bull's head,
With a threat as of gathering storm.

"And then twixt me and the new risen sun
It darkening poised i' the air,

Twas vain I strove the light to see
For the horror hanging there.

"Face to my face the grim thing kept,
And over Boghall Tower,
Instead of the blink of the morning light,
Twas dark at the morning hour.

"And yet methought twas not by might
That it quenched the sun of day,
But watchful aye it moved and turned,
As wile seeks noble prey.

"From the lift* at last the grim head passed, sky
And lo, the clear moon shone,
Yet I marveled why she stood in the sky,
When I looked for the morning sun.

"On a hazel glade her beams were shed,
In a hollow deep of the fell;
Soft and bright was her sparkle light
On the face of the Hunter's Well.

"And near it, methought, I saw a form
That knelt to the water fair,
And went and came as in trouble deep
For some one lying there.

"In the Well she bathed a new-cropt flower,
It seemed the strawberry pale,
Sadly she eyed its drooping face,
As in grief without avail.

"I knew the lady's face and form;
She lies in the sun-dark tomb,
But once she sat your well loved bride
In power of her youthful bloom.

"The Fleming wears the strawberry flower;
My lord, my life, take heed.
Drummelzier[1] bears the black bull's head,
Dark omen ye may read."

Lord Fleming's look was startled, strange,
Yet he mounted his horse and rode:
"I'll fare with the hawk this winter morn,
Recking nought night fancies' bode."

But as he passed oer the moorland fell,
Low words he muttering said,—

---

[1]The castle of Lord Fleming's enemy, James Tweedie, and thus a name for Tweedie himself.

Seemed as he spake to some one there,
"Is there ruth ev'n with my dead?"

He thought him of a clay-cold form
That lay in a chapel girth,
He marveled if but the loved in heaven
Keep watch oer the left on earth.

High they coursed oer the spreading fells,
Till late in the afternoon,
And far they rode by the lone burnheads,
Till up i' the east shot the moon.

Below from the Hope there seemed to come
As twere a dim cloud gleam;
Is this but the mist of the water-side
Struck bright by the glinting beam?

Out of that mist there sudden flashed,
A young face keen as flame;
Scant words but hot between them passed;
They bandied a lady's name.

One stealthy thrust from Drummelzier's sword,
And then a deep-drawn wail;
The strawberry white on the Fleming's breast
Grew red in the moonlight pale.

Dead he lay by the Hunter's Well,
Dead horse and hawk by his side;
Drummelzier and ten armed men
Rode late that eventide.

They rode by Chapel Kingledoors,
With clattering hoof they sped;
And well the priest in the lee moonlight
Knew omen of their tread.

All night on the moor Lord Fleming lay,
Face to the moonshine clear;
Next morn to Boghall they brought him slow
From the hill on a sauchen* bier. willow

His lady deemed him fair that morn,
When they brought him from the heath,
Soft pallor on his upturned face,—
Twas hard to think it death.

Pale and fair as his strawberry flower,
New snatched with drooping head;
For aye cut off from its quickening root,
Yet a grace is on it dead.

### Among the Hills, Away!

Far along the empurpled heights,
Where dews have wreathed the green,
The mists transfigured pass, sun-smit,
In folds of radiant sheen.
The north-west wind is up in might,
With clouds for speeding wings;
His gentle bride, the blue clear morn,
High oer the hills he brings.
Lo, strength and beauty rare are wed,
Wed in the sky to-day;
There's hurrying joy in heaven oerhead;
Among the hills, away!

High on the moors the sportive wind
Kisses the blooming heath;
He plays with the harebell's graceful form,
Steals the thyme's fragrant breath.
He speeds in gleam, he glides in shade,
Joy and grief are at play;
The blue clear morn looks loving on;
Among the hills, away!

## ALEXANDER SMITH (1830–1867)

### Squire Maurice

I threw from off me yesterday
The dull life I am doomed to wear—
A worn-out garment dim and bare,
And left it in my chambers gray:
The salt breeze wanders in my hair
Beside the splendor of the main:
Ere on the deep three sunsets burn,
To the old chambers I return,
And put it on again.
An old coat, worn for many a year,
No wonder it is something dear.

Ah, year by year life's fire burns out,
And year by year life's stream runs dry:
The wild deer dies within the blood,
The falcon in the eye.
And Hope, who sang miraculous songs
Of what should be, like one inspired,
How she should right the ancient wrongs,
(The generous fool!) grows hoarse and tired;
And turns from visions of a world renewed,
To dream of tripled rents, fair miles of stream and wood.
The savage horse, that leads
His tameless herd across the endless plain,
Is taught at last, with sullen heart, to strain

Beneath his load, nor quiver when he bleeds.
We cheat ourselves with our own lying eyes,
We chase a fleeting mirage oer the sand;
Across a grave the smiling phantom flies,
Oer which we fall with a vain-clutching hand.
What matter—-if we heave laborious breath,
And crack our hearts and sinews, groan and weep,
The pain of life but sweetens death,
The hardest labor brings the soundest sleep.

On bank and brae how thick they grow,
The self-same clumps, the self-same dyes,
The primroses of long ago—
But ah, the altered eyes!
I dream they are the very flowers,
Warm with the sun, wet with the showers
Which, years ago, I used to pull
Returning from the murmuring school.
Sweet Nature is a mother ever more;
A thousand tribes are breathing on the shore;
The pansy blows beside the rock,
The globe-flower, where the eddy swirls;
And on this withered human stock
Burst rosy boys and girls.
Sets Nature little store
On that which once she bore?
Does she forget the old, in rapture bear the new?
Are ye the flowers that grew
In other seasons? Do they e'er return,
The men who built the cities on the plain?—
Or must my tearless eyeballs burn
For ever oer that early urn,
Ne'er to be cooled by a delicious dew?
Let me take back my pain
Unto my heart again;
Before I can recover that I lack
The world must he rolled back.

Inland I wander slow,
Mute with the power the earth and heaven wield:
A black spot sails across the golden field,
And through the air a crow.
Before me wavers spring's first butterfly;
From out the sunny noon there starts the cuckoo's cry;
The daisied meads are musical with lambs;
Some play, some feed, some, white as snow-flakes, lie
In the deep sunshine, by their silent dams.
The road grows white and level to the feet;
The wandering woodbine through the hedge is drawn,
Unblown its streaky bugles dim and sweet;
Knee-deep in fern stand startled doe and fawn,
And lo, there gleams upon a spacious lawn
An Earl's marine retreat.

A little foot-path quivers up the height,
And what a vision for a townsman's sight!
A village, peeping from its orchard bloom,
With lowly roofs of thatch, blue threads of smoke,
O'erlooking all, a parsonage of white.
I hear the smithy's hammer, stroke on stroke;
A steed is at the door; the rustics talk,
Proud of the notice of the gaitered groom;
A shallow river breaks oer shallow falls.
Beside the ancient sluice that turns the mill
The lusty miller bawls;
The parson listens in his garden-walk,
The red-cloaked woman pauses on the hill.
This is a place, you say, exempt from ill,
A paradise, where, all the loitering day
Enamored pigeons coo upon the roof,
Where children ever play.
Alas, Time's webs are rotten warp and woof;
Rotten his cloth of gold, his coarsest wear.
Here, black-eyed Richard ruins red-cheeked Moll,
Indifferent as a lord to her despair.
The broken barrow hates the prosperous dray;
And, for a padded pew in which to pray,
The grocer sells his soul.

This cozy hostelry a visit craves.
Here will I sit awhile,
And watch the heavenly sunshine smile
Upon the village graves.
Strange is this little room in which I wait.
With its old table, rough with rustic names.
Tis summer now; instead of blinking flames,
Sweet-smelling ferns are hanging oer the grate.
With curious eyes I pore
Upon the mantle-piece, its precious wares,
Glazed Scripture prints in black lugubrious frames,
Filled with old Bible lore:
The whale is casting Jonah on the shore;
Pharaoh is drowning in the curly wave;
And to Elijah sitting at his cave,
The hospitable ravens fly in pairs,
Celestial food within their horny beaks;
On a slim David with great pinky cheeks,
A towered Goliath stares.
Here will I sit at peace:
While, piercing through the window's ivy veil,
A slip of sunshine smites the amber ale;
And the wreaths of fragrant smoke increase,
I'll read the letter which came down to-day:

> Ah, happy Maurice! while in chambers dun
> I pour over the deeds and parchments growing gray,
> Each glowing realm that spreads beneath the sun

Is but a paradise where you may play.
I am a bonded workman, you are free;
In your blood's hey-day—mine is early cold.
Life is rude furze at best; the sea-breeze wrings
And eats my branches on the bitter lea;
But you have root in dingle fat and old,
Fat with decayings of a hundred springs,
And blaze all splendid in your points of gold,
And in your heart a linnet sits and sings.

Unstable as the wind, infirm as foam,
I envy, Charles, your calmness and your peace;
The eye that marks its quarry from afar,
The heart that stoops on it and smiles it down.
I, struggling in a dim and obscure net,
Am but enmeshed the more. When you were here,
My spirit often burned to tell you all;
I urged the horse up to the leap, it shied
At something in the hedge. This must not last;
In shame and sorrow, ere I sleep to-night,
I'll shrive my inmost soul.
I have knelt, and sworn
By the sweet heavens—I have madly prayed
To be by them forsaken, when I forsake
A girl whose lot should be to sleep content
Upon a peasant's breast, and toil all day
Mong flaxen-headed children. She sits to-night,
When all the little town is lost in dream,
Her lax hands sunk in her neglected work,
Thinking of me. Smile not, my man of law,
Who, with a peering candle, walkest through
Black places in men's hearts, which only hear
The foot of conscience at the dead of night!
Her name might slip into my holiest prayer;
Her breath has come and gone upon my cheek,
Yet I dare stand before my mother's face,
Dare look into the heavenly eyes that yearn
For ever through a mist of golden hair,
With no shame on my brow. Tis not that way
My trouble looks. Yet, friend, in simple truth
Could this thing be obliterated quite,
Expunged for ever, like a useless cloak
I'd fling off my possessions, and go forth,
My roof the weeping heaven.
Though I would die
Rather than give her pain, I grimly smile
To think, were I assured this horrid dream
Which poisons day to me, would only prove
A breath upon the mirror of her mind—
A moment dim then gone (an issue which,
Could I have blotted out all memory,
Would let me freely breathe)—this love would turn
To bitterest gall of hate. O Vanity,

Thou god, who on the altar thou hast built
Pilest myrrh and frankincense, appliest the flame,
Then snuff'st the smoky incense, high and calm.
Thou nimble Proteus of all human shapes!
Malvolio, cross-gartered in the sun,
The dying martyr, gazing from his fire
Upon the opened heavens, filled with crowds
Of glorious angel-faces:—thou art all
We smile at, all we hymn! For thee we blush,
For thee shed noble tears! The glowing coal,
Oer which the frozen beggar spreads his hands,
Is of one essence with the diamond,
That on the haughty forehead of a queen
Trembles with dewy light. Could I, through pain,
Give back the peace I stole, my heart would leap;
Could she forget me and regain content—
How deeply I am wronged!

Is it the ancient trouble of my house
That makes the hours so terrible? Other men
Live to more purpose than those monstrous weeds
That drink a breath of sunshine, and give back
Nor hue nor fragrance; but my spirit droops,
A dead and idle banner from its staff,
Unstirred by any wind. Within a cell,
Without a straw to play with, or a nail
To carve my sorrow on the gloomy stone,
I sit and watch, from stagnant day to day,
The bloated spider hanging on its thread,
The dull fly on the wall. The blessed sleep
For which none are too poor; the sleep that comes
So sweetly to the weary laboring man,
The march-worn soldier on the naked ground,
The martyr in the pauses of the rack,
Drives me through forests full of dreadful eyes,
Flings me oer precipices, makes me kneel,
A sentenced man, before the dark platoon,
Or lays me helpless in the dim embrace
Of formless horror. Long ago, two foes
Lay in the yellow evening in their gore:
Like a malignant fury, that wild hour
Threw madness in the river of our blood:
Though it has run for thrice a century,
Been sweetened all the way by mothers' tears,
Tis poisoned until now.
                                        See how I stand
Delaying on the brink, like one who fears
And yet would meet the chill. When you were here
You saw a smoking-cap among my books;
A fond and fluttering letter badly spelt,
Each sentence headed with a little *i*,
Came with it, read with a blush, tossed in the fire,
Nor answered yet. Can you not now detect

The snail's slime on the rose?
                                        This miserable thing
Grew round me like the ivy round the oak;
Sweet were its early creeping rings, though now
I choke, from knotted root to highest bough.
In those too happy days I could not name
This strange new thing which came upon my youth,
But yielded to its sweetness. Fling it off?
Trample it clown? Bid me pluck out the eye
In which the sweet world dwells!—One night she wept;
It seemed so strange that I could make her weep;
Kisses may lie, but tears are surely true.
Then unbelief came back in solitude,
And love grew cruel; and to be assured
Cried out for tears, and with a shaking hand
And a wild heart that could have almost burst
With utter tenderness, yet would not spare,
He clutched her heart, and at the starting tears
Grew soft with all remorse. For those mad hours
Remembrance frets my heart in solitude,
As the lone mouse when all the house is still
Gnaws at the wainscot.
                                        Tis a haunting face,
Yet oftentimes I think I love her not;
Love's white hand flutters oer my spirit's keys
Unkissed by grateful music. Oft I think
The Lady Florence at the county ball,
Quenching the beauties as the lightning dims
The candles in a room, scarce smiles so sweet.
The one oppresses like a crown of gold,
The other gladdens like a beam in spring,
Stealing across a dim field, making blithe
Its daisies one by one.—I deemed that
I had broke my house of bondage, when one night
The memory of her face came back so sweet,
And stood between me and the printed page;
And phantoms of a thousand happy looks
Smiled from the dark. It was the old weak tale
Which time has told from Adam to this hour:
The slave comes back, takes up his broken chain.
I rode through storm toward the little town;
The minster, gleamed on by the flying moon,
Tolled midnight as I passed. I only sought
To see the line of light beneath her door,
The knowledge of her nearness was so sweet.
Hid in the darkness of the church, I watched
Her window like a shrine: a light came in
And a soft shadow broke along the roof;
She raised the window and leaned forth awhile.
I could have fallen down and kissed her feet;
The poor dear heart, I knew it could not rest;
I stood between her and the light—my shade
Fell 'cross her silver sphere. The window closed

When morn with cold bleak crimson laced the east,
Against a stream of raw and rainy wind
I rode back to the Hall.
The play-book tells
How Fortune's slippery wheel in Syracuse
Flung prosperous lordship to the chilly shades,
Heaved serfdom to the sun: in precious silks
Charwomen flounced, and scullions sat and laughed
In golden chairs, to see their fellows play
At football with a crown. Within my heart
In this old house, when all the fiends are here,
The story is renewed. Peace only comes
With a wild ride across the barren downs,
One look upon her face. She ne'er complains
Of my long absences, my hasty speech.—
"Crumbs from thy table are enough for me."
Her head against my breast a little while,
And she is paid for all. I choke with tears,
And think myself a devil from the pit
Loved by an angel. O that she would change
This tenderness and drooping-lily look,
The flutter when I come, the unblaming voice,
Wet eyes held up to kiss—one flash of fire,
A moment's start of keen and crimson scorn,
Would make me hers for ever!
I draw my birth
From a long line of gallant gentlemen,
Who only feared a lie—but what is this?
I dare not slight the daughter of a peer;
Her kindred could avenge. Yet I dare play
And palter with the pure soul of a girl
Without a friend, who, smitten, speaks no word,
But with a helpless face sinks in the grave
And takes her wrongs to God. Thou dark Sir Ralph,
Who lay with broken brand on Marston Moor,
What think you of this son?

This prison that I dwell in hath two doors,
Desertion, marriage; both are shut by shame,
And barred by cowardice. A stronger man
Would screw his heart up to the bitter wrench,
And break through either and regain the air.
I cannot give myself or others pain.
I wear a conscience nice and scrupulous,
Which, while it hesitates to draw a tear,
Lets a heart break. Conscience should be clear-eyed,

And look through years: conscience is tenderest oft
When clad in sternness, when it smites today,
To stay the ruin which it hears afar
Upon the wind. Pure womanhood is meek—
But which is nobler, the hysterical girl
Weeping oer flies huddling in slips of sun

On autumn sills, who has not heart enough
To crush a wounded grasshopper and end
Torture at once; or she, with flashing eyes,
Among the cannon, a heroic foot
Upon a fallen breast? My nerveless will
Is like a traitorous second, and deserts
My purpose in the very gap of need.
I groan beneath this cowardice of heart,
Which rolls the evil to be borne today
Upon tomorrow, loading it with gloom.
The man who clothes the stony moor with green,
In virtue of the beauty he creates,
Has there a right to dwell. And he who stands
Firm in this shifting sand and drift of things,
And rears from out the wasteful elements
An ordered home, in which the awful Gods,
The lighter Graces, serene Muses, dwell,
Holds in that masterdom the chartered right
To his demesne of Time. But I hold none;
I live by sufferance, am weak and vain
As a shed leaf upon a turbid stream,
Or an abandoned boat which can but drift
Whither the currents draw—to maelstrom, or
To green delicious shores. I should have had
My pendent cradle rocked by laughing winds
Within some innocent and idle isle
Where the sweet bread-fruit ripens and falls down,
Where the swollen pumpkin lolls upon the ground,
The lithe and slippery savage, drenched with oil,
Sleeps in the sun, and life is lazy ease.
But lamentation and complaint are vain:
The skies are stern and serious as doom;
The avalanche is loosened by a laugh;
And he who throws the dice of destiny,
Though with a sportive and unthinking hand,
Must bide the issue, be it life or death.
One path is clear before me. It may lead
Oer perilous rock, 'cross sands without a well,
Through deep and difficult chasms, but therein
The whiteness of the soul is kept, and that,
Not joy nor happiness, is victory.

Ah, she is not the creature who I dreamed
Should one day walk beside me dearly loved:
No fair majestic woman, void of fear,
And unabashed from purity of heart;
No girl with liquid eyes and shadowy hair,
To sing at twilight like a nightingale,
Or fill the silence with her glimmering smiles,
Deeper than speech or song. She has no birth,
No dowry, graces; no accomplishments,
Save a pure cheek, a fearless, innocent brow,
And a true-beating heart. She is no bank

Of rare exotics which oercome the sense
With perfumes—only fresh uncultured soil
With a wild-violet grace and sweetness born
Of Nature's teeming foison. Is this not
Enough to sweeten life? Could one not live
On brown bread, clearest water? Is this love
(What idle poets feign in fabling songs)
An unseen god, whose voice is heard but once
In youth's green valleys, ever dead and mute
Mong manhood's iron hills? A power that comes
On the instant, whelming, like the light that smote
Saul from his horse; never a thing that draws
Its exquisite being from the light of smiles
And low sweet tones and fond companionship?
Brothers and sisters grow up by our sides,
Unfelt and silently are knit to us,
And one flesh with our hearts; would love not grow
In the communion of long-wedded years,
Sweet as the dawning light, the greening spring?
Would not an infant be the marriage priest,
To stand between us and unite our hands,
And bid us love and be obeyed? its life,
A fountain, with a cooling fringe of green
Amid the arid sands, by which we twain
Could dwell in deep content? My sunshine drew
This odorous blossom from the bough; why then
With frosty fingers wither it, and seal up
Sun ripened fruit within its barren rind
Killing all sweet delights? I drew it forth:
If there is suffering, let me bear it all.

A very little goodness goes for much.
Walk mong my peasants—every urchin's face
Lights at my coming; girls at cottage-doors
Rise from their work and curtsey as I pass,
And old men bless me with their silent tears!
What have I done for this? I'm kind, they say,
Give coals in winter, cordials for the sick,
And once a fortnight stroke a curly head
Which hides half-frightened in a russet gown.
Tis easy for the sun to shine. My alms
Are to my riches like a beam to him.
They love me, these poor hinds, though I have ne'er
Resigned a pleasure, let a whim be crossed,
Pinched for an hour the stomach of desire
For one of them. Good Heaven! what am I
To be thus servitored? Am I to range
Like the discourseless creatures of the wood,
Without the common dignity of pain,
Without a pale or limit? To take up love
For its strange sweetness, and where're it tires,
Fling it aside as careless as I brush
A gnat from off my arm, and go my way

Untwinged with keen remorse? All this must end.
Firm land at last begins to peer above
The ebbing waves of hesitance and doubt.
Throughout this deepening spring my purpose grows
To flee with her to those young morning lands—
Australia, where the earth is gold, or where
The prairies roll toward the setting sun.
Not Lady Florence with her coronet,
Flinging white arms around me, murmuring
"Husband" upon my breast—not even that
Could make me happy, if I left a grave
On which the shadow of the village spire
Should rest at eve. The pain, if pain there be,
I'll keep locked up within my secret heart,
And wear what joy I have upon on my face;
And she shall live and laugh, and never know.

Come, Brother, at your earliest, down to me.
To-morrow night I sleep at Ferny-Chase:
There, shadowed by the memory of the dead,
We'll talk of this. My thought, mayhap, will take
A different hue, seen in your purer light,
Free from all stain of passion. Ere you come,
Break that false mirror of your ridicule,
Looking in which, the holiest saint beholds
A grinning Jackanapes, and hates himself.
More men hath Laughter driven from the right
Than Terror clad with fire. You have been young,
And know the mystery, that when we love,
We love the thing, not only for itself
But somewhat also for the love we give.
Think of the genial season of your youth
When you dwelt here, and come with serious heart.

---

So, in that bitter quarter sits the wind:
The village fool could tell, unless it shifts
Twill bring the rain in fiercest flaws and drifts.
How wise we are, yet blind,
Judging the wood's grain from the outer rind;
Wrapt in the twilight of this prison dim,
He envies me, I envy him!
The stream of my existence boils and leaps
Through broken rainbows mong the purple fells*, hills
And breaks its heart mid rocks, close-jammed, confined,
And plunges in a chasm black and blind,
To rage in hollow gulfs and iron hells,
And thence escaping, tamed and broken, creeps
Away in a wild sweat of beads and bells.
Though *his* slides lazy through the milky meads,
And once a week the sleepy slow-trailed barge
Rocks the broad water-lilies on its marge,

A dead face wavers from the oozy weeds.
It is but little matter where we dwell,
In fortune's center, on her utter verge;
Whether to death our weary steps we urge,
Or ride with ringing bridle, golden selle.
Life is one pattern wrought in different hues,
And there is nought to choose
Between its sad and gay—tis but to groan
Upon a rainy common or a throne,
Bleed neath the purple or the peasants' serge.

At his call I will go,
Though it is very little love can do;
In spite of all affection tried and true,
Each man alone must struggle with his woe.
He pities her, for he has done her wrong
And would repair the evil—noble deed,
To flash and tingle in a minstrel's song,
To move the laughter of our modern breed!
And yet the world is wise; each curve and round
Of custom's road is no result of chance;
It curves but to avoid some treacherous ground,
Some quagmire in the wilds of circumstance;
Nor safely left. The long-drawn caravan
Wavers through heat, then files oer Mecca's stones;
Far in the blinding desert lie the bones
Of the proud-hearted solitary man.
He marries her, but ere the year has died,—
Tis an old tale,—they wander to the grave
With hot revolting hearts, yet lashed and tied
Like galley-slave to slave.
Love should not stoop to Love, like prince to lord:
While oer their heads proud Cupid claps his wings;
Love should meet Love upon the marriage sward,
And kiss, like crowned kings.
If both are hurt, then let them bear the pain
Upon their separate paths; twill die at last:
The deed of one rash moment may remain
To darken all the future with the past.
And yet I cannot tell—the beam that kills
The gypsy's fire, kindles the desert flower;
Where he plucks blessings I may gather ills,
And in his sweetest sweet find sourest sour.
If what of wisdom and experience
My years have brought, be either guide or aid,
They shall be his, though to my mournful sense
The lights will steal away from wood and glade;
The garden will be sad with all its glows,
And I shall hear the glistening laurels talk
Of her, as I pass under in the walk,
And my light step will thrill each conscious rose.
The lark hangs high oer Ferny-Chase
In slant of sun, twinkle of rain;

Though loud and clear, the song I hear
Is half of joy, and half of pain.
I know by heart the dear old place,
The place where spring and summer meet—
By heart, like those old ballad rhymes,
Oer which I brood a million times,
And sink from sweet to deeper sweet.
I know the changes of the idle skies,
The idle shapes in which the clouds are blown;
The dear old place is now before my eyes,
Yea, to the daisy's shadow on the stone.
When through the golden furnace of the heat
The far-off landscape seems to shake and beat,
Within the lake I see old Hodge's cows
Stand in their shadows in a tranquil drowse,
While oer them hangs a restless steam of flies.
I see the clustered chimneys of the Hall
Stretch oer the lawn toward the blazing lake;
And in the dewy even-fall
I hear the mellow thrushes call
From tree to tree, from brake to brake.
Ah, when I thither go
I know that my joy-emptied eyes shall see
A white Ghost wandering where the lilies blow,
A Sorrow sitting by the trysting tree.
I kiss this soft curl of her living hair,
Tis full of light as when she did unbind
Her sudden ringlets, making bright the wind:
Tis here, but she is—where?
Why do I, like a child impatient, weep?
Delight dies like a wreath of frosted breath;
Though here I toil upon the barren deep,
I see the sunshine yonder lie asleep,
Upon the calm and beauteous shores of Death.
Ah, Maurice, let thy human heart decide,
The first best pilot through distracting jars.
The lowliest roof of love at least will hide
The desolation of the lonely stars.
Stretched on the painful rack of forty years,
I've learned at last the sad philosophy
Of the unhoping heart, unshrinking eye—
God knows; my icy wisdom and my sneers
Are frozen tears.

The day wears, and I go.
Farewell, Elijah, may you heartily dine.
I cannot, David, see your fingers twine
In the long hair of your foe.
Housewife, adieu, Heaven keep your ample form,
May custom never fail;
And may your heart, as sound as your own ale,
Be soured by never a storm.
Though I have traveled now for twice an hour

I have not heard a bird or seen a flower.
This wild road has a little mountain rill
To sing to it, ah, happier than I.
How desolate the region, and how still
The idle earth looks on the idle sky!
I trace the river by its wandering green;
The vale contracts to a steep pass of fear,
And through the midnight of the pines I hear
The torrent raging down the long ravine.
At last I've reached the summit high and bare;
I fling myself on heather dry and brown:
As silent as a picture lies the town,
Its peaceful smokes are curling in the air;
The bay is one delicious sheet of rose,
And round the far point of the tinted cliffs
I see the long strings of the fishing skiffs
Come home to roost like lines of evening crows.
I can be idle only one day more
As the nets drying on the sunny shore;
Thereafter, chambers, still mid thronged resorts,
Strewn books and littered parchments, nought to see,
Save a charwoman's face, a dingy tree,
A fountain plashing in the empty courts.

But let me hasten down this shepherd's track,
The Night is at my back.

## Glasgow

Sing, Poet, tis a merry world;
That cottage smoke is rolled and curled
In sport, that every moss
Is happy, every inch of soil;—
Before me runs a road of toil
With my grave cut across.
Sing, trailing showers and breezy downs—
I know the tragic heart of towns.

City! I am true son of thine;
Ne'er dwelt I where great mornings shine
Around the bleating pens;
Ne'er by the rivulets I strayed,
And ne'er upon my childhood weighed
The silence of the glens.
Instead of shores where ocean beats,
I hear the ebb and flow of streets.

Black Labor draws his weary waves,
Into their secret-moaning caves;
But with the morning light,
The sea again will overflow
With a long weary sound of woe,

Again to faint in night.
Wave am I in that sea of woes;
Which, night and morning, ebbs and flows.

I dwelt within a gloomy court
Wherein did never sunbeam sport;
Yet there my heart was stirred—
My very blood did dance and thrill,
When on my narrow window-sill,
Spring lighted like a bird.
Poor flowers—I watched them pine for weeks,
With leaves as pale as human cheeks.

Afar, one summer, I was borne;
Through golden vapors of the morn,
I heard the hills of sheep:
I trod with a wild ecstasy
The bright fringe of the living sea:
And on a ruined keep
I sat, and watched an endless plain
Blacken beneath the gloom of rain.

O fair the lightly sprinkled waste,
Oer which a laughing shower has raced!
O fair the April shoots!
O fair the woods on summer days,
While a blue hyacinthine haze
Is dreaming round the roots!
In thee, O City! I discern
Another beauty, sad and stern.

Draw thy fierce streams of blinding ore,
Smite on a thousand anvils, roar
Down to the harbor-bars;
Smolder in smoky sunsets, flare
On rainy nights, with street and square
Lie empty to the stars.
From terrace proud to alley base
I know thee as my mother's face.

When sunset bathes thee in his gold,
In wreaths of bronze thy sides are rolled,
Thy smoke is dusky fire;
And, from the glory round thee poured,
A sunbeam like an angel's sword
Shivers upon a spire.
Thus have I watched thee, Terror! Dream!
While the blue night crept up the stream.

The wild train plunges in the hills,
He shrieks across the midnight rills;
Streams through the shifting glare,
The roar and flap of foundry fires,

That shake with light the sleeping shires;
And on the moorlands bare,
He sees afar a crown of light
Hang oer thee in the hollow night.

At midnight, when thy suburbs lie
As silent as a noonday sky,
When larks with heat are mute,
I love to linger on thy bridge,
All lonely as a mountain ridge,
Disturbed but by my foot;
While the black lazy stream beneath,
Steals from its far-off wilds of heath.

And through my heart, as through a dream,
Flows on that black disdainful stream;
All scornfully it flows,
Between the huddled gloom of masts,
Silent as pines unvexed by blasts—
Tween lamps in streaming rows.
O wondrous sight! O stream of dread!
O long dark river of the dead!

Afar, the banner of the year
Unfurls: but dimly prisoned here,
Tis only when I greet
A dropt rose lying in my way,
A butterfly that flutters gay
Athwart the noisy street,
I know the happy Summer smiles
Around thy suburbs, miles on miles.

All raptures of this mortal breath,
Solemnities of life and death,
Dwell in thy noise alone:
Of me thou hast become a part—
Some kindred with my human heart
Lives in thy streets of stone;
For we have been familiar more
Than galley-slave and weary oar.

The beech is dipped in wine; the shower
Is burnished; on the swinging flower
The latest bee doth sit.
The low sun stares through dust of gold,
And oer the darkening heath and wold
The large ghost-moth doth flit.
In every orchard Autumn stands,
With apples in his golden hands.

But all these sights and sounds are strange;
Then wherefore from thee should I range?
Thou hast my kith and kin:

My childhood, youth, and manhood brave;
Thou hast an unforgotten grave
Within thy central din.
A sacredness of love and death
Dwells in thy noise and smoky breath.

While oer thy walls the darkness sails,
I lean against the churchyard rails;
Up in the midnight towers
The belfried spire, the street is dead,
I hear in silence overhead
The clang of iron hours:
It moves me not, I know her tomb
Is yonder in the shapeless gloom.

## Edinburgh

Edina, high in heaven wan,
Towered, templed, metropolitan,
Waited upon by hills,
River, and wide-spread ocean, tinged
By April light, or draped and fringed
As April vapor wills—
Thou hangest, like a Cyclops' dream,
High in the shifting weather-gleam.

Fair art thou when above thy head
The mistless firmament is spread;
But when the twilight's screen
Draws glimmering round thy towers and spires,
And thy lone bridge, uncrowned by fires,
Hangs in the dim ravine,
Thou art a very Persian tale—
Oh, Mirza's vision, Bagdad's vale.

The spring-time stains with emerald
Thy Castle's precipices bald.
Within thy streets and squares
The sudden summer camps, and blows
The plenteous chariot-shaken rose;
Or, lifting unawares
My eyes from out thy central strife,
Lo, far off, harvest-brazen Fife!

When rain-drops gemming tree and plant,
The rainbow is thy visitant,
Lovely as on the moors;
When sunset flecks with loving ray
Thy wilderness of gables gray,
And hoary embrasures;
When great Sir Walter's moon-blanched shrine,
Rich-carved, as Melrose, gleams divine,

I know thee; and I know thee, too
On winter nights, when gainst the blue
Thy high, gloom-wildered ridge
Breaks in a thousand splendors; lamps
Gleam broadly in the valley damps;
Thy air-suspended bridge
Shines steadfast; and the modern street
Looks on, star-fretted, loud with feet.

Fair art thou, City, to the eye,
But fairer to the memory.
There is no place that breeds—
Not Venice neath her mellow moons,
When the sea-pulse of full lagoons
Waves all her palace weeds—
Such wistful thoughts of far away,
Of the eternal yesterday.

Within thy high-piled Canongate
The air is of another date.
All speaks of ancient time:
Traces of gardens, dials, wells,
Thy dizzy gables, oyster-shells
Imbedded in the lime—
Thy shields above the doors of peers
Are old as Mary Stuart's tears.

Street haunted by the step of Knox;
Darnley's long, heavy-scented locks;
Ruthven's blood-freezing stare;
Dark Murray, dreaming of the crown—
His ride through fair Linlithgow town,
And the man waiting there
With loaded fuse, undreamed of—wiles
Of Mary, and her mermaid smiles.

Thou saw'st Montrose's passing face
Shame-strike the gloating silk and lace,
And jeering plumes that filled
The balcony oerhead; with pride
Thou saw'st Prince Charles bare-headed ride,
While bagpipes round him shrilled,
And far Culloden's smoky racks
Hid scaffold craped, and bloody ax.

What wine hast thou known brawl be-spilt,
What daggers ruddy to the hilt,
What stately minuets
Walked slowly oer thy oaken floors,
What hasty kisses at thy doors,
What banquetings and bets,
What talk, oer man that lives and errs,
Of double-chinned philosophers.

Great City, every morning I
See thy wild fringes in the sky,
Soft-blurred with smoky grace:
Each evening note the blazing sun
Flush luridly thy vapors dun—
A spire athwart his face.
Each night I watch thy wondrous feast,
Like some far city of the East.

But most I love thee faint and fair,
Dim-penciled in the April air,
When in the dewy bush
I hear from budded thick remote
The rapture of the blackbird's throat,
The sweet note of the thrush;
And all is shadowless and clear
In the uncolored atmosphere.

## Sea-Marge

The lark is singing in the blinding sky,
Hedges are white with May. The bride-groom sea
Is toying with the shore, his wedded bride,
And, in the fullness of his marriage joy,
He decorates her tawny brow with shells,
Retires a space, to see how fair she looks,
Then proud, runs up to kiss her. All is fair—
All glad, from grass to sun. Yet more I love
Than this, the shrinking day that sometimes comes
In Winter's front, so fair mong its dark peers,
It seems a straggler from the files of June,
Which in its wanderings had lost its wits,
And half its beauty; and, when it returned,
Finding its old companions gone away,
It joined November's troop, then marching past;
And so the frail thing comes, and greets the world
With a thin crazy smile, then bursts in tears,
And all the while it holds within its hand
A few half-withered flowers. I love and pity it.

## Beauty

Beauty still walketh on the earth and air,
Our present sunsets are as rich in gold
As ere the Iliad's music was out-rolled;
The roses of the Spring are ever fair,
Mong branches green still ring-doves coo and pair,
And the deep sea still foams its music old.
So, if we are at all divinely souled,
This beauty will unloose our bonds of care.
Tis pleasant, when blue skies are oer us bending
Within old starry-gated Poesy,

To meet a soul set to no worldly tune,
Like thine, sweet Friend. Oh, dearer this to me
Than are the dewy trees, the sun, the moon,
Or noble music with a golden ending.

## Lady Barbara

Earl Gawain wooed the Lady Barbara,
High-thoughted Barbara, so white and cold.
Mong broad-branched beeches in the summer shaw*, wood
In soft green light his passion he has told.
When rain-beat winds did shriek across the wold* upland field
The Earl to take her fair reluctant ear
Framed passion-trembled ditties manifold;
Silent she sat his amorous breath to hear,
With calm and steady eyes; her heart was otherwhere.

He sighed for her through all the summer weeks.
Sitting beneath a tree whose fruitful boughs
Bore glorious apples with smooth, shining cheeks,
Earl Gawain came and whispered, "Lady, rouse!
Thou art no vestal held in holy vows;
Out with our falcons to the pleasant heath."
Her father's blood leapt up into her brows,—
He who, exulting on the trumpet's breath,
Came charging like a star across the lists of death,

Trembled, and passed before her high rebuke:
And then she sat, her hands clasped round her knee.
Like one far-thoughted was the lady's look,
For in a morning cold as misery
She saw a lone ship sailing on the sea.
Before the north twas driven like a cloud,.
High on the poop a man sat mournfully.
The wind was whistling through mast and shroud,
And to the whistling wind thus did he sing aloud:—

"Didst look last night upon my native vales,
Thou Sun, that from the drenching sea hast clomb?
Ye demon winds, that glut my gaping sails,
Upon the salt sea must I ever roam,
Wander forever on the barren foam?
O, happy are ye, resting mariners.
O Death, that thou wouldst come and take me home.
A hand unseen this vessel onward steers,
And onward I must float through slow, moon-measured years.

"Ye winds, when like a curse ye drove us on,
Frothing the waters, and along our way,
Nor cape nor headland through red mornings shone,
One wept aloud, one shuddered down to pray,
One howled, 'Upon the deep we are astray.'

On our wild hearts his words fell like a blight.
In one short hour my hair was stricken gray,
For all the crew sank ghastly in my sight
As we went driving on through the cold starry night.

"Madness fell on me in my loneliness,
The sea foamed curses, and the reeling sky
Became a dreadful face which did oppress
Me with the weight of its unwinking eye.
It fled, when I burst forth into a cry,—
A shoal of fiends came on me from the deep;
I hid, but in all corners they did pry,
And dragged me forth, and round did dance and leap;
They mouthed on me in dream, and tore me from sweet sleep.

"Strange constellations burned above my head,
Strange birds around the vessel shrieked and flew,
Strange shapes, like shadows, through the clear sea fled,
As our lone ship, wide-winged, came rippling through,
Angering to foam the smooth and sleeping blue."
The lady sighed, "Far, far upon the sea,
My own Sir Arthur, could I die with you.
The wind blows shrill between my love and me."
Fond heart! the space between was but the apple-tree.

There was a cry of joy; with seeking hands
She fled to him, like worn bird to her nest;
Like washing water on the figured sands,
His being came and went in sweet unrest,
As from the mighty shelter of his breast
The Lady Barbara her head uprears
With a wan smile, "Methinks I'm but half blest:
Now when I've found thee, after weary years,
I cannot see thee, love, so blind I am with tears."

## A Minor Poet

He sat one winter neath a linden tree
In my bare orchard. "See, my friend," he said,
"The stars among the branches hang like fruit,
So, hopes were thick within me. When I'm gone
The world will like a valuator sit
Upon my soul, and say, 'I was a cloud
That caught its glory from a sunken sun,
And gradual burned into its native gray.'"
On an October eve, twas his last wish
To see again the mists and golden woods.
Upon his deathbed he was lifted up,
The slumb'rous sun within the lazy west
With their last gladness filled his dying eyes.
No sooner was he hence than critic-worms
Were swarming on the body of his fame,

And thus they judged the dead: "This poet was
An April tree whose vermeil-loaded boughs
Promised to Autumn apples juiced and red,
But never came to fruit." "He is to us
But a rich odor,—a faint music-swell."
"Poet he was not in the larger sense.
He could write pearls, but he could never write
A poem round and perfect as a star."
"Politic, i' faith. His most judicious act
Was dying when he did. The next five years
Had fingered all the fine dust from his wings,
And left him poor as we. He died—twas shrewd.
And came with all his youth and unblown hopes
On the world's heart, and touched it into tears."

## Dreamthorp

[Alexander Smith is primarily known as a poet, but he has claims to distinction as an essayist as well. He published a volume of twelve essays called *Dreamthorp* (1863), after one of its principal works. The volume was not particularly well received and he did not publish another, though a second collection appeared after his death. "Dreamthorp" is an example of the "familiar essay," that is, one to be valued for personality, and style.]

It matters not to relate how or when I became a denizen of Dreamthorp; it will be sufficient to say that I am not a born native, but that I came to reside in it a good while ago now. The several towns and villages in which, in my time, I have pitched a tent did not please, for one obscure reason or another: this one was too large, t'other too small; but when, on a summer evening about the hour of eight, I first beheld Dreamthorp, with its westward-looking windows painted by sunset, its children playing in the single straggling street, the mothers knitting at the open doors, the fathers standing about in long white blouses, chatting or smoking; the great tower of the ruined castle rising high into the rosy air, with a whole troop of swallows—by distance made as small as gnats—skimming about its rents and fissures;—when I first beheld all this, I felt instinctively that my knapsack might be taken off my shoulders, that my tired feet might wander no more, that at last, on the planet, I had found a home.

From that evening I have dwelt here, and the only journey I am like now to make, is the very inconsiderable one, so far at least as distance is concerned, from the house in which I live to the graveyard beside the ruined castle. There, with the former inhabitants of the place, I trust to sleep quietly enough, and nature will draw over our heads her coverlet of green sod, and tenderly tuck us in, as a mother her sleeping ones, so that no sound from the world shall ever reach us, and no sorrow trouble us any more.

The village stands far inland: and the streams that trot through the soft green valleys all about have as little knowledge of the sea, as the three-years' child of the storms and passions of manhood. The surrounding country is smooth and green, full of undulations; and pleasant country roads strike through it in every direction, bound for distant towns and villages, yet in no hurry to reach them.

On these roads the lark in summer is continually heard; nests are plentiful in the hedges and dry ditches; and on the grassy banks, and at the feet of the bowed dikes, the blue-eyed speedwell smiles its benison on the passing wayfarer.

On these roads you may walk for a year and encounter nothing more remarkable than the country cart, troops of tawny children from the woods, laden with primroses, and at long intervals— for people in this district live to a ripe age —a black funeral creeping in from some remote hamlet, and to this last the people reverently doff their hats and stand aside.

Death does not walk about here often, but when he does, he receives as much respect as the squire himself. Everything round one is unhurried, quiet, moss-grown, and orderly. Season follows in the track of season, and one year can hardly be distinguished from another. Time should be measured here by the silent dial, rather than by the ticking clock, or by the chimes of the church.

Dreamthorp can boast of a respectable antiquity, and in it the trade of the builder is unknown. Ever since I remember, not a single stone has been laid on the top of another. The castle, inhabited now by jackdaws and starlings, is old; the chapel which adjoins it is older still; and the lake behind both, and in which their shadows sleep, is, I suppose, as old as Adam. A fountain in the marketplace, all mouths and faces and curious arabesques—as dry, however, as the castle moat—has a tradition connected with it; and a great noble riding through the street one day several hundred years ago, was shot from a window by a man whom he had injured. The death of this noble is the chief link which connects the place with authentic history. The houses are old, and remote dates may yet be deciphered on the stones above the doors; the apple-trees are mossed and ancient; countless generations of sparrows have bred in the thatched roofs, and thereon have chirped out their lives. In every room of the place men have been born, men have died.

On Dreamthorp centuries have fallen, and have left no more trace than have last winter's snowflakes. This commonplace sequence and flowing on of life is immeasurably affecting. That winter morning when Charles lost his head in front of the banqueting-hall of his own palace, the icicles hung from the eaves of the houses here, and the clown kicked the snowballs from his clouted shoon, and thought but of his supper when, at three o'clock, the red sun set in the purple mist.

On that Sunday in June while Waterloo was going on, the gossips, after morning service, stood on the country roads discussing agricultural prospects, without the slightest suspicion that the day passing over their heads would be a famous one in the calendar.

Battles have been fought, kings have died, history has transacted itself; but, all-unheeding and untouched, Dreamthorp has watched apple-trees redden, and wheat ripen, and smoked its pipe, and quaffed its mug of beer, and rejoiced over its newborn children, and with proper solemnity carried its dead to the churchyard.

As I gaze on the village of my adoption, I think of many things very far removed and seem to get closer to them. The last setting sun that Shakespeare saw reddened the windows here, and struck warmly on the faces of the hinds coming home from the fields. The mighty storm that raged while Cromwell lay a-dying made all the oak-woods groan round about here, and tore the thatch from the very roofs I gaze upon. When I think of this, I can almost, so to speak, lay my hand on Shakespeare and on Cromwell. These poor walls were contemporaries of both, and I find something affecting in the thought. The mere soil is, of course, far older than either, but it does not touch one in the same way. A wall is the creation of a human hand, the soil is not.

This place suits my whim, and I like it better year after year. As with everything else, since I began to love it I find it gradually growing beautiful. Dreamthorp—a castle, a chapel, a lake, a straggling strip of gray houses, with a blue film of smoke over all—lies embosomed in emerald. Summer, with its daisies, runs up to every cottage door. From the little height where I am now sitting, I see it beneath me. Nothing could be more peaceful. The wind and the birds fly over it. A passing sunbeam makes brilliant a white gable-end, and brings out the colors of the blossomed apple-tree beyond, and disappears. I see figures in the street, but hear them not. The hands on the church clock seem always pointing to one hour. Time has fallen asleep in the afternoon sunshine; I make a frame of my fingers, and look at my picture. On the walls of the next Academy's Exhibition will hang nothing half so beautiful.

My village is, I think, a special favorite of summer's. Every window-sill in it she touches with color and fragrance; everywhere she wakens the drowsy murmurs of the hives: every place she scents with apple-blossom. Traces of her hand are to be seen on the weir beside the ruined mill: and even the canal, along which the barges come and go, has a great white water-lily asleep on its olive-colored face.

Never was velvet on a monarch's robe so gorgeous as the green mosses that beruff the roofs of farm and cottage, when the sunbeam slants on them and goes. The old road out towards the common, and the hoary dikes that might have been built in the reign of Alfred, have not been forgotten by the generous adorning season; for every fissure has its mossy cushion, and the old blocks themselves are washed by the loveliest gray-green lichens in the world, and the large loose stones lying on the ground have gathered to themselves the peacefulest mossy coverings. Some of these have not been disturbed for a century.

Summer has adorned my village as gaily, and taken as much pleasure in the task, as the people of old, when Elizabeth was queen, took in the adornment of the May-pole against a summer festival. And, just think, not only Dreamthorp, but every English village she has made beautiful after one fashion or another—making vivid green the hill slope on which straggling white Welsh hamlets hang right opposite the sea; drowning in apple-blossom the red Sussex ones in the fat valley. And think, once more, every spear of grass in England she has touched with a livelier green; the crest of every bird she has burnished; every old wall between the four seas has received her mossy and licheny attentions; every nook in every forest she has sown with pale flowers, every marsh she has dashed with the fires of the marigold. And in the wonderful night the moon knows, she hangs the planet on which so many millions of us fight, and sin, and agonize, and die—a sphere of glow-worm light.

Having discoursed so long about Dreamthorp, it is but fair that I should now introduce you to her lions. These are, for the most part, of a commonplace kind; and I am afraid that, if you wish to find romance in them you must bring it with you. I might speak of the old church tower, or of the church-yard beneath it, in which the village holds its dead, each resting-place marked by a simple stone, on which is inscribed the name and age of the sleeper, and a Scripture text beneath, in which live our hopes of immortality.

But, on the whole, perhaps it will be better to begin with the canal, which wears on its olive-colored face the big white water-lily already chronicled. Such a secluded place is Dreamthorp that the railway does not come near, and the canal is the only thing that connects it with the world. It stands high, and from it the undulating country may be seen stretching away into the gray of distance, with hills and woods, and stains of smoke which mark the sites of villages.

Every now and then a horse comes staggering along the towing-path, trailing a sleepy barge filled with merchandise. A quiet, indolent life these barge-men lead in the summer days. One lies stretched at his length on the sunheated plank; his comrade sits smoking in the little dog-hutch, which I suppose he calls a cabin. Silently they come and go; silently the wooden bridge lifts to let them through. The horse stops at the bridgehouse for a drink, and there I like to talk a little with the men. They serve instead of a newspaper, and retail with great willingness the news they have picked up in their progress from town to town. I am told they sometimes marvel who the old gentleman is who accosts them from beneath a huge umbrella in the sun, and that they think him either very wise or very foolish. Not in the least unnatural. We are great friends, I believe—evidence of which they occasionally exhibit by requesting me to disburse a trifle for drink-money.

This canal is a great haunt of mine of an evening. The water hardly invites one to bathe in it, and a delicate stomach might suspect the flavor of the eels caught therein; yet, to my thinking, it is not in the least destitute of beauty. A barge trailing up through it in the sunset is a pretty sight; and the heavenly crimsons and purples sleep quite lovingly upon its glossy ripples. Nor does the evening star disdain it, for as I walk along I see it mirrored therein as clearly as in the waters of the Mediterranean itself.

The old castle and chapel already alluded to are, perhaps, to a stranger, the points of attraction in Dreamthorp. Back from the houses is the lake, on the green sloping banks of which, with broken windows and tombs, the ruins stand. As it is noon, and the weather is warm, let us go and sit on a turret. Here, on these very steps, as old ballads tell, a queen sat once, day after day, looking southward for the light of returning spears.

I bethink me that yesterday, no further gone, I went to visit a consumptive shoemaker; seated here I can single out his very house, nay, the very window of the room in which he is lying. On that straw roof might the raven alight, and flap his sable wings. There, at this moment, is the supreme tragedy being enacted. A woman is weeping there, and little children are looking on with a sore bewilderment. Before nightfall the poor peaked face of the bowed artisan will have gathered its ineffable peace, and the widow will be led away from the bedside by the tenderness of neighbors, and the cries of the orphan brood will be stilled.

And yet this present indubitable suffering and loss does not touch me like the sorrow of the woman of the ballad, the phantom probably of a minstrel's brain. The shoemaker will be forgotten—I shall be forgotten; and long after visitors will sit here and look out on the landscape and murmur the simple lines. But why do death and dying obtrude themselves at the present moment?

On the turret opposite, about the distance of a gunshot, is as pretty a sight as eye could wish to see. Two young people, strangers apparently, have come to visit the ruin. Neither the ballad queen, nor the shoemaker down yonder, whose respirations are getting shorter and shorter, touches them in the least. They are merry and happy, and the graybeard turret has not the heart to thrust a foolish moral upon them. They would not thank him if he did, I daresay. Perhaps they could not understand him. Time enough! Twenty years hence they will be able to sit down at his feet, and count griefs with him, and tell him tale for tale. Human hearts get ruinous in so much less time than stone walls and towers. See, the young man has thrown himself down at the girl's feet on a little space of grass. In her scarlet cloak she looks like a blossom springing out of a crevice on the ruined steps. He gives her a flower, and she bows her face down over it almost to her knees. What did the flower say? Is it to hide a blush? He looks delighted; and I almost fancy I see a proud color on his brow. As I gaze, these young people make for me a perfect idyll. The generous, ungrudging sun, the melancholy ruin, decked, like mad Lear, with the flowers and ivies of forgetfulness and grief, and between them, sweet and evanescent, human truth and love.

Love!—does it yet walk the world, or is it imprisoned in poems and romances? Has not the circulating library become the sole home of the passion? Is love not become the exclusive property of novelists and playwrights, to be used by them only for professional purposes? Surely, if the men I see are lovers, or ever have been lovers, they would be nobler than they are. The knowledge that he is beloved should—*must* make a man tender, gentle, upright, pure.

While yet a youngster in a jacket, I can remember falling desperately in love with a young lady several years my senior—after the fashion of youngsters in jackets.

Could I have fibbed in these days? Could I have betrayed a comrade? Could I have stolen eggs or callow young from the nest? Could I have stood quietly by and seen the weak or the maimed bullied? Nay, verily. In these absurd days she lighted up the whole world for me. To sit in the same room with her was like the happiness of perpetual holiday; when she asked me to run a message for her, or to do any, the slightest, service for her, I felt as if a patent of nobility were conferred on me. I kept my passion to myself, like a cake, and nibbled it in private.

Juliet was several years my senior, and had a lover— was, in point of fact, actually engaged; and, in looking back, I can remember I was too much in love to feel the slightest twinge of jealousy. I remember also seeing Romeo for the first time, and thinking him a greater man than Caesar or Napoleon. The worth I credited him with, the cleverness, the goodness, the everything! He awed me by his manner and bearing. He accepted that girl's love coolly and as a matter of course: it put him no more about than a crown and scepter puts about a king. What I would have given my life to possess—being only fourteen, it was not much to part with after all— he wore lightly, as he wore his gloves or his cane. It did not seem a bit too good for him. His self-possession appalled me. If I had seen him take the sun out of the sky, and put it into his breeches' pocket, I don't think I should have been in the least degree surprised.

Well, years after, when I had discarded my passion with my jacket, I have assisted this middle-aged Romeo home from a roistering wine party, and heard him hiccup out his marital annoyances, with the strangest remembrances of old times, and the strangest deductions therefrom. Did that man with the idiotic laugh and the blurred utterance ever love? Was he ever capable of loving? I protest I have my doubts. But where are my young people? Gone! So it is always. We begin to moralize and look wise, and Beauty, who is something of a coquette, and of an exacting turn of mind, and likes attentions, gets disgusted with our wisdom or our stupidity, and goes off in a huff. Let the baggage go!

The ruined chapel adjoins the ruined castle on which I am now sitting, and is evidently a building of much older date. It is a mere shell now. It is quite roofless, ivy covers it in part; the stone tracery of the great western window is yet intact, but the colored glass is gone with the splendid vestments of the abbot, the fuming incense, the chanting choirs, and the patient, sad-eyed monks, who muttered *Aves,* shrived guilt, and illuminated missals.

Time was when this place breathed actual benedictions, and was a home of active peace. At present it is visited only by the stranger, and delights but the antiquary. The village people have so little respect for it, that they do not even consider it haunted. There are several tombs in the interior bearing knights' escutcheons, which time has sadly defaced. The dust you stand upon is noble. Earls have been brought here in dinted mail from battle, and earls' wives from the pangs of child-bearing. The last trumpet will break the slumber of a right honorable company.

One of the tombs—the most perfect of all in point of preservation—I look at often, and try to conjecture what it commemorates. With all my fancies, I can get no further than the old story of love and death. There, on the slab, the white figures sleep; marble hands, folded in prayer, on marble breasts. And I like to think that he was brave, she beautiful; that although the monument is worn by time, and sullied by the stains of the weather, the qualities which it commemorates—husbandly and wifely affection, courtesy, courage, knightly scorn of wrong and falsehood, meekness, penitence, charity—-are existing yet somewhere, recognizable by each other. The man who in this world can keep the whiteness of his soul, is not likely to lose it in any other.

In summer I spent a good deal of time floating about the lake. The landing-place to which my boat is tethered is ruinous, like the chapel and palace, and my embarkation causes quite a stir in the sleepy little village. Small boys leave their games and mud-pies, and gather round in silence; they have seen me get off a hundred times, but their interest in the matter seems always new. Not unfrequently an idle cobbler, in red nightcap and leathern apron, leans on a broken stile, and honors my proceedings with his attention. I shoot off, and the human knot dissolves.

The lake contains three islands, each with a solitary tree, and on these islands the swans breed. I feed the birds daily with bits of bread. See, one comes gliding towards me, with superbly arched neck, to receive its customary alms! How wildly beautiful its motions! How haughtily it begs! The green pasture lands run down to the edge of the water, and into it in the afternoons the red kine wade and stand knee-deep in their shadows, surrounded by troops of flies. Patiently the honest creatures abide the attacks of their tormentors. Now one swishes itself with its tail—now its neighbor flaps a huge ear.

I draw my oars alongside, and let my boat float at its own will. The soft blue heavenly abysses, the wandering streams of vapor, the long beaches of rippled cloud, are glassed and repeated in the lake. Dreamthorp is silent as a picture, the voices of the children are mute; and the smoke from the houses, the blue pillars all sloping in one angle, float upward as if in sleep. Grave and stern the old castle rises from its emerald banks, which long ago came down to the lake in terrace on terrace, gay with fruits and flowers, and with stone nymph and satyrs hid in every nook. Silent and empty enough today.

A flock of daws suddenly bursts out from a turret, and round and round they wheel, as if in panic. Has some great scandal exploded? Has a conspiracy been discovered? Has a revolution broken out? The excitement has subsided. and one of them, perched on the old banner-staff, chatters confidentially to himself as he, sideways, eyes the world beneath him. Floating about thus, time passes swiftly, for, before I know where I am, the kine have withdrawn from the lake to couch on the herbage, while one on a little height is lowing for the milkmaid and her pails. Along the road I see the laborers coming home for supper, while the sun setting behind me makes the village windows blaze; and so I take out my oars, and pull leisurely through waters faintly flushed with evening colors.

I do not think that Mr. Buckle could have written his *History of Civilization* in Dreamthorp, because in it books, conversation, and the other appurtenances of intellectual life, are not to be procured. I am acquainted with birds, and the building of nests—with wild-flowers, and the seasons in which they blow—but with the big world far away, with what men and women are thinking, and doing, and saying, I am acquainted only through the *Times,* and the occasional magazine or review, sent by friends whom I have not looked upon for years, but by whom, it seems, I am not yet forgotten. The village has but few intellectual wants, and the intellectual supply is strictly measured by the demand.

Still there is something. Down in the village, and opposite the curiously-carved fountain, is a schoolroom which can accommodate a couple of hundred people on a pinch. There are our public meetings held. Musical entertainments have been given there by a single performer. In that schoolroom last winter an American biologist terrified the villagers, and, to their simple understandings, mingled up the next world with this.

Now and again some rare bird of an itinerant lecturer covers dead walls with posters, yellow and blue, and to that schoolroom we flock to hear him. His rounded periods the eloquent gentleman devolves amidst a respectful silence. His audience do not understand him, but they see that the clergyman does, and the doctor does; and so they are content, and look as attentive and wise as possible.

Then, in connection with the schoolroom, there is a public library, where books are exchanged once a month. This library is a kind of Greenwich Hospital for disabled novels and romances. Each of these books has been in the wars; some are unquestionable antiques. The tears of three generations have fallen upon their dusky pages. The heroes and the heroines are of another age than ours. Sir Charles Grandison is standing with his hat under his arm. Tom Jones plops from the tree into the water, to the infinite distress of Sophia. Moses comes home from market with his stock of shagreen spectacles. Lovers, warriors, and villains—-as dead to the present generation of readers as Cambyses—-are weeping, fighting, and intriguing.

These books, tattered and torn as they are, are read with delight today. The viands are celestial if set forth on a dingy tablecloth. The gaps and chasms which occur in pathetic or perilous chapters are felt to be personal calamities. It is with a certain feeling of tenderness that I look upon these books; I think of the dead fingers that have turned over the leaves, of the dead eyes that have traveled along the lines.

An old novel has a history of its own. When fresh and new, and before it had breathed its secret, it lay on my lady's table. She killed the weary day with it, and when night came it was placed beneath her pillow. At the sea-side a couple of foolish heads have bent over it, hands have touched and tingled, and it has heard vows and protestations as passionate as any its pages contained. Coming down in the world, Cinderella in the kitchen has blubbered over it by the light of a surreptitious candle, conceiving herself the while the magnificent Georgiana, and Lord Mordaunt, Georgiana's lover, the pot-boy round the corner. Tied up with many a dingy brother, the auctioneer knocks the bundle down to the bidder of a few pence, and it finds its way to the quiet cove of some village library, where with some difficulty—-as if from want of teeth, and with numerous interruptions—-as if from lack of memory, it tells its old stories, and wakes tears, and blushes, and laughter as of yore. Thus it spends its age, and in a few years it will become unintelligible, and then, in the dust-bin, like poor human mortals in the grave, it will rest from all its labors.

It is impossible to estimate the benefit which such books have conferred. How often have they loosed the chain of circumstance. What unfamiliar tears—what unfamiliar laughter they have caused. What chivalry and tenderness they have infused into rustic loves. Of what weary hours they have cheated and beguiled their readers. The big, solemn history-books are in excellent preservation; the story-books are defaced and frayed, and their out-of-elbows condition is their pride, and the best justification of their existence. They are tashed, as roses are, by being eagerly handled and smelt. I observe, too, that the most ancient romances are not in every case the most severely worn. It is the pace that tells in horses, men, and books. There are Nestors wonderfully hale; there are juveniles in a state of dilapidation. One of the youngest books, *The Old Curiosity Shop*, is absolutely falling to pieces. That book, like Italy, is possessor of the fatal gift; but happily, in its case, everything can be rectified by a new edition. We have buried warriors and poets, princes and queens, but no one of these was followed to the grave by sincerer mourners than was little Nell.

Besides the itinerant lecturer, and the permanent library, we have the Sunday sermon. These sum up the intellectual aids and furtherances of the whole place. We have a church and a chapel, and I attend both. The Dreamthorp people are Dissenters, for the most part; why, I never could understand; because dissent implies a certain intellectual effort. But Dissenters they are, and Dissenters they are likely to remain. In an ungainly building, filled with hard gaunt pews, without an organ, without a touch of color in the windows, with nothing to stir the imagination or the devotional sense, the simple people worship. On Sunday, they are put upon a diet of spiritual bread-and-water. Personally, I should desire more generous food. But the laboring people listen attentively, till once they fall asleep, and they wake up to receive the benediction with a feeling of having done their duty. They know they ought to go to chapel, and they go.

I go likewise, from habit, although I have long ago lost the power of following a discourse. In my pew, and whilst the clergyman is going on, I think of the strangest things—of the tree at the window, of the congregation of the dead outside, of the wheat-fields and the corn-fields beyond and all around. And the odd thing is, that it is during sermon only that my mind flies off at a tangent and busies itself with things removed from the place and the circumstances. Whenever it is finished, fancy returns from her wanderings, and I am alive to the objects around me. The clergyman knows my humor, and is good Christian enough to forgive me; and he smiles good-humoredly when I ask him to let me have the chapel keys, that I may enter, when in the mood, and preach a sermon to myself. To my mind, an empty chapel is impressive; a crowded one, comparatively a commonplace affair. Alone, I could choose my own text, and my silent discourse would not be without its practical applications.

An idle life I live in this place, as the world counts it; but then I have the satisfaction of differing from the world as to the meaning of idleness. A windmill twirling its arms all day is admirable only when there is corn to grind. Twirling its arms for the mere barren pleasure of twirling them, or for the sake of looking busy, does not deserve any rapturous paean of praise. I must be made happy after my own fashion, not after the fashion of other people. Here I can live as I please, here I can throw the reins on the neck of my whim. Here I play with my own thoughts; here I ripen for the grave.

## ISA CRAIG KNOX (1831– ? )

### The Woodruffe

Thou art the flower of grief to me,
Tis in thy flavor.
Thou keepest the scent of memory,
A sickly savor.
In the moonlight, under the orchard tree,
Thou wert plucked and given to me,
For a love favor.

In the moonlight, under the orchard tree,
Ah, cruel flower,
Thou wert plucked and given to me,
While a fruitless shower
Of blossoms rained on the ground where grew
The woodruffe bed all wet with dew,
In the witching hour.

Under the orchard tree that night
Thy scent was sweetness,
And thou, with thy small star clusters bright
Of pure completeness,
Shedding a pearly luster bright,
Seemed, as I gazed in the meek moonlight,
A gift of meetness.

"It keeps the scent for years," said he,
(And thou hast kept it);

"And when you scent it, think of me."
(He could not mean thus bitterly.)
Ah, I had swept it
Into the dust where dead things rot,
Had I then believed his love was not
What I have wept it.

Between the leaves of this holy book,
O flower undying,
A worthless and withered weed in look
I keep thee lying.
The bloom of my life with thee was plucked,
And a close-pressed grief its sap hath sucked,
It strength updrying.

Thy circles of leaves, like pointed spears,
My heart pierce often;
They enter, it inly bleeds, no tears
The hid wounds soften;
Yet one will I ask to bury thee
In the soft white folds of my shroud with me,
Ere they close my coffin.

## The Way in the Wood

A wood lies on the shore,
Filled with murmurs, as each tree
Learned the music of the sea,
Which it heareth all the day,
Ever growing more and more,
Or fading far away.

And standing on that shore,
The past comes back to me,
In that music of the sea,
And that murmur of the wood,
Ever fading far away,
Yet evermore renewed.

In the weird and ancient wood,
There are fairy lights that fall,
Never by the sunshine made;
And a flicker and a shade,
Where no substance is at all.
There are thrilling touches laid

By no hand on head and shoulder;
Things that peep from leaf and blade
And blossom, when there's no beholder;
And we walk as in a story

Through the gloom and through the glory
Of the weird and ancient wood.

Through the gloom and through the glory
Of the ancient wood beheld,
Comes in glimpses, like her story,
A maiden of the times of Eld;
Like a young fawn, unafraid,
Straying through its own green glade.
Now a little rill she crosses,
Stealing through the velvet mosses,
From the hollow, where the trees
Stand in groups of twos and threes,
Wide-armed, bountiful, and spread
As for blessing overhead;
While the thick grass underfoot
Shelters violets round each root,
And on tender lap receives
Soft the fall of dying leaves.

All along the maiden's way,
Glades are opening, glad and green,
Ever tempting her to stray
From the bare brown path between.
Some one surely called her name!
Was it but the wood-dove cooing?
And that beck'ning, was't the same
As the plumy ferns are doing?
In each foxglove bell the bee
Swings himself right merrily,
Every bell by turns he tries,
He is buried head and thighs.
Now on that side, now on this,
Does a bird his song repeat,
Quivering at its close with bliss
Far too full and far too sweet
For the little throat to utter;
Here a whir, and there a flutter,
Here a coo, and there a call,
Here a dart, and there a spring,
Tokened happy creatures all.
Now and then awhile she stood,
Wishful that they might come near her,
Wistful half that they should fear her,
Silence in her attitude.

Now the sunny noon is high,
And upon a bank she sits,

Shade on shade around her flits—
On the bank's embroidery—
Star and heart of leaf inwrought,
Mazy as a poet's thought—
One doth rest beside the maid
In the mystic light and shade.
Into silence sweet subdued,
In the dim heart of the wood
Many paths together meet,
And companionship is sweet.

Sounds as of a river flowing
Through the forest depths are going,
And the distant murmurs seem
Like a river in a dream,
For the path is carried far
Over precipice and scaur*, steep hill
And beneath it runs the river,
Flowing onward, flowing ever,
Drawing down the little rills
From the rocks and from the hills,
To the bosom of the sea.
Here the daisies disappear,
Shadows on the pathway brown
Falling ever thicklier down,
Something like a thrill of fear
Touches trembling lip and limb,
And the violets in her eyes,
Blue beneath the open skies,
Seem to grow more large and dim.
Round and round, for rood on rood,
Trees are growing, trees are throwing
Shades of ill and shades of good,
Arms of shelter fondly flinging,
Arms of murder fiercely clinging,
Stifling in their close embraces,
Throes of terror and afright,
While some meekly in their places
Die of pining for the light.

Closely heart to heart will beat,
Closely lip with lip will meet,
Where the branch and bow embraces,
And the light and shade enlaces;
Hands of trust in his she places,
And her heaven is in his eyes,
Linked together as they rise
To go forward, but he chooses

Smoother than he would, refuses
Peril for her sake;—thus may
He be guarded still in guarding,
And be guided still in guiding,
Ill from the beloved warding,
Blessing to himself betiding.

In mid-forest oaks and beeches,
Thick and tow'ring, hold the ground;
By the river's winding reaches
Trees of every leaf are found;
Here the ash with arms all knotted,
Into anguished writhings grew;
Here the sickly alder rotted;
On a mound an ancient yew;
And the willows in the water
Trailed their tresses silver gray.
Aspen, when the low wind caught her,
Sighed through every trembling spray;
Lady birch so light and gay,
Something sad that wind had taught her,
For each slender limb would quiver:
While upon the moaning river,
Flags of drowned lilies lay.

In the forest depths unknown,
Once more is the maid alone;
And she hears the moaning river,
Hears the ivy near her shiver,
Hears the rain upon the leaves,
Beating with a sound that grieves;
On the path her feet are slipping,
Tween the river and the rock,
All the adder's-tongues are dripping,
Wet is every ruddy lock
Of her hair, and when she lays
Her small lily hand, and stays
Trembling steps, the worm is crawling,
Toads beneath her feet are sprawling,
And her very soul is faint
With the dank air's deathly taint.

She hath reached a tree whose head
Still is green, whose heart is dead;
Her wet robe about her clings,
And she sinks upon the ground,
Heedless of the loathly things,
Where her slain knight she hath found,

Lying white among the green
Of the ferns that strive to screen,
From the staring of the light,
Those dead eyes, a ghastly sight.

By the river sat the maiden,
With the burden of her pain.
Downward flowed the river laden
With the burden of the rain.
In that dark and swollen flood,
Who had known the little rill
At the entrance of the wood?
Who had known that maiden still?
When the dismal pall of night
Came and wrapt her grief from sight;
And there rose upon the blast,
In the dark hours wailing past,
Mingled groan and shriek and sigh—
More than mortal agony.

Ere long in that solitude
Rose the forest sanctuary,
Where the holy dead they bury,
Tween the murmur of the river,
And the murmur of the wood,
Filled with pleading sound for ever;
And a slain knight's moldering bones
Rest beneath its chancel stones.

Yellow, yellow leaves
All grown pale with sighing;—
For the sweet days dead,
For the sad days dying,
Yellow, yellow leaves,
How the parting grieves.

Yellow, yellow leaves,
Falling, falling, falling.
Death is best, when hope
There is no recalling;
Yet O, yellow leaves
How the parting grieves.

## JAMES MACFARLAN (1832–1862)

### The Midnight Train

Across the dull and brooding night
A giant flies with demon light,
And breath of wreathing smoke.
Around him whirls the reeling plain,
And with a dash of grim disdain
He cleaves the sundered rock.

In lonely swamps the low wind stirs
The belt of black funereal firs,
That murmur to the sky,
Till, startled by his mad career,
They seem to keep a hush of fear,
As if a god swept by.

Through many a dark wild heart of heath,
Oer booming bridges, where beneath
A midnight river brawls;
By ruins, remnants of the past,
Their ivies trembling in the blast;
By singing waterfalls;

The slumb'rer on his silent bed
Turns to the light his lonely head,
Divested of its dream.
Long leagues of gloom are hurried oer,
Through tunnel-sheaths, with iron roar,
And shrill night-rending scream.

Past huddling huts, past flying farms,
High furnace flames, whose crimson arms
Are grappling with the night,
He tears along receding lands,
To where the kingly city stands,
Wrapt in a robe of light.

Here, round each wide and gushing gate,
A crowd of eager faces wait,
And every smile is known.
We thank thee, O thou Titan train,
That in the city once again
We clasp our loved, our own.

## The Ruined City

The shadows of a thousand springs,
Unnumbered sunsets, sternly sleep
Above the dust of perished things
That form this city's blasted heap.
Dull watch the crumbling columns keep
Against the fierce relentless sky;
Hours, that no dial noteth, creep
Like unremembered phantoms by;
And still this city of the dead
Gives echo to no human tread.

A curse is writ on every stone.
The temple's latest pillar lies
Like some white mammoth's bleaching bone.
Its altars know no deities.
Fine columns of a palace rise,
And when the sun is red and low,
And glaring in the molten skies,
A shadow huge these columns throw,
That like some dark colossal hand
In silence creeps across the sand.

The senate slumbers, wondrous hive
Of counsels sage, of subtle schemes;
But does no lingering tone survive
To prove their presence more than dreams?
No light of revelation beams
Around that voiceless forum now,
Time bears upon his restless streams
No reflex of the haughty brow
That oft has frowned a nation's fate
Here—where dark reptiles congregate.

Where, where is now the regal rag
That clothed the monarch of yon tower,
On which the rank weed flaps its flag
Across the dusk this somber hour?
Alas, for pomp, alas, for power,
When time unveils their nakedness.
And valor's strength and beauty's flower
Find nought to echo their distress;
And flattery—fine delusive breath—
Melts in the iron grasp of death.

Day rises with an angry glance,
As if to blight the stagnant air,
And hurls his fierce and fiery lance

On that doomed city's forehead bare.
The sunset's wild and wandering hair
Streams backward like a comet's mane,
And from the deep and sullen glare
The shuddering columns crouch in vain,
And through the wreck of wrathful years
The grim hyena stalks and sneers.

## FRANCIS ERSKINE, EARL ROSSLYN (1833–1890)

### Memory

I still keep open memory's chamber: still
Drink from the fount of youth's perennial stream.
It may be in old age an idle dream
Of those dear children; but beyond my will
They come again, and dead affections thrill
My pulseless heart, for now once more they seem
To be alive, and wayward fancies teem
In my fond brain, and all my senses fill.
Come, Alice, leave your books; tis I who call.
Bind up your hair, and teasing—did you say
Kissing—that kitten? Evey, come with me.
Mary, grave darling, take my hand: yes, all.
I have three hands today, a holiday.
A holiday, Papa? Woe's me—tis memory.

## GEORGE MCCRAE (1833– ? )

[Born in Scotland, McCrae spent a good part of his life in Australia, and is sometimes considered an Australian poet. Much of his work is on Australian subjects, especially stories of its aborigines.]

### Forby Sutherland
A Story of Botany Bay—A.D. 1770

A lane of elms in June;—the air
Of eve is cool and calm and sweet.
See, straying here a youthful pair,
With sad and slowly moving feet,

On hand in hand to yon gray gate,
Oer which the rosy apples swing;
And there they vow a mingled fate,
One day when George the Third is king.

The ring scarce clasped her finger fair,
When, tossing in their ivied tower,
The distant bells made all the air
Melodious with that golden hour.

Then sank the sun out oer the sea,
Sweet day of courtship fond, . . . the last.
The holy hours of twilight flee
And speed to join the sacred past.

The house-dove on the moss-grown thatch
Is murmuring love songs to his mate,
As lovely Nell now lifts the latch
Beneath the apples at the gate.

A plighted maid she nears her home,
Those gentle eyes with weeping red.
Too soon her swain must breast the foam,
Alas, with that last hour he fled.

And, ah, that dust cloud on the road,
Yon heartless coach-guard's blaring horn;
But naught beside, that spoke or showed
Her sailor to poor Nell forlorn.

She dreams; and lo, a ship that plows
A foamy furrow through the seas,
As, plunging gaily, from her bows
She scatters diamonds on the breeze.

Swift, homeward bound, with flags displayed
In pennoned pomp, with drum and fife,
And all the proud old-world parade
That marks the man-o'-war man's life.

She dreams and dreams; her heart's at sea;
Dreams while she wears the golden ring.
Her spirit follows lovingly
One humble servant of the king.

And thus for years, since hope survives
To cheer the maid and nerve the youth.
"Forget-me-not"—how fair it thrives
Where planted in the soil of truth.

The skies are changed; and oer the sea,
Within a calm, sequestered nook,
Rests at her anchor thankfully
The tall-sterned ship of gallant Cook.

The emerald shores ablaze with flowers,
The sea reflects the smiling sky,
Soft breathes the air of perfumed bowers—
How sad to leave it all, and die.

To die, when all around is fair
And steeped in beauty;—ah, tis hard

When ease and joy succeed to care,
And rest, to watch and mounted guard.

But harder still, when one dear plan,
The end of all his life and cares,
Hangs by a thread; the dying man
Most needs our sympathy and prayers.

Twas thus with Forby as he lay
Wan in his narrow canvas cot;
Sole tenant of the lone sick bay.
Though mates came round, he heard them not.

For days his spirit strove and fought,
But, ah, the frame was all too weak.
Some phantom strange it seemed he sought,
And vainly tried to rise and speak.

At last he smiled and brightened up,
The noonday bugle went; and he
Drained (twas his last) the cooling cup
A messmate offered helpfully.

His tongue was loosed—"I hear the horn!
Ah, Nell, *my number's flying*. See—
The horses too;—they've had their corn.
Alas, dear love . . . I part from thee."

He waved his wasted hand, and cried,
"Sweet Nell, dear maid, my own true Nell.
The coach won't wait for me." . . . and died—
And this was Forby's strange farewell.

Next morn the barge, with muffled oars,
Pulls slowly forth, and leaves the slip
With flags half-mast, and gains the shores,
While silence seals each comrade's lip.

They bury him beneath a tree,
His treasure in his bosom hid.
What was that treasure? Go and see.
Long since it burst his coffin lid.

Nell gave to Forby, once in play,
Some hips of roses, with the seeds
Of hedgerow plants, and flowerets gay
(In England such might count for weeds).

"Take these," cries smiling Nell, "to sow
In foreign lands; and when folk see
The English roses bloom and grow,
Some one may bless an unknown me."

The turf lies green on Forby's bed,
A hundred years have passed, and more,
But twining over Forby's head
Are Nell's sweet roses on that shore.

The violet and the eglantine,
With sweet-breathed cowslips, deck the spot,
And nestling mid them in the shine,
The meek, blue-eyed forget-me not.

## JOHN NICHOL (1833–1894)

### Love Endures

My love, my love, the golden hours
Have come at last for you and me.
Fresh fragrance floats above the flowers,
A morning glory oer the sea.

The breeze long-lingering comes, and brings
The feeling of a new delight,
It comes with healing on its wings
To chase the shadows of the night.

Our honeymoon they say is oer,
And yet our walks are sweet as ever;
Whether we watch the purple shore,
Or ramble by the winding river.

The noontide in a sultry clime
Burns fiercely on the silent sands.
The cool of evening is the time
When song-birds sing in southern lands.

Thus, though my passion grows more calm,
That feverish pulse that throbs and dies,
Still from your lips I gather balm,
And inspiration from your eyes.

The world moves onward, but our love
Grows deeper, stronger, day by day,
Draws clearer accents from above,
And leads us by a nobler way.

My honeymoon they say is oer;
My happy years are but begun,
With thee to gleam a star before
My path, till all my work is done.

Good-night, my love, good-night.
The song that the sea is singing
Is gentle and soft tonight.

The luster the stars are flinging
On the bay is tender and bright.
The bark like a bird is springing
Along the waves tonight,
And a tune in my head keeps ringing
That makes my heart more light.
Goodnight, my love, goodnight.

### H. W. L.[1]

The roar of Niagara dies away,
The fever heats of war and traffic fade,
While the soft twilight melts the glare of day
In this new Helicon, the muses' glade.

The roof that sheltered Washington's retreat,
Thy home of homes, America, I find
In this memorial mansion, where we greet
The full-toned lyrist, with the gentle mind.

Here have thy chosen spirits met and flowered,
Season on season, neath magnetic spells
Of him who, in his refuge, rose-embowered,
Remote from touch of envious passion dwells.

Here Concord's sage and Harvard's wit contend:
The wise, the true, the learned of the land.
Grave thoughts, gay fantasies together blend
In subtle converse, neath his fostering hand.

With other forms than those of mortal guest
The house is haunted; visions of the morn,
Voices of night that soothe the soul to rest,
Attend the shapes, by aery wand reborn.

Serene companions of a vanished age,
Noiseless they tread the once familiar floors;
Or, later offspring of the poet's page,
They throng the threshold, crowd the corridors.

"Sweet Preciosa" beside the listening stair
Flutters expectant while Victorian sings.
Evangeline, with cloistral eyes of prayer,
Folds her white hands, in shade of angels' wings.

Conquistadors of Castile pace the hall;
Or red-skinned warriors pass the challenge round;
Or Minnehaha's laughter, as the fall
Of woodland waters, makes a silver sound.

---

[1]Henry Wadsworth Longfellow.

Thor rolls the thunders of his fiery vaunt,
The answering battle burns in Olaf's eyes;
Or love-crowned Elsie lures us with the chaunt
That lulled the waves, neath star-hung Genoan skies.

Here grim-faced captains of colonial days
Salute the builders of old German rhyme;
And choral troops of children hymn the praise
Of their own master minstrel of all time.

Fair shrine of pure creations, linger long
His bright example, may his fame increase:
Discord nor distance ever dim his song,
Whose ways are pleasantness, whose paths are peace.

Nor Hawthorne's manse, with ancient moss bespread,
Nor Irving's hollow, is with rest so rife
As this calm haven, where the leaves are shed
Round Indian summers of a golden life.

## JAMES THOMSON (1834–1882)

[James Thomson was born near Glasgow. His family moved to London when he was six and in England he lived most of the rest of his life. That life was unhappy, dominated by alcoholism and depression. Indeed his fame is that of the Poet of Despair. His great work is the long, nightmarish poem, "The City of Dreadful Night" (1874), a sustained mood-piece of melancholia and an at least implied condemnation of the spiritual malaise of Victorian society. The author seems to have picked up many of the images for this work from his own insomnia-induced nocturnal rambling about London.]

### The City of Dreadful Night

#### PROEM

Lo, thus, as prostrate, "In the dust I write.
My heart's deep languor and my soul's sad tears."
Yet why evoke the specters of black night
To blot the sunshine of exultant years?
Why disinter dead faith from moldering hidden?
Why break the seals of mute despair unbidden
And wail life's discords into careless ears?

Because a cold rage seizes one at whiles
To show the bitter old and wrinkled truth
Stripped naked of all vesture that beguiles,
False dreams, false hopes, false masks and modes of youth;
Because it gives some sense of power and passion
In helpless impotence to try to fashion
Our woe in living words howe'er uncouth.

Surely I write not for the hopeful young,
Or those who deem their happiness of worth,
Or such as pasture and grow fat among
The shows of life and feel nor doubt nor dearth,
Or pious spirits with a God above them
To sanctify and glorify and love them,
Or sages who foresee a heaven on earth.

For none of these I write, and none of these
Could read the writing if they deigned to try;
So may they flourish, in their due degrees
On our sweet earth and in their unplaced sky.
If any cares for the weak words here written,
It must be someone desolate, Fate-smitten,
Whose faith and hope are dead, and who would die.

Yes, here and there some weary wanderer
In that same city of tremendous night,
Will understand the speech, and feel a stir
Of fellowship in all-disastrous fight;
"I suffer mute and lonely, yet another
Uplifts his voice to let me know a brother
Travels the same wild paths though out of sight."

O sad Fraternity, do I unfold
Your dolorous mysteries shrouded from of yore?
Nay, be assured—no secret can be told
To any who divined it not before;
None uninitiate by many a presage
Will comprehend the language of the message,
Although proclaimed aloud for evermore.

1

The City is of Night; perchance of Death,
But certainly of Night; for never there
Can come the lucid morning's fragrant breath
After the dewy dawning's cold gray air;
The moon and stars may shine with scorn or pity;
The sun has never visited that city,
For it dissolveth in the daylight fair;

Dissolveth like a dream of night away,
Though present in distempered gloom of thought
And deadly weariness of heart all day.
But when a dream night after night is brought
Throughout a week, and such weeks few or many
Recur each year for several years, can any
Discern that dream from real life in aught?

For life is but a dream whose shapes return,
Some frequently, some seldom, some by night
And some by day, some night and day; we learn
The while all change and many vanish quite,

In their recurrence with recurrent changes
A certain seeming order; where this ranges
We count things real; such is memory's might.

A river girds the city west and south,
The main north channel of a broad lagoon,
Regurging with the salt tides from the mouth;
Waste marshes shine and glister to the moon
For leagues, then moorland black, then stony ridges;
Great piers and causeways, many noble bridges,
Connect the town and islet suburbs strewn.

Upon an easy slope it lies at large,
And scarcely overlaps the long curved crest
Which swells out two leagues from the river marge.
A trackless wilderness rolls north and west,
Savannahs, savage woods, enormous mountains,
Bleak uplands, black ravines with torrent fountains;
And eastward rolls the shipless sea's unrest.

The city is not ruinous, although
Great ruins of an unremembered past,
With others of a few short years ago,
More sad, are found within its precincts vast.
The street-lamps always burn; but scarce a casement
In house or palace front from roof to basement
Doth glow or gleam athwart the mirk air cast.

The street-lamps burn amidst the baleful glooms,
Amidst the soundless solitudes immense
Of ranged mansions dark and still as tombs.
The silence which benumbs or strains the sense
Fulfills with awe the soul's despair unweeping;
Myriads of habitants are ever sleeping,
Or dead, or fled from nameless pestilence.

Yet, as in some necropolis you find
Perchance one mourner to a thousand dead,
So there: worn faces that look deaf and blind
Like tragic masks of stone. With weary tread,
Each wrapped in his own doom, they wander, wander,
Or sit foredone and desolately ponder
Through sleepless hours with heavy drooping head.

Mature men chiefly, few in age or youth,
A woman rarely, now and then a child—
A child! If here the heart turns sick with ruth
To see a little one from birth defiled,
Or lame or blind, as preordained to languish
Through youthless life, think how it bleeds with anguish
To meet one erring in that homeless wild.

They often murmur to themselves, they speak
To one another seldom, for their woe
Broods maddening inwardly and scorns to wreak
Itself abroad; and if at whiles it grow
To frenzy which must rave, none heeds the clamor,
Unless there waits some victim of like glamour,
To rave in turn, who lends attentive show.

The City is of Night, but not of Sleep;
There sweet sleep is not for the weary brain;
The pitiless hours like years and ages creep,
A night seems termless hell. This dreadful strain
Of thought and consciousness, which never ceases,
Or which some moments' stupor but increases,
This, worse than woe, makes wretches there insane.

They leave all hope behind who enter there;[1]
One certitude while sane they cannot leave,
One anodyne for torture and despair—
The certitude of Death, which no reprieve
Can put off long; and which, divinely tender,
But waits the outstretched hand to promptly render
That draft whose slumber nothing can bereave.

2

Because he seemed to walk with an intent
I followed him; who, shadowlike and frail,
Unswervingly though slowly onward went,
Regardless, wrapped in thought as in a veil.
Thus step for step with lonely sounding feet
We traveled many a long dim silent street.

At length he paused—a black mass in the gloom,
A tower that merged into the heavy sky;
Around, the huddled stones of grave and tomb:
Some old God's-acre now corruption's sty:
He murmured to himself with dull despair,
"Here Faith died, poisoned by this charnel air."

Then, turning to the right, went on once more,
And traveled weary roads without suspense;
And reached at last a low wall's open door,
Whose villa gleamed beyond the foliage dense.
He gazed, and muttered with a hard despair,
"Here Love died, stabbed by its own worshipped pair."

Then, turning to the right, resumed his march,
And traveled streets and lanes with wondrous strength,
Until on stooping through a narrow arch
We stood before a squalid house at length.

---

[1]Words written above hell's gate, in Dante's *Inferno*, 3.1.9.

He gazed, and whispered with a cold despair,
"Here Hope died, starved out in its utmost lair."

When he had spoken thus, before he stirred,
I spoke, perplexed by something in the signs
Of desolation I had seen and heard
In this drear pilgrimage to ruined shrines:
"When Faith and Love and Hope are dead indeed,
Can Life still live? By what doth it proceed?"

As whom his one intense thought overpowers,
He answered coldly, "Take a watch, erase
The signs and figures of the circling hours,
Detach the hands, remove the dial-face;
The works proceed until run down, although
Bereft of purpose, void of use, still go."

Then, turning to the right, paced on again,
And traversed squares and traveled streets whose glooms
Seemed more and more familiar to my ken;
And reached that sullen temple of the tombs;
And paused to murmur with the old despair
"Here Faith died, poisoned by this charnel air."

I ceased to follow, for the knot of doubt
Was severed sharply with a cruel knife.
He circled thus forever tracing out
The series of the fraction left of life;
Perpetual recurrence in the scope
Of but three terms, dead Faith, dead Love, dead Hope.

3

Although lamps burn along the silent streets,
Even when moonlight silvers empty squares,
The dark holds countless lanes and close retreats;
But when the night its sphereless mantle wears,
The open spaces yawn with gloom abysmal,
The somber mansions loom immense and dismal,
The lanes are black as subterranean lairs.

And soon the eye a strange new vision learns:
The night remains for it as dark and dense,
Yet clearly in this darkness it discerns
As in the daylight with its natural sense;
Perceives a shade in shadow not obscurely,
Pursues a stir of black in blackness surely,
Sees specters also in the gloom intense.

The ear, too, with the silence vast and deep
Becomes familiar though unreconciled;
Hears breathings as of hidden life asleep,
And muffled throbs as of pent passions wild,
Far murmurs, speech of pity or derision;

But all more dubious than the things of vision,
So that it knows not when it is beguiled.

No time abates the first despair and awe,
But wonder ceases soon; the weirdest thing
Is felt least strange beneath the lawless law
Where Death-in-Life is the eternal king;
Crushed impotent beneath this reign of terror,
Dazed with such mysteries of woe and error,
The soul is too outworn for wondering.

4

He stood alone within the spacious square,
Declaiming from the central grassy mound,
With head uncovered and with streaming hair,
As if large multitudes were gathered round:
A stalwart shape, the gestures full of might,
The glances burning with unnatural light:

"As I came through the desert thus it was,
As I came through the desert: All was black,
In heaven no single star, on earth no track;
A brooding hush without a stir or note,
The air so thick it clotted in my throat;
And thus for hours; then some enormous things
Swooped past with savage cries and clanking wings.
But I strode on austere;
No hope could have no fear.

"As I came through the desert thus it was,
As I came through the desert: Eyes of fire
Glared at me throbbing with a starved desire.
The hoarse and heavy and carnivorous breath
Was hot upon me from deep jaws of death;
Sharp claws, swift talons, fleshless fingers cold
Plucked at me from the bushes, tried to hold.
But I strode on austere;
No hope could have no fear.

"As I came through the desert thus it was,
As I came through the desert: Lo you, there,
That hillock burning with a brazen glare;
Those myriad dusky flames with points a-glow
Which writhed and hissed and darted to and fro;
A Sabbath of the Serpents, heaped pell-mell
For Devil's roll-call and some fete of hell.
Yet I strode on austere;
No hope could have no fear.

"As I came through the desert thus it was,
As I came through the desert: Meteors ran
And crossed their javelins on the black sky-span;
The zenith opened to a gulf of flame,

The dreadful thunderbolts jarred earth's fixed frame;
The ground all heaved in waves of fire that surged
And weltered round me sole there unsubmerged.
Yet I strode on austere;
No hope could have no fear.

"As I came through the desert thus it was,
As I came through the desert: Air once more,
And I was close upon a wild seashore;
Enormous cliffs arose on either hand,
The deep tide thundered up a league-broad strand;
White foambelts seethed there, wan spray swept and flew;
The sky broke, moon and stars and clouds and blue.
And I strode on austere;
No hope could have no fear.

"As I came through the desert thus it was,
As I came through the desert: On the left
The sun arose and crowned a broad crag cleft;
There stopped and burned out black, except a rim,
A bleeding, eyeless socket, red and dim;
Whereon the moon fell suddenly southwest,
And stood above the right-hand cliffs at rest.
Still I strode on austere;
No hope could have no fear.

"As I came through the desert thus it was
As I came through the desert: From the right
A shape came slowly with a ruddy light;
A woman with a red lamp in her hand,
Bareheaded and barefooted on that strand;
O desolation moving with such grace!
O anguish with such beauty in thy face!
I fell as on my bier,
Hope travailed with such fear.

"As I came through the desert thus it was,
As I came through the desert: I was twain,
Two selves distinct that cannot join again;
One stood apart and knew but could not stir,
And watched the other stark in swoon and her;
And she came on, and never turned aside,
Between such sun and moon and roaring tide.
And as she came more near
My soul grew mad with fear.

"As I came through the desert thus it was,
As I came through the desert: Hell is mild
And piteous matched with that accursed wild;
A large black sign was on her breast that bowed,
A broad black band ran down her snow-white shroud;
That lamp she held was her own burning heart,
Whose blood-drops trickled step by step apart.

The mystery was clear;
Mad rage had swallowed fear.

"As I came through the desert thus it was,
As I came through the desert: By the sea
She knelt and bent above that senseless me;
Those lamp-drops fell upon my white brow there,
She tried to cleanse them with her tears and hair;
She murmured words of pity, love, and woe,
She heeded not the level rushing flow.
And mad with rage and fear,
I stood stonebound so near.

"As I came through the desert thus it was,
As I came through the desert: When the tide
Swept up to her there kneeling by my side,
She clasped that corpse-like me, and they were borne
Away, and this vile me was left forlorn;
I know the whole sea cannot quench that heart,
Or cleanse that brow, or wash those two apart.
They love; their doom is drear,
Yet they nor hope nor fear;
But I, what do I here?"

5

How he arrives there none can clearly know;
Athwart the mountains and immense wild tracts,
Or flung a waif upon that vast sea-flow,
Or down the river's boiling cataracts.
To reach it is as dying fever-stricken;
To leave it, slow faint birth intense pangs quicken;
And memory swoons in both the tragic acts.

But being there one feels a citizen;
Escape seems hopeless to the heart forlorn:
Can Death-in-Life be brought to life again?
And yet release does come; there comes a morn
When he awakes from slumbering so sweetly
That all the world is changed for him completely,
And he is verily as if new-born.

He scarcely can believe the blissful change,
He weeps perchance who wept not while accurst;
Never again will he approach the range
Infected by that evil spell now burst.
Poor wretch! who once hath paced that dolent city
Shall pace it often, doomed beyond all pity,
With horror ever deepening from the first.

Though he possess sweet babes and loving wife,
A home of peace by loyal friendships cheered,
And love them more than death or happy life,
They shall avail not; he must dree his weird*; "suffer his fate"

Renounce all blessings for that imprecation,
Steal forth and haunt that builded desolation,
Of woe and terrors and thick darkness reared.

6

I sat forlornly by the river-side,
And watched the bridge-lamps glow like golden stars
Above the blackness of the swelling tide,
Down which they struck rough gold in ruddier bars;
And heard the heave and splashing of the flow
Against the wall a dozen feet below.

Large elm-trees stood along that river-walk;
And under one, a few steps from my seat
I heard strange voices join in stranger talk
Although I had not heard approaching feet;
These bodiless voices in my waking dream
Flowed dark words blending with the somber stream:

"And you have after all come back; come back.
I was about to follow on your track.
And you have failed; our spark of hope is black."

"That I have failed is proved by my return;
The spark is quenched, nor ever more will burn.
But listen; and the story you shall learn.

"I reached the portal common spirits fear,
And read the words above it, dark yet clear,
'Leave hope behind, all ye who enter here,'

"And would have passed in, gratified to gain
That positive eternity of pain,
Instead of this insufferable inane.

"A demon warder clutched me, 'Not so fast;
First leave your hopes behind!'—'But years have passed
Since I left all behind me, to the last.

"'You cannot count for hope, with all your wit,
This bleak despair that drives me to the Pit;
How could I seek to enter void of it?'

"He snarled, 'What thing is this which apes a soul
And would find entrance to our gulf of dole
Without the payment of the settled toll?'

"Outside the gate he showed an open chest.
'Here pay their entrance fees the souls unblest;
Cast in some hope, you enter with the rest.

"'This is Pandora's box, whose lid shall shut,
And Hell-gate too, when hopes have filled it; but
They are so thin that it will never glut.'

"I stood a few steps backwards, desolate;
And watched the spirits pass me to their fate,
And fling off hope, and enter at the gate.

"When one casts off a load he springs upright,
Squares back his shoulders, breathes with all his might,
And briskly paces forward strong and light;

"But these, as if they took some burden, bowed;
The whole frame sank; however strong and proud
Before, they crept in quite infirm and cowed.

"And as they passed me, earnestly from each
A morsel of his hope I did beseech,
To pay my entrance; but all mocked my speech.

"Not one would cede a tittle of his store,
Though knowing that in instants three or four
He must resign the whole for evermore.

"So I returned. Our destiny is fell;
For in this Limbo we must ever dwell,
Shut out alike from heaven and earth and hell."

The other sighed back, "Yea; but if we grope
With care through all this Limbo's dreary scope,
We yet may pick up some minute lost hope;

"And, sharing it between us, entrance win,
In spite of fiends so jealous for gross sin.
Let us without delay our search begin."

7

Some say that phantoms haunt those shadowy streets,
And mingle freely there with sparse mankind;
And tell of ancient woes and black defeats,
And murmur mysteries in the grave enshrined.
But others think them visions of illusion,
Or even men gone far in self-confusion,
No man there being wholly sane in mind.

And yet a man who raves, however mad,
Who bares his heart and tells of his own fall,
Reserves some inmost secret good or bad;
The phantoms have no reticence at all;
The nudity of flesh will blush though tameless,
The extreme nudity of bone grins shameless,
The unsexed skeleton mocks shroud and pall.

I have seen phantoms there that were as men
And men that were as phantoms flit and roam;
Marked shapes that were not living to my ken,
Caught breathings acrid as with Dead Sea foam.
The City rests for man so weird and awful,
That his intrusion there might seem unlawful,
And phantoms there may have their proper home.

8

While I still lingered on that river-walk,
And watched the tide as black as our black doom,
I heard another couple join in talk,
And saw them to the left hand in the gloom
Seated against an elm bole on the ground,
Their eyes intent upon the stream profound.

"I never knew another man on earth
But had some joy and solace in his life,
Some chance of triumph in the dreadful strife;
My doom has been unmitigated dearth."
"We gaze upon the river, and we note
The various vessels large and small that float,
Ignoring every wrecked and sunken boat."

"And yet I asked no splendid dower, no spoil
Of sway or fame or rank or even wealth;
But homely love with common food and health,
And nightly sleep to balance daily toil."
"This all-too humble soul would arrogate
Unto itself some signalizing hate
From the supreme indifference of Fate!"

"Who is most wretched in this dolorous place?
I think myself; yet I would rather be
My miserable self than He, than He
Who formed such creatures to His own disgrace.

"The vilest thing must be less vile than Thou
From whom it had its being, God and Lord!
Creator of all woe and sin! abhorred,
Malignant and implacable, I vow

"That not for all Thy power furled and unfurled,
For all the temples to Thy glory built,
Would I assume the ignominious guilt
Of having made such men in such a world."

"As if a Being, God or Fiend, could reign,
At once so wicked, foolish, and insane,
As to produce men when He might refrain.

"The world rolls round forever like a mill;
It grinds out death and life and good and ill;
It has no purpose, heart or mind or will.

"While air of Space and Time's full river flow
The mill must blindly whirl unresting so;
It may be wearing out, but who can know?

"Man might know one thing were his sight less dim;
That it whirls not to suit his petty whim,
That it is quite indifferent to him.

"Nay, does it treat him harshly as he saith?
It grinds him some slow years of bitter breath,
Then grinds him back into eternal death."

9

It is full strange to him who hears and feels,
When wandering there in some deserted street,
The booming and the jar of ponderous wheels,
The trampling clash of heavy ironshod feet:
Who in this Venice of the Black Sea rideth?
Who in this city of the stars abideth
To buy or sell as those in daylight sweet?

The rolling thunder seems to fill the sky
As it comes on; the horses snort and strain,
The harness jingles, as it passes by;
The hugeness of an overburthened wain:
A man sits nodding on the shaft or trudges,
Three parts asleep beside his fellow-drudges;
And so it rolls into the night again.

What merchandise? whence, whither, and for whom?
Perchance it is a Fate-appointed hearse,
Bearing away to some mysterious tomb
Or Limbo of the scornful universe
The joy, the peace, the life-hope, the abortions
Of all things good which should have been our portions,
But have been strangled by that City's curse.

10

The mansion stood apart in its own ground;
In front thereof a fragrant garden-lawn,
High trees about it, and the whole walled round.
The massive iron gates were both withdrawn;
And every window of its front shed light,
Portentous in that City of the Night.

But though thus lighted, it was deadly still
As all the countless bulks of solid gloom;
Perchance a congregation to fulfill
Solemnities of silence in this doom,

Mysterious rites of dolor and despair
Permitting not a breath of chant or prayer?

Broad steps ascended to a terrace broad
Whereon lay still light from the open door;
The hall was noble, and its aspect awed,
Hung round with heavy black from dome to floor;
And ample stairways rose to left and right
Whose balustrades were also draped with night.

I paced from room to room, from hall to hall,
Nor any life throughout the maze discerned;
But each was hung with its funereal pall,
And held a shrine, around which tapers burned,
With picture or with statue or with bust,
All copied from the same fair form of dust—

A woman very young and very fair;
Beloved by bounteous life and joy and youth,
And loving these sweet lovers, so that care
And age and death seemed not for her in sooth.
Alike as stars, all beautiful and bright,
These shapes lit up that mausolean night.

At length I heard a murmur as of lips,
And reached an open oratory hung
With heaviest blackness of the whole eclipse;
Beneath the dome a fuming censer swung;
And one lay there upon a low white bed,
With tapers burning at the foot and head—

The Lady of the images. Supine,
Deathstill, lifesweet, with folded palms she lay;
And kneeling there, as at a sacred shrine,
A young man wan and worn who seemed to pray;
A crucifix of dim and ghostly white
Surmounted the large altar left in night:

"The chambers of the mansion of my heart,
In every one whereof thine image dwells,
Are black with grief eternal for thy sake.

"The inmost oratory of my soul,
Wherein thou ever dwellest quick or dead,
Is black with grief eternal for thy sake.

"I kneel beside thee and I clasp the cross
With eyes forever fixed upon that face,
So beautiful and dreadful in its calm.

"I kneel here patient as thou liest there;
As patient as a statue carved in stone,
Of adoration and eternal grief.

"Whilst thou dost not awake I cannot move;
And something tells me thou wilt never wake
And I alive feel turning into stone.

"Most beautiful were Death to end my grief,
Most hateful to destroy the sight of thee,
Dear vision better than all death or life.

"But I renounce all choice of life or death,
For either shall be ever at thy side,
And thus in bliss or woe be ever well."

He murmured thus and thus in monotone,
Intent upon that uncorrupted face,
Entranced except his moving lips alone.
I glided with hushed footsteps from the place.
This was the festival that filled with light
That palace in the City of the Night.

11

What men are they who haunt these fatal glooms,
And fill their living mouths with dust of death,
And make their habitations in the tombs,
And breathe eternal sighs with mortal breath,
And pierce life's pleasant veil of various error
To reach that void of darkness and old terror
Wherein expire the lamps of hope and faith?

They have much wisdom, yet they are not wise;
They have much goodness, yet they do not well
(The fools we know have their own paradise,
The wicked also have their proper hell);
They have much strength, but still their doom is stronger;
Much patience, but their time endureth longer;
Much valor, but life mocks it with some spell.

They are most rational and yet insane:
An outward madness, not to be controlled;
A perfect reason in the central brain,
Which has no power, but sitteth wan and cold,
And sees the madness, and foresees as plainly
The ruin in its path, and trieth vainly
To cheat itself refusing to behold.

And some are great in rank and wealth and power,
And some renowned for genius and for worth;
And some are poor and mean, who brood and cower
And shrink from notice, and accept all dearth
Of body, heart and soul, and leave to others
All boons of life; yet these and those are brothers,
The saddest and the weariest men on earth.

12

Our isolated units could be brought
To act together for some common end?
For one by one, each silent with his thought
I marked a long loose line approach and wend
Athwart the great cathedral's cloistered square,
And slowly vanish from the moonlit air.

Then I would follow in among the last;
And in the porch a shrouded figure stood,
Who challenged each one pausing ere he passed
With deep eyes burning through a blank white hood:
"Whence come you in the world of life and light
To this our City of Tremendous Night?"

"From pleading in a senate of rich lords
For some scant justice to our countless hordes
Who toil half-starved with scarce a human right—
I wake from daydreams to this real night."

"From wandering through many a solemn scene
Of opium visions, with a heart serene
And intellect miraculously bright—
I wake from daydreams to this real night."

"From making hundreds laugh and roar with glee
By my transcendent feats of mimicry,
And humor wanton as an elfish sprite—
I wake from daydreams to this real night."

"From prayer and fasting in a lonely cell,
Which brought an ecstasy ineffable
Of love and adoration and delight—
I wake from daydreams to this real night."

"From ruling on a splendid kingly throne
A nation which beneath my rule has grown
Year after year in wealth and arts and might—
I wake from daydreams to this real night."

"From preaching to an audience fired with faith
The Lamb who died to save our souls from death,
Whose blood hath washed our scarlet sins wool-white,
I wake from daydreams to this real night."

"From drinking fiery poison in a den
Crowded with tawdry girls and squalid men,
Who hoarsely laugh and curse and brawl and fight—
I wake from daydreams to this real night."

"From picturing with all beauty and all grace
First Eden and the parents of our race,

A luminous rapture unto all men's sight—
I wake from daydreams to this real night."

"From writing a great work with patient plan
To justify the ways of God to man,[1]
And show how ill must fade and perish quite—
I wake from daydreams to this real night."

"From desperate fighting with a little band
Against the powerful tyrants of our land,
To free our brethren in their own despite—
I wake from daydreams to this real night."

Thus, challenged by that warder sad and stern,
Each one responded with his countersign,
Then entered the cathedral; and in turn
I entered also, having given mine,
But lingered near until I heard no more,
And marked the closing of the massive door.

13

Of all things human which are strange and wild
This is perchance the wildest and most strange,
And showeth man most utterly beguiled,
To those who haunt that sunless City's range—
That he bemoans himself for aye, repeating
How time is deadly swift, how life is fleeting,
How naught is constant on the earth but change.

The hours are heavy on him and the days;
The burden of the months he scarce can bear;
And often in his secret soul he prays
To sleep through barren periods unaware,
Arousing at some longed-for date of pleasure;
Which having passed and yielded him small treasure,
He would outsleep another term of care.

Yet in his marvelous fancy he must make
Quick wings for Time, and see it fly from us—
This Time which crawleth like a monstrous snake,
Wounded and slow and very venomous;
Which creeps blindwormlike round the earth and ocean,
Distilling poison at each painful motion
And seems condemned to circle ever thus.

And since he cannot spend and use aright
The little time here given him in trust,
But wasteth it in weary undelight
Of foolish toil and trouble, strife and lust,
He naturally claimeth to inherit

---

[1] Milton's declared purpose in *Paradise Lost.*

The everlasting Future, that his merit
May have full scope—as surely is most just.

O length of the intolerable hours,
O nights that are as aeons of slow pain,
O Time, too ample for our vital powers,
O Life, whose woeful vanities remain
Immutable for all of all our legions
Through all the centuries and in all the regions,
Not of your speed and variance *we* complain.

*We* do not ask a longer term of strife,
Weakness and weariness and nameless woes;
We do not claim renewed and endless life
When this which is our torment here shall close
An everlasting conscious inanition!
We yearn for speedy death in full fruition,
Dateless oblivion and divine repose.

14

Large glooms were gathered in the mighty fane,
With tinted moongleams slanting here and there;
And all was hush—no swelling organ-strain,
No chant, no voice or murmuring of prayer;
No priests came forth, no tinkling censers fumed,
And the high altar space was unillumed.

Around the pillars and against the walls
Leaned men and shadows; others seemed to brood,
Bent or recumbent, in secluded stalls.
Perchance they were not a great multitude
Save in that city of so lonely streets
Where one may count up every face he meets.

All patiently awaited the event
Without a stir or sound, as if no less
Self-occupied, doomstricken, while attent.
And then we heard a voice of solemn stress
From the dark pulpit, and our gaze there met
Two eyes which burned as never eyes burned yet:

Two steadfast and intolerable eyes
Burning beneath a broad and rugged brow;
The head behind it of enormous size.
And as black fir-groves in a large wind bow,
Our rooted congregation, gloom-arrayed,
By that great sad voice deep and full were swayed:

"O melancholy Brothers, dark, dark, dark!
O battling in black floods without an ark!
O spectral wanderers of unholy Night!
My soul hath bled for you these sunless years,

With bitter blood-drops running down like tears;
Oh, dark, dark, dark, withdrawn from joy and light!

"My heart is sick with anguish for your bale;
Your woe hath been my anguish; yea, I quail
And perish in your perishing unblest.
And I have searched the heights and depths, the scope
Of all our universe, with desperate hope
To find some solace for your wild unrest.

"And now at last authentic word I bring,
Witnessed by every dead and living thing;
Good tidings of great joy for you, for all;
There is no God; no Fiend with names divine
Made us and tortures us; if we must pine,
It is to satiate no Being's gall.

"It was the dark delusion of a dream,
That living Person conscious and supreme,
Whom we must curse for cursing us with life;
Whom we must curse because the life He gave
Could not be buried in the quiet grave,
Could not be killed by poison or by knife.

"This little life is all we must endure,
The grave's most holy peace is ever sure,
We fall asleep and never wake again;
Nothing is of us but the moldering flesh,
Whose elements dissolve and merge afresh
In earth, air, water, plants, and other men.

"We finish thus; and all our wretched race
Shall finish with its cycle, and give place
To other beings, with their own time-doom;
Infinite aeons ere our kind began;
Infinite aeons after the last man
Has joined the mammoth in earth's tomb and womb.

"We bow down to the universal laws,
Which never had for man a special clause
Of cruelty or kindness, love or hate;
If toads and vultures are obscene to sight,
If tigers burn with beauty and with might,
Is it by favor or by wrath of fate?

"All substance lives and struggles evermore
Through countless shapes continually at war,
By countless interactions interknit;
If one is born a certain day on earth,
All times and forces tended to that birth,
Not all the world could change or hinder it.

"I find no hint throughout the Universe
Of good or ill, of blessing or of curse;
I find alone Necessity Supreme;
With infinite Mystery, abysmal, dark,
Unlighted ever by the faintest spark
For us the flitting shadows of a dream.

"O Brothers of sad lives! they are so brief;
A few short years must bring us all relief—
Can we not bear these years of laboring breath?
But if you would not this poor life fulfill,
Lo, you are free to end it when you will,
Without the fear of waking after death."

The organ-like vibrations of his voice
Thrilled through the vaulted aisles and died away;
The yearning of the tones which bade rejoice
Was sad and tender as a requiem lay;
Our shadowy congregation rested still
As brooding on that "End it when you will."

15

Wherever men are gathered, all the air
Is charged with human feeling, human thought;
Each shout and cry and laugh, each curse and prayer,
Are into its vibrations surely wrought;
Unspoken passion, wordless meditation,
Are breathed into it with our respiration;
It is with our life fraught and overfraught.

So that no man there breathes earth's simple breath,
As if alone on mountains or wide seas;
But nourishes warm life or hastens death
With joys and sorrows, health and foul disease,
Wisdom and folly, good and evil labors,
Incessant of his multitudinous neighbors;
He in his turn affecting all of these.

That City's atmosphere is dark and dense,
Although not many exiles wander there,
With many a potent evil influence,
Each adding poison to the poisoned air;
Infections of unutterable sadness,
Infections of incalculable madness,
Infections of incurable despair.

16

Our shadowy congregation rested still,
As musing on that message we had heard
And brooding on that "End it when you will";
Perchance awaiting yet some other word;
When keen as lightning through a muffled sky
Sprang forth a shrill and lamentable cry:

"The man speaks sooth, alas! the man speaks sooth;
We have no personal life beyond the grave;
There is no God; Fate knows nor wrath nor ruth.
Can I find here the comfort which I crave?

"In all eternity I had one chance,
One few years' term of gracious human life:
The splendors of the intellect's advance;
The sweetness of the home with babes and wife;

"The social pleasures with their genial wit;
The fascination of the worlds of art;
The glories of the worlds of nature, lit
By large imagination's glowing heart;

"The rapture of mere being, full of health;
The careless childhood and the ardent youth,
The strenuous manhood winning various wealth,
The reverend age serene with life's long truth—

"All the sublime prerogatives of Man;
The storied memories of the times of old,
The patient tracking of the world's great plan
Through sequences and changes myriadfold.

"This chance was never offered me before;
For me the infinite Past is blank and dumb.
This chance recurreth never, nevermore;
Blank, blank for me the infinite To-come.

"And this sole chance was frustrate from my birth,
A mockery, a delusion; and my breath
Of noble human life upon this earth
So racks me that I sigh for senseless death.

"My wine of life is poison mixed with gall,
My noonday passes in a nightmare dream,
I worse than lose the years which are my all;
What can console me for the loss supreme?

"Speak not of comfort where no comfort is,
Speak not at all; can words make foul things fair?
Our life's a cheat, our death a black abyss;
Hush and be mute, envisaging despair."

This vehement voice came from the northern aisle,
Rapid and shrill to its abrupt harsh close;
And none gave answer for a certain while,
For words must shrink from these most wordless woes;
At last the pulpit speaker simply said,
With humid eyes and thoughtful drooping head:

"My brother, my poor brothers, it is thus:
This life itself holds nothing good for us,
But it ends soon and nevermore can be;
And we knew nothing of it ere our birth,
And shall know nothing when consigned to earth.
I ponder these thoughts, and they comfort me."

17

How the moon triumphs through the endless nights!
How the stars throb and glitter as they wheel
Their thick processions of supernal lights
Around the blue vault obdurate as steel!
And men regard with passionate awe and yearning
The mighty marching and the golden burning,
And think the heavens respond to what they feel.

Boats gliding like dark shadows of a dream,
Are glorified from vision as they pass
The quivering moonbridge on the deep black stream;
Cold windows kindle their dead glooms of glass
To restless crystals; cornice, dome, and column
Emerge from chaos in the splendor solemn;
Like faery lakes gleam lawns of dewy grass.

With such a living light these dead eyes shine,
These eyes of sightless heaven, that as we gaze
We read a pity, tremulous, divine,
Or cold majestic scorn in their pure rays.
Fond man! they are not haughty, are not tender;
There is no heart or mind in all their splendor,
They thread mere puppets all their marvelous maze.

If we could near them with the flight unflown,
We should but find them worlds as sad as this,
Or suns all self-consuming like our own
Enringed by planet worlds as much amiss.
They wax and wane through fusion and confusion;
The spheres eternal are a grand illusion,
The empyrean is a void abyss.

18

I wandered in a suburb of the north,
And reached a spot whence three close lanes led down,
Beneath thick trees and hedgerows winding forth
Like deep brook channels, deep and dark and lown.
The air above was wan with misty light;
The dull gray south showed one vague blur of white.

I took the left-hand lane and slowly trod
Its earthen footpath, brushing as I went
The humid leafage; and my feet were shod
With heavy languor, and my frame downbent,

With infinite sleepless weariness outworn,
So many nights I thus had paced forlorn.

After a hundred steps I grew aware
Of something crawling in the lane below;
It seemed a wounded creature prostrate there
That sobbed with pangs in making progress slow,
The hind limbs stretched to push, the fore limbs then
To drag: for it would die in its own den.

But coming level with it I discerned
That it had been a man; for at my tread
It stopped in its sore travail and half turned,
Leaning upon its right, and raised its head,
And with the left hand twitched back as in ire
Long gray unreverend locks befouled with mire.

A haggard filthy face with bloodshot eyes,
An infamy for manhood to behold.
He gasped all trembling, "What, you want my prize?
You leave, to rob me, wine and lust and gold
And all that men go mad upon, since you
Have traced my sacred secret of the clue?

"You think that I am weak and must submit;
Yet I but scratch you with this poisoned blade,
And you are dead as if I clove with it
That false fierce greedy heart. Betrayed! betrayed!
I fling this phial if you seek to pass,
And you are forthwith shriveled up like grass."

And then with sudden change, "Take thought! take thought!
Have pity on me! it is mine alone.
If you could find, it would avail you naught;
Seek elsewhere on the pathway of your own.
For who of mortal or immortal race
The lifetrack of another can retrace?

"Did you but know my agony and toil!
Two lanes diverge up yonder from this lane;
My thin blood marks the long length of their soil;
Such clue I left, who sought my clue in vain.
My hands and knees are worn both flesh and bone;
I cannot move but with continual moan.

"But I am in the very way at last
To find the long-lost broken golden thread
Which reunites my present with my past,
If you but go your own way." And I said,
"I will retire as soon as you have told
Whereunto leadeth this lost thread of gold."

"And so you know it not!" he hissed with scorn;
"I feared you, imbecile! It leads me back
From this accursed night without a morn,
And through the deserts which have else no track,
And through vast wastes of horror-haunted time,
To Eden innocence in Eden's clime;

"And I become a nursling soft and pure,
An infant cradled on its mother's knee,
Without a past, love-cherished and secure;
Which if it saw this loathsome present Me
Would plunge its face into the pillowing breast,
And scream abhorrence hard to lull to rest."

He turned to grope, and I, retiring, brushed
Thin shreds of gossamer from off my face,
And mused, His life would grow, the germ uncrushed;
He should to antenatal night retrace
And hide his elements in that large womb
Beyond the reach of man-evolving Doom.

And even thus, what weary way were planned,
To seek oblivion through the far-off gate
Of birth, when that of death is close at hand!
For this is law, if law there be in Fate:
What never has been, yet may have its when;
The thing which has been, never is again.

19

The mighty river flowing dark and deep,
With ebb and flood from the remote seatides
Vague-sounding through the City's sleepless sleep,
Is named the River of the Suicides;
For night by night some lorn wretch over-weary,
And shuddering from the future yet more dreary,
Within its cold secure oblivion hides.

One plunges from a bridge's parapet,
As by some blind and sudden frenzy hurled;
Another wades in slow with purpose set
Until the waters are above him furled;
Another in a boat with dreamlike motion
Glides drifting down into the desert ocean,
To starve or sink from out the desert world.

They perish from their suffering surely thus,
For none beholding them attempts to save,
The while each thinks how soon, solicitous,
He may seek refuge in the selfsame wave;
Some hour when tired of ever-vain endurance
Impatience will forerun the sweet assurance
Of perfect peace eventual in the grave.

When this poor tragic-farce has palled us long,
Why actors and spectators do we stay?—
To fill our so-short *roles* out right or wrong;
To see what shifts are yet in the dull play
For our illusion; to refrain from grieving
Dear foolish friends by our untimely leaving—
But those asleep at home, how blest are they!

Yet it is but for one night after all;
What matters one brief night of dreary pain?
When after it the weary eyelids fall
Upon the weary eyes and wasted brain;
And all sad scenes and thoughts and feelings vanish
In that sweet sleep no power can ever banish,
That one best sleep which never wakes again.

20

I sat me weary on a pillar's base,
And leaned against the shaft; for broad moonlight
O'erflowed the peacefulness of cloistered space,
A shore of shadow slanting from the right.
The great cathedral's western front stood there
A wave-worn rock in that calm sea of air.

Before it, opposite my place of rest,
Two figures faced each other, large, austere;
A couchant sphinx in shadow to the breast,
An angel standing in the moonlight clear;
So mighty by magnificence of form,
They were not dwarfed beneath that mass enorm.

Upon the cross-hilt of a naked sword
The angel's hands, as prompt to smite, were held;
His vigilant, intense regard was poured
Upon the creature placidly unquelled,
Whose front was set at level gaze which took
No heed of aught, a solemn trance-like look.

And as I pondered these opposed shapes
My eyelids sank in stupor, that dull swoon
Which drugs and with a leaden mantle drapes
The outworn to worse weariness. But soon
A sharp and clashing noise the stillness broke
And from the evil lethargy I woke.

The angel's wings had fallen, stone on stone,
And lay there shattered; hence the sudden sound.
A warrior leaning on his sword alone
Now watched the sphinx with that regard profound;
The sphinx unchanged looked forthright, as aware
Of nothing in the vast abyss of air.

Again I sank in that repose unsweet,
Again a clashing noise my slumber rent;
The warrior's sword lay broken at his feet;
An unarmed man with raised hands impotent
Now stood before the sphinx, which ever kept
Such mien as if with open eyes it slept.

My eyelids sank in spite of wonder grown;
A louder crash upstartled me in dread—
The man had fallen forward, stone on stone,
And lay there shattered, with his trunkless head
Between the monster's large quiescent paws,
Beneath its grand front changeless as life's laws.

The moon had circled westward full and bright,
And made the temple-front a mystic dream,
And bathed the whole enclosure with its light,
The sworded angel's wrecks, the sphinx supreme.
I pondered long that cold majestic face
Whose vision seemed of infinite void space.

21

Anear the center of that northern crest
Stands out a level upland bleak and bare
From which the city east and south and west
Sinks gently in long waves; and throned there
An Image sits, stupendous, superhuman,
The bronze colossus of a winged Woman,
Upon a graded granite base foursquare.

Low-seated she leans forward massively,
With cheek on clenched left hand, the forearm's might
Erect, its elbow on her rounded knee;
Across a clasped book in her lap the right
Upholds a pair of compasses; she gazes
With full set eyes, but wandering in thick mazes
Of somber thought beholds no outward sight.

Words cannot picture her; but all men know
That solemn sketch the pure sad artist[1] wrought
Three centuries and threescore years ago,
With fantasies of his peculiar thought:
The instruments of carpentry and science
Scattered about her feet, in strange alliance
With the keen wolf-hound sleeping undistraught;

Scales, hour-glass, bell, and magic-square above;
The grave and solid infant perched beside,
With open winglets that might bear a dove,
Intent upon its tablets, heavy-eyed;

---

[1]Albrecht Durer (1471-1528), whose famous engraving *Melancholia* is here cited.

Her folded wings as of a mighty eagle,
But all too impotent to lift the regal
Robustness of her earth-born strength and pride;

And with those wings, and that light wreath which seems
To mock her grand head and the knotted frown
Of forehead charged with baleful thoughts and dreams,
The household bunch of keys, the housewife's gown
Voluminous indented, and yet rigid
As if a shell of burnished metal frigid,
The feet thick-shod to tread all weakness down;

The comet hanging oer the waste dark seas
The massy rainbow curved in front of it,
Beyond the village with the masts and trees;
The snaky imp, dog-headed, from the Pit,
Bearing upon its batlike leathern pinions
Her name unfolded in the sun's dominions,
The "MELENCOLIA" that transcends all wit.

Thus has the artist copied her, and thus
Surrounded to expound her form sublime,
Her fate heroic and calamitous;
Fronting the dreadful mysteries of Time,
Unvanquished in defeat and desolation,
Undaunted in the hopeless conflagration
Of the day setting on her baffled prime.

Baffled and beaten back she works on still,
Weary and sick of soul she works the more,
Sustained by her indomitable will;
The hands shall fashion and the brain shall pore,
And all her sorrow shall be turned to labor,
Till Death, the friend-foe, piercing with his saber
That mighty heart of hearts, ends bitter war.

But as if blacker night could dawn on night,
With tenfold gloom on moonless night unstarred
A sense more tragic than defeat and blight,
More desperate than strife with hope debarred,
More fatal than the adamantine Never
Encompassing her passionate endeavor,
Dawns glooming in her tenebrous regard—

The sense that every struggle brings defeat
Because Fate holds no prize to crown success;
That all the oracles are dumb or cheat
Because they have no secret to express;
That none can pierce the vast black veil uncertain
Because there is no light beyond the curtain;
That all is vanity and nothingness.

Titanic from her high throne in the north,
That City's somber Patroness and Queen,
In bronze sublimity she gazes forth.
Over her Capital of teen and threne,
Over the river with its isles and bridges,
The marsh and moorland, to the stern rockridges,
Confronting them with a coeval mien.

The moving moon and stars from east to west
Circle before her in the sea of air;
Shadows and gleams glide round her solemn rest.
Her subjects often gaze up to her there:
The strong to drink new strength of iron endurance,
The weak new terrors; all, renewed assurance
And confirmation of the old despair.

## Once in a Saintly Passion

Once in a saintly passion
I cried with desperate grief,
"O Lord, my heart is black with guile,
Of sinners I am chief."
Then stooped my guardian angel
And whispered from behind,
"Vanity, my little man,
You're nothing of the kind."

## L' Ancien Regime
### Or, The Good Old Rule

Who has a thing to bring
For a gift to our lord the king,
Our king all kings above?
A young girl brought him love;
And he dowered her with shame,
With a sort of infamous fame,
And then with lonely years
Of penance and bitter tears—
Love is scarcely the thing
To bring as a gift for our king.

Who has a thing to bring
For a gift to our lord the king?
A statesman brought him planned
Justice for all the land;
And he in recompense got
Fierce struggle with brigue* and plot, intrigue
Then a fall from lofty place
Into exile and disgrace—
Justice is never the thing
To bring as a gift for our king.

Who has a thing to bring
For a gift to our lord the king?
A writer brought him truth;
And first he imprisoned the youth,
And then he bestowed a free pyre
That the works might have plenty of fire,
And also to cure the pain
Of the headache called thought in the brain—
Truth is a very bad thing
To bring as a gift for our king.

Who has a thing to bring
For a gift to our lord the king?
The people brought their sure
Loyalty fervid and pure;
And he gave them bountiful spoil
Of taxes and hunger and toil,
Ignorance, brutish plight,
And wholesale slaughter in fight—
Loyalty's quite the worst thing
To bring as a gift for our king.

Who has a thing to bring
For a gift to our lord the king?
A courtier brought to his feet
Servility graceful and sweet,
With an ever ready smile
And an ever supple guile;
And he got in reward the place
Of the statesman in disgrace—
Servility's always a thing
To bring as a gift for our king.

Who has a thing to bring
For a gift to our lord the king?
A soldier brought him war,
*La gloire, la victoire,*
Ravage and carnage and groans,
For the pious *Te Deum* tones;
And he got in return for himself
Rank and honors and pelf—
War is a very fine thing
To bring as a gift for our king.

Who has a thing to bring
For a gift to our lord the king?
A harlot brought him her flesh,
Her lusts, and the maniford mesh
Of her wiles intervolved with caprice;
And he gave her his realm to fleece,
To corrupt, to ruin, and gave
Himself for her toy and her slave—

Harlotry's just the thing
To bring as a gift for our king.

Who has a thing to bring
For a gift to our lord the king,
Our king who fears to die?
A priest brought him a lie,
The blackness of hell uprolled
In heaven's shining gold;
And he got as guerdon for that
A see and a cardinal's hat—
A lie is an excellent thing
To bring as a gift for our king.

Has any one yet a thing
For a gift to our lord the king?
The country gave him a tomb,
A magnificent sleeping-room;
And for this it obtained some rest,
Clear riddance of many a pest,
And a hope which it much enjoyed
That the throne would continue void—
A tomb is the very best thing
For a gift to our lord the king.

## Give a Man a Horse He Can Ride

Give a man a horse he can ride,
Give a man a boat he can sail;
And his rank and wealth, his strength and health,
On sea nor shore shall fail.

Give a man a pipe he can smoke,
Give a man a book he can read;
And his home is bright with a calm delight,
Though the rooms be poor indeed.

Give a man a girl he can love,
As I, O my Love, love thee;
And his hand is great with the pulse of Fate,
At home, on land, on sea.

# THOMAS DAVIDSON (1838–1870)

## And There Will I Be Buried

Tell me not the good and wise
Care not where their dust reposes—
That to him in death who lies
Rocky beds are even as roses.

I've been happy above ground;
I can never be happy under
Out of gentle Teviot's sound—
Part us not, then far asunder.

Lay me here where I may see
Teviot round his meadows flowing,
And around and over me
Winds and clouds for ever going.

## The Auld Ash Tree

There grows an ash by my bour door,
And a' its boughs are buskit* braw,- dressed
In fairest weeds o' simmer green;
And birds sit singing on them a'.
But cease your sangs, ye blithesome birds;
An' o' your liltin' let me be:
Ye bring deid simmers frae their graves,
To weary me—to weary me.

There grows an ash by my bour door,
And a' its boughs are clad in snaw;
The ice-drap hangs at ilka twig,
And sad the nor' wind soughs* through' a'. swishes
Oh, cease thy mane, thou norlan' wind;
And o' thy wailin' let me be:
Thou brings deid winters frae their graves,
To weary me—to weary me.

Oh, I wad fain forget them a';
Remembered guid but deepens ill—
As gleids* o' licht far seen by nicht flashes
Mak' the near mirk but mirker still.
Then silent be, thou dear auld tree—
O' a' thy voices let me be;
They bring the deid years frae their graves,
To weary me—to weary me.

## On the Cheviots

Once more, once more upon the hills!
No more the splendor, quivering bright—
Which laid, at summer's height,
A finger on the lips of half the rills—
Pours on them; but the year's most mellow light.
Far through yon opening of the vale,
Upon the slopes of Teviotdale,
The green has ta'en a fainter tinge:
It is the time when flowers grow old,
And Summer trims her mantle fringe
With stray threads of autumnal gold.

The west Wind blows from Liddesdale;
And, as I sit—between the springs
Of Bowmont and of Kale—
To my half-listening ear it brings
All floating voices of the hill—
The hum of bees in heather bells,
And bleatings from the distant fells*, hills
The curlew's whistle far and shrill,
And babblings from the restless rill
That hastes to leave its lone hillside,
And hurries on to sleep in Till,
Or join the tremulous flow of Teviot's sunny tide.

It has not changed—the old hill tune,
And marks that years in me have wrought
Fade as its low familiar croon
Wakens by turns full many a thought,
And many an olden fancy brought
From glooms of long oblivion,—
Forlornest fragments, torn and strewn,
Of dreams which I have dreamed at noon,
Long since, when Summer led a fairer June,
And wealthier autumns spread the slopes,
And younger hearts nursed larger hopes
Of bounties that the years should bring,
Nor dreamed of all the care and all the war faring.

Oh, western wind, so soft and low,
Long-lingering by furze and fern,
Rise! From thy wing the languor throw,
And by the marge of mountain tarn,
By rushy brook, and lonely cairn,
Thy thousand bugles take, and blow
A wilder music up the fells! Thy whispered spells—
About my heart I feel them twined;
And all the landscape far around
Neath their still strength lies thralled and bound.
The sluggard clouds, the loitering streams,
And all the hills are dreaming dreams,
And I, too, dream with them, O western wind.

This morn, I thought to linger here
Till fall of evening and the dew—
To think some fresher thought perchance, or rear
Old hopes in forms and colors new;
Then homeward by the burn-side wend,
When over Cheviot, keen and clear,
The moon looked down upon the land.
But sad sweet spots hath each lost year—
As ruins have their crevice-flowers
That sprinkle beauty oer decay;
And I've been sitting hours on hours,

While those old seasons, hovering near,
Beguiled me of today.

I said that they were faded out,
The lines that years in me have wrought.
Alas, there is no hand to smooth
Life's gravel record from our brows;
Fate drives us from the fields of Youth,
And no returning step allows.
Let me no more, then, with reverted eyes—
Let me no more with covetous sighs
Gaze at the light that on them lies.
But come, assail me without ruth,
Pains of the life that's still my own.
Crowd out of sight the time that's gone:
Come, living cares; and come, the hour's anxieties.

## DAVID GRAY (1838–1861)

[Gray is noted as the author of a long, charming, if somewhat unfocused poem on a local river, *The Luggie*. He produced also a striking series of thirty sonnets called *In The Shadows*, written by the young man when he discovered he was shortly to die of tuberculosis. The first four poems below are taken from the sonnet sequence. The fifth selection, "The Dear Old Toiling One," is heartfelt, but in the sentimental vein of most popular poetry of the age.]

### If It Must Be

If it must be; if it must be, O God!
That I die young, and make no further moans;
That, underneath the unrespective sod,
In unescutcheoned privacy, my bones
Shall crumble soon,—then give me strength to bear
The last convulsive throe of too sweet breath.
I tremble from the edge of life, to dare
The dark and fatal leap, having no faith,
No glorious yearning for the Apocalypse;
But like a child that in the night-time cries
For light, I cry; forgetting the eclipse
Of knowledge and our human destinies.
   O peevish and uncertain soul, obey
   The law of life in patience till the Day.

### Last Night

Last night, on coughing slightly with sharp pain,
There came arterial blood, and with a sigh
Of absolute grief I cried in bitter vein,
That drop is my death-warrant: I must die.
Poor meager life is mine, meager and poor.
Rather a piece of childhood thrown away;
An adumbration faint; the overture

To stifled music; year that ends in May;
The sweet beginning of a tale unknown;
A dream unspoken; promise unfulfilled;
A morning with no noon, a rose unblown,—
All its deep rich vermilion crushed and killed
I' th' bud by frost:— Thus in false fear I cried,
Forgetting that to abolish death Christ died.

## The Daisy Flower

The daisy flower is to the summer sweet,
Though utterly unknown it live and die;
The spheral harmony were incomplete
Did the dewed laverock mount no more the sky,
Because her music's linked sorcery
Bewitched no mortal heart to heavenly mood.
This is the law of nature, that the deed
Should dedicate its excellence to God,
And in so doing find sufficient meed.
Then why should I make these heart-burning cries
In sickly rhyme with morbid feeling rife,
For fame and temporal felicities?
Forgetting that in holy labor lies
The scholarship severe of human life.

## Sometimes

Sometimes, when sunshine and blue sky prevail,
When spent winds sleep, and, from the budding larch,
Small birds, with incomplete, vague sweetness, hail
The unconfirmed yet quickening life of March,
Then say I to myself, half-eased of care,
Toying with hope as with a maiden's token,
"This glorious, invisible fresh air
Will clear my blood till the disease be broken."
But slowly, from the wild and infinite west,
Up-sails a cloud, full-charged with bitter sleet.
The omen gives my spirit much unrest;
I fling aside the hope, as indiscreet,
A false enchantment, treacherous and fair,
And sink into my habit of despair.

## The Dear Old Toiling One

Oh, many a leaf will fall tonight,
As she wanders through the wood.
And many an angry gust will break
The dreary solitude.
I wonder if she's past the bridge,
Where Luggie moans beneath,
While raindrops clash in planted lines
On rivulet and heath.

Disease hath laid his palsied palm
Upon my aching brow.
The headlong blood of twenty-one
Is thin and sluggish now.
Tis nearly ten, a fearful night,
Without a single star
To light the shadow on her soul
With sparkle from afar.
The moon is canopied with clouds,
And her burden it is sore.
What would wee Jackie do, if he
Should never see her more?
Ay, light the lamp, and hang it up
At the window fair and free.
Twill be a beacon on the hill
To let your mother see.
And trim it well, my little Ann,
For the night is wet and cold,
And you know the weary, winding way
Across the miry wold.
All drenched will be her simple gown,
And the wet will reach her skin.
I wish that I could wander down,
And the red quarry win,
To take the burden from her back,
And place it upon mine;
With words of cheerful condolence,
Not uttered to repine.
You have a kindly mother, dears,
As ever bore a child,
And heaven knows I love her well
In passion undefiled.

Ah me, I never thought that she
Would brave a night like this,
While I sat weaving by the fire
A web of fantasies.
How the winds beat this home of ours
With arrow-falls of rain.
This lonely home upon the hill
They beat with might and main.
And mid the tempest one lone heart
Anticipates the glow,
Whence, all her weary journey done,
Shall happy welcome flow.
Tis after ten. O, were she here,
Young man although I be,
I could fall down upon her neck,
And weep right gushingly.
I have not loved her half enough,
The dear old toiling one,
The silent watcher by my bed,
In shadow or in sun.

## The Harebell

Beneath a hedge of thorn, and near
Where Bothlin steals through light and shadow,
I saw its bell, so blue and clear—
That little beauty of the meadow.

It was a modest, tender flower—
So clearly blue, so sweetly tender;
No simpler offspring of the shower
And sunshine may July engender.

The "azure harebell," Shakespeare says—
And such a half-transparent azure
Was never seen in country ways
By poet in creative leisure.

But chiefly the beloved song—
The patriot ballad, fresh and olden—
The "Scottish Blue Bells," rose among
Some other memories, pure and golden.

And chiming oer one verse of power,
While in the chalice fondly peering,
A tear-drop fell upon the flower—
My blessing earnest and enduring.

The prize was mine!—but no, ah no—
To spare it was a poet's duty;
So in that spot I let it blow,
And left it in its lonely beauty.

# CHARLOTTE ELLIOT (1839–1880)

## The Wife of Loki[1]

Cursed by the gods and crowned with shame,
Fell father of a direful brood,
Whose crimes have filled the heaven with flame
And drenched the earth with blood;

Loki, the guileful Loki, stands
Within a rocky mountain gorge.
Chains gird his body, feet, and hands,
Wrought in no mortal forge.

[1] In Norse mythology, Loki was the most mischievous—or simply evil—of the gods. What is described below was his eternal punishment.

Coiled on the rock, a mighty snake
Above him, day and night, is hung,
With dull malignant eyes awake,
And poison-dropping tongue.

Drop follows drop in ceaseless flow,
Each falling where the other fell,
To lay upon his blistered brow
The liquid fire of hell.

But lo, beside the howling wretch
A woman stands, devoid of dread,
And one pale arm is seen to stretch
Above his tortured head.

All through the day is lifted up,
And all the weary nighttime through,
One patient hand that holds a cup
To catch the poison dew.

Sometimes the venom overfills
The cup, and she must pour it forth.
With Loki's curses then the hills
Are rent from south to north.

But she in answer only sighs,
And lays her lips upon his face,
And, with love's anguish in her eyes,
Resumes her constant place.

## ALEXANDER JAPP (1840–1905)

### A Music Lesson

Fingers on the holes, Johnny,
Fairly in a raw*. "row"
Lift this and then that,
And blaw, blaw, blaw.
That's hoo to play, Johnny,
On the pipes sae shrill.
Never was the piper yet
But needit a' his skill.

And lang and sair he tried it, tae,
Afore he wan the knack
O' making bag and pipe gie
His verra yearnin's back:
The echo tae his heart strings.
Frae sic a thing to come,
Oh, is it no a wonder—
Like a voice frae out the dumb?

Tak tentie*, noo, my Johnny lad, care
Ye maunna hurry through,
Tak time and try it owre again—
Sic a blast ye blew.
It's no alane by blawing strang,
But eke by blawing true,
That ye can mak the music
To thrill folk through and through.

The waik folk and the learnin',
Tis them that maks the din;
But for the finished pipers
They count it as a sin.
And maybe it's the verra same
A' the warld through,
The learners are the verra ones
That mak the most ado.

Ye ken the Southrons taunt us—
I sayna they're unfair—
Aboot oor squallin' music,
And their taunts hae hurt me sair.
But if they'd heard a piper true
At nicht come ower the hill,
Playin' up a pibroch
Upon the wind sae still:

Risin' noo, and fallin' noo,
And floatin' on the air,
The sounds come saftly on ye
Amaist ere ye're aware,
And wind themsels aboot the heart,
That hasna yet forgot
The witchery o' love and joy
Within some lanely spot.

I'm sure they wadna taunt us sae,
Nor say the bagpipe's wild,
Nor speak o' screachin' noises
Enuch to deave* a child. deafen
They would say the bagpipe only
Is the voice of hill and glen;
And would listen to it sorrowing,
Within the haunts of men.

Fingers on the holes, Johnny,
Fairly in a raw.
Lift this and then that,
And blaw, blaw, blaw.
That's hoo to play, Johnny,
On the pipes sae shrill.
Never was the piper yet
But needit a' his skill.

### Memories

My love he went to Burdon Fair,
And of all the gifts that he saw there
Was none could his great love declare.
So he brought me marjoram smelling rare—
Its sweetness filled all the air.
Oh, the days I dote on yet,
Marjoram, pansies, mignonette!

My love he sailed across the sea,
And all to make a home for me.
Oh, sweet his last kiss on the lea,
The pansies plucked beneath the tree,
When he said, "My love, I'll send for thee."
Oh, the days I dote on yet,
Marjoram, pansies, mignonette!

His mother sought for me anon;
So long my name she would not own.
Ah, gladly would she now atone,
For we together make our moan.
She brought the mignonette I've sown.
Oh, the days I dote on yet,
Marjoram, pansies, mignonette!

## HARRIET KING (1840– ? )

### The Crocus

Out of the frozen earth below,
Out of the melting of the snow,
No flower, but a film, I push to light;
No stem, no bud,—yet I have burst
The bars of winter, I am the first,
O sun, to greet thee out of the night.

Bare are the branches, cold is the air,
Yet it is fire at the heart I bear,
I come, a flame that is fed by none.
The summer hath blossoms for her delight,
Thick and dewy and waxen-white,
Thou seest me golden, O golden sun.

Deep in the warm sleep underground
Life is still, and the peace profound.
Yet a beam that pierced, and a thrill that smote
Called me and drew me from far away.
I rose, I came; to the open day
I have won, unsheltered, alone, remote.

No bee strays out to greet me at morn,
I shall die ere the butterfly is born,

I shall hear no note of the nightingale;
The swallow will come at the break of green,
He will never know that I have been
Before him here when the world was pale.

They will follow, the rose with the thorny stem,
The hyacinth stalk,—soft airs for them.
They shall have strength, I have but love.
They shall not be tender as I.
Yet I fought here first, to bloom, to die,
To shine in his face who shines above.

O glory of heaven, O ruler of morn,
O dream that shaped me, and I was born
In thy likeness, starry, and flower of flame;
I lie on the earth, and to thee look up,
Into thy image will grow my cup,
Till a sunbeam dissolve it into the same.

## WILLIAM BLACK (1841–1898)

[One of the leading Kailyard novelists, Black added to the expected sentimentality and rustic quaintness, a strong dose of melodrama and a Celtic Revival emphasis upon mood and Highland setting. "The Penance of John Logan," perhaps his best short work, is a restrained and powerful treatment of the theme of guilt and redemption.]

### The Penance of John Logan

*I The Temptation*

The summer sea was shining fair and calm, a perfect mirror of the almost cloudless heavens overhead, as a small rowing-boat, occupied by a single person, was slowly approaching a lonely little island in the Outer Hebrides. The solitary rower was neither fisherman nor sailor, but merely a holiday-maker—a well-known banker from London, in fact—who was seeking rest and recreation in the West Highlands, and who had rather a fancy for going about all by himself and for exploring out-of-the-way neighborhoods. He had heard a good deal of this *Eilean-na-Keal*—the Island of the Burying-place—of its sculptured tombstones, its ancient chapel, its Saints' Well, and other relics and traces of the time when the early Christians made their first settlements in these sea-solitudes; and on this pleasant morning, the water being like a sheet of glass, he thought he could not do better than hire a boat at the little village on the mainland where he chanced to be staying, and pull himself across. It is true that the nearer he got to the island he found that there was a heavy tide running, and his labor at the oars was a much more arduous task than he had bargained for; but eventually he managed to fight his way through, the boat at last shooting into a small and sheltered bay, well out of the current.

But when he stood up to reconnoiter the shore and select a landing-place, he found to his intense astonishment that the island was not so totally uninhabited as he had been informed it was. A pair of eyes were calmly regarding him; and those eyes belonged to a little old man who was seated on a rock some way along the beach—a little, bent, broad-shouldered old man, with long white hair and tanned and weather-worn face. A further glance showed him a cumbrous and dilapidated rowing-boat hauled up into a kind of creek, and also a number of lobster-traps lying about on the shingle. The new-comer therefore naturally concluded that he had not been forestalled by any such hateful being as a fellow tourist, but merely by an old lobster-fisherman who had come out to look after his traps.

The Englishman shoved his boat through the seaweed, jumped out, and hauled it up on the beach; and then walked along to the little old man, who had ceased mending his lobster-traps, and was still calmly regarding the stranger.

"Good morning!" the latter said, cheerfully—he was a good-humored-looking, middle-aged person, who had knocked about the world sufficiently, and who liked to converse with whomsoever he chanced to meet. "This is rather a lonely place for you to be in, isn't it?"

"Ay," said the old man, as he carefully scrutinized the other from head to heel, "there's not many comes here."

"But there used to be people living on the island?" Mr. Ramsden continued, chiefly for the sake of getting his new acquaintance to talk.

The old man paused for a moment or two; then he slowly made answer—

"Ay, I have heard that."

Was he half-witted, then, or was his English defective, or was it his lonely life that had made him thus chary and hesitating of speech? He seemed to ponder over the questions, his eyes all the while taking note of every detail of the stranger's features and dress.

"I saw some seals as I came along: are there many of them about here?"

"Ay, plenty."

"Don't people come and shoot them?"

"No."

"Doesn't anybody ever come here?"

"No."

"Do you ever have to pass the night here?"

"Ay."

"Where do you sleep, then—in your boat?"

He shook his head.

"Where then?"

"In the chaypel."

"Oh that's the chapel I've heard about: you must come and show me where it is, if you are not too busy. Have you been getting many lobsters lately?"

"Some."

"What do you do with them? You can't have many customers in Harivaig."

"To London," the old man said, laconically.

"Oh, you send them to London? To a fishmonger, or a fish dealer, perhaps?"

"Ay, do ye know him?" And then old John Logan seemed to wake up a little; indeed, he spoke almost eagerly, though he was continually hesitating for want of the proper word. "Do ye know him?—Corstorphine—Billingsgate—he sends me the boxes. Do ye know him?—bekass—bekass he is not giffing me enough—and if there wass another one now I would go aweh from him. Mebbe you know Corstorphine?"

"No; I'm sorry to say I don't. I should be very glad to help you if I could, but I'm afraid you would run a great risk in giving up a constant customer. I suppose he takes whatever you send?"

"Oh, ay; oh, ay," was the old man's answer, "but he does not gif enough! And—and I hef a young lass at home—she is the daughter of my daughter that's dead—and—and she is going to be married; and the young man—he is for buying a—a part of a herring-smack, and I am for helping him with the money. But Corstorphine should gif more."

"Well, I think so too. So your grand-daughter is going to be married; and you are going to help the young man to buy his share in the herring-smack as a kind of marriage-portion: is that it?"

"Ay, it's something like that," said old Logan—but doubtfully, for perhaps he had not quite understood.

"I should have thought now," Mr. Ramsden resumed—he had a knack of interesting himself in people—"that it would have been worth your while to take the young man into your own business, instead of buying him a share in a smack. You are getting up in years; and this is a very lonely life for you to lead; if the young man came in—with a little capital, perhaps—?"

Old Logan shook his head.

"It's not a good business at ahl. There's the coorse weather: and the things brekkin'; and—and then there's Corstorphine. He is not a fair man, Corstorphine. He should gif more—pless me, they hef plenty of money in London, as I wass being told many's the time."

"Yes, but they like to keep it, my friend," the banker replied. "Well, now, if you are not too busy, will you come and show me where the tombstones are, and the other things I have heard about?"

The old man slowly rose, and put aside the trap he had been mending. It was now apparent that, despite his short stature, his white hair, and his glazed eyes, he was a much stronger man—especially about the chest and shoulders—than he had appeared to be when sitting in a crouching position: there was no longer any mystery as to how that big, cumbrous boat had been got over.

"Mebbe you'll not be living in London?" the lobster fisherman asked thoughtfully, as he led the way for his companion along some rising slopes that were thickly matted with bracken.

"Yes, I live in London," was the answer.

"But you are not knowing Corstorphine?" was the next question.

"No, I don't know him; but surely you would not quarrel with him before getting another customer?"

"He is not a fair man; he should be giffing me more"—this was the refrain of the conversation, repeated again and again, as they made their way up to a rude little enclosure, the four-square wall of which had tumbled down until it was nearly level with the grass and the abundant nettles.

And now the banker-traveler found what he had come in search of—all kinds of sculptured gravestones, with memorial figures of knights in armor, lying scattered about among the tall weeds. In most cases he had to clear away this herbage before he could get a proper view of the stones; while his companion stood blankly gazing on, perhaps wondering at this curiosity about such familiar things but saying nothing. Nor did the stranger apparently expect to get from the old fisherman much information about the Culdees and their haunts, and the Irish princes and knights who were fain to choose for their burial-place one of those sacred islands in the northern seas.

He examined tombstone after tombstone, observing the curious emblems—elephants, two-handed swords, rude castles, and such smaller things as pincers and combs—that no doubt would have afforded to anyone sufficiently instructed some hint as to the dignity or office of the now-forgotten dead; and very singular it was to find these memorials of bygone ages in this silent little island set amid these lonely seas. Then they went to the chapel, a small building of hardly any architectural pretensions beyond some sculptured stones over the doorway; while inside the only noticeable feature was a lot of scattered hay—the old fisherman's bed when his business or the weather compelled him to pass a night on the island. Finally, they visited the Saints' Well, a considerable hole bored down through the solid rock; and here the exploration of this isolated little bit of no-man's-territory seemed to have come to an end.

But their last quest had brought them to the top of a ridge, from which they could look down on a tiny bay—a secluded small bay that appeared to be safe from the strong tides that were seen to be running a little further out.

"Not much of a current in here, is there?" the Englishman asked.

"No, not much," his companion answered.

"Well, look here, my friend, before setting out for home again, I think I should like to have a dip in the sea and this seems a very nice and likely place. In the meantime, if you go back to your boat, I wish you would pick me out two or three lobsters, and you shall have your own price for them—better than what Corstorphine gives you, I imagine. Do you understand?"

"Oh, ay," said the old man, beginning to move away; "I'll have their claws tied by the time you come."

These were the last words that this hapless traveler was ever to hear on this earth. The old fisherman went slowly back to his boat, to select the lobsters for his unexpected customer. He went leisurely about the task, thinking of nothing, most likely, but the price that would probably be paid for them. Then he lit his pipe, and sat waiting in the silence. An absolute silence it was, save for the noise of certain sea-swallows, that seemed to have been disturbed by the bather, and were now wheeling and darting overhead, uttering screams of alarm and resentment over the intrusion.

Suddenly the old man heard a cry—a call for help, as it seemed to be, from far away. He started up erect, and listened. That faint, boding sound was repeated. Instantly he threw aside the lobster trap that happened to be in his hand, and, with a speed that could hardly have been expected from one of his age, he made his way up the slopes of bracken, until he stood on a knoll commanding a view of the bay beside which he had left the stranger. The same moment he perceived whence had come that cry of anguish. The swimmer was some way out—perhaps the strong tide had caught him—perhaps cramp had struck him helpless—but just as old John Logan, entirely bewildered and unnerved, was hesitating as to what he ought to do, there was an arm raised from the surface of the water—as if in a last, pitiful appeal to the silent heavens overhead—and then the smooth plain of the sea was blank of any feature whatsoever. Nothing but this wide waste—and the voiceless air—and the warm sun shining abroad over an empty world.

Hardly knowing what he did, the old man rushed down the slopes again, and across the beach, and shoved off the stranger's boat, which was lighter than his own, jumping into it, and setting to work at the oars with a breathless and strenuous haste. But there were two small promontories intervening between this bay and that on the western side of the island; and his hurried pulling was not likely to be of any avail. Old Logan did his best—probably too much alarmed to have any time for the calculation of chances; and ever, as he came within view of the stretch of water where he had seen the drowning man go down, he kept glancing over his shoulder as he tugged away at the oars.

There was nothing visible at all—nothing but that wide blue plain of sea, and the lonely shore stretching in successive indentations away to the south. He relaxed his efforts now. He had reached, as well as he could judge, the very spot at which he had seen the stranger disappear. There was no sign of him, nor of any other living thing—even the screaming sea-fowl had departed. He took the oars into the boat, and stood up—looking all around. It was hopeless. If the swimmer had been seized with cramp, as seemed most likely, this strong tide would have swept him away with it long before Logan had come round to the point. Indeed, the current was so powerful that the old man had presently to take to the oars again, and pull hard into the quieter waters of the bay, where eventually he landed, dragging the boat a little bit up on the beach.

He was used to loneliness; but this loneliness had never been terrible to him before. That boding cry—that piteous call for aid—seemed still to linger in the air. It was so short a time since he had been familiarly speaking to this fellow-creature, who had been suddenly swept away out of the living and breathing world. In vain the old man, with long-accustomed eyes, swept that vast expanse of water; there was no sign—he knew there could be no sign. It was only a kind of mysterious fascination that kept him gazing on the wide watery plain where he had seen that arm thrown up as in a last despairing appeal for help. Help, he knew, there was none now; the stranger who had sought these solitary shores had vanished for ever from human ken.

There was nothing now for him but to go away back to the village of Harivaig, on the mainland, to acquaint the people there with what had happened; and so, with a parting glance at the empty waste of sea, he set out along the beach. And here, after he had gone some thirty or forty yards, he came upon the drowned man's clothes. He approached them with a morbid curiosity, and yet with a certain reluctance that was akin to fear. They looked strangely like a corpse. They were dead and mute, an unfamiliar and uncanny thing, lying dark on the white beach. And then, as he drew nearer—slowly and cautiously—he noticed that there was some small object there that glittered in the strong sunlight. It was a piece of jewelry, lying on the empty waistcoat.

He went close up, his eyes still fixed on those small stones that gleamed in the sun, and, although he did not quite know what this thing was—it was a locket, indeed, of considerable size, with initials on the outside composed of alternate rubies and diamonds—he recognized it as one of those adornments that rich people wore. And then—at what instigation, who can tell?—he bethought him of his granddaughter, Jeannie, the one sole creature in the world he cared for; she was to be married in the autumn, and she had nothing of this kind to give her value in the eyes of her husband. The young man who was going to marry her had made several voyages to foreign parts, and could talk bravely about the wonderful things he had seen: moreover, he was a smart young fellow and had saved up a little money; the neighbors seemed to consider that the granddaughter of the poor old lobster-fisherman was making a very good match. But if Jeannie were to wear this pretty thing on her wedding day, would not the young man prize her the more? For good looks there was none to beat her on mainland or island, and that everyone was ready to say; but her grandfather's hard-earned savings would be drawn upon rather to give the young couple a fair start in life; she would not have fine clothes to wear as a bride. But if she were to appear with this pretty thing at her neck, would not the young man be all the better pleased with her; and Jeannie would be proud to know that he thought something of her; and none of the neighbors would any longer be fancying that as regards the marriage between the two young people she was getting the best of the bargain?

Old John Logan turned slowly round—as if he feared to find someone watching him from afar. But his quick, furtive glance found nothing. The world was empty of all token of life. There were the trending lines of the bay, the placid mirror of the sea, the cloudless heavens; and he was alone with them. And he was alone with this pretty thing that would make his granddaughter of greater importance in the eyes of her husband. Of what use was it now to the drowned man? Doubtless there were other things of value in these clothes if he were to search—money, a gold watch, and so forth; but he would not touch any of these; for himself he wanted nothing; it was for Jeannie that he coveted this bit of adornment. He could hide it away somewhere. The drowning of the unfortunate man would soon be forgotten. And then the autumn would come; and as the wedding-day drew near he would present Jeannie with this pretty toy; and who could tell that he had not sent to Glasgow for it?

He turned round again towards the bauble that had tempted him, and stood there helpless and motionless for several seconds. Then he knelt down upon the shingle with both knees. But as he took up the locket—with a kind of pretense of only examining it—his hands were shaking as if he had been stricken with palsy. He pushed his scrutiny further. By accident—for he knew nothing of such trinkets—he happened to touch the yielding portion of the gold loop attaching the locket to the watch-chain; he pressed it, and saw how he could take the locket out. The next moment the prize that he had feared almost to look upon lay in the palm of his hand.

Then he slowly rose—his knees all shaking beneath him— and furtively his glance searched sea and shore for any sign of any living thing. Then, with many a backward look—for it seemed to him that there must be someone behind him, someone unseen, but watching—he crossed over the grassy ridges and went down to the creek in which his boat lay. His hand was shut now, with a nervous and tremulous grasp.

In the boat there was some old canvas that he sometimes used in patching up the lobster-traps; he cut off a piece, and wrapped up in it that fatal locket, with its glittering jewels; then he made his way up the hill and across to the old chapel. There was no difficulty in finding a hole in which to secrete his treasure; he chose one in the wall, close down to the ground; and then, having deposited the tiny packet there, he went and got some stones and dry earth and closed up the orifice in a rude sort of fashion. But there was little light in this small building; no one could have noticed that the wall had been meddled with.

And then old John Logan went down to the seaside again, and launched his boat. He might have taken the stranger's boat, which was a good deal lighter to pull; but he had left it on the shore of the other bay, and he dreaded to look again on the clothes lying there. So in his own cumbrous craft he set out for the mainland; and in due course of time he reached the small hamlet of Harivaig, which was speedily startled by the news that the Englishman who had recently come thither had been drowned, and that his clothes, and the boat in which he had rowed himself across, would be found on the beach at Eilean-na-Keal.

### *II Remorse*

Now, the chief public functionary of Harivaig and its neighborhood was the parish schoolmaster; and he it was who immediately took steps to apprise the relatives of the drowned man of what had happened. There was no difficulty about discovering who he was. His private address could not be found; but his papers showed clearly enough that he was a partner in the banking firm of Ramsden, Holt, and Smith, of London; and it was to them that the schoolmaster addressed his communication. Then the clothes of the stranger were brought back from the island, and also the boat in which he had rowed himself across. Finally, the owner of the nearest salmon-fishery sent four of his men as a search-party all along the coast; but although they labored at their task industriously for the better part of two days, no trace of the missing man could be found. Indeed, they worked without hope: it was matter almost of certainty that the body had been washed out to sea.

Meanwhile, old John Logan had more than once, and all by himself, been over to Eilean-na-Keal, and each time he had stealthily made his way to the small ruined chapel, and taken forth the locket from its secret repository, and regarded its gleaming white and red stones. Moreover, he had accidentally discovered that it would open; and inside he found the portrait of a pale faced, delicate-featured lady, apparently of middle age. On making this discovery, he had hurriedly shut the trinket again—for the pale face seemed to be looking strangely at him; and he had formed some dark resolution of removing it, either by gentle means or force, before the time came for presenting this pretty, bejeweled wedding-gift to his granddaughter.

But even when he restricted his contemplation to the outside—to the rich soft golden surface, and the glittering diamonds and rubies—there was not much joy in his heart. For one thing, a nameless terror seemed to seize him the moment he set foot on the island. He felt haunted by some mysterious presence; however his anxious scrutiny might satisfy him that these indented shores were devoid of human life, he appeared to be always expecting someone; when he walked across the lonely little knolls, on his way to the chapel, it was as if there were some living creature following him, close to his shoulder, unseen but felt.

And in the dusk of the chapel itself, when he was crouching down, ready to thrust back the locket into the hole in the wall, he would listen intently, as if fearing some footstep without; and then again, when he came forth into the daylight, his dazed eyes would furtively and swiftly look all around, to make sure that he was quite alone. If the time would but pass more quickly! If the days and weeks could be annihilated, and his granddaughter's wedding-morn be reached—then this precious thing would pass into her keeping, and would trouble his rest no more. For old John Logan had got into a perturbed and feverish state; the drowning of the stranger had made a great commotion in this quiet neighborhood; and Logan, as the last person who had seen him, had to answer innumerable questions—that sometimes seemed to bewilder and frighten him by their unexpectedness.

One morning the old man's granddaughter Jeannie was seated on the rude bench outside the cottage. She had got early finished with her household work, and now she was hemming some handkerchiefs—most likely part of her home-made trousseau—while she sung to herself the cheerful air of "I'll gang nae mair to yon town" without particular regard to the words. She was a good-looking lass of the darker Celtic type—coal-black hair, a complexion as fresh and clear as a June wild rose, dark blue-gray eyes with black lashes, and a pretty and smiling mouth. She was rather neatly dressed, and seemed very well content with herself; indeed, the neighbors were inclined to be indignant among themselves over the fashion in which old John Logan spoiled his pretty granddaughter. Nevertheless, Jeannie Logan (as she was called, though her name was properly Jeannie Carmichael) was a kind of favorite, and that despite the fact of her small house being kept a good deal more trim and tidy than any other in Harivaig.

The old man came out of the cottage, and was going off for the shore, when his granddaughter stopped him.

"Grandfather," said she (but she spoke in Gaelic), "will you not stay at home today? Archie is coming over from Usgary."

"What should I stay at home for?" was the answer (also in Gaelic). "When two young people are going to get married they have plenty to talk of by themselves; it does not need the old man of Ross to tell us that."

The young woman's cheeks flushed a little but she laughed all the same.

"I know," she said "that everyone thinks we talk of nothing but nonsense. Well, it is not of much consequence what any of them are thinking. But you remember, grandfather, that the valuing of the nets was to be done this week; and Archie was writing to me that he would like to have your opinion."

"My opinion!" the old man said, testily. "What is the use of my opinion? What do I know about herring-nets that I have not seen?"

Their conversation was interrupted. There was a sound of wheels—a most unusual sound in this unfrequented neighborhood—and presently there came in sight a waggonette and two horses. As the carriage drove past, a clear enough view of the occupant could be obtained; and these were seen to be a young lady of about seventeen or eighteen, fair-complexioned, and in deep mourning and a tall and elderly gentleman who sat opposite her in the body of the waggonette. The moment they had gone by, Jeannie Logan turned eagerly to her grandfather.

"Do you know who these are?" she said. "For I know. These must be the friends of the gentleman who was drowned. And they will be wanting to see you, grandfather—I am sure of it; so you must go indoors at once, and put on a white collar, and your black coat."

"But for what will they want to see me?" the old man said, with a quick look of apprehension on his face.

"Well, you brought the news over from Eilean-na-Keal; and you were the last that saw the gentleman, and spoke to him. I should not wonder if that was his daughter—poor young lady, this will be a sad day for her. Grandfather, go away and put on your black coat; for they will be coming to see you, or sending for you."

And she was right. Not a quarter of an hour had elapsed when a messenger came from the inn to say that the daughter of the gentleman who had been drowned was there, and that she wished to see John Logan, if he would be so kind as to come along. In the meantime, the old man had taken his granddaughter's advice—indeed, he allowed himself to be governed by her in all such matters—and put on his Sunday clothes. As he was setting out with the messenger, Jeannie Logan placed her hand on his arm for a moment, and said in a low voice,

"Grandfather, I think the young lady will be for going over to Eilean-na-Keal. Well, if the people have any sense, they will not allow her, for it will break her heart."

"Ay, ay!" he said, eagerly. "You are a wise lass, Jeannie, she should not go over to Eilean-na-Keal. No, no; what is the use of her going over to Eilean-na-Keal?"

And this is what he seemed to be pondering over all the way to the inn; for again and again he said in a half-muttering way to his companion.

"Ay, she is a wise lass is Jeannie. She has an old head on young shoulders. Why should the young lady be for going over to Eilean-na-Keal?"

But when at length he reached the inn, and was ushered into the parlor where the strangers were, there was no more speech left in him. This tall, fair-haired girl—whose face was wan and pale, and looked all the paler because of her deep mourning—when she came forward in a pathetic kind of way to take his hand, startled him beyond measure. Had he not seen her before, or someone strangely like her? And then in a bewildered fashion he thought of the face in the locket—the face that he had feared. This was the daughter, then: that, the mother. And he seemed incapable of meeting the steady glance of those plaintive eyes that regarded him so strangely; he was breathless, irresolute, nervous; he intertwisted his fingers; he had no answer for the questions which the elderly gentleman, the young lady's companion, put to him. The landlady, a placid-looking, middle-aged woman, had taken the liberty of remaining in the room.

"He is not used to the English, sir," she said. "He will tell you when he thinks over it."

"And will you not sit down?" the young lady said very gently to him; and she herself pulled out a chair from the wall. For her the violence of grief seemed over and gone; she was outwardly resigned and calm; it was only at times that tears swam into her eyes, and she appeared anxious to hide her emotion from these strangers.

"Yes, sit down, and take your own time," her companion, who was a Mr. Holt, said to old John Logan. "Just think over it, and tell us at your leisure how Mr. Ramsden came to the island, and what he said to you, and what was the last you saw of him. You can understand that his daughter is very anxious to know."

And then the old man, halting and hesitating at every few words, told his tale. Except for the matter of his English, it ought to have come readily enough to him, for he had narrated it, to the minutest circumstances, again and again among the neighbors. It was noticeable, however, that now he kept his eyes fixed on the ground, and that his narrative was a kind of appeal; he was as a culprit endeavoring to justify himself; and over and over he repeated that no man could have pulled harder than he did to try to reach the drowning swimmer.

"Oh, I am sure of that—I am sure of that!" the girl said piteously. "And—we will not forget it."

He did not appear to understand what she meant, so anxious was he to exonerate himself.

"There wass the two points to go round," he repeated once more. "When I wass on the top of the land I wass nearer to him—oh, yes—and I could hef run down to the waterside—and—and been nearer—but no use that would be. I hef not been sweeming since I wass a young man; I could not get out to him. And when I went back to the boat there wass the two points to go round—a long weh it was to pull, and the tide running strong—and I pulled as well as I could—I pulled as hard as ever I wass pulling ahl my life."

"Indeed, I am sure you did your best!" said she—for it seemed pitiable that this old man should think it needful to appeal to her and justify himself.

"Well," said her companion, seeing that Logan's narrative had come to an end, "we have sent for a boat. Miss Ramsden would like to go across to the island; and if you have time to come with us you could show her the place where you last saw her father. Will you add this further obligation to what we already owe you?"

Old Logan was stupefied. In Gaelic he might have remonstrated, and pointed out that it would only be harrowing the feelings of the young lady; but his English was not effective for any such purpose; he had merely to acquiesce in silence; and so it befell that when the salmon fisherman's boat, with a crew of four stalwart rowers, had been brought along, the orphaned girl and her friend, and old John Logan, too, went to the shore, and presently were being taken across the smooth plain of water to Eilean-na-Keal.

She was showing a wonderful fortitude. No sooner had she landed than she began asking the most particular questions—apparently anxious to construct for herself a complete picture of those last minutes of her father's life. Where did he pull his boat up on the beach? Where was he, Logan? What were her father's first words? In what direction did the two of them go to explore the island, and what was the subject of their talk?

Thus it was that the old man came to recall and repeat every single sentence that had been uttered between them. He told her of his complaints about Corstorphine. He told her of the approaching marriage of his granddaughter; of the young man who wanted to purchase a share in a herring-smack; of his own wish to help him in that matter; of the small prices he was getting for the lobsters; of his asking her father if he did not know Corstorphine, that perhaps he might remonstrate.

"But you need not let that trouble you," she said, gently; "I will take care you have enough money to buy the share in the boat."

He started somewhat, and stared at her.

"You, Mem? Oh, no, Mem! I could not be thinking of tekking money from you!" he said, with a curious earnestness that seemed to have something of dread in it.

For during all the time that they had been coming over in the boat, and all the time he had been talking to her on the island, the conviction was growing deeper in his heart that he had robbed this grief-stricken girl, and that without the possibility of restitution. When he had originally taken the locket it seemed the property of no one. Its owner was gone away out of this world; he could never come back to reclaim it; it did not belong to him any more. But now the old man knew that it belonged to this gentle spoken young lady, who was overwhelmed with her sorrow. That was her mother's portrait, sure enough.

And here—although he had robbed her of what must be of exceeding value to her—here she was proposing to do him some substantial act of kindness. The mere thought of it terrified him, somehow. It seemed to aggravate his guilt. Had he not done her enough wrong? And what would be the luck of the herring-smack if part of its purchase-money came through his hands that were stained with crime?

They were approaching the ruined chapel—he rather lingering behind her. He was reluctant to go near; he would not enter by the narrow porch; he would have dissuaded her from going further if only he had dared. And yet what could have been more simple if this anguish of remorse and contrition was becoming unbearable than for him to have gone courageously forward and taken out the locket from its hiding-place, confessed his fault, and begged for her forgiveness? She seemed a kind and sympathetic creature; she was profoundly grateful to him for the efforts, however futile, he had made to rescue her father. Surely she would accept this, all the reparation he could make, and grant him pardon?

But that was not at all how the matter appeared to old John Logan. In his mind the English were a great and powerful and terrible people. Sailors had told him again and again of the vast men-of-war coming into the Clyde, of their enormous cannon, and of the thunder that shook the world when the huge guns were fired. The dread powers of government were in England; the Queen was there, and the Parliament and the Tower that prisoners were thrown into. And if he confessed that he had robbed an English person, would he not be dragged away to that stranger country, and perhaps hanged? The English were a strong, terrible, and vindictive race—so he had heard many a time, in stories current in his boyhood's day. Not to them dared he appeal for mercy. If he made this confession, her forgiveness would avail him nothing; the inexorable powers of the law would seize him, and how would it be with his granddaughter Jeannie if he was taken away to the south and hanged?

He was less anxious and perturbed when the young lady came out of the chapel, and once more submitted to his guidance. In fact, they were following step by step the careless saunter that her father had little thought to be his last; until, finally, Logan took her to the ridge overlooking the fatal bay, and showed her, as well as he could, the precise spot at which the drowning man had disappeared.

It was so lonely, this outlook. She gazed upon it with a kind of shrinking terror. Calm as the sea was, it seemed a cruel, secret, dreadful thing. The silence was awful. She stood there a long while; and it was not until she was coming away that her forced composure entirely broke down. She had turned to cast one long, final, lingering glance towards these empty shores and the voiceless plain of the sea; and it was perhaps some sense of her complete orphanhood that was borne in upon her, or perhaps a feeling that this was a last farewell. But she gave way altogether, and, sinking to the ground, buried her head in her hands, and sobbed and cried passionately and bitterly.

"Edith!" her companion said to her, and he put his hand gently on her shoulder: "Edith, come away now! Indeed, you must come away!"

He assisted her to rise; and then, with bent head and uncertain footsteps, she made her way back to the boat. During the long pull to the mainland, she turned once or twice to regard the small island set amid the calm seas. This was indeed farewell.

Immediately on their arrival at the inn, Mr. Holt began to make preparations for their return to the south: for it was useless allowing the girl to remain in this sad neighborhood. He got his late partner's effects put together, and without much examination; for, finding watch, money, and papers all intact, he did not deem it necessary to make further inquiry, and it certainly never occurred to him at such a time to ask the bereaved daughter about trinkets. The men belonging to the salmon-fishery were liberally rewarded for their two days' search. Then came the question of Logan; and here it was fortunate that Archie MacEachran, who was to marry the old man's granddaughter, happened this very day to have come over from Usgary. Mr. Holt sent for him, and he came: a pleasant looking, light-haired young fellow he was, with a quick, alert eye, though he was somewhat bashful in manner. Mr. Holt had arranged to see him alone.

"I understand you are to marry John Logan's granddaughter," the banker said to him forthwith, "and there is some question of your buying a share in a herring-smack. Now, Miss Ramsden is very much interested in the old man—and grateful to him for having done what he could to rescue her father when he was drowning; and she would like to do something to show her gratitude. He seemed disturbed when she suggested money; I don't know why that should be so; but it has occurred to me that it might be managed in this way—he intends helping you to buy the share in the boat—"

"Ay, but there's the two ways of it," said this young man eagerly, and he could speak English freely enough, if still with a considerable accent; "he wass wanting me to tek the money ahltogether, and I did not like the look of that, for he has not mich, and the look of it would be that I was being paid for marrying his granddaughter. No, I said, I will tek a loan of the money, and I will pay you back. The Kate and Bella is a lucky boat; the Macdowell brothers that hef her, each one of them hass money in the savings-bank; and now that one of them thinks he can do better by buying sheep and tekking them to the trysts, it is a good chance for me to get his share in the smack. Old John Logan—well, he will be wanting his own savings when he gets too old to look after the lobster-traps; and besides that he will hef to be paying some young girl to mind the house for him, when Jeannie Logan comes to me. But if he will lend me the money, ferry well; and I will pay him back when I can."

"I think you take a very sensible view of the situation," the banker said. "How much is this loan that you require?"

"Well, I hef got ahl the money except about twenty-four pounds."

"Twenty-four pounds," Mr. Holt repeated. "Miss Ramsden thought of giving the old man something bigger than that. However, it can be managed in this way: we will make you a loan of fifty pounds, and you will covenant to pay it back to John Logan, in installments—extending over three years if you like. We will tell him that we have advanced you this loan on his account—to give you a fair start in your married life—and to preserve his small savings for his own need; and I dare say he won't mind taking the money in that indirect way."

"Not him, sir," the young man said, with a smile. "He knows the value of money as well as anyone. Some of them will be for saying that old John Logan is not ferry wise in the head; but I think he is clever enough about *that;* he can tell you ferry well what is due to him for interest, and how the book stands—that I know fine!"

"That's all right, then," Mr. Holt said, rising—and the other rose too, and stepped towards the door. "There will be some papers for you to sign. Write your full name and address on an envelope, and leave it for me with the landlady before you go. You will hear later on."

"I thank ye, sir; I thank ye," the young man said; but even with the door open he lingered, standing there shamefacedly.

"There's—there's something more," he stammered. "Maybe—I don't know how to say it, but if you were to tell the young lady that we thanked her for her kindness—and—and more than that—that there's not one of us—not one of us—but would rather not hef it at ahl if we could get her father back to her alive."

The banker stepped forward and took the young man's hand for a moment.

"I will give her the message. She is a kind-hearted girl. In this case I think her kindness has been well bestowed."

And so the strangers went away; and the little hamlet of Harivaig returned to its normal condition of slumberous quiet. But this peace brought no comfort to the mind of old John Logan. Ever before him was the remembrance of the grief-stricken young lady, pale and sad-eyed, who had accompanied him over the island; and he knew that the portrait of her mother, that by right belonged to her, was hidden away in the small chapel, and that he dared not bring it forth into the light. He had lost all intention now of giving the jeweled trinket to his granddaughter Jeannie, to adorn her on her wedding day. Even if the portrait were cut out, and deep buried in the earth, there would be something about the locket itself that he could not face. It was no longer flotsam and jetsam; it belonged to the beautiful, gentle-hearted girl who had been so kind to him and his: he had robbed her—as a requital of her bounty towards them.

The neighbors remarked that old John Logan was growing still more strange in his ways. He had hardly a word for anyone now. He seemed morose and depressed; he would not even talk about the purchase of the share in the Kate and Bella—though that was known to be a great thing for young MacEachran and Jeannie Logan; and he did not go over to Eilean-na-Keal as often as he used to do, even when the weather was quite fine.

Moreover, in the little Free Church building half-way on the road to Usgary, to which the Harivaig people walked every Sabbath morning, they noticed that, more than once, when the Minister was making a fervent appeal to the consciences of his people, John Logan, with downbent head, would answer with a perfectly audible moan. Some said that the old man was grown older than ever in his ways simply because of the solitary life that he led out at the lobster-baskets. Others hinted that the sight of the stranger drowning had frightened him, and that he had never been quite the same since. While others again maintained that it was merely the going away of his granddaughter that was preying on his mind, and that he would soon get accustomed to it, once the wedding was over.

"Grandfather," said Jeannie Logan to him one night—an open Bible was lying on the table before him, and she had heard him sigh heavily once or twice, as if in great distress or pain, "grandfather, is there anything wrong with you?"

"There is something wrong with me," he answered, in the Gaelic, "that will never be made right in this world."

"What is it, grandfather?" she asked, in sudden alarm.

But he would not speak; and as the days went by matters seemed to grow worse with him. The neighbors wondered; but his granddaughter could tell them nothing. At last there came one evening—he had got down the Bible, as usual, and as it was almost dark, she was just about to light the lamp.

"Jeannie," said he, "I have something to say to you."

"Yes, grandfather?"

"You have been a good lass to me in this house; and you will make a good wife. I could not wish to see you better married. The lad will do well. And you will say nothing to anyone to-night, nor yet in the morning; but to-morrow morning I am going away."

"Going away, grandfather!" she exclaimed. "Why, where are you going?"

"I am going away," he said—and as she lit the lamp at this moment, she was startled to find that there were tears running down the old man's face. "I am going away—to—to Greenock—and maybe further than that, and maybe I will never come back to Harivaig. But you have been a good lass—and you will make a good wife."

"Grandfather," said she, suddenly, "are you going away on my account? Is it because I am going to be married?"

"No, no; it is not that. I am glad that you will have a house of your own and a husband to look after you. It is not that; it is of no use for you to know; and if any of them ask you where I have gone you can say I am away by the Dunara Castle to the south. Be a good lass, Jeannie, be a good lass; you will have a house of your own now; and the lad will do well."

All her prayers and entreaties and expostulations were of no avail; she could get no further answer from him; nay, he enjoined her to silence; and early in the morning—long before the hamlet of Harivaig was awake—she heard him open the door and set out. He had started on his long and weary tramp to the nearest port at which the Dunara Castle called.

*III A Pilgrimage*

During that long sea-voyage to Greenock old John Logan saw many strange things, but nothing so strange as the termination of it, when, just after nightfall, the steamer slowly glided into its appointed berth alongside the quay. He had never beheld a large town before; and although this town was invisible, the amazing extent of it could be guessed from its bewildering glare—rows of points of yellow fire gleaming afar, as if along unknown hills, fiercer white lights, and green lamps, and red lamps, down here in the harbor, while the very heavens overhead were irradiated by a dull, somber, steady glow.

When Logan, with his small bundle in his hand, left the gangway, and found himself stranded on the quay—amid these hurrying black figures, and the bewildering gas lamps, and general confusion and noise—he knew not which way to turn. What he had in his mind was to find out the steamer that would carry him on to London; but how was he to discover her whereabouts in the dark? He had been told on board the Dunara Castle that there was such a steamer—the Anchor Line, they said. But he knew not where nor whom to ask; indeed, he was somewhat dazed, not to say frightened; he stood there irresolute, watching men and things pass by him as in some black and appalling nightmare.

And then, cautiously and fearfully, he began his quest, wandering like a ghost round the dimly-lit basins and docks. But all these vessels seemed dead. He made bold to ask one or two of the solitary passers-by; but they did not stay to answer this old man with his hesitating speech and unintelligible questions. At last one of them, more civil than his predecessors, did stop for a second to ascertain what the old man wanted; and then, with a curt "She'll be doon the morn," he went on his way again.

So there was the long night to be passed in this terrible place. He began to look at the houses, wondering whether he dared ask at any of them for a night's lodging. His stock of money was small; and he wished to hoard it; for what was yet before him was all unknown. Moreover, a night in the open was nothing to him—had it been on the sea, that is, or on the shores of an island; what a night in the streets of a town might be, he knew not.

He wandered on. He came upon a wider thoroughfare, where there was an amazing concourse of people—a double stream of people, passing along the pavement, under the gas-lamps, in front of the blazing windows of the shops. There were shouts and cries; there was a roar and rattle of wheels; the lights fell on all kinds of strange faces, many of them grimy and disfigured, some with unkempt hair and dissolute features, others loud-laughing with a ghastly mirth. It was like some kind of Pandemonium, into which he might fall, and be swept away; he shrank back from it; he hid himself in the gloom of one of the by-streets, and gazed forth upon it with an insatiable, terrified curiosity. And then he thought the neighborhood of the docks would be safer for him. He would feel more at his ease if he were near the water; so he turned his back upon that flaming, roaring, turbulent highway, and set out through the silence of the dark little thoroughfare to reach the harbor and the quays.

He had proceeded some way down this little by-street when the prevailing quietude was broken in upon by the distant raucous voice of someone bawling "Ye Banks and Braes" to the discordant accompaniment of a concertina. Presently two figures loomed in sight—one of them flinging his arms about as he made this hideous din with the concertina; the other growling and cursing at his companion for the noise he was making. They proved to be two great hulking fellows—loafers about the docks, most likely; and as they came up to old John Logan, one of them, a beetle-browed, surly-looking dog, angrily knocked the concertina out of his neighbor's hand, so as to ensure some kind of silence, while he proceeded, apparently from mere ill-temper, to cross-question John Logan as to how he came to be there and what he wanted. The old man, suspecting no ill, told him in his hesitating English that he was waiting for the steamer that was next day going to London, and that he was not sure whether to ask somewhere for a bed. By this time the brawling musician had quieted down, and seemed much interested in the stranger.

"Ye auld gomeril," said he, with rough jocularity, "what are ye aboot? Do ye no ken that my freen' here's the captain o' the verra steamer ye're gaun' in—ay, as sure's death: what for would I tell ye a lee? And dinna ye ken that she's already cam' doon frae Glesca—she's lying in the harbor, man, and what's to prevent yer ganging on board and getting a nicht's rest in yer ain berth?"

"Ay, could I do that?" old Logan said, eagerly: here was just the fulfillment of his most anxious wishes—to get on board the vessel at once, and know that he was safe bound for London.

"Of course ye can!" the other said, gaily; while the heavy browed ruffian stood silently by and watched. "There's my freen' the captain: speak him fair, and he'll put ye on board directly, and ye'll have yer ain bunk. Ye've got yer passage-money!"

"Ay," answered the old man.

"And maybe something ower?"

"Ay, ay—maybe," Logan said, with some hesitation.

"Ye'll have to pay yer passage-money afore ye gang on board—that's the rule in this line o' steamers," said the musician, who was gradually losing his boisterously facetious tone, and attending to this matter in a strictly business fashion. "And the best thing for ye will be to step round to the captain's house—it's no very far frae here—and we'll just settle up at once, and then ye'll gang strecht on board. It's no safe for an auld man like you to be wanderin' about Greenock streets: ye'll be far better on board the ship. Come on!"

Old Logan suspected nothing. He had seen captains of coasting vessels no better dressed than either of these men; and he was not likely to know the difference between the master of a trading smack and the master of an Anchor Liner. But, indeed, it was his extreme anxiety to get at once on board the steamer that induced him to consent. Without further scruple he accompanied the two strangers—down this street, across another, and along a third, until they stopped at a certain "close." This close or entrance was pitch-dark; but the concertina-player led the way, old Logan following, and groping with his hands along the wall, the surly-browed scoundrel bringing up the rear. Then they had to ascend a stair, also in absolute darkness; but at the second landing a door was opened, and that gave some small indication of their whereabouts.

They entered the house. It seemed empty, for there was not a sound of any kind; however, by the dull light of a small lamp in the lobby the old Highlander was ushered into a room, and there the leader of the party struck a match and lit a candle that was on the chimney-piece. It was a dingy little den; but Logan was not thinking of his surroundings: it was the steamer that concerned him.

The door was made fast behind them: the candle was placed on the table.

"Now, my decent old freen'," the concertina-player began, resuming his jocular manner, "we'll jist settle this business at once. Out wi' the little bits o' dibs. And ye may just as weel hand us over the lot: ye'll no want any money till ye get to London. Come on!—let's see what ye've got. Is't in a stocking? I'm vexed I canna offer ye a dram to croon the bargain; but never mind—just hand us ower what ye've got, and I'll gie ye a receipt at Marti'mas."

And now it was that old John Logan began to realize the position in which he found himself; and it was impossible to say which was the more disquieting—this bantering that was growing near to bullying, or the sinister silence with which the other confederate stood and looked on.

"I'll—I'll pay when I get on board the steamer," the old man said, and instinctively he turned and glanced towards the door.

"Will ye now?" the concertina-player rejoined, with a burst of laughter. "Weel, that's a guid ane! Ye're a funny auld deevle!" He put both elbows on the table, rested his head in his hands, and stared mockingly at old Logan. "Do ye no think this is a fine, quate place to do our wee bit o' business? We wadna disappoint the captain? If ye speak him fair, maybe he'll leave ye the price o' a dram. I'm getting awfu' dry mysel'; and I wish ye'd bring out they bonnie pound-notes—or is it a' in half-croons and shillins, in a nice wee bag?"

But here his accomplice broke in impatiently.

"Oh, stop your jaw!" he said; and then he turned to Logan: "Here, oot wi' that money!"

"Ay, that's it, Tam," the other said, complacently, "you get the money, and I'll just hae a look at the bundle—maybe there's a braw saytin waistcoat that'll dae for my weddin'."

He reached across, and would have seized the bundle, but that the old man—now thoroughly alarmed—snatched it out of his grasp and made forthwith for the door. Instantly the more taciturn of the two scoundrels placed himself in his way; whereupon Logan, wild with fright, dropped his bundle, and gripped the man with both hands, to hurl him on one side. The attack was so sudden—the strength of the old man so unexpected—that this heavy-built brute was taken aback—his one foot tripped over the other—he staggered a step or two and fell headlong before he had time to clutch at anything but the useless wall.

Logan turned in haste to pick up his bundle, only to find that the other bully was rushing at him with an uplifted poker. The blow would have fallen on his head, but that he warded it off with his arm; and then, in desperation, he drove at this fellow as he had driven at the other—with the whole weight of his heavy shoulders—sending him crashing against the table. In an instant everything was in blackness. The candle had been knocked over. And now, for a moment, it was just possible that the old man might have got safely away if he could have found the door at once; but instead of the door he stumbled against the more burly of the two ruffians, who seized and tried to hold him, while the other, with the most horrible threats and imprecations, was endeavoring to find a match to light the candle. And no sooner was the room lit again than the scrimmage recommenced; for the old man fought with the fury of a wild cat. It was not his money he was fighting for, nor yet his little bundle of clothes, but for the safety of a certain treasure sewn up in the lining of his coat, of the existence of which they little dreamed. Of course, such an unequal struggle could have but one end. A blow on the head with the poker knocked him senseless; and he knew no more.

When he came to himself—he had no idea how long thereafter—there was a fierce glare of yellow light striking into his dazed eyes. It was a policeman's lantern. He was lying on the pavement outside; and when the policeman helped him up to a sitting position, it was seen that his white hair was bedabbled with blood.

"Ye're an auld chap to hae been fechtin'," the policeman said, in no unkindly way. "How came ye to be in such a state as this? Ye're no drunk, too! Weel, ye'll hae to get up and gang wi' me to the office, and gie an account of yoursel'."

But the first thing that old John Logan did on regaining consciousness was quickly to put his hand to his side. It was enough. He felt the hard substance there under the cloth. They had robbed him of his little bundle of clothes, and plundered him of every penny, but they had not discovered the jeweled trinket, the restitution of which would make such reparation as was now possible, and perchance mitigate in some measure the remorse and anguish of his soul.

Obediently, like a child, he did what the policeman told him. He gave him what account he could of the circumstances leading up to the robbery, and of the robbery itself; but he could not say which of the "closes" in this dark little thoroughfare was the one he had been induced to enter, for the thieves had taken the precaution of dragging him some little way along the pavement after fetching him out. And obediently, if somewhat slowly—for he was faint and weak from want of blood—he accompanied the policeman to the station. Here he told his story over again, and had the wounds on his head dressed; and the inspector on duty, finding that the old man had been left without a farthing, would have allowed him to pass the night in one of the cells. But John Logan would not hear of that; nor would he listen to the proposal that he should remain in Greenock for a time to see whether the detectives could not discover the thieves who had robbed him, and perhaps get back some of the stolen property. His mind was set on London. The steamer was coming down the Clyde the next day. If he had no money, perhaps they would let him work his passage as a deck hand. So, as well as he was able, he thanked the people at the police-office for their kind treatment of him, and went forth again into the night.

But this time, while he was still anxious to get down to the harbor, with the vague instinct that he would somehow be safer near the water, he kept to the thoroughfares where he saw plenty of people. In this wise he made his way along Cathcart Street, and down the lane leading to the Custom House, until at length be found himself on the quay. Out there was the black water; and afar he could see the red and green sailing-lights of the steamers passing up and down the estuary. There was hardly anyone on this wide, open breadth of stone; so he wandered along, looking for some corner of a shed where he might rest for the night. For it was getting late; and the old man was weak and exhausted; moreover, there was a singing in his head that seemed to stupefy him; so that, when he happened in his wandering search to come upon a barrow that was chained to a post—it was dark here, and he thought no one would disturb him—he crept on to it, and lay down with his arm for a pillow, and with his other hand clasped over the jeweled toy that had brought him so much tribulation.

### *IV A Friend in Need*

But there was not much sleep for old John Logan. His circumstances were too desperate. He gave up the hope of being able to work his passage to London; they would not take an old white-haired man. Nor did he think of going by road; the distance, to his imagination, was immeasurable; he would die of hunger by the way. And if that were to be the end, there would be no restitution and atonement; his secret would be buried with him; there would be no chance of begging for forgiveness from the gentle voiced, sad-eyed young lady who had been so kind to them all.

Nay, on the awful day of Judgment, when he was arraigned as a thief, would she not be there, summoned to confront him as his accuser? How could he make known then what his contrition had been? She would stand opposite him; she would recognize him as the man for whose granddaughter she had done so much; and she would know him to be a thief. London seemed the width of worlds away. And so was Harivaig, too, to one who was penniless. He could not get back, if he had wished to get back. But he did not wish it. His life contained but one burning desire, and all things else were unregarded. So the night passed, in fruitless longings; in wild, pathetic visions of fulfillment; in the contemplation of failure, and leaden despair; and as he lay there, worn out and sleepless, with an aching head and a heavy heart, there gradually came into the eastern heavens a wan gray light that broadened and widened up until the new day was shining over land and sea.

He rose from his hard and restless couch and looked around him with dazed eyes. The wide waters of the Firth were all of a shimmering gray; far away on the other side was the wooded promontory of Roseneath, with the big castle on a clearance between the trees; there were white villages along the further shores, under the low-lying hills. The business of the work-a-day world had already begun; there were vessels going up and down—here a small tug towing after it a mass of floating timber, there a larger steamer taking a big three-master away up the river. Along the quays, too, near at hand, signs of life were becoming visible; so in case anyone should complain of his having appropriated this not very desirable bed, he got on his feet again and began to wander back in the direction of the town.

He had no thought of finding the two men who had robbed him—still less of recovering what they had taken from him. Indeed, he hardly knew what he was doing; only, the inspector at the police-office had spoken kindly to him, and he seemed to be drawn back thither, if he could but hit upon the way. There might be some word of advice. Anyhow, he wandered on.

He could not, however, discover the whereabouts of the police station, and his hopes in that direction were too vague to prompt him to ask his way of a stranger. But now that the activities of the streets were declaring themselves in every direction—the shops being opened, the passers-by increasing in number—each moment seemed to add to his dismay at the thought that the steamer would soon be arriving, and would leave the quay again and set forth on its long voyage to London, while he was left in this unknown town, among all these unknown people. The more he considered this probability, the more terrible it seemed. If only he could send to Harivaig for the money to pay his passage! It was impossible. Days—he knew not how many—would have to elapse before an answer could be got; and in the meantime how was he to live? But it was the thought of the steamer coming into the quay within the next few hours that rendered him almost desperate.

He began to look at the passers-by individually, wondering whether there was not some friendly soul amongst them who would lend him what he wanted. He had money at home. He would pay the loan twice over—if only he could get on at once to London. Even if he never returned to Harivaig—for as to what might befall him he was all uncertain—there were those there who would see that the money was honorably repaid.

But, as it chanced, Dame Fortune was bent this morning on making amends to old John Logan for her evil treatment of him on the previous night. As he was wandering along, regarding this one and that, he came upon a corner public-house that had just been opened, the proprietor of which was standing at the door, with his hands behind his back. He was a tall, thin man, with an aquiline nose, keen gray eyes, and light reddish-brown hair—in short, a Sutherlandshire-looking man; while there was an expression of easy good-nature about his features that was calculated to invite confidence. Old Logan hesitated—turned away—went back again—and finally, when this tall Highland-looking man retired into the shop, he followed, after a moment's pause. But when he entered, he could see no one but a young fellow who was busy polishing up the brass of the bar. Logan waited in silence. The young man turned to him.

"Weel, what is't?"

"I—I wass going to London," Logan began, in a breathless kind of way, "and—and—they hef stolen ahl my money; and I wass thinking that if I could get the loan of the money to tek me to London, I would pay it back—"

"Money to tak ye to London!" the barkeeper retorted, scornfully. "Yer heed's in a creel! Get oot o' this!"

John Logan was turning hopelessly away when the proprietor of the public-house came forth from the back premises.

"What's that, Jimmy?"

His assistant told him, with a laugh of derision. John Logan was still lingering there: the new-comer, with keen but not unkindly eyes, was scanning him from head to heel.

"Where do ye come from?" he asked.

"From Harivaig," Logan answered; "that is across the point from Usgary."

"Usgary?" the tall man repeated. "Then I suppose you have the Gaelic."

"Oh, yes, indeed—yes, indeed!" old Logan exclaimed, eagerly; and then, to his unspeakable surprise and rejoicing, he found this stranger talking to him in his native tongue.

"Tell me what has happened to you, and why you have come all the way from Usgary to Greenock, an old man like you."

There was no impediment now; with a sort of feverish haste old Logan told the story of what had befallen him—though he said nothing of the aim of his journey to London—and described his present straits; and if he did not directly beg for money to carry him on, he was eager to point out that the loan would be assuredly repaid.

"Well," said the other, continuing to talk in the Gaelic, "you are a foolish man to go into a house that you did not know; and if I were to lend you the money how should I be sure you would not fling it away in the same fashion?"

"But if I get enough to pay for the steamer, that is all I want," Logan said, with anxious eyes. "If I can get to London that is all I want. There is one Corstorphine there who knows me."

"If it comes to that, and you are so anxious to get to London, why do you not go in the train? You can leave Greenock to-night and be in London in the morning."

"The train?—I have heard about that, but I do not know it."

"Have you never seen a railway train?"

"No."

The tall, good-natured-looking publican seemed amused. He took down his Glengarry cap, and put it on his head.

"Come," said he, "and I will show you what a train is like."

Then, as they walked along the street, he said:

"And perhaps I will lend you the money, and you will find yourself in London to-morrow morning. For blood is thicker than water, as everyone knows; and I am sorry that one from the north, and a Highlander like myself, should have been robbed by these Lowland devils. It is a good thing to have the Gaelic when you meet with a Highlander; and that is the truth."

However, the publican's intentions were of no avail, in this direction at least. When they had climbed up the long flight of stairs, and entered the wide, hollow-sounding station, a train was just arriving at the platform—the huge black engine coming along with its ponderous clink-clank; and then, when it stopped, there was a sudden rush and roar of escaped steam, that caused old Logan to start back with terror on his face.

"Well, now you have seen a train," his companion said; "and do you know that it can take you to London in a dozen hours?"

Logan was silent for a moment or two; then he said— "God knows that I am anxious to go to London; and if it is on foot I must go, then it is on foot that I will be going; but it is not in *that* that I am going."

Nor would anything shake his resolution; and his newly-found friend, seeing that the old man could not be reasoned out of this unconquerable dread, good-naturedly assented to his taking the longer route by steamer, and said he should have enough money to pay his passage. Not only that, but, discovering that Logan had had no breakfast, he took him into a coffee-shop and gave him a substantial meal; he presented him with a supply of tobacco for the voyage; altogether, he played the part of good Samaritan; and the only receipt he took for the money he advanced was the address of Logan's relatives in the north. Moreover, he came down to the wharf to see the old man away; and as the big steamer stood out to the rippling waters of the Firth, he waved his Glengarry cap once or twice before turning and going back to his shop. That was the last of him that John Logan ever saw; but the old man did not forget his countryman, nor the help he had got from him in time of sore need.

The long voyage southward proved to be quite uneventful; and he was looking forward without any great apprehension to his landing in London, for he had been told that the St. Katharine Dock, where the steamer would reach her berth, was not far from Billingsgate.

He received this information from a wily-looking little foreign sailor, who, like himself, was one of the steerage-passengers, and who had attached himself to the old man, professing great friendship soon after their leaving Greenock. He was a small, yellow-faced, crop-haired creature, who wore rings in his ears, who had a sleek, insinuating manner, and looked of southern birth, though what English he knew sounded rather as if it had been picked up in the north of Europe. He had been all over the world, according to his own account; and was returning to London after having been summoned to Scotland to give evidence in a salvage case. He had a pack of cards with him, and would have beguiled the time in playing these with this new acquaintance, only that he found the old man had a superstitious horror of the "devil's books." Logan's refusal did not interrupt their intimacy; on the contrary, Vedroz, as he called himself, became more and more friendly, and showed his sympathetic concern by asking innumerable questions, that John Logan sometimes answered and sometimes did not answer.

One day, the shifty-eyed, dusky-faced little sailor said, in an offhand kind of fashion—

"My vrent, yo ave pain—no?—in your left side?"

John Logan, looking somewhat alarmed, said that he had no pain there.

"No?—vy you put up your hant so often? No pain? You ave no rheumatics dare? No? Vell, I vas make mistake. Das its nodings. Ver glad you ave no pain."

And then again, the same afternoon, he began to talk to the old Highlander about the best way of concealing valuables about one's person; and the straits he, Vedroz, had been put to in protecting himself against rogues and thieves. The waistband of his trousers seemed to be his favorite hiding-place. If you sewed the money into the lining of your coat—so he said, watching the old man's face the while—the coat might be torn off in a scuffle, or stolen when you were asleep.

The subject seemed to interest him; he returned to it again and again; but John Logan, though he looked more and more anxious, only held his peace. He made no confession; but sometimes he would ask, as if to be reassured, how far the St. Katherine's Docks were from Billingsgate.

When at last, after a voyage so long that it appeared to him that he had been carried away out of the world altogether, they arrived at their destination, and were free to leave the ship, Vedroz undertook to show the old man the way to Billingsgate Market, and would take no refusal. And indeed Logan was not a little terrified at the sight of the vastness of the place into which he was about to plunge; and was glad of this friendly escort. It was as yet early morning when they made their way into Upper East Smithfield; though already there were heavy vans and lorries, making a dull, continuous, distant roar through the solitude of the half-sleeping city.

Vedroz bent his steps eastward, talking lightly all the while. Old John Logan kept looking out for Billingsgate, which he expected to recognize by its piles of fish-boxes; but he saw nothing of the kind. Soon they had got into one of the lowest districts in Shadwell; and Vedroz was airily explaining, in his broken English, that the distances in London were so great that one had to exercise patience.

"And 'ere is my 'ouse," said he, "up this court 'ere. You vill come up vid me?—

No?—Vhy no?—one moment?—I keep you no one moment—den we go on to Billingsgate."

Logan followed him; but he was resolved upon entering no house. When they had got a little way up this narrow court, Vedroz knocked at a certain door; and that was immediately opened by a colossally tall, broad-shouldered, muscular-looking woman of hideous aspect, who glanced quickly from the one to the other of them.

"My vrent, dis is my vife," Vedroz said, leading the way into the passage. "Anna, dis is a vrent of mine from Scotland. Come in! No? No for one second? My Gott, why you no come in?"

But old John Logan resolutely declined; and for a moment Vedroz seemed disconcerted. Then he said—

"Ver' well. You stay there; I come back directly. You talk to my vife: Anna, see if my goot vrent will no come into the 'ouse."

He left, and was absent for several minutes, while the huge-limbed virago, instead of repeating the invitation, merely stood and stared at the old man in a stony silence. Then Vedroz made his appearance again, bearing in his hand a pewter tankard.

"'Ere, my vrent," said he, still standing within the passage; "'ere is a drink for you—oh, ver' good drink!—ver' good drink in the morning!"

But again John Logan declined, and firmly; and the little sallow faced sailor's eyes began to burn with concealed rage.

"My Gott, why you no drink? You dink it will do arm?—no arm!—ver' good for you—'ere, drink!"

And he held out the tankard again—inviting the old man to step into the passage. But John Logan was resolved. He would not drink—he would not enter the house. Then Vedroz, his eyes sparkling with anger, came to the door; he glanced up and down the court to see that there was no one about: then he said, in a low voice,

"Anna quick—bring him in!"

With a bound like a tigress the huge creature sprang upon the old man, and fixed both hands on his coat-collar; and the next moment he would have been dragged off his feet and into the house, but that with an extraordinary effort he pitched the whole weight of his shoulders against her chest so that they both reeled against the half-opened door. He sent up loud shouts of alarm; he fought and tore to get out of this terrible grip; and all at once he found himself thrown violently backwards—free as air—and the door shut in his face!

He made instant use of his liberty. He did not stay to ask what had frightened his assailants; he hastily picked up his cap, that had been knocked off in the struggle, ran down the court and out into the street, and looked wildly around for help. Well; there was plenty, if need were. But he was not pursued; and he had no wish to go back to that den, even with assistance; so he hurriedly walked on—he knew not in what direction; but only anxious to get away from this dreadful neighborhood.

As it chanced, he took pretty much the same route that he had come; and presently he was in the High-street of Shadwell, where, there being now plenty of people about, he could breathe a little more freely, and consider as to what he should do. His heart was beating with a frightful violence; but the treasure sewn in the lining of his coat was safe.

Well, it took him a considerable time to find his way from Shadwell to Billingsgate Market, for he walked slowly, and he carefully scanned the appearance of anyone whom he approached to ask his simple question. But he did get there in the end, without further peril or adventure; and to his own surprise—for the roar of traffic, the number of people, the mass of houses, and shops, and yards, and wagons were all bewildering to him—he was not long in finding out the place of his search. And then it was in a small counting-house at the back of some wide premises that old John Logan found himself at last face to face with the actual Corstorphine, who had for so many years been to him but a name.

*V Absolution*

Mr. Corstorphine was a jovial-looking, stout, rotund person, with a florid face, and bright, twinkling, small blue eyes.

"So you're John Logan?" said he, in a very friendly fashion. "Take a seat—take a seat. And what's brought ye to London? To collect your accounts? I dare say there's something in your favor in our books—I'll just see—"

"No," said the old man, "it is not that at ahl. I—hef come to London to—to speak to Mr. Holt—that wass the name. I wass thinking you would tell me where to find him."

"Holt?" said Mr. Corstorphine. "Holt? Oh, yes; by-the-bye, that was a sad business that happened up your way; I saw it all in the papers. You mean Holt, of Ramsden, Holt, don't you? Is it about the drowning of Mr. Ramsden you've come up to London?"

John Logan looked at the other straight in the face; he was not sure what to answer. Certain speeches of his own he had in a measure prepared; but he was not ready with replies to questions.

"Ay," said he, with deliberation, "it hass something to do with that."

Mr. Corstorphine waited for a moment, but the old man was silent; so, not caring to be too curious, he good-naturedly said:

"Oh, well, if you want to see Mr. Holt, I don't suppose there will be any difficulty. Their office is in Lombard-street."

"Ay?" said the old man looking rather downcast. "Is it far aweh?"

"Not at all; a few minutes walk. Are you going on there now?"

Logan hesitated; he hardly knew how to formulate the request that was in his mind.

"I am not knowing mich about towns," said he, slowly.

"Oh, but I'll send one of my lads with you," Corstorphine said at once.

"Ay, will ye do that?" the old man answered, looking up quickly and gratefully. "I wass thinking of it many's the time—maybe ye would do that. For I am not knowing mich about towns—and—and—my head is not quite right since they struck me in Greenock—and if there wass a young lad now to tek me to Mr. Holt—I would pay the young lad—"

"You will do nothing of kind," Corstorphine said, good—humoredly. "Come along, and I'll see you safe on the way to Lombard-street."

Thus it was that old John Logan found himself plunged into the very heart of the great city, in the busiest time of the forenoon. His guide soon discovered that he was a total stranger, and was so civil as to point out the Monument to him; but Logan took little notice of that—it was the dense, hurrying mass of people that overawed him. The lad with difficulty got him to cross to the western side of Gracechurch-street—he was afraid of venturing into that roaring Maelstrom; and, indeed he had to take the old man by the arm and haul him this way and that, or they would never have got safely through the surging stream of cabs and wagons and omnibuses.

Old Logan was quite breathless when they got to Lombard-street—not from physical exertion, but from the excitement caused by this strange, bewildering spectacle, and the mental contagion of all this eager haste. Indeed, when they reached the bank, and when his companion briefly informed him that this was Ramsden, Holt's, he hesitated about entering, for in this distracting whirl he had forgotten the speeches he had prepared during those idle days on board the steamer.

But here a fortunate circumstance happened. A brougham drove up, and there stepped from it no other than Mr. Holt himself, whose eye instantly fell on this unwonted figure that was near the door of the bank.

"Bless me!" he said, going up to Logan, "how have you come here? Do you bring any news? Has the body been found?"

John Logan was startled by so sudden an encounter; he regarded this tall, keen-looking man with a troubled eye.

"No," he managed to say at last, and he shook his head.

"But you have come to see me?" the other asked, promptly.

"Ay, ay," Logan made answer. "I—I wass wanting—"

"But come in, first of all," the banker said. "Come up to my room—then we'll hear what you've got to say," and he led the way into the bank, and upstairs to his own room, where he shut the door, and asked John Logan to be seated.

"Well, now, what can I do for you?" said he, pleasantly enough. "Was not that arrangement about the boat satisfactory? I thought the young man was very well content; and he seems an honest fellow—I think you may count on the installments being paid."

Old John Logan was looking all around him: this place in which he found himself was like a house; had he arrived at the goal of his long journey already!

"It's the young lady," said he, turning vaguely inquiring eyes upon the banker.

"What young lady? Miss Ramsden?"

"Ay, ay," the old man said, with a kind of breathless eagerness, "It's to see her I hef come ahl the way—and I was thinking you would tell me where to find her. If it is only for a moment—she was ferry, ferry kind to us—and—and if she would not think it trouble—only for a moment—"

"But what do you want to see her about?" Mr. Holt naturally asked: then directly something in the old man's face told him he had been indiscreet. "Ah. I see it is something you have got to say to herself. Very well; there can be no objection. I dare say it must be something of importance to have brought you so far; and I dare say, too, she will tell me all about it later on. However, if you want to see her, you will almost certainly find her at home this morning. If she is out, wait till she returns—she is pretty sure to be back by lunch-time. I will give you a card, and you will show it to the man who opens the door; and I will send a commissionaire with you to take you to the house, for I suppose you'd never make your way to Cornwall-gardens by yourself."

As well as he was able, the old man expressed his grateful thanks; and presently he was out once more in the wild Babel of confusion, under the guidance of this taciturn commissionaire. But now he felt that every step was taking him nearer and nearer to the end and aim of his journey. His heart shook within him as he thought of the ordeal before him; and his only wish was that it were well over and done with. He did not care what happened to him after that. The atonement once made to *her,* they might take him away and put him in gaol or hang him if they wished. It was of no consequence whether he ever went back to Harivaig. He was an old man; his days were about done anyway; and his granddaughter Jeannie would be well provided for and comfortably settled with her husband in their new home in Usgary.

Meanwhile the commissionaire who was acting as his guide had met with the same difficulty that the Greenock publican had experienced: old John Logan could not be induced to enter a train. Indeed, his dismay on being asked to go by an underground tunnel was even greater than before; so the commissionaire had to sacrifice the tickets he had purchased at the Mansion House Station, had to ascend to the upper air again, and take his charge down to Kensington on the top of an omnibus. Even that method of traveling seemed to the old fisherman to be fraught with imminent danger; but no doubt his fear of falling off helped in a measure to distract his mind from thinking of the trying interview that was now drawing near.

When they reached the large mansion in Cornwall-gardens to which they had been directed, the servant who opened the door stared with surprise and even resentment at this old man who had dared to ring the visitors' bell; but his manner changed somewhat when he was shown Mr. Holt's card. He said that Miss Ramsden was out riding just then, but that she would be back in half an hour or so; and would he step in and wait? The commissionaire, having seen his task accomplished, left; and old John Logan entered the house. The man-servant hesitated as to whether he should ask this odd-looking visitor, whose clothes and cap had suffered a good deal in his rough experiences of travel, to go any further than the hall. But Logan settled that matter for himself; he sat down on a chair that happened to be handy, and the footman, with another curious glance, disappeared, and left the old man alone.

The moment he had departed, John Logan whipped off his coat, took out his sailor's jackknife, and slit open a sewed patch in the inside lining. The locket that had cost him so much was in his hand. He undid the piece of canvas in which it was wrapped, and placed that in his pocket. He hastily put on his coat again, and then he sat still, waiting with the trinket that he had hardly dared to look on, clasped and hidden in his trembling fingers.

He heard the sound of horses' hoofs without. The servant who had let him in came along the hall and opened the door. There was a tall, fair-haired young lady in a black riding-habit coming up the steps. A young man, rather older than herself, immediately followed. The groom was leading away the horses. John Logan rose to his feet, though his heart was beating and his legs were shaking so that he could hardly stand. The world seemed to swim round him. He did not know that she turned very pale on catching sight of him, and came quickly forward, and asked him what he had come to tell her?

"Is it about my father?" she said, hurriedly.

For a moment he could not speak, he was all trembling so; then he said: "No, no, Mem. I wass come to gif you back something—something that wass yours—and it is a long weh I have come to—to—"

She saw that he was strongly agitated—and also that he glanced in a timorous fashion at her cousin, who was standing by.

"Mem," said the old man, in a sort of desperation, "will you be that kind—I wass thinking to see you by yourself—"

"Fred, wait for me in the drawing-room," she said instantly.

And then, quickly laying aside her hat and riding-whip, she took the old man gently by the hand. "Come in here," she said, leading him into the dining-room, and shutting the door behind them. "I see you are greatly distressed. What is it about? Can I help you? It is not about your granddaughter, is it, that was to be married? If I can help you, I'm sure I will!"

The old man stood helpless, bewildered, shaking from head to foot—his English was all gone from him—he could not explain: then, with a half-stifled cry of anguish, he threw himself at her feet, his two clenched hands on the floor, tears streaming from his eyes, his white head bowed with the violence of his sobbing.

*"Ma-an-nus!—ma-an-nus!—ma-an-nus!"*[1] was all he could say, in this overwhelming grief, in the despair of his appeal to her.

"But what is it?" she asked, in great alarm and commiseration, for it seemed so pitiable to see this white-haired old man so utterly stricken down.

He unclasped one of his hands, and put the locket at her feet.

"I hef brought it," he said—though his voice was so broken with his sobs that she could only make out a word or two here and there; "if you hef no pardon for me—I cannot tell what that will be for me—when I took it, I wass not thinking it wass anybody's—I had neffer seen you, Mem—God knows, I would not hef taken anything

---

[1]Mercy.

from you—but—but the clothes they were lying on the shore—and—and there wass no one—and I wass thinking of my lass Jeannie, and of her getting married, and not with the things that some of the young lasses hef for their wedding day—it—it is your pardon, Mem, I am asking—it is your pardon I am praying for—and if you hef no pardon for me, then God help me—for I—for I—"

But here he broke into another fit of passionate crying and sobbing, so that he could not proceed with his appeal to her for forgiveness. As for her, the tears were running down her own cheeks; this seemed so piteous a thing. She knelt down on one knee, and took up the locket.

"I think I understand you," she said, very gently. "Well; you have brought it back—what more could you do? I do forgive you—indeed, indeed I do forgive you!"

He seized the hem of her dress, and kissed it again and again.

"I wass not thinking," he continued, between his sobs, "that it belonged to any one. And there wass Jeannie, she wass going to be married—and—and I thought the young lad would be prouder of her. Mem, I did not know it wass yours—I did not; and when you wass coming to Harivaig—after that, there wass no peace for me, day or night; and I wass asking myself, day and night, if the young lady would gif me her pardon, if I went aweh to London—"

"And, indeed, indeed I do!" the girl said, in deep commiseration. "Come!" she said, putting her hand on his shoulder. "Come and tell me how you made such a long journey. I did miss the locket, and could not imagine where it had gone. But now you have brought it back—and come such a long way to restore it—well, now, you must not say a word more about it."

Old John Logan rose and wiped his wet cheeks with the back of his hand, and took a step towards the door.

"The long weh I hef come, Mem," said he, pausing now and again to gather his speech, "wass to gif back what I had taken—and—and to ask for your pardon. Now you hef been kind to me—more kind to me as I deserve—and—and that is ofer now—and God bless you for it, Mem. That is ofer now—but there's the other people—and I will tell them what I hef done—and if it is to be hanged I am, then it will not matter so much to be hanged now, since I hef your pardon. And now I will say good-bye to you Mem; and God bless you as you hef been merciful to me this day."

She guessed his meaning directly; and in an instant she had interposed herself between him and the door.

"No," said she, courageously, "you are not going like that, or with any such intention. What has been done has been settled and forgiven between you and me; and no one else has the right to interfere. *No one else* has got anything to do with it. If you like it will be a secret between you and me: not a word to be said. And I am not going to let you leave the house like this."

She put her hand on his arm. "Come," she said, quite cheerfully, so as to reassure him, and calm down his violent distress and agitation. "I want you to tell me all about your coming here, and I want to know what you are going to do before you go back. I suppose you have no friends in London—unless you will call me your friend? I want you to tell me about your granddaughter, and the marriage, and what you are going to buy in London to take to her for her wedding-day. If she would not be offended, I should like to send her some things; and perhaps she would rather be pleased to have them come all the way from London."

Her calm and soothing tones prevailed; he suffered himself to be led towards the window, and he took a seat there, she sitting opposite him in the embrasure. He understood that he was asked for the story of his adventures since leaving Harivaig, and he began and in the most simple fashion related the various incidents as well as his halting speech would allow. She was greatly concerned when he told her about the fighting in the Greenock den; and declared he must see a surgeon in London, to make sure his wounds had been properly dressed, and were healing satisfactorily; and then, when he brought his narrative down to this very day, and when she discovered that he had had nothing to eat or drink since very early that morning, she went promptly to the mantelpiece and rang the bell.

The footman appeared.

"Luncheon, Richard—and tell Mrs. Moulseley and Mr. Hare."

She turned to the old man.

"You will stay and have some lunch with me?" she said.

"Oh, no, Mem!" said he, glancing nervously at the table, which was already laid.

"But you must! Why, how many hours is it since you left the steamer this morning?"

Presently an elderly lady appeared, followed by the young man who had been out riding with Miss Ramsden—a tall young Englishman of the familiar blonde type. The moment young Hare perceived that the old fisherman was still in the dining-room, and apparently was going to stay to lunch, he said to his cousin—

"Edith!"

It was a kind of summons: she followed out into the hall.

"Why, what are you going to do now?" he said, by way of friendly remonstrance.

She stepped into the morning-room opposite, to be out of the way of the servants, and he accompanied her.

"This is an old man who has come a long way," she said to him; "and I am interested in him; and I have asked him to take lunch with me—that is all."

"How silly you are!" he said. "Why—"

She flushed up a little.

"You need not come in to luncheon unless you like!" she said, somewhat stiffly.

He looked at her, and smiled, and made bold to take her hand.

"So you want to quarrel, do you? My dear Edith, you don't know how. You haven't got it in you. You can't fight—you haven't got the weapons—what is it?—

*Un sourire qui dit: Bataille!*
*Un soupir qui dit: Je me rends!*[1]

that's the way you would fight, if you were to try."

She withdrew her hand none the less.

"You don't know how I am interested in this old man," she said, "and you don't know what a pitiable story he has just told me. But it is of no consequence. As I say, you need not come in to luncheon unless you like."

"Edith, don't be stupid!" he made answer, quite good-naturedly. "I was not thinking of myself at all; I was thinking of your ancient friend—whom you will make extremely uncomfortable. Do you imagine you are doing him any kindness? He would be a great deal happier if you would let him have his dinner in the servants' hall."

"Well, then, he is not going down to the servants' hall," was her reply.

"And I," said he, with a bit of a laugh, "am not going to be debarred from sitting next to you at luncheon simply because you choose to be cantankerous. Come along; if you keep Mrs. Moulseley waiting another minute she'll snap your head off," and with that he put his hand lightly on her shoulder and shoved her out of the room before him.

But old John Logan was far too preoccupied to be in any way embarrassed or uncomfortable when the young lady insisted on his taking a place next to her at table; nor did he seem to perceive how assiduous she was in paying him little friendly atten-

[1] A smile which says "Battle!"/ A sigh which says "I give up."

tions. His mind was intently fixed on quite other things. The servants placed various dishes before him; he paid no heed. The butler filled his glass; he did not look at it.

"But you are not eating anything!" his young hostess said.

"I wass not thinking of it," he answered, simply; and then he relapsed into a brooding silence, as if there was no outward world for him at all.

She began to wonder what this was that was weighing so heavily on his thoughts. Had she not fully satisfied him of her forgiveness? Had she not been explicit enough? Or was there still in his mind some dark imagining that quite outside the sphere of her acquittal there dwelt unknown terrors of punishment and vengeance? The moment that luncheon was over, she allowed her other two companions to leave, and desired the old man to remain with her. And then an adroit question or two soon made the matter more or less clear.

"It is you, Mem, who hef been kind to me," said he, fixing his eyes on the table before him, as if to seek out this that was troubling him; while she listened to him patiently and in silence, as he slowly constructed sentence after sentence. "And when I wass leaving Harivaig, I did not know whether I would ever be finding you; and now you wass giffing me your pardon; and what more is to happen to me, that I do not heed now, since you had mercy for me. But—but you said a secret. If I wass to go back to Harivaig, I would be thinking—ahl the day long, sometimes in the night too. I would be thinking there would be some one coming. He would say to me, 'You hef a secret, and that iss good as between the young lady and you; but the judges are not satisfied—there iss more to be done yet.' And now I am here in this town, where the judges are, I—I would sooner go to them. If they hef no pardon for me—well, I am an old man; it is not much matter now; and Jeannie would neffer know anything about it. When I wass coming through the streets I looked for them; but I wass not seeing them anywhere. And now, Mem, I will go. Whateffer happens there iss my thanks to you for your goodness to me; and I had no right to expect so mich from you. But I am not thinking of going back to Harivaig with a secret—and be waiting and waiting for the judges."

She was quick to perceive what all this meant.

"But you don't understand!" she said, with an almost pathetic eagerness. "It need not be a secret unless you like—that must be just as you wish—but I mentioned a secret merely because it is nobody else's business but yours and mine. No one can interfere now; it is settled. Surely you have suffered enough—surely you have made sufficient atonement: and if I say that—if I tell you that—who can interfere? The judges would not think of harming you. You might live all the rest of your life in London—you might walk through the streets every day—and nobody would think of meddling with you. Indeed," she said—for it suddenly occurred to her that the best way of assuring him of his safety would be to familiarize him with the London streets and the sight of the great official buildings and the repositories of power and authority, "I'm going to ask you to remain in London for a day or two, and go about, and see what the place is like. That is, until I can find some little presents for you to take home to your granddaughter, for the wedding. And there are a lot of things you have to do," she continued, in a brisk and matter-of-fact way, "before you can set out again for the North. You ought at once to send your friend in Greenock, who was so kind to you, the money he lent you— and if you haven't got it—"

"But, ay, ay!" he said, quickly; "there's Corstorphine! there's some money that Corstorphine is owing to me—"

"Well, we'll arrange about that later on," said she. "In the meantime I want you to see a little of London, and I'll get you some one who will take you about."

For so gentle-mannered and smooth-spoken a young lady she had a prompt and businesslike way of going about things. She rang the bell. The footman appeared.

"Tell Kemp I want to see him at once," she said. "If he is round at the stables send for him."

"Yes, Miss."

A few minutes thereafter she was told that Kemp was in the hall and immediately she left the room, shutting the door behind her.

"I shan't want the carriage this afternoon, Kemp," she said to this grave, stout, elderly person, who, in fact, was her coachman.

"Very well, Miss."

"But there is an old fisherman here, who has come from the North to see me, and you must look after him, and find lodgings for him for a night or two. Has your wife let that room that is next to yours?"

"No, Miss."

"That will do very well. You will see that the old man is comfortable. And in the meantime I want you to take him out now, and show him some of the sights of London—take him to see Buckingham Palace, and the Houses of Parliament, and the Horse Guards, and so on. And first of all you must persuade him to go somewhere and have some dinner; he has had nothing since early morning; be sure he has a good dinner; and when he comes back in the evening he must have some tea in his own room; and perhaps I may come round for a moment to see how he is getting on."

She took a sovereign from her purse.

"Mind you make him cheerful and comfortable, and talk to him and get everything he needs. Is there any Highland whiskey to be got in London refreshment-rooms?"

"They says so, Miss," the coachman answered, with grave caution.

"You must see what he would like with his dinner. His name is Mr. Logan. You must call him 'Mr.' Now I will give him over into your hands; and I hope to hear at night that he has spent a very pleasant afternoon."

And, strangely enough, this mere girl had hit upon the right way of going about this thing. Old John Logan, during the two or three days he spent in London. got to be convinced that he had nothing to fear—that no one wanted to harm him—that he was a free man—that the young lady's forgiveness of him was all sufficient. For one thing, Miss Ramsden took very good care not to say anything of what she had done or was doing to Mr. Holt. She had heard of such a phrase as "compounding a felony"; and while she felt in her heart that she was justified in assuring this old man that he had suffered enough and made ample expiation, she did not quite know how her conduct might strike a legal or commercial mind. She thought she would tell Mr. Holt all about it—after John Logan had gone home.

In the meantime, the old man's gratitude towards her was something extraordinary to witness. It was like the dumb gratitude of a dog, for he could not say much of what he felt. And when she showed him the pretty bits of finery that she had bought for his granddaughter, and that were to help to deck out the bride, tears rose to the old man's eyes, and he said—

"If you had the Gaelic, Mem, I could tell you what I was thinking of you, Mem, and—and your kindness—but I will never be able to tell you that."

His last speech to her, when the time came for his bidding her farewell, was of the same apologetic nature. She did not go down to the St. Katherine's Docks with him; but she put him in safe hands; and Mr. Holt, at her intercession, had made arrangement with one of the sub-officers on board the Anchor Liner, by which the old man would be taken care of if he had any time to wait in Greenock for the Dunara Castle. John Logan, as he was being driven down to St. Katherine's Docks in a four-wheeled cab, saw amongst the other things they passed, the Tower of London; and he beheld it without a qualm; the gentle-voiced young lady ha successfully banished all his fears.

But what was he to say to the people when, after the long, and as it chanced, uneventful voyage, he got back to Harivaig again—as one returned from the dead? Well; he said nothing at all. If anyone asked him, he answered that he had been away to the south, and had seen many strange sights. But when Jeannie Logan in mingled shyness and pride, began to show to her intimate, friends the beautiful things that the English young lady had sent her for her wedding-day, then the bruit got abroad that old John Logan was so insensately fond of his spoiled granddaughter that he had gone all the way to London to purchase adornments for her. Jeannie protested against this misapprehension, and even showed them the very grateful letter she was going to send to Miss Ramsden; but all was of no use.

Moreover, they made still another mistake when the wedding day came round. The marriage took place in the inn, as the custom holds in those parts; and in the evening all the people—some of them very remote kinsfolk, who had come from long distances—assembled at supper. It was a protracted feast; and there was a mighty babblement of laughter, and talking, and joking, to say nothing of the piper up at the fireplace end of the room, who was screaming away with "Hoop her and gird her" and "Follow her over the border"; so that, towards the end of the banquet, it was with difficulty the roaring guests could be got to understand that old John Logan—old John Logan, of all people in the world—was going to propose a health, with Highland honors too. Perhaps it was the excitement of the moment, perhaps it was an extra drop of Glendarroch that had put the idea into the old man's head; however, there was silence when he mounted on his chair, and raised his glass in his trembling hand.

"We are all friends here," said he, in the Gaelic, "and I ask all friends of me and mine to drink this: Blessings on her—and a hundred thousand blessings!—and long life and happiness to the *Roa-nam-ban!*" He put his right foot on the table.

*"Nish—nish! Suasa—suasa!"* he called; and therewith he tossed off the whiskey, and dashed the glass down to the floor, so that it should never be drunk out of again.

*"Roa-nam-ban!—Roa-nam-ban!"* they cried but they were all laughing at him; they thought it was a foolish thing for the infatuated old man to call his granddaughter the best of women, even on her wedding-day. For not one of them (except, perhaps, the granddaughter herself—who was not offended) guessed who it was whom old John Logan had in his mind, when he called on his friends to drink long life and happiness to the *Roa-nam-ban.*

## ROBERT BUCHANAN (1841–1901)

[Buchanan spent much of his life in London, making a living as a man of letters. He wrote a great deal, including many novels, almost all of which have been forgotten. He is remembered for a handful of poems—especially burlesques—and a notorious essay, "The Fleshly School of Poetry," attacking the Pre-Raphaelites.]

### The Wedding of Shon Maclean
A Bagpipe Melody

To the wedding of Shon Maclean,
Twenty Pipers together
Came in the wind and the rain
Playing across the heather;
Backward their ribbons flew,
Blast upon blast they blew,
Each clad in tartan new,
Bonnet, and blackcock feather:

And every Piper was fou*, "full" (drunk)
Twenty Pipers together!—

He's but a Sassenach* blind and vain Saxon (Englishman)
Who never heard of Shon Maclean—
The Duke's own Piper, called "Shon the Fair,"
From his freckled skin and his fiery hair.
Father and son, since the world's creation,
The Macleans had followed this occupation,
And played the pibroch to fire the Clan
Since the first Duke came and the earth began.
Like the whistling of birds, like the humming of bees,
Like the sough of the south-wind in the trees,
Like the singing of angels, the playing of shawms,
Like Ocean itself with its storms and its calms,
Were the strains of Shon, when with cheeks aflame
He blew a blast through the pipes of fame.
At last, in the prime of his playing life,
The spirit moved him to take a wife—
A lassie with eyes of Highland blue,
Who loves the pipes and the Piper too,
And danced to the sound with a foot and a leg
White as a lily and smooth as an egg.
So, twenty Pipers were coming together
Oer the moor and across the heather,
All in the wind and the rain:
Twenty Pipers so brawly dressed
Were flocking in from the east and west,
To bless the bedding and blow their best
At the wedding of Shon Maclean.

At the wedding of Shon Maclean
Twas wet and windy weather.
Yet through the wind and the rain
Came twenty Pipers together.
Earach and Dougal Dhu,
Sandy of Isla too,
Each with the bonnet o' blue,
Tartan, and blackcock feather;
And every Piper was fou,
Twenty Pipers together.

The knot was tied, the blessing said,
Shon was married, the feast was spread,
At the head of the table sat, huge and hoar,
Strong Sandy of Isla, age fourscore,
Whiskered, gray as a Haskeir seal,
And clad in crimson from head to heel.
Beneath and round him in their degree
Gathered the men of minstrelsy,
With keepers, gillies*, and lads and lasses, retainers
Mingling voices, and jingling glasses.
At soup and haggis, at roast and boiled,

Awhile the happy gathering toiled,—
While Shon and Jean at the table ends
Shook hands with a hundred of their friends.—
Then came a hush. Through the open door
A wee bright form flashed on the floor,—
The Duke himself, in the kilt and plaid,
With slim soft knees, like the knees of a maid,
And he took a glass, and he cried out plain—
"I drink to the health of Shon Maclean!
To Shon the Piper and Jean his wife,
A clean fireside and a merry life!"
Then out he slipt, and each man sprang
To his feet, and with "hooch" the chamber rang:
"Clear the tables!" shrieked out one—
A leap, a scramble,—and it was done.
And then the Pipers all in a row
Tuned their pipes and began to blow,
While all to dance stood fain:
Sandy of Isla and Earach More,
Dougal Dhu from Kilflannan shore,
Played up the company on the floor
At the wedding of Shon Maclean.

At the wedding of Shon Maclean,
Twenty Pipers together
Stood up, while all their train
Ceased to clatter and blether.
Full of the mountain-dew,
First in their pipes they blew,
Mighty of bone and thew,
Red-cheeked, with lungs of leather:
And every Piper was fou,
Twenty Pipers together.

Who led the dance? In pomp and pride
The Duke himself led out the bride.
Great was the joy of each beholder,
For the wee Duke only reached her shoulder.
And they danced, and turned, when the reel began,
Like a giantess and a fairie man.
But like an earthquake was the din
When Shon himself led the Duchess in.
And she took her place before him there,
Like a white mouse dancing with a bear.
So trim and tiny, so slim and sweet,
Her blue eyes watching Shon's great feet,
With a smile that could not be resisted,
She jigged, and jumped, and twirled, and twisted.
Sandy of Isla led off the reel,
The Duke began it with toe and heel,
Then all joined in amain.
Twenty Pipers ranged in a row,
From squinting Shamus to lame Kilcroe,

Their cheeks like crimson, began to blow,
At the wedding of Shon Maclean.

At the wedding of Shon Maclean
They blew with lungs of leather,
And blithsome was the strain
Those Pipers played together.
Moist with the mountain-dew,
Mighty of bone and thew,
Each with the bonnet o' blue,
Tartan, and blackcock feather:
And every Piper was fou,
Twenty Pipers together.

Oh for a wizard's tongue to tell
Of all the wonders that befell.
Of how the Duke, when the first stave died,
Reached up on tiptoe to kiss the bride,
While Sandy's pipes, as their mouths were meeting,
Skirled, and set every heart a-beating.
Then Shon took the pipes! and all was still,
As silently he the bags did fill,
With flaming cheeks and round bright eyes,
Till the first faint music began to rise.
Like a thousand laverocks singing in tune,
Like countless corn-craiks under the moon,
Like the smack of kisses, like sweet bells ringing,
Like a mermaid's harp, or a kelpie singing,
Blew the pipes of Shon: and the witching strain
Was the gathering song of the Clan Maclean.
Then slowly, softly, at his side,
All the Pipers around replied,
And swelled the solemn strain;
The hearts of all were proud and light,
To hear the music, to see the sight,
And the Duke's own eyes were dim that night,
At the wedding of Shon Maclean.

So to honor the Clan Maclean
Straight they began to gather,
Blowing the wild refrain,
"Blue bonnets across the heather."
They stamped, they strutted, they blew;
They shrieked; like cocks they crew;
Blowing the notes out true,
With wonderful lungs of leather:
And every Piper was fou,
Twenty Pipers together.

When the Duke and Duchess went away
The dance grew mad and the guests grew gay;
Man and maiden, face to face,
Leapt and footed and screamed apace.

Round and round the dancers whirled,
Shriller, louder, the Pipers skirled,
Till the soul seemed swooning into sound,
And all creation was whirling round.
Then, in a pause of the dance and glee,
The Pipers, ceasing their minstrelsy,
Draining the glass in groups did stand,
And passed the sneesh-box* from hand to hand. snuff-box
Sandy of Isla, with locks of snow,
Squinting Shamus, blind Kilmahoe,
Finlay Beg, and Earach More,
Dougal Dhu of Kilflannan shore,—
All the Pipers, black, yellow, and green,
All the colors that ever were seen,
All the Pipers of all the Macs,
Gathered together and took their cracks.
Then (no man knows how the thing befell
For none was sober enough to tell)
These heavenly Pipers from twenty places
Began disputing with crimson faces;
Each asserting, like one demented,
The claims of the Clan he represented.
In vain gray Sandy of Isla strove
To soothe their struggle with words of love,
Asserting there, like a gentleman,
The superior claims of his own great Clan;
Then, finding to reason is despair,
He seizes his pipes and he plays an air—
The gathering tune of his Clan—and tries
To drown in music the shrieks and cries.
Heavens! Every Piper, grown mad with ire,
Seizes his pipes with a fierce desire,
And blowing madly, with skirl and squeak,
Begins his particular tune to shriek.
Up and down the gamut they go,
Twenty Pipers, all in a row,
Each with a different strain.
Each tries hard to drown the first,
Each blows louder till like to burst.
Thus were the tunes of the Clan rehearst
At the wedding of Shon Maclean.

At the wedding of Shon Maclean,
Twenty Pipers together,
Blowing with might and main,
Through wonderful lungs of leather.
Wild was the hullabaloo!
They stamped, they screamed, they crew!
Twenty strong blasts they blew,
Holding the heart in tether:
And every Piper was fou,
Twenty Pipers together.

A storm of music! Like wild sleuth-hounds
Contending together, were the sounds.
At last a bevy of Eve's bright daughters
Poured oil—that's whisky—upon the waters;
And after another dram went down,
The Pipers chuckled and ceased to frown,
Embraced like brothers and kindred spirits,
And fully admitted each other's merits.

All bliss must end. For now the bride
Was looking weary and heavy-eyed
And soon she stole from the drinking chorus,
While the company settled to *deoch-an-dorus.*[1]
One hour—another—took its flight—
The clock struck twelve—the dead of night—
And still the bride like a rose so red
Lay lonely up in the bridal bed.
At half-past two the bridegroom, Shon,
Dropt on the table as heavy as stone,
But four strong Pipers across the floor
Carried him up to the bridal door,
Pushed him in at the open portal,
And left him snoring, serene and mortal.
The small stars twinkled over the heather,
As the Pipers wandered away together,
But one by one on the journey dropt,
Clutching his pipes, and there he stopt.
One by one on the dark hillside
Each faint blast of the bagpipes died,
Amid the wind and the rain.
And the twenty Pipers at break of day
In twenty different bogholes lay,
Serenely sleeping upon their way
From the wedding of Shon Maclean.

## Fra Giacomo

Alas, Fra Giacomo,
Too late—but follow me.
Hush! draw the curtain—so—
She is dead, quite dead, you see.
Poor little lady. She lies
With the light gone out of her eyes;
But her features still wear that soft
Gray meditative expression,
Which you must have noticed oft,
And admired too, at confession.
How saintly she looks, and how meek.
Though this be the chamber of death,
I fancy I feel her breath

[1] A Gaelic phrase, "a drink at the door," i.e. a farewell toast.

As I kiss her on the cheek.
With that pensive religious face,
She has gone to a holier place.
And I hardly appreciated her,—
Her praying, fasting, confessing,
Poorly, I own, I mated her.
I thought her too cold, and rated her
For her endless image-caressing.
Too saintly for me by far,
As pure and as cold as a star,
Not fashioned for kissing and pressing,—
But made for a heavenly crown.
Ay, father, let us go down,—
But first, if you please, your blessing.

Wine? No? Come, come, you must.
You'll bless it with your prayers,
And quaff a cup, I trust.
To the health of the saint up stairs?
My heart is aching so.
And I feel so weary and sad,
Through the blow that I have had,—
You'll sit, Fra Giacomo?
My friend! (and a friend I rank you
For the sake of that saint)—nay, nay,
Here's the wine—as you love me, stay.—
Tis Montepulciano!—Thank you.

Heigh-ho! Tis now six summers
Since I won that angel and married her.
I was rich, not old, and carried her
Off in the face of all comers.
So fresh, yet so brimming sith soul.
A tenderer morsel, I swear,
Never made the dull black coal
Of a monk's eye glitter and glare.
Your pardon!—nay, keep your chair.
I wander a little, but mean
No offense to the gray gabardine.
Of the church, Fra Giacomo,
I'm a faithful upholder, you know,
But (humor me) she was as sweet
As the saints in your convent windows,
So gentle, so meek, so discreet,
She knew not what lust does or sin does.
I'll confess, though, before we were one,
I deemed her less saintly, and thought
The blood in her veins had caught
Some natural warmth from the sun.
I was wrong—I was blind as a bat—
Brute that I was, how I blundered.
Though such a mistake as that
Might have occurred as pat

To ninety-nine men in a hundred.
Yourself, for example? you've seen her?
Spite her modest and pious demeanor,
And the manners so nice and precise,
Seemed there not color and light,
Bright motion and appetite,
That were scarcely consistent with *ice* ?
Externals implying, you see,
Internals less saintly than human?—
Pray speak, for between you and me
You're not a bad judge of a woman.
A jest—but a jest.—Very true,
Tis hardly becoming to jest,
And that saint up stairs at rest,—
Her soul may be listening, too.
I was always a brute of a fellow.
Well may your visage turn yellow—
To think how I doubted and doubted,
Suspected, grumbled at, flouted
That golden-haired angel,—and solely
Because she was zealous and holy.
Noon and night and morn
She devoted herself to piety.
Not that she seemed to scorn
Or dislike her husband's society,
But the claims of her *soul* superseded
All that I asked for or needed,
And her thoughts were far away
From the level of sinful clay,
And she trembled if earthly matters
Interfered with her *aves* and *paters*.
Poor dove, she so fluttered in flying
Above the dim vapors of hell—
Bent on self-sanctifying—
That she never thought of trying
To save her husband as well.
And while she was duly elected
For place in the heavenly roll,
I (brute that I was) suspected
Her manner of saving her soul.

So, half for the fun of the thing,
What did I (blasphemer!) but fling
On my shoulders the gown of a monk—
Whom I managed for that very day
To get safely out of the way—
And seat me, half sober, half drunk,
With the cowl thrown over my face,
In the father confessor's place.
*Eheu! benedicite!*
In her orthodox sweet simplicity,
With that pensive gray expression,
She sighfully knelt at confession

While I bit my lips till they bled,
And dug my nails in my hand,
And heard with averted head
What I'd guessed and could understand.
Each word was a serpent's sting,
But, wrapt in my gloomy gown,
I sat, like a marble thing,
As she told me all!—SIT DOWN.

More wine, Fra Giacomo?
One cup—if you love me. No?
What, have these dry lips drank
So deep of the sweets of pleasure—
*Sub rosa,* but quite without measure—
That Montepulciano tastes rank?
Come, drink, twill bring the streaks
Of crimson back to your cheeks.
Come, drink again to the saint
Whose virtues you loved to paint,
Who, stretched on her wifely bed,
With the tender, grave expression
You used to admire at confession,
Lies poisoned, overhead.

Sit still—or by heaven, you die!
Face to face, soul to soul, you and I
Have settled accounts, in a fine
Pleasant fashion, over our wine.
Stir not, and seek not to fly,—
Nay, whether or not, you are mine.
Thank Montepulciano for giving
You death in such delicate sips.
Tis not every monk ceases living
With so pleasant a taste on his lips.
But, lest Montepulciano unsurely should kiss,
Take this! and this! and this!

Cover him over, Pietro,
And bury him in the court below,—
You can be secret, lad, I know.
And, hark you, then to the convent go,—
Bid every bell of the convent toll,
And the monks say mass for your mistress' soul.

## Spring Song in the City

Who remains in London,
In the streets with me,
Now that Spring is blowing
Warm winds from the sea;
Now that trees grow green and tall,
Now the sun shines mellow,

And with moist primroses all
English lanes are yellow?

Little barefoot maiden,
Selling violets blue,
Hast thou ever pictured
Where the sweetlings grew?
Oh, the warm wild woodland ways,
Deep in dewy grasses,
Where the wind-blown shadow strays,
Scented as it passes.

Peddler breathing deeply,
Toiling into town,
With the dusty highway
You are dusky brown.
Hast thou seen by daisied leas,
And by rivers flowing,
Lilac ringlets which the breeze
Loosens lightly blowing?

Out of yonder wagon
Pleasant hay scents float,
He who drives it carries
A daisy in his coat.
Oh, the English meadows, fair
Far beyond all praises.
Freckled orchids everywhere
Mid the snow of daisies.

Now in busy silence
Broods the nightingale,
Choosing his love's dwelling
In a dimpled dale.
Round the leafy bower they raise
Rose trees wild are springing.
Underneath, through the green haze,
Bounds the brooklet singing.

And his love is silent
As a bird can be,
For the red buds only
Fill the red rose tree.
Just as buds and blossoms blow
He'll begin his tune,
When all is green and roses glow
Underneath the moon.

Nowhere in the valleys
Will the wind be still,
Everything is waving,
Wagging at his will.
Blows the milkmaid's kirtle clean

With her hand pressed on it.
Lightly oer the hedge so green
Blows the plowboys' bonnet.

Oh, to be a-roaming
In an English dell.
Every nook is wealthy,
All the world looks well,
Tinted soft the heavens glow,
Over earth and ocean,
Waters flow, breezes blow,
All is light and motion.

## The Summer Pool

There is a singing in the summer air,
The blue and brown moths flutter oer the grass,
The stubble bird is creaking in the wheat,
And perched upon the honeysuckle-hedge
Pipes the green linnet. Oh, the golden world:
The stir of life on every blade of grass,
The motion and the joy on every bough,
The glad feast everywhere, for things that love
The sunshine, and for things that love the shade.
Aimlessly wandering with weary feet,
Watching the wool-white clouds that wander by,
I come upon a lonely place of shade,
A still green pool, where with soft sound and stir
The shadows of oerhanging branches sleep,
Save where they leave one dreamy space of blue,
Oer whose soft stillness ever and anon
The feathery cirrus blows. Here unaware
I pause, and leaning on my staff I add
A shadow to the shadows; and behold:
Dim dreams steal down upon me, with a hum
Of little wings, a murmuring of boughs,
The dusky stir and motion dwelling here,
Within this small green world. Oershadowed
By dusky greenery, though all around
The sunshine throbs on fields of wheat and bean,
Downward I gaze into the dreamy blue,
And pass into a waking sleep, wherein
The green boughs rustle, feathery wreaths of cloud
Pass softly, piloted by golden airs.
The air is still—no birds sing any more,
And helpless as a tiny flying thing,
I am alone in all the world with God.
The wind dies—not a leaf stirs—on the pool
The fly scarce moves; earth seems to hold her breath
Until her heart stops, listening silently
For the far footsteps of the coming rain.

While thus I pause, it seems that I have gained
New eyes to see; my brain grows sensitive
To trivial things that, at another hour,
Had passed unheeded. Suddenly the air
Shivers, the shadows in whose midst I stand
Tremble and blacken—the blue eye o' the pool
Is closed and clouded; with a sudden gleam
Oiling its wings, a swallow darteth past,
And weedling flowers beneath my feet thrust up
Their leaves, to feel the fragrant shower. Oh, hark!
The thirsty leaves are troubled into sighs,
And up above me, on the glistening boughs,
Patters the summer rain.
Into a nook,
Screened by thick foliage of oak and beech,
I creep for shelter; and the summer shower
Murmurs around me. Oh, the drowsy sounds!
The pattering rain, the numerous sigh of leaves,
The deep, warm breathing of the scented air,
Sink sweet into my soul—until at last
Comes the soft ceasing of the gentle fall,
And lo, the eye of blue within the pool
Opens again, while with a silvern gleam
Dew-diamonds twinkle moistly on the leaves,
Or, shaken downward by the summer wind,
Fall melting on the pool in rings of light.

## The Churchyard

How slowly creeps the hand of time
On the old clock's green-mantled face.
Yea, slowly as those ivies climb,
The hours roll round with patient pace.
The drowsy rooks caw on the tower.
The tame doves hover round and round.
Below, the slow grass hour by hour
Makes green God's sleeping ground.

All moves, but nothing here is swift.
The grass grows deep, the green boughs shoot.
From east to west the shadows drift.
The earth feels heavenward underfoot.
The slow stream through the bridge doth stray
With water lilies on its marge,
And slowly, piled with scented hay,
Creeps by the silent barge.

All stirs, but nothing here is loud.
The cushat broods, the cuckoo cries.
Faint, far up, under a white cloud,
The lark trills soft to earth and skies;
And underneath the green graves rest;

And through the place, with slow footfalls,
With snowy cambric on his breast,
The old gray vicar crawls.

And close at hand, to see him come,
Clustering at the playground gate,
The urchins of the schoolhouse, dumb
And bashful, hang the head and wait.
The little maidens curtsey deep,
The boys their forelocks touch meanwhile;
The vicar sees them, half asleep,
And smiles a sleepy smile.

Slow as the hand on the clock's face,
Slow as the white cloud in the sky,
He cometh now with tottering pace
To the old vicarage hard by.
Smothered it stands in ivy leaves,
Laurels and yews make dark the ground;
The swifts that build beneath the eaves
Wheel in still circles round.

And from the portal, green and dark,
He glances at the church-clock old—
Gray soul, why seek his eyes to mark
The creeping of that finger cold?
He cannot see, but still as stone
He pauses, listening for the chime,
And hears from that green tower intone
The eternal voice of time.

## The Fleshly School of Poetry:
### Mr. D. G. Rossetti

[This article was published under an assumed name in the *Contemporary Review* in October, 1871, and is a review of the fifth edition of Rossetti's *Poems.* It was countered by Rossetti's "Stealthy School of Criticism" and Swinburne's *Under the Microscope.*]

If, on the occasion of any public performance of Shakespeare's great tragedy, the actors who perform the parts of Rosencranz and Guildenstern were, by a preconcerted arrangement and by means of what is technically known as "gagging," to make themselves fully as prominent as the leading character, and to indulge in soliloquies and business strictly belonging to Hamlet himself, the result would be, to say the least of it, astonishing; yet a very similar effect is produced on the unprejudiced mind when the "walking gentlemen" of the fleshly school of poetry, who bear precisely the same relation to Mr. Tennyson as Rosencranz and Guildenstern do to the Prince of Denmark in the play obtrude their lesser identities and parade their smaller idiosyncrasies in the front rank of leading performers.

In their own place, the gentlemen are interesting and useful. Pursuing still the theatrical analogy, the present drama of poetry might be cast as follows: Mr. Tennyson supporting the part of Hamlet, Mr. Matthew Arnold that of Horatio, Mr.

Bailey that of Voltimand, Mr. Buchanan that of Cornelius, Messrs. Swinburne and Morris the parts of Rosencranz and Guildenstern, Mr. Rossetti that of Osric, and Mr. Robert Lytton that of "A Gentleman." It will be seen that we have left no place for Mr. Browning, who may be said however, to play the leading character in his own peculiar fashion on alternate nights.

This may seem a frivolous and inadequate way of opening our remarks on a school of verse-writers which some people regard as possessing great merits; but in good truth, it is scarcely possible to discuss with any seriousness the pretensions with which foolish friends and small critics have surrounded the fleshly school which, in spite of its spasmodic ramifications in the erotic direction, is merely one of the many sub-Tennysonian schools expanded to supernatural dimensions, and endeavoring by affectations all its own to overshadow its connection with the great original.

In the sweep of one single poem, the weird and doubtful "Vivien," Mr. Tennyson has concentrated all the epicene force which, wearisomely expanded, constitutes the characteristic of the writers at present under consideration; and if in "Vivien" he has indicated for them the bounds of sensualism in art, he has in *Maud* in the dramatic person of the hero, afforded distinct precedent for the hysteric tone and overloaded style which is now so familiar to readers of Mr. Swinburne.

The fleshliness of "Vivien" may indeed be described as the distinct quality held in common by all the members of the last sub-Tennysonian school, and it is a quality which becomes unwholesome when there is no moral or intellectual quality to temper and control it. Fully conscious of this themselves, the fleshly gentlemen have bound themselves by solemn league and covenant to extol fleshliness as the distinct and supreme end of poetic and pictorial art; to aver that poetic expression is greater than poetic thought and by inference that the body is greater than the soul, and sound superior to sense, and that the poet, properly to develop his poetic faculty, must be an intellectual hermaphrodite, to whom the very facts of day and night are lost in a whirl of esthetic terminology.

After Mr. Tennyson has probed the depths of modern speculation in a series of commanding moods, all right and interesting in him as the reigning personage, the walking gentlemen, knowing that something of the sort is expected from all leading performers, bare their roseate bosoms and aver that *they* are creedless; the only possible question here being, if any disinterested person cares twopence whether Rosencranz, Guildenstern, and Osric are creedless or not—their self-revelation on that score being so perfectly gratuitous? But having gone so far it was and is too late to retreat. Rosencranz, Guildenstern, and Osric, finding it impossible to risk an individual bid for the leading business, have arranged all to play leading business together, and mutually to praise, extol, and imitate each other; and although by these measures they have fairly earned for themselves the title of the Mutual Admiration School, they have in a great measure succeeded in their object—-to the general stupefaction of a British audience.

It is time, therefore, to ascertain whether any of these gentlemen has actually in himself the making of a leading performer. When the *Athenaeum*—once more cautious in such matters—advertised nearly every week some interesting particular about Mr. Swinburne's health, Mr. Morris's holiday-making, or Mr. Rossetti's genealogy, varied with such startling statements as "We are informed that Mr. Swinburne dashed off his noble ode *at a sitting,*" or "Mr. Swinburne's songs have already reached a second edition," or "Good poetry seems to be in demand; the first edition of Mr. O'Shaughnessy's poems is exhausted," when the *Academy* informed us that "During the past year or two Mr. Swinburne has written several novels" (!), and that some review or other is to be praised for giving Mr. Rossetti's poems "the attentive study which they demand"—when we read these things we might or might not know pretty well how and where they originated; but to a provincial eye, perhaps, the whole thing really looked like leading business.

It would be scarcely worth while, however, to inquire into the pretensions of the writers on merely literary grounds, because sooner or later all literature finds its own level, whatever criticism may say or do in the matter; but it unfortunately happens in the present case that the fleshly school of verse-writers are, so to speak, public offenders, because they are diligently spreading the seeds of disease broadcast wherever they are read and understood. Their complaint too is catching, and carries off many young persons. What the complaint is, and how it works, may be seen on a very slight examination of the works of Mr. Dante Gabriel Rossetti, to whom we shall confine our attention in the present article.

Mr. Rossetti has been known for many years as a painter of exceptional powers, who, for reasons best known to himself, has shrunk from publicly exhibiting his pictures, and from allowing anything like a popular estimate to be formed of their qualities. He belongs, or is said to belong, to the so-called Pre-Raphaelite school, a school which is generally considered to exhibit much genius for color, and great indifference to perspective. It would be unfair to judge the painter by the glimpses we have had of his works, or by the photographs which are sold of the principal paintings. Judged by the photographs, he is an artist who conceives unpleasantly, and draws ill. Like Mr. Simeon Solomon, however, with whom he seems to have many points in common, he is distinctively a colorist, and of his capabilities in color we cannot speak, though we should guess that they are great; for if there is any good quality by which his poems are specially marked, it is a great sensitiveness to hues and tints as conveyed in poetic epithet.

These qualities, which impress the casual spectator of the photographs from his pictures, are to be found abundantly among his verses. There is the same thinness and transparence of design, the same combination of the simple and the grotesque, the same morbid deviation from healthy forms of life, the same sense of weary, wasting yet exquisite sensuality; nothing virile, nothing tender, nothing completely sane; a superfluity of extreme sensibility, of delight in beautiful forms, hues, and tints, and a deep-seated indifference to all agitating forces and agencies, all tumultuous griefs and sorrows all the thunderous stress of life, and all the straining storm of speculation.

Mr. Morris is often pure, fresh, and wholesome as his own great model; Mr. Swinburne startles us more than once by some fine flash of insight—but the mind of Mr. Rossetti is like a glassy mere, broken only by the dive of some water-bird or the hum of winged insects, and brooded over by an atmosphere of insufferable closeness, with a light blue sky above it, sultry depths mirrored within it and a surface so thickly sown with waterlilies that it retains its glassy smoothness even in the strongest wind. Judged relatively to his poetic associates, Mr. Rossetti must be pronounced inferior to either. He cannot tell a pleasant story like Mr. Morris, nor forge alliterative thunderbolts like Mr. Swinburne. It must be conceded, nevertheless, that he is neither so glibly imitative as the one, nor so transcendently superficial as the other.

Although he has been known for many years as a poet as well as a painter—as a painter and poet idolized by his own family and personal associates—and although he has once or twice appeared in print as a contributor to magazines, Mr. Rossetti did not formally appeal to the public until rather more than a year ago when he published a copious volume of poems, with the announcement that the book, although it contained pieces composed at intervals during a period of many years, "included nothing which the author believes to be immature." This work was inscribed to his brother, Mr. William Rossetti, who, having written much both in poetry and criticism, will perhaps be known to bibliographers as the editor of the worst edition of Shelley which has yet seen the light.

No sooner had the work appeared than the chorus of eulogy began. "The book is satisfactory from end to end," wrote Mr. Morris in the *Academy;* "I think these lyrics, with all their other merits, the most complete of their time, nor do I know what Lyrics of any time are to be called *great,* if we are to deny the title to these."

On the same subject Mr. Swinburne went into a hysteria of admiration: "golden affluence," "jewel-colored words," "chastity of form," "harmonious nakedness," "consummate fleshly sculpture," and so on in Mr. Swinburne's well-known manner when reviewing his friends.

Other critics, with a singular similarity of phrase, followed suit. Strange to say, moreover, no one accused Mr. Rossetti of naughtiness. What had been heinous in Mr. Swinburne was majestic exquisiteness in Mr. Rossetti. Yet we question if there is anything in the unfortunate *Poems and Ballads* quite so questionable on the score of thorough nastiness as many pieces in Mr. Rossetti's collection. Mr. Swinburne was wilder, more outrageous, more blasphemous, and his subjects were more atrocious in themselves; yet the hysterical tone slew the animalism, the furiousness of epithet lowered the sensation; and the first feeling of disgust at such themes as "Laus Veneris" and "Anactoria," faded away into comic amazement. It was only a little mad boy letting off squibs; not a great strong man, who might be really dangerous to society. "I *will* be naughty!" screamed the little boy; but, after all, what did it matter?

It is quite different, however, when a grown man, with the self-control and easy audacity of actual experience, comes forward to chronicle his amorous sensations, and, first proclaiming in a loud voice his literary maturity, and consequent responsibility, shamelessly prints and publishes such a piece of writing as this sonnet on "Nuptial Sleep";—

> At length their long kiss severed, with sweet smart:
> And as the last slow sudden drops are shed
> From sparkling eaves when all the storm has fled,
> So singly flagged the pulses of each heart.
> Their bosoms sundered, with the opening start
> Of married flowers to either side outspread
> From the knit stem; yet still their mouths, burnt red
> Fawned on each other where they lay apart.
>
> Sleep sank them lower than the tide of dreams,
> And their dreams watched them sink, and slid away.
> Slowly their souls swam up again, through gleams
> Of watered light and dull drowned waifs of day;
> Till from some wonder of new woods and streams
> He woke, and wondered more: for there she lay.

This, then, is "the golden affluence of words, the firm outline, the justice and chastity of form." Here is a full-grown man, presumably intelligent and cultivated, putting on record for other full-grown men to read, the most secret mysteries of sexual connection, and that with so sickening a desire to reproduce the sensual mood, so careful a choice of epithet to convey mere animal sensations, that we merely shudder at the shameless nakedness.

We are no purists in such matters. We hold the sensual part of our nature to be as holy as the spiritual or intellectual part, and we believe that such things must find their equivalent in all; but it is neither poetic, nor manly, nor even human, to obtrude such things as the themes of whole poems. It is simply nasty. Nasty as it is, we are very mistaken if many readers do not think it nice.

English society of one kind purchases the *Day's Doings.* English society of another kind goes into ecstasy over Mr. Solomon's pictures—pretty pieces of morality, such as "Love dying by the breath of Lust." There is not much to choose between the two objects of admiration, except that painters like Mr. Solomon lend actual genius to worthless subjects, and thereby produce veritable monsters—like the lovely devils that danced round Saint Anthony. Mr. Rossetti owes his so-called success to the same causes. In poems like "Nuptial Sleep," the man who is too sensitive to exhibit his pictures, and so modest that it takes him years to make up his mind to publish his poems, parades his private sensations before a coarse public, and is gratified by their applause.

It must not be supposed that all Mr. Rossetti's poems are made up of trash like this. Some of them are as noteworthy for delicacy of touch as others are for shamelessness of exposition. They contain some exquisite pictures of nature, occasional passages of real meaning, much beautiful phraseology, lines of peculiar sweetness, and epithets chosen with true literary cunning.

But the fleshly feeling is everywhere. Sometimes, as in "The Stream's Secret," it is deliciously modulated, and adds greatly to our emotion of pleasure at perusing a finely-wrought poem; at other times, as in the "Last Confession," it is fiercely held in check by the exigencies of a powerful situation and the strength of a dramatic speaker, but it is generally in the foreground, flushing the whole poem with unhealthy rose-color, stifling the senses with overpowering sickliness, as of too much civet. Mr. Rossetti is never dramatic, never impersonal—always attitudinizing, posturing, and describing his own exquisite emotions. He is the Blessed Damozel, leaning over the "gold bar of heaven," and seeing

> Time like a pulse shake fierce
> Through all the worlds.

He is "heaven-born Helen, Sparta's queen," whose "each twin breast is an apple sweet"; he is Lilith the first wife of Adam; he is the rosy Virgin of the poem called "Ave," and the Queen in the "Staff and Scrip"; he is "Sister Helen" melting her waxen man; he is all these, just as surely as he is Mr. Rossetti soliloquizing over Jenny in her London lodging, or the very nuptial person writing erotic sonnets to his wife. In petticoats or pantaloons, in modern times or in the middle ages, he is just Mr. Rossetti, a fleshly person, with nothing particular to tell us or teach us, with extreme self-control, a strong sense of color, and a careful choice of diction.

Amid all his "affluence of jewel-colored words," he has not given us one rounded and noteworthy piece of art, though his verses are all art; not one poem which is memorable for its own sake, and quite separable from the displeasing identity of the composer. The nearest approach to a perfect whole is the "Blessed Damozel," a peculiar poem, placed first in the book, perhaps by accident, perhaps because it is a key to the poems which follow. This poem appeared in a rough shape many years ago in the *Germ*, an unwholesome periodical started by the Pre-Raphaelites, and suffered, after gasping through a few feeble numbers, to die the death of all such publications. In spite of its affected title, and of numberless affectations throughout the text, the "Blessed Damozel" has great merits of its own, and a few lines of real genius. We have heard it described as the record of actual grief and love, or, in simple words, the apotheosis of one actually lost by the writer; but, without having any private knowledge of the circumstance of its composition, we feel that such an account of the poem is inadmissible. It does not contain one single note of sorrow. It is a "composition," and a clever one. Read the opening stanzas:—

> The blessed damozel leaned out
> From the gold bar of Heaven;
> Her eyes were deeper than the depth

Of water stilled at even;
She had three lilies in her hand
And the stars in her hair were seven.

Her robe, ungirt from clasp to hem
No wrought flowers did adorn,
But a white rose of Mary's gift,
For service meetly worn;
Her hair that lay along her back
Was yellow like ripe corn.

This is a careful sketch for a picture, which, worked into actual color by a master might have been worth seeing. The steadiness of hand lessens as the poem proceeds, and although there are several passages of considerable power,—such as that where, far down the void,

this earth
Spins like a fretful midge

or that other, describing how

the curled moon
Was like a little feather
Fluttering far down the gulf—

the general effect is that of a queer old painting in a missal, very affected and very odd. What moved the British critic to ecstasy in this poem seems to us very sad nonsense indeed, or, if not sad nonsense, very meretricious affectation. Thus, we have seen the following verses quoted with enthusiasm, as italicized—

And still she bowed herself and stooped
Out of the circling charm;
*Until her bosom must have made*
*The bar she leaned on warm,*
And the lilies lay as if asleep
Along her bended arm.

From the fixed place of Heaven she saw
*Time like a pulse shake fierce*
*Through all the worlds.* Her gaze still strove
Within the gulf to pierce
Its path; and now she spoke as when
The stars sang in their spheres.

It seems to us that all these lines are very bad with the exception of the two admirable lines ending the first verse, and that the italicized portions are quite without merit, and almost without meaning. On the whole, one feels disheartened and amazed at the poet who, in the nineteenth century, talks about "damozels," "citherns," and "citoles," and addresses the mother of Christ as the "Lady Mary,"—

With her five handmaidens, whose names
Are five sweet symphonies,
Cecily, Gertrude, Magdalen,

Margaret and Rosalys.

A suspicion is awakened that the writer is laughing at us. We hover uncertainly between picturesqueness and namby-pamby, and the effect, as Artemus Ward would express it, is "weakening to the intellect." The thing would have been almost too much in the shape of a picture, though the workmanship might have made amends. The truth is that literature, and more particularly poetry, is in a very bad way when one art gets hold of another, and imposes upon it its conditions and limitations. In the first few verses of the "Damozel" we have the subject, or part of the subject, of a picture, and the inventor should either have painted it or left it alone altogether; and, had he done the latter, the world would have lost nothing. Poetry is something more than painting; and an idea will not become a poem, because it is too smudgy for a picture.

In a short notice from a well-known pen, giving the best estimate we have seen of Mr. Rossetti's powers as a poet, the *North American Review* offers a certain explanation for affectation such as that of Mr. Rossetti. The writer suggests that "it may probably be the expression of genuine moods of mind in natures too little comprehensive." We would rather believe that Mr. Rossetti lacks comprehension than that he is deficient in sincerity, yet really to paraphrase the words which Johnson applied to Thomas Sheridan, Mr. Rossetti is affected, naturally affected, but it must have taken him a great deal of trouble to become what we now see him—such an excess of affectation is not in nature.

There is very little writing in the volume spontaneous in the sense that some of Swinburne's verses are spontaneous; the poems all look as if they had taken a great deal of trouble. The grotesque mediaevalism of "Stratton Water" and "Sister Helen," the medieval classicism of "Troy Town," the false and shallow mysticism of "Eden Bower," are one and all essentially imitative, and must have cost the writer much pains. It is time, indeed, to point out that Mr. Rossetti is a poet possessing great powers of assimilation and some faculty for concealing the nutriment on which he feeds. Setting aside the *Vita Nuova* and the early Italian poems, which are familiar to many readers by his own excellent translations, Mr. Rossetti may be described as a writer who has yielded to an unusual extent to the complex influences of the literature surrounding him at the present moment. He has the painter's imitative power developed in proportion to his lack of the poet's conceiving imagination.

He reproduces to a nicety the manner of an old ballad, a trick in which Mr. Swinburne is also an adept. Cultivated readers, moreover, will recognize in every one of these poems the tone of Mr. Tennyson broken up by the style of Mr. and Mrs. Browning, and disguised here and there by the eccentricities of the Pre-Raphaelites. The "Burden of Nineveh" is a philosophical edition of "Recollections of the Arabian Nights"; "A Last Confession" and "Dante at Verona" are, in the minutest trick and form of thought, suggestive of Mr. Browning; and that the sonnets have been largely molded and inspired by Mrs. Browning can be ascertained by any critic who will compare them with the *Sonnets from the Portuguese*. Much remains, nevertheless, that is Mr. Rossetti's own. We at once recognize as his own property such passages as this:—

I looked up
And saw where a brown-shouldered harlot leaned
Half through a tavern window thick with vine.
Some man had come behind her in the room
And caught her by her arms, and she had turned
With that coarse empty laugh on him, as now
He *munched her neck with kisses, while the vine*

*Crawled in her back.*

Or this:—

As I stooped, her own lips rising there
*Bubbled with brimming kisses at my mouth.*

Or this:—

Have seen your lifted silken skirt
Advertise dainties through the dirt!

Or this :—

What more prize than love to impel thee
*Grip* and *lip* my limbs as I tell thee.

Passages like these are the common stock of the walking gentlemen of the fleshly school. We cannot forbear expressing our wonder, by the way, at the kind of women whom it seems the unhappy lot of these gentlemen to encounter. We have lived as long in the world as they have, but never yet came across persons of the other sex who conduct themselves in the manner described. Females who bite, scratch, scream, bubble, munch, sweat, writhe, twist, wriggle, foam, and in a general way slaver over their lovers, must surely possess some extraordinary qualities to counteract their otherwise most offensive mode of conducting themselves.

It appears, however, on examination, that their poet-lovers conduct themselves in a similar manner. They, too, bite, scratch, scream, bubble, munch, sweat, writhe, twist, wriggle, foam, and slaver in a style frightful to hear of. Let us hope that it is only their fun, and that they don't mean half they say. At times, in reading such books as this, one cannot help wishing that things had remained for ever in the asexual state described in Mr. Darwin's great chapter on Palingenesis. We get very weary of this protracted hankering after a person of the other sex; it seems meat, drink, thought, sinew, religion for the fleshly school. There is no limit to the fleshliness, and Mr. Rossetti finds in it its own religious justification much in the same way as Holy Willie:—

Maybe thou let'st this fleshly thorn
Perplex thy servant night and morn,
'Cause he's so gifted.
If so, thy hand must e'en be borne,
Until thou lift it.

Whether he is writing of the holy Damozel, or of the Virgin herself, or of Lilith, or Helen, or of Dante, or of Jenny the street-walker, he is fleshly all over, from the roots of his hair to the tip of his toes, never a true lover merging his identity into that of the beloved one; never spiritual, never tender; always self-conscious and aesthetic. "Nothing," says a modern writer, "in human life is so utterly remorseless—not love, not hate, not ambition, not vanity—as the artistic or aesthetic instinct morbidly developed to the suppression of conscience and feeling"; and at no time do we feel more fully impressed with this truth than after the perusal of "Jenny," in some respects the finest poem in the volume, and in all respects the poem best indicative of the true quality of the writer's humanity. It is a production which bears signs of having been suggested by Mr. Buchanan's quasi-lyrical poems, which it copies in the style of title, and particularly by "Artist and Model"; but certainly Mr. Rossetti cannot be accused, as the Scottish writer has been accused, of maudlin sentiment and affected tenderness. The two first lines are perfect:—

> Lazy laughing languid Jenny,
> Fond of a kiss and fond of a guinea;

And the poem is a soliloquy of the poet— who has been spending the evening in dancing at a casino—over his partner, whom he has accompanied home to the usual style of lodgings occupied by such ladies, and who has fallen asleep with her head upon his knee, while he wonders, in a wretched pun—

> Whose person or whose purse may be
> The lodestar of your reverie?

The soliloquy is long, and in some parts beautiful, despite a very constant suspicion that we are listening to an emasculated Mr. Browning, whose whole tone and gesture, so to speak, is occasionally introduced with startling fidelity; and there are here and there glimpses of actual thought and insight, over and above the picturesque touches which belong to the writer's true profession, such as that where, at daybreak—

> lights creep in
> Past the gauze curtains half drawn to,
> And *the Lamp's doubled shade grows blue.*

What we object to in this poem is not the subject, which any writer may be fairly left to choose for himself; nor anything particularly vicious in the poetic treatment of it, nor any bad blood bursting through in special passages. But the whole tone, without being more than usually coarse, seems heartless. There is not a drop of piteousness in Mr. Rossetti. He is just to the outcast, even generous; severe to the seducer; sad even at the spectacle of lust in dimity and fine ribbons. Notwithstanding all this, and a certain delicacy and refinement of treatment unusual with this poet, the poem repels and revolts us, and we like Mr. Rossetti least after its perusal.

We are angry with the fleshly person at last.

The "Blessed Damozel" puzzled us, the "Song of the Bower" amused us, the love-sonnet depressed and sickened us, but "Jenny," though distinguished by less special viciousness of thought and style than any of these, fairly makes us lose patience. We detect its fleshliness at a glance, we perceive that the scene was fascinating less through its human tenderness than because it, like all the others, possessed an inherent quality of animalism.

"The whole work" ("Jenny") writes Mr. Swinburne, "is worthy to fill its place for ever as one of the most perfect poems of an age or generation. There is just the same life-blood and breadth of poetic interest in this episode of a London street and lodging as in the song of 'Troy Town' and the song of 'Eden Bower;' just as much, and no jot more,"

—to which last statement we cordially assent; for there is bad blood in all, and breadth of poetic interest in none. "Vengeance of Jenny's case," indeed!—when such a poet as this comes fawning over her, with tender compassion in one eye and aesthetic enjoyment in the other!

It is time that we permitted Mr. Rossetti to speak for himself, which we will do by quoting a fairly representative poem entire:—

Love-Lily

Between the hands, between the brows,
Between the lips of Love-Lily,
*A spirit is born whose birth endows*
*My blood with fire to burn through me;*
Who breathes upon my gazing eyes,
Who laughs and murmurs in mine ear,
At whose least touch my color flies,
And whom my life grows faint to hear.

Within the voice, within the heart
Within the mind of Love-Lily,
A spirit is born who lifts apart
His tremulous wings and looks at me;
Who on my mouth his finger lays,
And shows, while whispering lutes confer,
That Eden of Love's watered ways
Whose winds and spirits worship her.

Brows, hands, and lips, heart, mind, and voice,
Kisses and words of Love-Lily,—
Oh bid me with your joy rejoice
Till *riotous longing rest in me!*
Ah, let not hope be still distraught,
But find in her its gracious goal,
Whose speech Truth knows not from her thought,
Nor Love her body from her soul.

With the exception of the usual "riotous longing," which seems to make Mr. Rossetti a burthen to himself, there is nothing to find fault with in the extreme fleshliness of these verses, and to many people who live in the country they may even appear beautiful. Without pausing to criticize a thing so trifling—as well might we dissect a cobweb or anatomize a medusa—let us ask the reader's attention to a peculiarity to which all the students of the fleshly school must sooner or later give their attention—we mean the habit of accenting the last syllable in words which in ordinary speech are accentuated on the penultimate:—

Between the hands, between the brows,
Between the lips of Love-Lilee!

which may be said to give to the speaker's voice a sort of cooing tenderness just bordering on a loving whistle. Still better as an illustration are the lines —

Saturday night is market night
Everywhere, be it dry or wet,
And market night in the Haymar*ket!*

which the reader may advantageously compare with Mr. Morris's

Then said the king
Thanked be thou; *neither for nothing*
Shalt thou this good deed do to me;

or Mr. Swinburne's

> In either of the twain
> Red roses full of rain
> She hath for bond*women*
> All kinds of flowers.

It is unnecessary to multiply examples of an affectation which disfigures all these writers —Guildenstern, Rosencranz, and Osric; who, in the same spirit which prompts the ambitious nobodies that rent London theaters in the "empty" season to make up for their dullness by fearfully original "new readings," distinguish their attempt at leading business by affecting the construction of their grandfathers and great-grandfathers, and the accentuation of the poets of the court of James I. It is in all respects a sign of remarkable genius, from this point of view, to rhyme "was" with "grass," "death" with "lieth," "love" with "of," "once" with "suns," and so on *ad nauseam.*

We are far from disputing the value of bad rhymes used occasionally to break up the monotony of verse, but the case is hard when such blunders become the rule and not the exception, when writers deliberately lay themselves out to be as archaic and affected as possible. Poetry is perfect human speech, and these archaisms are the mere fiddlededeeing of empty heads and hollow hearts. Bad as they are, they are the true indication of falser tricks and affectations which lie far deeper. They are trifles, light as air, showing how the wind blows. The soul's speech and the heart's speech are clear, simple, natural, and beautiful, and reject the meretricious tricks to which we have drawn attention.

It is on the score that these tricks and affectations have procured the professors a number of imitators, that the fleshly school deliver their formula that great poets are always to be known because their manner is immediately reproduced by small poets, and that a poet who finds few imitators is probably of inferior rank—by which they mean to infer that they themselves are very great poets indeed.

It is quite true that they are imitated. On the stage, twenty provincial "stars" copy Charles Kean, while not one copies his father; there are dozens of actors who reproduce Mr. Charles Dillon, and not one who attempts to reproduce Macready. When we take up the poems of Mr. O'Shaughnessy, we are face to face with a second-hand Mr. Swinburne; when we read Mr. Payne's queer allegories, we remember Mr. Morris's early stage; and every poem of Mr. Marston's reminds us of Mr. Rossetti.

But what is really most droll and puzzling in the matter is that these imitators seem to have no difficulty whatever in writing nearly, if not quite, as well as their masters. It is not bad imitations they offer us, but poems which read just like the originals; the fact being that it is easy to reproduce sound when it has no strict connection with sense and simple enough to cull phraseology not hopelessly interwoven with thought and spirit. The fact that these gentlemen are so easily imitated is the most damning proof of their inferiority. What merits they have lie with their faults on the surface, and can be caught by any young gentleman as easily as the measles, only they are rather more difficult to get rid of.

All young gentlemen have animal faculties, though few have brains, and if animal faculties without brains will make poems, nothing is easier in the world. A great and good poet, however, is great and good irrespective of manner, and often in spite of manner; he is great because he brings great ideas and new light, because his thought is a revelation; and, although it is true that a great manner generally accompanies great matter, the manner of great matter is almost inimitable. The great poet is not Cowley, imitated and idolized and reproduced by every scribbler of his time;

nor Pope, whose trick of style was so easily copied that to this day we cannot trace his own hand with any certainty in the *Iliad;* nor Donne, nor Sylvester, nor the Della Cruscans. Shakespeare's blank verse is the most difficult and Jonson's the most easy to imitate of all the Elizabethan stock, and Shakespeare's verse is the best verse, because it combines the great qualities of all contemporary verse, with no individual affectations; and so perfectly does this verse, with all its splendor, intersect with the style of contemporaries at *their best,* that we would undertake to select passage after passage which would puzzle a good judge to tell which of the Elizabethans was the author—Marlowe, Beaumont, Dekker, Marston, Webster, or Shakespeare himself.

The great poet is Dante, full of the thunder of a great Idea; and Milton, unapproachable in the serene white light of thought and sumptuous wealth of style; and Shakespeare, all poets by turns, and all men in succession; and Goethe, always innovating, and ever indifferent to innovation for its own sake; and Wordsworth, clear as crystal and deep as the sea; and Tennyson, with his vivid range, far-piercing sight, and perfect speech; and Browning, great, not by virtue of his eccentricities but because of his close intellectual grasp. Tell *Paradise Lost,* the *Divine Comedy,* in naked prose; do the same by *Hamlet, Macbeth,* and *Lear;* read Mr. Hayward's translation of *Faust;* take up the *Excursion,* a great poem, though its speech is nearly prose already; turn the "Guinevere" into a mere story; reproduce Pompilia's last dying speech without a line of rhythm. Reduced to bald English, all these poems, and all great poems, lose much; but how much do they not retain? They are poems to the very roots and depths of being, poems born and delivered from the soul, and treat them as cruelly as you may, poems they will remain.

So it is with all good and thorough creations, however low in their rank, so it is with the "Ballot in a Wedding" and "Clever Tom Clinch," just as much as with the "Epistle of Karsheesh," or Goethe's torso of "Prometheus"; with Shelley's "Skylark," or Alfred de Musset's "A la Lune," as well as Racine's "Athalie," Victor Hugo's "Parricide," or Hood's "Last Man." A poem is a poem, first as to the soul, next as to the form. The fleshly persons who wish to create form for its own sake are merely pronouncing their own doom. But *such* form! If the PreRaphaelite fervor gains ground, we shall soon have popular songs like this:—

> When winds do roar, and rains do pour,
> Hard is the life of the sail*or.*
> He scarcely as he reels çan tell
> The side-lights from the binna*cle;*
> He looketh on the wild wat*er,* &c.,

and so on, till the English speech seems the speech of raving madmen. Of a piece with other affectations is the device of a burthen, of which the fleshly persons are very fond for its own sake, quite apart from its relevancy. Thus Mr. Rossetti sings:—

> Why did you melt your waxen man,
> Sister Helen?
> To-day is the third since you began.
> The time was long, yet the time ran,
> Little brother.
> *(O mother, Mary mother*
> *Three days to-day between Heaven and Hell)*

This burthen is repeated, with little or no alteration, through thirty-four verses, and might with as much music, and far more point, run as follows:—

Why did you melt your waxen man,
    Sister Helen?
To-day is the third since you began.
The time was long, yet the time ran,
    Little brother.
*(O Mr. Dante Rossetti*
*What stuff is this about Heaven and Hell?)*

About as much to the point is a burthen of Mr. Swinburne's, something to the following effect:—

We were three maidens in the green corn,
*Hey chickaleerie, the red cock and gray,*
Fairer maidens were never born,
*One o'clock, two o'clock, off and away.*

We are not quite certain of the words, as we quote from memory, but we are sure our version fairly represents the original, and is quite as expressive. Productions of this sort are "silly sooth" in good earnest, though they delight some newspaper critics of the day, and are copied by young gentlemen with animal faculties morbidly developed by too much tobacco and too little exercise. Such indulgence, however, would ruin the strongest poetical constitution, and it unfortunately happens that neither masters nor pupils were naturally very healthy.

In such a poem as "Eden Bower" there is not one scrap of imagination, properly so-called. It is a clever grotesque in the worst manner of Callot, unredeemed by a gleam of true poetry or humor. No good poet would have wrought into a poem the absurd tradition about Lilith; Goethe was content to glance at it merely, with a grim smile, in the great scene in the Brocken.

We may remark here that poems of this unnatural and morbid kind are only tolerable when they embody a profound meaning, as do Coleridge's "Ancient Mariner" and "Cristabel." Not that we would insult the memory of Coleridge by comparing his exquisitely conscientious work with this affected rubbish about "Eden Bower" and "Sister Helen," though his influence in their composition is unmistakable. Still more unmistakable is the influence of that most unwholesome poet, Beddoes, who, with all his great powers, treated his subjects in a thoroughly insincere manner, and is now justly forgotten.

The great strong current of English poetry rolls on, ever mirroring in its bosom new prospects of fair and wholesome thought. Morbid deviations are endless and inevitable; there must be marsh and stagnant mere as well as mountain and wood. Glancing backward into the shady places of the obscure, we see the once prosperous nonsense-writers each now consigned to his own little limbo—Skelton and Gower still playing fantastic tricks with the mother-tongue; Gascoigne outlasting the applause of all, and living to see his own works buried before him; Sylvester doomed to oblivion by his own fame as a translator; Carew the idol of the courts, and Donne the beloved of schoolmen, both buried in the same oblivion; the fantastic Fletchers winning the wonder of collegians, and fading out through sheer poetic impotence; Cowley shaking all England with his pindarics, and perishing with them; Waller, the famous, saved from oblivion by the natural note of one single song —and so on, through league after league of a flat and desolate country which once was prosperous, till we come again to these fantastic figures of the fleshly school, with their droll mediaeval garments, their funny archaic speech, and the fatal marks of literary consumption in every pale and delicate visage.

Our judgment on Mr. Rossetti, to whom we in the meantime confine our judgment, is substantially that of the *North American Reviewer,* who believes that "we have in him another poetical man, and a man markedly poetical, and of a kind apparently, though not radically, different from any of our secondary writers of poetry, but that we have not in him a new poet of any weight"; and that he is "so affected, sentimental, and painfully self-conscious, that the best to be done in his case is to hope that this book of his, having unpacked his bosom of so much that is unhealthy, may have done him more good than it has given others pleasure."

Such, we say, is our opinion, which might very well be wrong, and have to undergo modification, if Mr. Rossetti was younger and less self-possessed. His "maturity" is fatal.

## CRAMMOND KENNEDY (1841– ? )

### Greenwood Cemetery

How calm they sleep beneath the shade
Who once were weary of the strife,
And bent, like us, beneath the load
Of human life.

The willow hangs with sheltering grace
And benediction oer their sod,
And nature, hushed, assures the soul
They rest in God.

O weary hearts, what rest is here,
From all that curses yonder town.
So deep the peace, I almost long
To lay me down.

For, oh, it will be blest to sleep,
Nor dream, nor move, that silent night,
Till wakened in immortal strength
And heavenly light.

## ANDREW LANG (1844–1912)

[Andrew Lang was a "Man of Letters," who wrote much and in many fields—poetry, fiction, essays, children's literature, criticism, translations. Today he is remembered as a collector of fairy tales, as a notable translator of the *Odyssey*, a disciplined minor poet, and a writer of informal essays. The sketch below of Lang's friend, Robert Louis Stevenson, is one of many pleasing efforts in the last category.]

### Almae Matres

(St. Andrews, 1862. Oxford, 1865)

*St. Andrews by the Northern Sea,*
*A haunted town it is to me!*
A little city, worn and gray,
The gray North Ocean girds it round,
And oer the rocks, and up the bay,

The long sea-rollers surge and sound.
And still the thin and biting spray
Drives down the melancholy street,
And still endure, and still decay,
Towers that the salt winds vainly beat.
Ghost-like and shadowy they stand
Dim mirrored in the wet sea-sand.

St Leonard's chapel, long ago
We loitered idly where the tall
Fresh-budded mountain ashes blow
Within thy desecrated wall:
The tough roots rent the tomb below,
The April birds sang clamorous,
We did not dream, we could not know
How hardly Fate would deal with us!

O, broken minster*, looking forth cathedral
Beyond the bay, above the town,
O, winter of the kindly North,
O, college of the scarlet gown,
And shining sands beside the sea,
And stretch of links beyond the sand,
Once more I watch you, and to me
It is as if I touched his hand!
And therefore art thou yet more dear,
O, little city, gray and sere,
Though shrunken from thine ancient pride
And lonely by thy lonely sea,
Than these fair halls on Isis' side,
Where Youth and hour came back to me!
A land of waters green and clear,
Of willows and of poplars tall,
And, in the spring-time of the year,
The white may breaking over all,
And Pleasure quick to come at call.
And summer rides by marsh and wold,
And Autumn with her crimson pall
About the towers of Magdalen rolled;
And strange enchantments from the past,
And memories of the friends of old,
And strong Tradition, binding fast
The "flying terms" with bands of gold,—
All these hath Oxford: all are dear,
But dearer far the little town,
The drifting surge, the wintry year,
The college of the scarlet gown.
*St. Andrews by the Northern Sea,*
*That is a haunted town to me!*

## Of Life

Say, fair maids, maying
In gardens green,
In deep dells straying,
What end hath been
Two Mays between
Of the flowers that shone
And your own sweet queen?—
"They are dead and gone."

Say, grave priests, praying
In dule and teen,
From cells decaying,
What have ye seen
Of the proud and mean,
Of Judas and John,
Of the foul and clean?
"They are dead and gone."

Say, kings, arraying
Loud wars to win,
Of your manslaying
What gain ye glean?
"They are fierce and keen,
But they fall anon,
On the sword that lean,
They are dead and gone."

### Envoy

Through the mad world's scene
We are drifting on,
To this tune, I ween,
"They are dead and gone."

## Twilight on Tweed

Three crests against the saffron sky,
Beyond the purple plain,
The kind remembered melody
Of Tweed once more again.

Wan water from the border hills,
Dear voice from the old years,
Thy distant music lulls and stills,
And moves to quiet tears.

Like a loved ghost thy fabled flood
Fleets through the dusky land;
Where Scott, come home to die, has stood,
My feet returning stand.

A mist of memory broods and floats,
The border waters flow;
The air is full of ballad notes,
Borne out of long ago.

Old songs that sung themselves to me,
Sweet through a boy's day-dream,
While trout below the blossomed tree
Plashed in the golden stream.

Twilight, and Tweed, and Eildon Hill,
Fair and too fair you be;
You tell me that the voice is still
That should have welcomed me.

## Three Portraits of Prince Charles

1731

Beautiful face of a child,
Lighted with laughter and glee,
Mirthful and tender and wild,
My heart is heavy for thee.

1744

Beautiful face of a youth,
As an eagle poised to fly forth
To the old land loyal of truth,
To the hills and the sounds of the North:
Fair face, daring and proud,
Lo! the shadow of doom, even now,
The fate of thy line, like a cloud,
Rests on the grace of thy brow.

1773

Cruel and angry face!
Hateful and heavy with wine,
Where are the gladness, the grace,
The beauty, the mirth that were thine?

Ah, my Prince, it were well—
Hadst thou to the gods been dear—
To have fallen where Keppoch fell,
With the war-pipe loud in thine ear.
To have died with never a stain
On the fair White Rose of renown,
To have fallen, fighting in vain,
For thy father, thy faith, and thy crown.
More than thy marble pile,
With its women weeping for thee,
Were to dream in thine ancient isle,
To the endless dirge of the sea.
But the fates deemed otherwise;

Far thou sleepest from home,
From the tears of the northern skies,
In the secular dust of Rome.

A city of death and the dead,
But thither a pilgrim[1] came,
Wearing on weary head
The crowns of years and fame:
Little the Lucrine lake
Or Tivoli said to him,
Scarce did the memories wake
Of the far-off years and dim,
For he stood by Avernus' shore.
But he dreamed of a northern glen,
And he murmured, over and oer,
*"For Charlie and his men":*
And his feet, to death that went,
Crept forth to St. Peter's shrine,
And the latest minstrel bent
Oer the last of the Stuart line.

## Of His Choice of a Sepulchre

Here I'd come when weariest.
Here the breast
Of the Windberg's tufted over
Deep with bracken; here his crest
Takes the west,
Where the wide-winged hawk doth hover.

Silent here are lark and plover;
In the cover
Deep below, the cushat best
Loves his mate, and croons above her
Oer their nest,
Where the wide-winged hawk doth hover.

Bring me here, life's tired-out guest,
To the blest
Bed that waits the weary rover,—
Here should failure be confest;
Ends my quest,
Where the wide-winged hawk doth hover.

### Envoy

Friend, or stranger kind, or lover,
Ah, fulfill a last behest,
Let me rest
Where the wide-winged hawk doth hover.

---

[1] Walter Scott.

## The Odyssey

As one that for a weary space has lain
Lulled by the song of Circe and her wine
In gardens near the pale of Proserpine,
Where that Aeaean isle forgets the main,
And only the low lutes of love complain,
And only shadows of wan lovers pine—
As such an one were glad to know the brine
Salt on his lips, and the large air again—
So gladly, from the songs of modern speech
Men turn, and see the stars, and feel the free
Shrill wind beyond the close of heavy flowers,
And through the music of the languid hours
They hear like Ocean on the western beach
The surge and thunder of the Odyssey.

## Of Blue China

There's a joy without canker or cark,
There's a pleasure eternally new,
Tis to gloat on the glaze and the mark
Of china that's ancient and blue;
Unchipped, all the centuries through
It has passed, since the chime of it rang,
And they fashioned it, figure and hue,
In the reign of the Emperor Hwang.

These dragons (their tails, you remark,
Into bunches of gillyflowers grew),—
When Noah came out of the ark,
Did these lie in wait for his crew?
They snorted, they snapped, and they slew,
They were mighty of fin and of fang,
And their portraits Celestials drew
In the reign of the Emperor Hwang.

Here's a pot with a cot in a park,
In a park where the peach-blossoms blew,
Where the lovers eloped in the dark,
Lived, died, and were changed into two
Bright birds that eternally flew
Through the boughs of the may, as they sang;
Tis a tale was undoubtedly true
In the reign of the Emperor Hwang.

### Envoy

Come, snarl at my ecstasies, do,
Kind critic; your "tongue has a tang,"
But—a sage never heeded a shrew
In the reign of the Emperor Hwang.

## Telling the Bees[1]

Naiads, and ye pastures cold,
When the bees return with spring,
Tell them that Leucippus old
Perished in his hare-hunting,
Perished on a winter night.
Now no more shall he delight
In the hives he used to tend,
But the valley and the height
Mourn a neighbor and a friend.

## Romance

My Love dwelt in a Northern land.
A gray tower in a forest green
Was hers, and far on either hand
The long wash of the waves was seen,
And leagues on leagues of yellow sand,
The woven forest boughs between.

And through the silver Northern night
The sunset slowly died away,
And herds of strange deer, lily-white,
Stole forth among the branches gray;
About the coming of the light,
They fled like ghosts before the day.

I know not if the forest green
Still girdles around that castle gray.
I know not if the boughs between
The white deer vanish ere the day.
Above my Love the grass is green,
My heart is colder than the clay.

## A Dream

Why will you haunt my sleep?
You know it may not be.
The grave is wide and deep,
That sunders you and me.
In bitter dreams we reap
The sorrow we have sown,
And I would I were asleep,
Forgotten and alone.

We knew and did not know—
We saw and did not see,
The nets that long ago
Fate wove for you and me;
The cruel nets that keep

[1] Adapted from an anonymous Greek poem.

The birds that sob and moan;
And I would we were asleep,
Forgotten and alone.

## Melville and Coghill
(The Place of the Little Hand)

Dead, with their eyes to the foe,
Dead, with the foe at their feet;
Under the sky laid low
Truly their slumber is sweet,
Though the wind from the Camp of the Slain Men blow,
And the rain on the wilderness beat.
Dead, for they chose to die
When that wild race was run;
Dead, for they would not fly,
Deeming their work undone,
Nor cared to look on the face of the sky,
Nor loved the light of the sun.

Honor we give them and tears;
And the flag they died to save,
Rent from the rain of the spears,
Wet from the war and the wave,
Shall waft men's thoughts through the dust of the years,
Back to their lonely grave.

## On Calais Sands

On Calais Sands the gray began,
Then rosy red above the gray.
The morn with many a scarlet van
Leaped, and the world was glad with May.
The little waves along the bay
Broke white upon the shelving strands.
The sea-mews flitted white as they
On Calais Sands.

On Calais Sands must man with man
Wash honor clean in blood today.
On spaces wet from waters wan
How white the flashing rapiers play—
Parry, riposte, and lunge! The fray
Shifts for a while, then mournful stands
The victor. Life ebbs fast away
On Calais Sands.

On Calais Sands a little space
Of silence, then the splash and spray,
The sound of eager waves that ran
To kiss the perfumed locks astray,

To touch these lips that ne'er said "Nay,"
To dally with the helpless hands,
Till the deep sea in silence lay
On Calais Sands.

Between the lilac and the may
She waits her love from alien lands.
Her love is colder than the clay
On Calais Sands.

## Recollections of Robert Louis Stevenson

### TUSITALA[1]

We spoke of a rest in a Fairy hill of the north, but he
Far from the firths of the east and the racing tides of the west
Sleeps in the sight and the sound of the infinite southern sea,
Weary and well content, in his grave on the Vaea crest.

Tusitala, the lover of children, the teller of tales,
Giver of counsel and dreams, a wonder, a world's delight,
Looks oer the labor of men in the plain and the hill, and the sails
Pass and repass on the sea that he loved, in the day and the night.

Winds of the west and the east in the rainy season blow,
Heavy with perfume, and all his fragrant woods are wet,
Winds of the east and the west as they wander to and fro,
Bear him the love of the lands he loved, and the long regret.

Once we were kindest, he said, when leagues of the limitless sea,
Flowed between us, but now that no range of the refluent tides
Sunders us each from each, yet nearer we seem to be,
When only the unbridged stream of the River of Death divides.

Before attempting to give any "reminiscences" of Mr. Stevenson, it is right to observe that reminiscences of him can best be found in his own works. In his essay on "Child's Play," and in his "Child's Garden of Verse," he gave to the world his vivid recollections of his imaginative infancy; in other essays he spoke of his boyhood, his health, his dreams, his methods of work and study. "The Silverado Squatters" reveals part of his experience in America. The Parisian scenes in "The Wrecker" are inspired by his sojourn in French Bohemia; his journeys are recorded in "Travels with a Donkey" and "An Inland Voyage"; while his South Sea sketches, which appeared in periodicals, deal with his Oceanic adventures. He was the most autobiographical of authors, with an egoism nearly as complete, and to us as delightful, as the egoism of Montaigne. Thus, the proper sources of information about the author of "Kidnapped" are in his delightful books.

"John's own John," as Dr. Holmes says, may be very unlike his neighbor's John; but in the case of Mr. Stevenson, his Louis was very similar to my Louis; I mean that, as he presents his personality to the world in his writings, even so did that

[1] Louis Stevenson's name among the natives in Samoa.

personality appear to me in our intercourse. The man I knew was always a boy.

"Sing me a song of the lad that is gone,"

he wrote about Prince Charlie, but in his own case the lad was never "gone." Like Keats and Shelley, he was, and he looked, of the immortally young. He and I were at school together, but I was an elderly boy of seventeen, when he was lost in the crowd of "gytes," as the members of the lowest form are called. Like all Scotch people, we had a vague family connection; a great-uncle of his, I fancy, married an aunt of my own, called for her beauty, "The Flower of Ettrick." So we had both heard: but these things were before our day.

A lady of my kindred remembers carrying Stevenson about when he was "a rather peevish baby," and I have seen a beautiful photograph of him, like one of Raffael's children, taken when his years were three or four. But I never had heard of his existence till, in 1873, I think, I was at Mentone, in the interests of my health. Here I met Mr. Sidney Colvin, now of the British Museum, and, with Mr. Colvin, Stevenson. He looked as, in my eyes, he always did look, more like a lass than a lad, with a rather long, smooth oval face, brown hair worn at greater length than is common, large lucid eyes, but whether blue or brown I cannot remember, if brown, certainly light brown. On appealing to the authority of a lady, I learn that brown *was* the hue. His color was a trifle hectic, as is not unusual at Mentone, but he seemed, under his big blue cloak, to be of slender, yet agile frame. He was like nobody else whom I ever met. There was a sort of uncommon celerity in changing expression, in thought and speech. His cloak and Tyrolese hat (he would admit the innocent impeachment) were decidedly dear to him. On the frontier of Italy, why should he not do as the Italians do? It would have been well for me if I could have imitated the wearing of the cloak!

I shall not deny that my first impression was not wholly favorable. "Here," I thought, "is one of your aesthetic young men, though a very clever one." What the talk was about, I do not remember; probably of books. Mr. Stevenson afterwards told me that I had spoken of Monsieur Paul de St. Victor, as a fine writer, but added that "he was not a British sportsman." Mr. Stevenson himself, to my surprise, was unable to walk beyond a very short distance, and, as it soon appeared, he thought his thread of life was nearly spun. He had just written his essay, "Ordered South," the first of his published works, for his "Pentland Rising" pamphlet was unknown, a boy's performance.

On reading "Ordered South," I saw, at once, that here was a new writer, a writer indeed; one who could do what none of us, *nous autres,* could rival, or approach. I was instantly "sealed of the Tribe of Louis," an admirer, a devotee, a fanatic, if you please. At least my taste has never altered. From this essay it is plain enough that the author (as is so common in youth, but with better reason than many have) thought himself doomed. Most of us have gone through that, the Millevoye phase, but who else has shown such a wise and gay acceptance of the apparently inevitable? We parted; I remember little of our converse, except a shrewd and hearty piece of encouragement given me by my junior, who already knew so much more of life than his senior will ever do. For he ran forth to embrace life like a lover: *his* motto was never Lucy Ashton's—

"Vacant heart, and hand and eye,
Easy live and quiet die."

Mr. Stevenson came presently to visit me at Oxford. I make no hand of reminiscences; I remember nothing about what we did or said, with one exception, which is not going to be published. I heard of him, writing essays in the *Portfolio* and the *Cornhill,* those delightful views of life at twenty-five, so brave, so real, so vivid, so wise, so exquisite, which all should know. How we looked for "R. L. S." at the end of an article, and how devout was our belief, how happy our pride, in the young one!

About 1878, I think (I was now a slave of the quill myself), I received a brief note from Mr. Stevenson, introducing to me the person whom, in his essay on his old college magazine, he called "Glasgow Brown." What his real name was, whence he came, whence the money came, I never knew. G. B. was going to start a weekly Tory paper. Would I contribute? G. B. came to see me. Mr. Stevenson has described him, *not* as I would have described him: like Mr. Bill Sikes's dog, I have the Christian peculiarity of not liking dogs "as are not of my breed." G. B.'s paper, *London,* was to start next week. He had no writer of political leading articles. Would I do a "leader"? But I was *not* in favor of Lord Lytton's Afghan policy. How could I do a Tory leader? Well, I did a neutral-tinted thing, with citations from Aristophanes! I found presently *some other scribes for G. B.*

What a paper that was! I have heard that G. B. paid in handfuls of gold, in handfuls of bank-notes. Nobody ever read *London,* or advertised in it, or heard of it. It was full of the most wonderfully clever verses in old French forms. They were (it afterwards appeared) by Mr. W. E. Henley. Mr. Stevenson himself astonished and delighted *the public of London* (that is, the contributors) by *his* "New Arabian Nights." Nobody knew about them but ourselves, a fortunate few. Poor G. B. died and Mr. Henley became the editor. I may not name the contributors, the flower of the young lions, elderly lions now, there is a new race. But one lion, a distinguished and learned lion, said already that fiction, not essay, was Mr. Stevenson's field. Well, both fields were his, and I cannot say whether I would be more sorry to lose *Virginibus Puerisque* and "Studies of Men and Books," or "Treasure Island" and "Catriona." With the decease of G. B., Pactolus dried up in its mysterious sources, *London* struggled and disappeared.

Mr. Stevenson was in town, now and again, at the old Saville Club, in Saville Row, which had the tiniest and blackest of smoking-rooms. Here, or somewhere, he spoke to me of an idea of a tale, a Man who was Two Men. I said "'William Wilson' by Edgar Poe," and declared that it would never do. But his "Brownies," in a vision of the night, showed him a central scene, and he wrote "Jekyll and Hyde." My "friend of these days and of all days," Mr. Charles Longman, sent me the manuscript. In a very common-place London drawing-room, at 10.30 P.M., I began to read it. Arriving at the place where Utterson the lawyer, and the butler wait outside the Doctor's room, I threw down the manuscript and fled in a hurry. I had no taste for solitude any more. The story won its great success, partly by dint of the moral (whatever that may be), more by its terrible, lucid, visionary power. I remember Mr. Stevenson telling me, at this time, that he was doing some "regular crawlers," for this purist had a boyish habit of slang, and I *think* it was he who called Julius Caesar "the howlingest cheese who ever lived." One of the "crawlers" was "Thrawn Janet"; after "Wandering Willie's Tale" (but certainly *after* it); to my taste, it seems the most wonderful story of the "supernatural" in our language.

Mr. Stevenson had an infinite pleasure in Boisgobey, Montepin, and, of course, Gaboriau. There was nothing of the "cultured person" about him. Concerning a novel dear to culture, he said that he would die by my side, in the last ditch, proclaiming it the worst fiction in the world. I make haste to add that I have only known two men of letters as free as Mr. Stevenson, not only from literary jealousy, but from the writer's natural, if exaggerated, distaste for work which, though in his own line, is very different in aim and method from his own. I do not remember another case in which he dispraised any book. I do remember his observations on a novel then and now very popular, but not to his taste, nor, indeed, by any means, impeccable, though stirring; his censure and praise were both just. From his occasional fine efforts, the author of this romance, he said, should have cleared away acres of brushwood, of ineffectual matter. It was so, no doubt, as the writer spoken of would be ready to acknowledge. But he was an improviser of genius, and Mr. Stevenson was a conscious artist.

Of course we did by no means always agree in literary estimates; no two people do. But when certain works —in his line in one way—were stupidly set up as rivals of his, the person who was most irritated was not he, but his equally magnanimous contemporary. There was no thought of rivalry or competition in either mind. The younger romancists who arose after Mr. Stevenson went to Samoa were his friends by correspondence; from them, who never saw his face, I hear of his sympathy and encouragement. Every writer knows the special temptations of his tribe: they were temptations not even felt, I do believe, by Mr. Stevenson. His heart was far too high, his nature was in every way as generous as his hand was open. It is in thinking of these things that one feels afresh the greatness of the world's loss; for "a good heart is much more than style," writes one who knew him only by way of letters.

It is a trivial reminiscence that we once plotted a Boisgobesque story together. There was a prisoner in a Muscovite dungeon.

"We'll extract information from him," I said.

"How?"

"With corkscrews."

But the mere suggestion of such a process was terribly distasteful to him; not that I really meant to go to these extreme lengths. We never, of course, could really have worked together; and, his maladies increasing, he became more and more a wanderer, living at Bournemouth, at Davos, in the Grisons, finally, as all know, in Samoa. Thus, though we corresponded, not unfrequently, I never was of the inner circle of his friends. Among men there were school or college companions, or companions of Paris or Fontainebleau, cousins, like Mr. R. A. M. Stevenson, or a stray senior, like Mr. Sidney Colvin. From some of them, or from Mr. Stevenson himself, I have heard tales of "the wild Prince and Poins." That he and a friend traveled utterly without baggage, buying a shirt where a shirt was needed, is a fact, and the incident is used in "The Wrecker." Legend says that once he and a friend *did* possess a bag, and also, nobody ever knew why, a large bottle of scent. But there was no room for the bottle in the bag, so Mr. Stevenson spilled the whole contents over the other man's head, taking him unawares, that nothing might be wasted. I think the tale of the endless staircase, in "The Wrecker," is founded on fact, so are the stories of the *atelier,* which I have heard Mr. Stevenson narrate at the Oxford and Cambridge Club. For a nocturnal adventure, in the manner of the "New Arabian Nights," a learned critic already spoken of must be consulted. It is not my story. In Paris, at a cafe, I remember that Mr. Stevenson heard a Frenchman say the English were cowards. He got up and slapped the man's face.

*"Monsieur, vous m'avez frappe!"* said the Gaul.

*"A ce qu'il parait"*[1] said the Scot, and there it ended. He also told me that years ago he was present at a play, I forget what play, in Paris, where the moral hero exposes a woman "with a history." He got up and went out, saying to himself: "What a play! what a people! "

*"Ah, Monsieur, vous etes bien jeune"* [2] said an old French gentleman.

Like a right Scot, Mr. Stevenson was fond of "our auld ally of France," to whom our country and our exiled kings owed so much.

I rather vaguely remember another anecdote. He missed his train from Edinburgh to London, and his sole portable property was a return ticket, a meerschaum pipe, and a volume of Mr. Swinburne's poems. The last he found unmarketable; the pipe, I think, he made merchandise of, but somehow his provender for the day's journey consisted in one bath bun, which he could not finish.

---

[1]"Sir, you have struck me!"/ "So it would appear."

[2]"You are so young."

These trivial tales illustrate a period in his life and adventures which I only know by rumor. Our own acquaintance was, to a great degree, literary and bookish. Perhaps it began "with a slight aversion," but it seemed, like madeira, to be ripened and improved by his long sea voyage; and the news of his death taught me, at least, the true nature of the affection which he was destined to win. Indeed, our acquaintance was like the friendship of a wild singing bird and of a punctual, domesticated barn-door fowl, laying its daily "article" for the breakfast-table of the citizens. He often wrote to me from Samoa, sometimes with news of native manners and folklore. He sent me a devil-box, the "luck" of some strange island, which he bought at a great price. After parting with its "luck," or fetish (a shell in a curious wooden box), the island was unfortunate, and was ravaged by measles.

I occasionally sent out books needed for Mr. Stevenson's studies, of which more will be said. But I must make it plain that, in the body, we met but rarely. His really intimate friends were Mr. Colvin and Mr. Baxter (who managed the practical side of his literary business between them); Mr. Henley (in partnership with whom he wrote several plays); his cousin, Mr. R. A. M. Stevenson; and, among other *literati,* Mr. Gosse, Mr. Austin Dobson, Mr. Saintsbury, Mr. Walter Pollock, knew him well. The best portrait of Mr. Stevenson that I know is by Sir W. B. Richmond, R.A., and is in that gentleman's collection of contemporaries, with the effigies of Mr. Holman Hunt, Mr. William Morris, Mr. Browning, and others. It is unfinished, owing to an illness which stopped the sittings, and does not show the subject at his best, physically speaking. There is also a brilliant, slight sketch, almost a caricature, by Mr. Sargent. It represents Mr. Stevenson walking about the room in conversation.

The people I have named, or some of them, knew Mr. Stevenson more intimately than I can boast of doing. Unlike each other, opposites in a dozen ways, we always were united by the love of letters, and of Scotland, our dear country. He was a patriot, yet he spoke his mind quite freely about Burns, about that apparent want of heart in the poet's amours, which our countrymen do not care to hear mentioned. Well, perhaps, for some reasons, it had to be mentioned once, and so no more of it.

Mr. Stevenson possessed, more than any man I ever met, the power of making other men fall in love with him. I mean that he excited a passionate admiration and affection, so much so that I verily believe some men were jealous of other men's place in his liking. I once met a stranger who, having become acquainted with him, spoke of him with a touching fondness and pride, his fancy reposing, as it seemed, in a fond contemplation of so much genius and charm. What was so taking in him? and how is one to analyse that dazzling surface of pleasantry, that changeful shining humour, wit, wisdom, recklessness; beneath which beat the most kind and tolerant of hearts?

People were fond of him, and people were proud of him: his achievements, as it were, sensibly raised their pleasure in the world, and, to them, became parts of themselves. They warmed their hands at that center of light and heat. It is not every success which has these beneficent results. We see the successful sneered at, decried, insulted, even when success is deserved. Very little of all this, hardly aught of all this, I think, came in Mr. Stevenson's way. After the beginning (when the praises of his earliest admirers were irritating to dull scribes) he found the critics fairly kind, I believe, and often enthusiastic. He was so much his own severest critic that he probably paid little heed to professional reviewers. In addition to his "Rathillet," and other MSS. which he destroyed, he once, in the Highlands, long ago, lost a portmanteau with a batch of his writings. Alas, that he should have lost or burned anything! "King's chaff," says our country proverb, "is better than other folk's corn."

I have remembered very little, or very little that I can write, and about our last meeting, when he was so near death, in appearance, and so full of courage—how can I speak? His courage was a strong rock, not to be taken or subdued. When unable to utter a single word, his penciled remarks to his attendants were pithy and extremely characteristic. This courage and spiritual vitality made one hope that he would, if he desired it, live as long as Voltaire, that reed among oaks. There were of course, in so rare a combination of characteristics, some which were not equally to the liking of all. He was highly original in costume, but, as his photographs are familiar, the point does not need elucidation. Life was a drama to him, and he delighted, like his own British admirals, to do things with a certain air. He observed himself, I used to think, as he observed others, and "saw himself" in every part he played. There was nothing of the *cabotin* in this self-consciousness; it was the unextinguished childish passion for "playing at things" which remained with him. I have a theory that all children possess genius, and that it dies out in the generality of mortals, abiding only with people whose genius the world is forced to recognize. Mr. Stevenson illustrates, and perhaps partly suggested, this private philosophy of mine.

I have said very little; I have no skill in reminiscences, no art to bring the living aspect of the man before those who never knew him. I faintly seem to see the eager face, the light nervous figure, the fingers busy with rolling cigarettes; Mr. Stevenson talking, listening, often rising from his seat, standing, walking to and fro, always full of vivid intelligence, wearing a mysterious smile. I remember one pleasant dark afternoon, when he told me many tales of strange adventures, narratives which he had heard about a murderous lonely inn, somewhere in the States. He was as good to hear as to read. I do not recollect much of that delight in discussion, in controversy, which he shows in his essay on conversation, where he describes, I believe, Mr. Henley as "Burley," and Mr. Symonds as "Opalstein." He had great pleasure in the talk of the late Professor Fleeming Jenkin, which was both various and copious. But in these *noctes coenaeque deum* I was never a partaker.

In many topics, such as angling, golf, cricket, whereon I am willingly diffuse, Mr. Stevenson took no interest. He was very fond of boating and sailing in every kind; he hazarded his health by long expeditions among the fairy isles of ocean, but he "was not a British sportsman," though for his measure of strength a good pedestrian, a friend of the open air, and of all who live and toil therein.

As to his literary likings, they appear in his own confessions. He reveled in Dickens, but, about Thackeray —well, I would rather have talked to somebody else! To my amazement, he was of those (I think) who find Thackeray "cynical." "He takes you into a garden, and then pelts you with —horrid things!" Mr. Stevenson, on the other hand, had a free admiration of Mr. George Meredith. He did not so easily forgive the *longeurs* and lazinesses of Scott, as a Scot should do. He read French much; Greek only in translations.

Literature was, of course, his first love, but he was actually an advocate at the Scottish Bar, and, as such, had his name on a brazen door-plate. Once he was a competitor for a Chair of Modern History in Edinburgh University; he knew the romantic side of Scottish history very well. In his novel, "Catriona," the character of James Mohr Macgregor is wonderfully divined. Once I read some unpublished letters of Catriona's unworthy father, written when he was selling himself as a spy (and lying as he spied) to the Hanoverian usurper. Mr. Stevenson might have written these letters for James Mohr; they might be extracts from "Catriona."

In turning over old Jacobite pamphlets, I found a forgotten romance of Prince Charles's hidden years, and longed that Mr. Stevenson should retell it. There was a treasure, an authentic treasure; there were real spies, a real assassin; a real, or reported, rescue of a lovely girl from a fire at Strasbourg, by the Prince. The tale was to begin sur le *pont d' Avignon:* a young Scotch exile watching the Rhone, thinking how much of it he could cover with a salmon fly, thinking of the Tay or Beauly. To him enter another shady tramping exile, Blairthwaite, a murderer. And so it was to run on, as the author's fancy might lead him, with Alan Breck and the Master for characters.

At last, in unpublished MSS. I found an actual Master of Ballantrae, a Highland chief—noble, majestically handsome—and a paid spy of England! All these papers I sent out to Samoa, too late. The novel was to have been dedicated to me, and that chance of immortality is gone, with so much else.

Mr. Stevenson's last letters to myself were full of his concern for a common friend of ours, who was very ill. Depressed himself, Mr. Stevenson wrote to this gentleman—why should I not mention Mr. James Payn?— with consoling gaiety. I attributed his depression to any cause but his own health, of which he rarely spoke. He lamented the "ill-staged fifth act of life"; he, at least, had no long hopeless years of diminished force to bear.

I have known no man in whom the pre-eminently manly virtues of kindness, courage, sympathy, generosity, helpfulness, were more beautifully conspicuous than in Mr. Stevenson, no man so much loved—it is not too strong a word—by so many and such various people. He was as unique in character as in literary genius.

## ALEXANDER ANDERSON (1845–1909)

[Anderson was at one time a laborer for the railways. He wrote under the name "Surfaceman," a term which describes his former profession. He is noted both for railway poems and his verse for young people.]

### Toshie Norrie

O, Bonnie Toshie Norrie
To Inverard is gane,
An' wi' her a' the sunshine
That made us unco* fain*. very/happy
The win' is cauld an' gurly*, boisterous
An' winter's in the air,
But where dwells Toshie Norrie,
O, it's aye simmer there.

O, bonnie Toshie Norrie,
What made you leave us a'?
Your hame is no the Hielands,
Though there the hills are braw.
Come back wi' a' your daffin'*, fooling
An' walth o' gowden hair,
For where dwells Toshie Norrie,
O, it's aye simmer there.

O, bonnie Toshie Norrie,
The winter nichts are lang,
An' aft we sit an' weary
To hear an auld Scotch sang;
Come back, an' let your music,
Like sunshine, fill the air,
For where dwells Toshie Norrie,
O, it's aye simmer there.

## Jenny wi' the Airn Teeth

What a plague is this o' mine,
Winna steek* an e'e; — shut
Though I hap* him oer the heid, — clothe, cover
As cozy as can be.
Sleep an' let me to my wark—
A' thae claes to airn—
Jenny wi' the airn teeth,
Come an' tak the bairn.

Tak him to your ain den,
Whaur the bogie bides,
But first put baith your big teeth
In his wee plump sides;
Gie your auld gray pow* a shake, — head
Rive him frae my grup,
Tak him whaur nae kiss is gaun
When he waukens up.

Whatna noise is that I hear
Coomin' doon the street?
Weel I ken the dump, dump,
O' her beetle feet;
Mercy me, she's at the door!
Hear her lift the sneck*; — latch
Wheesht*, an' cuddle mammy noo, — (shush!)
Closer roun' the neck.

Jenny wi' the airn teeth,
The bairn has aff his claes;
Sleepin' safe an' soun', I think—
Dinna touch his taes.
Sleepin' bairns are no for you,
Ye may turn aboot,
An' tak' awa' wee Tam next door—
I hear him screichin' oot.

Dump, dump, awa' she gangs
Back the road she cam',
I hear her at the ither door,
Speirin'* after Tam; — asking
He's a crabbit, greetin'* thing— — crying
The warst in a' the toon,
Little like my ain wee wean—
Losh, he's sleepin' soun!

Mithers hae an awfu' wark
Wi' their bairns at nicht,
Chappin' on the chair wi' tangs,
To gie the rogues a fricht;
Aulder bairns are fleyed* wi' less, — frightened
Weel eneuch we ken,

Bigger bogies, bigger Jennies,
Frichten muckle men.

## Langsyne, When Life Was Bonnie

Langsyne, when life was bonnie,
An' a' the skies were blue,
When ilka thocht took blossom,
An' hung its heid wi' dew,
When winter wasna winter,
Though snaws cam' happin, doon,
Langyne, when life was bonnie,
Spring gaed a twalmonth roun'.

Langsyne, when life was bonnie,
An' a' the days were lang;
When through them ran the music
That comes to us in sang,
We never wearied liltin'
The auld love-laden tune;
Langsyne, when life was bonnie,
Love gaed a twalmonth roun'.

Langsyne, when life was bonnie,
An' a' the warld was fair,
The leaves were green wi' simmer,
For autumn wasna there.
But listen hoo they rustle,
Wi' an eerie, weary soun',
For noo, alas, tis winter
That gangs a twalmounth roun'.

## Cuddle Doon

The bairnies cuddle doon at nicht
Wi' muckle faught an' din;
"Oh try and sleep, ye waukrife* rogues, sleepless
Your faither's comin' in."
They never heed a word I speak.
I try to gie a froon,
But aye I hap* them up an' cry, dress, wrap
"Oh, bairnies, cuddle doon."

Wee Jamie wi' the curly heid—
He aye sleeps next the wa'—
Bangs up an' cries, "I want a piece."
The rascal starts them a'.
I rin an' fetch them pieces, drinks,
They stop awee the soun',
Then draw the blankets up an' cry,
"Noo, weanies, cuddle doon."

But, ere five minutes gang, wee Rab
Cries out, frae neath the claes,
"Mither, mak' Tam gie ower at ance,
He's kittlin' wi' his taes."
The mischief's in that Tam for tricks,
He'd bother half the toon;
But aye I hap them up and cry,
"Oh, bairnies, cuddle doon."

At length they hear their faither's fit*, "foot"
An', as he steeks* the door, shuts
They turn their faces to the wa',
While Tam pretends to snore.
"Hae a' the weans been gude?" he asks,
As he pits aff his shoon.
"The bairnies, John, are in their beds,
An' lang since cuddled doon."

An' just afore we bed oorsels,
We look at our wee lambs.
Tam has his airm roun' wee Rab's neck,
And Rab his airm round Tam's.
I lift wee Jamie up the bed,
An' as I straik each croon,
I whisper, till my heart fills up,
"Oh, bairnies, cuddle doon."

The bairnies cuddle doon at nicht
Wi' mirth that's dear to me;
But soon the big warl's cark* an' care weight
Will quaten doon their glee.
Yet, come what will to ilka ane,
May He who rules aboon
Aye whisper, though their pows* be bald, heads
"Oh, bairnies, cuddle doon."

## ARTHUR JAMES BALFOUR (1848–1930)

[Arthur Balfour was one of many Scotsmen who distinguished themselves in British politics. He was a Member of Parliament for many years and held many offices, including First Lord of the Treasury, Leader of the House of Commons, and finally Prime Minister from 1902–1905. He was Lord Rector of St. Andrews University and of Glasgow University. Balfour was a distinguished orator.]

### The Pleasure of Reading

Delivered at St. Andrews University, December 10, 1887

Truly it is a subject for astonishment that, instead of expanding to the utmost the employment of this pleasure-giving faculty, so many persons should set themselves to work to limit its exercise by all kinds of arbitrary regulations.

Some persons, for example, tell us that the acquisition of knowledge is all very well, but that it must be useful knowledge, meaning usually thereby that it must enable a man to get on in a profession, pass an examination, shine in conversation, or obtain a reputation for learning. But even if they mean something higher than this—even if they mean that knowledge, to be worth anything, must subserve ultimately, if not immediately, the material or spiritual interests of mankind, the doctrine is one which should be energetically repudiated.

I admit, of course, at once, that discoveries the most apparently remote from human concerns have often proved themselves of the utmost commercial or manufacturing value. But they require no such justification for their existence, nor were they striven for with any such object.

Navigation is not the final cause of astronomy, nor telegraphy of electro-dynamics, nor dye-works of chemistry. And if it be true that the desire of knowledge for the sake of knowledge was the animating motives of the great men who first wrested her secrets from nature, why should it not also be enough for us, to whom it is not given to discover, but only to learn as best we may what has been discovered by others?

Another maxim, more plausible but equally pernicious, is that superficial knowledge is worse than no knowledge at all. That "a little knowledge is a dangerous thing" is a saying which has now got currency as a proverb stamped in the mint of Pope's versification, of Pope who, with the most imperfect knowledge of Greek, translated Homer; with the most imperfect knowledge of the Elizabethan drama, edited Shakespeare; and with the most imperfect knowledge of philosophy, wrote the "Essay on Man."

But what is this "little knowledge" which is supposed to be so dangerous? What is it "little" in relation to?

If in relation to what there is to know, then all human knowledge is little. If in relation to what actually is known by somebody, then we must condemn as "dangerous" the knowledge which Archimedes possessed of mechanics, or Copernicus of astronomy; for a shilling primer and a few weeks' study will enable any student to outstrip in mere information some of the greatest teachers of the past.

No doubt that little knowledge which thinks itself to be great may possibly be a dangerous, as it certainly is a most ridiculous, thing. We have all suffered under that eminently absurd individual who, on the strength of one or two volumes, imperfectly apprehended by himself and long discredited in the estimation of every one else, is prepared to supply you on the shortest notice with a dogmatic solution of every problem suggested by this "unintelligible world"; or the political variety of the same pernicious genus whose statecraft consists in the ready application to the most complex question of national interest of some high-sounding commonplace which has done weary duty on a thousand platforms, and which even in its palmiest days was never fit for anything better than a peroration.

But in our dislike of the individual do not let us mistake the diagnosis of his disease. He suffers not from ignorance, but from stupidity. Give him learning, and you make him, not wise, but only more pretentious in his folly.

I say, then, that so far from a little knowledge being undesirable a little knowledge is all that on most subjects any of us can hope to attain, and that as a source, not of worldly profit, but of personal pleasure, it may be of incalculable value to its possessor. But it will naturally be asked, "How are we to select from among the infinite number of things which may be known those which it is best worth while for us to know?" We are constantly being told to concern ourselves with learning what is important, and not to waste our energies upon what is insignificant.

But what are the marks by which we shall recognize the important, and how is it to be distinguished from the insignificant? A precise and complete answer to this question which shall be true for all men cannot be given. I am considering knowledge, recollect, as it ministers to enjoyment, and from this point of view each unit of information is obviously of importance in proportion as it increases the general sum of enjoyment which we obtain from knowledge. This, of course, makes it impossible to lay down precise rules which shall be an equally sure guide to all sorts and conditions of men; for in this, as in other matters, tastes must differ, and against real difference of taste there is no appeal.

There is, however, one caution which it may be worth your while to keep in view: Do not be persuaded into applying any general proposition on this subject with a foolish impartiality to every kind of knowledge. There are those who tell you that it is the broad generalities and the far-reaching principles which govern the world, which are alone worthy of your attention.

A fact which is not an illustration of a law, in the opinion of these persons appears to lose all its value. Incidents which do not fit into some great generalization, events which are merely picturesque, details which are merely curious— they dismiss as unworthy the interest of a reasoning being.

Now, even in science, this doctrine in its extreme form does not hold good. The most scientific of men have taken profound interest in the investigation of facts from the determination of which they do not anticipate any material addition to our knowledge of the laws which regulate the universe. In these matters I need hardly say that I speak wholly without authority. But I have always been under the impression that an investigation which has cost hundreds of thousands of pounds; which has stirred on three occasions the whole scientific community throughout the civilized world; on which has been expended the utmost skill in the construction of instruments and their application to purposes of research (I refer to the attempts made to determine the distance of the sun by observations of the transit of Venus), would, even if they had been brought to a successful issue, have furnished mankind with the knowledge of no new astronomical principle.

The laws which govern the motions of the solar system, the proportions which the various elements in that system bear to one another, have long been known. The distance of the sun itself is known within limits of error, relatively speaking, not very considerable. Were the measuring-rod we apply to the heavens, based on an estimate of the sun's distance from the earth, which was wrong by (say) three per cent, it would not, to the lay mind, seem to affect very materially our view either of the distribution of the heavenly bodies or of their motions. And yet this information, this piece of celestial gossip, would seem to be that which was chiefly expected from the successful prosecution of an investigation in which whole nations have interested themselves.

But though no one can, I think, pretend that science does not concern itself, and properly concern itself, with facts which are not in themselves, to all appearance, illustrations of law, it is undoubtedly true that for those who desire to extract the greatest pleasure from science, a knowledge, however elementary, of the leading principles of investigation and the larger laws of nature, is the acquisition most to be desired. To him who is not a specialist, a comprehension of the broad outlines of the universe as it presents itself to the scientific imagination, is the thing most worth striving to attain.

But when we turn from science to what is rather vaguely called history, the same principles of study do not, I think, altogether apply, and mainly for this reason,—that while the recognition of the reign of law is the chief amongst the pleasures imparted by science, our inevitable ignorance makes it the least among the pleasures imparted by history.

It is no doubt true that we are surrounded by advisers who tell us that all study of the past is barren except in so far as it enables us to determine the laws by which the evolution of human societies is governed. How far such an investigation has been up to the present time fruitful in results I will not inquire. That it will ever enable us to trace with accuracy the course which states and nations are destined to pursue in the future, or to account in detail for their history in the past, I do not indeed believe.

We are borne along like travelers on some unexplored stream. We may know enough of the general configuration of the globe to be sure that we are making our way towards the ocean. We may know enough by experience or theory of the laws regulating the flow of liquids, to conjecture how the river will behave under the varying influences to which it may be subject. More than this we cannot know. It will depend largely upon causes which, in relation to any laws which we are ever likely to discover, may properly be called accidental, whether we are destined sluggishly to drift among fever-stricken swamps, to hurry down perilous rapids, or to glide gently through fair scenes of peaceful cultivation.

But leaving on one side ambitious sociological speculations, and even those more modest but hitherto more successful investigations into the causes which have in particular cases been principally operative in producing great political changes, there are still two modes in which we can derive what I may call "spectacular" enjoyment from the study of history.

There is first the pleasure which arises from the contemplation of some great historic drama, or some broad and well marked phase of social development. The story of the rise, greatness, and decay of a nation is like some vast epic which contains as subsidiary episodes the varied stories of the rise, greatness, and decay of creeds, of parties and of statesmen. The imagination is moved by the slow unrolling of this great picture of human mutability, as it is moved by the contrasted permanence of the abiding stars. The ceaseless conflict, the strange echoes of long-forgotten controversies, the confusion of purpose, the successes which lay deep the seeds of future evils, the failures that ultimately divert the otherwise inevitable danger, the heroism which struggles to the last for a cause foredoomed to defeat, the wickedness which sides with right, and the wisdom which huzzas at the triumph of folly— fate, meanwhile, through all this turmoil and perplexity, working silently toward the predestined end,—all these form together a subject the contemplation of which need surely never weary.

But there is yet another and very different species of enjoyment to be derived from the records of the past, which require a somewhat different method of study in order that it may be fully tasted. Instead of contemplating, as it were, from a distance, the larger aspects of the human drama, we may elect to move in familiar fellowship amid the scenes and actors of special periods.

We may add to the interest we derive from the contemplation of contemporary politics, a similar interest derived from a not less minute and probably more accurate knowledge of some comparatively brief passage in the political history of the past. We may extend the social circle in which we move—a circle perhaps narrowed and restricted through circumstances beyond our control—by making intimate acquaintances, perhaps even close friends, among a society long departed, but which, when we have once learnt the trick of it, it rests with us to revive.

It is this kind of historical reading which is usually branded as frivolous and useless, and persons who indulge in it often delude themselves into thinking that the real motive of their investigation into bygone scenes and ancient scandals is philosophy interest in an important historical episode, whereas in truth it is not the philosophy which glorifies the details, but the details which make tolerable the philosophy.

Consider, for example, the case of the French Revolution. The period from the taking of the Bastille to the fall of Robespierre is of about the same length as very commonly intervenes between two of our general elections. On these comparatively few months libraries have been written. The incidents of every week are matters of familiar knowledge. The character and the biography of every actor in the drama has been made the subject of minute study; and by common admission, there is no more fascinating page in the history of the world.

But the interest is not what is commonly called philosophy, it is personal. Because the Revolution is the dominant fact in modern history, therefore people suppose that the doings of this or that provincial lawyer, tossed into temporary eminence and eternal infamy by some freak of the revolutionary wave, or the atrocities committed by this or that mob, half-drunk with blood, rhetoric and alcohol, are of transcendent importance.

In truth their interest is great, but their importance is small. What we are concerned to know as students of the philosophy of history is not the character of each turn and eddy in the great social cataract, but the manner in which the currents of the upper stream drew surely in toward the final plunge, and slowly collected themselves after the catastrophe, again to pursue, at a different level, their renewed and comparatively tranquil course.

Now, if so much of the interest of the French Revolution depends upon our minute knowledge of each passing incident, how much more necessary is such knowledge when we are dealing with the quiet nooks and corners of history—when we are seeking an introduction, let us say, into the literary society of Johnson or the fashionable society of Walpole! Society, dead or alive, can have no charm without intimacy, and no intimacy without interest in trifles which I fear Mr. Harrison would describe as "merely curious."

If we would feel at our ease in any company, if we wish to find humor in its jokes and point in its repartees, we must know something of the beliefs and the prejudices of its various members—their loves and their hates, their hopes and their fears, their maladies, their marriages, and their flirtations. If these things are beneath our notice, we shall not be the less qualified to serve our queen and country, but need make no attempt to extract pleasure out of one of the most delightful departments of literature.

That there is such a thing as trifling information, I do not of course question; but the frame of mind in which the reader is constantly weighing the exact importance to the universe at large of each circumstance which the author presents to his notice, is not one conducive to the true enjoyment of a picture whose effect depends upon a multitude of slight and seemingly insignificant touches, which impress the mind often without remaining in the memory.

The best method of guarding against the danger of reading what is useless is to read only what is interesting, a truth which will seem a paradox to a whole class of readers, fitting objects of our commiseration, who may be often recognized by their habit of asking some adviser for a list of books, and then marking out a scheme of study in the course of which all these are to be conscientiously perused.

These unfortunate persons apparently read a book principally with the object of getting to the end of it. They reach the word "*Finis*" with the same sensation of triumph as an Indian feels who strings a fresh scalp to his girdle. They are not happy unless they mark by some definite performance each step in the weary path of self-improvement. To begin a volume and not to finish it would be to deprive themselves of this satisfaction; it would be to lose all the reward of their earlier self-denial by a lapse from virtue at the end. The skip, according to their literary code, is a form of cheating: it is a mode of obtaining credit for erudition on false pretenses; a plan by which the advantages of learning are surreptitiously obtained by those who have not won them by honest toil.

But all this is quite wrong. In matters literary, works have no saving efficacy. He has only half learned the art of reading who has not added to it the even more refined accomplishments of skipping and of skimming; and the first step has hardly been taken in the direction of making literature a pleasure, until interest in the subject, and not a desire to spare (so to speak) the author's feelings, or to accomplish an appointed task, is the prevailing motive of the reader.

## "HUGH HALIBURTON" (JAMES ROBERTSON 1849–1922)

[Primarily a pastoral poet, Robertson is best known for his "Hugh Haliburton" works, featuring a homespun observer named "Hughie." The latter poems, in fact, came to be called "Hughies" by their fairly large public.]

### Hughie's Advice to Dauvit

*Gratia cum nymphis geminisque sororibus audet ducere nuda choros.* —Horace, *Car. iv. 7.*

An' noo ance mair the Lomon'
Has donned his mantle green,
An' we may gang a-roamin'
Through the fields at e'en.

An' listen to the rustlin'
O' green leaves i' the shaw*, wood
An' hear the blackbird whistlin'
Winter weel awa'.

Sae mild's the weather, Dauvit,
That was but late sae bauld,
We gang withoot a grauvit* scarf
Careless o' the cauld.

An juist the ither nicht, man,
Twa barefit Mays* were seen maids
(It maun hae been a sicht, man.)
Dancin' on the green.

It sets a body thinkin'
Hoo quick the moments fly,
Hoo fast the days gang linkin'.
Spring 'ill soon be by;

Then Simmer wi' the roses,
Then Autumn wi' the grain;
Then Winter comes an' closes
A' thing ance again.

An' yet, though short her range is,
Dame Nature's never dune;
She just repeats the changes,
Just renews the tune.

The auld moon to her ruin
Gangs rowin' doon the sky,

When, swith*, a braw bran new ane quick
Cocks her horn on high.

Alas, when oor short mornin'
Slides doun the slope to nicht,
There's neither tide nor turnin'
Back to life an' licht.

We fa' as fell oor faithers
Into the narrow hame,
An' fog forgetfu' gaithers
Owre oor very name.

But what needs a' this grievin'
For griefs we dinna feel?
Let's leeve as lang's we're leevin',
Lauch as lang's we're weel.

An' if it's gude i' gloamin'
It's better soon than syne
To rise an' gang a-roamin'
Noo the weather's fine.

## Quem Tu, Melpomene

Wham at his birth wi' mournfu' smile
The Muse has ance regairdet,
Shall ne'er in field o' battle toil
To be with bays rewairdet.

Yet shall he haunt, a lanely ghost,
The placid battle plain—
To mourn the lives that there were lost,
The loves that there were slain.

Hoo caulder for thae stricken lives
Maun mony a hearth hae been;
Hoo blank to mony bairns an' wives
The social hoor at e'en.

Nae hunter on the heather hills
Bird-slaughterin' shall he be,
Nor fisher rivin' fra the gills
O' some puir troot his flee.

Yet shall he love the dusky pools
And speel* the mountain stairs, climb
Unburdened wi' the murderin' tools
O' gun an' gauds* an' snares,— rods

O'erjoyed to find attractions rife
In nature's ilka feature,

And share the brotherhood of life
With every happy creature.

Oh, what avails a victor's name
At close of battle clangor?
This warld is far owre sma' for fame,
And life owre short for anger.

## Spring on the Ochils

Fra whaur in fragrant woods ye bide
Secure fra winter care,
Come, gentle spring, to Ochilside
And Ochil valleys fair.
For sweet as ony pagan spring
Are Devon's waters clear;
And life wad be a lovely thing
Gif ye were only here.

She comes! the waffin' o' her wings
Wi' music fills the air;
An' wintry thochts o' men an' things
Vex human hearts nae mair.
On Devon banks wi' me she strays,
Her poet for the while,
And Ochil brooks and Ochil braes
Grow classic in her smile.

## An Ochil Farmer

Abune the braes I see him stand,
The tapmost corner o' his land,
An' scan wi' care, owre hill an' plain,
A prospect he may ca' his ain.

His yowes ayont the hillocks feed,
Weel herdit in by wakefu' Tweed;
An' canny through the bent* his kye     grass
Gang creepin' to the byre* doun-by.     barn

His hayfields lie fu' smoothly shorn,
An' ripenin' rise his rigs o' corn;
A simmer's evenin' glory fa's
Upon his hamestead's sober wa's.

A stately figure there he stands
An' rests upon his staff his hands:
Maist like some patriarch of eld,
In sic an evenin's calm beheld.

A farmer he of Ochilside,
For worth respectit far an' wide:

A friend of justice and of truth,
A favorite wi' age an' youth.

There's no' a bairn but kens him weel,
And ilka collie's at his heel;
Nor beast nor body e'er had ocht
To wyte* him wi', in deed or thocht. blame

Fu' mony a gloamin' may he stand
Abune the brae to bless the land.
Fu' mony a simmer rise an' fa'
In beauty owre his couthie* ha'. snug

For peacefu' aye, as simmer's air,
The kindly hearts that kindle there;
Whase friendship, sure an' aye the same,
For me maks Ochilside a hame.

## The Discovery of America
(Seen from the Ochils Through the Perspective of Four Centuries)

All the mill-horses of Europe
Were plodding round and round.
All the mills were droning
The same old sound.

The drivers were dozing, the millers
Were deaf—as millers will be;
When, startling them all, without warning
Came a great shout from the sea.

It startled them all. The horses,
Lazily plodding round,
Started and stopped; and the mills dropped
Like a mantle their sound.

The millers looked over their shoulders,
The drivers opened their eyes.
A silence, deeper than deafness,
Had fallen out of the skies.

"Halloa there!"—this time distinctly
It rose from the barren sea;
And Europe, turning in wonder,
Whispered, "What can it be?"

"Come down, come down to the shore here!"
And Europe was soon on the sand;—
It was the great Columbus
Dragging his prize to land.

## A Schule Laddie's Lament on the Lateness o' the Season

The east wind's whistlin' cauld an' shrill,
The snaw lies on the Lomont Hill.
It's simmer i' the almanac,
But when 'ill simmer days be back?

There's no' a bud on tree or buss.
The craws are at a sair nonplus,—
Hoo can they big*? Hoo can they pair? build
Wi' them sae cauld, and winds sae bare.

My faither cannot saw his seed,—
The hauf o' th' laund's to ploo, indeed;
The lambs are deein', an' the yowes
Are trauchled* wanderin' owre the knowes. tired

There's no' a swallow back as yet,
The robin doesna seek to flit;
There's no' a buckie*, nor a bud, shell
On ony brae, in ony wud.

It's no' a time for barefit feet
When it may be on-ding* o' sleet. pounding
The season's broken a' oor rules,—
It's no' the time o' year o' bools;

It's no' the time o' year o' peeries.
*I* think the year's gane tapsalteeries*. topsy-turvy
The farmers may be bad, nae doot—
It pits hiz laddies sair aboot.

## Hughie Refuses to Emigrate

Mattie, nae mair, ye'se gang your lane;
Tak my best wishes wi' ye,
An' may guid fortun' ower the main
An' snugly settled see ye.
I wuss ye weel. The kintra's lairge,
An' ye're but twa wi' Mary;
Ye'll shortly hae the owner's chairge
Nae doot o' half a prairie.
There's ample room in sic a park
To foond a score a' nations,
An' flourish like a patriarch
Amon' your generations.

But me may Scotland's bonnie hills
Maintain to utmost auld age,
Leadin' my flocks by quiet rills,
An' lingerin' through the gold age;
Untemptit wi' a foreign gain
That maks ye merely laird o't,

An' thinkin' Scotland a' min' ain
Though' ownin' ne'er a yaird o't.

What hills are like the Ochil hills?
There's nane sae green, though grander;
What rills are like the Ochil rills?
Nane, nane on earth that wander.
There Spring returns amon' the sleet,
Ere Winter's tack* be near through; lease
There Spring an' Simmer fain wad meet
To tarry a' the year through.

An' there in green Glendevon's shade
A grave at last be found me,
Wi' daisies growin' at my head
An' Devon lingerin' round me.
Nae stane disfigurement o' grief
Wi' lang narration rise there;
A line wad brawly serve, if brief,
To tell the lave* wha lies there. rest
But ony sculptured wecht o' stane
Wad only overpow'r me;
A shepherd, musin' there his lane*, (alone)
Were meeter bendin' owre me.

## A Winter View

The rime lies cauld on ferm an' fauld,
The lift's a drumlie* gray; somber
The hill-taps a' are white wi' snaw,
An' dull an' dour's the day.
The canny sheep thegither creep,
The govin'* cattle glower; staring
The plooman staunds to chap his haunds
An' wuss the storm were ower.

But ance the snaw's begoud to fa'
The cauld's no' near sae sair:
'Neth stingin' drift oor herts we lift
The winter's warst to dare.
Wi' frost an' cauld we battle bauld,
Nor fear a passin' fa'
But warstle up wi' warmer grup
O' life an' hope, an' a'.

An' sae my frien', when to oor een
Oor warldly ills appear
In prospect mair than we can bear,
An outlook cauld and drear;
Let's bear in mind—an' this, ye'll find
Has heartened not a few—

When ance we're in the battle's din
We'll find we're half gate* through. way

## IAN MACLAREN (JOHN WATSON 1850–1907)

[Watson, a minister in the Scottish Free Church, was one of the most successful and most notorious Kailyarders. He wrote a series of sentimental and often humorous sketches ("idylls" is his term) of small-town Scottish life, set in the mythical village of "Drumtochty." His most notable collections are in *Beside the Bonnie Brier Bush* (1894), and *The Days of Auld Lang Syne* (1895). "Domsie," one of his best stories, is an example of his sentiment, unabashed evangelical piety, "local color" and humor of character.]

### Domsie

#### I. A LAD O' PAIRTS[1]

The Revolution reached our parish years ago, and Drumtochty has a School Board, with a chairman and a clerk, besides a treasurer and an officer. Young Hillocks, who had two years in a lawyer's office, is clerk, and summons meetings by post, although he sees every member at the market or the kirk. Minutes are read with much solemnity, and motions to expend ten shillings upon a coal-cellar door passed, on the motion of Hillocks, seconded by Drumsheugh, who are both severely prompted for the occasion, and move uneasily before speaking.

Drumsheugh was at first greatly exalted by his poll, and referred freely on market days to his "plumpers," but as time went on the irony of the situation laid hold upon him. "Think o' you and me, Hillocks, veesitin' the schule and sittin' wi' bukes in oor hands watchin' the Inspector. Keep's a', it' eneuch to mak' the auld Dominie turn in his grave. Twa meenisters cam' in his time, and Domsie put Geordie Hoo or some ither gleg[2] laddie, that was makin' for college, through his facin's, and maybe some bit lassie brocht her copybuke. Syne they had their dinner, and Domsie tae, wi' the Doctor. Man, a've often thocht it was the prospeck o' the Schule Board and its weary bit rules that feenished Domsie. He wasna maybe sae shairp at the elements as this pirjinct body we hae noo, but a'body kent he was a terrible scholar and a credit tae the parish. Drumtochty was a name in thae days wi' the lads he sent tae college. It was maybe juist as weel he slippit awa' when he did, for he wud hae taen ill with thae new fikes, and nae college lad to warm his hert."

The present school-house stands in an open place beside the main road to Muirtown. Treeless and comfortless, built of red, staring stone, with a playground for the boys and another for the girls, and a trim, smug-looking teacher's house, all very neat and symmetrical, and well regulated. The local paper had a paragraph headed "Drumtochty," written by the Muirtown architect, describing the whole premises in technical language that seemed to compensate the ratepayers for the cost, mentioning the contractor's name, and concluding that "this handsome building of the Scoto-Grecian style was one of the finest works that had ever come from the accomplished architect's hands." It has pitch-pine benches and map-cases, and a thermometer to be kept at not less than 58 and not more than 62°, and ventilators

---

[1] A famous Scottish term for a Scottish phenomenon, the able but poor scholar who is nevertheless able to attend a university through great sacrifice by himself, his parents and often his community.

[2] Quick in perception.

which the Inspector is careful to examine. When I stumbled in last week the teacher was drilling the children in Tonic Sol-fa with a little harmonium, and I left on tiptoe.

It is difficult to live up to this kind of thing, and my thoughts drift to the auld schulehouse and Domsie. Some one with the love of God in his heart had built it long ago, and chose a site for the bairns in the sweet pine-woods at the foot of the cart road to Whinnie Knowe and the upland farms. It stood in a clearing with the tall Scotch firs round three sides, and on the fourth a brake of gorse and bramble bushes, through which there was an opening to the road. The clearing was the playground, and in summer the bairns annexed as much wood as they liked, playing tig among the trees, or sitting down at dinner-time on the soft, dry spines that made an elastic carpet everywhere. Domsie used to say there were two pleasant sights for his old eyes every day. One was to stand in the open at dinner-time and see the flitting forms of the healthy, rosy sonsie[1] bairns in the wood, and from the door in the afternoon to watch the schule skail[2] till each group was lost in the kindly shadow, and the merry shouts died away in this quiet place.

Then the Dominie took a pinch of snuff and locked the door, and went to his house beside the school. One evening I came on him listening bare-headed to the voices, and he showed so kindly that I shall take him as he stands. A man of middle height, but stooping below it, with sandy hair turning to gray, and bushy eye-brow covering keen, shrewd gray eyes. You will notice that his linen is coarse but spotless, and that, though his clothes are worn almost threadbare, they are well brushed and orderly. But you will be chiefly arrested by the Dominie's coat, for the like of it was not in the parish. It was a black dress coat, and no man knew when it had begun its history; in its origin and its continuance it resembled Melchisedek. Many were the myths that gathered round that coat, but on this all were agreed, that without it we could not have realized the Dominie, and it became to us the sign and trappings of learning. He had taken a high place at the University, and won a good degree, and I've heard the Doctor say that he had a career before him.

But something happened in his life, and Domsie buried himself among the woods with the bairns of Drumtochty. No one knew the story, but after he died I found a locket on his breast, with a proud, beautiful face within, and I have fancied it was a tragedy. It may have been in substitution that he gave all his love to the children, and nearly all his money too, helping lads to college, and affording an inexhaustible store of peppermints for the little ones.

Perhaps one ought to have been ashamed of that school-house, but yet it had its own distinction, for scholars were born there, and now and then to this day some famous man will come and stand in the deserted playground for a space. The door was at one end, and stood open in summer, so that the boys saw the rabbits come out from their holes on the edge of the wood, and birds sometimes flew in unheeded. The fireplace was at the other end, and was fed in winter with the sticks and peats brought by the scholars. On one side Domsie sat with the half-dozen lads he hoped to send to college, to whom he grudged no labor, and on the other gathered the very little ones, who used to warm their bare feet at the fire, while down the sides of the room the other scholars sat at their rough old desks, working sums and copying.

Now and then a class came up and did some task, and at times a boy got the tawse[3] for his negligence, but never a girl. He kept the girls in as their punishment, with a brother to take them home, and both had tea in Domsie's house, with a bit of his best honey, departing much torn between an honest wish to please Domsie and a

---

[1]Jolly, healthy.

[2]Scatter.

[3]Strap.

pardonable longing for another tea.

"Domsie," as we called the schoolmaster, behind his back in Drumtochty, because we loved him, was true to the tradition of his kind, and had an unerring scent for "pairts" in his laddies. He could detect a scholar in the egg, and prophesied Latinity from a boy that seemed fit only to be a cowherd. It was believed that he had never made a mistake in judgment, and it was not his blame if the embryo scholar did not come to birth.

"Five and thirty years have I been minister at Drumtochty," the Doctor used to say at school examinations, "and we have never wanted a student at the University, and while Dominie Jamieson lives we never shall." Whereupon Domsie took snuff, and assigned his share of credit to the Doctor, "who gave the finish in Greek to every lad of them, without money and without price, to make no mention of the 'higher mathematics.' Seven ministers, four schoolmasters, four doctors, one professor, and three civil service men had been sent out by the auld schule in Domsie's time, besides many that "had given themselves to mercantile pursuits."

He had a leaning to classics and the professions, but Domsie was catholic in his recognition of "pairts," and when the son of Hillocks' foreman made a collection of the insects of Drumtochty, there was a council at the manse. "Bumbee Willie," as he had been pleasantly called by his companions, was rescued from ridicule and encouraged to fulfill his bent. Once a year a long letter came to Mr. Patrick Jamieson, M.A., Schoolmaster, Drumtochty, N.B., and the address within was the British Museum. When Domsie read this letter to the school, he was always careful to explain that "Dr. Graham is the greatest living authority on beetles," and, generally speaking, if any clever lad did not care for Latin, he had the alternative of beetles.

But it was Latin Domsie hunted for as for fine gold, and when he found the smack of it in a lad he rejoiced openly. He counted it a day in his life when he knew certainly that he had hit on another scholar, and the whole school saw the identification of George Howe. For a winter Domsie had been "at point," racing George through Caesar, stalking him behind irregular verbs, baiting traps with tit-bits of Virgil. During these exercises Domsie surveyed George from above his spectacles with a hope that grew every day in assurance, and came to its height over a bit of Latin prose. Domsie tasted it visibly, and read it again in the shadow of the firs at mealtime, slapping his leg twice.

"He'll dae! he'll dae!" cried Domsie aloud, ladling in the snuff. "George, ma mannie, tell yir father that I am comin' up to Whinnie Knowe the nicht on a bit o' business."

Then the "schule" knew that Geordie Hoo was marked for college, and pelted him with fir cones in great gladness of heart.

"Whinnie" was full of curiosity over the Dominie's visit, and vexed Marget sorely, to whom Geordie had told wondrous things in the milk-house. "It canna be coals at he's wantin' frae the station, for there's a fell puckle left."

"And it'll no be seed taties," she said, pursuing the principle of exhaustion, "for he hes some Perthshire reds himsel'. I doot it's somethin' wrang with Geordie," and Whinnie started on a new track.

"He's been playin' truant maybe. A' mind gettin' ma paiks for birdnestin' masel. I'll wager that's the verra thing."

"Weel, yir wrang, Weelum," broke in Marget, Whinnie's wife, a tall, silent woman, with a speaking face; "it's naither the ae thing nor the ither, but something I've been prayin' for since Geordie was a wee bairn. Clean yirsel and meet Domsie on the road, for nae man deserves more honor in Drumtochty, naither laird nor farmer."

Conversation with us was a leisurely game, with slow movements and many pauses, and it was our custom to handle all the pawns before we brought the queen into action.

Domsie and Whinnie discussed the weather with much detail before they came in sight of George, but it was clear that Domsie was charged with something weighty, and even Whinnie felt that his own treatment of the turnip crop was wanting in repose.

At last Domsie cleared his throat and looked at Marget, who had been in and out, but ever within hearing.

"George is a fine laddie, Mrs. Howe."

An ordinary Drumtochty mother, although bursting with pride, would have responded, "He's weel eneuch, if he hed grace in his heart," in a tone that implied it was extremely unlikely, and that her laddie led the reprobates of the parish. As it was, Marget's face lightened, and she waited.

"What do you think of making him?" and the Dominie dropped the words slowly, for this was a moment in Drumtochty. There was just a single ambition in those humble homes, to have one of its members at college, and if Domsie approved a lad, then his brothers and sisters would give their wages, and the family would live on skim milk and oat cake, to let him have his chance.

Whinnie glanced at his wife and turned to Domsie.

"Marget's set on seein' Geordie a minister, Dominie."

"If he's worthy o't, no otherwise. We haena the means though; the farm is highly rented, and there's barely a penny over at the end o' the year."

"But you are willing George should go and see what he can do. If he disappoint you, then I dinna know a lad o' pairts when I see him, and the Doctor is with me."

"Maister Jamieson," said Marget, with great solemnity, "ma hert's desire is to see George a minister, and if the Almichty spared me to hear ma only bairn open his mooth in the Evangel, I wud hae naething mair to ask . . . but I doot sair it canna be managed."

Domsie had got all he asked, and he rose in his strength.

"If George Howe disna get to college, then he's the first scholar I've lost in Drumtochty . . . ye 'ill manage his keep and sic like?"

"Nae fear o' that," for Whinnie was warming, "though I haena a steek (stitch) o' new claithes for four years. But what aboot his fees and ither ootgaeins?"

"There's ae man in the parish can pay George's fees without missing a penny, and I'll warrant he 'ill dae it."

"Are ye meanin' Drumsheugh?" said Whinnie, "for ye 'ill never get a penny piece oot o' him. Did ye no hear hoo the Frees[1] wiled him in tae their kirk, Sabbath past a week, when Netherton's sister's son frae Edinboro' wes preaching the missionary sermon, expectin' a note, and if he didna change a shillin' at the public-hoose and pit in a penny. Sall, he's a lad Drumsheugh; a'm thinking ye may save yir journey, Dominie."

But Marget looked away from her into the past, and her eyes had a tender light. "He hed the best hert in the pairish aince."

Domsie found Drumsheugh inclined for company, and assisted at an exhaustive and caustic treatment of local affairs. When the conduct of Piggie Walker, who bought Drumsheugh's potatoes and went into bankruptcy without paying for a single tuber, had been characterized in language that left nothing to be desired, Drumsheugh began to soften and show signs of reciprocity.

"Hoo's yir laddies, Dominie?" whom the farmers regarded as a risky turnip crop

---

[1]Supporters of the "Free Kirk," a fundamentalist offsplitting from the Presbyterian Church of Scotland.

in a stiff clay that Domsie had "to fecht awa in." "Are ony o' them shaping weel?"

Drumsheugh had given himself away, and Domsie laid his first parallel with a glowing account of George Howe's Latinity, which was well received.

"Weel, I'm gled tae hear sic accoonts o' Marget Hoo's son; there's naething in Whinnie but what the spoon puts in."

But at the next move Drumsheugh scented danger and stood at guard. "Na, na, Dominie, I see what yir aifter fine; ye mind hoo ye got three notes oot o' me at Perth market Martinmas a year past for ane o' yir college laddies. Five punds for four years; my word, yir no blate (modest).[1] And what for sud I educat Marget Hoo's bairn? If ye kent a' ye wudna ask me; it's no reasonable, Dominie. So there's an end o't."

Domsie was only a pedantic old parish schoolmaster, and he knew little beyond his craft, but the spirit of the Humanists awoke within him, and he smote with all his might, bidding good-bye to his English as one flings away the scabbard of a sword.

"Ye think that a'm asking a great thing when I plead for a pickle[2] notes to give a puir laddie a college education. I tell ye, man, a'm honorin' ye and givin' ye the fairest chance ye'll ever hae o' winning wealth. Gin ye store the money ye hae scrapit by mony a hard bargain, some heir ye never saw 'ill gar it flee in chambering and wantonness. Gin ye hed the heart to spend it on a lad o' pairts like Geordie Hoo, ye wud hae twa rewards nae man could tak fra ye. Ane wud be the honest gratitude o' a laddie whose desire for knowledge ye hed sateesfied, and the second wud be this—anither scholar in the land; and a'm thinking with auld John Knox that ilka scholar is something added to the riches of the commonwealth. And what 'ill it cost ye? Little mair than the price o' a cattle beast. Man, Drumsheugh, ye poverty-stricken cratur, I've naethin' in this world but a handfu' o' books and a tenpund note for my funeral, and yet, if it wasna I have all my brither's bairns tae keep, I wud pay every penny mysel'. But I'll no see Geordie sent to the plow, though I gang frae door to door. Na, na, the grass 'ill no grow on the road atween the college and the schulehoose o' Drumtochty till they lay me in the auld kirkyard."

"Sall, Domsie was roosed," Drumsheugh explained in the Muirtown inn next market. "'Miserly wratch' was the ceevilest word on his tongue. He wud naither sit nor taste, and was half way doon the yaird afore I cud quiet him. An' a'm no sayin' he hed na reason if I'd been meanin' a' I said. It wud be a scan'al to the pairish if a likely lad cudna win tae college for the want o' siller. Na, na, neeburs, we hae oor faults, but we're no sae dune mean as that in Drumtochty."

As it was, when Domsie did depart he could only grip Drumsheugh's hand, and say Maecenas,[3] and was so intoxicated, but not with strong drink, that he explained to Hillocks on the way home that Drumsheugh would be a credit to Drumtochty, and that his Latin style reminded him of Cicero. He added as an afterthought that Whinnie Knowe had promised to pay Drumsheugh's fees for four years at the University of Edinburgh.

## II. HOW WE CARRIED THE NEWS TO WHINNIE KNOWE

Domsie was an artist, and prepared the way for George's University achievement with much cunning. Once every Sabbath in the kirk-yard, where he laid down the law beneath an old elm tree, and twice between Sabbaths, at the post-office and by the wayside, he adjured us not to expect beyond measure, and gave us reasons.

"Ye see, he has a natural talent for learning, and took to Latin like a duck to

---

[1]The parenthetical glosses are in Maclaren's text.

[2]Few.

[3]Virgil's wealthy patron, and so by extension any generous supporter of the arts.

water. What could be done in Drumtochty was done for him, and he's working night and day, but he'll have a sore fight with the lads from the town schools. Na, na, neighbors," said the Dominie, lapsing into dialect, "we daurna luik for a prize. No the first year, at ony rate."

"Man, Dominie. A'm clean astonished at ye," Drumsheugh used to break in, who, since he had given to George's support, outran us all in his faith, and had no patience with Domsie's devices, "a' tell ye if Geordie disna get a first in every class he's entered for, the judges 'ill be a puir lot," with a fine confusion of circumstances.

"Losh, Drumsheugh, be quiet, or ye'll dae the laddie an injury," said Domsie, with genuine alarm. "We maunna mention prizes, and first is fair madness. A certificate of honor now, that will be aboot it, may be next to the prizemen."

Coming home from market he might open his heart. "George 'ill be amang the first sax, or my name is no Jamieson," but generally he prophesied a moderate success. There were times when he affected indifference, and talked cattle. We then regarded him with awe, because this was more than mortal.

It was my luck to carry the bulletin to Domsie, and I learned what he had been enduring. It was good manners in Drumtochty to feign amazement at the sight of a letter, and to insist that it must be intended for some other person. When it was finally forced upon one, you examined the handwriting at various angles and speculated about the writer. Some felt emboldened, after these precautions, to open the letter, but this haste was considered indecent. When Posty handed Drumsheugh the factor's letter, with the answer to his offer for the farm, he only remarked, "It'll be frae the factor," and harked back to a polled Angus bull he had seen at the show. "Sall," said Posty in the kirkyard with keen relish, "ye'll never flurry Drumsheugh." Ordinary letters were read in leisurely retirement, and, in case of urgency, answered within the week.

Domsie clutched the letter, and would have torn off the envelope. But he could not; his hand was shaking like an aspen. He could only look, and I read:

"DEAR MR. JAMIESON,—The class honor lists are just out, and you will be pleased to know that I have got the medal both in the Humanity and the Greek."

There was something about telling his mother, and his gratitude to his schoolmaster, but Domsie heard no more. He tried to speak and could not, for a rain of tears was on his hard old face. Domsie was far more a pagan than a saint, but somehow he seemed to me that day as Simeon, who had at last seen his heart's desire, and was satisfied.

When the school had dispersed with a joyful shout, and disappeared in the pine woods, he said, "Ye'll come too," and I knew he was going to Whinnie Knowe. He did not speak one word upon the way, but twice he stood and read the letter which he held fast in his hand. His face was set as he climbed the cart track. I saw it set again as we came down that road one day, but it was well that we could not pierce beyond the present.

Whinnie left his plow in the furrow, and. came to meet us, taking two drills at a stride, and shouting remarks on the weather yards off.

Domsie only lifted the letter. "Frae George."

"Ay, ay, and what's he gotten noo?"

Domsie solemnly unfolded the letter, and brought down his spectacles. "Edinburgh, April 7th." Then he looked at Whinnie, and closed his mouth.

"We'll tell it first to his mither."

"Yer richt, Dominie. She weel deserves it. I'm thinking she's seen us by this time." So we fell into a procession, Dominie leading by two yards; and then a strange thing happened. For the first and last time in his life Domsie whistled, and the tune was "A hundred pipers and a' and a'," and as he whistled he seemed to dilate before our eyes, and he struck down thistles with his stick—a thistle at every stroke.

"Domsie's fair carried," whispered Whinnie, "it cowes a'."

Marget met us at the end of the house beside the brier bush, where George was to sit on summer afternoons before he died, and a flash passed between Domsie and the lad's mother. Then she knew that it was well, and fixed her eyes on the letter, but Whinnie, his thumbs in his armholes, watched the wife. Domsie now essayed to read the news, but between the shaking of his hands and his voice he could not.

"It's nae use," he cried, "he's first in the Humanity oot o' a hundred and seeventy lads, first o' them a', and he's first in the Greek too; the like o' this is hardly known, and it has na been seen in Drumtochty since there was a schule. That's the word he's sent, and he bade me tell his mother without delay, and I am here as fast as my old feet could carry me."

I glanced round, although I did not myself see very clearly.

Marget was silent for the space of five seconds; she was a good woman, and I knew that better afterwards. She took the Dominie's hand, and said to him, "Under God this was your doing, Maister Jamieson, and for your reward ye'ill get naither silver nor gold, but ye hae a mither's gratitude."

Whinnie gave a hoarse chuckle and said to his wife, "It was frae you, Marget, he got it a'."

When we settled in the parlor Domsie's tongue was loosed, and he lifted up his voice and sang the victory of Geordie Hoo.

"It's ten years ago at the brak up o' the winter ye brought him down to me, Mrs. Hoo, and ye said at the schule-hoose door, 'Dinna be hard on him, Maister Jamieson, he's my only bairn, and a wee thingie quiet.' Div ye mind what I said, 'There's something ahint that face,' and my heart warmed to George that hour. Two years after the Doctor examined the schule, and he looks at George. 'That's a likely lad, Dominie. What think ye?' And he was only eight years auld, and no big for his size. 'Doctor, I daurna prophesy till we turn him into the Latin, but a've my thoughts.' So I had a' the time, but I never boasted, na, na, that's dangerous. Didna I say, 'Ye hev a promisin' laddie, Whinnie,' ae day in the market?"

"It's a fac'," said Whinnie, "it wes the day I bocht the white coo." But Domsie swept on.

"The first year o' Latin was enough for me. He juist nippet up his verbs. Caesar could na keep him going; he wes into Virgil afore he wes eleven, and the Latin prose, man, as sure as a'm living, it tasted o' Cicero frae the beginning."

Whinnie wagged his head in amazement. "It was the verra nicht o' the Latin prose I cam up to speak aboot the college, and ye thocht Geordie hed been playing truant."

Whinnie laughed uproariously, but Domsie heeded not.

"It was awfu' work the next twa years, but the Doctor stood in weel wi' the Greek. Ye mind hoo Geordie tramped ower the muir to the manse through the weet an' the snaw, and there wes aye dry stockings for him in the kitchen afore he had his Greek in the Doctor's study."

"And a warm drink tae," put in Marget, "and that's the window I pit the licht in to guide him hame in the dark winter nichts, and mony a time when the sleet played swish on the glass I wes near wishin'—" Domsie waved his hand.

"But that's dune wi' noo, and he was worth a' the toil and trouble. First in the Humanity and first in the Greek, sweepit the field, Lord preserve us. A' can hardly believe it. Eh, I was feared o' thae High School lads. They had terrible advantages. Maisters frae England, and tutors, and whatna', but Drumtochty carried aff the croon. It'll be fine reading in the papers—

*Humanity.*—First Prize (and Medal), George Howe, Drumtochty, Perthshire.
*Greek.*—First Prize (and Medal), George Howe, Drumtochty, Perthshire."

"It'll be michty," cried Whinnie, now fairly on fire.

"And Philosophy and Mathematics to come. Geordie's no bad at Euclid. I'll wager he'll be first there too. When he gets his hand in there's naething he's no fit for wi' time. My ain laddie—and the Doctor's—we maunna forget him—it's his classics he hes, every book o' them. The Doctor 'ill be lifted when he comes back on Saturday. A'm thinkin' we'll hear o't on Sabbath. And Drumsheugh, he'll be naither to had nor bind in the kirkyard. As for me, I wad na change places wi' the Duke o' Athole," and Domsie shook the table to its foundation.

Then he awoke, as from a dream, and the shame of boasting that shuts the mouths of self-respecting Scots descended upon him.

"But this is fair nonsense. Ye'll no mind the havers[1] o' an auld dominie."

He fell back on a recent roup, and would not again break away, although sorely tempted by certain of Whinnie's speculations,

When I saw him last, his coat-tails were waving victoriously as he leaped a dyke on his way to tell our Drumtochty Maecenas that the judges knew their business.

### III. IN MARGET'S GARDEN

The cart track to Whinnie Knowe was commanded by a gable window, and Whinnie boasted that Marget had never been taken unawares. Tramps, finding every door locked, and no sign of life anywhere, used to express their mind in the "close," and return by the way they came, while ladies from Kildrummie, fearful lest they should put Mrs. Howe out, were met at the garden gate by Marget in her Sabbath dress, and brought into a set tea as if they had been invited weeks before.

Whinnie gloried most in the discomfiture of the Tory agent, who had vainly hoped to coerce him in the stack yard without Marget's presence, as her intellectual contempt for the Conservative party knew no bounds.

"Sall she saw him slip aff the road afore the last stile, and wheep roond the fit o' the gairden wa' like a tod (fox) aifter the chickens.

'It's a het day, Maister Anderson,' says Marget frae the gairden, lookin' doon on him as calm as ye like. 'Yir surely no gaein' to pass oor hoose without a gless o' milk?"

"Wud ye believe it, he wes that upset he left withoot sayin' 'vote,' and Drumsheugh telt me next market that his langidge aifterwards cudna be printed."

When George came home for the last time, Marget went back and forward all afternoon from his bedroom to the window, and hid herself beneath the laburnum to see his face as the cart stood before the stile. It told her plain what she had feared, and Marget passed through her Gethsemane with the gold blossoms falling on her face. When their eyes met, and before she helped him down, mother and son understood.

"Ye mind what I told ye, o' the Greek mothers, the day I left. Weel, I wud hae liked to have carried my shield, but it wasna to be, so I've come home on it." As they went slowly up the garden walk, "I've got my degree, a double first, mathematics and classics."

"Ye've been a gude soldier, George, and faithfu'."

"Unto death, a'm dootin, mother."

"Na," said Marget, "unto life."

Drumtochty was not a heartening place in sickness, and Marget, who did not think our thoughts, endured much consolation at her neighbor's hands. It is said that in cities visitors congratulate a patient on his good looks, and deluge his family with instances of recovery. This would have seemed to us shallow and unfeeling, besides

[1]Nonsense.

being a "temptin' o' Providence," which might not have intended to go to extremities, but on a challenge of this kind had no alternative. Sickness was regarded as a distinction tempered with judgment, and favored people found it difficult to be humble. I always thought more of Peter MacIntosh when the mysterious "tribble" that needed the Perth doctor made no difference in his manner, and he passed his snuff box across the seat before the long prayer as usual. But in this indifference to privileges Peter was exceptional.

You could never meet Kirsty Stewart on equal terms, although she was quite affable to any one who knew his place.

"Ay," she said, on my respectful allusion to her experience, "a've seen mair than most. It doesna become me to boast, but though I say it as sudna, I hae buried a' my ain fouk."

Kirsty had a "way" in sick visiting, consisting in a certain cadence of the voice and arrangement of the face, which was felt to be soothing and complimentary.

"Yir aboot again, a'm glad to see," to me after my accident, "but yir no dune wi' that leg; na, na, Jeems, that was ma second son, scrapit his shin aince, though no so bad as ye've dune a'm hearing (for I had denied Kirsty the courtesy of an inspection). It's sax year syne noo, and he got up and wes traivellin' fell hearty like yersel. But he begood to dwam (sicken) in the end of the year, and soughed awa' in the spring. Ay, ay, when tribble comes ye never ken hoo it 'ill end. A' thocht I wud come up and speir[1] for ye. A body needs comfort gin he's sober (ill)." When I found George wrapped in his plaid beside the brier bush whose roses were no whiter than his cheeks, Kirsty was already installed as comforter in the parlor, and her drone came through the open window.

"Ay, ay, Marget, sae it's come to this. Weel, we daurna complain, ye ken. Be thankfu' ye haena lost your man and five sons, besides twa sisters and a brither, no to mention cousins. That wud be something to speak aboot, and Losh keep's, there's nae saying but he micht hang on a whilie. Ay, ay, it's a sair blow aifter a' that wes in the papers. I wes feared when I heard o' the papers; 'Lat weel alane,' says I to the Dominie; 'ye 'ill bring a judgment on the laddie wi' yir blawing.' But ye micht as weel hae spoken to the hills. Domsie's a thraun body at the best, and he was clean infatuat' wi' George. Ay, ay, it's an awfu' lesson, Marget, no to mak' idols o' our bairns, for that's naethin' else than provokin' the Almichty."

It was at this point that Marget gave way and scandalized Drumtochty, which held that obtrusive prosperity was an irresistible provocation to the higher powers, and that a skillful depreciation of our children was a policy of safety.

"Did ye say the Almichty? I'm thinkin' that's ower grand a name for your God, Kirsty. What wud ye think o' a faither that brocht hame some bonnie thing frae the fair for ane o' his bairns, and when the puir bairn wes pleased wi' it tore it oot o' his hand and flung it into the fire? Eh, woman, he wud be a meeserable cankered jealous body. Kirsty, wumman, when the Almichty sees a mither bound up in her laddie, I tell ye He is sair pleased in His heaven, for mind ye hoo He loved His ain Son. Besides, a'm judgin' that nane o' us can love anither withoot lovin' Him, or hurt anither withoot hurtin' Him. Oh, I ken weel that George is gaein' to leave us; but it's no because the Almichty is jealous o' him or me, no likely. It cam' to me last nicht that He needs my laddie for some grand wark in the ither world, and that's hoo George has his bukes brocht oot tae the garden and studies a' the day. He wants to be ready for his kingdom, just as he trachled in the bit schule o' Drumtochty for Edinboro'. I hoped he wud hae been a minister o' Christ's Gospel here, but he 'ill be judge over many cities yonder. A'm no denyin', Kirsty, that it's a trial, but I hae licht

[1] Ask.

on it, and naethin' but gude thochts o' the Almichty."

Drumtochty understood that Kirsty had dealt faithfully with Marget for pride and presumption, but all we heard was, "Losh keep us a'."

When Marget came out and sat down beside her son, her face was shining. Then she saw the open window.

"I didna ken."

"Never mind, mither, there's nae secrets atween us, and it garred my heart leap to hear ye speak up like yon for God, and to know yir content. Div ye mind the nicht I called for ye, mother, and ye gave me the Gospel aboot God?"

Marget slipped her hand into George's, and he let his head rest on her shoulder. The likeness flashed upon me in that moment, the earnest deep-set gray eyes, the clean-cut firm jaw, and the tender mobile lips, that blend of apparent austerity and underlying romance that make the pathos of a Scottish face.

"There had been a Revival man, here," George explained to me, "and he was preaching on hell. As it grew dark a candle was lighted, and I can still see his face as in a picture, a hard-visaged man. He looked down at us laddies in the front, and asked us if we knew what like hell was. By this time we were that terrified none of us could speak, but I whispered 'No.'

"Then he rolled up a piece of paper and held it in the flame, and we saw it burn and glow and shrivel up and fall in black dust.

"'Think,' said he, and he leaned over the desk, and spoke in a gruesome whisper which made the cold run down our backs, 'that yon paper was your finger, one finger only of your hand, and it burned like that for ever and ever, and think of your hand and your arm and your whole body all on fire, never to go out.' We shuddered that you might have heard the form creak. 'That is hell, and that is where ony laddie will go who does not repent and believe.'

"It was like Dante's Inferno, and I dared not take my eyes off his face. He blew out the candle, and we crept to the door trembling, not able to say one word.

"That night I could not sleep, for I thought I might be in the fire before morning. It was harvest time, and the moon was filling the room with cold clear light. From my bed I could see the stooks standing in rows upon the field, and it seemed like the judgment day.

"I was only a wee laddie, and I did what we all do in trouble, I cried for my mother.

"Ye hae na forgotten, mither, the fricht that was on me that nicht."

"Never," said Marget, "and never can; it's hard wark for me to keep frae hating that man, dead or alive. Geordie gripped me wi' baith his wee airms round my neck, and he cries over and over and over again, 'Is yon God?'"

"Ay, and ye kissed me, mither, and ye said (it's like yesterday), 'Yir safe with me,' and ye telt me that God micht punish me to mak me better if I was bad, but that he wud never torture ony puir soul, for that cud dae nae guid, and was the Devil's wark. Ye asked me:

"'Am I a guid mother tae ye?' and when I could dae naethin' but hold, ye said, 'Be sure God maun be a hantle kinder.'

"The truth came to me as with a flicker, and I cuddled down into my bed, and fell asleep in His love as in my mother's arms.

"Mither," and George lifted up his head, "that was my conversion, and, mither dear, I hae longed a' through thae college studies for the day when ma mooth wud be opened wi' this evangel."

Marget's was an old-fashioned garden, with pinks and daisies and forget-me-nots, with sweet-scented wall-flower and thyme and moss roses, where nature had her way, and gracious thoughts could visit one without any jarring note. As George's voice softened to the close, I caught her saying, "His servants shall see His face," and the peace of Paradise fell upon us in the shadow of death.

The night before the end George was carried out to his corner and Domsie, whose heart was nigh unto the breaking, sat with him the afternoon. They used to fight the College battles over again, with their favorite classics beside them, but this time none of them spoke of books. Marget was moving about the garden, and she told me that George looked at Domsie wistfully, as if he had something to say and knew not how to do it.

After a while he took a book from below his pillow, and began, like one thinking over his words:

"Maister Jamieson, ye hae been a gude freend tae me, the best I ever hed aifter my mither and faither. Wull ye tak this buik for a keepsake o' yir grateful scholar? It's a Latin 'Imitation,' Dominie, and it's bonnie printin'. Ye mind hoo ye gave me yir ain Virgil, and said he was a kind o' Pagan sanct. Noo here is my sanct, and div ye ken I've often thocht Virgil saw His day afar off, and was glad. Wull ye read it, Dominie, for my sake, and maybe ye 'ill come to see—" and George could not find words for more.

But Domsie understood. "Ma laddie, ma laddie, that I luve better than onythin' on earth, I'll read it till I die, and, George, I'll tell ye what livin' man does na ken. When I was your verra age I had a cruel trial, and ma heart was turned frae faith. The classics hae been my bible, though I said naethin' to ony man against Christ. He aye seemed beyond man, and noo the veesion o' Him has come to me in this gairden. Laddie, ye hae dune far mair for me than I ever did for you. Wull ye mak a prayer for yir auld dominie afore we pairt?" There was a thrush singing in the birches and a sound of bees in the air, when George prayed in a low, soft voice, with a little break in it.

"Lord Jesus, remember my dear maister, for he's been a kind freend to me and mony a puir laddie in Drumtochty. Bind up his sair heart and give him licht at eventide, and may the maister and his scholars meet some mornin' where the schule never skails, in the kingdom o' oor Father."

Twice Domsie said Amen, and it seemed as the voice of another man, and then he kissed George upon the forehead; but what they said Marget did not wish to hear.

When he passed out at the garden gate, the westering sun was shining golden, and the face of Domsie was like unto that of a little child.

## IV. A SCHOLAR'S FUNERAL

Drumtochty never acquitted itself with credit at a marriage, having no natural aptitude for gaiety, and being haunted with anxiety lest any "hicht" should end in a "howe,"[1] but the parish had a genius for funerals. It was long mentioned with a just sense of merit that an English undertaker, chancing on a "beerial" with us, had no limits to his admiration. He had been disheartened to despair all his life by the ghastly efforts of chirpy little Southerners to look solemn on occasion, but his dreams were satisfied at the sight of men like Drumsheugh and Hillocks in their Sabbath blacks. Nature lent an initial advantage in face, but it was an instinct in the blood that brought our manner to perfection, and nothing could be more awful than a group of those austere figures, each man gazing into vacancy without a trace of expression, and refusing to recognize his nearest neighbor by word or look. Drumtochty gave itself to a "beerial" with chastened satisfaction, partly because it lay near to the sorrow of things, and partly because there was nothing of speculation in it. "Ye can hae little rael pleesure in a merrige," explained our gravedigger, in whom the serious side had been perhaps abnormally developed, "for ye never ken hoo it will end; but

[1] "High" should end in a "low" (hole, depression).

there's nae risk about a 'beerial.'"

It came with a shock upon townsmen that the ceremony began with a "service o' speerits," and that an attempt of the Free Kirk minister to replace this by the reading of Scripture was resisted as an "innovation." Yet every one admitted that the seriousness of Drumtochty pervaded and sanctified this function. A tray of glasses was placed on a table with great solemnity by the "wricht," who made no sign and invited none. You might have supposed that the circumstance had escaped the notice of the company, so abstracted and unconscious was their manner, had it not been that two graven images a minute later are standing at the table.

"Ye 'ill taste, Tammas," with settled melancholy.

"Na, na; I've nae incleenation the day; it's an awfu' dispensation this, Jeems. She wud be barely saxty."

"Ay, ay, but we maun keep up the body sae lang as we're here, Tammas."

"Weel, puttin' it that way, a'm not sayin' but yir richt," yielding unwillingly to the force of circumstance.

"We're here the day and there the morn, Tammas. She wes a fine wumman—Mistress Stirton—a weel-livin' wumman; this 'ill be a blend, a'm thinkin'."

"She slippit aff sudden in the end; a'm judgin' it's frae the Muirtown grocer; but a body canna discreeminate on a day like this."

Before the glasses are empty all idea of drinking is dissipated, and one has a vague impression that he is at church.

It was George Howe's funeral that broke the custom and closed the "service." When I came into the garden where the neighbors were gathered, the "wricht" was removing his tray, and not a glass had been touched. Then I knew that Drumtochty had a sense of the fitness of things, and was stirred to its depths.

"Ye saw the wricht carry in his tray," said Drumsheugh, as we went home from the kirkyard. "Weel, yon's the last sicht o't ye 'ill get, or a'm no Drumsheugh. I've nae objection ma'sel to a nee'bur tastin' at a funeral, a' the mair if he's come frae the upper end o' the pairish, and ye ken I dinna hold wi' thae teetotal fouk. A'm ower auld in the horn to change noo. But there's times and seasons, as the gude Buik says, and it wud hae been an awfu' like business tae luik at a gless in Marget's gairden, and puir Domsie standing in ahent the brier bush as if he cud never lift his heid again. Ye may get shairper fouk in the uptak', but ye 'ill no get a pairish with better feelin's. It 'ill be a kind o' sateesfaction tae Marget when she hears o't. She was aye against tastin', and a'm judgin' her tribble has ended it at beerials."

"Man, it was hard on some o' yon lads the day, but there wesna ane o' them made a mudge[1]. I keepit my eye on Posty, but he never lookit the way it wes. He's a drouthy[2] body, but he hes his feelin's, hes Posty."

Before the Doctor began the prayer, Whinnie took me up to the room.

"There's twa o' Geordie's College freends with Marget, grand scholars a'm telt, and there's anither I canna weel mak oot. He's terrible cast doon, and Marget speaks as if she kent him."

It was a low-roofed room, with a box bed and some pieces of humble furniture, fit only for a laboring man. But the choice treasures of Greece and Rome lay on the table, and on a shelf beside the bed College prizes and medals, while everywhere were the roses he loved. His peasant mother stood beside the body of her scholar son, whose hopes and thoughts she had shared, and through the window came the bleating of distant sheep. It was the idyll of Scottish University life.

George's friends were characteristic men, each of his own type, and could only

---

[1]Stir, movement.

[2]Thirsty.

have met in the commonwealth of letters. One was of an ancient Scottish house which had fought for Mary against the Lords of the Congregation, followed Prince Charlie to Culloden, and were High Church and Tory to the last drop of their blood. Ludovic Gordon left Harrow with the reputation of a classic, and had expected to be first at Edinboro'. It was Gordon, in fact, that Domsie feared in the great war, but he proved second to Marget's son, and being of the breed of Prince Jonathan, which is the same the world over, he came to love our David as his own soul. The other, a dark little man, with a quick, fiery eye, was a Western Celt, who had worried his way from a fishing croft in Barra to be an easy first in Philosophy at Edinboro', and George and Ronald Maclean were as brothers because there is nothing so different as Scottish and Highland blood.

"Maister Gordon," said Marget, "this is George's Homer, and he bade me tell you that he coonted yir freendship ain o' the gifts o' God."

For a brief space Gordon was silent, and, when he spoke, his voice sounded strange in that room.

"Your son was the finest scholar of my time, and a very perfect gentleman. He was also my true friend, and I pray God to console his mother." And Ludovic Gordon bowed low over Marget's worn hand as if she had been a queen.

Marget lifted Plato, and it seemed to me that day as if the dignity of our Lady of Sorrows had fallen upon her.

"This is the buik George chose for you, Maister Maclean, for he aye said to me ye hed been a prophet and shown him mony deep things."

The tears sprang to the Celt's eyes.

"It wass like him to make all other men better than himself," with the soft, sad Highland accent; "and a proud woman you are to hef been his mother."

The third man waited at the window till the scholars left, and then I saw he was none of that kind, but one who had been a slave of sin and now was free.

"Andra Chaumers, George wished ye tae hev his Bible, and he expecks ye tae keep the tryst."

"God helping me, I will," said Chalmers, hoarsely; and from the garden ascended a voice, "O God, who art a very present help in trouble."

The Doctor's funeral prayer was one of the glories of the parish, compelling even the Free Kirk to reluctant admiration, although they hinted that its excellence was rather of the letter than the spirit, and regarded its indiscriminate charity with suspicion. It opened with a series of extracts from the Psalms, relieved by two excursions into the minor prophets, and led up to a sonorous recitation of the problem of immortality from Job, with its triumphant solution in the peroration of the fifteenth chapter of 1 Corinthians. Drumtochty men held their breath till the Doctor reached the crest of the hill (Hillocks disgraced himself once by dropping his staff at the very moment when the Doctor was passing from Job to Paul), and then we relaxed while the Doctor descended to local detail. It was understood that it took twenty years to bring the body of this prayer to perfection, and any change would have been detected and resented.

The Doctor made a good start, and had already sighted Job, when he was carried out of his course by a sudden current, and began to speak to God about Marget and her son, after a very simple fashion that brought a lump to the throat, till at last, as I imagine, the sight of the laddie working at his Greek in the study of a winter night came up before him, and the remnants of the great prayer melted like an iceberg in the Gulf Stream.

"Lord, hae peety upon us, for we a' luved him, and we were a' prood o' him."

After the Doctor said "Amen" with majesty, one used to look at his neighbor, and the other would shut his eyes and shake his head, meaning, "There's no use asking me, for it simply can't be better done by living man." This time no one remembered his neighbor, because every eye was fixed on the Doctor. Drumtochty was identifying its new minister.

"It may be that I hef judged him hardly," said Lachlan Campbell, one of the Free Kirk Highlanders, and our St. Dominic. "I shall never again deny that the root of the matter is in the man, although much choked with the tars of worldliness and Arminianism."

"He is a goot man, Lachlan," replied Donald Menzies, another Celt, and he was our St. Francis, for 'every one that loveth is born of God.'"

There was no hearse in Drumtochty, and we carried our dead by relays of four, who waded every stream unless more than knee deep, the rest following in straggling, picturesque procession over the moor and across the stepping stones. Before we started, Marget came out and arranged George's white silken hood upon the coffin with roses in its folds.

She swept us into one brief flush of gratitude, from Domsie to Posty.

"Neeburs, ye were a' his freends, and he wanted ye tae ken hoo yir trust wes mickle help tae him in his battle."

There was a stir within us, and it came to birth in Drumsheugh of all men:

"Marget Hoo, this is no the day for mony words, but there's juist ae heart in Drumtochty, and it's sair."

No one spoke to Domsie as we went down the cart track, with the ripe corn standing on either side, but he beckoned Chalmers to walk with him. "Ye hae heard him speak o' me, then, Maister Jamieson?"

"Ay, oftentimes, and he said once that ye were hard driven, but that ye had trampled Satan under yir feet."

"He didna tell ye all, for if it hadna been for George Howe I wudna been worth callin' a man this day. One night when he was workin' hard for his honors examination and his disease was heavy upon him, puir fellow, he sought me oot where I was, and wouldna leave till I cam' wi him.

"'Go home,' I said, 'Howe; it's death for ye to be oot in this sleet and cold. Why not leave me to lie in the bed I hae made?'"

"He took me by the arm into a passage. I see the gaslicht on his white face, and the shining o' his eyes."

"Because I have a mother."

"Dominie, he pulled me oot o' hell."

"Me tae, Andra, but no your hell. Ye mind the Roman Triumph, when a general cam' hame wi' his spoils. Laddie, we're the captives that go with his chariot up the Capitol."

Donald Menzies was a man of moods, and the Doctor's prayer had loosed his imagination so that he saw visions.

"Look," said he, as we stood on a ridge, "I hef seen it before in the book of Joshua."

Below the bearers had crossed a burn on foot, and were ascending the slope where an open space of deep green was fringed with purple heather.

"The ark hass gone over Jordan, and George will have come into the Land of Promise."

The September sunshine glinted on the white silk George won with his blood, and fell like a benediction on the two figures that climbed tha hard ascent close after the man they loved.

Strangers do not touch our dead in Drumtochty, but the eight of nearest blood lower the body into the grave. The order of precedence is keenly calculated, and the loss of a merited cord can never be forgiven. Marget had arranged everything with Whinnie, and all saw the fitness. His father took the head, and the feet (next in honor) he gave to Domsie.

"Ye maun dae it. Marget said ye were o' his ain bluid."

On the right side the cords were handed to the Doctor, Gordon, and myself; and on the left to Drumsheugh, Maclean, and Chalmers. Domsie lifted the hood for Marget, but the roses he gently placed on George's name. Then with bent, uncovered heads, and in unbroken silence, we buried all that remained of our scholar.

We always waited till the grave was filled and the turf laid down, a trying quarter of an hour. Ah me! the thud of the spade on your mother's grave! None gave any sign of what he felt save Drumsheugh, whose sordid slough had slipped off from a tender heart, and Chalmers, who went behind a tombstone and sobbed aloud. Not even Posty asked the reason so much as by a look, and Drumtochty, as it passed, made as though it did not see. But I marked that the Dominie took Chalmers home, and walked all the way with him to Kildrummie station next morning. His friends erected a granite cross over George's grave, and it was left to Domsie to choose the inscription. There was a day when it would have been "Whom the gods love die young." Since then Domsie had seen the kingdom of God, and this is graven where the roses bloomed fresh every summer for twenty years till Marget was laid with her son:

GEORGE HOWE, M.A.,
Died September 22nd, 1869,
Aged 21.
"They shall bring the glory and honor of the
nations into it."

It was a late November day when I went to see George's memorial, and the immortal hope was burning low in my heart; but as I stood before that cross, the sun struggled from behind a black watery bank of cloud, and picked out every letter of the Apocalypse in gold.

## ROBERT LOUIS STEVENSON (1850–1894)

[Robert Louis Stevenson is one of the most beloved of Scottish writers. His place in the literary pantheon is, however, still being argued. What disturbs a number of modern Scottish critics about Stevenson is (a) his huge popularity among the general—and presumably undiscriminating—readership, (b) the common perception that many of his works are most appropriately enjoyed by boys, and (c) that he writes most of his works in standard English. The judgment here is that he is one of the finest Scottish writers of his century, with strong work in the novel, especially *Kidnapped* (1886). His *Dr. Jekyll and Mr. Hyde* is the finest novelette by any Scottish writer, and for all its setting in London, one only a Scot is likely to have written. Also, Stevenson has done solid work as a poet. Finally, a painstaking stylist, he is one of the best essayists of his century. Stevenson is represented here by *Jekyll and Hyde*, by a brilliant short story in Scots, "Thrawn Janet," by two of his most famous essays, and by carefully polished verse in both Scots and English.]

### Whole Duty of Children

A child should always say what's true
And speak when he is spoken to,
And behave mannerly at table—
At least as far as he is able.

## Nest Eggs

Birds all the sunny day
Flutter and quarrel,
Here in the arbor-like
Tent of the laurel.

Here in the fork
The brown nest is seated;
Four little blue eggs
The mother keeps heated.

While we stand watching her,
Staring like gabies*, chatterers
Safe in each egg are the
Bird's little babies.

Soon the frail eggs they shall
Chip, and upspringing
Make all the April woods
Merry with singing.

Younger than we are,
O children, and frailer,
Soon in blue air they'll be
Singer and sailor.

We so much older,
Taller and stronger,
We shall look down on the
Birdies no longer.

They shall go flying
With musical speeches
High overhead in the
Tops of the beeches.

In spite of our wisdom
And sensible talking,
We on our feet must go
Plodding and walking.

## A Mile an' a Bittock

A mile an' a bittock, a mile or twa,
Abune the burn, ayont* the law* beyond/hill
Davie an' Donal' an' Cherlie an' a',
An' the moon was shinin' clearly.

Ane went hame wi' the ither, an' then
The ither went hame wi' the ither twa men,
An' baith wad return him the service again,
An' the moon was shinin' clearly.

The clocks were chappin' in house an' ha',
Eleeven, twal' an' ane an' twa;
An' the guidman's face was turnt to the wa',
An' the moon was shinin' clearly.

A wind got up frae affa the sea,
It blew the stars as clear's could be,
It blew in the een of a' o' the three,
An' the moon was shinin clearly.

Noo, Davie was first to get sleep in his head,
"The best o' frien's maun twine," he said;
"I'm weariet, an' here I'm awa' to my bed,"
An' the moon was shinin' clearly.

Twa o' them walkin' an' crackin'* their lane,[1] chattering
The mornin' licht cam gray an' plain,
An' the birds they yammert on stick an' stane,
An' the moon was shinin' clearly.

O years ayont, O years awa',
My lads, ye'll mind whate'er befa'—
My lads, ye'll mind on the bield* o' the law shelter
When the moon was shinin' clearly.

## To N.V. De G. S.[2]

The unfathomable sea, and time, and tears,
The deeds of heroes and the crimes of kings
Dispart us; and the river of events
Has, for an age of years, to east and west
More widely borne our cradles. Thou to me
Art foreign, as when seamen at the dawn
Descry a land far off and know not which.
So I approach uncertain; so I cruise
Round thy mysterious islet, and behold
Surf and great mountains and loud river-bars,
And from the shore hear inland voices call.
Strange is the seaman's heart; he hopes, he fears;
Draws closer and sweeps wider from that coast;
Last, his rent sail refits, and to the deep
His shattered prow uncomforted puts back.
Yet as he goes he ponders at the helm
Of that bright island; where he feared to touch,
His spirit readventures; and for years,
Where by his wife he slumbers safe at home,
Thoughts of that land revisit him; he sees
The eternal mountains beckon, and awakes
Yearning for that far home that might have been.

---

[1]"Their lane" = by themselves.

[2]Nelly Van De Grift Sanchez, R.L.S.'s sister-in law.

## The Spaewife[1]

O I wad like to ken—to the beggar-wife says I—
Why chops are guid to brander* and nane sae guid to fry. broil
An' siller, that's sae braw to keep, is brawer still to gie.
*It's gey* an' easy spierin'**, says the beggar-wife to me. very/asking

O, I wad like to ken—to the beggar wife says I—
Hoo a' things come to be whaur we find them when we try,
The lasses in their claes an' the fishes in the sea.
*—It's gey an' easy speirin',* says the beggar-wife to me.

O, I wad like to ken—to the beggar-wife says I—
Why lads are a' to sell an' lasses a' to buy;
An' naebody for dacency but barely twa or three.
*—It's gey an' easy speirin',* says the beggar-wife to me.

O, I wad like to ken—to the beggar-wife says I—
Gin death's as shure to men as killin' is to kye,
Why God has filled the yearth sae fu' o' tasty things to pree*. prove, taste
*—It's gey an' easy speirin* says the beggar-wife to me.

O, I wad like to ken—to the beggar-wife says I—
The reason o' the cause an' the wherefore o' the why,
Wi' mony anither riddle brings the tear into my e'e.
*—It's gey an' easy speirin',* says the beggar-wife to me.

## When I Am Grown to Man's Estate

When I am grown to man's estate
I shall be very proud and great,
And tell the other girls and boys
Not to meddle with my toys.

## The Celestial Surgeon

If I have faltered more or less
In my great task of happiness;
If I have moved among my race
And shown no glorious morning face;
If beams from happy human eyes
Have moved me not; if morning skies,
Books, and my food, and summer rain
Knocked on my sullen heart in vain—
Lord, thy most pointed pleasure take
And stab my spirit broad awake;
Or, Lord, if too obdurate I,
Choose thou, before that spirit die,
A piercing pain, a killing sin,
And to my dead heart run them in.

---

[1]Fortune teller.

## The Vagabond

To an Air of Schubert

Give to me the life I love,
Let the lave* go by me, rest
Give the jolly heaven above
And the byway nigh me.
Bed in the bush with stars to see,
Bread I dip in the river—
There's the life for a man like me,
There's the life for ever.

Let the blow fall soon or late,
Let what will be oer me;
Give the face of earth around
And the road before me.
Wealth I seek not, hope nor love,
Nor a friend to know me;
All I seek, the heaven above
And the road below me.

Or let autumn fall on me
Where afield I linger,
Silencing the bird on tree,
Biting the blue finger.
White as meal the frosty field—
Warm the fireside haven—
Not to autumn will I yield,
Not to winter even.

Let the blow fall soon or late,
Let what will be oer me;
Give the face of earth around,
And the road before me.
Wealth I ask not, hope nor love,
Nor a friend to know me;
All I ask the heaven above,
And the road below me.

## In the Highlands

In the highlands, in the country places,
Where the old plain men have rosy faces,
And the young fair maidens
Quiet eyes;
Where essential silence cheers and blesses,
And for ever in the hill-recesses
*Her* more lovely music
Broods and dies.

O to mount again where erst I haunted;
Where the old red hills are bird-enchanted,

And the low green meadows
Bright with sward;
And when even dies, the million-tinted,
And the night has come, and planets glinted,
Lo, the valley hollow
Lamp-bestarred.

O to dream, O to awake and wander
There, and with delight to take and render,
Through the trance of silence,
Quiet breath;
Lo! for there, among the flowers and grasses,
Only the mightier movement sounds and passes;
Only winds and rivers,
Life and death.

## Ille Terrarum

Frae nirly, nippin', Eas'lan' breeze,
Frae Norlan' snaw, an' haar* o' seas, mist
Weel happit* in your gairden trees, dressed
A bonny bit,
Atween the muckle Pentland's knees,
Secure ye sit.

Beeches an' aiks entwine their theek*, thatch
An' firs, a stench, auld-farrant* clique, old-fashioned
A' simmer day, your chimleys reek*, smoke
Couthy and bien*, snug
An' here an' there your windies keek* peek
Amang the green.

A pickle* plats an' paths an' posies, few
A wheen auld gillyflowers an' roses:
A ring o' wa's the hale encloses
Frae sheep or men;
An' there the auld housie beeks* an' dozes, "bakes"
A' by her lane.

The gairdner crooks his weary back
A' day in the pitaty-track,
Or mebbe stops awhile to crack* chat
Wi' Jane the cook,
Or at some buss, worm-eaten-black,
To gie a look.

Frae the high hills the curlew ca's;
The sheep gang baaing by the wa's;
Or whiles a clan o' roosty craws
Cangle thegether;
The wild bees seek the gairden raws,
Weariet wi' heather.

Or in the gloamin' douce* an' gray    sober
The sweet-throat mavis tunes her lay;
The herd comes linkin' doun the brae;
    An' by degrees
The muckle siller moon maks way
    Amang the trees.

Here aft hae I, wi' sober heart,
For meditation sat apairt,
When orra* loves or kittle art    odd, occasional
    Perplexed my mind;
Here socht a balm for ilka smart
    O' humankind.

Here aft, weel neukit by my lane,
Wi' Horace, or perhaps Montaigne,
The mornin' hours hae come an' gane
    Abune my heid—
I wadnae gi'en a chucky-stane
    For a' I'd read.

But noo the auld city, street by street,
An' winter fu' o' snaw an' sleet,
Awhile shut in my gangrel* feet    wandering
    An' goavin'* mettle;    staring
Noo is the soopit* ingle sweet,    "swept"
    An' liltin' kettle.

An' noo the winter winds complain;
Cauld lies the glaur in ilka lane;
On draigled hizzie, tautit* wean    arguing
    An' drucken lads,
In the mirk nicht, the winter rain
    Dribbles an' blads*.    splashes

Whan bugles frae the Castle rock,
An' beaten drums wi' dowie* shock,    sad
Wauken, at cauld-rife sax o' clock,
    My chitterin' frame,
I mind me on the kintry cock,
    The kintry hame.

I mind me on yon bonny bield*;    cottage, shelter
An' Fancy traivels far afield
To gaither a' that gairdens yield
    O' sun an' simmer:
To hearten up a dowie chield*,    fellow
    Fancy's the limmer*!    sweetheart

## The House Beautiful

*A naked house, a naked moor,*
*A shivering pool before the door,*
*A garden bare of flowers and fruit*
*And poplars at the garden foot;*
*Such is the place that I live in,*
*Bleak without and bare within.*

Yet shall your ragged moor receive
The incomparable pomp of eve.
And the cold glories of the dawn
Behind your shivering trees be drawn;
And when the wind from place to place
Doth the unmoored cloud-galleons chase,
Your garden gloom and gleam again,
With leaping sun, with glancing rain.
Here shall the wizard moon ascend
The heavens, in the crimson end
Of day's declining splendor; here
The army of the stars appear.
The neighbor hollows dry or wet,
Spring shall with tender flowers beset;
And oft the morning muser see
Larks rising from the broomy lea,
And every fairy wheel and thread
Of cobweb dew-bediamonded.
When daisies go, shall winter time
Silver the simple grass with rime;
Autumnal frosts enchant the pool
And make the cart-ruts beautiful;
And when snow-bright the moor expands,
How shall your children clap their hands!
To make this earth our hermitage,
A cheerful and a changeful page,
God's bright and intricate device
Of days and seasons doth suffice.

## Sing Me a Song

Sing me a song of a lad that is gone,
Say, could that lad be I?
Merry of soul he sailed on a day
Over the sea to Skye.

Mull was astern, Rum on the port,
Egg on the starboard bow;
Glory of youth glowed in his soul—
Where is that glory now?

Sing me a song of a lad that is gone,
Say, could that lad be I?

Merry of soul he sailed on a day
Over the sea to Skye.

Give me again all that was there,
Give me the sun that shone.
Give me the eyes, give me the soul,
Give me the lad that's gone.

Sing me a song of a lad that is gone,
Say, could that lad be I?
Merry of soul he sailed on a day
Over the sea to Skye.

Billow and breeze, islands and seas,
Mountains of rain and sun,
All that was good, all that was fair,
All that was me is gone.

## To S. R. Crockett
### (In Reply to a Dedication)

Blows the wind to-day, and the sun and the rain are flying,
Blows the wind on the moors to-day and now,
Where about the graves of the martyrs the whaups[1] are crying,
My heart remembers how.

Gray recumbent tombs of the dead in desert places,
Standing-stones on the vacant wine-red moor,
Hills of sheep, and the homes of the silent vanquished races,
And winds, austere and pure:

Be it granted me to behold you again in dying,
Hills of home, and I hear again the call;
Hear about the graves of the martyrs the peewees crying,
And hear no more at all.

## Romance

I will make you brooches and toys for your delight,
Of bird-song at morning and star-shine at night.
I will make a palace fit for you and me,
Of green days in forests and blue days at sea.

I will make my kitchen, and you shall keep your room,
Where white flows the river and bright blows the bloom,
And you shall wash your linen and keep your body white
In rainfall at morning and dewfall at night.

---

[1] A sea bird.

And this shall be for music when no one else is near,
The fine song for singing, the rare song to hear!
That only I remember, that only you admire,
Of the broad road that stretches and the roadside fire.

## On His Pitiable Transformation

I who was young so long,
Young and alert and gay,
Now that my hair is gray,
Begin to change my song.

Now I know right from wrong,
Now I know *pay* and *pray*—
I who was young so long,
Young and alert and gay.

Now I follow the throng,
Walk in the beaten way,
Hear what the elders say,
And own that I was wrong—
I who was young so long.

## Bright Is the Ring of Words

Bright is the ring of words
When the right man rings them,
Fair the fall of songs
When the singer sings them.
Still they are caroled and said—
On wings they are carried—
After the singer is dead
And the maker buried.

Low as the singer lies
In the field of heather,
Songs of his fashion bring
The swains together.
And when the west is red
With the sunset embers,
The lover lingers and sings,
And the maid remembers.

## Plain as the Glistering Planets Shine

Plain as the Glistering Planets Shine
When winds have cleaned the skies,
Her love appeared, appealed for mine,
And wantoned in her eyes.

Clear as the shining tapers burned
On Cytherea's shrine,

Those brimming, lustrous beauties turned,
And called and conquered mine.

The beacon-lamp that Hero lit
No fairer shone on sea,
No plainlier summoned will and wit,
Than hers encouraged me.

I thrilled to feel her influence near,
I struck my flag at sight.
Her starry silence smote my ear
Like sudden drums at night.

I ran as, at the cannon's roar,
The troops the ramparts man—
As in the holy house of yore
The willing Eli ran.

Here, lady, lo, that servant stands
You picked from passing men,
And should you need nor heart nor hands
He bows and goes again.

## Heather Ale: A Galloway Legend

From the bonny bells of heather
They brewed a drink long-syne,
Was sweeter far than honey,
Was stronger far than wine.
They brewed it and they drank it,
And lay in a blessed swound
For days and days together
In their dwellings underground.

There rose a king in Scotland,
A fell man to his foes,
He smote the Picts in battle,
He hunted them like roes.
Over miles of the red mountain
He hunted as they fled,
And strewed the dwarfish bodies
Of the dying and the dead.

Summer came in the country,
Red was the heather bell;
But the manner of the brewing
Was none alive to tell.
In graves that were like children's
On many a mountain head,
The brewsters of the heather
Lay numbered with the dead.

The king in the red moorland
Rode on a summer's day;
And the bees hummed, and the curlews
Cried beside the way.
The king rode, and was angry;
Black was his brow and pale,
To rule in a land of heather
And lack the heather ale.

It fortuned that his vassals,
Riding free on the heath,
Came on a stone that was fallen
And vermin hid beneath.
Rudely plucked from their hiding,
Never a word they spoke:
A son and his aged father—
Last of the dwarfish folk.

The king sat high on his charger,
He looked on the little men;
And the dwarfish and swarthy couple
Looked at the king again.
Down by the shore he had them;
And there on the giddy brink—
"I will give you life, ye vermin,
For the secret of the drink."

There stood the son and father
And they looked high and low.
The heather was red around them,
The sea rumbled below.
And up and spoke the father,
Shrill was his voice to hear:
"I have a word in private,
A word for the royal ear.

"Life is dear to the aged,
And honor a little thing;
I would gladly sell the secret,"
Quoth the Pict to the King.
His voice was small as a sparrow's,
And shrill and wonderful clear:
"I would gladly sell my secret,
Only my son I fear.

"For life is a little matter,
And death is nought to the young;
And I dare not sell my honor
Under the eye of my son.
Take him, O king, and bind him,
And cast him far in the deep;
And it's I will tell the secret
That I have sworn to keep."

They took the son and bound him,
Neck and heels in a thong,
And a lad took him and swung him,
And flung him far and strong,
And the sea swallowed his body,
Like that of a child of ten;—
And there on the cliff stood the father,
Last of the dwarfish men.

"True was the word I told you:
Only my son I feared;
For I doubt the sapling courage
That goes without the beard.
But now in vain is the torture,
Fire shall never avail.
Here dies in my bosom
The secret of heather ale."

## In the Season

It is the season now to go
About the country high and low,
Among the lilacs hand in hand,
And two by two in fairy land.

The brooding boy, the sighing maid,
Wholly fain and half afraid,
Now meet along the hazelled brook
To pass and linger, pause and look.

A year ago, and blithely paired,
Their rough-and-tumble play they shared;
They kissed and quarreled, laughed and cried,
A year ago at Eastertide.

With bursting heart, with fiery face,
She strove against him in the race;
He unabashed her garter saw,
That now would touch her skirts with awe.

Now by the stile ablaze she stops,
And his demurer eyes he drops;
Now they exchange averted sighs
Or stand and marry silent eyes.

And he to her a hero is
And sweeter she than primroses;
Their common silence dearer far
Than nightingale and mavis are.

Now when they sever wedded hands,
Joy trembles in their bosom-strands,

And lovely laughter leaps and falls
Upon their lips in madrigals.

## If This Were Faith

God, if this were enough,
That I see things bare to the buff
And up to the buttocks in mire;
That I ask nor hope nor hire,
Nut in the husk,
Nor dawn beyond the dusk,
Nor life beyond death—
God, if this were faith?

Having felt thy wind in my face
Spit sorrow and disgrace,
Having seen thine evil doom
In Golgotha and Khartoum,
And the brutes, the work of thine hands,
Fill with injustice lands
And stain with blood the sea;
If still in my veins the glee
Of the black night and the sun
And the lost battle, run;
If, an adept,
The iniquitous lists I still accept
With joy, and joy to endure and be withstood,
And still to battle and perish for a dream of good—
God, if that were enough?

If to feel, in the ink of the slough,
And the sink of the mire,
Veins of glory and fire
Run through and transpierce and transpire,
And a secret purpose of glory in every part,
And the answering glory of battle fill my heart;
To thrill with the joy of girded men
To go on forever and fail and go on again,
And be mauled to the earth and arise,
And contend for the shade of a word and a thing not seen with the eyes,
With the half of a broken hope for a pillow at night,
That somehow the right is the right
And the smooth shall bloom from the rough—
Lord, if that were enough?

## Evensong

The embers of the day are red
Beyond the murky hill.
The kitchen smokes; the bed
In the darkling house is spread;

The great sky darkens overhead,
And the great woods are shrill.
So far have I been led,
Lord, by thy will;
So far I have followed, Lord, and wondered still.

The breeze from the embalmed land
Blows sudden toward the shore,
And claps my cottage door.
I hear the signal, Lord—I understand.
The night at Thy command
Comes. I will eat and sleep and will not question more.

## Go, Little Book

Go, little book, and wish to all
Flowers in the garden, meat in the hall,
A bin of wine, a spice of wit,
A house with lawns enclosing it,
A living river by the door,
A nightingale in the sycamore.

## Requiem[1]

Under the wide and starry sky,
Dig the grave and let me lie,
Glad did I live and gladly die,
And I laid me down with a will.

This be the verse you grave for me:
*Here he lies where he longed to be,*
*Home is the sailor, home from sea,*
*And the hunter home from the hill.*

## Aes Triplex

[This famous essay was first printed in 1872. The title ("triple brass") is taken from a Horatian ode. (I.3.9–12)

Illi robur et aes triplex
Circapectus erat qui fragilem truci
Commisit pelago ratem
Primus

"Oak and triple brass encircled the breast of the man who first trusted his fragile boat to the wild sea."

Stevenson's title thus implies resolution. Stevenson suffered from poor health all his life—he spent his days in a constant search for a salubrious climate. Among his friends he was a byword for courage and patient forbearance.]

---

[1] Latin for "rest," taken from the mass for the dead.

The changes wrought by death are in themselves so sharp and final, and so terrible and melancholy in their consequences, that the thing stands alone in man's experience, and has no parallel upon earth. It outdoes all other accidents because it is the last of them. Sometimes it leaps suddenly upon its victims, like a Thug; sometimes it lays a regular siege and creeps upon their citadel during a score of years. And when the business is done, there is sore havoc made in other people's lives, and a pin knocked out by which many subsidiary friendships hung together. There are empty chairs, solitary walks, and single beds at night.

Again, in taking away our friends, death does not take them away utterly, but leaves behind a mocking, tragical, and soon intolerable residue, which must be hurriedly concealed. Hence a whole chapter of sights and customs striking to the mind, from the pyramids of Egypt to the gibbets and dule trees of medieval Europe. The poorest persons have a bit of pageant going towards the tomb; memorial stones are set up over the least memorable; and, in order to preserve some show of respect for what remains of our old loves and friendships, we must accompany it with much grimly ludicrous ceremonial, and the hired undertaker parades before the door.

All this, and much more of the same sort, accompanied by the eloquence of poets, has gone a great way to put humanity in error; nay, in many philosophies the error has been embodied and laid down with every circumstance of logic; although in real life the bustle and swiftness, in leaving people little time to think, have not left them time enough to go dangerously wrong in practice.

As a matter of fact, although few things are spoken of with more fearful whisperings than this prospect of death, few have less influence on conduct under healthy circumstances. We have all heard of cities in South America built upon the side of fiery mountains, and how, even in this tremendous neighborhood, the inhabitants are not a jot more impressed by the solemnity of mortal conditions than if they were delving gardens in the greenest corner of England. There are serenades and suppers and much gallantry among the myrtles overhead; and meanwhile the foundation shudders underfoot, the bowels of the mountain growl, and at any moment living ruin may leap sky-high into the moonlight, and tumble man and his merrymaking in the dust.

In the eyes of very young people, and very dull old ones, there is something indescribably reckless and desperate in such a picture. It seems not credible that respectable married people, with umbrellas, should find appetite for a bit of supper within quite a long distance of a fiery mountain; ordinary life begins to smell of high-handed debauch when it is carried on so close to a catastrophe; and even cheese and salad, it seems, could hardly be relished in such circumstances without something like a defiance of the Creator. It should be a place for nobody but hermits dwelling in prayer and maceration, or mere born devils drowning care in a perpetual carouse.

And yet, when one comes to think upon it calmly, the situation of these South American citizens forms only a very pale figure for the state of ordinary mankind. This world itself, traveling blindly and swiftly in overcrowded space, among a million other worlds traveling blindly and swiftly in contrary directions, may very well come by a knock that would set it into explosion like a penny squib.

And what, pathologically looked at, is the human body, with all its organs, but a mere bagful of petards? The least of these is as dangerous to the whole economy as the ship's powder-magazine to the ship; and with every breath we breathe, and every meal we eat, we are putting one or more of them in peril. If we clung as devotedly as some philosophers pretend we do to the abstract idea of life, or were half as frightened as they make out we are, for the subversive accident that ends it all, the trumpets might sound by the hour and no one would follow them into battle—the blue peter might fly at the truck, but who would climb into a seagoing ship?

Think (if these philosophers were right) with what a preparation of spirit we should affront the daily peril of the dinner table— a deadlier spot than any battlefield in history, where the far greater proportion of our ancestors have miserably left their bones! What woman would ever be lured into marriage, so much more dangerous than the wildest sea?

And what would it be to grow old? for, after a certain distance, every step we take in life we find the ice growing thinner below our feet, and all around us and behind us we see our contemporaries going through. By the time a man gets well into the seventies, his continued existence is a mere miracle—and when he lays his old bones in bed for the night, there is an overwhelming probability that he will never see the day. Do the old men mind it, as a matter of fact? Why, no. They were never merrier; they have their grog at night, and tell the raciest stories; they hear of the death of people about their own age, or even younger, not as if it was a grisly warning, but with a simple childlike pleasure at having outlived someone else; and when a draft might puff them out like a guttering candle, or a bit of a stumble shatter them like so much glass, their old hearts keep sound and unaffrighted, and they go on, bubbling with laughter, through years of man's age compared to which the valley of Balaklava was as safe and peaceful as a village cricket-green on Sunday. It may fairly be questioned (if we look to the peril only) whether it was a much more daring feat for Curtius to plunge into the gulf, than for any old gentleman of ninety to doff his clothes and clamber into bed.

Indeed, it is a memorable subject for consideration, with what unconcern and gaiety mankind pricks on along the Valley of the Shadow of Death. The whole way is one wilderness of snares, and the end of it, for those who fear the last pinch, is irrevocable ruin. And yet we go spinning through it all, like a party for the Derby. Perhaps the reader remembers one of the humorous devices of the deified Caligula: how he encouraged a vast concourse of holiday-makers on to his bridge over Baiae bay; and when they were in the height of their enjoyment, turned loose the Praetorian guards among the company, and had them tossed into the sea. This is no bad miniature of the dealings of nature with the transitory race of man. Only, what a checkered picnic we have of it, even while it lasts! and into what great waters, not to be crossed by any swimmer, God's pale Praetorian throws us over in the end!

We live the time that a match flickers; we pop the cork of a ginger-beer bottle, and the earthquake swallows us on the instant. Is it not odd, is it not incongruous, is it not, in the highest sense of human speech, incredible, that we should think so highly of the ginger-beer, and regard so little the devouring earthquake?

The love of Life and the fear of Death are two famous phrases that grow harder to understand the more we think about them. It is a well-known fact that an immense proportion of boat accidents would never happen if people held the sheet in their hands instead of making it fast; and yet, unless it be some martinet of a professional mariner or some landsman with shattered nerves, every one of God's creatures makes it fast. A strange instance of man's unconcern and brazen boldness in the face of death!

We confound ourselves with metaphysical phrases, which we import into daily talk with noble inappropriateness. We have no idea of what death is, apart from its circumstances and some of its consequences to others—and, although we have some experience of living, there is not a man on earth who has flown so high into abstraction as to have any practical guess at the meaning of the word *life*.

All literature from Job and Omar Khayyam to Thomas Carlyle or Walt Whitman, is but an attempt to look upon the human state with such largeness of view as shall enable us to rise from the consideration of living to the Definition of Life. And our sages give us about the best satisfaction in their power when they say that it is a vapor, or a show, or made of the same stuff with dreams. Philosophy, in its more rigid sense, has been at the same work for ages; and after a myriad bald heads have wagged over the problem, and piles of words have been heaped one upon another into dry and cloudy volumes without end, philosophy has the honor of laying before us, with modest pride, her contribution toward the subject: that life is a Permanent Possibility of Sensation.

Truly a fine result! A man may very well love beef, or hunting, or a woman; but surely, surely, not a Permanent Possibility of Sensation! He may be afraid of a precipice, or a dentist, or a large enemy with a club, or even an undertaker's man; but not certainly of abstract death. We may trick with the word life in its dozen senses until we are weary of tricking; we may argue in terms of all the philosophies on earth, but one fact remains true throughout—that we do not love life, in the sense that we are greatly preoccupied about its conservation—that we do not, properly speaking, love life at all, but living.

Into the views of the least careful there will enter some degree of providence, no man's eyes are fixed entirely on the passing hour; but although we have some anticipation of good health, good weather, wine, active employment, love, and self-approval, the sum of these anticipations does not amount to anything like a general view of life's possibilities and issues; nor are those who cherish them most vividly, at all the most scrupulous of their personal safety. To be deeply interested in the accidents of our existence, to enjoy keenly the mixed texture of human experience, rather leads a man to disregard precautions, and risk his neck against a straw. For surely the love of living is stronger in an Alpine climber roping over a peril, or a hunter riding merrily at a stiff fence, than in a creature who lives upon a diet and walks a measured distance in the interest of his constitution.

There is a great deal of very vile nonsense talked upon both sides of the matter—tearing divines reducing life to the dimensions of a mere funeral procession, so short as to be hardly decent; and melancholy unbelievers yearning for the tomb as if it were a world too far away. Both sides must feel a little ashamed of their performances now and again when they draw in their chairs to dinner.

Indeed, a good meal and a bottle of wine is an answer to most standard works upon the question. When a man's heart warms to his viands, he forgets a great deal of sophistry, and soars into a rosy zone of contemplation. Death may be knocking at the door, like the Commander's statue; we have something else in hand, thank God, and let him knock.

Passing bells are ringing all the world over. All the world over, and every hour, someone is parting company with all his aches and ecstasies. For us also the trap is laid. But we are so fond of life that we have no leisure to entertain the terror of death. It is a honeymoon with us all through, and none of the longest. Small blame to us if we give our whole hearts to this glowing bride of ours, to the appetites, to honor, to the hungry curiosity of the mind, to the pleasure of the eyes in nature, and the pride of our own nimble bodies.

We all of us appreciate the sensations; but as for caring about the Permanence of the Possibility, a man's head is generally very bald, and his senses very dull, before he comes to that. Whether we regard life as a lane leading to a dead wall—a mere bag's end, as the French say—or whether we think of it as a vestibule or gymnasium, where we wait our turn and prepare our faculties for some more noble destiny; whether we thunder in a pulpit, or pule in little atheistic poetry-books, about its vanity and brevity; whether we look justly for years of health and vigor, or are about to mount into a Bath chair, as a step towards the hearse—in each and all of these views and situations there is but one conclusion possible—that a man should stop his ears against paralyzing terror, and run the race that is set before him with a single mind.

No one surely could have recoiled with more heartache and terror from the thought of death than our respected lexicographer; and yet we know how little it affected his conduct, how wisely and boldly he walked, and in what a fresh and lively vein he spoke of life. Already an old man, he ventured on his Highland tour—and his heart, bound with triple brass, did not recoil before twenty-seven individual cups of tea. As courage and intelligence are the two qualities best worth a good man's cultivation, so it is the first part of intelligence to recognize our precarious estate in life, and the first part of courage to be not at all abashed before the fact. A frank and somewhat headlong carriage, not looking too anxiously before, not dallying in maudlin regret over the past, stamps the man who is well armored for this world.

And not only well armored for himself, but a good friend and a good citizen to boot. We do not go to cowards for tender dealing; there is nothing so cruel as panic—the man who has least fear for his own carcass, has most time to consider others. That eminent chemist who took his walks abroad in tin shoes, and subsisted wholly upon tepid milk, had all his work cut out for him in considerate dealings with his own digestion. So soon as prudence has begun to grow up in the brain, like a dismal fungus, it finds its first expression in a paralysis of generous acts. The victim begins to shrink spiritually; he develops a fancy for parlors with a regulated temperature, and takes his morality on the principle of tin shoes and tepid milk. The care of one important body or soul becomes so engrossing that all the noises of the outer world begin to come thin and faint into the parlor with the regulated temperature; and the tin shoes go equably forward over blood and rain.

To be overwise is to ossify—and the scruple-monger ends by standing stock-still. Now the man who has his heart on his sleeve, and a good whirling weathercock of a brain, who reckons his life as a thing to be dashingly used and cheerfully hazarded, makes a very different acquaintance of the world, keeps all his pulses going true and fast, and gathers impetus as he runs, until, if he be running towards anything better than wildfire, he may shoot up and become a constellation in the end.

Lord look after his health, Lord have a care of his soul, says he; and he has at the key of the position, and swashes through incongruity and peril towards his aim. Death is on all sides of him with pointed batteries, as he is on all sides of all of us; unfortunate surprises gird him round; mimmouthed friends and relations hold up their hands in quite a little elegiacal synod about his path—and what cares he for all this? Being a true lover of living, a fellow with something pushing and spontaneous in his inside, he must, like any other soldier, in any other stirring, deadly warfare, push on at his best pace until he touch the goal.

"A peerage or Westminster Abbey!" cried Nelson in his bright, boyish, heroic manner. These are great incentives; not for any of these, but for the plain satisfaction of living, of being about their business in some sort or other, do the brave, serviceable men of every nation tread down the nettle danger, and pass flyingly over all the stumbling blocks of prudence.

Think of the heroism of Johnson, think of that superb indifference to mortal limitation that set him upon his dictionary, and carried him through triumphantly until the end! Who, if he were wisely considerate of things at large, would ever embark upon any work much more considerable than a halfpenny post card? Who would project a serial novel, after Thackeray and Dickens had each fallen in mid-course? Who would find heart enough to begin to live, if he dallied with the consideration of death?

And, after all, what sorry and pitiful quibbling all this is! To forego all the issues of living in a parlor with the regulated temperature—as if that were not to die a hundred times over, and for ten years at a stretch! As if it were not to die in one's own lifetime, and without even the sad immunities of death! As if it were not to die, and yet be the patient spectators of our own pitiable change!

The Permanent Possibility is preserved but the sensations carefully held at arm's length, as if one kept a photographic plate in a dark chamber. It is better to lose health like a spendthrift than to waste it like a miser. It is better to live and be done with it, than to die daily in the sick room.

By all means begin your folio; even if the doctor does not give you a year, even if he hesitates about a month, make one brave push and see what can be accomplished in a week.

It is not only in finished undertakings that we ought to honor useful labor. A spirit goes out of the man who means execution, which outlives the most untimely ending. All who have meant good work with their whole hearts, have done good work, although they may die before they have the time to sign it. Every heart that has beat, strong and cheerfully has left a hopeful impulse behind it in the world, and bettered the tradition of mankind. And even if death catch people, like an open pitfall, and in mid-career, laying out vast projects, and planning monstrous foundations, flushed with hope, and their mouths full of boastful language, they should be at once tripped up and silenced—is there not something brave and spirited in such a termination? and does not life go down with a better grace, foaming in full body over a precipice, than miserably straggling to an end in sandy deltas?

When the Greeks made their fine saying that those whom the gods love die young, I cannot help believing they had this sort of death also in their eye. For surely, at whatever age it overtake the man, this is to die young. Death has not been suffered to take so much as an illusion from his heart. In the hotfit of life, a-tiptoe on the highest point of being, he passes at a bound on to the other side. The noise of the mallet and chisel is scarcely quenched, the trumpets are hardly done blowing, when trailing with him clouds of glory, this happy starred, full-blooded spirit shoots into the spiritual land.

## Pulvis et Umbra[1]

We look for some reward of our endeavors and are disappointed; not success, not happiness, not even peace of conscience, crowns our ineffectual efforts to do well. Our frailties are invincible, our virtues barren; the battle goes sore against us to the going down of the sun. The canting moralist tells us of right and wrong; and we look abroad, even on the face of our small earth, and find them change with every climate, and no country where some action is not honored for a virtue and none where it is not branded for a vice; and we look in our experience, and find no vital congruity in the wisest rules, but at the best a municipal fitness.

It is not strange if we are tempted to despair of good. We ask too much. Our religions and moralities have been trimmed to flatter us, till they are all emasculate and sentimentalized, and only please and weaken. Truth is of a rougher strain. In the harsh face of life, faith can read a bracing gospel. The human race is a thing more ancient than the ten commandments; and the bones and revolutions of the Cosmos, in whose joints we are but moss and fungus, more ancient still.

### I

Of the Cosmos in the last resort, science reports many doubtful things and all of them appalling. There seems no substance to this solid globe on which we stamp,—nothing but symbols and ratios. Symbols and ratios carry us and bring us forth and beat us down; gravity, that swings the incommensurable suns and worlds through space, is but a figment varying inversely as the squares of distances; and the suns and worlds themselves, imponderable figures of abstraction—$NH_3$ and $H_2O$. Consideration dares not dwell upon this view; that way madness lies; science carries us into zones of speculation where there is no habitable city for the mind of man.

---

[1]Dust and shadow.

But take the Cosmos with a grosser faith, as our senses give it us. We behold space sown with rotatory islands, suns and worlds and the shards and wrecks of systems; some, like the sun, still blazing; some rotting, like the earth; others, like the moon, stable in desolation. All of these we take to be made of something we call matter,—a thing which no analysis can help us to conceive, to whose incredible properties no familiarities can reconcile our minds. This stuff, when not purified by the lustration of fire, rots uncleanly into something we call life; seized through all its atoms with a pediculous malady; swelling in tumors that become independent, sometimes even (by an abhorrent prodigy) locomotory; one splitting into millions, millions cohering into one, as the malady proceeds through varying stages.

This vital putrescence of the dust, used as we are to it, yet strikes us with occasional disgust, and the profusion of worms in a piece of ancient turf, or the air of a marsh darkened with insects, will some times check our breathing so that we aspire for cleaner places. But none is clean: the moving sand is infected with lice; the pure spring, where it bursts out of the mountain, is a mere issue of worms; even in the hard rock the crystal is forming.

In two main shapes this eruption covers the countenance of the earth: the animal and the vegetable: one in some degree the inversion of the other: the second rooted to the spot; the first coming detached out of its natal mud, and scurrying abroad with the myriad feet of insects, or towering into the heavens on the wings of birds, —a thing so incomprehensible that, if it be well considered, the heart stops. To what passes with the anchored vermin, we have little clue: doubtless they have their joys and sorrows, their delights and killing agonies,—it appears not how.

But of the locomotory, to which we ourselves belong, we can tell more. These share with us a thousand miracles: the miracles of sight, of hearing, of the projection of sound, things that bridge space; the miracles of memory and reason, by which the present is conceived, and when it is gone its image kept living in the brains of man and brute; the miracle of reproduction, with its imperious desires and staggering consequences.

And to put the last touch upon this mountain mass of the revolting and the inconceivable, all these prey upon each other, lives tearing other lives in pieces, cramming them inside themselves, and by that summary process growing fat: the vegetarian, the whale, perhaps the tree, not less than the lion of the desert,—for the vegetarian is only the eater of the dumb.

Meanwhile our rotatory island loaded with predatory life, and more drenched with blood, both animal and vegetable, than ever mutinied ship, scuds through space with unimaginable speed, and turns alternate cheeks to the reverberation of a blazing world ninety million miles away.

## II

What a monstrous specter is this man, the disease of the agglutinated dust, lifting alternate feet or lying drugged with slumber; killing, feeding, growing, bringing forth small copies of himself; grown upon with hair like grass, fitted with eyes that move and glitter in his face; a thing to set children screaming;—and yet looked at nearlier, known as his fellows know him, how surprising are his attributes! Poor soul, here for so little, cast among so many hardships, filled with desires so incommensurate and so inconsistent, savagely surrounded, savagely descended, irremediably condemned to prey upon his fellow lives: who should have blamed him had he been of a piece with his destiny and a being merely barbarous?

And we look and behold him instead filled with imperfect virtues: infinitely childish, often admirably valiant, often touchingly kind; sitting down, amidst his momentary life, to debate of right and wrong and the attributes of the deity; rising up to do battle for an egg or die for an idea; singling out his friends and his mate with cordial affection; bringing forth in pain, rearing with long-suffering solicitude, his young.

To touch the heart of his mystery, we find in him one thought, strange to the point of lunacy: the thought of duty; the thought of something owing to himself, to his neighbor, to his God; an ideal of decency, to which he would rise if it were possible; a limit of shame below which, if it be possible, he will not stoop.

The design in most men is one of conformity; here and there, in picked natures, it transcends itself and soars on the other side, arming martyrs with independence; but in all, in their degrees, it is a bosom thought:—not in man alone, for we trace it in dogs and cats whom we know fairly well, and doubtless some similar point of honor sways the elephant, the oyster, and the louse, of whom we know so little:—but in man, at least, it sways with so complete an empire that merely selfish things come second, even with the selfish; that appetites are starved, fears are conquered, pains supported; that almost the dullest shrinks from the reproof of a glance, although it were a child's; and all but the most cowardly stand amid the risks of war; and the more noble, having strongly conceived an act as due to their ideal, affront and embrace death.

Strange enough if, with their singular origin and perverted practice, they think they are to be rewarded in some future life; stranger still, if they are persuaded of the contrary, and think this blow which they solicit will strike them senseless for eternity. I shall be reminded what a tragedy of misconception and misconduct man at large presents, —of organized injustice, cowardly violence, and treacherous crime, and of the damning imperfections of the best. They cannot be too darkly drawn. Man is indeed marked for failure in his efforts to do right. But where the best consistently miscarry, how tenfold more remarkable that all should continue to strive; and surely we should find it both touching and inspiriting, that in a field from which success is banished, our race should not cease to labor.

If the first view of this creature, stalking in his rotatory isle, be a thing to shake the courage of the stoutest, on this nearer sight he startles us with an admiring wonder. It matters not where we look, under what climate we observe him, in what state of society, in what depth of ignorance, burthened with what erroneous morality; by camp-fires in Assiniboia, the snow powdering his shoulders, the wind plucking his blanket, as he sits, passing the ceremonial calumet and uttering his grave opinions like a Roman senator; in ships at sea, a man inured to hardship and vile pleasures, his brightest hope a fiddle in a tavern and a bedizened trull who sells herself to rob him, and he for all that simple, innocent, cheerful, kindly like a child, constant to toil, brave to drown, for others; in the slums of cities, moving among indifferent millions to mechanical employments, without hope of change in the future, with scarce a pleasure in the present, and yet true to his virtues, honest up to his lights, kind to his neighbors, tempted perhaps in vain by the bright gin palace, perhaps long-suffering with the drunken wife that ruins him; in India (a woman this time) kneeling with broken cries and streaming tears, as she drowns her child in the sacred river; in the brothel, the discard of society, living mainly on strong drink, fed with affronts, a fool, a thief, the comrade of thieves, and even here keeping the point of honor and the touch of pity, often repaying the world's scorn with service, often standing firm upon a scruple, and at a certain cost rejecting riches —everywhere some virtue cherished or affected, everywhere some decency of thought and carriage, everywhere the ensign of man's ineffectual goodness.

Ah! if I could show you this! If I could show you these men and women, all the world over, in every stage of history, under every abuse of error, under every circumstance of failure, without hope, without help, without thanks, still obscurely fighting the lost fight of virtue, still clinging, in the brothel or on the scaffold, to some rag of honor, the poor jewel of their souls! They may seek to escape, and yet they cannot;

it is not alone their privilege and glory, but their doom; they are condemned to some nobility, all their lives long, the desire of good is at their heels, the implacable hunter.

Of all earth's meteors, here at least is the most strange and consoling: that this ennobled lemur, this hair-crowned bubble of the dust, this inheritor of a few years and sorrows, should yet deny himself his rare delights, and add to his frequent pains, and live for an ideal, however misconceived.

Nor can we stop with man. A new doctrine, received with screams a little while ago by canting moralists, and still not properly worked into the body of our thoughts, lights us a step farther into the heart of this rough but noble universe. For nowadays the pride of man denies in vain his kinship with the original dust. He stands no longer like a thing apart. Close at his heels we see the dog, prince of another genus; and in him too we see dumbly testified the same cultus of an unattainable ideal, the same constancy in failure.

Does it stop with the dog? We look at our feet where the ground is blackened with the swarming ant; a creature so small, so far from us in the hierarchy of brutes, that we can scarce trace and scarce comprehend his doings; and here also, in his ordered polities and rigorous justice, we see confessed the law of duty and the fact of individual sin.

Does it stop, then, with the ant? Rather this desire of well-doing and this doom of frailty run through all the grades of life: rather is this earth, from the frosty top of Everest to the next margin of the internal fire, one stage of ineffectual virtues and one temple of pious tears and perseverance. The whole creation groaneth and travaileth together. It is the common and the god-like law of life. The browsers, the biters, the barkers, the hairy coats of field and forest, the squirrel in the oak, the thousand-footed creeper in the dust, as they share with us the gift of life, share with us the love of an ideal; strive like us—like us are tempted to grow weary of the struggle—to do well; like us receive at times unmerited refreshment, visitings of support, returns of courage; and are condemned like us to be crucified between that double law of the members and the will.

Are they like us, I wonder, in the timid hope of some reward, some sugar with the drug? do they, too, stand aghast at unrewarded virtues, at the sufferings of those whom, in our partiality, we take to be just, and the prosperity of such as in our blindness we call wicked? It may be, and yet God knows what they should look for. Even while they look, even while they repent, the foot of man treads them by thousands in the dust, the yelping hounds burst upon their trail, the bullet speeds, the knives are heating in the den of the vivisectionist, or the dew falls, and the generation of a day is blotted out. For these are creatures compared with whom our weakness is strength, our ignorance wisdom, our brief span eternity.

And as we dwell, we living things, in our isle of terror and under the imminent hand of death, God forbid it should be man the erected, the reasoner, the wise in his own eyes—God forbid it should be man that wearies in well-doing, that despairs of unrewarded effort, or utters the language of complaint. Let it be enough for faith, that the whole creation groans in mortal frailty, strives with unconquerable constancy: surely not all in vain.

## New York

from *The Amateur Immigrant* (1895)

As we drew near to New York I was at first amused, and then somewhat staggered, by the cautions and the grisly tales that went the round. You would have thought we were to land upon a cannibal island. You must speak to no one in the streets, as they would not leave you till you were rooked and beaten. You must enter a hotel with military precautions; for the least you had to apprehend was to awake next morning without money or baggage, or necessary raiment, a lone forked radish in a bed; and if the worst befell, you would instantly and mysteriously disappear from the ranks of mankind.

I have usually found such stories correspond to the least modicum of fact. Thus I was warned, I remember, against the roadside inns of the Cevennes, and that by a learned professor; and when I reached Pradelles the warning was explained; it was but the far-away rumor and reduplication of a single terrifying story already half a century old, and half forgotten in the theater of the events. So I was tempted to make light of these reports against America. But we had on board with us a man whose evidence it would not do to put aside. He had come near these perils in the body; he had visited a robber inn. The public has an old and well-grounded favor for this class of incident, and shall be gratified to the best of my power.

My fellow-passenger, whom we shall call M'Naughten, had come from New York to Boston with a comrade, seeking work. They were a pair of rattling blades; and, leaving their baggage at the station, passed the day in beer-saloons, and with congenial spirits, until midnight struck. Then they applied themselves to find a lodging, and walked the streets till two, knocking at houses of entertainment and being refused admittance, or themselves declining the terms. By two the inspiration of their liquor had begun to wear off; they were weary and humble, and after a great circuit found themselves in the same street where they had begun their search, and in front of a French hotel where they had already sought accommodation. Seeing the house still open, they returned to the charge. A man in a white cap sat in an office by the door. He seemed to welcome them more warmly than when they had first presented themselves, and the charge for the night had somewhat unaccountably fallen from a dollar to a quarter. They thought him ill looking, but paid their quarter apiece, and were shown upstairs to the top of the house. There, in a small room, the man in the white cap wished them pleasant slumbers.

The room was furnished with a bed, a chair, and some conveniences. The door did not lock on the inside; and the only sign of adornment was a couple of framed pictures, one close above the head of the bed, and the other opposite the foot, and both curtained, as we may sometimes see valuable watercolors, or the portraits of the dead, or works of art more than usually skittish in the subject.

It was perhaps in the hope of finding something of this last description that M'Naughten's comrade pulled aside the curtain of the first. He was startlingly disappointed. There was no picture. The frame surrounded, and the curtain was designed to hide, an oblong aperture in the partition, through which they looked forth into the dark corridor. A person standing without could easily take a purse from under the pillow, or even strangle a sleeper as he lay abed. M'Naughten and his comrade stared at each other like Balboa and his men, "with a wild surmise"; and then the latter, catching up the lamp, ran to the other frame and roughly raised the curtain. There he stood, petrified; and M'Naughten, who had followed, grasped him by the wrist in terror. They could see into another room, larger in size than that which they occupied, where three men sat crouching and silent in the dark. For a second or so these five persons looked each other in the eyes, then the curtain was dropped, and M'Naughten and his friend made but one bolt of it out of the room and down the stairs.

The man in the white cap said nothing as they passed him; and they were so pleased to be once more in the open night that they gave up all notion of a bed, and walked the streets of Boston till the morning.

No one seemed much cast down by these stories, but all inquired after the address of a respectable hotel; and I, for my part, put myself under the conduct of Mr. Jones. Before noon of the second Sunday we sighted the low shores outside of New

York harbor; the steerage passengers must remain on board to pass through Castle Garden on the following morning; but we of the second cabin made our escape along with the lords of the saloon; and by six o'clock Jones and I issued into West Street, sitting on some straw in the bottom of an open baggage-wagon.

It rained miraculously; and from that moment till on the following night I left New York, there was scarce a lull, and no cessation of the downpour. The roadways were flooded; a loud strident noise of falling water filled the air; the restaurants smelt heavily of wet people and wet clothing.

It took us but a few minutes, though it cost us a good deal of money, to be rattled along West Street to our destination: "Reunion House, No. 10 West Street, one minute's walk from Castle Garden; convenient to Castle Garden, the Steamboat Landings, California Steamers and Liverpool Ships; Board and Lodging per day I dollar, single meals 25 cents, lodging per night 25 cents; private rooms for families; no charge for storage or baggage; satisfaction guaranteed to all persons; Michael Mitchell, Proprietor."

Reunion House was, I may go the length of saying, a humble hostelry. You entered through a long barroom, thence passed into a little dining-room, and thence into a still smaller kitchen. The furniture was of the plainest; but the bar was hung in the American taste, with encouraging and hospitable mottoes. (There is something youthful in this fashion which pleases me; it runs into the advertisements; they do not merely offer you your money's worth of perfunctory attendance, but hold out golden prospects and welcome you with both hands; such a proprietor defies black care to follow you into his saloon; such another, touching the keynote with precision, invites you to his bar "to have a good time with the boys." So they not only insure their own attention but the wit and friendly spirit of their guests.)

Jones was well known; we were received warmly; and two minutes afterwards I had refused a drink from the proprietor, and was going on, in my plain European fashion, to refuse a cigar, when Mr. Mitchell sternly interposed, and explained the situation. He was offering to treat me, it appeared; whenever an American bar-keeper proposes anything, it must be borne in mind that he is offering to treat; and if I did not want a drink, I must at least take the cigar. I took it bashfully, feeling I had begun my American career on the wrong foot. I did not enjoy that cigar; but this may have been from a variety of reasons, even the best cigar often failing to please if you smoke three-quarters of it in a drenching rain.

For many years America was to me a sort of promised land. "Westward the march of empire holds its way"; the race is for the moment to the young; what has been and what is we imperfectly and obscurely know; what is to be yet lies beyond the flight of our imaginations. Greece, Rome, and Judea are gone by for ever, leaving to generations the legacy of their accomplished work; China still endures, an old inhabited house in the brand-new city of nations; England has already declined, since she has lost the States; and to these States, therefore, yet undeveloped, full of dark possibilities, and grown, like another Eve, from one rib out of the side of their own old land, the minds of young men in England turn naturally at a certain hopeful period of their age.

It will be hard for an American to understand the spirit. But let him imagine a young man who shall have grown up in an old and rigid circle, following bygone fashions and taught to distrust his own fresh instincts, and who now suddenly hears of a family of cousins, all about his own age, who keep house together by themselves and live far from restraint and tradition; let him imagine this, and he will have some imperfect notion of the sentiment with which spirited English youths turn to the thought of the American Republic. It seems to them as if, out west, the war of life was still conducted in the open air, and on free barbaric terms; as if it had not yet been narrowed into parlors, nor begun to be conducted, like some unjust and dreary arbitration, by compromise, costume, forms of procedure, and sad, senseless self-denial. Which of these two he prefers, a man with any youth still left in him will decide rightly for himself. He would rather be houseless than denied a pass-key; rather go without food than partake of a stalled ox in stiff, respectable society; rather be shot out of hand than direct his life according to the dictates of the world.

He knows or thinks nothing of the Maine Laws, the Puritan sourness, the fierce, sordid appetite for dollars, or the dreary existence of country towns. A few wild story-books which delighted his childhood form the imaginative basis of his picture of America. In course of time, there is added to this a great crowd of stimulating details—vast cities that grow up as by enchantment; the birds, that have gone south in autumn, returning with the spring to find thousands camped upon their marshes, and the lamps burning far and near along populous streets; forests that disappear like snow; countries larger than Britain that are cleared and settled, one man running forth with his household gods before another, while the bear and the Indian are yet scarce aware of their approach; oil that gushes from the earth; gold that is washed or quarried in the brooks or glens of the Sierras; and all that bustle, courage, action, and constant kaleidoscopic change that Walt Whitman has seized and set forth in his vigorous, cheerful, and loquacious verses.

Even the shot-gun, the navy revolver and the bowie knife, seem more connected with courage than with cruelty. I remember a while ago when Chicago was burned, hearing how a man, ere he began to rebuild his house, put up a board with some such inscription as the following: "All lost. Have a wife and three children. Have the world to begin again"; and then in large capitals the word: "Energy." The pluck and the expansion are alike youthful, and go straight to a young heart. Yes, it seemed to me, here was the country after all; here the undaunted stock of mankind, worthy to earn a new world.

I think Americans are scarce aware of this romantic attraction exercised by their land upon their cousins over sea. Perhaps they are unable to detect it under a certain jealousy and repentant soreness with which we regard a prosperity that might have been ours but for our own misconduct. Perhaps, too, we purposely conceal it; for we do not yet despair of the old ship. And perhaps the feeling flourishes more freely in the absence of any embodied and gently disappointing Uncle Sam. Europe is visited yearly by a crowd of preposterous fellows who, stung by some inattention or merely sick with patriotism, decline their titles of superiority in our ears and insult us with statistics by the page. From some such excursion, they return full of bitterness because the English show so small an interest and so modified a pleasure in the progress of the States.

Truly; but perhaps we should please them better, if they would measure the growth of America on some different standard from the decline of England. That capital essayist, Mr. Lowell, suffered much from "a certain condescension in foreigners," by which they made him feel that America was still young and incomplete; there is, I fear, a certain assumption in the American, by which he manages to taunt us with our age and debility.

And since I am on this subject, let me courteously invite each American citizen who purposes traveling in Europe, either to hold his peace upon the subject of the Alabama claims;[1] or if he must discuss the matter, to first refund from his own pocket the money which was paid by the one party and accepted by the other to conclude and definitively bury the dispute. The first American I ever encountered after I had begun to adore America, quarreled with me, or else I quarreled with him,

---

[1]Relative to the Confederate warship built in Britain which had done so much damage to Northern shipping.

about the Alabama claims. He has not been the last. Yet I never started the subject; indeed I know nothing about it, except that the money was paid; and fight for my flag in ignorance like a man before the mast.

It is possible that some people are always best at home, though the reverse is scandalously true of others. I have just been reading Mr. Charles Reade's *Woman Hater* (for which I wish to thank him), and I am reminded of Zoe Vizard's remark: "What does that matter? We are abroad." Sedentary, respectable people seem to leave some vital qualities behind them when they travel: *non omnia sua secum;* they are not themselves, and with all that mass of baggage, have forgotten to put up their human virtues. A Bohemian may not have much to recommend him, but what he has, is at least his own and indefeasible. You may rely as surely upon his virtues as upon his vices, for they are both bred in the bone. Neither have been assumed to suit the temper of society, or depend in any degree on the vicinity of Portman Square.

But respectable people, transplanted from their own particular zone of respectability, too often lose their manners, their good sense, and a considerable part of their religion. For instance I have not yet seen the Sabbatarian who did not visibly relax upon the continent. Hence perhaps the difference between the American abroad and the American at home. If one thing were deeply written on my mind, it was this: that the American dislikes England and the English; and yet I had no sooner crossed the Atlantic, than I began to think it an unfounded notion. The old country—so they called it with an accent of true kindliness—was plainly not detested; they spoke of it with a certain emotion, as of a father from whom they had parted in anger and who was since dead; and wherever I went, I found my nationality an introduction. I am old-fashioned enough to be patriotic, particularly when away from home; and thus the change delighted and touched me. Up to the moment of my arrival, I had connected Americans with hostility, not to me indeed, but to my land; from that moment forward, I found that was a link which I had thought to be a barrier, and knew that I was among blood relations.

So much had I written some time ago, with great good sense, as I thought, and complete catholicity of view. But it began at first to dawn upon me slowly, and was then forced upon me in a thunderclap, that I had myself become one of those uncivil travelers whom I so heartily condemned: that while here I was, kindly received, I could not find a good word nor so much as a good thought for the land that harbored me; that I was eager to spy its faults and shrank from the sight of virtues as if they were injustices to England.

Such was the case; explain it how you may. It was too like my home, and yet not like enough. It stood to me like a near relation who is scarce a friend, and who may disgrace us by his misconduct and yet cannot greatly please by his prosperity. I can bear to read the worst word of a Frenchman about England, and can do so smiling; but let an American take up the tale, and I am all quivering susceptibility from head to foot. There is still a sense of domestic treachery when we fall out, and a sense of unwarrantable coolness even when we agree.

Did you ever read the parable of the Prodigal Son? Or do you fancy, if things had been reversed and the prodigal come home in broadcloth and a chaise and four, that his brother who had stayed at home and stood by the old concern, would be better satisfied with the result? He might have been; not I. I have not enough justice in me for a case so trying. And then in one version of the parable, the prodigal was driven from home with barbarous usage; and O! what a bitterness is added to the cup!

Your own Benjamin Franklin has foreseen my case. "Were it possible for us to forget and forgive," he wrote, "it is not possible for you (I mean the British nation) to forgive the people you have so heavily injured."

Incisive Franklin! Yours is the prophecy, mine the ill-feeling. I have all the faults of my forefathers on my stomach; I have historical remorse; I cannot see

America but through the jaundiced spectacles of criminality.

And surely if jealousy be, as I believe it is, only the most radical, primeval and naked form of admiration—admiration in war paint, so to speak—then every word of my confession proves a delicate flattery like incense. Sail on, O mighty Union! God knows I wish you a noble career. Only somehow, when I was younger, I used to feel as if I had some portion in your future; but first I began to meet Americans in my own home, and they did not run to greet me as I hoped; and then I came myself into these states, and found my own heart not pure of ancient hatred. With that I knew I was a stranger, and you did but justice to refuse me copyright. Yet it is with disappointed tenderness that I behold you steaming off to glory in your new and elegant turret ship, while I remain behind to go down with the old three decker. We have feelings that will not be uttered in prose; and where poetry is absent, jingle must serve the turn.

With half a heart I wander here
As from an age gone by,
A brother—yet, though young in years,
An elder brother I!

You speak another tongue from mine,
Though both were English born.
I towards the night of time decline:
You mount into the morn.

Youth shall grow great and strong and free
But age must still decay.
Tomorrow for the States—for me
England and yesterday!

Here I was at last in America, and was soon out upon New York streets, spying for things foreign. The place had to me an air of Liverpool; but such was the rain that not Paradise itself would have looked inviting. We were a party of four, under two umbrellas; Jones and I and two Scots lads, recent immigrants, and not indisposed to welcome a compatriot. They had been six weeks in New York, and neither of them had yet found a single job or earned a single halfpenny. Up to the present they were exactly out of pocket by the amount of the fare.

The lads soon left us. Now I had sworn by all my gods to have such a dinner as would rouse the dead; there was scarce any expense at which I should have hesitated; the devil was in it but Jones and I should dine like heathen emperors. I set to work, asking after a restaurant; and I chose the wealthiest and most gastronomical-looking passers-by to ask from. Yet, although I had told them I was willing to pay anything in reason, one and all sent me off to cheap, fixed-price houses where I would not have eaten that night for the cost of twenty dinners. I do not know if this were characteristic of New York, or whether it was only Jones and I who looked undinerly and discouraged enterprising suggestions.

But at length, by our own sagacity, we found a French restaurant, where there was a French waiter, some fair French cooking, some so-called French wine, and French coffee to conclude the whole. I never entered into the feelings of Jack on land so completely as when I tasted that coffee.

I suppose we had one of the "private rooms for families" at Reunion House. It was very small; furnished with a bed, a chair, and some clothes-pegs; and it derived all that was necessary for the life of the human animal through two borrowed lights; one, looking into the passage, and the second opening, without sash, into another apartment, where three men fitfully snored, or, in intervals of wakefulness, drearily mumbled to each other all night long.

It will be observed that this was almost exactly the disposition of the room in M'Naughten's story. Jones had the bed; I pitched my camp upon the floor; he did not sleep until near morning, and I, for my part, never closed an eye. (Some of this wakefulness was due to the change from shipboard; but the better part, in my case, to a certain distressing malady which had been growing on me during the last few days and of which more anon.)

At sunrise I heard a cannon fired; and shortly afterwards the men in the next room gave over snoring for good, and began to rustle over their toilettes. The sound of their voices as they talked was low and moaning, like that of people watching by the sick. Jones, who had at last begun to doze, tumbled and murmured, and every now and then opened unconscious eyes upon me where I lay. I found myself growing eerier and eerier, for I daresay I was a little fevered by my restless night, and hurried to dress and get down-stairs.

You had to pass through the rain, which still fell thick and resonant, to reach a lavatory on the other side of the court. There were three basin-stands, and a few crumpled towels and pieces of wet soap, white and slippery like fish; nor should I forget a looking-glass and a pair of questionable combs. Another Scots lad was here, scrubbing his face with a good will. He had been three months in New York and had not yet found a single job nor earned a single halfpenny. Up to the present, he also was exactly out of pocket by the amount of the fare. I began to grow sick at heart for my fellow-emigrants.

Of my nightmare wanderings in New York I spare to tell. I had a thousand and one things to do; only the day to do them in, and a journey across the continent before me in the evening. It rained with patient fury; every now and then I had to get under cover for a while in order, so to speak, to give my mackintosh a rest; for under this continued drenching it began to grow damp on the inside. I went to banks, post-offices, railway-offices, restaurants, publishers, booksellers, moneychangers, and wherever I went a pool would gather about my feet, and those who were careful of their floors would look on with an unfriendly eye.

Wherever I went, too, the same traits struck me: the people were all surprisingly rude and surprisingly kind. The money-changer cross-questioned me like a French commissary, asking my age, my business, my average income, and my destination, beating down my attempts at evasion, and receiving my answers in silence; and yet when all was over, he shook hands with me up to the elbows, and sent his lad nearly a quarter of a mile in the rain to get me books at a reduction.

Again, in a very large publishing and bookselling establishment, a man, who seemed to be the manager, received me as I had certainly never before been received in any human shop, indicated squarely that he put no faith in my honesty, and refused to look up the names of books or give me the slightest help or information, on the ground, like the steward, that it was none of his business.

I lost my temper at last, said I was a stranger in America and not learned in their etiquette; but I would assure him, if he went to any bookseller in England, of more handsome usage. The boast was perhaps exaggerated; but like many a long shot, it struck the gold. The manager passed at once from one extreme to the other; I may say that from that moment he loaded me with kindness; he gave me all sorts of good advice, wrote me down addresses, and came bareheaded into the rain to point me out a restaurant where I might lunch, nor even then did he seem to think that he had done enough.

These are (it is as well to be bold in statement) the manners of America. It is this same opposition that has most struck me in people of almost all classes and from east to west. By the time a man had about strung me up to be the death of him by his insulting behavior, he himself would be just upon the point of melting into confidence and serviceable attentions. Yet I suspect, although I have met with the like in so many parts, that this must be the character of some particular State or group of States; for in America, and this again in all classes, you will find some of the softest-mannered gentlemen in the world.

I returned to Mitchell's to write some letters, and then made the acquaintance of his stripling daughter. She was a slip of a girl at that attractive period of life when the girl just begins to put on the forms of the woman, and yet retains an accent and character of her own. Her looks were dark, strange and comely. Her eyes had a caressing fixity, which made you inclined to turn aside your own. She was what is called a reading girl, and it was because she saw books in my open knapsack as I sat writing at a table near the bar, that she plucked up courage to address me. Had I any songs? she asked me, touching a volume with her finger. I told her I had not; but she still hovered by, and again inquired, if any of the books were nice? I gave her a volume of my own, not because I thought it so nice, but because it had a likeness of myself in the frontispiece, which I thought it would amuse the child to recognize. She was delighted beyond measure, and read a good many pages aloud to her sister as I sat writing; the sister, I must confess, soon wearied and ran away; but the other child, with admirable courage, persevered till it was time for me to go. I wish her a kind husband who will have, without my wishing it, a most desirable wife, particularly for an author.

I went to a chemist's in Broadway, a great temple near the Post office, where I was examined and prescribed for by a fine gentleman in fine linen and with the most insinuative manners. My wrists were a mass of sores; so were many other parts of my body. The itching was at times overwhelming; at times, too, it was succeeded by furious stinging pains, like so many cuts with a carriage whip. There were moments when even a stoic or an Indian Gymnosophist might have been excused for some demonstration of interest; and for my part, I was ready to roll upon the floor in my paroxysms.

The gentleman in fine linen told me, with admirable gravity, that my liver was out of order, and presented me with a blue pill, a seidlitz powder and a little bottle of some salt and colorless fluid to take night and morning on the journey. He might as well have given me a cricket bat and a copy of Johnson's dictionary, I might have lived exclusively on blue pills and been none the better. But the diagnosis of the gentleman in fine linen was hopelessly at fault. Perhaps he had moved too exclusively in elegant circles; perhaps he was too noble-minded to suspect me of anything disgraceful.

The true name of my complaint, I will never divulge, for I know what is due to the reader and to myself; but there is every reason to believe that I am not the only emigrant who has arrived in the Western world with similar symptoms. It is indeed a piece of emigrant experience, though one which I had not desired to share. Should any person be so intoxicated by my descriptions of an emigrant's career, as to desire to follow in my footsteps, here is a consideration which may modify if not eradicate the wish. But I have since been told that with a ring of red sublimate about the wrist, a man may plunge into the vilest company unfearing. I had no red sublimate: that is my story; hence these tears.

I was so wet when I got back to Mitchell's towards the evening, that I had simply to divest myself of my shoes, socks, and trousers, and leave them behind for the benefit of New York city. No fire could have dried them ere I had to start; and to pack them in their present condition was to spread ruin among my other possessions. With a heavy heart I said farewell to them as they lay a pulp in the middle of a pool upon the floor of Mitchell's kitchen. I wonder if they are dry by now. Mitchell hired a man to carry my baggage to the station, which was hard by, accompanied me thither himself, and recommended me to the particular attention of the officials. No one could have been kinder. Those who are out of pocket may go safely to Reunion House, where they will get decent meals and find an honest and obliging landlord. I owed him this word of thanks, before I enter fairly on the second chapter of my emigrant experience.

## The Scot Abroad
### from *The Silverado Squatters* (1883)

A few pages back I wrote that a man belonged, in these days, to a variety of countries; but the old land is still the true love, the others are but pleasant infidelities. Scotland is indefinable; it has no unity except upon the map. Two languages, many dialects, innumerable forms of piety, and countless local patriotisms and prejudices, part us among ourselves more widely than the extreme east and west of that great continent of America. When I am at home, I feel a man from Glasgow to be something like a rival, a man from Barra to be more than half a foreigner. Yet let us meet in some far country, and, whether we hail from the braes of Manor or the braes of Mar, some ready-made affection joins us on the instant. It is not race. Look at us. One is Norse, one Celtic, and another Saxon. It is not community of tongue. We have it not among ourselves; and we have it, almost to perfection, with English, or Irish, or American. It is no tie of faith, for we detest each other's errors. And yet somewhere, deep down in the heart of each one of us, something yearns for the old land and the old kindly people.

Of all mysteries of the human heart this is perhaps the most inscrutable. There is no special loveliness in that gray country, with its rainy, sea-beat archipelago; its fields of dark mountains; its unsightly places, black with coal; its treeless, sour, unfriendly-looking corn-lands; its quaint, gray, castled city, where the bells clash of a Sunday, and the wind squalls, and the salt showers fly and beat. I do not even know if I desire to live there; but let me hear, in some far land, a kindred voice sing out, "O why left I my hame?" and it seems at once as if no beauty under the kind heavens, and no society of the wise and good, can repay me for my absence from my country. And though I think I would rather die elsewhere, yet in my heart of hearts I long to be buried among good Scots clods. I will say it fairly, it grows on me with every year: there are no stars so lovely as Edinburgh street-lamps. When I forget thee, Auld Reekie, may my right hand forget its cunning!

The happiest lot on earth is to be born a Scotsman. You must pay for it in many ways, as for all other advantages on earth. You have to learn the Paraphrases and the Shorter Catechism; you generally take to drink; your youth, as far as I can find out, is a time of louder war against society, of more outcry and tears and turmoil, than if you had been born, for instance, in England. But somehow life is warmer and closer; the hearth burns more redly; the lights of home shine softer on the rainy street; the very names, endeared in verse and music, cling nearer round our hearts. An Englishman may meet an Englishman to-morrow, upon Chimborazo, and neither of them cares; but when the Scots wine-grower told me of Mons Meg it was like magic.

> "From the dim shieling on the misty island
> Mountains divide us, and a world of seas;
> Yet still our hearts are true, our hearts are Highland,
> And we, in dreams, behold the Hebrides."[1]

And, Highland and Lowland, all our hearts are Scottish.

---

[1]From the "Canadian Boat Song," somewhat misquoted. The poem is printed on page 530.

Only a few days after I had seen M'Eckron, a message reached me in my cottage. It was a Scotsman who had come down a long way from the hills to market. He had heard there was a countryman in Calistoga, and came round to the hotel to see him. We said a few words to each other; we had not much to say—should never have seen each other had we stayed at home, separated alike in space and in society; and then we shook hands, and he went his way again to his ranch among the hills, and that was all.

Another Scotsman there was, a resident, who for the mere love of the common country, douce,[1] serious, religious man, drove me all about the valley, and took as much interest in me as if I had been his son: more, perhaps; for the son has faults too keenly felt, while the abstract countryman is perfect—like a whiff of peats.

And there was yet another. Upon him I came suddenly, as he was calmly entering my cottage, his mind quite evidently bent on plunder: a man of about fifty, filthy, ragged, roguish, with a chimney-pot hat and a tail-coat, and a pursing of his mouth that might have been envied by an elder of the kirk. He had just such a face as I have seen a dozen times behind the plate.

"Hullo, sir!" I cried. "Where are you going?" He turned round without a quiver.

"You're a Scotsman, sir?" he said gravely. "So am I; I come from Aberdeen. This is my card," presenting me with a piece of pasteboard which he had raked out of some gutter in the period of the rains. "I was just examining this palm," he continued, indicating the misbegotten plant before our door, "which is the largest specimen I have yet observed in California."

There were four or five larger within sight. But where was the use of argument? He produced a tape-line, made me help him to measure the tree at the level of the ground, and entered the figures in a large and filthy pocket-book, all with the gravity of Solomon. He then thanked me profusely, remarking that such little services were due between countrymen; shook hands with me, "for auld lang syne," as he said; and took himself solemnly away, radiating dirt and humbug as he went.

A month or two after this encounter of mine, there came a Scot to Sacramento—perhaps from Aberdeen. Anyway, there never was any one more Scottish in this wide world. He could sing and dance—and drink, I presume; and he played the pipes with vigor and success. All the Scots in Sacramento became infatuated with him, and spent their spare time and money driving him about in an open cab, between drinks, while he blew himself scarlet at the pipes. This is a very sad story. After he had borrowed money from every one, he and his pipes suddenly disappeared from Sacramento, and when I last heard, the police were looking for him.

I cannot say how this story amused me, when I felt myself so thoroughly ripe on both sides to he duped in the same way.

It is at least a curious thing, to conclude, that the races which wander widest, Jews and Scots, should be the most clannish in the world. But perhaps these two are cause and effect: "For ye were strangers in the land of Egypt."

## Thrawn Janet

The Reverend Murdoch Soulis was long minister of the moorland parish of Balweary, in the vale of Dule. A severe, bleak-faced old man, dreadful to his hearers, he dwelt in the last years of his life, without relative or servant or any human company, in the small and lonely manse under the Hanging Shaw. In spite of the iron composure of his features, his eye was wild, scared, and uncertain; and when he dwelt, in private admonition, on the future of the impenitent, it seemed as if his eye

[1]Sober, respectable.

pierced through the storms of time to the terrors of eternity. Many young persons, coming to prepare themselves against the season of the Holy Communion, were dreadfully affected by his talk. He had a sermon on 1st Peter, v. and 8th, "The devil as a roaring lion," on the Sunday after every seventeenth of August, and he was accustomed to surpass himself upon that text both by the appalling nature of the matter and the terror of his bearing in the pulpit. The children were frightened into fits, and the old looked more than usually oracular, and were, all that day, full of those hints that Hamlet deprecated.

The manse itself, where it stood by the water of Dule among some thick trees, with the Shaw overhanging it on the one side, and on the other many cold, moorish hill-tops rising toward the sky, had begun, at a very early period of Mr. Soulis's ministry, to be avoided in the dusk hours by all who valued themselves upon their prudence; and guidmen sitting at the clachan[1] alehouse shook their heads together at the thought of passing late by that uncanny neighborhood. There was one spot, to be more particular, which was regarded with especial awe. The manse stood between the highroad and the water of Dule, with a gable to each; its back was towards the kirk-town of Balweary, nearly half a mile away; in front of it, a bare garden, hedged with thorn, occupied the land between the river and the road. The house was two stories high, with two large rooms on each. It opened not directly on the garden, but on a causewayed path, or passage, giving on the road on the one hand, and closed on the other by the tall willows and elders that bordered on the stream. And it was this strip of causeway that enjoyed among the young parishioners of Balweary so infamous a reputation. The minister walked there often after dark, sometimes groaning aloud in the instancy of his unspoken prayers; and when he was from home, and the manse door was locked, the more daring school-boys ventured, with beating hearts, to "follow my leader" across that legendary spot.

This atmosphere of terror, surrounding, as it did, a man of God of spotless character and orthodoxy, was a common cause of wonder and subject of inquiry among the few strangers who were led by chance or business into that unknown, outlying country. But many even of the people of the parish were ignorant of the strange events which had marked the first year of Mr. Soulis's ministrations; and among those who were better informed, some were naturally reticent, and others shy of that particular topic. Now and again, only, one of the older folk would warm into courage over his third tumbler, and recount the cause of the minister's strange looks and solitary life.

Fifty years syne, when Mr. Soulis cam' first into Ba'weary, he was still a young man—a callant,[2] the folk said—fu' o' book-learnin' an' grand at the exposition, but, as was natural in sae young a man, wi' nae leevin' experience in religion. The younger sort were greatly taken wi' his gifts and his gab; but auld, concerned, serious men and women were moved even to prayer for the young man, whom they took to be a self deceiver, and the parish that was like to be sae ill-supplied. It was before the days o' the moderates—weary fa' them; but ill things are like guid—they baith come bit by bit, a pickle[3] at a time; and there were folk even then that said the Lord had left the college professors to their ain devices, an' the lads that went to study wi' them wad hae done mair an' better sittin' in a peat-bog, like their forbears of the persecution, wi' a Bible under their oxter an' a speerit o' prayer in their heart. There was nae doubt onyway, but that Mr. Soulis had been ower lang at the college. He was careful and troubled for mony things besides the ae thing needful. He had a feck o'

---

[1]Village.

[2]Youth.

[3]Few.

books wi' him—mair than had ever been seen before in a' that presbytery; and a sair wark the carrier had wi' them, for they were a' like to have smoored[1] in the De'il's Hag between this and Kilmackerlie. They were books o' divinity, to he sure, or so they ca'd them; but the serious were o' opinion there was little service for sae mony, when the hail o' God's Word would gang in the neuk o' a plaid. Then he wad sit half the day and half the nicht forbye, which was scant decent—writin', nae less; an' first they were feared he wad read his sermons; an' syne it proved he was writin' a book himsel', which was surely no' fittin' for ane o' his years an' sma' experience.

Onyway it behooved him to get an auld, decent wife to keep the manse for him an' see to his bit deeners; an' he was recommended to an auld limmer[2]—Janet M'Clour they ca'd her—an' sae far left to himsel' as to be ower persuaded. There was mony advised him to the contrar, for Janet was mair than suspeckit by the best folk in Ba'weary. Lang or that, she had had a wean to a dragoon; she hadna come forrit[3] for maybe thretty year; and bairns had seen her mumblin' to hersel' up on Key's Loan in the gloamin', whilk was an unco time an' place for a Godfearin' woman. Howsoever, it was the laird himsel' that had first tauld the minister o' Janet; an' in thae days he wad hae gane a far gate to pleesure the laird. When folk tauld him that Janet was sib to the de'il, it was a' superstition by his way o' it; an' when they cast up the Bible to him an' the witch of Endor, he wad threep it doun their thrapples[4] that thir days were a' gane by, an' the de'il was mercifully restrained.

Weel, when it got about the clachan that Janet M'Clour was to be servant at the manse, the folk were fair mad wi' her an' him thegither; an' some o' the guidwives had nae better to dae than get round her door-cheeks and chairge her wi' a' that was ken't again' her, frae the sodger's bairn to John Tamson's twa kye. She was nae great speaker; folk usually let her gang her ain gate, an' she let them gang theirs, wi' neither Fair-guid-een nor Fair-guid-day; but when she buckled to, she had a tongue to deave[5] the miller. Up she got, an' there wasna an auld story in Ba'weary but she gart somebody lowp for it that day; they couldna say ae thing but she could say twa to it; till, at the hinder end, the guidwives up an' claught haud of her, an' clawed the coats aff her back, and pu'd her doun the clachan to the water o' Dule, to see if she were a witch or no, soom or droun. The carline[6] skirled till ye could hear her at the Hangin' Shaw, an' she focht like ten; there was mony a guidwife bure the mark o' her neist day an' mony a lang day after; an' just in the hettest o' the collieshangie, wha suld come up (for his sins) but the new minister!

"Women," said he (an' he had a grand voice), "I charge you in the Lord's name to let her go."

Janet ran to him—she was fair wud wi' terror —an' clang to him, an' prayed him, for Christ's sake, save her frae the cummers;[7] an' they, for their pairt, tauld him a' that was ken't, an' maybe mair.

"Woman," says he to Janet, "is this true?"

"As the Lord sees me," says she, "as the Lord made me, no' a word o't. Forbye the bairn," says she, "I've been a decent woman a' my days."

"Will you," says Mr. Soulis, "in the name of God, and before me, His unworthy minister, renounce the devil and his works?"

---

[1]"Smothered."

[2]Jade.

[3]Taken communion.

[4]Gullets.

[5]Deafen.

[6]Old woman, witch.

[7]Women, housewives.

Weel, it wad appear that when he askit that, she gave a girn that fairly frichtit them that saw her, an' they could hear her teeth play dirl thegither in her chafts; but there was naething for it but the ae way or the ither; an' Janet lifted up her hand an' renounced the de'il before them a'.

"And now," says Mr. Soulis to the guidwives, "home with ye, one and all, and pray to God for His forgiveness."

An' he gied Janet his arm, though she had little on her but a sark, and took her up the clachan to her ain door like a leddy o' the land; an' her screighin' an' laughin' as was a scandal to be heard.

There were mony grave folk lang ower their prayers that nicht; but when the morn cam' there was sic a fear fell upon a' Ba'weary that the bairns hid theirsels, an' even the men-fouk stood an' keekit[1] frae their doors. For there was Janet comin' doun the clachan—her or her likeness, nane could tell—wi' her neck thrawn,[2] an' her heid on ae side, like a body that has been hangit, an' a girn on her face like an unstreakit corp. By an' by they got used wi' it, an' even speered[3] at her to ken what was wrang; but frae that day forth she couldna speak like a Christian woman, but slavered an' played click wi' her teeth like a pair o' shears; an' frae that day forth the name o' God cam' never on her lips. Whiles she wad try to say it, but it michtna be. Them that kenned best said least; but they never gied that Thing the name o' Janet M'Clour; for the auld Janet, by their way o't, was in muckle hell that day. But the minister was neither to haud nor to bind; he preached about naething but the folk's cruelty that had gi'en her a stroke of the palsy; he skelpit the bairns that meddled her; an' he had her up to the manse that same nicht, an' dwalled there a' his lane wi' her under the Hangin' Shaw.

Weel, time gaed by: and the idler sort commenced to think mair lichtly o' that black business. The minister was weel thocht o'; he was aye late at the writing, folk wad see his can'le doon by the Dule water after twal' at e'en; and he seemed pleased wi' himsel' an' upsitten as at first, though a' body could see that he was dwining. As for Janet she cam' an' she gaed; if she didna speak muckle afore, it was reason she should speak less then; she meddled naebody; but she was an eldritch thing to see, an' nane wad hae mistrysted wi' her for Ba'weary glebe.

About the end o' July there cam' a spell o' weather, the like o't never was in that countryside; it was lown an' het an' heartless; the herds couldna win up the Black Hill, the bairns were ower weariet to play; an' yet it was gousty too, wi' claps o' het wund that rumm'led in the glens, and bits o' shouers that slockened naething. We aye thocht it but to thun'er on the morn; but the morn cam', an' the morn's morning, an' it was aye the same uncanny weather, sair on folks and bestial. O' a' that were the waur, nane suffered like Mr. Soulis; he could neither sleep nor eat, he tauld his elders; an' when he wasna writin' at his weary book, he wad be stravaguin'[4] ower a' the country-side like a man possessed, when a' body else was blithe to keep caller ben the house.

Abune Hangin' Shaw, in the bield[5] o' the Black Hill, there's a bit enclosed grund wi' an iron yett;[6] an' it seems, in the auld days, that was the kirkyaird o' Ba'weary, an' consecrated by the Papists before the blessed licht shone upon the

---

[1]Peeked.

[2]Twisted, wrung.

[3]Asked.

[4]Wandering.

[5]Shelter.

[6]Gate.

kingdom. It was a great howff[1] o' Mr. Soulis's onyway; there he wad sit an' consider his sermons; an' indeed it's a bieldy bit. Weel, as he cam' ower the wast end o' the Black Hill, ae day, he saw first twa, an' syne fower, an' syne seeven corbie craws fleein' round an' round abune the auld kirkyaird. They flew laigh an' heavy, an' squawked to ither as they gaed; an' it was clear to Mr. Soulis that something had put them frae their ordinar. He wasna easy fleyed, an' gaed straucht up to the wa's; an' what suld he find there but a man, or the appearance o' a man, sittin' in the inside upon a grave. He was of a great stature, an' black as hell, and his e'en were singular to see. Mr. Soulis had heard tell o' black men, mony's the time; but there was something unco about this black man that daunted him. Het as he was, he took a kind o' cauld grue in the marrow o' his banes; but up he spak for a' that; an' says he: "My friend, are you a stranger in this place?" The black man answered never a word; he got upon his feet, an' begoud on to hirsle to the wa' on the far side; but he aye lookit at the minister; an' the minister stood an' lookit back; till a' in a meenit the black man was ower the wa' an' rinnin' for the bield o' the trees. Mr. Soulis, he hardly kenned why, ran after him; but he was fair forjeskit wi' his walk an' the het, unhalesome weather; an' rin as he likit, he got nae mair than a glisk o' the black man amang the birks, till he won doun to the foot o' the hillside, an' there he saw him ance mair, gaun, hap-step-an'-lawp, ower Dule water to the manse.

Mr. Soulis wasna weel pleased that this fearsome gangrel suld mak' sae free wi' Ba'weary manse; an' he ran the harder, an', wet shoon, ower the burn, an' up the walk; but the deil a black man was there to see. He stepped out upon the road, but there was naebody there; he gaed a' ower the gairden, but na, nae black man. At the hinder end, an' a bit feared as was but natural, he lifted the hasp an' into the manse; and there was Janet M'Clour before his e'en, wi' her thrawn craig,[2] an' nane sae pleased to see him. An' he aye minded sinsyne, when first he set his e'en upon her, he had the same cauld and deidly grue.

"Janet," says he, "have you seen a black man?"

"A black man!" quo' she. "Save us a'! Ye're no wise, minister. There's nae black man in a' Ba'weary."

But she didna speak plain, ye maun understand; but yam-yammered, like a powney wi' the bit in its moo.

"Weel," says he, "Janet, if there was nae black man, I have spoken with the Accuser of the Brethren."

An' he sat doun like ane wi' a fever, an' his teeth chittered in his heid.

"Hoots," says she, "think shame to yoursel', minister"; an' gied him a drap brandy that she keept aye by her.

Syne Mr. Soulis gaed into his study amang a' his books. It's a lang, laigh, mirk chalmer, perishin' cauld in winter, an' no' very dry even in the top o' the simmer, for the manse stands near the burn. Sae doun he sat, and thocht of a' that had come an' gane since he was in Ba'weary, an' his hame, an' the days when he was a bairn an' ran daffin' on the braes; an' that black man aye ran in his heid like the owercome of a sang. Aye the mair he thocht, the mair he thocht o' the black man.

He tried the prayer, an' the words wouldna come to him; an' he tried, they say, to write at his book, but he couldna mak' nae mair o' that. There was whiles he thocht the black man was at his oxter,[3] an' the swat stood upon him cauld as well-water; and there was ither whiles, when he cam' to himsel like a christened bairn an' minded naething.

---

[1] Haunt.
[2] Neck.
[3] Arm.

The upshot was that he gaed to the window an' stood glowrin' at Dule water. The trees are unco thick, an' the water lies deep an' black under the manse; an' there was Janet washin' the cla'es wi' her coats kilted. She had her back to the minister, an' he, for his pairt, hardly kenned what he was lookin' at. Syne she turned round, an' shawed her face; Mr. Soulis had the same cauld grue as twice that day afore, an' it was borne in upon him what folk said, that Janet was deid lang syne, an' this was a bogle in her clay-cauld flesh. He drew back a pickle and he scanned her narrowly. She was tramp-trampin' in the cla'es croonin' to hersel'; and eh! Gude guide us, but it was a fearsome face. Whiles she sang louder, but there was nae man born o' woman that could tell the words o' her sang; an' whiles she lookit side-lang doun, but there was naething there for her to look at. There gaed a scunner[1] through the flesh upon his banes; an' that was Heeven's advertisement. But Mr. Soulis just blamed himsel', he said, to think sae ill o' a puir, auld afflicted wife that hadna a freend forbye himsel'; an' he put up a bit prayer for him an' her, an' drank a little caller water—for his heart rose again' the meat—an' gaed up to his naked bed in the gloamin'.

That was a nicht that has never been forgotten in Ba'weary, the nicht o' the seeventeenth o' August, seeventeen hun'er' an' twal'. It had been het afore, as I hae said, but that nicht it was hetter than ever. The sun gaed doun amang unco-lookin' clouds; it fell as mirk as the pit; no' a star, no' a breath o' wund; ye couldna see your han' afore your face, an' even the auld folk cuist the covers frae their beds an' lay pechin' for their breath. Wi' a' that he had upon his mind, it was gey an' unlikely Mr. Soulis wad get muckle sleep. He lay an' he tummled; the gude, caller bed that he got into brunt his very banes; whiles he slept, an' whiles he waukened; whiles he heard the time o' nicht, an' whiles a tyke yowlin' up the muir, as if somebody was deid; whiles he thocht he heard bogles claverin' in his lug,[2] an' whiles he saw spunkies[3] in the room. He behoved, he judged, to be sick; an' sick he was—little he jaloosed the sickness.

At the hinder end, he got a clearness in his mind, sat up in his sark on the bed-side, an' fell thinkin' ance mair o' the black man an' Janet. He couldna weel tell how—maybe it was the cauld to his feet—but it cam' in upon him wi' a spate that there was some connection between thir twa, an' that either or baith o' them were bogles. An' just at that moment, in Janet's room, which was neist to his, there cam' a stramp o' feet as if men were wars'lin', an' then a loud bang; an' then a wund gaed reishling round the fower quarters o' the house; an' then a' was ance mair as seelent as the grave.

Mr. Soulis was feared for neither man nor de'il. He got his tinder-box, an' lit a can'le, an' made three steps o't ower to Janet's door. It was on the hasp, an' he pushed it open, an' keeked bauldly in. It was a big room, as big as the minister's ain, an' plenished wi' grand, auld solid gear, for he had naething else. There was a fower-posted bed wi' auld tapestry; an' a braw cabinet o' aik, that was fu' o' the minister's divinity books, an' put there to be out o' the gate; an' a wheen[4] duds o' Janet's lying here an' there about the floor. But nae Janet could Mr. Soulis see; nor ony sign o' a contention. In he gaed (an' there's few that wad hae followed him) an' lookit a' round, an' listened. But there was naething to be heard, neither inside the manse nor in a' Ba'weary parish, an' naething to be seen but the muckle shadows turnin' round the can'le. An' then, a' at aince, the minister's heart played dunt an' stood stock-still;

[1] Disgust ("shiver").

[2] Ear.

[3] Fireflies.

[4] Few.

an' a cauld wund blew amang the hairs o' his heid. Whaten a weary sicht was that for the puir man's e'en! For there was Janet hangin' frae a nail beside the auld aik cabinet: her heid aye lay on her shouther, her e'en were steekit, the tongue projected frae her mouth, an' her heels were twa feet clear abune the floor.

"God forgive us all" thocht Mr. Soulis, "poor Janet's dead."

He cam' a step nearer to the corp; an' then his heart fair whammled in his inside. For by what cantrip[1] it wad ill beseem a man to judge, she was hangin' frae a single nail an' by a single wursted thread for darnin' hose.

It's a awfu' thing to be your lane at nicht wi' siccan prodigies o' darkness; but Mr. Soulis was strong in the Lord. He turned an' gaed his ways oot o' that room, an' lockit the door ahint him; an' step by step, doun the stairs, as heavy as leed; and set doun the can'le on the table at the stairfoot. He couldna pray, he couldna think, he was dreepin' wi' caul' swat, an' naething could he hear but the dunt-dunt-duntin' o' his ain heart. He micht maybe hae stood there an hour, or maybe twa, he minded sae little; when a' o' a sudden, he heard a laigh, uncanny steer up-stairs; a foot gaed to an' fro in the chalmer whaur the corp was hangin'; syne the door was opened, though he minded weel that he had lockit it; an' syne there was a step upon the landin', an' it seemed to him as if the corp was lookin' ower the rail and doun upon him whaur he stood.

He took up the can'le again (for he couldna want the licht), an' as saftly as ever he could, gaed straucht out o' the manse an' to the far end o' the causeway. It was aye pit-mirk; the flame o' the can'le, when he set it on the grund, brunt steedy and clear as in a room; naething moved, but the Dule water seepin' and sabbin' doun the glen, an' yon unhaly footstep that cam' ploddin' doun the stairs inside the manse. He kenned the foot ower weel, for it was Janet's; an' at ilka step that cam' a wee thing nearer, the cauld got deeper in his vitals. He commended his soul to Him that made an' keepit him; "and, O Lord," said he, "give me strength this night to war against the powers of evil."

By this time the foot was comin' through the passage for the door; he could hear a hand skirt alang the wa', as if the fearsome thing was feelin' for its way. The saughs[2] tossed an' maned thegither, a long sigh cam' ower the hills, the flame o' the can'le was blawn aboot; an' there stood the corp of Thrawn Janet, wi' her grogram goun an' her black mutch,[3] wi' the heid aye upon the shouther, an' the girn still upon the face o't— leevin', ye wad hae said—deid, as Mr. Soulis weel kenned—upon the threshold o' the manse.

It's a strange thing that the soul of man should be that thirled into his perishable body; but the minister saw that, an' his heart didna break.

She didna stand there lang; she began to move again an' cam' slowly towards Mr. Soulis whaur he stood under the saughs. A' the life o' his body, a' the strength o' his speerit, were glowerin' frae his e'en. It seemed she was gaun to speak, but wanted words, an' made a sign wi' the left hand. There cam' a clap o' wund, like a cat's fuff; oot gaed the can'le, the saughs skreighed like folk; an' Mr. Soulis kenned that, live or die, this was the end o't.

"Witch, beldame, devil!" he cried, "I charge you, by the power of God, begone if you be dead, to the grave—if you be damned, to hell."

An' at that moment the Lord's ain hand out o' the Heevens struck the Horror whaur it stood; the auld, deid, desecrated corp o' the witch-wife, sae lang keepit frae the grave and hirsled round by de'ils, lowed up like a brunstane spunk an' fell in

---

[1]Trick.

[2]Willows.

[3]Cap.

ashes to the grund; the thunder followed, peal on dirling peal, the rairin' rain upon the back o' that; and Mr. Soulis lowped through the garden hedge, an' ran, wi' skelloch upon skelloch, for the clachan.

That same mornin', John Christie saw the Black Man pass the Muckle Cairn as it was chappin' six; before eicht, he gaed by the changehouse at Knockdow; an' no' lang after, Sandy M'Lellan saw him gaun linkin' doun the braes frae Kilmackerlie. There's little doubt but it was him that dwalled sae lang in Janet's body; but he was awa' at last; an' sinsyne the de'il has never fashed[1] us in Ba'weary.

But it was a sair dispensation for the minister; lang, lang he lay ravin' in his bed; an' frae that hour to this, he was the man ye ken the day.

## Dr. Jekyll and Mr. Hyde

[Louis Stevenson's "shilling shocker" appeared in 1886 and was instantly successful. Its thesis—that every man is many men, that each of us contains the potential for both good and evil—is one of Stevenson's major themes. We see it in almost all of his novels. It is also a major preoccupation in Scottish literature in general, the other great example of it being James Hogg's brilliant anti-Calvinist novel, *Confessions of a Justified Sinner.*

The original of Stevenson's Dr. Jekyll is usually agreed to be Deacon Brodie, a respectable eighteenth century Edinburgh cabinet maker who led a gang of housebreakers on the side, and who was eventually hanged for his nocturnal activities. Stevenson had collaborated with the English poet Earnest Henley upon an unsuccessful stage version of Brodie's story. Now he transferred the tale to London (still very recognizably Edinburgh) and universalized the experience. The story has become one of the seminal myths of Western literature.

(Another splendid Scottish contribution to the Brodie story and the theme of the bifurcated man is Muriel Spark's brilliant novel, *The Prime of Miss Jean Brodie* [1961]. In this work, perhaps the most successful Scottish novel of our generation, an Edinburgh schoolteacher, a direct descendant of Deacon Brodie, as she proudly informs her charges, displays simultaneously almost every conceivable contradiction in the Scottish national character.)]

### *Story of the Door*

Mr. Utterson the lawyer was a man of a rugged countenance that was never lighted by a smile; cold, scanty and embarrassed in discourse; backward in sentiment; lean, long, dusty, dreary and yet somehow lovable. At friendly meetings, and when the wine was to his taste, something eminently human beaconed from his eye; something indeed which never found its way into his talk, but which spoke not only in these silent symbols of the after-dinner face, but more often and loudly in the acts of his life. He was austere with himself; drank gin when he was alone, to mortify a taste for vintages; and though he enjoyed the theater, had not crossed the doors of one for twenty years. But he had an approved tolerance for others; sometimes wondering, almost with envy, at the high pressure of spirits involved in their misdeeds; and in any extremity inclined to help rather than to reprove. "I incline to Cain's heresy," he used to say quaintly: "I let my brother go to the devil in his own way." In this character, it was frequently his fortune to be the last reputable acquaintance and the last good influence in the lives of downgoing men. And to such as these, so long as they came about his chambers, he never marked a shade of change in his demeanor.

---

[1]Troubled.

No doubt the feat was easy to Mr. Utterson; for he was undemonstrative at the best, and even his friendship seemed to be founded in a similar catholicity of good nature. It is the mark of a modest man to accept his friendly circle ready-made from the hands of opportunity; and that was the lawyer's way. His friends were those of his own blood or those whom he had known the longest; his affections, like ivy, were the growth of time, they implied no aptness in the object. Hence, no doubt, the bond that united him to Mr. Richard Enfield, his distant kinsman, the well-known man about town. It was a nut to crack for many, what these two could see in each other, or what subject they could find in common. It was reported by those who encountered them in their Sunday walks, that they said nothing, looked singularly dull, and would hail with obvious relief the appearance of a friend. For all that, the two men put the greatest store by these excursions, counted them the chief jewel of each week, and not only set aside occasions of pleasure, but even resisted the calls of business, that they might enjoy them uninterrupted.

It chanced on one of these rambles that their way led them down a by-street in a busy quarter of London. The street was small and what is called quiet, but it drove a thriving trade on the week-days. The inhabitants were all doing well, it seemed, and all emulously hoping to do better still, and laying out the surplus of their gains in coquetry; so that the shop fronts stood along that thoroughfare with an air of invitation, like rows of smiling saleswomen. Even on Sunday, when it veiled its more florid charms and lay comparatively empty of passage, the street shone out in contrast to its dingy neighborhood, like a fire in a forest; and with its freshly painted shutters, well-polished brasses, and general cleanliness and gaiety of note, instantly caught and pleased the eye of the passenger.

Two doors from one corner, on the left hand going east, the line was broken by the entry of a court; and just at that point, a certain sinister block of building thrust forward its gable on the street. It was two storeys high; showed no window, nothing but a door on the lower storey and a blind forehead of discolored wall on the upper; and bore in every feature, the marks of prolonged and sordid negligence. The door, which was equipped with neither bell nor knocker, was blistered and distained. Tramps slouched into the recess and struck matches on the panels; children kept shop upon the steps; the schoolboy had tried his knife on the moldings; and for close on a generation, no one had appeared to drive away these random visitors or to repair their ravages.

Mr. Enfield and the lawyer were on the other side of the by-street; but when they came abreast of the entry, the former lifted up his cane and pointed.

"Did you ever remark that door," he asked; and when his companion had replied in the affirmative, "It is connected in my mind," added he, "with a very odd story."

"Indeed?" said Mr. Utterson, with a slight change of voice, "and what was that?"

"Well, it was this way," returned Mr. Enfield: "I was coming home from some place at the end of the world, about three o'clock of a black winter morning, and my way lay through a part of town where there was literally nothing to be seen but lamps. Street after street, and all the folks asleep—street after street, all lighted up as if for a procession and all as empty as a church—till at last I got into that state of mind when a man listens and listens and begins to long for the sight of a policeman. All at once, I saw two figures: one a little man who was stumping along eastwards at a good walk, and the other a girl of maybe eight or ten was running as hard as she was able down a cross street. Well, sir, the two ran into one another naturally enough at the corner; and then came the horrible part of the thing; for the man trampled calmly over the child's body and left her screaming on the ground. It sounds nothing to hear, but it was hellish to see. It wasn't like a man; it was like some damned Juggernaut. I gave a view halloa, took to my heels, collared my gentleman, and brought him back to where there was already quite a group about the screaming child. He was perfectly cool and made no resistance, but gave me one look, so ugly that it brought out the sweat on me like running. The people who had turned out were the girl's own family; and pretty soon, the doctor, for whom she had been sent, put in his appearance. Well, the child was not much the worse, more frightened, according to the sawbones; and there you might have supposed would be an end to it. But there was one curious circumstance. I had taken a loathing to my gentleman at first sight. So had the child's family, which was only natural. But the doctor's case was what struck me. He was the usual cut and dry apothecary, of no particular age and color, with a strong Edinburgh accent, and about as emotional as a bagpipe. Well, sir, he was like the rest of us; every time he looked at my prisoner, I saw that sawbones turn sick and white with the desire to kill him, I knew what was in his mind, just as he knew what was in mine; and killing being out of the question, we did the next best. We told the man we could and would make such a scandal out of this, as should make his name stink from one end of London to the other. If he had any friends or any credit, we undertook that he should lose them.

"And all the time, as we were pitching it in red hot, we were keeping the women off him as best we could, for they were as wild as harpies. I never saw a circle of such hateful faces; and there was the man in the middle, with a kind of black, sneering coolness—frightened too, I could see that—but carrying it off, sir, really like Satan. 'If you choose to make capital out of this accident,' said he, 'I am naturally helpless. No gentleman but wishes to avoid a scene,' says he. 'Name your figure.' Well, we screwed him up to a hundred pounds for the child's family; he would have clearly liked to stick out; but there was something about the lot of us that meant mischief, and at last he struck.

"The next thing was to get the money; and where do you think he carried us but to that place with the door?—whipped out a key, went in, and presently came back with the matter of ten pounds in gold and a cheque for the balance on Coutts's, drawn payable to bearer and signed with a name that I can't mention, though it's one of the points of my story, but it was a name at least very well known and often printed. The figure was stiff; but the signature was good for more than that, if it was only genuine. I took the liberty of pointing out to my gentleman that the whole business looked apocryphal, and that a man does not, in real life, walk into a cellar door at four in the morning and come out of it with another man's cheque for close upon a hundred pounds. But he was quite easy and sneering. 'Set your mind at rest,' says he, 'I will stay with you till the banks open and cash the cheque myself.' So we all set off, the doctor, and the child's father, and our friend and myself, and passed the rest of the night in my chambers—and next day, when we had breakfasted, went in a body to the bank. I gave in the cheque myself, and said I had every reason to believe it was a forgery. Not a bit of it. The cheque was genuine."

"Tut-tut," said Mr. Utterson.

"I see you feel as I do," said Mr. Enfield. "Yes, it's a bad story. For my man was a fellow that nobody could have to do with, a really damnable man; and the person that drew the cheque is the very pink of the proprieties, celebrated too, and (what makes it worse) one of your fellows who do what they call good. Blackmail, I suppose; an honest man paying through the nose for some of the capers of his youth. Blackmail House is what I call that place with the door, in consequence. Though even that, you know, is far from explaining all," he added, and with the words fell into a vein of musing.

From this he was recalled by Mr. Utterson asking rather suddenly: "And you don't know if the drawer of the cheque lives there?"

"A likely place, isn't it," returned Mr. Enfield. "But I happen to have noticed his address; he lives in some square or another."

"And you never asked about the—place with the door," said Mr. Utterson.

"No, sir: I had a delicacy," was the reply. "I feel very strongly about putting questions; it partakes too much of the style of the day of judgment. You start a question, and it's like starting a stone. You sit quietly on the top of a hill; and away the stone goes, starting others; and presently some bland old bird (the last you would have thought of) is knocked on the head in his own back garden and the family have to change their name. No sir, I make it a rule of mine: the more it looks like Queer Street, the less I ask."

"A very good rule, too," said the lawyer.

"But I have studied the place for myself," continued Mr. Enfield. "It seems scarcely a house. There is no other door, and nobody goes in or out of that one but, once in a great while, the gentleman of my adventure. There are three windows looking on the court on the first floor; none below; the windows are always shut but they're clean. And then there is a chimney which is generally smoking; so somebody must live there. And yet it's not so sure; for the buildings are so packed together about the court, that it's hard to say where one ends and another begins."

The pair walked on again for a while in silence; and then "Enfield," said Mr. Utterson, "that's a good rule of yours."

"Yes, I think it is," returned Enfield.

"But for all that," continued the lawyer, "there's one point I want to ask: I want to ask the name of that man who walked over the child."

"Well," said Mr. Enfield, "I can't see what harm it would do. It was a man of the name of Hyde."

"Hm," said Mr. Utterson. "What sort of a man is he to see?"

"He is not easy to describe. There is something wrong with his appearance; something displeasing, something down-right detestable. I never saw a man I so disliked, and yet I scarce know why. He must be deformed somewhere; he gives a strong feeling of deformity, although I couldn't specify the point. He's an extraordinary looking man, and yet I really can name nothing out of the way. No, sir; I can make no hand of it; I can't describe him. And it's not want of memory; for I declare I can see him this moment."

Mr. Utterson again walked some way in silence and obviously under a weight of consideration. "You are sure he used a key?" he inquired at last.

"My dear sir . . ." began Enfield, surprised out of himself.

"Yes, I know," said Utterson; "I know it must seem strange. The fact is, if I do not ask you the name of the other party, it is because I know it already. You see, Richard, your tale has gone home. If you have been inexact in any point, you had better correct it."

"I think you might have warned me," returned the other with a touch of sullenness. "But I have been pedantically exact, as you call it. The fellow had a key, and what's more, he has it still. I saw him use it, not a week ago."

Mr. Utterson sighed deeply but said never a word; and the young man presently resumed. "Here is another lesson to say nothing," said he. "I am ashamed of my long tongue. Let us make a bargain never to refer to this again."

"With all my heart," said the lawyer. "I shake hands on that, Richard."

### *Search for Mr. Hyde*

That evening Mr. Utterson came home to his bachelor house in somber spirits and sat down to dinner without relish. It was his custom of a Sunday, when this meal was over, to sit close by the fire, a volume of some dry divinity on his reading desk, until the clock of the neighboring church rang out the hour of twelve, when he would go soberly and gratefully to bed. On this night, however, as soon as the cloth was taken away, he took up a candle and went into his business room. There he opened his safe, took from the most private part of it a document endorsed on the envelope as Dr. Jekyll's Will, and sat down with a clouded brow to study its contents. The will was holograph, for Mr. Utterson, though he took charge of it now that it was made, had refused to lend the least assistance in the making of it; it provided not only that, in case of the decease of Henry Jekyll, M.D., D.C.L., L.L.D., F.R.S., etc., all his possessions were to pass into the hands of his "friend and benefactor Edward Hyde," but that in case of Dr. Jekyll's "disappearance or unexplained absence for any period exceeding three calendar months," the said Edward Hyde should step into the said Henry Jekyll's shoes without further delay and free from any burthen or obligation, beyond the payment of a few small sums to the members of the doctor's household.

This document had long been the lawyer's eyesore. It offended him both as a lawyer and as a lover of the sane and customary sides of life, to whom the fanciful was the immodest. And hitherto it was his ignorance of Mr. Hyde that had swelled his indignation: now, by a sudden turn, it was his knowledge. It was already bad enough when the name was but a name of which he could learn no more. It was worse when it began to be clothed upon with detestable attributes; and out of the shifting, insubstantial mists that had no long baffled his eye, there leaped up the sudden, definite presentment of a fiend.

"I thought it was madness," he said, as he replaced the obnoxious paper in the safe, "and now I begin to fear it disgrace."

With that he blew out his candle, put on a greatcoat and set forth in the direction of Cavendish Square, that citadel of medicine, where his friend, the great Dr. Lanyon, had his house and received his crowding patients. "If anyone knows, it will be Lanyon," he had thought.

The solemn butler knew and welcomed him; he was subjected to no stage of delay, but ushered direct from the door to the dining-room where Dr. Lanyon sat alone over his wine. This was a hearty, healthy, dapper, red-faced gentleman, with a shock of hair prematurely white, and a boisterous and decided manner. At sight of Mr. Utterson, he sprang up from his chair and welcomed him with both hands. The geniality, as was the way of the man, was somewhat theatrical to the eye; but it reposed on genuine feeling. For these two were old friends, old mates both at school and college, both thorough respectors of themselves and of each other, and what does not always follow, men who thoroughly enjoyed each other's company.

After a little rambling talk, the lawyer led up to the subject which so disagreeably preoccupied his mind.

"I suppose, Lanyon," said he, "you and I must be the two oldest friends that Henry Jekyll has?"

"I wish the friends were younger," chuckled Dr. Lanyon. "But I suppose we are. And what of that? I see little of him now."

"Indeed?" said Utterson. "I thought you had a bond of common interest."

"We had," was the reply. "But it is more than ten years since Henry Jekyll became too fanciful for me. He began to go wrong, wrong in mind; and though of course I continue to take an interest in him for old sake's sake, as they say, I see and I have seen devilish little of the man. Such unscientific balderdash," added the doctor, flushing suddenly purple, "would have estranged Damon and Pythias."

This little spirit of temper was somewhat of a relief to Mr. Utterson. "They have only differed on some point of science," he thought; and being a man of no scientific passions (except in the matter of conveyancing), he even added: "It is nothing worse than that." He gave his friend a few seconds to recover his composure, and then approached the question he had come to put. "Did you ever come across a protégé of his—one Hyde?" he asked.

"Hyde?" repeated Lanyon. "No. Never heard of him. Since my time."

That was the amount of information that the lawyer carried back with him to the great, dark bed on which he tossed to and fro, until the small hours of the morning began to grow large. It was a night of little ease to his toiling mind, toiling in mere darkness and besieged by questions

Six o'clock struck on the bells of the church that was so conveniently near to Mr. Utterson's dwelling. and still he was digging at the problem. Hitherto it had touched him on the intellectual side alone; but now his imagination was also engaged, or rather enslaved; and as he lay and tossed in the gross darkness of the night and the curtained room Mr. Enfield's tale went by before his mind in a scroll of lighted pictures. He would be aware of the great field of lamps of a nocturnal city; then of the figure of a man walking swiftly; then of a child running from the doctor's and then these met, and that human Juggernaut trod the child down and passed on regardless of her screams. Or else he would see a room in a rich house, where his friend lay asleep, dreaming and smiling at his dreams; and then the door of that room would be opened, the curtains of the bed plucked apart, the sleeper recalled, and lo! there would stand by his side a figure to whom power was given, and even at that dead hour, he must rise and do its bidding.

The figure in these two phases haunted the lawyer all night; and if at any time he dozed over, it was but to see it glide more stealthily through sleeping houses, or move the more swiftly and still the more swiftly, even to dizziness, through wider labyrinths of lamp-lighted city, and at every street corner crush a child and leave her screaming. And still the figure had no face by which he might know it; even in his dreams, it had no face, or one that baffled him and melted before his eyes; and thus it was that there sprang up and grew apace in the lawyer's mind a singularly strong, almost an inordinate, curiosity to behold the features of the real Mr. Hyde.

If he could but once set eyes on him, he thought the mystery would lighten and perhaps roll altogether away, as was the habit of mysterious things when well examined. He might see a reason for his friend's strange preference or bondage (call it which you please) and even for the startling clause of the will. At least it would be a face worth seeing: the face of a man who was without bowels of mercy: a face which had but to show itself to raise up, in the mind of the unimpressionable Enfield, a spirit of enduring hatred.

From that time forward, Mr. Utterson began to haunt the door in the by-street of shops. In the morning before office hours, at noon when business was plenty, and time scarce, at night under the face of the fogged city moon, by all lights and at all hours of solitude or concourse, the lawyer was to be found on his chosen post.

"If he be Mr. Hyde," he had thought, "I shall be Mr. Seek."

And at last his patience was rewarded. It was a fine dry night; frost in the air; the streets as clean as a ballroom floor; the lamps, unshaken by any wind, drawing a regular pattern of light and shadow. By ten o'clock, when the shops were closed, the by-street was very solitary and, in spite of the low growl of London from all round, very silent. Small sounds carried far; domestic sounds out of the houses were clearly audible on either side of the roadway; and the rumor of the approach of any passenger preceded him by a long time. Mr. Utterson had been some minutes at his post, when he was aware of an odd, light footstep drawing near. In the course of his nightly patrols, he had long grown accustomed to the quaint effect with which the footfalls of a single person, while he is still a great way off, suddenly spring out distinct from the vast hum and clatter of the city. Yet his attention had never before been so sharply and decisively arrested, and it was with a strong, superstitious prevision of success that he withdrew into the entry of the court.

The steps drew swiftly nearer, and swelled out suddenly louder as they turned the end of the street. The lawyer, looking forth from the entry, could soon see what manner of man he had to deal with. He was small and very plainly dressed, and the look of him, even at that distance, went somehow strongly against the watcher's inclination. But he made straight for the door, crossing the roadway to save time; and as he came, he drew a key from his pocket like one approaching home.

Mr. Utterson stepped out and touched him on the shoulder as he passed. "Mr. Hyde, I think."

Mr. Hyde shrank back with a hissing intake of the breath. But his fear was only momentary; and though he did not look the lawyer in the face, he answered coolly enough: "That is my name. What do you want?"

"I see you are going in," returned the lawyer. "I am an old friend of Dr. Jekyll's—Mr. Utterson of Gaunt Street—you must have heard of my name; and meeting you so conveniently, I thought you might admit me."

"You will not find Dr. Jekyll; he is from home," replied Mr. Hyde, blowing in the key. And then suddenly, but still without looking up, "How did you know me?" he asked.

"On your side," said Mr. Utterson, "will you do me a favor?"

"With pleasure," replied the other. "What shall it be?"

"Will you let me see your face?" asked the lawyer.

Mr. Hyde appeared to hesitate, and then, as if upon some sudden reflection, fronted about with an air of defiance—and the pair stared at each other pretty fixedly for a few seconds. "Now I shall know you again," said Mr. Utterson. "It may be useful."

"Yes," returned Mr. Hyde, "it is as well we have met; and *a propos,* you should have my address." And he gave a number of a street in Soho.

"Good God!" thought Mr. Utterson, "can he, too, have been thinking of the will?" But he kept his feelings to himself and only grunted in acknowledgment of the address.

"And now," said the other, "how did you know me?"

"By description," was the reply.

"Whose description?"

"We have common friends," said Mr. Utterson.

"Common friends" echoed Mr. Hyde, a little hoarsely. "Who are they?"

"Jekyll, for instance," said the lawyer.

"He never told you," cried Mr. Hyde, with a flush of anger. "I did not think you would have lied."

"Come," said Mr. Utterson, "that is not fitting language."

The other snarled aloud into a savage laugh; and the next moment with extraordinary quickness, he had unlocked the door and disappeared into the house.

The lawyer stood awhile when Mr. Hyde had left him, the picture of disquietude. Then he began slowly to mount the street, pausing every step or two and putting his hand to his brow like a man in mental perplexity. The problem he was thus debating as he walked, was one of a class that is rarely solved. Mr. Hyde was pale and dwarfish, he gave an impression of deformity without any nameable malformation, he had a displeasing smile, he had borne himself to the lawyer with a sort of murderous mixture of timidity and boldness, and he spoke with a husky, whispering and somewhat broken voice; all these were points against him, but not all of these together could explain the hitherto unknown disgust, loathing and fear with which Mr. Utterson regarded him. "There must be something else," said the perplexed gentleman. "There *is* something more, if I could find a name for it. God bless me, the man seems hardly human. Something troglodytic, shall we say? or can it be the old story of Dr. Fell? or is it the mere radiance of a foul soul that thus transpires through, and transfigures, its clay continent? The last I think; for, O my poor old Harry Jekyll, if ever I read Satan's signature upon a face, it is on that of your new friend."

Round the corner from the by-street, there was a square of ancient, handsome houses, now for the most part decayed from their high estate and let in flats and chambers to all sorts and conditions of men; map-engravers, architects, shady lawyers and the agents of obscure enterprises. One house, however, second from the corner, was still occupied entire; and at the door of this, which wore a great air of wealth and comfort, though it was now plunged in darkness except for the fanlight, Mr. Utterson stopped and knocked. A well-dressed, elderly servant opened the door.

"Is Dr. Jekyll at home, Poole?" asked the lawyer.

"I will see, Mr. Utterson," said Poole, admitting the visitor, as he spoke, into a large, low-roofed, comfortable hall, paved with flags, warmed (after the fashion of a country house) by a bright, open fire, and furnished with costly cabinets of oak. "Will you wait here by the fire, sir? or shall I give you a light in the dining-room?"

"Here, thank you," said the lawyer, and he drew near and leaned on the tall fender. This hall, in which he was now left alone, was a pet fancy of his friend the doctor's; and Utterson himself was wont to speak of it as the pleasantest room in London. But tonight there was a shudder in his blood; the face of Hyde sat heavy on his memory; he felt (what was rare with him) a nausea and distaste of life; and in the gloom of his spirits, he seemed to read a menace in the flickering of the firelight on the polished cabinets and the uneasy starting of the shadow on the roof. He was ashamed of his relief, when Poole presently returned to announce that Dr. Jekyll was gone out.

"I saw Mr. Hyde go in by the old dissecting-room door, Poole," he said. "Is that right, when Dr. Jekyll is from home?"

"Quite right, Mr. Utterson, sir," replied the servant. "Mr. Hyde has a key."

"Your master seems to repose a great deal of trust in that young man, Poole," resumed the other musingly.

"Yes, sir, he do indeed," said Poole. "We have all orders to obey him."

"I do not think I ever met Mr. Hyde?" asked Utterson.

"O, dear no, sir. He never *dines* here," replied the butler. "Indeed we see very little of him on this side of the house; he mostly comes and goes by the laboratory."

"Well, good-night, Poole."

"Good-night, Mr. Utterson."

And the lawyer set out homeward with a very heavy heart. "Poor Harry Jekyll," he thought, "my mind misgives me he is in deep waters! He was wild when he was young; a long while ago to be sure; but in the law of God, there is no statute of limitations. Ay, it must be that; the ghost of some old sin, the cancer of some concealed disgrace: punishment coming, *pede claudo,* years after memory has forgotten and self-love condoned the fault."

And the lawyer, scared by the thought, brooded awhile on his own past, groping in all the corners of memory, lest by chance some Jack-in-the-Box of an old iniquity should leap to light there. His past was fairly blameless; few men could read the rolls of their life with less apprehension; yet he was humbled to the dust by the many ill things he had done, and raised up again into a sober and fearful gratitude by the many that he had come so near to doing, yet avoided. And then by a return on his former subject, he conceived a spark of hope. "This Master Hyde, if he were studied," thought he, "must have secrets of his own; black secrets, by the look of him; secrets compared to which poor Jekyll's worst would be like sunshine. Things cannot continue as they are. It turns me cold to think of this creature stealing like a thief to Harry's bedside; poor Harry, what a wakening. And the danger of it; for if this Hyde suspects the existence of the will, he may grow impatient to inherit. Ah, I must put my shoulders to the wheel—if Jekyll will but let me," he added, "if Jekyll will only let me." For once more he saw before his mind's eye, as clear as a transparency, the strange clauses of the will.

*Dr. Jekyll Was Quite at Ease*

A fortnight later, by excellent good fortune, the doctor gave one of his pleasant dinners to some five or six old cronies, all intelligent, reputable men and all judges of good wine; and Mr. Utterson so contrived that he remained behind after the others had departed. This was no new arrangement, but a thing that had befallen many scores of times. Where Utterson was liked, he was liked well. Hosts loved to detain the dry lawyer, when the lighthearted and loose-tongued had already their foot on the threshold; they liked to sit awhile in his unobtrusive company, practicing for solitude, sobering their minds in the man's rich silence after the expense and strain of gaiety. To this rule, Dr. Jekyll was no exception; and as he now sat on the opposite side of the fire, a large, well-made, smooth-faced man of fifty, with something of a slyish cast perhaps, but every mark of capacity and kindness—you could see by his looks that he cherished for Mr. Utterson a sincere and warm affection.

"I have been wanting to speak to you, Jekyll," began the latter. "You know that will of yours?"

A close observer might have gathered that the topic was distasteful; but the doctor carried it off gaily. "My poor Utterson," said he, "you are unfortunate in such a client. I never saw a man so distressed as you were by my will; unless it were that hide-bound pedant, Lanyon, at what he called my scientific heresies. Oh, I know he's a good fellow—you needn't frown—an excellent fellow, and I always mean to see more of him; but a hide-bound pedant for all that; an ignorant, blatant pedant. I was never more disappointed in any man than Lanyon."

"You know I never approved of it," pursued Utterson, ruthlessly disregarding the fresh topic.

"My will? Yes, certainly, I know that," said the doctor, a trifle sharply. "You have told me so."

"Well, I tell you so again," continued the lawyer. "I have been learning something of young Hyde."

The large handsome face of Dr. Jekyll grew pale to the very lips, and there came a blackness about his eyes. "I do not care to hear more," said he. "This is a matter I thought we had agreed to drop."

"What I heard was abominable," said Utterson.

"It can make no change. You do not understand my position," returned the doctor, with a certain incoherency of manner. "I am painfully situated, Utterson; my position is a very strange one—a very strange one. It is one of those affairs that cannot be mended by talking."

"Jekyll," said Utterson, "you know me: I am a man to be trusted. Make a clean breast of this in confidence—and I make no doubt I can get you out of it."

"My good Utterson," said the doctor, "this is very good of you, this is downright good of you, and I cannot find words to thank you in. I believe you fully; I would trust you before any man alive, ay, before myself, if I could make the choice; but indeed it isn't what you fancy; it is not so bad as that; and just to put your good heart at rest, I will tell you one thing: the moment I choose, I can be rid of Mr. Hyde. I give you my hand upon that; and I thank you again and again; and I will just add one little word, Utterson, that I'm sure you'll take in good part: this is a private matter, and I beg of you to let it sleep."

Utterson reflected a little, looking in the fire.

"I have no doubt you are perfectly right," he said at last, getting to his feet.

"Well, but since we have touched upon this business and for the last time I hope," continued the doctor, "there is one point I should like you to understand. I have really a very great interest in poor Hyde. I know you have seen him; he told me so; and I fear he was rude. But I do sincerely take a great, a very great interest in that young man; and if I am taken away, Utterson, I wish you to promise me that you will bear with him and get his rights for him. I think you would, if you knew all: and it would be a weight off my mind if you would promise."

"I can't pretend that I shall ever like him," said the lawyer.

"I don't ask that," pleaded Jekyll, laying his hand upon the other's arm; "I only ask for justice; I only ask you to help him for my sake, when I am no longer here."

Utterson heaved an irrepressible sigh. "Well," said he, "I promise."

*The Carew Murder Case*

Nearly a year later, in the month of October, 18—, London was startled by a crime of singular ferocity and rendered all the more notable by the high position of the victim. The details were few and startling. A maid servant living alone in a house not far from the river, had gone upstairs to bed about eleven. Although a fog rolled over the city in the small hours, the early part of the night was cloudless, and the lane, which the maid's window overlooked, was brilliantly lit by the full moon. It seems she was romantically given, for she sat down upon her box, which stood immediately under the window, and fell into a dream of musing. Never (she used to say, with streaming tears, when she narrated that experience), never had she felt more at peace with all men or thought more kindly of the world.

And as she so sat she became aware of an aged and beautiful gentleman with white hair, drawing near along the lane; and advancing to meet him, another and very small gentleman, to whom at first she paid less attention. When they had come within speech (which was just under the maid's eyes) the older man bowed and accosted the other with a very pretty manner of politeness. It did not seem as if the subject of his address were of great importance; indeed, from his pointing, it sometimes appeared as if he were only inquiring his way; but the moon shone on his face as he spoke, and the girl was pleased to watch it, it seemed to breathe such an innocent and old-world kindness of disposition, yet with something high too, as of a well-founded self-content.

Presently her eye wandered to the other, and she was surprised to recognize in him a certain Mr. Hyde, who had once visited her master and for whom she had conceived a dislike. He had in his hand a heavy cane, with which he was trifling; but he answered never a word, and seemed to listen with an ill-contained impatience. And then all of a sudden he broke out in a great flame of anger, stamping with his foot, brandishing the cane, and carrying on (as the maid described it) like a madman. The old gentleman took a step back, with the air of one very much surprised and a trifle hurt; and at that Mr. Hyde broke out of all bounds and clubbed him to the earth. And next moment, with ape-like fury, he was trampling his victim under foot and hailing down a storm of blows, under which the bones were audibly shattered and the body jumped upon the roadway. At the horror of these sights and sounds, the maid fainted.

It was two o'clock when she came to herself and called for the police. The murderer was gone long ago; but there lay his victim in the middle of the lane, incredibly mangled. The stick with which the deed had been done, although it was of some rare and very tough and heavy wood, had broken in the middle under the stress of this insensate cruelty; and one splintered half had rolled in the neighboring gutter—the other, without doubt, had been carried away by the murderer. A purse and a gold watch were found upon the victim: but no cards or papers, except a sealed and stamped envelope, which he had been probably carrying to the post, and which bore the name and address of Mr. Utterson.

This was brought to the lawyer the next morning, before he was out of bed; and he had no sooner seen it, and been told the circumstances, than he shot out a solemn lip. "I shall say nothing till I have seen the body," said he; "this may be very serious. Have the kindness to wait while I dress." And with the same grave countenance he hurried through his breakfast and drove to the police station, whither the body had been carried. As soon as he came into the cell, he nodded.

"Yes," said he, "I recognize him. I am sorry to say that this is Sir Danvers Carew."

"Good God, sir," exclaimed the officer, "is it possible?" And the next moment his eye lighted up with professional ambition. "This will make a deal of noise," he said. "And perhaps you can help us to the man." And he briefly narrated what the maid had seen, and showed the broken stick.

Mr. Utterson had already quailed at the name of Hyde; but when the stick was laid before him, he could doubt no longer; broken and battered as it was, he recognized it for one that he had himself presented many years before to Henry Jekyll.

"Is this Mr. Hyde a person of small stature?" he inquired.

"Particularly small and particularly wicked-looking, is what the maid calls him," said the officer.

Mr. Utterson reflected; and then, raising his head, "If you will come with me in my cab," he said, "I think I can take you to his house."

It was by this time about nine in the morning, and the first fog of the season. A great chocolate-colored pall lowered over heaven, but the wind was continually charging and routing these embattled vapors; so that as the cab crawled from street to street, Mr. Utterson beheld a marvelous number of degrees and hues of twilight; for here it would be dark like the backend of evening; and there would be a glow of a rich, lurid brown. like the light of some strange conflagration; and here, for a moment, the fog would be quite broken up, and a haggard shaft of daylight would glance in between the swirling wreaths. The dismal quarter of Soho seen under these changing glimpses, with its muddy ways, and slatternly passengers, and its lamps, which had never been extinguished or had been kindled afresh to combat this mournful reinvasion of darkness, seemed, in the lawyer's eyes, like a district of some city in a nightmare. The thoughts of his mind, besides. were of the gloomiest dye; and when he glanced at the companion of his drive, he was conscious of some touch of that terror of the law and the law's officers, which may at times assail the most honest.

As the cab drew up before the address indicated, the fog lifted a little and showed him a dingy street, a gin palace, a low French eating house, a shop for the retail of penny numbers and twopenny salads, many ragged children huddled in the doorways, and many women of many different nationalities passing out, key in band, to have a morning glass; and the next moment the fog settled down again upon that part, as brown as umber, and cut him off from his blackguardly surroundings. This was the home of Henry Jekyll's favorite; of a man who was heir to a quarter of a million sterling.

An ivory-faced and silvery-haired old woman opened the door. She had an evil face, smoothed by hypocrisy: but her manners were excellent. Yes, she said, this was Mr. Hyde's, but he was not at home; he had been in that night very late, but he had gone away again in less than an hour; there was nothing strange in that; his habits were very irregular, and he was often absent; for instance, it was nearly two months since she had seen him till yesterday.

"Very well, then, we wish to see his room," said the lawyer; and when the woman began to declare it was impossible, "I had better tell you who this person is," he added. "This is Inspector Newcomen of Scotland Yard."

A flash of odious joy appeared upon the woman's face.

"Ah!" said she, "he is in trouble. What has he done?"

Mr. Utterson and the inspector exchanged glances. "He don't seem a very popular character," observed the latter. "And now, my good woman, just let me and this gentleman have a look about us."

In the whole extent of the house, which but for the old woman remained otherwise empty, Mr. Hyde had only used a couple of rooms; but these were furnished with luxury and good taste. A closet was filled with wine; the plate was of silver, and napery elegant; a good picture hung upon the walls, a gift (as Utterson supposed) from Henry Jekyll who was much of a connoisseur; and the carpets were of many piles and agreeable in color. At this moment, however, the rooms bore every mark of having been recently and hurriedly ransacked; clothes lay about the floor, with their pockets inside out; lock-fast drawers stood open; and on the hearth there lay a pile of gray ashes, as though many papers had been burned. From these embers the inspector disinterred the butt end of a green cheque book, which had resisted the action of the fire; the other half of the stick was found behind the door; and as this clinched his suspicions, the officer declared himself delighted. A visit to the bank, where several thousand pounds were found to be lying to the murderer's credit, completed his gratification.

"You may depend upon it, sir." he told Mr. Utterson: "I have him in my hand. He must have lost his head, or he never would have left the stick or, above all, burned the cheque book. Why, money's life to the man. We have nothing to do but wait for him at the bank, and get out the handbills."

This last, however, was not so easy of accomplishment; for Mr. Hyde had numbered few familiars—even the master of the servant maid had only seen him twice; his family could nowhere be traced; he had never been photographed; and the few who could describe him differed widely, as common observers will. Only on one point were they agreed; and that was the haunting sense of unexpressed deformity with which the fugitive impressed his beholders.

### *Incident of the Letter*

It was late in the afternoon, when Mr. Utterson found his way to Dr. Jekyll's door, where he was at once admitted by Poole, and carried down by the kitchen offices and across a yard which had once been a garden, to the building which was indifferently known as the laboratory or the dissecting rooms. The doctor had bought the house from the heirs of a celebrated surgeon; and his own tastes being rather chemical than anatomical, had changed the destination of the block at the bottom of the garden. It was the first time that the lawyer had been received in that part of his friend's quarters; and he eyed the dingy, windowless structure with curiosity, and gazed round with a distasteful sense of strangeness as he crossed the theater, once crowded with eager students and now lying gaunt and silent, the tables laden with chemical apparatus, the floor strewn with crates and littered with packing straw, and the light falling dimly through the foggy cupola.

At the further end, a flight of stairs mounted to a door covered with red baize; and through this, Mr. Utterson was at last received into the doctor's cabinet. It was a large room fitted round with glass presses, furnished, among other things, with a cheval-glass and a business table, and looking out upon the court by three dusty windows barred with iron. The fire burned in the grate; a lamp was set lighted on the chimney shelf, for even in the houses the fog began to lie thickly; and there, close up to the warmth, sat Dr. Jekyll, looking deadly sick. He did not rise to meet his visitor, but held out a cold hand and bade him welcome in a changed voice.

"And now," said Mr. Utterson, as soon as Poole had left them, "you have heard the news?"

The doctor shuddered. "They were crying it in the square," he said. "I heard them in my dining-room."

"One word," said the lawyer. "Carew was my client, but so are you, and I want to know what I am doing. You have not been mad enough to hide this fellow?"

"Utterson, I swear to God," cried the doctor, "I swear to God I will never set eyes on him again. I bind my honor to you that I am done with him in this world. It is all at an end. And indeed he does not want my help; you do not know him as I do; he is safe, he is quite safe; mark my words, he will never more he heard of."

The lawyer listened gloomily; he did not like his friend's feverish manner.

"You seem pretty sure of him," said he; "and for your sake, I hope you may be right. If it came to a trial, your name might appear."

"I am quite sure of him," replied Jekyll; "I have grounds for certainty that I cannot share with anyone. But there is one thing on which you may advise me. I have received a letter; and I am at a loss whether I should show it to the police. I should like to leave it in your hands, Utterson; you would judge wisely, I am sure; I have so great a trust in you."

"You fear, I suppose, that it might lead to his detection?" asked the lawyer.

"No," said the other. "I cannot say that I care what becomes of Hyde; I am quite done with him. I was thinking of my own character, which this hateful business has rather exposed."

Utterson ruminated awhile; he was surprised at his friend's selfishness, and yet relieved by it. "Well," said he, at last, "let me see the letter."

The letter was written in an odd, upright hand and signed "Edward Hyde": and it signified, briefly enough, that the writer's benefactor, Dr. Jekyll, whom he had long so unworthily repaid for a thousand generosities, need labor under no qualm for his safety, as he had means of escape on which he placed a sure dependence. The lawyer liked this letter well enough; it put a better color on the intimacy than he had looked for; and he blamed himself for some of his past suspicions.

"Have you the envelope?" he asked.

"I burned it," replied Jekyll, "before I thought what I was about. But it bore no postmark. The note was handed in."

"Shall I keep this and sleep upon it?" asked Utterson.

"I wish you to judge for me entirely," was the reply. "I have lost confidence in myself."

"Well, I shall consider," returned the lawyer. "And now one word more: it was Hyde who dictated the terms in your will about that disappearance?"

The doctor seemed seized with a qualm of faintness; he shut his mouth tight and nodded.

"I knew it," said Utterson. "He meant to murder you. You had a fine escape."

"I have had what is far more to the purpose," returned the doctor solemnly: "I have had a lesson—O God, Utterson, what a lesson I have had!" And he covered his face for a moment with his hands.

On his way out, the lawyer stopped and had a word or two with Poole. "By the bye," said he, "there was a letter handed in today: what was the messenger like?" But Poole was positive nothing had come except by post; "and only circulars by that," he added.

This news sent off the visitor with his fears renewed. Plainly the letter had come by the laboratory door; possibly, indeed, it had been written in the cabinet; and if that were so, it must be differently judged, and handled with the more caution. The newsboys, as he went, were crying themselves hoarse along the footways: "Special edition. Shocking murder of an M.P." That was the funeral oration of one friend and client; and he could not help a certain apprehension lest the good name of another should be sucked down in the eddy of the scandal. It was, at least, a ticklish decision that he had to make; and self-reliant as he was by habit, he began to cherish a longing for advice. It was not to be had directly; but perhaps, he thought, it might be fished for.

Presently after, he sat on one side of his own hearth, with Mr. Guest, his head clerk, upon the other, and midway between, at a nicely calculated distance from the fire, a bottle of a particular old wine that had long dwelt unsunned in the foundations of his house. The fog still slept on the wing above the drowned city, where the lamps glimmered like carbuncles; and through the muffle and smother of these fallen clouds, the procession of the town's life was still rolling in through the great arteries with a sound as of a mighty wind. But the room was gay with firelight. In the bottle the acids were long ago resolved; the imperial dye had softened with time, as the color grows richer in stained windows; and the glow of hot autumn afternoons on hillside vineyards, was ready to be set free and to disperse the fogs of London.

Insensibly the lawyer melted. There was no man from whom he kept fewer secrets than Mr. Guest; and he was not always sure that he kept as many as he meant. Guest had often been on business to the doctors; he knew Poole; he could scarce have failed to hear of Mr. Hyde's familiarity about the house; he might draw conclusions: was it not as well, then, that he should see a letter which put that mystery to rights? and above all since Guest, being a great student and critic of handwriting, would consider the step natural and obliging? The clerk, besides, was a man of counsel; he would scarce read so strange a document without dropping a remark; and by that remark Mr. Utterson might shape his future course.

"This is a sad business about Sir Danvers," he said.

"Yes, sir, indeed. It has elicited a great deal of public feeling," returned Guest. "The man, of course, was mad."

"I should like to hear your views on that," replied Utterson. "I have a document here in his handwriting; it is between ourselves, for I scarce know what to do about it; it is an ugly business at the best. But there it is; quite in your way: a murderer's autograph."

Guest's eyes brightened, and he sat down at once and studied it with passion. "No sir," he said: "not mad; but it is an odd hand."

"And by all accounts a very odd writer," added the lawyer.

Just then the servant entered with a note.

"Is that from Dr. Jekyll, sir?" inquired the clerk. "I thought I knew the writing. Anything private, Mr. Utterson?"

"Only an invitation to dinner. Why? Do you want to see it?"

"One moment. I thank you, sir," and the clerk laid the two sheets of paper alongside and sedulously compared their contents. "Thank you, sir," he said at last, returning both; "it's a very interesting autograph."

There was a pause, during which Mr. Utterson struggled with himself. "Why did you compare them, Guest?" he inquired suddenly.

"Well, sir," returned the clerk, "there's a rather singular resemblance; the two hands are in many points identical: only differently sloped."

"Rather quaint," said Utterson.

"It is, as you say, rather quaint," returned Guest.

"I wouldn't speak of this note, you know," said the master.

"No, sir," said the clerk. "I understand."

But no sooner was Mr. Utterson alone that night, than he locked the note into his safe, where it reposed from that time forward. "What!" he thought. "Henry Jekyll forge for a murderer!" and his blood ran cold in his veins.

*Remarkable Incident of Dr. Lanyon*

Time ran on; thousands of pounds were offered in reward, for the death of Sir Danvers was resented as a public injury; but Mr. Hyde had disappeared out of the ken of the police as though he had never existed. Much of his past was unearthed, indeed, and all disreputable: tales came out of the man's cruelty, at once so callous and violent; of his vile life, of his strange associates, of the hatred that seemed to have surrounded his career, but of his present whereabouts, not a whisper. From the time he had left the house in Soho on the morning of the murder, he was simply blotted out; and gradually, as time drew on, Mr. Utterson began to recover from the hotness of his alarm, and to grow more at quiet with himself. The death of Sir Danvers was, to his way of thinking, more than paid for by the disappearance of Mr. Hyde.

Now that that evil influence had been withdrawn, a new life began for Dr. Jekyll. He came out of his seclusion, renewed relations with his friends, became once more their familiar guest and entertainer; and whilst he had always been known for charities, he was now no less distinguished for religion. He was busy, he was much in the open air, he did good; his face seemed to open and brighten, as if with an inward consciousness of service; and for more than two months, the doctor was at peace.

On the 8th of January Utterson had dined at the doctor's with a small party; Lanyon had been there; and the face of the host had looked from one to the other as in the old days when the trio were inseparable friends. On the 12th, and again on the 14th, the door was shut against the lawyer. "The doctor was confined to the house," Poole said, "and saw no one." On the 15th, he tried again, and was again refused; and having now been used for the last two months to see his friend almost daily, he found this return of solitude to weigh upon his spirits. The fifth night he had in Guest to dine with him; and the sixth he betook himself to Dr. Lanyon's.

There at least he was not denied admittance; but when he came in, he was shocked at the change which had taken place in the doctor's appearance. He had his death warrant written legibly upon his face. The rosy man had grown pale; his flesh had fallen away; he was visibly balder and older; and yet it was not so much these tokens of a swift physical decay that arrested the lawyer's notice, as a look in the eye and quality of manner that seemed to testify to some deep-seated terror of the mind. It was unlikely that the doctor should fear death; and yet that was what Utterson was tempted to suspect. "Yes," he thought; "he is a doctor, he must know his own state and that his days are counted; and the knowledge is more than he can bear." And yet when Utterson remarked on his ill-looks, it was with an air of great firmness that Lanyon declared himself a doomed man.

"I have had a shock," he said, "and I shall never recover. It is a question of weeks. Well, life has been pleasant; I liked it; yes, sir, I used to like it. I sometimes think if we knew all, we should be more glad to get away."

"Jekyll is ill, too," observed Utterson. "Have you seen him?"

But Lanyon's face changed, and he held up a trembling hand. "I wish to see or hear no more of Dr. Jekyll," he said in a loud, unsteady voice. "I am quite done with that person; and I beg that you will spare me any allusion to one whom I regard as dead."

"Tut-tut," said Mr. Utterson, and then after a considerable pause, "Can't I do anything?" he inquired. "We are three very old friends, Lanyon; we shall not live to make others."

"Nothing can be done," returned Lanyon; "ask himself."

"He will not see me," said the lawyer.

"I am not surprised at that," was the reply. "Some day, Utterson, after I am dead, you may perhaps come to learn the right and wrong of this. I cannot tell you. And in the meantime, if you can sit and talk with me of other things, for God's sake, stay and do so; but if you cannot keep clear of this accursed topic, then in God's name, go, for I cannot bear it."

As soon as he got home, Utterson sat down and wrote to Jekyll, complaining of his exclusion from the house, and asking the cause of this unhappy break with Lanyon; and the next day brought him a long answer, often very pathetically worded, and sometimes darkly mysterious in drift. The quarrel with Lanyon was incurable. "I do not blame our old friend," Jekyll wrote, "but I share his view that we must never meet. I mean from henceforth to lead a life of extreme seclusion; you must not be surprised, nor must you doubt my friendship, if my door is often shut even to you. You must suffer me to go my own dark way. I have brought on myself a punishment and a danger that I cannot name. If I am the chief of sinners, I am the chief of sufferers also. I could not think that this earth contained a place for sufferings and terrors so unmanning; and you can do but one thing, Utterson, to lighten this destiny, and that is to respect my silence."

Utterson was amazed; the dark influence of Hyde had been withdrawn, the doctor had returned to his old tasks and amities; a week ago, the prospect had smiled with every promise of a cheerful and an honored age; and now in a moment, friendship, and peace of mind, and the whole tenor of his life were wrecked. So great and unprepared a change pointed to madness; but in view of Lanyon's manner and words, there must lie for it some deeper ground.

A week afterwards Dr. Lanyon took to his bed, and in something less than a fortnight he was dead. The night after the funeral, at which he had been sadly affected, Utterson locked the door of his business room, and sitting there by the light of a melancholy candle, drew out and set before him an envelope addressed by the hand and sealed with the seal of his dead friend. "PRIVATE: for the hands of G.J. Utterson ALONE, and in case of his predecease to *be destroyed unread,"* So it was emphatically superscribed; and the lawyer dreaded to behold the contents. "I have buried one friend to-day," he thought: "what if this should cost me another?" And then he condemned the fear as a disloyalty, and broke the seal. Within there was another enclosure, likewise sealed, and marked upon the cover as "not to be opened till the death or disappearance of Dr. Henry Jekyll."

Utterson could not trust his eyes. Yes, it was disappearance; here again, as in the mad will which he had long ago restored to its author, here again were the idea of a disappearance and the name of Henry Jekyll bracketed. But in the will, that idea had sprung from the sinister suggestion of the man Hyde; it was set there with a purpose all too plain and horrible. Written by the hand of Lanyon, what should it mean? A great curiosity came on the trustee, to disregard the prohibition and dive at once to the bottom of these mysteries; but professional honor and faith to his dead friend were stringent obligations; and the packet slept in the inmost corner of his private safe.

It is one thing to mortify curiosity, another to conquer it; and it may be doubted if, from that day forth, Utterson desired the society of his surviving friend with the same eagerness. He thought of him kindly; but his thoughts were disquieted and fearful. He went to call indeed; but he was perhaps relieved to be denied admittance; perhaps, in his heart, he preferred to speak with Poole upon the doorstep and surrounded by the air and sounds of the open city, rather than to be admitted into that house of voluntary bondage, and to sit and speak with its inscrutable recluse. Poole had, indeed, no very pleasant news to communicate. The doctor, it appeared, now more than ever confined himself to the cabinet over the laboratory, where he would sometimes even sleep; he was out of spirits, he had grown very silent, he did not read; it seemed as if he had something on his mind. Utterson became so used to the unvarying character of these reports, that he fell off little by little in the frequency of his visits.

### *Incident at the Window*

It chanced on Sunday, when Mr. Utterson was on his usual walk with Mr. Enfield, that their way lay once again through the by-street; and that when they came in front of the door, both stopped to gaze on it.

"Well," said Enfield, "that story's at an end at least. We shall never see more of Mr. Hyde."

"I hope not," said Utterson. "Did I ever tell you that I once saw him, and shared your feeling of repulsion?"

"It was impossible to do the one without the other," returned Enfield. "And by the way, what an ass you must have thought me, not to know that this was a back way to Dr. Jekyll's! It was partly your own fault that I found it out, even when I did."

"So you found it out, did you?" said Utterson. "But if that be so, we may step into the court and take a look at the windows. To tell you the truth, I am uneasy about poor Jekyll, and even outside, I feel as if the presence of a friend might do him good."

The court was very cool and a little damp, and full of premature twilight, although the sky, high up overhead, was still bright with sunset. The middle one of the three windows was half-way open; and sitting close beside it, taking the air with an infinite sadness of mien, like some disconsolate prisoner, Utterson saw Dr. Jekyll.

"What! Jekyll," he cried. "I trust you are better."

"I am very low, Utterson," replied the doctor, drearily, "very low. It will not last long, thank God."

"You stay too much indoors," said the lawyer. "You should be out, whipping up the circulation like Mr. Enfield and me. (This is my cousin—Mr. Enfield—Dr. Jekyll.) Come now; get your hat and take a quick turn with us."

"You are very good," sighed the other. "I should like to very much; but no, no, no, it is quite impossible; I dare not. But indeed, Utterson, I am very glad to see you; this is really a great pleasure; I would ask you and Mr. Enfield up, but the place is really not fit."

"Why, then," said the lawyer, good-naturedly, "the best thing we can do is to stay down here and speak with you from where we are."

"That is just what I was about to venture to propose," returned the doctor with a smile. But the words were hardly uttered, before the smile was struck out of his face and succeeded by an expression of such abject terror and despair, as froze the very blood of the two gentlemen below. They saw it but for a glimpse for the window was instantly thrust down; but that glimpse had been sufficient, and they turned and left the court without a word. In silence, too, they traversed the by-street; and it was not until they had come into a neighboring thoroughfare, where even upon a Sunday there were still some stirrings of life, that Mr. Utterson at last turned and looked at his companion. They were both pale; and there was an answering horror in their eyes.

"God forgive us, God forgive us," said Mr. Utterson.

But Mr. Enfield only nodded his head very seriously, and walked on once more in silence.

### *The Last Night*

Mr. Utterson was sitting by his fireside one evening after dinner, when he was surprised to receive a visit from Poole.

"Bless me, Poole, what brings you here?" he cried; and then taking a second look at him, "What ails you?" he added, "is the doctor ill?"

"Mr. Utterson," said the man, "there is something wrong."

"Take a seat, and here is a glass of wine for you," said the lawyer. "Now, take your time, and tell me plainly what you want."

"You know the doctor's ways, sir," replied Poole, "and how he shuts himself up. Well, he's shut up again in the cabinet; and I don't like it, sir—I wish I may die if I like it. Mr. Utterson, sir, I'm afraid."

"Now, my good man," said the lawyer, "be explicit. What are you afraid of?"

"I've been afraid for about a week," returned Poole, doggedly disregarding the question, "and I can bear it no more."

The man's appearance amply bore out his words; his manner was altered for the worse; and except for the moment when he had first announced his terror, he had not once looked the lawyer in the face. Even now, he sat with the glass of wine untasted on his knee, and his eyes directed to a corner of the floor. "I can bear it no more," he repeated.

"Come," said the lawyer, "I see you have some good reason, Poole; I see there is something seriously amiss. Try to tell me what it is."

"I think there's been foul play," said Poole, hoarsely.

"Foul play!" cried the lawyer, a good deal frightened and rather inclined to be irritated in consequence. "What foul play? What does the man mean?"

"I daren't say, sir," was the answer; "but will you come along with me and see for yourself?"

Mr. Utterson's only answer was to rise and get his hat and greatcoat; but he observed with wonder the greatness of the relief that appeared upon the butler's face, and perhaps with no less, that the wine was still untasted when he set it down to follow.

It was a wild, cold, seasonable night of March, with a pale moon, lying on her back as though the wind had tilted her, and a flying wrack of the most diaphanous and lawny texture. The wind made talking difficult, and flecked the blood into the face. It seemed to have swept the streets unusually bare of passengers, besides; for Mr. Utterson thought he had never seen that part of London so deserted. He could have wished it otherwise; never in his life had he been conscious of so sharp a wish to see and touch his fellow-creatures; for struggle as he might, there was borne in upon his mind a crushing anticipation of calamity. The square, when they got there, was all full of wind and dust, and the thin trees in the garden were lashing themselves along the railing. Poole, who had kept all the way a pace or two ahead, now pulled up in the middle of the pavement, and in spite of the biting weather, took off his hat and mopped his brow with a red pocket handkerchief. But for all the hurry of his coming, these were not the dews of exertion that he wiped away, but the moisture of some strangling anguish; for his face was white and his voice, when he spoke, harsh and broken.

"Well, sir," he said, "here we are, and God grant there be nothing wrong."

"Amen, Poole," said the lawyer.

Thereupon the servant knocked in a very guarded manner; the door was opened on the chain; and a voice asked from within, "Is that you, Poole?"

"It's all right," said Poole. "Open the door."

The hall, when they entered it, was brightly lighted up; the fire was built high; and about the hearth the whole of the servants, men and women, stood huddled together like a flock of sheep. At the sight of Mr. Utterson, the housemaid broke into hysterical whimpering; and the cook, crying out "Bless God! it's Mr. Utterson," ran forward as if to take him in her arms.

"What, what? Are you all here?" said the lawyer peevishly. "Very irregular, very unseemly; your master would be far from pleased."

"They're all afraid," said Poole.

Blank silence followed, no one protesting; only the maid lifted up her voice and now wept loudly.

"Hold your tongue!" Poole said to her, with a ferocity of accent that testified to his own jangled nerves; and indeed, when the girl had so suddenly raised the note of her lamentation, they had all started and turned towards the inner door with faces of dreadful expectation. "And now," continued the butler, addressing the knife-boy, "reach me a candle, and we'll get this through hands at once." And then he begged Mr. Utterson to follow him, and led the way to the back garden.

"Now, sir," said he, "you come as gently as you can. I want you to hear, and I don't want you to be heard. And see here, sir, if by any chance he was to ask you in, don't go."

Mr. Utterson's nerves, at this unlooked-for-termination, gave a jerk that nearly threw him from his balance; but he recollected his courage and followed the butler into the laboratory building and through the surgical theater, with its lumber of crates and bottles, to the foot of the stair. Here Poole motioned him to stand on one side and listen; while he himself, setting down the candle and making a great and obvious call on his resolution, mounted the steps and knocked with a somewhat uncertain hand on the red baize of the cabinet door.

"Mr. Utterson, sir, asking to see you," he called; and even as he did so, once more violently signed to the lawyer to give ear.

A voice answered from within: "Tell him I cannot see anyone," it said complainingly.

"Thank you, sir," said Poole, with a note of something like triumph in his voice; and taking up his candle, he led Mr. Utterson back across the yard and into the great kitchen, where the fire was out and the beetles were leaping on the floor.

"Sir," he said, looking Mr. Utterson in the eyes, "was that my master's voice?"

"It seems much changed," replied the lawyer, very pale, but giving look for look.

"Changed? Well, yes, I think so," said the butler. "Have I been twenty years in this man's house, to be deceived about his voice? No, sir; master's made away with; he was made away with eight days ago, when we heard him cry out upon the name of God; and *who's* in there instead of him, and *why* it stays there, is a thing that cries to Heaven, Mr. Utterson."

"This is a very strange tale, Poole; this is rather a wild tale, my man," said Mr. Utterson, biting his finger. "Suppose it were as you suppose, supposing Dr. Jekyll to have been—well, murdered, what could induce the murderer to stay? That won't hold water; it doesn't commend itself to reason."

"Well, Mr. Utterson, you are a hard man to satisfy, but I'll do it yet," said Poole. "All this last week (you must know) him, or it, or whatever it is that lives in that cabinet, has been crying night and day for some sort of medicine and cannot get it to his mind. It was sometimes his way— the master's, that is—to write his orders on a sheet of paper and throw in on the stair. We've had nothing else this week back; nothing but papers, and a closed door, and the very meals left there to be smuggled in when nobody was looking. Well, sir, every day, ay, and twice and thrice in the same day, there have been orders and complaints, and I have been sent flying to all the wholesale chemists in town. Every time I brought the stuff back, there would be another paper telling me to return it, because it was not pure, and another order to a different firm. This drug is wanted bitter bad, sir, whatever for."

"Have you any of these papers?" asked Mr. Utterson.

Poole felt in his pocket and handed out a crumpled note, which the lawyer, bending nearer to the candle, carefully examined. Its contents ran thus: "Dr. Jekyll presents his compliments to Messrs. Maw. He assures them that their last sample is impure and quite useless for his present purpose. In the year 18—, Dr. J. purchased a somewhat large quantity from Messrs. M. He now begs them to search with the most sedulous care, and should any of the same quality be left, to forward it to him at once. Expense is no consideration. The importance of this to Dr. J. can hardly be exaggerated." So far the letter had run composedly enough, but here with a sudden splutter of the pen, the writer's emotion had broken loose. "For God's sake," he had added, "find me some of the old."

"This is a strange note," said Mr. Utterson; and then sharply, "How do you come to have it open?"

"The man at Maw's was main angry, sir, and he threw it back to me like so much dirt," returned Poole.

"This is unquestionably the doctor's hand, do you know?" resumed the lawyer.

"I thought it looked like it," said the servant rather sulkily; and then, with another voice, "But what matters hand of writer?" he said. "I've seen him!"

"Seen him?" repeated Mr. Utterson. "Well?"

"That's it!" said Poole. "It was this way. I came suddenly into the theater from the garden. It seems he had slipped out to look for this drug or whatever it is; for the cabinet door was open, and there he was at the far end the room digging among the crates. He looked up when I came in, gave a kind of cry, and whipped upstairs into the cabinet. It was but for one minute that I saw him, but the hair stood upon my head like quills. Sir, if that was my master why had he a mask upon his face? If it was my master why did he cry out like a rat, and run from me? I have served him long enough. And then—" The man paused and passed his hand over his face.

"These are all very strange circumstances," said Mr. Utterson, "but I think I begin to see daylight. Your master, Poole, is plainly seized with one of those maladies that both torture and deform the sufferer; hence, for aught I know, the alteration of his voice, hence the mask and his avoidance of his friends; hence his eagerness to find this drug, by means of which the poor soul retains some hope of ultimate recovery—God grant that he be not deceived! There is my explanation; it is sad enough, Poole, ay, and appalling to consider; but it is plain and natural, hangs well together, and delivers us from all exorbitant alarms."

"Sir," said the butler, turning to a sort of mottled pallor, "that thing was not my master, and there's the truth. My master"—here he looked round him and began to whisper—"is a tall, fine build of a man, and this was more of a dwarf." Utterson attempted to protest. "Oh, sir," cried Poole, "do you think I do not know my master after twenty years? Do you think I do not know where his head comes to in the cabinet door, where I saw him every morning of my life? No, sir, that thing in the mask was never Dr. Jekyll. God knows what it was, but it was never Dr. Jekyll; and it is the belief of my heart that there was murder done."

"Poole," replied the lawyer, "if you say that, it will become my duty to make certain. Much as I desire to spare your master's feelings, much as I am puzzled by this note which seems to prove him to be still alive, I shall consider it my duty to break in that door."

"Ah, Mr. Utterson, that's talking!" cried the butler.

"And now comes the second question," resumed Utterson: "Who is going to do it?"

"Why, you and me, sir," was the undaunted reply.

"That's very well said," returned the lawyer; "and whatever comes of it, I shall make it my business to see you are no loser."

"There is an ax in the theater," continued Poole; "and you might take the kitchen poker for yourself."

The lawyer took that rude but weighty instrument into his hand, and balanced it. "Do you know, Poole," he said, looking up, "that you and I are about to place ourselves in a position of some peril?"

"You may say so, sir, indeed," returned the butler.

"It is well, then, that we should be frank," said the other. "We both think more than we have said; let us make a clean breast. This masked figure that you saw, did you recognize it?"

"Well, sir, it went so quick, and the creature was so doubled up, that I could hardly swear to that," was the answer. "But if you mean, was it Mr. Hyde?—why, yes, I think it was. You see, it was much of the same bigness; and it had the same quick, light way with it; and then who else could have got in by the laboratory door? You have not forgot, sir, that at the time of the murder he had still the key with him? But that's not all. I don't know, Mr. Utterson, if you ever met this Mr. Hyde?"

"Yes," said the lawyer. "I once spoke with him."

"Then you must know as well as the rest of us that there was something queer about that gentleman—something that gave a man a turn—I don't know rightly how to say it, sir, beyond this: that you felt in your marrow kind of cold and thin."

"I own I felt something of what you describe," said Mr. Utterson.

"Quite so, sir," returned Poole. "Well, when that masked thing like a monkey jumped from among the chemicals and whipped into the cabinet, it went down my spine like ice. O, I know it's not evidence, Mr. Utterson, I'm book-learned enough for that; but a man has his feelings, and I give you my bible-word it was Mr. Hyde."

"Ay, ay," said the lawyer. "My fears incline to the same point. Evil, I fear, founded—evil was sure to come—of that connection. Ay truly, I believe you; I believe poor Harry is killed; and I believe his murderer (for what purpose, God alone can tell) is still lurking in his victim's room. Well, let our name be vengeance. Call Bradshaw."

The footman came at the summons, very white and nervous.

"Pull yourself together, Bradshaw," said the lawyer. "This suspense, I know, is telling upon all of you; but it is now our intention to make an end of it. Poole, here, and I are going to force our way into the cabinet. If all is well, my shoulders are broad enough to bear the blame. Meanwhile, lest anything should really be amiss, or any malefactor seek to escape by the back, you and the boy must go round the corner with a pair of good sticks and take your post at the laboratory door. We give you ten minutes, to get to your stations."

As Bradshaw left, the lawyer looked at his watch. "And now, Poole, let us get to ours," he said; and taking the poker under his arm, he led the way into the yard. The scud had banked over the moon, and it was now quite dark. The wind, which only broke in puffs and draughts into that deep well of building, tossed the light of the candle to and fro about their steps, until they came into the shelter of the theater, where they sat down silently to wait. London hummed solemnly all around; but nearer at hand, the stillness was only broken by the sounds of a footfall moving to and fro along the cabinet floor.

"So it will walk all day, sir," whispered Poole; "ay, and the better part of the night. Only when a new sample comes from the chemist there's a bit of a break. Ah, it's an ill conscience that's such an enemy to rest. Ah, sir, there's blood foully shed in every step of it. But hark again, a little closer—put your heart in your ears, Mr. Utterson, and tell me, is that the doctor's foot?"

The steps fell lightly and oddly, with a certain swing for all they went so slowly; it was different indeed from the heavy creaking tread of Henry Jekyll. Utterson sighed. "Is there never anything else?" he asked.

Poole nodded. "Once," he said. "Once I heard it weeping!"

"Weeping? how that?" said the lawyer, conscious of a sudden chill of horror.

"Weeping like a woman or a lost soul," said the butler. "I came away with that upon my heart, that I could have wept too."

But now the ten minutes drew to an end. Poole disinterred the ax from under a stack of packing straw; the candle was set upon the nearest table to light them to the attack; and they drew near with bated breath to where that patient foot was still going up and down, up and down, in the quiet of the night.

"Jekyll," cried Utterson, with a loud voice, "I demand to see you." He paused a moment, but there came no reply. "I give you fair warning, our suspicions are aroused, and I must and shall see you," he resumed; "if not by fair means, then by foul—if not of your consent, then by brute force."

"Utterson," said the voice, "for God's sake, have mercy!"

"Ah, that's not Jekyll's voice—it's Hyde's!" cried Utterson. "Down with the door, Poole!"

Poole swung the ax over his shoulder; the blow shook the building, and the red baize door leaped against the lock and hinges. A dismal screech, as of mere animal terror, rang from the cabinet. Up went the ax again, and again the panels crashed and the frame bounded; four times the blow fell, but the wood was tough and the fittings were of excellent workmanship; and it was not until the fifth, that the lock burst in sunder, and the wreck of the door fell inwards on the carpet.

The besiegers, appalled by their own riot and the stillness that had succeeded, stood back a little and peered in. There lay the cabinet before their eyes in the quiet lamplight, a good fire glowing and chattering on the hearth, the kettle singing its thin strain, a drawer or two open, papers neatly set forth on the business table, and nearer the fire, the things laid out for tea; the quietest room, you would have said, and, but for the glazed presses full of chemicals, the most commonplace that night in London.

Right in the midst there lay the body of a man sorely contorted and still twitching. They drew near on tiptoe, turned it on its back and beheld the face of Edward Hyde. He was dressed in clothes far too large for him, clothes of the doctor's bigness; the cords of his face still moved with a semblance of life, but life was quite gone: and by the crushed phial in the hand and the strong smell of kernels that hung upon the air, Utterson knew that he was looking on the body of a self-destroyer.

"We have come too late," he said sternly, "whether to save or punish. Hyde is gone to his account; and it only remains for us to find the body of your master."

The far greater proportion of the building was occupied by the theater, which filled almost the whole ground storey and was lighted from above, and by the cabinet, which formed an upper storey at one end and looked upon a court. A corridor joined the theater to the door on the bystreet; and with this the cabinet communicated separately by a second flight of stairs. There were besides a few dark closets and a spacious cellar. All these they now thoroughly examined. Each closet needed but a glance, for all were empty, and all, by the dust that fell from their doors, had stood long unopened. The cellar, indeed, was filled with crazy lumber, mostly dating from the time of the surgeon who was Jekyll's predecessor; but even as they opened the door they were advertised of the uselessness of further search, by the fall of a perfect mat of cobweb which had for years sealed up the entrance. Nowhere was there any trace of Henry Jekyll, dead or alive.

Poole stamped on the flags of the corridor. "He must be buried here," he said, hearkening to the sound.

"Or he may have fled," said Utterson, and he turned to examine the door in the by-street. It was locked; and lying near by on the flags, they found the key, already stained with rust.

"This does not look like use," observed the lawyer.

"Use!" echoed Poole. "Do you not see, sir, it is broken? much as if a man had stamped on it."

"Ay," continued Utterson, "and the fractures, too, are rusty." The two men looked at each other with a scare. "This is beyond me, Poole," said the lawyer. "Let us go back to the cabinet."

They mounted the stair in silence, and still with an occasional awestruck glance at the dead body, proceeded more thoroughly to examine the contents of the cabinet. At one table, there were traces of chemical work, various measured heaps of some white salt being laid on glass saucers, as though for an experiment in which the unhappy man had been prevented.

"That is the same drug that I was always bringing him," said Poole; and even as he spoke, the kettle with a startling noise boiled over.

This brought them to the fireside, where the easy chair was drawn cozily up, and the tea things stood ready to the sitter's elbow, the very sugar in the cup. There were several books on a shelf; one lay beside the tea things open, and Utterson was amazed to find it a copy of a pious work, for which Jekyll had several times expressed a great esteem, annotated, in his own hand, with startling blasphemies.

Next, in the course of their review of the chamber, the searchers came to the cheval-glass, into whose depths they looked with an involuntary horror. But it was so turned as to show them nothing but the rosy glow playing on the roof, the fire sparkling in a hundred repetitions along the glazed front of the presses, and their own pale and fearful countenances stooping to look in.

"This glass has seen some strange things, sir," whispered Poole.

"And surely none stranger than itself," echoed the lawyer in the same tones. "For what did Jekyll"—he caught himself up at the word with a start, and then conquering the weakness—"what could Jekyll want with it?" he said.

"You may say that!" said Poole.

Next they turned to the business table. On the desk, among the neat array of papers, a large envelope was uppermost, and bore, in the doctor's hand, the name of Mr. Utterson. The lawyer unsealed it, and several enclosures fell to the floor. The first was a will, drawn in the same eccentric terms as the one which he had returned six months before, to serve as a testament in case of death and as a deed of gift in case of disappearance; but in place of the name of Edward Hyde, the lawyer, with indescribable amazement, read the name of Gabriel John Utterson. He looked at Poole, and then back at the paper, and last of all at the dead malefactor stretched upon the carpet.

"My head goes round," he said. "He has been all these days in possession; he had no cause to like me; he must have raged to see himself displaced; and he has not destroyed this document."

He caught up the next paper; it was a brief note in the doctor's hand and dated at the top. "O Poole!" the lawyer cried, "he was alive and here this day. He cannot have been disposed of in so short a space; he must be still alive, he must have fled! And then, why fled! and how? and in that case, can we venture to declare this suicide? O, we must be careful. I foresee that we may yet involve your master in some dire catastrophe."

"Why don't you read it, sir?" asked Poole.

"Because I fear," replied the lawyer solemnly. "God grant I have no cause for it!" And with that he brought the paper to his eyes and read as follows:

> My dear Utterson,—When this shall fall into your hands, I shall have disappeared, under what circumstances I have not the penetration to foresee, but my instincts and all the circumstances of my nameless situation tell me that the end is sure and must be early. Go then, and first read the narrative which Lanyon warned me he was to place in your hands; and if you care to hear more, turn to the confession of
>
> Your unworthy and unhappy friend,
>
> Henry Jekyll

"There was a third enclosure?" asked Utterson.

"Here, sir," said Poole, and gave into his hands a considerable packet sealed in several places.

The lawyer put it in his pocket. "I would say nothing of this paper. If your master has fled or is dead, we may at least save his credit. It is now ten; I must go home and read these documents in quiet; but I shall be back before midnight, when we shall send for the police."

They went out, locking the door of the theater behind them; and Utterson, once more leaving the servants gathered about the fire in the hall, trudged back to his office to read the two narratives in which this mystery was now to be explained.

*Dr. Lanyon's Narrative*

On the ninth of January, now four days ago, I received by the evening delivery a registered envelope, addressed in the hand of my colleague and old school companion, Henry Jekyll. I was a good deal surprised by this; for we were by no means in the habit of correspondence; I had seen the man, dined with him, indeed, the night before; and I could imagine nothing in our intercourse that should justify the formality of registration. The contents increased my wonder; for this is how the letter ran:

10th December, 18—

Dear Lanyon,—You are one of my oldest friends and although we may have differed at times on scientific questions, I cannot remember, at least on my side, any break in our affection. There was never a day when, if you had said to me, "Jekyll, my life, my honor, my reason, depend upon you," I would not have sacrificed fortune or my left hand to help you. Lanyon, my life, my honor, my reason, are all at your mercy; if you fail me to-night, I am lost. You might suppose, after this preface, that I am going to ask you for something dishonorable to grant. Judge for yourself.

I want you to postpone all other engagements for to-night—ay, even if you were summoned to the bedside of an emperor; to take a cab, unless your carriage should be actually at the door; and with this letter in your hand for consultation, to drive straight to my house. Poole, my butler, has his orders; you will find him waiting your arrival with a locksmith. The door of my cabinet is then to be forced: and you are to go in alone; to open the glazed press (letter E) on the left hand, breaking the lock if it be shut; and to draw out, *with all its contents as they stand,* the fourth drawer from the top or (which is the same thing) the third from the bottom. In my extreme distress of mind, I have a morbid fear of misdirecting you; but even if I am in error, you may know the right drawer by its contents: some powders, a phial and a paper book. This drawer I beg of you to carry back with you to Cavendish Square exactly as it stands.

That is the first part of the service: now for the second. You should be back, if you set out at once on the receipt of this, long before midnight; but I will leave you that amount of margin, not only in the fear of one of those obstacles that can neither be prevented nor foreseen, but because an hour when your servants are in bed is to be preferred for what will then remain to do. At midnight, then, I have to ask you to be alone in your consulting room, to admit with your own hand into the house a man who will present himself in my name, and to place in his hands the drawer that you will have brought with you from my cabinet. Then you will have played your part and earned my gratitude completely. Five minutes afterwards, if you insist upon an explanation, you will have understood that these arrangements are of capital importance and that by the neglect of one of them, fantastic as they must appear, you might have charged your conscience with my death or the shipwreck of my reason.

Confident as I am that you will not trifle with this appeal, my heart sinks and my hand trembles at the bare thought of such a possibility. Think of me at this hour, in a strange place, laboring under a blackness of distress that no fancy can exaggerate, and yet well aware that, if you will but punctually serve me, my troubles will roll away like a story that is told. Serve me, my dear Lanyon, and save

Your friend,

H. J.

P.S.—I had already sealed this up when a fresh terror struck upon my soul. It is possible that the post-office may fail me, and this letter not come into your hands until tomorrow morning. In that case, dear Lanyon, do my errand when it shall be most convenient for you in the course of the day; and once more expect my messenger at midnight. It may then already be too late; and if that night passes without event, you will know that you have seen the last of Henry Jekyll.

Upon the reading of this letter, I made sure my colleague was insane; but till that was proved beyond the possibility of doubt, I felt bound to do as he requested. The less I understood of this farrago, the less I was in a position to judge of its importance; and an appeal so worded could not be set aside without a grave responsibility. I rose accordingly from table, got into a hansom, and drove straight to Jekyll's house. The butler was awaiting my arrival; he had received by the same post as mine a registered letter of instruction, and had sent at once for a locksmith and a carpenter. The tradesmen came while we were yet speaking; and we moved in a body to old Dr. Denman's surgical theater, from which (as you are doubtless aware) Jekyll's private cabinet is most conveniently entered. The door was very strong, the lock excellent; the carpenter avowed he would have great trouble and have to do much damage, if force were to be used; and the locksmith was near despair. But this last was a handy fellow, and after two hours' work, the door stood open. The press marked E was unlocked; and I took out the drawer, had it filled up with straw and tied in a sheet, and returned with it to Cavendish Square.

Here I proceeded to examine its contents. The powders were neatly enough made up, but not with the nicety of the dispensing chemist; so that it was plain they were of Jekyll's private manufacture: and when I opened one of the wrappers I found what seemed to me a simple crystalline salt of a white color. The phial, to which I next turned my attention, might have been about half full of a blood-red liquor, which was highly pungent to the sense of smell and seemed to me to contain phosphorus and some volatile ether. At the other ingredients I could make no guess. The book was an ordinary version book and contained little but a series of dates. These covered a period of many years, but I observed that the entries ceased nearly a year ago and quite abruptly. Here and there a brief remark was appended to a date, usually no more than a single word: "double" occurring perhaps six times in a total of several hundred entries; and once very early in the list and followed by several marks of exclamation, "total failure!"

All this, though it whetted my curiosity, told me little that was definite. Here were a phial of some tincture, a paper of some salt, and the record of a series of experiments that had led (like too many of Jekyll's investigations) to no end of practical usefulness. How could the presence of these articles in my house affect either the honor, the sanity, or the life of my flighty colleague? If his messenger could go to one place, why could ho not go to another? And even granting some impediment, why was this gentleman to be received by me in secret? The more I reflected the more convinced I grew that I was dealing with a case of cerebral disease; and though I dismissed my servants to bed, I loaded an old revolver, that I might be found in some posture of self-defense.

Twelve o'clock had scarce rung out over London, ere the knocker sounded very gently on the door. I went myself at the summons, and found a small man crouching against the pillars of the portico.

"Are you come from Dr. Jekyll?" I asked.

He told me "yes" by a constrained gesture; and when I had bidden him enter, he did not obey me without a searching backward glance into the darkness of the square. There was a policeman not far off, advancing with his bull's eye open; and at the sight, I thought my visitor started and made greater haste.

These particulars struck me, I confess, disagreeably; and as I followed him into the bright light of the consulting room, I kept my hand ready on my weapon. Here, at last, I had a chance of clearly seeing him. I had never set eyes on him before, so much was certain. He was small, as I have said; I was struck besides with the shocking expression of his face, with his remarkable combination of great muscular activity and great apparent debility of constitution, and—last but not least—with the odd, subjective disturbance caused by his neighborhood. This bore some resemblance to incipient rigor, and was accompanied by a marked sinking of the pulse. At the time, I set it down to some idiosyncratic, personal distaste, and merely wondered at the acuteness of the symptoms; but I have since had reason to believe the cause to lie much deeper in the nature of man, and to turn on some nobler hinge than the principle of hatred.

This person (who had thus, from the first moment of his entrance, struck in me what I can only describe as a disgustful curiosity) was dressed in a fashion that would have made an ordinary person laughable; his clothes, that is to say, although they were of rich and sober fabric, were enormously too large for him in every measurement—the trousers hanging on his legs and rolled up to keep them from the ground, the waist of the coat below his haunches, and the collar sprawling wide upon his shoulders. Strange to relate, this ludicrous accouterment was far from moving me to laughter. Rather, as there was something abnormal and misbegotten in the very essence of the creature that now faced me—something seizing, surprising and revolting—this fresh disparity seemed but to fit in with and to reinforce it; so that to my interest in the man's nature and character, there was added a curiosity as to his origin, his life, his fortune and status in the world.

These observations, though they have taken so great a space to be set down in, were yet the work of a few seconds. My visitor was, indeed, on fire with somber excitement.

"Have you got it?" he cried. "Have you got it?" And so lively was his impatience that he even laid his hand upon my arm and sought to shake me.

I put him back, conscious at his touch of a certain icy pang along my blood. "Come, sir," said I. "You forget that I have not yet the pleasure of your acquaintance. Be seated, if you please." And I showed him an example, and sat down myself in my customary seat and with as fair an imitation of my ordinary manner to a patient, as the lateness of the hour, the nature of my preoccupations, and the horror I had of my visitor, would suffer me to muster.

"I beg your pardon, Dr. Lanyon," he replied civilly enough. "What you say is very well founded; and my impatience has shown its heels to my politeness. I come here at the instance of your colleague, Dr. Henry Jekyll, on a piece of business of some moment; and I understood . . ."

He paused and put his hand to his throat, and I could see, in spite of his collected manner, that he was wrestling against the approaches of the hysteria—"I understood, a drawer . . ."

But here I took pity on my visitor's suspense, and some perhaps on my own growing curiosity.

"There it is, sir," said I, pointing to the drawer, where it lay on the floor behind a table and still covered with the sheet.

He sprang to it, and then paused, and laid his hand upon his heart: I could hear his teeth grate with the convulsive action of his jaws; and his face was so ghastly to see that I grew alarmed both for his life and reason.

"Compose yourself," said I.

He turned a dreadful smile to me, and as if with the decision of despair, plucked away the sheet. At sight of the contents, he uttered one loud sob of such immense relief that I sat petrified. And the next moment, in a voice that was already fairly well under control, "Have you a graduated glass?" he asked.

I rose from my place with something of an effort and gave him what he asked.

He thanked me with a smiling nod, measured out a few minims of the red tincture and added one of the powders. The mixture, which was at first of a reddish hue, began, in proportion as the crystals melted, to brighten in color, to effervesce audibly, and to throw off small fumes of vapor. Suddenly and at the same moment, the ebullition ceased and the compound changed to a dark purple, which faded again more slowly to a watery green. My visitor, who had watched these metamorphoses with a keen eye smiled, set down the glass upon the table, and then turned and looked upon me with an air of scrutiny.

"And now," said he, "to settle what remains. Will you be wise? will you be guided? will you suffer me to take this glass in my hand and to go forth from your house without further parley? or has the greed of curiosity too much command of you? Think before you answer, for it shall be done as you decide. As you decide, you shall be left as you were before, and neither richer nor wiser, unless the sense of service rendered to a man in mortal distress may be counted as a kind of riches of the soul. Or, if you shall so prefer to choose, a new province of knowledge and new avenues to fame and power shall be laid open to you, here in this room, upon the instant; and your sight shall be blasted by a prodigy to stagger the unbelief of Satan."

"Sir," said I, affecting a coolness that I was far from truly possessing, "you speak enigmas, and you will perhaps not wonder that I hear you with no very strong impression of belief. But I have gone too far in the way of inexplicable services to pause before I see the end."

"It is well," replied my visitor. "Lanyon, you remember your vows: what follows is under the seal of our profession. And now, you who have so long been bound to the most narrow and material views, you who have denied the virtue of transcendental medicine, you who have derided your superiors—behold!"

He put the glass to his lips and drank at one gulp. A cry followed; he reeled, staggered, clutched at the table and held on, staring with injected eyes, gasping with open mouth; and as I looked there came, I thought, a change—he seemed to swell—his face became suddenly black and the features seemed to melt and alter—and the next moment, I had sprung to my feet and leaped back against the wall, my arm raised to shield me from that prodigy, my mind submerged in terror.

"O God!" I screamed, and "O God!" again and again; for there before my eyes—pale and shaken, and half fainting, and groping before him with his hands, like a man restored from death—there stood Henry Jekyll!

What he told me in the next hour, I cannot bring my mind to set on paper. I saw what I saw, I heard what I heard, and my soul sickened at it; and yet now when that sight has faded from my eyes, I ask myself if I believe it, and I cannot answer. My life is shaken to its roots; sleep has left me; the deadliest terror sits by me at all hours of the day and night; and I feel that my days are numbered, and that I must die; and yet I shall die incredulous. As for the moral turpitude that man unveiled to me, even with tears of penitence, I cannot, even in memory, dwell on it without a start of horror. I will say but one thing, Utterson, and that (if you can bring your mind to credit it) will be more than enough. The creature who crept into my house that night was, on Jekyll's own confession, known by the name of Hyde and hunted for in every corner of the land as the murderer of Carew.

Hastie Lanyon

### *Henry Jekyll's Full Statement of the Case*

I was born in the year 18— to a large fortune, endowed besides with excellent parts, inclined by nature to industry, fond of the respect of the wise and good among my fellow men, and thus, as might have been supposed, with every guarantee of an honorable and distinguished future. And indeed the worst of my faults was a certain impatient gaiety of disposition, such as has made the happiness of many, but such as I found it hard to reconcile with my imperious desire to carry my head high, and wear a more than commonly grave countenance before the public. Hence it came about that I concealed my pleasures; and that when I reached years of reflection, and began to look round me and take stock of my progress and position in the world, I stood already committed to a profound duplicity of life.

Many a man would have even blazoned such irregularities as I was guilty of; but from the high views that I had set before me, I regarded and hid them with an almost morbid sense of shame. It was thus rather the exacting nature of my aspirations than any particular degradation in my fault, that made me what I was, and, with even a deeper trench than in the majority of men, severed in me those provinces of good and evil which divide and compound man's dual nature. In this case, I was driven to reflect deeply and inveterately on that hard law of life, which lies at the root of religion and is one of the most plentiful springs of distress. Though so profound a double-dealer, I was in no sense a hypocrite—both sides of me were in dead earnest; I was no more myself when I laid aside restraint and plunged in shame, than when I labored, in the eye of day, at the furtherance of knowledge or the relief of sorrow and suffering. And it chanced that the direction of my scientific studies, which led wholly towards the mystic and the transcendental, reacted and shed a strong light on this consciousness of the perennial war among my members. With every day, and from both sides of my intelligence, the moral and the intellectual, I thus drew steadily nearer to that truth, by whose partial discovery I have been doomed to such a dreadful ship wreck: that man is not truly one, but truly two.

I say two because the state of my own knowledge does not pass beyond that point. Others will follow, others will outstrip me on the same lines; and I hazard the guess that man will be ultimately known for a mere polity of multifarious, incongruous and independent denizens. I, for my part, from the nature of my life, advanced infallibly in one direction and in one direction only. It was on the moral side, and in my own person, that I learned to recognize the thorough and primitive duality of man; I saw that, of the two natures that contended in the field of my consciousness, even if could rightly be said to be either, it was only because I was radically both; and from an early date, even before, the course of my scientific discoveries had begun to suggest the most naked possibility of such a miracle, I had learned to dwell with pleasure, as a beloved daydream, on the thought of the separation of these elements.

If each, I told myself, could but be housed in separate identities, life would be relieved of all that was unbearable; the unjust might go his way, delivered from the aspirations and remorse of his more upright twin; and the just could walk steadfastly and securely on his upward path, doing the good things in which he found his pleasure, and no longer exposed to disgrace and penitence by the hands of his extraneous evil. It was the curse of mankind that these incongruous faggots were thus bound together—that in the agonized womb of consciousness, these polar twins should be continuously struggling. How, then, were they dissociated?

I was so far in my reflections when, as I have said, a side light began to shine upon the subject from the laboratory table. I began to perceive more deeply than it has ever yet been stated, the trembling immateriality, the mist like transience, of this seemingly so solid body in which we walk attired. Certain agents I found to have the power to shake and pluck back that fleshly vestment, even as a wind might toss the curtains of a pavilion. For two good reasons, I will not enter deeply into this scientific branch of my confession. First, because I have been made to learn that the doom and burthen of our life is bound for ever on man's shoulder, and when the attempt is made to cast it off, it but returns upon us with more unfamiliar and more awful pressure. Second, because, as my narrative will make, alas too evident, my discoveries were incomplete. Enough then, that I not only recognized my natural body from the mere aura and effulgence of certain of the powers that made up my spirit, but managed to compound a drug by which these powers should be dethroned from their supremacy, and a second form and countenance substituted, none the less natural to me because they were the expression, and bore the stamp of lower elements in my soul.

I hesitated long before I put this theory to the test of practice. I knew well that I risked death; for any drug that so potently controlled and shook the very fortress of identity, might, by the least scruple of an overdose or at the least inopportunity in the moment of exhibition, utterly blot out that immaterial tabernacle which I looked to it to change. But the temptation of a discovery so singular and profound at last overcame the suggestions of alarm. I had long since prepared my tincture; I purchased at once, from a firm of wholesale chemists, a large quantity of a particular salt which I knew, from my experiments, to be the last ingredient required; and late one accursed night, I compounded the elements, watched them boil and smoke together in the glass, and when the ebullition had subsided, with a strong glow of courage, drank off the potion.

The most racking pangs succeeded: a grinding in the bones, deadly nausea, and a horror of the spirit that cannot be exceeded at the hour of birth or death. Then these agonies began swiftly to subside, and I came to myself as if out of a great sickness. There was something strange in my sensations, something indescribably new and, from its very novelty, incredibly sweet. I felt younger, lighter, happier in body; within I was conscious of a heady recklessness, a current of disordered sensual images running like a millrace in my fancy, a solution of the bonds of obligation, an unknown but not an innocent freedom of the soul. I knew myself, at the first breath of this new life, to be more wicked, tenfold more wicked, sold a slave to my original evil; and the thought, in that moment, braced and delighted me like wine. I stretched out my hands, exulting in the freshness of these sensations; and in the act, I was suddenly aware that I had lost in stature.

There was no mirror, at that date, in my room; that which stands beside me as I write, was brought there later on and for the very purpose of those transformations. The night, however, was far gone into the morning—the morning, black as it was, was nearly ripe for the conception of the day—the inmates of my house were locked in the most rigorous hours of slumber; and I determined, flushed as I was with hope and triumph, to venture in my new shape as far as to my bedroom. I crossed the yard, wherein the constellations looked down upon me, I could have thought, with wonder, the first creature of that sort that their unsleeping vigilance had yet disclosed to them; I stole through the corridors, a stranger in my own house; and coming to my room, I saw for the first time the appearance of Edward Hyde.

I must here speak by theory alone, saying not that which I know, but which I suppose to be most probable. The evil side of my nature, to which I had now transferred the stamping efficacy, was less robust and less developed than the good which I had just deposed. Again, in the course of my life, which had been, after all, nine tenths a life of effort, virtue and control, it had been much less exercised and much less exhausted. And hence, as I think, it came about that Edward Hyde was so much smaller, slighter and younger than Henry Jekyll.

Even as good shone upon the countenance of the one, evil was written broadly and plainly on the face of the other. Evil besides (which I must still believe to be the lethal side of man) had left on that body an imprint of deformity and decay. And yet when I looked upon that ugly idol in the glass, I was conscious of no repugnance, rather of a leap of welcome. This, too, was myself. It seemed natural and human. In my eyes it bore a livelier image of the spirit, it seemed more express and single, than the imperfect and divided countenance I had been hitherto accustomed to call mine. And in so far I was doubtless right. I have observed that when I wore the semblance of Edward Hyde, none could come near to me at first without a visible misgiving of the flesh. This, as I take it, was because all human beings, as we meet them, are commingled out of good and evil: and Edward Hyde, alone in the ranks of mankind, was pure evil.

I lingered but a moment at the mirror: the second and conclusive experiment had yet to be attempted; it yet remained to be seen if I had lost my identity beyond redemption and must flee before daylight from a house that was no longer mine; and hurrying back to my cabinets, I once more prepared and drank the cup, once more suffered the pangs of dissolution, and came to myself once more with the character, the stature and face of Henry Jekyll.

That night I had come to the fatal cross-roads. Had I approached my discovery in a more noble spirit, had I risked the experiment while under the empire of generous or pious aspirations, all must have been otherwise, and from these agonies of death and birth, I had come forth an angel instead of a fiend. The drug had no discriminating action; it was neither diabolical nor divine; it but shook the doors of the prison house of my disposition; and like the captives of Philippi, that which stood within ran forth. At that time my virtue slumbered; my evil, kept awake by ambition, was alert and swift to seize the occasion; and the thing that was projected was Edward Hyde. Hence, although I had now two characters as well as two appearances, one was wholly evil, and the other was still the old Henry Jekyll, that incongruous compound of whose reformation and improvement I had already learned to despair. The movement was thus wholly toward the worse.

Even at that time, I had not conquered my aversions to the dryness of a life of study. I would still be merrily disposed at times; and as my pleasures were (to say the least) undignified, and I was not only well known and highly considered, but growing towards the elderly man, this incoherency of my life was daily growing more unwelcome. It was on this side that my new power tempted me until I fell in slavery. I had but to drink the cup, to doff at once the body of the noted professor, and to assume, like a thick cloak, that of Edward Hyde. I smiled at the notion. It seemed to me at the time to be humorous; and I made my preparations with the most studious care. I took and furnished that house in Soho, to which Hyde was tracked by the police; and engaged as a housekeeper a creature whom I knew well to be silent and unscrupulous. On the other side, I announced to my servants that a Mr. Hyde (whom I described) was to have full liberty and power about my house in the square; and to parry mishaps, I even called and made myself a familiar object, in my second character. I next drew up that will to which you so much objected; so that if anything befell me in the person of Dr. Jekyll, I could enter on that of Edward Hyde without pecuniary loss. And thus fortified, as I supposed, on every side, I began to profit by the strange immunities of my position.

Men have before hired bravos to transact their crimes, while their own person and reputation sat under shelter. I was the first that ever did so for his pleasures. I was the first that could thus plod in the public eye with a load of genial respectability, and in a moment, like a schoolboy, strip off these lendings and spring headlong into the sea of liberty. But for me, in my impenetrable mantle, the safety was complete. Think of it—I did not even exist. Let me but escape into my laboratory door, give me but a second or two to mix and swallow the draught that I had always standing ready; and whatever he had done, Edward Hyde would pass away like the stain of breath upon a mirror; and there in his stead, quietly at home, trimming the midnight lamp in his study, a man who could afford to laugh at suspicion, would be Henry Jekyll.

The pleasures which I made haste to seek in my disguise were, as I have said, undignified; I would scarce use a harder term. But in the hands of Edward Hyde, they soon began to turn toward the monstrous. When I would come back from these excursions, I was often plunged into a kind of wonder at my vicarious depravity. This familiar that I called out of my own soul, and sent forth alone to do his good pleasure, was a being inherently malign and villainous, his every act and thought centered on self; drinking pleasure with bestial avidity from any degree of torture to another; relentless like a man of stone. Henry Jekyll stood at times aghast before the acts of Edward Hyde; but the situation was apart from ordinary laws, and insidiously relaxed the grasp of conscience. It was Hyde, after all, and Hyde alone, that was guilty. Jekyll was no worse; he woke again to his good qualities seemingly unimpaired; he would even make haste, where it was possible, to undo the evil done by Hyde. And thus his conscience slumbered.

Into the details of the infamy at which I thus connived (for even now I can scarce grant that I committed it) I have no design of entering; I mean but to point out the warnings and the successive steps with which my chastisement approached. I met with one accident which, as it brought on no consequence, I shall no more than mention. An act of cruelty to a child aroused against me the anger of a passer-by, whom I recognized the other day in the person of your kinsman; the doctor and the child's family joined him; there were moments when I feared for my life; and at last, in order to pacify their too just resentment, Edward Hyde had to bring them to the door, and pay them in a cheque drawn in the name of Henry Jekyll. But this danger was easily eliminated from the future, by opening an account at another bank in the name of Edward Hyde himself; and when, by sloping my own hand backwards, I had supplied my double with a signature, I thought I sat beyond the reach of fate.

Some two months before the murder of Sir Danvers, I had been out for one of my adventures, had returned at a late hour, and woke the next day in bed with somewhat odd sensations. It was in vain I looked about me; in vain I saw the decent furniture and tall proportions of my room in the square; in vain that I recognized the pattern of the bed curtains and the design of the mahogany frame; something still kept insisting that I was not where I was, that I had not wakened where I seemed to be, but in the little room in Soho where I was accustomed to sleep in the body of Edward Hyde. I smiled to myself, and, in my psychological way, began lazily to inquire into the elements of this illusion, occasionally, even as I did so, dropping back into a comfortable morning doze. I was still so engaged when, in one of my more wakeful moments, my eye fell upon my hand. Now the hand of Henry Jekyll (as you have often remarked) was professional in shape and size: it was large, firm, white and comely. But the hand which I now saw, clearly enough, in the yellow light of a mid-London morning, lying half shut on the bedclothes, was lean, corded, knuckly, of a dusky pallor and thickly shaded with a swart growth of hair. It was the hand of Edward Hyde.

I must have stared upon it for near half a minute, sunk as I was in the mere stupidity of wonder, before terror woke up in my breast as sudden and startling as the crash of cymbals; and bounding from my bed, I rushed to the mirror. At the sight that met my eyes, my blood was changed into something exquisitely thin and icy. Yes, I had gone to bed Henry Jekyll, I had awakened Edward Hyde.

How was this to be explained? I asked myself; and then, with another bound of terror—how was it to be remedied? It was well on in the morning; the servants were up; all my drugs were in the cabinet—a long journey down two pair of stairs, through the back passage, across the open court and through the anatomical theater, from where I was then standing horror-struck. It might indeed be possible to cover my face; but of what use was that, when I was unable to conceal the alteration of my stature? And then with an overpowering sweetness of relief, it came back upon my mind that the servants were already used to the coming and going of my second self. I had soon dressed, as well as I was able, in clothes of my own size: had soon passed through the house, where Bradshaw stared and drew back at seeing Mr. Hyde at such an hour and in such a strange array; and ten minutes later, Dr. Jekyll had returned to his own shape and was sitting down, with a darkened brow, to make a feint of breakfasting.

Small indeed was my appetite. This inexplicable incident, this reversal of my previous experience, seemed, like the Babylonian finger on the wall, to be spelling out the letters of my judgment; and I began to reflect more seriously than ever before on the issues and possibilities of my double existence. That part of me which I had the power of projecting, had lately been much exercised and nourished; it had seemed to me of late as though the body of Edward Hyde had grown in stature, as though (when I wore that form) I were conscious of a more generous tide of blood; and I began to spy a danger that, if this were much prolonged, the balance of my nature might be permanently overthrown, the power of voluntary change be forfeited, and the character of Edward Hyde become irrevocably mine.

The power of the drug had not been always equally displayed. Once, very early in my careers, it had totally failed me; since then I had been obliged on more than one occasion to double, and once, with infinite risk of death, to treble the amount; and these rare uncertainties had cast hitherto the sole shadow on my contentment. Now, however, and in the light of that morning's accident, I was led to remark that whereas, in the beginning, the difficulty had been to throw off the body of Jekyll, it had of late gradually but decidedly transferred itself to the other side. All things therefore seemed to point to this; that I was slowly losing hold of my original and better self, and becoming slowly incorporated with my second and worse.

Between these two, I now felt I had to choose. My two natures had memory in common, but all other faculties were most unequally shared between them. Jekyll (who was composite) now with the most sensitive apprehensions, now with a greedy gusto, projected and shared in the pleasures and adventures of Hyde; but Hyde was indifferent to Jekyll, or but remembered him as the mountain bandit remembers the cavern in which he conceals himself from pursuit. Jekyll had more than a father's interest; Hyde had more of a son's indifference. To cast in my lot with Jekyll, was to die to those appetites which I had long secretly indulged and had of late begun to pamper. To cast it in with Hyde, was to die to a thousand interests and aspirations, and to become, at a blow and forever, despised and friendless.

The bargain might appear unequal; but there was still another consideration in the scales; for while Jekyll would suffer smartingly in the fires of abstinence, Hyde would be not even conscious of all that he had lost. Strange as my circumstances were, the terms of this debate are as old and commonplace as man; much the same inducements and alarms cast the die for any tempted and trembling sinner; and it fell out with me, as it falls with so vast a majority of my fellows, that I chose the better part and was found wanting in the strength to keep to it.

Yes, I preferred the elderly and discontented doctor surrounded by friends and cherishing honest hopes; and bade a resolute farewell to the liberty, the comparative youth, the light step, leaping impulses and secret pleasures, that I had enjoyed in the disguise of Hyde. I made this choice perhaps with some unconscious reservation, for I neither gave up the house in Soho, nor destroyed the clothes of Edward Hyde, which still lay ready in my cabinet. For two months, however, I was true to my determination; for two months, I led a life of such severity as I had never before attained to, and enjoyed the compensations of an approving conscience. But time began at last to obliterate the freshness of my alarm; the praises of conscience began to grow into a thing of course; I began to be tortured with throes and longings, as of Hyde struggling for freedom; and at last, in an hour of moral weakness, I once again compounded and swallowed the transforming draught.

I do not suppose that, when a drunkard reasons with himself upon his vice, he is once out of five hundred times affected by the dangers that he runs through his brutish, physical insensibility; neither had I, long as I had considered my position, made enough allowance for the complete moral insensibility and insensate readiness to evil, which were the leading characters of Edward Hyde. Yet it was by these that I was punished. My devil had been long caged, he came out roaring. I was conscious, even when I took the draught, of a more unbridled, a more furious propensity to ill. It must have been this, I suppose, that stirred in my soul that tempest of impatience with which I listened to the civilities of my unhappy victim; I declare, at least, before God, no man morally sane could have been guilty of that crime upon so pitiful a provocation; and that I struck in no more reasonable spirit than that in which a sick child may break a plaything. But I had voluntarily stripped myself of all those balancing instincts by which even the worst of us continues to walk with some degree of steadiness among temptations; and in my case, to be tempted, however slightly, was to fall.

Instantly the spirit of hell awoke in me and raged. With a transport of glee, I mauled the unresisting body, tasting delight from every blow; and it was not till weariness had begun to succeed, that I was suddenly, in the top fit of my delirium, struck through the heart by a cold thrill of terror. A mist dispersed; I saw my life to be forfeit; and fled from the scene of these excesses, at once glorying and trembling, my lust of evil gratified and stimulated, my love of life screwed to the topmost peg. I ran to the house in Soho, and (to make assurance doubly sure) destroyed my papers; thence I set out through the lamplit streets, in the same divided ecstasy of mind, gloating on my crime, light-headedly devising others in the future, and yet still hastening and still hearkening in my wake for the steps of the avenger.

Hyde had a song upon his lips as he compounded the draught, and as he drank it, pledged the dead man. The pangs of transformation had not done tearing him, before Henry Jekyll, with streaming tears of gratitude and remorse, had fallen upon his knees and lifted his clasped hands to God. The veil of self-indulgence was rent from head to foot. I saw my life as a whole: I followed it up from the days of childhood, when I had walked with my father's hand, and through the self-denying toils of my professional life, to arrive again and again, with the same sense of unreality, at the damned horrors of the evening. I could have screamed aloud; I sought with tears and prayers to smother down the crowd of hideous images and sounds with which my memory swarmed against me; and still, between the petitions, the ugly face of my iniquity stared into my soul.

As the acuteness of this remorse began to die away, it was succeeded by a sense of joy. The problem of my conduct was solved. Hyde was thenceforth impossible; whether I would or not, I was now confined to the better part of my existence; and O, how I rejoiced to think it! with what willing humility I embraced anew the restrictions of natural life! with what sincere renunciation I locked the door by which I had so often gone and come, and ground the key under my heel.

The next day, came the news that the murder had been overlooked, that the guilt of Hyde was patent to the world, and that the victim was a man high in public estimation. It was not only a crime, it had been a tragic folly. I think I was glad to know it; I think I was glad to have my better impulses thus buttressed and guarded by the terrors of the scaffold. Jekyll was now my city of refuge; let but Hyde peep out an instant, and the hands of all men would be raised to take and slay him.

I resolved in my future conduct to redeem the past; and I can say with honesty that my resolve was fruitful of some good. You know yourself how earnestly, in the last months of the last year, I labored to relieve suffering; you know that much was done for others, and that the days passed quietly, almost happily for myself. Nor can I truly say that I wearied of this beneficent and innocent life; I think instead that I daily enjoyed it more completely but I was still cursed with my duality of purpose; and as the first edge of my penitence wore off, the lower side of me, so long indulged, so recently chained down, began to growl for license. Not that I dreamed of resuscitating Hyde—the bare idea of that would startle me to frenzy: no, it was in my own person that I was once more tempted to trifle with my conscience; and it was as an ordinary secret sinner that I at last fell before the assaults of temptation.

There comes an end to all things; the most capacious measure is filled at last; and this brief condescension to my evil finally destroyed the balance of my soul. And yet I was not alarmed; the fall seemed natural, like a return to the old days before I had made my discovery.

It was a fine, clear, January day, wet under foot where the frost had melted, but cloudless overhead; and the Regent's Park was full of winter chirrupings and sweet with spring odor. I sat in the sun on a bench; the animal within me licking the chops of memory; the spiritual side a little drowsed, promising subsequent penitence, but not yet moved to begin. After all, I reflected, I was like my neighbors; and then I smiled, comparing myself with the other men, comparing my active good-will with the lazy cruelty of their neglect. And at the very moment of that vainglorious thought, a qualm came over me, a horrid nausea and the most deadly shuddering. These passed away, and left me faint; and then as in its turn faintness subsided, I began to be aware of a change in the temper of my thoughts, a greater boldness, a contempt of danger, a solution of the bonds of obligation. I looked down; my clothes hung formlessly on my shrunken limbs; the hand that lay on my knee was corded and hairy. I was once more Edward Hyde. A moment before I had been safe of all men's respect, wealthy, beloved—the cloth laying for me in the dining-room at home; and now I was the common quarry of mankind, hunted, houseless, a known murderer, thrall to the gallows.

My reason wavered, but it did not fail me utterly. I have more than once observed that, in my second character, my faculties seemed sharpened to a point and my spirits more tensely elastic; thus it came about that, where Jekyll perhaps might have succumbed, Hyde rose to the importance of the moment. My drugs were in one of the presses of my cabinet; how was I to reach them? That was the problem that (crushing my temples in my hands) I set myself to solve. The laboratory door I had closed. If I sought to enter by the house, my own servants would consign me to the gallows. I saw I must employ another hand, and thought of Lanyon.

How was he to be reached? how persuaded? Supposing that I escaped capture in the streets, how was I to make my way into his presence? and how should I, an unknown and displeasing visitor, prevail on the famous physician to rifle the study of his colleague, Dr. Jekyll? Then I remembered that of my original character, one part remained to me: I could write my own hand; and once I had conceived that kindling spark, the way that I must follow became lighted up from end to end.

Thereupon, I arranged my clothes as best I could, and summoning a passing hansom, drove to an hotel in Portland Street, the name of which I chanced to remember. At my appearance (which was indeed comical enough, however tragic a fate these garments covered) the driver could not conceal his mirth. I gnashed my teeth upon him with a gust of devilish fury; and the smile withered from his face—happily for him—yet more happily for myself, for in another instant I had certainly dragged him from his perch. At the inn, as I entered, I looked about me with so black a countenance as made the attendants tremble; not a look did they exchange in my presence; but obsequiously took my orders, led me to a private room, and brought me wherewithal to write.

Hyde in danger of his life was a creature new to me; shaken with inordinate anger, strung to the pitch of murder, lusting to inflict pain. Yet the creature was astute; mastered his fury with a great effort of the will; composed two important letters, one to Lanyon and one to Poole; and that he might receive actual evidence of their being posted, sent them out with directions that they should be registered. Thenceforward, he sat all day over the fire in the private room, gnawing his nails; there he dined, sitting alone with his fears, the waiter visibly quailing before his eye; and thence, when the night was fully come, he set forth in the corner of a closed cab, and was driven to and fro about the streets of the city. He, I say—I cannot say, I. That child of Hell had nothing human; nothing lived in him but fear and hatred. And when at last, thinking the driver had begun to grow suspicious, he discharged the cab and ventured on foot, attired in his misfitting clothes, an object marked out for observation, into the midst of the nocturnal passengers, these two base passions raged within him like a tempest. He walked fast, hunted by his fears, chattering to himself, skulking through the less frequented thoroughfares, counting the minutes that still divided him from midnight. Once a woman spoke to him, offering, I think, a box of lights. He smote her in the face, and she fled.

When I came to myself at Lanyon's, the horror of my old friend perhaps affected me somewhat: I do not know; it was at least but a drop in the sea to the abhorrence with which I looked back upon these hours. A change had come over me. It was no longer the fear of the gallows, it was the horror of being Hyde that racked me. I received Lanyon's condemnation partly in a dream; it was partly in a dream that I came home to my own house and got into bed. I slept after the prostration of the day, with a stringent and profound slumber which not even the nightmare that wrung me could avail to break, I awoke in the morning shaken, weakened, but refreshed. I still hated and feared the thought of the brute that slept within me, and I had not of course forgotten the appalling dangers of the day before; but I was once more at home, in my own house and close to my drugs; and gratitude for my escape shone so strong in my soul that it almost rivaled the brightness of hope.

I was stepping leisurely across the court after breakfast, drinking the chill of the air with pleasure, when I was seized again with those indescribable sensations that heralded the change, and I had but the time to gain the shelter of my cabinet, before I was once again raging and freezing with the passions of Hyde. It took on this occasion a double dose to recall me to myself; and alas six hours after, as I sat looking sadly in the fire, the pangs returned, and the drug had to be re-administered. In short, from that day forth it seemed only by a great effort as of gymnastics, and only under the immediate stimulation of the drug, that I was able to wear the countenance of Jekyll. At all hours of the day and night, I would be taken with the premonitory shudder; above all, if I slept, or even dozed for a moment in my chair, it was always as Hyde that I awakened.

Under the strain of this continually impending doom and by the sleeplessness to which I now condemned myself, ay, even beyond what I had thought possible to man, I became, in my own person, a creature eaten up and emptied by fever, languidly weak both in body and mind, and solely occupied by one thought: the horror of my other self. But when I slept, or when the virtue of the medicine wore off, I would leap almost without transition (for the pangs of transformation grew daily less marked) into the possession of a fancy brimming with images of terror, a soul boiling with causeless hatreds, and a body that seemed not strong enough to contain the raging energies of life.

The powers of Hyde seemed to have grown with the sickliness of Jekyll. And certainly the hate that now divided them was equal on each side. With Jekyll, it was a thing of vital instinct. He had now seen the full deformity of that creature that shared with him some of the phenomena of consciousness, and was co-heir with him to death: and beyond these links of community, which in themselves made the most poignant part of his distress, he thought of Hyde, for all his energy of life, as of something not only hellish but inorganic. This was the shocking thing; that the slime of the pit seemed to utter cries and voices; that the amorphous dust gesticulated and sinned; that what was dead, and had no shape, should usurp the offices of life. And this again, that that insurgent horror was knit to him closer than a wife, closer than an eye; lay caged in his flesh, where he heard it mutter and felt it struggle to be born; and at every hour of weakness, and in the confidence of slumber, prevailed against him, and deposed him out of life.

The hatred of Hyde for Jekyll was of a different order. His terror of the gallows drove him continually to commit temporary suicide, and return to his subordinate station of a part instead of a person; but he loathed the necessity, he loathed the despondency into which Jekyll was now fallen, and he resented the dislike with which he was himself regarded. Hence the ape-like tricks that he would play me, scrawling in my own hand blasphemies on the pages of my books, burning the letters and destroying the portrait of my father; and indeed, had it not been for his fear of death, he would long ago have ruined himself in order to involve me in the ruin. But his love of life is wonderful; I go further: I, who sicken and freeze at the mere thought of him, when I recall the abjection and passion of this attachment, and when I know how he fears my power to cut him off by suicide, I find it in my heart to pity him.

It is useless, and the time awfully fails me, to prolong this description; no one has ever suffered such torments, let that suffice; and yet even to these, habit brought—no, not alleviation—but a certain callousness of soul, a certain acquiescence of despair; and my punishment might have gone on for years, but for the last calamity which has now befallen, and which has finally severed me from my own face and nature. My provision of the salt, which had never been renewed since the date of the first experiment, began to run low. I sent out for a fresh supply and mixed the draught; the ebullition followed, and the first change of color, not the second; I drank it and it was without efficiency. You will learn from Poole how I have had London ransacked; it was in vain; and I am now persuaded that my first supply was impure, and that it was that unknown impurity which lent efficacy to the draught.

About a week has passed, and I am now finishing this statement under the influence of the last of the old powders. This, then, is the last time, short of a miracle, that Henry Jekyll can think his own thoughts or see his own face (now had sadly altered!) in the glass. Nor must I delay too long to bring my writing to an end; for if my narrative has hitherto escaped destruction, it has been by a combination of great prudence and great good luck.

Should the throes of change take me in the act of writing it, Hyde will tear it in pieces; but if some time shall have elapsed after I have laid it by, his wonderful selfishness and circumscription to the moment will probably save it once again from the action of his ape-like spite. And indeed the doom that is closing on us both has already changed and crushed him. Half an hour from now, when I shall again and forever reindue that hated personality, I know how I shall sit shuddering and weeping in my chair or continue, with the most strained and fearstruck ecstasy of listening, to pace up and down this room (my last earthly refuge) and give ear to every sound of menace. Will Hyde die upon the scaffold? or will he find the courage to release himself at the last moment? God knows; I am careless; this is my true hour of death, and what is to follow concerns another than myself.

Here then, as I lay down the pen and proceed to seal up my confession, I bring the life of that unhappy Henry Jekyll to an end.

## F. WYVILLE HOME (1851– ? )

### Dover Cliff

Last April, when the winds had lost their chill,
I lay down dreamily upon the verge
Of Shakespeare's Cliff, where sea and sea-wind scourge
The eternal barrier that withstands them still.
I heard the billows break beneath and fill
The wide air with the thunder of the surge;
And near my cheek, half fearful to emerge,
A violet grew upon the grassy hill.
There while I lay, Poet, I dreamed of thee.

Thy very voice, whose matchless music yet
O'ermasters all the world's, surrounded me,
Singing, and in the sound of it there met
With all the might and passion of the sea
The utter sweetness of the violet.

## In a September Night

There the moon leans out and blesses
All the dreamy hills below.
Here the willows wash their tresses
Where the water-lilies blow
In the stream that glideth slow.

High in heaven, in serried ranges,
Cloud-wreaths float through pallid light,
Like a flock of swans that changes
In the middle Autumn night
North for South in ordered flight.

What know ye, who hover yonder,
More than I, or that veiled good
Whither all things tend, I wonder,
That ye follow the wind's mood
In such patient quietude?

## An English Girl

Speak, quiet lips, and utter forth my fate.
Before thy beauty I bow down, I kneel,
Girl, and to thee my life I dedicate,
And seal the past up with a dateless seal.

What delicate hours and seasons without storm
Have nursed thee, and what happy English dale?
For tenderer is thy light and gracile form
Than any snowy wind-flower of the vale.

O wild-flower, though the bee that drinks thy wine
Must soar past crags that front the leaping sea,
I climb to thee; thy beauty shall be mine;
Or let the cold green wave go over me.

# ROBERT CUNNINGHAME GRAHAM (1852–1936)

## Beattock for Moffat

The bustle on the Euston platform stopped for an instant to let the men who carried him to the third class compartment pass along the train. Gaunt and emaciated, he looked just at death's door, and, as they propped him in the carriage between two pillows, he faintly said, "Jock, do ye think I'll live as far as Moffat? I should na' like to die in London in the smoke."

His cockney wife, drying her tears with a cheap, hem-stitched, pocket handkerchief, her scanty town-bred hair looking like wisps of tow beneath her hat, bought from some window in which each individual article was marked at seven-and-sixpence, could only sob. His brother, with the country sun and wind burn still upon his face, and his huge hands hanging like hams in front of him, made answer.

"Andra'," he said, "gin ye last as far as Beattock, we'll gie ye a braw hurl back to the farm, syne the bask air, ye ken, and the milk, and, and—but can ye last as far as Beattock, Andra'?"

The sick man, sitting with the cold sweat upon his face, his shrunken limbs looking like sticks inside his ill-made black slop suit, after considering the proposition on its merits, looked up, and said, "I should na' like to bet I feel fair boss,[1] God knows; but there, the mischief of it is, he will na' tell ye, so that, as ye may say, his knowledge has na commercial value. I ken I look as gash[2] as Garscadden.' Ye mind, Jock in the braw auld times, when the auld laird just slipped awa' whiles they were birlin'[3] at the clairet. A braw death, Jock . . . do ye think it'll be rainin' aboot Ecclefechan? Aye . . . sure to be rainin' aboot Lockerbie. Nae Christians there, Jock a' Johnstones and Jardines, ye mind?"

The wife, who had been occupied with an air cushion, and having lost the bellows, had been blowing into it till her cheeks seemed almost bursting, and her false teeth were loosened in her head, left off her toil to ask her husband "If 'e could pick a bit of something, a porkpie, or a nice sausage roll, or something tasty," which she could fetch from the refreshment room. The invalid having declined to eat, and his brother having drawn from his pocket a dirty bag, in which were peppermints, gave him a "drop," telling him that he "minded he aye used to like them weel, when the meenister had fairly got into his prelection in the auld kirk outby."

The train slid almost imperceptibly away, the passengers upon the platform looking after it with that half foolish, half astonished look with which men watch a disappearing train. Then a few sandwich papers rose with the dust almost to the level of the platform, sank again, the clock struck twelve, and the station fell into a half quiescence, like a volcano in the interval between the lava showers. Inside the third class carriage all was quiet until the lights of Harrow shone upon the left, when the sick man, turning himself with difficulty, said, "Good-bye, Harrow-on-the-Hill. I aye liked Harrow for the hill's sake, though ye can scarcely ca' yon wee bit mound a hill, Jean."

His wife, who, even in her grief, still smarted under the Scotch variant of her name, which all her life she had pronounced as "Jayne," and who, true cockney as she was, bounded her world within the lines of Plaistow, Peckham Rye, the Welch 'Arp ('Endon way), and Willesden, moved uncomfortably at the depreciation of the chief mountain in her cosmos, but held her peace. Loving her husband in a sort of half antagonistic fashion, born of the difference of type between the hard, unyielding, yet humorous and sentimental Lowland Scot, and the conglomerate of all races of the island which meet in London and produce the weedy, shallow breed, almost incapable of reproduction, and yet high strung and nervous, there had arisen between them that intangible veil of misconception which, though not excluding love, is yet impervious to respect. Each saw the other's failings, or, perhaps, thought the good qualities which each possessed were faults, for usually men judge each other by their good points, which, seen through prejudice of race, religion and surroundings, appear to them defects.

---

[1] Destitute, empty.

[2] Ghostly, grim.

[3] Whirling.

The brother, who but a week ago had left his farm unwillingly, just when the "neeps were wantin' heughin'[1] and a feck o' things requirin' to be done, forby a puckle[2] sheep waitin' for keelin',[3] to come and see his brother for the last time, sat in that dour and seeming apathetic attitude which falls upon the country man, torn from his daily toil and plunged into a town. Most things in London, during the brief intervals he had passed away from the sick bed, seemed foolish to him, and of a nature such as a self-respecting Moffat man, in the hebdomadal[4] enjoyment of the "prelections" of a Free Church minister could not authorize.

"Man, saw ye e'er a carter sittin' on his cart, and drivin' at a trot, instead o' walkin' in a proper manner alangside his horse?" had been his first remark.

The short-tailed sheep dogs, and the way they worked, the inferior quality of the cart horses, their shoes with hardly any calkins worth the name, all was repugnant to him.

On Sabbath, too, he had received a shock for, after walking miles to sit under the "brither of the UP. minister at Symington," he had found Erastian hymn books in the pews, and noticed with stern reprobation that the congregation stood to sing, and that, instead of sitting solidly whilst the "man wrastled in prayer," stooped forward in the fashion called the Nonconformist lounge.

His troubled spirit had received refreshment from the sermon, which, though short, and extending to but some five-and-forty minutes, had still been powerful, for he said:

"When yon wee, shilpit[5] meenister—brither, ye ken, of rantin' Ferguson, out by Symington—shook the congregation ower the pit mouth, ye could hae fancied that the very sowls in hell just girned. Man, he garred the very stour[6] to flee aboot the kirk, and, hadna' the big Book been weel brass banded, he would hae dang[7] the haricles fair oot."

So the train slipped past Watford, swaying round the curves like a gigantic serpent, and jolting at the facing points as a horse "pecks" in his gallop at an obstruction in the ground.

The moon shone brightly into the compartment, extinguishing the flickering of the half-candle power electric light. Rugby, the station all lit up, and with its platforms occupied but by a few belated passengers, all muffled up like race horses taking their exercise, flashed past. They slipped through Cannock Chase, which stretches down with heath and firs, clear brawling streams, and birch trees, an outpost of the north lost in the midland clay. They crossed the oily Trent, flowing through alder copses, and with its backwaters all overgrown with lilies, like an *aguapey* in Paraguay or in Brazil.

The sick man, wrapped in cheap rugs, and sitting like Guy Fawkes, in the half comic, half pathetic way that sick folk sit, making them sport for fools, and, at the same time, moistening the eye of the judicious, who reflect that they themselves may one day sit as they do, bereft of all the dignity of strength, looked listlessly at nothing as the train sped on. His loving, tactless wife, whose cheap "sized" handkerchief had long since become a rag with mopping up her tears, endeavored to bring round her husband's thoughts to paradise, which she conceived a sort of music

[1]Thinning.

[2]Few (here meaning "many").

[3]Marking.

[4]Weekly.

[5]Puny-looking.

[6]Dust.

[7]Knock, strike.

hall, where angels sat with their wings folded, listening to sentimental songs.

Her brother-in-law, reared on the fiery faith of Moffat Calvinism, eyed her with great disfavor, as a terrier eyes a rat imprisoned in a cage.

"Jean, wumman," he burst out, "to hear ye talk I would jist think your meenister had been a perfectly illeeterate man, pairadise here, pairadise there, what do ye think a man like Andra' could dae daunderin' aboot a gairden naked, pu'in soor aipples frae the trees?"

Cockney and Scotch conceit, impervious alike to outside criticism, and each so bolstered in its pride as to be quite incapable of seeing that any thing existed outside the purlieus of their sight, would soon have made the carriage into a battle-field, had not the husband, with the authority of approaching death, put in his word.

"Whist, Jeanie wumman. Jock, dae ye no ken that the *odium theologicum*[1] is just a curse—pairadise—set ye baith up—pairadise. I dinna' even richly ken if I can last as far as Beattock."

Stafford, its iron furnaces belching out flames which burned red holes into the night, seemed to approach, rather than be approached, so smoothly ran the train. The mingled moonlight and the glare of iron-works lit the canal beside the railway, and from the water rose white vapors as from Styx or Periphlegethon. Through Cheshire ran the train, its timbered houses showing ghastly in the frost which coated all the carriage windows, and rendered them opaque. Preston, the Catholic city, lay silent in the night, its river babbling through the public park and then the hills of Lancashire loomed lofty in the night. Past Garstang, with its water-lily-covered ponds, Garstang where, in the days gone by, Catholic squires, against their will, were forced on Sundays to "take wine" in Church on pain of fine, the puffing serpent slid.

The talk inside the carriage had given place to sleep, that is, the brother-in-law and wife slept fitfully, but the sick man looked out, counting the miles to Moffat, and speculating on his strength. Big drops of sweat stood on his forehead, and his breath came double, whistling through his lungs.

They passed by Lancaster, skirting the sea on which the moon shone bright, setting the fishing boats in silver as they lay scarcely moving on the waves. Then, so to speak, the train set its face up against Shap Fell, and, puffing heavily, drew up into the hills, the scattered gray stone houses of the north, flanked by their gnarled and twisted ash trees, hanging upon the edge of the streams, as lonely, and as cut off from the world (except the passing train) as if they had been in Central Africa. The moorland roads, winding amongst the heather, showed that the feet of generations had marked them out, and not the line, spade, and theodolite, with all the circumstance of modern road makers. They, too, looked white and unearthly in the moonlight, and now and then a sheep, aroused by the snorting of the train, moved from the heather into the middle of the road, and stood there motionless, its shadow filling the narrow track, and flickering on the heather at the edge. The keen and penetrating air of the hills and night roused the two sleepers, and they began to talk, after the Scottish fashion, of the funeral, before the anticipated corpse.

"Ye ken, we've got a braw new hearse outby, sort of Epescopalian lookin', we' gless a'roond, so's ye can see the kist.[2] Very conceity too, they mak the hearses noo-a-days. I min' when they were jist auld sort o' ruckly boxes, awfu' licht, ye ken, upon the springs, and just went dodderin' alang, the body swinging to and fro, as if it would flee richt oot. The roads, ye ken, were no nigh and so richtly metalled in thae days."

The subject of the conversation took it cheerfully, expressing pleasure at the advance of progress as typified in the new hearse, hoping his brother had a decent

[1]"Theological hatred."

[2]Chest (coffin).

"stan' o' black," and looking at his death, after the fashion of his kind, as it were something outside himself, a fact indeed, on which, at the same time, he could express himself with confidence as being in some measure interested. His wife, not being Scotch, took quite another view, and seemed to think that the mere mention of the word was impious, or, at the least, of such a nature as to bring on immediate dissolution, holding the English theory that unpleasant things should not be mentioned, and that, by this means, they can be kept at bay. Half from affection, half from the inborn love of cant, inseparable from the true Anglo-Saxon, she endeavored to persuade her husband that he looked better, and yet would mend, once in his native air.

"At Moffit, ye'd 'ave the benefit of the 'ill breezes, and that 'ere country milk, which never 'as no cream in it, but 'olesome, as you say. Why yuss, in about eight days at Moffit, you'll be as 'earty as you ever was. Yuss, you will, you take my word."

Like a true Londoner, she did not talk religion, being too thin in mind and body even to have grasped the dogma of any of the sects. Her Heaven a music 'all, her paradise to see the king drive through the streets, her literary pleasure to read lies in newspapers or pore on novelettes which showed her the pure elevated lives of duchesses, placing the knaves and prostitutes within the limits of her own class; which view of life she accepted as quite natural, and as a thing ordained to be by the bright stars who write.

Just at the Summit they stopped an instant to let a goods train pass, and, in a faint voice, the consumptive said, "I'd almost lay a wager now I'd last to Moffat, Jock The Shap, ye ken, I aye looked as at the beginning of the run home. The hills, ye ken, are sort o' heartsome. No that they're bonny hills like Moffat hills, na', na', ill-shapen sort of things, just like Borunty tatties, awfu' puir names too, Shap Fell and Rowbad Edge, Hutton Roof Crags, and Arnside Fell. Heard ever onybody sich like names for hills? Naething to fill the mooth. Man, the Scotch hills jist grap ye in the mooth for a' the world like speerits."

They stopped at Penrith, which the old castle walls make even meaner, in the cold morning light, than other stations look. Little Salkeld, and Armathwaite, Cotehill, and Scotby all rushed past, and the train, slackening, stopped with a jerk upon the platform at Carlisle. The sleepy porters bawled out "Change for Maryport," some drovers slouched into carriages, kicking their dogs before them, and, slamming to the doors, exchanged the time of day with others of their tribe, all carrying ash or hazel sticks, all red-faced and keen-eyed, their caps all crumpled, and their great-coat tails all creased, as if their wearers had laid down to sleep full dressed, so as to lose no time in getting to the labors of the day. The old red sandstone church, with something of a castle in its look, as well befits a shrine close to a frontier where in days gone by the priest had need to watch and pray, frowned on the passing train, and on the manufactories whose banked-up fires sent poisonous fumes into the air, withering the trees which, in the public park a careful council had hedged round about with wire.

The Eden ran from bank to bank its water swirling past as wildly as when "The Bauld Buccleugh" and his moss-troopers, bearing "the Kinmount" fettered in their midst, plunged in and passed it, whilst the keen Lord Scroope stood on the brink amazed and motionless. Gretna, so close to England, and yet a thousand miles away in speech and feeling, found the sands now flying through the glass. All through the mosses which once were the "Debateable Land" on which the moss-troopers of the clan Graeme were used to hide the cattle stolen from the "auncient enemy," the now repatriated Scotchman murmured feebly "that it was bonny scenery" although a drearier prospect of "moss hags" and stunted birch trees is not to be found. At Ecclefechan he just raised his head, and faintly spoke of "yon auld carle, Caryle, ye ken, a dour thrawn[1] body, but a gran' pheelosopher," and then lapsed into silence, broken by frequent struggles to take breath.

His wife and brother sat still, and eyed him as a cow watches a locomotive engine pass, amazed and helpless, and he himself had but the strength to whisper "Jock, I'm dune, I'll no' see Moffat, blast it, yon smoke, ye ken, yon London smoke has been ower muckle for ma lungs."

The tearful, helpless wife, not able even to pump up the harmful and unnecessary conventional lie, which, after all, consoles only the liar, sat pale and limp, chewing the fingers of her Berlin gloves. Upon the weather-beaten cheek of Jock glistened a tear, which he brushed off as angrily as it had been a wasp.

"Aye, Andra'," he said, "I would hae liket awfu' weel that ye should win to Moffat. Man, the rowan-trees are a' in bloom, and there's a bonny breer upon the corn—aye, ou aye, the reid bogs are lookin' gran' the year—but Andra', I'll tak' ye east to the auld kirk-yaird, ye'll no' ken onything aboot it, but we'll hae a heartsome funeral."

Lockerbie seemed to fly towards them, and the dying Andra' smiled as his brother pointed out the place and said, "Ye mind, there are no ony Christians in it," and answered, "Aye, I mind, naething but Jardines," as he fought for breath.

The death dews gathered on his forehead as the train shot by Nethercleugh, passed Wamphray, and Dinwoodie, and with a jerk pulled up at Beattock just at the summit of the pass.

So in the cold spring morning light, the fine rain beating on the platform, as the wife and brother got their almost speechless care out of the carriage, the brother whispered, "Dam't, ye've done it, Andra', here's Beattock. I'll tak' ye east to Moffat yet to dee."

But on the platform, huddled on the bench to which he had been brought, Andra' sat speechless and dying in the rain. The doors banged to, the guard stepped in lightly as the train flew past, and a belated porter shouted, "Beattock, Beattock for Moffat," and then, summoning his last strength, Andra' smiled, and whispered faintly in his brother's ear, "Aye, Beattock—for Moffat?" Then his head fell back, and a faint bloody foam oozed from his pallid lips. His wife stood crying helplessly, the rain beating upon the flowers of her cheap hat, rendering it shapeless and ridiculous. But Jock, drawing out a bottle, took a short dram and saying, "Andra', man, ye made a richt gude fecht o' it," snorted an instant in a red pocket handkerchief, and calling up a boy, said, "Ring, Jamie, to the toon, and tell McNicol to send up and fetch a corp." Then, after helping to remove the body to the waiting room, walked out into the rain, and, whistling "Corn Rigs" quietly between his teeth, lit up his pipe, and muttered as he smoked "A richt gude fecht—man aye, ou aye, a game yin Andra', puir felly. Weel, weel, he'll hae a braw hurl onyway in the new Moffat hearse."

## With the North-East Wind

A north-east haar[2] had hung the city with a pall of gray. It gave an air of hardness to the stone-built houses, blending them with the stonepaved streets, till you could scarce see where the houses ended and the street began. A thin gray dust hung in the air. It colored everything, and people's faces all looked pinched with the first touch of autumn cold. The wind, boisterous and gusty, whisked the soot-grimed city leaves about in the high suburb at the foot of a long range of hills, making one think it would be easy to have done with life on such an uncongenial day. Tramways were

[1] Twisted.

[2] Wind, mist.

packed with people of the working class, all of them of the alert, quick-witted type only to be seen in the great city on the Clyde, in all our Empire, and comparable alone to the dwellers in Chicago for dry vivacity.

By the air they wore of chastened pleasure, all those who knew them saw that they were intent upon a funeral. To serious-minded men such as they are, for all their quickness, nothing is so soul-filling, for it is of the nature of a fact that no one can deny. A wedding has its possibilities, for it may lead to children, or divorce, but funerals are in another category. At them the Scottish people is at its best, for never more than then does the deep underlying tenderness peep through the hardness of the rind. On foot and in the tramways, but most especially on foot, converged long lines of men and women, though fewer women, for the national prejudice that in years gone by thought it not decent for a wife to follow to the grave her husband's coffin, still holds a little in the north. Yet there was something in the crowd that showed it was to attend no common funeral, that they were "stepping west." No one wore black, except a minister or two, who looked a little like the belated rook you sometimes see amongst a flock of seagulls, in that vast ocean of gray tweed.

They tramped along, the whistling north-east wind pinching their features, making their eyes run, and as they went, almost unconsciously they fell into procession, for beyond the tramway line, a country lane that had not quite put on the graces of a street, though straggling houses were dotted here and there along it, received the crowd and marshaled it, as it were mechanically, without volition of its own. Kept in between the walls, and blocked in front by the hearse and long procession of the mourning-coaches, the people slowly surged along. The greater portion of the crowd were townsmen, but there were miners washed and in their Sunday best. Their faces showed the blue marks of healed-up scars into which coal dust or gunpowder had become tattooed, scars gained in the battle of their lives down in the pits, remembrances of falls of rock or of occasions when the mine had "fired upon them."

Many had known Keir Hardie in his youth, had "wrocht wi' him out-by," at Blantyre, at Hamilton, in Ayrshire, and all of them had heard him speak a hundred times. Even to those who had not heard him, his name was as a household word. Miners predominated, but men of every trade were there. Many were members of that black-coated proletariat, whose narrow circumstances and daily struggle for appearances make their life harder to them than is the life of any working man before he has had to dye his hair. Women tramped, too, for the dead leader had been a champion of their sex. They all respected him, loving him with that half-contemptuous gratitude that women often show to men who make the "woman question" the object of their lives.

After the Scottish fashion at a funeral, greetings were freely passed, and Reid, who hadna' seen his friend Mackinder since the time of the Mid-Lanark fight, greeted him with "Ye mind when first Keir Hardie was puttin' up for Parliament," and wrung his hand, hardened in the mine, with one as hardened, and instantly began to recall elections of the past.

"Ye mind yon Wishaw meeting?"

"Aye, ou aye;" ye mean when a' they Irish wouldna' hear John Ferguson. Man, he almost grat[1] after the meeting aboot it."

"Aye, but they gied Hardie himself a maist respectful hearing . . . aye, ou aye."

Others remembered him a boy, and others in his home at Cumnock, but all spoke of him with affection, holding him as something of their own apart from other politicians, almost apart from men.

Old comrades who had been with him either at this election or that meeting, had

---

[1]Wept.

helped or had intended to have helped at the crises of his life, fought their old battles over, as they tramped along, all shivering in the wind.

The procession reached a long dip in the road, and the head of it, full half a mile away, could be seen gathered round the hearse, outside the chapel of the crematorium, whose ominous tall chimney, through which the ashes, and perchance the souls of thousands have escaped towards some empyrean or another, towered up starkly. At last all had arrived, and the small open space was crowded, the hearse and carriages appearing stuck amongst the people, like raisins in a cake, so thick they pressed upon them. The chapel, differing from the ordinary chapel of the faiths as much as does a motor driver from a cabman, had an air as of modernity about it, which contrasted strangely with the ordinary looking crowd, the adjacent hills, the decent mourning coaches and the black-coated undertakers who bore the coffin up the steps. Outside, the wind whistled and swayed the soot-stained trees about; but inside the chapel the heat was stifling.

When all was duly done, and long exordiums passed upon the man who in his life had been the target for the abuse of Press and pulpit, the coffin slid away to its appointed place. One thought one heard the roaring of the flames, and somehow missed the familiar lowering of the body . . . earth to earth . . . to which the centuries of use and wont have made us all familiar, though dust to dust in this case was the more appropriate.

In either case, the book is closed for ever, and the familiar face is seen no more.

So, standing just outside the chapel in the cold, waiting till all the usual greetings had been exchanged, I fell a-musing on the man whom I had known so well. I saw him as he was thirty years ago, outlined against a bing[1] or standing in a quarry in some mining village, and heard his once familiar address of "Men." He used no other in those days, to the immense disgust of legislators and other worthy but unimaginative men whom he might chance to meet. About him seemed to stand a shadowy band, most of whom now are dead or lost to view, or have gone under in the fight.

John Ferguson was there, the old-time Irish leader, the friend of Davitt and of Butt. Tall and erect he stood, dressed in his long frock-coat, his roll of papers in one hand, and with the other stuck into his breast, with all the air of being the last Roman left alive. Tom Mann, with his black hair, his flashing eyes, and his tumultuous speech peppered with expletives. Beside him, Sandy Haddow, of Parkhead, massive and Doric in his speech, with a gray woolen comforter rolled round his neck, and hands like panels of a door. Champion, pale, slight, and interesting, still the artillery officer, in spite of Socialism. John Burns; and Small, the miners' agent, with his close brown beard and taste for literature. Smillie stood near, he of the seven elections, and then check weigher at a pit, either at Cadzow or Larkhall. There, too, was silver-tongued Shaw Maxwell and Chisholm Robertson, looking out darkly on the world through tinted spectacles; with him Bruce Glasier, girt with a red sash and with an aureole of fair curly hair around his head, half poet and half revolutionary.

They were all young and ardent, and as I mused upon them and their fate, and upon those of them who have gone down into the oblivion that waits for those who live before their time, I shivered in the wind.

Had he, too, lived in vain, he whose scant ashes were no doubt by this time all collected in an urn, and did they really represent all that remained of him?

Standing amongst the band of shadowy comrades I had known, I saw him, simple and yet with something of the prophet in his air, and something of the seer. Effective and yet ineffectual, something there was about him that attracted little

[1] Slag-heap.

children to him, and I should think lost dogs. He made mistakes, but then those who make no mistakes seldom make anything. His life was one long battle, so it seemed to me that it was fitting that at his funeral the north-east wind should howl amongst the trees, tossing and twisting them as he himself was twisted and storm-tossed in his tempestuous passage through the world.

As the crowd moved away, and in the hearse and mourning-coaches the spavined horses limped slowly down the road, a gleam of sun-shine, such as had shone too little in his life, lighted up everything.

The swaying trees and dark, gray houses of the ugly suburb of the town were all transfigured for a moment. The chapel door was closed, and from the chimney of the crematorium a faint blue smoke was issuing, which, by degrees, faded into the atmosphere, just as the soul, for all I know, may melt into the air.

When the last stragglers had gone, and bits of paper scurried uneasily along before the wind, the world seemed empty, with nothing friendly in it, but the shoulder of Ben Lomond peeping out shyly over the Kilpatrick Hills.

## WILLIAM SHARP (1855–1905)

[William Sharp was born at Paisley near the Highlands, the latter becoming his spiritual home, though he spent most of his life in Glasgow and London. He is known chiefly for the dreamy "Celtic revival" poems which he wrote under the name of "Fiona Macleod," a Highland girl he had once known. In fact, he went to elaborate lengths to maintain the authorial fiction, in part by producing a steady stream of works under his own name as well.]

### The Last Aboriginal

I see him sit, wild-eyed, alone,
Amidst gaunt, spectral, moonlit gums;
He waits for death: not once a moan
From out his rigid fixed lips comes;
His lank hair falls adown a face
Haggard as any wave-worn stone,
And in his eyes I dimly trace
The memory of a vanished race.

The lofty ancient gum-trees stand,
Each gray and ghostly in the moon,
The giants of an old strange land
That was exultant in its noon
When all our Europe was o'erturned
With deluge and with shifting sand,
With earthquakes that the hills inurned
And central fires that fused and burned.

The moon moves slowly through the vast
And solemn skies; the night is still,
Save when a warrigal* springs past  wild dog
With dismal howl, or when the shrill
Scream of a parrot rings which feels
A twining serpent's fangs fixed fast,

Or when a gray opossum squeals—
Or long iguana, as it steals

From bole to bole, disturbs the leaves.
But hushed and still he sits—who knows
That all is o'er for him who weaves
With inner speech, malign, morose,
A curse upon the whites who came
And gathered up his race like sheaves
Of thin wheat, fit but for the flame—
Who shot or spurned them without shame.

He knows he shall not see again
The creeks whereby the lyre-birds sing;
He shall no more upon the plain,
Sun-scorched, and void of water-spring,
Watch the dark cassowaries sweep
In startled flight, or, with spear lain
In ready poise, glide, twist, and creep
Where the brown kangaroo doth leap.

No more in silent dawns he'll wait
By still lagoons, and mark the flight
Of black swans near; no more elate
Whirl high the boomerang aright
Upon some foe. He knows that now
He too must share his race's night—
He scarce can know the white man's plow
Will one day pass above his brow.

Last remnant of the Austral race,
He sits and stares, with failing breath;
The shadow deepens on his face,
For 'midst the spectral gums waits death:
A dingo's sudden howl swells near—
He stares once with a startled gaze,
As half in wonder, half in fear,
Then sinks back on his unknown bier.

## The Valley of the Pale Blue Flowers

In a hidden valley a pale blue flower grows.
It is so pale that in the moonshine it is dimmer than dim gold,
And in the starshine paler than the palest rose.

It is the flower of dream. Who holds it is never old.
It is the flower of forgetfulness—and oblivion is youth;
Breathing it, flame is not empty air, dust is not cold.

Lift it, and there is no memory of sorrow or any ruth;
The gray monotone of the low sky is filled with light;
The dim, terrible, impalpable lie wears the raiment of truth.

I lift it now, for somewhat in the heart of the night
Fills me with dread. It may be that, as a tiger in his lair,
Memory, crouching, waits to spring into the light.

No, I will clasp it close to my heart, overdroop with my hair;
I will breathe thy frail faint breath, O pale blue flower,
And then . . . and then . . . nothing shall take me unaware.

Nothing: no thought; no fear, only the invisible power
Of the vast deeps of night, wherein down a shadowy stair
My soul slowly, slowly, slowly, will sink to its ultimate hour.

## The Wasp

Where the ripe pears droop heavily
The yellow wasp hums loud and long
His hot and drowsy autumn song:
A yellow flame he seems to be,
When darting suddenly from high
He lights where fallen peaches lie:

Yellow and black, this tiny thing's
A tiger-soul on elfin wings.

## Wild Roses

Against the dim hot summer blue
Yon wave of white wild-roses lies,
Watching with listless golden eyes
The green leaves shutting out their view,
The tiny leaves whose motions bright
Are like small wings of emerald light:
White butterflies like snow-flakes fall
And brown bees drone their honey-call.

## Susurro

Breath o' the grass;
Ripple of wandering wind,
Murmur of tremulous leaves:
A moonbeam moving white
Like a ghost across the plain:
A shadow on the road:
And high up, high,
From the cypress-bough;
A long sweet melancholy note.
Silence.
And the topmost spray
Of the cypress-bough is still
As a wavelet in a pool:
The road lies duskily bare:
The plain is a misty gloom:

Still are the tremulous leaves;
Scarce a last ripple of wind,
Scarce a breath i' the grass.
Hush: the tired wind sleeps.
Is it the wind's breath; or
Breath o' the grass.

## White Rose

Far in the inland valleys
The Spring her secret tells;
The roses lift on the bushes;
The lilies shake their bells.

To a lily of the valley
A white rose leans from above;
"Little white flower o' the valley,
Come up and be my love."

To the lily of the valley
A speedwell whispers, "No!
Where the roses live are thorns;
'Tis safe below.

The lily clomb to the rose-bush;
A thorn in her side:
The white rose has wedded a red rose;
And the lily died.

## On a Nightingale in April

The yellow moon is a dancing phantom
Down secret ways of the flowing shade;
And the waveless stream has a murmuring whisper
Where the alders wade.

Not a breath, not a sigh, save the slow stream's whisper:
Only the moon is a dancing blade
That leads a host of the Crescent warriors
To a phantom raid.

Out of the lands of Faerie a summons,
A long strange cry that thrills through the glade—
The gray-green glooms of the elm are stirring,
Newly afraid.

Last heard, white music, under the olives
Where once Theocritus sang and played—
Thy Thracian song is the old new wonder—
O moon-white maid.

## The Isle of Lost Dreams

There is an isle beyond our ken,
Haunted by dreams of weary men.
Gray hopes enshadow it with wings
Weary with burdens of old things.
There the insatiate water-springs
Rise with the tears of all who weep:
And deep within it—deep, oh, deep—
The furtive voice of sorrow sings.
There evermore,
Till time be oer,
Sad, oh, so sad, the dreams of men
Drift through the isle beyond our ken.

## Red Poppies

In the Sabine Valleys Near Rome

Through the seeding grass,
And the tall corn,
The wind goes:
With nimble feet,
And blithe voice,
Calling, calling,
The wind goes
Through the seeding grass,
And the tall corn.

What calleth the wind,
Passing by—
The shepherd-wind?
Far and near
He laugheth low,
And the red poppies
Lift their heads
And toss i' the sun.
A thousand thousand blooms
Tossed i' the air,
Banners of joy,
For tis the shepherd-wind
Passing by,
Singing and laughing low
Through the seeding grass
And the tall corn.

## The Weaver of Snow

In Polar noons when the moonshine glimmers,
And the frost-fans whirl,
And whiter than moonlight the ice-flowers grow,
And the lunar rainbow quivers and shimmers,
And the Silent Laughers dance to and fro,

A stooping girl
As pale as pearl
Gathers the frost-flowers where they blow:
And the fleet-foot fairies smile, for they know
The Weaver of Snow.

And she climbs at last to a berg set free,
That drifteth slow;
And she sails to the edge of the world we see,
And waits till the wings of the north wind lean
Like an eagle's wings o'er a lochan* of green, pond
And the pale stars glow
On berg and floe . . .
Then down on our world with a wild laugh of glee
She empties her lamp full of shimmer and sheen.
And that is the way in a dream I have seen
The Weaver of Snow.

## The Valley of Silence

In the secret Valley of Silence
No breath doth fall;
No wind stirs in the branches;
No bird doth call.
As on a white wall
A breathless lizard is still,
So silence lies in the valley
Breathlessly still.

In the dusk-grown heart of the valley
An altar rises white.
No rapt priest bends in awe
Before its silent light;
But sometimes a flight
Of breathless words of prayer
White-winged enclose the altar,
Eddies of prayer.

## The White Peace

It lies not on the sunlit hill
Nor on the sunlit plain;
Nor ever on any running stream
Nor on the unclouded main—

But sometimes, through the Soul of Man,
Slow moving o'er his pain,
The moonlight of a perfect peace
Floods heart and brain.

## At the Last

She cometh no more;
Time, too, is dead.
The last tide is led
From the last shore.
Eternity—
What is Eternity?
But the sea coming,
The sea going,
For evermore.

## INDEX OF AUTHORS AND TITLES